Principles With Promise

Old Testament
New Testament

by
Vincent DiGirolamo

Principles with Promise

Old Testament
New Testament

© Copyright 2007 Vincent DiGirolamo

Library of Congress Control Number: 2008900133

ISBN-13: 978-0-9786815-4-8
ISBN-10: 0-9786815-4-1

First Printing, December 2007

Printed in the United States of America

Celestine Publishing, LLC
9660 Falls of Neuse Road
Suite 138, #146
Raleigh, North Carolina 27615

www.CelestinePublishing.com

Cover design by David DiGirolamo
Website by Jonathan (Chad) DiGirolamo

Dedicated to

the honorable men and women of the

United States Armed Forces and to all First Responders

whom with their families have sacrificed much

to establish and ensure the continuation

of our God given freedoms, inaliable rights and liberties

which were founded upon these very principles

and from which our forefathers forged this great nation.

In God We Trust

Acknowledgements

Principles with Promise is a series of concordances that have been developed over a twenty-five period of collecting and cataloging principles from holy writ. Each new release has been developed and edited by those family, friends and associates closest to me, many of whom have been recognized in the first publication.

Regarding this publication, I would like to thank my wife Dana for doing the final edits on each page for the indexing of this book which allows the easy location of subject material. Your continued love and devotion has kept the Principles with Promise series alive and well.

I wish to acknowledge all those whom I have served with and continue to serve with, both in uniform and civilian attire – it is the same, for the protection and welfare of our freedoms and liberties. However, this book is also dedicated to another valiant group of men and women who serve every day on the front lines – our first responders; those unsung heroes who put themselves in harms way to protect life and property in times of crisis and need. Your personal sacrifices and devotion to duty are as noble as those to whom serve in our armed forces. Thank You.

One of my favorite songs, *Eternal Father, Strong to Save*, comes to mind when I think of the camaraderie, bonds of friendship, and love experienced though the unfailing service and sacrifices made by those who not only defend these principles, but those who scribed them from the Father of all. May we all therefore show our deepest gratitude by living these principles each day to the best of our ability. God Speed.

Author's Note

Principles with Promise: Old Testament and New Testament catalogs gospel principles found in the Authorized King James Version (KJV) of the Bible. Special care was taken to ensure that scriptural meanings were not compromised when taken out of context, however the reader is encouraged in all cases to read the verse in context during a sincere study of the principles to gain the more accurate meaning for which it was intended. With this publishing, I hope to pursue the development of its equivalent using the New International Version (NIV) of the Bible for those who prefer or accept more readily its translation.

Unlike many undertakings in my life, this adventure did not start with an end in mind. What began as the answer to a simple question, *"What are the commandments that I might keep them?"* matured into this lifelong labor of love – a labor that discovered much more than the commandments. During this journey I have often felt a personal guidance regarding its development. Everything from its contents to layout to cross referencing and key word selection has been guided by the quiet assurance to go in that direction.

I have also felt what I believe to have been the loving intimations of those who originally scribed these words, encouraging me to press on during endless hours of quiet retreat in my studies and as this manuscript went through its rigorous development. It is their words, not mine that make *Principles with Promise* another beacon, a promise that God loves us and governs our lives according to laws established for our ultimate joy and salvation.

Collectively, these principles seem to have a natural organization or order, and though each principle is independently declared at times, they are all interrelated in some way. I have often described that order as being analogous to a rainbow with its many colors blending one into another – only this rainbow begins with a white light emanating outward from the center to the magnificent colors representing the principles that govern our world and our relationships.

While *Principles with Promise* has captured thousands of principles cataloged under more than eighteen hundred key words, the work is not finished when this book is published – rather, it is like the rainbow with its endless array of colors and whose end you can never quite see. The Lord willing, I will continue working on its next edition, a multi-hued version filled with all of the feedback received from you, the reader, on how to make it better, more complete, more correct. And, though interpretation and practice of these principles may vary from one religious denomination to the next, these are the principles that have been identified according to the processes explained in the Introduction and Foreward.

So here it is, a new kind of concordance to help you navigate your own sweet journey through the scriptures to understand the principles that govern life – God given principles that are unchanging, universal and eternal. It is my own personal experience that each opportunity taken to review, study or search these principles is another step towards learning, and more especially knowing for yourself what treasures of truth are there for you to discover.

May God bless you with grace divine along your way.   Vinny DiGirolamo

And he gave some, apostles;
and some, prophets;
and some, evangelists;
and some, pastors and teachers;
For the perfecting of the saints, for
the work of the ministry,
for the edifying of the body of
Christ: Till we all come in the unity
of the faith, and of the knowledge
of the Son of God, unto a perfect
man, unto the measure of the
stature of the fulness of Christ.

Eph. 4:11-13

TABLE OF CONTENTS

If any of you lack wisdom,
let him ask of God,
that giveth to all men liberally,
and upbraideth not;
and it shall be given him.

James 1:5

Introduction

What is Principles with Promise?

Principles with Promise is a new kind of scriptural concordance – a principle based topical guide. It is a compilation of action-based principles and their associated promises found in the King James Version (KJV) of the Old and New Testaments. Principles of all kinds have been extracted and catalogued from the laws, ordinances, commandments, and doctrines regarding our personal journey here on the earth and also the life to come.

Principles with Promise is something quite different from most concordances, but familiar at the same time. *Principles with Promise* primarily catalogs principles of action – the things we should do or should not do – all according to the gospel of Jesus Christ as taught by His disciples, the prophets of God, and God himself.

What are principles and how were they selected?

Principles are unchanging, universal, God given laws that govern human behavior and growth, both spiritual and temporal. They are fundamental truths that characterize our relationships with God and our fellowman, the world we live in, and the heavens above. They consist of everything from the physical laws of nature to all of the laws, ordinances, commandments, and guidance intended by God for the welfare, happiness, perfection, and salvation of man.

Principles exist as simple statements of truth or as self-evident statements of fact. They are found as directives like commandments that require action or as guidelines that follow the *cause and effect* construct, the *if-then* principle, or simply, the *principle with promise*. Many of the principles catalogued in *Principles with Promise* include these *if-then* principles. *If* you do something (the principle), *then* you will realize some benefit or consequence for your action (the promise).

We are guided by the scriptures and counseled by our leaders and teachers to live gospel principles more fully. This is often said in summary about the topic being presented or declared as more general, overarching guidance. However, at times we may have wondered which principles they are referring to, and of course, what are they that we might live them more fully? With this in mind, Dr. Steven R. Covey has said, *"When we value correct principles, we have truth - a knowledge of things as they are."* Therefore, I am certain that I am not alone in listing these principles to know them better – seeking a knowledge of things as they truly are.

Each principle was extracted from the scriptures with the greatest of care – one verse at a time, and cataloged under one or more key words using the conventions found in typical scriptural concordances or topical guides. If a particular verse appeared to be an action statement, a statement that described something we should to be doing, it was catalogued under the primary topic it addressed. For example, if an action statement was referring to *faith*, it was filed under a collection of verses that also spoke to some aspect of *faith* – what it is, how to obtain it, exercise it, experiment with it, grow it, etc.

Later, having accumulated several thousand principles under more than eighteen hundred key words, similar principles and references were grouped together as seemed appropriate. Very rarely did a single verse address only one topic area or one action, and therefore, more often than not, principles are catalogued and cross referenced under several of the key topic areas they address (nouns) as well as the associated actions required (verbs). Promises are then found as part of the verse or more often in the supporting references listed.

Principles cataloged in this publication include the statements of action along with their associated promises, while others are simple facts about a topic. Some principles are explained in lengthy dissertations about different aspects of that topic, and that same dissertation may also include several related principles as well. Other principles are represented as commandments, simple declarations of truth, or are worded as corollary statements of the actual principle – statements of what not to do rather than statements of what to do.

Often times, the scriptures describe the principles that are being practiced by the people of that day and they are presented here as examples of the principle in action. Some principles are presented in the form of a question – prompting introspection, or they are found in a story, parable or in songs; all designed to teach us these precious truths. Other principles are more hidden and harder to find, scattered throughout the scriptures, and must be pieced together to make sense and sometimes are the treasures we find for ourselves. Lastly, several principles are fragmented beyond recognition and leave room for debate and interpretation.

How do I use Principles with Promise?

These principles are not new. They have been set forth throughout the dispensations of time by God and His servants, all for our benefit if we but choose to follow them. Some of the best talks I have heard have addressed specific principles that are accompanied by that noticeable Spirit of testimony. To me, these are further witnesses that the principles are indeed true and worthy of our consideration.

Principles with Promise can be used in several different ways. We often seek out specific principles when we are asked to prepare a talk on a particular subject or give a lesson in church. We use our familiar resources and scores of good references to search for the scriptures that support our topic, and we locate the desired scriptures via an index of key words. There are also very capable computer programs that do the same thing, find the scriptures related to the topic – then the rest is up to us, to develop the message we are inspired to deliver.

This book can also be used like any other topical guide or concordance in this manner. If you want to research a particular topic, you similarly enter *Principles with Promise* under that topical word, like *charity*, *grace*, or *hope*, and identify the principle or set of principles you wish to understand or include in your research, whether it be for personal edification or in preparation for a talk on Sunday or other teaching assignment.

At one baptism I was asked to speak on the gift of the *Holy Ghost*, so I listed out all of the principles on that topic and determined which three or four principles I would present that day. This simplified my research by having the principles sorted out for me already, and the rest was relatively easy as the topic focused on those principles as the message was delivered.

Another way to use *Principles with Promise*, a way in which I have benefited the most in my studies is by listing the principles on a particular topic beforehand, and by having them collectively in front of me at one time, I am better able to ponder that subject area in a more focused manner. As I review and ponder each principle, then move from one cross-referenced subject to another, a new level of understanding evolves as ideas and thoughts come to light that may not have been previously known – even new meanings.

This method of studying gospel principles is where I have found that the promises of searching, pondering and praying yields its sweetest fruit. And, I have often said to my friends, that when this book is published, I will finally have the time to study it in this manner of prayerful consideration. Much of this research cataloging is already done and the opportunity to focus on your selected topic area is here. And as a friend of mine once said, *"Some of us may think we know what the principles means, but isn't it more important to know what the Lord means about the principle?"*

Principles with Promise gathers them together in one place and provides an easier way to research, learn and understand these eternal truths. It is like peeling back the layers of an onion; as we sincerely seek to know things as they truly are, we will find new understandings and truths according to the laws that govern our lives, even eternal life.

Finally, if you desire to get the most benefit using *Principles with Promise*, as well as with the scriptures themselves, the rest is up to you.

That's where the adventure really begins...

Foreword

Navigating Principles with Promise

Principles with Promise serves as a ready reference book to assist you in your study of the principles, prepare talks and lessons, and contribute to your knowledge and testimony of the gospel. Principles are grouped alphabetically by *key words* found in each principle. While most principles are action oriented, there are many principles included in these lists that are statements of fact or simply stated eternal truths. There are several illustrations following this discussion to help you navigate this book.

- The sample page illustrates how the principles and the supporting reference verses are arranged.

- Following the sample page is an example of a principle layout with an illustration of the types of supporting references that are associated with each principle. Supporting references include the principle itself, dissertations on that topic, examples of the principle in action and other related material on the topic.

- Finally, as with most concordances, a Topical Index is provided at the end to help you more quickly locate principles by a key word search and page numbers. Principles are all interrelated in some way – remember the analogous rainbow described in the preceding Author's Note.

The selection of key words for each principle was based on the topic that the principle and its references primarily addressed. You may find a principle listed under several key words because of the rich associations with multiple topics, but to save space, the principle's supporting references are only listed under one of the more dominant key words. In cases where the principle contains several key topics, you will find them repeated under the other key words listed in the parenthesis that follow the principle. For example, a principle found under the topic of *Faith* may be followed by (*see also* Hope, Charity) indicating this principle is also found under the topics of *Hope* and *Charity*.

Key words themselves are related to other key words. For example, the key word *Charity* is also related topically to other words like *Alms, Benevolence, Compassion, Generosity, Love, Mercy,* and *Welfare.* If the key word is followed instead by (*see* Hope, Charity) and there are no principles following that key word, it is simply redirecting you, suggesting other similar or related key words that may have principles and references listed under them. Cataloging principles under multiple key words was one of the greatest challenges for this compilation and you are encouraged to search the related topic areas to get a more complete picture for better understanding. Having cataloged the principles under multiple topics gives you the option to pursue their information in multiple ways – both with key word topics and additional principle related topics.

Principles have been extracted directly from the scriptures in their many forms. In some cases the promises are mentioned as part of the principle itself. In other cases, the promises will be found in the supporting references. The abbreviated, concordance styled supporting references are meant to serve only as a pointer, indicating where you will find the more complete text, and you are encouraged to refer to those scriptures to learn more about the meaning and setting of the selected verses.

Another convention to save space and avoid repetition without loosing meaning is to abbreviate key words and italicize them within the supporting references. For example, the supporting references to principles under the topic of *Faith, Faithful, Faithfulness* will have these words abbreviated and italicized as *f.* in all of the supporting references. If there is a series of words that are repeated often in the references, they will be similarly abbreviated. For example, under the key word *Commandments*, the phrase *keep my commandments* is abbreviated as *k.m.c.* because the number of times the phrase is repeated in the references.

Several blank pages are provided at the end of the book so that you might add other principles and references you will discover in you own personal study of the scriptures, during General, Stake and Ward Conferences, and from other good books and publications that you feel are worth remembering.

Feedback

The author assumes all editorial responsibilities and apologizes beforehand for any errors in spelling, text, formatting or scripture references – they are there. Most publishers would not have taken on this project due to the enormous amount of editorial resources needed to insure its accuracy. Therefore, you are further encouraged to provide feedback regarding recommended corrections and changes for future editions. To do this, feel free to send your comments to Celestine Publishing, LLC at 9660 Falls of Neuse Rd, STE 138, #146, Raleigh, NC 27615 or by logging on to www.celestinepublishing.com or www.principleswithpromise.com.

Principles with Promise
Sample Page

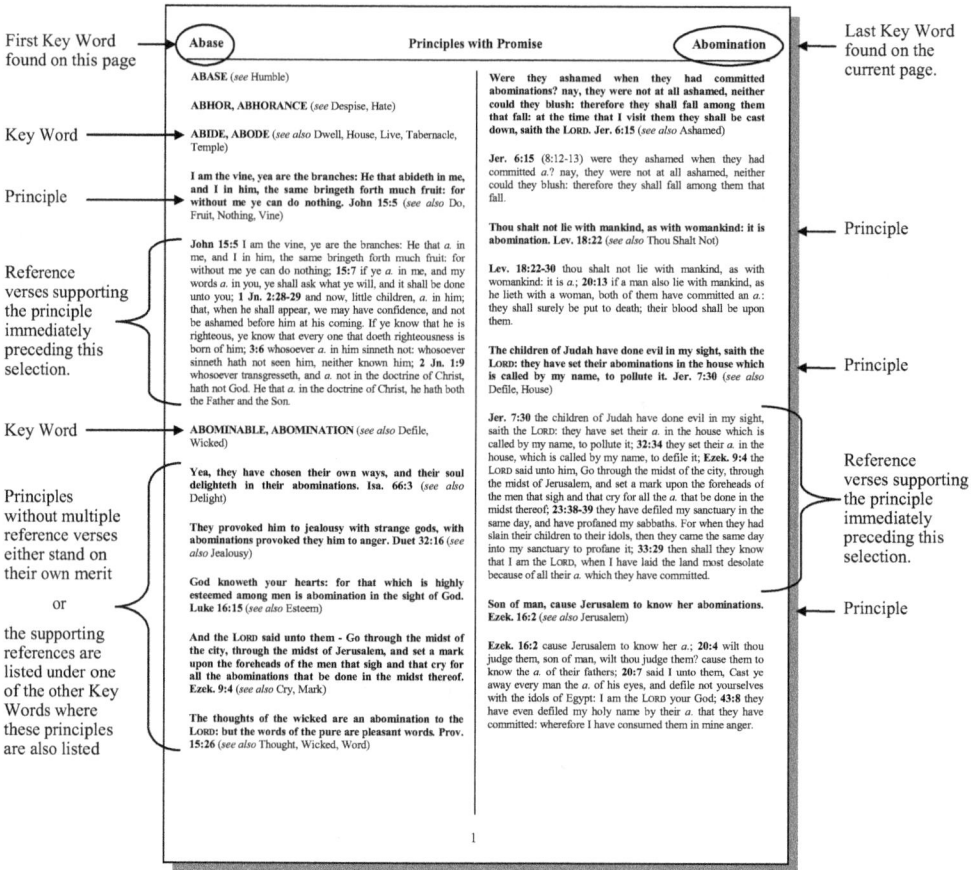

First Key Word found on this page → **Abase**

Principles with Promise

Abomination ← **Last Key Word found on the current page.**

ABASE (*see* Humble)

ABHOR, ABHORANCE (*see* Despise, Hate)

Key Word → **ABIDE, ABODE** (*see also* Dwell, House, Live, Tabernacle, Temple)

Principle → I am the vine, yea are the branches: He that abideth in me, and I in him, the same bringeth forth much fruit: for without me ye can do nothing. John 15:5 (*see also* Do, Fruit, Nothing, Vine)

Reference verses supporting the principle immediately preceding this selection. → John **15:5** I am the vine, ye are the branches: He that *a.* in me, and I in him, the same bringeth forth much fruit; for without me ye can do nothing; **15:7** if ye *a.* in me, and my words *a.* in you, ye shall ask what ye will, and it shall be done unto you; **1 Jn. 2:28-29** and now, little children, *a.* in him; that, when he shall appear, we may have confidence, and not be ashamed before him at his coming. If ye know that he is righteous, ye know that every one that doeth righteousness is born of him; **3:6** whosoever *a.* in him sinneth not: whosoever sinneth hath not seen him, neither known him; **2 Jn. 1:9** whosoever transgresseth, and *a.* not in the doctrine of Christ, hath not God. He that *a.* in the doctrine of Christ, hath both the Father and the Son.

Key Word → **ABOMINABLE, ABOMINATION** (*see also* Defile, Wicked)

Principles without multiple reference verses either stand on their own merit

or

the supporting references are listed under one of the other Key Words where these principles are also listed

Yea, they have chosen their own ways, and their soul delighteth in their abominations. Isa. **66:3** (*see also* Delight)

They provoked him to jealousy with strange gods, with abominations provoked they him to anger. Duet **32:16** (*see also* Jealousy)

God knoweth your hearts: for that which is highly esteemed among men is abomination in the sight of God. Luke **16:15** (*see also* Esteem)

And the LORD said unto them - Go through the midst of the city, through the midst of Jerusalem, and set a mark upon the foreheads of the men that sigh and that cry for all the abominations that be done in the midst thereof. **Ezek. 9:4** (*see also* Cry, Mark)

The thoughts of the wicked are an abomination to the LORD: but the words of the pure are pleasant words. Prov. **15:26** (*see also* Thought, Wicked, Word)

Were they ashamed when they had committed abominations? nay, they were not at all ashamed, neither could they blush: therefore they shall fall among them that fall: at the time that I visit them they shall be cast down, saith the LORD. Jer. **6:15** (*see also* Ashamed)

Jer. **6:15** (8:12-13) were they ashamed when they had committed *a*.? nay, they were not at all ashamed, neither could they blush: therefore they shall fall among them that fall. ← **Principle**

Thou shalt not lie with mankind, as with womankind: it is abomination. Lev. **18:22** (*see also* Thou Shalt Not)

Lev. **18:22-30** thou shalt not lie with mankind, as with womankind: it is *a.*; **20:13** if a man also lie with mankind, as he lieth with a woman, both of them have committed an *a.*: they shall surely be put to death; their blood shall be upon them.

The children of Judah have done evil in my sight, saith the LORD: they have set their abominations in the house which is called by my name, to pollute it. Jer. **7:30** (*see also* Defile, House) ← **Principle**

Jer. **7:30** the children of Judah have done evil in my sight, saith the LORD: they have set their *a.* in the house which is called by my name, to pollute it; **32:34** they set their *a.* in the house, which is called by my name, to defile it; **Ezek. 9:4** the LORD said unto him, Go through the midst of the city, through the midst of Jerusalem, and set a mark upon the foreheads of the men that sigh and that cry for all the *a.* that be done in the midst thereof; **23:38-39** they have defiled my sanctuary in the same day, and have profaned my sabbaths. For when they had slain their children to their idols, then they came the same day into my sanctuary to profane it; **33:29** then shall they know that I am the LORD, when I have laid the land most desolate because of all their *a.* which they have committed. ← **Reference verses supporting the principle immediately preceding this selection.**

Son of man, cause Jerusalem to know her abominations. Ezek. **16:2** (*see also* Jerusalem) ← **Principle**

Ezek. **16:2** cause Jerusalem to know her *a.*; **20:4** wilt thou judge them, son of man, wilt thou judge them? cause them to know the *a.* of their fathers; **20:7** said I unto them, Cast ye away every man the *a.* of his eyes, and defile not yourselves with the idols of Egypt: I am the LORD your God; **43:8** they have even defiled my holy name by their *a.* that they have committed: wherefore I have consumed them in mine anger.

1

Note: Key words are listed in alphabetical order and grouped according to different spellings or variations of the word.

The following diagram represents a typical principle layout using concordance conventions, and the types of information that support the selected or primary principle. The primary principle illustrated below is "If thou wilt enter into life, *keep the commandments*" was extracted from Matthew 19:17. It is used as an example to illustrate what type of information you may find related to the principle as listed in its supporting references.

The supporting references will include a reiteration of the principle and examples of the principle being practiced, some amplifying facts or dissertation about the principle, testimonies or witnesses of the principle, admonitions and encouragements to live the principle, and the promises or consequences for obedience or disobedience to the principle.

Even though a principle may be listed under several different key words, the supporting references generally appear only once under the most appropriate key word, or the first time the principle is listed alphabetically (mostly to limit the size of this concordance). If there are no related reference verses, a particular principle may simply stand on its own merit, or the references are listed with that principle under another key word.

Sample Principle

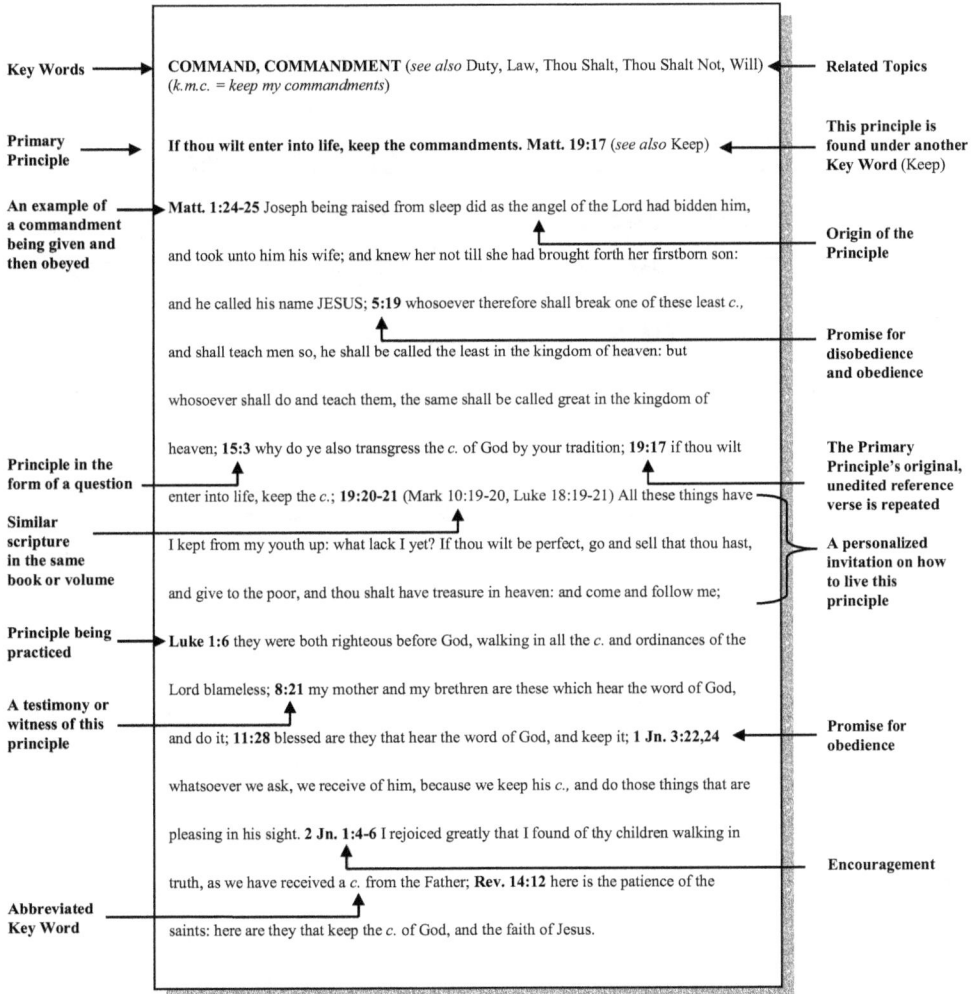

Key Words →

COMMAND, COMMANDMENT (*see also* Duty, Law, Thou Shalt, Thou Shalt Not, Will) ← **Related Topics**
(*k.m.c. = keep my commandments*)

Primary Principle →

This principle is found under another Key Word (Keep)

If thou wilt enter into life, keep the commandments. Matt. 19:17 (*see also* Keep) ←

An example of a commandment being given and then obeyed →

Matt. 1:24-25 Joseph being raised from sleep did as the angel of the Lord had bidden him,

Origin of the Principle

and took unto him his wife; and knew her not till she had brought forth her firstborn son:

and he called his name JESUS; **5:19** whosoever therefore shall break one of these least *c.*,

Promise for disobedience and obedience

and shall teach men so, he shall be called the least in the kingdom of heaven: but

whosoever shall do and teach them, the same shall be called great in the kingdom of

heaven; **15:3** why do ye also transgress the *c.* of God by your tradition; **19:17** if thou wilt

Principle in the form of a question →

The Primary Principle's original, unedited reference verse is repeated

enter into life, keep the *c.*; **19:20-21** (Mark 10:19-20, Luke 18:19-21) All these things have

Similar scripture in the same book or volume →

I kept from my youth up: what lack I yet? If thou wilt be perfect, go and sell that thou hast,

A personalized invitation on how to live this principle

and give to the poor, and thou shalt have treasure in heaven: and come and follow me;

Principle being practiced →

Luke 1:6 they were both righteous before God, walking in all the *c.* and ordinances of the

Lord blameless; **8:21** my mother and my brethren are these which hear the word of God,

A testimony or witness of this principle →

and do it; **11:28** blessed are they that hear the word of God, and keep it; **1 Jn. 3:22,24** ←

Promise for obedience

whatsoever we ask, we receive of him, because we keep his *c.*, and do those things that are

pleasing in his sight. **2 Jn. 1:4-6** I rejoiced greatly that I found of thy children walking in

truth, as we have received a *c.* from the Father; **Rev. 14:12** here is the patience of the

Encouragement

Abbreviated Key Word →

saints: here are they that keep the *c.* of God, and the faith of Jesus.

*All scripture is given by
inspiration of God,
and is profitable for doctrine,
for reproof, for correction,
for instruction in righteousness:
That the man of God may be
perfect, thoroughly furnished
unto all good works.*

2 Timothy 3:16-17

The following standard scriptural abbreviation conventions apply.

THE OLD TESTAMENT

Genesis	Gen.	Ecclesiastes	Eccl.
Exodus	Ex.	The Song of Solomon	Song
Leviticus	Lev.	Isaiah	Isa.
Numbers	Num.	Jeremiah	Jer.
Deuteronomy	Deut.	Lamentations	Lam.
Joshua	Josh.	Ezekiel	Ezek.
Judges	Judg.	Daniel	Dan.
Ruth	Ruth	Hosea	Hosea
1 Samuel	1 Sam.	Joel	Joel
2 Samuel	2 Sam.	Amos	Amos
1 Kings	1 Kgs.	Obadiah	Obad.
2 Kings	2 Kgs.	Jonah	Jonah
1 Chronicles	1 Chr.	Micah	Micah
2 Chronicles	2 Chr.	Nahum	Nahum
Ezra	Ezra	Habakkuk	Hab.
Nehemiah	Neh.	Zephaniah	Zeph.
Esther	Esth.	Haggai	Hag.
Job	Job	Zechariah	Zech.
Psalms	Ps.	Malachi	Mal.
Proverbs	Prov.		

THE NEW TESTAMENT
OF OUR LORD AND SAVIOUR JESUS CHRIST

Matthew	Matt.	1 Timothy	1 Tim.
Mark	Mark	2 Timothy	2 Tim.
Luke	Luke	Titus	Titus
John	John	Philemon	Philem.
The Acts	Acts	Hebrews	Heb.
Romans	Rom.	James	James
1 Corinthians	1 Cor.	1 Peter	1 Pet.
2 Corinthians	2 Cor.	2 Peter	2 Pet.
Galatians	Gal.	1 John	1 Jn.
Ephesians	Eph.	2 John	2 Jn.
Philippians	Philip.	3 John	3 Jn.
Colossians	Col.	Jude	Jude
1 Thessalonians	1 Thes.	Revelation	Rev.
2 Thessalonians	2 Thes		

ABASE (*see* Humble)

ABHOR, ABHORRENCE (*see* Despise, Hate)

ABIDE, ABODE (*see also* Dwell, House, Live, Tabernacle, Temple)

I am the vine, yea are the branches: He that abideth in me, and I in him, the same bringeth forth much fruit: for without me ye can do nothing. John 15:5 (*see also* Do, Fruit, Nothing, Vine)

John 15:5 I am the vine, ye are the branches: He that *a.* in me, and I in him, the same bringeth forth much fruit: for without me ye can do nothing; **15:7** if ye *a.* in me, and my words *a.* in you, ye shall ask what ye will, and it shall be done unto you; **1 Jn. 2:28-29** and now, little children, *a.* in him; that, when he shall appear, we may have confidence, and not be ashamed before him at his coming. If ye know that he is righteous, ye know that every one that doeth righteousness is born of him; **3:6** whosoever *a.* in him sinneth not: whosoever sinneth hath not seen him, neither known him; **2 Jn. 1:9** whosoever transgresseth, and *a.* not in the doctrine of Christ, hath not God. He that *a.* in the doctrine of Christ, he hath both the Father and the Son.

ABOMINABLE, ABOMINATION (*see also* Defile, Wicked)

Yea, they have chosen their own ways, and their soul delighteth in their abominations. Isa. 66:3 (*see also* Delight)

They provoked him to jealousy with strange gods, with abominations provoked they him to anger. Duet 32:16 (*see also* Jealousy)

God knoweth your hearts: for that which is highly esteemed among men is abomination in the sight of God. Luke 16:15 (*see also* Esteem)

And the LORD said unto them - Go through the midst of the city, through the midst of Jerusalem, and set a mark upon the foreheads of the men that sigh and that cry for all the abominations that be done in the midst thereof. Ezek. 9:4 (*see also* Cry, Mark)

The thoughts of the wicked are an abomination to the LORD: but the words of the pure are pleasant words. Prov. 15:26 (*see also* Thought, Wicked, Word)

Were they ashamed when they had committed abominations? nay, they were not at all ashamed, neither could they blush: therefore they shall fall among them that fall: at the time that I visit them they shall be cast down, saith the LORD. Jer. 6:15 (*see also* Ashamed)

Jer. 6:15 (8:12-13) were they ashamed when they had committed *a.*? nay, they were not at all ashamed, neither could they blush: therefore they shall fall among them that fall.

Thou shalt not lie with mankind, as with womankind: it is abomination. Lev. 18:22 (*see also* Thou Shalt Not)

Lev. 18:22-30 thou shalt not lie with mankind, as with womankind: it is *a.*; **20:13** if a man also lie with mankind, as he lieth with a woman, both of them have committed an *a.*: they shall surely be put to death; their blood shall be upon them.

The children of Judah have done evil in my sight, saith the LORD: they have set their abominations in the house which is called by my name, to pollute it. Jer. 7:30 (*see also* Defile, House)

Jer. 7:30 the children of Judah have done evil in my sight, saith the LORD: they have set their *a.* in the house which is called by my name, to pollute it; **32:34** they set their *a.* in the house, which is called by my name, to defile it; **Ezek. 9:4** the LORD said unto him, Go through the midst of the city, through the midst of Jerusalem, and set a mark upon the foreheads of the men that sigh and that cry for all the *a.* that be done in the midst thereof; **23:38-39** they have defiled my sanctuary in the same day, and have profaned my sabbaths. For when they had slain their children to their idols, then they came the same day into my sanctuary to profane it; **33:29** then shall they know that I am the LORD, when I have laid the land most desolate because of all their *a.* which they have committed.

Son of man, cause Jerusalem to know her abominations. Ezek. 16:2 (*see also* Jerusalem)

Ezek. 16:2 cause Jerusalem to know her *a.*; 20:4 wilt thou judge them, son of man, wilt thou judge them? cause them to know the *a.* of their fathers; 20:7 said I unto them, Cast ye away every man the *a.* of his eyes, and defile not yourselves with the idols of Egypt: I am the LORD your God; 43:8 they have even defiled my holy name by their *a.* that they have committed: wherefore I have consumed them in mine anger.

ABSTAIN, ABSTINENCE

Now the Spirit speaketh expressly, that in the latter times some shall depart from the faith, giving heed to seducing spirits, and doctrines of devils; Speaking lies in hypocrisy; having their conscience seared with a hot iron; Forbidding to marry, and commanding to abstain from meats, which God hath created to be received with thanksgiving of them which believe and know the truth. 1 Tim. 4:1-3 (*see also* Conscience, Food, Latter Day, Marriage, Meat, Thanksgiving)

ABUNDANCE, ABUNDANT

[Serve] the Lord thy God with joyfulness, and with gladness of heart, for the abundance of all things. Deut. 28:47 (*see also* Serve)

Ye shall serve the LORD your God, and he shall bless thy bread, and thy water; and I will take sickness away from the midst of thee. Ex. 23:25 (*see also* Serve)

He which soweth sparingly shall reap also sparingly; and he which soweth bountifully shall reap also bountifully. 2 Cor. 9:6 (*see also* Reap, Sow, Sparingly)

ACCOMPLISH (*see* Accountable, Diligence, Do, Fulfill, Perform)

ACCOUNTABLE, ACCOUNTABILITY (*see also* Record, Steward)

For it is written, As I live, saith the Lord, every knee shall bow to me, and every tongue shall confess to God. So then every one of us shall give account of himself to God. Rom. 14:12

His lord said unto him: Well done, thou good and faithful servant: thou hast been faithful over a few things, I will make thee ruler over many things: enter thou into the joy of thy lord. Matt. 25:21 (*see also* Steward)

ACCUSATION, ACCUSE (*see also* Charge, Judge)

Accuse not a servant unto his master, lest he curse thee, and thou be found guilty. Prov. 30:10

Against an elder, receive not an accusation but before two or three witnesses. 1 Tim. 5:19 (*see also* Elder, Witness)

A false witness shall not be unpunished, and he that speaketh lies shall not escape. Prov. 19:5 (*see also* Deceive, False Witness, Liar)

Do violence to no man, neither accuse any falsely; and be content with your wages. Luke 3:14 (*see also* False, Speak)

Matt. 15:11 not that which goeth into the mouth defileth a man; but that which cometh out of the mouth, this defileth a man; **Luke 3:14** the soldiers likewise demanded of him, saying, And what shall we do? And he said unto them, Do violence to no man, neither *a.* any falsely; and be content with your wages; **19:8-9** if I have taken any thing from any man by false *a.*, I restore him fourfold; **Acts 25:7** laid many and grievous complaints against Paul, which they could not prove; **Eph. 4:29** let no corrupt communication proceed out of your mouth, but that which is good to the use of edifying, that it may minister grace unto the hearers; **Titus 3:2** speak evil of no man, to be no brawlers, but gentle, shewing all meekness unto all men; **James 4:11-12** speak not evil one of another, brethren. He that speaketh evil of his brother, and judgeth his brother, speaketh evil of the law, and judgeth the law: but if thou judge the law, thou art not a doer of the law, but a judge.

ACKNOWLEDGE (*see also* Confess)

Hear, ye that are far off, what I have done; and, ye that are near, acknowledge my might. Isa. 33:13

LORD, thou art our father; we are the clay, and thou our potter; and we all are the work of thy hand. Isa. 64:8

Ps. 138:8 the LORD will perfect that which concerneth me: thy mercy, O LORD, endureth for ever: forsake not the works of thine own hands; **139:13** thou hast possessed my reins: thou hast covered me in my mothers womb; **Isa. 57:16** I will not contend for ever, neither will I be always wroth: for the spirit should fail before me, and the souls which I have made; **64:8** LORD, thou art our father; we are the clay, and thou our potter; and we all are the work of thy hand; **Jer. 18:2-6** the word of the LORD came to me, saying, O house of Israel, cannot I do with you as this potter? saith the LORD. Behold, as the clay is in the potters hand, so are ye in mine hand.

In all thy ways acknowledge him, and he shall direct thy paths. Prov. 3:6 (*see also* Direct, Way)

Prov. 3:6 in all thy ways *a.* him, and he shall direct thy paths; **4:11-12** I have taught thee in the way of wisdom; I have led thee in right paths. When thou goest, thy steps shall not be straitened; and when thou runnest, thou shalt not stumble; **4:18** the path of the just is as the shining light, that shineth more and more unto the perfect day; **Hosea 5:15** I will go and return to my place, till they *a.* their offence, and seek my face: in their affliction they will seek me early.

Acknowledge thine iniquity that thou hast transgressed against the LORD thy God, and hast scattered thy ways to the strangers under every green tree, and ye have not obeyed my voice, saith the LORD. Jer. 3:13 (*see also* Iniquity)

Jer. 3:13 *a.* thine iniquity, that thou hast transgressed against the LORD thy God, and hast scattered thy ways to the strangers under every green tree, and ye have not obeyed my voice, saith the LORD.

ADD, ADDITIONAL (*see also* Increase)

Ye shall not add unto the word which I command you, neither shall ye diminish ought from it, that ye may keep the commandments of the LORD your God which I command you. Deut. 4:2 (*see also* Diminish, Word)

Which of you by taking thought can add one cubit unto his stature? Matt. 6:27 (*see also* Faith)

ADMONISH, ADMONITION (*see also* Rebuke, Warn)

Ye fathers, provoke not your children to wrath: but bring them up in the nurture and admonition of the Lord. Eph. 6:4 (*see also* Children, Nurture)

Eph. 6:4 ye fathers, provoke not your children to wrath: but bring them up in the nurture and *a.* of the Lord; **Col. 3:22** Fathers, provoke not your children to anger, lest they be discouraged.

Let the word of Christ dwell in you richly in all wisdom; teaching and admonishing one another in psalms and hymns and spiritual songs, singing with grace in your hearts to the Lord. Col. 3:16 (*see also* Grace, Hymn, Psalm, Sing, Wisdom, Word)

Rom. 15:14 ye also are full of goodness, filled with all knowledge, able also to *a.* one another; **1 Cor. 4:14-17** I write not these things to shame you, but as my beloved sons I warn you; **Eph. 5:19-20** speaking to yourselves in psalms and hymns and spiritual songs, singing and making melody in your heart to the Lord; Giving thanks always for all things unto God and the Father in the name of our Lord Jesus Christ; **Col. 3:16** let the word of Christ dwell in you richly in all wisdom; teaching and *a.* one another in psalms and hymns and spiritual songs, singing with grace in your hearts to the Lord; **James 5:13** is any merry? let him sing psalms.

ADOPT, ADOPTION

For as many as are led by the Spirit of God, they are the sons of God. For ye have not received the spirit of bondage again to fear; but ye have received the Spirit of adoption, whereby we cry, Abba, Father. Rom 8:14-18 (*see also* Father, Heir)

ADULTERY (*see also* Chastity, Fornication, Whoredom)

Thou shalt not lie carnally with thy neighbour's wife, to defile thyself with her. Lev. 18:20-24 (*see also* Defile)

Whosoever putteth away his wife, and marrieth another, committeth adultery: and whosoever marrieth her that is put away from her husband committeth adultery. Luke 16:18 (*see also* Divorce)

Thou shalt not commit adultery. Ex. 20:14 (*see also* Thou Shalt Not, Mosiah 13:22)

Gen. 20:3 thou art but a dead man, for the woman which thou hast taken; for she is a mans wife; **20:5** she, even she herself said, He is my brother: in the integrity of my heart and innocency of my hands have I done this; **20:7** restore the man his wife; for he is a prophet, and he shall pray for thee, and thou shalt live; **39:9** neither hath he kept back any thing from me but thee, because thou art his wife: how then can I do this great wickedness, and sin against God; **39:12** she caught him by his garment, saying, Lie with me: and he left his garment in her hand, and fled, and got him out; **Ex. 20:14** thou shalt not commit adultery; **Lev. 18:20** thou shalt not lie carnally with thy neighbour's wife, to defile thyself with her; **20:10-12** the man that committeth *a.* with another mans wife, even he that committeth *a.* with his neighbour's wife, the adulterer and the adulteress shall surely be put to death; **Num. 5:19-22** if thou hast gone aside to another instead of thy husband, and if thou be defiled, and some man have lain with thee beside thine husband: Then the priest shall charge the woman with an oath of cursing; **5:28-31** if the woman be not defiled, but be clean; then she shall be free, and shall conceive seed; **Deut. 5:18** neither shalt thou commit *a.*; **Job 24:15** the eye also of the adulterer waiteth for the twilight, saying, No eye shall see me: and disguiseth his face; **Prov. 6:24-29** he that goeth in to his neighbours wife; whosoever toucheth her shall not be innocent; **6:32-35** whoso committeth *a.* with a woman lacketh understanding: he that doeth it destroyeth his own soul; **7:6-27** with her much fair speech she caused him to yield, with the flattering of her lips she forced him. He goeth after her straightway, as an ox goeth to the slaughter; **30:20** such is the way of an adulterous woman; she eateth, and wipeth her mouth, and saith, I have done no wickedness; **Jer. 3:8** I saw, when for all the causes whereby backsliding Israel committed *a.* I had put her away, and given her a bill of divorce; **5:7** how shall I pardon thee for this? thy children have forsaken me... when I had fed them to the full, they then committed *a.*; **7:9** will ye steal, murder, and commit *a.*, and swear falsely,

and burn incense unto Baal, and walk after other gods whom ye know not; **9:2** for they be all adulterers, an assembly of treacherous men; **13:27** I have seen thine *a.*, and thy neighings, the lewdness of thy whoredom, and thine abominations; **23:10** the land is full of adulterers; for because of swearing the land mourneth; the pleasant places of the wilderness are dried up, and their course is evil; **23:14** I have seen... an horrible thing: they commit *a.*, and walk in lies: they strengthen also the hands of evildoers, that none doth return from his wickedness; **29:23** they have committed villany in Israel, and have committed *a.* with their neighbour's wives, and have spoken lying words in my name, which I have not commanded them; **30:14-15** all thy lovers have forgotten thee; they seek thee not; for I have wounded thee with the wound of an enemy, with the chastisement of a cruel one, for the multitude of thine iniquity; **Ezek. 16:32** as a wife that committeth *a.*, which taketh strangers instead of her husband; **18:6** hath not eaten upon the mountains, neither hath lifted up his eyes to the idols of the house of Israel, neither hath defiled his neighbour's wife; **18:15** that hath not eaten upon the mountains, neither hath lifted up his eyes to the idols of the house of Israel, hath not defiled his neighbour's wife; **22:11** one hath committed abomination with his neighbour's wife; and another hath lewdly defiled his daughter in law; **23:37** they have committed *a.*, and blood is in their hands, and with their idols have they committed *a.*; **23:43-48** said I unto her that was old in *a.*, Will they now commit whoredoms with her, and she with them; **Hosea 2:3-13** I will not have mercy upon her children; for they be the children of whoredoms. For their mother hath played the harlot: she that conceived them hath done shamefully; **4:1-5** the LORD hath a controversy with the inhabitants of the land, because there is no truth, nor mercy, nor knowledge of God in the land. By swearing, and lying, and killing, and stealing, and committing *a.*; **4:13** therefore your daughters shall commit whoredom, and your spouses shall commit *a.*; **7:4** they are all adulterers, as an oven heated by the baker, who ceaseth from raising after he hath kneaded the dough; **Mal. 3:5** I will be a swift witness against the sorcerers, and against the *a.,* and against false swearers, and against those that oppress; **Mark 10:19** thou knowest the commandments, Do not commit *a.*; **Rom. 13:9** thou shalt not commit adultery.

ADVERSARY (*see also* Devil, Enemy, Satan)

Be sober, be vigilant; because your adversary the devil, as a roaring lion, walketh about, seeking whom he may devour: 1 Pet. 5:8 (*see also* Sober, Vigilant)

Give none occasion to the adversary to speak reproachfully. 1 Tim. 5:14

Agree with thine adversary quickly, whiles thou art in the way with him; lest at any time the adversary deliver thee to the judge, and the judge deliver thee to the officer, and thou be cast into prison. Matt. 5:25 (*see also* Agree, Contend)

Matt. 5:25-26 agree with thine *a.* quickly, whiles thou art in the way with him; lest at any time the *a.* deliver thee to the judge, and the judge deliver thee to the officer, and thou be cast into prison. Verily I say unto thee, Thou shalt by no means come out thence, till thou hast paid the uttermost farthing; **5:38-40** ye have heard that it hath been said, An eye for an eye, and a tooth for a tooth: But I say unto you, That ye resist not evil: but whosoever shall smite thee on thy right cheek, turn to him the other also. And if any man will sue thee at the law, and take away thy coat, let him have thy cloke also.

ADVERSITY (*see* Afflict, Suffer, Trouble)

AFFAIRS

A good man sheweth favour, and lendeth: he will guide his affairs with discretion. Ps. 112:5

Ps. 112:5-6 a good man sheweth favour, and lendeth: he will guide his *a.* with discretion; **Prov. 1:4** to give subtilty to the simple, to the young man knowledge and discretion; **2:11** discretion shall preserve thee, understanding shall keep thee; **5:2** that thou mayest regard discretion, and that thy lips may keep knowledge; **11:22** as a jewel of gold in a swines snout, so is a fair woman which is without discretion.

AFFECTION (*see also* Charity, Friendship, Kindness, Love)

Set your affection on things above, not on things on the earth. Col. 3:2

AFFLICT, AFFLICTION (*see also* Adversity, Chasten, Oppress, Persecute, Sorrow, Suffer, Trouble)

O LORD, my strength, and my fortress, and my refuge in the day of affliction. Jer. 16:19

To him that is afflicted, pity should be shewed from his friend. Job 6:14 (*see also* Pity)

Behold, I have refined thee, but not with silver; I have chosen thee in the furnace of affliction. Isa. 48:10 (*see also* Furnace, Refine)

If thou draw out thy soul to the hungry, and satisfy the afflicted soul; then shall thy light rise in obscurity, and thy darkness be as the noonday: And the LORD shall guide thee continually. Isa. 58:10 (*see also* Hunger, Soul)

I know your manifold transgressions and your mighty sins: they afflict the just, they take a bribe, and they turn aside the poor in the gate from their right. Amos 5:12 (*see also* Bribe, Just)

Many are the afflictions of the righteous: but the LORD delivereth him out of them all Ps. 34:19 (*see also* Patience)

Ps. 34:19-20 many are the *a.* of the righteous: but the LORD delivereth him out of them all; **44:17-18** all this is come upon us; yet have we not forgotten thee, neither have we dealt falsely in thy covenant. Our heart is not turned back, neither have our steps declined from thy way; **44:22** for thy sake are we killed all the day long; we are counted as sheep for the slaughter; **71:20-21** thou, which hast shewed me great and sore troubles, shalt quicken me again, and shalt bring me up again from the depths of the earth. Thou shalt increase my greatness, and comfort me on every side; **102:8-12** thou hast lifted me up, and cast me down. My days are like a shadow that declineth; and I am withered like grass. But thou, O LORD, shalt endure for ever; and thy remembrance unto all generations; **105:19** until the time that his word came: the word of the LORD tried him; **Eccl. 7:8** better is the end of a thing than the beginning thereof: and the patient in spirit is better than the proud in spirit; **Isa. 54:11** O thou *a.*, tossed with tempest, and not comforted, behold, I will lay thy stones with fair colours, and lay thy foundations with sapphires.

The poor man cried, and the LORD heard him, and saved him out of all his troubles. Ps. 34:6 (*see also* Cry)

2 Chron. 14:11 Asa cried unto the LORD his God, and said, LORD, it is nothing with thee to help, whether with many, or with them that have no power: help us, O LORD our God; for we rest on thee; **15:4** when they in their trouble did turn unto the LORD God of Israel, and sought him, he was found of them; **20:9** if, when evil cometh upon us... we stand before this house, and in thy presence, [for thy name is in this house,] and cry unto thee in our *a.*, then thou wilt hear and help; **33:12** when he was in *a.*, he besought the LORD his God, and humbled himself greatly before the God of his fathers; **34:27** because thine heart was tender, and thou didst humble thyself before God... and didst rend thy clothes, and weep before me; I have even heard thee also, saith the LORD; **Ezra 8:21-23** I proclaimed a fast there, at the river of Ahava, that we might *a.* ourselves before our God, to seek of him a right way for us, and for our little ones, and for all our substance; **9:6** O my God, I am ashamed and blush to lift up my face to thee, my God: for our iniquities are increased over our head, and our trespass is grown up unto the heavens; **Neh. 9:4** then stood up upon the stairs, of the Levites, Jeshua, and Bani, Kadmiel, Shebaniah, Bunni, Sherebiah, Bani, and Chenani, and cried with a loud voice unto the LORD their God; **Job 5:6-9** I would seek unto God, and unto God would I commit my cause: Which doeth great things and unsearchable; marvellous things without number; **23:10** he knoweth the way that I take: when he hath tried me, I shall come forth as gold; **34:28** they cause the cry of the poor to come unto him, and he heareth the cry of the *a.*; **36:8-9** if they be bound in fetters, and be holden in cords of *a.*; Then he sheweth them their work, and their transgressions that they have exceeded; **36:15** he delivereth the poor in his *a.*, and openeth their ears in oppression; **Ps. 3:4** I cried unto the LORD with my voice, and he heard me out of his holy hill; **6:6-8** depart from me, all ye workers of iniquity; for the LORD hath heard the voice of my weeping; **11:4** the LORD is in his holy temple, the LORD's throne is in heaven: his eyes behold, his eyelids try, the children of men; **18:6** in my distress I called upon the LORD, and cried unto my God: he heard my voice out of his temple, and my cry came before him, even into his ears; **18:27** thou wilt save the *a.* people; but wilt bring down high looks; **22:2** O my God, I cry in the daytime, but thou hearest not; and in the night season, and am not silent; **22:5** they cried unto

thee, and were delivered: they trusted in thee, and were not confounded; **22:24** he hath not despised nor abhorred the *a.* of the afflicted; neither hath he hid his face from him; but when he cried unto him, he heard; **25:16-18** turn thee unto me, and have mercy upon me; for I am desolate and *a.*. The troubles of my heart are enlarged: O bring thou me out of my distresses. Look upon mine *a.* and my pain; and forgive all my sins; **28:1-2** unto thee will I cry, O LORD my rock; be not silent to me: lest, if thou be silent to me, I become like them that go down into the pit. Hear the voice of my supplications, when I cry unto thee; **30:2** O LORD my God, I cried unto thee, and thou hast healed me; **30:5** his anger endureth but a moment; in his favour is life: weeping may endure for a night, but joy cometh in the morning; **30:8** I cried to thee, O LORD; and unto the LORD I made supplication; **30:10-11** hear, O LORD, and have mercy upon me: LORD, be thou my helper; **31:7** I will be glad and rejoice in thy mercy: for thou hast considered my trouble; thou hast known my soul in adversities; **31:9** have mercy upon me, O LORD, for I am in trouble: mine eye is consumed with grief, yea, my soul and my belly; **31:22** I said in my haste, I am cut off from before thine eyes: nevertheless thou heardest the voice of my supplications when I cried unto thee; **32:3-4** when I kept silence, my bones waxed old through my roaring all the day long. For day and night thy hand was heavy upon me: my moisture is turned into the drought of summer; **34:6** this poor man cried, and the LORD heard him, and saved him out of all his troubles; **34:15-17** the eyes of the LORD are upon the righteous, and his ears are open unto their cry... The righteous cry, and the LORD heareth, and delivereth them out of all their troubles; **39:12** hear my prayer, O LORD, and give ear unto my cry; hold not thy peace at my tears; **40:1** I waited patiently for the LORD; and he inclined unto me, and heard my cry; **42:4** when I remember these things, I pour out my soul in me: for I had gone with the multitude, I went with them to the house of God, with the voice of joy and praise; **44:25-26** our soul is bowed down to the dust: our belly cleaveth unto the earth. Arise for our help, and redeem us for thy mercies sake; **55:1-2** give ear to my prayer, O God; and hide not thyself from my supplication. Attend unto me, and hear me: I mourn in my complaint, and make a noise; **55:17** evening, and morning, and at noon, will I pray, and cry aloud: and he shall hear my voice; **56:9** when I cry unto thee, then shall mine enemies turn back: this I know; for God is for me; **57:2** I will cry unto God most high; unto God that performeth all things for me; **61:1-2** hear my cry, O God; attend unto my prayer. From the end of the earth will I cry unto thee, when my heart is overwhelmed: lead me to the rock that is higher than I; **66:11** thou broughtest us into the net; thou laidst *a.* upon our loins; **66:17** I cried unto him with my mouth, and he was extolled with my tongue; **66:19-20** verily God hath heard me; he hath attended to the voice of my prayer. Blessed be God, which hath not turned away my prayer, nor his mercy from me; **72:12** he shall deliver the needy when he crieth; the poor also, and him that hath no helper; **84:2** my soul longeth, yea, even fainteth for the courts of the LORD: my heart and my flesh crieth out for the living God; **88:6-9** I am shut up, and I cannot come forth. Mine eye mourneth by reason of *a.*: LORD, I have called daily upon thee, I have stretched out my hands unto thee; **89:26** he shall cry unto me, Thou art my father, my God, and the rock of my salvation; **102:1-2** hear my prayer, O LORD, and let my cry come unto thee. Hide not thy face from me in the day when I am in trouble; incline thine ear unto me: in the day when I call answer me speedily; **106:44** he regarded their *a.*, when he heard their cry; **107:6** they cried unto the LORD in their trouble, and he delivered them out of their distresses; **107:10** such as sit in darkness and in the shadow of death, being bound in *a.* and iron; **107:13** they cried unto the LORD in their trouble, and he saved them out of their distresses; **107:19** they cry unto the LORD in their trouble, and he saveth them out of their distresses; **107:28** they cry unto the LORD in their trouble, and he bringeth them out of their distresses; **107:39** they are minished and brought low through oppression, *a.*, and sorrow; **107:41** setteth he the poor on high from *a.*, and maketh him families like a flock; **116:1-10** I love the LORD, because he hath heard my voice and my supplications. Because he hath inclined his ear unto me, therefore will I call upon him as long as I live; **116:13** I will take the cup of salvation, and call upon the name of the LORD; **116:17** I will offer to thee the sacrifice of thanksgiving, and will call upon the name of the LORD; **118:5** I called upon the LORD in distress: the LORD answered me, and set me in a large place; **118:25** save now, I beseech thee, O LORD: O LORD, I beseech thee, send now prosperity; **119:49-50** remember the word unto thy servant, upon which thou hast caused me to hope. This is my comfort in my *a.*: for thy word hath quickened me; **119:71-72** it is good for me that I have been *a.*; that I might learn thy statutes; **119:75** I know, O LORD, that thy judgments are right, and that thou in faithfulness hast *a.* me;

119:86 all thy commandments are faithful: they persecute me wrongfully; help thou me; **119:107-108** I am *a.* very much: quicken me, O LORD, according unto thy word. Accept, I beseech thee, the freewill offerings of my mouth, O LORD, and teach me thy judgments; **119:145** I cried with my whole heart; hear me, O LORD: I will keep thy statutes; **119:169** let my cry come near before thee, O LORD: give me understanding according to thy word; **120:1** in my distress I cried unto the LORD, and he heard me; **121:1-2** I will lift up mine eyes unto the hills, from whence cometh my help. My help cometh from the LORD, which made heaven and earth; **126:5-6** they that sow in tears shall reap in joy. He that goeth forth and weepeth, bearing precious seed, shall doubtless come again with rejoicing; **130:1-2** out of the depths have I cried unto thee, O LORD. Lord, hear my voice: let thine ears be attentive to the voice of my supplications; **138:3** in the day when I cried thou answeredst me, and strengthenedst me with strength in my soul; **138:7-8** though I walk in the midst of trouble, thou wilt revive me: thou shalt stretch forth thine hand against the wrath of mine enemies, and thy right hand shall save me; **140:6-7** I said unto the LORD, Thou art my God: hear the voice of my supplications, O LORD. O GOD the Lord, the strength of my salvation; **140:12** I know that the LORD will maintain the cause of the *a.*, and the right of the poor; **141:1-2** LORD, I cry unto thee: make haste unto me; give ear unto my voice, when I cry unto thee. Let my prayer be set forth before thee as incense; and the lifting up of my hands as the evening sacrifice; **142:1** I cried unto the LORD with my voice; with my voice unto the LORD did I make my supplication; **142:6** attend unto my cry; for I am brought very low: deliver me from my persecutors; for they are stronger than I; **143:1** hear my prayer, O LORD, give ear to my supplications: in thy faithfulness answer me, and in thy righteousness; **145:18-19** the LORD is nigh unto all them that call upon him, to all that call upon him in truth. He will fulfil the desire of them that fear him: he also will hear their cry, and will save them; **Prov. 17:3** the fining pot is for silver, and the furnace for gold: but the LORD trieth the hearts; **18:14** the spirit of a man will sustain his infirmity; but a wounded spirit who can bear; **Eccl. 7:3** sorrow is better than laughter: for by the sadness of the countenance the heart is made better; **7:14** in the day of prosperity be joyful, but in the day of adversity consider: God also hath set the one over against the other, to the end that man should find nothing after him;

8:6-7 to every purpose there is time and judgment,therefore the misery of man is great upon him. For he knoweth not that which shall be: for who can tell him when it shall be; **Isa. 30:19** thou shalt weep no more: he will be very gracious unto thee at the voice of thy cry; when he shall hear it, he will answer thee; **33:2** O LORD, be gracious unto us; we have waited for thee: be thou their arm every morning, our salvation also in the time of trouble; **33:7** their valiant ones shall cry without: the ambassadors of peace shall weep bitterly; **43:16** thus saith the LORD, which maketh a way in the sea, and a path in the mighty waters; **48:10** I have refined thee, but not with silver; I have chosen thee in the furnace of *a.*; **48:15** I, even I, have spoken; yea, I have called him: I have brought him, and he shall make his way prosperous; **48:17** I am the LORD thy God which teacheth thee to profit, which leadeth thee by the way that thou shouldest go; **54:11** O thou *a.*, tossed with tempest, and not comforted, behold, I will lay thy stones with fair colours, and lay thy foundations with sapphires; **63:9** in all their *a.* he was *a.*, and the angel of his presence saved them: in his love and in his pity he redeemed them; and he bare them, and carried them all the days of old; **Jer. 11:20** O LORD of hosts, that judgest righteously, that triest the reins and the heart, let me see thy vengeance on them: for unto thee have I revealed my cause; **12:3** thou, O LORD, knowest me: thou hast seen me, and tried mine heart toward thee: pull them out like sheep for the slaughter, and prepare them for the day of slaughter; **16:19** O LORD, my strength, and my fortress, and my refuge in the day of *a.*; **18:19** give heed to me, O LORD, and hearken to the voice of them that contend with me; **20:12** O LORD of hosts, that triest the righteous, and seest the reins and the heart, let me see thy vengeance on them: for unto thee have I opened my cause; **Lam. 2:18-20** arise, cry out in the night: in the beginning of the watches pour out thine heart like water before the face of the Lord: lift up thy hands toward him for the life of thy young children; **Dan. 12:10** many shall be purified, and made white, and tried; but the wicked shall do wickedly: and none of the wicked shall understand; but the wise shall understand; **Hosea 5:15** I will go and return to my place, till they acknowledge their offence, and seek my face: in their *a.* they will seek me early; **7:14** they have not cried unto me with their heart, when they howled upon their beds: they assemble themselves for corn and wine, and they rebel against me; **Joel 1:14** sanctify ye a fast, call a solemn assembly, gather the elders and all the inhabitants of the land into the house

of the LORD your God, and cry unto the LORD; **1:19** O LORD, to thee will I cry: for the fire hath devoured the pastures of the wilderness, and the flame hath burned all the trees of the field; **Jonah 1:14** we beseech thee, O LORD, we beseech thee, let us not perish for this mans life, and lay not upon us innocent blood: for thou, O LORD, hast done as it pleased thee; **2:2** I cried by reason of mine *a.* unto the LORD, and he heard me; out of the belly of hell cried I, and thou heardest my voice; **Nahum 1:7** the LORD is good, a strong hold in the day of trouble; and he knoweth them that trust in him; **1:9** what do ye imagine against the LORD? he will make an utter end: *a.* shall not rise up the second time; **1:12** I have *a.* thee, I will *a.* thee no more.

AFRAID (*see also* Fear)

Be ye afraid of the sword: for wrath bringeth the punvishments of the sword, that ye may know there is a judgment. Job 19:29 (*see also* Sword)

Be strong and of a good courage; be not afraid, neither be thou dismayed; for the LORD thy God is with thee whithersoever thou goest. Josh. 1:9 (*see also* Courage, Dismayed)

Be not afraid, only believe. Mark 5:36 (*see also* Belief)

Mark 5:36 be not *a.*, only believe; **6:50** immediately he talked with them, and saith unto them, Be of good cheer: it is I; be not *a.*; **Acts 18:9** then spake the Lord to Paul in the night by a vision, Be not *a.*, but speak, and hold not thy peace.

Be not afraid of sudden fear, neither of the desolation of the wicked, when it cometh. For the LORD shall be thy confidence, and shall keep thy foot from being taken. Prov. 3:25-26

Prov. 3:25-26 be not *a.* of sudden fear, neither of the desolation of the wicked, when it cometh. For the LORD shall be thy confidence, and shall keep thy foot from being taken; **Isa. 57:21** there is no peace, saith my God, to the wicked; **Ezek. 18:18** because he cruelly oppressed, spoiled his brother by violence, and did that which is not good among his people, lo, even he shall die in his iniquity.

AGAINST (*see also* Contend, Oppose)

Have we not all one father? hath not one God created us? why do we deal treacherously every man against his brother, by profaning the covenant of our fathers? Mal. 2:10 (*see also* Deal)

Magnify not thyself against the Lord. Jer. 48:26 (*see also* Magnify)

Jer. 48:26 make ye him drunken: for he magnified himself *a.* the LORD: Moab also shall wallow in his vomit, and he also shall be in derision; 48:42 Moab shall be destroyed from being a people, because he hath magnified himself *a.* the LORD; 50:24 I have laid a snare for thee, and thou art also taken, O Babylon, and thou wast not aware: thou art found, and also caught, because thou hast striven *a.* the LORD; 50:29-32 recompense her according to her work; according to all that she hath done, do unto her: for she hath been proud *a.* the LORD, *a.* the Holy One of Israel; 51:1-4 I will raise up *a.* Babylon, and *a.* them that dwell in the midst of them that rise up *a.* me, a destroying wind; And will send unto Babylon fanners, that shall fan her, and shall empty her land; Ezek. 14:13 when the land sinneth *a.* me by trespassing grievously, then will I stretch out mine hand upon it, and will break the staff of the bread thereof, and will send famine upon it; Dan. 6:5 we shall not find any occasion against this Daniel, except we find it *a.* him concerning the law of his God; Hosea 4:7 as they
were increased, so they sinned *a.* me: therefore will I change their glory into shame; 5:7 they have dealt treacherously *a.* the LORD: for they have begotten strange children: now shall a month devour them with their portions; 6:7 they like men have transgressed the covenant: there have they dealt treacherously *a.* me; 7:13 destruction unto them! because they have transgressed against me: though I have redeemed them, yet they have spoken lies *a.* me; 7:15 though I have bound and strengthened their arms, yet do they imagine mischief *a.* me; Nahum 1:9 what do ye imagine *a.* the LORD? he will make an utter end: affliction shall not rise up the second time; 1:11 there is one come out of thee, that imagineth evil *a.* the LORD, a wicked counsellor; Mal. 3:13 your words have been stout *a.* me, saith the LORD. Yet ye say, What have we spoken so much *a.* thee.

AGREE (*see also* Approve)

Agree with thine adversary quickly, whiles thou art in the way with him; lest at any time the adversary deliver thee to the judge, and the judge deliver thee to the officer, and thou be cast into prison. Matt. 5:25 (*see also* Adversary)

Matt. 5:25 *a.* with thine adversary quickly, whiles thou art in the way with him; lest at any time the adversary deliver thee to the judge, and the judge deliver thee to the officer, and thou be cast into prison.

Friend, I do thee no wrong: didst not thou agree with me for a penny? Take that thine is, and go thy way: I will give unto this last, even as unto thee. Matt. 20:1-14 (*see also* Take)

Matt. 20:1-14 the kingdom of heaven is like unto a man that is an householder, which went out early in the morning to hire labourers into his vineyard... Friend, I do thee no wrong: didst not thou *a.* with me for a penny? Take that thine is, and go thy way: I will give unto this last, even as unto thee.

ALIVE (*see also* Eternal Life, Live)

Knowing that Christ being raised from the dead dieth no more; death hath no more dominion over him. For in that he died, he died unto sin once: but in that he liveth, he liveth unto God. Likewise reckon ye also yourselves to be dead indeed unto sin, but alive unto God through Jesus Christ our Lord. Rom. 6:9-11 (*see also* Jesus Christ, Reckon, Sin)

ALL THINGS (*see also* Things)

Let all things be done decently and in order. 1 Cor. 14:40 (*see also* Order)

Evil men understand not judgment: but they that seek the LORD understand all things. Prov. 28:5 (*see also* Seek, Understand)

I can do all things through Christ which strengtheneth me. Philip. 4:13 (*see also* Strength)

Every man that striveth for the mastery is temperate in all things. 1 Cor. 9:25 (*see also* Temperance)

These things have I spoken unto you, being yet present with you. But the Comforter, which is the Holy Ghost, whom the Father will send in my name, he shall teach you all things, and bring all things to your remembrance, whatsoever I have said unto you. John 14:25-26 (*see also* Comforter, Holy Ghost, Remembrance)

Do all things without murmurings and disputings: That ye may be blameless and harmless, the sons of God, without rebuke, in the midst of a crooked and perverse nation, among whom ye shine as lights in the world. Philip. 2:14-15 (*see also* Dispute, Murmur)

He that overcometh shall inherit all things; and I will be his God, and he shall be my son. But the fearful, and unbelieving, and the abominable, and murderers, and whore-mongers, and sorcerers, and idolaters, and all liars, shall have their part in the lake which burneth with fire and brimstone: which is the second death. Rev. 21:7 (*see also* Death, Inherit, Second, Unbelief)

Lord, thou hast searched me, and known me. Thou knowest my downsitting and mine uprising, thou understandest my thought afar off. Thou compassest my path and my lying down, and art acquainted with all my ways. For there is not a word in my tongue, but, lo, O Lord, thou knowest it altogether. Ps. 139:1-5 (*see also* Know)

According as his divine power hath given unto us all things that pertain unto life and godliness, through the knowledge of him that hath called us to glory and virtue: Whereby we are given unto us exceeding great and precious promises: that by these ye might be partakers of the divine nature, having escaped the corruption that is in the world through lust. 2 Pet. 1:3-4 (*see also* Divine Nature, Knowledge, Lust, Promise)

The woman saith unto him, I know that Messias cometh, which is called Christ: when he is come, he will tell us all things. John 4:25 (*see also* Messiah)

Matt. 10:29-31 are not two sparrows sold for a farthing? and one of them shall not fall on the ground without your Father. But the very hairs of your head are all numbered. Fear ye not therefore, ye are of more value than many sparrows; Mark 11:2-3 (Luke 19:30-31) go your

way into the village over against you: and as soon as ye be entered into it, ye shall find a colt tied; Luke 22:8-13 go ye into the city, and there shall meet you a man bearing a pitcher of water: follow him. And wheresoever he shall go in, say ye to the goodman of the house, The Master saith, Where is the guestchamber, where I shall eat the passover with my disciples?; 14:18-19 one of you which eateth with me shall betray me; Luke 9:51 when the time was come that he should be received up, he stedfastly set his face to go to Jerusalem; 12:6 are not five sparrows sold for two farthings, and not one of them is forgotten before God; 13:33 must walk to day, and to morrow, and the day following: for it cannot be that a prophet perish out of Jerusalem; 16:15 God knoweth your hearts: for that which is highly esteemed among men is abomination in the sight of God; 18:31-32 he took unto him the twelve, and said unto them, Behold, we go up to Jerusalem, and *a.t.* that are written by the prophets concerning the Son of man shall be accomplished; 19:5-6 when Jesus came to the place, he looked up, and saw him, and said unto him, Zacchaeus, make haste, and come down; for to day I must abide at thy house. And he made haste, and came down, and received him joyfully; 20:26 they could not take hold of his words before the people: and they marvelled at his answer, and held their peace; 22:21-22 the hand of him that betrayeth me is with me on the table; John 1:48 Nathanael saith unto him, Whence knowest thou me? Jesus answered and said unto him, Before that Philip called thee, when thou wast under the fig tree, I saw thee; 4:17-18 the woman answered and said, I have no husband. Jesus said unto her, Thou hast well said, I have no husband: For thou hast had five husbands; and he whom thou now hast is not thy husband: in that saidst thou truly; 4:25 the woman saith unto him, I know that Messias cometh, which is called Christ: when he is come, he will tell us *a.t.*; 6:15 when Jesus therefore perceived that they would come and take him by force, to make him a king, he departed again into a mountain himself alone; 7:8 go ye up unto this feast: I go not up yet unto this feast; for my time is not yet full come; 13:1 Jesus knew that his hour was come that he should depart out of this world unto the Father, having loved his own which were in the world, he loved them unto the end; 16:30 now are we sure that thou knowest *a.t.*, and needest not that any man should ask thee: by this we believe that thou camest forth from God; 18:4 Jesus therefore, knowing *a.t.* that should immediately the cock crew; 19:28 Jesus knowing come upon him, went forth, and said unto them, Whom seek ye; **18:27** Peter then denied again: and that *a.t.* were now accomplished, that the scripture might be fulfilled, saith, I thirst; **2 Cor. 11:31** God and Father of our Lord Jesus Christ, which is blessed for evermore, knoweth that I lie not; **Eph. 1:11** in whom also we have obtained an inheritance, being predestinated according to the purpose of him who worketh *a.t.* after the counsel of his own will.

The things which are impossible with men are possible with God. Luke 18:27 (*see also* Possible)

Matt. 3:9 think not to say within yourselves, We have Abraham to our father: for I say unto you, that God is able of these stones to raise up children unto Abraham; **9:28** Jesus saith unto them, Believe ye that I am able to do this; **9:35** Jesus went about all the cities and villages, teaching in their synagogues, and preaching the gospel of the kingdom, and healing every sickness and every disease among the people; **15:28** O woman, great is thy faith: be it unto thee even as thou wilt. And her daughter was made whole from that very hour; **15:35-39** (Mark 8:2-9) he took the seven loaves and the fishes, and gave thanks, and brake them, and gave to his disciples, and the disciples to the multitude. And they did all eat, and were filled; **19:26** with men this is impossible; but with God *a.t.* are possible; **26:53-54** thinkest thou that I cannot now pray to my Father, and he shall presently give me more than twelve legions of angels; **28:18** all power is given unto me in heaven and in earth; **Mark 4:39-41** he arose, and rebuked the wind, and said unto the sea, Peace, be still. And the wind ceased, and there was a great calm; **5:43** straightway the damsel arose, and walked; **6:47-50** they saw him walking upon the sea, they supposed it had been a spirit, and cried out: For they all saw him, and were troubled. And immediately he talked with them, and saith unto them, Be of good cheer: it is I; be not afraid; **7:37** were beyond measure astonished, saying, He hath done *a.t.* well: he maketh both the deaf to hear, and the dumb to speak; **9:23** if thou canst believe, *a.t.* are possible to him that believeth; **10:27** with men it is impossible, but not with God: for with God *a.t.* are possible; **14:36** Abba, Father, *a.t.* are possible unto thee; take away this cup from me: nevertheless not what I will, but what thou wilt; **Luke 1:37** for with God nothing shall be impossible; **5:23-24** whether is easier, to say, Thy sins be forgiven thee; or to say, Rise up and walk? But that ye

may know that the Son of man hath power upon earth to forgive sins, (he said unto the sick of the palsy,) I say unto thee, Arise, and take up thy couch, and go into thine house; **7:21** in that same hour he cured many of their infirmities and plagues, and of evil spirits; and unto many that were blind he gave sight; **8:25** what manner of man is this! for he commandeth even the winds and water, and they obey him; **8:30-36** And Jesus asked him, saying, What is thy name? And he said, Legion: because many devils were entered into him. And they then went the devils out of the man, and entered into the swine: and the herd ran violently down a steep place into the lake, and were choked; **8:49** fear not: believe only, and she shall be made whole; **9:42-43** they were all amazed at the mighty power of God. But while they wondered every one at *a.t.* which Jesus did; **18:27** (Matt. 19:26) the things which are impossible with men are possible with God; **21:33** heaven and earth shall pass away: but my words shall not pass away; **23:46** Father, into thy hands I commend my spirit:and having said thus, he gave up the ghost; **24:15-16** while they communed together and reasoned, Jesus himself drew near, and went with them. But their eyes were holden that they should not know him; **24:45** then opened he their understanding, that they might understand the scriptures; **John 1:51** hereafter ye shall see heaven open, and the angels of God ascending and descending upon the Son of man; **5:20-21** the Father loveth the Son, and sheweth him *a.t.* that himself doeth: and he will shew him greater works than these, that ye may marvel. For as the Father raiseth up the dead, and quickeneth them; even so the Son quickeneth whom he will; **6:19** they see Jesus walking on the sea, and drawing nigh unto the ship: and they were afraid; **11:15** I am glad for your sakes that I was not there, to the intent ye may believe; **13:3** Jesus knowing that the Father had given *a.t.* into his hands, and that he was come from God, and went to God; **14:29** I have told you before it come to pass, that, when it is come to pass, ye might believe; **19:11** thou couldest have no power at all against me, except it were given thee from above: therefore he that delivered me unto thee hath the greater sin; **Rom. 11:36** for of him, and through him, and to him, are *a.t.*: to whom be glory for ever; **2 Cor. 9:8** God is able to make all grace abound toward you; that ye, always having all sufficiency in *a.t.*, may abound to every good work; **Eph. 1:3** blessed be the God and Father of our Lord Jesus Christ, who hath blessed us with all spiritual blessings in heavenly places in Christ; **3:9** to make all men see what is the fellowship of the mystery, which from the beginning of the world hath been hid in God, who created *a.t.* by Jesus Christ; **3:20** unto him that is able to do exceeding abundantly above all that we ask or think, according to the power that worketh in us; **Philip. 3:20-21** for our conversation is in heaven; from whence also we look for the Saviour, the Lord Jesus Christ: Who shall change our vile body, that it may be fashioned like unto his glorious body, according to the working whereby he is able even to subdue *a.t.* unto himself; **Heb. 3:4** every house is builded by some man; but he that built *a.t.* is God; **4:13** neither is there any creature that is not manifest in his sight: but *a.t.* are naked and opened unto the eyes of him with whom we have to do; **11:19** God was able to raise him up, even from the dead.

ALMS, ALMSGIVING (*see also* Charity)

Cornelius, a centurion of the band called the Italian band, a devout man, and one that feared God with all his house, which gave much alms to the people, and prayed to God alway. Acts 10:2

Acts 10:2 a devout man, and one that feared God with all his house, which gave much *a.* to the people, and prayed to God alway; **10:31** thy prayer is heard, and thine *a.* are had in remembrance in the sight of God.

When thou doest alms let not thy left hand know what thy right hand doeth; That thine alms may be in secret: and thy Father which seeth in secret himself shall reward thee openly. Matt 6:4

Matt. 6:1 take heed that ye do not your *a.* before men, to be seen of them: otherwise ye have no reward of your Father which is in heaven; **6:2** when thou doest thine *a.,* do not sound a trumpet before thee, as the hypocrites do in the synagogues and in the streets, that they may have glory of men. Verily I say unto you, They have their reward; **6:3-4** when thou doest *a.,* let not thy left hand know what thy right hand doeth: That thine *a.* may be in secret: and thy Father which seeth in secret himself shall reward thee openly; **6:6** when thou prayest, enter into thy closet, and when thou hast shut thy door, pray to thy Father which is in secret; and thy Father which seeth in secret shall reward thee openly; **6:18** that thou appear not unto men to fast, but unto thy Father which is in secret: and thy

Father, which seeth in secret, shall reward thee openly; **Mark 12:40** for a pretence make long prayers: these shall receive greater damnation; **Acts 10:4** thy prayers and thine *a.* are come up for a memorial before God.

ALPHA (*see also* Beginning, Jesus Christ)

I am Alpha and Omega, the beginning and the ending, saith the Lord, which is, and which was, and which is to come, the Almighty. Rev. 1:8 (*see also* Omega)

ALWAYS (*see also* Continue, Diligence)

Men ought always to pray, and not to faint. Luke 18:1 (*see also* Pray, Faint)

AMBASSADOR (*see also* Disciple, Minister, Prophet, Servant)

A wicked messenger falleth into mischief: but a faithful ambassador is health. Prov. 13:17

AMEND (*see also* Change, Repair)

Thus saith the Lord of hosts, the God of Israel, Amend your ways and your doings, and I will cause you to dwell in this place. Jer. 7:3 (*see also* Way)

Jer. 7:3 thus saith the Lord of hosts, the God of Israel, *A.* your ways and your doings, and I will cause you to dwell in this place; **7:5** throughly *a.* your ways and your doings... throughly execute judgment between a man and his neighbour; **26:13** *a.* your ways and your doings, and obey the voice of the Lord your God; and the Lord will repent him of the evil that he hath pronounced against you.

ANGEL (*see also* Minister, Servant)

When we cried unto the Lord, he heard our voice, and sent an angel. Num. 20:16 (*see also* Cried)

Let no man beguile you of your reward in a voluntary humility and worshiping of angels, intruding into those things which he hath not seen, vainly puffed up by his fleshly mind. Col. 2:18 (*see also* Beguile, Vain)

I saw another sign in heaven, great and marvellous, seven angels having the seven last plagues; for in them is filled up the wrath of God. **Rev. 15:1** (*see also* Plague, Seven, Sign)

Blessed be the God of Shadrach, Meshach, and Abed-nego, who hath sent his angel, and delivered his servants that trusted in him, and have changed the king's word, and yielded their bodies, that they might not serve nor worship any god, except their own God. **Dan. 3:28** (*see also* Courage, Idol, Serve, Worship)

Be not forgetful to entertain strangers: for thereby some have entertained angels unawares. **Heb. 13:2** (*see also* Stranger)

Gen. 16:7-11 the *a.* of the LORD found her by a fountain of water in the wilderness; **19:1-5** there came two *a.* to Sodom at even; and Lot sat in the gate of Sodom: and Lot seeing them rose up to meet them; **21:17** the *a.* of God called to Hagar out of heaven, and said unto her, What aileth thee, Hagar? fear not; **22:11** the *a.* of the LORD called unto him out of heaven, and said, Abraham, Abraham; **22:15** the *a.* of the LORD called unto Abraham out of heaven the second time; **24:7** the LORD God of heaven, which took me from my fathers house, and from the land of my kindred, and which spake unto me; **24:40** the LORD, before whom I walk, will send his *a.* with thee, and prosper thy way; **28:12** he dreamed, and behold a ladder set up on the earth, and the top of it reached to heaven: and behold the *a.* of God ascending and descending on it; **31:11** the *a.* of God spake unto me in a dream; **32:1** Jacob went on his way, and the *a.* of God met him; **Ex. 3:2** the *a.* of the LORD appeared unto him in a flame of fire out of the midst of a bush; **14:19** the *a.* of God, which went before the camp of Israel, removed and went behind them; **23:20** I send an *a.* before thee, to keep thee in the way, and to bring thee into the place which I have prepared; **23:23** mine *a.* shall go before thee, and bring thee in; **32:34** mine *a.* shall go before thee; **33:2** I will send an *a.* before thee; **Num. 20:16** when we cried unto the LORD, he heard our voice, and sent an *a.*, and hath brought us forth; **22:22-35** the LORD opened the eyes of Balaam, and he saw the *a.* of the LORD standing in the way, and his sword drawn in his hand; **Judg. 2:1** an *a.* of the LORD came up... and said, I made you to go up out of Egypt, and have brought you unto the land which I sware unto your fathers; **2:4** when the *a.* of the LORD spake these words unto all the children of Israel... the people lifted up their voice, and wept; **5:23** curse ye... said the

a. of the LORD, curse ye bitterly the inhabitants thereof; because they came not to the help of the LORD; **6:11-12** there came an *a.* of the LORD, and sat under an oak... And the *a.* of the LORD appeared unto him, and said unto him, The LORD is with thee; **6:20-22** when Gideon perceived that he was an *a.* of the LORD, Gideon said, Alas, O Lord GOD! for because I have seen an *a.* of the LORD face to face; **13:3** the *a.* of the LORD appeared unto the woman, and said unto her, Behold now, thou art barren, and bearest not: but thou shalt conceive, and bear a son; **13:6** the woman came and told her husband, saying, A man of God came unto me, and his countenance was like the countenance of an *a.* of God; **13:9** the *a.* of God came again unto the woman as she sat in the field; **13:13** the *a.* of the LORD said unto Manoah, Of all that I said to the woman let her beware; **13:15-21** when the flame went up toward heaven... the *a.* of the LORD ascended in the flame of the altar... Then Manoah knew that he was an *a.* of the LORD; **1 Sam. 29:9** I know that thou art good in my sight, as an *a.* of God; **2 Sam. 14:17** the word of my lord the king shall now be comfortable: for as an *a.* of God, so is my lord the king to discern good and bad; **14:20** Joab [hath] done this thing: and my lord is wise, according to the wisdom of an *a.* of God; **19:27** my lord the king is as an *a.* of God: do therefore what is good in thine eyes; **24:16-17** when the *a.* stretched out his hand upon Jerusalem to destroy it, the LORD repented him of the evil, and said to the *a.* that destroyed the people, It is enough: stay now thine hand; **1 Kgs. 13:18** an *a.* spake unto me by the word of the LORD, saying, Bring him back with thee into thine house; **19:5-7** an *a.* touched him, and said unto him, Arise and eat; **2 Kgs. 1:3** the *a.* of the LORD said to Elijah the Tishbite, Arise, go up to meet the messengers of the king; **1:15** the *a.* of the LORD said unto Elijah, Go down with him: be not afraid of him; **19:35** the *a.* of the LORD went out, and smote in the camp of the Assyrians; **1 Chron. 21:12** the *a.* of the LORD destroying throughout all the coasts of Israel; **21:15-16** God sent an *a.* unto Jerusalem to destroy it: and as he was destroying, the LORD beheld, and he repented him of the evil, and said to the *a.* that destroyed, It is enough, stay now thine hand; **21:18-20** the *a.* of the LORD commanded Gad to say to David; **2 Chron. 32:21** the LORD sent an *a.*, which cut off all the mighty men of valour, and the leaders and captains in the camp; **Ps. 34:7** the *a.* of the LORD encampeth round about them that fear him, and delivereth them; **35:5-6** let the *a.* of the LORD chase them. Let their way be dark and slippery: and let the *a.* of the LORD persecute them; **68:17** the chariots of God are twenty thousand, even thousands of *a*.: the Lord is among them; **91:11** he shall give his *a*. charge over thee, to keep thee in all thy ways; **103:20** bless the LORD, ye his *a*., that excel in strength, that do his commandments; **104:4** who maketh his *a*. spirits; his ministers a flaming fire; **148:2** praise ye him, all his *a*.: praise ye him, all his hosts; **Isa. 37:36** the *a*. of the LORD went forth, and smote in the camp of the Assyrians; **Dan. 3:28** blessed be the God of Shadrach, Meshach, and Abed-nego, who hath sent his *a*., and delivered his servants that trusted in him; **6:22** God hath sent his *a*., and hath shut the lions mouths, that they have not hurt me; **Zech. 1:9-14** the *a*. that talked with me said unto me, I will shew thee what these be; **3:1** he shewed me Joshua the high priest standing before the *a*. of the LORD; **3:5-7** the *a*. of the LORD stood by. And the *a*. of the LORD protested unto Joshua; **4:1-5** the *a*. that talked with me came again, and waked me, as a man that is wakened out of his sleep; **12:8** the house of David shall be as God, as the *a*. of the LORD before them; **Matt. 4:6** he shall give his *a*. charge concerning thee: and in their hands they shall bear thee up, lest at any time thou dash thy foot against a stone; **13:39-41** the Son of man shall send forth his *a*., and they shall gather out of his kingdom all things that offend, and them which do iniquity; **13:49** so shall it be at the end of the world: the *a*. shall come forth, and sever the wicked from among the just; **18:10** in heaven their *a*. do always behold the face of my Father which is in heaven; **22:30** for in the resurrection they neither marry, nor are given in marriage, but are as the *a*. of God in heaven; **24:31** he shall send his *a*. with a great sound of a trumpet, and they shall gather together his elect from the four winds, from one end of heaven to the other; **26:53** thinkest thou that I cannot now pray to my Father, and he shall presently give me more than twelve legions of *a*.; **Mark 8:38** when he cometh in the glory of his Father with the holy *a*.; **Luke 2:15** as the *a*. were gone away from them into heaven, the shepherds said one to another, Let us now go even unto Bethlehem; **15:10** there is joy in the presence of the *a*. of God over one sinner that repenteth; **John 1:51** hereafter ye shall see heaven open, and the *a*. of God ascending and descending upon the Son of man; **1 Cor. 6:2-3** know ye not that we shall judge *a*.? how much more things that pertain to this life; **Heb. 13:2** be not forgetful to entertain strangers: for thereby some have entertained *a*. unaware; **Rev. 18:1** after these things I saw another *a*. come down from heaven, having great power; and the earth was lightened with his glory; **19:17** I saw an *a*. standing in the sun; and he cried with a loud voice, saying to all the fowls that fly in the midst of heaven, Come and gather yourselves together unto the supper of the great God; **20:1** I saw an *a*. come down from heaven, having the key of the bottomless pit and a great chain in his hand; **22:8-9** I fell down to worship before the feet of the *a*. which shewed me these things. Then saith he unto me, See thou do it not: for I am thy fellowservant, and of thy brethren the prophets, and of them which keep the sayings of this book: worship God.

ANGER, ANGRY (*see also* Provoke, Wrath)

He that is slow to anger is better than the mighty; and he that ruleth his spirit than he that taketh a city. Prov. 16:32 (*see also* Rule, Spirit)

Do [no] evil in the sight of the LORD, to provoke him to anger. 2 Kgs. 17:17 (*see also* Evil)

Make no friendship with an angry man; and with a furious man thou shalt not go: Lest thou learn his ways, and get a snare to thy soul. Prov. 22:24-25 (*see also* Way)

A gift in secret pacifieth anger: and a reward in the bosom strong wrath. Prov. 21:14 (*see also* Gift)

Whosoever is angry with his brother without a cause shall be in danger of the judgment: and whosoever shall say to his brother, Raca, shall be in danger of the council: but whosoever shall say, Thou fool, shall be in danger of hell fire. Matt. 5:22 (*see also* Danger)

Be ye angry, and sin not: let not the sun go down upon your wrath: Neither give place to the devil. Eph. 4:26 (*see also* Go)

Eph 4:26 be ye *a*., and sin not: let not the sun go down upon your wrath; **4:31** let all bitterness, and wrath, and *a*., and clamour, and evil speaking, be put away from you, with all malice; **Col. 3:8** put off all these; *a*., wrath, malice, blasphemy, filthy communication out of your mouth.

Cease from anger, and forsake wrath: fret not thyself in any wise to do evil. Ps. 37:8 (*see also* Wrath)

Ps. 37:8 cease from *a*., and forsake wrath: fret not thyself in any wise to do evil; **Prov. 14:17** he that is soon *a*. dealeth foolishly: and a man of wicked devices is hated; **19:11** the discretion of a man deferreth his *a*.; and it is his glory to pass over a transgression.

Be not hasty in thy spirit to be angry: for anger resteth in the bosom of fools. Eccl. 7:9

Prov. 15:18 a wrathful man stirreth up strife: but he that is slow to *a*. appeaseth strife; **16:32** he that is slow to *a*. is better than the mighty; and he that ruleth his spirit than he that taketh a city; **19:11** the discretion of a man deferreth his *a*.; and it is his glory to pass over a transgression; **Eccl. 7:9** be not hasty in thy spirit to be *a*.: for *a*. resteth in the bosom of fools; **Ezek. 35:11** as I live, saith the Lord GOD, I will even do according to thine *a*., and according to thine envy which thou hast used out of thy hatred against them.

He wrought much wickedness in the sight of the LORD, to provoke him to anger. 2 Kgs. 21:6

2 Kgs. 17:11 they burnt incense in all the high places, as did the heathen whom the LORD carried away before them; and wrought wicked things to provoke the LORD to *a*.; **21:6** he wrought much wickedness in the sight of the LORD, to provoke him to *a*.; **2 Chron. 33:6** he wrought much evil in the sight of the LORD, to provoke him to *a*.; **Ps. 106:7** our fathers understood not thy wonders in Egypt; they remembered not the multitude of thy mercies; but provoked him at the sea; **106:29** they provoked him to *a*. with their inventions: and the plague brake in upon them; **Prov. 20:2** the fear of a king is as the roaring of a lion: whoso provoketh him to *a*. sinneth against his own soul; **Isa. 1:4** sinful nation, a people laden with iniquity, a seed of evildoers, children that are corrupters: they have forsaken the LORD, they have provoked the Holy One of Israel unto *a*.; **Jer. 7:19-20** do they provoke me to *a*.? saith the LORD... Behold, mine *a*. and my fury shall be poured out upon this place; **32:29-32** the children of Israel have only provoked me to *a*. with the work of their hands, saith the LORD. For this city hath been to me as a provocation of mine *a*. and of my fury from the day that they built it; **Ezek. 8:17** they have filled the land with violence, and have returned to provoke me to *a*.

ANOINT, ANOINTING (*see also* Called)

Is any sick among you? let him call for the elders of the church; and let them pray over him, anointing him with oil in the name of the Lord: And the prayer of faith shall save the sick, and the Lord shall raise him up; and if he have committed sins, they shall be forgiven him. James 5:14-15 (*see also* Elder, Heal, Oil)

Mark 6:13 *a*. with oil many that were sick, and healed them; **James 5:14-15** is any sick among you? let him call for the elders of the church; and let them pray over him, *a*. him with oil in the name of the Lord: And the prayer of faith shall save the sick, and the Lord shall raise him up; and if he have committed sins, they shall be forgiven him.

ANSWER

A man hath joy by the answer of his mouth: and a word spoken in due season, how good is it. Prov. 15:23 (*see also* Season, Word)

Answer not a fool according to his folly, lest thou also be like unto him. Answer a fool according to his folly, lest he be wise in his own conceit. Prov. 26:4-5 (*see also* Fool)

Sanctify the Lord God in your heats; and be ready always to give an answer to every man that asketh you a reason of the hope that is in you with meekness and fear: Having a good conscience; that, whereas they speak evil of you, as of evildoers, they may be ashamed that falsely accuse your good conversation in Christ. 1 Pet. 3:15-16 (*see also* Conversation, Hope, Ready, Reason, Sanctify)

He that answereth a matter before he heareth it, it is folly and shame unto him. Prov. 18:13 (*see also* Matter)

I will make there an altar unto God, who answered me in the day of my distress, and was with me in the way which I went. Gen. 35:3

Gen. 25:21-23 Isaac intreated the LORD for his wife, because she was barren: and the LORD was intreated of him, and Rebekah his wife conceived; **35:3** I will make there an altar unto God, who *a*. me in the day of my distress, and was with me in the way which I went.

A SOFT answer turneth away wrath: but grievous words stir up anger. Prov. 15:1 (*see also* Wrath)

Prov. 15:1 a SOFT *a.* turneth away wrath: but grievous words stir up anger; 18:23 the poor useth intreaties; but the rich *a.* roughly.

The heart of the righteous studieth to answer: but the mouth of the wicked poureth out evil things. Prov. 15:28 (*see also* Heart, Study)

Prov. 15:28 the heart of the righteous studieth to *a.*: but the mouth of the wicked poureth out evil things; 16:1 the preparations of the heart in man, and the *a.* of the tongue, is om the LORD.

APOSTASY (*see also* Fall, Falling Away, Rebel, Reject, Sin)

Let no man deceive you by any means: for that day shall not come, except there come a falling away first, and that man of sin be revealed, the son of perdition; who opposeth and exalteth himself above all that is called God, or that is worshiped; so that he as God sitteth in the temple of God, shewing himself that he is God. 2 Thes. 2:3-4 (*see also* Falling Away, Second Coming)

APOSTLE (*see also* Disciple, Messenger, Priesthood, Witness)

Ye are no more strangers and foreigners, but fellowcitizens with the saints, and of the household of God; And are built upon the foundation of the apostles and prophets, Jesus Christ himself being the chief corner stone. Eph. 2:19-20 (*see also* Cornerstone, Jesus Christ, Prophet, Saint)

And he gave some, apostles; and some, prophets; and some, evangelists; and some, pastors and teachers; For the perfecting of the saints, for the work of the ministry, for the edifying of the body of Christ: Till we all come in the unity of the faith, and of the knowledge of the Son of God, unto a perfect man, unto the measure of the stature of the fulness of Christ. Eph. 4:11-13 (*see also* Perfection, Prophet, Unity)

Gal 1:1 Paul, an apostle, (not of men, neither by man, but by Jesus Christ, and God the Father, who raised him from the dead); Eph. 1:1 Paul, an apostle of Jesus Christ by the will of God, to the saints which are at Ephesus, and to the

faithful in Christ Jesus; 2:20 built upon the foundation of the *a.* and prophets, Jesus Christ himself being the chief corner stone; 3:5 which in other ages was not made known unto the sons of men, as it is now revealed unto his holy *a.* and prophets by the Spirit; 4:11 and he gave some, *a.*; and some, prophets; and some, evangelists; and some, pastors and teachers Col. 1:1 Paul, an apostle of Jesus Christ by the will of God, and Timotheus our brother; 1 Tim. 1:1 Paul, an apostle of Jesus Christ by the commandment of God our Saviour, and Lord Jesus Christ, which is our hope; 2:7 whereunto I am ordained a preacher, and an apostle, (I speak the truth in Christ and lie not); Titus 1:1 Paul, a servant of God, and an apostle of Jesus Christ, according to the faith of God's elect, and the acknowledging of the truth which is after godliness.

APPAREL (*see also* Garment)

In like manner also, that women adorn themselves in modest apparel, with shamefacedness and sobriety; not with broided hair, or gold, or pearls, or costly array; but (which becometh women professing godliness) with good works. 1 Tim. 2:9-10 (*see also* Modest)

APPEAR, APPEARANCE, APPEARING

When thou fasteth, anoint thine head, and wash thy face; That thou appear not unto men to fast, but unto thy Father which is in secret; and thy Father, which seeth in secret, shall reward thee openly. Matt. 6:17-18 (*see also* Fast, Secret)

Do ye look on things after the outward appearance? 2 Cor. 10:7

Judge not according to the appearance, but judge righteous judgment. John 7:24 (*see also* Judge)

We must all appear before the judgment seat of Christ; that every one may receive the things done in his body, according to that he hath done, whether it be good or bad. 2 Cor. 5:10 (*see also* Bad, Body, Judge)

When the chief Shepherd shall appear, ye shall receive a crown of glory that fadeth not away. 1 Pet. 5:4 (*see also* Crown, Shepherd)

Abstain from all appearance of evil. 1 Thes. 5:22

1 Thes 5:22 abstain from all *a.* of evil; **1 Tim. 5:14** give none occasion to the adversary to speak reproachfully.

APPETITE (*see also* Carnal, Food, Lust, Tempt)

When thou sittest to eat with a ruler, consider diligently what is before thee: And put a knife to thy throat, if thou be a man given to appetite. Prov. 23:1-2

APPLY (*see also* Liken)

I applied mine heart to know, and to search, and to seek out wisdom, and the reason of things, and to know the wickedness of folly, even of foolishness and madness. Eccl. 7:25 (*see also* Heart, Know, Reason, Seek, Wisdom)

Incline thine ear unto wisdom, and apply thine heart to understanding. Prov. 2:2 (*see also* Understanding, Wisdom)

Prov. 2:2-5 incline thine ear unto wisdom, and *a.* thine heart to understanding; Yea, if thou criest after knowledge, and liftest up thy voice for understanding... Then shalt thou understand the fear of the LORD; **2:10** wisdom entereth into thine heart, and knowledge is pleasant unto thy soul; **23:12** apply thine heart unto instruction, and thine ears to the words of knowledge.

APPOINT, APPOINTMENT (*see also* Call)

Exact no more than that which is appointed you. Luke 3:13 (*see also* Exact)

APPROACH

They seek me daily, and delight to know my ways, as a nation that did righteousness, and forsook not the ordinance of their God: they ask of me the ordinances of justice; they take delight in approaching to God. Isa. 58:2 (*see also* Delight)

Isa. 58:2 they seek me daily, and delight to know my ways, as a nation that did righteousness, and forsook not the ordinance of their God: they ask of me the ordinances of justice; they take delight in *a.* to God.

APPROVE, APPROVED (*see also* Agree, Call)

Approve things that are excellent; that ye may be sincere and without offense till the day of Christ. Philip. 1:10 (*see also* Excellent, Offense, Sincere)

Study to shew thyself approved unto God, a workman that needeth not to be ashamed, rightly dividing the word of truth. 2 Tim. 2:15 (*see also* Study)

ARISE (*see also* Rise)

Arise, shine; for thy light is come, and the glory of the LORD is risen upon thee. Isa. 60:1 (*see also* Light)

Isa. 60:1-6 (62:10) *a.*, shine; for thy light is come, and the glory of the LORD is risen upon thee.

Arise ye, and let us go up to Zion unto the LORD our God. Jer. 31:6 (*see also* Zion)

Jer. 31:6 there shall be a day, that the watchmen upon the mount Ephraim shall cry, *A.* ye, and let us go up to Zion unto the LORD our God.

ARM, ARMED (*see* Might, Strength, Trust)

ARMOR (*see also* Righteousness)

Let us therefore cast off the works of darkness, and let us put on the armor of light. Rom. 13:12 (*see also* Light)

Rom. 13:11-12 knowing the time, that now it is high time to awake out of sleep: for now is our salvation nearer than when we believed. The night is far spent, the day is at hand: let us therefore cast off the works of darkness, and let us put on the *a.* of light; **Eph. 6:11-14** put on the whole *a.* of God, that ye may be able to stand against the wiles of the devil.

ARROGANCE, ARROGANCY, ARROGANT (*see also* Highminded, Pride, Stiffnecked)

The fear of the LORD is to hate evil: pride, and arrogancy, and the evil way, and the froward mouth, do I hate. Prov. 8:13 (*see also* Evil, Fear, Hate)

ASCRIBE

Ascribe ye strength unto God; his excellency is over Israel, and his strength is in the clouds. Ps. 68:34 (*see also* Glorify, Strength)

ASHAMED

Were they ashamed when they had committed abominations? nay, they were not at all ashamed, neither could they blush: therefore they shall fall among them that fall: at the time that I visit them they shall be cast down, saith the LORD. Jer. 6:15 (*see also* Abomination)

Be not thou therefore ashamed of the testimony of our Lord. 2 Tim. 1:8 (*see also* Testimony)

I will speak of thy testimonies also before kings, and will not be ashamed. Ps. 119:46 (*see also* Testify)

O my God, I trust in thee: let me not be ashamed, let not mine enemies triumph over me. Yea, let none that wait on thee be ashamed: let them be ashamed which transgress without cause Ps. 25:2 (*see also* Trust)

Ps. 25:2-3 O my God, I trust in thee: let me not be *a.*, let not mine enemies triumph over me. Yea, let none that wait on thee be *a.*: let them be *a.* which transgress without cause; **31:1** in thee, O LORD, do I put my trust; let me never be *a.*; **31:17** let me not be *a.*, O LORD; for I have called upon thee: let the wicked be *a.*; **69:6** let not them that wait on thee, O Lord GOD of hosts, be *a.* for my sake: let not those that seek thee be confounded for my sake, O God of Israel; **74:21** let not the oppressed return *a.*: let the poor and needy praise thy name; **119:80** let my heart be sound in thy statutes; that I be not *a.*; **119:116** uphold me according unto thy word, that I may live: and let me not be *a.* of my hope.

Whosoever shall be ashamed of me and of my words, of him shall the Son of man be ashamed, when he shall come in his own glory, and in his Father's, and of the holy angels. Luke 9:26 (*see also* Offend)

Mark 8:38 whosoever therefore shall be *a.* of me and of my words in this adulterous and sinful generation; of him also shall the Son of man be *a.*, when he cometh in the glory of his Father

with the holy angels; **Luke 9:26** whosoever shall be *a.* of me and of my words, of him shall the Son of man be *a.*, when he shall come in his own glory, and in his Father's, and of the holy angels; **Rom. 1:16** I am not *a.* of the gospel of Christ: for it is the power of God unto salvation to every one that believeth; to the Jew first, and also to the Greek; **9:33** I lay in Sion a stumblingstone and rock of offence: and whosoever believeth on him shall not be *a.*; **Philip. 1:20** according to my earnest expectation and my hope, that in nothing I shall be *a.*, but that with all boldness, as always, so now also Christ shall be magnified in my body, whether it be by life, or by death.

ASK (*see also* Beseech, Cry, Entreat, Inquire, Plead, Pray, Seek)

Thus saith the LORD, the Holy One of Israel, and his Maker, Ask me of things to come concerning my sons, and concerning the work of my hands command ye me. Isa. 45:11

If any of you lack wisdom, let him ask of God, that giveth to all men liberally, and upbraideth not; and it shall be given him. But let him ask in faith, nothing wavering. For he that wavereth is like a wave of the sea driven with the wind and tossed. James 1:5-6 (*see also* Lack, Waver, Wisdom)

Ye ask, and receive not, because ye ask amiss, that ye may consume it upon your lusts. James 4:3 (*see also* Consume, Lust)

They shall ask the way to Zion with their faces thitherward, *saying,* **Come, and let us join ourselves to the LORD in a perpetual covenant that shall not be forgotten. Jer. 50:5** (*see also* Covenant, Zion)

Ask, and it shall be given you; seek, and ye shall find; knock, and it shall be opened unto you. Luke 11:9 (*see also* Knock, Seek)

Matt. 6:8 be not ye therefore like unto them: for your Father knoweth what things ye have need of, before ye *a.* him; **7:7-9** *a.*, and it shall be given you; seek, and ye shall find; knock, and it shall be opened unto you: For every one that *a.* receiveth; and he that seeketh findeth; and to him that knocketh it shall be opened. Or what man is there of you, whom if his son *a.* bread, will he give him a stone; **7:11** if ye then, being evil, know how to give good gifts unto your children, how much more shall your Father which is in heaven give good things to them that *a.* him; **18:19-20** if two of you shall agree on earth as touching any thing that they shall *a.,* it shall be done for them of my Father which is in heaven. For where two or three are gathered together in my name, there am I in the midst of them; **21:22** all things, whatsoever ye shall *a.* in prayer, believing, ye shall receive; **Mark 7:26** she besought him that he would cast forth the devil out of her daughter; **10:35-36** Master, we would that thou shouldest do for us whatsoever we shall desire. And he said unto them, What would ye that I should do for you; **11:24** what things soever ye desire, when ye pray, believe that ye receive them, and ye shall have them; **13:3-4** tell us, when shall these things be? and what shall be the sign when all these things shall be fulfilled; **Luke 11:8-9-13** *a.,* and it shall be given you; seek, and ye shall find; knock, and it shall be opened unto you. For every one that *a.* receiveth; and he that seeketh findeth; and to him that knocketh it shall be opened. If a son shall *a.* bread of any of you that is a father, will he give him a stone? or if he *a.* a fish, will he for a fish give him a serpent? Or if he shall *a.* an egg, will he offer him a scorpion? If ye then, being evil, know how to give good gifts unto your children: how much more shall your heavenly Father give the Holy Spirit to them that *a.* him; **John 14:13-14** whatsoever ye shall *a.* in my name, that will I do, that the Father may be glorified in the Son. If ye shall *a.* any thing in my name, I will do it; **15:16** ye have not chosen me, but I have chosen you, and ordained you, that ye should go and bring forth fruit, and that your fruit should remain: that whatsoever ye shall *a.* of the Father in my name, he may give it you; **16:23-24** in that day ye shall *a.* me nothing. Verily, verily, I say unto you, Whatsoever ye shall *a.* the Father in my name, he will give it you. Hitherto have ye *a.* nothing in my name: *a.,* and ye shall receive, that your joy may be full; **Eph. 3:12** in whom we have boldness and access with confidence by the faith of him; **James 4:2-4** ye *a.,* and receive not, because ye *a.* amiss, that ye may consume it upon your lusts. Ye adulterers and adulteresses, know ye not that the friendship of the world is enmity with God? whosoever therefore will be a friend of the world is the enemy of God; **1 Jn. 3:22** whatsoever we *a.,* we receive of him, because we keep his commandments, and do those things that are pleasing in his sight; **5:14-15** this is the confidence that we have in him, that, if we *a.* any thing according to his will, he heareth us: And if we know that he hear us, whatsoever we *a.,* we know that we have the petitions that we desired of him.

ASSEMBLE, ASSEMBLIES (*see also* Gather, Meet, Sabbath, Worship)

Come ye near unto me, hear ye this; I have not spoken in secret from the beginning; from the time that it was, there *am* I: and now the Lord God, and his Spirit, hath sent me. Isa. 48:16 (*see also* Hear)

If two of you shall agree on earth as touching any thing that they shall ask, it shall be done for them of my Father which is in heaven. For where two or three are gathered together in my name, there am I in the midst of them. Matt. 18:19-20 (*see also* Gather)

Matt. 18:19-20 if two of you shall agree on earth as touching any thing that they shall ask, it shall be done for them of my Father which is in heaven. For where two or three are gathered together in my name, there am I in the midst of them; **Acts 11:26** a whole year they *a.* themselves with the church, and taught much people; **Heb. 10:25** not forsaking the *a.* of ourselves together, as the manner of some is; but exhorting one another: and so much the more, as ye see the day approaching.

ASSURANCE, ASSURE (*see also* Belief, Comfort, Faith, Know)

Let us draw near with a true heart in full assurance of faith, having our hearts sprinkled from an evil conscience, and our bodies washed with pure water. Heb. 10:22 (*see also* Draw, Heart)

Let all the house of Israel know assuredly, that God hath made that same Jesus, whom ye have crucified, both Lord and Christ. Acts 2:36 (*see also* Jesus Christ, Testify)

ASTRAY (*see also* Wander)

Whoso causeth the righteous to go astray in an evil way, he shall fall himself into his own pit; but the upright shall have good things in possession. Prov. 28:10 (*see also* Righteous, Way)

Prov. 28:10 whoso causeth the righteous to go *a.* in an evil way, he shall fall himself into his own pit: but the upright shall have good things in possession; **Ezek. 7:4** mine eye shall not spare thee, neither will I have pity: but I will recompense thy ways upon thee; **48:11** it shall be for the priests that are sanctified of the sons of Zadok; which have kept my charge, which went not *a.* when the children of Israel went *a.*

ASTROLOGER, ASTROLOGY (*see also* Sorcery, Superstitious)

Now the wise men, the astrologers, have been brought in before me, that they should read this writing, and make known unto me the interpretation thereof: but they could not shew the interpretation of the thing. **Dan 5:15** (*see also* Dream, Interpret, Magician)

ATONE, ATONEMENT (*see also* Redeem, Save)

We also joy in God through our Lord Jesus Christ, by whom we have now received the atonement. **Rom. 5:11** (*see also* Rejoice)

ATTEND (*see also*Meeting)

My son, attend to my words; incline thine ear unto my sayings. Let them not depart from thine eyes; keep them in the midst of thine heart. For they are life unto those that find them, and health to all their flesh. **Prov. 4:20-22** (*see also* Incline, Say, Word)

AUTHOR (*see also* Creator)

God is not the author of confusion, but of peace, as in all churches of the saints. **1 Cor. 14:33** (*see also* Confusion)

[Look] unto Jesus the author and finisher of our faith; who for the joy that was set before him endured the cross, despising the shame, and is set down at the right hand of the throne of God. **Heb. 12:2** (*see also* Faith, Finisher, Jesus Christ)

AUTHORITY (*see also* Called, Laying on of Hands, Keys, Priesthood)

He called his twelve disciples together, and gave them power and authority over all devils, and to cure diseases. And he sent them to preach the kingdom of God, and to heal the sick. **Luke 9:1-2** (*see also* Preach)

When the righteous are in authority, the people rejoice: but when the wicked beareth rule, the people mourn. **Prov. 29:2** (*see also* Mourn, Righteous, Rule, Wicked)

By what authority doest thou these things? and who gave thee this authority to do these things? And Jesus answered and said unto them, I will also ask of you one question, and answer me, and I will tell you by what authority I do these things. **Mark 11:28** (*see also* Do)

Mark 11:28-33 (Luke 20:2-8) By what *a.* doest thou these things? and who gave thee this *a.* to do these things? And Jesus answered and said unto them, I will also ask of you one question, and answer me, and I will tell you by what *a.* I do these things. The baptism of John, was it from heaven, or of men? answer me. And they reasoned with themselves, saying, If we shall say, From heaven; he will say, Why then did ye not believe him? But if we shall say, Of men; they feared the people: for all men counted John, that he was a prophet indeed. And they answered and said unto Jesus, We cannot tell. And Jesus answering saith unto them, Neither do I tell you by what *a.* I do these things.

Paul, being grieved, turned and said to the spirit, I command thee in the name of Jesus Christ to come out of her. And he came out the same hour. **Acts 16:18** (*see also* Unclean)

Luke 7:21 in that same hour he cured many of their infirmities and plagues, and of evil spirits; **8:2** Mary called Magdalene, out of whom went seven devils; **Acts 8:7** unclean spirits, crying with loud voice, came out of many that were possessed with them; **16:18** Paul, being grieved, turned and said to the spirit, I command thee in the name of Jesus Christ to come out of her. And he came out the same hour; **19:13-17** certain of the vagabond Jews, exorcists, took upon them to call over them which had evil spirits the name of the Lord Jesus, saying, We adjure you by Jesus whom Paul preacheth.

Therefore leaving the principles of the doctrine of Christ, let us go on unto perfection; not laying again the foundation of repentance from dead works, and of faith toward God, Of the doctrine of baptisms, and of laying on of hands, and of resurrection of the dead, and of eternal judgment. **Heb. 6:1-2** (*see also* Call, Laying on of Hands)

Acts 6:6-7 whom they set before the apostles: and when they had prayed, they laid their hands on them; **13:3** when they had fasted and prayed, and laid their hands on them, they sent them away; **14:23** when they had ordained them elders in every church, and had prayed with fasting, they commended them to the Lord, on whom they believed; **Rom. 1:1** Paul, a servant of Jesus Christ, called to be an apostle, separated unto the gospel of God; **Heb. 6:2** of the doctrine of baptisms, and of laying on of hands, and of resurrection of the dead, and of eternal judgment.

AVENGE (*see also* Recompense, Revenge, Vengeance)

Thou shalt not avenge, nor bear any grudge against the children of thy people, but thou shalt love thy neighbour as thyself: I *am* the LORD. Lev. 19:18 (*see also* Grudge)

AVOID

Avoid foolish questions, and genealogies, and contentions, and strivings about the law; for they are unprofitable and vain. Titus 3:9 (*see also* Fool)

Enter not into the paths of the wicked, and go not in the way of evil men. Avoid it, pass not by it, turn from it, and pass away. Prov. 4:14-15 (*see also* Enter, Path)

AWAKE, AWAKEN (*see also* Rise)

Awake thou that sleepest, and arise from the dead, and Christ shall give thee light. Eph. 5:14

Awake, awake; put on thy strength, O Zion; put on thy beautiful garments, O Jerusalem, the holy city. Isa. 52:1

Isa. 51:17 *a., a.*, stand up, O Jerusalem, which hast drunk at the hand of the LORD the cup of his fury; **52:1** *a., a.*; put on thy strength, O Zion; put on thy beautiful garments, O Jerusalem, the holy city.

BABBLE, BABBLING

Keep that which is committed to thy trust, avoiding profane and vain babblings, and oppositions of science falsely called: Which some professing have erred concerning the faith. 1 Tim. 6:20

1 Tim 6:20 keep that which is committed to thy trust, avoiding profane and vain *b.*, and oppositions of science falsely so called; **2 Tim. 2:16-17** shun profane and vain *b.*: for they will increase unto more ungodliness. And their word will eat as doth a canker; **3:6** for of this sort are they which creep into houses, and lead captive silly women laden with sins, led away with divers lusts.

BACKBITE, BACKBITING (*see also* Gossip, Mock, Slander)

He that backbiteth not with his tongue, nor doeth evil to his neighbour, nor taketh up a reproach against his neighbour [shall abide in thy tabernacle]. Ps. 15:3 (*see also* Reproach)

Ps. 15:3 he that *b.* not with his tongue, nor doeth evil to his neighbour, nor taketh up a reproach against his neighbour; **39:1** I will take heed to my ways, that I sin not with my tongue: I will keep my mouth with a bridle, while the wicked is before me; **Prov. 2.1:23** whoso keepeth his mouth and his tongue keepeth his soul from troubles.

BAD (*see also* Evil, Oppose, Wicked)

We must all appear before the judgment seat of Christ; that every one may receive the things done in his body, according to that he hath done, whether it be good or bad. 2 Cor. 5:10 (*see also* Appear, Body, Judge)

BALANCE (*see also* Weight)

A false balance is abomination to the LORD: but a just weight is his delight. Prov. 11:1 (*see also* Just, Weight)

Prov. 11:1 a false *b.* is abomination to the LORD: but a just weight is his delight; **12:22** lying lips are abomination to the LORD: but they that deal truly are his delight; **16:11** a just weight and *b.* are the LORD s: all the weights of the bag are his work; **20:10** divers weights, and divers measures, both of them are alike abomination to the LORD; **20:23** divers weights are an abomination unto the LORD; and a false *b.* is not good; **Ezek. 6:11** smite with thine hand, and stamp with thy foot, and say, Alas for all the evil abominations of the house of Israel! for they shall fall by the sword, by the famine, and by the pestilence; **45:10** ye shall have just *b.*, and a just ephah, and a just bath; **Amos 8:5-10** when will the new moon be gone, that we may sell corn?... falsifying the *b.* by deceit? That we may buy the poor for silver, and the needy for a pair of shoes; yea, and sell the refuse of the wheat? The LORD hath sworn... Surely I will never forget any of their works.

BAPTISM, BAPTIZE (*see also* Immersion, Ordinance, Principle)

Enter ye in at the strait gate: for wide is the gate, and broad is the way, that leadeth to destruction, and many there be which go in thereat: Because strait is the gate, and narrow is the way, which leadeth unto life, and few there be that find it. Matt. 7:13-14 (*see also* Way)

Repent, and be baptized every one of you in the name of Jesus Christ for the remission of sins, and ye shall receive the gift of the Holy Ghost. Acts 2:38 (*see also* Remission, Repent)

Matt. 3:6 were *b.* of him in Jordan, confessing their sins; **3:11** I indeed *b.* you with water unto repentance; **3:13** then cometh Jesus from Galilee to Jordan unto John, to be *b.* of him; **3:15-16** suffer it to be so now: for thus it becometh us to fulfil all righteousness. Then he suffered him. And Jesus, when he was *b.,* went up straightway out of the water: and, lo, the heavens were opened unto him, and he saw the Spirit of God descending like a dove, and lighting upon him; **28:19** go ye therefore, and teach all nations, *b.* them in the name of the Father, and of the Son, and of the Holy Ghost; **Mark 1:4** John did *b.* in the wilderness, and preach the *b.* of repentance for the remission of sins; **1:5** and were all *b.* of him in the river of Jordan, confessing their sins; **1:8** I indeed have *b.* you with water: but he shall *b.* you with the Holy Ghost; **1:9-11** Jesus came from Nazareth of Galilee, and was *b.* of John in Jordan. And straightway coming up out of the water, he saw the heavens opened, and the Spirit like a dove descending upon him: And there came a voice from heaven, saying, Thou art my beloved Son, in whom I am well pleased; **10:38-39** be *b.* with the *b.* that I am *b.* with? And they said unto him, We can. And Jesus said unto them, Ye shall indeed drink of the cup that I drink of; and with the *b.* that I am *b.* withal shall ye be *b.;* **Luke 3:3** he came into all the country about Jordan, preaching the *b.* of repentance for the remission of sins; **3:7** the multitude that came forth to be *b.* of him, O generation of vipers, who hath warned you to flee from the wrath to come; **3:12** then came also publicans to be *b.,* and said unto him, Master, what shall we do; **3:15-16** I

indeed *b.* you with water; but one mightier than I cometh, the latchet of whose shoes I am not worthy to unloose: he shall *b.* you with the Holy Ghost and with fire; **3:21** now when all the people were *b.,* it came to pass, that Jesus also being *b.,* and praying, the heaven was opened; **7:29-30** being *b.* with the *b.* of John. But the Pharisees and lawyers rejected the counsel of God against themselves, being not *b.* of him; **13:24** strive to enter in at the strait gate: for many, I say unto you, will seek to enter in, and shall not be able; **John 1:25** why *b.* thou then, if thou be not that Christ, nor Elias, neither that prophet; **1:28** these things were done in Bethabara beyond Jordan, where John was *b.;* **1:30-32** this is he of whom I said, After me cometh a man which is preferred before me: for he was before me. And I knew him not: but that he should be made manifest to Israel, therefore am I come *b.* with water. And John bare record, saying, I saw the Spirit descending from heaven like a dove, and it abode upon him; **3:22-23** there he tarried with them, and *b..* And John also was *b.* in Aenon near to Salim, because there was much water there: and they came, and were *b.;* **3:26** he that was with thee beyond Jordan, to whom thou barest witness, behold, the same *b.,* and all men come to him; **4:1-2** Jesus made and *b.* more disciples than John, Though Jesus himself *b.* not, but his disciples; **10:1** he that entereth not by the door into the sheepfold, but climbeth up some other way, the same is a thief and a robber; **Acts 2:38** repent, and be *b.* every one of you in the name of Jesus Christ for the remission of sins, and ye shall receive the gift of the Holy Ghost; **2:41** they that gladly received his word were *b.;* **8:12** when they believed Philip preaching the things concerning the kingdom of God, and the name of Jesus Christ, they were *b.,* both men and women; **8:16-17** they were *b.* in the name of the Lord Jesus; **8:36-39** they went down both into the water, both Philip and the eunuch; and he *b.* him. And when they were come up out of the water, the Spirit of the Lord caught away Philip, that the eunuch saw him no more: and he went on his way rejoicing; **9:18** immediately there fell from his eyes as it had been scales: and he received sight forthwith, and arose, and was *b.;* **10:37** after the *b.* which John preached; **10:47-48** he commanded them to be *b.* in the name of the Lord; **13:24** John had first preached before his coming the *b.* of repentance to all the people of Israel; **16:15** she was *b.,* and her household; **16:33** he took them the same hour of the night, and washed their stripes; and was *b.;* **18:8** many of the Corinthians hearing believed, and were *b.;* **19:4-5** John verily *b.* with the *b.* of repentance, saying unto the people, that they should believe on him which should come after him; **22:16** why tarriest thou? arise, and be *b.*, and wash away thy sins, calling on the name of the Lord; **Rom. 6:3-10** we are buried with him by *b.* into death: that like as Christ was raised up from the dead by the glory of the Father, even so we also should walk in newness of life; **Gal. 3:27**as many of you as have been *b.* into Christ have put on Christ; **Eph. 4:5** one Lord, one faith, one *b.*; **Col. 2:12** buried with him in *b.*, wherein also ye are risen with him through the faith of the operation of God; **1 Pet. 3:21** even *b.* doth also now save us.

BATTLE (*see also* Fight, Strife, War)

The horse is prepared against the day of battle; but safety is of the LORD. Prov. 21:31 (*see also* Prepare)

Prov. 21:31 the horse is prepared against the day of *b.*: but safety is of the LORD; **Nahum 2:1-5** keep the munition, watch the way, make thy loins strong, fortify thy power mightily. For the LORD hath turned away the excellency of Jacob, as the excellency of Israel.

BE (*see also* Become)

Be ye therefore wise as serpents and harmless as doves. Matt. 10:16 (*see also* Harmless, Wise)

Be not among winebibbers; among riotous eaters of flesh: for the drunkard and the glutton shall come to poverty: and drowsiness shall clothe a man with rags. Prov. 23:20-21 (*see also* Drunk, Wine)

Be ye not as the horse, or as the mule, which have no understanding: whose mouth must be held in with bit and bridle, lest they come near unto thee. Ps. 32:9 (*see also* Understanding)

BEAR, BORE, BORNE (*see also* Carry, Endure, Strive)

There hath no temptation. taken you but such as is common to man: but God is faithful, who will not suffer you to be tempted above that ye are able; but will with the temptation also make a way to escape, that ye may be able to bear it. 1 Cor. 10:13 (*see also* Escape, Tempt)

Charity suffereth long, and is kind; charity envieth not; charity vaunteth not itself, is not puffed up, Doth not behave itself unseemly, seeketh not her own, is not easily provoked, thinketh no evil; Rejoiceth not in iniquity, but rejoiceth in the truth; Beareth all things, believeth all things, hopeth all things, endureth all things. 1 Cor. 13:4-7 (*see also* All Things, Believe, Charity, Endure, Hope, Provoke, Rejoice, Seek, Suffer, Think)

I will bear the indignation of the LORD, because I have sinned against him, until he plead my cause, and execute judgment for me: he will bring me forth to the light, and I shall behold his righteousness. Micah 7:9-10 (*see also* Indignation, Lord)

BEAST

A righteous man regardeth the life of his beast: but the tender mercies of the wicked are cruel. Prov. 12:10

BEAUTIFUL, BEAUTIFY, BEAUTY (*see also* Pure)

Thine heart was lifted up because of thy beauty, thou hast corrupted thy wisdom by reason of thy brightness: I will cast thee to the ground. Ezek. 28:17 (*see also* Lift)

Beautify the house of the LORD which is in Jerusalem. Ezra 7:27 (*see also* House)

How beautiful upon the mountains are the feet of him that bringeth good tidings, that publisheth peace; that bringeth good tidings of good, that publisheth salvation; that saith unto Zion, Thy God reigneth! Isa. 52:7 (*see also* Good, Mountain, Peace, Publish, Zion)

Give unto the LORD the glory due unto his name: bring an offering, and come before him: worship the LORD in the beauty of holiness. 1 Chron. 16:29 (*see also* Glory, Offer)

BECOME (*see also* Be)

Though I speak with the tongues of men and of angels, and have not charity, I am become as sounding brass, or a tinkling cymbal. 1 Cor. 13:1 (*see also* Brass, Charity, Speak)

Let your conversation be as it becometh the gospel of Christ: that whether I come and see you, or else be absent, I may hear of your affairs, that ye stand fast in one spirit, with one mind striving together for the faith of the gospel. **Philip. 1:27** (*see also* Conversation, Gospel, One)

Moreover, thou son of man, take thee one stick, and write upon it, For Judah, and for the children of Israel his companions: then take another stick, and write upon it For Joseph, the stick of Ephraim, and for all the house of Israel his companions: And join them one to another into one stick; and they shall become one in thine hand. **Ezek. 37:16-17** (*see also* Bible, Stick)

Except ye be converted, and become as little children, ye shall not enter into the kingdom of heaven. **Matt. 18:3** (*see also* Child, Convert, Kingdom)

BEG, BEGGAR (*see* Ask, Beseech, Entreat, Petition, Request)

BEGAT, BEGET, BEGOTTEN (*see also* Born)

For God so loved the world, that he gave his only begotten Son, that whosoever believeth in him should not perish, but have everlasting life. **John 3:16** (*see also* Everlasting Life)

Grace be unto you, and peace, from him which is, and which was, and which is to come; and from the seven Spirits which are before his throne; And from Jesus Christ, who is the faithful witness, and the first begotten of the dead, and the prince of the kings of the earth. Unto him that loved us, and washed us from our sins in his own blood, And hath made us kings and priests unto God and his Father; to him be glory and dominion for ever and ever. Amen. **Rev. 1:4-6** (*see also* Blood, Glory, Jesus Christ)

BEGIN, BEGINNING (*see also* Create, Establish, Start)

The fear of the LORD is the beginning of knowledge: but fools despise wisdom and and instruction. **Prov. 1:7** (*see also* Instruction, Wisdom)

In the beginning was the Word, and the Word was with God, and the Word was God. **John 1:1** (*see also* God, Word)

BEGUILE (*see also* Deceive, Feign)

Let no man beguile you of your reward in a voluntary humility and worshiping of angels, intruding into those things which he hath not seen, vainly puffed up by his fleshly mind. **Col. 2:18** (*see also* Angel, Vain)

BEHAVE, BEHAVIOR (*see also* Act, Accountable, Responsible)

Thou oughtest to behave thyself in the house of God, which is the church of the living God, the pillar and ground of the truth. **1 Tim. 3:15** (*see also* House, Temple)

Be of good courage, and let us behave ourselves valiantly for our people, and for the cities of our God: and let the LORD do *that which* is good in his sight. **1 Chron. 19:13** (*see also* Courage)

1 Chron. 19:13 be of good courage, and let us *b.* ourselves valiantly for our people, and for the cities of our God: and let the LORD do that which is good in his sight; **2 Chron. 32:8** with him is an arm of flesh; but with us is the LORD our God to help us, and to fight our battles; **Ps. 60:12** through God we shall do valiantly: for he it is that shall tread down our enemies; **Jer. 9:3** they bend their tongues like their bow for lies: but they are not valiant for the truth upon the earth; for they proceed from evil to evil, and they know not me, saith the LORD.

BEHOLD (*see* Look, Observe, See)

BELIEF, BELIEVE (*see also* Assure, Confidence, Faith, Trust)

Believest thou the prophets? **Acts 26:27** (*see also* Prophet)

Be not afraid, only believe. **Mark 5:36** (*see also* Afraid)

But without faith it is impossible to please him: for he that cometh to God must believe that he is, and that he is a rewarder of them that diligently seek him. **Heb. 11:6** (*see also* Diligently, Faith, Impossible, Reward, Seek)

God hath from the beginning chosen you to salvation through sanctification of the Spirit and belief of the truth. **2 Thes. 2:13** (*see also* Salvation, True)

He commanded us to preach unto the people, and to testify that it is he which was ordained of God to be the Judge of quick and dead. To him give all the prophets witness, that through his name whosoever believeth in him shall receive remission of sins. **Acts 10:43** (*see also* Judge, Remission)

Charity suffereth long, and is kind; charity envieth not; charity vaunteth not itself, is not puffed up, Doth not behave itself unseemly, seeketh not her own, is not easily provoked, thinketh no evil; Rejoiceth not in iniquity, but rejoiceth in the truth; Beareth all things, believeth all things, hopeth all things, endureth all things. **1 Cor. 13:4-7** (*see also* All Things, Bear, Charity, Endure, Hope, Provoke, Rejoice, Seek, Suffer, Think)

Trust in the living God, who is the Saviour of all men, specially of those that believe. **1 Tim. 4:10** (*see also* Savior, Trust)

When therefore he was risen from the dead, his disciples remembered that he had said this unto them; and they believed the scripture, and the word which Jesus had said. **John 2:22** (*see also* Scripture)

Many other signs truly did Jesus in the presence of his disciples, which are not written in this book: But these are written, that ye might believe that Jesus is the Christ, the Son of God; and that believing ye might have life through his name. **John 20:30-31** (*see also* Record)

We will not serve thy gods, nor worship the golden image which thou hast set up. **Dan. 3:18** (*see also* False)

I know that thou canst do every thing, and that no thought can be withholden from thee. **Job 42:2** (*see also* Think)

Where be all his miracles which our fathers told us? **Judg. 6:13** (*see also* Miracle)

The simple believeth every word: but the prudent man looketh well to his going. **Prov. 14:15** (*see also* Word)

Let no man despise thy youth; but be thou an example of the believers, in word, in conversation, in charity, in spirit, in faith, in purity. **1 Tim. 4:12** (*see also* Charity, Conversation, Despise, Example, Pure)

1 Tim. 4:12 let no man despise thy youth; but be thou an example of the believers, in word, in conversation, in charity, in spirit, in faith, in purity.

For what knowest thou, O wife, whether thou shalt save thy husband? or how knowest thou, O man, whether thou shalt save thy wife? **1 Cor. 7:16** (*see also* Tolerance)

1 Cor 7:12-16 if any brother hath a wife that *b.* not, and she be pleased to dwell with him, let him not put her away. And the woman which hath an husband that *b.* not, and if he be pleased to dwell with her, let her not leave him. For the unbelieving husband is sanctified by the wife, and the unbelieving wife is sanctified by the husband: else were your children unclean; but now are they holy. But if the unbelieving depart, let him depart. A brother or a sister is not under bondage in such cases: but God hath called us to peace. For what knowest thou, O wife, whether thou shalt save thy husband? or how knowest thou, O man, whether thou shalt save thy wife?

These are written, that ye might believe that Jesus is the Christ, the Son of God; and that believing ye might have life through his name. **John 20:31** (*see also* Jesus Christ)

Mark 9:6-7 there was a cloud that overshadowed them: and a voice came out of the cloud, saying, This is my beloved Son: hear him; **Luke 3:16** I indeed baptize you with water; but one mightier than I cometh, the latchet of whose shoes I am not worthy to unloose: he shall baptize you with the Holy Ghost and with fire; **22:67** art thou the Christ? tell us. And he said unto them, If I tell you, ye will not *b.*; **John 1:12** as many as received him, to them gave he power to become the sons of God, even to them that *b.* on his name; **2:11** this beginning of miracles did Jesus in Cana of Galilee, and manifested forth his glory; and his disciples *b.* on him; **2:23**

many *b.* in his name, when they saw the miracles which he did; **3:15** whosoever *b.* in him should not perish, but have eternal life; **3:16-18** for God so loved the world, that he gave his only begotten Son, that whosoever *b.* in him should not perish, but have everlasting life. For God sent not his Son into the world to condemn the world; but that the world through him might be saved. He that *b.* on him is not condemned: but he that *b.* not is condemned already, because he hath not *b.* in the name of the only begotten Son of God; **3:36** he that *b.* on the Son hath everlasting life: and he that *b.* not the Son shall not see life; but the wrath of God abideth on him; **4:41** many more *b.* because of his own word; **5:37-38** the Father himself, which hath sent me, hath borne witness of me. Ye have neither heard his voice at any time, nor seen his shape. And ye have not his word abiding in you: for whom he hath sent, him ye *b.* not; **5:43** I am come in my Father's name, and ye receive me not: if another shall come in his own name, him ye will receive; **6:29** this is the work of God, that ye *b.* on him whom he hath sent; **6:35** I am the bread of life: he that cometh to me shall never hunger; and he that *b.* on me shall never thirst; **6:40** this is the will of him that sent me, that every one which seeth the Son, and *b.* on him, may have everlasting life: and I will raise him up at the last day; **6:47** he that *b.* on me hath everlasting life; **6:69** we *b.* and are sure that thou art that Christ, the Son of the living God; **7:38-39** he that *b.* on me, as the scripture hath said, out of his belly shall flow rivers of living water. this spake he of the Spirit, which they that *b.* on him should receive: for the Holy Ghost was not yet given; because that Jesus was not yet glorified; **8:24** I said therefore unto you, that ye shall die in your sins: for if ye *b.* not that I am he, ye shall die in your sins; **8:30** as he spake these words, many *b.* on him; **8:36** if the Son therefore shall make you free, ye shall be free indeed; **9:35-38** Jesus heard that they had cast him out; and when he had found him, he said unto him, Dost thou *b.* on the Son of God? He answered and said, Who is he, Lord, that I might *b.* on him? And Jesus said unto him, Thou hast both seen him, and it is he that talketh with thee. And he said, Lord, I *b.*. And he worshipped him; **10:9** I am the door: by me if any man enter in, he shall be saved, and shall go in and out, and find pasture; **10:25-26** Jesus answered them, I told you, and ye *b.* not: the works that I do in my Father's name, they bear witness of me. But ye *b.* not, because ye are not of my sheep, as I said unto you; **10:37** if I do not the works of my Father, *b.* me not; **10:41-42**all things that John spake of this man were

true. And many *b.* on him there; **11:21** said Martha unto Jesus, Lord, if thou hadst been here, my brother had not died; **11:25-26** Jesus said unto her, I am the resurrection, and the life: he that *b.* in me, though he were dead, yet shall he live: And whosoever liveth and *b.* in me shall never die. *b.* thou this; **11:40** said I not unto thee, that, if thou wouldest *b.*, thou shouldest see the glory of God; **11:45** had seen the things which Jesus did, *b.* on him; **12:10-11** the chief priests consulted that they might put Lazarus also to death; Because that by reason of him many of the Jews went away, and *b.* on Jesus; **12:36-37** while ye have light, *b.* in the light, that ye may be the children of light. These things spake Jesus, and departed, and did hide himself from them. But though he had done so many miracles before them, yet they *b.* not on him; **12:42** among the chief rulers also many *b.* on him; but because of the Pharisees they did not confess him, lest they should be put out of the synagogue; **12:44-48** Jesus cried and said, He that *b.* on me, *b.* not on me, but on him that sent me. And he that seeth me seeth him that sent me. I am come a light into the world, that whosoever *b.* on me should not abide in darkness. And if any man hear my words, and *b.* not, I judge him not: for I came not to judge the world, but to save the world. He that rejecteth me, and receiveth not my words, hath one that judgeth him: the word that I have spoken, the same shall judge him in the last day; **14:1** let not your heart be troubled: ye *b.* in God, *b.* also in me; **14:4-6** Lord, we know not whither thou goest; and how can we know the way? Jesus saith unto him, I am the way, the truth, and the life: no man cometh unto the Father, but by me; **14:12** he that *b.* on me, the works that I do shall he do also; and greater works than these shall he do; because I go unto my Father; **14:14** if ye shall ask any thing in my name, I will do it; **16:27** the Father himself loveth you, because ye have loved me, and have *b.* that I came out from God; **16:33** these things I have spoken unto you, that in me ye might have peace. In the world ye shall have tribulation: but be of good cheer; I have overcome the world; **17:8** I have given unto them the words which thou gavest me; and they have received them, and have known surely that I came out from thee, and they have *b.* that thou didst send me; **17:20** neither pray I for these alone, but for them also which shall *b.* on me through their word; **19:35** he that saw it bare record, and his record is true: and he knoweth that he saith true, that ye might *b.*; **20:29-31** Thomas, because thou hast seen me, thou hast *b.*: blessed are they that have not seen, and yet have *b.* And many other signs truly did Jesus in the presence of his disciples, which are not written in this book: But these are written, that ye might *b.* that Jesus is the Christ, the Son of God; and that *b.* ye might have life through his name; **Acts 2:36** let all the house of Israel know assuredly, that God hath made that same Jesus, whom ye have crucified, both Lord and Christ; **4:12** neither is there salvation in any other: for there is none other name under heaven given among men, whereby we must be saved; **8:37** if thou *b.* with all thine heart, thou mayest. And he answered and said, I *b.* that Jesus Christ is the Son of God; **10:42-43** he commanded us to preach unto the people, and to testify that it is he which was ordained of God to be the Judge of quick and dead. To him give all the prophets witness, that through his name whosoever *b.* in him shall receive remission of sins; **11:17** God gave them the like gift as he did unto us, who *b.* on the Lord Jesus Christ; what was I, that I could withstand God; **13:12** the deputy, when he saw what was done, *b.,* being astonished at the doctrine of the Lord; **13:39** all that *b.* are justified from all things, from which ye could not be justified by the law of Moses; **14:23** when they had ordained them elders in every church, and had prayed with fasting, they commended them to the Lord, on whom they *b.*; **16:31** *b.* on the Lord Jesus Christ, and thou shalt be saved, and thy house; **17:2-3** Paul, as his manner was, went in unto them, and three sabbath days reasoned with them out of the scriptures, Opening and alleging, that Christ must needs have suffered, and risen again from the dead; and that this Jesus, whom I preach unto you, is Christ; **17:27-28** seek the Lord, if haply they might feel after him, and find him, though he be not far from every one of us: For in him we live, and move, and have our being; as certain also of your own poets have said, For we are also his offspring; **17:31** he hath appointed a day, in the which he will judge the world in righteousness by that man whom he hath ordained; whereof he hath given assurance unto all men, in that he hath raised him from the dead; **18:5** Paul was pressed in the spirit, and testified to the Jews that Jesus was Christ; **18:8** Crispus, the chief ruler of the synagogue, *b.* on the Lord with all his house; and many of the Corinthians hearing *b.,* and were baptized; **24:24** Felix came with his wife Drusilla, which was a Jewess, he sent for Paul, and heard him concerning the faith in Christ; **Rom. 4:24** if we *b.* on him that raised up Jesus our Lord from the dead; **5:8** God commendeth his love toward us, in that, while we were yet sinners, Christ died for us; **5:11** we also joy in God through our Lord Jesus Christ, by whom we

have now received the atonement; **5:17** for if by one man's offence death reigned by one; much more they which receive abundance of grace and of the gift of righteousness shall reign in life by one, Jesus Christ; **6:23** the wages of sin is death; but the gift of God is eternal life through Jesus Christ our Lord; **9:33** I lay in Sion a stumblingstone and rock of offence: and whosoever *b.* on him shall not be ashamed; **10:4** Christ is the end of the law for righteousness to every one that *b.*; **10:11** the scripture saith, Whosoever *b.* on him shall not be ashamed; **10:14** how then shall they call on him in whom they have not *b.*? and how shall they *b.* in him of whom they have not heard? and how shall they hear without a preacher; **14:8** whether we live, we live unto the Lord; and whether we die, we die unto the Lord: whether we live therefore, or die, we are the Lord's; **15:8** Jesus Christ was a minister of the circumcision for the truth of God, to confirm the promises made unto the fathers; **1 Cor. 1:24** Christ the power of God, and the wisdom of God; **8: 6** to us there is but one God, the Father, of whom are all things, and we in him; and one Lord Jesus Christ, by whom are all things, and we by him; **10:4** they drank of that spiritual Rock that followed them: and that Rock was Christ; **15:20-22** for since by man came death, by man came also the resurrection of the dead. For as in Adam all die, even so in Christ shall all be made alive; **15:57** thanks be to God, which giveth us the victory through our Lord Jesus Christ; **2 Cor. 3:14** until this day remaineth the same vail untaken away in the reading of the old testament; which vail is done away in Christ; **5:15** he died for all, that they which live should not henceforth live unto themselves, but unto him which died for them, and rose again; **5:21** he hath made him to be sin for us, who knew no sin; that we might be made the righteousness of God in him; **8:9** ye know the grace of our Lord Jesus Christ, that, though he was rich, yet for your sakes he became poor, that ye through his poverty might be rich; **Gal. 1:4** who gave himself for our sins, that he might deliver us from this present evil world, according to the will of God and our Father; **2:16** knowing that a man is not justified by the works of the law, but by the faith of Jesus Christ, even we have *b.* in Jesus Christ, that we might be justified by the faith of Christ, and not by the works of the law: for by the works of the law shall no flesh be justified; **2:20** I am crucified with Christ: nevertheless I live; yet not I, but Christ liveth in me: and the life which I now live in the flesh I live by the faith of the Son of God, who loved me, and gave himself for me; **Gal. 3:6** even as

Abraham *b*. God, and it was accounted to him for righteous-ness; **3:14** the blessing of Abraham might come on the Gentiles through Jesus Christ; that we might receive the promise of the Spirit through faith; **3:16** to Abraham and his seed were the promises made. He saith not, And to seeds, as of many; but as of one, And to thy seed, which is Christ; **3:22** the scripture hath concluded all under sin, that the promise by faith of Jesus Christ might be given to them that *b*.; **3:29** if ye be Christ's, then are ye Abraham's seed, and heirs according to the promise; **4:4** when the fulness of the time was come, God sent forth his Son, made of a woman, made under the law; **Eph. 1:7** in whom we have redemption through his blood, the forgiveness of sins, according to the riches of his grace; **1:13** in whom ye also trusted, after that ye heard the word of truth, the gospel of your salvation: in whom also after that ye *b*., ye were sealed with that holy Spirit of promise; **1:19-22** what is the exceeding greatness of his power to us-ward who *b*., according to the working of his mighty power, Which he wrought in Christ, when he raised him from the dead, and set him at his own right hand in the heavenly places, Far above all principality, and power, and might, and dominion, and every name that is named, not only in this world, but also in that which is to come: And hath put all things under his feet, and gave him to be the head over all things to the church; **2:6** hath raised us up together, and made us sit together in heavenly places in Christ Jesus; **2:13-14** in Christ Jesus ye who sometimes were far off are made nigh by the blood of Christ. For he is our peace, who hath made both one, and hath broken down the middle wall of partition between us; **2:18** through him we both have access by one Spirit unto the Father; **2:20** are built upon the foundation of the apostles and prophets, Jesus Christ himself being the chief corner stone; **3:9** to make all men see what is the fellowship of the mystery, which from the beginning of the world hath been hid in God, who created all things by Jesus Christ; **3:20** unto him that is able to do exceeding abundantly above all that we ask or think, according to the power that worketh in us; **4:5** One Lord, one faith, one baptism; **5:2** walk in love, as Christ also hath loved us, and hath given himself for us an offering and a sacrifice to God for a sweetsmelling savour; **Philip. 1:29** unto you it is given in the behalf of Christ, not only to *b*. on him, but also to suffer for his sake; **2:6-7** who, being in the form of God, thought it not robbery to be equal with God: But made himself of no reputation, and took upon him the form of a servant, and was made in the likeness of men; **2:10-11** at the name of Jesus every knee should bow, of things in heaven, and things in earth, and things under the earth; And that every tongue should confess that Jesus Christ is Lord, to the glory of God the Father; **3:20-21** our conversation is in heaven; from whence also we look for the Saviour, the Lord Jesus Christ: Who shall change our vile body, that it may be fashioned like unto his glorious body, according to the working whereby he is able even to subdue all things unto himself; **Col. 1:14-22** In whom we have redemption through his blood, even the forgiveness of sins: Who is the image of the invisible God, the firstborn of every creature: For by him were all things created, that are in heaven, and that are in earth, visible and invisible, whether they be thrones, or dominions, or principalities, or powers: all things were created by him, and for him: And he is before all things, and by him all things consist. And he is the head of the body, the church: who is the beginning, the firstborn from the dead; that in all things he might have the preeminence. For it pleased the Father that in him should all fulness dwell; And, having made peace through the blood of his cross, by him to reconcile all things unto himself; by him, I say, whether they be things in earth, or things in heaven. And you, that were sometime alienated and enemies in your mind by wicked works, yet now hath he reconciled. In the body of his flesh through death, to present you holy and unblameable and unreproveable in his sight; **1:27** God would make known what is the riches of the glory of this mystery among the Gentiles; which is Christ in you, the hope of glory; **2:2** their hearts might be comforted, being knit together in love, and unto all riches of the full assurance of understanding, to the acknowledgment of the mystery of God, and of the Father, and of Christ; **2:9-11** in him dwelleth all the fulness of the Godhead bodily. And ye are complete in him, which is the head of all principality and power: In whom also ye are circumcised with the circumcision made without hands, in putting off the body of the sins of the flesh by the circumcision of Christ; **3:3-4** ye are dead, and your life is hid with Christ in God. When Christ, who is our life, shall appear, then shall ye also appear with him in glory; **3:11** where there is neither Greek nor Jew, circumcision nor uncircumcision, Barbarian, Scythian, bond nor free: but Christ is all, and in all; **1 Thes. 2:20** For ye are our glory and joy; **4:14-16** if we *b*. that Jesus died and rose again, even so them also which sleep in Jesus will God bring with him. For this we say unto you by the word of the Lord, that we which are alive and remain unto the coming of the Lord shall not prevent them which are asleep. For the Lord himself shall descend from heaven with a shout, with the voice of the archangel, and with the trump of God: and the dead in Christ shall rise first**; 2 Thes. 2:16** our Lord Jesus Christ himself, and God, even our Father, which hath loved us, and hath given us everlasting consolation and good hope through grace; **3:4-6** we have confidence in the Lord touching you, that ye both do and will do the things which we command you. And the Lord direct your hearts into the love of God, and into the patient waiting for Christ; **1 Tim. 1:1** Paul, an apostle of Jesus Christ by the commandment of God our Saviour, and Lord Jesus Christ, which is our hope; **1:12** I thank Christ Jesus our Lord, who hath enabled me, for that he counted me faithful, putting me into the ministry; **1:15** this is a faithful saying, and worthy of all acceptation, that Christ Jesus came into the world to save sinners; of whom I am chief; **2:5-6** there is one God, and one mediator between God and men, the man Christ Jesus; Who gave himself a ransom for all, to be testified in due time; **3:16** great is the mystery of godliness: God was manifest in the flesh, justified in the Spirit, seen of angels, preached unto the Gentiles, *b.* on in the world, received up into glory; **6:15** in his times he shall shew, who is the blessed and only Potentate, the King of kings, and Lord of lords; **2 Tim. 1:10** appearing of our Saviour Jesus Christ, who hath abolished death, and hath brought life and immortality to light through the gospel; **1:12** I am not ashamed: for I know whom I have *b.,* and am persuaded that he is able to keep that which I have committed unto him against that day; **2:8** remember that Jesus Christ of the seed of David was raised from the dead according to my gospel; **2:11** It is a faithful saying: For if we be dead with him, we shall also live with him; **2:19** the foundation of God standeth sure, having this seal, The Lord knoweth them that are his. And, Let every one that nameth the name of Christ depart from iniquity; **3:15** from a child thou hast known the holy scriptures, which are able to make thee wise unto salvation through faith which is in Christ Jesus; **4:1** I charge thee therefore before God, and the Lord Jesus Christ, who shall judge the quick and the dead at his appearing and his kingdom; **4:17** the Lord stood with me, and strengthened me; that by me the preaching might be fully known, and that all the Gentiles might hear: and I was delivered out of the mouth of the lion; **Titus 2:13-14** looking for

that blessed hope, and the glorious appearing of the great God and our Saviour Jesus Christ; Who gave himself for us, that he might redeem us from all iniquity, and purify unto himself a peculiar people, zealous of good works; **3:5** not by works of righteousness which we have done, but according to his mercy he saved us, by the washing of regeneration, and renewing of the Holy Ghost; **3:7** being justified by his grace, we should be made heirs according to the hope of eternal life; **Heb. 1:2** hath in these last days spoken unto us by his Son, whom he hath appointed heir of all things, by whom also he made the worlds; **2:9** Jesus, who was made a little lower than the angels for the suffering of death, crowned with glory and honour; that he by the grace of God should taste death for every man; **3:1** holy brethren, partakers of the heavenly calling, consider the Apostle and High Priest of our profession, Christ Jesus; **4:13-14** neither is there any creature that is not manifest in his sight: but all things are naked and opened unto the eyes of him with whom we have to do. Seeing then that we have a great high priest, that is passed into the heavens, Jesus the Son of God, let us hold fast our profession; **5:9** being made perfect, he became the author of eternal salvation unto all them that obey him; **6:20** Jesus, made an high priest for ever after the order of Melchisedec; **8:1** Now of the things which we have spoken this is the sum: We have such an high priest, who is set on the right hand of the throne of the Majesty in the heavens; **9:15** for this cause he is the mediator of the new testament, that by means of death, for the redemption of the transgressions that were under the first testament, they which are called might receive the promise of eternal inheritance; **9:26** then must he often have suffered since the foundation of the world: but now once in the end of the world hath he appeared to put away sin by the sacrifice of himself; **9:28** Christ was once offered to bear the sins of many; and unto them that look for him shall he appear the second time without sin unto salvation; **10:10-11** we are sanctified through the offering of the body of Jesus Christ once for all. And every priest standeth daily ministering and offering oftentimes the same sacrifices, which can never take away sins; **11:26** esteeming the reproach of Christ greater riches than the treasures in Egypt: for he had respect unto the recompence of the reward; **1 Pet. 1:3-4** blessed be the God and Father of our Lord Jesus Christ, which according to his abundant mercy hath begotten us again unto a lively hope by the resurrection of Jesus Christ from the dead, To an inheritance incorruptible, and undefiled, and that fadeth not away, reserved in heaven for you; **1:8** Whom having not seen, ye love; in whom, though now ye see him not, yet believing, ye rejoice with joy unspeakable and full of glory; **1:20** who verily was foreordained before the foundation of the world, but was manifest in these last times for you; **2:6** it is contained in the scripture, Behold, I lay in Sion a chief corner stone, elect, precious: and he that *b.* on him shall not be confounded; **2:24-25** who his own self bare our sins in his own body on the tree, that we, being dead to sins, should live unto righteousness: by whose stripes ye were healed. For ye were as sheep going astray; but are now returned unto the Shepherd and Bishop of your souls; **3:18** Christ also hath once suffered for sins, the just for the unjust, that he might bring us to God, being put to death in the flesh, but quickened by the Spirit; **3:22** who is gone into heaven, and is on the right hand of God; angels and authorities and powers being made subject unto him; **5:7** casting all your care upon him; for he careth for you; **2 Pet. 1:17** he received from God the Father honour and glory, when there came such a voice to him from the excellent glory, This is my beloved Son, in whom I am well pleased; **1 Jn. 2:2** he is the propitiation for our sins: and not for ours only, but also for the sins of the whole world; **3:5** he was manifested to take away our sins; and in him is no sin; **3:8** for this purpose the Son of God was manifested, that he might destroy the works of the devil; **3:23** this is his commandment, That we should *b.* on the name of his Son Jesus Christ, and love one another, as he gave us commandment; **4:4** ye are of God, little children, and have overcome them: because greater is he that is in you, than he that is in the world; **4:9-10** in this was manifested the love of God toward us, because that God sent his only begotten Son into the world, that we might live through him. Herein is love, not that we loved God, but that he loved us, and sent his Son to be the propitiation for our sins; **5:1** whosoever *b.* that Jesus is the Christ is born of God: and every one that loveth him that begat loveth him also that is begotten of him; **5:5** who is he that overcometh the world, but he that *b.* that Jesus is the Son of God; **5:10** he that *b.* on the Son of God hath the witness in himself: he that *b.* not God hath made him a liar; because he *b.* not the record that God gave of his Son; **5:12-13** he that hath the Son hath life; and he that hath not the Son of God hath not life. These things have I written unto you that *b.* on the name of the Son of God; that ye may know that ye have eternal life, and that ye may *b.* on the name of the Son of

God; **Jude 1:24** him that is able to keep you from falling, and to present you faultless before the presence of his glory with exceeding joy; **Rev. 5:9** they sung a new song, saying, Thou art worthy to take the book, and to open the seals thereof: for thou wast slain, and hast redeemed us to God by thy blood out of every kindred, and tongue, and people, and nation; **7:14** these are they which came out of great tribulation, and have washed their robes, and made them white in the blood of the Lamb; **11:15** there were great voices in heaven, saying, The kingdoms of this world are become the kingdoms of our Lord, and of his Christ; and he shall reign for ever and ever; **11:18** the nations were angry, and thy wrath is come, and the time of the dead, that they should be judged, and that thou shouldest give reward unto thy servants the prophets, and to the saints, and them that fear thy name, small and great; and shouldest destroy them which destroy the earth; **12:10** I heard a loud voice saying in heaven, Now is come salvation, and strength, and the kingdom of our God, and the power of his Christ: for the accuser of our brethren is cast down, which accused them before our God day and night; **17:13** these have one mind, and shall give their power and strength unto the beast; **19:11-16** I saw heaven opened, and behold a white horse; and he that sat upon him was called Faithful and True, and in righteousness he doth judge and make war. His eyes were as a flame of fire, and on his head were many crowns; and he had a name written, that no man knew, but he himself. And he was clothed with a vesture dipped in blood: and his name is called The Word of God. And the armies which were in heaven followed him upon white horses, clothed in fine linen, white and clean. And out of his mouth goeth a sharp sword, that with it he should smite the nations: and he shall rule them with a rod of iron: and he treadeth the winepress of the fierceness and wrath of Almighty God. And he hath on his vesture and on his thigh a name written, KING OF KINGS, AND LORD OF LORDS.

Believeth all things. 1 Cor. 13:7 (*see also* All Things)

Matt. 13:3-8 behold, a sower went forth to sow; **13:15** they should see with their eyes, and hear with their ears, and should understand with their heart, and should be converted, and I should heal them; **13:58** he did not many mighty works there because of their unbelief; **Mark 6:5-6** he marvelled because of their unbelief; **9:23-27** Jesus said unto him, If thou canst *b.,* all things are possible to him that *b.*. And straightway the father of the child cried out, and said with tears, Lord, I *b.*; help thou mine unbelief; **16:10-11** when they had heard that he was alive, and had been seen of her, *b.* not; **16:12-14** he appeared in another form unto two of them, as they walked, and went into the country. And they went and told it unto the residue: neither *b.* they them. Afterward he appeared unto the eleven as they sat at meat, and upbraided them with their unbelief and hardness of heart, because they *b.* not them which had seen him after he was risen; **16:16** he that *b.* and is baptized shall be saved; but he that *b.* not shall be damned; **16:17** these signs shall follow them that *b.*; In my name shall they cast out devils; they shall speak with new tongues; **Luke 1:1** forasmuch as many have taken in hand to set forth in order a declaration of those things which are most surely *b.* among us; **1:18** Zacharias said unto the angel, Whereby shall I know this? for I am an old man, and my wife well stricken in years; **8:12** those by the way side are they that hear; then cometh the devil, and taketh away the word out of their hearts, lest they should *b.* and be saved; **8:50** when Jesus heard it, he answered him, saying, Fear not: *b.* only, and she shall be made whole; **12:29** seek not ye what ye shall eat, or what ye shall drink, neither be ye of doubtful mind; **John 1:7** the same came for a witness, to bear witness of the Light, that all men through him might *b.*; **1:50** Jesus answered and said unto him, Because I said unto thee, I saw thee under the fig tree, believest thou? thou shalt see greater things than these; **4:39** many of the Samaritans of that city *b.* on him for the saying of the woman, which testified, He told me all that ever I did; **4:41** many more *b.* because of his own word; **5:44** how can ye *b.*, which receive honour one of another, and seek not the honour that cometh from God only; **20:29** Jesus saith unto him, Thomas, because thou hast seen me, thou hast *b.*: blessed are they that have not seen, and yet have *b.*; **20:31** these are written, that ye might *b.* that Jesus is the Christ, the Son of God; and that *b.* ye might have life through his name; **Acts 13:12** when he saw what was done, *b.*, being astonished at the doctrine of the Lord; **13:46** it was necessary that the word of God should first have been spoken to you: but seeing ye put it from you, and judge yourselves unworthy of everlasting life, lo, we turn to the Gentiles; **13:48** when the Gentiles heard this, they were glad, and glorified the word of the Lord: and as many as were ordained to eternal life *b.*; **14:1** a great multitude both of the Jews and also of the Greeks *b.*; **16:34** when he had brought them into

his house, he set meat before them, and rejoiced, *b.* in God with all his house; **17:4** some of them *b.*, and consorted with Paul and Silas; and of the devout Greeks a great multitude, and of the chief women not a few; **24:14** this I confess unto thee, that after the way which they call heresy, so worship I the God of my fathers, *b.* all things which are written in the law and in the prophets; **Rom. 3:3-4** what if some did not *b.*? shall their unbelief make the faith of God without effect; **4:11** he might be the father of all them that *b.*, though they be not circumcised; that righteousness might be imputed unto them also; **4:20** he staggered not at the promise of God through unbelief; but was strong in faith, giving glory to God; **10:10** with the heart man *b.* unto righteousness; **15:13** the God of hope fill you with all joy and peace in *b.*, that ye may abound in hope, through the power of the Holy Ghost; **1 Cor. 13:7** beareth all things, *b.* all things, hopeth all things, endureth all things; **2 Thes. 2:13** God hath from the beginning chosen you to salvation through sanctification of the Spirit and belief of the truth; **Heb. 3:16-19** some, when they had heard, did provoke: howbeit not all that came out of Egypt by Moses. But with whom was he grieved forty years? was it not with them that had sinned, whose carcases fell in the wilderness? And to whom sware he that they should not enter into his rest, but to them that *b.* not? So we see that they could not enter in because of unbelief; **4:3** we which have *b.* do enter into rest; **11:1** faith is the substance of things hoped for, the evidence of things not seen; **11:6** without faith it is impossible to please him: for he that cometh to God must *b.* that he is, and that he is a rewarder of them that diligently seek him; **1 Pet. 2:6** I lay in Sion a chief corner stone, elect, precious: and he that *b.* on him shall not be confounded; **Rev. 21:8** the fearful, and unbelieving, and the abominable, and murderers, and whoremongers, and sorcerers, and idolaters, and all liars, shall have their part in the lake which burneth with fire and brimstone.

Believe in the Lord your God, so shall ye be established; believe his prophets, so shall ye prosper. 2 Chron. 20:20 (*see also* Establish, Hearken, Prophet, Prosper)

Gen. 15:6 he *b.* in the LORD; and he counted it to him for righteousness; **Deut. 1:32** in this thing ye did not *b.* the LORD your God; **2 Kgs. 17:14** they would not hear, but hardened their necks, like to the neck of their fathers, that did not *b.* in the LORD their God; **2 Chron. 20:20** *b.* in the LORD your God, so shall ye be established;

b. his prophets, so shall ye prosper; **Ps. 22:31** they shall come, and shall declare his righteousness unto a people that shall be born, that he hath done this; **23:1** the LORD is my shepherd; I shall not want; **33:12** blessed is the nation whose God is the LORD: and the people whom he hath chosen for his own inheritance; **78:22** they *b.* not in God, and trusted not in his salvation; **106:12** believed they his words; they sang his praise; **116:10** I believed, therefore have I spoken: I was greatly afflicted; **119:105** thy *w.* is a lamp unto my feet, and a light unto my path; **Isa. 43:10** ye may know and *b.* me, and understand that I am he: before me there was no God formed, neither shall there be after me; **53:1** who hath believed our report? and to whom is the arm of the LORD revealed; **Jonah 3:5** [they] *b.* God, and proclaimed a fast.

He staggered not at the promise of God through unbelief; but was strong in faith, giving glory to God; And being fully persuaded that, what he had promised, he was able also to perform. And therefore it was imputed to him for righteousness. Rom. 4:20-22 (*see also* Promise)

Rom. 4:17-22 when he was about an hundred years old, neither yet the deadness of Sara's womb: He staggered not at the promise of God through unbelief; but was strong in faith, giving glory to God; And being fully persuaded that, what he had promised, he was able also to perform. And therefore it was imputed to him for righteousness.

Say not, I am a child: for thou shalt go to all that I shall send thee, and whatsoever I command thee thou shalt speak. Be not afraid of their faces: for I am with thee to deliver thee, saith the LORD. Jer. 1:7-8 (*see also* Speak)

Jer. 1:2-19 the LORD said unto me, Say not, I am a child: for thou shalt go to all that I shall send thee, and whatsoever I command thee thou shalt speak. Be not afraid of their faces: for I am with thee to deliver thee; **2:1-2** the word of the LORD came to me, saying, Go and cry in the ears of Jerusalem, saying, Thus saith the LORD; I remember thee, the kindness of thy youth; **19:1-2** thus saith the LORD... go forth unto the valley of the son of Hinnom, which is by the entry of the east gate, and proclaim there the words that I shall tell thee; **19:14-15** then came Jeremiah from Tophet, whither the LORD had sent him to prophesy; and he stood in the court of the LORD's

house; and said to all the people, Thus saith the LORD of hosts, the God of Israel.

If ye will not believe, surely ye shall not be established. Isa. 7:9 (*see also* Establish)

Ps. 116:10 I believed, therefore have I spoken: I was greatly afflicted; **119:66** teach me good judgment and knowledge: for I have *b.* thy commandments; **Isa. 7:9** if ye will not *b.*, surely ye shall not be established.

When I speak with thee, I will open thy mouth, and thou shalt say unto them, Thus saith the Lord GOD; He that heareth, let him hear; and he that forbeareth, let him forbear. Ezek. 3:27 (*see also* Talk)

Jer. 13:1-7 thus saith the LORD unto me... And the word of the LORD came unto me the second time... And it came to pass after many days, that the LORD said unto me; **13:12** thou shalt speak unto them this word; Thus saith the LORD God of Israel; **26:2** thus saith the LORD; Stand in the court of the Lord's house, and speak unto all the cities of Judah, which come to worship in the LORD's house, all the words that I command thee to speak unto them; **27:1-4** came this word unto Jeremiah from the LORD, saying, Thus saith the LORD to me; Make thee bonds and yokes; **32:1** the word that came to Jeremiah from the LORD; **32:6** Jeremiah said, The word of the LORD came unto me; **39:16** thus saith the LORD of hosts, the God of Israel; Behold, I will bring my words upon this city for evil, and not for good; and they shall be accomplished in that day before thee; **47:2** thus saith the LORD; Behold, waters rise up out of the north, and shall be an overflowing flood, and shall overflow the land, and all that is therein; **49:34** the word of the LORD that came to Jeremiah the prophet; **Ezek. 1:3** the word of the LORD came expressly unto Ezekiel the priest... and the hand of the LORD was there upon him; **1:24-28** I heard the noise of their wings, like the noise of great waters, as the voice of the Almighty, the voice of speech, as the noise of an host... This was the appearance of the likeness of the glory of the LORD. And when I saw it, I fell upon my face, and I heard a voice of one that spake; **2:1-3** he said unto me, Son of man, stand upon thy feet, and I will speak unto thee. And the spirit entered into me when he spake unto me, and set me upon my feet, that I heard him that spake unto me; **3:1** he said unto me, Son of man, eat that thou findest; eat this roll, and go speak unto the house of Israel; **3:4** he said unto me, Son of man, go, get thee unto the house of Israel, and speak with my words unto them; **3:10** he said unto me, Son of man, all my words that I shall speak unto thee receive in thine heart, and hear with thine ears; **3:22-23** the hand of the LORD was there upon me; and he said unto me, Arise, go forth into the plain, and I will there talk with thee; **3:27** when I speak with thee, I will open thy mouth, and thou shalt say unto them, Thus saith the Lord GOD; He that heareth, let him hear; and he that forbeareth, let him forbear; **7:1** the word of the LORD came unto me, saying; **8:1-5** as I sat in mine house... the hand of the Lord GOD fell there upon me... And, behold, the glory of the God of Israel was there, according to the vision that I saw in the plain. Then said he unto me, Son of man, lift up thine eyes; **10:5** the sound of the cherubims wings was heard even to the outer court, as the voice of the Almighty God when he speaketh; **11:5** the Spirit of the LORD fell upon me, and said unto me, Speak; Thus saith the LORD; Thus have ye said, O house of Israel: for I know the things that come into your mind, every one of them; **12:8** in the morning came the word of the LORD unto me; **12:26** the word of the LORD came to me; **13:1** the word of the LORD came unto me; **15:1** the word of the LORD came unto me; **17:1-3** the word of the LORD came unto me, saying, Son of man, put forth a riddle, and speak a parable unto the house of Israel; **20:35** I will bring you into the wilderness of the people, and there will I plead with you face to face; **21:1** the word of the LORD came unto me; **21:7** thou shalt answer, For the tidings; because it cometh: and every heart shall melt, and all hands shall be feeble, and every spirit shall faint, and all knees shall be weak as water: behold, it cometh, and shall be brought to pass, saith the Lord GOD; **21:18** the word of the LORD came unto me again; **22:1** the word of the LORD came unto me; **22:17** the word of the LORD came unto me; **22:23** the word of the LORD came unto me; **23:1** the word of the LORD came again unto me; **24:1** the word of the LORD came unto me; **25:1-4** the word of the LORD came again unto me, saying, Son of man, set thy face against the Ammonites, and prophesy against them; And say unto the Ammonites, Hear the word of the Lord GOD; **26:1** the word of the LORD came unto me; **28:1** the word of the LORD came again unto me; **28:11** (28:20, 29:1, 30:1, 30:20, 33:1, 33:23, 34:1, 35:1, 36:16) the word of the LORD came unto me; **40:1** in the selfsame

day the hand of the LORD was upon me; **Amos 7:15** the LORD took me as I followed the flock, and the LORD said unto me, Go, prophesy unto my people Israel; **8:1-2** thus hath the Lord GOD shewed unto me: and behold a basket of summer fruit. And he said, Amos, what seest thou; **9:1** I saw the Lord standing upon the altar: and he said, Smite the lintel of the door, that the posts may shake; **Jonah 1:1-3** the word of the LORD came unto Jonah the son of Amittai, saying, Arise, go to Nineveh, that great city, and cry against it; for their wickedness is come up before me; **3:1-2** the word of the LORD came unto Jonah the second time, saying, Arise, go unto Nineveh, that great city, and preach unto it the preaching that I bid thee; **Micah 1:1** the word of the LORD that came to Micah the Morasthite.

BESEECH, BESOUGHT (*see also* Ask, Beg, Entreat, Petition, Plead, Request)

Beseech God that he will be gracious unto us. Mal. 1:9 (*see also* Gracious)

Mal. 1:9 *b.* God that he will be gracious unto us: this hath been by your means: will he regard your persons? saith the LORD of hosts; **Jer. 26:19** did he not fear the LORD, and *b.* the LORD, and the LORD repented him of the evil which he had pronounced against them? Thus might we procure great evil against our souls.

BESET (*see also* Hinder)

Seeing we also are compassed about with so great a cloud of witnesses, let us lay aside every weight, and the sin which doth so easily beset us, and let us run with patience the race that is set before us. Heb. 12:1 (*see also* Patience, Run, Sin, Weight, Witness)

BEST (*see also* Greatest)

But covet earnestly the best gifts: and yet shew I unto you a more excellent way. 1 Cor. 12:31 (*see also* Best, Covet, Gift)

BESTOW (*see also* Administer, Appoint, Give)

Though I bestow all my goods to feed the poor, an though I give my body to be burned, and have not charity, it profiteth me nothing. 1 Cor. 13:3 (*see also* Charity)

BETRAY, BETRAYAL (*see also* Deceive)

All these are the beginning of sorrows. Then shall they deliver you up to be afflicted, and shall kill you: and ye shall be hated of all nations for my name's sake. And then shall many be offended, and shall betray one another, and shall hate one another. Matt. 24:8-10 (*see also* Sorrow)

Matt. 24:8-10 these are the beginning of sorrows. Then shall they deliver you up to be afflicted, and shall kill you: and ye shall be hated of all nations for my name's sake. And then shall many be offended, and shall *b.* one another, and shall hate one another; 26:15-16 what will ye give me, and I will deliver him unto you? And they covenanted with him for thirty pieces of silver. And from that time he sought opportunity to *b.* him; 26:23-24 (Matt. 26:21, Mark 14:21) he that dippeth his hand with me in the dish, the same shall *b.* me. The Son of man goeth as it is written of him: but woe unto that man by whom the Son of man is *b.*! it had been good for that man if he had not been born; 26:45-46 (Mark 14:41-42) the hour is at hand, and the Son of man is *b.* into the hands of sinners. Rise, let us be going: behold, he is at hand that doth *b.* me; 27:3-4 Judas, which had *b.* him, when he saw that he was condemned, repented himself, and brought again the thirty pieces of silver to the chief priests and elders, Saying, I have sinned in that I have *b.* the innocent blood; **Mark 14:10-11** Judas Iscariot, one of the twelve, went unto the chief priests, to *b.* him unto them. And when they heard it, they were glad, and promised to give him money. And he sought how he might conveniently *b.* him; **14:18** one of you which eateth with me shall *b.* me; **Luke 22:48** Judas, *b.* thou the Son of man with a kiss; **John 13:18** he that eateth bread with me hath lifted up his heel against me; **13:21** that one of you shall *b.* me.

BETTER (*see also* Good, Heal)

Say not thou, What is the cause that the former days were better than these? Eccl. 7:10 (*see also* Former Days)

Thine own friend, and thy father's friend, forsake not; neither go into thy brother's house in the day of thy calamity: for better is a neighbour *that* is near than a brother far off. Prov. 27:10 (*see also* Calamity, Forsake)

He that is slow to anger is better than the mighty; and he that ruleth his spirit than he that taketh a city. Prov. 16:32 (*see also* Anger, Rule, Spirit)

It were better for him that a millstone were hanged about his neck, and he cast into the sea, than that he should offend one of these little ones. Luke 17:2 (*see also* Child)

Choose the things that please me, and take hold of my covenant; Even unto them will I give in mine house and within my walls a place and a name better than of sons and of daughters. Isa. 56:4-5 (*see also* Choose, Covenant)

It is better to dwell in the wilderness, than with a contentious and an angry woman. Prov. 21:19 (*see also* Contend)

It is better to hear the rebuke of the wise, than for a man to hear the song of fools. Eccl. 7:5 (*see also* Rebuke)

Let nothing be done through strife or vainglory; but in lowliness of mind let each esteem other better than themselves. Philip. 2:3 (*see also* Esteem. Low)

For wisdom is better than rubies; and all the things that may be desired are not to be compared to it. Prov. 8:11 (*see also* Desire, Wisdom)

If after they have escaped the pollutions of the world through the knowledge of the Lord and Savior Jesus Christ, they are again entangled therein, and overcome, the latter end is worse with them than the beginning. For it had been better for them not to have known the way of righteousness, than, after they have known it, to turn from the holy commandment delivered unto them. But it is happened unto them according to the true proverb, The dog is turned to his own vomit again; and the sow that was washed to her wallowing in the mire. 2 Pet. 2:20-22 (*see also* Vomit, Way)

Wherefore if thy hand or thy foot offend thee, cut them off, and cast them from thee: it is better for thee to enter into life halt or maimed, rather than having two hands or two feet to be cast into everlasting fire. Matt. 18:8 (*see also* Cut, Everlasting Fire, Offend)

BIBLE (*see also* Record, Scripture, Stick, Word, Write)

Moreover, thou son of man, take thee one stick, and write upon it, For Judah, and for the children of Israel his companions: then take another stick, and write upon it For Joseph, the stick of Ephraim, and for all the house of Israel his companions: And join them one to another into one stick; and they shall become one in thine hand. Ezek. 37:16-17 (*see also* Become, Stick)

BIND, BOUND, BOUNDS (*see also* Covenant)

Let not mercy and truth forsake thee: bind them about thy neck: write them upon the table of thine heart; So shalt thou find favour and good understanding in the sight of God and man. Prov. 3:3-4 (*see also* Heart, Merciful, True, Write)

Prov. 3:3-4 let not mercy and truth forsake thee: b. them about thy neck; write them upon the table of thine heart: So shalt thou find favour and good understanding in the sight of God and man; 21:21 he that followeth after righteousness and mercy findeth life, righteousness, and honour.

BIRTH, BIRTHRIGHT (*see* Born Again, Conceive, Genealogy, Heir, Inherit, Lineage)

BISHOP (*see also* Judge, Priesthood)

A bishop then must be blameless, the husband of one wife, vigilant, sober, of good behaviour, given to hospitality, apt to teach. 1 Tim. 3:2 (*see also* Vigilant, Wife)

BITTER, BITTERNESS (*see also* Hate)

The heart knoweth his own bitterness; and a stranger doth not intermeddle with his joy. Prov. 14:10 (*see also* Heart)

BLAME (*see* Accuse)

BLASPHEME, BLASPHEMOUS, BLASPHEMY (*see also* False Doctrine, Profane, Swear)

He that shall blaspheme against the Holy Ghost hath never forgiveness, but is in danger of eternal damnation. Mark 3:29 (*see also* Danger, Holy Ghost)

Do not they blaspheme that worthy name by the which ye are called? James 2:7

Lev. 24:11-16 he that b. the name of the LORD, he shall surely be put to death, and all the congregation shall certainly stone him: as well the stranger, as he that is born in the land, when he b. the name of the LORD, shall be put to death; 1 Kgs. 21:10 set two men... before him, to bear witness against him, saying, Thou didst b. God and the king. And then carry him out, and stone him, that he may die; 21:13 the men of Belial witnessed against him... in the presence of the people, saying, Naboth did b. God and the king. Then they carried him forth out of the city, and stoned him with stones; 2 Kgs. 19:6-7 thus saith the LORD, Be not afraid of the words which thou hast heard, with which the servants of the king of Assyria have b. me. Behold, I will send a blast upon him; Ps. 74:10 O God, how long shall the adversary reproach? shall the enemy b. thy name for ever; 74:18 remember this, that the enemy hath reproached, O LORD, and that the foolish people have b. thy name; Isa. 36:15 neither let Hezekiah make you trust in the LORD, saying, The LORD will surely deliver us; 36:21 they held their peace, and answered him not a word: for the kings commandment was, saying, Answer him not; 37:1 when king Hezekiah heard it, that he rent his clothes, and covered himself with sackcloth, and went into the house of the LORD; 37:3 this day is a day of trouble, and of rebuke, and of b.: for the children are come to the birth, and there is not strength to bring forth; 37:6-7 be not afraid of the words that thou hast heard, wherewith the servants of the king of Assyria have b. me. Behold, I will send a blast upon him; 37:17 incline thine ear, O LORD, and hear; open thine eyes, O LORD, and see: and hear all the words of Sennacherib, which hath sent to reproach the living God; 37:23-24 whom hast thou reproached and b.? and against whom hast thou exalted thy voice, and lifted up thine eyes on high? even against the Holy One of Israel; 37:33 thus saith the LORD concerning the king of Assyria, He shall not come into this city, nor shoot an arrow there, nor come before it with shields, nor cast a bank against it; 52:5 what have I here, saith the LORD, that my people is taken away for nought? they that rule over them make them to howl, saith the LORD; and my name continually every day is b.; 65:7 your iniquities, and the iniquities of your fathers together, saith the LORD, which have burned incense upon the mountains, and b. me upon the hills; Ezek. 20:27 thus saith the Lord GOD; Yet in this your fathers have b.

me, in that they have committed a trespass against me; **35:12** thou shalt know that I am the LORD, and that I have heard all thy *b.* which thou hast spoken against the mountains of Israel; **Matt. 15:19-20** for out of the heart proceed evil thoughts, murders, adulteries, fornications, thefts, false witness, *b.*: These are the things which defile a man; **Mark 7:22-23** thefts, covetousness, wickedness, deceit, lasciviousness, an evil eye, *b.*, pride, foolishness: All these evil things come from within, and defile the man; **Luke 22:65** many other things *b.* spake they against him; **Acts 13:45** when the Jews saw the multitudes, they were filled with envy, and spake against those things which were spoken by Paul, contradicting and *b.*; **18:6** when they opposed themselves, and *b.*, he shook his raiment, and said unto them, Your blood be upon your own heads; I am clean: from henceforth I will go unto the Gentiles; **Rom. 2:24** the name of God is *b.* among the Gentiles through you, as it is written; **Col. 3:8** put off all these; anger, wrath, malice, *b.*, filthy communication out of your mouth; **1 Tim. 1:20** Hymenaeus and Alexander; whom I have delivered unto Satan, that they may learn not to *b.*; **6:1** let as many servants as are under the yoke count their own masters worthy of all honour, that the name of God and his doctrine be not *b.*; **2 Tim. 3:2** men shall be lovers of their own selves, covetous, boasters, proud, *b.*, disobedient to parents, unthankful, unholy; **James 2:7** do not they *b.* that worthy name by the which ye are called; **Rev. 13:5** there was given unto him a mouth speaking great things and *b.*

BLESS, BLESSED, BLESSING (*see also* Administer, Praise, Reward, Wage)

The blessing of the LORD be upon you: we bless you in the name of the LORD. Ps. 129:8

Blessed are they that keep judgment, and he that doeth righteousness at all times. Ps. 106:3 (*see also* Righteous)

If thou shalt hearken diligently unto the voice of the LORD thy God, to observe and to do all his commandments which I command thee this day, that the LORD thy God will sit thee on high above all nations of the earth; And all these blessings shall come on thee, and overtake thee, if thou shalt hearken unto the voice of the LORD thy God. Deut. 28:1-2 (*see also* Commandment, Hearken)

Now bless the LORD your God. 1 Chron. 29:20

Gen. 24:48 I bowed down my head, and worshipped the LORD, and *b.* the LORD God of my master Abraham, which had led me in the right way; **Ex. 15:2** the LORD is my strength and song, and he is become my salvation: he is my God, and I will prepare him an habitation; my fathers God, and I will exalt him; **Deut. 8:10** when thou hast eaten and art full, then thou shalt *b.* the LORD thy God for the good land which he hath given thee; **1 Kgs. 5:7** *b.* be the LORD this day, which hath given unto David a wise son over this great people; **1 Chron. 23:13** sanctify the most holy things, he and his sons for ever, to burn incense before the LORD, to minister unto him, and to *b.* in his name for ever; **29:10** David *b.* the LORD before all the congregation: and David said, *b.* be thou, LORD God of Israel our father, for ever and ever; **29:20** David said to all the congregation, Now *b.* the LORD your God. And all the congregation *b.* the LORD God of their fathers, and bowed down their heads, and worshipped the LORD, and the king; **2 Chron. 20:26** on the fourth day they assembled themselves in the valley of Berachah; for there they *b.* the LORD; **Neh. 8:6** Ezra *b.* the LORD, the great God. And all the people answered, Amen, Amen, with lifting up their hands: and they bowed their heads, and worshipped the LORD with their faces to the ground; **9:5** stand up and *b.* the LORD your God for ever and ever: and *b.* be thy glorious name, which is exalted above all *b.* and praise; **Job 1:21** naked came I out of my mothers womb, and naked shall I return thither: the LORD gave, and the LORD hath taken away; *b.* be the name of the LORD; **Ps. 16:7** I will *b.* the LORD, who hath given me counsel: my reins also instruct me in the night seasons; **18:46** the LORD liveth; and *b.* be my rock; and let the God of my salvation be exalted; **26:12** my foot standeth in an even place: in the congregations will I *b.* the LORD; **28:6** *b.* be the LORD, because he hath heard the voice of my supplications; **34:1** I will *b.* the LORD at all times: his praise shall continually be in my mouth; **63:4** thus will I *b.* thee while I live: I will lift up my hands in thy name; **66:8** O *b.* our God, ye people, and make the voice of his praise to be heard; **68:26** *b.* ye God in the congregations, even the Lord, from the fountain of Israel; **72:17-18** all nations shall call him *b.*. *b.* be the LORD God, the God of Israel, who only doeth wondrous things; **103:1** *b.* the LORD, O my soul: and all that is within me, *b.* his holy name; **103:20-22** *b.* the LORD, ye his angels, that excel in strength, that do his commandments, hearkening unto the voice of his word. *b.* ye the LORD, all ye his hosts; ye ministers of his, that do his pleasure. *b.* the LORD, all his works in all places of his dominion: *b.* the LORD, O my soul; **104:1** *b.* the LORD, O my soul. O LORD my God, thou art very great; thou art clothed with honour and majesty; **115:18** we will *b.* the LORD from this time forth and for evermore. Praise the LORD; **134:1-2** *b.* ye the LORD, all ye servants of the LORD, which by night stand in the house of the LORD. Lift up your hands in the sanctuary, and *b.* the LORD; **135:19-21** *b.* the LORD, O house of Israel: *b.* the LORD, O house of Aaron: *b.* the LORD, O house of Levi: ye that fear the LORD, *b.* the LORD. *b.* be the LORD out of Zion, which dwelleth at Jerusalem. Praise ye the LORD; **145:1-2** I will extol thee, my God, O king; and I will *b.* thy name for ever and ever. Every day will I *b.* thee; and I will praise thy name for ever and ever; **145:10** all thy works shall praise thee, O LORD; and thy saints shall *b.* thee; **145:21** my mouth shall speak the praise of the LORD: and let all flesh *b.* his holy name for ever and ever.

BLIND, BLINDNESS (*see also* Bondage, Darkness, Deceit, Evil)

He that hateth his brother is in darkness, and walketh in darkness, and knoweth not whither he goeth, because that darkness hath blinded his eyes. 1 Jn. 2:11 (*see also* Hate)

BLOOD, BLOODSHED (*see also* Atone, Innocent, Murder)

Shed not innocent blood. Jer. 7:6 (*see also* Innocent)

Almost all things are by the law purged with blood; and without shedding of blood is no remission. Heb. 9:22 (*see also* Remission)

Grace be unto you, and peace, from him which is, and which was, and which is to come; and from the seven Spirits which are before his throne; And from Jesus Christ, who is the faithful witness, and the first begotten of the dead, and the prince of the kings of the earth. Unto him that loved us, and washed us from our sins in his own blood, And hath made us kings and priests unto God and his Father; to him be glory and dominion for ever and ever. Amen. Rev. 1:4-6 (*see also* Begotten, Glory, Jesus Christ)

And he took the cup, and gave thanks, and gave it to them, saying, Drink ye all of it; For this is my blood of the new testament, which is shed for many for the remission of sins. Matt. 26:28 (*see also* Remission)

Therefore also said the wisdom of God, I will send them prophets and apostles, and some of them they shall slay and persecute: That the blood of all the prophets, which was shed from the foundation of the world, may be required of this generation. Luke 11:49-50 (*see also* Persecute, Prophet, Wisdom)

BOAST, BOASTING (*see also* Glory, Haughty, Pride)

In God we boast all the day long, and praise thy name for ever. Ps. 44:8 (*see also* Praise)

Let another man praise thee, and not thine own mouth; a stranger, and not thine own lips. Prov. 27:2 (*see also* Praise)

They that trust in their wealth, and boast themselves in the multitude of their riches; None of them can by any means redeem his brother. Ps. 49:6-7 (*see also* Redeem, Rich)

Now ye rejoice in your boastings: all such rejoicing is evil. James 4:16

Mark 7:36 he charged them that they should tell no man: but the more he charged them, so much the more a great deal they published it; **8:30** he charged them that they should tell no man of him; **Luke 8:56** her parents were astonished: but he charged them that they should tell no man what was done; **Rom. 1:22** professing themselves to be wise, they became fools; **11:18** *b.* not against the branches. But if thou boast, thou bearest not the root, but the root thee; **Eph. 2:8-10** by grace are ye saved through faith; and that not of yourselves: it is the gift of God: Not of works, lest any man should *b.*; **2 Tim. 3:2** men shall be lovers of their own selves, covetous, *b.*, proud, blasphemers, disobedient to parents, unthankful, unholy; **James 4:16** now ye rejoice in your *b.*: all such rejoicing is evil.

Whoso boasteth himself of a false gift *is like* clouds and wind without rain. Prov. 25:14 (*see also* Gift)

Prov. 25:14 whoso *b.* himself of a false gift is like clouds and wind without rain; **Dan. 4:30-31** the king spake, and said, Is not this great Babylon, that I have built for the house of the kingdom by the might of my power, and for the honour of my majesty?... there fell a voice from heaven, saying, O king Nebuchadnezzar, to thee it is spoken; The kingdom is departed from thee.

Boast not thyself of tomorrow; for thou knowest not what a day may bring forth. Prov. 27:1 (*see also* Tomorrow)

Prov. 27:1 *b.* not thyself of tomorrow; for thou knowest not what a day may bring forth; **Isa. 10:15** shall the axe *b.* itself against him that heweth therewith?

With your mouth ye have boasted against me, and have multiplied your words against me: I have heard *them*. Thus saith the Lord GOD; When the whole earth rejoiceth, I will make thee desolate. Ezek. 35:13-14

Ezek. 29:9-11 the land of Egypt shall be desolate and waste; and they shall know that I am the LORD: because he hath said, The river is mine, and I have made it; **35:13-14** with your mouth ye have *b.* against me, and have multiplied your words against me: I have heard them. Thus saith the Lord GOD; When the whole earth rejoiceth, I will make thee desolate; **Dan. 5:23** thou hast praised the gods of silver, and gold, of brass, iron, wood, and stone, which see not, nor hear, nor know: and the God in whose hand thy breath is, and whose are all thy ways, hast thou not glorified.

BODY (*see also* Flesh, Spirit)

If any man offend not in word, the same is a perfect man, and able also to bridle the whole body. James 3:2 (*see also* Bridle, Offend, Perfect)

I keep under my body, and bring it into subjection: lest that by any means, when I have preached to others, I myself should be a castaway. 1 Cor. 9:27 (*see also* Flesh, Subject, Will)

What? Know ye not that your body is a temple of the Holy Ghost which is in you, which ye have of God, and ye are not your own? For ye are bought with a price: therefore glorify God in your body, and in your spirit, which are God's. 1 Cor. 6:20 (*see also* Holy Ghost, Temple)

We must all appear before the judgment seat of Christ; that every one may receive the things done in his body, according to that he hath done, whether it be good or bad. 2 Cor. 5:10 (*see also* Appear, Bad, Judge)

BOLD, BOLDLY, BOLDNESS (*see also* Courage)

BOND, BONDAGE (*see also* Blind)

After that ye have known God, or rather are known of God, how turn ye again to the weak and beggarly elements, whereunto ye desire again to be in bondage? Gal. 4:9 (*see also* Fall)

There is neither Jew nor Greek, there is neither bond nor free, there is neither male nor female: for ye are all one in Christ Jesus. Gal. 3:28 (*see also* Equality, Female, Male, One)

BOOK, BOOKS (*see also* Record, Scripture)

This book of the law shall not depart out of thy mouth; but thou shalt meditate therein day and night, that thou mayest observe to do according to all that is written therein: for then thou shalt make thy way prosperous, and then thou shalt have good success. Josh. 1:8 (*see also* Do, Meditate, Prosperous, Success)

If any man shall take away from the words of the book of this prophecy, God shall take away his part out of the book of life, and out of the holy city, and from the things which are written in this book Rev. 22:19 (*see also* Book, Part)

BORN, BORN AGAIN, BORN OF GOD (*see also* Baptism, Conversion, Heart, Holy Ghost, New)

Jesus answered, Verily, verily, I say unto thee, Except a man be born of water and of the Spirit, he cannot enter into the kingdom of God. John 3:5 (*see also* Enter, Spirit, Water)

Marvel not that I said unto thee, Ye must be born again. The wind bloweth where it listeth, and thou hearest the sound thereof, but canst not tell whence it cometh, and whither it goeth: so is every one that is born of the Spirit. John 3:7-8 (*see also* Holy Spirit)

John 1:13 which were *b.*, not of blood, nor of the will of the flesh, nor of the will of man, but of God; **3:3** except a man be *b.a.*, he cannot see the kingdom of God; **3:5** Jesus answered, Verily, verily, I say unto thee, Except a man be *b.* of water and of the Spirit, he cannot enter into the kingdom of God; **3:7-8** marvel not that I said unto thee, Ye must be *b.a.*. The wind bloweth where it listeth, and thou hearest the sound thereof, but canst not tell whence it cometh, and whither it goeth: so is every one that is *b.* of the Spirit; **1 Pet. 1:23** being *b.a.*, not of corruptible seed, but of incorruptible, by the word of God, which liveth and abideth for ever; **1 Jn. 3:9** whosoever is *b.* of God doth not commit sin; for his seed remaineth in him: and he cannot sin, because he is *b.* of God; **5:4** for whatsoever is *b.* of God overcometh the world: and this is the victory that overcometh the world, even our faith; **5:18** we know that whosoever is *b.* of God sinneth not; but he that is begotten of God keepeth himself, and that wicked one toucheth him not.

BORROW (*see also* Bondage, Debt, Owe)

The rich ruleth over the poor, and the borrower is servant to the lender. **Prov. 22:7**

The wicked borroweth, and payeth not again: but the righteous sheweth mercy, and giveth. **Ps. 37:21** (*see also* Mercy)

Give to him that asketh thee, and from him that would borrow of thee turn not thou away. **Matt. 5:42 9** (*see also* Give)

Matt. 5:42 9 give to him that asketh thee, and from him that would *b.* of thee turn not thou away.

BOW (verb) (*see also* Yield)

Come, let us worship and bow down: let us kneel before the LORD our maker. **Ps. 95:6** (*see also* Kneel, Worship)

Bow down thine ear, and hear the words of the wise, and apply thine heart unto my knowledge. **Prov. 22:17** (*see also* Know, Wise)

Prov. 22:17 *b.* down thine ear, and hear the words of the wise, and apply thine heart unto my knowledge; **22:21** I might make thee know the certainty of the words of truth; that thou mightest answer the words of truth to them that send unto thee.

BRASS

Though I speak with the tongues of men and of angels, and have not charity, I am become as sounding brass, or a tinkling cymbal. **1 Cor. 13:1** (*see also* Become, Charity, Speak)

His head and his hairs were white like wool, as white as snow; and his eyes were as a flame of fire; And his feet like unto fine brass, as if they burned in a furnace; and his voice as the sound of many waters. **Rev. 1:15** (*see also* Jesus Christ, Voice)

BREAD (*see also* Life, Word)

He humbled thee, and suffered thee to hunger, and fed thee with manna, which thou knewest not, neither did thy fathers know; that he might make thee know that man doth not live by bread only, but by every word that proceedeth out of the mouth of the LORD doth man live. **Deut. 8:3** (*see also* Proceed, Word)

Man shall not live by bread alone, but by every word that proceedeth out of the mouth of God. **Matt. 4:4** (*see also* Live, Proceed, Word)

Eateth not the bread of idleness. **Prov. 31:27** (*see also* Idle)

Jesus took bread, and blessed it, and brake it, and gave it to the disciples, and said, Take, eat; this is my body. **Matt 26:26** (*see also* Sacrament)

Matt. 26:26 (Mark 14:22, Luke 22:19, 1 Cor. 11:23) Jesus took bread, and blessed it, and brake it, and gave it to the disciples, and said, Take, eat; this is my body; **Acts 2:42** they continued stedfastly in the apostles' doctrine and fellowship, and in breaking of bread, and in prayers; **1 Cor. 10:16** the bread which we break, is it not the communion of the body of Christ?

He that hath a bountiful eye shall be blessed; for he giveth of his bread to the poor. **Prov. 22:9**

Job 22:5-11 is not thy wickedness great?... thou hast not given water to the weary to drink, and thou hast withholden *b.* from the hungry; **Prov. 22:9** he that hath a bountiful eye shall be blessed; for he giveth of his *b.* to the poor; **Isa. 58:7-9** is it not to deal thy *b.* to the hungry, and that thou bring the poor that are cast out to thy house; **Ezek. 18:7** hath not oppressed any, but hath restored to the debtor his pledge, hath spoiled none by violence, hath given his *b.* to the hungry, and hath covered the naked with a garment; **18:18** because he cruelly oppressed, spoiled his brother by violence, and did that which is not good among his people, lo, even he shall die in his iniquity.

BREAK, BROKEN (*see also* Contrite, Loose)

The LORD is nigh unto them that are of a broken heart; and saveth such as be of a contrite spirit. Ps. 34:18 (*see also* Contrite, Heart)

BRETHREN, BROTHER

He stretched forth his hand toward his disciples, and said, Behold my mother and my brethren! For whosoever shall do the will of m Father which is in heaven, the same is my brother, and sister, and mother. Matt. 12:49-50 (*see also* Sister, Will, Mark 3:35)

BRIBE, BRIBERY (*see also* Gift)

I know your manifold transgressions and your mighty sins: they afflict the just, they take a bribe, and they turn aside the poor in the gate from their right. Amos 5:12 (*see also* Afflict, Just)

BRIDLE (*see also* Refrain)

If any man offend not in word, the same is a perfect man, and able also to bridle the whole body. James 3:2 (*see also* Body, Offend, Perfect)

BRING, BROUGHT (*see also* Gather)

Hear the word, and receive it, and bring forth fruit. Mark 4:20 (*see also* Fruit, Word)

BROKENHEARTED (*see also* Contrite, Heart)

The LORD hath anointed me to preach good tidings unto the meek; he hath sent me to bind up the brokenhearted, to proclaim liberty to the captives, and the opening of the prison to them that are bound. Isa. 61:1

Isa. 61:1 the Spirit of the Lord GOD is upon me; because the LORD hath anointed me to preach good tidings unto the meek; he hath sent me to bind up the *b.*; **61:3** appoint unto them that mourn in Zion, to give unto them beauty for ashes, the oil of joy for mourning, the garment of praise for the spirit of heaviness; that they might be called trees of righteousness, the planting of the LORD, that he might be glorified.

BUILD, BUILT (*see* Edify, Establish)

BURDEN, BURDENSOME (*see also* Afflict, Oppress, Suffer)

We then that are strong ought to bear the infirmities of the weak, and not to please ourselves. Rom. 15:1 (*see also* Poor)

Cast thy burden upon the LORD, and he shall sustain thee: he shall never suffer the righteous to be moved. Ps. 55:22 (*see also* Moved)

Ps. 55:22 cast thy *b.* upon the LORD, and he shall sustain thee: he shall never suffer the righteous to be moved; **58:11** verily there is a reward for the righteous: verily he is a God that judgeth in the earth.

In all things I have kept myself from being burdensome unto you, and so will I keep myself. 2 Cor. 11:9

Acts 15:28 it seemed good to the Holy Ghost, and to us, to lay upon you no greater *b.* than these necessary things; **20:34** these hands have ministered unto my necessities, and to them that were with me; **2 Cor. 11:9** in all things I have kept myself from being *b.* unto you, and so will I keep myself; **12:13-14** ye were inferior to other churches, except it be that I myself was not *b.* to you? forgive me this wrong; **1 Thes. 2:5-6** or of men sought we glory, neither of you, nor yet of others, when we might have been *b.,* as the apostles of Christ.

BURN

They said one to another, Did not our heart burn within us, while he talked with us by the way, and while he opened to us the scriptures? Luke 24:32 (see also Opened)

BUSYBODY (see also Gossip, Talebearer)

But let none of you suffer as a murderer, or as a thief, or as an evildoer, or as a busybody in other men's matters. 1 Pet. 4:15 (see also Matter)

BUY, BOUGHT

What? Know ye not that your body is a temple of the Holy Ghost which is in you, which ye have of God, and ye are not your own? For ye are bought with a price: therefore glorify God in your body, and in your spirit, which are God's. 1 Cor. 6:20 (see also Body, Holy Ghost, Temple)

CALAMITIES, CALAMITY (see also Sign, World)

Whoso mocketh the poor reproacheth his Maker: and he that is glad at calamities shall not be unpunished. Prov. 17:5

Thine own friend, and thy father's friend, forsake not; neither go into thy brother's house in the day of thy calamity: for better is a neighbour that is near than a brother far off. Prov. 27:10 (see also Better, Forsake)

CALL, CALLED, CALLING (see also Appoint, Authority, Election, Foreordain, Priesthood)

Be not ye called Rabbi: for one is your Master, even Christ; and all ye are brethren. Matt. 23:8 (see also Rabbi)

Call unto me, and I will answer thee, and shew thee great and mighty things, which thou knowest not. Jer. 33:3 (see also Mysteries, Reveal)

Call no man your father upon the earth: for one is your Father which is in heaven. Matt. 23:9 (see also Father)

Neither be ye called masters: for one is your Master, even Christ. Matt. 23:10 (see also Master)

Ye that is called in the Lord, being a servant is the Lord's freeman: likewise also he that is called, being free, is Christ's servant. Ye are bought with a price; be not ye the servants of men. 1 Cor 7:22-23 (see also Price, Servant)

Fight the good fight of faith, lay hold on eternal life, whereunto thou art also called, and hast professed a good profession before many witnesses. 1 Tim. 6:12 (see also Eternal)

Call upon the name of the LORD, to serve him with one consent. Zeph. 3:9

Whosoever shall call on the name of the Lord shall be saved. Acts 2:21

Walk worthy of the vocation wherewith ye are called. Eph. 4:1 (see also Vocation)

Therefore leaving the principles of the doctrine of Christ, let us go on unto perfection; not laying again the foundation of repentance from dead works, and of faith toward God, Of the doctrine of baptisms, and of laying on of hands, and of resurrection of the dead, and of eternal judgment. Heb. 6:1-2 (see also Authority, Laying on of Hands)

Give thanks unto the LORD, call upon his name, make known his deeds among the people. 1 Chron. 16:8 (see also Make Known, Thank)

Praise the LORD, call upon his name, declare his doings among the people, make mention that his name is exalted. Isa. 12:4 (see also Declare, Praise)

Offer unto God thanksgiving; and pay thy vows unto the most High: And call upon me in the day of trouble: I will deliver thee, and thou shalt glorify me. Ps. 50:14-15 (see also Thank)

In the day of my trouble I will call upon thee: for thou wilt answer me. Ps. 86:7 (see also Call, Seek, Trouble)

Take heed to the ministry which thou hast received in the Lord, that thou fulfill it. Col. 4:17 (see also Ministry)

Acts 6:2-4 look ye out among you seven men of honest report, full of the Holy Ghost and wisdom, whom we may appoint over this business. But we will give ourselves continually to prayer, and to the ministry of the word; **12:25** And Barnabas and Saul returned from Jerusalem, when they had fulfilled their ministry, and took with them John, whose surname was Mark; **Rom. 11:13** inasmuch as I am the apostle of the Gentiles, I magnify mine office; **15:16-17** I have therefore whereof I may glory through Jesus Christ in those things which pertain to God; **1 Cor. 4:9** I think that God hath set forth us the apostles last, as it were appointed to death: for we are made a spectacle unto the world, and to angels, and to men; **7:17** as God hath distributed to every man, as the Lord hath *c.* every one, so let him walk; **7:20-22** let every man abide in the same *c.* wherein he was *c..* Art thou *c.* being a servant? care not for it: but if thou mayest be made free, use it rather. For he that is *c.* in the Lord, being a servant, is the Lord's freeman: likewise also he that is *c.,* being free, is Christ's servant; **7:24** let every man, wherein he is *c.,* therein abide with God; **9:2** if I be not an apostle unto others, yet doubtless I am to you: for the seal of mine apostleship are ye in the Lord; **2 Cor. 6:4** in all things approving ourselves as the ministers of God, in much patience, in afflictions, in necessities, in distresses; **Eph. 4:4** there is one body, and one Spirit, even as ye are *c.* in one hope of your *c.*; **Col. 4:17** take heed to the ministry which thou hast received in the Lord, that thou fulfil it; **1 Tim. 3:13** the office of a deacon well purchase to themselves a good degree, and great boldness in the faith which is in Christ Jesus; **2 Tim. 1:9-11** who hath saved us, and *c.* us with an holy *c.,* not according to our works, but according to his own purpose and grace, which was given us in Christ Jesus before the world began, But is now made manifest by the appearing of our Saviour Jesus Christ, who hath abolished death, and hath brought life and immortality to light through the gospel: Whereunto I am appointed a preacher, and an apostle, and a teacher of the Gentiles.

In my distress I call upon the LORD, and cried to my God: and he did hear my voice out of his temple, and my cry did enter into his ears. 1 Sam. 22:7

Gen. 4:26 to Seth, to him also there was born a son; and he *c.* his name Enos: then began men to *c.* upon the name of the LORD; **12:8** there he builded an altar unto the LORD, and *c.* upon the name of the LORD; **13:4** there Abram *c.* on the name of the LORD; **16:13** she *c.* the name of the LORD that spake unto her, Thou God seest me: for she said, Have I also here looked after him

that seeth me; **21:33** Abraham... *c.* there on the name of the LORD, the everlasting God; **Judg. 15:18** he was sore athirst, and *c.* on the LORD, and said, Thou hast given this great deliverance into the hand of thy servant: and now shall I die for thirst; **16:28** Samson *c.* unto the LORD, and said, O Lord GOD, remember me, I pray thee, and strengthen me, I pray thee, only this once, O God; **1 Sam. 12:17-18** I will *c.* unto the LORD, and he shall send thunder and rain; that ye may perceive and see that your wickedness is great; **2 Sam. 22:4** I will *c.* on the LORD, who is worthy to be praised: so shall I be saved from mine enemies; **22:7** in my distress I *c.* upon the LORD, and cried to my God: and he did hear my voice out of his temple, and my cry did enter into his ears; **1 Kgs. 18:24** *c.* ye on the name of your gods, and I will *c.* on the name of the LORD: and the God that answereth by fire, let him be God; **2 Kgs. 19:15** Hezekiah prayed before the LORD, and said, O LORD God of Israel, which dwellest between the cherubims, thou art the God, even thou alone; **20:2-3** he turned his face to the wall, and prayed unto the LORD, saying, I beseech thee, O LORD, remember now how I have walked before thee in truth and with a perfect heart; **1 Chron. 4:10** Jabez *c.* on the God of Israel, saying, Oh that thou wouldest bless me indeed... and that thine hand might be with me... And God granted him that which he requested; **16:8** give thanks unto the LORD, *c.* upon his name, make known his deeds among the people; **21:26** David built there an altar unto the LORD, and offered burnt offerings and peace offerings, and *c.* upon the LORD; and he answered him; **Ps. 14:4** have all the workers of iniquity no knowledge? who eat up my people as they eat bread, and *c.* not upon the LORD; **17:6-7** I have *c.* upon thee, for thou wilt hear me, O God: incline thine ear unto me, and hear my speech; **18:3** I will *c.* upon the LORD, who is worthy to be praised: so shall I be saved from mine enemies; **18:6** I *c.* upon the LORD, and cried unto my God: he heard my voice out of his temple, and my cry came before him, even into his ears; **31:17** let me not be ashamed, O LORD; for I have *c.* upon thee; **50:15** *c.* upon me in the day of trouble: I will deliver thee, and thou shalt glorify me; **53:4** have the workers of iniquity no knowledge? who eat up my people as they eat bread: they have not *c.* upon God; **55:16** I will *c.* upon God; and the LORD shall save me; **86:5-7** thou, Lord, art good, and ready to forgive; and plenteous in mercy unto all them that *c.* upon thee... In the day of my trouble I will *c.* upon thee: for thou wilt answer me; **99:6** they *c.* upon the LORD, and he answered them; **105:1** give thanks unto the LORD; *c.* upon his name: make known his deeds among the people; **116:1-2** I love the LORD, because he hath heard my voice and my supplications. Because he hath inclined his ear unto me, therefore will I *c.* upon him as long as I live; **116:13** I will take the cup of salvation, and *c.* upon the name of the LORD; **116:17** I will offer to thee the sacrifice of thanksgiving, and will *c.* upon the name of the LORD; **118:5** I *c.* upon the LORD in distress: the LORD answered me; **145:18** the LORD is nigh unto all them that *c.* upon him, to all that *c.* upon him in truth; **Prov. 1:24** I have *c.*, and ye refused; I have stretched out my hand, and no man regarded; **Isa. 12:4** praise the LORD, *c.* upon his name, declare his doings among the people, make mention that his name is exalted; **55:6** seek ye the LORD while he may be found, *c.* ye upon him while he is near; **62:7** give him no rest, till he establish, and till he make Jerusalem a praise in the earth; **65:12** ye shall all bow down to the slaughter: because when I *c.*, ye did not answer; when I spake, ye did not hear; but did evil before mine eyes; **65:24** before they *c.*, I will answer; and while they are yet speaking, I will hear; **Jer. 10:25** pour out thy fury upon the heathen that know thee not, and upon the families that *c.* not on thy name; **29:12** [ye shall] *c.* upon me, and ye shall go and pray unto me, and I will hearken unto you; **33:3** *c.* unto me, and I will answer thee, and shew thee great and mighty things, which thou knowest not; **Lam. 3:55-57** I *c.* upon thy name, O LORD, out of the low dungeon. Thou hast heard my voice: hide not thine ear at my breathing, at my cry; **Dan. 9:3-6** I set my face unto the Lord God, to seek by prayer and supplications, with fasting, and sackcloth, and ashes: And I prayed unto the LORD my God, and made my confession; **Hosea 7:7** all their kings are fallen: there is none among them that *c.* unto me; **Joel 2:32** whosoever shall *c.* on the name of the LORD shall be delivered; **Zeph. 3:9** then will I turn to the people a pure language, that they may all *c.* upon the name of the LORD, to serve him with one consent; **Zech. 13:9** they shall *c.* on my name, and I will hear them: I will say, It is my people: and they shall say, The LORD is my God. **Acts 2:21** whosoever shall *c.* on the name of the Lord shall be saved; **1 Cor. 1:2** to them that are sanctified in Christ Jesus, called to be saints, with all that in every place *c.* upon the name of Jesus Christ our Lord, both theirs and ours; **Rom. 10:12** the same Lord over all is rich unto all that *c.* upon him. For whosoever shall *c.* upon the name of the Lord shall be saved.

CANDLE (*see also* Light)

Let your light so shine before men, that they may see your good works, and glorify your Father which is in heaven. Matt. 5:16 (*see also* Example, Light)

The spirit of man is the candle of the LORD, searching all the inward parts of the belly. Prov. 20:27

No man, when he hath lighted a candle, covereth it with a vessel, or putteth it under a bed; but setteth it on a candlestick, that they which enter in may see the light. Luke 8:16 (*see also* Light)

Luke 8:16 No man, when he hath lighted a candle, covereth it with a vessel, or putteth it under a bed; but setteth it on a candlestick, that they which enter in may see the light; **Luke 11:33** No man, when he hath lighted a candle, putteth *it* in a secret place, neither under a bushel, but on a candlestick, that they which come in may see the light.

CANKER, CANKERED (*see also* Corrupt)

Your gold and silver is cankered; and the rust of them shall be a witness against you, and shall eat your flesh as it were fire. Ye have heaped treasure together for the last days. James 5:3

CARE, CAREFUL, CAREFULLY (*see also* Nurture)

He that is unmarried careth for the things that belong to the Lord, how he may please the Lord: But he that is married careth for the things that are of the world, how he may please his wife. 1 Cor. 7:32-33 (*see also* Wife)

CARELESS (*see also* Foolish)

Hear now this, thou that art given to pleasures, that dwellest carelessly, that sayest in thine heart, I am, and none else beside me. Isa. 47:8 (*see also* Dwell)

CAST (*see also* Persecute, Reject)

Cast out the scorner, and contention shall go out; yea, strife and reproach shall cease. Prov. 22:10 (*see also* Contend, Scorn)

Is it not to deal thy bread to the hungry, and that thou bring the poor that are cast out to thy house? When thou seest the naked, that thou cover him; and that thou hide not thyself from thine own flesh? Isa. 58:7 (*see also* Cover, Naked)

These signs shall follow them that believe; In my name shall they cast out devils; they shall speak with new tongues; They shall take up serpents; and if they drink any deadly thing it shall not hurt them; they shall lay hands on the sick and they shall recover. Mark 16:17-18 (*see also* Deadly, Devil, Name, Sign, Tongues)

CATCH, CAUGHT

We which are alive and remain shall be caught up together with them in the clouds, to meet the Lord in the air: and so shall we ever be with the Lord. 1 Thes. 4:17 (*see also* Second Coming)

Jesus said unto Simon, Fear not; from henceforth thou shalt catch men. Luke 5:10

CAUSE (*see also* Reason)

Let them shout for joy, and be glad, that favour my righteous cause: yea, let them say continually, Let the LORD be magnified, which hath pleasure in the prosperity of his servant. Ps. 35:27 (*see also* Righteous)

Strive not with a man without cause, if he have done thee no harm. Prov. 3:30 (*see also* Harm)

Prov. 3:30 strive not with a man without *c.*, if he have done thee no harm; 17:14 the beginning of strife is as when one letteth out water: therefore leave off contention, before it be meddled with.

CELESTIAL (*see also* Heaven, Save)

There are also celestial bodies, and bodies terrestrial: but the glory of the celestial is one, and the glory of the terrestrial is another. There is one glory of the sun, and another glory of the moon, and another glory of the stars: for one star differeth from another star in glory. So also is the resurrection of the dead. 1 Cor. 15:40-42 (*see also* Dead, Glory, Terrestrial, Resurrection)

CHANGE (*see also* Alter, Born Again, Conversion, New, Sanctified)

Fear thou the LORD and the king: and meddle not with them that are given to change: For their calamity shall rise suddenly; and who knoweth the ruin of them both? Prov. 24:21 (*see also* Meddle)

CHARGE (*see also* Accuse, Command)

In all this Job sinned not, nor charged God foolishly. Job 1:22

CHARITY (*see also* Alms, Benevolence, Compassion, Love, Mercy)

Though I speak with the tongues of men and of angels, and have not charity, I am become as sounding brass, or a tinkling cymbal. 1 Cor. 13:1 (*see also* Brass, Speak)

Though I bestow all my goods to feed the poor, an though I give my body to be burned, and have not charity, it profiteth me nothing. 1 Cor. 13:3 (*see also* Bestow)

Let no man despise thy youth; but be thou an example of the believers, in word, in conversation, in charity, in spirit, in faith, in purity. 1 Tim. 4:12 (*see also* Believe, Conversation, Despise, Example, Pure)

Charity suffereth long, and is kind; charity envieth not; charity vaunteth not itself, is not puffed up, Doth not behave itself unseemly, seeketh not her own, is not easily provoked, thinketh no evil; Rejoiceth not in iniquity, but rejoiceth in the truth; Beareth all things, believeth all things, hopeth all things, endureth all things. 1 Cor. 13:4-7 (*see also* All Things, Bear, Believe, Endure, Hope, Provoke, Rejoice, Seek, Suffer, Think)

And above all things have fervent charity among yourselves: for charity shall cover the multitude of sins. 1 Pet 4:8 (*see also* Multitude, Sin)

Above all things, put on charity, which is the bond of perfectness. Col. 3:14 (*see also* Perfect)

Matt. 24:12 because iniquity shall abound, the love of many shall wax cold; Luke 11:42 woe unto you, Pharisees! for ye tithe mint and rue and all manner of herbs, and pass over judgment and the love of God: these ought ye to have done, and not to leave the other undone; **John 5:42** I know you, that ye have not the love of God in you; **17:24** Father, I will that they also, whom thou hast given me, be with me where I am; that they may behold my glory, which thou hast given me: for thou lovedst me before the foundation of the world; **17:26** I have declared unto them thy name, and will declare it: that the love wherewith thou hast loved me may be in them, and I in them; **Rom. 5:5** hope maketh not ashamed; because the love of God is shed abroad in our hearts by the Holy Ghost which is given unto us; **12:9** let love be without dissimulation; **13:8** owe no man any thing, but to love one another: for he that loveth another hath fulfilled the law; **13:10** love worketh no ill to his neighbour: therefore love is the fulfilling of the law; **1 Cor. 8:1** knowledge puffeth up, but *c.* edifieth; **13:1-3** though I speak with the tongues of men and of angels, and have not *c.,* I am become as sounding brass, or a tinkling cymbal. And though I have the gift of prophecy, and understand all mysteries, and all knowledge; and though I have all faith, so that I could remove mountains, and have not *c.,* I am nothing. And though I bestow all my goods to feed the poor, and though I give my body to be burned, and have not *c.,* it profiteth me nothing; **13:8** *c.* never faileth: but whether there be prophecies, they shall fail; whether there be tongues, they shall cease; whether there be knowledge, it shall vanish away; **13:13** now abideth faith, hope, *c.,* these three; but the greatest of these is *c.*; **14:1** follow after *c.,* and desire spiritual gifts, but rather that ye may prophesy; **2 Cor. 6:6** by pureness, by knowledge, by longsuffering, by kindness, by the Holy Ghost, by love unfeigned; **6:11** our mouth is open unto you, our heart is enlarged; **Gal. 5:6** in Jesus Christ neither circumcision availeth any thing, nor uncircumcision; but faith which worketh by love; **5:13** ye have been called unto liberty; only use not liberty for an occasion to the flesh, but by love serve one another; **Eph. 1:15** I heard of your faith in the Lord Jesus, and love unto all the saints; **3:17** Christ may dwell in your hearts by faith; that ye, being rooted and grounded in love; **3:19** to know the love of Christ, which passeth knowledge, that ye might be filled with all the fulness of God; **4:2-3** with all lowliness and meekness, with long-suffering, forbearing one another in love; Endeavouring to keep the unity of the Spirit in the bond of peace; **4:15-16** speaking the truth in love, may grow up into him in all things, which is the head, even Christ: From whom the whole body fitly joined together

and compacted by that which every joint supplieth, according to the effectual working in the measure of every part, maketh increase of the body unto the edifying of itself in love; **5:2** walk in love, as Christ also hath loved us, and hath given himself for us an offering and a sacrifice to God for a sweetsmelling savour; **6:23** peace be to the brethren, and love with faith, from God the Father and the Lord Jesus Christ; **Philip. 1:9** I pray, that your love may abound yet more and more in knowledge and in all judgment; **Col. 2:2** their hearts might be comforted, being knit together in love, and unto all riches of the full assurance of understanding, to the acknowledge-ment of the mystery of God, and of the Father, and of Christ; **3:14** above all these things put on *c.,* which is the bond of perfectness; **1 Thes. 1:3** remembering without ceasing your work of faith, and labour of love, and patience of hope in our Lord Jesus Christ, in the sight of God and our Father; **3:6** brought us good tidings of your faith and *c.,* and that ye have good remembrance of us always; **3:11-12** the Lord make you to increase and abound in love one toward another, and toward all men, even as we do toward you; **4:9** as touching brotherly love ye need not that I write unto you: for ye yourselves are taught of God to love one another; **5:8** be sober, putting on the breastplate of faith and love; and for an helmet, the hope of salvation; **2 Thes. 1:3** your faith groweth exceedingly, and the *c.* of every one of you all toward each other aboundeth; **1 Tim. 1:5** now the end of the commandment is *c.* out of a pure heart, and of a good conscience, and of faith unfeigned; **4:12** let no man despise thy youth; but be thou an example of the believers, in word, in conversation, in *c.,* in spirit, in faith, in purity; **6:11** follow after righteousness, god-liness, faith, love, patience, meekness; **2 Tim. 1:7** God hath not given us the spirit of fear; but of power, and of love, and of a sound mind; **1:13** hold fast the form of sound words, which thou hast heard of me, in faith and love which is in Christ Jesus; **2:22** flee also youthful lusts: but follow righteousness, faith, *c.,* peace, with them that call on the Lord out of a pure heart; **3:10** thou hast fully known my doctrine, manner of life, purpose, faith, long-suffering, *c.,* patience; **Titus 2:2** be sober, grave, temperate, sound in faith, in *c.,* in patience; **Heb. 6:10** God is not unrighteous to forget your work and labour of love, which ye have shewed toward his name, in that ye have ministered to the saints, and do minister; **10:24** let us consider one another to provoke unto love and to good works; **1 Pet. 4:8** above all things have fervent *c.* among yourselves: for *c.* shall cover the multitude of sins; **5:14** greet ye one another with a kiss of *c..* Peace be with you all that are in Christ Jesus; **2 Pet. 1:7** and to godliness brotherly kindness; and to brotherly kindness *c.*; **1 Jn. 2:5** whoso keepeth his word, in him verily is the love of God perfected: hereby know we that we are in him; **3:1** what manner of love the Father hath bestowed upon us, that we should be called the sons of God: therefore the world knoweth us not, because it knew him not; **3:16** hereby perceive we the love of God, because he laid down his life for us: and we ought to lay down our lives for the brethren; **4:16** God is love; and he that dwelleth in love dwelleth in God, and God in him; **4:17** herein is our love made perfect, that we may have boldness in the day of judgment: because as he is, so are we in this world; **4:18** there is no fear in love; but perfect love casteth out fear: because fear hath torment. He that feareth is not made perfect in love; **4:19** we love him, because he first loved us; **5:1** whosoever believeth that Jesus is the Christ is born of God: and every one that loveth him that begat loveth him also that is begotten of him; **5:3** for this is the love of God, that we keep his command-ments: and his commandments are not grievous; **2 Jn. 1:6** this is love, that we walk after his commandments. This is the commandment, That, as ye have heard from the beginning, ye should walk in it; **3 Jn. 1:5-8** beloved, thou doest faithfully whatsoever thou doest to the brethren, and to strangers; Which have borne witness of thy *c.* before the church... We therefore ought to receive such, that we might be fellowhelpers to the truth; **Jude 1:21** keep yourselves in the love of God, looking for the mercy of our Lord Jesus Christ unto eternal life; **2:19** I know thy works, and *c.,* and service, and faith, and thy patience, and thy works.

CHASTE, CHASTITY (*see also* Clean, Holy, Modest, Pure, Sanctify, Virtue)

Be discreet, chaste, keepers at home, good, obedient to their own husbands, that the word of God be not blasphemed. Titus 2:5 (*see also* Discrete)

CHASTEN, CHASTENING, CHASTISE (*see also* Afflict, Correct, Exhort, Punish, Rebuke, Warn)

Despise not the chastening of the Lord, nor faint when thou art rebuked of him. Heb. 12:5

In trouble have they visited thee, they poured out a prayer when thy chastening was upon them. Isa. 26:16 (*see also* Pray)

Chasten thy son while there is hope, and let not thy soul spare for his crying. Prov. 19:18

From the first day that thou didst set thine heart to understand, and to chasten thyself before thy God, thy words were heard, and I am come for thy words. Dan. 10:12 (*see also* Understand)

Dan. 10:12 fear not, Daniel: for from the first day that thou didst set thine heart to understand, and to chasten thyself before thy God, thy words were heard, and I am come for thy words.

Behold, happy is the man whom God correcteth: therefore despise not thou the chastening of the Almighty: For he maketh sore, and bindeth up; he woundeth, and his hands make whole. Job 5:17-18 (*see also* Despise)

Job 5:17-27 happy is the man whom God correcteth: therefore despise not thou the *c.* of the Almighty; **34:31-32** it is meet to be said unto God, I have borne *c.,* I will not offend any more: That which I see not teach thou me: if I have done iniquity, I will do no more; **Ps. 7:9** let the wickedness of the wicked come to an end; but establish the just: for the righteous God trieth the hearts and reins; **11:5** the LORD trieth the righteous: but the wicked and him that loveth violence his soul hateth; **17:3** thou hast proved mine heart; thou hast visited me in the night; thou hast tried me, and shalt find nothing; I am purposed that my mouth shall not transgress; **94:12-13** blessed is the man whom thou *c.,* O LORD, and teachest him out of thy law; That thou mayest give him rest from the days of adversity; **Prov. 3:11-12** despise not the *c.* of the LORD; neither be weary of his correction: For whom the LORD loveth he correcteth; even as a father the son in whom he delighteth; **13:24** he that spareth his rod hateth his son: but he that loveth him *c.* him betimes; **Isa. 26:16-18** LORD, in trouble have they visited thee, they poured out a prayer when thy *c.* was upon them.

CHEEK (*see* Forgive)

I say unto you, That ye resist not evil: but whosoever shall smite thee on thy right cheek, turn to him the other also. Matt. 5:39 (*see also* Smite)

CHEER, CHEERFUL, CHEERFULNESS (*see also* Glad, Happiness, Joy, Merry, Rejoice, Wonderful)

Be of good cheer. Mark 6:50 (*see also* Good)

Mark 6:50 they all saw him, and were troubled. And immediately he talked with them, and saith unto them, Be of good *c.*: it is I; be not afraid; **John 16:33** I have spoken unto you, that in me ye might have peace. In the world ye shall have tribulation: but be of good *c.*; I have overcome the world; **Acts 23:11** the night following the Lord stood by him, and said, Be of good *c.*; **27:22** I exhort you to be of good *c.*

All the days of the afflicted are evil: but he that is of a merry heart hath a continual feast. Prov. 15:15

Prov. 15:13 a merry heart maketh a *c.* countenance: but by sorrow of the heart the spirit is broken; **15:15** all the days of the afflicted are evil: but he that is of a merry heart hath a continual feast.

CHIEF (*see also* Lead)

Whosoever will be chief among you, let him be your servant. Matt. 20:27 (*see also* Servant)

CHILD, CHILDREN (*see also* Daughter, Family)

And these words, which I command thee this day, shall be in thine heart: And thou shalt teach them diligently unto thy children, and shalt talk of them when thou sittest in thine house, and when thou walkest by the way and when thou liest down, and when thou risest up. And thou shalt bind them for a sign upon thine hand, and they shalt be as frontlets between thine eyes. And thou shalt write them upon the posts of thy house, and on thy gates. Deut. 6:6-9 (*see also* Diligence, Teach, Word)

Withhold not correction from the child. Prov. 23:13 (*see also* Correct)

Blessed are the peacemakers: for they shall be called the children of God. Matt. 5:9 (*see also* Peace)

He that spareth his rod hateth his son: but he that loveth him chasteneth him betimes. Prov. 13:24 (*see also* Betimes)

Jesus said, Suffer little children, and forbid them not to come unto me, for of such is the kingdom of heaven. Matt. 19:14

It were better for him that a millstone were hanged about his neck, and he cast into the sea, than that he should offend one of these little ones. Luke 17:2 (*see also* Better)

Ye fathers, provoke not your children to wrath: but bring them up in the nurture and admonition of the Lord. Eph. 6:4 (*see also* Admonition, Nurture)

Children, obey your parents in all things: for this is well pleasing unto the Lord. Col. 3:20 (*see also* Obey)

Eph 6:1 *c.,* obey your parents in the Lord: for this is right; **Col. 3:20** *c.,* obey your parents in all things: for this is well pleasing unto the Lord.

Suffer the little children to come unto me, and forbid them not. Mark 10:14

Mark 10:14 when Jesus saw it, he was much displeased, and said unto them, Suffer the little *c.* to come unto me, and forbid them not: for of such is the kingdom of God; **Luke 18:15-16** Jesus called them unto him, and said, Suffer little *c.* to come unto me, and forbid them not: for of such is the kingdom of God; **Eph. 5:1** be ye therefore followers of God, as dear *c.*

Train up a child in the way he should go: and when he is old, he will not depart from it. Prov. 22:6 (*see also* Depart, Train, Way)

Prov. 22:6 train up a *c.* in the way he should go: and when he is old, he will not depart from it; **22:15** foolishness is bound in the heart of a *c.*; but the rod of correction shall drive it far from him; **23:13** withhold not correction from the *c.*: for if thou beatest him with the rod, he shall not die.

Thou shalt not bow down thyself to them, nor serve them: for I the LORD thy God am a jealous God, visiting the iniquities of the fathers upon the children unto the third and fourth generation of them that hate me. Ex. 20:5 (*see also* Thou Shalt Not, Jealous)

Except ye be converted, and become as little children, ye shall not enter into the kingdom of heaven. Matt. 18:3 (*see also* Become, Convert, Kingdom)

Matt. 11:25 (Luke 10:21) I thank thee, O Father, Lord of heaven and earth, because thou hast hid these things from the wise and prudent, and hast revealed them unto babes; **18:1-6** except ye be converted, and become as little *c.,* ye shall not enter into the kingdom of heaven. Whosoever therefore shall humble himself as this little *c.,* the same is greatest in the kingdom of heaven. And whoso shall receive one such little *c.* in my name receiveth me. But whoso shall offend one of these little ones which believe in me, it were better for him that a millstone were hanged about his neck, and that he were drowned in the depth of the sea; **18:10** take heed that ye despise not one of these little ones; for I say unto you, That in heaven their angels do always behold the face of my Father which is in heaven; **19:14** suffer little *c.,* and forbid them not, to come unto me: for of such is the kingdom of heaven; **21:16** out of the mouth of babes and sucklings thou hast perfected praise; **Mark 10:15** whosoever shall not receive the kingdom of God as a little *c.,* he shall not enter therein; **Luke 9:48** whosoever shall receive this *c.* in my name receiveth me: and whosoever shall receive me receiveth him that sent me: for he that is least among you all, the same shall be great; **18:17** whosoever shall not receive the kingdom of God as a little *c.* shall in no wise enter therein; **Gal. 4:1** now I say, That the heir, as long as he is a *c.,* differeth nothing from a servant, though he be lord of all.

CHOICE, CHOOSE, CHOSEN (*see also* Act)

If it seem evil unto you to serve the LORD, choose you this day whom ye will serve; whether the gods which your fathers served that *were* on the other side of the flood, or the gods of the Amorites, in whose land ye dwell: but as for me and my house, we will serve the LORD. Josh. 24:15 (*see also* Serve)

Choose the things that please me, and take hold of my covenant; Even unto them will I give in mine house and within my walls a place and a name better than of sons and of daughters. Isa. 56:4-5 (*see also* Better, Covenant)

So the last shall be first, and the first last: for many be called, but few chosen. Matt 20:16 (*see also* Few)

Jesus answered and said unto her, Martha, Martha, thou art careful and troubled about many things: But one thing is needful: and Mary hath chosen that good part, which shall not be taken away from her. Luke 10:41-42 (*see also* Good)

Matt. 13:22 (Mark 4:19, Luke 8:14) he also that received seed among the thorns is he that heareth the word; and the care of this world, and the deceitfulness of riches, choke the word, and he becometh unfruitful; **Luke 10:41-42** Jesus answered and said unto her, Martha, Martha, thou art careful and troubled about many things: But one thing is needful: and Mary hath chosen that good part, which shall not be taken away from her; **14: 17-24** sent his servant at supper time to say to them that were bidden, Come; for all things are now ready. And they all with one consent began to make excuse... And the lord said unto the servant, Go out into the highways and hedges, and compel them to come in, that my house may be filled. For I say unto you, That none of those men which were bidden shall taste of my supper.

O that they were wise, that they understood this, that they would consider their latter end! Deut. 32:29 (*see also* End)

Deut. 32:29 O that they were wise, that they understood this, that they would consider their latter end; **1 Kgs. 18:21** Elijah came unto all the people, and said, How long halt ye between two opinions? if the LORD be God, follow him: but if Baal, then follow him; **Isa. 47:7** thou didst not lay these things to thy heart, neither didst remember the latter end of it.

I have set before you life and death, blessing and cursing, therefore choose life, that both thou and thy seed may live, That thou mayest love the LORD thy God, and that thou mayest obey his voice, and that thou mayest cleave unto him, for he is thy life, and the length of thy days. Deut. 30:19-20

Deut. 30:15 I have set before thee this day life and good, and death and evil; **30:19-20** I have set before you life and death, blessing and cursing: therefore c. life, that both thou and thy seed may live: That thou mayest love the Lord thy God; **Prov. 11:19** as righteousness tendeth to life: so he that pursueth evil pursueth it to his own death; **12:28** in the way of righteousness is life; and in the pathway thereof there is no death; **13:14** the law of the wise is a fountain of life, to depart from the snares of death; **14:27** the fear of the Lord is a fountain of life, to depart from the snares of death; **15:24** the way of life is above to the wise, that he may depart from hell beneath; **Jer. 21:8** thus saith the Lord; Behold, I set before you the way of life, and the way of death.

CHRIST (*see also* Jesus Christ, Lord, Savior)

If any man shall say unto you, Lo, here is Christ, or there; believe it not. For there shall arise false Christs, and false prophets, and shall shew great signs and wonders; insomuch that, if it were possible, they shall deceive the very elect. Matt. 24:23-24 (*see also* Deceive, False Christ, False Prophet)

CHURCH (*see also* Assemble, Kingdom, Meet, Temple, Zion)

Husbands, love your wives, even as Christ also loved the church, and gave himself for it. That he might sanctify and cleanse it with the washing of water by the word, That he might present it to himself a glorious church, not having spot, or wrinkle, or any such thing; but that it should be holy and without blemish. So ought men to love their wives as their own bodies. He that loveth his wife loveth himself. Eph. 5:25-28 (*see also* Husband, Love)

CIRCUMCISE, CIRCUMCISION (*see also* Purify)

Circumcise yourselves to the Lord, and take away the foreskins of your heart. Jer. 4:4 (*see also* Heart)

Thus saith the Lord GOD; No stranger uncircumcised in heart, nor circumcised in flesh, shall enter into my sanctuary, of any strangers that is among the children of Israel. Ezek. 44:9 (*see also* Sanctuary, Uncircumcised)

Circumcision is that of the heart, in the spirit, and not in the letter; whose praise is not of men, but of God. Rom. 2:28-29 (*see also* Heart)

Rom. 2:28-29 he is not a Jew, which is one outwardly; neither is that c., which is outward in the flesh: But he is a Jew, which is one inwardly; and c. is that of the heart, in the spirit, and not in the letter; whose praise is not of men, but of God; **3:30** seeing it is one God, which shall justify the c. by faith, and uncircumcision through faith; **4:8-12** cometh this blessedness then upon the c. only, or upon the uncircumcision also.

CLEAN, CLEANSED. CLEANLINESS (*see also* Baptize, Chastity, Forgive, Pure, Sanctify, Virtue, Worthiness)

Depart ye, depart ye, go ye out from thence, touch no unclean *thing*; go ye out of the midst of her; be ye clean, that bear the vessels of the Lord. Isa. 52:11 (*see also* Unclean, Vessels)

Truly God is good to Israel, *even* to such as are of a clean heart. Ps. 73:1 (*see also* Heart)

The Lord rewarded me according to my righteousness; according to the cleanness of my hands hath he recompensed me. Ps. 18:20 (*see also* Hand, Reward, Righteous)

Ps. 18:20 the Lord rewarded me according to my righteousness; according to the c. of my hands hath he recompensed me; **18:24** therefore hath the Lord recompensed me according to my righteousness, according to the c. of my hands in his eyesight; **24:4** he that hath c. hands, and a pure heart; who hath not lifted up his soul unto vanity, nor sworn deceitfully.

Teach my people the difference between the holy and profane, and cause them to discern between the unclean and the clean. Ezek. 44:23 (*see also* Holy, Teach, Unclean)

Ezek. 22:26 her priests have violated my law, and have profaned mine holy things: they have put no difference between the holy and profane, neither have they shewed difference between the unclean and the c.; **44:23** teach my people the difference between the holy and profane, and cause them to discern between the unclean and the c.

What God hath cleansed, that call not thou common. Acts 10:15

Acts 10:15 what God hath *c.*, that call not thou common; **10:28** God hath shewed me that I should not call any man common or unclean; **10:34-35** I perceive that God is no respecter of persons: But in every nation he that feareth him, and worketh righteousness, is accepted with him; **10:45** they of the circumcision which believed were astonished, as many as came with Peter, because that on the Gentiles also was poured out the gift of the Holy Ghost.

CLEAR (*see also* Clean, Pure)

Thou hypocrite, first cast out the beam out of thine own eye; and then shalt thou see clearly to cast out the mote out of thy brother's eye. Matt. 7:3-5 (*see also* Hypocrite)

CLEAVE (*see also* Hold, Join)

[Barnabas] exhorted them all, that with purpose of heart they would cleave unto the Lord. Acts 11:23 (*see also* Heart)

Acts 11:23 who, when he came, and had seen the grace of God, was glad, and exhorted them all, that with purpose of heart they would *c.* unto the Lord.

Therefore shall a man leave his father and his mother, and shall cleave unto his wife: and they shall be one flesh. Gen. 2:24 (*see also* Wife, Moses 3:24, Mark 10:6-10)

Gen. 2:24 therefore shall a man leave his father and his mother, and shall *c.* unto his wife: and they shall be one flesh; **4:1** Adam knew Eve his wife; and she conceived, and bare Cain; **4:17** Cain knew his wife; and she conceived, and bare Enoch; **4:25** Adam knew his wife again; and she bare a son, and called his name Seth; **Prov. 5:15-21** let thy fountain be blessed: and rejoice with the wife of thy youth; **Eccl. 4:9-12** two are better than one; because they have a good reward for their labour. For if they fall, the one will lift up his fellow; **Mark 10:6-8** from the beginning of the creation God made them male and female. For this cause shall a man leave his father and mother, and *c.* to his wife; And they twain shall be one flesh: so then they are no more twain, but one flesh; **1 Cor. 11:10-12** neither is the man without the woman, neither the woman without the man, in the Lord. For as the woman is of the man, even so is the man also by the woman; but all things of God.

CLOSET (*see* Prayer)

When thou prayest, enter into thy closet, and when thou hast shut thy door, pray to thy Father which is in secret; and thy Father which seeth in secret shall reward thee openly. Matt. 6:6 (*see also* Prayer, Secret)

COME (*see also* Follow)

Come ye, and let us go to the mountain of the LORD to the house of the God of Jacob; and he will teach us of his ways and we will walk in his paths: for out of Zion shall go forth the law, and the word of the LORD from Jerusalem. Isa. 2:3 (*see also* Go, House, Path, Way)

Come unto me, all ye that labour and are heavy laden, and I will give you rest. Take my yoke upon you, and learn of me; for I am meek and lowly in heart: and ye shall find rest unto your souls. For my yoke is easy, and my burden is light. Matt. 11:28-30 (*see also* Labor, Rest, Yoke)

COMFORT (*see also* Assure, Compassion, Empathize)

Proclaim the acceptable year of the LORD, and the day of vengeance of our God, to comfort all that mourn. Isa. 61:2 (*see also* Mourn, Proclaim, Year)

Blessed be God, even the Father of our Lord Jesus Christ, the Father of mercies, and the God of all comfort; Who comforteth us in all our tribulation, that we may be able to comfort them which are in any trouble, by the comfort wherewith we ourselves are comforted of God. For as the sufferings of Christ abound in us, so our consolation also aboundeth by Christ. 2 Cor. 1:3-5 (*see also* Empathize, Tribulation)

Be of good comfort. 2 Cor. 13:11

Mark 10:49 be of good *c.*, rise; he calleth thee; **Acts 9:31** walking in the fear of the Lord, and in the *c.* of the Holy Ghost, were multiplied; **Rom. 15:4** we through patience and *c.* of the scriptures might have hope; **2 Cor. 1:3-7** blessed be God, even the Father of our Lord Jesus Christ, the Father of mercies, and the God of all *c.*; Who *c.* us in all our tribulation, that we may be able to *c.* them which are in any trouble, by the *c.* wherewith we ourselves are *c.* of God; **13:11** Be perfect, be of good *c.,* be of one mind, live in peace; and the God of love and peace shall be with you; **1 Thes. 4:18** *c.* one another with these words; **5:14** warn them that are unruly, *c.* the feebleminded, support the weak, be patient toward all men.

COMFORTER (*see also* Holy Ghost, Holy Spirit, Spirit)

Nevertheless I tell you the truth; It is expedient for you that I go away; for if I go not away, the Comforter will not come unto you; but if I depart, I will send him unto you. **John 16:7**

These things have I spoken unto you, being yet present with you. But the Comforter, which is the Holy Ghost, whom the Father will send in my name, he shall teach you all things, and bring all things to your remembrance, whatsoever I have said unto you. **John 14:25-26** (*see also* All Things, Holy Ghost, Remembrance)

COMMAND, COMMANDMENT (*see also* Law, Thou Shalt, Thou Shalt Not, Will) (*k.m.c. = keep my commandments*)

Thou shalt love the Lord thy God with all thy heart, and with all thy soul, and with all thy mind, and with all thy strength: this is the first commandment. **Mark 12:30** (*see also* Love, Thou Shalt)

What thing soever I command you, observe to do it: thou shalt not add thereto, nor diminish from it. **Deut. 12:32**

I will give them one heart, and I will put a new spirit within you; and I will take the stony heart out of their flesh, and will give them an heart of flesh: That they may walk in my statutes, and keep mine ordinances, and do them: and they shall be my people, and I will be their God. **Ezek. 11:19-20** (*see also* Heart, One)

Jesus said unto him, Thous shalt love the Lord thy God with all thy heart, and with all thy soul, and with all thy mind. This is the first and great commandment. And the second is like unto it, Thou shalt love thy neighbour as thyself. On these two commandments, hang all the law and the prophets. **Matt 22:37-40** (*see also* Hang, Love, Thous Shalt)

Obey my voice, and I will be your God, and ye shall be my people: and walk ye in all the ways that I have commanded you, that it may be well unto you. **Jer. 7:23** (*see also* Obey)

If thou shalt hearken diligently unto the voice of the LORD thy God, to observe and to do all his commandments which I command thee this day, that the LORD thy God will set thee on high above all nations of the earth; And all these blessings shall come on thee, and overtake thee, if thou shalt hearken unto the voice of the LORD thy God. **Deut. 28:1-2** (*see also* Bless, Hearken)

Remember ye the law of Moses my servant, which I commanded unto him in Horeb for all Israel, with the statutes and judgments. **Mal. 4:4** (*see also* Remember)

If thou wilt enter into life, keep the commandments. **Matt. 19:17** (*see also* Keep)

Matt. 1:24-25 Joseph being raised from sleep did as the angel of the Lord had bidden him, and took unto him his wife; and knew her not till she had brought forth her firstborn son: and he called his name JESUS; **2:14** he took the young child and his mother by night, and departed into Egypt; **2:20-22** saying, Arise, and take the young child and his mother, and go into the land of Israel: for they are dead which sought the young child's life; he arose, and took the young child and his mother, and came into the land of Israel; **5:19** whosoever therefore shall break one of these least *c.,* and shall teach men so, he shall be called the least in the kingdom of heaven: but whosoever shall do and teach them, the same shall be called great in the kingdom of heaven; **7:24-27** whosoever heareth these sayings of mine, and doeth them, I will liken him unto a wise man, which built his house upon a rock; **15:3** why do ye also transgress the *c.* of God by your tradition; **17:9** Jesus charged them, saying, Tell the vision to no man, until the Son of man be risen again from the dead; **19:17** if thou wilt enter into life, keep the *c.*; **19:20-21** (Mark 10:19-20, Luke 18:19-21) All these things have I kept from my youth up: what lack I yet? If thou wilt be perfect, go and sell that thou hast, and give to the poor, and thou shalt have treasure in heaven: and come and follow me; **Mark 5:19-20** tell them how great things the Lord hath done for thee, and hath had compassion on thee.

And he departed, and began to publish in Decapolis how great things Jesus had done for him; **Luke 1:6** they were both righteous before God, walking in all the *c.* and ordinances of the Lord blameless; **2:39** when they had performed all things according to the law of the Lord, they returned into Galilee; **8:15** an honest and good heart, having heard the word, keep it, and bring forth fruit with patience; **8:21** my mother and my brethren are these which hear the word of God, and do it; **11:28** blessed are they that hear the word of God, and keep it; **17:9-10** when ye shall have done all those things which are *c.* you, say, We are unprofitable servants: we have done that which was our duty to do; **John 12:50** I know that his *c.* is life everlasting **15:10-11** if ye *k.m.c.,* ye shall abide in my love; even as I have kept my Father's *c.,* and abide in his love **15:14-15** ye are my friends, if ye do whatsoever I *c.* you; **Acts 10:33** now therefore are we all here present before God, to hear all things that are *c.* thee of God; **10:42** he *c.* us to preach unto the people, and to testify that it is he which was ordained of God to be the Judge of quick and dead; **Rom. 11:22** if thou continue in his goodness: otherwise thou also shalt be cut off; **1 Cor. 7:19** circumcision is nothing, and uncircumcision is nothing, but the keeping of the *c.* of God; **11:2** remember me in all things, and keep the ordinances, as I delivered them to you; **James 2:10-11** whosoever shall keep the whole law, and yet offend in one point, he is guilty of all; **1 Jn. 2:3-5** hereby we do know that we know him, if we keep his *c..* He that saith, I know him, and keepeth not his *c.,* is a liar, and the truth is not in him. But whoso keepeth his word, in him verily is the love of God perfected: hereby know we that we are in him; **2:7-8** a new *c.* I write unto you, which thing is true in him and in you: because the darkness is past, and the true light now shineth; **3:22,24** whatsoever we ask, we receive of him, because we keep his *c.,* and do those things that are pleasing in his sight. And he that keepeth his *c.* dwelleth in him, and he in him. And hereby we know that he abideth in us, by the Spirit which he hath given us; **5:2-3** by this we know that we love the children of God, when we love God, and keep his *c..* For this is the love of God, that we keep his *c.:* and his *c.* are not grievous; **2 Jn. 1:4-6** I rejoiced greatly that I found of thy children walking in truth, as we have received a *c.* from the Father; **Rev. 1:3** blessed is he that readeth, and they that hear the words of this prophecy, and keep those things which are written therein: for the time is at hand; **2:26** he that overcometh, and keepeth my works unto the end, to him will I give power over the

nations; **3:8** I know thy works: behold, I have set before thee an open door, and no man can shut it: for thou hast a little strength, and hast kept my word, and hast not denied my name; **3:10** because thou hast kept the word of my patience, I also will keep thee from the hour of temptation, which shall come upon all the world, to try them that dwell upon the earth; **12:17** the dragon was wroth with the woman, and went to make war with the remnant of her seed, which keep the *c.* of God, and have the testimony of Jesus Christ; **14:12** here is the patience of the saints: here are they that keep the *c.* of God, and the faith of Jesus.

I love thy commandments above gold; yea, above fine gold. Ps. 119:127 (*see also* Gold)

Ps. 19:10 more to be desired are they than gold, yea, than much fine gold: sweeter also than honey and the honeycomb; **119:127** I love thy *c.* above gold; yea, above fine gold; **119:140** thy word is very pure: therefore thy servant loveth it; **119:142** thy righteousness is an everlasting righteousness, and thy law is the truth; **119:161** princes have persecuted me without a cause: but my heart standeth in awe of thy word; **119:163** I hate and abhor lying: but thy law do I love; **Prov. 13:13** whoso despiseth the word shall be destroyed: but he that feareth the *c.* shall be rewarded.

If ye walk in my statutes and keep my commandments, and do them; Then I will give you rain in due season, and the land shall yield her increase, and the trees of the field shall yield her fruit. Lev. 26:3-4 (*see also* Fruit, Season)

Gen. 2:16-17 the LORD God *c.* the man; **6:22** according to all that God *c.* him, so did he; **7:5** Noah did according unto all that the LORD *c.* him; **17:23** Abraham [did], as God had said unto him; **19:26** his wife looked back from behind him, and she became a pillar of salt; **26:4-5** I will make thy seed to multiply as the stars of heaven, and will give unto thy seed all these countries; and in thy seed shall all the nations of the earth be blessed; Because that Abraham obeyed my voice, and kept my charge, my *c.,* my statutes, and my laws; **31:16** whatsoever God hath said unto thee, do; **Ex. 4:18** Moses went and returned to Jethro his father in law, and said unto him, Let me go, I pray thee, and return unto my brethren which are in Egypt, and see whether they be yet alive. And Jethro said to Moses, Go in peace; **7:6** Moses and Aaron did as the LORD *c.* them; **12:28**

the children of Israel did as the LORD had *c.*; **15:26** If thou wilt diligently hearken to the voice of the LORD thy God, I will put none of these diseases upon thee; **16:28** how long refuse ye to *k.m.c.* and my laws; **20:6** shewing mercy unto them that *k.m.c.*; **23:22** if thou shalt indeed obey his voice, and do all that I speak; then I will be an enemy unto thine enemies; **24:12** the LORD said... I will give thee tables of stone, and a law, and *c.* which I have written; that thou mayest teach them; **34:4** Moses rose up early in the morning, and went up unto mount Sinai, as the LORD had *c.* him; **34:32** he gave them in *c.* all that the LORD had spoken with him in mount Sinai; **35:10** make all that the LORD hath *c.*; **35:29** the children of Israel brought a willing offering unto the LORD, which the LORD had *c.* to be made by the hand of Moses; **36:1** in whom the LORD put wisdom and understanding according to all that the LORD had *c.*; **39:5** the curious girdle of his ephod, was according to the work thereof; as the LORD *c.* Moses; **39:31-32** the children of Israel did according to all that the LORD *c.* Moses, so did they; **39:42-43** according to all that the LORD *c.* Moses, so the children of Israel made all the work... they had done it as the LORD had *c.*; **40:16-33** thus did Moses: according to all that the LORD *c.* him; **Lev. 4:2-3** if a soul shall sin through ignorance against any of the *c.* of the LORD concerning things which ought not to be done, and shall do against any of them: [make an offering] unto the LORD for a sin offering; **4:13-14** they have done somewhat against any of the *c.* of the LORD concerning things which should not be done; **4:22-23** when a ruler hath sinned, and done somewhat through ignorance against any of the *c.* of the LORD his God concerning things which should not be done, and is guilty; [he shall make an offering]; **4:27** while he doeth somewhat against any of the *c.* of the LORD; **7:38** in the day that he *c.* the children of Israel to offer their oblations unto the LORD; **8:13** Moses [did] as the LORD *c.*; **8:21** as the LORD *c.* Moses; **8:36** Aaron and his sons did all things which the LORD *c.* by the hand of Moses; **9:6** this is the thing which the LORD *c.* that ye should do: and the glory of the LORD shall appear unto you; **10:1-2** [they] offered strange fire before the LORD, which he *c.* them not; **10:13** [ye shall do this]: for so I am *c.*; **20:22** keep all my statutes, and all my judgments, and do them; **22:31** *k.m.c.*, and do them: I am the LORD; **25:18-19** ye shall do my statutes, and keep my judgments, and do them; and ye shall dwell in the land in safety; **26:3-12** *k.m.c.*, and do them; And I will walk among you, and will be your God, and ye shall be my people; **26:14-20** if

ye will not hearken unto me, and will not do all these *c.*; then I will punish you seven times more for your sins; **26:21-25** if ye walk contrary unto me, and will not hearken unto me; I will bring seven times more plagues upon you according to your sins; **Num. 1:19** the LORD *c.* Moses; **1:54** the children of Israel did according to all that the LORD *c.* Moses; **2:34** the children of Israel did according to all that the LORD *c.*; **8:20** all the congregation of the children of Israel, did... according unto all that the LORD *c.*; **15:39-40** remember all the *c.* of the LORD, and do them; **20:27** Moses did as the LORD *c.*; **22:38** the word that God putteth in my mouth, that shall I speak; **23:12** must I not take heed to speak that which the LORD hath put in my mouth; **23:26** all that the LORD speaketh, that I must do; **24:13** I cannot go beyond the *c.* of the LORD, to do either good or bad of mine own mind; **32:23** if ye will not do Moses; **9:6** this is the thing which the LORD *c.* that ye should do: and the glory of the LORD shall appear unto you; **10:1-2** [they] offered strange fire before the LORD, which he *c.* them not; **10:13** [ye shall do this]: for so I am *c.*; **20:22** keep all my statutes, and all my judgments, and do them; **22:31** *k.m.c.*, and do them: I am the LORD; **25:18-19** ye shall do my statutes, and keep my judgments, and do them; and ye shall dwell in the land in safety; **26:3-12** *k.m.c.*, and do them; And I will walk among you, and will be your God, and ye shall be my people; **26:14-20** if ye will not hearken unto me, and will not do all these *c.*; then I will punish you seven times more for your sins; **26:21-25** if ye walk contrary unto me, and will not hearken unto me; I will bring seven times more plagues upon you according to your sins; **Num. 1:19** the LORD *c.* Moses; **1:54** the children of Israel did according to all that the LORD *c.* Moses; **2:34** the children of Israel did according to all that the LORD *c.*; **8:20** all the congregation of the children of Israel, did... according unto all that the LORD *c.*; **15:39-40** remember all the *c.* of the LORD, and do them; **20:27** Moses did as the LORD *c.*; **22:38** the word that God putteth in my mouth, that shall I speak; **23:12** must I not take heed to speak that which the LORD hath put in my mouth; **23:26** all that the LORD speaketh, that I must do; **24:13** I cannot go beyond the *c.* of the LORD, to do either good or bad of mine own mind; **32:23** if ye will not do so, behold, ye have sinned against the LORD; **Deut. 1:3** Moses spake unto the children of Israel, according unto all that the LORD had given him in *c.* unto them; **4:2** that ye may keep the *c.* of the LORD your God which I *c.* you; **4:13** he declared unto you his covenant, which he *c.* you to perform; **4:40** thou shalt keep therefore his statutes, and his *c.*, which I *c.* thee this day, that it may go well with thee; **5:1** Moses said unto them, Hear, O Israel, the statutes and judgments that ye may learn them, and keep, and do them; **5:10** shewing mercy unto them that *k.m.c.*; **5:27** all that the LORD our God shall speak... we will hear it, and do it; **5:29** O that there were such an heart in them, that they would fear me, and keep all my *c.* always; **6:2** keep all his statutes and his *c.*, which I *c.* thee, that thy days may be prolonged; **6:17** keep the *c.* of the LORD your God, and his testimonies, and his statutes, which he hath *c.* thee; **6:24-25** the LORD *c.* us to do all these statutes, for our good always, it shall be our righteousness, if we observe to do all these *c.* before the LORD our God, as he hath *c.* us; **7:9** know that the LORD thy God... keepeth covenant and mercy with them that keep his *c.* to a thousand generations; **7:11-12** thou shalt therefore keep the *c.*, and the statutes, and the judgments, which I *c.* thee this day, to do them; **8:1** the *c.* shall ye observe to do, that ye may live; **8:6** thou shalt keep the *c.* of the LORD thy God; **9:16** ye had turned aside quickly out of the way which the LORD had *c.* you; **10:13** keep the *c.* of the LORD, and his statutes; **11:1** keep his charge, and his statutes, and his judgments, and his *c.*, alway; **11:8** keep all the *c.* which I *c.* you this day, that ye may be strong; **11:13-15** if ye shall hearken diligently unto my *c.* which I *c.* you this day... I will give you the rain of your land; **11:27-28** a blessing, if ye obey the *c.* of the LORD your God... a curse, if ye will not obey the *c.* of the LORD; **12:28** observe and hear all these words which I *c.* thee, that it may go well with thee; **12:32** what thing soever I *c.* you, observe to do it; **13:18** thou shalt hearken to the voice of the LORD thy God, to keep all his *c.* which I *c.* thee this day, to do that which is right in the eyes of the LORD thy God; **15:5** observe to do all these *c.* which I *c.* thee this day; **17:19** that he may learn to keep all the words of this law and these statutes, to do them; **18:19** whosoever will not hearken unto my words which he shall speak in my name, I will require it of him; **19:9** keep all these *c.* to do them, which I *c.* thee this day, to love the LORD thy God, and to walk ever in his ways; **26:13-18** I have [done] according to all thy *c.* which thou hast *c.* me: I have not transgressed thy *c.*, neither have I forgotten them; **27:1** keep all the *c.* which I *c.* you this day; **27:17** [avouch] the LORD this day to be thy God, and to walk in his ways, and to keep his statutes, and his *c.*, and his judgments, and to hearken unto his voice; **28:1** hearken diligently unto the voice of the LORD thy God, to observe and to do all his *c.* which I *c.* thee this day; **28:9**

keep the *c.* of the LORD thy God, and walk in his ways; **28:13-15** thou shalt be above only, and thou shalt not be beneath; if that thou hearken unto the *c.* of the LORD thy God, which I *c.* thee this day, to observe and to do them; **28:45** all these curses shall come upon thee, and shall pursue thee, and overtake thee, till thou be destroyed; because thou hearkenedst not unto the voice of the LORD thy God, to keep his *c.* and his statutes which he *c.* thee; **29:9** keep therefore the words of this covenant, and do them, that ye may prosper in all that ye do; **29:29** do all the words of this law; **30:2** return unto the LORD thy God, and... obey his voice according to all that I *c.* thee this day, thou and thy children, with all thine heart, and with all thy soul; **30:8** return and obey the voice of the LORD, and do all his *c.* which I *c.* thee this day; **30:10** hearken unto the voice of the LORD thy God, to keep his *c.* and his statutes which are written in this book of the law; **30:16** I *c.* thee this day to love the LORD thy God, to walk in his ways, and to keep his *c.* and his statutes and his judgments; **31:5** the LORD shall give them up before your face, that ye may do unto them according unto all the *c.* which I have *c.* you; **Josh.14:9** the land whereon thy feet have trodden shall be thine inheritance, and thy childrens for ever, because thou hast wholly followed the LORD my God; **22:5** take diligent heed to do the *c.* and the law, which Moses the servant of the LORD charged you, to love the LORD your God, and to walk in all his ways, and to keep his *c.*; **Judg. 2:17** they turned quickly out of the way which their fathers walked in, obeying the *c.* of the LORD; but they did not so; **3:4** they were to prove Israel by them, to know whether they would hearken unto the *c.* of the LORD, which he *c.* their fathers; **1 Kgs. 2:3** keep the charge of the LORD thy God, to walk in his ways, to keep his statutes, and his *c.*, and his judgments, and his testimonies; **3:14** if thou wilt walk in my ways, to keep my statutes and my *c.*...then I will lengthen thy days; **6:12** if thou wilt walk in my statutes, and execute my judgments, and keep all my *c.* to walk in them; then will I perform my word with thee; **8:58** incline our hearts unto him, to walk in all his ways, and to keep his *c.*, and his statutes, and his judgments; **8:61** let your heart therefore be perfect with the LORD our God, to walk in his statutes, and to keep his *c.*; **9:6** *k.m.c.* and my statutes which I have set before you; **11:34** I will make him prince all the days of his life for David my servants sake... because he kept my *c.* and my statutes; **11:38** hearken unto all that I *c.* thee, and... walk in my ways, and do that is right in my sight, to keep my statutes and my *c.*; **13:21-**

22 forasmuch as thou hast disobeyed the mouth of the LORD, and hast not kept the *c.* which the LORD thy God *c.* thee... thy carcase shall not come unto the sepulchre of thy fathers; **14:8** thou hast not been as my servant David, who kept my *c.*, and who followed me with all his heart, to do that only which was right in mine eyes; **15:5** David did that which was right in the eyes of the LORD, and turned not aside from any thing that he *c.* him all the days of his life; **22:14** as the LORD liveth, what the LORD saith unto me, that will I speak; **2 Kgs. 17:13** turn ye from your evil ways, and *k.m.c.* and my statutes, according to all the law which I *c.* your fathers, and which I sent to you by my servants the prophets; **17:16** they left all the *c.* of the LORD their God, and made them molten images... and worshiped all the host of heaven, and served Baal; **17:19** Judah kept not the *c.* of the LORD their God, but walked in the statutes of Israel which they made; **17:34-36** they fear not the LORD, neither do they after their statutes, or after their ordinances, or after the law and *c.* which the LORD *c.* the children of Jacob; **18:6** he clave to the LORD, and departed not from following him, but kept his *c.*; **1 Chron. 15:15** the children of the Levites bare the ark of God upon their shoulders with the staves thereon, as Moses *c.* according to the word of the LORD; **16:40** do according to all that is written in the law of the LORD, which he *c.* Israel; **22:12-13** keep the law of the LORD thy God. Then shalt thou prosper, if thou takest heed to fulfil the statutes and judgments which the LORD charged; **28:7-8** be constant to do my *c.* and my judgments... keep and seek for all the *c.* of the LORD your God: that ye may possess this good land; **28:8** keep and seek for all the *c.* of the LORD your God: that ye may possess this good land; **29:19** keep thy *c.*, thy testimonies, and thy statutes, and to do all these things; **2 Chron. 14:4** *c.*...to seek the LORD God of their fathers, and to do the law and the *c.*; **17:4** [he] sought to the LORD God of his father, and walked in his *c.*; **24:20-21** thus saith God, Why transgress ye the *c.* of the LORD, that ye cannot prosper? because ye have forsaken the LORD, he hath also forsaken you; **30:12** the hand of God was to give them one heart to do the *c.* of the king and of the princes, by the word of the LORD; **31:3-4** he [did according to] the law of the LORD. Moreover he *c.* the people [to live accordingly,] that they might be encouraged in the law of the LORD; **33:8** take heed to do all that I have *c.* them, according to the whole law and the statutes and the ordinances; **34:21** great is the wrath of the LORD that is poured out upon us, because our fathers have not kept the word of the LORD;

34:31 walk after the LORD, and... keep his *c.*, and his testimonies, and his statutes; **35:17-18** the children of Israel that were present kept the passover at that time, and the feast of unleavened bread seven days; **Ezra 3:2** [they] builded the altar of the God of Israel, to offer burnt offerings thereon, as it is written in the law of Moses the man of God; **6:14** they builded, and finished it, according to the *c.* of the God of Israel; **7:10** Ezra had prepared his heart to seek the law of the LORD, and to do it, and to teach in Israel statutes and judgments; **9:10-12** O our God, what shall we say after this? for we have forsaken thy *c.*, Which thou hast *c.* by thy servants the prophets; **Neh. 1:5** O LORD God of heaven, the great and terrible God, that keepeth covenant and mercy for them that love him and observe his *c.*; **1:7-9** we have dealt very corruptly against thee, and have not kept the *c.*, nor the statutes, nor the judgments, which thou *c.*; **8:14** they found written in the law which the LORD had *c.* by Moses; **9:13** thou camest down... and spakest with them from heaven, and gavest them right judgments, and true laws, good statutes and *c.*; **9:16** they and our fathers dealt proudly, and hardened their necks, and hearkened not to thy *c.*; **9:29** they dealt proudly, and hearkened not unto thy *c.*, but sinned against thy judgments; **10:29** They... entered... into an oath, to walk in Gods law, which was given by Moses the servant of God, and to observe and do all the *c.* of the LORD our Lord, and his judgments and his statutes; **10:34** [we made an offering], to burn upon the altar of the LORD our God, as it is written in the law; LORD **Ps. 19:11** by them is thy servant warned: and in keeping of them there is great reward; **89:31-32** if they break my statutes, and keep not my *c.*; Then will I visit their transgression with the rod, and their iniquity with stripes; **103:20** bless the LORD, ye his angels, that excel in strength, that do his *c.*, hearkening unto the voice of his word; **105:45** observe his statutes, and keep his laws; **111:7** the works of his hands are verity and judgment; all his *c.* are sure; **111:10** the fear of the LORD is the beginning of wisdom: a good understanding have all they that do his *c.*: his praise endureth for ever; **119:10** O let me not wander from thy *c.*. Thy word have I hid in mine heart, that I might not sin against thee; **119:33** teach me, O LORD, the way of thy statutes; and I shall keep it unto the end; **119:44** so shall I keep thy law continually for ever and ever; **119:60** I made haste, and delayed not to keep thy *c.*; **119:66-68** I have believed thy *c.*. Before I was afflicted I went astray: but now have I kept thy word;

119:96-98 I have seen an end of all perfection: but thy *c.* is exceeding broad. O how love I thy law! it is my meditation all the day; **119:100** I understand more than the ancients, because I keep thy precepts; **119:115** depart from me, ye evildoers: for I will keep the *c.* of my God; **119:131** I opened my mouth, and panted: for I longed for thy *c.*; **119:166-168** LORD, I have hoped for thy salvation, and done thy *c.* My soul hath kept thy testimonies; and I love them exceedingly. I have kept thy precepts and thy testimonies: for all my ways are before thee; **119:172** my tongue shall speak of thy word: for all thy *c.* are righteousness; **145:20** the LORD preserveth all them that love him: but all the wicked will he destroy; **199:73** thy hands have made me and fashioned me: give me understanding, that I may learn thy *c.*; **Prov. 3:1-2** forget not my law; but let thine heart *k.m.c.*: For length of days, and long life, and peace, shall they add to thee; **4:4** let thine heart retain my words: *k.m.c.*, and live; **7:1-3** keep my words, and lay up my *c.* with thee. Keep my *c.*, and live; and my law as the apple of thine eye; **10:8** the wise in heart will receive *c.*: but a prating fool shall fall; **Eccl. 12:13** fear God, and keep his *c.*: for this is the whole duty of man; **Isa. 26:2** open ye the gates, that the righteous nation which keepeth the truth may enter in; **48:18-19** O that thou hadst hearkened to my *c.*; **Jer. 32:23** they obeyed not thy voice, neither walked in thy law; they have done nothing of all that thou *c.* them to do; **35:8-10** we have... obeyed, and done according to all that Jonadab our father *c.* us; **35:16** [they] have performed the *c.* of their father, which he *c.* them; **35:18-19** ye have obeyed the *c.* of Jonadab your father, and kept all his precepts, and done according unto all that he hath *c.* you; **Ezek. 18:9** [he that] hath walked in my statutes, and hath kept my judgments, to deal truly; he is just, he shall surely live; **18:17** [he that] hath executed my judgments, hath walked in my statutes; he shall not die for the iniquity of his father, he shall surely live; **20:11** I gave them my statutes, and shewed them my judgments, which if a man do, he shall even live in them; **20:19** I am the LORD your God; walk in my statutes, and keep my judgments, and do them; **20:21** the children rebelled against me: they walked not in my statutes, neither kept my judgments to do them, which if a man do, he shall even live in them; **20:24** they had not executed my judgments, but had despised my statutes, and had polluted my sabbaths, and their eyes were after their fathers idols; **24:18** I did in the morning as I was *c.*; **36:27-28** I will put my spirit within you, and cause you to walk in my statutes, and ye shall keep my judgments, and do them; **37:24-26** they shall also walk in my judgments, and observe my statutes, and do them; **44:24** they shall keep my laws and my statutes in all mine assemblies; and they shall hallow my sabbaths; **Dan. 6:2-4** Daniel was preferred above the presidents and princes, because [he was faithful in obeying *c.*]; and the king thought to set him over the whole realm; **Amos 2:4** they have despised the law of the LORD, and have not kept his *c.*

COMMIT, COMMITMENT (*see also* Dedicate, Diligence)

Commit thy way unto the Lord; trust also in Him; and He shall bring it to pass. And he shall bring forth thy righteousness as the light, and thy judgment as the noonday. Ps. 37:5-6 (*see also* Light, Trust, Way)

COMMUNICATE, COMMUNICATION (*see also* Ask, Confess, Contend, Conversation, Cry, Declare, Gossip, Language, Pray, Preach, Speak, Teach, Testify)

Be rich in good works, ready to distribute, willing to communicate. 1 Tim. 6:18 (*see also* Rich)

COMPASSION, COMPASSIONATE (*see also* Charity, Love, Mercy)

Some have compassion, making a difference. Jude 1:22

Luke 10:33-34 he had *c.* on him, And went to him, and bound up his wounds, pouring in oil and wine, and set him on his own beast, and brought him to an inn, and took care of him; **16:20-22** it came to pass, that the beggar died, and was carried by the angels into Abraham's bosom; **Philip. 4:15-16** no church communicated with me as concerning giving and receiving, but ye only. For even in Thessalonica ye sent once and again unto my necessity; **Heb. 5:2** who can have *c.* on the ignorant, and on them that are out of the way; for that he himself also is compassed with infirmity; **Jude 1:22** some have *c.*, making a difference.

COMPEL (*see also* Bondage, Force, Liberty)

Whosoever shall compel thee to go a mile, go with him twain. **Matt. 5:41** (*see also* Mile)

CONCEIT, CONCEITED (*see also* Arrogant, Haughty, Highminded, Pride, Vain)

The rich man is wise in his own conceit; but the poor that hath understanding searcheth him out. **Prov. 28:11** (*see also* Search)

Answer a fool according to his folly, lest he be wise in his own conceit. **Prov. 26:5**

Prov. 26:5 answer a fool according to his folly, lest he be wise in his own *c.*; **26:12** seest thou a man wise in his own *c.*? there is more hope of a fool than of him; **26:16** the sluggard is wiser in his own *c.* than seven men that can render a reason.

CONCEIVE (*see also* Birth, Child)

None calleth for justice, nor any pleadeth for truth: they trust in vanity, and speak lies; they conceive mischief, and bring forth iniquity. **Isa. 59:4** (*see also* Mischief)

CONDEMN, CONDEMNATION (*see also* Accuse, Judge)

He that justifieth the wicked, and he that condemneth the just, even they both are abomination to the LORD. **Prov. 17:15** (*see also* Just, Wicked)

CONFESS, CONFESSION (*see also* Acknowledge, Testify, Witness)

If they shall confess their iniquity, and the iniquity of their fathers, with their trespass which they trespassed against me, and that also they have walked contrary unto me; And that I also have walked contrary unto them, and have brought them into the land of their enemies; if then their uncircumcised hearts be humbled, and they then accept of the punishment of their iniquity: Then will I remember my covenant with Jacob, and also my covenant with Isaac, and also my covenant with Abraham will I remember; and I will remember the land. **Lev. 26:40-42** (*see also* Iniquity, Remember, Repent)

I was speaking, and praying, and confessing my sin and the sin of my people Israel, and presenting my supplication before the LORD my God for the holy mountain of my God. **Dan. 9:20**

For it is written, As I live, saith the Lord, every knee shall bow to me, and every tongue shall confess to God. **Rom 14:11** (*see also* Knee)

He that covereth his sins shall not prosper: but whoso confesseth and forsaketh them shall have mercy. **Prov. 28:13** (*see also* Forsake, Mercy, Sin)

Whosoever shall confess that Jesus is the Son of God, God dwelleth in him, and he in God. **1 Jn. 4:15** (*see also* Dwell, Testify)

I acknowledged my sin unto thee, and mine iniquity have I not hid. I said, I will confess my transgressions unto the LORD; and thou forgavest the iniquity of my sin. **Ps. 32:5**

2 Chron. 30:22 they did eat throughout the feast seven days, offering peace offerings, and making *c.* to the LORD God of their fathers; **Ezra 10:11** make *c.* unto the LORD God of your fathers, and do his pleasure: and separate yourselves from the people of the land, and from the strange wives; **Neh. 9:2-3** the seed of Israel separated themselves from all strangers, and stood and *c.* their sins, and the iniquities of their fathers; **Ps. 32:5** I acknowledged my sin unto thee, and mine iniquity have I not hid. I said, I will *c.* my transgressions unto the LORD; and thou forgavest the iniquity of my sin.

Confess your faults one to another, and ray one for another, that ye may be healed. The effectual fervent prayer of a righteous man availeth much. **James 5:16** (*see also* Heal, Pray)

Mark 1:5 were all baptized of him in the river of Jordan, *c.* their sins; **Rom. 14:11** every knee shall bow to me, and every tongue shall *c.* to God. So then every one of us shall give account of himself to God; **James 5:16** *c.* your faults one to another, and pray one for another, that ye may be healed. The effectual fervent prayer of a righteous man availeth much; **1 Jn. 1:9** if we *c.* our sins, he is faithful and just to forgive us our sins, and to cleanse us from all unrighteousness.

CONFIDENCE (*see also* Assurance, Believe, Faith, Know, Trust)

Confidence in an unfaithful man in time of trouble is like a broken tooth, and a foot out of joint. Prov. 25:19

Prov. 25:19 *c.* in an unfaithful man in time of trouble is like a broken tooth, and a foot out of joint; **Isa. 30:15** thus saith the Lord GOD, the Holy One of Israel; In returning and rest shall ye be saved; in quietness and in *c.* shall be your strength: and ye would not.

CONFIRM (*see* Baptism, Holy Ghost, Laying on of Hands)

Let them all be confounded and turned back that hate Zion. Ps. 129:5 (*see also* Zion)

CONFUSE, CONFUSION

God is not the author of confusion, but of peace, as in all churches of the saints. 1 Cor. 14:33 (*see also* Author)

For where envying and strife is, there is confusion and every evil work. James 3:16 (*see also* Envy, Strife)

CONSCIENCE (*see also* Inspiration, Light, Mind)

I exercise myself, to have always a conscience void of offense toward God, and toward men. Acts 24:16 (*see also* Offend)

Now the Spirit speaketh expressly, that in the latter times some shall depart from the faith, giving heed to seducing spirits, and doctrines of devils; Speaking lies in hypocrisy; having their conscience seared with a hot iron; Forbidding to marry, and commanding to abstain from meats, which God hath created to be received with thanksgiving of them which believe and know the truth. 1 Tim. 4:1-3 (*see also* Abstain, Food, Latter Day, Marriage, Meat, Thanksgiving)

CONSENT, CONTENTMENT (*see also* One, United, Voice)

If sinners entice thee, consent thou not. Prov. 1:10 (*see also* Entice)

Prov. 1:10-15 if sinners entice thee, *c.* thou not. If they say, Come with us... walk not thou in the way with them; refrain thy foot from their path.

CONSEQUENCE (*see* Choice, Promise, Punish, Reward)

CONSIDER (*see also* Choice, Ponder, Think)

Thus saith the Lord of Hosts; Consider your ways. Hag. 1:4-5 (*see also* Ways)

Stand still, and consider the wondrous works of God. Job 37:14 (*see also* Work)

Job 37:14 stand still, and *c.* the wondrous works of God; **Ps. 46:8-9** come, behold the works of the LORD, what desolations he hath made in the earth; **Eccl. 7:13** *c.* the work of God: for who can make that straight, which he hath made crooked; **Isa. 41:17-20** that they may see, and know, and *c.*, and understand together, that the hand of the LORD hath done this, and the Holy One of Israel hath created it; **Ezek. 12:3-5** it may be they will *c.*, though they be a rebellious house.

CONSOLATION, CONSOLE (*see* Care, Comfort, Compassion)

CONSUME (*see also* Lust)

Ye ask, and receive not, because ye ask amiss, that ye may consume it upon your lusts. James 4:3 (*see also* Ask, Lust)

CONTEND, CONTENTION, CONTENTIOUS (*see also* Argue, Dispute, Harden, Persecute, Strife)

Agree with thine adversary quickly, whiles thou art in the way with him; lest at any time the adversary deliver thee to the judge, and the judge deliver thee to the officer, and thou be cast into prison. Matt. 5:25 (*see also* Agree, Adversary)

Cast out the scorner, and contention shall go out; yea, strife and reproach shall cease. Prov. 22:10 (*see also* Cast, Scorn)

Shall he that contendeth with the Almighty instruct him? he that reproveth God, let him answer it. Job 40:2

Unto them that are contentious, and do not obey the truth, but obey unrighteousness, indignation and wrath. Rom. 2:8 (*see also* Obedience)

If a wise man contendeth with a foolish man, whether he rage or laugh, there is no rest. Prov. 29:9

Beloved, when I gave all diligence to write unto you of the common salvation, it was needful for me to write unto you, and exhort you that ye should earnestly contend for the faith which was once delivered unto the saints. Jude 1:3 (*see also* Earnestly, Saints)

A brother offended is harder to be won than a strong city: and their contentions are like the bars of a castle. Prov. 18:19 (*see also* Offend)

Let there be no strife, I pray thee, between me and thee, and between my herdmen and thy herdmen; for we be brethren. Gen. 13:8 (*see also* Strife)

The lot causeth contensions to cease, and parteth between the mighty. Prov. 18:18 (*see also* Lot)

Grudge not one against another, brethren, lest ye be condemned: behold, the judge standeth before the door. James 5:9

Acts 15:39 the *c.* was so sharp between them, that they departed asunder one from the other; 1 Cor. 11:16 if any man seem to be *c.,* we have no such custom, neither the churches of God; Gal. 5:15 if ye bite and devour one another, take heed that ye be not consumed one of another; 1 Tim. 6:20 keep that which is committed to thy trust, avoiding profane and vain babblings, and oppositions of science falsely so called; James 5:9 grudge not one against another, brethren, lest ye be condemned: behold, the judge standeth before the door; 1 Pet. 2:1 wherefore laying aside all malice, and all guile, and hypocrisies, and envies, and all evil speakings.

It is better to dwell in the wilderness, than with a contentious and an angry woman. Prov. 21:19 (*see also* Better)

Prov. 19:13 a foolish son is the calamity of his father: and the *c.* of a wife are a continual dropping; 21:9 it is better to dwell in a corner of the housetop, than with a brawling woman in a

wide house; 21:19 it is better to dwell in the wilderness, than with a *c.* and an angry woman.

CONTINUALLY, CONTINUE (*see also* Diligent)

Continue in the faith grounded and settled, and be not moved away from the hope of the gospel, which ye have heard, and which was preached to every creature which is under heaven. Col. 1:23 (*see also* Hope)

John 8:31-32 if ye *c.* in my word, then are ye my disciples indeed; And ye shall know the truth, and the truth shall make you free; Acts 14:22 confirming the souls of the disciples, and exhorting them to *c.* in the faith, and that we must through much tribulation enter into the kingdom of God; 23:1 men and brethren, I have lived in all good conscience before God until this day; 24:16 I exercise myself, to have always a conscience void of offence toward God, and toward men; Gal. 5:7 ye did run well; who did hinder you that ye should not obey the truth; Philip. 1:5 your fellowship in the gospel from the first day until now; Col. 1:23 *c.* in the faith grounded and settled, and be not moved away from the hope of the gospel, which ye have heard, and which was preached to every creature which is under heaven; 2 Tim. 3:14 *c.* thou in the things which thou hast learned and hast been assured of, knowing of whom thou hast learned them.

CONTRIBUTE, CONTRIBUTION (*see also* Alms, Charity, Give, Serve)

It hath pleased them of Macedonia and Achaia to make a certain contribution for the poor saints which are at Jerusalem Rom. 15:26

CONTRITE (*see also* Humble, Meek, Repent, Teach)

The LORD is nigh unto them that are of a broken heart; and saveth such as be of a contrite spirit. Ps. 34:18 (*see also* Broken, Heart)

CONVERSATION, CONVERSE (*see also* Communicate, Speak)

Let your conversation be without covetousness; and be content with such things as ye have. Heb. 13:5

Let no man despise thy youth; but be thou an example of the believers, in word, in conversation, in charity, in spirit, in faith, in purity. 1 Tim. 4:12 (*see also* Believe, Charity, Despise, Example, Pure)

Let your conversation be as it becometh the gospel of Christ: that whether I come and see you, or else be absent, I may hear of your affairs, that ye stand fast in one spirit, with one mind striving together for the faith of the gospel. Philip. 1:27 (*see also* Become, Gospel, One)

Sanctify the Lord God in your heats; and be ready always to give an answer to every man that asketh you a reason of the hope that is in you with meekness and fear: Having a good conscience; that, whereas they speak evil of you, as of evildoers, they may be ashamed that falsely accuse your good conversation in Christ. 1 Pet. 3:15-16 (*see also* Answer, Hope, Ready, Reason, Sanctify)

Ye know that ye were not redeemed with corruptible things, as silver and gold, from your vain conversation received by tradition from your fathers. 1 Pet. 1:18 (*see also* Corrupt, Redeem, Tradition)

A wholesome tongue is a tree of life: but perverseness therein is a breach in the spirit. Prov. 15:4

Prov. 15:4 a wholesome tongue is a tree of life: but perverseness therein is a breach in the spirit; 26:21 as coals are to burning coals, and wood to fire; so is a contentious man to kindle strife.

CONVERT, CONVERSION, CONVERTED
(*see also* Born Again, Change, Heart, New, Soul)

Except ye be converted, and become as little children, ye shall not enter into the kingdom of heaven. Matt. 18:3 (*see also* Child, Kingdom)

Make the heart of this people fat, and make their ears heavy, and shut their eyes; lest they see with their eyes, and hear with their ears, and understand with their heart, and convert, and be healed. Isa. 6:10 (*see also* Heal, See)

When thou are converted, strengthen thy brethren. Luke 22:32

Luke 22:32 I have prayed for thee, that thy faith fail not: and when thou art c., strengthen thy brethren; Acts 12:11 when Peter was come to himself, he said, Now I know of a surety, that the Lord hath sent his angel, and hath delivered me out of the hand of Herod, and from all the expectation of the people of the Jews; 18:23 after he had spent some time there, he departed, and went over all the country of Galatia and Phrygia in order, strengthening all the disciples; 28:27 they should see with their eyes, and hear with their ears, and understand with their heart, and should be c., and I should heal them; Philip. 4:15 no church communicated with me as concerning giving and receiving, but ye only; 4:17-19 not because I desire a gift: but I desire fruit that may abound to your account. But I have all, and abound: I am full, having received of Epaphroditus the things which were sent from you, an odour of a sweet smell, a sacrifice acceptable, well pleasing to God. But my God shall supply all your need according to his riches in glory by Christ Jesus; 3 Jn. 1:2 I wish above all things that thou mayest prosper and be in health, even as thy soul prospereth; Jude 1:2 mercy unto you, and peace, and love, be multiplied.

CORD (*see also* Bind)

Enlarge the place of thy tent, and let them stretch forth the curtains of thine habitations; spare not, lengthen the cords, and strengthen thy stakes. Isa. 54:2-3 (*see also* Stake, Strengthen)

CORNER, CORNERSTONE (*see also* Foundation, Jesus Christ, Rock, Stone)

Ye are no more strangers and foreigners, but fellowcitizens with the saints, and of the household of God; And are built upon the foundation of the apostles and prophets, Jesus Christ himself being the chief corner stone. Eph. 2:19-20 (*see also* Apostle, Jesus Christ, Prophet, Saint)

Wherefore also it is contained in the scripture, Behold, I lay in Sion a chief corner stone, elect, precious: and he that believeth on him shall not be confounded. 1 Pet. 2:6 (*see also* Jesus Christ, Zion)

Be it known unto you all, and to all the people of Israel, that by the name of Jesus Christ of Nazareth, whom ye crucified, whom God raised from the dead, even by him doth this man stand here before you whole. This is the stone which was set at nought of you builders, which is become the head of the corner. Neither is there salvation in any other: for there is none other name under heaven given among men, whereby we must be saved. Acts 4:10-12 (*see also* Israel, Jesus Christ, Name, Saved, Stone)

Have ye not read this scripture; The stone which the builders rejected is become the head of the corner? Mark 12:10 (*see also* Stone)

Mark 12:10 have ye not read this scripture; The stone which the builders rejected is become the head of the corner; Luke 20:17 what is this then that is written, The stone which the builders rejected, the same is become the head of the corner?

CORRECT, CORRECTION (*see also* Chasten, Punish)

Withhold not correction from the child. Prov. 23:13 (*see also* Child)

Correct thy son, and he shall give thee rest; yea he shall give delight unto thy soul. Prov. 29:17

Whoso loveth instruction loveth knowledge: but he that hateth reproof is brutish. Prov. 12:1 (*see also* Instruct, Know)

Jer. 7:28 this is a nation that obeyeth not the voice of the LORD their God, nor receiveth *c.*: truth is perished, and is cut off from their mouth; Zeph. 3:2 she received not *c.*; she trusted not in the LORD; she drew not near to her God; Prov. 12:1 whoso loveth instruction loveth knowledge: but he that hateth reproof is brutish; 17:10 a reproof entereth more into a wise man than an hundred stripes into a fool.

CORRUPT, CORRUPTIBLE (*see also* Defile, Pervert, Wicked)

Ye know that ye were not redeemed with corruptible things, as silver and gold, from your vain conversation received by tradition from your fathers. 1 Pet. 1:18 (*see also* Conversation, Redeem, Tradition)

COUNSEL, COUNSELOR (*see also* Communicate, Edify, Meet)

For unto us a child is born, unto us a son is given: and the government shall be upon his shoulder: and his name shall be called, Wonderful, Counsellor, The mighty God, The everlasting Father, The Prince of Peace. Isa. 9:6 (*see also* Father, Government, Peace, Wonderful)

Remember the former things of old: for I am God, and there is none else; I am God, and there is none like me, Declaring the end from the beginning, and from ancient times the things that are not yet done, saying, My counsel shall stand, and I will do all my pleasure: Calling a ravenous bird from the east, the man that executeth my counsel from a far county: yea, I have spoken it, I will also bring it to pass; I have purposed it, I will also do it. Isa. 46:9-11 (*see also* Remember)

Then went the Pharisees, and took counsel how they might entangle him in his talk. Matt. 22:15 (*see also* Entangle, Evil)

Hearken now unto my voice, I will give thee counsel, and God shall be with thee. Ex. 18:19 (*see also* Hearken)

Ex. 18:19 hearken now unto my voice, I will give thee *c.*, and God shall be with thee; Deut. 32:29 O that they were wise, that they understood this, that they would consider their latter end; Josh.9:14 the men took of their victuals, and asked not *c.* at the mouth of the LORD; Judg. 18:5 ask *c.*, we pray thee, of God, that we may know whether our way which we go shall be prosperous; 20:18 (20:23) the children of Israel arose, and went up to the house of God, and asked *c.* of God; 1 Sam. 14:37 Saul asked *c.* of God, Shall I go down after the Philistines?; Ps. 16:7 I will bless the LORD, who hath given me *c.*; 20:4 grant thee according to thine own heart, and fulfil all thy *c.*; 33:10-11 the LORD bringeth the *c.* of the heathen to nought: he maketh the devices of the people of none effect. The *c.* of the LORD standeth for ever, the thoughts of his heart to all generations; 81:12 I gave them up unto their own hearts lust: and they walked in their own *c.*; 119:24 thy testimonies also are my delight and my *c.*; Prov. 11:14

where no *c.* is, the people fall: but in the multitude of *c.* there is safety; **19:21** there are many devices in a mans heart; nevertheless the *c.* of the LORD, that shall stand; **Isa. 30:1-3** woe to the rebellious children, saith the LORD, that take *c.*, but not of me; **30:6-7** they will carry their riches upon the shoulders of young asses, and their treasures upon the bunches of camels, to a people that shall not profit them. For the Egyptians shall help in vain, and to no purpose; **37:14-16** Hezekiah prayed unto the LORD, saying, O LORD of hosts, God of Israel, that dwellest between the cherubims, thou art the God, even thou alone, of all the kingdoms of the earth: thou hast made heaven and earth; **Jer. 23:18** who hath stood in the *c.* of the LORD, and hath perceived and heard his word? who hath marked his word, and heard it; **50:45** hear ye the *c.* of the LORD, that he hath taken against Babylon; and his purposes; **Hosea 8:4** they have set up kings, but not by me: they have made princes, and I knew it not: of their silver and their gold have they made them idols, that they may be cut off; **Zech. 10:1** ask ye of the LORD rain in the time of the latter rain; so the LORD shall make bright clouds.

A wise man will hear, and will increase learning; and a man of understanding shall attain unto wise counsels. Prov. 1:5 (*see also* Wisdom)

Prov. 1:5 a wise man will hear, and will increase learning; and a man of understanding shall attain unto wise *c.*; **11:14** where no *c.* is, the people fall: but in the multitude of *c.* there is safety; **12:15** the way of a fool is right in his own eyes: but he that hearkeneth unto *c.* is wise; **15:22** without *c.* purposes are disappointed: but in the multitude of *c.* they are established; **19:20** hear *c.*, and receive instruction, that thou mayest be wise in thy latter end; **22:17** bow down thine ear, and hear the words of the wise, and apply thine heart unto my knowledge; **24:6** by wise *c.* thou shalt make thy war: and in multitude of *c.* there is safety; **27:9** ointment and perfume rejoice the heart: so doth the sweetness of a mans friend by hearty *c.*; **Isa. 44:26-28** confirmeth the word of his servant, and performeth the *c.* of his messengers.

Woe unto them that seek deep to hide their counsel from the LORD and their works are in the dark, and they say, Who seeth us? and who knoweth us? Isa. 29:15 (*see also* Hide, Seek)

Prov. 1:25-31 ye have set at nought all my *c.*, and would none of my reproof: I also will laugh at your calamity; I will mock when your fear cometh; **Isa. 29:15** woe unto them that seek deep to hide their *c.* from the LORD, and their works are in the dark, and they say, Who seeth us? and who knoweth us.

COUNTENANCE (*see also* Face, Image)

Blessed is the people that know the joyful sound: they shall walk, O LORD, in the light of thy countenance. Ps. 89:15 (*see also* Joy)

Ps. 89:15-17 blessed is the people that know the joyful sound: they shall walk, O LORD, in the light of thy *c.*; **90:17** let the beauty of the LORD our God be upon us: and establish thou the work of our hands upon us; yea, the work of our hands establish thou it.

COURAGE, COURAGEOUS (*see also* Endure, Strength)

Be of good courage, and let us behave ourselves valiantly for our people, and for the cities of our God: and let the LORD do *that* which is good in his sight. 1 Chron. 19:13 (*see also* Behave)

Be of good courage, and he shall strengthen your heart, all ye that hope in the LORD. Ps. 31:24 (*see also* Hope)

Blessed be the God of Shadrach, Meshach, and Abed-nego, who hath sent his angel, and delivered his servants that trusted in him, and have changed the king's word, and yielded their bodies, that they might not serve nor worship any god, except their own God. Dan. 3:28 (*see also* Angel, Idol, Serve, Worship)

Be strong and of a good courage; be not afraid, neither be thou dismayed; for the Lord thy God is with thee whithersoever thou goest. Josh. 1:9 (*see also* Afraid, Dismayed)

Num. 13:20 be ye of good *c.*, and bring of the fruit of the land; **Deut. 11:8** therefore shall ye keep all the commandments which I command you this day, that ye may be strong, and go in and possess the land; **31:6-7** be strong and of a good *c.*, fear not, nor be afraid of them: for the LORD thy God, he it is that doth go with thee; he will not fail thee, nor forsake thee; **31:23** be strong and of a good *c.*: for thou shalt bring the children of Israel into the land which I sware unto them: and I will be with thee; **Josh. 1:6-7** be strong and of a good *c*.: for unto this people shalt thou divide for an inheritance the land, which I sware unto their fathers to give them. Only be thou strong and very *c*., that thou mayest observe to do according to all the law; **1:9** be strong and of a good *c*.; be not afraid, neither be thou dismayed: for the LORD thy God is with thee whithersoever thou goest; **10:25** fear not, nor be dismayed, be strong and of good *c*.: for thus shall the LORD do to all your enemies against whom ye fight; **1 Sam. 17:45-46** thou comest to me with a sword, and with a spear, and with a shield: but I come to thee in the name of the LORD of hosts, the God of the armies of Israel, whom thou hast defied. This day will the LORD deliver thee into mine hand; **2 Sam. 10:12** be of good *c*., and let us play the men for our people, and for the cities of our God: and the LORD do that which seemeth him good; **3 Nephi 14:11** If ye then, being evil, know how to give good gifts unto your children, how much more shall your Father who is in heaven give good things to them that ask him; **1 Chron. 19:13** be of good *c*., and let us behave ourselves valiantly for our people, and for the cities of our God: and let the LORD do that which is good in his sight; **28:10** take heed now; for the LORD hath chosen thee to build an house for the sanctuary: be strong, and do it; **28:20** (22:13) be strong and of good *c*., and do it: fear not, nor be dismayed: for the LORD God, even my God, will be with thee; he will not fail thee; **2 Chron. 15:7** be ye strong therefore, and let not your hands be weak: for your work shall be rewarded; **19:11** deal *c*., and the LORD shall be with the good; **20:15** be not afraid nor dismayed by reason of this great multitude; for the battle is not yours, but Gods; **32:7** be strong and *c*., be not afraid nor dismayed for the king of Assyria, nor for all the multitude that is with him: for there be more with us than with him; **Ezra 10:4** arise; for this matter belongeth unto thee: we also will be with thee: be of good *c*., and do it; **Job 13:21** withdraw thine hand far from me: and let not thy dread make me afraid; **Ps. 27:14** wait on the LORD: be of good *c*., and he shall strengthen thine heart; **31:24** be of good *c*., and he shall strengthen your heart, all ye that hope in the LORD; **Isa. 24:15** glorify ye the LORD in the fires, even the name of the LORD God of Israel in the isles of the sea; **32:20** blessed are ye that sow beside all waters, that send forth thither the feet of the ox and the ass; **35:4** be strong, fear not: behold, your God will come with vengeance, even God with a recompence; he will come and save you; **41:6-7**

they helped every one his neighbour; and every one said to his brother, Be of good *c*.; **61:8** I the LORD love judgment, I hate robbery for burnt offering; and I will direct their work in truth, and I will make an everlasting covenant with them; **Jer. 1:8** be not afraid of their faces: for I am with thee to deliver thee, saith the LORD; **Dan. 10:19** fear not: peace be unto thee, be strong, yea, be strong. And when he had spoken unto me, I was strengthened; **Hag. 2:4** be strong, all ye people of the land, saith the LORD, and work: for I am with you, saith the LORD of hosts.

COVENANT (*see also* Oath, Priesthood, Promise)

Choose the things that please me, and take hold of my covenant; Even unto them will I give in mine house and within my walls a place and a name better than of sons and of daughters. Isa. 56:4-5 (*see also* Choice)

They shall ask the way to Zion with their faces thitherward, *saying,* Come, and let us join ourselves to the LORD in a perpetual covenant that shall not be forgotten. Jer. 50:5 (*see also* Ask, Zion)

Obey my voice indeed, and keep my covenant. Ex. 19:5 (*see also* Obey)

And God said, This is the token of the covenant which I make between me and you and every living creature that is with you, for perpetual generations: I do set my bow in the cloud, and it shall be for a token of a covenant between me and the earth. And it shall come to pass, when I bring a cloud over the earth, that the bow shall be seen in the cloud: And I will remember my covenant, which is between me and you and every living creature of all flesh; and the waters shall no more become a flood to destroy all flesh. Gen. 9:13 (*see also* Rainbow)

Remember his holy covenant. Luke 1:72 (*see also* Remember)

Luke 1:72 to perform the mercy promised to our fathers, and to remember his holy *c*.; **Acts 7:25-26** ye are the children of the prophets, and of the *c*. which God made with our fathers, saying unto Abraham, And in thy seed shall all the kindreds of the earth be blessed. Unto you first God, having raised up his Son Jesus, sent him to bless you, in turning away every one of you from his iniquities; **Gal. 3:17** the *c.*, that was confirmed before of God in Christ, the law, which was four hundred and thirty years after, cannot disannul, that it should make the promise of none effect; **Heb. 8:5-13** Who serve unto the example and shadow of heavenly things, as Moses was admonished of God when he was about to make the tabernacle: for, See, saith he, that thou make all things according to the pattern shewed to thee in the mount. But now hath he obtained a more excellent ministry, by how much also he is the mediator of a better *c.*, which was established upon better promises. For if that first *c.* had been faultless, then should no place have been sought for the second. For finding fault with them, he saith, Behold, the days come, saith the Lord, when I will make a new *c.* with the house of Israel and with the house of Judah: Not according to the *c.* that I made with their fathers in the day when I took them by the hand to lead them out of the land of Egypt; because they continued not in my *c.*, and I regarded them not, saith the Lord. For this is the *c.* that I will make with the house of Israel after those days, saith the Lord; I will put my laws into their mind, and write them in their hearts: and I will be to them a God, and they shall be to me a people. And they shall not teach every man his neighbour, and every man his brother, saying, Know the Lord: for all shall know me, from the least to the greatest. For I will be merciful to their unrighteousness, and their sins and their iniquities will I remember no more. In that he saith, A new *c.*, he hath made the first old. Now that which decayeth and waxeth old is ready to vanish away.

Be ye mindful always of his covenant; the word which he commanded to a thousand generations; Even of the covenant which he made with Abraham, and of his oath unto Isaac; And hath confirmed the same to Jacob for a law, and to Israel for an everlasting covenant. 1 Chron. 16:15-17 (*see also* Everlasting)

1 Chron. 16:15-17 be ye mindful always of his *c.*; the word which he commanded to a thousand generations; **2 Chron. 29:10** it is in mine heart to make a *c.* with the LORD God of Israel, that his fierce wrath may turn away from us; **34:31** the king stood in his place, and made a *c.* before the LORD, to walk after the LORD, and to keep his commandments, and his testimonies, and his statutes, with all his heart, and with all his soul; **Ps. 25:10** all the paths of the LORD are mercy

and truth unto such as keep his *c.* and his testimonies; **25:14** the secret of the LORD is with them that fear him; and he will shew them his *c.*; **50:5** gather my saints together unto me; those that have made a *c.* with me by sacrifice; **Prov. 2:17** which forsaketh the guide of her youth, and forgetteth the *c.* of her God.

Thou shalt keep my covenant therefore, thou, and thy seed after thee in their generations. Gen. 17:9 (*see also* Thou Shalt)

Gen. 6:18 with thee will I establish my *c.*; and thou shalt come into the ark, thou, and thy sons, and thy wife, and thy sons wives with thee; **9:9-17** I will establish my *c.* with you; neither shall all flesh be cut off any more by the waters of a flood; neither shall there any more be a flood to destroy the earth; **15:18** the LORD made a *c.* with Abram, saying, Unto thy seed have I given this land; **17:2-4** I will make my *c.* between me and thee, and will multiply thee exceedingly; **17:7** I will establish my *c.* between me and thee and thy seed after thee in their generations for an everlasting *c.*; **17:9-14** thou shalt keep my *c.* therefore, thou, and thy seed after thee in their generations. This is my *c.*, which ye shall keep, between me and you and thy seed after thee; **17:19** I will establish my *c.* with him for an everlasting *c.*, and with his seed after him; **17:21** my *c.* will I establish with Isaac, which Sarah shall bear unto thee at this set time in the next year; **26:28** the LORD was with thee: and we said, Let there be now an oath betwixt us, even betwixt us and thee, and let us make a *c.* with thee; **Ex. 2:24-25** God remembered his *c.* with Abraham, with Isaac, and with Jacob. And God looked upon the children of Israel, and God had respect unto them; **6:4-5** I have also established my *c.* with them, to give them the land of Canaan... I have remembered my *c.*; **19:5** if ye will obey my voice indeed, and keep my *c.*, then ye shall be a peculiar treasure unto me above all people; **31:16** the children of Israel shall keep the sabbath, to observe the sabbath throughout their generations, for a perpetual *c.*; **Lev. 24:8** every sabbath he shall set it in order before the LORD continually, being taken from the children of Israel by an everlasting *c.*; **26:9** I will have respect unto you, and make you fruitful, and multiply you, and establish my *c.* with you; **26:15** [do not] despise my statutes, or... abhor my judgments, so that ye will not do all my commandments, but that ye break my *c.*; **26:42** I [will] remember my *c.* with Jacob, and also my *c.* with Isaac, and also my *c.* with Abraham will I remember; **26:44-45** I will not cast them away, neither will I abhor them, to destroy them utterly, and to break my *c.* with them: for I am the LORD their God; **Num. 18:19** the heave offerings... have I given thee, and thy sons and thy daughters with thee, by a statute for ever: it is a *c.* of salt for ever before the LORD; **25:12-13** I give unto him my *c.* of peace: And he shall have it, and his seed after him, even the *c.* of an everlasting priesthood; **Deut. 4:13** he declared unto you his *c.*, which he commanded you to perform, even ten commandments; **4:23** take heed unto yourselves, lest ye forget the *c.* of the LORD your God, which he made with you; **4:31** the LORD thy God is a merciful God;] he will not forsake thee, neither destroy thee, nor forget the *c.* of thy fathers which he sware unto them; **5:2-3** the LORD our God made a *c.* with us... The LORD made not this *c.* with our fathers, but with us, even us; **7:9** the LORD thy God, he is God, the faithful God, which keepeth *c.* and mercy with them that love him and keep his commandments to a thousand generations; **7:12** if ye hearken to these judgments, and keep, and do them, that the LORD thy God shall keep unto thee the *c.* and the mercy which he sware unto thy fathers; **8:18** thou shalt remember the LORD thy God: for it is he that giveth thee power to get wealth, that he may establish his *c.* which he sware unto thy fathers; **17:2** if there be found among you... that hath wrought wickedness in the sight of the LORD thy God, in transgressing his *c.*; **29:1** these are the words of the *c.*, which the LORD commanded Moses to make with the children of Israel; **29:9** keep therefore the words of this *c.*, and do them, that ye may prosper in all that ye do; **29:12** thou shouldest enter into *c.* with the LORD thy God, and into his oath, which the LORD thy God maketh with thee this day; **33:9** they have observed thy word, and kept thy *c.*; **Josh. 7:11** they have also transgressed my *c.* which I commanded them: for they have even taken of the accursed thing; **7:15** he that is taken with the accursed thing shall be burnt with fire, he and all that he hath: because he hath transgressed the *c.* of the LORD; **23:16** when ye have transgressed the *c.* of the LORD your God, which he commanded you... then shall the anger of the LORD be kindled against you; **Judg. 2:20** the anger of the LORD was hot against Israel; and he said, Because that this people hath transgressed my *c.* which I commanded their fathers; **1 Sam. 23:18** they two made a *c.* before the LORD; **2 Sam. 23:5** he hath made with me an everlasting *c.*, ordered in all things, and sure: for this is all my salvation, and all my desire; **1 Kgs. 8:9** the

LORD made a *c.* with the children of Israel, when they came out of the land of Egypt; **8:21** I have set there a place for the ark, wherein is the *c.* of the LORD, which he made with our fathers; **8:23** LORD God of Israel, there is no God like thee, in heaven above, or on earth beneath, who keepest *c.* and mercy with thy servants that walk before thee with all their heart; **11:11** forasmuch as this is done of thee, and thou hast not kept my *c.* and my statutes, which I have commanded thee, I will surely rend the kingdom from thee; **1 Chron. 11:3** David made a *c.* with them in Hebron before the LORD; and they anointed David king over Israel; **16:15-17** be ye mindful always of his *c.*; the word which he commanded to a thousand generations; **2 Chron. 6:14** O LORD God of Israel, there is no God like thee in the heaven, nor in the earth; which keepest *c.*, and shewest mercy unto thy servants, that walk before thee with all their hearts; **15:12-15** they entered into a *c.* to seek the LORD God of their fathers with all their heart and with all their soul; **21:7** the LORD would not destroy the house of David, because of the *c.* that he had made with David; **29:10** it is in mine heart to make a *c.* with the LORD God of Israel, that his fierce wrath may turn away from us; **Neh. 1:5** I beseech thee, O LORD God of heaven, the great and terrible God, that keepeth *c.* and mercy for them that love him and observe his commandments; **9:32** our God, the great, the mighty, and the terrible God, who keepest *c.* and mercy, let not all the trouble seem little before thee; **Ps. 25:10** all the paths of the LORD are mercy and truth unto such as keep his *c.* and his testimonies; **78:10** they kept not the *c.* of God, and refused to walk in his law; **78:37** their heart was not right with him, neither were they stedfast in his *c.*; **89:34** my *c.* will I not break, nor alter the thing that is gone out of my lips; **103:17-18** the mercy of the LORD is from everlasting to everlasting upon them that fear him, and his righteousness unto childrens children; To such as keep his *c.*; **132:12** if thy children will keep my *c.* and my testimony that I shall teach them, their children shall also sit upon thy throne for evermore; **Isa. 54:10** my kindness shall not depart from thee, neither shall the *c.* of my peace be removed; **59:21** this is my *c.* with them, saith the LORD; My spirit that is upon thee, and my words which I have put in thy mouth, shall not depart out of thy mouth; **61:8** I the LORD love judgment, I hate robbery for burnt offering; and I will direct their work in truth, and I will make an everlasting *c.* with them; **Jer. 11:2-6** thus saith the LORD God of Israel; Cursed be the man that obeyeth not the words of this *c.*, Which I commanded your fathers... Hear ye the words of this *c.*, and do them; **14:20-21** do not abhor us, for thy names sake, do not disgrace the throne of thy glory: remember, break not thy *c.* with us; **32:40** I will make an everlasting *c.* with them, that I will not turn away from them, to do them good; **33:20-21** if ye can break my *c.* of the day, and my *c.* of the night, and that there should not be day and night in their season; Then may also my *c.* be broken with David my servant; **Ezek. 16:8** I sware unto thee, and entered into a *c.* with thee, saith the Lord GOD, and thou becamest mine; **16:59-62** I will even deal with thee as thou hast done, which hast despised the oath in breaking the *c.*. Nevertheless I will remember my *c.* with thee in the days of thy youth; **37:26** I will make a *c.* of peace with them; it shall be an everlasting *c.* with them; **Dan. 9:4** O Lord, the great and dreadful God, keeping the *c.* and mercy to them that love him, and to them that keep his commandments; **Hosea 8:1** he shall come as an eagle against the house of the LORD, because they have transgressed my *c.*, and trespassed against my law.

COVER (*see also* Hide)

Is it not to deal thy bread to the hungry, and that thou bring the poor that are cast out to thy house? When thou seest the naked, that thou cover him; and that thou hide not thyself from thine own flesh? Isa. 58:7 (*see also* Cast, Naked)

Isa. 58:7-12 is it not to deal thy bread to the hungry, and that thou bring the poor that are cast out to thy house? when thou seest the naked, that thou *c.* him; and that thou hide not thyself from thine own flesh; **Ezek. 18:7** hath not oppressed any, but hath restored to the debtor his pledge, hath spoiled none by violence, hath given his bread to the hungry, and hath *c.* the naked with a garment; **18:16** neither hath oppressed any, hath not withholden the pledge, neither hath spoiled by violence, but hath given his bread to the hungry, and hath *c.* the naked with a garment.

COVET, COVETOUS, COVETOUSNESS
(*see also* Desire, Envy, Greed, Jealous, Lust)

But covet earnestly the best gifts: and yet shew I unto you a more excellent way. 1 Cor. 12:31 (*see also* Best, Gift)

Thou shat not covet thy neighbour's house, thou shalt not covet thy neighbour's wife, nor his manservant, nor his maidservant, nor his ox, nor his ass, nor anything that is thy neighbour's. Ex. 20:17 (*see also* Pledge, Thou Shalt Not, Mosiah 13:24)

Ex. 18:21 thou shalt provide out of all the people able men, such as fear God, men of truth, hating *c.* and place such over them, to be rulers of thousands; **20:17** thou shalt not *c.* thy neighbour's house, thou shalt not *c.* thy neighbour's wife, nor his manservant, nor his maidservant, nor his ox, nor his ass, nor any thing that is thy neighbour's; **Deut. 5:21** neither shalt thou desire thy neighbour's wife, neither shalt thou *c.* thy neighbour's house, his field, or his manservant, or his maidservant, his ox, or his ass, or any thing that is thy neighbour's; **Ps. 119:36** incline my heart unto thy testimonies, and not to *c.*; **Prov. 28:16** the prince that wanteth understanding is also a great oppressor: but he that hateth *c.* shall prolong his days; **Isa. 57:17** for the iniquity of his *c.* was I wroth, and smote him; **Jer. 5:8** they were as fed horses in the morning: every one neighed after his neighbour's wife; **6:13** from the least of them even unto the greatest of them every one is given to *c.*; **8:10** for every one from the least even unto the greatest is given to *c.*; **22:17** thine eyes and thine heart are not but for thy *c.*, and for to shed innocent blood, and for oppression, and for violence, to do it; **51:13** O thou that dwellest upon many waters, abundant in treasures, thine end is come, and the measure of thy *c.*; **Ezek. 33:26-27** ye stand upon your sword, ye work abomination, and ye defile every one his neighbour's wife: and shall ye possess the land; **33:31** with their mouth they shew much love, but their heart goeth after their *c.*; **Micah 2:2** they *c.* fields, and take them by violence; and houses, and take them away; **Haba 2:9** woe to him that *c.* an evil *c.* to his house, that he may set his nest on high; **Luke 12:15-20** take heed, and beware of *c.*: for a man's life consisteth not in the abundance of the things which he possesseth; **16:14-15** the Pharisees also, who were *c.*, heard all these things: and they derided him. And he said unto them, Ye are they which justify yourselves before men; but God knoweth your hearts: for that which is highly esteemed among men is abomination in the sight of God; **Acts 20:33** I have *c.* no man's silver, or gold, or apparel; **Rom. 7:7** the law had said, Thou shalt not *c.*; **1 Cor. 6:10** nor thieves, nor *c.*, nor drunkards, nor revilers, nor extortioners, shall inherit the kingdom of God; **Eph. 5:3** fornication, and all uncleanness, or *c.*, let it not be once named among you, as becometh saints; **Col. 3:5-6** mortify therefore your members which are upon the earth; fornication, uncleanness, inordinate affection, evil concupiscence, and *c.,* which is idolatry: For which things sake the wrath of God cometh on the children of disobedience; **1 Tim. 3:2-3** A bishop then must be... patient, not a brawler, not *c.*; **6:10** while some coveted after, they have erred from the faith, and pierced themselves through with many sorrows; **Heb. 13:5-6** let your conversation be without *c.*; and be content with such things as ye have.

CREATE, CREATED, CREATION (*see also* Establish, Faith, Jesus Christ, Labor, Works)

God created the heaven and the earth. Gen. 1:1

Gen1:21 God *c.* great whales, and every living creature that moveth, after their kind, and every winged fowl after his kind; **Gen. 1:1** God *c.* the heaven and the earth; **1:27** God *c.* man in his own image, in the image of God *c.* he him; male and female *c.* he them; **2:3-4** God blessed the seventh day, and sanctified it: because that in it he had rested from all his work which God *c.* and made; **5:1-2** God *c.* man, in the likeness of God made he him; Male and female *c.* he them; and blessed them, and called their name Adam; **6:7** I will destroy man whom I have *c.* from the face of the earth; both man, and beast, and the creeping thing, and the fowls of the air; for it repenteth me that I have made them; **Ex. 1:19-20** God dealt well with the midwives: and the people multiplied; **Deut. 4:32** ask from the one side of heaven unto the other, whether there hathbeen any such thing as this great thing is, or hath been heard like it; **Job 42:2** I know that thou canst do every thing, and that no thought can be withholden from thee; **Ps. 104:30** thou sendest forth thy spirit, they are *c.*: and thou renewest the face of the earth; **148:5** let them praise the name of the LORD: for he commanded, and they were *c.*; **Isa. 40:26** lift up your eyes on high, and behold who hath *c.* these things; **41:20** that they may see, and know, and consider, and understand together, that the hand of the LORD hath done this, and the Holy One of Israel hath *c.* it; **42:5** God the LORD, he that *c.* the heavens, and stretched them out; he that spread forth the earth, and that which cometh out of it; he that giveth breath unto the people upon it, and spirit to them that walk therein; **43:1** the LORD

that *c.* thee; **43:7** every one that is called by my name: for I have *c.* him for my glory, I have formed him; yea, I have made him; **45:7-8** I form the light, and create darkness: I make peace, and create evil: I the LORD do all these things; **45:12** I have made the earth, and *c.* man upon it: I, even my hands, have stretched out the heavens, and all their host have I commanded; **45:18** God himself that formed the earth and made it; he hath established it, he *c.* it not in vain, he formed it to be inhabited; **54:16** I have *c.* the smith that bloweth the coals in the fire, and that bringeth forth an instrument for his work; and I have *c.* the waster to destroy; **Jer. 31:22** the LORD hath *c.* a new thing in the earth, A woman shall compass a man; **Ezek. 28:13** thou hast been in Eden the garden of God; every precious stone was thy covering: the workmanship of thy tabrets and of thy pipes was prepared in thee in the day that thou wast *c.*; **28:15** thou wast perfect in thy ways from the day that thou wast *c.*, till iniquity was found in thee; **Mal. 2:10** have we not all one father? hath not one God *c.* us? why do we deal treacherously every man against his brother.

CRIME (*see* Bribe, Evil, Murder, Sin, Transgress, Wicked)

CROOKED (*see also* Path, Way)

I will go before thee, and make the crooked places straight: I will break in pieces the gates of brass, and cut in sunder the bars of iron. Isa. 45:2 (*see also* Go, Straight)

CROSS (*see also* Adversity, Burden)

He said unto them all, If any man will come after me, let him deny himself, and take up his cross daily, and follow me. Luke 9:23 (*see also* Daily, Deny, Follow)

CROWN (*see also* Glory)

Fear none of those things which thou shalt suffer: behold, the devil shall cast some of you into prison, that ye may be tried; and ye shall have tribulation ten days: be thou faithful unto death, and I will give thee a crown of life. Rev. 2:10 (*see also* Fear, Trial, Tribulation)

When the chief Shepherd shall appear, ye shall receive a crown of glory that fadeth not away. 1 Pet. 5:4 (*see also* Appear, Shepherd)

CRUEL, CRUELTY (*see also* Oppress, Persecute)

The merciful man doeth good to his own soul: but he that is cruel troubleth his own flesh. Prov. 11:17 (*see also* Merciful, Rule)

Prov. 11:17 the merciful man doeth good to his own soul: but he that is *c.* troubleth his own flesh; **12:10** a righteous man regardeth the life of his beast: but the tender mercies of the wicked are *c.*; **Lam. 4:3-5** even the sea monsters draw out the breast, they give suck to their young ones: the daughter of my people is become *c.*, like the ostriches in the wilderness; **Ezek. 34:4** the diseased have ye not strengthened, neither have ye healed that which was sick... neither have ye sought that which was lost; but with force and with *c.* have ye ruled them.

CRIED, CRY (*see also* Mourn, Pray)

The poor man cried, and the LORD heard him, and saved him out of all his troubles. Ps. 34:6 (*see also* Afflict)

Be merciful unto me, O Lord: for I cry unto thee daily. Rejoice the soul of thy servant: for unto thee, O Lord, do I lift up my soul. Ps. 86:3-5 (*see also* Daily, Pray)

And the LORD said unto them- Go through the midst of the city, through the midst of Jerusalem, and set a mark upon the foreheads of the men that sigh and that cry for all the abominations that be done in the midst thereof. Ezek. 9:4 (*see also* Abomination)

Cry aloud, spare not, lift up thy voice like a trumpet, and shew my people their transgression, and the house of Jacob their sins. Isa. 58:1 (*see also* Sin, Voice)

When we cried unto the LORD, he heard our voice, and sent an angel. Num. 20:16 (*see also* Angel)

Gen. 21:16 he sat over against him, and lift up her voice, and wept; **Ex. 8:12** Moses *c.* unto the LORD; **15:25** he *c.* unto the LORD; and the LORD shewed him a tree; **17:4** Moses *c.* unto the LORD, saying, What shall I do unto this people; **Num. 12:13** Moses *c.* unto the LORD, saying, Heal her now, O God, I beseech thee; **20:16** when we *c.* unto the LORD, he heard our voice, and sent an angel; **Deut. 26:7** when we *c.* unto the LORD God of our fathers, the LORD heard our voice, and

looked on our affliction; **Josh. 24:7** when they *c.* unto the LORD, he put darkness between you and the Egyptians; **Judg. 3:9** when the children of Israel *c.* unto the LORD, the LORD raised up a deliverer to the children of Israel; **3:15** when the children of Israel *c.* unto the LORD, the LORD raised them up a deliverer; **4:3** (6:6-7, 10:10) the children of Israel *c.* unto the LORD; **1 Sam. 7:9** Samuel *c.* unto the LORD for Israel; and the LORD heard him; **12:8** your fathers *c.* unto the LORD; **12:10** they *c.* unto the LORD, and said, We have sinned, because we have forsaken the LORD; **15:11** it grieved Samuel; and he *c.* unto the LORD all night; **1 Kgs. 17:20-21** he *c.* unto the LORD; **2 Kgs. 20:11** Isaiah the prophet *c.* unto the LORD; **2 Chron. 13:14** they *c.* unto the LORD, and the priests sounded with the trumpets; **14:11** Asa *c.* unto the LORD his God, and said, LORD, it is nothing with thee to help; **Job 33:26** he shall pray unto God, and he will be favourable unto him; **Ps. 3:4** I *c.* unto the LORD with my voice, and he heard me out of his holy hill; **107:6** they *c.* unto the LORD in their trouble, and he delivered them out of their distresses; **107:13** they *c.* unto the LORD in their trouble, and he saved them out of their distresses; **120:1** in my distress I *c.* unto the LORD, and he heard me; **142:1** I *c.* unto the LORD with my voice; with my voice unto the LORD did I make my supplication; **Lam. 2:18** their heart *c.* unto the Lord; **Jonah 1:14** they *c.* unto the LORD, and said, We beseech thee, O LORD, we beseech thee, let us not perish for this mans life.

Cease not to cry unto the Lord. 1 Sam. 7:8

Ex. 2:23 the children of Israel sighed by reason of the bondage, and they *c.*, and their *c.* came up unto God by reason of the bondage; **8:12** Moses *c.* unto the LORD because of the frogs which he had brought against Pharaoh; **14:10** they were sore afraid: and the children of Israel *c.* out unto the LORD; **15:25** he *c.* unto the LORD; and the LORD shewed him a tree; **17:4** Moses *c.* unto the LORD, saying, What shall I do unto this people? they be almost ready to stone me; **22:23** if thou afflict them in any wise, and they *c.* at all unto me, I will surely hear their *c.*; **Num. 12:13** Moses *c.* unto the LORD, saying, Heal her now, O God, I beseech thee; **20:16** when we *c.* unto the LORD, he heard our voice, and sent an angel, and hath brought us forth out of Egypt; **Deut. 26:7** when we *c.* unto the LORD God of our fathers, the LORD heard our voice, and looked on our affliction, and our labour, and our oppression; **Josh. 24:7** when they *c.* unto the LORD, he put darkness between you and the Egyptians, and brought the sea upon them, and covered them; **Judg. 3:9** when the children of Israel *c.* unto the LORD, the LORD raised up a deliverer to the children of Israel, who delivered them; **3:15** when the children of Israel *c.* unto the LORD, the LORD raised them up a deliverer; **4:3** the children of Israel *c.* unto the LORD: for he had nine hundred chariots of iron; and twenty years he mightily oppressed the children of Israel; **6:6-7** Israel was greatly impoverished because of the Midianites; and the children of Israel *c.* unto the LORD; **10:10** the children of Israel *c.* unto the LORD, saying, We have sinned against thee; **1 Sam. 7:8** cease not to *c.* unto the LORD our God for us, that he will save us out of the hand of the Philistines; **2 Chron. 6:19** have respect therefore to the prayer of thy servant, and to his supplication, O LORD my God, to hearken unto the *c.* and the prayer which thy servant prayeth before thee; **30:27** the priests the Levites arose and blessed the people: and their voice was heard, and their prayer came up to his holy dwelling place, even unto heaven; **32:24** Hezekiah was sick to the death, and prayed unto the LORD: and he spake unto him; **Job 16:20** my friends scorn me: but mine eye poureth out tears unto God; **Ps. 4:1** hear me when I call, O God of my righteousness: thou hast enlarged me when I was in distress; have mercy upon me, and hear my prayer; **4:3** they are all gone aside, they are all together become filthy: there is none that doeth good, no, not one; **25:4-7** shew me thy ways, O LORD; teach me thy paths. Lead me in thy truth, and teach me: for thou art the God of my salvation; on thee do I wait all the day; **32:6** every one that is godly pray unto thee in a time when thou mayest be found; **54:1-2** hear my prayer, O God; give ear to the words of my mouth; **69:13** as for me, my prayer is unto thee, O LORD, in an acceptable time: O God, in the multitude of thy mercy hear me; **86:3** be merciful unto me, O Lord: for I *c.* unto thee daily; **102:17** he will regard the prayer of the destitute, and not despise their prayer; **107:19** they *c.* unto the LORD in their trouble, and he saveth them out of their distresses; **107:28** they *c.* unto the LORD in their trouble, and he bringeth them out of their distresses; **Isa. 19:20** they shall *c.* unto the LORD because of the oppressors, and he shall send them a saviour, and a great one, and he shall deliver them; **37:15-17** Hezekiah prayed unto the LORD, saying, O LORD of hosts, God of Israel, that dwellest between the cherubims, thou art the God... Incline thine ear, O LORD, and hear; open thine eyes, O LORD, and see; **Dan. 6:10** he kneeled upon his knees three times a day, and prayed, and gave thanks before his God, as he did aforetime; **9:13** all this evil is come upon us: yet made we not our prayer before the LORD our God, that we might turn from our iniquities; **Joel 1:14** sanctify ye a fast, call a solemn assembly, gather the elders and all the inhabitants of the land into the house of the LORD your God, and *c.* unto the LORD; **Micah 3:4** then shall they *c.* unto the LORD, but he will not hear them: he will even hide his face from them at that time, as they have behaved themselves ill in their doings; **Zech. 8:21-23** let us go speedily to pray before the LORD, and to seek the LORD of hosts.

Hear my cry, O God; attend unto my prayer. From the end of the earth will I cry unto thee, when my heart is overwhelmed. Ps. 61:1-2

Ps. 61:1-2 hear my *c.*, O God; attend unto my prayer. From the end of the earth will I *c.* unto thee, when my heart is overwhelmed; **62:8** trust in him at all times; ye people, pour out your heart before him: God is a refuge for us; **77:3** I remembered God, and was troubled: I complained, and my spirit was overwhelmed; **142:3** when my spirit was overwhelmed within me, then thou knewest my path; **143:3-4** therefore is my spirit overwhelmed within me; my heart within me is desolate; **145:18** the LORD is nigh unto all them that call upon him, to all that call upon him in truth.

CUNNING

Be no more children, tossed to and fro, and carried about with every wind of doctrine, by the sleight of men, and cunning craftiness, whereby they lie in wait to deceive. Eph. 4:14 (*see also* Deceit, Doctrine)

CUP

Jesus answered and said, Ye know not what ye ask. Are ye able to drink of the cup that I shall drink of, and to be baptized with the baptism that I am baptized with? They say unto him, We are able. Matt. 20:22 (*see also* Mark 10:38)

CURE (*see* Bless, Heal, Miracle, Restore, Sanctify, Save)

CURSE (*see also* Blaspheme, Condemn)

Thou shalt not curse the deaf, nor put a stumblingblock before the blind, but shalt fear thy God: I am the LORD. Lev. 19:14

Love your enemies, bless them that curse you, do good to them that hate you, and pray for them which despitefully use you, and persecute you. Matt. 5:44 (*see also* Enemy, Love, Persecute, Spite)

Curse not the king, no not in thy thought; and curse not the rich in thy bedchamber: for a bird of the air shall carry the voice, and that which hath wings shall tell the matter. Eccl. 10:20

Said his wife unto him, Dost thou still retain thine integrity? curse God, and die. Job 2:9

Job 1:5 Job sent and sanctified them, and rose up early in the morning, and offered burnt offerings according to the number of them all: for Job said, It may be that my sons have sinned, and *c.* God in their hearts. Thus did Job continually; 1:11 put forth thine hand now, and touch all that he hath, and he will *c.* thee to thy face; 2:5 put forth thine hand now, and touch his bone and his flesh, and he will *c.* thee to thy face; 2:9 said his wife unto him, Dost thou still retain thine integrity? *c.* God, and die; 6:8-9 oh that I might have my request; and that God would grant me the thing that I long for! Even that it would please God to destroy me; that he would let loose his hand, and cut me off.

Whoso curseth his father or his mother, his lamp shall be put out in obscure darkness. Prov. 20:20 (*see also* Father, Mother)

Prov. 20:20 whoso *c.* his father or his mother, his lamp shall be put out in obscure darkness; 30:11 there is a generation that *c.* their father, and doth not bless their mother; 30:17 the eye that mocketh at his father, and despiseth to obey his mother, the ravens of the valley shall pick it out, and the young eagles shall eat it.

CUT, CUT OFF

Wherefore if thy hand or thy foot offend thee, cut them off, and cast them from thee: it is better for thee to enter into life halt or maimed, rather than having two hands or two feet to be cast into everlasting fire. Matt. 18:8 (*see also* Better, Everlasting Fire, Offend)

Matt. 5:30 if thy right hand offend thee, cut it off, and cast it from thee: for it is profitable for thee that one of thy members should perish, and not that thy whole body should be cast into hell; Matt. 18:8 if thy hand or thy foot offend thee, cut them off, and cast them from thee: it is better for thee to enter into life halt or maimed, rather than having two hands or two feet to be cast into everlasting fire.

DAILY (*see also* Day, Diligent, Time)

He said unto them all, If any man will come after me, let him deny himself, and take up his cross daily, and follow me. Luke 9:23 (*see also* Cross, Deny, Follow)

Be merciful unto me, O Lord: for I cry unto thee daily. Rejoice the soul of thy servant: for unto thee, O Lord, do I lift up my soul. Ps. 86:3-5 (*see also* Cry, Pray)

They received the word with all readiness of mind, and searched the scriptures daily, whether those things were so. Acts 17:11 (*see also* Mind, Readiness, Receive, Scripture, Search, Word)

Exhort one another daily; while it is called To day; lest any of you be hardened through the deceitfulness of sin. Heb. 3:13 (*see also* Exhort)

DANGER, DANGEROUS (*see also* Peril)

He that shall blaspheme against the Holy Ghost hath never forgiveness, but is in danger of eternal damnation. Mark 3:29 (*see also* Blaspheme, Holy Ghost)

Whosoever is angry with his brother without a cause shall be in danger of the judgment: and whosoever shall say to his brother, Raca, shall be in danger of the council: but whosoever shall say, Thou fool, shall be in danger of hell fire. Matt. 5:22 (*see also* Anger)

DARK, DARKEN, DARKNESS (*see also* Night, Spirit)

Discretion shall preserve thee, understanding shall keep thee; To deliver thee from the way of the evil man, from the man that speaketh froward things; who leave the paths of righteousness, to walk in the ways of darkness. Prov. 2:11-13 (*see also* Leave, Righteous, Walk, Way)

The LORD hath a controversy with the inhabitants of the land, because there is no truth, nor mercy, nor knowledge of God in the land. By swearing, and lying, and killing, and stealing, and committing adultery, they break out, and blood toucheth blood. Hosea 4:1-2 (*see also* Swear)

When thine eye is evil, thy body also is full of darkness. Take heed therefore that the light which is in thee be not darkness. Luke 11:34-35 (*see also* Evil)

DAUGHTER (*see* Child, Family, Sister, Parent)

DAY, DAYS (*see also* Daily, Time)

I must work the works of him that sent me, while it is day: the night cometh, when no man can work. John. 9:4 (*see also* Night, Work)

Teach us to number our days, that we may apply our hearts unto wisdom. Ps. 90:12 (*see also* Wisdom)

Heaven and earth shall pass away, but my words shall not pass away. But of that day and hour knoweth no man, no, not the angels of heaven, by my Father only. Matt 24:36 (*see also* Hour, Second Coming)

Blow ye the trumpet in Zion, and sound an alarm in my holy mountain: let all the inhabitants of the land tremble: for the day of the Lord cometh, for it is nigh at hand. Joel 2:1 (*see also* Zion)

As the partridge sitteth on eggs, and hatcheth them not; so he that getteth riches, and not by right, shall leave them in the midst of his days, and at his end shall be a fool. Jer. 17:11 (*see also* Rich, Right)

Hold thy peace at the presence of the LORD God: for the day of the LORD is at hand: for the LORD hath prepared a sacrifice, he hath bid his guests. Zeph. 1:7 (*see also* Peace, Presence)

This is the day which the LORD hath made; we will rejoice and be glad in it. Ps. 118:24 (*see also* Rejoice, Today)

Ye shall walk in all the ways which the LORD your God hath commanded you, that ye may live, and that ye may prolong your days in the land which ye shall posses. Deut. 5:33 (*see also* Prolong, Walk, Way)

DEACON (*see also* Priesthood)

Likewise must the deacons be grave, not doubletongued, not given to much wine, not greedy of filthy lucre; Holding the mystery of faith in a pure conscience. 1 Tim. 3:8 (*see also* Greed)

DEAD, DEADLY (*see also* Death)

There are also celestial bodies, and bodies terrestrial: but the glory of the celestial is one, and the glory of the terrestrial is another. There is one glory of the sun, and another glory of the moon, and another glory of the stars: for one star differeth from another star in glory. So also is the resurrection of the dead. 1 Cor. 15:40-42 (*see also* Celestial, Glory, Terrestrial, Resurrection)

These signs shall follow them that believe; In my name shall they cast out devils; they shall speak with new tongues; They shall take up serpents; and if they drink any deadly thing it shall not hurt them; they shall lay hands on the sick and they shall recover. Mark 16:17-18 (*see also* Cast, Devil, Name, Sign, Tongues)

DEAF (*see also* Hear)

[They] were beyond measure astonished, saying, He hath done all things well: he maketh both the deaf to hear, and the dumb to speak. Mark 7:37 (*see also* Dumb, Miracle)

When Jesus saw that the people came running together, he rebuked the foul spirit, saying unto him, Thou dumb and deaf spirit, I charge thee, come out of him, and enter no more into him. Mark 9:25 (*see also* Dumb, Rebuke)

DEAL, DEALING (*see also* Give, Work)

Ye shall not steal, neither deal falsely, neither lie one to another. Lev. 19:11 (*see also* Deceive)

Deal not foolishly. Ps. 75:4 (*see also* Fool)

Have we not all one father? hath not one God created us? why do we deal treacherously every man against his brother, by profaning the covenant of our fathers? Mal. 2:10 (*see also* Against)

Isa. 33:1 woe to thee that spoilest, and thou wast not spoiled; and *d.* treacherously, and they *d.* not treacherously with thee; Jer. 5:11-13 the house of Israel and the house of Judah have *d.* very treacherously against me, saith the LORD. They have belied the LORD, and said, It is not he; neither shall evil come upon us; 12:1 righteous art thou, O LORD, when I plead with thee: yet let me talk with thee of thy judgments: Wherefore doth the way of the wicked prosper? wherefore are all they happy that *d.* very treacherously; 12:6 even thy brethren, and the house of thy father, even they have *d.* treacherously with thee; yea, they have called a multitude after thee: believe them not, though they speak fair words unto thee; Mal. 2:10 have we not all one father? hath not one God created us? why do we *d.* treacherously every man against his brother, by profaning the covenant of our fathers; 2:15-16 take heed to your spirit, and let none *d.* treacherously against the wife of his youth. For the LORD, the God of Israel, saith that he hateth putting away.

DEATH, DIED (*see also* Bury, Dead, Fall)

I know that he shall rise again in the resurrection at the last day. Jesus said unto her, I am the resurrection, and the life: he that believeth in me, though he were dead, yet shall he live. John 11:24-25 (*see also* Jesus Christ, Resurrection)

He that overcometh shall inherit all things; and I will be his God, and he shall be my son. But the fearful, and unbelieving, and the abominable, and murderers, and whore-mongers, and sorcerers, and idolaters, and all liars, shall have their part in the lake which burneth with fire and brimstone: which is the second death. Rev. 21:7 (*see also* All Things, Inherit, Second, Unbelief)

When a righteous man turneth away from his right-eousness, and committeth iniquity, and dieth in them; for his iniquity that he hath done shall he die. Ezek. 18:26 (*see also* Iniquity, Righteousness, Turn)

DEBATE (*see also* Argue, Communicate, Contend)

Debate thy cause with thy neighbour *himself*; and discover not a secret to another: lest he that heareth *it* put thee to shame, and thine infamy turn not away. Prov. 25:9-10 (*see also* Gossip, Secret)

DEBT, DEBTOR (*see also* Lend, Bind, Bondage)

Owe no man any thing, but to love one another: for he that loveth another hath fulfilled the law. Rom. 13:8 (*see also* Love, Owe)

Be not thou one of them that strike hands, or of them that are sureties for debts. Prov. 22:26 (*see also* Strike)

DECEIT, DECEITFULLY, DECEIVE (*see also* False, Hypocrisy, Lie)

A false witness shall not be unpunished, and he that speaketh lies shall not escape. Prov. 19:5 (*see also* Accusation, False Witness, Liar)

Wine is a mocker, strong drink is raging: and whosoever is deceived thereby is not wise. Prov. 20:1 (*see also* Strong Drink, Wine)

Beware of false prophets, which come to you in sheep's clothing, but inwardly they are ravening wolves. Ye shall know them by their fruits. Matt. 7:15-16 (*see also* False Prophet, Wolves)

By thy sorceries were all nations deceived. Rev. 18:23 (*see also* Sorcery)

Be not deceived; God is not mocked: for whatsoever a man soweth, that shall he also reap. Galtians 6:7 (*see also* Sow)

Be not a witness against thy neighbour without cause; and deceive not with thy lips. Prov. 24:28 (*see also* False Witness)

Cursed be he that doeth the the work of the LORD deceitfully. Jer. 48:10 (*see also* Work)

Ye shall not steal, neither deal falsely, neither lie one to another. Lev. 19:11 (*see also* Deal)

Ex. 8:29 let not Pharaoh deal *d.* any more in not letting the people go to sacrifice to the LORD; **Lev. 19:11** ye shall not steal, neither deal falsely, neither lie one to another; **2 Chron. 32:15** let not Hezekiah *d.* you, nor persuade you on this manner, neither yet believe him; **Job 6:15** my brethren have dealt *d.* as a brook, and as the stream of brooks they pass away; **6:27** ye overwhelm the fatherless, and ye dig a pit for your friend; **27:4** my lips shall not speak wickedness, nor my tongue utter *d.*; **31:5** if I have walked with vanity, or if my foot hath hasted to *d.*; **Ps. 5:6** the LORD will abhor the bloody and *d.* man; **24:4** he that hath clean hands, and a pure heart; who hath not lifted up his soul unto vanity, nor sworn *d.*; **28:3** the workers of iniquity, which speak peace to their neighbours, but mischief is in their hearts; **52:2-5** thy tongue deviseth mischiefs; like a sharp razor, working *d.*. Thou lovest evil more than good; and lying rather than to speak righteousness. Selah. Thou lovest all devouring words, O thou *d.* tongue. God shall likewise destroy thee for ever, he shall take thee away, and pluck thee out of thy dwelling place, and root thee out of the land of the living; **55:23** God, shalt bring them down into the pit of destruction: bloody and *d.* men shall not live out half their days; but I will trust in thee; **78:57** dealt unfaithfully like their fathers: they were turned aside like a *d.* bow; **101:7** he that worketh *d.* shall not dwell within my house: he that telleth lies shall not tarry in my sight; **Prov. 11:18** the wicked worketh a *d.* work; **12:5** the thoughts of the righteous are right: but the counsels of the wicked are *d.*; **12:20** *d.* is in the heart of them that imagine evil; **14:8-9** the folly of fools is *d.*. Fools make a mock at sin; **14:25** a *d.* witness speaketh lies; **20:14** it is naught, it is naught, saith the buyer: but when he is gone his way, then he boasteth; **24:28** be not a witness against thy neighbour without cause; and *d.* not with thy lips; **Isa. 36:14** let not Hezekiah *d.* you: for he shall not be able to deliver you; **Jer. 6:13** from the least of them even unto the greatest of them every one is given to covetousness; and from the prophet even unto the priest every one dealeth falsely; **8:5** why then is this people of Jerusalem slidden back by a perpetual backsliding? they hold fast *d.*, they refuse to return; **8:10** therefore will I give their wives unto others, and their fields to them that shall inherit them: for every one from the least even unto the greatest is given to covetousness, from the

prophet even unto the priest every one dealeth falsely; **9:5-8** they will *d.* every one his neighbour, and will not speak the truth: they have taught their tongue to speak lies, and weary themselves to commit iniquity. Thine habitation is in the midst of *d.*; through *d.* they refuse to know me, saith the LORD. Therefore thus saith the LORD of hosts, Behold, I will melt them, and try them; for how shall I do for the daughter of my people? Their tongue is as an arrow shot out; it speaketh *d.*: one speaketh peaceably to his neighbour with his mouth, but in heart he layeth his wait; **29:8** let not your prophets and your diviners, that be in the midst of you, *d.* you, neither hearken to your dreams which ye cause to be dreamed; **Ezek. 18:9** hath walked in my statutes, and hath kept my judgments, to deal truly; he is just, he shall surely live; **Zeph. 3:13** neither shall a *d.* tongue be found in their mouth: for they shall feed and lie down, and none shall make them afraid; **Mal. 1:14** cursed be the *d.*, which hath in his flock a male, and voweth, and sacrificeth unto the Lord a corrupt thing.

Be no more children, tossed to and fro, and carried about with every wind of doctrine, by the sleight of men, and cunning craftiness, whereby they lie in wait to deceive. Eph. 4:14 (*see also* Cunning, Doctrine)

Matt. 23:27-28 woe unto you, scribes and Pharisees, hypocrites! for ye are like unto whited sepulchres, which indeed appear beautiful outward, but are within full of dead men's bones, and of all uncleanness. Even so ye also outwardly appear righteous unto men, but within ye are full of hypocrisy and iniquity; **Gal. 2:4** because of false brethren unawares brought in, who came in privily to spy out our liberty which we have in Christ Jesus, that they might bring us into bondage; **Eph. 4:14** we henceforth be no more children, tossed to and fro, and carried about with every wind of doctrine, by the sleight of men, and cunning craftiness, whereby they lie in wait to deceive; **Philip. 3:2** beware of dogs, beware of evil workers, beware of the concision; **1 Tim. 4:13** till I come, give attendance to reading, to exhortation, to doctrine; **2 Tim. 3:5** having a form of godliness, but denying the power thereof: from such turn away; **Titus 1:16** they profess that they know God; but in works they deny him, being abominable, and disobedient, and unto every good work reprobate; **1 Jn. 2:18** little children, it is the last time: and as ye have heard that antichrist shall come, even now are there many antichrists; whereby we know that it is the last time.

If any man shall say unto you, Lo, here is Christ, or there; believe it not. For there shall arise false Christs, and false prophets, and shall shew great signs and wonders; insomuch that, if it were possible, they shall deceive the very elect. Matt. 24:23-24 (*see also* False Christ, False Prophet)

Matt. 24:4-5 (Mark 13:5-6) take heed that no man *d.* you. For many shall come in my name, saying, I am Christ; and shall *d.* many; 24:23-27 if any man shall say unto you, Lo, here is Christ, or there; believe it not. For there shall arise false Christs, and false prophets, and shall shew great signs and wonders; insomuch that, if it were possible, they shall *d.* the very elect; Mark 13:21 if any man shall say to you, Lo, here is Christ; or, lo, he is there; believe him not: For false Christs and false prophets shall rise, and shall shew signs and wonders, to seduce, if it were possible, even the elect; Luke 21:8 And he said, Take heed that ye be not *d.*: for many shall come in my name, saying, I am Christ; and the time draweth near: go ye not therefore after them; 1 Cor. 6: 9 know ye not that the unrighteous shall not inherit the kingdom of God? Be not *d.*; Eph. 4:14 we henceforth be no more children, tossed to and fro, and carried about with every wind of doctrine, by the sleight of men, and cunning craftiness, whereby they lie in wait to *d.*; 5:6 let no man *d.* you with vain words: for because of these things cometh the wrath of God upon the children of disobedience; 2 Thes. 2:3 let no man *d.* you by any means: for that day shall not come, except there come a falling away first, and that man of sin be revealed, the son of perdition; Titus 1:11 whose mouths must be stopped, who subvert whole houses, teaching things which they ought not, for filthy lucre's sake; Heb. 13:9 be not carried about with divers and strange doctrines. For it is a good thing that the heart be established with grace; not with meats, which have not profited them that have been occupied therein; 1 Jn. 2:19 they went out from us, but they were not of us; 2:26 these things have I written unto you concerning them that seduce you; 3:7 little children, let no man *d.* you: he that doeth righteousness is righteous, even as he is righteous; 2 Jn. 1:7 many *d.* are entered into the world, who confess not that Jesus Christ is come in the flesh. This is a *d.* and an antichrist; 1:10 if there come any unto you, and bring not this doctrine, receive him not into your house,

neither bid him God speed; Rev 12:9 the great dragon was cast out, that old serpent, called the Devil, and Satan, which *d.* the whole world: he was cast out into the earth, and his angels were cast out with him; 13:6 he opened his mouth in blasphemy against God, to blaspheme his name, and his tabernacle, a nd them that dwell in heaven; 19:20 the beast was taken, and with him the false prophet that wrought miracles before him, with which he *d.* them that had received the mark of the beast, and them that worshipped his image.

DECLARE (*see also* Cry, Preach, Publish, Testify, Witness)

Declare in Zion the vengeance of the LORD our God, the vengeance of His temple. Jer. 50:28 (*see also* Vengeance, Zion)

All the multitude kept silence, and gave audience to Barnabas and Paul, declaring what miracles and wonders God had wrought among the Gentiles by them. Acts 15:12 (*see also* Miracle)

Let us declare in Zion the work of the LORD our God. Jer. 51:10 (*see also* Zion)

Praise the LORD, call upon his name, declare his doings among the people, make mention that his name is exalted. Isa. 12:4 (*see also* Call, Praise)

Isa. 12:4 praise the LORD, call upon his name, *d.* his doings among the people, make mention that his name is exalted; 21:10 that which I have heard of the LORD of hosts, the God of Israel, have I *d.* unto you.

DECREE, DECREED (*see also* Command, Law, Statute)

WOE unto them that decree unrighteous decrees, and that write grievousness which they have prescribed. Isa. 10:1

Isa. 10:1-2 woe unto them that *d.* unrighteous *d.*, and that write grievousness which they have prescribed; To turn aside the needy from judgment, and to take away the right from the poor of my people.

DEFER (*see also* Delay)

When thou vowest a vow unto God, defer not to pay it; for he hath no pleasure in fools: pay that which thou hast vowed. Eccl. 5:4 (*see also* Pay, Vow)

DEFILE (*see also* Corrupt, Pollute, Profane, Unclean)

The children of Judah have done evil in my sight, saith the LORD: they have set their abominations in the house which is called by my name, to pollute it. Jer. 7:30 (*see also* Abomination, House)

That which cometh out of the man, that defileth the man. For from within, out of the heart of men, proceed evil thoughts, adulteries, fornications, murders, Thefts, covetousness, wickedness, deceit, lasciviousness, an evil eye, blasphemy, pride, foolishness: All these evil things come from within, and defile the man. Mark 7:20-23 (*see also* Evil, Lasciviousness, Think)

Do not ye yet understand, that whatsoever entereth in at the mouth goeth into the belly, and is cast out into the draught? But those things which proceed out of the mouth come froth from the heart; and they defile the man. For out of the heart proceed evil thoughts, murders, adulteries, fornications, thefts, false witness, blasphemies: These are the things which defile a man: but to eat with unwashen hands defileth not a man. Matt: 17-20 (*see also* Heart, Mouth, Proceed)

There shall in no wise enter into [the temple] any thing that defileth, neither whatsoever worketh abomination, or maketh a lie: but they which are written in the Lamb's book of life. Rev. 21:27 (*see also* Lie, Temple)

Thou hast defiled thy sanctuaries by the multitude of thine iniquities, by the iniquity of thy traffick; therefore will I bring forth a fire from the midst of thee, it shall devour thee. Ezek. 28:18-19 (*see also* Iniquity, Sanctuary)

Ezek. 28:18-19 thou hast *d.* thy sanctuaries by the multitude of thine iniquities, by the iniquity of thy traffick; therefore will I bring forth a fire from the

midst of thee, it shall devour thee; **44:7** ye have brought into my sanctuary strangers, uncircumcised in heart, and uncircumcised in flesh, to be in my sanctuary, to pollute it, even my house.

Thou shalt not lie carnally with thy neighbour's wife, to defile thyself with her. Lev. 18:20-24 (*see also* Adultery)

Gen. 34:2-7 he took her, and lay with her, and *d.* her; **Lev. 18:20-24** thou shalt not lie carnally with thy neighbour's wife, to *d.* thyself with her; **Ps. 119:1** blessed are the undefiled in the way, who walk in the law of the LORD; **Jer. 2:7** I brought you into a plentiful country, to eat the fruit thereof and the goodness thereof; but when ye entered, ye *d.* my land; **Ezek. 18:6** neither hath *d.* his neighbour's wife; **28:18** thou hast *d.* thy sanctuaries by the multitude of thine iniquities, by the iniquity of thy traffick; therefore will I bring forth a fire from the midst of thee, it shall devour thee; **33:26** ye *d.* every one his neighbour's wife.

Neither shalt thou lie with any beast to defile thyself therewith. Lev. 18:23

Lev. 18:22-30 neither shalt thou lie with any beast to *d.* thyself therewith; **20:15-16** if a man lie with a beast, he shall surely be put to death: and ye shall slay the beast. And if a woman approach unto any beast, and lie down thereto, thou shalt kill the woman, and the beast; **Ps. 119:1** blessed are the undefiled in the way, who walk in the law of the LORD; **Jer. 2:7** I brought you into a plentiful country, to eat the fruit thereof and the goodness thereof; but when ye entered, ye *d.* my land, and made mine heritage an abomination.

DEFRAUD (*see also* False Witness)

[Let] no man go beyond and defraud his brother in any matter: because that the Lord is the avenger of all such, as we also have forewarned you and testified. 1 Thes. 4:6

Mark 10:19 thou knowest the commandments, Do not commit adultery, Do not kill, Do not steal, Do not bear false witness, Defraud not, Honour thy father and mother; **1 Thes. 4:6** no man go beyond and defraud his brother in any matter: because that the Lord is the avenger of all such, as we also have forewarned you and testified.

Thou shalt not defraud thy neighbour, neither rob him. Lev. 19:13 (*see also* Thou Shalt Not)

Lev. 19:13 thou shalt not *d.* thy neighbour, neither rob him; **1 Sam. 12:3-4** whose ox have I taken? or whose ass have I taken? or whom have I *d.*? whom have I oppressed? or of whose hand have I received any bribe to blind mine eyes therewith? and I will restore it you; **Prov. 22:22** rob not the poor, because he is poor: neither oppress the afflicted in the gate.

DELIGHT (*see also* Joy, Pleasure)

I delight to do thy will, O my God: yea, thy law is within my heart. Ps. 40:8 (*see also* Law)

Delight thyself also in the LORD; and he shall give thee the desires of thine heart. Ps. 37:4 (*see also* Desire, Righteous)

They seek me daily, and delight to know my ways, as a nation that did righteousness, and forsook not the ordinance of their God: they ask of me the ordinances of justice; they take delight in approaching to God. Isa. 58:2 (*see also* Approach)

If thou turn away thy foot from the sabbath, from doing thy pleasure on my holy day; and call the sabbath a delight, the holy of the LORD, honorable; and shalt honor him, not doing thy own ways, nor finding thine own pleasure, nor speaking thine own words: Then shalt thou delight thyself in the LORD; and I will cause thee to ride upon the high places of the earth, and feed thee with the heritage of Jacob thy father: for the mouth of the LORD hath spoken it. Isa. 58:13-14 (*see also* Honor, Sabbath)

Yea, they have chosen their own ways, and their soul delighteth in their abominations. Isa. 66:3 (*see also* Abomination)

DELIVER, DELIVERANCE (*see also* Save, Salvation)

If ye do return unto the LORD with all your hearts, then put away the strange gods and Ashtaroth from among you, and prepare your hearts unto the LORD, and serve him only: and he will deliver you out of the hand of the Philistines. 1 Sam. 7:3 (*see also* Return)

Thy God whom thou servest continually, he will deliver thee. Dan. 6:16 (*see also* Serve)

2 Chron. 20:12 our God, wilt thou not judge them? for we have no might against this great company that cometh against us; neither know we what to do: but our eyes are upon thee; **Isa. 8:17** I will wait upon the LORD, that hideth his face from the house of Jacob, and I will look for him; **31:1** woe to them that go down to Egypt for help... because they are very strong; but they look not unto the Holy One of Israel, neither seek the LORD; **42:18** hear, ye deaf; and look, ye blind, that ye may see; **Dan. 6:16** the king commanded, and they brought Daniel, and cast him into the den of lions. Now the king spake and said unto Daniel, Thy God whom thou servest continually, he will *d.* thee; **6:20-24** said Daniel unto the king, O king, live for ever. My God hath sent his angel, and hath shut the lions mouths, that they have not hurt me: forasmuch as before him innocency was found in me; and also before thee, O king, have I done no hurt; **6:27-28** he *d.* and rescueth, and he worketh signs and wonders in heaven and in earth, who hath *d.* Daniel from the power of the lions; **Zech. 9:1** the burden of the word of the LORD in the land of Hadrach, and Damascus shall be the rest thereof: when the eyes of man, as of all the tribes of Israel, shall be toward the LORD.

DENY (*see also* Reject)

He said unto them all, If any man will come after me, let him deny himself, and take up his cross daily, and follow me. Luke 9:23 (*see also* Cross, Daily, Follow)

Who is a liar but he that denieth that Jesus is the Christ? He is antichrist, that denieth the Father and the Son. 1 Jn. 2:22-23 (*see also* Liar)

Matt. 10:33 whosoever shall *d.* me before men, him will I also *d.* before my Father which is in heaven; **26:34-35** this night, before the cock crow, thou shalt *d.* me thrice. Peter said unto him, Though I should die with thee, yet will I not *d.* thee. Likewise also said all the disciples; **26:56** all the disciples forsook him, and fled; **26:69-73** Peter sat without in the palace: and a damsel came unto him, saying, Thou also wast with Jesus of Galilee. But he *d.* before them all, saying, I know not what thou sayest. And when he was gone out into the porch, another maid saw him, and said unto them that were there, This fellow was also with Jesus of Nazareth.

And again he *d.* with an oath, I do not know the man. And after a while came unto him they that stood by, and said to Peter, Surely thou also art one of them; for thy speech betrayeth thee; **26:75** Peter remembered the word of Jesus, which said unto him, Before the cock crow, thou shalt *d.* me thrice. And he went out, and wept bitterly; **Mark 14:30-31** before the cock crow twice, thou shalt *d.* me thrice. But he spake the more vehemently, If I should die with thee, I will not *d.* thee in any wise; **14:66-72** And as Peter was beneath in the palace, there cometh one of the maids of the high priest: And when she saw Peter warming himself, she looked upon him, and said, And thou also wast with Jesus of Nazareth. But he *d.,* saying, I know not, neither understand I what thou sayest. And he went out into the porch; and the cock crew. And a maid saw him again, and began to say to them that stood by, This is one of them. And he *d.* it again. And a little after, they that stood by said again to Peter, Surely thou art one of them: for thou art a Galilaean, and thy speech agreeth thereto. But he began to curse and to swear, saying, I know not this man of whom ye speak. And the second time the cock crew. And Peter called to mind the word that Jesus said unto him, Before the cock crow twice, thou shalt *d.* me thrice. And when he thought thereon, he wept; **Luke 12:9** he that *d.* me before men shall be *d.* before the angels of God; **22:34** Peter, the cock shall not crow this day, before that thou shalt thrice *d.* that thou knowest me; **Acts 3:13-14** the God of Abraham, and of Isaac, and of Jacob, the God of our fathers, hath glorified his Son Jesus; whom ye delivered up, and *d.* him in the presence of Pilate, when he was determined to let him go. But ye *d.* the Holy One and the Just, and desired a murderer to be granted unto you; **2 Tim. 2:12-13** if we *d.* him, he also will *d.* us: If we believe not, yet he abideth faithful: he cannot *d.* himself; **Titus 1:16** they profess that they know God; but in works they *d.* him, being abominable, and disobedient, and unto every good work reprobate; **1 Jn. 2:22-23** who is a liar but he that *d.* that Jesus is the Christ? He is antichrist, that *d.* the Father and the Son. Whosoever *d.* the Son, the same hath not the Father: [but] he that acknowledgeth the Son hath the Father also; **Rev. 3:8** I know thy works: behold, I have set before thee an open door, and no man can shut it: for thou hast a little strength, and hast kept my word, and hast not *d.* my name.

DEPART (*see also* Leave)

Train up a child in the way he should go: and when he is old, he will not depart from it. Prov. 22:6 (*see also* Child, Train, Way)

Depart from evil, and do good; seek peace, and pursue it. Ps. 34:14 (*see also* Evil, Good)

Ps. 34:14 *d.* from evil, and do good; seek peace, and pursue it; **37:27** *d.* from evil, and do good; and dwell for evermore; **Prov. 3:7** be not wise in thine own eyes: fear the LORD, and *d.* from evil.

DEPEND, DEPENDABILITY, DEPENDABLE (*see also* Accountable, Diligence, Rely, Responsible, Trust)

DESIRE (*see also* Covet, Lust)

For wisdom is better than rubies; and all the things that may be desired are not to be compared to it. Prov. 8:11 (*see also* Better, Wisdom)

Let us not be desirous of vain glory, provoking one another, envying one another. Gal. 5:26 (*see also* Envious)

Delight thyself also in the LORD; and he shall give thee the desires of thine heart. Ps. 37:4 (*see also* Delight, Righteous)

Ps. 37:4 delight thyself also in the LORD; and he shall give thee the *d.* of thine heart; **Prov. 13:19** the *d.* accomplished is sweet to the soul: but it is abomination to fools to depart from evil.

Yea, in the way of thy judgments, O LORD, have we waited for thee; the desire of our soul is to thy name, and to the remembrance of thee. Isa. 26:8 (*see also* Name)

Isa. 26:8-9 in the way of thy judgments, O LORD, have we waited for thee; the *d.* of our soul is to thy name, and to the remembrance of thee; **43:26** put me in remembrance: let us plead together: declare thou, that thou mayest be justified.

As newborn babes, desire the sincere milk of the word, that ye may grow thereby. 1 Pet. 2:2 (*see also* Word)

1 Cor 3:2-3 I have fed you with milk, and not with meat: for hitherto ye were not able to bear it, neither yet now are ye able. For ye are yet carnal: for whereas there is among you envying, and strife, and divisions, are ye not carnal, and walk as men; Heb. 5:12-13 for the time ye ought to be teachers, ye have need that one teach you again which be the first principles of the oracles of God; and are become such as have need of milk, and not of strong meat. For every one that useth milk is unskilful in the word of righteousness: for he is a babe; 1 Pet. 2:2-3 as newborn babes, *d.* the sincere milk of the word, that ye may grow thereby: If so be ye have tasted that the Lord is gracious.

DESPAIR, DESPAIRING (*see* Anguish, Sorrow, Troubled)

DESPISE (*see also* Abhor, Hate)

Ye despisers, and wonder, and perish: for I work a work in your days, a work which ye shall in no wise believe, though a man declare it unto you. Acts 13:41

Because ye despise this word, and trust in oppression or perverseness, and stay thereon: Therefore this iniquity shall be to you as a breach ready to fall, swelling out in a high wall, whose breaking cometh suddenly at an instant. Isa. 30:12-13 (*see also* Oppress, Perverse, Word)

Let not him that eateth despise him that eateth not; and let not him which eateth not judge him that eateth. Rom. 14:3 (*see also* Eat)

Matt. 18:10 take heed that ye *d.* not one of these little ones; for I say unto you, That in heaven their angels do always behold the face of my Father which is in heaven; Luke 18:9 he spake this parable unto certain which trusted in themselves that they were righteous, and *d.* others; Rom. 14:1-3 him that is weak in the faith receive ye, but not to doubtful disputations. For one believeth that he may eat all things: another, who is weak, eateth herbs. Let not him that eateth *d.* him that eateth not; and let not him which eateth not judge him that eateth: for God hath received him; 1 Thes. 4:8 he therefore that *d., d.* not man, but God, who hath also given unto us his holy Spirit; 1 Tim. 6:2 let them not *d.*

them, because they are brethren; but rather do them service, because they are faithful and beloved, partakers of the benefit.

Behold, happy is the man whom God correcteth: therefore despise not thou the chastening of the Almighty: For he maketh sore, and bindeth up; he woundeth, and his hands make whole. Job 5:17-18 (*see also* Chasten)

Let no man despise thy youth; but be thou an example of the believers, in word, in conversation, in charity, in spirit, in faith, in purity. 1 Tim. 4:12 (*see also* Believe, Charity, Conversation, Example, Pure)

The LORD saith, Be it far from me; for them that honour me I will honour, and they that despise me shall be lightly esteemed. 1 Sam. 2:30 (*see also* Honor)

Lev. 26:15 if ye shall *d.* my statutes, or if your soul abhor my judgments, so that ye will not do all my commandments, but that ye break my covenant; Num. 11:20 it be loathsome unto you: because that ye have *d.* the LORD which is among you, and have wept before him; 15:31 because he hath *d.* the word of the LORD, and hath broken his commandment, that soul shall utterly be cut off; 1 Sam. 2:30 the LORD saith, Be it far from me; for them that honour me I will honour, and they that *d.* me shall be lightly esteemed; 2 Sam. 12:9-10 wherefore hast thou *d.* the commandment of the LORD, to do evil in his sight; 2 Chron. 36:16 they mocked the messengers of God, and *d.* his words, and misused his prophets, until the wrath of the LORD arose against his people; Job 5:17 happy is the man whom God correcteth: therefore *d.* not thou the chastening of the Almighty; Prov. 3:11 *d.* not the chastening of the LORD; neither be weary of his correction; 19:16 he that keepeth the commandment keepeth his own soul; but he that *d.* his ways shall die; Isa. 30:12 thus saith the Holy One of Israel, Because ye *d.* this word, and trust in oppression and perverseness; 53:3 he is *d.* and rejected of men; a man of sorrows, and acquainted with grief: and we hid as it were our faces from him; he was *d.,* and we esteemed him not; Jer. 23:17 they say still unto them that *d.* me, The LORD hath said, Ye shall have peace; and they say unto every one that walketh after the imagination of his own heart, No evil shall come upon you; Ezek. 7:16-19 thus saith the Lord GOD; As I live, surely mine oath that he hath *d.*, and my covenant that he hath broken, even it will I recompense upon his own head; **20:13** they walked not in my statutes, and they *d.* my judgments, which if a man do, he shall even live in them; **20:16** they *d.* my judgments, and walked not in my statutes, but polluted my sabbaths: for their heart went after their idols; **20:24** they had not executed my judgments, but had *d.* my statutes, and had polluted my sabbaths, and their eyes were after their fathers idols; **22:8** thou hast *d.* mine holy things, and hast profaned my sabbaths; **Amos 2:4** for three transgressions of Judah, and for four, I will not turn away the punishment thereof; because they have *d.* the law of the LORD, and have not kept his commandments; **Mal. 1:6-7** if then I be a father, where is mine honour? and if I be a master, where is my fear? saith the LORD of hosts unto you, O priests, that *d.* my name.

He that is void of wisdom despiseth his neighbour: but a man of understanding holdeth his peace. Prov. 11:12

Prov. 11:12 he that is void of wisdom *d.* his neighbour: but a man of understanding holdeth his peace; **14:21** he that *d.* his neighbour sinneth: but he that hath mercy on the poor, happy is he; **Zeph. 1:9** I [will] punish all those that leap on the threshold, which fill their masters houses with violence and deceit.

DESTROY, DESTROYER, DESTRUCTION (*see also* Kill, Perish, Persecute, Waste)

Woe be unto the pastors that destroy and scatter the sheep of my pasture! saith the LORD. Jer. 23:1 (*see also* Persecute, Scatter, Sheep)

Concerning the works of men, by the word of thy lips I have kept me from the paths of the destroyer. Ps. 17:4 (*see also* Path)

The destruction of the transgressors and of the sinners shall be together, and they that forsake the LORD shall be consumed. Isa. 1:28 (*see also* Forget)

Thou shouldest not have looked on the day of thy brother in the day that he became a stranger; neither shouldest thou have rejoiced over the children of Judah in the day of their destruction; neither shouldest thou have spoken proudly in the day of distress. Obad. 1:12 (*see also* Rejoice)

Job 31:29 if I rejoiced at the *d.* of him that hated me, or lifted up myself when evil found him; **Obad. 1:12-14** thou shouldest not have looked on the day of thy brother in the day that he became a stranger; neither shouldest thou have rejoiced over the children of Judah in the day of their *d.*; neither shouldest thou have spoken proudly in the day of distress.

DEVICE

They said, There is no hope: but we will walk after our own devices, and we will every one do the imagination of his evil heart. Jer. 18:12 (*see also* Imagine, Walk)

DEVISE (*see also* Create, Imagine)

WOE to them that devise iniquity, and work evil upon their beds! Micah 2:1 (*see also* Iniquity)

Micah 2:1 woe to them that *d.* iniquity, and work evil upon their beds! when the morning is light, they practise it, because it is in the power of their hand; **3:4** they [shall] cry unto the LORD, but he will not hear them: he will even hide his face from them at that time, as they have behaved themselves ill in their doings.

Devise not evil against thy neighbour, seeing he dwelleth securely by thee. Prov. 3:29 (*see also* Evil)

Ps. 31:13 I have heard the slander of many: fear was on every side: while they took counsel together against me, they *d.* to take away my life; **35:4** let them be confounded and put to shame that seek after my soul: let them be turned back and brought to confusion that *d.* my hurt; **35:15** in mine adversity they rejoiced, and gathered themselves together: yea, the abjects gathered themselves together against me, and I knew it not; **35:19-21** let not them that are mine enemies wrongfully rejoice over me: neither let them wink with the eye that hate me without a cause. For they speak not peace: but they *d.* deceitful matters; **35:26** let them be ashamed and brought to confusion together that rejoice at mine hurt: let them be clothed with shame and dishonour that magnify themselves against me; **37:12** the wicked plotteth against the just, and gnasheth upon him with his teeth; **37:14-15** the wicked have drawn out the sword, and have bent their bow, to cast down the poor and needy, and to slay such as be of upright conversation; **37:32** the wicked watcheth the righteous, and seeketh to slay him; **38:12** they also that seek after my life lay snares for me: and they that seek my hurt speak mischievous things, and imagine deceits; **40:14** let them be ashamed and confounded together that seek after my soul to destroy it; let them be driven backward and put to shame that wish me evil; **41:7** all that hate me whisper together against me: against me do they *d.* my hurt; **41:9** mine own familiar friend, in whom I trusted, which did eat of my bread, hath lifted up his heel against me; **56:6** they gather themselves together, they hide themselves, they mark my steps, when they wait for my soul; **57:6** they have prepared a net for my steps; my soul is bowed down: they have digged a pit before me, into the midst whereof they are fallen themselves; **62:3** how long will ye imagine mischief against a man? ye shall be slain all of you: as a bowing wall shall ye be, and as a tottering fence; **63:9-10** those that seek my soul, to destroy it, shall go into the lower parts of the earth. They shall fall by the sword: they shall be a portion for foxes; **64:2-6** they encourage themselves in an evil matter: they commune of laying snares privily; they say, Who shall see them? They search out iniquities; they accomplish a diligent search; **71:10-13** mine enemies speak against me; and they that lay wait for my soul take counsel together, Saying, God hath forsaken him: persecute and take him; for there is none to deliver him; **71:24** my tongue also shall talk of thy righteousness all the day long: for they are confounded, for they are brought unto shame, that seek my hurt; **83:3-5** they have taken crafty counsel against thy people, and consulted against thy hidden ones. They have said, Come, and let us cut them off from being a nation; **86:14** O God, the proud are risen against me, and the assemblies of violent men have sought after my soul; and have not set thee before them; **140:4-5** keep me, O LORD, from the hands of the wicked; preserve me from the violent man; who have purposed to overthrow my goings. The proud have hid a snare for me; **140:8-11** grant not, O LORD, the desires of the wicked: further not his wicked device; lest they exalt themselves... Let not an evil speaker be established in the earth; **141:9-10** keep me from the snares which they have laid for me, and the gins of the workers of iniquity. Let the wicked fall into their own nets, whilst that I withal escape; **142:3** when my spirit was overwhelmed within me, then thou knewest my path. In the way wherein I walked have they privily laid a snare for me; **143:3** the enemy hath persecuted my soul; he hath smitten my life down to the ground; he hath made me to dwell in darkness, as those that have been long dead; **143:7** hear me speedily, O LORD: my spirit faileth: hide not thy face from me, lest I be like unto them that go down into the pit; **Prov. 3:29** *d.* not evil against thy neighbour, seeing he dwelleth securely by thee; **26:27** whoso diggeth a pit shall fall therein: and he that rolleth a stone, it will return upon him; **Eccl. 10:8** he that diggeth a pit shall fall into it; and whoso breaketh an hedge, a serpent shall bite him; **Isa. 7:5** Syria, Ephraim, and the son of Remaliah, have taken evil counsel against thee; **Dan. 6:4-7** we shall not find any occasion against this Daniel, except we find it against him concerning the law of his God; **6:11-15** then answered they and said before the king, That Daniel, which is of the children of the captivity of Judah, regardeth not thee, O king, nor the decree that thou hast signed, but maketh his petition three times a day; **Micah 7:2-7** the good man is perished out of the earth: and there is none upright among men: they all lie in wait for blood; they hunt every man his brother with a net.

DEVIL, DEVILISH (*see also* Adversary, Evil, Hell, Lucifer, Satan, Wicked)

These signs shall follow them that believe; In my name shall they cast out devils; they shall speak with new tongues; They shall take up serpents; and if they drink any deadly thing it shall not hurt them; they shall lay hands on the sick and they shall recover. Mark 16:17-18 (*see also* Cast, Deadly, Name, Sign, Tongues)

DILIGENCE, DILIGENT, DILIGENTLY (*see also* Daily, Depend, Labor, Time, Work)

Whatsoever is commanded by the God of heaven, let it be diligently done for the house of the God of heaven. Ezra 7:23 (*see also* House)

And these words, which I command thee this day, shall be in thine heart: And thou shalt teach them diligently unto thy children, and shalt talk of them when thou sittest in thine house, and when thou walkest by the way and when thou liest down, and when thou risest up. And thou shalt bind them for a sign upon thine hand, and they shalt be as frontlets between thine eyes. And thou shalt write them upon the posts of thy house, and on thy gates. Deut. 6:6-9 (*see also* Children, Teach, Word)

Give diligence to make your calling and election sure. 2 Pet. 1:10 (*see also* Election)

Be thou diligent to know the state of thy flocks, and look well to thy herds. For riches are not for ever: and doth the crown endure to every generation. Prov. 27:23-24 (*see also* Flock)

But without faith it is impossible to please him: for he that cometh to God must believe that he is, and that he is a rewarder of them that diligently seek him. Heb. 11:6 (*see also* Believe, Faith, Impossible, Reward, Seek)

The soul of the sluggard desireth, and hath nothing: but the soul of the diligent shall be made fat. Prov. 13:4

Prov. 13:4 the soul of the sluggard desireth, and hath nothing: but the soul of the *d.* shall be made fat; 21:5 the thoughts of the *d.* tend only to plenteousness; but of every one that is hasty only to want; 22:29 seest thou a man *d.* in his business? he shall stand before kings; he shall not stand before mean men.

DIMINISH

What thing soever I command you, observe to do it: thou shalt not add thereto, nor diminish from it. Deut. 12:32 (*see also* Command)

Ye shall not add unto the word which I command you, neither shall ye diminish ought from it, that ye may keep the commandments of the LORD your God which I command you. Deut. 4:2 (*see also* Add, Word)

DIRECT (*see also* Call, Guide, Lead, Order, Priesthood)

In all thy ways acknowledge him, and he shall direct thy paths. Prov. 3:6 (*see also* Acknowledge, Way)

DISCERN (*see also* Judge, Know, See)

Discern the signs of the times. Matt. 16:3 (*see also* Sign)

DISCIPLE (*see* Apostle, Follower, Messenger, Priesthood, Prophet, Servant)

DISCORD (*see also* Contend, Dispute, Strife)

These six things doth the LORD hate: yea, seven are an abomination unto him: A proud look, a lying tongue, and hands that shed innocent blood, An heart that deviseth wicked imaginations, feet that be swift in running to mischief, A false witness that speaketh lies, and he that soweth discord among brethren. Prov. 6:16-19 (*see also* False Witness, Imagine, Innocent, Liar, Mischief, Pride)

Prov. 6:19 a false witness that speaketh lies, and he that soweth *d.* among brethren; Eccl. 11:6 in the morning sow thy seed, and in the evening withhold not thine hand: for thou knowest not whether shall prosper, either this or that, or whether they both shall be alike good.

DISCRETE, DISCRETION (*see also* Careful, Choice)

Be discreet, chaste, keepers at home, good, obedient to their own husbands, that the word of God be not blasphemed. Titus 2:5 (*see also* Chaste)

My son, attend unto my wisdom, and bow thine ear to my understanding: That thou mayest regard discretion and *that* thy lips may keep knowledge. Prov. 5:2 (*see also* Lips, Mouth)

Keep sound wisdom and discretion: So shall they be life unto thy soul, and grace to thy neck. Prov. 3:21-22 (*see also* Wisdom)

DISHONOR (*see also* Reproach)

God also gave them up to uncleanness through the lusts of their own hearts, to dishonour their own bodies between themselves. Rom. 1:24 (*see also* Lust)

Rom. 1:24 God also gave them up to uncleanness through the lusts of their own hearts, to *d.* their own bodies between themselves; 1:26 for this cause God gave them up unto vile affections: for even their women did change the natural use into that which is against nature.

DISMAY, DISMAYED (*see also* Transgress, Unbelief)

Be strong and of good courage, and do it: fear not, nor be dismayed: for the LORD GOD, even my GOD, will be with thee; he will not fail thee, nor forsake thee. 1 Chron. 28:20 (*see also* Fear)

Be strong and of a good courage; be not afraid, neither be thou dismayed; for the Lord thy God is with thee whithersoever thou goest. Josh. 1:9 (*see also* Fear)

Deut. 1:21 fear not, neither be discouraged; **20:3-4** let not your hearts faint, fear not, and do not tremble, neither be ye terrified because of them; For the LORD your God is he that goeth with you; **31:6-8** be strong and of a good courage, fear not, nor be afraid of them: for the LORD thy God, he it is that doth go with thee; he will not fail thee, nor forsake thee; **Josh. 1:9** be strong and of a good courage; be not afraid, neither be thou dismayed; for the Lord thy God is with thee whithersoever thou goest; **8:1** fear not, neither be thou *d.*; **10:25** fear not, nor be *d.*, be strong and of good courage; **1 Kgs. 17:13** fear not; go and do as thou hast said; **2 Kgs. 6:15-17** fear not: for they that be with us are more than they that be with them; **1 Chron. 28:20** be strong and of good courage, and do it: fear not, nor be *d.*: for the LORD God, even my God, will be with thee; he will not fail thee, nor forsake thee; **2 Chron. 20:17** fear not, nor be *d.*; to morrow go out against them: for the LORD will be with you; **Ps. 27:3** though an host should encamp against me, my heart shall not fear: though war should rise against me, in this will I be confident; **Isa. 7:4** take heed, and be quiet; fear not, neither be fainthearted; **8:12** neither fear ye their fear, nor be afraid; **12:2** I will trust, and not be afraid: for the LORD JEHOVAH is my strength and my song; **Jer. 46:27** fear not thou, O my servant Jacob, and be not *d.*, O Israel: for, behold, I will save thee from afar off; **Ezek. 2:6** be not afraid of them, neither be afraid of their words... nor be *d.* at their looks, though they be a rebellious house; **3:9** fear them not, neither be *d.* at their looks, though they be a rebellious house.

DISOBEDIENCE, DISOBEY (*see* Rebel, Reject, Sin, Wickedness)

DISORDERLY (*see also* Rebellious, Unruly)

We command you, brethren, in the name of our Lord Jesus Christ, that ye withdraw yourselves from every brother that walketh disorderly, and not after the tradition which he received of us. 2 Thes. 3:6 (*see also* Tradition)

2 Thes 3:6 we command you, brethren, in the name of our Lord Jesus Christ, that ye withdraw yourselves from every brother that walketh *d.*, and not after the tradition which he received of us; **3:11** we hear that there are some which walk among you *d.*, working not at all, but are busybodies; **2 Tim. 3:8** these also resist the truth: men of corrupt minds, reprobate concerning the faith.

DISPUTE (*see also* Contend, Dissension, Strife)

Do all things without murmurings and disputings: That ye may be blameless and harmless, the sons of God, without rebuke, in the midst of a crooked and perverse nation, among whom ye shine as lights in the world. Philip. 2:14-15 (*see also* All Things, Murmur)

DISSENSION (*see also* Backbite, Contend, Dispute, False Doctrine, Fight, Gossip, Rebel)

DISTRIBUTE, DISTRIBUTION

Now when Jesus heard these things, he said unto him, Yet lackest thou one thing: sell all that thou hast, and distribute unto the poor, and thou shalt have treasure in heaven: and come, follow me. Luke 18:22 (*see also* Lack, Treasure)

[Distribute] to the necessity of saints; given to hospitality. Rom. 12:13 (*see also* Hospitality)

DIVINATION (*see also* Enchantment, Sorcery, Superstitious, Wizardry)

There shall be no more any vain vision nor flattering divination within the house of Israel. Ezek. 12:24 (*see also* Israel, Vision)

Ezek. 12:24 there shall be no more any vain vision nor flattering *d.* within the house of Israel; **13:6-10** they have seen vanity and lying *d.*, saying, The LORD saith: and the LORD hath not sent them: and they have made others to hope that they would confirm the word; **13:16**

the prophets of Israel which prophesy concerning Jerusalem, and which see visions of peace for her, and there is no peace; **13:19** will ye pollute me among my people for handfuls of barley and for pieces of bread, to slay the souls that should not die, and to save the souls alive that should not live, by your lying to my people that hear your lies; **13:22-23** with lies ye have made the heart of the righteous sad, whom I have not made sad; and strengthened the hands of the wicked, that he should not return from his wicked way, by promising him life; **14:9-11** if the prophet be deceived when he hath spoken a thing, I the LORD have deceived that prophet, and I will stretch out my hand upon him, and will destroy him from the midst of my people Israel; **22:28** her prophets have daubed them with untempered morter, seeing vanity, and *d.* lies unto them, saying, Thus saith the Lord GOD, when the LORD hath not spoken.

DIVINE NATURE (*see also* Be, Become, Born Again, Charity, Righteous)

According as his divine power hath given unto us all things that pertain unto life and godliness, through the knowledge of him that hath called us to glory and virtue: Whereby we are given unto us exceeding great and precious promises: that by these ye might be partakers of the divine nature, having escaped the corruption that is in the world through lust. 2 Pet. 1:3-4 (*see also* All Things, Knowledge, Lust, Promise)

Rom. 1:28 God gave them over to a reprobate mind, to do those things which are not convenient; **Philip. 4:8** if there be any virtue, and if there be any praise, think on these things; **Col. 3:16** let the word of Christ dwell in you richly in all wisdom; teaching and admonishing one another in psalms and hymns and spiritual songs, singing with grace in your hearts to the Lord; **2 Pet. 1:3-4** according as his divine power hath given unto us all things that pertain unto life and godliness, through the knowledge of him that hath called us to glory and virtue: Whereby are given unto us exceeding great and precious promises: that by these ye might be partakers of the divine nature, having escaped the corruption that is in the world through lust.

DIVORCE, DIVORCEMENT (*see also* Excommunicate, Marriage)

What therefore God hath joined together, let not man put asunder. Mark 10:9

Whosoever putteth away his wife, and marrieth another, committeth adultery: and whosoever marrieth her that is put away from her husband committeth adultery. Luke 16:18 (*see also* Adultery)

Unto the married I command, yet not I, but the Lord, Let not the wife depart from her husband: But and if she depart, let her remain unmarried, or be reconciled to her husband: and let not the husband put away his wife. 1 Cor. 7:10-11 (*see also* Reconcile)

DO, DOINGS, DOER (*see also* Act, Diligence, Exercise, Labor, Use, Works)

For with God nothing shall be impossible. Luke 1:37 (*see also* Impossible, Nothing)

Do after the will of your God. Ezra 7:18 (*see also* Will)

Whether therefore ye eat, or drink, or whatsoever ye do, do all to the glory of God. 1 Cor. 10:31 (*see also* Eat, Glorify)

I am the vine, yea are the branches: He that abideth in me, and I in him, the same bringeth forth much fruit: for without me ye can do nothing. John 15:5 (*see also* Abide, Fruit, Nothing, Vine)

He did that which was right in the sight of the LORD. 2 Chron. 29:2 (*see also* Right)

This one thing I do, forgetting those things which are behind, and reaching forth unto those things which are before, I press toward the mark for the prize of the high calling of God in Christ Jesus. Philip 3:13-14 (*see also* Mark, Prize, Reach)

O inhabitants of Jerusalem, and men of Judah, judge, I pray you, betwixt me and my vineyard. What could have been done more to my vineyard, that I have not done in it? Isa. 5:3-4 (*see also* Judge)

Work the works of God. John 6:28 (*see also* God, Work)

If I then, your Lord and Master, have ashed your feet; ye also ought to wash one another's feet. For I have given you an example, that ye should do as I have done to you. John 13:14-15 (*see also* Example, Feet, Wash)

Those things, which ye have both learned, and received, and heard, and seen in me, do: and the God of peace shall be with you. Philip. 4:9 (*see also* Example)

Say not, I will do so to him as he hath done to me; I will render to the man according to his work. Prov. 24:29 (*see also* Render, Work)

Be ye doers of the word, and not hearers only, deceiving your own selves. For if any be a hearer of the word, and not a doer, he is like unto a man beholding his natural face in a glass: For he beholdeth himself, and goeth his way, and straightway forgetteth what manner of man he was. James 1:22-24 (*see also* Hear, Word)

This book of the law shall not depart out of thy mouth; but thou shalt meditate therein day and night, that thou mayest observe to do according to all that is written therein: for then thou shalt make thy way prosperous, and then thou shalt have good success. Josh. 1:8 (*see also* Book, Meditate, Prosperous, Success)

So is the will of God, that with well doing ye may put to silence the ignorance of foolish men: As free, and not using your liberty for a cloke of maliciousness, but as the servants of God. 1 Pet. 2:15-16 (*see also* Liberty, Servant, Will)

To him that knoweth to do good, and doeth it not, to him it is sin. James 4:17 (*see also* Good)

Do well on the sabbath days. Matt. 12:12 (*see also* Sabbath)

Whatsoever ye do in word or deed, do all in the name of the Lord Jesus, giving thanks to God and the Father by him. Col. 3:17 (*see also* Name)

Learn to do well; seek judgment, relieve the oppressed, judge the fatherless, plead for the widow. Isa. 1:17 (*see also* Learn, Judge, Plead, Relieve)

Thus shall ye do in the fear of the LORD, faithfully, and with a perfect heart. 2 Chron. 19:9

2 Chron. 19:9 he charged them, saying, Thus shall ye *d.* in the fear of the LORD, faithfully, and with a perfect heart; 25:2 he did that which was right in the sight of the LORD, but not with a perfect heart; Neh. 9:8 foundest his heart faithful before thee, and madest a covenant with him to give the land of the Canaanites, the Hittites, the Amorites, and the Perizzites, and the Jebusites, and the Girgashites, to give it, I say, to his seed, and hast performed thy words; for thou art righteous; Ps. 31:23 love the LORD, all ye his saints: for the LORD preserveth the faithful, and plentifully rewardeth the proud *d.*; 102:15 the heathen shall fear the name of the LORD, and all the kings of the earth thy glory; Dan. 6:4 they could find none occasion nor fault; forasmuch as he was faithful, neither was there any error or fault found in him.

By what authority doest thou these things? and who gave thee this authority to do these things? And Jesus answered and said unto them, I will also ask of you one question, and answer me, and I will tell you by what authority I do these things. Mark 11:28 (*see also* Authority)

DOCTRINE (*see also* Gospel, Principle, Truth, Way)

Be no more children, tossed to and fro, and carried about with every wind of doctrine, by the sleight of men, and cunning craftiness, whereby they lie in wait to deceive. Eph. 4:14 (*see also* Cunning, Deceive)

For the time will come when they will not endure sound doctrine; but after their own lusts shall they heap to themselves teachers, having itching ears; And they shall turn away their ears from the truth, and shall be turned unto fables. 2 Tim. 4:3-4 (*see also* Ear, Fable)

Be not carried about with divers and strange doctrines. For it is a good thing that the heart be established with grace; not with meats, which have not profited them that have been occupied therein. **Heb. 13:9** (*see also* False Doctrine, Teach)

All scripture is given by inspiration of God, and is profitable for doctrine, for reproof, for correction, for instruction in righteousness: That the man of God may be perfect, throughly furnished unto all good works. **2 Tim. 3:16-17** (*see also* Inspiration, Perfect, Scripture, Works)

Speak thou the things which become sound doctrine: That the aged men be sober, grave, temperate, sound in faith, in charity, in patience. **Titus 2:1-2** (*see also* Sound)

Titus 2:1 speak thou the things which become sound *d.*; **2:7** in all things shewing thyself a pattern of good works: in *d.* shewing uncorruptness, gravity, sincerity.

This people draweth nigh unto me with their mouth, and honoureth me with their lips; but their heart is far from me. But in vain they do worship me, teaching for doctrines the commandments of men. **Matt. 15:8-9** (*see also* Teach)

Matt. 15:4-6 God commanded, saying, Honour thy father and mother: and, He that curseth father or mother, let him die the death. But ye say, Whosoever shall say to his father or his mother, It is a gift, by whatsoever thou mightest be profited by me; And honour not his father or his mother, he shall be free. Thus have ye made the commandment of God of none effect by your tradition; **15:8-9** this people draweth nigh unto me with their mouth, and honoureth me with their lips; but their heart is far from me. But in vain they do worship me, teaching for *d.* the commandments of men; **Mark 7:7-8** in vain do they worship me, teaching for *d.* the commandments of men. For laying aside the commandment of God, ye hold the tradition of men, as the washing of pots and cups: and many other such like things ye do; **Acts 15:1** except ye be circumcised after the manner of Moses, ye cannot be saved; **15:24** certain which went out from us have troubled you with words, subverting your souls, saying, Ye must be circumcised, and keep the law: to whom we gave

no such commandment; **Rom. 15:18** I will not dare to speak of any of those things which Christ hath not wrought by me, to make the Gentiles obedient, by word and deed; **Col. 2:21-23** touch not; taste not; handle not; Which all are to perish with the using; after the commandments and *d.* of men; **1 Tim. 1:3-4** thou mightest charge some that they teach no other *d.*, Neither give heed to fables and endless genealogies, which minister questions, rather than godly edifying which is in faith: so do; **6:21** some professing have erred concerning the faith; **2 Tim. 2:18** who concerning the truth have erred, saying that the resurrection is past already; and overthrow the faith of some; **4:3** the time will come when they will not endure sound *d.*; but after their own lusts shall they heap to themselves teachers, having itching ears; **Titus 1:11-14** mouths must be stopped, who subvert whole houses, teaching things which they ought not, for filthy lucre's sake. One of themselves, even a prophet of their own, said, The Cretians are alway liars, evil beasts, slow bellies. This witness is true. Wherefore rebuke them sharply, that they may be sound in the faith; Not giving heed to Jewish fables, and commandments of men, that turn from the truth; **Heb. 13:9** be not carried about with divers and strange *d.* For it is a good thing that the heart be established with grace; not with meats, which have not profited them; **Rev. 2:15** so hast thou also them that hold the *d.* of the Nicolaitans, which thing I hate.

DOMINION (*see also* Call, Come, Compel, Follow, Lead, Unrighteous Dominion)

Let not any iniquity have dominion over me. **Ps. 119:133** (*see also* Iniquity)

Have dominion over the fish of the sea, and over the fowl of the air, and over the cattle, and over all the earth, and over every creeping thing that creepeth upon the earth. **Gen. 1:26**

DOOR (*see also* Gate, Way)

I am the door: by me if any man enter in, he shall be saved, and shall go in and out, and find pasture. **John 10:9**

Behold, I stand at the door, and knock: if any man hear my voice, and open the door, I will come in to him, and will sup with him, and he with me. **Rev. 3:20** (*see also* Open)

DOUBLE, DOUBLE MINDED (*see also* Unsteady, Waiver)

A double minded man is unstable in all his ways. **James 1:8** (*see also* Mind, Unsteady, Way)

They speak vanity every one with his neighbour: with flattering lips and with a double heart. **Ps. 12:2** (*see also* Heart, Speak)

DOUBT, DOUBTFUL (*see also* Unbelief)

Have faith, and doubt not. Matt. 21:21

Matt. 14:29-31 when Peter was come down out of the ship, he walked on the water, to go to Jesus. But when he saw the wind boisterous, he was afraid; and beginning to sink, he cried, saying, Lord, save me. And immediately Jesus stretched forth his hand, and caught him, and said unto him, O thou of little faith, wherefore didst thou *d.*; **21:21** if ye have faith, and *d.* not, ye shall not only do this which is done to the fig tree, but also if ye shall say unto this mountain, Be thou removed, and be thou cast into the sea; it shall be done; **Mark 11:23** whosoever shall say unto this mountain, Be thou removed, and be thou cast into the sea; and shall not *d.* in his heart, but shall believe that those things which he saith shall come to pass; he shall have whatsoever he saith; **Luke 1:18-20** Zacharias said unto the angel, Whereby shall I know this? for I am an old man, and my wife well stricken in years. And the angel answering said unto him, I am Gabriel, that stand in the presence of God; and am sent to speak unto thee, and to shew thee these glad tidings. And, behold, thou shalt be dumb, and not able to speak, until the day that these things shall be performed, because thou believest not my words, which shall be fulfilled in their season; **12: 45-46** if that servant say in his heart, My lord delayeth his coming; and shall begin to beat the menservants and maidens, and to eat and drink, and to be drunken; The lord of that servant will come in a day when he looketh not for him, and at an hour when he is not aware, and will cut him in sunder, and will appoint him his portion with the unbelievers; **Acts 11:12** the Spirit bade me go with them, nothing *d.* Moreover these six brethren accompanied me, and we entered into the man's.

DRAW NEAR

Draw nigh to God, and he will draw nigh to you. James 4:8 (*see also* Seek)

Let us draw near with a true heart in full assurance of faith, having our hearts sprinkled from an evil conscience, and our bodies washed with pure water. **Heb. 10:22** (*see also* Assurance, Heart)

It is good for me to draw near to God: I have put my trust in the Lord GOD. **Ps. 73:28**

Ps. 73:28 it is good for me to *d.* near to God: I have put my trust in the Lord GOD; **Zeph. 3:2** she obeyed not the voice; she received not correction; she trusted not in the LORD; she *d.* not near to her God.

DREAM (*see also* Prophecy, Reveal, Vision)

The prophet that hath a dream, let him tell a dream. **Jer. 23:28** (*see also* Prophet)

Now the wise men, the astrologers, have been brought in before me, that they should read this writing, and make known unto me the interpretation thereof: but they could not shew the interpretation of the thing. **Dan 5:15** (*see also* Astrologer, Interpretation, Magician)

The secret which the king hath demanded cannot the wise men, the astrologers, the magicians, the soothsayers, shew unto the king; But there is a God in heaven that revealeth secrets, and maketh known to the king Nebuchadnezzar what shall be in the latter days. **Dan. 1:27-28** (*see also* Interpretation, Secret)

I will pour out my spirit upon all flesh; and your sons and your daughters shall prophesy, your old men shall dream dreams, your young men shall see visions. **Joel 2:28** (*see also* Reveal, Vision)

Gen. 28:12-16 he *d.*, and behold a ladder set up on the earth, and the top of it reached to heaven: and behold the angels of God ascending and descending on it. And, behold, the LORD stood above it, and said, I am the LORD God of Abraham thy father, and the God of Isaac; **31:10-12** I lifted up mine eyes, and saw in a *d.*, and, behold, the rams which leaped upon the cattle were ringstraked, speckled, and grisled; **31:24** God came to Laban the Syrian in a *d.* by night, and said unto him, Take heed that thou speak not to Jacob either good or bad; **40:5** they *d.* a *d.* both of them, each man his *d.* in one night, each man according to the interpretation of his *d.*, the butler and the baker of the king of Egypt, which were bound in the prison; **40:8-14** we have *d.* a *d.*, and there is no interpreter of it. And Joseph said unto them, Do not interpretations belong to God? tell me them, I pray you; **40:16-19** the chief baker saw that the interpretation was good, he said unto Joseph, I also was in my *d.*; **40:20-23** he hanged the chief baker: as Joseph had interpreted to them. Yet did not the chief butler remember Joseph, but forgat him; **41:1-8** Pharaoh *d.*: and, behold, he stood by the river; **41:9-13** an Hebrew, servant to the captain of the guard; and we told him, and he interpreted to us our *d.*s; to each man according to his *d.* he did interpret. And it came to pass, as he interpreted to us, so it was; me he restored unto mine office, and him he hanged; **41:15-32** Pharaoh said unto Joseph, I have *d.* a *d.*, and there is none that can interpret it: and I have heard say of thee, that thou canst understand a *d.* to interpret it. And Joseph answered Pharaoh, saying, It is not in me: God shall give Pharaoh an answer of peace; **46:2-4** God spake unto Israel in the visions of the night; **Num. 12:6** if there be a prophet among you, I the Lord will make myself known unto him in a vision, and will speak unto him in a *d.*; **Judg. 7:13** I *d.* a *d.*, and, lo, a cake of barley bread tumbled into the host of Midian, and came unto a tent, and smote it that it fell, and overturned it, that the tent lay along; **1Kings 3:5** the Lord appeared to Solomon in a *d.* by night: and God said, Ask what I shall give thee; **2 Chron. 26:5** understanding in the visions of God: and as long as he sought the Lord, God made him to prosper; **Job 33:14-17** in a *d.*, in a vision of the night, when deep sleep falleth upon men, in slumberings upon the bed; Then he openeth the ears of men, and sealeth their instruction, That he may withdraw man from his purpose, and hide pride from man; **Eccl. 5:3** a *d.* cometh through the multitude of business; and a fools voice is known by multitude of words; **Isa. 1:1** the vision of Isaiah the son of Amoz, which he saw concerning Judah and Jerusalem; **22:14** it was revealed in mine ears by the Lord of hosts; **Isa. 29:7** even all that fight against her and her munition, and that distress her, shall be as a *d.* of a night; **Jer. 23:28** the prophet that hath a *d.*, let him tell a *d.*; and he that hath my word, let him speak my word faithfully. What is the chaff to the wheat? saith the Lord; **25:4** the Lord hath sent unto you all his servants the prophets, rising early and sending them; **Ezek. 1:1-28** the heavens were opened, and I saw visions of God; **8:1-4** the glory of the God of Israel was there, according to the vision that I

saw in the plain; **10:1-22** in the firmament that was above the head of the cherubims there appeared over them as it were a sapphire stone, as the appearance of the likeness of a throne; **11:1** the spirit lifted me up, and brought me unto the east gate of the Lord's house, which looketh eastward; **11:24** the spirit took me up, and brought me in a vision by the Spirit of God into Chaldea, to them of the captivity. So the vision that I had seen went up from me; **40:1-5** the visions of God brought he me into the land of Israel, and set me upon a very high mountain; **40:20-23** he hanged the chief baker: as Joseph had interpreted to them. Yet did not the chief butler remember Joseph, but forgat him; **41:9-13** an Hebrew, servant to the captain of the guard; and we told him, and he interpreted to us our *d.*s; to each man according to his *d.* he did interpret. And it came to pass, as he interpreted to us, so it was; me he restored unto mine office, and him he hanged; **41:15-32** Pharaoh said unto Joseph, I have *d.* a *d.*, and there is none that can interpret it: and I have heard say of thee, that thou canst understand a *d.* to interpret it. And Joseph answered Pharaoh, saying, It is not in me: God shall give Pharaoh an answer of peace;**Dan. 2:1-6** the king commanded to call the magicians, and the astrologers, and the sorcerers, and the Chaldeans, for to shew the king his *d.* So they came and stood before the king; **2:16** Daniel went in, and desired of the king that he would give him time, and that he would shew the king the interpretation; **2:29-30** thy thoughts came into thy mind upon thy bed, what should come to pass hereafter: and he that revealeth secrets maketh known to thee what shall come to pass. But as for me, this secret is not revealed to me for any wisdom that I have more than any living, but for their sakes that shall make known the interpretation to the king, and that thou mightest know the thoughts of thy heart; **2:45** the great God hath made known to the king what shall come to pass hereafter: and the *d.* is certain, and the interpretation thereof sure; **4:8-23** before him I told the *d.*, saying, O Belteshazzar, master of the magicians, because I know that the spirit of the holy gods is in thee, and no secret troubleth thee, tell me the visions of my *d.* that I have seen, and the interpretation thereof; **5:12** an excellent spirit, and knowledge, and understanding, interpreting of *d.*, and shewing of hard sentences, and dissolving of doubts, were found in the same Daniel, whom the king named Belteshazzar: now let Daniel be called, and he will shew the interpretation; **5:16-17** let thy gifts be to thyself, and give thy rewards to another; yet I will read the writing unto the king, and make known to him the interpretation; **7:1-7** Daniel had a *d.* and visions of his head upon his bed: then he wrote the *d.*, and told the sum of the matters. Daniel spake and said, I saw in my vision by night, and, behold, the four winds of the heaven strove upon the great sea; **7:15-16** I Daniel was grieved in my spirit in the midst of my body, and the visions of my head troubled me. I came near unto one of them that stood by, and asked him the truth of all this. So he told me, and made me know the interpretation of the things; **7:28** my cogitations much troubled me, and my countenance changed in me: but I kept the matter in my heart; **8:1-27** I Daniel fainted, and was sick certain days; afterward I rose up, and did the kings business; and I was astonished at the vision, but none understood it; **9:23-24** at the beginning of thy supplications the commandment came forth, and I am come to shew thee; for thou art greatly beloved: therefore understand the matter, and consider the vision; **10:1** the thing was true, but the time appointed was long: and he understood the thing, and had understanding of the vision; **10:5** I lifted up mine eyes, and looked, and behold a certain man clothed in linen, whose loins were girded with fine gold of Uphaz; **Joel 2:28** I will pour out my spirit upon all flesh; and your sons and your daughters shall prophesy, your old men shall *d. d.*, your young men shall see visions; **Haba 2:3** the vision is yet for an appointed time, but at the end it shall speak, and not lie: though it tarry, wait for it; because it will surely come, it will not tarry; **Zech. 1:7-11** the prophet, saying, I saw by night, and, behold a man riding upon a red horse, and he stood among the myrtle trees that were in the bottom; **1:19-21** I said unto the angel that talked with me, What be these? And he answered me, These are the horns which have scattered Judah, Israel, and Jerusalem; **4:1-5** the angel that talked with me came again, and waked me, as a man that is wakened out of his sleep, And said unto me, What seest thou; **6:1-15** I turned, and lifted up mine eyes, and looked, and, behold, there came four chariots out from between two mountains; and the mountains were mountains of brass.

DRINK, DRUNK, DRUNKENNESS

Be not among winebibbers; among riotous eaters of flesh: for the drunkard and the glutton shall come to poverty: and drowsiness shall clothe a man with rags. Prov. 23:20-21 (*see also* Be, Wine)

Be not drunk with wine, wherein is excess; but be filled with the Spirit. Eph. 5:18 (*see also* Excess, Spirit, Wine)

DROSS

Take away the dross from the silver, and there shall come forth a vessel for the finer. Prov. 25:4

DUE (*see also* Owe, Promise)

Withhold not good from them to whom it is due, when it is in the power of thine hand to do it. Prov. 3:27 (*see also* Good)

DUMB

[They] were beyond measure astonished, saying, He hath done all things well: he maketh both the deaf to hear, and the dumb to speak. Mark 7:37 (*see also* Deaf, Miracle)

When Jesus saw that the people came running together, he rebuked the foul spirit, saying unto him, Thou dumb and deaf spirit, I charge thee, come out of him, and enter no more into him. Mark 9:25 (*see also* Deaf, Rebuke)

DUST

And the LORD God formed man of the dust of the ground, and breathed into his nostrils the breath of life; and man became a living soul. Gen 2:7 (*see also* Man)

DWELL (*see also* Abide)

Hear now this, thou that art given to pleasures, that dwellest carelessly, that sayest in thine heart, I am, and none else beside me. Isa. 47:8 (*see also* Care, Pleasure)

How good and how pleasant it is for brethren to dwell together in unity! Ps. 133:1 (*see also* Unite)

Whosoever shall confess that Jesus is the Son of God, God dwelleth in him, and he in God. 1 Jn. 4:15 (*see also* Confess, Testify)

EAR (*see also* Listen)

For the time will come when they will not endure sound doctrine; but after their own lusts shall they heap to themselves teachers, having itching ears; And they shall turn away their ears from the truth, and shall be turned unto fables. 2 Tim. 4:3-4 (*see also* Doctrine, Fable)

Give ear, O my people, to my law: incline your ears to the words of my mouth. Ps. 78:1 (*see also* Word)

Ps. 78:1 give ear, O my people, to my law: incline your *e.* to the words of my mouth; **Isa. 55:3** incline your *e.*, and come unto me: hear, and your soul shall live; and I will make an everlasting covenant with you; **Jer. 7:24** they hearkened not, nor inclined their *e.*, but walked in the counsels and in the imagination of their evil heart; **7:26** they hearkened not unto me, nor inclined their *e.*, but hardened their neck; **Ezek. 3:10** all my words that I shall speak unto thee receive in thine heart, and hear with thine *e.*

The eyes of them that see shall not be dim, and the ears of them that hear shall hearken. **Isa. 32:3** (*see also* Eye, Word)

Prov. 20:12-13 the hearing *e.*, and the seeing eye, the LORD hath made even both of them; **Isa. 32:3** the eyes of them that see shall not be dim, and the *e.* of them that hear shall hearken.

EARLY (*see also* Time)

O GOD, thou art my God; early will I seek thee: my soul thirsteth for thee. Ps. 63:1

Ps. 63:1 O God, thou art my God; *e.* will I seek thee: my soul thirsteth for thee; **108:2** awake, psaltery and harp: I myself will awake *e.*; **Prov. 8:17-21** I love them that love me; and those that seek. me *e.* shall find me; **Isa. 26:9** with my soul have I desired thee in the night; yea, with my spirit within me will I seek thee *e.*

EARNEST, EARNESTLY (*see also* Diligence)

We ought to give the more earnest heed to the things which we have heard, lest at any time we should let them slip. **Heb. 2:1** (*see also* Heed, Word)

Beloved, when I gave all diligence to write unto you of the common salvation, it was needful for me to write unto you, and exhort you that ye should earnestly contend for the faith which was once delivered unto the saints. **Jude 1:3** (*see also* Contend, Saints)

EARTH (*see also* Creation, Dust, World)

It is a light thing that thou shouldest be my servant to raise up the tribes of Jacob, and to restore the preserved of Israel: I will also give thee for a light to the Gentiles, that thou mayest be my salvation unto the end of the earth. **Isa. 49:6** (*see also* Gentile, Light, Salvation)

But the LORD is in his holy temple: let all the earth keep silence before him. **Hab. 2:20** (*see also* Silence, Temple)

EASE, EASIER, EASINESS, EASY (*see also* Simple)

Woe to them that are at ease in Zion. **Amos 6:1**

EAT, EATEN (*see also* Consume)

Let not him that eateth despise him that eateth not; and let not him which eateth not judge him that eateth. **Rom. 14:3** (*see also* Despise)

If thine enemy be hungry, give him bread to eat; and if he be thirsty, give him water to drink: for thou shalt heap coals of fire upon his head, and the LORD shall reward thee. **Prov. 25:21-22** (*see also* Enemy)

For even when we were with you, this we commanded you, that if any would not work, neither should he eat. **2 Thes. 3:10** (*see also* Work)

Eat thou not the bread of him that hath an evil eye, neither desire thou his dainty meats. **Prov. 23:6-8** (*see also* Evil)

They, continuing daily with one accord in the temple, and breaking bread from house to house, did eat their meat with gladness and singleness of heart. **Acts 2:46** (*see also* Temple)

Whether therefore ye eat, or drink, or whatsoever ye do, do all to the glory of God. **1 Cor. 10:31** (*see also* Do, Glorify)

Eat so much as is sufficient for thee, lest thou be filled therewith, and vomit it. **Prov. 25:16** (*see also* Sufficient)

EDIFICATION, EDIFIED, EDIFY (*see also* Build, Enlighten, Instruct, Teach)

Teach no other doctrine, Neither give heed to fables and endless genealogies, which minister questions, rather than godly edifying which is in faith: so do. **1 Tim. 1:3-4** (*see also* Fables)

Follow after the things which make for peace, and things wherewith one may edify another. **Rom. 14:19** (*see also* Peace)

Let no corrupt communication proceed out of your mouth, but that which is good to the use of edifying, that it may minister grace unto the hearers. **Eph. 4:29** (*see also* Grace, Speak)

Acts 20:7 Paul preached unto them, ready to depart on the morrow; and continued his speech until midnight; **Eph. 3:8** unto me, who am less than the least of all saints, is this grace given, that I should preach among the Gentiles the unsearchable riches of Christ; **4:29** let no corrupt communication proceed out of your mouth, but that which is good to the use of *e.,* that it may minister grace unto the hearers; **Col. 3:8** put off all these; anger, wrath, malice, blasphemy, filthy communication out of your mouth; **2 Tim. 3:8** so do these also resist the truth: men of corrupt minds, reprobate concerning the faith; **1 Pet. 1:15** he which hath called you is holy, so be ye holy in all manner of conversation; **1:18** as ye know that ye were not redeemed with corruptible things, as silver and gold, from your vain conversation received by tradition from your fathers.

ELDER (*see also* Priesthood)

Against an elder, receive not an accusation but before two or three witnesses. **1 Tim. 5:19** (*see also* Accuse, Witness)

Rebuke not an elder, but intreat him as a father; and the younger men as brethren; The elder women as mothers; the younger as sisters, with all purity. **1 Tim. 5 1-2** (*see also* Entreat, Rebuke, Young)

Is any sick among you? let him call for the elders of the church; and let them pray over him, anointing him with oil in the name of the Lord: And the prayer of faith shall save the sick, and the Lord shall raise him up; and if he have committed sins, they shall be forgiven him. **James 5:14-15** (*see also* Anoint, Heal, Oil)

Acts 3:6-7 Peter said, Silver and gold have I none; but such as I have give I thee: In the name of Jesus Christ of Nazareth rise up and walk. And he took him by the right hand, and lifted him up: and immediately his feet and ankle bones received strength; **3:12** ye men of Israel, why marvel ye at this? or why look ye so earnestly on us, as though by our own power or holiness we had made this man to walk; **3:16** his name through faith in his name hath made this man strong, whom ye see and know: yea, the faith which is by him hath given him this perfect soundness in the presence of you all; **5:15-16** insomuch that they brought forth the sick into the streets, and laid them on beds and couches, that at the least the shadow of Peter passing by might overshadow some of them. There came also a multitude out of the cities round about unto Jerusalem, bringing sick folks, and them which were vexed with unclean spirits: and they were healed every one; **8:7** unclean spirits, crying with loud voice, came out of many that were possessed with them: and many taken with palsies, and that were lame, were healed; **9:12** hath seen in a vision a man named Ananias coming in, and putting his hand on him, that he might receive his sight; **9:17** brother Saul, the Lord, even Jesus, that appeared unto thee in the way as thou camest, hath sent me, that thou mightest receive thy sight, and be filled with the Holy Ghost; **9:34** Jesus Christ maketh thee whole: arise, and make thy bed. And he arose immediately; **10:37** how God anointed Jesus of Nazareth with the Holy Ghost and with power: who went about doing good, and healing all that were oppressed of the devil; for God was with him; **14:8-10** Paul speak: who stedfastly beholding him, and perceiving that he had faith to be healed, Said with a loud voice, Stand upright on thy feet. And he leaped and walked; **16:18** I command thee in the name of Jesus Christ to come out of her. And he came out the same hour; **28:8-9** Paul entered in, and prayed, and laid his hands on him, and healed him. So when this was done, others also, which had diseases in the island, came, and were healed; **James 5:14-15** is any sick among you? let him call for the *e.* of the church; and let them pray over him, anointing him with oil in the name of

The Lord: And the prayer of faith shall save the sick, and the Lord shall raise him up; and if he have committed sins, they shall be forgiven him.

ELECT, ELECTION (*see also* Call, Chosen, Exalt)

False Christs and false prophets shall rise, and shall shew signs and wonders, to seduce, if it were possible, even the elect. Mark 13:22 (*see also* False Christ, False Prophet, Seduce, Sign, Wonder)

Give diligence to make your calling and election sure. 2 Pet. 1:10 (*see also* Diligence)

2 Peter 1:10-11 give diligence to make your calling and *e.* sure: for if ye do these things, ye shall never fall: For so an entrance shall be ministered unto you abundantly into the everlasting kingdom of our Lord and Saviour Jesus Christ.

EMPATHIZE, EMPATHY (*see also* Comfort, Compassion)

Blessed be God, even the Father of our Lord Jesus Christ, the Father of mercies, and the God of all comfort; Who comforteth us in all our tribulation, that we may be able to comfort them which are in any trouble, by the comfort wherewith we ourselves are comforted of God. For as the sufferings of Christ abound in us, so our consolation also aboundeth by Christ. 2 Cor. 1:3-5 (*see also* Comfort, Tribulation)

ENCHANTMENT (*see also* Divination, Sorcery, Superstitious, Witchcraft)

Hearken not ye to your prophets, nor to your diviners, nor to your dreamers, nor to your enchantments, nor to your sorcerers, which speak unto you, saying, Ye shall not serve the king of Babylon: For they prophesy a lie unto you. Jer. 27:9-10 (*see also* Sorcery)

Isa. 47:9 these two things shall come to thee in a moment in one day, the loss of children, and widowhood: they shall come upon thee in their perfection for the multitude of thy sorceries, and for the great abundance of thine *e.*; **47:12-15** stand now with thine *e.*, and with the multitude of thy sorceries, wherein thou hast laboured from thy youth; **Jer. 27:9-10** hearken not ye to your

prophets, nor to your diviners, nor to your dreamers, nor to your *e.*, nor to your sorcerers, which speak unto you, saying, Ye shall not serve the king of Babylon: For they prophesy a lie unto you.

END (*see also* Last Days)

O that they were wise, that they understood this, that they would consider their latter end! Deut. 32:29 (*see also* Consider)

Hold fast the confidence and the rejoicing of the hope firm unto the end. Heb. 3:6 (*see also* Hope)

1 Thes 4:17 we which are alive and remain shall be caught up together with them in the clouds, to meet the Lord in the air: and so shall we ever be with the Lord; **2 Tim. 4:7-8** I have fought a good fight, I have finished my course, I have kept the faith: Henceforth there is laid up for me a crown of righteousness, which the Lord, the righteous judge, shall give me at that day: and not to me only, but unto all them also that love his appearing; **Heb. 3:6** Christ as a son over his own house; whose house are we, if we hold fast the confidence and the rejoicing of the hope firm unto the end; **3:14** we are made partakers of Christ, if we hold the beginning of our confidence steadfast unto the end; **6:15** after he had patiently *e.*, he obtained the promise; **James 5:11** we count them happy which *e.*. Ye have heard of the patience of Job, and have seen the end of the Lord; that the Lord is very pitiful, and of tender mercy.

ENDURE, ENDURANCE (*see also* Adversity, End, Faithful, Obey, Persevere, Steadfast)

Endureth temptation. James 1:12-15 (*see also* Temptation)

I gave my back to the smiters and my cheeks to them that plucked off the hair: I hid not my face from shame and spitting. For the Lord GOD will help me; therefore shall I not be confounded. Isa. 50:6-7 (*see also* Endure, Persecute, Smite)

Endureth to the end. Matt. 10:22

Matt. 10:21-22 the brother shall deliver up the brother to death, and the father the child: and the children shall rise up against their parents, and cause them to be put to death. And ye shall be hated of all men for my name's sake: but he that *e.* to the end shall be saved; **24:13** he that shall *e.* unto the end, the same shall be saved; **Mark 13:13** ye shall be hated of all men for my name's sake: but he that shall *e.* unto the end, the same shall be saved; **2 Thes. 1:4-5** we ourselves glory in you in the churches of God for your patience and faith in all your persecutions and tribulations that ye *e.*: Which is a manifest token of the righteous judgment of God, that ye may be counted worthy of the kingdom of God, for which ye also suffer; **2 Tim. 2:3** thou therefore *e.* hardness, as a good soldier of Jesus Christ; **2:10** I *e.* all things for the elect's sakes, that they may also obtain the salvation which is in Christ Jesus with eternal glory. It is a faithful saying: For if we be dead with him, we shall also live with him: If we suffer, we shall also reign with him: if we deny him, he also will deny us; **Heb. 12:7** if ye *e.* chastening, God dealeth with you as with sons; for what son is he whom the father chasteneth not; **James 5:11** we count them happy which *e.*. Ye have heard of the patience of Job, and have seen the end of the Lord; that the Lord is very pitiful, and of tender mercy.

ENEMIES, ENEMY (*see also* Adversary)

Love your enemies, bless them that curse you, do good to them that hate you, and pray for them which despitefully use you, and persecute you. Matt. 5:44 (*see also* Curse, Love, Persecute, Spite)

Rejoice not when thine enemy falleth, and let not thine heart be glad when he stumbleth: Lest the Lord see it, and it displease him, and he turn away his wrath from him. Prov. 24:17-18 (*see also* Fail, Rejoice)

We made our prayer unto our God, and set a watch against them day and night. Neh. 4:9 (*see also* Watch)

If thine enemy be hungry, give him bread to eat; and if he be thirsty, give him water to drink: for thou shalt heap coals of fire upon his head, and the Lord shall reward thee. Prov. 25:21-22 (*see also* Eat)

O Israel, ye approach this day unto battle against your enemies; let not your hearts faint, fear not and do not tremble of them neither be ye terrified because of them; for the Lord your God is he that goeth with you, to fight for you against your enemies, to save you. Deut. 20:3-4 (*see also* Fight)

Ex. 14:13-14 fear ye not, stand still, and see the salvation of the Lord, which he will shew to you to day: for the Egyptians whom ye have seen to day, ye shall see them again no more for ever. The Lord shall fight for you; **Deut. 1:29-30** dread not, neither be afraid of them. The Lord your God which goeth before you, he shall fight for you; **3:22** ye shall not fear them: for the Lord your God he shall fight for you; **20:1-4** let not your hearts faint, fear not, and do not tremble, neither be ye terrified because of them; For the Lord your God is he that goeth with you, to fight for you against your *e.* to save you; **Isa. 41:10-12** fear thou not; for I am with thee: be not dismayed; for I am thy God: I will strengthen thee; yea, I will help thee; yea, I will uphold thee with the right hand of my righteousness.

ENLARGE (*see* Increase)

ENLIGHTEN, ENLIGHTENED (*see also* Discern, Edify, Study, Teach, Understand)

For it is impossible for those who were once enlightened, and have tasted of the heavenly gift, and were made partakers of the Holy Ghost, And have tasted the good word of God, and the powers of the world to come, If they shall fall away, to renew them again unto repentance; seeing they crucify to themselves the Son of God afresh, and put him to an open shame. Heb. 6:4 (*see also* Holy Ghost, Impossible, Second Death)

ENMITY (*see* Contention, Hate)

ENTANGLE

Then went the Pharisees, and took counsel how they might entangle him in his talk. Matt. 22:15 (*see also* Counsel, Evil)

Matt. 22:15 then went the Pharisees, and took counsel how they might entangle him in his talk; **Acts 14:2** the unbelieving Jews stirred up the Gentiles, and made their minds evil affected against the brethren.

If after they have escaped the pollutions of the world through the knowledge of the Lord and Savior Jesus Christ, they are again entangled therein, and overcome, the latter end is worse with them than the beginning. For it had been better for them not to have known the way of righteousness, than, after they have known it, to turn from the holy commandment delivered unto them. But it is happened unto them according to the true proverb, The dog is turned to his own vomit again; and the sow that was washed to her wallowing in the mire. 2 Pet. 2:20-22 (*see also* Better, Vomit, Way)

ENTER, ENTRANCE (*see also* Baptism, Gate, Way)

Not every one that saith unto me, Lord, Lord, shall enter into the kingdom of heaven; but he that doeth the will of my Father who is in heaven. Many will say to me in that day: Lord, Lord, have we not prophesied in thy name, and in thy name have cast out devils, and in thy name done many wonderful works? And then will I profess unto them: I never knew you; depart from me, ye that work iniquity. Matt. 7:21-23 (*see also* Father, Priestcraft, Will, Wonderful)

Strive to enter in at the strait gate: for many, I say unto you, will seek to enter in, and shall not be able. Luke 13:24 (*see also* Gate, Strait, Strive)

Enter not into the paths of the wicked, and go not in the way of evil men. Avoid it, pass not by it, turn from it, and pass away. Prov. 4:14-15 (*see also* Avoid, Path)

Open ye the gates, that the righteous nation which keepeth the truth may enter in. Isa. 26:2 (*see also* Gate, Nation, Righteous)

Jesus answered, Verily, verily, I say unto thee, Except a man be born of water and of the Spirit, he cannot enter into the kingdom of God. John 3:5 (*see also* Born, Spirit, Water)

It is easier for a camel to go through the eye of a needle, than for a rich man to enter into the kingdom of God. Matt 19:24 (*see also* Rich)

Eye hath not seen, nor ear heard, neither have entered into the heart of man, the things which God hath prepared for them that love him. But God hath reveled them unto us by his Spirit; for the Spirit searcheth all things, yea, the deep things of God. 1 Cor. 2:9-10 (*see also* Mysteries, Search, Spirit)

1 Cor. 2:9-10 eye hath not seen, nor ear heard, neither have entered into the heart of man, the things which God hath prepared for them that love him. But God hath reveled them unto us by his Spirit; for the Spirit searcheth all things, yea, the deep things of God.

ENTICE (*see also* Tempt)

If sinners entice thee, consent thou not. Prov. 1:10 (*see also* Consent)

ENTREAT, ENTREATED (*see also* Ask, Beg, Beseech, Inquire, Invite, Plead)

Rebuke not an elder, but intreat him as a father; and the younger men as brethren; The elder women as mothers; the younger as sisters, with all purity. 1 Tim. 5 1-2 (*see also* Elder, Rebuke, Young)

ENVIOUS, ENVY (*see also* Covet, Jealous)

Let us not be desirous of vain glory, provoking one another, envying one another. Gal. 5:26 (*see also* Desire)

For where envying and strife is, there is confusion and every evil work. James 3:16 (*see also* Confusion, Strife)

Wrath killeth the foolish man, and envy slayeth the silly one. Job 5:2 (*see also* Wrath)

Job 5:2 wrath killeth the foolish man, and *e.* slayeth the silly one; **Ps. 73:3** I was *e.* at the foolish, when I saw the prosperity of the wicked; **Prov. 14:30** a sound heart is the life of the flesh: but *e.* the rottenness of the bones; **Isa. 26:11** LORD, when thy hand is lifted up, they will not see: but they shall see, and be ashamed for their *e.* at the people; yea, the fire of thine enemies shall devour them; **Ezek. 35:11** as I live, saith the Lord GOD, I will even do according to thine anger, and according to thine *e.* which thou hast used out of thy hatred against them; and I will make myself known among them.

Fret not thyself because of evil doers, neither be thou envious against the workers of iniquity. Ps. 37:1 (*see also* Iniquity)

Ps. 37:1 fret not thyself because of evildoers, neither be thou *e.* against the workers of iniquity; **37:7** rest in the LORD, and wait patiently for him: fret not thyself because of him who prospereth in his way, because of the man who bringeth wicked devices to pass; **Prov. 21:15** it is joy to the just to do judgment: but destruction shall be to the workers of iniquity; **23:17** let not thine heart *e.* sinners: but be thou in the fear of the LORD all the day long; **24:19** fret not thyself because of evil men, neither be thou *e.* at the wicked; **Ezek. 7:13** neither shall any strengthen himself in the iniquity of his life.

Envy not the oppressor, and choose none of his ways. Prov. 3:31-32 (*see also* Way)

Prov. 3:31-32 *e.* thou not the oppressor, and choose none of his ways; **16:25** there is a way that seemeth right unto a man, but the end thereof are the ways of death.

Let not thine heart envy sinners: but be thou in the fear of the LORD all the day long. Prov. 23:17 (*see also* Fear)

Prov. 23:17 let not thine heart *e.* sinners: but be thou in the fear of the LORD all the day long; **24:1-2** be not thou *e.* against evil men, neither desire to be with them. For their heart studieth destruction, and their lips talk of mischief; **24:19-20** fret not thyself because of evil men, neither be thou *e.* at the wicked; **27:4** wrath is cruel, and anger is outrageous; but who is able to stand before *e.*

Walk honestly, as in the day; not in rioting and drunkenness, not in chambering and wantonness, not in strife and envying. Rom. 13:13 (*see also* Strife)

Matt. 27:18 he knew that for *e.* they had delivered him; **Mark 15:10** the chief priests had delivered him for *e.*; **Acts 13:45** when the Jews saw the multitudes, they were filled with *e.,* and spake against those things which were spoken by Paul, contradicting and blaspheming; **Rom. 13:13** let us walk honestly, as in the day; not in rioting and drunkenness, not in chambering and wantonness, not in strife and *e.*; **1 Cor. 13:4** charity suffereth long, and is kind; charity *e.* not; **Gal. 5:26** let us not be desirous of vain glory, provoking one another, *e.* one another; **James**

3:14-16 if ye have bitter *e.* and strife in your hearts, glory not, and lie not against the truth. This wisdom descendeth not from above, but is earthly, sensual, devilish. For where *e.* and strife is, there is confusion and every evil work.

EQUAL, EQUALITY, EQUITY (*see also* Judge, Justice, One, Righteous, United)

Regardest not the person of men. Matt. 22:16 (*see also* Respect)

Matt. 22:16 master, we know that thou art true, and teachest the way of God in truth, neither carest thou for any man: for thou regardest not the person of men; **Rom. 12:16** be of the same mind one toward another.

The law of truth was in his mouth, and iniquity was not found in his lips: he walked with me in peace and equity, and did turn many away from iniquity. Mal. 2:6 (*see also* Peace)

How much less to him that accepteth not the persons of princes, nor regard the rich more than the poor? for they all are the work of his hands. Job 34:19 (*see also* Regard)

There is neither Jew nor Greek, there is neither bond nor free, there is neither male nor female: for ye are all one in Christ Jesus. Gal. 3:28 (*see also* Bond, Female, Male, One)

I charge thee before God, and the Lord Jesus Christ, and the elect angels, that thou observe these things without preferring one before another, doing nothing by partiality. 1 Tim. 5:21 (*see also* Partial, Respect)

Luke 20:21 we know that thou sayest and teachest rightly, neither acceptest thou the person of any, but teachest the way of God truly; **Rom. 2:11** for there is no respect of persons with God; **10:12** there is no difference between the Jew and the Greek: for the same Lord over all is rich unto all that call upon him; **14:11** as I live, saith the Lord, every knee shall bow to me, and every tongue shall confess to God; **1 Cor. 4:6** learn in us not to think of men above that which is written, that no one of you be puffed up for one against another; **Col. 3:12** where there is neither Greek nor Jew, circumcision nor uncircumcision, Barbarian, Scythian, bond nor free: but Christ is all, and in all; **1 Tim. 5:21** I charge thee before God, and the Lord Jesus Christ, and the elect angels, that thou observe these things without preferring one before another, doing nothing by partiality; **James 2:1-4** have not the faith of our Lord Jesus Christ, the Lord of glory, with respect of persons. For if there come unto your assembly a man with a gold ring, in goodly apparel, and there come in also a poor man in vile raiment; And ye have respect to him that weareth the gay clothing, and say unto him, Sit thou here in a good place; and say to the poor, Stand thou there, or sit here under my footstool: Are ye not then partial in yourselves, and are become judges of evil thoughts; **2:8-9** if ye fulfil the royal law according to the scripture, Thou shalt love thy neighbour as thyself, ye do well: But if ye have respect to persons, ye commit sin, and are convinced of the law as transgressors; **3:17** the wisdom that is from above is first pure, then peaceable, gentle, and easy to be intreated, full of mercy and good fruits, without partiality, and without hypocrisy.

ERR, ERROR (*see also* False, Sin, Transgress)

The leaders of this people cause them to err; and they that are led of them are destroyed. **Isa. 9:16** (*see also* Lead)

It is a people that do err in their heart, and they have not known my ways. **Ps. 95:10** (*see also* Heart, Ways)

The vile person will speak villany, and his heart will work iniquity, to practise hypocrisy, and to utter error against the LORD, to make empty the soul of the hungry. **Isa. 32:6** (*see also* Utter)

ESCAPE (*see also* Deliver, Flee, Save)

How shall we escape, if we neglect so great salvation; which at the first began to be spoken by the Lord, and was confirmed unto us by them that heard him; God also bearing them witness, both with signs and wonders, and with divers miracles, and gifts of the Holy Ghost, according to his own will? **Heb. 2:3-4** (*see also* Escape, Miracle, Salvation, Witness)

There hath no temptation. taken you but such as is common to man: but God is faithful, who will not suffer you to be tempted above that ye are able; but will with the temptation also make a way to escape, that ye may be able to bear it. **1 Cor. 10:13** (*see also* Bear, Tempt)

ESCHEW (*see also* Reject)

Let him eschew evil, and do good; let him seek peace, and ensue it. **1 Pet. 3:11** (*see also* Peace)

ESTABLISH, ESTABLISHED (*see also* Begin, Build, Foundation)

If ye will not believe, surely ye shall not be established. **Isa. 7:9** (*see also* Beleive)

Ye that make mention of the LORD, keep not silence, And give him no rest, till he establish, and till he make Jerusalem a praise in the earth. **Isa. 62:6-7** (*see also* Jerusalem, Mention)

We thought it good to be left at Athens alone; and sent Timotheus, our brother, and minister of God, and our fellowlabourer in the gospel of Christ, to establish you, and to comfort you concerning your faith. **1 Thes. 3:1-2**

He shall not be afraid of evil tidings: his heart is fixed, trusting in the LORD. His heart is established, he shall not be afraid. **Ps. 112:7-8** (*see also* Evil, Trust)

Ponder the path of thy feet and let all thy ways be established. **Prov. 4:26** (*see also* Feet, Ponder, Way)

Believe in the Lord your God, so shall ye be established; believe his prophets, so shall ye prosper. **2 Chron. 20:20** (*see also* Believe, Hearken, Prophet, Prosper)

ESTEEM (*see also* Love, Regard, Respect)

Let nothing be done through strife or vainglory; but in lowliness of mind let each esteem other better than themselves. **Philip. 2:3** (*see also* Better, Low)

God knoweth your hearts: for that which is highly esteemed among men is abomination in the sight of God. **Luke 16:15** (*see also* Abomination)

ETERNAL, ETERNAL LIFE, ETERNALLY, ETERNITY (*see also* Everlasting Life, Exalt, Salvation, Save)

This is life eternal, that they might know thee the only true God, and Jesus Christ, whom thou hast sent. **John 17:3** (*see also* Jesus Christ)

Search the scriptures; for in them ye think ye have eternal life: and they are they which testify of me. **John 5:39** (*see also* Scripture, Search)

My sheep hear my voice, and I know them, and they follow me; And I give unto them eternal life; and they shall never perish, neither shall any man pluck them our of my hand. **John 10:27** (*see also* Sheep, Voice)

Fight the good fight of faith, lay hold on eternal life, whereunto thou art also called, and hast professed a good profession before many witnesses. **1 Tim. 6:12** (*see also* Call)

1 Tim. 6:12 fight the good fight of faith, lay hold on *e.l.,* whereunto thou art also called, and hast professed a good profession before many witnesses.

EVERLASTING COVENANT (*see also* Covenant)

Be ye mindful always of his covenant; the word which he commanded to a thousand generations; Even of the covenant which he made with Abraham, and of his oath unto Isaac; And hath confirmed the same to Jacob for a law, and to Israel for an everlasting covenant. **1 Chron. 16:15-17** (*see also* Covenant)

The earth also is defiled under the inhabitants thereof; because they have transgressed the laws, changed the ordinance, broken the everlasting covenant. **Isa. 24:5** (*see also* Ordinance)

EVERLASTING FIRE (*see also* Hell)

Wherefore if thy hand or thy foot offend thee, cut them off, and cast them from thee: it is better for thee to enter into life halt or maimed, rather than having two hands or two feet to be cast into everlasting fire. **Matt. 18:8** (*see also* Better, Cut, Offend)

EVERLASTING LIFE (*see also* Life)

He that heareth my word, and believeth on him that sent me, hath everlasting life, and shall not come into condemnation; but is passed from death unto life. **John 5:24** (*see also* Father)

Labour not for the meat which perisheth, but for that meat which endureth unto everlasting life. **John 6:27** (*see also* Labor)

But whosoever drinketh of the water that I shall give him shall never thirst; but the water that I shall give him shall be in him a well of water springing up into everlasting life. **John 4:14** (*see also* Springing, Thirst)

For God so loved the world, that he gave his only begotten Son, that whosoever believeth in him should not perish, but have everlasting life. **John 3:16** (*see also* Begotten)

John 3:16 for God so loved the world, that he gave his only begotten Son, that whosoever believeth in him should not perish, but have everlasting life.

EVERYWHERE

Whither shall I go from thy spirit? or whither shall I flee from thy presence? **Ps. 139:4-7** (*see also* Flee)

Ps. 139:4-13 whither shall I go from thy spirit? or whither shall I flee from thy presence? If I ascend up into heaven, thou art there: if I make my bed in hell, behold, thou art there. If I take the wings of the morning, and dwell in the uttermost parts of the sea; Even there shall thy hand lead me, and thy right hand shall hold me.

EVIL (*see also* Abomination, Bad, Carnal, Filthy, Iniquity, Sin, Transgress, Wickedness)

Do no evil. **2 Cor. 13:7**

The love of money is the root of all evil: which while some coveted after, they have erred from the faith, and pierced themselves through with many sorrows. **1 Tim. 6:9** (*see also* Money, Sorrow)

That which cometh out of the man, that defileth the man. For from within, out of the heart of men, proceed evil thoughts, adulteries, fornications, murders, Thefts, covetousness, wickedness, deceit, lasciviousness, an evil eye, blasphemy, pride, foolishness: All these evil things come from within, and defile the man. **Mark 7:20-23** (*see also* Defile, Think)

Turn not to the right hand nor to the left: remove thy foot from evil. **Prov. 4:27** (*see also* Foot, Remove)

Then went the Pharisees, and took counsel how they might entangle him in his talk. **Matt. 22:15** (*see also* Cause, Entangle)

Though I walk through the valley of the shadow of death, I will fear no evil: for thou art with me. **Ps. 23:4** (*see also* Fear)

Evil shall slay the wicked: and they that hate the righteous shall be desolate. **Ps. 34:21** (*see also* Hate)

He shall not be afraid of evil tidings: his heart is fixed, trusting in the LORD. His heart is established, he shall not be afraid. **Ps. 112:7-8** (*see also* Establish, Trust)

Rejoice [not] to do evil, and delight in the frowardness of the wicked. **Prov. 2:14** (*see also* Rejoice)

The fear of the LORD is to hate evil: pride, and arrogancy, and the evil way, and the froward mouth, do I hate. **Prov. 8:13** (*see also* Arrogance, Fear, Hate)

Eat thou not the bread of him that hath an evil eye, neither desire thou his dainty meats. **Prov. 23:6-8** (*see also* Eat)

If thou hast done foolishly in lifting up thyself, or if thou has thought evil, lay thine hand upon thy mouth. **Prov. 30:32** (*see also* Think)

Woe unto them that call evil good, and good evil; that put darkness for light, and light for darkness; that put bitter for sweet and sweet for bitter! **Isa. 5:20** (*see also* Good, Sweet)

Ye have wearied the LORD with your words. Yet ye say, Wherein have we wearied him? When ye say, Every one that doeth evil is good in the sight of the LORD. **Mal. 2:17** (*see also* Good, Weary, Word)

Be ye not as your fathers, unto whom the former prophets have cried, saying, Thus saith the LORD of hosts; Turn ye now from your evil ways, and from your evil doings: but they did not hear, nor hearken unto me, saith the LORD. **Zech. 1:4** (*see also* Hear, Way)

Be not overcome of evil, but overcome evil with good. **Rom. 12:21**

Return ye now every one from his evil way, and make your ways and your doings good. **Jer. 18:11** (*see also* Good, Way)

It shall come to pass at that time, that I will search Jerusalem with candles, and punish the men that are settled on their lees: that say in their heart, The LORD will not do good, neither will he do evil. **Zeph. 1:12** (*see also* Good, Say)

Devise not evil against thy neighbour, seeing he dwelleth securely by thee. **Prov. 3:29** (*see also* Devise)

Do [no] evil in the sight of the LORD, to provoke him to anger. **2 Kgs. 17:17** (*see also* Anger)

Gen. 44:4-5 wherefore have ye rewarded *e.* for good? Is not this it in which my lord drinketh, and whereby indeed he divineth? ye have done *e.* in so doing; **Ex. 23:2** thou shalt not follow a multitude to do *e.*; neither shalt thou speak in a cause to decline after many to wrest judgment; **Num. 32:13** the LORD's anger was kindled against Israel, and he made them wander in the wilderness forty years, until all the generation, that had done *e.* in the sight of the LORD, was consumed; **Deut. 4:25-26** when thou shalt... do *e.* in the sight of the LORD thy God, to provoke him to anger: I call heaven and earth to witness against you this day, that ye shall soon utterly perish from off the land; **31:29** ye will utterly corrupt yourselves, and turn aside from the way which I have commanded you; and *e.* will befall you in the latter days; because ye will do *e.* in the sight of the LORD; **Judg. 2:11** the children of Israel did *e.* in the sight of the LORD; **3:7** the children of Israel did *e.* in the sight of the LORD, and forgat the LORD their God; **6:1** (3:12, 4:1) the children of Israel did *e.* in the sight of the LORD: and the LORD delivered them into the hand of Midian seven years; **10:6** the children of Israel did *e.* again in the sight of the LORD... and forsook the LORD, and served not him; **13:1** the children of Israel did *e.* again in the sight of the LORD; and the LORD delivered them into the hand of the Philistines forty years; **1 Sam. 15:19** wherefore then didst thou not obey the voice of the LORD, but didst fly upon the spoil, and didst *e.* in the sight of the LORD; **24:17-19** thou art more righteous than I: for thou hast rewarded me good, whereas I have rewarded thee *e*. And thou hast shewed this day how that thou hast dealt well with me; **25:28** my lord fighteth the battles of the LORD, and *e*. hath not been found in thee all thy days; **2 Sam. 12:9** wherefore hast thou despised the commandment of the LORD, to do *e*. in his sight; **13:16** this *e*. in sending me away is greater than the other that thou didst unto me; **1 Kgs. 11:6** Solomon did *e*. in the sight of the LORD, and went not fully after the LORD, as did David his father; **13:33** after this thing Jeroboam returned not from his *e*. way, but made again of the lowest of the people priests of the high places; **14:9** hast done *e*. above all that were before thee: for thou hast gone and made thee other gods, and molten images, to provoke me to anger; **14:22** Judah did *e*. in the sight of the LORD, and they provoked him to jealousy with their sins which they had committed; **15:26** he did *e*. in the sight of the LORD, and walked in the way of his father, and in his sin wherewith he made Israel to sin; **15:34** he did *e*. in the sight of the LORD, and walked in the way of Jeroboam, and in his sin wherewith he made Israel to sin; **16:7** by the hand of the prophet... came the word of the LORD against Baasha, and against his house, even for all the *e*. that he did in the sight of the LORD, in provoking him to anger; **16:19** for his sins which he sinned in doing *e*. in the sight of the LORD, in walking in the way of Jeroboam, and in his sin which he did, to make Israel to sin; **16:25** Omri wrought *e*. in the eyes of the LORD, and did worse than all that were before him; **16:30** Ahab the son of Omri did *e*. in the sight of the LORD above all that were before him; **21:20** I have found thee: because thou hast sold thyself to work *e*. in the sight of the LORD; **22:52** he did *e*. in the sight of the LORD, and walked in the way of his father, and in the way of his mother; **2 Kgs. 3:2-3** he wrought *e*. in the sight of the LORD; but not like his father, and like his mother; **8:18** he did *e*. in the sight of the LORD; **8:27** he walked in the way of the house of Ahab, and did *e*. in the sight of the LORD; **13:2** he did that which was *e*. in the sight of the LORD, and followed the sins of Jeroboam the son of Nebat, which made Israel to sin; he departed not therefrom; **13:11** (14:24) he did that which was *e*. in the sight of the LORD; he departed not from all the sins of Jeroboam the son of Nebat, who made Israel sin; **15:9** (15:18, 24, 28) he did that which was *e*. in the sight of the LORD, as his fathers had done: he departed not from the sins of Jeroboam; **17:13** turn ye from your *e*. ways, and keep my commandments and my statutes, according to all the law which I commanded your fathers; **17:17** they caused their sons and their daughters to pass through the fire, and used divination and enchantments, and sold themselves to do *e*. in the sight of the LORD, to provoke him to anger; **21:2** he did that which was *e*. in the sight of the LORD, after the abominations of the heathen; **21:9** Manasseh seduced them to do more *e*. than did the nations whom the LORD destroyed; **21:15** they have done that which was *e*. in my sight, and have provoked me to anger; **23:32** he did that which was *e*. in the sight of the LORD, according to all that his fathers had done; **23:37** he did that which was *e*. in the sight of the LORD, according to all that his fathers had done; **24:9** he did that which was *e*. in the sight of the LORD, according to all that his father had done; **24:19** he did that which was *e*. in the sight of the LORD, according to all that Jehoiakim had done; **1 Chron. 2:3** Er, the firstborn of Judah, was *e*. in the sight of the LORD; and he slew him; **4:10** oh that thou wouldest bless me indeed, and enlarge my coast, and that thine hand might be with me, and that thou wouldest keep me from *e*.; **10:13** Saul died for his transgression which he committed against the LORD, even against the word of the LORD, which he kept not; **21:17** I it is that have sinned and done *e*. indeed; but as for these sheep, what have they done? let thine hand, I pray thee, O LORD my God, be on me, and on my fathers house; but not on thy people; **2 Chron. 29:6-9** our fathers have trespassed, and done that which was *e*. in the eyes of the LORD our God, and have forsaken him, and have turned away their faces from the habitation of the LORD, and turned their backs; **33:2-6** [he] did that which was *e*. in the sight of the LORD, like unto the abominations of the heathen, whom the LORD had cast out before the children of Israel; **Job 1:1** there was a man... whose name was Job; and that man was perfect and upright, and one that feared God, and eschewed *e*.; **1:8** (2:3) hast thou considered my servant Job, that there is none like him in the earth, a perfect and an upright man, one that feareth God, and escheweth *e*.; **Ps. 37:9** evildoers shall be cut off: but those that wait upon the LORD, they shall inherit the earth; **Prov. 24:8** he that deviseth to do *e*. shall be called a mischievous person; **Isa. 1:16** wash you, make you clean; put away the *e*. of your doings from before mine eyes; cease to do *e*.; **14:20** the seed of evildoers shall never be renowned; **56:2-7** blessed is the man that doeth this, and the son of man that layeth hold on it; that keepeth the sabbath from polluting it, and keepeth his hand from doing any *e*.; **Jer. 7:30** the children of Judah have done *e*. in my sight, saith the LORD: they have set their abominations in the house which is called by my name, to pollute it;

52:2 he did that which was *e.* in the eyes of the LORD.

I have not sat with vain persons, neither will I go in with dissemblers. I have hated the congregation of evil doers; and will not sit with the wicked. Ps. 26:4-5 (*see also* Vain)

Ps. 26:4-5 I have not sat with vain persons, neither will I go in with dissemblers. I have hated the congregation of evil doers; and will not sit with the wicked; **37:12** the wicked plotteth against the just, and gnasheth upon him with his teeth; **141:4** incline not my heart to any *e.* thing, to practise wicked works with men that work iniquity; **Prov. 12:12** the wicked desireth the net of *e.* men: but the root of the righteous yieldeth fruit; **30:8** remove far from me vanity and lies: give me neither poverty nor riches.

Depart from evil, and do good; seek peace, and pursue it. Ps. 34:14 (*see also* Depart, Good)

Ps. 34:14 depart from *e.*, and do good; seek peace, and pursue it; **37:27** depart from *e.*, and do good; and dwell for evermore; **Prov. 14:16** a wise man feareth, and departeth from *e.*: but the fool rageth, and is confident; **14:22** do they not err that devise *e.*? but mercy and truth shall be to them that devise good; **16:17** the highway of the upright is to depart from *e.*: he that keepeth his way preserveth his soul; **Eccl. 3:12** I know that there is no good in them, but for a man to rejoice, and to do good in his life.

As righteousness tendeth to life: so he that pursueth evil pursueth it to his own death. Prov. 11:19

Prov. 11:19 as righteousness tendeth to life: so he that pursueth *e.* pursueth it to his own death; **18:1** through desire a man, having separated himself, seeketh and intermeddleth with all wisdom.

I have refrained my feet from every evil way, that I might keep thy word. Ps. 119:101 (*see also* Keep, Word)

Ps. 119:101 I have refrained my feet from every *e.* way, that I might keep thy word; **Prov. 8:13** the fear of the LORD is to hate *e.*: pride, and arrogancy, and the *e.* way, and the froward mouth; **27:8** as a bird that wandereth from her nest, so is a man that wandereth from his place; **27:12** a prudent man foreseeth the *e.*, and hideth

himself; but the simple pass on, and are punished.

They are not valiant for the truth upon the earth, for they proceed from evil to evil, and they know not me, saith the LORD. Jer. 9:3 (*see also* Valiant)

Turn ye again now every one from his evil way, and from the evil of your doings, and dwell in the land that the LORD hath given unto you and to your fathers for ever and ever. Jer. 25:5 (*see also* Turn, Way)

Jer. 25:5 turn ye again now every one from his *e.* way, and from the *e.* of your doings, and dwell in the land that the LORD hath given unto you and to your fathers for ever and ever; **26:3** if so be they will hearken, and turn every man from his *e.* way, that I may repent me of the *e.*, which I purpose to do unto them because of the *e.* of their doings; **36:3** it may be that the house of Judah will hear all the *e.* which I purpose to do unto them; that they may return every man from his *e.* way; that I may forgive their iniquity and their sin; **Ezek. 33:11** as I live, saith the Lord GOD, I have no pleasure in the death of the wicked; but that the wicked turn from his way and live: turn ye, turn ye from your *e.* ways; for why will ye die, O house of Israel; **33:15** if the wicked restore the pledge, give again that he had robbed, walk in the statutes of life, without committing iniquity; he shall surely live, he shall not die; **33:19** if the wicked turn from his wickedness, and do that which is lawful and right, he shall live thereby; **Mal. 2:6** the law of truth was in his mouth, and iniquity was not found in his lips: he walked with me in peace and equity, and did turn many away from iniquity.

Abhor that which is evil; cleave to that which is good. Rom. 12:9 (*see also* Good)

Matt. 7:17-19 every tree that bringeth not forth good fruit is hewn down, and cast into the fire; **7:23** then will I profess unto them, I never knew you: depart from me, ye that work iniquity; **13:41-42** The Son of man shall send forth his angels, and they shall gather out of his kingdom all things that offend, and them which do iniquity; And shall cast them into a furnace of fire: there shall be wailing and gnashing of teeth; **13:49-50** at the end of the world: the angels shall come forth, and sever the wicked from among the just, And shall cast them into the furnace of fire: there shall be wailing and gnashing of teeth; **18:7-9** if thy hand or thy foot offend thee, cut them off, and cast them from thee: it is better for thee to enter into life halt or maimed, rather than having two hands or two feet to be cast into everlasting fire; **24:12** because iniquity shall abound, the love of many shall wax cold; **24:48-51** in an hour that he is not aware of, And shall cut him asunder, and appoint him his portion with the hypocrites: there shall be weeping and gnashing of teeth; **Luke 6:49** he that heareth, and doeth not, is like a man that without a foundation built an house upon the earth; against which the stream did beat vehemently, and immediately it fell; and the ruin of that house was great; **12:5** I will forewarn you whom ye shall fear: Fear him, which after he hath killed hath power to cast into hell; yea, I say unto you, Fear him; **13: 27-28** depart from me, all ye workers of iniquity. There shall be weeping and gnashing of teeth, when ye shall see Abraham, and Isaac, and Jacob, and all the prophets, in the kingdom of God, and you yourselves thrust out; **John 5:14** sin no more, lest a worse thing come unto thee; **8:34** whosoever committeth sin is the servant of sin; **Acts 3:26** God, having raised up his Son Jesus, sent him to bless you, in turning away every one of you from his iniquities; **Rom. 2:8-9** unto them that are contentious, and do not obey the truth, but obey unrighteousness, indignation and wrath, Tribulation and anguish, upon every soul of man that doeth *e.*; **3:11-12** there is none that understandeth, there is none that seeketh after God. They are all gone out of the way, they are together become unprofitable; there is none that doeth good, no, not one; **6:11-13** neither yield ye your members as instruments of unrighteousness unto sin; **6:19** ye have yielded your members servants to uncleanness and to iniquity unto iniquity; **7:23** I see another law in my members, warring against the law of my mind, and bringing me into captivity to the law of sin which is in my members; **8:5** they that are after the flesh do mind the things of the flesh; **12:9** let love be without dissimulation. Abhor that which is *e.*; cleave to that which is good; **12:21** be not overcome of *e.,* but overcome *e.* with good; **13:4** he is the minister of God, a revenger to execute wrath upon him that doeth *e.*; **2 Cor. 7:1** let us cleanse ourselves from all filthiness of the flesh and spirit, perfecting holiness in the fear of God; **Eph. 5:11-13** have no fellowship with the unfruitful works of darkness, but rather reprove them. For it is a shame even to speak of those things which are done of them in secret; **Col. 3:25** he that doeth wrong shall receive for the wrong which he hath done: and there is no respect of persons; **1 Tim. 5:24-25** some men's sins are open beforehand,

going before to judgment; and some men they follow after; **2 Tim. 2:19** let every one that nameth the name of Christ depart from iniquity; **3:13** *e.* men and seducers shall wax worse and worse, deceiving, and being deceived; **Heb. 10:26-27** if we sin willfully after that we have received the knowledge of the truth, there remaineth no more sacrifice for sins, But a certain fearful looking for of judgment and fiery indignation, which shall devour the adversaries; **12:3-4** consider him that endured such contradiction of sinners against himself, lest ye be wearied and faint in your minds; **James 1:27** pure religion and undefiled before God and the Father is this, To visit the fatherless and widows in their affliction, and to keep himself unspotted from the world; **4:7** resist the devil, and he will flee from you; **5:1-6** weep and howl for your miseries that shall come upon you. Your riches are corrupted, and your garments are motheaten. Your gold and silver is cankered; and the rust of them shall be a witness against you, and shall eat your flesh as it were fire. Ye have heaped treasure together for the last days. Behold, the hire of the labourers who have reaped down your fields, which is of you kept back by fraud, crieth: and the cries of them which have reaped are entered into the ears of the Lord of sabaoth. Ye have lived in pleasure on the earth, and been wanton; ye have nourished your hearts, as in a day of slaughter. Ye have condemned and killed the just; and he doth not resist you; **1 Pet. 4:2-5** he no longer should live the rest of his time in the flesh to the lusts of men, but to the will of God. For the time past of our life may suffice us to have wrought the will of the Gentiles, when we walked in lasciviousness, lusts, excess of wine, revellings, banquetings, and abominable idolatries: Wherein they think it strange that ye run not with them to the same excess of riot, speaking *e.* of you: Who shall give account to him that is ready to judge the quick and the dead; **4:15** let none of you suffer as a murderer, or as a thief, or as an evildoer, or as a busybody in other men's matters; **2 Pet. 2:5-7** bringing in the flood upon the world of the ungodly; And turning the cities of Sodom and Gomorrha into ashes condemned them with an overthrow, making them an ensample unto those that after should live ungodly; **2:9-14** the Lord knoweth how to deliver the godly out of temptations, and to reserve the unjust unto the day of judgment to be punished: But chiefly them that walk after the flesh in the lust of uncleanness, and despise government. Presumptuous are they, selfwilled, they are not afraid to speak *e.* of dignities. Whereas angels, which are greater in power and might, bring not railing accusation against them before the Lord. But these, as natural brute beasts, made to be taken and destroyed, speak *e.* of the things that they understand not; and shall utterly perish in their own corruption; And shall receive the reward of unrighteousness, as they that count it pleasure to riot in the day time. Spots they are and blemishes, sporting themselves with their own deceivings while they feast with you; Having eyes full of adultery, and that cannot cease from sin; beguiling unstable souls: an heart they have exercised with covetous practices; cursed children; **2:15-16** was rebuked for his iniquity: the dumb ass speaking with man's voice forbad the madness of the prophet; **2:17-19** the servants of corruption: for of whom a man is overcome, of the same is he brought in bondage; **1 Jn. 1:8** if we say that we have no sin, we deceive ourselves, and the truth is not in us; **2:2** my little children, these things write I unto you, that ye sin not; **3:4** whosoever committeth sin transgresseth also the law: for sin is the transgression of the law; **3:8** he that committeth sin is of the devil; for the devil sinneth from the beginning. For this purpose the Son of God was manifested, that he might destroy the works of the devil; **3:12** Not as Cain, who was of that wicked one, and slew his brother. And wherefore slew he him? Because his own works were *e.,* and his brother's righteous; **2 Jn. 1:9** whosoever transgresseth, and abideth not in the doctrine of Christ, hath not God. He that abideth in the doctrine of Christ, he hath both the Father and the Son; **Jude 1:4** ungodly men, turning the grace of our God into lasciviousness, and denying the only Lord God, and our Lord Jesus Christ; **1:8** also these filthy dreamers defile the flesh, despise dominion, and speak *e.* of dignities; **1:11-13** woe unto them! for they have gone in the way of Cain, and ran greedily after the error of Balaam for reward, and perished in the gainsaying of Core; **1:15-16** execute judgment upon all, and to convince all that are ungodly among them of all their ungodly deeds which they have ungodly committed, and of all their hard speeches which ungodly sinners have spoken against him. These are murmurers, complainers, walking after their own lusts; and their mouth speaketh great swelling words, having men's persons in admiration because of advantage; **1:19** these be they who separate themselves, sensual, having not the Spirit; **3:4** thou hast a few names even in Sardis which have not defiled their garments; and they shall walk with me in white: for they are worthy; **14:10-11** the same shall drink of the wine of the wrath of God, which is poured out without mixture into

the cup of his indignation; **16:2** the first went, and poured out his vial upon the earth; and there fell a noisome and grievous sore upon the men which had the mark of the beast, and upon them which worshipped his image; **17:1-2** I will shew unto thee the judgment of the great whore that sitteth upon many waters: With whom the kings of the earth have committed fornication, and the inhabitants of the earth have been made drunk with the wine of her fornication; **18:9-10** the kings of the earth, who have committed fornication and lived deliciously with her, shall bewail her, and lament for her, when they shall see the smoke of her burning; **18:17-19** cried, weeping and wailing, saying, Alas, alas, that great city, wherein were made rich all that had ships in the sea by reason of her costliness! for in one hour is she made desolate; **18:21-24** with violence shall that great city Babylon be thrown down, and shall be found no more at all. And in her was found the blood of prophets, and of saints, and of all that were slain upon the earth; **19:20-21** the beast was taken, and with him the false prophet that wrought miracles before him, with which he deceived them that had received the mark of the beast, and them that worshipped his image; **20:2** he laid hold on the dragon, that old serpent, which is the Devil, and Satan, and bound him a thousand years; **20:10** the beast and the false prophet are, and shall be tormented day and night for ever and ever; **20:15** whosoever was not found written in the book of life was cast into the lake of fire; **21:27** any thing that defileth, neither whatsoever worketh abomination, or maketh a lie.

Do men gather grapes of thorns, or figs of thistles? Even so every good tree bringeth forth good fruit; but a corrupt tree bringeth forth evil fruit. A good tree cannot bring forth evil fruit, neither can a corrupt tree bring forth good fruit. Every tree that bringeth not forth good fruit is hewn down, and cast into the fire. Wherefore by their fruits ye shall know them. Matt. 7:16-20 (*see also* Good)

Matt. 7:16 ye shall know them by their fruits. Do men gather grapes of thorns, or figs of thistles? Even so every good tree bringeth forth good fruit; but a corrupt tree bringeth forth *e.* fruit. A good tree cannot bring forth *e.* fruit, neither can a corrupt tree bring forth good fruit. Every tree that bringeth not forth good fruit is hewn down, and cast into the fire. Wherefore by their fruits ye shall know them; **9:33-34** but the Pharisees said, He casteth out devils through the prince of the devils; **11:18** for John came neither eating nor drinking, and they say, He hath a devil; **12:5-7** in this place is one greater than the temple. But if ye had known what this meaneth, I will have mercy, and not sacrifice, ye would not have condemned the guiltless; **12:24** when the Pharisees heard it, they said, This fellow doth not cast out devils, but by Beelzebub the prince of the devils; **20:14-15** take that thine is, and go thy way: I will give unto this last, even as unto thee. Is it not lawful for me to do what I will with mine own? Is thine eye e., because I am good; **21:15** when the chief priests and scribes saw the wonderful things that he did, and the children crying in the temple, and saying, Hosanna to the Son of David; they were sore displeased; **21:45-46** when they sought to lay hands on him, they feared the multitude, because they took him for a prophet; **26:55** are ye come out as against a thief with swords and staves for to take me? I sat daily with you teaching in the temple, and ye laid no hold on me; **26:65** the high priest rent his clothes, saying, He hath spoken blasphemy; what further need have we of witnesses? behold, now ye have heard his blasphemy; **27:20** the chief priests and elders persuaded the multitude that they should ask Barabbas, and destroy Jesus; **Mark 3:4** is it lawful to do good on the sabbath days, or to do e.? to save life, or to kill?; **3:22** the scribes which came down from Jerusalem said, He hath Beelzebub, and by the prince of the devils casteth he out devils; **14:4-8** there were some that had indignation within themselves, and said, Why was this waste of the ointment made? For it might have been sold for more than three hundred pence, and have been given to the poor; **14:63-64** the high priest rent his clothes, and saith, What need we any further witnesses? Ye have heard the blasphemy: what think ye? And they all condemned him to be guilty of death; **15:14** Pilate said unto them, Why, what e. hath he done? And they cried out the more exceedingly, Crucify him; **Luke 7:30** the Pharisees and lawyers rejected the counsel of God against themselves, being not baptized of him; **7:31-34** John the Baptist came neither eating bread nor drinking wine; and ye say, He hath a devil. The Son of man is come eating and drinking; and ye say, Behold a gluttonous man, and a winebibber, a friend of publicans and sinners; **11:15** some of them said, He casteth out devils through Beelzebub the chief of the devils; **11:17-19** if Satan also be divided against

himself, how shall his kingdom stand? because ye say that I cast out devils through Beelzebub. And if I by Beelzebub cast out devils, by whom do your sons cast them out? therefore shall they be your judges; **John 5:43** I am come in my Father's name, and ye receive me not: if another shall come in his own name, him ye will receive; **6:41-42** the Jews then murmured at him, because he said, I am the bread which came down from heaven. And they said, Is not this Jesus, the son of Joseph, whose father and mother we know? how is it then that he saith, I came down from heaven; **7:12** there was much murmuring among the people concerning him: for some said, He is a good man: others said, Nay; but he deceiveth the people; **10:19-21** he hath a devil, and is mad; why hear ye him? Others said, These are not the words of him that hath a devil. Can a devil open the eyes of the blind; **10:32** Jesus answered them, Many good works have I shewed you from my Father; for which of those works do ye stone me; **16:2-3** the time cometh, that whosoever killeth you will think that he doeth God service; **16:20** ye shall weep and lament, but the world shall rejoice: and ye shall be sorrowful, but your sorrow shall be turned into joy; **18:23** if I have spoken e., bear witness of the e.: but if well, why smitest thou me; **19:7** the Jews answered him, We have a law, and by our law he ought to die, because he made himself the Son of God; **5:38** refrain from these men, and let them alone: for if this counsel or this work be of men, it will come to nought; **6:12-13** set up false witnesses, which said, This man ceaseth not to speak blasphemous words against this holy place, and the law; **7:39** to whom our fathers would not obey, but thrust him from them, and in their hearts turned back again into Egypt; **13:27-28** though they found no cause of death in him, yet desired they Pilate that he should be slain; **13:45** when the Jews saw the multitudes, they were filled with envy, and spake against those things which were spoken by Paul, contradicting and blaspheming; **17:5** the Jews which believed not, moved with envy, took unto them certain lewd fellows of the baser sort, and gathered a company, and set all the city on an uproar, and assaulted the house of Jason, and sought to bring them out to the people; **1 Cor. 8: 8** but meat commendeth us not to God: for neither, if we eat, are we the better; neither, if we eat not, are we the worse.

See that none render evil for evil unto any man; but ever follow that which is good, both among yourselves, and to all men. 1 Thes. 5:15 (*see also* Render)

Rom. 12:17 recompense to no man *e*. for *e*.; **12:19** avenge not yourselves, but rather give place unto wrath: for it is written, Vengeance is mine; I will repay, saith the Lord; **1 Thes. 5:15** see that none render *e*. for *e*. unto any man; but ever follow that which is good, both among yourselves, and to all men; **2 Tim. 4:14** Alexander the coppersmith did me much *e*.: the Lord reward him according to his works; **1 Pet. 3:9** not rendering *e*. for *e*., or railing for railing: but contrariwise blessing; knowing that ye are thereunto called, that ye should inherit a blessing.

When thine eye is evil, thy body also is full of darkness. Take heed therefore that the light which is in thee be not darkness. Luke 11:34-35 (*see also* Dark)

Matt. 2:3,7,8,16 then Herod, when he saw that he was mocked of the wise men, was exceeding wroth, and sent forth, and slew all the children that were in Bethlehem, and in all the coasts thereof, from two years old and under, according to the time which he had diligently enquired of the wise men; **12:14** Pharisees went out, and held a council against him, how they might destroy him; **12:43-45** when the unclean spirit is gone out of a man, he walketh through dry places, seeking rest, and findeth none. Then he saith, I will return into my house from whence I came out; and when he is come, he findeth it empty, swept, and garnished. Then goeth he, and taketh with himself seven other spirits more wicked than himself, and they enter in and dwell there: and the last state of that man is worse than the first. Even so shall it be also unto this wicked generation; **13:24-30** the kingdom of heaven is likened unto a man which sowed good seed in his field: But while men slept, his enemy came and sowed tares among the wheat, and went his way. But when the blade was sprung up, and brought forth fruit, then appeared the tares also. So the servants of the householder came and said unto him, Sir, didst not thou sow good seed in thy field? from whence then hath it tares? He said unto them, An enemy hath done this; **13:38** the field is the world; the good seed are the children of the kingdom; but the tares are the children of the wicked one; **13:41-42** the Son of man shall send forth his angels, and they shall gather out of his kingdom all things that offend,

and them which do iniquity; And shall cast them into a furnace of fire: there shall be wailing and gnashing of teeth; **14:3-10** Herodias danced before them, and pleased Herod. Whereupon he promised with an oath to give her whatsoever she would ask. And she, being before instructed of her mother, said, Give me here John Baptist's head in a charger; **15:19-20** out of the heart proceed evil thoughts, murders, adulteries, fornications, thefts, false witness, blasphemies: These are the things which defile a man: but to eat with unwashen hands defileth not a man; **16:4** a wicked and adulterous generation seeketh after a sign; and there shall no sign be given unto it, but the sign of the prophet Jonas. And he left them, and departed; **22:13** bind him hand and foot, and take him away, and cast him into outer darkness; there shall be weeping and gnashing of teeth; **23:33** ye serpents, ye generation of vipers, how can ye escape the damnation of hell; **24:10** then shall many be offended, and shall betray one another, and shall hate one another; **25:41** depart from me, ye cursed, into everlasting fire, prepared for the devil and his angels; **25:46** these shall go away into everlasting punishment: but the righteous into life eternal; **Mark 7:21-23** out of the heart of men, proceed evil thoughts, adulteries, fornications, murders;... All these evil things come from within, and defile the man; **14:1** the chief priests and the scribes sought how they might take him by craft, and put him to death; **15:11-13** the chief priests moved the people, that he should rather release Barabbas unto them. And Pilate answered and said again unto them, What will ye then that I shall do unto him whom ye call the King of the Jews? And they cried out again, Crucify him; **Luke 3:17** Whose fan is in his hand, and he will throughly purge his floor, and will gather the wheat into his garner; but the chaff he will burn with fire unquenchable; **3:19** Herod the tetrarch, being reproved by him for Herodias his brother Philip's wife, and for all the evils which Herod had done; **4:12-13** thou shalt not tempt the Lord thy God. And when the devil had ended all the temptation, he departed from him for a season; **6:11** they were filled with madness; and communed one with another what they might do to Jesus; **11:34-35** when thine eye is evil, thy body also is full of darkness. Take heed therefore that the light which is in thee be not darkness; **24:20** the chief priests and our rulers delivered him to be condemned to death, and have crucified him; **John 6:71** he it was that should betray him, being one of the twelve; **8:44** ye are of your father the devil, and the lusts of your father ye will do. He was a murderer from the beginning, and abode not in the truth, because there is no truth in him. When he speaketh a lie, he speaketh of his own: for he is a liar, and the father of it; **Rom. 3:14** whose mouth is full of cursing and bitterness; **3:16** destruction and misery are in their ways; **6:19** I speak after the manner of men because of the infirmity of your flesh: for as ye have yielded your members servants to uncleanness and to iniquity unto iniquity; even so now yield your members servants to righteousness unto holiness; **6:23** the wages of sin is death; but the gift of God is eternal life through Jesus Christ our Lord; **11:8-10** God hath given them the ears that they should not hear;) unto this day. And David saith, Let their table be made a snare, and a trap, and a stumblingblock, and a recompence unto them: Let their eyes be darkened, that they may not see, and bow down their back alway. I say then, Have they stumbled that they should fall? God forbid: but rather through their fall salvation is come unto the Gentiles, for to provoke them to jealousy; **2 Thes. 2:8-11** then shall that wicked be revealed, whom the Lord shall consume with the spirit of his mouth, and shall destroy with the brightness of his coming:Even him, whose coming is after the working of Satan with all power and signs and lying wonders, And with all deceivableness of unrighteousness in them that perish; because they received not the love of the truth, that they might be saved. And for this cause God shall send them strong delusion, that they should believe a lie; **Rev. 16:2** there fell a noisome and grievous sore upon the men which had the mark of the beast, and upon them which worshipped his image.

EXACT

Exact no more than that which is appointed you. Luke 3:13 (*see also* Appoint)

EXALT, EXALTATION (*see also* Eternal Life, Magnify, Praise)

Let not the rebellious exalt themselves. Ps. 66:7 (*see also* Rebel)

Exalt the LORD our God, and worship at his holy hill; for the LORD our God is holy. Ps. 99:9 (*see also* Holy)

EXAMINE (*see also* Prove, Try)

Whosoever shall eat this bread, and drink this cup of the Lord, unworthily, shall be guilty of the body and blood of the Lord. But let a man examine himself, and so let him eat of that bread, and drink of that cup. For he that eateth and drinketh unworthily, eateth and drinketh damnation to himself, not discerning the Lord's body. 1 Cor. 11:27-29 (*see also* Sacrament, Unworthiness, Worthy)

EXAMPLE, ENSAMPLE (*see also* Light, Pattern, Standard)

Those things, which ye have both learned, and received, and heard, and seen in me, do: and the God of peace shall be with you. Philip. 4:9 (*see also* Do)

He that saith he abideth in him ought himself also so to walk, even as he walked. 1 Jn. 2:6 (*see also* Walk)

If I then, your Lord and Master, have ashed your feet; ye also ought to wash one another's feet. For I have given you an example, that ye should do as I have done to you. John 13:14-15 (*see also* Do, Feet, Wash)

Let your light so shine before men, that they may see your good works, and glorify your Father which is in heaven. Matt. 5:16 (*see also* Candle, Light)

Matt. 5:15-16 neither do men light a candle, and put it under a bushel, but on a candlestick; and it giveth light unto all that are in the house. Let your light so shine before men, that they may see your good works, and glorify your Father which is in heaven; **Luke 1:79** give light to them that sit in darkness and in the shadow of death, to guide our feet into the way of peace; **8:16-17** no man, when he hath lighted a candle, covereth it with a vessel, or putteth it under a bed; but setteth it on a candlestick, that they which enter in may see the light. For nothing is secret, that shall not be made manifest; neither any thing hid, that shall not be known and come abroad; **11:33-36** the light of the body is the eye: therefore when thine eye is single, thy whole body also is full of light; but when thine eye is evil, thy body also is full of darkness; **12:35-36** let your loins be girded about, and your lights burning; And ye yourselves like unto men that wait for their lord, when he will return from the wedding; that when he cometh and knocketh, they may open unto him immediately.

Let no man despise thy youth; but be thou an example of the believers, in word, in conversation, in charity, in spirit, in faith, in purity. 1 Tim. 4:12 (*see also* Believe, Charity, Conversation, Despise, Pure)

1 Thes 3:9 not because we have not power, but to make ourselves an ensample unto you to follow us; **1 Tim. 4:12** be thou an example of the believers, in word, in conversation, in charity, in spirit, in faith, in purity; **Titus 2:6-7** in all things shewing thyself a pattern of good works; **1 Pet. 5:3** neither as being lords over God's heritage, but being ensamples to the flock.

EXCEL, EXCELLENT

God hath set some in the church, first apostles, secondarily prophets, thirdly teachers, after that miracles, then gifts of healings, helps, governments, diversities of tongues. Are all apostles? are all prophets? are all teachers? are all workers of miracles? Have all the gifts of healing? do all speak with tongues? do all interpret? But covet earnestly the best gifts: and yet shew I unto you a more excellent way. 1 Cor. 12:28-31 (*see also* Gift, Prophet, Way)

Approve things that are excellent; that ye may be sincere and without offense till the day of Christ. Philip. 1:10 (*see also* Approve, Offense)

EXCESS

Be not drunk with wine, wherein is excess; but be filled with the Spirit. Eph. 5:18 (*see also* Drunk, Spirit, Wine)

EXERCISE (*see also* Choose, Do)

Exercise thyself rather unto godliness. 1 Tim. 4:7 (*see also* Godliness)

EXHORT (*see* Plead, Preach, Warn)

[Hold] fast the faithful word as he hath been taught, that he may be able by sound doctrine both to exhort and to convince the gainsayers. Titus 1:9

I have written briefly, exhorting, and testifying that this is the true grace of God wherein ye stand. 1 Pet. 5:12 (*see also* Grace)

They that have believeing masters, let them not despise them, because they are brethren; but rather do them service, because they are faithful and beloved, partakers of the benefit. These things teach and exhort. 1 Tim 6:3 (*see also* Teach)

Exhort one another daily; while it is called To day; lest any of you be hardened through the deceitfulness of sin. Heb. 3:13 (*see also* Daily)

EXIST, EXISTENCE

The fool hath said in his heart, There is no God. They are corrupt, they have done abominable works, there is none that doeth good. Ps. 14:1 (*see also* Fool)

EXPERIMENT (*see* Prove, Try)

EXPLAIN, EXPOUND (*see* Preach, Teach)

EXTORT (*see also* False)

Know ye not that the unrighteous shall not inherit the kingdom of God? Be not deceived: neither fornicators, nor idolaters, nor adulterers, nor effeminate, nor abusers of themselves with mankind, Nor thieves, nor covetous, nor drunkards, nor revilers, nor extortioners, shall inherit the kingdom of God. 1 Cor. 6:9-10 (*see also* Inherit, Unrighteous)

Thou hast taken usury and increase, and thou hast greedily gained of thy neighbours by extortion, and hast forgotten me, saith the Lord GOD. Ezek. 22:12 (*see also* Greed)

EYE (*see also* See)

The eyes of them that see shall not be dim, and the ears of them that hear shall hearken. Isa. 32:3 (*see also* Word)

Unto thee lift I up mine eyes, O thou that dwellest in the heavens. Ps. 123:1

Ps. 123:1 unto thee lift I up mine *e.*, O thou that dwellest in the heavens; **Isa. 40:26** Lift up your *e.* on high, and behold who hath created these things, that bringeth out their host by number; **Lam. 3:41** let us lift up our heart with our hands unto God in the heavens.

FABLES

For the time will come when they will not endure sound doctrine; but after their own lusts shall they heap to themselves teachers, having itching ears; And they shall turn away their ears from the truth, and shall be turned unto fables. 2 Tim. 4:3-4 (*see also* Doctrine, Ear)

Teach no other doctrine, Neither give heed to fables and endless genealogies, which minister questions, rather than godly edifying which is in faith: so do. 1 Tim. 1:3-4 (*see also* Edify)

FACE

Seek the LORD, and his strength: seek his face evermore. Ps. 105:3-4 (*see also* Seek)

Your iniquities have separated between you and your God, and your sins have hid his face from you, that he will not hear. Isa. 59:2 (*see also* Iniquity, Separate)

I have seen God face to face, and my life is preserved. Gen. 32:24-30 (*see also* Wrestle)

FAIL (*see also* Adversity, Despair, Faint, Oppose)

Rejoice not when thine enemy falleth, and let not thine heart be glad when he stumbleth: Lest the LORD see it, and it displease him, and he turn away his wrath from him. Prov. 24:17-18 (*see also* Enemy, Rejoice)

FAINT (*see also* Endure, Fail)

Men ought always to pray, and not to faint. Luke 18:1 (*see also* Always, Pray)

Wait on the LORD: be of good courage, and he shall strengthen thine heart: wait, I say, on the LORD. Ps. 27:14 (*see also* Wait)

FAITH, FAITHFUL, FAITHFULLY, FAITHFULNESS (*see also* Assure, Belief, Obey, Trust)

He that hath my word, let him speak my word faithfully. Jer. 23:28 (*see also* Speak, Word)

What doth it profit, my brethren, though a man say he hath faith, and have not works? can faith save him? James. 2:14 (*see also* Profit, Save, Works)

If ye have faith as a grain of mustard seed, ye shall say unto this mountain, Remove hence to yonder place; and it shall remove; and nothing shall be impossible unto you. Matt. 17:20 (*see also* Impossible, Seed)

[Look] unto Jesus the author and finisher of our faith; who for the joy that was set before him endured the cross, despising the shame, and is set down at the right hand of the throne of God. Heb. 12:2 (*see also* Author, Finisher, Jesus Christ)

For unto us was the gospel preached, as well as unto them: but the word preached did not profit them, not being mixed with faith in them that heard it. Heb. 4:2 (*see also* Profit)

But without faith it is impossible to please him: for he that cometh to God must believe that he is, and that he is a rewarder of them that diligently seek him. Heb. 11:6 (*see also* Believe, Diligently, Impossible, Reward, Seek)

So must their wives be grave, not slanderers, sober, faithful in all things. 1 Tim. 3:11

I will sing of the mercies of the LORD for ever: with my mouth will I make known thy faithfulness to all generations. Ps. 89:1

Ps. 89:1 I will sing of the mercies of the LORD for ever: with my mouth will I make known thy *f.* to all generations; **89:5** the heavens shall praise thy wonders, O LORD: thy *f.* also in the congregation of the saints; **89:8** O LORD God of hosts, who is a strong LORD like unto thee? or to thy *f.* round about thee; **Isa. 11:5** righteousness shall be the girdle of his loins, and *f.* the girdle of his reins.

For as the body without the spirit is dead, so faith without works is dead also. James 2:26 (*see also* Work)

James 2:14-26 what doth it profit, my brethren, though a man say he hath *f.* and have not works? can *f.* save him... For as the body without the spirit is dead, so *f.* without works is dead also.

Have faith in God. Mark 11:22

Matt. 6:24-32 O ye of little *f.*? Therefore take no thought, saying, What shall we eat? or, What shall we drink? or, Wherewithal shall we be clothed? (For after all these things do the Gentiles seek:) for your heavenly Father knoweth that ye have need of all these things; **8:6-10** I have not found so great *f.*, no, not in Israel; **8:24-26** why are ye fearful, O ye of little *f.*? Then he arose, and rebuked the winds and the sea; and there was a great calm; **9:18** my daughter is even now dead: but come and lay thy hand upon her, and she shall live; **9:20-22** daughter, be of good comfort; thy *f.* hath made thee whole. And the woman was made whole from that hour; **9:27-28** Jesus saith unto them, Believe ye that I am able to do this? They said unto him, Yea, Lord; **14:28-31** immediately Jesus stretched forth his hand, and caught him, and said unto him, O thou of little *f.*, wherefore didst thou doubt; **15:22-28** truth, Lord: yet the dogs eat of the crumbs which fall from their masters' table. Then Jesus answered and said unto her, O woman, great is thy *f.*: be it unto thee even as thou wilt. And her daughter was made whole from that very hour; **16:8-11** O ye of little *f.*, why reason ye among yourselves, because ye have brought no bread; **17:14-20** O faithless and perverse generation, how long shall I be with you? how long shall I suffer you? bring him hither to me. And Jesus rebuked the devil; and he departed out of him: and the child was cured from that very hour; **21:18-21** if ye have *f.*, and doubt not, ye shall not only do this which is done to the fig tree, but also if ye shall say unto this mountain, Be thou removed, and be thou cast into the sea; it shall be done; **24:45** who then is a *f.* and wise servant, whom his lord hath made ruler over his household, to give them meat in due season; **Mark 1:40-42, Luke 5:12-13** If thou wilt, thou canst make me clean. And Jesus, moved with compassion, put forth his hand, and touched him, and saith unto him, I will; be thou clean. And as soon as he had spoken, immediately the leprosy departed from him, and he was cleansed; **2:4-5** when Jesus saw their *f.*, he said unto the sick of the palsy, Son, thy sins be forgiven thee; **4:35-41** why are ye so fearful? how is it that ye have no *f.*? And they feared exceedingly, and said one to another, What manner of man is this, that even the wind and the sea obey him; **5:22-23** my little daughter lieth at the point of death: I pray thee, come and lay thy hands on her, that she may be healed; and she shall live; **5:25-43** he took the damsel by the hand, and said unto her, Talitha cumi; which is,

being interpreted, Damsel, I say unto thee, arise. And straightway the damsel arose, and walked; for she was of the age of twelve years; **6:55-56** besought him that they might touch if it were but the border of his garment: and as many as touched him were made whole; **7:25-30** the devil is gone out of thy daughter. And when she was come to her house, she found the devil gone out, and her daughter laid upon the bed; **8:22-25** after that he put his hands again upon his eyes, and made him look up: and he was restored, and saw every man clearly; **9:17-19** O faithless generation, how long shall I be with you? how long shall I suffer you? bring him unto me; **9:24-29** Jesus took him by the hand, and lifted him up; and he arose. And when he was come into the house, his disciples asked him privately, Why could not we cast him out? And he said unto them, This kind can come forth by nothing, but by prayer and fasting; **10:48-52** Jesus said unto him, Go thy way; thy *f.* hath made thee whole. And immediately he received his sight, and followed Jesus in the way; **11:22-23** have *f.* in God. For verily I say unto you, That whosoever shall say unto this mountain, Be thou removed, and be thou cast into the sea; and shall not doubt in his heart, but shall believe that those things which he saith shall come to pass; he shall have whatsoever he saith; **Luke 1:38** behold the handmaid of the Lord; be it unto me according to thy word. And the angel departed from her; **5:5** master, we have toiled all the night, and have taken nothing: nevertheless at thy word I will let down the net; **5:20** when he saw their *f.*, he said unto him, Man, thy sins are forgiven thee; **6:17** came to hear him, and to be healed of their diseases; **7:2-3** a great multitude of people out of all Judaea and Jerusalem, and from the sea coast of Tyre and Sidon, which came to hear him, and to be healed of their diseases; **7:9** when Jesus heard these things, he marvelled at him, and turned him about, and said unto the people that followed him, I say unto you, I have not found so great *f.*, no, not in Israel; **7:50** he said to the woman, Thy *f.* hath saved thee; go in peace; **8:23-25** where is your *f.*? And they being afraid wondered, saying one to another, What manner of man is this! for he commandeth even the winds and water, and they obey him; **8:41-48** a woman having an issue of blood twelve years, which had spent all her living upon physicians, neither could be healed of any, Came behind him, and touched the border of his garment: and immediately her issue of blood stanched; **8:49-55** thy daughter is dead; trouble not the Master. But when Jesus heard it, he answered him, saying, Fear not: believe only, and she shall be made whole. And when he came into the house, he suffered no man to go in, save Peter, and James, and John, and the father and the mother of the maiden; **9:38-42** O faithless and perverse generation, how long shall I be with you, and suffer you? Bring thy son hither. And as he was yet a coming, the devil threw him down, and tare him. And Jesus rebuked the unclean spirit, and healed the child, and delivered him again to his father; **12:28** if then God so clothe the grass, which is to day in the field, and to morrow is cast into the oven; how much more will he clothe you, O ye of little f.; **14:4** they held their peace. And he took him, and healed him, and let him go; **16:10-12** if ye have not been f. in that which is another man's, who shall give you that which is your own; **17:5-6** Lord, Increase our f.. And the Lord said, If ye had f. as a grain of mustard seed, ye might say unto this sycamine tree, Be thou plucked up by the root, and be thou planted in the sea; and it should obey you; **17:13-14** it came to pass, that, as they went, they were cleansed; **17:19** Arise, go thy way: thy f. hath made thee whole; **18:8** when the Son of man cometh, shall he find f. on the earth; **18:35-42** what wilt thou that I shall do unto thee? And he said, Lord, that I may receive my sight. And Jesus said unto him, Receive thy sight: thy f. hath saved thee; **22:31-32** Simon, behold, Satan hath desired to have you, that he may sift you as wheat: But I have prayed for thee, that thy f. fail not: and when thou art converted, strengthen thy brethren; **John 4:46-47** besought him that he would come down, and heal his son: for he was at the point of death; **4:50-54** thy son liveth: and himself believed, and his whole house. This is again the second miracle that Jesus did; **5:4-9** wilt thou be made whole? The impotent man answered him, Sir, I have no man, when the water is troubled, to put me into the pool: but while I am coming, another steppeth down before me. Jesus saith unto him, Rise, take up thy bed, and walk. And immediately the man was made whole, and took up his bed, and walked; **11:22** I know, that even now, whatsoever thou wilt ask of God, God will give it thee; **20:27** Thomas, Reach hither thy finger, and behold my hands; and reach hither thy hand, and thrust it into my side: and be not faithless, but believing; **Acts 3:16** his name through f. in his name hath made this man strong, whom ye see and know: yea, the f. which is by him hath given him this perfect soundness in the presence of you all; **6:5** they chose Stephen, a man full of f. and of the Holy Ghost; **14:9** beholding him, and perceiving that he had f. to be healed; **14:22** exhorting them to continue in the f., and that we

must through much tribulation enter into the kingdom of God; **14:27** how he had opened the door of f. unto the Gentiles; **15:9** put no difference between us and them, purifying their hearts by f.; **20:21-22** I go bound in the spirit unto Jerusalem, not knowing the things that shall befall me there; **24:24** heard him concerning the f. in Christ; **26:18** to open their eyes, and to turn them from darkness to light, and from the power of Satan unto God, that they may receive forgiveness of sins, and inheritance among them which are sanctified by f. that is in me; **Rom. 1:8** I thank my God through Jesus Christ for you all, that your f. is spoken of throughout the whole world; **1:12** that I may be comforted together with you by the mutual f. both of you and me; **1:16-17** For therein is the righteousness of God revealed from f. to f.: as it is written, The just shall live by f.; **3:3-4** what if some did not believe? shall their unbelief make the f. of God without effect? God forbid; **3:22** even the righteousness of God which is by f. of Jesus Christ unto all and upon all them that believe: for there is no difference; **3:25-31** seeing it is one God, which shall justify the circumcision by f., and uncircumcision through f.. Do we then make void the law through f.? God forbid: yea, we establish the law; **4:9** cometh say that f. was reckoned to Abraham for righteousness; **4:12-15** if they which are of the law be heirs, f. is made void, and the promise this blessedness then upon the circumcision only, or upon the uncircumcision also? for we made of none effect: Because the law worketh wrath: for where no law is, there is no transgression; **4:16** it is of f., that it might be by grace; to the end the promise might be sure to all the seed; not to that only which is of the law, but to that also which is of the f. of Abraham; who is the father of us all; **4:19** being not weak in f., he considered not his own body now dead, when he was about an hundred years old; **5:1-2** being justified by f., we have peace with God through our Lord Jesus Christ: By whom also we have access by f. into this grace wherein we stand, and rejoice in hope of the glory of God; **9:30** the Gentiles, which followed not after righteousness, have attained to righteousness, even the righteousness which is of f.; **9:31-32** Israel, which followed after the law of righteousness, hath not attained to the law of righteousness. Wherefore? Because they sought it not by f., but as it were by the works of the law. For they stumbled at that stumblingstone; **10:6** the righteousness which is of f. speaketh on this wise, Say not in thine heart, Who shall ascend into heaven; **10:8** in thy heart: that is, the word of f., which we preach; **10:17** f. cometh by hearing, and hearing by the word of God; **12:6** let us prophesy according to the proportion of *f*.; **14:22-23** whatsoever is not of *f*. is sin; **1 Cor. 2:5** your *f*. should not stand in the wisdom of men, but in the power of God; **4:2** it is required in stewards, that a man be found *f*.; **16:13** watch ye, stand fast in the *f*., quit you like men, be strong; **2 Cor. 10:15** when your *f*. is increased, that we shall be enlarged by you according to our rule abundantly; **Gal. 2:16** a man is not justified by the works of the law, but by the *f*. of Jesus Christ, even we have believed in Jesus Christ, that we might be justified by the *f*. of Christ, and not by the works of the law: for by the works of the law shall no flesh be justified; **2:20** I now live in the flesh I live by the *f*. of the Son of God, who loved me, and gave himself for me; **3:2** received ye the Spirit by the works of the law, or by the hearing of *f*.; **3:5** he therefore that ministereth to you the Spirit, and worketh miracles among you, doeth he it by the works of the law, or by the hearing of *f*.; **3:7-9** they which are of *f*., the same are the children of Abraham; **3:11-12** the just shall live by *f*.; **3:14** the blessing of Abraham might come on the Gentiles through Jesus Christ; that we might receive the promise of the Spirit through *f*.; **3:22-26** the scripture hath concluded all under sin, that the promise by *f*. of Jesus Christ might be given to them that believe. But before *f*. came, we were kept under the law, shut up unto the *f*. which should afterwards be revealed. Wherefore the law was our schoolmaster to bring us unto Christ, that we might be justified by *f*.. But after that *f*. is come, we are no longer under a schoolmaster. For ye are all the children of God by *f*. in Christ Jesus; **5:6** in Jesus Christ neither circumcision availeth any thing, nor uncircumcision; but *f*. which worketh by love; **Eph. 1:15** I heard of your *f*. in the Lord Jesus, and love unto all the saints; **3:12** in whom we have boldness and access with confidence by the *f*. of him; **3:17** Christ may dwell in your hearts by *f*.; that ye, being rooted and grounded in love; **4:5** one Lord, one *f*., one baptism; **4:13** till we all come in the unity of the *f*., and of the knowledge of the Son of God, unto a perfect man, unto the measure of the stature of the fulness of Christ; **6:16** above all, taking the shield of *f*., wherewith ye shall be able to quench all the fiery darts of the wicked; **6:23** peace be to the brethren, and love with *f*., from God the Father and the Lord Jesus Christ; **Philip. 3:9** that which is through the *f*. of Christ, the righteousness which is of God by *f*.; **Col. 1:4** we heard of your *f*. in Christ Jesus, and of the love which ye have to all the saints; **1:23** if ye continue in the *f*. grounded and settled, and be

not moved away from the hope of the gospel; **2:5** I with you in the spirit, joying and beholding your order, and the stedfastness of your *f*. in Christ; **2:7** rooted and built up in him, and stablished in the *f*., as ye have been taught, abounding therein with thanksgiving; **2:12** ye are risen with him through the *f*. of the operation of God, who hath raised him from the dead; **4:9** a *f*. and beloved brother, who is one of you. They shall make known unto you all things which are done here; **1 Thes. 1:3** remembering without ceasing your work of *f*.; **1:8** in every place your *f*. to God-ward is spread abroad; so that we need not to speak any thing; **3:6** brought us good tidings of your *f*. and charity, and that ye have good remembrance of us always, desiring greatly to see us, as we also to see you; **5:8** let us, who are of the day, be sober, putting on the breastplate of *f*. and love; and for an helmet, the hope of salvation; **2 Thes. 1:3** your *f*. groweth exceedingly, and the charity of every one of you all toward each other aboundeth; **3:2** we may be delivered from unreasonable and wicked men: for all men have not *f*.; **1 Tim. 1:12** I thank Christ Jesus our Lord, who hath enabled me, for that he counted me *f*., putting me into the ministry; **2:15** she shall be saved in childbearing, if they continue in *f*. and charity and holiness with sobriety; **3:9** holding the mystery of the *f*. in a pure conscience; **4:12** let no man despise thy youth; but be thou an example of the believers, in word, in conversation, in charity, in spirit, in *f*., in purity; **6:10-11** follow after righteousness, godliness, *f*., love, patience, meekness; **2 Tim. 1:5** I call to remembrance the unfeigned *f*. that is in thee; **2:22** flee also youthful lusts: but follow righteousness, *f*., charity, peace, with them that call on the Lord out of a pure heart; **3:10** thou hast fully known my doctrine, manner of life, purpose, *f*., longsuffering, charity, patience; **3:15** from a child thou hast known the holy scriptures, which are able to make thee wise unto salvation through *f*. which is in Christ Jesus; **4:7** I have fought a good fight, I have finished my course, I have kept the *f*.; **Philem. 1:6** the communication of thy *f*. may become effectual by the acknowledging of every good thing which is in you in Christ Jesus; **Heb. 4:2** the word preached did not profit them, not being mixed with *f*. in them that heard it; **6:12** ye be not slothful, but followers of them who through *f*. and patience inherit the promises; **10:22-23** let us draw near with a true heart in full assurance of *f*., having our hearts sprinkled from an evil conscience, and our bodies washed with pure water. Let us hold fast the profession of our *f*. without wavering;

(for he is *f.* that promised); **10:38-39** the just shall live by *f.*: but if any man draw back, my soul shall have no pleasure in him; **11:1-40** *f.* is the substance of things hoped for, the evidence of things not seen; **12:2** looking unto Jesus the author and finisher of our *f.*; **1:2-3** the trying of your *f.* worketh patience; **1:6** let him ask in *f.*, nothing wavering. For he that wavereth is like a wave of the sea driven with the wind and tossed; **2:14-26** what doth it profit, my brethren, though a man say he hath *f.*, and have not works; **1 Pet. 1:5-7** the trial of your *f.*, being much more precious than of gold that perisheth, though it be tried with fire, might be found unto praise and honour and glory at the appearing of Jesus Christ; **1:9** receiving the end of your *f.*, even the salvation of your souls; **1:21** that your *f.* and hope might be in God; **2 Pet. 1:1** to them that have obtained like precious *f.* with us through the righteousness of God and our Saviour Jesus Christ; **1:5** add to your *f.* virtue; and to virtue knowledge; **Rev. 2:19** I know thy works, and charity, and service, and *f.*, and thy patience, and thy works; and the last to be more than the first; **14:12** here is the patience of the saints: here are they that keep the commandments of God, and the *f.* of Jesus.

FAITHLESS (*see also* Unbelief)

Then saith he to Thomas, Reach hither thy finger, and behold my hands; and reach hither thy hand, and thrust it into my side: and be not faithless, but believing. John 20:27 (*see also* Unbelief)

FALL, FALLEN, FELL (*see also* Apostasy, Carnal, Death)

Stand fast therefore in the liberty wherewith Christ hath made us free, and be not entangled again with the yoke of bondage. Gal. 5:1 (*see also* Liberty, Stand)

After that ye have known God, or rather are known of God, how turn ye again to the weak and beggarly elements, whereunto ye desire again to be in bondage? Gal. 4:9 (*see also* Bondage)

Rom. 1:18-19 the wrath of God is revealed from heaven against all ungodliness and unrighteousness of men, who hold the truth in unrighteousness; Because that which may be known of God is manifest in them; for God hath shewed it unto them; **1:21** when they knew God, they glorified

him not as God, neither were thankful; but became vain in their imaginations, and their foolish heart was darkened; **2:8-9** But unto them that are contentious, and do not obey the truth, but obey unrighteousness, indignation and wrath, Tribulation and anguish, upon every soul of man that doeth evil, of the Jew first, and also of the Gentile; **2:12-13** as many as have sinned without law shall also perish without law: and as many as have sinned in the law shall be judged by the law; (For not the hearers of the law are just before God, but the doers of the law shall be justified; **1 Cor. 8:10-12** if any man see thee which hast knowledge sit at meat in the idol's temple, shall not the conscience of him which is weak be emboldened to eat those things which are offered to idols; And through thy knowledge shall the weak brother perish, for whom Christ died? But when ye sin so against the brethren, and wound their weak conscience, ye sin against Christ; **10:12** let him that thinketh he standeth take heed lest he *f.*; **2 Cor. 6:1** we then, as workers together with him, beseech you also that ye receive not the grace of God in vain; **10:5** casting down imaginations, and every high thing that exalteth itself against the knowledge of God, and bringing into captivity every thought to the obedience of Christ; **Gal. 3:1-4** are ye so foolish? having begun in the Spirit, are ye now made perfect by the flesh? Have ye suffered so many things in vain? if it be yet in vain; **4:9** now, after that ye have known God, or rather are known of God, how turn ye again to the weak and beggarly elements, whereunto ye desire again to be in bondage; **5:1** stand fast therefore in the liberty wherewith Christ hath made us free, and be not entangled again with the yoke of bondage; **5:7** ye did run well; who did hinder you that ye should not obey the truth; **Col 1:23** if ye continue in the faith grounded and settled, and be not moved away from the hope of the gospel, which ye have heard, and which was preached to every creature which is under heaven; **1 Thes. 5:19** quench not the Spirit; **2 Tim. 3:14** continue thou in the things which thou hast learned and hast been assured of, knowing of whom thou hast learned them; **Titus 1:9** holding fast the faithful word as he hath been taught, that he may be able by sound doctrine both to exhort and to convince the gainsayers; **Heb. 2:1-3** we ought to give the more earnest heed to the things which we have heard, lest at any time we should let them slip. For if the word spoken by angels was stedfast, and every transgression and disobedience received a just recompence of reward; How shall we escape, if we neglect so great salvation; which at the first began to be spoken by the Lord, and was confirmed unto us by them that heard him; **3:12-14** take heed, brethren, lest there be in any of you an evil heart of unbelief, in departing from the living God. But exhort one another daily, while it is called To day; lest any of you be hardened through the deceitfulness of sin. For we are made partakers of Christ, if we hold the beginning of our confidence stedfast unto the end; **6:4-8** it is impossible for those who were once enlightened, and have tasted of the heavenly gift, and were made partakers of the Holy Ghost, And have tasted the good word of God, and the powers of the world to come, If they shall *f.* away, to renew them again unto repentance; seeing they crucify to themselves the Son of God afresh, and put him to an open shame; **10:26-27** if we sin wilfully after that we have received the knowledge of the truth, there remaineth no more sacrifice for sins, But a certain fearful looking for of judgment and fiery indignation, which shall devour the adversaries; **10:29** of how much sorer punishment, suppose ye, shall he be thought worthy, who hath trodden under foot the Son of God, and hath counted the blood of the covenant, wherewith he was sanctified, an unholy thing, and hath done despite unto the Spirit of grace; **10:35** cast not away therefore your confidence, which hath great recompence of reward; **12:3** consider him that endured such contradiction of sinners against himself, lest ye be wearied and faint in your minds; **James 4:17** to him that knoweth to do good, and doeth it not, to him it is sin; **1 Pet. 1:14** obedient children, not fashioning yourselves according to the former lusts in your ignorance; **2 Pet. 1:9** he that lacketh these things is blind, and cannot see afar off, and hath forgotten that he was purged from his old sins; **2:20-22** if after they have escaped the pollutions of the world through the knowledge of the Lord and Saviour Jesus Christ, they are again entangled therein, and overcome, the latter end is worse with them than the beginning. For it had been better for them not to have known the way of righteousness, than, after they have known it, to turn from the holy commandment delivered unto them. But it is happened unto them according to the true proverb, The dog is turned to his own vomit again; and the sow that was washed to her wallowing in the mire; **3:17** seeing ye know these things before, beware lest ye also, being led away with the error of the wicked, *f.* from your own stedfastness; **1 Jn. 2:24-25** if that which ye have heard from the beginning shall remain in you, ye also shall continue in the Son,

and in the Father. And this is the promise that he hath promised us, even eternal life; **2 Jn. 1:8** look to yourselves, that we lose not those things which we have wrought, but that we receive a full reward; **Jude 1:6** the angels which kept not their first estate, but left their own habitation, he hath reserved in everlasting chains under darkness unto the judgment of the great day; **Rev. 2:24-25** as many as have not this doctrine, and which have not known the depths of Satan, as they speak; I will put upon you none other burden. But that which ye have already hold fast till I come; **3:3** remember therefore how thou hast received and heard, and hold fast, and repent. If therefore thou shalt not watch, I will come on thee as a thief, and thou shalt not know what hour I will come upon thee; **3:11** behold, I come quickly: hold that fast which thou hast, that no man take thy crown.

FALLING AWAY (*see also* Apostasy)

Let no man deceive you by any means: for that day shall not come, except there come a falling away first, and that man of sin be revealed, the son of perdition; who opposeth and exalteth himself above all that is called God, or that is worshiped; so that he as God sitteth in the temple of God, shewing himself that he is God. 2 Thes. 2:3-4 (*see also* Apostasy, Second Coming)

FALSE, FALSEHOOD, FALSELY (*see also* Deceit, Gossip, Hypocrisy, Lie, Wrong)

Do violence to no man, neither accuse any falsely; and be content with your wages. Luke 3:14 (*see also* Accuse)

There shall be false teachers among you, who privily shall bring in damnable heresies. 2 Pet. 2:1 (*see also* Teacher)

When ye offer your gifts, when ye make your sons to pass through the fire, ye pollute yourselves with all your idols, even unto this day. Ezek. 20:31 (*see also* Sacrifice)

Be not a witness against thy neighbour without cause; and deceive not with thy lips. Prov. 24:28 (*see also* Deceive)

A false witness shall not be unpunished, and he that speaketh lies shall not escape. Prov. 19:5 (*see also* Accusation, Deceive, Liar)

As for our iniquities, we know them: in transgressing and lying against the LORD, and departing away from our God, speaking oppression and revolt, conceiving and uttering from the heart words of falsehood. Isa. 59:12-13 (*see also* Heart, Word)

We will not serve thy gods, nor worship the golden image which thou hast set up. Dan. 3:18 (*see also* Belief)

Jer. 10:5-6 be not afraid of them; for they cannot do evil, neither also is it in them to do good. Forasmuch as there is none like unto thee, O LORD; thou art great, and thy name is great in might; 10:11 the gods that have not made the heavens and the earth, even they shall perish from the earth, and from under these heavens; 19:4 they have forsaken me, and have estranged this place, and have burned incense in it unto other gods, whom neither they nor their fathers have known; 22:9-12 they have forsaken the covenant of the LORD their God, and worshipped other gods, and served them; 25:6 go not after other gods to serve them, and to worship them, and provoke me not to anger with the works of your hands; and I will do you no hurt; 32:29 [they] shall come and set fire on this city, and burn it with the houses, upon whose roofs they have offered incense unto Baal, and poured out drink offerings unto other gods, to provoke me to anger; 32:31 this city hath been to me as a provocation of mine anger and of my fury from the day that they built it even unto this day; that I should remove it from before my face; 44:3 they have committed to provoke me to anger, in that they went to burn incense, and to serve other gods, whom they knew not, neither they, ye, nor your fathers; Dan. 3:18 be it known unto thee, O king, that we will not serve thy gods, nor worship the golden image which thou hast set up.

Hearken not unto the words of [false] prophets that prophecy unto you; they make you vain; they speak a vision of their own heart and not out of the mouth of the LORD. Jer. 23:16 (*see also* False Prophet)

Jer. 23:16 hearken not unto the words of the prophets that prophesy unto you: they make you vain: they speak a vision of their own heart, and not out of the mouth of the LORD; 26:15 if ye put me to death, ye shall surely bring innocent blood upon yourselves, and upon this city, and upon the inhabitants thereof: for of a truth the LORD hath sent me unto you to speak all these words

in your ears; 29:21 thus saith the LORD of hosts, the God of Israel, of [those] which prophesy a lie unto you in my name; Behold, I will deliver them into the hand of Nebuchadrezzar king of Babylon; and he shall slay them; 50:6-7 my people hath been lost sheep: their shepherds have caused them to go astray, they have turned them away on the mountains: they have gone from mountain to hill, they have forgotten their restingplace.

This is thy lot, the portion of thy measures from me, saith the LORD; because thou hast forgotten me, and trusted in falsehood. Jer. 13:25 (*see also* Trust)

Jer. 13:22 if thou say in thine heart, Wherefore come these things upon me? For the greatness of thine iniquity are thy skirts discovered, and thy heels made bare; 13:25 this is thy lot, the portion of thy measures from me, saith the LORD; because thou hast forgotten me, and trusted in f.; 43:9 take great stones in thine hand, and hide them in the clay in the brickkiln, which is at the entry of Pharaohs house in Tahpanhes, in the sight of the men of Judah; Ezek. 12:24 there shall be no more any vain vision nor flattering divination within the house of Israel.

FALSE CHRIST

If any man shall say unto you, Lo, here is Christ, or there; believe it not. For there shall arise false Christs, and false prophets, and shall shew great signs and wonders; insomuch that, if it were possible, they shall deceive the very elect. Matt. 24:23-24 (*see also* Christ, Deceive, False Prophet)

False Christs and false prophets shall rise, and shall shew signs and wonders, to seduce, if it were possible, even the elect. Mark 13:22 (*see also* Elect, False Prophet, Seduce, Sign, Wonder)

FALSE DOCTRINE (*see also* False)

Be not carried about with divers and strange doctrines. For it is a good thing that the heart be established with grace; not with meats, which have not profited them that have been occupied therein. Heb. 13:9 (*see also* Doctrine, Teach)

Matt. 16:11-12 ye should beware of the leaven of the Pharisees and of the Sadducees? Then understood they how that he bade them not beware of the leaven of bread, but of the doctrine of the Pharisees and of the Sadducees; **Acts 13:8** Elymas the sorcerer (for so is his name by interpretation) withstood them, seeking to turn away the deputy from the faith; **1 Tim. 4:1-2** the Spirit speaketh expressly, that in the latter times some shall depart from the faith, giving heed to seducing spirits, and doctrines of devils; Speaking lies in hypocrisy; having their conscience seared with a hot iron; **6:21** some professing have erred concerning the faith; **Heb. 13:9** be not carried about with divers and strange doctrines. For it is a good thing that the heart be established with grace; not with meats, which have not profited them that have been occupied therein; **1 Jn. 2:19** they went out from us, but they were not of us; for if they had been of us, they would no doubt have continued with us: but they went out, that they might be made manifest that they were not all of us; **4:3** very spirit that confesseth not that Jesus Christ is come in the flesh is not of God: and this is that spirit of antichrist, whereof ye have heard that it should come; and even now already is it in the world; **2 Jn. 1:10-11** if there come any unto you, and bring not this doctrine, receive him not into your house, neither bid him God speed.

FALSE PROPHET (*see also* Priestcraft)

False Christs and false prophets shall rise, and shall shew signs and wonders, to seduce, if it were possible, even the elect. Mark 13:22 (*see also* Elect, False Christ, Seduce, Sign, Wonder)

If any man shall say unto you, Lo, here is Christ, or there; believe it not. For there shall arise false Christs, and false prophets, and shall shew great signs and wonders; insomuch that, if it were possible, they shall deceive the very elect. Matt. 24:23-24 (*see also* Christ, Deceive, False Christ)

Not every one that saith unto me, Lord, Lord, shall enter into the kingdom of heaven; but he that doeth the will of my Father who is in heaven. Many will say to me in that day: Lord, Lord, have we not prophesied in thy name, and in thy name have cast out devils, and in thy name done many wonderful works? And then will I profess unto them: I never knew you; depart from me, ye that work iniquity. Matt. 7:21-23 (*see also* Father, Priestcraft, Will, Wonderful)

Beware of false prophets, which come to you in sheep's clothing, but inwardly they are ravening wolves. Ye shall know them by their fruits. Matt. 7:15-16 (*see also* Deceive)

Matt. 7:15-20 beware of *f.p.*, which come to you in sheep's clothing, but inwardly they are ravening wolves. Ye shall know them by their fruits. Do men gather grapes of thorns, or figs of thistles? Even so every good tree bringeth forth good fruit; but a corrupt tree bringeth forth evil fruit. A good tree cannot bring forth evil fruit, neither can a corrupt tree bring forth good fruit. Every tree that bringeth not forth good fruit is hewn down, and cast into the fire. Wherefore by their fruits ye shall know them; **24:11** many *f.p.* shall rise, and shall deceive many; **24:24** there shall arise *f.* Christs, and *f.p.*, and shall shew great signs and wonders; Insomuch that, if it were possible, they shall deceive the very elect; **Mark 13:22** *f.* Christs and *f.p.* shall rise, and shall shew signs and wonders, to seduce, if it were possible, even the elect; **Luke 6:26** woe unto you, when all men shall speak well of you! for so did their fathers to the *f.p.*; **Acts 13:6** they found a certain sorcerer, a *f.p.*, a Jew, whose name was Bar-jesus; **20:29-30** after my departing shall grievous wolves enter in among you, not sparing the flock. Also of your own selves shall men arise, speaking perverse things, to draw away disciples after them; **2 Cor. 11:4** if he that cometh preacheth another Jesus, whom we have not preached, or if ye receive another spirit, which ye have not received, or another gospel, which ye have not accepted, ye might well bear with him; **11:13-15** such are *f.* apostles, deceitful workers, transforming themselves into the apostles of Christ. And no marvel; for Satan himself is transformed into an angel of light. Therefore it is no great thing if his ministers also be transformed as the ministers of righteousness; whose end shall be according to their works; **Col. 2:4-8** beware lest any man spoil you through philosophy and vain deceit, after the tradition of men, after the rudiments of the world, and not after Christ; **2 Pet. 2:1-4** there were *f.p.* also among the people, even as there shall be *f.* teachers among you, who privily shall bring in damnable heresies, even denying the Lord that bought them, and bring upon themselves swift destruction. And many shall follow their pernicious ways; by reason of whom the way of truth shall be evil spoken of. And through covetousness shall they with feigned words make merchandise of you: whose judgment now of a long time lingereth not, and their damnation slumbereth not. For if God spared not the angels that sinned, but cast them down to hell, and delivered them into chains of darkness, to be reserved unto judgment; **1 Jn. 4:1** believe not every spirit, but try the spirits whether they are of God: because many *f.p.* are gone out into the world; **Rev. 2:20** I have a few things against thee, because thou sufferest that woman Jezebel, which calleth herself a prophetess, to teach and to seduce my servants to commit fornication, and to eat things sacrificed unto idols; **19:20** the beast was taken, and with him the *f.p.* that wrought miracles before him, with which he deceived them that had received the mark of the beast, and them that worshipped his image. These both were cast alive into a lake of fire burning with brimstone.

FALSE WITNESS (*see also* False, Lie, Slander)

These six things doth the LORD hate: yea, seven are an abomination unto him: A proud look, a lying tongue, and hands that shed innocent blood, An heart that deviseth wicked imaginations, feet that be swift in running to mischief, A false witness that speaketh lies, and he that soweth discord among brethren. Prov. 6:16-19 (*see also* Discord, Imagine, Innocent, Mischief, Pride)

Thou shalt not bear false witness against thy neighbour. Ex. 20:16 (*see also* Neighbor, Thous Shalt Not, Witness)

Ex. 20:16 thou shalt not bear false witness against thy neighbour; **23:1** thou shalt not raise a *f.* report: put not thine hand with the wicked to be an unrighteous witness; **Lev. 6:2-5** if a soul sin, and commit a trespass against the **LORD**, and lie unto his neighbour in that which was delivered him to keep, or in fellowship, or in a thing taken away by violence, or hath deceived his neighbour; Or have found that which was lost, and lieth concerning it, and sweareth *f.*; in any of all these that a man doeth, sinning therein: Then it shall be, because he hath sinned, and is guilty, that he shall restore that which he took violently away; **Deut. 5:20** neither shalt thou bear *f.w.* against thy neighbour; **19:16-19** if a *f.w.* rise up against any man to testify against him that which is wrong; Then both the men, between whom the controversy is, shall stand before the **LORD**; **Ps. 35:11** *f.w.* did rise up; they

laid to my charge things that I knew not; **Prov. 6:19** a *f.w.* that speaketh lies, and he that soweth discord among brethren; **12:17** he that speaketh truth sheweth forth righteousness: but a *f.w.* deceit; **14:5** a faithful witness will not lie: but a *f.w.* will utter lies; **19:5** a *f.w.* shall not be unpunished, and he that speaketh lies shall not escape; **19:9** a *f.w.* shall not be unpunished, and he that speaketh lies shall perish; **19:28** an ungodly witness scorneth judgment: and the mouth of the wicked devoureth iniquity; **21:28** a *f.w.* shall perish: but the man that heareth speaketh constantly; **25:18** a man that beareth *f.w.* against his neighbour is a maul, and a sword, and a sharp arrow; **Matt. 15:19-20** for out of the heart proceed evil thoughts, murders, adulteries, fornications, thefts, *f.w.*, blasphemies: These are the things which defile a man; **19:18** Thou shalt not bear *f.w.*; **26:59-62** the chief priests, and elders, and all the council, sought *f.w.* against Jesus, to put him to death; But found none: yea, though many *f.w.* came, yet found they none. At the last came two *f.w.*; **27:13** hearest thou not how many things they witness against thee; **Mark 10:19** do not bear *f.w.*; **14:55-59** the chief priests and all the council sought for witness against Jesus to put him to death; and found none. For many bare *f.w.* against him, but their witness agreed not together. And there arose certain, and bare *f.w.* against him, saying, We heard him say, I will destroy this temple that is made with hands, and within three days I will build another made without hands. But neither so did their witness agree together; **14:60** asked Jesus, saying, Answerest thou nothing? what is it which these witness against thee; **Luke 18:20** do not bear *f.w.*; **23:2** they began to accuse him, saying, We found this fellow perverting the nation, and forbidding to give tribute to Caesar, saying that he himself is Christ a King; **23:9-10** he questioned with him in many words; but he answered him nothing. And the chief priests and scribes stood and vehemently accused him; **23:14** Ye have brought this man unto me, as one that perverteth the people: and, behold, I, having examined him before you, have found no fault in this man touching those things whereof ye accuse him; **Rom. 13:9** Thou shalt not bear *f.w.*, Thou shalt not covet; and if there be any other commandment, it is briefly comprehended in this saying, namely, Thou shalt love thy neighbour as thyself.

FAMILIAR (*see also* Evil, Superstitious, Unclean)

When they shall say unto you, Seek unto them that have familiar spirits, and unto wizards that peep, and that mutter: should not a people seek unto their God? Isa. 8:19 (*see also* Seek, Wizards)

Isa. 8:19-22 when they shall say unto you, Seek unto them that have familiar spirits, and unto wizards that peep, and that mutter: should not a people seek unto their God; **19:3** the spirit of Egypt shall fail in the midst thereof; and I will destroy the counsel thereof: and they shall seek to the idols, and to the charmers, and to them that have *f.* spirits, and to the wizards.

Regard not them that have familiar spirits, neither seek after wizards, to be defiled by them: I am the LORD your God. Lev. 19:31

Lev. 19:31 regard not them that have *f.* spirits, neither seek after wizards, to be defiled by them: I am the LORD your God; **20:6** the soul that turneth after such as have *f.* spirits, and after wizards, to go a whoring after them, I will even set my face against that soul, and will cut him off from among his people; **20:27** a man also or woman that hath a *f.* spirit, or that is a wizard, shall surely be put to death; **Deut. 18:10-12** there shall not be found among you any one that maketh his son or his daughter to pass through the fire, or that useth divination, or an observer of times, or an enchanter, or a witch, Or a charmer, or a consulter with *f.* spirits, or a wizard, or a necromancer. For all that do these things are an abomination unto the LORD; **1 Sam. 28:3** Saul had put away those that had *f.* spirits, and the wizards, out of the land; **28:9** he hath cut off those that have *f.* spirits, and the wizards, out of the land: wherefore then layest thou a snare for my life, to cause me to die; **2 Kgs. 21:6** he made his son pass through the fire, and observed times, and used enchantments, and dealt with *f.* spirits and wizards: he wrought much wickedness in the sight of the LORD, to provoke him to anger; **23:24** the workers with *f.* spirits, and the wizards, and the images, and the idols, and all the abominations that were spied in the land of Judah and in Jerusalem, did Josiah put away; **1 Chron. 10:13** Saul died for his transgression which he committed against the LORD, even against the word of the LORD, which he kept not, and also for asking counsel of one that had a *f.*

spirit, to enquire of it; **2 Chron. 33:6** he observed times, and used enchantments, and used witchcraft, and dealt with a *f.* spirit, and with wizards: he wrought much evil in the sight of the LORD, to provoke him to anger; **Ps. 119:1** blessed are the undefiled in the way, who walk in the law of the LORD; **Isa. 8:19** seek unto them that have *f.* spirits, and unto wizards that peep, and that mutter: should not a people seek unto their God; **19:3** they shall seek to the idols, and to the charmers, and to them that have *f.* spirits, and to the wizards; **47:9** the loss of children, and widowhood: they shall come upon thee in their perfection for the multitude of thy sorceries, and for the great abundance of thine enchantments; **47:12** stand now with thine enchantments, and with the multitude of thy sorceries, wherein thou hast laboured from thy youth; **Jer. 2:7** I brought you into a plentiful country, to eat the fruit thereof and the goodness thereof; but when ye entered, ye defiled my land, and made mine heritage an abomination; **Ezek. 36:17** when the house of Israel dwelt in their own land, they defiled it by their own way and by their doings; **Micah 5:12** I will cut off witchcrafts out of thine hand; and thou shalt have no more soothsayers; **Mal. 3:5** I will come near to you to judgment; and I will be a swift witness against the sorcerers, and against the adulterers, and against false swearers.

FAMILY (*see* Children, Father, Genealogy, Marriage, Mother)

FASHION

The fashion of this world passeth away. 1 Cor. 7:31

FAST, FASTING (*see also* Sacrifice)

When thou fasteth, anoint thine head, and wash thy face; That thou appear not unto men to fast, but unto thy Father which is in secret; and thy Father, which seeth in secret, shall reward thee openly. Matt. 6:17-18 (*see also* Appear, Secret)

When they were sick, my clothing was sackcloth: I humbled my soul with fasting; and my prayer returned into mine own bosom. I behaved myself as though he had been my friend or brother: I bowed down heavily, as one that mourneth for his mother. Ps. 35:13-14 (*see also* Humble)

[She] served God with fasting and prayers night and day. Luke 2:37 (*see also* Pray)

Turn ye even to me with all your heart, and with fasting, and with weeping, and with mourning: And rend your heart, and not your garments, and turn unto the LORD your God: for he is gracious and merciful, slow to anger, and of great kindness, and repenteth him of the evil. Joel 2:12-13 (*see also* Heart, Turn)

When ye fast, be not, as the hypocrites, of a sad countenance: for they disfigure their faces, that they may appear unto men to fast. Verily I say unto you, They have their reward. Matt. 6:16 (*see also* Pray)

Matt. 6:16 moreover when ye *f.*, be not, as the hypocrites, of a sad countenance: for they disfigure their faces, that they may appear unto men to *f.*. Verily I say unto you, They have their reward; **9:14-15** (Mark 2:18-20, Luke 5:33-35) why do we and the Pharisees *f.* oft, but thy disciples *f.* not? And Jesus said unto them, Can the children of the bridechamber mourn, as long as the bridegroom is with them? but the days will come, when the bridegroom shall be taken from them, and then shall they *f.*; **17:21** (Mark 9:29) howbeit this kind goeth not out but by prayer and *f.*; **Luke 2:37** she was a widow of about fourscore and four years, which departed not from the temple, but served God with *f.* and prayers night and day; **Acts 10:30** I was *f.* until this hour; and at the ninth hour I prayed in my house, and, behold, a man stood before me in bright clothing; **14:23** when they had ordained them elders in every church, and had prayed with *f.*, they commended them to the Lord, on whom they believed; **27:33** Paul besought them all to take meat, saying, This day is the fourteenth day that ye have tarried and continued *f.*, having taken nothing; **1 Cor. 7:5** defraud ye not one the other, except it be with consent for a time, that ye may give yourselves to *f.* and prayer; and come together again, that Satan tempt you not for your incontinency.

I proclaimed a fast there, at the river of Ahava, that we might afflict ourselves before our God, to seek of him a right way for us, and for our little ones, and for all our substance. Ezra 8:21-23 (*see also* Way)

Judg. 20:26 all the children of Israel, and all the people, went up, and came unto the house of God, and wept, and sat there before the LORD, and fasted that day until even; **1 Sam. 1:7** when she went up to the house of the LORD, so she provoked her; therefore she wept, and did not eat; **7:6** they gathered together... and *f.* on that day, and said there, We have sinned against the LORD; **31:13** they took their bones, and buried them under a tree at Jabesh, and *f.* seven days; **2 Sam. 1:12** they mourned, and wept, and *f.* until even, for Saul, and for Jonathan his son, and for the people of the LORD, and for the house of Israel; **12:16** David therefore besought God for the child; and David *f.*, and went in, and lay all night upon the earth; **12:21-23** while the child was yet alive, I *f.* and wept: for I said, Who can tell whether GOD will be gracious to me, that the child may live? But now he is dead, wherefore should I *f.*? can I bring him back again; **1 Kgs. 21:9** proclaim a *f.*, and set Naboth on high among the people; **21:12** they proclaimed a *f.*, and set Naboth on high among the people; **21:27** he rent his clothes, and put sackcloth upon his flesh, and *f.*, and lay in sackcloth, and went softly; **1 Chron. 10:12** they arose, all the valiant men, and took away the body of Saul, and the bodies of his sons, and brought them to Jabesh, and buried their bones under the oak in Jabesh, and *f.* seven days; **2 Chron. 20:3** Jehoshaphat feared, and set himself to seek the LORD, and proclaimed a *f.* throughout all Judah; **Ezra 8:21-23** I proclaimed a *f.* there, at the river of Ahava, that we might afflict ourselves before our God, to seek of him a right way for us, and for our little ones, and for all our substance; **Neh. 1:4** I sat down and wept, and mourned certain days, and *f.*, and prayed before the God of heaven; **Esth. 4:3** whithersoever the kings commandment and his decree came, there was great mourning among the Jews, and *f.*, and weeping, and wailing; **4:16** *f.* ye for me, and neither eat nor drink three days, night or day: I also and my maidens will *f.* likewise; and so will I go in unto the king, which is not according to the law; **Ps. 109:24** my knees are weak through *f.*; and my flesh faileth of fatness; **Isa. 58:3-12** wilt thou call this a *f.*, and an acceptable day to the LORD? Is not this the *f.* that I have chosen? to loose the bands of wickedness, to undo the heavy burdens, and to let the oppressed go free, and that ye break every yoke? Is it not to deal thy bread to the hungry, and that thou bring the poor that are cast out to thy house; **Jer. 14:12** when they *f.*, I will not hear their cry; and when they offer burnt offering and an oblation, I will not accept them: but I will consume them; **36:9** they proclaimed a *f.* before the LORD to all the people in Jerusalem, and to all the people that came from the cities of Judah unto Jerusalem; **Dan. 6:18** the king went to his palace, and passed the night *f*.: neither were instruments of musick brought before him: and his sleep went from him; **Joel 1:14** sanctify ye a *f*., call a solemn assembly, gather the elders and all the inhabitants of the land into the house of the LORD your God, and cry unto the LORD; **2:15** blow the trumpet in Zion, sanctify a *f*., call a solemn assembly; **Jonah 3:5-7** the people of Nineveh believed God, and proclaimed a *f*....by the decree of the king and his nobles, saying, Let neither man nor beast, herd nor flock, taste any thing: let them not feed, nor drink water; **Zech. 7:5-6** when ye *f*. and mourned in the fifth and seventh month, even those seventy years, did ye at all *f*. unto me, even to me; **8:19** the *f*. of the fourth month, and the *f*. of the fifth, and the *f*. of the seventh, and the *f*. of the tenth, shall be to the house of Judah joy and gladness, and cheerful feasts.

FATHER (*see also* Marriage, Parent)

He that heareth my word, and believeth on him that sent me, hath everlasting life, and shall not come into condemnation; but is passed from death unto life. John 5:24 (*see also* Everlasting Life)

The God of our Lord Jesus Christ, the Father of glory, may give unto you the spirit of wisdom and revelation in the knowledge of him: The eyes of your understanding being enlightened; that ye may know what is the hope of his calling, and what the riches of the glory of his inheritance in the saints. Eph. 1:17-18 (*see also* Hope, Reveal, Wisdom)

Not every one that saith unto me, Lord, Lord, shall enter into the kingdom of heaven; but he that doeth the will of my Father who is in heaven. Many will say to me in that day: Lord, Lord, have we not prophesied in thy name, and in thy name have cast out devils, and in thy name done many wonderful works? And then will I profess unto them: I never knew you; depart from me, ye that work iniquity. Matt. 7:21-23 (*see also* False Prophets, Priestcraft, Will, Wonderful)

For unto us a child is born, unto us a son is given: and the government shall be upon his shoulder: and his name shall be called, Wonderful, Counsellor, The mighty God, The everlasting Father, The Prince of Peace. Isa. 9:6 (*see also* Counselor, Government, Peace, Wonderful)

For as many as are led by the Spirit of God, they are the sons of God. For ye have not received the spirit of bondage again to fear; but ye have received the Spirit of adoption, whereby we cry, Abba, Father. The Spirit itself beareth witness with our spirit, that we are the children of God: And if children, then heirs; heirs of God, and joint-heirs with Christ; if so be that we suffer with him, that we may be also glorified together. For I reckon that the sufferings of this present time are not worthy to be compared with the glory which shall be revealed in us. Rom 8:14-18 (*see also* Adopt, Heir)

Call no man your father upon the earth: for one is your Father, which is in heaven. Matt. 23:9 (*see also* Call)

Come out from among them, and be ye separate, saith the Lord, and touch not the unclean thing; and I will receive you, And will be a Father unto you, and ye shall be my sons and daughters. 2 Cor. 6:17 (*see also* Unclean)

Be ye therefore perfect, even as your Father in heaven is perfect. Matt. 5:48 (*see also* Perfect)

Whoso curseth his father or his mother, his lamp shall be put out in obscure darkness. Prov. 20:20 (*see also* Curse, Mother)

These things have I spoken unto you in proverbs: but the time cometh, when I shall no more speak unto you in proverbs, but I shall shew you plainly of the Father. John 16:25 (*see also* Plain, Speak)

Honour thy father and thy mother, as the LORD thy God hath commanded thee; that thy days may be prolonged, and that it may go well with thee, in the land which the LORD thy God giveth thee. Deut. 5:16 (*see also* Go, Honor, Mother)

FATHERLESS

Pure religion and undefiled before God and the Father is this, To visit the fatherless and widows in their affliction, and to keep himself unspotted from the world. James 1:27 (*see also* Widow)

Oppress not the widow, nor the fatherless, the stranger, nor the poor; and let none of you imagine evil against his brother in your heart. Zech. 7:10 (*see also* Oppress, Stranger, Widow)

Isa. 1:23 every one loveth gifts, and followeth after rewards: they judge not the fatherless, neither doth the cause of the widow come unto them; **Jer. 7:6-7** oppress not the stranger, the fatherless, and the widow, and shed not innocent blood in this place, neither walk after other gods to your hurt; **Ezek. 22:7** in thee have they vexed the fatherless and the widow; **22:29** the people of the land have used oppression, and exercised robbery, and have vexed the poor and needy: yea, they have oppressed the stranger wrongfully; **Zech. 7:10** oppress not the widow, nor the *f.*, the stranger, nor the poor; and let none of you imagine evil against his brother in your heart; **Mal. 3:5** I will come near to you to judgment; and I will be a swift witness against the sorcerers, and against the adulterers, and against false swearers, and against those that oppress the hireling in his wages, the widow, and the *f.*

FAVOR, FAVORED

Whoso findeth a wife findeth a good thing, and obtaineth favour of the LORD. Prov. 18:22 (*see also* Wife)

Jesus increased in wisdom and stature, and in favour with God and man. Luke 2:52 (*see also* Increase, Jesus Christ, Stature, Wisdom)

FEAR, FEARFUL, FEARFULNESS (*see also* Afraid, Evil, Wicked)

Teach me thy way, O LORD; I will walk in thy truth: unite my heart to fear thy name. Ps. 86:11 (*see also* Truth, Way)

Fear none of those things which thou shalt suffer: behold, the devil shall cast some of you into prison, that ye may be tried; and ye shall have tribulation ten days: be thou faithful unto death, and I will give thee a crown of life. Rev. 2:10 (*see also* Crown, Trial, Tribulation)

The fear of the LORD is to hate evil: pride, and arrogancy, and the evil way, and the froward mouth, do I hate. Prov. 8:13 (*see also* Arrogance, Evil, Hate)

Many of the brethren in the Lord, waxing confident by my bonds, are much more bold to speak the word without fear. Philip. 1:14

Let not thine heart envy sinners: but be thou in the fear of the LORD all the day long. Prov. 23:17 (*see also* Envy)

Be not wise in thine own eyes: fear the LORD and depart from evil. It shall be health to thy navel, and marrow to thy bones. Prov. 3:7-8 (*see also* Wise)

Let not thine heart envy sinners: but be thou in the fear of the LORD all the day long. Prov. 23:17 (*see also* Envy)

Though I walk through the valley of the shadow of death, I will fear no evil: for thou art with me. Ps. 23:4 (*see also* Evil)

Fear not them which kill the body, but are not able to kill the soul: but rather fear him which is able to destroy both soul and body in hell. Matt. 10:28 (*see also* Soul)

Matt. 10:24-26 fear them not therefore: for there is nothing covered, that shall not be revealed; and hid, that shall not be known; **10:28** fear not them which kill the body, but are not able to kill the soul: but rather fear him which is able to destroy both soul and body in hell; **Luke 12:4-5** be not afraid of them that kill the body, and after that have no more that they can do; **Heb. 13:6** so that we may boldly say, The Lord is my helper, and I will not fear what man shall do unto me; **1 Pet. 3:14** if ye suffer for righteousness' sake, happy are ye: and be not afraid of their terror, neither be troubled.

Fear God. 1 Pet. 2:17

Acts 10:2 a devout man, and one that feared God with all his house, which gave much alms to the people, and prayed to God alway; **10:22** a just man, and one that feareth God, and of good report among all the nation of the Jews, was warned from God by an holy angel to send for thee into his house, and to hear words of thee; **13:16** men of Israel, and ye that fear God, give audience; **13:26** whosoever among you feareth God, to you is the word of this salvation sent; **Rom. 3:18** there is no fear of God before their eyes; **Heb. 4:1** let us therefore fear, lest, a promise being left us of entering into his rest, any of you should seem to come short of it;

1 Pet. 1:17 if ye call on the Father, who without respect of persons judgeth according to every man's work, pass the time of your sojourning here in fear; **2:17** honour all men. Love the brotherhood. Fear God. Honour the king; **Rev. 14:7** Fear God, and give glory to him; for the hour of his judgment is come: and worship him that made heaven, and earth, and the sea, and the fountains of waters; **15:4** who shall not fear thee, O Lord, and glorify thy name? for thou only art holy: for all nations shall come and worship before thee; for thy judgments are made manifest; **19:5** a voice came out of the throne, saying, Praise our God, all ye his servants, and ye that fear him, both small and great.

Let not your hearts be troubled, neither let it be afraid. John 14:27 (*see also* Trouble)

Matt. 28:10 then said Jesus unto them, Be not afraid: go tell my brethren that they go into Galilee, and there shall they see me; **Luke 8:50** fear not: believe only, and she shall be made whole; **9:33-34** while he thus spake, there came a cloud, and overshadowed them: and they feared as they entered into the cloud; **9:45** they understood not this saying, and it was hid from them, that they perceived it not: and they feared to ask him of that saying; **12:32** fear not, little flock; for it is your Father's good pleasure to give you the kingdom; **John 14:27** peace I leave with you, my peace I give unto you: not as the world giveth, give I unto you. Let not your heart be troubled, neither let it be afraid; **2 Tim. 1:7** for God hath not given us the spirit of fear; but of power, and of love, and of a sound mind.

Fear ye not the reproach of men, neither be ye afraid of their revilings. Isa. 51:7 (*see also* Reproach)

Isa. 51:7-8 *f.* ye not the reproach of men, neither be ye afraid of their revilings. For the moth shall eat them up like a garment, and the worm shall eat them like wool: but my righteousness shall be for ever; **51:12** I, am he that comforteth you: who art thou, that thou shouldest be afraid of a man that shall die, and of the son of man which shall be made as grass.

Be strong and of good courage, and do it: fear not, nor be dismayed: for the LORD GOD, even my GOD, will be with thee; he will not fail thee, nor forsake thee. 1 Chron. 28:20 (*see also* Dismay)

Gen. 15:1 *f.* not... I am thy shield, and thy exceeding great reward; **21:17** *f.* not; for God hath heard the voice of the lad where he is; **26:24** I am the God of Abraham thy father: *f.* not, for I am with thee, and will bless thee; **43:23** peace be to you, *f.* not: your God, and the God of your father, hath given you treasure in your sacks; **50:19-21** *f.* ye not: I will nourish you, and your little ones. And he comforted them, and spake kindly unto them; **Ex. 20:20** *f.* not: for God is come to prove you, and that his *f.* may be before your faces, that ye sin not; **Deut. 1:21** *f.* not, neither be discouraged; **20:3-4** let not your hearts faint, *f.* not, and do not tremble, neither be ye terrified because of them; For the LORD your God is he that goeth with you; **31:6-8** be strong and of a good courage, *f.* not, nor be afraid of them: for the LORD thy God, he it is that doth go with thee; he will not fail thee, nor forsake thee; **Josh. 8:1** *f.* not, neither be thou dismayed; **10:25** fear not, nor be dismayed, be strong and of good courage; **1 Kgs. 17:13** *f.* not; go and do as thou hast said; **2 Kgs. 6:15-17** *f.* not: for they that be with us are more than they that be with them; **1 Chron. 28:20** be strong and of good courage, and do it: *f.* not, nor be dismayed: for the LORD God, even my God, will be with thee; he will not fail thee, nor forsake thee; **2 Chron. 20:17** *f.* not, nor be dismayed; to morrow go out against them: for the LORD will be with you; **Ps. 27:3** though an host should encamp against me, my heart shall not *f.*: though war should rise against me, in this will I be confident; **78:53** he led them on safely, so that they *f.* not; **Isa. 7:4** take heed, and be quiet; *f.* not, neither be fainthearted; **8:12** neither *f.* their *f.*, nor be afraid; **12:2** I will trust, and not be afraid: for the LORD JEHOVAH is my strength and my song; **35:4** be strong, *f.* not: behold, your God will come with vengeance, even God with a recompence; he will come and save you; **41:13-14** *f.* not; I will help thee... saith the LORD, and thy redeemer, the Holy One of Israel; **43:1-2** *f.* not: for I have redeemed thee, I have called thee by thy name; thou art mine; **43:5** *f.* not: for I am with thee: I will bring thy seed from the east, and gather thee from the west; **44:2** fear *f.*. whom I have chosen; **44:8** *f.* ye not, neither be afraid: have not I told thee from that time, and have declared it; **Jer. 46:27** *f.* not thou, O my servant Jacob, and be not dismayed, O Israel: for, behold, I will save thee from afar off; **Ezek. 2:6** be not afraid of them, neither be afraid of their words... nor be dismayed at their looks, though they be a rebellious house; **3:9** *f.* them, neither be dismayed at their looks, though they be a rebellious house; **Joel 2:21-22** *f.* not, O land; be glad and rejoice: for the LORD will do great things. Be not afraid; **Hag. 2:5** according to the word that I covenanted with you... so my spirit remaineth among you: *f.* ye not; **Zech. 8:13** as ye were a curse among the heathen... so will I save you, and ye shall be a blessing: *f.* not, but let your hands be strong; **8:15** *f.* ye not.

Thou shalt fear the LORD thy GOD; him shalt thou serve, and to him shalt thou cleave, and swear by his name. Deut. 10:20 (*see also* Serve)

Gen. 20:11 surely the *f.* of God is not in this place; and they will slay me for my wifes sake; **22:12** I know that thou *f.* God, seeing thou hast not withheld thy son, thine only son from me; **Ex. 10:7-8** let the men go, that they may serve the LORD their God; **10:11** go now ye that are men, and serve the LORD; for that ye did desire; **10:24** go ye, serve the LORD; **10:26** thereof must we take to serve the LORD our God; and we know not with what we must serve the LORD, until we come thither; **12:31** tise up, and get you forth from among my people, both ye and the children of Israel; and go, serve the LORD, as ye have said; **23:25** ye shall serve the LORD your God, and he shall bless thy bread, and thy water; **Deut. 4:10** gather me the people together, and I will make them hear my words, that they may learn to *f.* me all the days that they shall live upon the earth; **6:2** that thou mightest *f.* the LORD thy God, to keep all his statutes and his commandments, which I command thee; **6:13** thou shalt *f.* the LORD thy God, and serve him; **8:6** thou shalt keep the commandments of the LORD thy God, to walk in his ways, and to *f.* him; **10:12-13** what doth the LORD thy God require of thee, but to *f.* the LORD thy God, to walk in all his ways, and to love him, and to serve the LORD thy God; **10:20** thou shalt *f.* the LORD thy God; him shalt thou serve; **13:4** ye shall walk after the LORD your God, and *f.* him, and keep his commandments, and obey his voice, and ye shall serve him, and cleave unto him; **14:23** thou mayest learn to *f.* the LORD thy God always;

17:19 that he may learn to *f.* the LORD his God, to keep all the words of this law and these statutes, to do them; **20:1** be not afraid of them: for the LORD thy God is with thee; **28:58-59** if thou wilt not observe to do all the words of this law that are written in this book, that thou mayest *f.* this glorious and *f.* name, THE LORD THY GOD; Then the LORD will make thy plagues wonderful; **31:12-13** *f.* the LORD your God, and observe to do all the words of this law; **Josh. 4:24** that all the people of the earth might know the hand of the LORD, that it is mighty: that ye might *f.* the LORD your God for ever; **24:14** *f.* the LORD, and serve him in sincerity and in truth; **1 Sam. 12:14-15** *f.* the LORD, and serve him, and obey his voice; **12:24** *f.* the LORD, and serve him in truth with all your heart; **15:24** I have transgressed the commandment of the LORD, and thy words: because I *f.* the people, and obeyed their voice; **1 Kgs. 8:40** that they may *f.* thee all the days that they live; **8:43** that all people of the earth may know thy name, to *f.* thee; **18:12** I thy servant *f.* the LORD from my youth; **2 Kgs. 4:1** thou knowest that thy servant did *f.* the LORD: and the creditor is come to take unto him my two sons to be bondmen; **17:25** so it was at the beginning of their dwelling there, that they *f.* not the LORD: therefore the LORD sent lions among them, which slew some of them; **17:28** one of the priests... taught them how they should *f.* the LORD; **17:33** they *f.* the LORD, and served their own gods, after the manner of the nations whom they carried away from thence; **17:39** the LORD your God ye shall *f.*; and he shall deliver you out of the hand of all your enemies; **1 Chron. 16:25-26** great is the LORD, and greatly to be praised: he also is to be *f.* above all gods; **16:30** *f.* before him, all the earth; **2 Chron. 19:7** let the *f.* of the LORD be upon you; take heed and do it: for there is no iniquity with the LORD our God; **20:29** the *f.* of God was on all the kingdoms of those countries; **Ezra 9:4** then were assembled unto me every one that trembled at the words of the God of Israel; **Neh. 1:11** O Lord, I beseech thee, let now thine ear be attentive to the prayer of thy servant, and to the prayer of thy servants, who desire to *f.* thy name; **Job 1:1** there was a man... whose name was Job; and that man was perfect and upright, and one that *f.* God; **1:8** hast thou considered my servant Job, that there is none like him in the earth, a perfect and an upright man, one that *f.* God, and escheweth evil; **2:3** hast thou considered my servant Job, that there is none like him in the earth, a perfect and an upright man, one that *f.* God, and escheweth evil; **37:24** men do therefore *f.* him: he respecteth not any that are wise of heart; **Ps. Ps. 2:11** serve the LORD with *f.*, and rejoice with trembling; **15:4** he honoureth them that *f.* the LORD; **22:23** ye that *f.* the LORD, praise him; all ye the seed of Jacob, glorify him; and *f.* him, all ye the seed of Israel; **25:12-13** what man is he that *f.* the LORD? him shall he teach in the way that he shall choose; **27:1** the LORD is my light and my salvation; whom shall I *f.?* the LORD is the strength of my life; of whom shall I be afraid; **31:19** how great is thy goodness, which thou hast laid up for them that *f.* thee; **33:8** let all the earth *f.* the LORD: let all the inhabitants of the world stand in awe of him; **33:18** the eye of the LORD is upon them that *f.* him, upon them that hope in his mercy; **34:7** the angel of the LORD encampeth round about them that *f.* him, and delivereth them; **34:9** O *f.* the LORD, ye his saints: for there is no want to them that *f.* him; **36:1** the transgression of the wicked saith within my heart, that there is no *f.* of God before his eyes; **60:4** thou hast given a banner to them that *f.* thee, that it may be displayed because of the truth; **67:7** all the ends of the earth shall *f.* him; **72:5** they shall *f.* thee as long as the sun and moon endure; **85:9** his salvation is nigh them that *f.* him; that glory may dwell in our land; **86:11** teach me thy way, O LORD; I will walk in thy truth: unite my heart to *f.* thy name; **96:4** the LORD is great, and greatly to be praised: he is to be *f.* above all gods; **96:9** worship the LORD in the beauty of holiness: *f.* before him, all the earth; **103:13** the LORD pitieth them that *f.* him; **111:5-6** he hath given meat unto them that *f.* him: he will ever be mindful of his covenant; **111:10** the *f.* of the LORD is the beginning of wisdom; **115:11-14** ye that *f.* the LORD, trust in the LORD: he is their help and their shield; **118:4** let them now that *f.* the LORD say, that his mercy endureth for ever; **119:38-39** stablish thy word unto thy servant, who is devoted to thy *f.*; **128:1-6** blessed is every one that *f.* the LORD; that walketh in his ways; **135:20** ye that *f.* the LORD, bless the LORD; **147:11** the LORD taketh pleasure in them that *f.* him, in those that hope in his mercy; **Prov. 3:7** be not wise in thine own eyes: *f.* the LORD, and depart from evil; **9:10** the *f.* of the LORD is the beginning of wisdom; **14:26-27** in the *f.* of the LORD is strong confidence: and his children shall have a place of refuge. The *f.* of the LORD is a fountain of life; **15:16** better is little with the *f.* of the LORD than great treasure and trouble therewith; **15:33** the *f.* of the LORD is the instruction of wisdom; **16:6** by the *f.* of the LORD men depart from evil; **19:23** the *f.* of the LORD tendeth to life: and he that hath it shall abide satisfied; **22:4** by humility and the *f.* of the LORD

are riches, and honour, and life; **23:17-18** be thou in the *f.* of the LORD all the day long; **24:21** *f.* thou the LORD and the king; **28:14** happy is the man that *f.* alway; **31:30** a woman that *f.* the LORD, she shall be praised; **Eccl. 3:14** God doeth it, that men should *f.* before him; **5:7** in the multitude of dreams and many words there are also divers vanities: but *f.* thou God; **7:16-18** he that *f.* God shall come forth of them all; **8:12-13** I know that it shall be well with them that *f.* God, which *f.* before him; **12:13** *f.* God, and keep his commandments: for this is the whole duty of man; **Isa. 2:10** enter into the rock, and hide thee in the dust, for *f.* of the LORD, and for the glory of his majesty; **2:19** they shall go into the holes of the rocks, and into the caves of the earth, for *f.* of the LORD, and for the glory of his majesty; **2:21** go into the clefts of the rocks, and into the tops of the ragged rocks, for *f.* of the LORD, and for the glory of his majesty; **8:10** speak the word, and it shall not stand: for God is with us; **8:13-16** sanctify the LORD of hosts himself; and let him be your *f.*, and let him be your dread; **9:18-19** through the wrath of the LORD of hosts is the land darkened, and the people shall be as the fuel of the fire; **29:13** their *f.* toward me is taught by the precept of men; **29:23** they shall sanctify my name, and sanctify the Holy One of Jacob, and shall *f.* the God of Israel; **33:22** the LORD is our judge, the LORD is our lawgiver, the LORD is our king; he will save us; **41:5** the isles saw it, and *f.*; the ends of the earth were afraid; **50:10** who is among you that *f.* the LORD, that obeyeth the voice of his servant, that walketh in darkness, and hath no light; **59:19** they [shall] *f.* the name of the LORD from the west, and his glory from the rising of the sun; **60:5** thine heart shall *f.*, and be enlarged; because the abundance of the sea shall be converted unto thee; **64:2** when the melting fire burneth, the fire causeth the waters to boil, to make thy name known to thine adversaries, that the nations may tremble at thy presence; **Jer. 5:22** *f.* ye not me? saith the LORD: will ye not tremble at my presence; **5:24** let us now *f.* the LORD our God, that giveth rain, both the former and the latter; **10:6** O LORD; thou art great, and thy name is great in might; **26:19** did he not *f.* the LORD, and besought the LORD, and the LORD repented him of the evil which he had pronounced against them; **32:38-41** I will be their God: And I will give them one heart, and one way, that they may *f.* me for ever, for the good of them; **33:9** they shall *f.* and tremble for all the goodness and for all the prosperity that I procure unto it; **36:24** they were not afraid, nor rent their garments, neither the king, nor any of his servants that heard all these words; **44:10-11** they are not humbled even unto this day, neither have they *f.*, nor walked in my law, nor in my statutes, that I set before you; **48:43-44** *f.*, and the pit, and the snare, shall be upon thee; **Dan. 6:26** in every dominion of my kingdom men tremble and *f.* before the God of Daniel: for he is the living God, and stedfast for ever; **Hosea 3:5** the children of Israel... shall *f.* the LORD and his goodness in the latter days; **10:3** we have no king, because we *f.* not the LORD; what then should a king do to us; **Jonah 1:9** I *f.* the LORD, the God of heaven, which hath made the sea and the dry land; **1:16** the men *f.* the LORD exceedingly, and offered a sacrifice unto the LORD; **Micah 7:5-8** I will look unto the LORD; I will wait for the God of my salvation: my God will hear me. Rejoice not against me, O mine enemy: when I fall, I shall arise; **7:17** they shall be afraid of the LORD our God, and shall *f.* because of thee; **Haba 3:2** O LORD, I have heard thy speech, and was afraid; **3:16** when I heard, my belly trembled; my lips quivered at the voice: rottenness entered into my bones, and I trembled in myself; **Zeph. 3:7** surely thou wilt *f.* me, thou wilt receive instruction; so their dwelling should not be cut off, howsoever I punished them; **3:12** I will also leave in the midst of thee an afflicted and poor people, and they shall trust in the name of the LORD; **Hag. 1:12** [they] obeyed the voice of the LORD their God... and the people did *f.* before the LORD; **Zech. 10:5** they shall be as mighty men, which tread down their enemies in the mire of the streets in the battle: and they shall fight, because the LORD is with them; **Mal. 1:6** if I be a master, where is my *f.*? saith the LORD of hosts unto you; **1:14** I am a great King, saith the LORD of hosts, and my name is dreadful among the heathen; **2:5-6** I gave them to him for the *f.* wherewith he *f.* me, and was afraid before my name; **3:5** I will be a swift witness against... [those] that turn aside the stranger from his right, and *f.* not me, saith the LORD of hosts; **3:16-17** they that *f.* the LORD spake often one to another: and the LORD hearkened, and heard it, and a book of remembrance was written before him for them that *f.* the LORD; **4:2-3** unto you that *f.* my name shall the Sun of righteousness arise with healing in his wings.

In God I will praise his word, in God I have put my trust; I will not fear what flesh can do unto me. Ps. 56:4

Num. 14:9 rebel not ye against the LORD, neither *f.* ye the people of the land; for they are bread for us: their defence is departed from them, and the

LORD is with us: *f.* them not; **Deut. 20:3-4** let not your hearts faint, *f.* not, and do not tremble, neither be ye terrified because of them; For the LORD your God is he that goeth with you; **Josh. 10:8** the LORD said unto Joshua, *F.* them not: for I have delivered them into thine hand; there shall not a man of them stand before thee; **1 Sam. 15:24** I have sinned: for I have transgressed the commandment of the LORD, and thy words: because I *f.* the people, and obeyed their voice; **21:10** David arose, and fled that day for *f.* of Saul; **2 Kgs. 6:15-16** his servant said unto him, Alas, my master! how shall we do? And he answered, *F.* not: for they that be with us are more than they that be with them; **Ps. 3:6** I will not be afraid of ten thousands of people, that have set themselves against me round about; **27:1-3** the LORD is my light and my salvation; whom shall I *f.*? the LORD is the strength of my life; of whom shall I be afraid; **56:4** in God I will praise his word, in God I have put my trust; I will not *f.* what flesh can do unto me; **56:11** in God have I put my trust: I will not be afraid what man can do unto me; **118:6** the LORD is on my side; I will not *f.*: what can man do unto me; **Prov. 29:25** the *f.* of man bringeth a snare: but whoso putteth his trust in the LORD shall be safe; **Isa. 51:12** I, even I, am he that comforteth you: who art thou, that thou shouldest be afraid of a man that shall die; **Ezek. 3:9** *f.* them not, neither be dismayed at their looks, though they be a rebellious house.

FEAST (*see also* Eat, Feed)

Keep thy solemn feasts, perform thy vows. Nahum 1:15 (*see also* Keep, Vow)

FEEBLE

Strengthen ye the weak hands, and confirm the feeble knees. Say to them that are of a fearful heart, Be strong, fear not: behold, your God will come with vengeance, even God with a recompense; he will come and save you. Isa. 35:3-4 (*see also* Save, Strengthen)

FEED, FED (*see also* Eat)

Feed thy people with thy rod, the flock of thine heritage, which dwell solitarily in the wood. Micah 7:14 (*see also* Rod, Word)

Feed the flock of God which is among you, taking the oversight thereof, not by constraint, but willingly; not for filthy lucre, but of a ready mind. 1 Pet. 5:2

Acts 13:15 after the reading of the law and the prophets the rulers of the synagogue sent unto them, saying, Ye men and brethren, if ye have any word of exhortation for the people, say on; **14:22** exhorting them to continue in the faith, and that we must through much tribulation enter into the kingdom of God; **15:32** being prophets also themselves, exhorted the brethren with many words, and confirmed them; **1 Thes. 2:11-12** ye know how we exhorted and comforted and charged every one of you, as a father doth his children, That ye would walk worthy of God, who hath called you unto his kingdom and glory; **1 Tim. 4:13** till I come, give attendance to reading, to exhortation, to doctrine; **2 Tim. 4:2** preach the word; be instant in season, out of season; reprove, rebuke, exhort with all longsuffering and doctrine; **Titus 2:6** young men likewise exhort to be sober minded; **Heb. 3:13** exhort one another daily, while it is called To day; lest any of you be hardened through the deceitfulness of sin; **13:22** suffer the word of exhortation: for I have written a letter unto you in few words; **1 Pet. 5:1-2** the elders which are among you I exhort, who am also an elder, and a witness of the sufferings of Christ, and also a partaker of the glory that shall be revealed: Feed the flock of God which is among you, taking the oversight thereof, not by constraint, but willingly; not for filthy lucre, but of a ready mind; **2 Pet. 1:12** I will not be negligent to put you always in remembrance of these things, though ye know them, and be established in the present truth; **2 Jn. 1:12** having many things to write unto you, I would not write with paper and ink: but I trust to come unto you, and speak face to face, that our joy may be full.

FEEL, FEELING, FELT (*see* Heart, Holy Ghost, Testimony, Witness)

FEET (*see also* Foot)

If I then, your Lord and Master, have ashed your feet; ye also ought to wash one another's feet. For I have given you an example, that ye should do as I have done to you. John 13:14-15 (*see also* Do, Example, Wash)

[She] stood at his feet behind him weeping, and began to wash his feet with tears, and did wipe them with the hairs of her head, and kissed his feet, and anointed them with the ointment. Luke 7:38 (*see also* Kiss)

Ponder the path of thy feet and let all thy ways be established. Prov. 4:26 (*see also* Establish, Ponder, Way)

FEIGN, FEIGNED, FEIGNEDLY (*see also* Lie)

O Lord, attend unto my cry, give ear unto my prayer, that goeth not out of feigned lips. Ps. 17:1 (*see also* Pray)

Ps. 17:1 hear the right, O Lord, attend unto my cry, give ear unto my prayer, that goeth not out of *f.* lips; **Jer. 3:10** for all this her treacherous sister Judah hath not turned unto me with her whole heart, but *f.*, saith the Lord.

FELLOWSHIP, FELLOWSHIPPING (*see also* Brother, Friend, Sister)

Be ye not unequally yoked together with unbelievers: for what fellowship hath righteousness with unrighteousness? and what communion hath light with darkness. 2 Cor. 6:14 (*see also* Yoke)

FEMALE (*see also* Mother, Wife)

There is neither Jew nor Greek, there is neither bond nor free, there is neither male nor female: for ye are all one in Christ Jesus. Gal. 3:28 (*see also* Bond, Equality, Male, One)

FEW

So the last shall be first, and the first last: for many be called, but few chosen. Matt 20:16 (*see also* Chosen)

Matt 20:16 So the last shall be first, and the first last: for many be called, but few chosen; **22:14** many are called, but few are chosen.

FIELD (*see* World)

Lift up your eyes, and look on the fields; for they are white already to harvest. John 4:35 (*see also* Harvest)

FIGHT, FOUGHT (*see also* Battle, Contend, Strife, War)

Be not ye afraid of them: remember the Lord, which is great and terrible, and fight for your brethren, your sons, and your daughters, your wives, and your houses. Neh. 4:14

It shall even be as when an hungry man dreameth, and, behold, he eateth; but he awaketh, and his soul is empty: or as when a thirsty man dreameth, and, behold, he drinketh; but he awaketh, and, behold, he is faint, and his soul hath appetite: so shall the multitude of all the nations be, that fight against mount Zion. Isa. 29:8 (*see also* Zion)

O Israel, ye approach this day unto battle against your enemies; let not your hearts faint, fear not and do not tremble of them neither be ye terrified because of them; for the LORD your GOD is he that goeth with you, to fight for you against your enemies, to save you. Deut. 20:3-4 (*see also* Enemy)

Fight ye not against the Lord God of your fathers; for ye shall not prosper. 2 Chron. 13:12 (*see also* Prosper)

2 Chron. 13:12 *f.* ye not against the LORD God of your fathers; for ye shall not prosper; **14:4** commanded Judah to seek the LORD God of their fathers, and to do the law and the commandment; **Ps. 98:6** with trumpets and sound of cornet make a joyful noise before the LORD, the King.

FILL

I am the LORD thy God, which brought thee out of the land of Egypt: open thy mouth wide, and I will fill it. Ps. 81:10

FILTH, FILTHINESS, FILTHY (*see also* Corrupt, Defile, Pollute, Unclean, Wicked)

The children of Israel, which were come again out of captivity, and all such as had separated themselves unto them from the filthiness of the heathen of the land, to seek the LORD God of Israel, did eat. Ezra 6:21

There is a generation that are pure in their own eyes, an yet is not washed from their filthiness. Prov. 30:12 (*see also* Pure, Wash)

Prov. 30:12 there is a generation that are pure in their own eyes, and yet is not washed from their *f.*; **Zeph. 3:1** woe to her that is *f.* and polluted, to the oppressing city.

FIND, FOUND (*see also* Look, Seek)

Come unto me, all ye that labour and are heavy laden, and I will give you rest. Take my yoke upon you, and learn of me; for I am meek and lowly in heart: and ye shall find rest unto your souls. Matt. 11:28-29 (*see also* Come, Heavy, Lowly, Meek, Seek)

Thou shalt seek the LORD thy God, thou shalt find him, if thou seek him with all thy heart and with all thy soul. Deut. 4:29 (*see also* Seek, Thou Shalt)

Ask, and it shall be given you; seek, and ye shall find; knock, and it shall be opened unto you. Luke 11:9 (*see also* Ask, Knock, Seek)

FINISHER (*see also* Author)

[Look] unto Jesus the author and finisher of our faith; who for the joy that was set before him endured the cross, despising the shame, and is set down at the right hand of the throne of God. Heb. 12:2 (*see also* Author, Faith, Jesus Christ)

FLATTER, FLATTERY (*see also* False, Glory, Hypocrisy, Praise)

Neither at any time used we flattering words, as ye know, nor a cloke of covetousness; God is witness. 1 Thes. 2:5

He that speaketh flattery to his friends, even the eyes of his children shall fail. Job 17:5 (*see also* Speak)

Job 17:5 he that speaketh *f.* to his friends, even the eyes of his children shall fail; **32:21-22** let me not, I pray you, accept any mans person, neither let me give *f.* titles unto man. For I know not to give *f.* titles; in so doing my maker would soon take me away; **Ps. 5:9** there is no faithfulness in their mouth; their inward part is very wickedness; their throat is an open sepulchre; they *f.* with their tongue; **12:2-3** they speak vanity every one with his neighbour: with *f.* lips and with a double heart do they speak. The LORD shall cut off all *f.* lips, and the tongue that speaketh proud things; **Prov. 2:16** (6:24) deliver thee from the strange woman, even from the stranger which *f.* with her words; **7:5** keep thee from the strange woman, from the stranger which *f.* with her words; **20:19** he that goeth about as a talebearer revealeth secrets: therefore meddle not with him that *f.* with his lips; **26:28** a lying tongue hateth those that are afflicted by it; and a *f.* mouth worketh ruin; **29:5** a man that *f.* his neighbour spreadeth a net for his feet.

FLEE, FLED (*see also* Escape)

Whither shall I go from thy spirit? or whither shall I flee from thy presence? Ps. 139:4-7 (*see also* Everywhere)

Flee fornication. 1 Cor. 6:18 (*see also* Fornication)

Flee also youthful lusts: but follow righteousness, faith, charity, peace, with them that call on the Lord out of a pure heart. 2 Tim. 2:22 (*see also* Lust, Peace, Pure)

FLESH (*see also* Arm, Blood, Body, Fallen, Lust, Mortal)

Vain is the help of man. Ps. 60:11 (*see also* Trust)

Put ye on the Lord Jesus Christ, and make not provision for the flesh, to fulfil the lusts thereof. Rom. 13:14 (*see also* Jesus Christ, Lust)

They that are after the flesh do mind the things of the flesh; but they that are after the Spirit the things of the Spirit. For to be carnally minded is death; but to be spiritually minded is life and peace. Rom. 8:5-6 (*see also* Mind, Spirit)

He that soweth to his flesh shall of the flesh reap corruption; but he that soweth to the Spirit shall of the Spirit reap life everlasting. Gal. 6:8 (*see also* Sow, Spirit)

Cursed be the man that trusteth in man, and maketh flesh his arm, and whose heart departeth from the LORD. Jer. 17:5 (*see also* Heart, Trust)

Though we walk in the flesh, we do not war after the flesh: Casting down imaginations, and every high thing that exalteth itself against the knowledge of God, and bringing into captivity every thought to the obedience of Christ. 2 Cor. 10:3,5 (*see also* Imagination, Obedient, Thought)

I keep under my body, and bring it into subjection: lest that by any means, when I have preached to others, I myself should be a castaway. 1 Cor. 9:27 (*see also* Body, Subject, Will)

Have ye not read, that he which made them at the beginning made them male and female, And said, For this cause shall a man leave father and mother, and shall cleave to his wife: and they twain shall be one flesh? Wherefore they are no more twain, but one flesh. What therefore God hath joined together, let not man put asunder. Matt. 19:4-6 (*see also* Join, Marriage)

Walk not after the flesh, but after the Spirit. Rom. 8:4 (*see also* Walk)

Rom. 8:3-5 for what the law could not do, in that it was weak through the *f.*, God sending his own Son in the likeness of sinful *f.*, and for sin, condemned sin in the *f.*: That the righteousness of the law might be fulfilled in us, who walk not after the *f.*, but after the Spirit. For they that are after the *f.* do mind the things of the *f.*; but they that are after the Spirit the things of the Spirit; **8:7-9** the carnal mind is enmity against God: for it is not subject to the law of God, neither indeed can be. So then they that are in the *f.* cannot please God. But ye are not in the *f.*, but in the Spirit, if so be that the Spirit of God dwell in you. Now if any man have not the Spirit of Christ, he is none of his; **8:12-13** brethren, we are debtors, not to the *f.*, to live after the *f.*. For if ye live after the *f.*, ye shall die: but if ye through the Spirit do mortify the deeds of the body, ye shall live; **1 Cor. 1:20** where is the wise? where is the scribe? where is the disputer of this world? hath not God made foolish the wisdom of this world; **1:27-29** God hath chosen the foolish things of the world to confound the wise; and God hath chosen the weak things of the world to confound the things which are mighty; And base things of the world, and things which are despised, hath God chosen, yea, and things which are not, to bring to nought things that are: That no *f.* should glory in his presence; **Gal. 5:16-18** walk in the Spirit, and ye shall no fulfil the lust of the *f.*. For the *f.* lusteth against the Spirit, and the Spirit against the *f.*: and these are contrary the one to the other: so that ye cannot do the things that ye would; **5:22-25** the fruit of the Spirit is love, joy, peace, longsuffering, gentle-ness, goodness, faith, Meekness, temperance: against such there is no law. And they that are Christ's have crucified the *f.* with the affections and lusts. If we live in the Spirit, let us also walk in the Spirit; **Philip. 3:3** we are the circumcision, which worship God in the spirit, and rejoice in Christ Jesus, and have no confidence in the *f.*; **2 Tim. 3:4** traitors, heady, highminded, lovers of pleasures more than lovers of God; **3:8-9** so do these also resist the truth: men of corrupt minds, reprobate concerning the faith. But they shall proceed no further: for their folly shall be manifest unto all men, as theirs also was; **1 Pet. 1:24-25** all *f.* is as grass, and all the glory of man as the flower of grass. The grass withereth, and the flower thereof falleth away: But the word of the Lord endureth for ever; **2:11** dearly beloved, I beseech you as strangers and pilgrims, abstain from *f.* lusts, which war against the soul; **1 Jn. 1:7** if we walk in the light, as he is in the light, we have fellowship one with another, and the blood of Jesus Christ his Son cleanseth us from all sin; **2 Jn. 1:4** I rejoiced greatly that I found of thy children walking in truth; **3 Jn. 1:4** I have no greater joy than to hear that my children walk. in truth; **Jude 1:18** there should be mockers in the last time, who should walk after their own ungodly lusts.

FLOCK (*see also* Church, Sheep)

Be thou diligent to know the state of thy flocks, and look well to thy herds. Prov. 27:23-27 (*see also* Diligence)

FOLLOW, FOLLOWER, FOLLOWING

He said unto them all, If any man will come after me, let him deny himself, and take up his cross daily, and follow me. Luke 9:23 (*see also* Cross, Daily, Deny)

He that followeth after righteousness and mercy, findeth life, righteousness, and honour. Prov. 21:21 (*see also* Life, Mercy, Righteousness)

Then Jesus beholding him loved him, and said unto him, One thing thou lackest: go thy way, sell whatsoever thou hast, and give to the poor, and thou shalt have treasure in heaven: and come, take up the cross, and follow me. Mark 10:21 (*see also* Lack, Treasure)

If thou wilt be perfect, go and sell that thou hast, and give to the poor, and thou shalt have treasure in heaven: and come and follow me. Matt. 19:21-22 (*see also* Perfect, Sacrifice, Treasure)

Turn not aside from following the Lord, but serve the Lord with all your heart. 1 Sam 12:20 (*see also* Serve, Turn)

Num. 32:10-12 the Lords anger was kindled the same time, and he sware, saying, Surely none of the men that came up out of Egypt... shall see the land which I sware unto Abraham, unto Isaac, and unto Jacob; because they have not wholly *f.* me; **Deut. 1:36** to him will I give the land that he hath trodden upon, and to his children, because he hath wholly *f.* the Lord; **7:4** they will turn away thy son from *f.* me, that they may serve other gods: so will the anger of the Lord be kindled against you, and destroy thee suddenly; **Josh. 14:8-9** surely the land whereon thy feet have trodden shall be thine inheritance, and thy childrens for ever, because thou hast wholly *f.* the Lord my God; **14:14** Hebron therefore became the inheritance of Caleb the son of Jephunneh the Kenezite unto this day, because that he wholly *f.* the Lord God of Israel; **22:16-18** what trespass is this that ye have committed against the God of Israel, to turn away this day from *f.* the Lord, in that ye have builded you an altar, that ye might rebel this day against the Lord; **22:23** we have built us an altar to turn from *f.* the Lord, or if to offer thereon burnt offering or meat offering, or if to offer peace offerings thereon, let the Lord himself require it; **22:29** God forbid that we should rebel against the Lord, and turn this day from *f.* the Lord; **1 Sam. 12:14** if ye will fear the Lord, and serve him, and obey his voice, and not rebel against the commandment of the Lord, then shall both ye and also the king that reigneth over you continue *f.* the Lord your God; **12:20** fear not: ye have done all this wickedness: yet turn not aside from *f.* the Lord, but serve the Lord with all your heart; **15:10-11** it repenteth me that I have set up Saul to be king: for he is turned back from *f.* me, and hath not performed my commandments; **25:27** this blessing which thine handmaid hath brought unto my lord, let it even be given unto the young men that *f.* my lord; **1 Kgs. 9:6** [do not] turn from *f.* me, ye or your children, and will not keep my commandments and my statutes which I have set before you, but go and serve other gods; **14:8** thou hast not been as my servant David, who kept my commandments, and who *f.* me with all his heart, to do that only which was right in mine eyes; **18:21** if the Lord be God, *f.* him; **2 Kgs. 17:21** Jeroboam drave Israel from *f.* the Lord, and made them sin a great sin; **18:6** he clave to the Lord, and departed not from *f.* him, but kept his commandments; **2 Chron. 25:27** after the time that Amaziah did turn away from *f.* the LORD they made a conspiracy against him in Jerusalem; **34:33** all his days they departed not from *f.* the LORD, the God of their fathers; **Prov. 21:21** he that *f.* after righteousness and mercy findeth life, righteousness, and honour; **Isa. 51:1-2** hearken to me, ye that *f.* after righteousness, ye that seek the LORD; **Jer. 17:16** I have not hastened from being a pastor to *f.* thee.

Come, follow me. Luke 18:22

Matt. 4:19-22 he saith unto them, *F.* me, and I will make you fishers of men. And they straightway left their nets, and *f.* him; **8:19-23** Master, I will *f.* thee whithersoever thou goest; **9:9** he saith unto him, *F.* me. And he arose, and *f.* him; **10:38-39** (16:24-25, Mark 8:34-38, Luke 9:23-24) he that taketh not his cross, and *f.* after me, is not worthy of me. He that findeth his life shall lose it: and he that loseth his life for my sake shall find it; **11:2-3** art thou he that should come, or do we look for another; **11:28** come unto me, all ye that labour and are heavy laden, and I will give you rest; **12:15** great multitudes *f.* him, and he healed them all; **15:29-30** great multitudes came unto him, having with them those that were lame, blind, dumb, maimed, and many others, and cast them down at Jesus' feet; and he healed them; **19:21-22** if thou wilt be perfect, go and sell that thou hast, and give to the poor, and thou shalt have treasure in heaven: and come and *f.* me; **20:34** Jesus had compassion on them, and touched their eyes: and immediately their eyes received sight, and they *f.* him; **Mark 1:16-18** come ye after me, and I will make you to become fishers of men. And straightway they forsook their nets, and *f.* him; **1:19-20** straightway he called them: and they left their father Zebedee in the ship with the hired servants, and went after him; **2:14** *f.* me. And he arose and *f.* him; **3:7-8** they had heard what great things he did, came unto him; **5:24** much people *f.* him, and thronged him; **6:1** his disciples *f.* him; **10:20-21** one thing thou lackest: go thy way, sell whatsoever thou hast, and give to the poor, and thou shalt have treasure in heaven: and come, take up the cross, and *f.* me; **10:28** Peter began to say unto him, Lo, we have left all, and have *f.* thee; **10:52** go thy way; thy faith hath made thee whole. And immediately he received his sight, and *f.* Jesus in the way; **Luke 4:42** he departed and went into a desert place: and the people sought him, and came unto him, and stayed him, that he should not depart from them; **5:8-11** they had brought their ships to land, they forsook all, and *f.* him; **5:27-28** *f.* me. And he left all, rose

up, and *f.* him; **6:47-49** whosoever cometh to me, and heareth my sayings, and doeth them, I will shew you to whom he is like: He is like a man which built an house, and digged deep, and laid the foundation on a rock: and when the flood arose, the stream beat vehemently upon that house, and could not shake it: for it was founded upon a rock; **8:40** when Jesus was returned, the people gladly received him: for they were all waiting for him; **9:11** when they knew it, *f.* him: and he received them, and spake unto them of the kingdom of God, and healed them that had need of healing; **9:57-58** a certain man said unto him, Lord, I will *f.* thee whithersoever thou goest. And Jesus said unto him, Foxes have holes, and birds of the air have nests; but the Son of man hath not where to lay his head; **14:25-33** if any man come to me, and hate not his father, and mother, and wife, and children, and brethren, and sisters, yea, and his own life also, he cannot be my disciple. And whosoever doth not bear his cross, and come after me, cannot be my disciple… whosoever he be of you that forsaketh not all that he hath, he cannot be my disciple; **18:22** yet lackest thou one thing: sell all that thou hast, and distribute unto the poor, and thou shalt have treasure in heaven: and come, *f.* me; **John 6:35** Jesus said unto them, I am the bread of life: he that cometh to me shall never hunger; and he that believeth on me shall never thirst; **7:37** in the last day, that great day of the feast, Jesus stood and cried, saying, If any man thirst, let him come unto me, and drink; **8:12** I am the light of the world: he that *f.* me shall not walk in darkness, but shall have the light of life; **10:4-5** when he putteth forth his own sheep, he goeth before them, and the sheep *f.* him: for they know his voice. And a stranger will they not *f.*, but will flee from him: for they know not the voice of strangers; **10:7-9** I am the door of the sheep. All that ever came before me are thieves and robbers: but the sheep did not hear them. I am the door: by me if any man enter in, he shall be saved, and shall go in and out, and find pasture; **10:27-29** my sheep hear my voice, and I know them, and they *f.* me: And I give unto them eternal life; and they shall never perish, neither shall any man pluck them out of my hand; **12:32** if I be lifted up from the earth, will draw all men unto me; **15:4-5** abide in me, and I in you. As the branch cannot bear fruit of itself, except it abide in the vine; no more can ye, except ye abide in me. I am the vine, ye are the branches: He that abideth in me, and I in him, the same bringeth forth much fruit: for without me ye can do nothing; **21:19** signifying by what death he should glorify God. And when he had spoken this, he saith unto him, *f.* me; **21:22** if I will that he tarry till I come, what is that to thee? *f.* thou me; **1 Cor. 11:1** be ye *f.* of me, even as I also am of Christ; **Eph. 5:1** be ye therefore *f.* of God, as dear children; **Col. 2:6** ye have therefore received Christ Jesus the Lord, so walk ye in him; **1 Thes. 1:6** ye became *f.* of us, and of the Lord, having received the word in much affliction, with joy of the Holy Ghost; **Heb. 10:22** let us draw near with a true heart in full assurance of faith, having our hearts sprinkled from an evil conscience, and our bodies washed with pure water; **13:13** let us go forth therefore unto him without the camp, bearing his reproach; **James 4:7** submit yourselves therefore to God. Resist the devil, and he will flee from you; **1 Pet. 3:13** who is he that will harm you, if ye be *f.* of that which is good; **1 Jn. 1:6** if we say that we have fellowship with him, and walk in darkness, we lie, and do not the truth; **2:6** he that saith he abideth in him ought himself also so to walk, even as he walked; **2:28** now, little children, abide in him; that, when he shall appear, we may have confidence, and not be ashamed before him at his coming; **3 Jn. 1:11** *f.* not that which is evil, but that which is good. He that doeth good is of God: but he that doeth evil hath not seen God; **Rev. 22:17** come. And let him that heareth say, Come. And let him that is athirst come. And whosoever will, let him take the water of life freely.

FOLLY (*see also* Foolish, Rebel, Wicked)

Hear what God the LORD will speak: for he will speak peace unto his people, and to his saints: but let them not turn again to folly. Ps. 85:8 (*see also* Turn)

Ps. 85:8 I will hear what God the LORD will speak: for he will speak peace unto his people, and to his saints: but let them not turn again to *f.*; **Prov. 15:21** *f.* is joy to him that is destitute of wisdom: but a man of understanding walketh uprightly; **18:13** he that answereth a matter before he heareth it, it is *f.* and shame unto him; **26:11** as a dog returneth to his vomit, so a fool returneth to his *f.*; **Eccl. 1:17** I gave my heart to know wisdom, and to know madness and *f.*; **2:3** I sought in mine heart to give myself unto wine, yet acquainting mine heart with wisdom; and to lay hold on *f.*, till I might see what was that good for the sons of men; **2:13** I saw that wisdom excelleth folly, as far as light excelleth darkness; **Isa. 9:17** the Lord shall have no joy in their

young men, neither shall have mercy on their fatherless and widows: for every one is an hypocrite and an evildoer, and every mouth speaketh *f.*

FOOD (*see also* Herb, Meat)

Now the Spirit speaketh expressly, that in the latter times some shall depart from the faith, giving heed to seducing spirits, and doctrines of devils; Speaking lies in hypocrisy; having their conscience seared with a hot iron; Forbidding to marry, and commanding to abstain from meats, which God hath created to be received with thanksgiving of them which believe and know the truth. 1 Tim. 4:1-3 (*see also* Abstain, Conscience, Latter Day, Marriage, Meat, Thanksgiving)

He causeth the grass to grow for the cattle, and herb for the service of man; that he may bring forth food out of the earth. Ps. 104:14 (*see also* Herb)

Every creature of God is good, and nothing to be refused, if it be received with thanksgiving: For it is sanctified by the word of God and prayer. 1 Tim. 4:4-5 (*see also* Thank)

Mark 8:6 he took the seven loaves, and gave thanks, and brake, and gave to his disciples to set before them; and they did set them before the people; **1 Tim. 4:1-4** for every creature of God is good, and nothing to be refused, if it be received with thanksgiving: For it is sanctified by the word of God and prayer; **6:8** having food and raiment let us be therewith content.

FOOL, FOOLISH, FOOLISHLY, FOOLISHNESS (*see also* Folly)

The fool hath said in his heart, There is no God. They are corrupt, they have done abominable works, there is none that doeth good. Ps. 14:1 (*see also* Existance)

He that walketh with wise men shall be wise: but a companion of fools shall be destroyed. Prov. 13:20 (*see also* Walk, Wise)

Surely these are poor; they are foolish: for they know not the way of the LORD, nor the judgment of their God. Jer. 5:4 (*see also* Way)

Avoid foolish questions, and genealogies, and contentions, and strivings about the law; for they are unprofitable and vain. Titus 3:9 (*see also* Avoid)

Answer not a fool according to his folly, lest thou also be like unto him. Answer a fool according to his folly, lest he be wise in his own conceit. Prov. 26:4-5 (*see also* Answer)

The natural man receiveth not the things of the Spirit of God: for they are foolishness unto him: neither can he know them, because they are spiritually discerned. 1 Cor. 2:14 (*see also* Natural Man, Spirit)

Be not over much wicked, neither be thou foolish: why shouldest thou die before thy time? Eccl. 7:17 (*see also* Time, Wicked)

Go from the presence of a foolish man, when thou preceivest not in him the lips of knowledge. Prov. 14:7 (*see also* Know)

Prov. 14:7 go from the presence of a *f.* man, when thou perceivest not in him the lips of knowledge; **14:16-17** a wise man feareth, and departeth from evil: but the *f.* rageth, and is confident. He that is soon angry dealeth *f.*: and a man of wicked devices is hated; **15:7** the lips of the wise disperse knowledge: but the heart of the *f.* doeth not so.

Speak not in the ears of a fool: for he will despise the wisdom of thy words. Prov. 23:9 (*see also* Wisdom)

Prov. 23:9 speak not in the ears of a *f.*: for he will despise the wisdom of thy words; **24:7** wisdom is too high for a *f.*: he openeth not his mouth in the gate; **26:1-12** answer not a *f.* according to his folly, lest thou also be like unto him. Answer a *f.* according to his folly, lest he be wise in his own conceit. He that sendeth a message by the hand of a *f.* cutteth off the feet, and drinketh damage.

Deal not foolishly. Ps. 75:4 (*see also* Deal)

Ps. 75:4 deal not *f.*: and to the wicked, Lift not up the horn; **Prov. 3:35** the wise shall inherit glory: but shame shall be the promotion of *f.*; **10:8** the wise in heart will receive commandments: but a prating *f.* shall fall; **10:10** he that winketh with the eye causeth sorrow: but a prating *f.* shall fall; **10:14** wise men lay up knowledge: but the mouth of the *f.* is near

destruction; **11:29** he that troubleth his own house shall inherit the wind: and the *f.* shall be servant to the wise of heart; **12:16** a *f.* wrath is presently known: but a prudent man covereth shame; **13:16** every prudent man deal with knowledge: but a *f.* layeth open his folly; **13:19-20** he that walketh with wise men shall be wise: but a companion of *f.* shall be destroyed; **14:3** in the mouth of the *f.* is a rod of pride: but the lips of the wise shall preserve them; **14:24** the crown of the wise is their riches: but the *f.* of *f.* is folly; **15:14** the heart of him that hath understanding seeketh knowledge: but the mouth of *f.* feedeth on *f.*; **27:3** a stone is heavy, and the sand weighty; but a *f.* wrath is heavier than them both; **Jer. 4:22** my people is *f.*, they have not known me; they are sottish children, and they have none understanding: they are wise to do evil, but to do good they have no knowledge.

Forsake the foolish, and live; and go in the way of understanding. Prov. 9:6 (*see also* Understand, Way)

Prov. 9:6 forsake the *f.*, and live; and go in the way of understanding; **9:13-18** a *f.* woman is clamorous: she is simple, and knoweth nothing; **10:1** a wise son maketh a glad father: but a *f.* son is the heaviness of his mother; **10:18** he that hideth hatred with lying lips, and he that uttereth a slander, is a *f.*; **10:21** the lips of the righteous feed many: but *f.* die for want of wisdom; **12:15** the way of a *f.* is right in his own eyes: but he that hearkeneth unto counsel is wise; **12:23** a prudent man concealeth knowledge: but the heart of *f.* proclaimeth *f.*; **14:33** wisdom resteth in the heart of him that hath understanding: but that which is in the midst of *f.* is made known; **15:2** the tongue of the wise useth knowledge aright: but the mouth of *f.* poureth out *f.*; **15:20** a wise son maketh a glad father: but a *f.* man despiseth his mother; **16:22** understanding is a wellspring of life unto him that hath it: but the instruction of *f.* is folly; **17:10** a reproof entereth more into a wise man than an hundred stripes into a *f.*; **17:12** let a bear robbed of her whelps meet a man, rather than a *f.* in his folly; **17:16** is there a price in the hand of a *f.* to get wisdom, seeing he hath no heart to it; **17:21** he that begetteth a *f.* doeth it to his sorrow: and the father of a *f.* hath no joy; **17:24-25** wisdom is before him that hath understanding; but the eyes of a *f.* are in the ends of the earth. A *f.* son is a grief to his father, and bitterness to her that bare him; **18:2** a *f.* hath no delight in understanding, but that his heart may discover itself; **18:6-7** a *f.* lips enter into contention, and his mouth calleth for strokes.

A *f.* mouth is his destruction, and his lips are the snare of his soul; **19:1** better is the poor that walketh in his integrity, than he that is perverse in his lips, and is a *f.*; **19:3** the *f.* of man perverteth his way: and his heart fretteth against the LORD; **19:10** delight is not seemly for a *f.*; much less for a servant to have rule over princes; **19:13** a *f.* son is the calamity of his father: and the contentions of a wife are a continual dropping; **19:29** judgments are prepared for scorners, and stripes for the back of *f.*; **20:3** it is an honour for a man to cease from strife: but every *f.* will be meddling; **24:9** the thought of *f.* is sin; **27:22** though thou shouldest bray a *f.* in a mortar among wheat with a pestle, yet will not his *f.* depart from him; **Eccl. 4:5** the *f.* foldeth his hands together, and eateth his own flesh; **4:13** better is a poor and a wise child than an old and *f.* king; **5:3** a *f.* voice is known by multitude of words; **7:6** as the crackling of thorns under a pot, so is the laughter of the *f.*: this also is vanity; **7:17** be not over much wicked, neither be thou *f.*; **10:2-3** a wise mans heart is at his right hand; but a *f.* heart at his left. Yea also, when he that is a *f.* walketh by the way, his wisdom faileth him, and he saith to every one that he is a *f.*; **10:13-15** the beginning of the words of his mouth is *f.*: and the end of his talk is mischievous madness. A *f.* also is full of words.

FOOT (*see also* Feet)

Turn not to the right hand nor to the left: remove thy foot from evil. Prov. 4:27 (*see also* Evil, Remove)

FORCE (*see also* Evil, Unrighteous Dominion, Wicked)

The merciful man doeth good to his own soul: but he that is cruel troubleth his own flesh. Prov. 11:17 (*see also* Cruel, Rule)

Surely the churning of milk bringeth forth butter, and the wringing of the nose bringeth forth blood: so the forcing of wrath bringeth forth strife. Prov. 30:33 (*see also* Wrath)

Prov. 30:33 surely the churning of milk bringeth forth butter, and the wringing of the nose bringeth forth blood: so the forcing of wrath bringeth forth strife.

FORGAT, FORGET, FORGOT, FORGOTTEN (*see also* Forgive)

Zion said, the LORD hath forsaken me, and my LORD hath forgotten me. Can a woman forget her sucking child, that she should not have compassion on the son of her womb? yea, they may forget, yet will I not forget thee. Isa. 49:14-15 (*see also* Forsake, Say)

Only take heed to thyself, and keep thy soul diligently, lest thou forget the things which thine eyes have seen, and lest they depart from thine heart all the days of thy life: but teach them thy sons, and thy sons sons. Deut. 4:9 (*see also* Testify)

Deut. 4:9 take heed to thyself, and keep thy soul diligently, lest thou *f.* the things which thine eyes have seen, and lest they depart from thy heart all the days of thy life; **8:19** if thou do at all *f.* the LORD thy God, and walk after other gods, and serve them, and worship them, I testify against you this day that ye shall surely perish; **Job 8:12-13** so are the paths of all that *f.* God; and the hypocrites hope shall perish; **Ps. 44:17-18** yet have we not *f.* thee, neither have we dealt falsely in thy covenant. Our heart is not turned back, neither have our steps declined from thy way; **44:20** if we have *f.* the name of our God, or stretched out our hands to a strange god; **106:13** they soon forgat his works; they waited not for his counsel; **106:21** they *f.* God their saviour, which had done great things in Egypt; **119:16** I will delight myself in thy statutes: I will not *f.* thy word; **119:139** my zeal hath consumed me, because mine enemies have *f.* thy words; **119:141** I am small and despised: yet do not I *f.* thy precepts; **119:153** consider mine affliction, and deliver me: for I do not *f.* thy law; **Prov. 10:4** he becometh poor that dealeth with a slack hand: but the hand of the diligent maketh rich; **12:24** the hand of the diligent shall bear rule: but the slothful shall be under tribute; **12:27** the slothful man roasteth not that which he took in hunting: but the substance of a diligent man is precious; **Isa. 17:10** thou hast *f.* the God of thy salvation, and hast not been mindful of the rock of thy strength; **Hosea 4:10** they shall eat, and not have enough: they shall commit whoredom, and shall not increase: because they have left off to take heed to the LORD; **13:6-8** they were filled, and their heart was exalted; therefore have they *f.* me.

The wicked shall be turned into hell, and all the nations that forget God. Ps. 9:17 (*see also* Wicked)

Ps. 9:17 the wicked shall be turned into hell, and all the nations that *f.* God; **9:20** put them in fear, O LORD: that the nations may know themselves to be but men; **50:22** consider this, ye that *f.* God, lest I tear you in pieces, and there be none to deliver; **119:141** I am small and despised: yet do not I *f.* thy precepts; **119:153** consider mine affliction, and deliver me: for I do not *f.* thy law; **Isa. 17:10-11** thou hast *f.* the God of thy salvation, and hast not been mindful of the rock of thy strength; **51:13** *f.* the LORD thy maker, that hath stretched forth the heavens, and laid the foundations of the earth; and hast feared continually every day because of the fury of the oppressor, as if he were ready to destroy; **Jer. 2:32** my people have *f.* me days without number; **13:25** this is thy lot, the portion of thy measures from me, saith the LORD; because thou hast *f.* me, and trusted in falsehood; **18:15** my people hath *f.* me, they have burned incense to vanity, and they have caused them to stumble in their ways from the ancient paths, to walk in paths, in a way not cast up; **18:17** I will scatter them as with an east wind before the enemy: I will shew them the back, and not the face, in the day of their calamity; **Ezek. 22:12** in thee have they taken gifts to shed blood; thou hast taken usury and increase, and thou hast greedily gained of thy neighbours by extortion, and hast *f.* me, saith the Lord GOD; **23:35** thou hast *f.* me, and cast me behind thy back, therefore bear thou also thy lewdness and thy whoredoms.

FORGIVE, FORGIVENESS (*see also* Atone, Confess, Forget, Repentance, Redeem, Remission)

Then came Peter to him, and said, Lord, how oft shall my brother sin against me, and I forgive him? till seven times? Jesus saith unto him, I say not unto thee, Until seven times: but, until seventy times seven. Matt. 18:21-22 (*see also* Seven)

If thy brother shall trespass against thee, go and tell him his faults between thee and him alone. Matt. 18:15 (*see also* Trespass)

Be ye kind one to another, tenderhearted, forgiving one another, even as God for Christ's sake hath forgiven you. Eph. 4:32 (*see also* Kind)

Forgive if ye have ought against any. Mark 11:25

Matt. 5:23-24 if thou bring thy gift to the altar, and there rememberest that thy brother hath ought against thee; Leave there thy gift before the altar, and go thy way; first be reconciled to thy brother, and then come and offer thy gift. **6:12** forgive us our debts, as we forgive our debtors; **6:14** if ye forgive men their trespasses, your heavenly Father will also forgive you; **6:15** if ye forgive not men their trespasses, neither will your Father forgive your trespasses; **18:21-23** then came Peter to him, and said, Lord, how oft shall my brother sin against me, and I forgive him? till seven times? Jesus saith unto him, I say not unto thee, Until seven times: but, Until seventy times seven; **18:35** so likewise shall my heavenly Father do also unto you, if ye from your hearts forgive not every one his brother their trespasses; **Mark 11:25-26** when ye stand praying, forgive, if ye have ought against any: that your Father also which is in heaven may forgive you your trespasses; But if ye do not forgive, neither will your Father which is in heaven forgive your trespasses; **Luke 6:37** judge not, and ye shall not be judged: condemn not, and ye shall not be condemned: forgive, and ye shall be forgiven; **15:11-18** a certain man had two sons: And the younger of them said to his father, Father, give me the portion of goods that falleth to me. And he divided unto them his living. And not many days after the younger son gathered all together, and took his journey into a far country, and there wasted his substance with riotous living; **15: 30-32** as soon as this thy son was come, which hath devoured thy living with harlots, thou hast killed for him the fatted calf. And he said unto him, Son, thou art ever with me, and all that I have is thine. It was meet that we should make merry, and be glad: for this thy brother was dead, and is alive again; and was lost, and is found; **17:3-4** take heed to yourselves: If thy brother trespass against thee, rebuke him; and if he repent, forgive him. And if he trespass against thee seven times in a day, and seven times in a day turn again to thee, saying, I repent; thou shalt forgive him; **23:34** then said Jesus, Father, forgive them; for they know not what they do; **2 Cor. 2:10-11** to whom ye forgive any thing, I forgive also: for if I forgave any thing, to whom I forgave it, for your sakes forgave I it in the person of Christ; Lest Satan should get an advantage of us: for we are not ignorant of his devices; **Col. 3:13** forbearing one another, and forgiving one another, if any man have a quarrel against any: even as Christ forgave you, so also do ye.

FORMER DAYS

Say not thou, What is the cause that the former days were better than these? Eccl. 7:10 (*see also* Better)

FORNICATION (*see also* Adultery, Chastity, Lust, Whoredom)

Flee fornication. 1 Cor. 6:18 (*see also* Flee)

Matt. 15:19-20 out of the heart proceed evil thoughts, murders, adulteries, *f.*, thefts, false witness, blasphemies: These are the things which defile a man; **Mark 7:21** out of the heart of men, proceed evil thoughts, adulteries, *f.*, murders; **7:23** all these evil things come from within, and defile the man; **Acts 15:20** abstain from pollutions of idols, and from *f.*, and from things strangled, and from blood; **15:29** abstain from meats offered to idols, and from blood, and from things strangled, and from *f.*: from which if ye keep yourselves, ye shall do well; **21:25** keep themselves from things offered to idols, and from blood, and from strangled, and from *f.*; **1 Cor. 5:1** it is reported commonly that there is *f.* among you, and such *f.* as is not so much as named among the Gentiles, that one should have his father's wife; **6:9** know ye not that the unrighteous shall not inherit the kingdom of God? Be not deceived: neither fornicators, nor idolaters, nor adulterers, nor effeminate, nor abusers of themselves with mankind; **6:13** the body is not for *f.*, but for the Lord; and the Lord for the body; **6:15** know ye not that your bodies are the members of Christ? shall I then take the members of Christ, and make them the members of an harlot? God forbid; **6:18-19** flee *f.*. Every sin that a man doeth is without the body; but he that committeth *f.* sinneth against his own body. What? know ye not that your body is the temple of the Holy Ghost which is in you, which ye have of God, and ye are not your own; **7:1-2** it is good for a man not to touch a woman. Nevertheless, to avoid *f.*, let every man have his own wife, and let every woman have her own husband; **7:8-9** I say therefore to the unmarried and widows, It is good for them if they abide even as *i*. But if they cannot contain, let them marry: for it is better to marry than to burn; **10:8** neither let us commit *f.*, as some of them committed, and fell in one day three and twenty thousand; **Eph. 5:5** this ye know, that no whoremonger, nor unclean person, nor covetous

man, who is an idolater, hath any inheritance in the kingdom of Christ and of God; **Col. 3:5-6** mortify therefore your members which are upon the earth; *f.*, uncleanness, inordinate affection, evil concupiscence, and covetousness, which is idolatry: For which things' sake the wrath of God cometh on the children of disobedience; **1 Thes. 4:3-4** this is the will of God, even your sanctification, that ye should abstain from *f.*: That every one of you should know how to possess his vessel in sanctification and honour; **Jude 1:7** even as Sodom and Gomorrha, and the cities about them in like manner, giving themselves over to *f.*, and going after strange flesh, are set forth for an example, suffering the vengeance of eternal fire; **Rev. 2:14** to cast a stumblingblock before the children of Israel, to eat things sacrificed unto idols, and to commit *f.*; **2:21-23** I gave her space to repent of her *f.*; and she repented not. Behold, I will cast her into a bed, and them that commit adultery with her into great tribulation, except they repent of their deeds. And I will kill her children with death; and all the churches shall know that I am he which searcheth the reins and hearts: and I will give unto every one of you according to your works; **9:21** neither repented they of their murders, nor of their sorceries, nor of their *f.*, nor of their thefts; **14:8** Babylon is fallen, is fallen, that great city, because she made all nations drink of the wine of the wrath of her *f.*; **18:3** all nations have drunk of the wine of the wrath of her *f.*, and the kings of the earth have committed *f.* with her.

FORSAKE, FORSAKEN, FORSOOK (*see also* Despair)

Thine own friend, and thy father's friend, forsake not; neither go into thy brother's house in the day of thy calamity: for better is a neighbour *that* is near than a brother far off. Prov. 27:10 (*see also* Better, Calamity)

Zion said, the LORD hath forsaken me, and my LORD hath forgotten me. Can a woman forget her sucking child, that she should not have compassion on the son of her womb? yea, they may forget, yet will I not forget thee. Isa. 49:14-15 (*see also* Forget, Say)

He that covereth his sins shall not prosper: but whoso confesseth and forsaketh them shall have mercy. Prov. 28:13 (*see also* Confess, Mercy, Sin)

Let the wicked forsake his way, and the unrighteous man his thoughts: and let him return unto the LORD, and he will have mercy upon him; and to our God, for he will abundantly pardon. Isa. 55:7 (*see also* Forsake, Pardon, Return)

The destruction of the transgressors and of the sinners shall be together, and they that forsake the LORD shall be consumed. Isa. 1:28 (*see also* Destruction)

Isa. 1:28 the destruction of the transgressors and of the sinners shall be together, and they that *f.* the LORD shall be consumed; **Jer. 2:13** my people have committed two evils; they have forsaken me the fountain of living waters, and hewed them out cisterns, broken cisterns, that can hold no water; **2:17** hast thou not procured this unto thyself, in that thou hast *f.* the LORD thy God, when he led thee by the way; **2:19** thine own wickedness shall correct thee, and thy backslidings shall reprove thee: know therefore and see that it is an evil thing and bitter, that thou hast *f.* the LORD thy God, and that my fear is not in thee; **3:21** a voice was heard upon the high places, weeping and supplications of the children of Israel: for they have perverted their way, and they have forgotten the LORD their God; **15:6** thou hast *f.* me, saith the LORD, thou art gone backward: therefore will I stretch out my hand against thee, and destroy thee; I am weary with repenting; **15:8-9** I have brought upon them against the mother of the young men a spoiler at noonday: I have caused him to fall upon it suddenly, and terrors upon the city... she hath been ashamed and confounded: and the residue of them will I deliver to the sword before their enemies, saith the LORD; **16:11** your fathers have *f.* me, saith the LORD, and have walked after other gods, and have served them, and have worshipped them, and have *f.* me, and have not kept my law; **16:13** I [will] cast you out of this land into a land that ye know not, neither ye nor your fathers; and there shall ye serve other gods day and night; where I will not shew you favour; **17:13** LORD, the hope of Israel, all that *f.* thee shall be ashamed, and they that depart from me shall be written in the earth, because they have *f.* the LORD.

FOUNDATION (*see* Cornerstone, Jesus Christ, Rock)

FRIEND, FRIENDSHIP (*see also* Brother, Sister, Fellowship)

A man that hath friends must shew himself friendly: and there is a friend that sticketh closer than a brother. Prov. 18:24

FROWARD (*see also* Evil, Rebellious, Wicked)

Thorns and snares are in the way of the froward: he that doth keep his soul shall be far from them. Prov. 22:5 (*see also* Soul, Way)

He that hath a froward heart findeth no good: and he that hath a perverse tongue falleth into mischief. Prov 17:20 (*see also* Heart, Tongue)

Ps. 101:4-5 a *f.* heart shall depart from me: I will not know a wicked person. Whoso privily slandereth his neighbour, him will I cut off: him that hath an high look and a proud heart will not I suffer; **138:6** though the LORD be high, yet hath he respect unto the lowly: but the proud he knoweth afar off; **Prov. 10:31-32** the mouth of the just bringeth forth wisdom: but the *f.* tongue shall be cut out. The lips of the righteous know what is acceptable: but the mouth of the wicked speaketh *f.*; **11:20** they that are of a *f.* heart are abomination to the LORD: but such as are upright in their way are his delight; **17:20** he that hath a *f.* heart findeth no good: and he that hath a perverse tongue falleth into mischief; **21:4** an high look, and a proud heart, and the plowing of the wicked, is sin; **22:5** thorns and snares are in the way of the *f.*: he that doth keep his soul shall be far from them; **Isa. 10:12** I will punish the fruit of the stout heart of the king of Assyria, and the glory of his high looks; **57:17** for the iniquity of his covetousness was I wroth, and smote him: I hid me, and was wroth, and he went on *f.* in the way of his heart.

Put away from thee a froward mouth, and perverse lips put far from thee. Prov. 4:24 (*see also* Lips, Perverse)

Prov. 4:24 put away from thee a *f.* mouth, and perverse lips put far from thee; **6:12-15** a naughty person, a wicked man, walketh with a *f.* mouth... *F.* is in his heart, he deviseth mischief continually; he soweth discord. Therefore shall his calamity come suddenly; **8:7-8** my mouth shall speak truth; and wickedness is an abomination to my lips. All the words of my mouth are in righteousness; there is nothing *f.* or perverse in them; **8:13** the fear of the LORD is to hate evil: pride, and arrogancy, and the evil way, and the *f.* mouth, do I hate; **10:32** the lips of the righteous know what is acceptable: but the mouth of the wicked speaketh *f.*; **11:3** the integrity of the upright shall guide them: but the perverseness of transgressors shall destroy them; **12:8** a man shall be commended according to his wisdom: but he that is of a perverse heart shall be despised; **12:13** the wicked is snared by the transgression of his lips: but the just shall come out of trouble; **13:2-3** he that keepeth his mouth keepeth his life: but he that openeth wide his lips shall have destruction; **14:2** he that walketh in his uprightness feareth the LORD: but he that is perverse in his ways despiseth him; **14:23** in all labour there is profit: but the talk of the lips tendeth only to penury; **15:28** the heart of the righteous studieth to answer: but the mouth of the wicked poureth out evil things; **17:20** he that hath a *f.* heart findeth no good: and he that hath a perverse tongue falleth into mischief; **18:7** a fools mouth is his destruction, and his lips are the snare of his soul; **21:23** whoso keepeth his mouth and his tongue keepeth his soul from troubles; **28:18** whoso walketh uprightly shall be saved: but he that is perverse in his ways shall fall at once; **Isa. 30:12** thus saith the Holy One of Israel... ye despise this word, and trust in oppression and perverseness; **59:3** your hands are defiled with blood, and your fingers with iniquity; your lips have spoken lies, your tongue hath muttered perverseness; **Ezek. 9:9** the iniquity of the house of Israel and Judah is exceeding great, and the land is full of blood, and the city full of perverseness.

FRUIT, FRUITFUL (*see also* Good, Love, Eternal Life, Works)

If ye walk in my statutes and keep my commandments, and do them; Then I will give you rain in due season, and the land shall yield her increase, and the trees of the field shall yield her fruit. Lev. 26:3-4 (*see also* Commandment, Season)

I am the vine, yea are the branches: He that abideth in me, and I in him, the same bringeth forth much fruit: for without me ye can do nothing. John 15:5 (*see also* Abide, Do, Nothing, Vine)

Hear the word, and receive it, and bring forth fruit. Mark 4:20 (*see also* Bring, Word)

Honour the Lord with thy substance, and with the first fruits of all thine increase. Prov. 3:9-10 (*see also* Substance)

They should repent and turn to God, and do works meet for repentance. Acts 26:20 (*see also* Repent)

Matt. 3:7-8 O generation of vipers, who hath warned you to flee from the wrath to come? Bring forth therefore *f.* meet for repentance; **3:10** (Luke 3:9) the axe is laid unto the root of the trees: therefore every tree which bringeth not forth good fruit is hewn down, and cast into the fire; **Luke 3:8** bring forth therefore fruits worthy of repentance, and begin not to say within yourselves, We have Abraham to our father: for I say unto you, That God is able of these stones to raise up children unto Abraham. **Acts 26:20** they should repent and turn to God, and do works meet for repentance; **Rom. 2:4** despisest thou the riches of his goodness and forbearance and longsuffering; not knowing that the goodness of God leadeth thee to repentance.

FULFILL (*see* Accomplish, Diligence, Do, Endure, Perform)

FURNACE (*see also* Afflict, Persecute)

Behold, I have refined thee, but not with silver; I have chosen thee in the furnace of affliction. Isa. 48:10 (*see also* Afflict, Refine)

Isa. 48:10 I have refined thee, but not with silver; I have chosen thee in the furnace of affliction.

GAIN (*see also* Increase, Obtain)

For what is a man profited, if he shall gain the whole world, and lose his own soul? or what shall a man give in exchange for his soul? Matt.16:26 (*see also* Profit, Soul, World)

Whosoever will save his life shall lose it; but whosoever shall lose his life for my sake and the gospel's, the same shall save it. For what shall it profit a man, if he shall gain the whole world, and lose his own soul? Mark 8:36 (*see also* Life, Save, Soul)

What is the hope of the hypocrite, though he hath gained, when God taketh away his soul? Will God hear his cry when trouble cometh upon him? Job 27:8-9 (*see also* Hypocrite)

He that walketh righteously, and speaketh uprightly; he that despiseth the gain of oppressions, that shaketh his hands from holding of bribes, that stoppeth his ears from hearing of blood, and shutteth his eyes from seeing evil; He shall dwell on high: his defence shall be the munitions of rocks: bread shall be given him; his waters shall be sure. Isa. 33:15-16 (*see also* Oppress, Righteous, See, Speak, Uprightly, Walk)

GARMENTS (*see also* Apparel)

The woman shall not wear that which pertaineth unto a man, neither shall a man put on a women's garment: for all that do so are abomination unto the LORD thy God. Deut. 22:5 (*see also* Woman)

I will greatly rejoice in the LORD, my soul shall be joyful in my God; for he hath clothed me with the garments of salvation, he hath covered me with the robe of righteousness. Isa. 61:10 (*see also* Righteous, Robe)

Isa. 61:10 I will greatly rejoice in the LORD, my soul shall be joyful in my God; for he hath clothed me with the g. of salvation, he hath covered me with the robe of righteousness; 62:1 for Zions sake will I not hold my peace, and for Jerusalems sake I will not rest, until the righteousness thereof go forth as brightness, and the salvation thereof as a lamp that burneth; Ezek. 42:14 when the priests enter therein, then shall they not go out of the holy place into the utter court, but there they shall lay their g. wherein they minister; for they are holy.

GATE (*see also* Entrance, Path, Way)

Open ye the gates, that the righteous nation which keepeth the truth may enter in. Isa. 26:2 (*see also* Nation, Righteous, Truth)

Enter ye in at the strait gate; for wide is the gate, and broad is the way, that leadeth to destruction, and many there be which go in thereat; Because strait is the gate, and narrow is the way, which leadeth to life, and few be there that find it. Matt. 7:13-14 (*see also* Few, Narrow, Strait, Work)

Strive to enter in at the strait gate: for many, I say unto you, will seek to enter in, and shall not be able. Luke 13:24 (*see also* Enter, Strait, Strive)

GATHER, GATHERING (*see also* Bring)

And before him shall be gathered all nations: and he shall separate them one from another, as a shepherd divideth his sheep from the goats. Matt. 25:32 (*see also* Nation, Separate, Sheep)

If two of you shall agree on earth as touching any thing that they shall ask, it shall be done for them of my Father which is in heaven. For where two or three are gathered together in my name, there am I in the midst of them. Matt. 18:19-20 (*see also* Assemble)

GENEALOGY (*see also* Birthright, Family, Inheritance)

My God put into mine heart to gather together the nobles, and the rulers, and the people, that they might be reckoned by genealogy. Neh. 7:5 (*see also* Reckon)

1 Chron. 9:1 all Israel were reckoned by g.; and, behold, they were written in the book of the kings of Israel and Judah; 2 Chron. 31:16-19 both to the g. of the priests by the house of their fathers, and the Levites from twenty years old and upward, in their charges by their courses; And to the g. of all their little ones, their wives, and their sons, and their daughters, through all the congregation; Neh. 7:5 my God put into mine heart to gather together the nobles, and the rulers, and the people, that they might be reckoned by g.

GENERATION (*see also* Time)

Save yourselves from this untoward generation. Acts 2:40 (*see also* Save)

GENTILE (*see also* Israel)

It is a light thing that thou shouldest be my servant to raise up the tribes of Jacob, and to restore the preserved of Israel: I will also give thee for a light to the Gentiles, that thou mayest be my salvation unto the end of the earth. Isa. 49:6 (*see also* Earth, Light, Salvation)

Isa. 49:6 it is a light thing that thou shouldest be my servant to raise up the tribes of Jacob, and to restore the preserved of Israel: I will also give thee for a light to the G., that thou mayest be my salvation; 60:3 the g. shall come to thy light, and kings to the brightness of thy rising; 62:2 the g.

shall see thy righteousness, and all kings thy glory: and thou shalt be called by a new name, which the mouth of the LORD shall name.

GENTLE, GENTLENESS (*see also* Kind, Meek, Merciful)

The servant of the Lord must not strive; but be gentle unto all men, apt to teach, patient. 2 Tim. 2:24 (*see also* Teach)

2 Cor 10:1 now I Paul myself beseech you by the meekness and gentleness of Christ, who in presence am base among you, but being absent am bold toward you; **1 Thes. 2:7** we were gentle among you, even as a nurse cherisheth her children; **2 Tim. 2:24-26** the servant of the Lord must not strive; but be gentle unto all men, apt to teach, patient; **Titus 3:2** speak evil of no man, to be no brawlers, but gentle, shewing all meekness unto all men.

GIFT (*see also* Bribe, Holy Ghost, Offer, Sacrifice, Talent)

Every man should eat and drink, and enjoy the good of all his labor, it is the gift of God. Eccl. 3:13 (*see also* Labor)

But covet earnestly the best gifts: and yet shew I unto you a more excellent way. 1 Cor. 12:31 (*see also* Best, Covet)

I would that ye all spake with tongues, but rather that ye prophesied: for greater is he that prophesieth than he that speaketh with tongues, except he interpret, that the church may receive edifying. 1 Cor. 14:5 (*see also* Prophecy, Tongues)

If thou bring thy gift to the altar, and there rememberest that thy brother hath ought against thee; Leave there thy gift before the altar, and go thy way; first be reconciled to thy brother, and then come and offer thy gift. Matt. 5:23-24 (*see also* Offer, Reconcile)

A gift in secret pacifieth anger: and a reward in the bosom strong wrath. Prov. 21:14 (*see also* Anger)

Having then gifts differing according to the grace that is given to us, whether prophecy, let us prophesy according to the proportion of faith. Rom. 12:6 (*see also* Prophecy)

Whoso boasteth himself of a false gift is like clouds and wind without rain. Prov. 25:14 (*see also* Boast)

Neglect not the gift that is in thee. 1 Tim. 4:14 (*see also* Neglect)

1 Tim 4:14 Neglect not the g. that is in thee, which was given thee by prophecy, with the laying on of the hands of the presbytery; **2 Tim. 1:6** I put thee in remembrance that thou stir up the g of God, which is in thee by the putting on of my hands.

A gift is as a precious stone in the eyes of him that hath it: whithersoever it turneth, it prospereth. Prov. 17:8

Prov. 17:8 a g. is as a precious stone in the eyes of him that hath it: whithersoever it turneth, it prospereth; **18:16** a mans g. maketh room for him, and bringeth him before great men; **19:6** many will intreat the favour of the prince: and every man is a friend to him that giveth g.

God hath set some in the church, first apostles, secondarily prophets, thirdly teachers, after that miracles, then gifts of healings, helps, governments, diversities of tongues. Are all apostles? are all prophets? are all teachers? are all workers of miracles? Have all the gifts of healing? do all speak with tongues? do all interpret? But covet earnestly the best gifts: and yet shew I unto you a more excellent way. 1 Cor. 12:28-31 (*see also* Excellent, Prophet, Way)

1 Cor 1:7 so that ye come behind in no g; waiting for the coming of our Lord Jesus Christ; **7:7** I would that all men were even as I myself. But every man hath his proper g. of God, one after this manner, and another after that; **12:8** to one is given by the Spirit the word of wisdom; to another the word of knowledge by the same Spirit; **12:28-31** God hath set some in the church, first apostles, secondarily prophets, thirdly teachers, after that miracles, then g. of healings, helps, governments, diversities of tongues. Are all apostles? A re all prophets? are all teachers? are all workers of miracles? Have all the g. of healing? do all speak with tongues? do all interpret? But covet earnestly the best g.: and yet shew I unto you a more excellent way; **14:1** follow after charity, and desire spiritual g., but rather that ye may prophesy; **14:12** forasmuch as ye are zealous of spiritual g., seek that ye may excel to the edifying of the church; **14:39** wherefore, brethren, covet to prophesy, and forbid not to speak with tongues; **Eph. 4:11-12** and he gave some, apostles; and some, prophets; and some, evangelists; and some, pastors and teachers; For the perfecting of the saints, for the work of the ministry, for the edifying of the body of Christ; **Heb. 11:4** by faith Abel offered unto God a more excellent sacrifice than Cain, by which he obtained witness that he was righteous, God testifying of his *g.*: and by it he being dead yet speaketh; **James 1:17** every good *g.* and every perfect *g.* is from above, and cometh down from the Father of lights, with whom is no variableness, neither shadow of turning; **1 Pet. 4:10-11** as every man hath received the *g.*, even so minister the same one to another, as good stewards of the manifold grace of God. If any man speak, let him speak as the oracles of God; if any man minister, let him do it as of the ability which God giveth: that God in all things may be glorified through Jesus Christ, to whom be praise and dominion for ever and ever.

GIRD UP (*see also* Bind, Courage)

Thou therefore gird up thy loins, and arise, and speak unto them all that I command thee: be not dismayed at their faces, lest I confound thee before them. Jer. 1:17

Jer. 1:7 the LORD said unto me, Say not, I am a child: for thou shalt go to all that I shall send thee, and whatsoever I command thee thou shalt speak; **1:17** *g.u.* thy loins, and arise, and speak unto them all that I command thee: be not dismayed at their faces, lest I confound thee.

Gird up now thy loins like a man; for I will demand of thee, and answer thou me. Job 38:3

Job 38:3 *g.u.* now thy loins like a man; for I will demand of thee, and answer thou me; **40:7** *g.u.* thy loins now like a man: I will demand of thee, and declare thou unto me.

GAVE, GIVE, GIVEN (*see also* Alms, Bestow, Charity, Offer, Sacrifice)

He coveteth greedily all the day long: but the righteous giveth and spareth not. Prov. 21:26 (*see also* Greed)

Meditate upon these things; give thyself wholly to them; that thy profiting may appear to all. 1 Tim. 4:15 (*see also* Meditate, Ponder)

Give to him that asketh thee, and from him that would borrow of thee turn not thou away. Matt. 5:42 9 (*see also* Borrow)

Matt. 5:42 give to him that asketh thee, and from him that would borrow of thee turn not thou away; **Luke 6:30** give to every man that asketh of thee; and of him that taketh away thy goods ask them not again; **6:34-35** if ye lend to them of whom ye hope to receive, what thank have ye? for sinners also lend to sinners, to receive as much again. But love ye your enemies, and do good, and lend, hoping for nothing again; and your reward shall be great, and ye shall be the children of the Highest: for he is kind unto the unthankful and to the evil; **6:38** give, and it shall be given unto you; good measure, pressed down, and shaken together, and running over, shall men give into your bosom. For with the same measure that ye mete withal it shall be measured to you again; **11:7-8** trouble me not: the door is now shut, and my children are with me in bed; I cannot rise and give thee. I say unto you, Though he will not rise and give him, because he is his friend, yet because of his importunity he will rise and give him as many as he needeth; **2 Cor. 9:7** every man according as he purposeth in his heart, so let him give; not grudgingly, or of necessity: for God loveth a cheerful giver.

GLAD, GLADNESS (*see* Cheerful, Happy, Joy)

GLORIFY, GLORIOUS, GLORY (*see also* Exalt, Honor, Praise)

There are also celestial bodies, and bodies terrestrial: but the glory of the celestial is one, and the glory of the terrestrial is another. There is one glory of the sun, and another glory of the moon, and another glory of the stars: for one star differeth from another star in glory. So also is the resurrection of the dead. 1 Cor. 15:40-42 (*see also* Celestial, Dead, Terrestrial, Resurrection)

Give unto the LORD the glory due unto his name: bring an offering, and come before him: worship the LORD in the beauty of holiness. 1 Chron. 16:29 (*see also* Beauty, Offer)

Give unto the LORD the glory due unto his name; worship the LORD in the beauty of holiness. Ps. 29:2 (*see also* Worship)

Ascribe ye strength unto God; his excellency is over Israel, and his strength is in the clouds. Ps. 68:34 (*see also* Ascribe, Strength)

Thus saith the LORD, Let not the wise man glory in his wisdom, neither let the mighty man glory in his might, let not the rich man glory in his riches: But let him that glorieth glory in this, that he understandeth and knoweth me Jer. 9:23-24 (*see also* Wisdom)

It is not good to eat much honey: so for men to search their own glory is not glory. Prov. 25:27

Who is this King of glory? The LORD of hosts, he is the King of glory. Ps. 24:8 (*see also* One)

My people have changed their glory for that which doth not profit. Jer. 2:8 (*see also* Profit, Walk)

Grace be unto you, and peace, from him which is, and which was, and which is to come; and from the seven Spirits which are before his throne; And from Jesus Christ, who is the faithful witness, and the first begotten of the dead, and the prince of the kings of the earth. Unto him that loved us, and washed us from our sins in his own blood, And hath made us kings and priests unto God and his Father; to him be glory and dominion for ever and ever. Amen. Rev. 1:4-6 (*see also* Begotten, Blood, Jesus Christ)

Declare his glory among the heathen; his marvelous works among all nations. 1 Chron. 16:24 (*see also* Declare)

1 Chron. 16:24 declare his *g.* among the heathen; his marvellous works among all nations; Ps. 75:9 I will declare for ever; I will sing praises to the God of Jacob; 96:3 declare his *g.* among the heathen, his wonders among all people; 102:21 declare the name of the LORD in Zion, and his praise in Jerusalem; 107:22 let them sacrifice the sacrifices of thanksgiving, and declare his works with rejoicing; 118:17 I shall not die, but live, and declare the works of the LORD; 145:4-6 one generation shall praise thy works to another, and shall declare thy mighty acts. I will speak of the glorious honour of thy majesty, and of thy wondrous works; Isa. 66:19 I

will set a sign among them, and I will send those that escape of them unto the nations... that have not heard my fame, neither have seen my *g.*; and they shall declare my *g.* among the Gentiles; Jer. 4:2 thou shalt swear, The LORD liveth, in truth, in judgment, and in righteousness; and the nations shall bless themselves in him, and in him shall they *g.*; 9:12 who is he to whom the mouth of the LORD hath spoken, that he may declare it, for what the land perisheth and is burned up like a wilderness, that none passeth through.

Give unto the LORD, ye kindreds of the people, give unto the LORD glory and strength. Give unto the LORD the glory due unto his name. 1 Chron. 16:28-29

1 Chron. 16:28-29 give unto the LORD, ye kindreds of the people, give unto the LORD *g.* and strength. Give unto the LORD the *g.* due unto his name; Ps. 22:23 ye that fear the LORD, praise him; all ye the seed of Jacob, *g.* him; and fear him, all ye the seed of Israel; 29:1-2 give unto the LORD, O ye mighty, give unto the LORD *g.* and strength. Give unto the LORD the *g.* due unto his name; worship the LORD in the beauty of holiness; 30:1 I will extol thee, O LORD; for thou hast lifted me up, and hast not made my foes to rejoice over me; 30:12 to the end that my *g.* may sing praise to thee, and not be silent. O LORD my God, I will give thanks unto thee for ever; 86:9 all nations whom thou hast made shall come and worship before thee, O Lord; and shall *g.* thy name; 86:12 I will praise thee, O Lord my God, with all my heart: and I will *g.* thy name for evermore; 96:7-8 O ye kindreds of the people, give unto the LORD *g.* and strength. Give unto the LORD the *g.* due unto his name; 115:1 not unto us, but unto thy name give *g.*, for thy mercy, and for thy truths sake; Isa. 42:12 let them give *g.* unto the LORD, and declare his praise in the islands; 60:7 they shall come up with acceptance on mine altar, and I will *g.* the house of my *g.*; 60:9 bring thy sons from far, their silver and their gold with them, unto the name of the LORD thy God, and to the Holy One of Israel, because he hath *g.* thee; Jer. 4:2 thou shalt swear, The LORD liveth, in truth, in judgment, and in righteousness; and the nations shall bless themselves in him, and in him shall they *g.*; 13:16 give *g.* to the LORD your God, before he cause darkness; Dan. 5:23 thou hast praised the gods of silver, and gold, of brass, iron, wood, and stone, which see not, nor hear, nor know: and the God in whose hand thy breath is, and whose are all thy ways, hast thou not *g.*

Whether therefore ye eat, or drink, or whatsoever ye do, do all to the glory of God. 1 Cor. 10:31 (*see also* Do, Eat)

Matt. 9:8 when the multitudes saw it, they marvelled, and *g.* God, which had given such power unto men; **15:31** they saw the dumb to speak, the maimed to be whole, the lame to walk, and the blind to see: and they *g.* the God of Israel; **21:7-9** the multitudes that went before, and that followed, cried, saying, Hosanna to the Son of David: Blessed is he that cometh in the name of the Lord; Hosanna in the highest; **23:39** ye shall not see me henceforth, till ye shall say, Blessed is he that cometh in the name of the Lord; **Mark 2:12** immediately he arose, took up the bed, and went forth before them all; insomuch that they were all amazed, and *g.* God; **7:6** Esaias prophesied of you hypocrites, as it is written, This people honoureth me with their lips, but their heart is far from me; **Luke 1:46-47** my soul doth magnify the Lord, And my spirit hath rejoiced in God my Saviour; **5:25-26** immediately he rose up before them, and took up that whereon he lay, and departed to his own house, *g.* God. And they were all amazed, and they *g.* God, and were filled with fear; **7:16** there came a fear on all: and they *g.* God; **17:15** when he saw that he was healed, turned back, and with a loud voice *g.* God; **17:18** there are not found that returned to give *g.* to God, save this stranger; **18:43** immediately he received his sight, and followed him, *g.* God: and all the people, when they saw it, gave praise unto God; **John 7:18** he that speaketh of himself seeketh his own *g.*: but he that seeketh his *g.* that sent him, the same is true, and no unrighteousness is in him; **15:8** herein is my Father *g.*, that ye bear much fruit; so shall ye be my disciples; **17:10** all mine are thine, and thine are mine; and I am *g.* in them; **Acts 11:18** when they heard these things, they held their peace, and *g.* God, saying, Then hath God also to the Gentiles granted repentance unto life; **12:23** immediately the angel of the Lord smote him, because he gave not God the *g.*: and he was eaten of worms, and gave up the ghost; **1 Cor. 10:31** whether therefore ye eat, or drink, or whatsoever ye do, do all to the *g.* of God; **Philip. 2:11** every tongue should confess that Jesus Christ is Lord, to the *g.* of God the Father; **2 Thes. 1:12** that the name of our Lord Jesus Christ may be *g.* in you, and ye in him, according to the grace of our God and the Lord Jesus Christ; **3:1** pray for us, that the word of the Lord may have free course, and be *g.*, even as it is with you; **Titus 2:10** not purloining, but shewing all good fidelity; that they may adorn the doctrine of God our Saviour in all things; **Rev. 1:6** hath made us kings and priests unto God and his Father; to him be *g.* and dominion for ever and ever.

How can ye believe, which receive honour one of another, and seek not the honour that cometh from God only? John 5:44 (*see also* Honor, Praise)

Mark 12:38-40 beware of the scribes, which love to go in long clothing, and love salutations in the marketplaces, And the chief seats in the synagogues, and the uppermost rooms at feasts: Which devour widows' houses, and for a pretence make long prayers: these shall receive greater damnation; **Luke 9:25** what is a man advantaged, if he gain the whole world, and lose himself, or be cast away; **11:43** for ye love the uppermost seats in the synagogues, and greetings in the markets; **11:46** woe unto you also, ye lawyers! for ye lade men with burdens grievous to be borne, and ye yourselves touch not the burdens with one of your fingers; **John 5:44** how can ye believe, which receive honour one of another, and seek not the honour that cometh from God only; **7:18** he that speaketh of himself seeketh his own *g.*: but he that seeketh his *g.* that sent him, the same is true, and no unrighteousness is in him; **12:43** for they loved the praise of men more than the praise of God; **17:14** I have given them thy word; and the world hath hated them, because they are not of the world, even as I am not of the world; **1 Cor. 9:15-16** I have used none of these things: neither have I written these things, that it should be so done unto me: for it were better for me to die, than that any man should make my *g.* void. For though I preach the gospel, I have nothing to *g.* of: for necessity is laid upon me; yea, woe is unto me, if I preach not the gospel; **1 Thes. 2:6** nor of men sought we *g.*, neither of you, nor yet of others, when we might have been burdensome, as the apostles of Christ; **James 4:4** whosoever therefore will be a friend of the world is the enemy of God.

GO, GOING (*see also* Proceed)

Come ye, and let us go to the mountain of the LORD to the house of the God of Jacob; and he will teach us of his ways and we will walk in his paths: for out of Zion shall go forth the law, and the word of the LORD from Jerusalem. Isa. 2:3 (*see also* House, Path, Way)

Enter ye in at the strait gate: for wide is the gate, and broad is the way, that leadeth to destruction, and many there be which go in thereat: Because strait is the gate, and narrow is the way, which leadeth unto life, and few there be that find it. Matt. 7:13-14 (*see also* Baptism, Way)

Let us go into the house of the LORD. Ps. 122:1 (*see also* House)

Go in the strength of the Lord GOD: I will make mention of thy righteousness, even of thine only. Ps. 71:16 (*see also* Righteous, Strength)

I will go before thee, and make the crooked places straight: I will break in pieces the gates of brass, and cut in sunder the bars of iron. Isa. 45:2 (*see also* Crooked, Straight)

Ye shut up the kingdom of heaven against men: for ye neither go in yourselves, neither suffer ye them that are entering to go in. Matt. 23:13 (*see also* Kingdom)

Thou shalt do that which is right and good in the sight of the LORD: that it may be well with thee, and that thou mayest go in and possess the good land which the LORD swear unto thy fathers, To cast out all thine enemies from before thee, as the LORD hath spoken. Deut. 6:18-19 (*see also* Right, Thous Shalt)

Honour thy father and thy mother, as the LORD thy God hath commanded thee; that thy days may be prolonged, and that it may go well with thee, in the land which the LORD thy God giveth thee. Deut. 5:16 (*see also* Father, Honor, Mother)

Be ye angry, and sin not: let not the sun go down upon your wrath: Neither give place to the devil. Eph. 4:26 (*see also* Anger)

Therefore leaving the principles of the doctrine of Christ, let us go on unto perfection; not laying again the foundation of repentance from dead works, and of faith toward God, Of the doctrine of baptisms, and of laying on of hands, and of resurrection of the dead, and of eternal judgment. Heb. 6:1-2 (*see also* Authority, Call, Laying on of Hands, Principle)

GOD, GODHEAD (*see also* Father, Holy Ghost, Jesus Christ, Lord, Savior)

In the beginning was the Word, and the Word was with God, and the Word was God. John 1:1 (*see also* Beginning, Word)

The LORD is the true God, he is the living God, and an everlasting king: at his wrath the earth shall tremble, and the nations shall not be able to abide his indignation. Jer. 10:10 (*see also* King, True)

Work the works of God. John 6:28 (*see also* Do, Work)

I am the LORD thy God from the land of Egypt, and thou shalt know no god but me: for there is no saviour beside me. Hosea 13:4 (*see also* Savior)

Hosea 13:4 I am the LORD thy God from the land of Egypt, and thou shalt know no *g*. but me: for there is no saviour beside me; 13:9 O Israel, thou hast destroyed thyself; but in me is thine help.

Thou shalt have no other gods before me. Ex. 20:3 (*see also* Idol, Thous Shalt)

Gen. 35:2 put away the strange *g*. that are among you, and be clean, and change your garments; Ex. 20:3 thou shalt have no other *g*. before me; 22:20 he that sacrificeth unto any *g*., save unto the LORD only, he shall be utterly destroyed; 23:13 be circumspect: and make no mention of the name of other *g*., neither let it be heard out of thy mouth; 23:32-33 thou shalt make no covenant with them, nor with their *g*.. They shall not dwell in thy land, lest they make thee sin against me: for if thou serve their *g*., it will surely be a snare unto thee; 32:31 Moses returned unto the LORD, and said, Oh, this people have sinned a great sin, and have made them *g*. of gold; Deut. 5:7 thou shalt have none other *g*. before me; 6:14 ye shall not go after other *g*., of the *g*. of the people which are round about you; 7:4 they will turn away thy son from following me, that they may serve other *g*.: so will the anger of the LORD be kindled against you, and destroy thee suddenly; 8:19 if thou do at all forget the LORD thy *G*., and walk after other *g*., and serve them, and worship them, I testify against you this day that ye shall surely perish; 11:16 take heed to yourselves, that your heart be not deceived, and ye turn aside, and serve other g., and worship them; **11:28** if ye will not obey the commandments of the LORD your *G.*, but turn aside out of the way which I command you this day, to go after other *g.*, which ye have not known; **17:3** hath gone and served other *g.*, and worshipped them, either the sun, or moon, or any of the host of heaven, which I have not commanded; **29:26** they went and served other *g.*, and worshipped them, *g.* whom they knew not, and whom he had not given unto them; **1 Kgs. 11:4** when Solomon was old, that his wives turned away his heart after other *g.*: and his heart was not perfect with the LORD his *G.*, as was the heart of David his father; **14:9** thou hast gone and made thee other *g.*, and molten images, to provoke me to anger, and hast cast me behind thy back; **18:27-29** cut themselves after their manner with knives and lancets, till the blood gushed out upon them. And it came to pass, when midday was past, and they prophesied until the time of the offering of the evening sacrifice, that there was neither voice, nor any to answer, nor any that regarded; **19:18** I have left me seven thousand in Israel, all the knees which have not bowed unto Baal, and every mouth which hath not kissed him; **2 Kgs. 22:17** because they have forsaken me, and have burned incense unto other *g.*, that they might provoke me to anger with all the works of their hands; therefore my wrath shall be kindled against this place, and shall not be quenched; **Ps. 16:4** their sorrows shall be multiplied that hasten after another *g.*: their drink offerings of blood will I not offer, nor take up their names into my lips; **81:9** there shall no strange *g.* be in thee; neither shalt thou worship any strange *g.*; **Jer. 7:6-9** will ye steal, murder, and commit adultery, and swear falsely, and burn incense unto Baal, and walk after other *g.* whom ye know not; **11:10** they are turned back to the iniquities of their forefathers, which refused to hear my words; and they went after other *g.* to serve them: the house of Israel and the house of Judah have broken my covenant which I made with their fathers; **13:10** this evil people, which refuse to hear my words, which walk in the imagination of their heart, and walk after other *g.*, to serve them, and to worship them, shall even be as this girdle, which is good for nothing; **16:11** your fathers have forsaken me, saith the LORD, and have walked after other *g.*, and have served them, and have worshipped them, and have forsaken me, and have not kept my law; **16:13** shall ye serve other *g.* day and night; where I will not shew you favour.

GODLINESS (*see also* Charity, Golden Rule, Holiness, Perfect)

Lead a quiet and peaceable life in all godliness and honesty. 1 Tim. 2:2 (*see also* Honest, Life, Peace)

Exercise thyself rather unto godliness. 1 Tim. 4:7 (*see also* Exercise)

1 Tim 4:7-9 refuse profane and old wives' fables, and exercise thyself rather unto *g.* For bodily exercise profiteth little: but *g.* is profitable unto all things, having promise of the life that now is, and of that which is to come. This is a faithful saying and worthy of all acceptation; **6:5** perverse disputings of men of corrupt minds, and destitute of the truth, supposing that gain is *g.*: from such withdraw thyself; **6:11** O man of God, flee these things; and follow after righteousness, *g.*, faith, love, patience, meekness; **Titus 2:12** teaching us that, denying ungodliness and worldly lusts, we should live soberly, righteously, and *g.*, in this present world; **2 Pet. 1:3-4** his divine power hath given unto us all things that pertain unto life and *g.*, through the knowledge of him that hath called us to glory and virtue: Whereby are given unto us exceeding great and precious promises: that by these ye might be partakers of the divine nature, having escaped the corruption that is in the world through lust; **1:6-7** and to knowledge temperance; and to temperance patience; and to patience *g.*; And to *g.* brotherly kindness; and to brotherly kindness charity; **3:11** what manner of persons ought ye to be in all holy conversation and *g.*

GOLD (*see also* Riches, Silver, Treasure)

I love thy commandments above gold; yea, above fine gold. Ps. 119:127 (*see also* Commandment)

GOLDEN RULE (*see* Charity, Do, Kindness, Love)

Therefore all things whatsoever ye would that men should do to you, do ye even so to them: for this is the law and the prophets. Matt. 7:12 (*see also* Do)

GOOD, GOODNESS (*see also* Bless, Jesus Christ, Righteous, Works)

Rejoice in goodness. 2 Chron. 6:41 (*see also* Rejoice)

Trust in the LORD, and do good. Ps. 37:3 (*see also* Do, Trust)

Ye have wearied the LORD with your words. Yet ye say, Wherein have we wearied him? When ye say, Every one that doeth evil is good in the sight of the LORD. Mal. 2:17 (*see also* Evil, Weary)

In all things shewing thyself a pattern of good works: in doctrine shewing uncorruptness, gravity, sincerity, Sound speech, that cannot be condemned; that he that is of the contrary part may be ashamed, having no evil thing to say of you. Titus 2:7-8 (*see also* Pattern, Speak, Works)

To him that knoweth to do good, and doeth it not, to him it is sin. James 4:17 (*see also* Do)

Be of good cheer. Mark 6:50 (*see also* Cheer)

Jesus answered and said unto her, Martha, Martha, thou art careful and troubled about many things: But one thing is needful: and Mary hath chosen that good part, which shall not be taken away from her. Luke 10:41-42 (*see also* Choose)

Do men gather grapes of thorns, or figs of thistles? Even so every good tree bringeth forth good fruit; but a corrupt tree bringeth forth evil fruit. A good tree cannot bring forth evil fruit, neither can a corrupt tree bring forth good fruit. Every tree that bringeth not forth good fruit is hewn down, and cast into the fire. Wherefore by their fruits ye shall know them. Matt. 7:16 (*see also* Evil)

Abhor that which is evil; cleave to that which is good. Rom. 12:9 (*see also* Evil)

Depart from evil, and do good; seek peace, and pursue it. Ps. 34:14 (*see also* Depart, Evil)

Because of the house of the LORD our God I will seek thy good. Ps. 122:9 (*see also* House)

The LORD is good to all: and his tender mercies are over all his works. Ps. 145:9 (*see also* Mercy)

Walk in the ways of good men, and keep the paths of the righteous. Prov. 2:20 (*see also* Walk, Way)

Heaviness in the heart of man maketh it stoop: but a good word maketh it glad. Prov. 12:25 (*see also* Heart)

Woe unto them that call evil good, and good evil; that put darkness for light, and light for darkness; that put bitter for sweet and sweet for bitter! Isa. 5:20 (*see also* Evil, Sweet)

Return ye now every one from his evil way, and make your ways and your doings good. Jer. 18:11 (*see also* Evil, Way)

Ye have wearied the LORD with your words. Yet ye say, Wherein have we wearied him? When ye say, Every one that doeth evil is good in the sight of the LORD, and he delighteth in them. Mal. 2:17 (*see also* Evil)

Most men will proclaim every one his own goodness: but a faithful man who can find? Prov. 20:6 (*see also* Proclaim)

It shall come to pass at that time, that I will search Jerusalem with candles, and punish the men that are settled on their lees: that say in their heart, The LORD will not do good, neither will he do evil. Zeph. 1:12 (*see also* Evil, Say)

How beautiful upon the mountains are the feet of him that bringeth good tidings, that publisheth peace; that bringeth good tidings of good, that publisheth salvation; that saith unto Zion, Thy God reigneth! (*see also* Beautiful, Mountain, Peace, Publish, Zion)

Isa. 52:7 how beautiful upon the mountains are the feet of him that bringeth *g.* tidings, that publisheth peace; that bringeth *g.* tidings of *g.*, that publisheth salvation; that saith unto Zion, Thy God reigneth; **Nahum 1:15** behold upon the mountains the feet of him that bringeth *g.* tidings, that publisheth peace! O Judah, keep thy solemn feasts, perform thy vows: for the wicked shall no more pass through thee.

Withhold not good from them to whom it is due, when it is in the power of thine hand to do it. Prov. 3:27 (*see also* Due)

Prov. 3:27 withhold not *g.* from them to whom it is due, when it is in the power of thine hand to do it; **11:24-26** there is that scattereth, and yet increaseth; and there is that withholdeth more than is meet, but it tendeth to poverty... He that withholdeth corn, the people shall curse him: but blessing shall be upon the head of him that selleth it.

Thou shalt do that which is right and good in the sight of the LORD: that it may be well with thee, and that thou mayest go in and possess the good land which the LORD sware unto thy fathers, To cast out all thine enemies from before thee, as the LORD hath spoken. Deut. 6:18-19 (*see also* Go, Right)

Deut. 6:18 thou shalt do that which is right and *g.* in the sight of the LORD: that it may be well with thee; **Josh.21:45** there failed not ought of any *g.* thing which the LORD had spoken unto the house of Israel; **Judg. 3:7** the children of Israel did evil in the sight of the LORD, and forgat the LORD their God; **2 Kgs. 12:2** Jehoash did that which was right in the sight of the LORD all his days; **13:2** he did that which was evil in the sight of the LORD, and followed the sins of Jeroboam; **13:11** he did that which was evil in the sight of the LORD; he departed not from all the sins; **14:3** he did that which was right in the sight of the LORD; **15:3** he did that which was right in the sight of the LORD; **15:34** he did that which was right in the sight of the LORD; **16:2** twenty years old was Ahaz when he began to reign, and reigned sixteen years in Jerusalem, and did not that which was right in the sight of the LORD his God; **17:9** the children of Israel did secretly those things that were not right against the LORD their God; **18:3** he did that which was right in the sight of the LORD; **2 Chron. 6:41** let thy priests, O LORD God, be clothed with salvation, and let thy saints rejoice in *g.*; **20:32** he walked in the way of Asa his father, and departed not from it, doing that which was right in the sight of the LORD; **26:4** he did that which was right in the sight of the LORD; **31:20** thus did Hezekiah throughout all Judah, and wrought that which was *g.* and right and truth before the LORD his God; **34:2** he did that which was right in the sight of the LORD, and walked in the ways of David his father, and declined neither to the right hand, nor to the left; **Neh. 5:19** think upon me, my God, for *g.*, according to all that I have done for this people; **Ps. 31:23** O love the LORD, all ye his saints: for the LORD preserveth the faithful, and plentifully rewardeth the proud doer; **34:14** depart from evil, and do *g.*; seek peace, and pursue it; **37:3** trust in the LORD, and do *g.*; **37:24-25** though he fall, he shall not be utterly cast down: for the LORD upholdeth him with his hand; **112:5** a *g.* man sheweth favour,

and lendeth: he will guide his affairs with discretion; **122:9** because of the house of the LORD our God I will seek thy *g.*; **126:6** he that goeth forth and weepeth, bearing precious seed, shall doubtless come again with rejoicing; **Prov. 11:27** he that diligently seeketh *g.* procureth favour: but he that seeketh mischief, it shall come unto him; **12:2** a *g.* man obtaineth favour of the LORD: but a man of wicked devices will he condemn; **14:14** the backslider in heart shall be filled with his own ways: and a *g.* man shall be satisfied from himself; **15:30** the light of the eyes rejoiceth the heart: and a *g.* report maketh the bones fat; **31:12** she will do him *g.* and not evil all the days of her life; **Isa. 38:3-6** remember now, O LORD, I beseech thee, how I have walked before thee in truth and with a perfect heart, and have done that which is *g.* in thy sight; **Amos 5:14-15** seek *g.*, and not evil, that ye may live: and so the LORD, the God of hosts, shall be with you.

Prove all things; hold fast that which is good. 1 Thes. 5:21 (*see also* Prove)

1 Thes 5:21 prove all things; hold fast that which is *g.*; **1 Tim. 1:18-19** according to the prophecies which went before on thee, that thou by them mightest war a *g.* warfare; Holding faith, and a *g.* conscience; which some having put away concerning faith have made shipwreck; **4:16** take heed unto thyself, and unto the doctrine; continue in them: for in doing this thou shalt both save thyself, and them that hear thee; **2 Tim. 1:13** hold fast the form of sound words, which thou hast heard of me; **Titus 1:9** holding fast the faithful word as he hath been taught, that he may be able by sound doctrine both to exhort and to convince the gainsayers; **1 Cor. 3:14** we are made partakers of Christ, if we hold the beginning of our confidence stedfast unto the end.

As we have therefore opportunity, let us do good unto all men, especially unto them who are of the household of faith. Gal. 6:10

Matt. 5:44-45 love your enemies, bless them that curse you, do *g.* to them that hate you, and pray for them which despitefully use you, and persecute you; That ye may be the children of your Father which is in heaven: for he maketh his sun to rise on the evil and on the *g.*, and sendeth rain on the just and on the unjust; **7:17-19** every *g.* tree bringeth forth *g.* fruit; but a corrupt tree bringeth forth evil fruit. A *g.* tree cannot bring forth evil fruit, neither can a corrupt tree bring forth g. fruit. Every tree that bringeth not forth g. fruit is hewn down, and cast into the fire; **10:1** he gave them power against unclean spirits, to cast them out, and to heal all manner of sickness and all manner of disease; **12:12** how much then is a man better than a sheep? Wherefore it is lawful to do well on the sabbath days; **12:33-35,** (Luke 6:43-45) either make the tree g., and his fruit g.; or else make the tree corrupt, and his fruit corrupt: for the tree is known by his fruit. O generation of vipers, how can ye, being evil, speak g. things? for out of the abundance of the heart the mouth speaketh. A g. man out of the g. treasure of the heart bringeth forth g. things: and an evil man out of the evil treasure bringeth forth evil things; **16:27** for the Son of man shall come in the glory of his Father with his angels; and then he shall reward every man according to his works; **19:17** (Mark 10:17-18) why callest thou me g.? there is none g. but one, that is, God: but if thou wilt enter into life, keep the commandments; **Mark 3:4** is it lawful to do g. on the sabbath days, or to do evil? to save life, or to kill; **Luke 6:27** love your enemies, do g. to them which hate you; **6:33** if ye do g. to them which do g. to you, what thank have ye? for sinners also do even the same; **6:35** love ye your enemies, and do g., and lend, hoping for nothing again; and your reward shall be great, and ye shall be the children of the Highest: for he is kind unto the unthankful and to the evil;**10:33-35** a certain Samaritan, as he journeyed, came where he was: and when he saw him, he had compassion on him, And went to him, and bound up his wounds, pouring in oil and wine, and set him on his own beast, and brought him to an inn, and took care of him. And on the morrow when he departed, he took out two pence, and gave them to the host, and said unto him, Take care of him; and whatsoever thou spendest more, when I come again, I will repay thee; **12:36-38** blessed are those servants, whom the Lord when he cometh shall find watching: verily I say unto you, that he shall gird himself, and make them to sit down to meat, and will come forth and serve them. And if he shall come in the second watch, or come in the third watch, and find them so, blessed are those servants; **John 5:29** they that have done g., unto the resurrection of life; and they that have done evil, unto the resurrection of damnation; **13:17** if ye know these things, happy are ye if ye do them; **Rom. 2:7** to them who by patient continuance in well doing seek for glory and honour and immortality, eternal life; **2:10** glory, honour, and peace, to every man that worketh g., to the Jew first, and also to the Gentile; **13:3** rulers are not a

terror to g. works, but to the evil. Wilt thou then not be afraid of the power? do that which is g., and thou shalt have praise of the same; **2 Cor. 5:10** we must all appear before the judgment seat of Christ; that every one may receive the things done in his body, according to that he hath done, whether it be g. or bad; **9:8** God is able to make all grace abound toward you; that ye, always having all sufficiency in all things, may abound to every g. work; **Gal. 4:18** it is g. to be zealously affected always in a g. thing, and not only when I am present with you; **6:9** (2 Thes 3:13) let us not be weary in well doing: for in due season we shall reap, if we faint not; **Eph. 2:10** we are his workmanship, created in Christ Jesus unto g. works, which God hath before ordained that we should walk in them; **4:28** let him labour, working with his hands the thing which is g., that he may have to give to him that needeth; **6:8** knowing that whatsoever g. thing any man doeth, the same shall he receive of the Lord, whether he be bond or free; **Gal. 6:9-10** let us not be weary in well doing: for in due season we shall reap, if we faint not. As we have therefore opportunity, let us do g. unto all men, especially unto them who are of the household of faith; **1 Thes. 5:15** see that none render evil for evil unto any man; but ever follow that which is g., both among yourselves, and to all men; **2 Thes. 2:17** comfort your hearts, and stablish you in every g. word and work; **1 Tim. 2:10** but (which becometh women professing godliness) with g. works; **5:10** well reported of for g. works; if she have brought up children, if she have lodged strangers, if she have washed the saints' feet, if she have relieved the afflicted, if she have diligently followed every g. work; **6:18** they do g., that they be rich in g. works, ready to distribute, willing to communicate; **2 Tim. 2:21** if a man therefore purge himself from these, he shall be a vessel unto honour, sanctified, and meet for the master's use, and prepared unto every g. work; **Titus 3:1** put them in mind to be subject to principalities and powers, to obey magistrates, to be ready to every g. work; **3:8** they which have believed in God might be careful to maintain g. works. These things are g. and profitable unto men; **3:14** let ours also learn to maintain g. works for necessary uses, that they be not unfruitful; **Heb. 10:24** let us consider one another to provoke unto love and to g. works; **13:16** do g. and to communicate forget not: for with such sacrifices God is well pleased; **James 4:17** to him that knoweth to do g., and doeth it not, to him it is sin; **1 Pet. 2:12** as evildoers, they may by your g. works, which they shall behold, glorify God in the day of visitation; **2:15** so is the will of God, that with well doing ye may put to silence the ignorance of foolish men; **3:11** let him eschew evil, and do g.; let him seek peace, and ensue it; **1 Jn. 3:18-21** my little children, let us not love in word, neither in tongue; but in deed and in truth. And hereby we know that we are of the truth, and shall assure our hearts before him. For if our heart condemn us, God is greater than our heart, and knoweth all things. Beloved, if our heart condemn us not, then have we confidence toward God; **3 Jn. 1:11** follow not that which is evil, but that which is g.. He that doeth g. is of God: but he that doeth evil hath not seen God; **Rev. 2:23** I am he which searcheth the reins and hearts: and I will give unto every one of you according to your works; **20:12** I saw the dead, small and great, stand before God; and the books were opened: and another book was opened, which is the book of life: and the dead were judged out of those things which were written in the books, according to their works; **20:13** the sea gave up the dead which were in it; and death and hell delivered up the dead which were in them: and they were judged every man according to their works; **22:12** I come quickly; and my reward is with me, to give every man according as his work shall be.

GOSPEL (*see also* Jesus Christ, Record, Restore, Salvation, Scripture, Truth, Word)

To you who are troubled rest with us, when the Lord Jesus shall be revealed from heaven with his mighty angels, In flaming fire taking vengeance on them that know not God, and that obey not the gospel of our Lord Jesus Christ. 2 Thes. 1:7-8 (*see also* Jesus Christ)

Take heed unto thyself, and unto the doctrine; continue in them: for in doing this thou shalt both save thyself, and them that hear thee. 1 Tim. 4:16 (*see also* Obey)

Let your conversation be as it becometh the gospel of Christ: that whether I come and see you, or else be absent, I may hear of your affairs, that ye stand fast in one spirit, with one mind striving together for the faith of the gospel. Philip. 1:27 (*see also* Conversation, One)

I marvel that ye are so soon removed from him that called you into the grace of Christ unto another gospel. Gal. 1:6 (*see also* Turn)

The time is fulfilled, and the kingdom of God is at hand: repent ye, and believe the gospel. Mark 1:15 (*see also* Repent)

Mark 1:15 the time is fulfilled, and the kingdom of God is at hand: repent ye, and believe the *g.*; **16:17-18** these signs shall follow them that believe; In my name shall they cast out devils; they shall speak with new tongues; They shall take up serpents; and if they drink any deadly thing, it shall not hurt them: they shall lay hands on the sick, and they shall recover; **Acts 13:12** the deputy, when he saw what was done, believed, being astonished at the doctrine of the Lord; **15:7** ye know how that a good while ago God made choice among us, that the Gentiles by my mouth should hear the word of the *g.*, and believe; **2 Cor. 4:4** the god of this world hath blinded the minds of them which believe not, lest the light of the glorious *g.* of Christ, who is the image of God, should shine unto them.

Go ye into all the world, and preach the gospel to every creature. Mark 16:15 (*see also* Preach)

Matt. 3:1 In those days came John the Baptist, preaching in the wilderness of Judaea; **4:23** Jesus went about all Galilee, teaching in their synagogues, and preaching the *g.* of the kingdom; **5:2** he opened his mouth, and taught them; **5:19** whosoever shall do and teach them, the same shall be called great in the kingdom of heaven; **7:28-29** when Jesus had ended these sayings, the people were astonished at his doctrine: For he taught them as one having authority, and not as the scribes; **9:35** Jesus went about all the cities and villages, teaching in their synagogues, and preaching the *g.* of the kingdom, and healing every sickness and every disease among the people; **10:5-15** go rather to the lost sheep of the house of Israel. And as ye go, preach, saying, The kingdom of heaven is at hand; **10:27** what I tell you in darkness, that speak ye in light: and what ye hear in the ear, that preach ye upon the housetops; **10:32-33** whosoever therefore shall confess me before men, him will I confess also before my Father which is in heaven; **11:1** [Jesus] departed thence to teach and to preach in their cities; **11:5** the poor have the *g.* preached to them; **13:1-2** great multitudes were gathered together unto him, so that he went into a ship, and sat; and the whole multitude stood on the shore; **13:34** all these things spake Jesus unto the multitude in parables; and without a parable spake he not unto them; **21:23** the chief priests and the elders of the people came unto him as he was teaching; **24:14** this *g.* of the kingdom shall be preached in all the world for a witness unto all nations; and then shall the end come; **26:55** I sat daily with you teaching in the temple, and ye laid no hold on me; **28:19** go ye therefore, and teach all nations, baptizing them in the name of the Father, and of the Son, and of the Holy Ghost; **Mark 1:1-2** the beginning of the *g.* of Jesus Christ, the Son of God; As it is written in the prophets, Behold, I send my messenger before thy face, which shall prepare thy way before thee; **1:14** Jesus came into Galilee, preaching the *g.* of the kingdom of God; **1:21** on the sabbath day he entered into the synagogue, and taught; **1:38-39** let us go into the next towns, that I may preach there also: for therefore came I forth. And he preached in their synagogues throughout all Galilee, and cast out devils; **1:45** he went out, and began to publish it much, and to blaze abroad the matter, insomuch that Jesus could no more openly enter into the city, but was without in desert places: and they came to him from every quarter; **2:2** many were gathered together, insomuch that there was no room to receive them, no, not so much as about the door: and he preached the word unto them; **2:13** he went forth again by the sea side; and allthe multitude resorted unto him, and he taught them; **4:1-2** he began again to teach by the sea side: and there was gathered unto him a great multitude, so that he entered into a ship, and sat in the sea; and the whole multitude was by the sea on the land. And he taught them many things by parables, and said unto them in his doctrine; **4:34** without a parable spake he not unto them: and when they were alone, he expounded all things to his disciples; **4:44** he preached in the synagogues of Galilee; **6:2** when the sabbath day was come, he began to teach in the synagogue: and many hearing him were astonished, saying, From whence hath this man these things? and what wisdom is this which is given unto him, that even such mighty works are wrought by his hands; **6:6** he marvelled because of their unbelief. And he went round about the villages, teaching; **6:8-12** commanded them that they should take nothing for their journey, save a staff only; no scrip, no bread, no money in their purse: But be shod with sandals; and not put on two coats; **6:30** the apostles gathered themselves together unto Jesus, and told him all things, both what they had done, and what they had taught; **6:34** Jesus, when he came out, saw much people, and was moved with compassion toward them, because they were as sheep not having a shepherd: and he began to teach them many things; **10:1** the people resort unto him again;

and, as he was wont, he taught them again; **11:18** the scribes and chief priests heard it, and sought how they might destroy him: for they feared him, because all the people was astonished at his doctrine; **12:28** one of the scribes came, and having heard them reasoning together, and perceiving that he had answered them well; **12:35** while he taught in the temple, How say the scribes that Christ is the Son of David; **13:10** the *g.* must first be published among all nations; **14:9** wheresoever this *g.* shall be preached throughout the whole world, this also that she hath done shall be spoken of for a memorial of her; **14:49** I was daily with you in the temple teaching, and ye took me not: but the scriptures must be fulfilled; **16:15** go ye into all the world, and preach the *g.* to every creature; **16:20** they went forth, and preached every where, the Lord working with them, and confirming the word with signs following; **Luke 1:76-77** to give knowledge of salvation unto his people by the remission of their sins; **2:46** it came to pass, that after three days they found him in the temple, sitting in the midst of the doctors, both hearing them, and asking them questions; **3:18** many other things in his exhortation preached he unto the people; **4:15-16** he taught in their synagogues, being glorified of all; **4:18-19** the Spirit of the Lord is upon me, because he hath anointed me to preach the *g.* to the poor... To preach the acceptable year of the Lord; **4:43** I must preach the kingdom of God to other cities also: for therefore am I sent; **5:1-3** the people pressed upon him to hear the word of God; **5:10** Jesus said unto Simon, Fear not; from henceforth thou shalt catch men; **7:22** go your way, and tell John what things ye have seen and heard... to the poor the *g.* is preached; **8:4** much people were gathered together, and were come to him out of every city, he spake by a parable; **9:2-6** he sent them to preach the kingdom of God... and they departed, and went through the towns, preaching the *g.,* and healing every where; **9:59-60** Jesus said unto him, Let the dead bury their dead: but go thou and preach the kingdom of God; **10:1-12** the Lord appointed other seventy also, and sent them two and two before his face into every city and place, whither he himself would come; **12:22-24** take no thought for your life, what ye shall eat; neither for the body, what ye shall put on. The life is more than meat, and the body is more than raiment; **13:10** he was teaching in one of the synagogues on the sabbath; **13:22-23** he went through the cities and villages, teaching, and journeying toward Jerusalem; **19:47-48** he taught daily in the temple; **20:1** as he taught the people in the temple, and preached the *g.,* the chief priests and the scribes came upon him with the elders; **21:37-38** in the day time he was teaching in the temple; and at night he went out, and abode in the mount that is called the mount of Olives. And all the people came early in the morning to him in the temple, for to hear him; **24:47** repentance and remission of sins should be preached in his name among all nations, beginning at Jerusalem; **John 6:45** it is written in the prophets, And they shall be all taught of God. Every man therefore that hath heard, and hath learned of the Father, cometh unto me; **7:14** Jesus went up into the temple, and taught; **8:2** early in the morning he came again into the temple, and all the people came unto him; and he sat down, and taught them; **Acts 3:25** ye are the children of the prophets, and of the covenant which God made with our fathers, saying unto Abraham, And in thy seed shall all the kindreds of the earth be blessed; **5:42** daily in the temple, and in every house, they ceased not to teach and preach Jesus Christ; **8:5** Philip... preached Christ unto them; **8:25** testified and preached the word of the Lord, preached the *g.* in many villages of the Samaritans; **Philip. 9:15** go thy way: for he is a chosen vessel unto me, to bear my name before the Gentiles, and kings, and the children of Israel; **9:20** straightway he preached Christ in the synagogues, that he is the Son of God; **10:42** he commanded us to preach unto the people, and to testify that it is he which was ordained of God to be the Judge of quick and dead; **11:1** the apostles and brethren that were in Judaea heard that the Gentiles had also received the word of God; **11:20-22** preaching the Lord Jesus; **11:26** that a whole year they assembled themselves with the church, and taught much people; **13:47** the Lord commanded us, saying, I have set thee to be a light of the Gentiles, that thou shouldest be for salvation unto the ends of the earth; **14:7** there they preached the *g.*; **14:21** when they had preached the *g.* to that city, and had taught many; **14:25** when they had preached the word in Perga, they went down into Attalia; **15:7** Peter rose up, and said unto them, Men and brethren, ye know how that a good while ago God made choice among us, that the Gentiles by my mouth should hear the word of the *g.*, and believe; **15:35** teaching and preaching the word of the Lord, with many others also; **16:32** they spake unto him the word of the Lord, and to all that were in his house; **17:18** he preached unto them Jesus, and the resurrection; **18:11** he continued there a year and six months, teaching the word of God among them; **18:23** strengthening all the disciples; **19:10** this continued by the space of two years; so that all they which dwelt in Asia

heard the word of the Lord Jesus, both Jews and Greeks; **20:20** I kept back nothing that was profitable unto you, but have shewed you, and have taught you publickly, and from house to house; **21:19** he declared particularly what things God had wrought among the Gentiles by his ministry; **22:15** thou shalt be his witness unto all men of what thou hast seen and heard; **22:21** I will send thee far hence unto the Gentiles; **26:18** open their eyes, and to turn them from darkness to light, and from the power of Satan unto God, that they may receive forgiveness of sins, and inheritance among them which are sanctified by faith that is in me; **Rom. 1:15** as much as in me is, I am ready to preach the *g.* to you; **10:8** the word is nigh thee, even in thy mouth, and in thy heart: that is, the word of faith, which we preach; **10:14-15** how then shall they call on him in whom they have not believed? and how shall they believe in him of whom they have not heard? and how shall they hear without a preacher? And how shall they preach, except they be sent? as it is written, How beautiful are the feet of them that preach the *g.* of peace, and bring glad tidings of good things; **10:21** all day long I have stretched forth my hands unto a disobedient and gainsaying people; **12:6-7** having then gifts differing according to the grace that is given to us, whether prophecy, let us prophesy according to the proportion of faith; Or ministry, let us wait on our ministering: or he that teacheth, on teaching; Or he that exhorteth, on exhortation: he that giveth, let him do it with simplicity; he that ruleth, with diligence; he that sheweth mercy, with cheerfulness; **15:19-20** through mighty signs and wonders, by the power of the Spirit of God; so that from Jerusalem, and round about unto Illyricum, I have fully preached the *g.* of Christ; **1 Cor. 1:17** Christ sent me not to baptize, but to preach the *g.*: not with wisdom of words, lest the cross of Christ should be made of none effect; **1:23** we preach Christ crucified; **9:13** they which minister about holy things live of the things of the temple; **9:18** when I preach the *g.*, I may make the *g.* of Christ without charge, that I abuse not my power in the *g.*; **9:20-23** I became as a Jew, that I might gain the Jews; to them that are under the law, as under the law, that I might gain them that are under the law; To them that are without law, as without law, (being not without law to God, but under the law to Christ,) that I might gain them that are without law. To the weak became I as weak, that I might gain the weak: I am made all things to all men, that I might by all means save some. And this I do for the *g.* sake, that I might be partaker thereof with you; **15:1** I declare unto you the *g.*

which I preached unto you, which also ye have received, and wherein ye stand; **2 Cor. 2:12** I came to Troas to preach Christ's *g.,* and a door was opened unto me of the Lord; **2:14** thanks be unto God, which always causeth us to triumph in Christ, and maketh manifest the savour of his knowledge by us in every place; **4:4-5** the god of this world hath blinded the minds of them which believe not, lest the light of the glorious *g.* of Christ, who is the image of God, should shine unto them. For we preach not ourselves, but Christ Jesus the Lord; **4:10-14** I believed, and therefore have I spoken; we also believe, and therefore speak; Knowing that he which raised up the Lord Jesus shall raise up us also by Jesus, and shall present us with you; **9:6** he which soweth sparingly shall reap also sparingly; and he which soweth bountifully shall reap also bountifully; **9:13** the experiment of this ministration they glorify God for your professed subjection unto the *g.* of Christ; **10:16** to preach the *g.* in the regions beyond you, and not to boast in another man's line of things made ready to our hand; **11:7** have I committed an offence in abasing myself that ye might be exalted, because I have preached to you the *g.* of God freely; **Gal. 2:2** I went up by revelation, and communicated unto them that *g.* which I preach among the Gentiles, but privately to them which were of reputation, lest by any means I should run, or had run, in vain; **2:9** James, Cephas, and John, who seemed to be pillars, perceived the grace that was given unto me, they gave to me and Barnabas the right hands of fellowship; that we should go unto the heathen, and they unto the circumcision; **Eph. 3:6** the Gentiles should be fellowheirs, and of the same body, and partakers of his promise in Christ by the *g.*; **Philip. 1:18** notwithstanding, every way, whether in pretence, or in truth, Christ is preached; and I therein do rejoice, yea, and will rejoice; **Col. 1:28** whom we preach, warning every man, and teaching every man in all wisdom; that we may present every man perfect in Christ Jesus; **1 Thes. 1:8** from you sounded out the word of the Lord... in every place your faith to God-ward is spread abroad; **2:3** our exhortation was not of deceit, nor of uncleanness, nor in guile; **2:8-9** remember, brethren, our labour and travail: for labouring night and day... we preached unto you the *g.* of God; **2 Tim. 2:2** the things that thou hast heard of me among many witnesses, the same commit thou to faithful men, who shall be able to teach others also; **4:2** preach the word; be instant in season, out of season; reprove, rebuke, exhort with all longsuffering and doctrine; **1 Pet. 4:6** for

this cause was the *g.* preached also to them that are dead, that they might be judged according to men in the flesh, but live according to God in the spirit; **Rev. 14:6** I saw another angel fly in the midst of heaven, having the everlasting *g.* to preach unto them that dwell on the earth, and to every nation, and kindred, and tongue, and people; **14:15-20** thrust in thy sickle, and reap: for the time is come for thee to reap; for the harvest of the earth is ripe.

GOSSIP (*see also* Communicate, False, Hypocrisy, Lie, Speak, Talebearer)

Debate thy cause with thy neighbour *himself*; **and discover not a secret to another: lest he that heareth** *it* **put thee to shame, and thine infamy turn not away. Prov. 25:9-10** (*see also* Debate, Secret)

They learn to be idle, wandering about from house to house; and not only idle, but tattlers also and busybodies, speaking things which they ought not. 1 Tim. 5:13 (*see also* Idle)

Thou shalt not go up and down as a talebearer among thy people. Lev. 19:16 (*see also* Talebearer)

Speak evil of no man, to be no brawlers, but gentle, shewing all meekness unto all men. Titus 3:2 (*see also* Meek, Speak)

GOVERN, GOVERNMENT (*see also* Kingdom, Law, Lead, Liberty, Order)

For unto us a child is born, unto us a son is given: and the government shall be upon his shoulder: and his name shall be called, Wonderful, Counsellor, The mighty God, The everlasting Father, The Prince of Peace. Isa. 9:6 (*see also* Counselor, Father, Peace, Wonderful)

God hath set some in the church, first apostles, secondarily prophets, thirdly teachers, after that miracles, then gifts of healings, helps, governments, diversities of tongues. Are all apostles? are all prophets? are all teachers? are all workers of miracles? Have all the gifts of healing? do all speak with tongues? do all interpret? But covet earnestly the best gifts: and yet shew I unto you a more excellent way. 1 Cor. 12:28-31 (*see also* Excellent, Gift, Prophet, Way)

After the wisdom of thy God, that is in thine hand, set magistrates and judges, which may judge all the people that are beyond the river, all such as know the laws of thy God; and teach ye them that know them not. Ezra 7:25 (*see also* Judge)

GRACE (*see also* Gift, Holy Ghost, Knowledge, Mysteries, Salvation, Save)

God resisteth the proud, but giveth grace unto the humble. James 4:6 (*see also* Humble, Pride)

Let the word of Christ dwell in you richly in all wisdom; teaching and admonishing one another in psalms and hymns and spiritual songs, singing with grace in your hearts to the Lord. Col. 3:16 (*see also* Admonish, Hymn, Psalm, Sing, Wisdom, Word)

I have written briefly, exhorting, and testifying that this is the true grace of God wherein ye stand. 1 Pet. 5:12 (*see also* Exhort)

Likewise, ye younger, submit yourselves unto the elder. Yea, all of you be subject one to another, and be clothed with humility: for God resisteth the proud, and giveth grace to the humble. 1 Pet. 5:5 (*see also* Humble, Submit, Young)

Let no corrupt communication proceed out of your mouth, but that which is good to the use of edifying, that it may minister grace unto the hearers. Eph. 4:29 (*see also* Edify, Speak)

Gird up the loins of your mind, be sober, and hope to the end for the grace that is to be brought unto you at the revelation of Jesus Christ. 1 Pet. 1:13 (*see also* Hope, Jesus Christ, Mind)

Let your speech be alway with grace, seasoned with salt, that ye may know how ye ought to answer every man. Col. 4:6 (*see also* Speak)

Matt. 15:11 not that which goeth into the mouth defileth a man; but that which cometh out of the mouth, this defileth a man; 15:17-18 do not ye yet understand, that whatsoever entereth in at the mouth goeth into the belly, and is cast out into the draught? But those things which proceed out of the mouth come forth from the heart; and they defile the man; Col. 4:6 let your speech be alway with *g.,* seasoned with salt, that ye may know how ye ought to answer every man.

We believe that through the grace of the Lord Jesus Christ we shall be saved, even as they. Acts 15:11

Luke 2:40 he child grew, and waxed strong in spirit, filled with wisdom: and the *g.* of God was upon him; John 1:15-17 his fulness have all we received, and *g.* for *g..* For the law was given by Moses, but *g.* and truth came by Jesus Christ; Acts 4:33 with great power gave the apostles witness of the resurrection of the Lord Jesus: and great *g.* was upon them all; 11:23 who, when he came, and had seen the *g.* of God, was glad, and exhorted them all, that with purpose of heart they would cleave unto the Lord; 13:43 speaking to them, persuaded them to continue in the *g.* of God; 14:3 long time therefore abode they speaking boldly in the Lord, which gave testimony unto the word of his *g.,* and granted signs and wonders to be done by their hands; 14:26 from whence they had been recommended to the *g.* of God for the work which they fulfilled; 15:11 we believe that through the *g.* of the Lord Jesus Christ we shall be saved, even as they; 18:27 who, when he was come, helped them much which had believed through *g.*; 20:24 none of these things move me, neither count I my life dear unto myself, so that I might finish my course with joy, and the ministry, which I have received of the Lord Jesus, to testify the gospel of the *g.* of God; 20:32 I commend you to God, and to the word of his *g.,* which is able to build you up, and to give you an inheritance among all them which are sanctified; Rom. 1:5 by whom we have received *g.* and apostleship, for obedience to the faith among all nations, for his name; 3:23-24 all have sinned, and come short of the glory of God; Being justified freely by his *g.* through the redemption that is in Christ Jesus; 4:16 it is of faith, that it might be by *g.*; to the end the promise might be sure to all the seed; not to that only which is of the law, but to that also which is of the faith of Abraham; who is the father of us all; 5:15 if through the offence of one many be dead, much more the *g.* of God, and the gift by *g.,* which is by one man, Jesus Christ, hath abounded unto many; 5:21 as sin hath reigned unto death, even so might *g.* reign through righteousness unto eternal life by Jesus Christ our Lord; 6:15 what then? shall we sin, because we are not under the law, but under *g.*? God forbid; 11:6-7 if by *g.,* then is it no more of works: otherwise *g.* is no more *g..* But if it be of works, then is it no more *g.*: otherwise work is no more work; 12:6 having then gifts differing according to the *g.* that is given to us, whether prophecy, let us prophesy according to the proportion of faith; **15:15** I have written the more boldly unto you in some sort, as putting you in mind, because of the *g.* that is given to me of God; **1 Cor. 1:3** (16:23, Gal. 1:3, Philip. 1:2, 4:23, Col. 1:2, 1 Thes. 5:28) *g.* be unto you, and peace, from God our Father, and from the Lord Jesus Christ; **15:10** by the *g.* of God I am what I am: and his *g.* which was bestowed upon me was not in vain; but I laboured more abundantly than they all: yet not I, but the *g.* of God which was with me; **2 Cor. 1:12** the testimony of our conscience, that in simplicity and godly sincerity, not with fleshly wisdom, but by the *g.* of God, we have had our conversation in the world, and more abundantly to you-ward; **6:1** as workers together with him, beseech you also that ye receive not the *g.* of God in vain; **8:7** as ye abound in every thing, in faith, and utterance, and knowledge, and in all diligence, and in your love to us, see that ye abound in this *g.* also; **9:8** God is able to make all *g.* abound toward you; that ye, always having all sufficiency in all things, may abound to every good work; **12:9** my *g.* is sufficient for thee: for my strength is made perfect in weakness. Most gladly therefore will I rather glory in my infirmities, that the power of Christ may rest upon me; **2:21** do not frustrate the *g.* of God: for if righteousness come by the law, then Christ is dead in vain; **Eph. 1:17** the God of our Lord Jesus Christ, the Father of glory, may give unto you the spirit of wisdom and revelation in the knowledge of him; **2:5** even when we were dead in sins, hath quickened us together with Christ, (by *g.* ye are saved); **2:8** for by *g.* are ye saved through faith; and that not of yourselves: it is the gift of God; **3:7** I was made a minister, according to the gift of the *g.* of God given unto me by the effectual working of his power; **4:7-8** unto every one of us is given *g.* according to the measure of the gift of Christ. Wherefore he saith, When he ascended up on high, he led captivity captive, and gave gifts unto men; **4:13** till we all come in the unity of the faith, and of the knowledge of the Son of God, unto a perfect man, unto the measure of the stature of the fulness of Christ; **6:24** *g.* be with all them that love our Lord Jesus Christ in sincerity; **Col. 1:6** the day ye heard of it, and knew the *g.* of God in truth; **1:10** that ye might walk worthy of the Lord unto all pleasing, being fruitful in every good work, and increasing in the knowledge of God; **3:16** let the word of Christ dwell in you richly in all wisdom; teaching and admonishing one another in psalms and hymns and spiritual songs, singing with *g.* in your hearts to the Lord; **4:6** let your speech be alway with *g.,* seasoned with salt, that ye may know how ye

ought to answer every man; **2 Thes. 1:12** that the name of our Lord Jesus Christ may be glorified in you, and ye in him, according to the *g.* of our God and the Lord Jesus Christ; **1 Tim. 1:14** the *g.* of our Lord was exceeding abundant with faith and love which is in Christ Jesus; **2 Tim. 2:1** be strong in the *g.* that is in Christ Jesus; **Heb. 4:16** let us therefore come boldly unto the throne of *g.,* that we may obtain mercy, and find *g.* to help in time of need; **12:28** let us have *g.,* whereby we may serve God acceptably with reverence and godly fear; **13:9** be not carried about with divers and strange doctrines. For it is a good thing that the heart be established with *g.*; not with meats, which have not profited them that have been occupied therein; **James 4:6** he giveth more *g.*. Wherefore he saith, God resisteth the proud, but giveth *g.* unto the humble; **1 Pet. 1:10** of which salvation the prophets have enquired and searched diligently, who prophesied of the *g.* that should come unto you; **1:13** gird up the loins of your mind, be sober, and hope to the end for the *g.* that is to be brought unto you at the **Rev.** of Jesus Christ; **5:5** all of you be subject one to another, and be clothed with humility: for God resisteth the proud, and giveth *g.* to the humble; **2 Pet 1:2** *g.* and peace be multiplied unto you through the knowledge of God, and of Jesus our Lord; **1:4** given unto us exceeding great and precious promises: that by these ye might be partakers of the divine nature; **1:8** if these things be in you, and abound, they make you that ye shall neither be barren nor unfruitful in the knowledge of our Lord Jesus Christ; **3:18** grow in *g.,* and in the knowledge of our Lord and Saviour Jesus Christ; **2 Jn. 1:3** *g.* be with you, mercy, and peace, from God the Father, and from the Lord Jesus Christ, the Son of the Father, in truth and love; **Jude 1:4** there are certain men crept in unawares, who were before of old ordained to this condemnation, ungodly men, turning the *g.* of our God into lasciviousness, and denying the only Lord God, and our Lord Jesus Christ.

GRACIOUS, GRATEFUL, GRATEFULNESS (*see also* Kind, Merciful, Thankful)

A gracious woman retaineth honour. Prov. 11:16

Beseech God that he will be gracious unto us. Mal. 1:9 (*see also* Beseech)

GRAIN (*see also* Food, Herb)

If ye have faith as a grain of mustard seed, ye shall say unto this mountain, Remove hence to yonder place; and it shall remove; and nothing shall be impossible unto you. Matt. 17:20 (*see also* Impossible, Seed, Luke 17:6)

Another parable put he forth unto them, saying, The kingdom of heaven is like to a grain of mustard seed, which a man took, and sowed in his field. Matt. 13:31 (*see also* Kingdom, Sow)

GRAVEN IMAGE (*see also* Idol)

They provoked him to anger with their high places, and moved him to jealousy with their graven images. Ps. 78:58 (*see also* Jealousy)

Thy graven images also will I cut off, and thy standing images out of the midst of thee; and thou shalt no more worship the work of thine hands. Micah 5:13 (*see also* Hand, Worship)

Micah 5:13 thy graven images also will I cut off, and thy standing images out of the midst of thee; and thou shalt no more worship the work of thine hands; **Nahum 1:14** no more of thy name be sown: out of the house of thy gods will I cut off the graven image and the molten image: I will make thy grave; for thou art vile.

Thou shalt not make unto thee any graven image, or any likeness of any thing that is in heaven above, or that is in the earth beneath, or that is in the water under the earth. Thou shalt not bow down thyself to them, nor serve them: For I the LORD thy God am a jealous God, visiting the iniquity of the fathers upon the children unto the third and fourth generation of them that hate me; And shewing mercy unto thousands of them that love me, and keep my commandments. Ex. 20:4-6 (*see also* Idol, Thous Shalt Not)

Ex. 20:4-6 thou shalt not make unto thee any graven image, or any likeness of any thing that is in heaven above, or that is in the earth beneath, or that is in the water under the earth. Thou shalt not bow down thyself to them, nor serve them.

GREAT, GREATER, GREATNESS (*see also* Best, Mighty)

I will publish the name of the LORD: ascribe ye greatness unto our God. Deut. 32:3 (*see also* Great, Publish)

Ex. 15:6-7 thy right hand, O LORD, is become glorious in power: thy right hand, O LORD, hath dashed in pieces the enemy. And in the g. of thine excellency thou hast overthrown them that rose up against thee; **15:16** fear and dread shall fall upon them; by the g. of thine arm they shall be as still as a stone; till thy people pass over, O LORD; **Num. 14:19** pardon, I beseech thee, the iniquity of this people according unto the g. of thy mercy; **Deut. 3:24** O Lord GOD, thou hast begun to shew thy servant thy g., and thy mighty hand: for what God is there in heaven or in earth, that can do according to thy works, and according to thy might; **5:24** the LORD our God hath shewed us his glory and his g.; **9:26** O Lord GOD, destroy not thy people and thine inheritance, which thou hast redeemed through thy g.; **11:2** I speak not with your children which have not known, and which have not seen the chastisement of the LORD your God, his g., his mighty hand, and his stretched out arm; **32:3** I will publish the name of the LORD: ascribe ye g. unto our God; **1 Chron. 29:11** thine, O LORD, is the g., and the power, and the glory, and the victory, and the majesty; **2 Chron. 2:5** the house which I build is g.: for g. is our God above all gods; **Neh. 13:22** remember me, O my God, concerning this also, and spare me according to the g. of thy mercy; **Ps. 66:3** how terrible art thou in thy works! through the g. of thy power shall thine enemies submit themselves unto thee; **68:34** ascribe ye strength unto God: his excellency is over Israel, and his strength is in the clouds; **71:21** thou shalt increase my g., and comfort me on every side; **79:11** let the sighing of the prisoner come before thee; according to the g. of thy power preserve thou those that are appointed to die; **145:3** g. is the LORD, and g. to be praised; and his g. is unsearchable; **145:6** men shall speak of the might of thy terrible acts: and I will declare thy g.; **150:2** praise him for his mighty acts: praise him according to his excellent g.; **Isa. 40:26** lift up your eyes on high, and behold who hath created these things, that bringeth out their host by number: he calleth them all by names by the g. of his might.

GREED, GREEDINESS, GREEDY (*see also* Covet, Lust, Selfish)

Thou hast taken usury and increase, and thou hast greedily gained of thy neighbours by extortion, and hast forgotten me, saith the Lord GOD. Ezek. 22:12 (*see also* Extort)

He coveteth greedily all the day long: but the righteous giveth and spareth not. Prov. 21:26 (*see also* Give)

Likewise must the deacons be grave, not doubletongued, not given to much wine, not greedy of filthy lucre; Holding the mystery of faith in a pure conscience. 1 Tim. 3:8 (*see also* Deacon)

Eph 4:19 who being past feeling have given themselves over unto lasciviousness, to work all uncleanness with *g.*; **1 Tim. 3:3** not given to wine, no striker, not *g.* of filthy lucre; but patient, not a brawler, not covetous; **3:8** likewise must the deacons be grave, not doubletongued, not given to much wine, not *g.* of filthy lucre; Holding the mystery of faith in a pure conscience.

He that is greedy of gain troubleth his own house; but he that hateth gifts shall live. Prov. 15:27

Prov. 15:27 he that is *g.* of gain troubleth his own house; but he that hateth gifts shall live; **28:8** he that by usury and unjust gain increaseth his substance, he shall gather it for him that will pity the poor; **Ezek. 22:12** thou hast taken usury and increase, and thou hast *g.* gained of thy neighbours by extortion, and hast forgotten me, saith the Lord GOD.

GREET

Greet ye one another with an holy kiss. 1 Cor. 16:20

1 Cor 16:20 all the brethren greet you. Greet ye one another with an holy kiss; **2 Cor. 13:12** greet one another with an holy kiss; **Philip. 4:21** salute every saint in Christ Jesus. The brethren which are with me greet you; **1 Thes. 5:26** greet all the brethren with an holy kiss; **Heb. 13:24** salute all them that have the rule over you, and all the saints.

GRIEF, GRIEVE (*see also* Despair, Mourn, Sorrow)

Grieve not the holy Spirit of God, whereby ye are sealed unto the day of redemption. Eph. 4:30 (*see also* Holy Spirit, Seal)

Let the lying lips be put to silence; which speak grievous things proudly and contemptuously against the righteous. Ps. 31:18 (*see also* Liar)

GRUDGE (*see also* Hate, Offend)

Thou shalt not avenge, nor bear any grudge against the children of thy people, but thou shalt love thy neighbour as thyself: I *am* the LORD. Lev. 19:18 (*see also* Avenge)

Use hospitality one to another without grudging. 1 Pet. 4:9 (*see also* Hospitality)

GUARD (*see also* Watch)

Be thou prepared, and prepare for thyself, thou, and all thy company that are assembled unto thee, and be thou a guard unto them. Ezek. 38:7 (*see also* Prepare)

GUIDANCE, GUIDE (*see also* Counsel, Direct, Lead, Order, Reveal, Spirit)

Hear thou, my son, and be wise, and guide thine heart in the way. Prov. 23:19 (*see also* Hear, Heart, Way, Wise)

Woe unto you, ye blind guides, which say, Whosoever shall swear by the temple, it is nothing; but whosoever shall swear by the gold of the temple, he is a debtor! Ye fools and blind: for whether is greater, the gold, or the temple that sanctifieth the gold? And, Whosoever shall swear by the altar, it is nothing; but whosoever sweareth by the gift that is upon it, he is guilty. Matt. 23:16-18 (*see also* Swear)

Matt. 23:16-18 woe unto you, ye blind guides, which say, Whosoever shall swear by the temple, it is nothing; but whosoever shall swear by the gold of the temple, he is a debtor! Ye fools and blind: for whether is greater, the gold, or the temple that sanctifieth the gold? And, Whosoever shall swear by the altar, it is nothing; but whosoever sweareth by the gift that is upon it, he is guilty; **23:24** ye blind guides, which strain at a gnat, and swallow a camel.

GUILE (*see also* Deceit, Hypocrisy)

Blessed is the man unto whom the LORD imputeth not iniquity, and in whose spirit there is no guile. **Ps. 32:2**

Keep thy tongue from evil, and thy lips from speaking guile. **Ps. 34:13** (*see also* Iniquity, Speak, Tongue)

For he that will love life, and see good days, let him refrain his tongue from evil, and his lips that they speak no guile: Let him eschew evil, and do good; let him seek peace, and ensue it. **1 Pet. 3:10-11** (*see also* Peace, Speak)

Mark 7:22-23 thefts, covetousness, wickedness, deceit, lasciviousness, an evil eye, blasphemy, pride, foolishness: All these evil things come from within, and defile the man; **John 1:47** Jesus saw Nathanael coming to him, and saith of him, Behold an Israelite indeed, in whom is no *g.*; **2 Cor. 7:2** we have defrauded no man; **1 Pet. 2:22** who did no sin, neither was *g.* found in his mouth; **3:10** he that will love life, and see good days, let him refrain his tongue from evil, and his lips that they speak no *g.*; **Rev. 14:5** in their mouth was found no *g.*: for they are without fault before the throne of God.

HALLOW, HALLOWED (*see also* Holy, Pure, Sanctify)

Hallow the sabbath day, to do no work therein. **Jer. 17:24** (*see also* Sabbath)

HAND (*see* Laying on of Hands)

The LORD rewarded me according to my righteousness; according to the cleanness of my hands hath he recompensed me. **Ps. 18:20** (*see also* Clean, Reward, Righteous)

I stretch forth my hands unto thee: my soul thirsteth after thee, as a thirsty land. Shela. **Ps. 143:6** (*see also* Thirst)

For the poor shall never cease out of the land: therefore I command thee, saying, thou shalt open thine hand wide unto thy brother, to thy poor, and to thy needy, in the land. **Deut. 15:11** (*see also* Needy, Poor)

Whatever thy hand findeth to do, do it with thy might; for there is no work, nor device, nor knowledge, nor wisdom, in the grave, whither thou goest. **Eccl. 9:10** (*see also* Might)

They regard not the work of the LORD, neither consider the operation of his hands. **Isa. 5:12** (*see also* Work)

Thy graven images also will I cut off, and thy standing images out of the midst of thee; and thou shalt no more worship the work of thine hands. **Micah 5:13** (*see also* Graven Images, Worship)

In that day it shall be said to Jerusalem, Fear thou not: and to Zion, Let not thine hands be slack. **Zeph. 3:16** (*see also* Slack)

Zeph. 3:16 fear thou not: and to Zion, Let not thine *h.* be slack; **Zech. 8:9** let your *h.* be strong, ye that hear in these days these words by the mouth of the prophets, which were in the day that the foundation of the house of the LORD of hosts was laid; **8:13** it shall come to pass, that as ye were a curse among the heathen, O house of Judah, and house of Israel; so will I save you, and ye shall be a blessing: fear not, but let your *h.* be strong.

HANG

Jesus said unto him, Thous shalt love the Lord thy God with all thy heart, and with all thy soul, and with all thy mind. This is the first and great commandment. And the second is like unto it, Thou shalt love thy neighbour as thyself. On these two commandments, hang all the law and the prophets. **Matt 22:37-40** (*see also* Commandment, Love, Thous Shalt)

HAPPINESS, HAPPY (*see also* Abundant, Bless, Cheerful, Glad, Joy, Merry, Pleasure, Sing)

Happy is that people, that is in such a case: yea, happy is that people, whose God is the LORD. **Ps. 144:15** (*see also* Jesus Christ)

If ye know these things, happy are ye if ye do them. **John 13:17** (*see also* Know)

HARD, HARDEN, HARDHEARTED, HARNESS (*see also* Doubt, Hate, Heart, Pride, Rebel, Stiffnecked, Unbelief, Wicked)

Harden not your heart, as in the provocation, and as in the day of temptation in the wilderness:When your fathers tempted me, proved me, and saw my work. **Ps. 95:9** (*see also* Prove)

Is any thing too hard for the LORD? Gen. 18:14

Gen. 18:14 is any thing too hard for the LORD; **Ex. 4:7-8** it shall come to pass, if they will not believe thee, neither hearken to the voice of the first sign, that they will believe the voice of the latter sign; **6:1-2** now shalt thou see what I will do to Pharaoh... And God spake unto Moses, and said unto him, I am the LORD; **9:29** as soon as I am gone out of the city, I will spread abroad my hands unto the LORD; and the thunder shall cease, neither shall there be any more hail; that thou mayest know how that the earth is the LORD s; **Deut. 1:31-32** thou hast seen how that the LORD thy God bare thee, as a man doth bear his son, in all the way that ye went, until ye came into this place. Yet in this thing ye did not believe the LORD your God; **Job 42:2** I know that thou canst do every thing, and that no thought can be withholden from thee.

HARLOT (*see also* Adultery, Fornication, Whore)

Whoso loveth wisdom rejoiceth his father: but he that keepeth company with harlots spendeth his substance. Prov. 29:3

Prov. 29:3 whoso loveth wisdom rejoiceth his father: but he that keepeth company with *h.* spendeth his substance; **Jer. 3:1** thou hast played the *h.* with many lovers; yet return again to me, saith the LORD; **3:3** the showers have been withholden, and there hath been no latter rain; and thou hadst a whores forehead, thou refusedst to be ashamed; **3:8** I saw, when for all the causes whereby backsliding Israel committed adultery I had put her away, and given her a bill of divorce; yet her treacherous sister Judah feared not, but went and played the *h.*; **22:22-23** the wind shall eat up all thy pastors, and thy lovers shall go into captivity: surely then shalt thou be ashamed and confounded for all thy wickedness; **Ezek. 16:15-16** thou didst trust in thine own beauty, and playedst the *h.* because of thy renown, and pouredst out thy fornications on every one that passed by.

HARM (*see also* Mischief, Persecute)

Strive not with a man without cause, if he have done thee no harm. Prov. 3:30 (*see also* Cause)

HARMLESS

Be ye therefore wise as serpents and harmless as doves. Matt. 10:16 (*see also* Be, Wise)

HARVEST (*see also* Gather, Promise, Reap, Reward, Sow)

Lift up your eyes, and look on the fields; for they are white already to harvest. John 4:35 (*see also* Field)

John 4:35-37 say not ye, There are yet four months, and then cometh harvest? behold, I say unto you, Lift up your eyes, and look on the fields; for they are white already to harvest. And he that reapeth receiveth wages, and gathereth fruit unto life eternal: that both he that soweth and he that reapeth may rejoice together. And herein is that saying true, One soweth, and another reapeth.

HASTE, HASTEN, HASTY

Be not rash with thy mouth, and let not thine heart be hasty to utter any thing before God: for God is in heaven, and thou upon earth: therefore let thy words be few. Eccl. 5:2-3 (*see also* Mouth)

Go not hastily to strive, lest thou know not what to do in the end thereof, when thy neighbour hath put thee to shame. Prov. 25:8 (*see also* Strive)

An inheritance may be gotten hastily at the beginning; but the end thereof shall not be blessed. Prov. 20:21 (*see also* Inheritance)

Seest thou a man that is hasty in his words? there is more hope of a fool than of him. Prov. 29:20 (*see also* Word)

A faithful man shall abound with blessings: but he that maketh haste to be rich shall not be innocent. Prov. 28:20 (*see also* Rich)

He that hasteth to be rich hath an evil eye, and considereth not that poverty shall come upon him. Prov. 28:22 (*see also* Rich)

He that is slow to wrath is of great understanding: but he that is hasty of spirit exalteth folly. Prov. 14:29 (*see also* Patience)

Prov. 14:29 he that is slow to wrath is of great understanding: but he that is *h.* of spirit exalteth folly; **21:5** the thoughts of the diligent tend only to plenteousness; but of every one that is *h.* only to want; **25:8** go not forth *h.* to strive, lest thou know not what to do in the end thereof; **Isa. 28:16** I lay in Zion for a foundation a stone, a tried stone, a precious corner stone, a sure foundation: he that believeth shall not make *h.*

HATE, HATED, HATRED (*see also* Abhor, Despise, Persecute, Revile)

He that sinneth against me wrongeth his own soul: all they that hate me love death. **Prov. 8:36** (*see also* Sin)

No man can serve two masters: for either he will hate the one, and love the other; or else he will hold to the one, and despise the other. Ye cannot serve God and mammon. **Matt. 6:24** (*see also* Master, Serve)

The fear of the LORD is to hate evil: pride, and arrogancy, and the evil way, and the froward mouth, do I hate. **Prov. 8:13** (*see also* Arrogance, Evil, Fear)

Better is a dinner of herbs where love is, than a stalled ox and hatred therewith. **Prov. 15:17** (*see also* Love)

Evil shall slay the wicked: and they that hate the righteous shall be desolate. **Ps. 34:21** (*see also* Evil)

Ps. 34:21 evil shall slay the wicked: and they that hate the righteous shall be desolate; **109:3-4** they compassed me about also with words of *h.*; and fought against me without a cause. For my love they are my adversaries.

Through thy precepts I get understanding: therefore I hate every false way. **Ps. 119:104** (*see also* Way)

Ps. 119:104 I *h.* every false way; **119:128** I esteem all thy precepts concerning all things to be right; and I *h.* every false way.

Do not I hate them, O LORD, that hate thee? **Ps. 139:21**

Ps. 139:21-22 do not I *h.* them, O LORD, that *h.* thee? and am not I grieved with those that rise up against thee? I *h.* them with perfect *h.*: I count them mine enemies.

Thou shalt not hate thy brother in thine heart: thou shalt in any wise rebuke thy neighbour and not suffer sin upon him. **Lev. 19:17** (*see also* Thou Shalt Not)

Lev. 19:17 thou shalt not *h.* thy brother in thine heart; **Deut. 19:11** if any man *h.* his neighbour, and lie in wait for him, and rise up against him, and smite him mortally that he die, and fleeth into one of these cities; **Prov. 10:12** *h.* stirreth up strifes: but love covereth all sins; **14:21** he that despiseth his neighbour sinneth: but he that hath mercy on the poor, happy is he; **Ezek. 35:5-6** Because thou hast had a perpetual *h.*, and hast shed the blood of the children of Israel... I will prepare thee unto blood, and blood shall pursue thee; **35:11** I will even do according to thine anger, and according to thine envy which thou hast used out of thy *h.* against them.

He that hateth his brother is in darkness, and walketh in darkness, and knoweth not whither he goeth, because that darkness hath blinded his eyes. **1 Jn. 2:11** (*see also* Blind)

Matt. 24:10 then shall many be offended, and shall betray one another, and shall hate one another; **1 Jn. 2:11** he that hateth his brother is in darkness, and walketh in darkness, and knoweth not whither he goeth, because that darkness hath blinded his eyes; **3:15** whosoever hateth his brother is a murderer: and ye know that no murderer hath eternal life abiding in him; **Rev. 18:2** Babylon the great is fallen, is fallen, and is become the habitation of devils, and the hold of every foul spirit, and a cage of every unclean and hateful bird.

He that hideth hatred with lying lips, and he that uttereth a slander, is a fool. **Prov. 10:18** (*see also* Liar, Slander)

Prov. 10:18 he that hideth *h.* with lying lips, and he that uttereth a slander, is a fool; **26:23-27** he that *h.* dissembleth with his lips, and layeth up deceit within him; When he speaketh fair, believe him not: for there are seven abominations in his heart; **Ezek. 7:4** mine eye shall not spare thee, neither will I have pity: but I will recompense thy ways upon thee, and thine abominations shall be in the midst of thee; **7:8** I [will] shortly pour out my fury upon thee, and accomplish mine anger upon thee: and I will judge thee according to thy ways, and will recompense thee for all thine abominations.

HAUGHTINESS, HAUGHTY (see also Arrogance, Boast, Conceit, Highminded, Pride, Vanity)

Pride goeth before destruction, and an haughty spirit before a fall. Prov. 16:18 (see also Pride)

HEAD

His mischief shall return upon his own head, and his violent dealing shall come down upon his own pate. Ps. 7:16 (see also Mischief, Return, Violent)

HEAL, HEALING (see also Administer, Laying on of Hands, Miracle, Restore, Save, Sanctify)

Wilt thou be made whole? John. 5:6 (see also Whole)

Make the heart of this people fat, and make their ears heavy, and shut their eyes; lest they see with their eyes, and hear with their ears, and understand with their heart, and convert, and be healed. Isa. 6:10 (see also Convert, See)

Is any sick among you? let him call for the elders of the church; and let them pray over him, anointing him with oil in the name of the Lord: And the prayer of faith shall save the sick, and the Lord shall raise him up; and if he have committed sins, they shall be forgiven him. James 5:14-15 (see also Anoint, Oil, Elder)

All they that had any sick with divers diseases brought them unto him; and he laid his hands on every one of them, and healed them. Luke 4:40 (see also Laying on of Hands)

Confess your faults one to another, and ray one for another, that ye may be healed. The effectual fervent prayer of a righteous man availeth much. James 5:16 (see also Confess, Pray)

HEAR, HEARD (see also Hearken)

Cease, my son, to hear the instruction that causeth to err from the words of knowledge. Prov. 19:27 (see also Instruct, Know)

Hear thou, my son, and be wise, and guide thine heart in the way. Prov. 23:19 (see also Guide, Heart, Wise)

Let every man be swift to hear, slow to speak, slow to wrath. James 1:19 (see also Speak, Wrath)

Hear ye, and give ear; be not proud: for the LORD hath spoken. Jer. 13:15 (see also Pride)

All ye inhabitants of the world, and dwellers on the earth, see ye, when he lifted up an ensign on the mountains; and when he bloweth a trumpet, hear ye. Isa. 18:3 (see also See)

Be ye not as your fathers, unto whom the former prophets have cried, saying, Thus saith the LORD of hosts; Turn ye now from your evil ways, and from your evil doings: but they did not hear, nor hearken unto me, saith the LORD. Zech. 1:4 (see also Evil, Way)

This is a rebellious people, lying children, children that will not hear the law of the LORD. Isa. 30:9

Rise up, ye women that are at ease; hear my voice, ye careless daughters; give ear unto my speech. Many days and years shall ye be troubled, ye careless women: for the vintage shall fail, the gathering shall not come. Isa. 32:9-10 (see also Rise)

Keep thy foot when thou goest to the house of God, and be more ready to hear than to give the sacrifice of fools: for they consider not that they do evil. Eccl. 5:1 (see also House)

He that walketh righteously, and speaketh uprightly; he that despiseth the gain of oppressions, that shaketh his hands from holding of bribes, that stoppeth his ears from hearing of blood, and shutteth his eyes from seeing evil; He shall dwell on high: his defence shall be the munitions of rocks: bread shall be given him; his waters shall be sure. Isa. 33:15-16 (see also Oppress, Righteous, See, Speak, Uprightly, Walk)

Should ye not hear the words which the LORD hath cried by the former prophets, when Jerusalem was inhabited and in prosperity, and the cities thereof round about her, when men inhabited the south and the plain? Zech. 7:7 (see also Prophet, Word)

Be ye doers of the word, and not hearers only, deceiving your own selves. For if any be a hearer of the word, and not a doer, he is like unto a man beholding his natural face in a glass: For he beholdeth himself, and goeth his way, and straightway forgetteth what manner of man he was. James 1:22-24 (*see also* Do, Word)

Luke 8:21 my mother and my brethren are these which *h.* the word of God, and do it; **James 1:22** be ye doers of the word, and not hearers only, deceiving your own selves.

O earth, earth, earth, hear the word of the LORD. Jer. 22:29

Neh. 8:2 Ezra the priest brought the law before the congregation both of men and women, and all that could *h.* with understanding; **8:8** they read in the book in the law of God distinctly, and gave the sense, and caused them to understand the reading; **Job 28:28** unto man he said, Behold, the fear of the Lord, that is wisdom; and to depart from evil is understanding; **Ps. 95:7** he is our God; and we are the people of his pasture, and the sheep of his hand. To day if ye will *h.* his voice; **138:4** all the kings of the earth shall praise thee, O LORD, when they *h.* the words of thy mouth; **Prov. 5:7** *h.* me now therefore, O ye children, and depart not from the words of my mouth; **Isa. 1:10** *h.* the word of the LORD, ye rulers of Sodom; give ear unto the law of our God, ye people of Gomorrah; **42:18** *h.,* ye deaf; and look, ye blind, that ye may see; **66:5** *h.* the word of the LORD, ye that tremble at his word; your brethren that hated you, that cast you out for my names sake; **Jer. 9:20** *h.* the word of the LORD, O ye women, and let your ear receive the word of his mouth, and teach your daughters wailing, and every one her neighbour lamentation; **10:1** *h.* ye the word which the LORD speaketh unto you, O house of Israel; **11:10** they are turned back to the iniquities of their forefathers, which refused to *h.* my words; and they went after other gods to serve them; **13:10-11** this evil people, which refuse to *h.* my words, which walk in the imagination of their heart, and walk after other gods, to serve them, and to worship them, shall even be as this girdle, which is good for nothing; **19:15** I will bring upon this city and upon all her towns all the evil that I have pronounced against it, because they have hardened their necks, that they might not *h.* my words; **22:29** O earth, earth, earth, *h.* the word of the LORD; **25:8-11** because ye have not *h.* my words, Behold, I will send and take all the

families of the north, saith the LORD, and Nebuchadrezzar the king of Babylon, my servant, and will bring them against this land; **Ezek. 3:11** go, get thee to them of the captivity, unto the children of thy people, and speak unto them, and tell them, Thus saith the Lord GOD; whether they will *h.,* or whether they will forbear; **6:3** *h.* the word of the Lord GOD; Thus saith the Lord GOD to the mountains, and to the hills, to the rivers, and to the valleys; Behold, I, even I, will bring a sword upon you, and I will destroy your high places; **36:4** *h.* the word of the Lord GOD; Thus saith the Lord GOD to the mountains, and to the hills, to the rivers, and to the valleys, to the desolate wastes, and to the cities that are forsaken; **Hosea 4:1-5** *h.* the word of the LORD, ye children of Israel: for the LORD hath a controversy with the inhabitants of the land, because there is no truth, nor mercy, nor knowledge of God in the land; **Micah 6:1-2** *h.* ye now what the LORD saith; Arise, contend thou before the mountains, and let the hills *h.* thy voice. *h.* ye, O mountains, the LORD's controversy, and ye strong foundations of the earth.

Hear ye the word of the LORD, O house of Jacob, and all the families of the house of Israel. Jer. 2:4 (*see also* Word)

Jer. 2:4 *h.* ye the word of the LORD, O house of Jacob, and all the families of the house of Israel; **2:31** O generation, see ye the word of the LORD. Have I been a wilderness unto Israel? a land of darkness? wherefore say my people, We are lords; we will come no more unto thee.

Come ye near unto me, hear ye this; I have not spoken in secret from the beginning; from the time that it was, there am I: and now the Lord GOD, and his Spirit, hath sent me. Isa. 48:16 (*see also* Assemble)

Isa. 48:14 assemble yourselves, and *h.;* which among them hath declared these things? The LORD hath loved him: he will do his pleasure; **48:16** come ye near unto me, *h.* ye this; I have not spoken in secret from the beginning; from the time that it was, there am I: and now the Lord GOD, and his Spirit, hath sent me.

My mother and my brethren are these which hear the word of God, and do it. Luke 8:21 (*see also* Word)

Matt. 13:9 (13:23) who hath ears to *h.,* let him *h.;* **Mark 4:20** he that received seed into the good ground is he that *h.* the word, and understandeth it; which also beareth fruit, and bringeth forth, some an hundredfold, some sixty, some thirty; **15:10** *h.,* and understand; **17:5** while he yet spake, behold, a bright cloud overshadowed them: and behold a voice out of the cloud, which said, This is my beloved Son, in whom I am well pleased; *h.* ye him; **Luke 6:17** which came to *h.* him, and to be healed of their diseases; **8:8** he that hath ears to *h.,* let him *h.*; **8:12** those by the way side are they that *h.*; then cometh the devil, and taketh away the word out of their hearts, lest they should believe and be saved; **11:28** blessed are they that *h.* the word of God, and keep it; **John 5:23-24** he that *h.* my word, and believeth on him that sent me, hath everlasting life, and shall not come into condemnation; but is passed from death unto life; **18:37** to this end was I born, and for this cause came I into the world, that I should bear witness unto the truth. Every one that is of the truth *h.* my voice; **Acts 10:33** we all here present before God, to *h.* all things that are commanded thee of God; **10:44** while Peter yet spake these words, the Holy Ghost fell on all them which *h.* the word; **13:7** desired to *h.* the word of God; **13:44** the next sabbath day came almost the whole city together to *h.* the word of God; **1 Thes. 2:13** thank we God without ceasing, because, when ye received the word of God which ye *h.* of us, ye received it not as the word of men, but as it is in truth, the word of God, which effectually worketh also in you that believe; **2 Tim. 2:15** study to shew thyself approved unto God, a workman that needeth not to be ashamed, rightly dividing the word of truth; **Rev. 2:7** he that hath an ear, let him *h.* what the Spirit saith unto the churches.

He that received seed into the good ground is he that heareth the word, and understandeth it; which also beareth fruit, and bringeth forth, some an hundredfold, some sixty, some thirty. Matt. 13:23 (*see also* Understand)

Matt. 13:3-8 they sprung up, because they had no deepness of earth: And when the sun was up, they were scorched; and because they had no root, they withered away; **13:15** this people's heart is waxed gross, and their ears are dull of *h.,* and their eyes they have closed; lest at any time they should see with their eyes, and *h.* with their ears, and should understand with their heart, and should be converted, and I should heal them; **13:19** when any one *h.* the word of the kingdom, and understandeth it not, then cometh the wicked one, and catcheth away that which was sown in

his heart. This is he which received seed by the way side; **13:23** he that received seed into the good ground is he that *h.* the word, and understandeth it; which also beareth fruit, and bringeth forth, some an hundredfold, some sixty, some thirty; **15:16** are ye also yet without understanding; **24:15** whoso readeth, let him understand; **Mark 4:9** he that hath ears to *h.,* let him *h.*; **4:11-12** unto you it is given to know the mystery of the kingdom of God: but unto them that are without, all these things are done in parables: That seeing they may see, and not perceive; and *h.* they may *h.,* and not understand; lest at any time they should be converted, and their sins should be forgiven them; **4:24-25** take heed what ye *h.*: with what measure ye mete, it shall be measured to you: and unto you that *h.* shall more be given. For he that hath, to him shall be given: and he that hath not, from him shall be taken even that which he hath; **4:33-34** with many such parables spake he the word unto them, as they were able to *h.* it. But without a parable spake he not unto them: and when they were alone, he expounded all things to his disciples; **7:14** when he had called all the people unto him, he said unto them, Hearken unto me every one of you, and understand; **7:16-19** if any man have ears to *h.,* let him *h.* And when he was entered into the house from the people, his disciples asked him concerning the parable. And he saith unto them, Are ye so without understanding also; **8:17** why reason ye, because ye have no bread? perceive ye not yet, neither understand? have ye your heart yet hardened; **8:21** how is it that ye do not understand; **9:32** they understood not that saying, and were afraid to ask him; **Luke 1:3** it seemed good to me also, having had perfect understanding of all things from the very first; **2:47** all that *h.* him were astonished at his understanding and answers; **8:8** he that hath ears to *h.,* let him *h.*; **8:10** unto you it is given to know the mysteries of the kingdom of God: but to others in parables; that seeing they might not see, and *h.* they might not understand; **9:44** let these sayings sink down into your ears: for the Son of man shall be delivered into the hands of men; **10:24** many prophets and kings have desired to see those things which ye see, and have not seen them; and to *h.* those things which ye *h.,* and have not *h.* them; **John 8:43** why do ye not understand my speech? even because ye cannot *h.* my word; **8:47** he that is of God *h.* God's words: ye therefore *h.* them not, because ye are not of God; **10:6** they understood not what things they were which he spake unto them; **12:40** he hath blinded their eyes, and hardened their heart; that they should not see with their eyes, nor understand with their heart, and be converted, and I should heal them; **Acts 28:27** the heart of this people is waxed gross, and their ears are dull of *h.,* and their eyes have they closed; lest they should see with their eyes, and *h.* with their ears, and understand with their heart, and should be converted, and I should heal them; **1 Cor. 3:2-3** I have fed you with milk, and not with meat: for hitherto ye were not able to bear it, neither yet now are ye able. For ye are yet carnal; **Eph. 1:18** the eyes of your understanding being enlightened; that ye may know what is the hope of his calling, and what the riches of the glory of his inheritance in the saints; **3:18-19** may be able to comprehend with all saints what is the breadth, and length, and depth, and height; And will make with them after those days, saith the Lord, I will put my laws into their hearts, and in their minds will I write them.

HEARKEN (*see also* Do, Hear, Heed, Obey)

Thou hast avouched the Lord this day to be thy God, and to walk in his ways, and to keep his statutes, and his commandments, and his judgments, and to hearken unto his voice. **Deut. 26:17** (*see also* Keep, Way)

Believe in the Lord your God, so shall ye be established; believe his prophets, so shall ye prosper. **2 Chron. 20:20** (*see also* Belief, Establish, Prophet, Prosper)

If thou shalt hearken diligently unto the voice of the Lord thy God, to observe and to do all his commandments which I command thee this day, that the Lord thy God will sit thee on high above all nations of the earth; And all these blessings shall come on thee, and overtake thee, if thou shalt hearken unto the voice of the Lord thy God. **Deut. 28:1-2** (*see also* Bless, Commandment)

Hearken now unto my voice, I will give thee counsel, and God shall be with thee. **Ex. 18:19** (*see also* Counsel)

If a ruler hearken to lies, all his servants are wicked. **Prov. 29:12** (*see also* Liar)

Hearken unto me, ye stouthearted, that are far from righteousness. **Isa. 46:12** (*see also* Righteous, Stouthearted)

Hearken to the words of my servants the prophets, whom I sent unto you, both rising up early, and sending *them,* but ye have not hearkened. **Jer. 26:5** (*see also* Prophet)

HEART (*see also* Born Again, Change, Conversion, Feel, Hardness)

Trust not in oppression, and become not vain in robbery: if riches increase, set not your heart upon them. **Ps. 62:10** (*see also* Increase, Oppress, Rich, Rob, Trust)

Let us draw near with a true heart in full assurance of faith, having our hearts sprinkled from an evil conscience, and our bodies washed with pure water. **Heb. 10:22** (*see also* Assurance, Draw)

Do not ye yet understand, that whatsoever entereth in at the mouth goeth into the belly, and is cast out into the draught? But those things which proceed out of the mouth come froth from the heart; and they defile the man. For out of the heart proceed evil thoughts, murders, adulteries, fornications, thefts, false witness, blasphemies: These are the things which defile a man: but to eat with unwashen hands defileth not a man. **Matt: 17-20** (*see also* Defile, Mouth, Proceed)

It is a people that do err in their heart, and they have not known my ways. **Ps. 95:10** (*see also* Err, Ways)

Heaviness in the heart of man maketh it stoop: but a good word maketh it glad. **Prov. 12:25** (*see also* Good)

Examine me, O Lord, and prove me; try my reins and my heart. **Ps. 26:2** (*see also* Prove)

Circumcision is that of the heart, in the spirit, and not in the letter; whose praise is not of men, but of God. **Rom. 2:28-29** (*see also* Circumcise)

Therefore shall ye lay up these my words in your heart and in your soul, and bind them for a sign upon your hand, that they may be as frontlets between your eyes. **Deut. 11:18** (*see also* Sign, Word)

He scorneth the scorners: but he giveth grace unto the lowly. **Prov. 3:34** (*see also* Lowly)

I will give them an heart to know me, that I am the LORD: and they shall be my people, and I will be their God: for they shall return unto me with their whole heart. Jer. 24:7 (*see also* Return)

Blessed are they that keep his testimonies, and that seek him with the whole heart. Ps. 119:2 (*see also* Testimony)

[Barnabas] exhorted them all, that with purpose of heart they would cleave unto the Lord. Acts 11:23 (*see also* Cleave)

They speak vanity every one with his neighbour: with flattering lips and with a double heart. Ps. 12:2 (*see also* Double, Speak)

Who can say, I have made my heart clean, I am pure from my sin? Prov. 20:9 (*see also* Pure)

Truly God is good to Israel, *even* to such as are of a clean heart. Ps. 73:1 (*see also* Clean)

He that hath a froward heart findeth no good: and he that hath a perverse tongue falleth into mischief. Prov 17:20 (*see also* Froward, Tongue)

Let not mercy and truth forsake thee: bind them about thy neck: write them upon the table of thine heart; So shalt thou find favour and good understanding in the sight of God and man. Prov. 3:3-4 (*see also* Bind, Merciful, True, Write)

Be ye of an understanding heart. Prov. 8:5 (*see also* Understand)

The wise in heart will receive commandments: but a prating fool shall fall. Prov. 10:8 (*see also* Wise)

The heart knoweth his own bitterness; and a stranger doth not intermeddle with his joy. Prov. 14:10 (*see also* Bitterness)

The heart of the righteous studieth to answer: but the mouth of the wicked poureth out evil things. Prov. 15:28 (*see also* Answer, Study)

Hear thou, my son, and be wise, and guide thine heart in the way. Prov. 23:19 (*see also* Guide, Hear, Wise)

He that trusteth in his own heart is a fool: but whoso walketh wisely, he shall be delivered. Prov. 28:26 (*see also* Trust)

As for our iniquities, we know them: in transgressing and lying against the LORD, and departing away from our God, speaking oppression and revolt, conceiving and uttering from the heart words of falsehood. Isa. 59:12-13 (*see also* False, Word)

Cursed be the man that trusteth in man, and maketh flesh his arm, and whose heart departeth from the LORD. Jer. 17:5 (*see also* Flesh, Trust)

Set thee up waymarks, make thee high heaps: set thine heart toward the highway, even the way which thou wentest: turn again. Jer. 31:21 (*see also* Turn, Way)

The eyes of the LORD run to and fro throughout the whole earth, to shew himself strong in the behalf of them whose heart is perfect toward him. 2 Chron. 16:9 (*see also* Perfect)

He shall turn the heart of the fathers to the children, and the heart of the children to their fathers, lest I come and smite the earth with a curse. Mal. 4:6 (*see also* Turn)

Lay not up for yourselves treasures upon earth, where moth and rust doth corrupt, and where thieves break through and steal: But lay up for yourselves treasures in heaven, where neither moth nor rust doth corrupt, and where thieves do not break through nor steal: For where your treasure is, there will your heart be also. Matt. 6:19-21 (*see also* Heaven, Lay Up, Steal, Treasure)

Oppress not the widow, nor the fatherless, the stranger, nor the poor; and let none of you imagine evil against his brother in your heart. Zech. 7:10 (*see also* Imagine, Mischief)

Ps. 140:2 which imagine mischiefs in their *h.*; continually are they gathered together for war; Zech. 7:10 oppress not the widow, nor the fatherless, the stranger, nor the poor; and let none of you imagine evil against his brother in your *h.*

I will walk within my house with a perfect heart. Ps. 101:2 (*see also* Perfect)

Ps. 101:2 I will walk within my house with a perfect *h.*; **Prov. 28:26** he that trusteth in his own *h.* is a fool: but whoso walketh wisely, he shall be delivered.

Trust in the LORD with all thine heart; and lean not unto thine own understanding. Prov. 3:5 (*see also* Trust, Understand)

Prov. 3:5 trust in the LORD with all thine *h.*; and lean not unto thine own understanding; **Isa. 48:2** they call themselves of the holy city, and stay themselves upon the God of Israel; The LORD of hosts is his name.

Keep thy heart with all diligence; for out of it are the issues of life. Prov. 4:23

Prov. 4:23 keep thy *h.* with all diligence; for out of it are the issues of life; **22:5** thorns and snares are in the way of the froward: he that doth keep his soul shall be far from them.

The LORD is nigh unto them that are of a broken heart; and saveth such as be of a contrite spirit. Ps. 34:18 (*see also* Broken, Contrite)

Ps. 34:18 the LORD is nigh unto them that are of a broken *h.*; and saveth such as be of a contrite spirit; **51:16-17** the sacrifices of God are a broken spirit: a broken and a contrite *h.*, O God, thou wilt not despise; **68:10** thy congregation hath dwelt therein: thou, O God, hast prepared of thy goodness for the poor; **69:29** I am poor and sorrowful: let thy salvation, O God, set me up on high; **69:33** the LORD heareth the poor, and despiseth not his prisoners; **109:22** I am poor and needy, and my *h.* is wounded within me; **147:3** he healeth the broken in *h.*, and bindeth up their wounds; **Isa. 62:6** ye that make mention of the LORD, keep not silence; **66:2** all those things hath mine hand made, and all those things have been, saith the LORD: but to this man will I look, even to him that is poor and of a contrite spirit.

I applied mine heart to know, and to search, and to seek out wisdom, and the reason of things, and to know the wickedness of folly, even of foolishness and madness. Eccl. 7:25 (*see also* Apply, Know, Reason, Seek, Wisdom)

Eccl. 7:25 I applied mine *h.* to know, and to search, and to seek out wisdom, and the reason of things, and to know the wickedness of folly, even of foolishness and madness; **8:9** all this have I seen, and applied my *h.* unto every work that is done under the sun; **8:16-17** I applied mine *h.* to know wisdom, and to see the business that is done upon the earth... then I beheld all the work of God, that a man cannot find out the work that is done under the sun; **9:1** I considered in my *h.* even to declare all this, that the righteous, and the wise, and their works, are in the hand of God: no man knoweth either love or hatred by all that is before them.

Hear now this, thou that art given to pleasures, that dwellest carelessly, that sayest in thine heart, I am, and none else beside me. Isa. 47:8

Neither shall they walk any more after the imagination of their evil heart. Jer. 3:17 (*see also* Imagine, Walk)

Jer. 3:17 they shall call Jerusalem the throne of the LORD; and all the nations shall be gathered unto it, to the name of the LORD, to Jerusalem: neither shall they walk any more after the imagination of their evil *h.*; **16:12-13** ye walk every one after the imagination of his evil *h.*, that they may not hearken unto me: Therefore will I cast you out of this land into a land that ye know not; **18:12** they said, There is no hope: but we will walk after our own devices, and we will every one do the imagination of his evil *h.*

Circumcise yourselves to the LORD, and take away the foreskins of your heart. Jer. 4:4 (*see also* Circumcise)

Jer. 4:4 circumcise yourselves to the LORD, and take away the foreskins of your *h.*... lest my fury come forth like fire, and burn that none can quench it, because of the evil of your doings; **9:26** all that are in the utmost corners, that dwell in the wilderness: for all these nations are uncircumcised, and all the house of Israel are uncircumcised in the *h.*

As for them whose heart walketh after the heart of their detestable things and their abominations, I will recompense their way upon their own heads, saith the Lord GOD. Ezek. 11:21 (*see also* Walk)

Ezek. 11:21 as for them whose *h.* walketh after the *h.* of their detestable things and their abominations, I will recompense their way upon their own heads, saith the Lord GOD; **16:50-51** they were haughty, and committed abomination before me: therefore I took them away as I saw good. Neither hath Samaria committed half of thy sins; but thou hast multiplied thine abominations more than they; **20:7-8** cast ye away every man the abominations of his eyes, and defile not yourselves with the idols of Egypt: I am the LORD your God. But they rebelled against me, and would not hearken unto me; **23:36** the LORD said moreover unto me; Son of man, wilt thou judge Aholah and Aholibah? yea, declare unto them their abominations.

Cast away from you all your transgressions, whereby ye have transgressed; and make you a new heart and a new spirit; for why will ye die, O house of Israel? Ezek. 18:31 (*see also* Transgression)

Ezek. 18:31 cast away from you all your transgressions, whereby ye have transgressed; and make you a new *h*. and a new spirit: for why will ye die, O house of Israel; **20:7** cast ye away every man the abominations of his eyes, and defile not yourselves with the idols of Egypt: I am the LORD your God.

I will give them one heart, and I will put a new spirit within you; and I will take the stony heart out of their flesh, and will give them an heart of flesh: That they may walk in my statutes, and keep mine ordinances, and do them: and they shall be my people, and I will be their God. Ezek. 11:19-20 (*see also* Commandment, One)

2 Chron. 30:12 the hand of God was to give them one *h*. to do the commandment of the king and of the princes, by the word of the LORD; **Ezek. 11:19-20** I will give them one *h*., and I will put a new spirit within you; and I will take the stony *h*. out of their flesh, and will give them an *h*. of flesh: That they may walk in my statutes, and keep mine ordinances, and do them: and they shall be my people, and I will be their God.

Consider it in thine heart, that the LORD he is God in heaven above, and upon the earth beneath: there is none else. Deut. 4:39 (*see also* One)

Gen. 35:11 I am God Almighty: be fruitful and multiply; **46:3** I am God, the God of thy father: fear not to go down into Egypt; for I will there make of thee a great nation; **Deut. 4:39** know

therefore this day, and consider it in thine *h*., that the LORD he is God in heaven above, and upon the earth beneath: there is none else; **1 Kgs. 8:60** all the people of the earth may know that the LORD is God, and that there is none else; **2 Chron. 20:6** O LORD God of our fathers, art not thou God in heaven? and rulest not thou over all the kingdoms of the heathen? and in thine hand is there not power and might, so that none is able to withstand thee; **Ps. 46:10** be still, and know that I am God: I will be exalted among the heathen, I will be exalted in the earth; **50:7** I will testify against thee: I am God, even thy God; **Isa. 43:12** ye are my witnesses, saith the LORD, that I am God; **45:5-6** I am the LORD, and there is none else, there is no God beside me; **45:18** I am the LORD; and there is none else; **45:22** look unto me, and be ye saved, all the ends of the earth: for I am God, and there is none else; **46:9** I am God, and there is none else; I am God, and there is none like me; **Jer. 30:21** I will cause him to draw near, and he shall approach unto me: for who is this that engaged his *h*. to approach unto me? saith the LORD; **Hosea 11:9** I am God, and not man; the Holy One in the midst of thee.

Come unto me, all ye that labour and are heavy laden, and I will give you rest. Take my yoke upon you, and learn of me; for I am meek and lowly in heart: and ye shall find rest unto your souls. Matt. 11:28-29 (*see also* Find, Heavy, Lowly, Meek, Seek)

Blessed are the pure in heart: for they shall see God. Matt. 5:8 (*see also* Pure)

Matt. 5:8 blessed are the pure in *h*.: for they shall see God; **1 Tim. 1:5** now the end of the commandment is charity out of a pure *h*., and of a good conscience, and of faith unfeigned; **2 Tim. 22** flee also youthful lusts: but follow righteousness, faith, charity, peace, with them that call on the Lord out of a pure *h*.; **Titus 1:15** unto the pure all things are pure: but unto them that are defiled and unbelieving is nothing pure; but even their mind and conscience is defiled; **Heb. 10:22** let us draw near with a true *h*. in full assurance of faith, having our *h*. sprinkled from an evil conscience, and our bodies washed with pure water; **James 3:17** wisdom that is from above is first pure, then peaceable, gentle, and easy to be intreated, full of mercy and good fruits, without partiality, and without hypocrisy; **1 Pet. 1:23** Seeing ye have purified your souls in obeying the truth through the Spirit unto unfeigned love of the brethren, see that ye love one another with a pure *h*.

fervently: Being born again, not of corruptible seed, but of incorruptible, by the word of God, which liveth and abideth for ever; **1 Jn. 3:3** are we the sons of God, and it doth not yet appear what we shall be: but we know that, when he shall appear, we shall be like him; for we shall see him as he is. And every man that hath this hope in him purifieth himself, even as he is pure.

Harden not your hearts, as in the provocation, in the day of temptation in the wilderness: When your fathers tempted me, proved me, and saw my works forty years. Heb. 3:8 (*see also* Tempt)

Matt. 19:8 Moses because of the hardness of your *h.* suffered you to put away your wives: but from the beginning it was not so; **Mark 3:5** being grieved for the hardness of their *h.*, he saith unto the man, Stretch forth thine hand. And he stretched it out: and his hand was restored whole as the other; **6:51-52** he went up unto them into the ship; and the wind ceased: and they were sore amazed in themselves beyond measure, and wondered. For they considered not the miracle of the loaves: for their *h.* was hardened; **8:17** why reason ye, because ye have no bread? perceive ye not yet, neither understand? have ye your *h.* yet hardened; **10:2-5** Jesus answered and said unto them, For the hardness of your *h.* he wrote you this precept; **16:14** afterward he appeared unto the eleven as they sat at meat, and upbraided them with their unbelief and hardness of *h.*, because they believed not them which had seen him after he was risen; **Acts 7:51** ye stiffnecked and uncircumcised in *h.* and ears, ye do always resist the Holy Ghost: as your fathers did, so do ye; **Rom. 2:5** after thy hardness and impenitent *h.* treasurest up unto thyself wrath against the day of wrath and **Rev.** of the righteous judgment of God; **Heb. 3:8** Harden not your *h.*, as in the provocation, in the day of temptation in the wilderness; **3:13** exhort one another daily, while it is called To day; lest any of you be hardened through the deceitfulness of sin; **3:15** to day if ye will hear his voice, harden not your *h.*, as in the provocation; **4:7** To day, after so long a time; as it is said, To day if ye will hear his voice, harden not your *h.*; **5:11** of whom we have many things to say, and hard to be uttered, seeing ye are dull of hearing.

Put away, said he, the strange gods which are among you, and incline your heart unto the LORD God of Israel. Josh. 24:23 (*see also* Incline)

Josh.24:23 put away, said he, the strange gods which are among you, and incline your *h.* unto the LORD God of Israel; **1 Kgs. 8:58** that he may incline our *h.* unto him, to walk in all his ways, and to keep his commandments, and his statutes,

and his judgments, which he commanded our fathers; **Ps. 119:36** incline my *h.* unto thy testimonies, and not to covetousness; **119:112** I have inclined mine *h.* to perform thy statutes alway, even unto the end; **141:4** incline not my *h.* to any evil thing, to practise wicked works with men that work iniquity; **Jer. 25:4** the LORD hath sent unto you all his servants the prophets, rising early and sending them; but ye have not hearkened, nor inclined your ear to hear; **Ezek. 3:10** all my words that I shall speak unto thee receive in thine *h.*, and hear with thine ears.

If there be among you a poor man of one of thy brethren within any of thy gates in thy land which the LORD thy God giveth thee, thou shalt not harden thine heart, nor shut thine hand from thy poor brother. Deut. 15:7 (*see also* Poor)

Ex. 4:21 I will harden his *h.*, that he shall not let the people go; **7:3** I will harden Pharaohs *h.*, and multiply my signs and my wonders in the land of Egypt; **14:4** I will harden Pharaohs *h.*, that he shall follow after them; and I will be honoured upon Pharaoh, and upon all his host; that the Egyptians may know that I am the LORD; **14:17** I will harden the *h.* of the Egyptians; and upon his horsemen; **Deut. 15:7** if there be among you a poor man of one of thy brethren within any of thy gates in thy land which the LORD thy God giveth thee, thou shalt not harden thine *h.*, nor shut thine hand from thy poor brother; **Josh. 11:20** it was of the LORD to harden their *h.*, that they should come against Israel in battle, that he might destroy them utterly; **1 Sam. 6:6** wherefore then do ye harden your *h.*, as the Egyptians and Pharaoh hardened their *h.*; **Ps. 95:8** harden not your *h.*, as in the provocation, and as in the day of temptation in the wilderness; **Prov. 28:14** happy is the man that feareth alway: but he that hardeneth his *h.* shall fall into mischief.

Walk before me, as David thy father walked, in integrity of heart, and in uprightness, to do according to all that I have commanded thee, and wilt keep my statutes and my judgments. 1 Kgs. 9:4 (*see also* Integrity)

Gen. 20:5-6 in the integrity of my *h.* and innocency of my hands have I done this; **1 Sam. 29:6** thou hast been upright, and thy going out and thy coming in with me in the host is good in my sight: for I have not found evil in thee since the day of thy coming unto me; **2 Sam. 22:24-26** I was also upright before him, and have kept myself from mine iniquity. Therefore the LORD hath recompensed me according to my righteousness; **1 Kgs. 3:6** thou hast shewed unto thy servant David my father great mercy, according as he walked before thee in truth, and in righteousness, and in uprightness of *h.* with thee; **9:4** walk before me, as David thy father walked, in integrity of *h.*, and in uprightness, to do according to all that I have commanded thee, and wilt keep my statutes and my judgments; **11:38** if thou wilt hearken unto all that I command thee, and wilt walk in my ways, and do that is right in my sight, to keep my statutes and my commandments, as David my servant did; that I will be with thee; **15:14** Asas *h.* was perfect with the LORD all his days; **22:43** he walked in all the ways of Asa his father; he turned not aside from it, doing that which was right in the eyes of the LORD; **1 Chron. 29:17** thou triest the *h.*, and hast pleasure in uprightness. As for me, in the uprightness of mine *h.* I have willingly offered all these things; **2 Chron. 6:14** there is no God like thee in the heaven, nor in the earth; which keepest covenant, and shewest mercy unto thy servants, that walk before thee with all their *h.*; **6:16** here shall not fail thee a man in my sight to sit upon the throne of Israel; yet so that thy children take heed to their way to walk in my law, as thou hast walked before me; **29:34** the Levites were more upright in *h.* to sanctify themselves than the priests; **Job 1:1** that man was perfect and upright, and one that feared God, and eschewed evil; **1:8** hast thou considered my servant Job, that there is none like him in the earth, a perfect and an upright man, one that feareth God, and escheweth evil; **2:3** the LORD said unto Satan, Hast thou considered my servant Job, that there is none like him in the earth, a perfect and an upright man, one that feareth God, and escheweth evil; **2:9** dost thou still retain thine integrity? **4:6** is not this thy fear, thy confidence, thy hope, and the uprightness of thy ways; **27:5** God forbid that I should justify you: till I die I will not remove mine integrity

from me; **33:3** my words shall be of the uprightness of my *h.*: and my lips shall utter knowledge clearly; **Ps. 7:8** the LORD shall judge the people: judge me, O LORD, according to my righteousness, and according to mine integrity that is in me; **7:10** my defence is of God, which saveth the upright in *h.*; **11:2-3** the integrity of the upright shall guide them: but the perverseness of transgressors shall destroy them; **11:7** the righteous LORD loveth righteousness; his countenance doth behold the upright; **15:2** he that walketh uprightly, and worketh righteousness, and speaketh the truth in his *h.*; **18:23** I was also upright before him, and I kept myself from mine iniquity; **18:25** with the merciful thou wilt shew thyself merciful; with an upright man thou wilt shew thyself upright; **19:13** then shall I be upright, and I shall be innocent from the great transgression; **25:21** let integrity and uprightness preserve me; for I wait on thee; **26:1** judge me, O LORD; for I have walked in mine integrity: I have trusted also in the LORD; therefore I shall not slide; **26:11** as for me, I will walk in mine integrity: redeem me, and be merciful unto me; **32:11** be glad in the LORD, and rejoice, ye righteous: and shout for joy, all ye that are upright in *h.*; **36:10** continue thy lovingkindness unto them that know thee; and thy righteousness to the upright in *h.*; **37:18-19** the LORD knoweth the days of the upright: and their inheritance shall be for ever; **37:22** such as be blessed of him shall inherit the earth; and they that be cursed of him shall be cut off; **37:37** mark the perfect man, and behold the upright: for the end of that man is peace; **41:12** as for me, thou upholdest me in mine integrity, and settest me before thy face for ever; **64:10** the righteous shall be glad in the LORD, and shall trust in him; and all the upright in *h.* shall glory; **78:72** he fed them according to the integrity of his *h.*; and guided them by the skilfulness of his hands; **84:11** the LORD God is a sun and shield: the LORD will give grace and glory: no good thing will he withhold from them that walk uprightly; **94:15** judgment shall return unto righteousness: and all the upright in *h.* shall follow it; **97:11** light is sown for the righteous, and gladness for the upright in *h.*; **112:2-4** unto the upright there ariseth light in the darkness: he is gracious, and full of compassion, and righteous; **125:4** do good, O LORD, unto those that be good, and to them that are upright in their *h.*; **Prov. 2:7** he layeth up sound wisdom for the righteous: he is a buckler to them that walk uprightly; **2:9** then shalt thou understand righteousness, and judgment, and equity; yea, every good path; **2:21** the upright shall dwell in the land, and the perfect shall remain in it; **10:9** he that walketh uprightly walketh surely: but he that perverteth his ways shall be known; **10:29** the way of the LORD is strength to the upright: but destruction shall be to the workers of iniquity; **11:3** the integrity of the upright shall guide them: but the perverseness of transgressors shall destroy them; **11:6** the righteousness of the upright shall deliver them: but transgressors shall be taken in their own naughtiness; **11:11** by the blessing of the upright the city is exalted: but it is overthrown by the mouth of the wicked; **11:20** they that are of a froward *h.* are abomination to the LORD: but such as are upright in their way are his delight; **12:6** the words of the wicked are to lie in wait for blood: but the mouth of the upright shall deliver them; **13:6** righteousness keepeth him that is upright in the way: but wickedness overthroweth the sinner; **14:2** he that walketh in his uprightness feareth the LORD: but he that is perverse in his ways despiseth him; **14:11** the house of the wicked shall be overthrown: but the tabernacle of the upright shall flourish; **15:8** the sacrifice of the wicked is an abomination to the LORD: but the prayer of the upright is his delight; **15:21** folly is joy to him that is destitute of wisdom: but a man of understanding walketh uprightly; **20:7** the just man walketh in his integrity: his children are blessed after him; **21:29** a wicked man hardeneth his face: but as for the upright, he directeth his way; **28:6** better is the poor that walketh in his uprightness, than he that is perverse in his ways, though he be rich; **28:18** whoso walketh uprightly shall be saved: but he that is perverse in his ways shall fall at once; **29:10** the bloodthirsty hate the upright: but the just seek his soul; **29:27** an unjust man is an abomination to the just: and he that is upright in the way is abomination to the wicked; **Eccl. 7:29** this only have I found, that God hath made man upright; but they have sought out many inventions; **Isa. 26:7** the way of the just is uprightness: thou, most upright, dost weigh the path of the just; **57:2** he shall enter into peace: they shall rest in their beds, each one walking in his uprightness.

Turn ye even to me with all your heart, and with fasting, and with weeping, and with mourning: And rend your heart, and not your garments, and turn unto the LORD your God: for he is gracious and merciful, slow to anger, and of great kindness, and repenteth him of the evil. Joel 2:12-13 (*see also* Fast, Turn)

2Kngs 23:25 like unto him was there no king before him, that turned to the LORD with all his *h.*, and with all his soul, and with all his might; **2 Chron. 30:5-6** turn again unto the LORD God of Abraham, Isaac, and Israel, and he will return to the remnant of you, that are escaped out of the hand of the kings of Assyria; **30:9** turn again unto the LORD... for the LORD your God is gracious and merciful, and will not turn away his face from you, if ye return unto him; **Ps. 22:27** all the ends of the world shall remember and turn unto the LORD: and all the kindreds of the nations shall worship before thee; **Isa. 31:6** turn ye unto him from whom the children of Israel have deeply revolted; **Hosea 12:6** turn thou to thy God: keep mercy and judgment, and wait on thy God continually; **14:2-4** turn to the LORD: say unto him, Take away all iniquity, and receive us graciously: so will we render the calves of our lips; **Joel 2:12-13** turn ye even to me with all your *h.*, and with fasting, and with weeping, and with mourning: And rend your *h.*, and not your garments, and turn unto the LORD your God.

Sow to yourselves in righteousness, reap in mercy; break up your fallow ground: for it is time to seek the LORD, till he come and rain righteousness upon you. Hosea 10:12 (*see also* Seek)

2 Chron. 12:14 he did evil, because he prepared not his *h.* to seek the LORD; **14:7** we have sought the LORD our God, we have sought him, and he hath given us rest on every side. So they built and prospered; **15:2** the LORD is with you, while ye be with him; and if ye seek him, he will be found of you; but if ye forsake him, he will forsake you; **19:3** there are good things found in thee, in that thou hast taken away the groves out of the land, and hast prepared thine *h.* to seek God; **20:33** the high places were not taken away: for as yet the people had not prepared their *h.* unto the God of their fathers; **30:19** that prepareth his *h.* to seek God, the LORD God of his fathers, though he be not cleansed according to the purification of the sanctuary; **Ezra 7:10** Ezra had prepared his *h.* to seek the law of the LORD, and to do it, and to teach in Israel statutes and judgments; **Lam. 3:25** the LORD is good unto them that wait for him, to the soul that seeketh him; **Hosea 10:12** sow to yourselves in righteousness, reap in mercy; break up your fallow ground: for it is time to seek the LORD, till he come and rain righteousness upon you.

HEATHEN (*see also* Gentile, Nation, World)

Thus saith the Lord, learn not the way of the heathen, and be not dismayed at the signs of heaven; for the heathen are dismayed at them. Jer. 10:2 (*see also* Heaven, Sign, Way)

HEAVEN (*see also* Celestial, Kingdom, Zion)

Lay not up for yourselves treasures upon earth, where moth and rust doth corrupt, and where thieves break through and steal: But lay up for yourselves treasures in heaven, where neither moth nor rust doth corrupt, and where thieves do not break through nor steal: For where your treasure is, there will your heart be also. Matt. 6:19-21 (*see also* Heart, Lay Up, Steal, Treasure)

Thus saith the Lord, learn not the way of the heathen, and be not dismayed at the signs of heaven; for the heathen are dismayed at them. Jer. 10:2 (*see also* Heathen, Sign, Way)

HEAVY (*see also* Burden)

A stone is heavy, and the sand weighty; but a fool's wrath is heavier than them both. Prov. 27:3 (*see also* Wrath)

Come unto me, all ye that labour and are heavy laden, and I will give you rest. Take my yoke upon you, and learn of me; for I am meek and lowly in heart: and ye shall find rest unto your souls. Matt. 11:28-29 (*see also* Heart, Lowly, Meek, Seek)

HEED (*see also* Follow, Hearken, Regard, Respect)

We ought to give the more earnest heed to the things which we have heard, lest at any time we should let them slip. Heb. 2:1 (*see also* Earnest, Word)

HEIR (*see also* Birthright, Genealogy, Inherit)

For as many as are led by the Spirit of God, they are the sons of God. For ye have not received the spirit of bondage again to fear; but ye have received the Spirit of adoption, whereby we cry, Abba, Father. The Spirit itself beareth witness with our spirit, that we are the children of God: And if children, then heirs; heirs of God, and joint-heirs with Christ; if so be that we suffer with him, that we may be also glorified together. For I reckon that the sufferings of this present time are not worthy to be compared with the glory which shall be revealed in us. Rom 8:14-18 (*see also* Adopt, Father)

HELL (*see also* Death, Sin, Transgress)

If thy hand offend thee, cut it off: it is better for thee to enter into life maimed, than having two hands to go into hell, into the fire that never shall be quenched. Mark 9:43 (*see also* Offend)

HELP (*see* Serve)

HERB (*see also* Eat)

He causeth the grass to grow for the cattle, and herb for the service of man; that he may bring forth food out of the earth. Ps. 104:14 (*see also* Food)

HID, HIDDEN, HIDE (*see also* Mystery)

Woe unto them that seek deep to hide their counsel from the LORD and their works are in the dark, and they say, Who seeth us? and who knoweth us? Isa. 29:15 (*see also* Counsel, Seek)

HIGHMINDED (*see also* Arrogance, Haughty, Pride)

Be not highminded, nor trust in uncertain riches, but in the living God, who giveth us richly all things to enjoy. 1 Tim. 6:17-19 (*see also* Rich, Trust)

Be not highminded. Rom. 11:20

Rom. 11:20 be not *h.*, but fear; **11:25** for I would not, brethren, that ye should be ignorant of this mystery, lest ye should be wise in your own conceits; that blindness in part is happened to Israel, until the fulness of the Gentiles be come in; **12:16** mind not high things, but condescend to men of low estate. Be not wise in your own conceits; **Gal.** 6:3 for if a man think himself to be something, when he is nothing, he deceiveth himself.

Charge them that are rich in this world, that they be not highminded, nor trust in uncertain riches, but in the living God, who giveth us richly all things to enjoy. 1 Tim. 6:17 (*see also* Rich)

1 Tim 6:17 charge them that are rich in this world, that they be not *h.*, nor trust in uncertain riches, but in the living God, who giveth us richly all things to enjoy; **2 Tim. 3:1-4** This know also, that in the last days perilous times shall come. For men shall be lovers of their own selves, covetous, boasters, proud, blasphemers, disobedient to parents, unthankful, unholy, without natural affection, trucebreakers, false accusers, incontinent, fierce, despisers of those that are good, traitors, heady, *h.*, lovers of pleasures more than lovers of God.

HIGH PRIEST (*see also* Melchisedec, Priesthood)

That by two immutable things, in which it was impossible for God to lie, we might have a strong consolation, who have fled for refuge to lay hold upon the hope set before us: Which hope we have as an anchor of the soul, both sure and stedfast, and which entereth into that within the veil; Whither the forerunner is for us entered, even Jesus, made an high priest for ever after the order of Melchisedec. Heb. 6:18-19 (*see also* Hope, Impossible, Melchisedec)

HINDER (*see also* Stumbling Block)

Woe unto you, lawyers! for ye have taken away the key of knowledge: ye entered not in yourselves, and them that were entering in ye hindered. Luke 11:52 (*see also* Key)

HOLD, HOLD FAST (*see also* Cleave, Retain)

Hold fast the form of sound words, which thou hast heard of me, in faith and love which is in Christ Jesus. 2 Tim. 1:13 (*see also* Sound, Word)

HOLINESS, HOLIER, HOLY (*see also* Clean, Hallow, Pure, Righteous, Sacred, Sanctify)

Teach my people the difference between the holy and profane, and cause them to discern between the unclean and the clean. Ezek. 44:23 (*see also* Clean, Teach)

Be silent, O all flesh, before the LORD: for he is raised up out of his holy habitation. Zech. 2:13 (*see also* Silence)

An abomination is committed in Israel and in Jerusalem; for Judah hath profaned the holiness of the LORD which he loved, and hath married the daughter of a strange god. Mal. 2:11 (*see also* Profane)

Exalt the LORD our God, and worship at his holy hill; for the LORD our God is holy. Ps. 99:9 (*see also* Exalt)

Ye shall be holy: for I the LORD God *am* holy. Lev. 19:2

Ex. 22:31 ye shall be *h.* men unto me; **Lev. 11:44** I am the LORD your God: ye shall therefore sanctify yourselves, and ye shall be *h.*; for I am *h.*; **19:2** ye shall be *h.*: for I the LORD your God am *h.*; **20:26** ye shall be *h.* unto me: for I the LORD am *h.*, and have severed you from other people, that ye should be mine; **21:6** they shall be *h.* unto their God, and not profane the name of their God; **Isa. 4:3** he that remaineth in Jerusalem, shall be called *h.*, even every one that is written among the living; **65:5** stand by thyself, come not near to me; for I am *h.* than thou.

Thou hast despised mine holy things, and hast profaned my sabbaths. Ezek. 22:8 (*see also* Sabbath)

Ezek. 22:8 thou hast despised mine *h.* things, and hast profaned my sabbaths; **22:25-26** her priests have violated my law, and have profaned mine *h.* things: they have put no difference between the *h.* and profane, neither have they shewed difference between the unclean and the clean, and have hid their eyes from my sabbaths; **44:8** ye have not kept the charge of mine *h.* things: but ye have set keepers of my charge in my sanctuary for yourselves.

The place of my throne, and the place of the soles of my feet, where I will dwell in the midst of the children of Israel for ever, and my holy name, shall the house of Israel no more defile. Ezek. 43:7 (*see also* Name)

Ezek. 39:7 make my *h.* name known in the midst of my people Israel; and I will not let them pollute my *h.* name any more; **43:7** the place of my throne, and the place of the soles of my feet, where I will dwell in the midst of the children of Israel for ever, and my *h.* name, shall the house of Israel no more defile.

Follow peace with all men, and holiness, without which no man shall see the Lord. Heb. 12:14 (*see also* Peace)

1 Thes 4:7 God hath not called us unto uncleanness, but unto *h.*; **1 Tim. 2:15** she shall be saved in childbearing, if they continue in faith and charity and *h.* with sobriety; **Titus 2:3** the aged women likewise, that they be in behaviour as becometh *h.*, not false accusers, not given to much wine, teachers of good things; **Heb. 12:14** follow peace with all men, and *h.*, without which no man shall see the Lord.

Give not that which is holy unto the dogs, neither cast ye your pearls before swine, lest they trample them under their feet, and turn again and rend you. Matt. 7:6 (*see also* Pearl)

Matt. 7:6 give not that which is holy unto the dogs, neither cast ye your pearls before swine, lest they trample them under their feet, and turn again and rend you; **22:5** but they made light of it, and went their ways, one to his farm, another to his merchandise.

HOLY GHOST (*see also* Baptism, Comforter, Gift, Holy Ghost, Know, Testimony)

For it is impossible for those who were once enlightened, and have tasted of the heavenly gift, and were made partakers of the Holy Ghost, And have tasted the good word of God, and the powers of the world to come, If they shall fall away, to renew them again unto repentance; seeing they crucify to themselves the Son of God afresh, and put him to an open shame. Heb. 6:4 (*see also* Enlightened, Impossible, Second Death)

For the prophecy came not in old time by the will of man: but holy men of God spake as they were moved by the Holy Ghost. 2 Pet. 1:21 (*see also* Moved, Prophecy)

What? Know ye not that your body is a temple of the Holy Ghost which is in you, which ye have of God, and ye are not your own? For ye are bought with a price: therefore glorify God in your body, and in your spirit, which are God's. 1 Cor. 6:20 (*see also* Body, Bought, Temple)

These things have I spoken unto you, being yet present with you. But the Comforter, which is the Holy Ghost, whom the Father will send in my name, he shall teach you all things, and bring all things to your remembrance, whatsoever I have said unto you. John 14:25-26 (*see also* All Things, Comforter, Remembrance)

He that shall blaspheme against the Holy Ghost hath never forgiveness, but is in danger of eternal damnation. Mark 3:29 (*see also* Blaspheme, Danger)

[Peter and John] then laid they their hands on them, and they received the Holy Ghost. Acts 8:17 (*see also* Laying on of Hands)

Matt. 3:11 I indeed baptize you with water unto repentance: but he that cometh after me is mightier than I, whose shoes I am not worthy to bear: he shall baptize you with the *H.G.*, and with fire; **Mark 1:8** I indeed have baptized you with water: but he shall baptize you with the *H.G.*; **Luke 1:67** Zacharias was filled with the *H.G.*, and prophesied; **2:25** the same man was just and devout, waiting for the consolation of Israel: and the *H.G.* was upon him; **2:26** it was revealed unto him by the *H.G.*, that he should not see death, before he had seen the Lord's Christ; **4:1** And Jesus being full of the *H.G.* returned from Jordan, and was led by the Spirit into the wilderness; **12:11-12** the *H.G.* shall teach you in the same hour what ye ought to say; **John 1:33-34** upon whom thou shalt see the Spirit descending, and remaining on him, the same is he which baptizeth with the *H.G.*. And I saw, and bare record that this is the Son of God; **7:39** (But this spake he of the Spirit, which they that believe on him should receive: for the *H.G.* was not yet given; because that Jesus was not yet glorified); **14:26** the Comforter, which is the *H.G.*, whom the Father will send in my name, he shall teach you all things, and bring all things to your remembrance, whatsoever I have said unto you; **15:26** when the Comforter is come, whom I will send unto you from the Father, even the Spirit of truth, which proceedeth from the Father, he shall testify of me; **16:7** it is expedient for you that I go away: for if I go not away, the Comforter will not come unto you; but if I depart, I will send him unto you; **16:13** when he, the Spirit of truth, is come, he will guide you into all truth: for he shall not speak of himself; but whatsoever he shall hear, that shall he speak: and he will shew you things to come; **Acts 1:2** until the day in which he was taken up, after that he through the *H.G.* had given commandments unto the apostles whom he had chosen; **1:4-5** John truly baptized with water; but ye shall be baptized with the *H.G.* not many days hence; **1:8** ye shall receive power, after that the *H.G.* is come upon you: and ye shall be witnesses unto me both in Jerusalem, and in all Judaea, and in Samaria, and unto the uttermost part of the earth; **2:2-4** suddenly there came a sound from heaven as of a rushing mighty wind, and it filled all the house where they were sitting. And there appeared unto them cloven tongues like as of fire, and it sat upon each of them. And they were all filled with the *H.G.*, and began to speak with other tongues, as the Spirit gave them utterance; **2:17** it shall come to pass in the last days, saith God, I will pour out of my Spirit upon all flesh: and your sons and your daughters shall prophesy, and your young men shall see visions, and your old men shall dream dreams; **2:37-38** Repent, and be baptized every one of you in the name of Jesus Christ for the remission of sins, and ye shall receive the gift of the *H.G.*; **7:55-56** he, being full of the *H.G.*, looked up stedfastly into heaven, and saw the glory of God, and Jesus standing on the right hand of God, And said, Behold, I see the heavens opened, and the Son of man standing on the right hand of God; **8:17** then laid they their hands on them, and they received the *H.G.*; **11:24** he was a good man, and full of the *H.G.* and of faith: and much people was added unto the Lord; **19:2-3** have ye received the *H.G.* since ye believed? And they said unto him, We have not so much as heard whether there be any *H.G.*; **19:6** when Paul had laid his hands upon them, the *H.G.* came on them; and they spake with tongues, and prophesied; **Rom. 15:16** ministering the gospel of God, that the offering up of the Gentiles might be acceptable, being sanctified by the *H.G.*; **1 Cor. 6:19** know ye not that your body is the temple of the *H.G.* which is in you, which ye have of God, and ye are not your own; **2 Cor. 9:15** thanks be unto God for his unspeakable gift; **Gal. 5:22-23** the fruit of the Spirit is love, joy, peace, longsuffering, gentleness, goodness, faith, Meekness, temperance: against such there is no law; **Eph. 2:21-22** all the building fitly framed together groweth unto an holy temple in the Lord: In whom ye also are builded together for an habitation of God through the Spirit; **3:5** in other ages was not made known unto the sons of men, as it is now revealed unto his holy apostles and prophets by the Spirit; **3:16** he

would grant you, according to the riches of his glory, to be strengthened with might by his Spirit in the inner man; **Heb. 2:4** God also bearing them witness, both with signs and wonders, and with divers miracles, and gifts of the *H.G.*, according to his own will; **6:4** it is impossible for those who were once enlightened, and have tasted of the heavenly gift, and were made partakers of the *H.G.*, and have tasted the good word of God, and the powers of the world to come; **10:15** the *H.G.* also is a witness to us: for after that he had said before; **1 Pet. 1:12** now reported unto you by them that have preached the gospel unto you with the *H.G.* sent down from heaven; which things the angels desire to look into; **1 Jn. 4:13** know we that we dwell in him, and he in us, because he hath given us of his Spirit; **5:6-7** it is the Spirit that beareth witness, because the Spirit is truth. For there are three that bear record in heaven, the Father, the Word, and the *H.G.*; **Jude 1:18-21** there should be mockers in the last time, who should walk after their own ungodly lusts. These be they who separate themselves, sensual, having not the Spirit. But ye, beloved, building up yourselves on your most holy faith, praying in the *H.G.*, Keep yourselves in the love of God, looking for the mercy of our Lord Jesus Christ unto eternal life.

Whosoever speaketh a word against the Son of man, it shall be forgiven him: but whosoever speaketh against the Holy Ghost, it shall not be forgiven him, neither in this world, neither in the world to come. Matt. 12:32

Matt. 12:31-32 all manner of sin and blasphemy shall be forgiven unto men: but the blasphemy against the *H.G.* shall not be forgiven unto men. And whosoever speaketh a word against the Son of man, it shall be forgiven him: but whosoever speaketh against the *H.G.*, it shall not be forgiven him, neither in this world, neither in the world to come; **Mark 3:29** he that shall blaspheme against the *H.G.* hath never forgiveness, but is in danger of eternal damnation; **Luke 12:10** whosoever shall speak a word against the Son of man, it shall be forgiven him: but unto him that blasphemeth against the *H.G.* it shall not be forgiven; **1 Jn. 2:22** who is a liar but he that denieth that Jesus is the Christ? He is antichrist, that denieth the Father and the Son.

HOLY SPIRIT (*see also* Holy Ghost, Seal, Spirit)

Grieve not the holy Spirit of God, whereby ye are sealed unto the day of redemption. **Eph. 4:30** (*see also* Grieve, Seal)

Marvel not that I said unto thee, Ye must be born again. The wind bloweth where it listeth, and thou hearest the sound thereof, but canst not tell whence it cometh, and whither it goeth: so is every one that is born of the Spirit. **John 3:7-8** (*see also* Born Again)

As many as are led by the Spirit of God, they are the sons of God. **Rom. 8:14** (*see also* Lead)

Acts 8:29 then the Spirit said unto Philip, Go near, and join thyself to this chariot; **16:6-7** when they had gone throughout Phrygia and the region of Galatia, and were forbidden of the Holy Ghost to preach the word in Asia, After they were come to Mysia, they assayed to go into Bithynia: but the Spirit suffered them not; **20:22** I go bound in the spirit unto Jerusalem, not knowing the things that shall befall me there; **Rom. 8:11** if the Spirit of him that raised up Jesus from the dead dwell in you, he that raised up Christ from the dead shall also quicken your mortal bodies by his Spirit that dwelleth in you; **8:14** for as many as are led by the Spirit of God, they are the sons of God; **1 Cor. 2:10-14** God hath revealed them unto us by his Spirit: for the Spirit searcheth all things, yea, the deep things of God. For what man knoweth the things of a man, save the spirit of man which is in him? even so the things of God knoweth no man, but the Spirit of God. Now we have received, not the spirit of the world, but the spirit which is of God; that we might know the things that are freely given to us of God. Which things also we speak, not in the words which man's wisdom teacheth, but which the Holy Ghost teacheth; comparing spiritual things with spiritual. But the natural man receiveth not the things of the Spirit of God: for they are foolishness unto him: neither can he know them, because they are spiritually discerned; **12:2-3** no man speaking by the Spirit of God calleth Jesus accursed: and that no man can say that Jesus is the Lord, but by the Holy Ghost; **2 Cor. 3:6** who also hath made us able ministers of the new testament; not of the letter, but of the spirit: for the letter killeth, but the spirit giveth life; **Eph. 5:9** the fruit of the Spirit is in all goodness and righteousness and truth.

HONEST, HONESTLY, HONESTY (*see also* Depend, Integrity, Sincere, True, Trust, Truth)

Lead a quiet and peaceable life in all godliness and honesty. **1 Tim. 2:2** (*see also* Godliness, Life, Peace)

Let us walk honestly, as in the day; not in rioting and drunkenness, not in chambering and wantonness, not in strife and envying. **Rom. 13:13** (*see also* Walk)

Luke 8:15 on the good ground are they, which in an *h.* and good heart, having heard the word, keep it, and bring forth fruit with patience; **Rom. 12:17** recompense to no man evil for evil. Provide things *h.* in the sight of all men; **13:13** let us walk *h.*, as in the day; not in rioting and drunkenness, not in chambering and wantonness, not in strife and envying; **2 Cor. 4:2** have renounced the hidden things of dishonesty, not walking in craftiness, nor handling the word of God deceitfully; but by manifestation of the truth commending ourselves to every man's conscience in the sight of God; **Philip. 4:8** whatsoever things are true, whatsoever things are *h.*, whatsoever things are just, whatsoever things are pure, whatsoever things are lovely, whatsoever things are of good report; if there be any virtue, and if there be any praise, think on these things; **1 Tim. 2:2** kings, and for all that are in authority; that we may lead a quiet and peaceable life in all godliness and *h.*; **Heb. 13:18** we trust we have a good conscience, in all things willing to live *h.*; **1 Pet. 2:12** having your conversation *h.* among the Gentiles: that, whereas they speak against you as evildoers, they may by your good works, which they shall behold, glorify God in the day of visitation.

HONOR, HONORABLE (*see also* Glory, Praise)

Honour all men. Love the brotherhood. Fear God. Honour the king. **1 Pet. 2:17**

How can ye believe, which receive honour one of another, and seek not the honour that cometh from God only? **John 5:44** (*see also* Glorify, Praise)

The LORD saith, Be it far from me; for them that honour me I will honour, and they that despise me shall be lightly esteemed. **1 Sam. 2:30** (*see also* Despise)

If thou turn away thy foot from the sabbath, from doing thy pleasure on my holy day; and call the sabbath a delight, the holy of the LORD, honorable; and shalt honor him, not doing thy own ways, nor finding thine own pleasure, nor speaking thine own words: Then shalt thou delight thyself in the LORD; and I will cause thee to ride upon the high places of the earth, and feed thee with the heritage of Jacob thy father: for the mouth of the LORD hath spoken it. Isa. 58:13-14 (*see also* Delight, Sabbath)

Honour thy father and thy mother. Matt. 19:19

Matt. 15:4-6 God commanded, saying, *H.* thy father and mother: and, He that curseth father or mother, let him die the death. But ye say, Whosoever shall say to his father or his mother, It is a gift, by whatsoever thou mightest be profited by me; And *h.* not his father or his mother, he shall be free; **19:19** *h.* thy father and thy mother; **Mark 7:10** *H.* thy father and thy mother; and, Whoso curseth father or mother, let him die the death; **Luke 18:20** *H.* thy father and thy mother; **Eph. 6:2-3** *h.* thy father and mother; (which is the first commandment with promise;) That it may be well with thee, and thou mayest live long on the earth.

All men should honour the Son, even as they honour the Father. John 5:23

John 5:23 all men should *h.* the Son, even as they honour the Father. He that *h.* not the Son *h.* not the Father which hath sent him.

Honoureth them that fear the Lord. Ps. 15:4

Ps. 15:4 he *h.* them that fear the LORD; **Prov. 8:13** the fear of the LORD is to hate evil: pride, and arrogancy, and the evil way, and the froward mouth, do I hate.

Honour thy father and thy mother, as the LORD thy God hath commanded thee; that thy days may be prolonged, and that it may go well with thee, in the land which the LORD thy God giveth thee. Deut. 5:16 (*see also* Father, Go, Mother)

Ex. 20:12 *h.* thy father and thy mother: that thy days may be long upon the land which the LORD thy God giveth thee; **21:15** he that smiteth his father, or his mother, shall be surely put to death; **21:17** he that curseth his father, or his mother,

shall surely be put to death; **Lev. 20:9** every one that curseth his father or his mother shall be surely put to death: he hath cursed his father or his mother; his blood shall be upon him; **Deut. 5:16** *h.* thy father and thy mother, as the LORD thy God hath commanded thee; that thy days may be prolonged, and that it may go well with thee, in the land which the LORD thy God giveth thee; **Prov. 31:28** her children arise up, and call her blessed.

Honour the LORD with thy substance, and with the firstfruits of all thine increase. Prov. 3:9 (*see also* Tithe)

1 Sam. 2:30 the LORD saith, Be it far from me; for them that *h.* me I will *h.*, and they that despise me shall be lightly esteemed; **Ps. 71:8** let my mouth be filled with thy praise and with thy *h.* all the day; **Prov. 3:9** *h.* the LORD with thy substance, and with the firstfruits of all thine increase; **Isa. 29:13** forasmuch as this people draw near me with their mouth, and with their lips do *h.* me, but have removed their heart far from me, and their fear toward me is taught by the precept of men; **43:20** the beast of the field shall *h.* me, the dragons and the owls: because I give waters in the wilderness, and rivers in the desert, to give drink to my people, my chosen; **Dan. 4:37** I Nebuchadnezzar praise and extol and *h.* the King of heaven, all whose works are truth, and his ways judgment.

Wives shall give to their husbands honour, both to great and small. Esth. 1:20

Esth. 1:17 this deed of the queen shall come abroad unto all women, so that they shall despise their husbands in their eyes, when it shall be reported; **1:20** when the kings decree which he shall make shall be published throughout all his empire, [for it is great,] all the wives shall give to their husbands *h.*, both to great and small; **Ezek. 14:20** as I live, saith the Lord GOD, they shall deliver neither son nor daughter; they shall but deliver their own souls by their righteousness; **14:23** they shall comfort you, when ye see their ways and their doings: and ye shall know that I have not done without cause all that I have done in it, saith the Lord GOD.

HOPE (*see also* Belief, Faith, Know, Reason, Truth)

Hold fast the confidence and the rejoicing of the hope firm unto the end. Heb. 3:6 (*see also* End)

Hope deferred maketh the heart sick. Prov. 13:12

The God of our Lord Jesus Christ, the Father of glory, may give unto you the spirit of wisdom and revelation in the knowledge of him: The eyes of your understanding being enlightened; that ye may know what is the hope of his calling, and what the riches of the glory of his inheritance in the saints. Eph. 1:17-18 (see also Father, Reveal, Wisdom)

Continue in the faith grounded and settled, and be not moved away from the hope of the gospel, which ye have heard, and which was preached to every creature which is under heaven. Col. 1:23 (see also Continue)

Charity suffereth long, and is kind; charity envieth not; charity vaunteth not itself, is not puffed up, Doth not behave itself unseemly, seeketh not her own, is not easily provoked, thinketh no evil; Rejoiceth not in iniquity, but rejoiceth in the truth; Beareth all things, believeth all things, hopeth all things, endureth all things. 1 Cor. 13:4-7 (see also All Things, Bear, Believe, Charity, Endure, Provoke, Rejoice, Seek, Suffer, Think)

That by two immutable things, in which it was impossible for God to lie, we might have a strong consolation, who have fled for refuge to lay hold upon the hope set before us: Which hope we have as an anchor of the soul, both sure and stedfast, and which entereth into that within the veil; Whither the forerunner is for us entered, even Jesus, made an high priest for ever after the order of Melchisedec. Heb. 6:18-19 (see also High Priest, Impossible, Melchisedec)

Gird up the loins of your mind, be sober, and hope to the end for the grace that is to be brought unto you at the revelation of Jesus Christ. 1 Pet. 1:13 (see also Grace, Jesus Christ, Mind)

Be of good courage, and he shall strengthen your heart, all ye that hope in the LORD. Ps. 31:24 (see also Courage)

Num. 14:1-4 all the congregation lifted up their voice, and cried; and the people wept that night. And all the children of Israel murmured; Ps. 31:24 be of good courage, and he shall strengthen your heart, all ye that hope in the LORD; 119:81-83 my soul fainteth for thy

salvation: but I hope in thy word. Mine eyes fail for thy word, saying, When wilt thou comfort me.

My soul fainteth for thy salvation: but I hope in thy word. Ps. 119:81 (see also Word)

Ps. 119:49 remember the word unto thy servant, upon which thou hast caused me to h.; 119:58 I intreated thy favour with my whole heart: be merciful unto me according to thy word; 119:74 they that fear thee will be glad when they see me; because I have h. in thy word; 119:81 my soul fainteth for thy salvation: but I h. in thy word; 119:114 thou art my hiding place and my shield: I h. in thy word; 119:147 I prevented the dawning of the morning, and cried: I h. in thy word; 130:5 I wait for the LORD, my soul doth wait, and in his word do I h.

Sanctify the Lord God in your heats; and be ready always to give an answer to every man that asketh you a reason of the hope that is in you with meekness and fear: Having a good conscience; that, whereas they speak evil of you, as of evildoers, they may be ashamed that falsely accuse your good conversation in Christ. 1 Pet. 3:15-16 (see also Answer, Conversation, Ready, Reason, Sanctify)

1 Peter 3:15-16 sanctify the Lord God in your hearts: and be ready always to give an answer to every man that asketh you a reason of the h. that is in you with meekness and fear: Having a good conscience; that, whereas they speak evil of you, as of evildoers, they may be ashamed that falsely accuse your good conversation in Christ; Rev. 3:3 if therefore thou shalt not watch, I will come on thee as a thief, and thou shalt not know what hour I will come upon thee.

Hope thou in God. Ps. 42:5

Job 7:6 my days are swifter than a weavers shuttle, and are spent without h.; Ps. 39:7-8 Lord, what wait I for? my h. is in thee. Deliver me from all my transgressions: make me not the reproach of the foolish; 42:5 (42:11) why art thou cast down, O my soul? and why art thou disquieted in me? h. thou in God: for I shall yet praise him for the help of his countenance; 43:5 why art thou cast down, O my soul? and why art thou disquieted within me? h. in God: for I shall yet praise him, who is the health of my countenance, and my God; 71:5 thou art my h., O Lord GOD: thou art my trust from my youth; 78:7 that they might set their h. in God, and not forget the works of God, but keep his commandments; **130:7** let Israel *h.* in the LORD: for with the LORD there is mercy, and with him is plenteous redemption; **131:3** let Israel *h.* in the LORD from henceforth and for ever; **146:5** happy is he that hath the God of Jacob for his help, whose *h.* is in the LORD his God; **146:7** which executeth judgment for the oppressed: which giveth food to the hungry. The LORD looseth the prisoners; **147:10-11** the LORD taketh pleasure in them that fear him, in those that *h.* in his mercy; **Prov. 14:32** the wicked is driven away in his wickedness: but the righteous hath *h.* in his death; **Jer. 17:13** O LORD, the *h.* of Israel, all that forsake thee shall be ashamed, and they that depart from me shall be written in the earth; **17:17** be not a terror unto me: thou art my *h.* in the day of evil; **Lam. 3:21-29** the LORD is my portion, saith my soul; therefore will I *h.* in him. The LORD is good unto them that wait for him, to the soul that seeketh him. It is good that a man should both *h.* and quietly wait for the salvation of the LORD; **Joel 3:16-17** the LORD will be the *h.* of his people, and the strength of the children of Israel. So shall ye know that I am the LORD your God dwelling in Zion, my holy mountain: then shall Jerusalem be holy; **Zech. 9:11-12** turn you to the strong hold, ye prisoners of *h.*: even to day do I declare that I will render double unto thee.

Have hope. Rom. 15:4

Acts 2:26 therefore did my heart rejoice, and my tongue was glad; moreover also my flesh shall rest in hope; **23:6** the *h.* and resurrection of the dead I am called in question; **24:15** have *h.* toward God, which they themselves also allow, that there shall be a resurrection of the dead, both of the just and unjust; **Rom. 4:18** who against *h.* believed in hope, that he might become the father of many nations; **5:2** we have access by faith into this grace wherein we stand, and rejoice in *h.* of the glory of God; **5:5** *h.* maketh not ashamed; because the love of God is shed abroad in our hearts by the Holy Ghost which is given unto us; **8:24-25** we are saved by hope: but *h.* that is seen is not hope: for what a man seeth, why doth he yet *h.* for? But if we *h.* for that we see not, then do we with patience wait for it; **12:12** rejoicing in hope; patient in tribulation; continuing instant in prayer; **15:4** whatsoever things were written aforetime were written for our learning, that we through patience and comfort of the scriptures might have hope; **15:13** the God of *h.* fill you with all joy and peace in believing, that ye may abound in hope, through

the power of the Holy Ghost; **1 Cor. 9:10** this is written: that he that ploweth should plow in hope; and that he that thresheth in *h.* should be partaker of his hope; **13:7** beareth all things, believeth all things, hopeth all things, endureth all things; **2 Cor. 3:12** we have such hope, we use great plainness of speech; **5:6** we are always confident, knowing that, whilst we are at home in the body, we are absent from the Lord; **10:15** not boasting of things without our measure, that is, of other men's labours; but having hope, when your faith is increased, that we shall be enlarged by you according to our rule abundantly; **Gal. 5:5** we through the Spirit wait for the *h.* of righteousness by faith; **Eph. 2:12** ye were without Christ, being aliens from the commonwealth of Israel, and strangers from the covenants of promise, having no hope, and without God in the world; **Col. 1:5** the *h.* which is laid up for you in heaven, whereof ye heard before in the word of the truth of the gospel; **1:23** if ye continue in the faith grounded and settled, and be not moved away from the *h.* of the gospel, which ye have heard; **1 Thes. 1:3** without ceasing your work of faith, and labour of love, and patience of *h.* in our Lord Jesus Christ, in the sight of God and our Father; **5:8** let us, who are of the day, be sober, putting on the breastplate of faith and love; and for an helmet, the *h.* of salvation; **2 Thes. 2:16** our Lord Jesus Christ himself, and God, even our Father, which hath loved us, and hath given us everlasting consolation and good *h.* through grace; **Heb. 6:18-19** lay hold upon the *h.* set before us: Which *h.* we have as an anchor of the soul, both sure and stedfast, and which entereth into that within the veil; **1 Pet. 1:3** blessed be the God and Father of our Lord Jesus Christ, which according to his abundant mercy hath begotten us again unto a lively *h.* by the resurrection of Jesus Christ from the dead; **1:13** gird up the loins of your mind, be sober, and *h.* to the end for the grace that is to be brought unto you at the **Rev.** of Jesus Christ; **1:21** believe in God, that raised him up from the dead, and gave him glory; that your faith and *h.* might be in God; **1 Jn. 3:2-3** beloved, now are we the sons of God, and it doth not yet appear what we shall be: but we know that, when he shall appear, we shall be like him; for we shall see him as he is. And every man that hath this *h.* in him purifieth himself, even as he is pure.

HOSPITALITY (*see also* Charity, Kindness, Neighbor)

[Distribute] to the necessity of saints; given to hospitality. Rom. 12:13 (*see also* Distribute)

Use hospitality one to another without grudging. **1 Pet. 4:9** (*see also* Grudge)

1 Tim. 3:2 a bishop then must be blameless, the husband of one wife, vigilant, sober, of good behaviour, given to *h.,* apt to teach; **Titus 1:8** but a lover of *h.,* a lover of good men, sober, just, holy, temperate; **Heb. 13:2** be not forgetful to entertain strangers: for thereby some have entertained angels unawares; **1 Pet. 4:9** use *h.* one to another without grudging.

HOUR (*see also* Time)

Heaven and earth shall pass away, but my words shall not pass away. But of that day and hour knoweth no man, no, not the angels of heaven, by my Father only. **Matt 24:36** (*see also* Day, Second Coming)

Paul, being grieved, turned and said to the spirit, I command thee in the name of Jesus Christ to come out of her. And he came out the same hour. **Acts 16:18** (*see also* Command, Jesus Christ, Unclean)

Take no thought how or what ye shall speak: for it shall be given you in that same hour what ye shall speak. For it is not ye that speak, but the Spirit of your Father which speaketh in you. **Matt. 10:19-20** (*see also* Speak, Spirit, Thought)

Watch therefore: for ye know not what hour your Lord doth come. **Matt. 24:42** (*see also* Sign, Watch)

HOUSE, HOUSEHOLD (*see also* Church, Family, Temple)

Because of the house of the Lord our God I will seek thy good. **Ps. 122:9** (*see also* Good)

Blessed be he that cometh in the name of the Lord: we have blessed you out of the house of the Lord. **Ps. 118:26** (*see also* Servant)

Through wisdom is an house builded; and by understanding it is established: And by knowledge shall the chambers be filled with all precious and pleasant riches. **Prov. 24:3-4** (*see also* Understand, Wisdom)

Thou oughtest to behave thyself in the house of God, which is the church of the living God, the pillar and ground of the truth. **1 Tim. 3:15** (*see also* Behave, Temple)

Peace be within thy walls, and prosperity within thy palaces. For my bretheren and companions' sakes, I will now say, Peace be within thee. **Ps. 122:7-8** (*see also* Peace)

Whoso rewardeth evil for good, evil shall not depart from his house. **Prov. 17:13** (*see also* Reward)

Keep thy foot when thou goest to the house of God, and be more ready to hear than to give the sacrifice of fools: for they consider not that they do evil. **Eccl. 5:1** (*see also* Hear)

Beautify the house of the Lord which is in Jerusalem. **Ezra 7:27** (*see also* Beautify)

Stand in the gate of the Lord's house, and proclaim there this word, and say, Hear the word of the Lord. **Jer. 7:2** (*see also* Proclaim, Word)

Bring an offering in a clean vessel into the house of the Lord. **Isa. 66:20** (*see also* Offer)

Woe unto him that buildeth his house in unrighteousness, and his chambers by wrong; that useth his neighbour's service without wages, and giveth him not for his work. **Jer. 22:13** (*see also* Serve, Wage, Work)

The children of Judah have done evil in my sight, saith the Lord: they have set their abominations in the house which is called by my name, to pollute it. **Jer. 7:30** (*see also* Abomination, Defile, Pollute)

We are confounded, because we have heard reproach: shame hath covered our faces: for strangers are come into the sanctuaries of the Lord 's house. **Jer. 51:51** (*see also* Sanctuary)

Let us go into the house of the Lord. **Ps. 122:1** (*see also* Go)

Ps. 122:1 let us go into the *h.* of the Lord; **122:9** because of the *h.* of the Lord our God I will seek thy good.

I had rather be a doorkeeper in the house of my God, than to dwell in the tents of wickedness. **Ps. 84:10**

Ps. 27:4 (84:4) I may dwell in the *h.* of the Lord all the days of my life, to behold the beauty of the Lord, and to enquire in his temple; **84:10** a day in thy courts is better than a thousand. I had rather be a doorkeeper in the *h.* of my God, than to dwell in the tents of wickedness.

Come, and let us go up to the mountain of the LORD, and to the house of the God of Jacob; and he will teach us of his ways, and we will walk in his paths; for the law shall go forth of Zion, and the word of, the LORD from Jerusalem. Micah 4:2 (*see also* Jerusalem, Law, Mountain, Ways, Word, Zion)

Isa. 2:3 let us go up to the mountain of the LORD, to the *h.* of the God of Jacob; and he will teach us of his ways, and we will walk in his paths: for out of Zion shall go forth the law, and the word of the LORD from Jerusalem; **55:1** every one that thirsteth, come ye to the waters, and he that hath no money; come ye, buy, and eat; yea, come, buy wine and milk without money and without price.

Solomon determined to build an house for the name of the LORD, and an house for his kingdom. 2 Chron. 2:1 (*see also* Kingdom, Name)

2 Chron. 2:1 Solomon determined to build an *h.* for the name of the LORD, and an *h.* for his kingdom; **2:4** I build an *h.* to the name of the LORD my God, to dedicate it to him, and to burn before him sweet incense, and for the continual shewbread, and for the burnt offerings; **2:12** blessed be the LORD God of Israel, that made heaven and earth, who hath given to David the king a wise son, endued with prudence and understanding, that might build an *h.* for the LORD; **3:1** Solomon began to build the *h.* of the LORD at Jerusalem in mount Moriah, where the LORD appeared unto David his father; **4:19-20** Solomon made all the vessels that were for the *h.* of God, the golden altar also, and the tables whereon the shewbread was set; Moreover the candlesticks with their lamps, that they should burn after the manner before the oracle, of pure gold; **5:1-2** all the work that Solomon made for the *h.* of the LORD was finished: and Solomon brought in all the things that David his father had dedicated; **Ezra 1:2-3** the LORD God of heaven hath given me all the kingdoms of the earth; and he hath charged me to build him an *h.* at Jerusalem; **1:5** then rose up the chief of the fathers of Judah and Benjamin, and the priests, and the Levites, with all them whose spirit God had raised, to go up to build the *h.* of the LORD; **3:11-12** all the people shouted with a great shout, when they praised the LORD, because the foundation of the *h.* of the LORD was laid; **4:1**

the children of the captivity builded the temple unto the LORD God of Israel; **4:3** ye have nothing to do with us to build an *h.* unto our God; but we ourselves together will build unto the LORD God of Israel; **4:24** then ceased the work of the *h.* of God which is at Jerusalem; **5:2** then rose up Zerubbabel the son of Shealtiel, and Jeshua the son of Jozadak, and began to build the *h.* of God which is at Jerusalem: and with them were the prophets of God helping them; **5:11** we are the servants of the God of heaven and earth, and build the *h.* that was builded these many years ago, which a great king of Israel builded and set up; **6:3-16** the king made a decree concerning the *h.* of God at Jerusalem, Let the *h.* be builded, the place where they offered sacrifices, and let the foundations thereof be strongly laid; **Prov. 24:3** through wisdom is an *h.* builded; and by understanding it is established; **Zech. 6:13** he shall build the temple of the LORD; and he shall bear the glory, and shall sit and rule upon his throne; **6:15** they that are far off shall come and build in the temple of the LORD, and ye shall know that the LORD of hosts hath sent me unto you.

He set the porters at the gates of the house of the LORD, that none which was unclean in any thing should enter in. 2 Chron. 23:19 (*see also* Unclean)

2 Chron. 23:19 he set the porters at the gates of the *h.* of the LORD, that none which was unclean in any thing should enter in; **29:5** sanctify now yourselves, and sanctify the *h.* of the LORD God of your fathers, and carry forth the filthiness out of the holy place; **29:16** the priests went into the inner part of the *h.* of the LORD, to cleanse it, and brought out all the uncleanness that they found in the temple of the LORD into the court of the *h.* of the LORD; **29:36** Hezekiah rejoiced, and all the people, that God had prepared the people: for the thing was done suddenly; **36:14** all the chief of the priests, and the people, transgressed very much after all the abominations of the heathen; and polluted the *h.* of the LORD which he had hallowed in Jerusalem; **Isa. 35:8** an highway shall be there, and a way, and it shall be called The way of holiness; the unclean shall not pass over it; but it shall be for those: the wayfaring men, though fools, shall not err therein; **52:1** awake, awake; put on thy strength, O Zion; put on thy beautiful garments, O Jerusalem, the holy city: for henceforth there shall no more come into thee the uncircumcised and the unclean; **Jer. 7:11** is this house, which is called by my name, become a den of robbers in your eyes? Behold, even I have seen it, saith the LORD; **Ezek. 5:11-12** saith the Lord GOD; Surely, because thou hast defiled my sanctuary with all thy detestable things, and with all thine abominations, therefore will I also diminish thee; neither shall mine eye spare, neither will I have any pity.

Gather of all Israel money to repair the house of your God from year to year. 2 Chron. 24:4-5 (*see also* Repair)

2 Chron. 24:4-5 Joash was minded to repair the *h.* of the LORD. And he gathered together the priests and the Levites, and said to them, Go out unto the cities of Judah, and gather of all Israel money to repair the *h.* of your God from year to year; **24:12** the king and Jehoiada gave it to such as did the work of the service of the *h.* of the LORD, and hired masons and carpenters to repair the *h.* of the LORD, and also such as wrought iron and brass to mend the *h.* of the LORD; **29:35** the burnt offerings were in abundance, with the fat of the peace offerings, and the drink offerings for every burnt offering. So the service of the *h.* of the LORD was set in order; **34:8** he sent Shaphan the son of Azaliah, and Maaseiah the governor of the city, and Joah the son of Joahaz the recorder, to repair the *h.* of the LORD his God; **34:10** they put it in the hand of the workmen that had the oversight of the *h.* of the LORD, and they gave it to the workmen that wrought in the *h.* of the LORD, to repair and amend the *h.*; **34:12** the men did the work faithfully: and the overseers of them were Jahath and Obadiah, the Levites, of the sons of Merari; and Zechariah and Meshullam, of the sons of the Kohathites, to set it forward.

Whatsoever is commanded by the God of heaven, let it be diligently done for the house of the God of heaven. Ezra 7:23 (*see also* Diligent)

Ezra 7:23 whatsoever is commanded by the God of heaven, let it be diligently done for the *h.* of the God of heaven; **Jer. 50:21** go up against the land of Merathaim, even against it, and against the inhabitants of Pekod: waste and utterly destroy after them, saith the LORD, and do according to all that I have commanded thee; **Ezek. 12:7** I did so as I was commanded: I brought forth my stuff by day, as stuff for captivity, and in the even I digged through the wall with mine hand; **Hag. 1:8** go up to the mountain, and bring wood, and build the *h.*; and I will take pleasure in it, and I will be glorified, saith the LORD; **1:14** the LORD stirred up the spirit of Zerubbabel the son of Shealtiel, governor of Judah, and the spirit of Joshua the son of Josedech, the high priest, and the spirit of all the remnant of the people; and they came and did work in the *h.* of the LORD; **2:7-9** I will shake all nations, and the desire of all nations shall come: and I will fill this *h.* with glory, saith the LORD of hosts. The silver is mine, and the gold is mine, saith the LORD of hosts. The glory of this latter *h.* shall be greater than of the former.

HUMBLE, HUMILITY (*see also* Meek, Submit)

God resisteth the proud, but giveth grace unto the humble. James 4:6 (*see also* Grace, Pride)

Likewise, ye younger, submit yourselves unto the elder. Yea, all of you be subject one to another, and be clothed with humility: for God resisteth the proud, and giveth grace to the humble. 1 Pet. 5:5 (*see also* Grace, Submit, Young)

The mean man shall be brought down, and the mighty man shall be humbled, and the eyes of the lofty shall be humbled. Isa. 5:15 (*see also* Lofty, Mean)

When they were sick, my clothing was sackcloth: I humbled my soul with fasting; and my prayer returned into mine own bosom. I behaved myself as though he had been my friend or brother: I bowed down heavily, as one that mourneth for his mother. Ps. 35:13-14 (*see also* Fast)

O man, what is good; and what doth the LORD require of thee, but to do justly, and to love mercy, and to walk humbly with thy God? Micah 6:8 (*see also* Just, Merciful)

Humble yourselves therefore under the mighty hand of God, that he may exalt you in due time. 1 Pet. 5:5-6 (*see also* Time)

Ex. 10:3 how long wilt thou refuse to *h.* thyself before me? let my people go, that they may serve me; **34:8** Moses made haste, and bowed his head toward the earth, and worshipped; **Deut. 8:2** thou shalt remember all the way which the LORD thy God led thee these forty years in the wilderness, to *h.* thee, and to prove thee, to know what was in thine heart; **8:16** who fed thee in the wilderness with manna, which thy fathers knew not, that he might *h.* thee, and that he might prove thee, to do thee good at thy latter end;

Judg. 19:24 them I will bring out now, and *h.* ye them, and do with them what seemeth good unto you; **1 Sam. 15:17** when thou wast little in thine own sight, wast thou not made the head of the tribes of Israel, and the LORD anointed thee king over Israel; **2 Kgs. 22:19** thine heart was tender, and thou hast *h.* thyself before the LORD, when thou heardest what I spake against this place; **2 Chron. 7:14** i my people, which are called by my name, shall *h.* themselves, and pray, and seek my face, and turn from their wicked ways; then will I hear from heaven, and will forgive their sin; **12:6-7** the princes of Israel and the king *h.* themselves; and they said, The LORD is righteous. And when the LORD saw that they *h.* themselves, the word of the LORD came; **12:12** when he *h.* himself, the wrath of the LORD turned from him, that he would not destroy him altogether; **32:26** Hezekiah *h.* himself for the pride of his heart, both he and the inhabitants of Jerusalem, so that the wrath of the LORD came not upon them; **33:12** when he was in affliction, he besought the LORD his God, and *h.* himself greatly before the God of his fathers; **33:23** [he] *h.* not himself before the LORD, as Manasseh his father had *h.* himself; **34:27** thine heart was tender, and thou didst *h.* thyself before God, when thou heardest his words against this place, and against the inhabitants thereof, and *h.* thyself before me; **36:12** and he did that which was evil in the sight of the LORD his God, and *h.* not himself; **Job 22:29** when men are cast down, then thou shalt say, There is lifting up; and he shall save the *h.* person; **Ps. 6:2** have mercy upon me, O LORD; for I am weak: O LORD, heal me; for my bones are vexed; **9:12** he remembereth them: he forgetteth not the cry of the *h.*; **10:12** arise, O LORD; O God, lift up thine hand: forget not the *h.*; **10:17** LORD, thou hast heard the desire of the *h.*: thou wilt prepare their heart, thou wilt cause thine ear to hear; **34:2** my soul shall make her boast in the LORD: the *h.* shall hear thereof, and be glad; **69:32** the *h.* shall see this, and be glad: and your heart shall live that seek God; **145:14** the LORD upholdeth all that fall, and raiseth up all those that be bowed down; **146:8** the LORD raiseth them that are bowed down; **Prov. 6:3** go, *h.* thyself, and make sure thy friend; **15:33** the fear of the LORD is the instruction of wisdom; and before honour is humility; **16:19** better it is to be of an *h.* spirit with the lowly, than to divide the spoil with the proud; **18:12** before destruction the heart of man is haughty, and before honour is humility; **22:4** by humility and the fear of the LORD are riches, and honour, and life; **29:23** a mans pride shall bring him low: but honour shall uphold the *h.* in

spirit; **Isa. 2:9** the mean man boweth down, and the great man *h.* himself; **2:11** the lofty looks of man shall be *h.*, and the haughtiness of men shall be bowed down, and the LORD alone shall be exalted in that day; **57:15** I dwell in the high and holy place, with him also that is of a contrite and *h.* spirit; **Jer. 13:18** *h.* yourselves, sit down: for your principalities shall come down, even the crown of your glory; **Lam. 3:20** my soul hath them still in remembrance, and is *h.* in me; **Zech. 9:9** thy King cometh unto thee: he is just, and having salvation; lowly, and riding upon an ass, and upon a colt the foal of an ass; **Mal. 3:14** ye have said, It is vain to serve God: and what profit is it that we have kept his ordinance, and that we have walked mournfully before the LORD of hosts; **Matt. 5:3** blessed are the poor in spirit: for theirs is the kingdom of heaven; **11:11** among them that are born of women there hath not risen a greater than John the Baptist: notwithstanding he that is least in the kingdom of heaven is greater than he; **18:4** whosoever therefore shall *h.* himself as this little child, the same is greatest in the kingdom of heaven; **23:12** (Luke 14:7-11, 18:13-14) whosoever shall exalt himself shall be abased; and he that shall *h.* himself shall be exalted; **Mark 1:7** there cometh one mightier than I after me, the latchet of whose shoes I am not worthy to stoop down and unloose; **Luke 1:52** he hath put down the mighty from their seats, and exalted them of low degree; **5:8** depart from me; for I am a sinful man, O Lord; **9:48** whosoever shall receive this child in my name receiveth me: and whosoever shall receive me receiveth him that sent me: for he that is least among you all, the same shall be great; **1 Cor. 15:9** I am the least of the apostles, that am not meet to be called an apostle, because I persecuted the church of God; **Gal. 6:3-4** if a man think himself to be something, when he is nothing, he deceiveth himself. But let every man prove his own work, and then shall he have rejoicing in himself alone, and not in another; **Eph. 3:8** am less than the least of all saints, is this grace given, that I should preach among the Gentiles the unsearchable riches of Christ; **3:14** for this cause I bow my knees unto the Father of our Lord Jesus Christ; **Philip. 2:8-9** being found in fashion as a man, he *h.* himself, and became obedient unto death, even the death of the cross; **Col. 3:12** put on therefore, as the elect of God, holy and beloved, bowels of mercies, kindness, *h.* of mind, meekness, longsuffering; **James 1:9** let the brother of low degree rejoice in that he is exalted; **4:6** he giveth more grace. Wherefore he saith, God resisteth the proud, but giveth grace unto the *h.;* **4:10** *h.* yourselves in the sight of the

Lord, and he shall lift you up; **1 Pet. 5:5-6** be clothed with humility: for God resisteth the proud, and giveth grace to the *h.. h.* yourselves therefore under the mighty hand of God, that he may exalt you in due time.

HUNGER, HUNGRY (*see also* Alms, Poor, Seek, Thirst)

If thou draw out thy soul to the hungry, and satisfy the afflicted soul; then shall thy light rise in obscurity, and thy darkness be as the noonday: And the LORD shall guide thee continually. Isa. 58:10 (*see also* Afflict, Soul)

Blessed are they which do hunger and thirst after righteousness: for they shall be filled. Matt. 5:6 (*see also* Righteousness, Thirst)

HUSBAND (*see also* Family, Marriage)

Let the husband render unto the render unto the wife due benevolence: and likewise also the wife unto the husband. 1 Cor. 7:3-5 (*see also* Wife, Treatment)

Husbands, love your wives, even as Christ also loved the church, and gave himself for it. That he might sanctify and cleanse it with the washing of water by the word, That he might present it to himself a glorious church, not having spot, or wrinkle, or any such thing; but that it should be holy and without blemish. So ought men to love their wives as their own bodies. He that loveth his wife loveth himself. Eph. 5:25-28 (*see also* Church, Love)

Eph 5:25-33 *h.,* love your wives, even as Christ also loved the church, and gave himself for it; That he might sanctify and cleanse it with the washing of water by the word, That he might present it to himself a glorious church, not having spot, or wrinkle, or any such thing; but that it should be holy and without blemish. So ought men to love their wives as their own bodies. He that loveth his wife loveth himself. For no man ever yet hated his own flesh; but nourisheth and cherisheth it, even as the Lord the church: For we are members of his body, of his flesh, and of his bones. For this cause shall a man leave his father and mother, and shall be joined unto his wife, and they two shall be one flesh. This is a great mystery: but I speak concerning Christ and the church. Nevertheless let every one of you in particular so love his wife even as himself; and the wife see that she

reverence her *h.;* **Col. 3:19** *h.,* love your wives, and be not bitter against them; **1 Pet. 3:7** likewise, ye *h.,* dwell with them according to knowledge, giving honour unto the wife, as unto the weaker vessel, and as being heirs together of the grace of life; that your prayers be not hindered.

HYMN (*see also* Praise, Prayer, Psalms, Song)

Let the word of Christ dwell in you richly in all wisdom; teaching and admonishing one another in psalms and hymns and spiritual songs, singing with grace in your hearts to the Lord. Col. 3:16 (*see also* Admonish, Grace, Psalm, Sing, Wisdom, Word)

HYPOCRISY, HYPOCRITE (*see also* Deceive, Evil, False, Flatter, Guile, Lie, Mock)

Woe unto you, scribes and Pharisees, hypocrites! for ye pay tithe of mint and anise and cummin, and have omitted the weightier matters of the law, judgment, mercy, and faith: these ought ye to have done, and not to leave the other undone. Matt. 23:23 (*see also* Law, Worth)

Thou hypocrite, first cast out the beam out of thine own eye; and then shalt thou see clearly to cast out the mote out of thy brother's eye. Matt. 7:3-5 (*see also* Clear)

Matt. 7:3-5 (Luke 6:41-42) why beholdest thou the mote that is in thy brother's eye, but considerest not the beam that is in thine own eye? Or how wilt thou say to thy brother, Let me pull out the mote out of thine eye; and, behold, a beam is in thine own eye? Thou hypocrite, first cast out the beam out of thine own eye; and then shalt thou see clearly to cast out the mote out of thy brother's eye; **23:25-26** woe unto you, scribes and Pharisees, hypocrites! for ye make clean the outside of the cup and of the platter, but within they are full of extortion and excess. Thou blind Pharisee, cleanse first that which is within the cup and platter, that the outside of them may be clean also.

What is the hope of the hypocrite, though he hath gained, when God taketh away his soul? Will God hear his cry when trouble cometh upon him? Job 27:8-9 (*see also* Gain)

Job 8:12-15 so are the paths of all that forget God; and the *h.* hope shall perish: Whose hope shall be cut off, and whose trust shall be a spiders web; **13:16** he also shall be my salvation: for an *h.* shall not come before him; **15:34** the congregation of *h.* shall be desolate, and fire shall consume the tabernacles of bribery; **20:5-9** the triumphing of the wicked is short, and the joy of the *h.* but for a moment; **27:8-9** what is the hope of the *h.*, though he hath gained, when God taketh away his soul? Will God hear his cry when trouble cometh upon him; **34:30** [let] the *h.* reign not, lest the people be ensnared; **36:13-14** the *h.* in heart heap up wrath: they cry not when he bindeth them. They die in youth, and their life is among the unclean; **Ps. 28:3** draw me not away with the wicked, and with the workers of iniquity, which speak peace to their neighbours, but mischief is in their hearts; **62:4** they only consult to cast him down from his excellency: they delight in lies: they bless with their mouth, but they curse inwardly; **Prov. 11:9** an *h.* with his mouth destroyeth his neighbour: but through knowledge shall the just be delivered; **Isa. 32:6** the vile person will speak villany, and his heart will work iniquity, to practise *h.*, and to utter error against the LORD; **33:14** the sinners in Zion are afraid; fearfulness hath surprised the *h.*; **Jer. 7:9-10** will ye steal, murder, and commit adultery, and swear falsely... and walk after other gods whom ye know not; And come and stand before me in this house, which is called by my name, and say, We are delivered to do all these abominations.

Ye hypocrites, well did Esaias prophesy of you, saying, This people draweth nigh unto me with their mouth, and honoureth me with their lips; but their heart is far from me. Matt. 15:7-8 (*see also* Mouth)

Matt. 6:16 when ye fast, be not, as the *h.*, of a sad countenance: for they disfigure their faces, that they may appear unto men to fast. Verily I say unto you, They have their reward; **15:7-8** ye *h.*, well did Esaias prophesy of you, saying, This people draweth nigh unto me with their mouth, and honoureth me with their lips; but their heart is far from me; **22:17** Jesus perceived their wickedness, and said, Why tempt ye me, ye *h.*; **23:3** whatsoever they bid you observe, that observe and do; but do not ye after their works: for they say, and do not; **23:4** they bind heavy burdens and grievous to be borne, and lay them on men's shoulders; but they themselves will not move them with one of their fingers; **23:13-16** woe unto you, scribes and Pharisees, *h.*! for ye shut up the kingdom of heaven against men:

for ye neither go in yourselves, neither suffer ye them that are entering to go in. Woe unto you, scribes and Pharisees, *h.*! for ye devour widows' houses, and for a pretence make long prayer: therefore ye shall receive the greater damnation. Woe unto you, scribes and Pharisees, *h.*! for ye compass sea and land to make one proselyte, and when he is made, ye make him twofold more the child of hell than yourselves; **23:28** even so ye also outwardly appear righteous unto men, but within ye are full of *h.* and iniquity; **23:31** ye be witnesses unto yourselves, that ye are the children of them which killed the prophets; **24:51** and shall cut him asunder, and appoint him his portion with the *h.*: there shall be weeping and gnashing of teeth; **Mark 7:5-6** well hath Esaias prophesied of you *h.*, as it is written, This people honoureth me with their lips, but their heart is far from me; **Luke 6:42** thou *h.*, cast out first the beam out of thine own eye, and then shalt thou see clearly to pull out the mote that is in thy brother's eye; **11:37-44** woe unto you, scribes and Pharisees, *h.*! for ye are as graves which appear not, and the men that walk over them are not aware of them; **12:1-2** beware ye of the leaven of the Pharisees, which is *h.* For there is nothing covered, that shall not be revealed; neither hid, that shall not be known; **12:56** ye *h.*, ye can discern the face of the sky and of the earth; but how is it that ye do not discern this time; **13:15** thou *h.*, doth not each one of you on the sabbath loose his ox or his ass from the stall, and lead him away to watering; **20:46-47** beware of the scribes, which desire to walk in long robes, and love greetings in the markets, and the highest seats in the synagogues, and the chief rooms at feasts; Which devour widows' houses, and for a shew make long prayers: the same shall receive greater damnation; **Rom. 2:21-22** thou therefore which teachest another, teachest thou not thyself? thou that preachest a man should not steal, dost thou steal? Thou that sayest a man should not commit adultery, dost thou commit adultery? thou that abhorrest idols, dost thou commit sacrilege; **1 Tim. 4:2** speaking lies in *h.*; having their conscience seared with a hot iron; **Titus 1:16** they profess that they know God; but in works they deny him, being abominable, and disobedient, and unto every good work reprobate; **1 Jn. 1:6** if we say that we have fellowship with him, and walk in darkness, we lie, and do not the truth; **2:4** he that saith, I know him, and keepeth not his commandments, is a liar, and the truth is not in him.

IDLE, IDLENESS, IDLER (*see also* Laziness, Sleep, Slothful, Thou Shalt Not)

Eateth not the bread of idleness. Prov. 31:27 (*see also* Bread)

Prov. 19:15 slothfulness casteth into a deep sleep; and an *i.* soul shall suffer hunger; **31:27** she looketh well to the ways of her household, and eateth not the bread of *i.*; **Eccl. 10:18** by much slothfulness the building decayeth; and through *i.* of the hands the house droppeth through; **Ezek. 16:49** this was the iniquity of thy sister Sodom, pride, fulness of bread, and abundance of *i.* was in her and in her daughters.

They learn to be idle, wandering about from house to house; and not only idle, but tattlers also and busybodies, speaking things which they ought not. 1 Tim. 5:13 (*see also* Gossip)

1 Tim 5:13 withal they learn to be *i.*, wandering about from house to house; and not only *i.*, but tattlers also and busybodies, speaking things which they ought not; **6:20** keep that which is committed to thy trust, avoiding profane and vain babblings, and oppositions of science falsely so called; **2 Tim. 3:6** lead captive silly women laden with sins, led away with divers lusts.

IDOL, IDOLATER, IDOLATRY (*see also* False, Image, Superstitious, Worship)

Thou shalt have no other gods before me. Ex. 20:3 (*see also* God, Thou Shalt)

For rebellion is as the sin of witchcraft, and stubbornness is as iniquity and idolatry. Because thou hast rejected the word of the LORD, he hath also rejected thee from being king. 1 Sam 15:23 (*see also* Rebellion, Stubborn, Witchcraft)

Their land also is full of idols; they worship the work of their own hands, that which their own fingers have made own fingers have made. Isa. 2:8 (*see also* Work, Worship)

Blessed be the God of Shadrach, Meshach, and Abed-nego, who hath sent his angel, and delivered his servants that trusted in him, and have changed the king's word, and yielded their bodies, that they might not serve nor worship any god, except their own God. Dan. 3:28 (*see also* Angel, Courage, Serve, Trust, Worship)

Shall I not, as I have done unto Samaria and her idols, so do to Jerusalem and her idols? Isa. 10:11 (*see also* Liken)

Repent, and turn yourselves from your idols. Ezek. 14:6 (*see also* Repent)

Ezek. 14:6 say unto the house of Israel, Thus saith the Lord GOD; Repent, and turn yourselves from your *i.*; and turn away your faces from all your abominations.

Thou shalt not make unto thee any graven image, or any likeness of any thing that is in heaven above, or that is in the earth beneath, or that is in the water under the earth. Thou shalt not bow down thyself to them, nor serve them: For I the LORD thy God am a jealous God, visiting the iniquity of the fathers upon the children unto the third and fourth generation of them that hate me; And shewing mercy unto thousands of them that love me, and keep my commandments. Ex. 20:4-6 (*see also* Graven Image, Thous Shalt Not)

Ex. 20:4-5 thou shalt not make unto thee any graven image, or any likeness of any thing that is in heaven above, or that is in the earth beneath, or that is in the water under the earth: Thou shalt not bow down thyself to them, nor serve them; **20:23** ye shall not make with me gods of silver, neither shall ye make unto you gods of gold; **32:4** he received them at their hand, and fashioned it with a graving tool, after he had made it a molten calf: and they said, These be thy gods; **32:7-8** thy people... have corrupted themselves: They have turned aside quickly out of the way which I commanded them: they have made them a molten calf, and have worshipped it; **32:31** this people have sinned a great sin, and have made them gods of gold; **Lev. 19:4** turn ye not unto *i.*, nor make to yourselves molten gods: I am the LORD your God; **26:1** ye shall make you no *i.* nor graven image, neither rear you up a standing image, neither shall ye set up any image of stone in your land, to bow down unto it; **Deut. 4:16** lest ye corrupt yourselves, and make you a graven image, the similitude of any figure, the likeness of male or female; **4:23-26** take heed unto yourselves, lest ye forget the covenant of the LORD your God, which he made with you, and make you a graven image, or the likeness of any thing, which the LORD thy God hath forbidden; **5:8-9** thou shalt not make thee any graven image, or any likeness of any thing that is in heaven above, or that is in the earth beneath, or that is in the waters beneath the earth: Thou shalt not bow down thyself unto them, nor serve them; **7:25-26** the graven images of their gods shall ye burn with fire: thou shalt not desire the silver or gold that is on them, nor take it unto thee, lest thou be snared therein: for it is an abomination to the LORD thy God; **8:19** if thou do at all forget the LORD thy God, and walk after other gods, and serve them, and worship them, I testify against you this day that ye shall surely perish; **9:16** ye had sinned against the LORD your God, and had made you a molten calf: ye had turned aside quickly out of the way which the LORD had commanded you; **11:16-17** take heed to yourselves, that your heart be not deceived, and ye turn aside, and serve other gods, and worship them; And then the LORD's wrath be kindled against you; **16:22** neither shalt thou set thee up any image; which the LORD thy God hateth; **29:17** ye have seen their abominations, and their *i.*, wood and stone, silver and gold, which were among them; **29:26-27** they went and served other gods, and worshipped them, gods whom they knew not, and whom he had not given unto them: And the anger of the LORD was kindled against this land; **30:17** if thine heart turn away, so that thou wilt not hear, but shalt be drawn away, and worship other gods, and serve them; **31:20-21** then will they turn unto other gods, and serve them, and provoke me, and break my covenant; **32:16-17** they provoked him to jealousy with strange gods, with abominations provoked they him to anger; **32:37** where are their gods, their rock in whom they trusted; **Josh.23:7** come not among these nations, these that remain among you; neither make mention of the name of their gods, nor cause to swear by them, neither serve them, nor bow yourselves unto them; **24:14-16** fear the LORD, and serve him in sincerity and in truth: and put away the gods which your fathers served on the other side of the flood; **24:19-20** if ye forsake the LORD, and serve strange gods, then he will turn and do you hurt, and consume you, after that he hath done you good; **Judg. 2:12** they forsook the LORD God of their fathers, which brought them out of the land of Egypt, and followed other gods; **2:17** they would not hearken unto their judges, but they went a whoring after other gods, and bowed themselves unto them; **2:19** they returned, and corrupted themselves more than their fathers, in following other gods to serve them, and to bow down unto them; **3:6-7** the children of Israel did evil in the sight of the LORD, and forgat the LORD their God, and served Baalim and the groves; **6:10** I am the LORD your God; fear not the gods of the Amorites, in whose land ye dwell: but ye have not obeyed my voice; **8:33** the children of Israel turned again, and went a whoring after Baalim, and made Baal-berith their god; **16:23** the lords of the Philistines gathered them together for to offer a great sacrifice unto Dagon their god, and to rejoice; **17:3-4** I had wholly dedicated the silver unto the LORD from my hand for my son, to make a graven image and a molten image: now therefore I will restore it unto thee; **18:17** the five men that went to spy out the land went up, and came in thither, and took the graven image, and the ephod, and the teraphim, and the molten image; **18:31** they set them up Micahs graven image, which he made, all the time that the house of God was in Shiloh; **1 Kgs. 15:12-13** he took away the sodomites out of the land, and removed all the *i.* that his fathers had made. And also Maachah his mother, even her he removed from being queen, because she had made an *i.* in a grove; **21:26** he did very abominably in following *i.*, according to all things as did the Amorites, whom the LORD cast out; **2 Kgs. 17:7** the children of Israel had sinned against the LORD their God, which had brought them up out of the land of Egypt, from under the hand of Pharaoh king of Egypt, and had feared other gods; **17:10-12** they set them up images and groves in every high hill, and under every green tree: And there they burnt incense in all the high places, as did the heathen whom the LORD carried away before them; **17:16** they left all the commandments of the LORD their God, and made them molten images, even two calves, and made a grove, and worshipped all the host of heaven; **17:29** every nation made gods of their own, and put them in the houses of the high places; **17:33-36** they feared the LORD, and served their own gods, after the manner of the nations whom they carried away from thence; **17:41** these nations feared the LORD, and served their graven images, both their children, and their childrens children: as did their fathers; **19:18** they were no gods, but the work of mens hands, wood and stone: therefore they have destroyed them; **21:21** he walked in all the way that his father walked in, and served the *i.* that his father served, and worshipped them; **1 Chron. 5:25-26** they transgressed against the God of their fathers, and went a whoring after the gods of the people of the land, whom God destroyed before them; **2 Chron. 14:2** Asa did that which was good and right in the eyes of the LORD his God; **15:8** he took courage, and put away the abominable *i.* out of all the land of Judah and Benjamin, and out of the cities which he had taken from mount Ephraim, and renewed the altar of the LORD; **24:18** they left the house of the LORD God of their fathers, and served groves and *i.*: and wrath came upon Judah and Jerusalem for this their trespass; **25:14-15** he brought the gods of the children of Seir, and set them up to be his gods, and bowed down himself before them, and burned incense unto them. Wherefore the anger of the LORD was kindled against Amaziah; **25:20** it came of God, that he might deliver them into the hand of their enemies, because they sought after the gods of Edom; **28:2-5** he walked in the ways of the kings of Israel, and made also molten images for Baalim. Moreover he burnt incense in the valley of the son of Hinnom, and burnt his children in the fire, after the abominations of the heathen whom the LORD had cast out before the children of Israel; **28:25** in every several city of Judah he made high places to burn incense unto other gods, and provoked to anger the LORD God of his fathers; **31:1** all Israel that were present went out to the cities of Judah, and brake the images in pieces, and cut down the groves, and threw down the high places and the altars; **32:19** they spake against the God of Jerusalem, as against the gods of the people of the earth, which were the work of the hands of man; **33:7** he set a carved image, the *i.* which he had made, in the house of God; **33:22** he did that which was evil in the sight of the LORD, as did Manasseh his father: for Amon sacrificed unto all the carved images which Manasseh his father had made, and served them; **34:4** they brake down the altars of Baalim in his presence; and the images, that were on high above them, he cut down; and the groves, and the carved images, and the molten images, he brake in pieces; **34:7** he had broken down the altars and the groves, and had beaten the graven images into powder, and cut down all the *i.*; **Neh. 9:18** they had made them a molten calf, and said, This is thy God that brought thee up out of Egypt, and had wrought great provocations; **Ps. 16:4** their sorrows shall be multiplied that hasten after another god; **44:20** we have forgotten the name of our God, or stretched out our hands to a strange god; **78:58** they provoked him to anger with their high places, and moved him to jealousy with their graven images; **96:5** all the gods of the nations are *i.*: but the LORD made the heavens; **97:7** confounded be all they that serve graven images, that boast themselves of *i.*: worship him, all ye gods; **106:28** they joined themselves also unto Baal-peor, and ate the sacrifices of the dead; **106:36-38** they served their *i.*: which were a snare unto them. Yea, they sacrificed their sons and their daughters unto devils, And shed innocent blood; **115:2** wherefore should the heathen say, Where is now their God; **115:4** their

i. are silver and gold, the work of mens hands; **135:15-18** the *i.* of the heathen are silver and gold, the work of mens hands... They that make them are like unto them: so is every one that trusteth in them; **Isa. 2:8** their land also is full of *i.*; they worship the work of their own hands, that which their own fingers have made; **2:18** the *i.* he shall utterly abolish; **2:20** a man shall cast his *i.* of silver, and his *i.* of gold, which they made each one for himself to worship, to the moles and to the bats; **10:11** shall I not, as I have done unto Samaria and her *i.*, so do to Jerusalem and her *i.*; **17:8-9** he shall not look to the altars, the work of his hands, neither shall respect that which his fingers have made, either the groves, or the images; **19:1-2** the LORD rideth upon a swift cloud, and shall come into Egypt: and the *i.* of Egypt shall be moved at his presence, and the heart of Egypt shall melt in the midst of it; **19:5-9** they that work in fine flax, and they that weave networks, shall be confounded; **31:7** every man shall cast away his *i.* of silver, and his *i.* of gold, which your own hands have made unto you for a sin; **40:19-20** the workman melteth a graven image, and the goldsmith spreadeth it over with gold, and casteth silver chains; **41:29** they are all vanity; their works are nothing: their molten images are wind and confusion; **42:8** I am the LORD: that is my name: and my glory will I not give to another, neither my praise to graven images; **42:17** they shall be greatly ashamed, that trust in graven images, that say to the molten images, Ye are our gods; **44:9-20** they that make a graven image are all of them vanity; and their delectable things shall not profit; and they are their own witnesses; they see not, nor know; that they may be ashamed; **45:16** they shall be ashamed, and also confounded, all of them: they shall go to confusion together that are makers of *i.*; **46:1-2** their *i.* were upon the beasts, and upon the cattle: your carriages were heavy loaden; they are a burden to the weary beast; **46:6-7** they lavish gold out of the bag, and weigh silver in the balance, and hire a goldsmith; and he maketh it a god: they fall down, yea, they worship; **57:5** enflaming yourselves with *i.* under every green tree, slaying the children in the valleys under the clifts of the rocks; **Jer. 1:16** I will utter my judgments against them touching all their wickedness, who have forsaken me, and have burned incense unto other gods, and worshipped the works of their own hands; **2:20** thus saith the Lord GOD; Behold, mine anger and my fury shall be poured out upon this place, upon man, and upon beast, and upon the trees of the field, and upon the fruit of the ground; **2:28** where are thy gods that thou hast made thee? let them arise, if they can save thee in the time of thy trouble: for according to the number of thy cities are thy gods; **5:7** how shall I pardon thee for this? thy children have forsaken me, and sworn by them that are no gods; **5:19** like as ye have forsaken me, and served strange gods in your land, so shall ye serve strangers in a land that is not yours; **6:20-21** your burnt offerings are not acceptable, nor your sacrifices sweet unto me. Therefore thus saith the LORD; **7:9** will ye steal, murder, and commit adultery, and swear falsely, and burn incense unto Baal, and walk after other gods whom ye know not; **7:18** the children gather wood, and the fathers kindle the fire, and the women knead their dough, to make cakes to the queen of heaven, and to pour out drink offerings unto other gods; **8:19** why have they provoked me to anger with their graven images, and with strange vanities; **10:3-6** the customs of the people are vain: for one cutteth a tree out of the forest, the work of the hands of the workman, with the axe. They deck it with silver and with gold; they fasten it with nails and with hammers, that it move not; **10:14** every man is brutish in his knowledge: every founder is confounded by the graven image: for his molten image is falsehood, and there is no breath in them; **10:17** gather up thy wares out of the land, O inhabitant of the fortress; **11:10-13** they are turned back to the iniquities of their forefathers, which refused to hear my words; and they went after other gods to serve them; **13:10** this evil people, which refuse to hear my words, which walk in the imagination of their heart, and walk after other gods, to serve them, and to worship them, shall even be as this girdle; **13:21** what wilt thou say when he shall punish thee? for thou hast taught them to be captains, and as chief over thee: shall not sorrows take thee; **16:11** because your fathers have forsaken me, saith the LORD, and have walked after other gods, and have served them, and have worshipped them, and have forsaken me; **16:13** I [will] cast you out of this land into a land that ye know not, neither ye nor your fathers; and there shall ye serve other gods day and night; where I will not shew you favour; **16:18** I will recompense their iniquity and their sin double; because they have defiled my land, they have filled mine inheritance with the carcases of their detestable and abominable things; **16:20** shall a man make gods unto himself, and they are no gods; **50:2** her *i.* are confounded, her images are broken in pieces; **50:38-42** they shall be dried up: for it is the land of graven images, and they are mad upon their *i.*; **51:17-18** every founder is confounded by the graven image: for his molten image is falsehood,

and there is no breath in them. They are vanity, the work of errors: in the time of their visitation they shall perish; **51:47** I will do judgment upon the graven images of Babylon: and her whole land shall be confounded, and all her slain shall fall in the midst of her; **51:52** I will do judgment upon her graven images: and through all her land the wounded shall groan; **Ezek. 6:4-7** your altars shall be desolate, and your images shall be broken: and I will cast down your slain men before your *i.*. And I will lay the dead carcases of the children of Israel before their *i.*; **6:9** I am broken with their whorish heart, which hath departed from me, and with their eyes, which go a whoring after their *i.*: and they shall lothe themselves for the evils which they have committed; **6:12-13** then shall ye know that I am the LORD, when their slain men shall be among their *i.* round about their altars... the place where they did offer sweet savour to all their *i.*; **7:16-20** they shall cast their silver in the streets, and their gold shall be removed: their silver and their gold shall not be able to deliver them in the day of the wrath of the LORD; **7:25** destruction cometh; and they shall seek peace, and there shall be none; **8:10-12** I went in and saw; and behold every form of creeping things, and abominable beasts, and all the *i.* of the house of Israel, pourtrayed upon the wall round about; **8:16** between the porch and the altar, were about five and twenty men, with their backs toward the temple of the LORD, and their faces toward the east; and they worshipped the sun toward the east; **14:3-8** every man of the house of Israel that setteth up his *i.* in his heart, and putteth the stumblingblock of his iniquity before his face, and cometh to the prophet; I the LORD will answer him that cometh according to the multitude of his *i.*; **16:17-21** thou hast also taken thy fair jewels of my gold and of my silver, which I had given thee, and madest to thyself images of men, and didst commit whoredom with them; **16:36-39** because thy filthiness was poured out, and thy nakedness discovered through thy whoredoms with thy lovers, and with all the *i.* of thy abominations... I will also give thee into their hand, and they shall throw down thine eminent place, and shall break down thy high places; **18:6** hath not eaten upon the mountains, neither hath lifted up his eyes to the *i.* of the house of Israel, neither hath defiled his neighbour's wife, neither hath come near to a menstruous woman; **18:12-13** [if he] hath lifted up his eyes to the *i.*, hath committed abomination, Hath given forth upon usury... he shall not live: he hath done all these abominations; he shall surely die; his blood shall be upon him; **18:15** that hath not eaten upon the mountains, neither hath lifted up his eyes to the *i.* of the house of Israel; **20:7-8** cast ye away every man the abominations of his eyes, and defile not yourselves with the *i.* of Egypt: I am the LORD your God; **20:16** they despised my judgments, and walked not in my statutes, but polluted my sabbaths: for their heart went after their *i.*; **20:18** walk ye not in the statutes of your fathers, neither observe their judgments, nor defile yourselves with their *i.*; **20:24** they had not executed my judgments, but had despised my statutes, and had polluted my sabbaths, and their eyes were after their fathers *i.*; **20:31-32** when ye offer your gifts, when ye make your sons to pass through the fire, ye pollute yourselves with all your *i.*, even unto this day; **20:39** go ye, serve ye every one his *i.*, and hereafter also, if ye will not hearken unto me: but pollute ye my holy name no more with your gifts, and with your *i.*; **21:21** he made his arrows bright, he consulted with images, he looked in the liver; **22:3-4** the city sheddeth blood in the midst of it, that her time may come, and maketh *i.* against herself to defile herself. Thou art become guilty in thy blood that thou hast shed; and hast defiled thyself in thine *i.* which thou hast made; **23:7** she committed her whoredoms with them, with all them that were the chosen men of Assyria, and with all on whom she doted: with all their *i.* she defiled herself; **23:30** I will do these things unto thee, because thou hast gone a whoring after the heathen, and because thou art polluted with their *i.*; **23:37** they have committed adultery, and blood is in their hands, and with their *i.* have they committed adultery; **23:39** when they had slain their children to their *i.*, then they came the same day into my sanctuary to profane it; **23:49** they shall recompense your lewdness upon you, and ye shall bear the sins of your *i.*: and ye shall know that I am the Lord GOD; **33:25** ye eat with the blood, and lift up your eyes toward your *i.*, and shed blood: and shall ye possess the land; **33:27** as I live, surely they that are in the wastes shall fall by the sword, and him that is in the open field will I give to the beasts to be devoured, and they that be in the forts and in the caves shall die of the pestilence; **36:18** I poured my fury upon them for the blood that they had shed upon the land, and for their *i.* wherewith they had polluted it; **37:23** neither shall they defile themselves any more with their *i.*, nor with their detestable things, nor with any of their transgressions; **44:10-12** Israel went astray, which went astray away from me after their *i.*; they shall even bear their iniquity; **Dan. 3:1** the king made an image of gold, whose height was threescore cubits, and the breadth thereof six cubits; **3:5-6** ye fall down and worship the golden image that Nebuchadnezzar the king hath set up; **3:10-18** there are certain Jews whom thou hast set over the affairs of the province of Babylon, Shadrach, Meshach, and Abed-nego; these men, O king, have not regarded thee: they serve not thy gods, nor worship the golden image which thou hast set up; **5:4-5** they drank wine, and praised the gods of gold, and of silver, of brass, of iron, of wood, and of stone; **Hosea 3:1** go yet, love a woman beloved of her friend, yet an adulteress, according to the love of the LORD toward the children of Israel, who look to other gods, and love flagons of wine; **4:17** Ephraim is joined to *i.*: let him alone; **8:4-6** of their silver and their gold have they made them *i.*, that they may be cut off. Thy calf, O Samaria, hath cast thee off; mine anger is kindled against them; **10:1-2** according to the goodness of his land they have made goodly images. Their heart is divided; now shall they be found faulty: he shall break down their altars, he shall spoil their images; **11:2** they sacrificed unto Baalim, and burned incense to graven images; **13:2-3** they sin more and more, and have made them molten images of their silver, and *i.* according to their own understanding, all of it the work of the craftsmen; **13:8** I will meet them as a bear that is bereaved of her whelps, and will rend the caul of their heart, and there will I devour them like a lion; **14:8** what have I to do any more with *i.*? I have heard him, and observed him: I am like a green fir tree. From me is thy fruit found; **Amos 5:26-27** ye have borne the tabernacle of your Moloch and Chiun your images, the star of your god, which ye made to yourselves. Therefore will I cause you to go into captivity beyond Damascus; **Micah 1:7** all the graven images thereof shall be beaten to pieces, and all the hires thereof shall be burned with the fire, and all the *i.* thereof will I lay desolate; **5:13** thy graven images also will I cut off, and thy standing images out of the midst of thee; and thou shalt no more worship the work of thine hands; **Nahum 1:14** out of the house of thy gods will I cut off the graven image and the molten image: I will make thy grave; for thou art vile; **Haba 2:18** what profiteth the graven image that the maker thereof hath graven it; the molten image, and a teacher of lies, that the maker of his work trusteth therein, to make dumb *i.*; **Zeph. 2:11** the LORD will be terrible unto them: for he will famish all the gods of the earth; and men shall worship him, every one from his place; **Zech. 13:2** I will cut off the names of the *i.* out of the land, and they shall no more be remembered; **Mal. 2:11-13** an abomination is committed in

Israel and in Jerusalem; for Judah hath profaned the holiness of the LORD which he loved, and hath married the daughter of a strange god.

Know that an idol is nothing in the world, and that there is none other God but one. 1 Cor. 8:4 (*see also* World)

Acts 4:12 neither is there salvation in any other: for there is none other name under heaven given among men, whereby we must be saved; **7:41** they made a calf in those days, and offered sacrifice unto the *i.*, and rejoiced in the works of their own hands; **15:29** that ye abstain from meats offered to *i.*, and from blood, and from things strangled, and from fornication: from which if ye keep yourselves, ye shall do well; **17:29** we are the offspring of God, we ought not to think that the Godhead is like unto gold, or silver, or stone, graven by art and man's device; **19:26** Paul hath persuaded and turned away much people, saying that they be no gods, which are made with hands; **21:25** we have written and concluded that they observe no such thing, save only that they keep themselves from things offered to *i.*; **Rom. 1:23** changed the glory of the uncorruptible God into an image made like to corruptible man, and to birds, and fourfooted beasts, and creeping things; **11:4** I have reserved to myself seven thousand men, who have not bowed the knee to the image of Baal; **1 Cor. 6:9** know ye not that the unrighteous shall not inherit the kingdom of God? Be not deceived: neither fornicators, nor *i.*, nor adulterers, nor effeminate, nor abusers of themselves with mankind; **8:1** now as touching things offered unto *i.*; **8: 4** as concerning therefore the eating of those things that are offered in sacrifice unto *i.*, we know that an *i.* is nothing in the world, and that there is none other God but one; **10:7** neither be ye *i.*, as were some of them; **10:14** my dearly beloved, flee from *i.*; **10:18-21** that the *i.* is any thing, or that which is offered in sacrifice to *i.* is any thing? But I say, that the things which the Gentiles sacrifice, they sacrifice to devils, and not to God: and I would not that ye should have fellowship with devils. Ye cannot drink the cup of the Lord, and the cup of devils: ye cannot be partakers of the Lord's table, and of the table of devils; **10:28** if any man say unto you, This is offered in sacrifice unto *i.*, eat not for his sake that shewed it, and for conscience sake: for the earth is the Lord's, and the fulness thereof; **Eph. 5:5** no whoremonger, nor unclean person,

nor covetous man, who is an *i.*, hath any inheritance in the kingdom of Christ and of God; **Col. 3:6-7** for which things' sake the wrath of God cometh on the children of disobedience: In the which ye also walked some time, when ye lived in them; **1 Thes. 1:9** ye turned to God from *i.* to serve the living and true God; **1 Jn. 2:17** the world passeth away, and the lust thereof: but he that doeth the will of God abideth for ever; **5:21** little children, keep yourselves from *i.*; **Rev. 9:20** the rest of the men which were not killed by these plagues yet repented not of the works of their hands, that they should not worship devils, and *i.* of gold, and silver, and brass, and stone, and of wood: which neither can see, nor hear, nor walk; **13:15** he had power to give life unto the image of the beast, that the image of the beast should both speak, and cause that as many as would not worship the image of the beast should be killed; **16:2** there fell a noisome and grievous sore upon the men which had the mark of the beast, and upon them which worshipped his image; **19:20** the beast was taken, and with him the false prophet that wrought miracles before him, with which he deceived them that had received the mark of the beast, and them that worshipped his image. These both were cast alive into a lake of fire burning with brimstone; **21:8** the fearful, and unbelieving, and the abominable, and murderers, and whoremongers, and sorcerers, and *i.*, and all liars, shall have their part in the lake which burneth with fire and brimstone: which is the second death.

IMAGE (*see also* Graven Image, Idol, Likeness)

As we have borne the image of the earthly, we shall also bear the image of the heavenly. 1 Cor. 15:49

He shall not look to the altars, the work of his hands, neither shall respect that which his fingers have made, either the groves, or the images. Isa. 17:8 (*see also* Look)

Isa. 17:8-9 he shall not look to the altars, the work of his hands, neither shall respect that which his fingers have made, either the groves, or the *i.*; **19:1** the idols of Egypt shall be moved at his presence, and the heart of Egypt shall melt in the midst of it; **21:9** all the graven *i.* of her gods he hath broken unto the ground; **Micah 5:13** thy graven *i.* also will I cut off, and thy standing *i.* out of the midst of thee; and thou shalt no more worship the work of thine hands.

IMAGINE, IMAGINATION (*see also* Vain Imagination)

GOD saw that the wickedness of man was great in the earth, and that every imagination of the thoughts of his heart was only evil continually. Gen. 6:5 (*see also* Think)

Let none of you imagine evil in your hearts against his neighbour; and love no false oath: for all these are things that I hate, saith the LORD. Zech. 8:17 (*see also* Love, Oath)

Though we walk in the flesh, we do not war after the flesh: Casting down imaginations, and every high thing that exalteth itself against the knowledge of God, and bringing into captivity every thought to the obedience of Christ. 2 Cor. 10:3,5 (*see also* Flesh, Obedient, Thought)

These six things doth the LORD hate: yea, seven are an abomination unto him: A proud look, a lying tongue, and hands that shed innocent blood, An heart that deviseth wicked imaginations, feet that be swift in running to mischief, A false witness that speaketh lies, and he that soweth discord among brethren. Prov. 6:16-19 (*see also* Discord, False Witness, Innocent, Mischief, Pride)

Know thou the God of thy father, and serve him with a perfect heart and with a willing mind: for the LORD searcheth all hearts, and understandeth all the imaginations of the thoughts. 1 Chron. 28:9 (*see also* Perfect)

They said, There is no hope: but we will walk after our own devices, and we will every one do the imagination of his evil heart. Jer. 18:12 (*see also* Device, Walk)

Oppress not the widow, nor the fatherless, the stranger, nor the poor; and let none of you imagine evil against his brother in your heart. Zech. 7:10 (*see also* Heart, Mischief)

Neither shall they walk any more after the imagination of their evil heart. Jer. 3:17 (*see also* Heart, Walk)

Gen. 8:21 the LORD said in his heart, I will not again curse the ground any more for mans sake; for the *i.* of mans heart is evil from his youth; Deut. 29:19 he bless himself in his heart, saying, I shall have peace, though I walk in the *i.* of mine heart, to add drunkenness to thirst; 1

Chron. 29:18-19 keep this for ever in the *i.* of the thoughts of the heart of thy people, and prepare their heart unto thee; Jer. 3:17 neither shall they walk any more after the *i.* of their evil heart; 7:24 they hearkened not, nor inclined their ear, but walked in the counsels and in the *i.* of their evil heart; 9:14-15 [they] have walked after the *i.* of their own heart; 11:8 they obeyed not, nor inclined their ear, but walked every one in the *i.* of their evil heart: therefore I will bring upon them all the words of this covenant; 13:10 this evil people, which refuse to hear my words, which walk in the *i.* of their heart, and walk after other gods, to serve them, and to worship them, shall even be as this girdle; 16:12 ye have done worse than your fathers; for, behold, ye walk every one after the *i.* of his evil heart; 18:12 there is no hope: but we will walk after our own devices, and we will every one do the *i.* of his evil heart; 23:17 the LORD hath said, Ye shall have peace; and they say unto every one that walketh after the *i.* of his own heart, No evil shall come upon you.

IMPART (*see* Almsgiving, Charity, Give, Serve)

IMPOSSIBLE

For with God nothing shall be impossible. Luke 1:37 (*see also* Do, Nothing)

For it is impossible for those who were once enlightened, and have tasted of the heavenly gift, and were made partakers of the Holy Ghost, And have tasted the good word of God, and the powers of the world to come, If they shall fall away, to renew them again unto repentance; seeing they crucify to themselves the Son of God afresh, and put him to an open shame. Heb. 6:4 (*see also* Enlightened, Holy Ghost, Second Death)

That by two immutable things, in which it was impossible for God to lie, we might have a strong consolation, who have fled for refuge to lay hold upon the hope set before us: Which hope we have as an anchor of the soul, both sure and stedfast, and which entereth into that within the veil; Whither the forerunner is for us entered, even Jesus, made an high priest for ever after the order of Melchisedec. Heb. 6:18-19 (*see also* High Priest, Hope, Melchisedec)

If ye have faith as a grain of mustard seed, ye shall say unto this mountain, Remove hence to yonder place; and it shall remove; and nothing shall be impossible unto you. **Matt. 17:20** (*see also* Faith, Seed)

But without faith it is impossible to please him: for he that cometh to God must believe that he is, and that he is a rewarder of them that diligently seek him. **Heb. 11:6** (*see also* Believe, Diligently, Faith, Reward, Seek)

INCENSE

Burn no incense unto other gods. **Jer. 44:5**

Jer. 19:4 they have forsaken me, and have estranged this place, and have burned *i.* in it unto other gods... and have filled this place with the blood of innocents; **19:13** the houses of Jerusalem, and the houses of the kings of Judah, shall be defiled as the place of Tophet, because of all the houses upon whose roofs they have burned *i.* unto all the host of heaven; **44:5** they hearkened not, nor inclined their ear to turn from their wickedness, to burn no *i.* unto other gods; **44:8** ye provoke me unto wrath with the works of your hands, burning *i.* unto other gods in the land of Egypt; **44:16-19** we will certainly do whatsoever thing goeth forth out of our own mouth, to burn *i.* unto the queen of heaven, and to pour out drink offerings unto her; **44:23** because ye have burned *i.*, and because ye have sinned against the LORD... therefore this evil is happened unto you, as at this day; **44:25-26** we will surely perform our vows that we have vowed, to burn *i.* to the queen of heaven, and to pour out drink offerings unto her; **46:25** the LORD of hosts, the God of Israel, saith; Behold, I will punish the multitude of No, and Pharaoh, and Egypt, with their gods, and their kings; even Pharaoh, and all them that trust in him; **48:35-38** I will cause to cease in Moab, saith the LORD, him that offereth in the high places, and him that burneth *i.* to his gods; **48:41-42** Moab shall be destroyed from being a people, because he hath magnified himself against the LORD; **48:46** woe be unto thee, O Moab! the people of Chemosh perisheth: for thy sons are taken captives, and thy daughters captives.

INCLINE (*see also* Hearken, Heed, Listen, Open)

Put away, said he, the strange gods which are among you, and incline your heart unto the LORD God of Israel. **Josh. 24:23** (*see also* Heart)

Incline not my heart to any evil thing, to practice wicked works with men that work iniquity. **Ps. 141:4** (*see also* Iniquity)

My son, attend to my words; incline thine ear unto my sayings. Let them not depart from thine eyes; keep them in the midst of thine heart. For they are life unto those that find them, and health to all their flesh. **Prov. 4:20-22** (*see also* Attend, Say, Word)

INCREASE (*see also* Enlarge, Gain)

Jesus increased in wisdom and stature, and in favour with God and man. **Luke 2:52** (*see also* Favor, Jesus Christ, Stature, Wisdom)

Trust not in oppression, and become not vain in robbery: if riches increase, set not your heart upon them. **Ps. 62:10** (*see also* Heart, Oppress, Rich, Rob, Trust)

INDEBTED (*see* Debt, Owe)

INDIGNATION (*see also* Anger, Hate, Offended, Punish, Wrath)

I will bear the indignation of the LORD, because I have sinned against him, until he plead my cause, and execute judgment for me: he will bring me forth to the light, and I shall behold his righteousness. **Micah 7:9-10** (*see also* Bear, Lord)

INDUSTRIOUS, INDUSTRY (*see* Diligence, Labor, Work)

INHERIT, INHERITANCE (*see also* Birthright, Genealogy)

Blessed are the meek: for they shall inherit the earth. **Matt. 5:5** (*see also* Meek)

An inheritance may be gotten hastily at the beginning; but the end thereof shall not be blessed. **Prov. 20:21** (*see also* Haste)

Know ye not that the unrighteous shall not inherit the kingdom of God? Be not deceived: neither fornicators, nor idolaters, nor adulterers, nor effeminate, nor abusers of themselves with mankind, Nor thieves, nor covetous, nor drunkards, nor revilers, nor extortioners, shall inherit the kingdom of God. 1Cor. 6:9-10(*see also* Extort, Unrighteous)

He that overcometh shall inherit all things; and I will be his God, and he shall be my son. But the fearful, and unbelieving, and the abominable, and murderers, and whore-mongers, and sorcerers, and idolaters, and all liars, shall have their part in the lake which burneth with fire and brimstone: which is the second death. Rev. 21:7 (*see also* All Things, Death, Second, Unbelief)

INIQUITY (*see also* Evil, Sin, Transgress, Trespass, Wicked)

Your iniquities have separated between you and your God, and your sins have hid his face from you, that he will not hear. Isa. 59:2 (*see also* Face, Separate)

Not every one that saith unto me, Lord, Lord, shall enter into the kingdom of heaven; but he that doeth the will of my Father who is in heaven. Many will say to me in that day: Lord, Lord, have we not prophesied in thy name, and in thy name have cast out devils, and in thy name done many wonderful works? And then will I profess unto them: I never knew you; depart from me, ye that work iniquity. Matt. 7:21-23 (*see also* Enter, False Prophets, Father, Will, Wonderful)

When a righteous man turneth away from his right-eousness, and committeth iniquity, and dieth in them; for his iniquity that he hath done shall he die. Ezek. 18:26 (*see also* Death, Righteousness, Turn)

WOE to them that devise iniquity, and work evil upon their beds! Micah 2:1 (*see also* Devise)

Acknowledge thine iniquity that thou hast transgressed against the LORD thy God, and hast scattered thy ways to the strangers under every green tree, and ye have not obeyed my voice, saith the LORD. Jer. 3:13 (*see also* Acknowledge)

Because iniquity shall abound, the love of many shall wax cold. Matt. 24:12

Thou hast defiled thy sanctuaries by the multitude of thine iniquities, by the iniquity of thy traffick; therefore will I bring forth a fire from the midst of thee, it shall devour thee. Ezek. 28:18-19 (*see also* Defile, Sanctuary)

If they shall confess their iniquity, and the iniquity of their fathers, with their trespass which they trespassed against me, and that also they have walked contrary unto me; And that I also have walked contrary unto them, and have brought them into the land of their enemies; if then their uncircumcised hearts be humbled, and they then accept of the punishment of their iniquity: Then will I remember my covenant with Jacob, and also my covenant with Isaac, and also my covenant with Abraham will I remember; and I will remember the land. Lev. 26:40-42 (*see also* Confess, Remember, Repent)

Fret not thyself because of evil doers, neither be thou envious against the workers of iniquity. Ps. 37:1 (*see also* Envy)

I will declare mine iniquity; I will be sorry for my sin. Ps. 38:18 (*see also* Repent, Sin)

If I regard iniquity in my heart, the Lord will not hear me. Ps. 66:18

Let not any iniquity have dominion over me. Ps. 119:133 (*see also* Dominion)

All this evil is come upon us: yet made we not our prayer before the LORD our God, that we might turn from our iniquities and understand thy truth. Dan. 9:13 (*see also* Pray)

He that soweth iniquity shall reap vanity: and the rod of his anger shall fail. Prov. 22:8 (*see also* Sow)

I will get me unto the great men, and will speak unto them; for they have known the way of the LORD, and the judgment of their God: but these have altogether broken the yoke, and burst the bonds. Jer. 5:5 (*see also* Way)

Do no iniquity. Ps. 119:3

Ps. 119:3 do no *i.*; **125:3** the rod of the wicked shall not rest upon the lot of the righteous; lest the righteous put forth their hands unto *i.*

Keep thy tongue from evil, and thy lips from speaking guile. Ps. 34:13 (*see also* Guile, Speak, Tongue)

Job 6:30 is there *i.* in my tongue? cannot my taste discern perverse things; **36:10** he openeth also their ear to discipline, and commandeth that they return from *i.*; **Ps. 34:13** keep thy tongue from evil, and thy lips from speaking guile; **Prov. 8:7** my mouth shall speak truth; and wickedness is an abomination to my lips; **18:21** death and life are in the power of the tongue: and they that love it shall eat the fruit thereof; **Zeph. 3:13** the remnant of Israel shall not do *i.*, nor speak lies; neither shall a deceitful tongue be found in their mouth.

Incline not my heart to any evil thing, to practice wicked works with men that work iniquity. Ps. 141:4 (*see also* Incline)

Ps. 141:4 incline not my heart to any evil thing, to practise wicked works with men that work *i.*; **Isa. 31:2-3** [he] will arise against the house of the evildoers, and against the help of them that work *i.*...When the LORD shall stretch out his hand, both he that helpeth shall fall, and he that is holpen shall fall down; **57:21** there is no peace, saith my God, to the wicked; **Hosea 4:8** they eat up the sin of my people, and they set their heart on their *i.*

Flee out of the midst of Babylon, and deliver every man his soul; be not cut off in her iniquity; for this is the time of the LORD's vengeance; he will render unto her a recompense. Jer. 51:6 (*see also* Recompense)

Jer. 51:6-12 flee out of the midst of Babylon, and deliver every man his soul: be not cut off in her *i.*; for this is the time of the LORD's vengeance; he will render unto her a recompence; **51:20-33** I will render unto Babylon and to all the inhabitants of Chaldea all their evil that they have done in Zion in your sight, saith the LORD; **51:45** my people, go ye out of the midst of her, and deliver ye every man his soul from the fierce anger of the LORD.

Be ashamed and confounded for your own ways, O house of Israel. Ezek. 36:32 (*see also* Way)

Ezek. 36:31-32 ye [shall] remember your own evil ways, and your doings that were not good, and shall lothe yourselves in your own sight for your *i.* and for your abominations... be ashamed and confounded for your own ways; **43:10-11** shew the house to the house of Israel, that they may be ashamed of their *i.*: and let them measure the pattern.

INJURE, INJURY (*see* Afflict, Offend, Persecute, Suffer)

INJUSTICE (*see* Accuse, False Witness, Oppress, Persecute)

INNOCENCE, INNOCENT (*see also* Harmless, Judge)

These six things doth the LORD hate: yea, seven are an abomination unto him: A proud look, a lying tongue, and hands that shed innocent blood, An heart that deviseth wicked imaginations, feet that be swift in running to mischief, A false witness that speaketh lies, and he that soweth discord among brethren. Prov. 6:16-19 (*see also* Discord, False Witness, Imagine, Mischief, Pride)

Shed not innocent blood. Jer. 7:6 (*see also* Blood)

Gen. 9:6 whoso sheddeth mans blood, by man shall his blood be shed; **37:22** shed no blood, but cast him into this pit that is in the wilderness, and lay no hand upon him; **Lev. 17:3-4** he hath shed blood; and that man shall be cut off from among his people; **Deut. 19:10** that *i.* blood be not shed in thy land, which the LORD thy God giveth thee for an inheritance, and so blood be upon thee; **19:13** thine eye shall not pity him, but thou shalt put away the guilt of *i.* blood from Israel; **21:8** lay not *i.* blood unto thy people of Israels charge; **1 Sam. 19:5** wherefore then wilt thou sin against *i.* blood; **25:26** the LORD hath withholden thee from coming to shed blood, and from avenging thyself with thine own hand; **25:31** that this shall be no grief unto thee, nor offence of heart unto my lord, either that thou hast shed blood causeless; **25:33** blessed be thy advice, and blessed be thou, which hast kept me this day from coming to shed blood, and from avenging myself with mine own hand; **1 Kgs.**

2:31-32 bury him; that thou mayest take away the *i.* blood, which Joab shed, from me, and from the house of my father; **2 Kgs. 21:16** Manasseh shed *i.* blood very much, till he had filled Jerusalem from one end to another; beside his sin wherewith he made Judah to sin; **24:3-4** for the *i.* blood that he shed: for he filled Jerusalem with *i.* blood; which the LORD would not pardon; **Ps. 106:37-38** they sacrificed their sons and their daughters unto devils, And shed *i.* blood, even the blood of their sons and of their daughters; **Prov. 1:16** their feet run to evil, and make haste to shed blood; **6:17** a proud look, a lying tongue, and hands that shed *i.* blood; **Isa. 59:7** their feet run to evil, and they make haste to shed *i.* blood; **Jer. 2:34-35** in thy skirts is found the blood of the souls of the poor *i.*; **7:6-7** shed not *i.* blood in this place; **19:4-10** they have forsaken me... and have filled this place with the blood of *i.*; **22:3** do no wrong, do no violence to the stranger, the fatherless, nor the widow, neither shed *i.* blood in this place; **22:17** thine eyes and thine heart are not but for thy covetousness, and for to shed *i.* blood, and for oppression, and for violence, to do it; **26:15-16** know ye for certain, that if ye put me to death, ye shall surely bring *i.* blood upon yourselves, and upon this city, and upon the inhabitants thereof; **Lam. 4:13** for the sins of her prophets, and the iniquities of her priests, that have shed the blood of the just in the midst of her; **Ezek. 22:12-13** they [have] taken gifts to shed blood; thou hast taken usury and increase, and thou hast greedily gained of thy neighbours by extortion, and hast forgotten me, saith the Lord GOD; **22:27** her princes in the midst thereof are like wolves ravening the prey, to shed blood, and to destroy souls, to get dishonest gain; **33:25** ye eat with the blood, and lift up your eyes toward your idols, and shed blood: and shall ye possess the land; **35:5** thou hast had a perpetual hatred, and hast shed the blood of the children of Israel by the force of the sword in the time of their calamity; **36:18** I poured my fury upon them for the blood that they had shed upon the land; **Joel 3:19** Egypt shall be a desolation, and Edom shall be a desolate wilderness, for the violence against the children of Judah, because they have shed *i.* blood in their land; **Jonah 1:14** they cried unto the LORD, and said, We beseech thee, O LORD, we beseech thee, let us not perish for this mans life, and lay not upon us *i.* Blood.

INQUIRE (*see also* Ask, Entreat, Petition, Pray, Seek)

They returned and enquired early after God. Ps. 78:34

One thing have I desired of the LORD, that will I seek after; that I may dwell in the house of the LORD all the days of my life, to behold the beauty of the LORD, and to enquire in his temple. **Ps. 27:4** (*see also* Temple)

Is there not here a prophet of the LORD, that we may inquire of the LORD by him? **2 Kgs. 3:11** (*see also* Prophet)

Judg. 20:27 the children of Israel *i.* of the LORD; **2 Sam. 5:19** David *i.* of the LORD, saying, Shall I go up to the Philistines? Wilt thou deliver them into mine hand; **5:22-23** when David *i.* of the LORD, he said, Thou shalt not go up; but fetch a compass behind them, and come upon them; **2 Kgs. 3:11** is there not here a prophet of the LORD, that we may *i.* of the LORD by him; **Job 8:8** *i.*, I pray thee, of the former age, and prepare thyself to the search of their fathers.

Inquire of the Lord. Gen. 25:22

Gen. 25:22 she went to *i.* of the LORD; **Ex. 14:10** they were sore afraid: and the children of Israel cried out unto the LORD; **34:9** if now I have found grace in thy sight, O Lord, let my Lord, I pray thee, go among us; for it is a stiffnecked people; and pardon our iniquity and our sin, and take us for thine inheritance; **34:13-17** thou shalt worship no other god: for the LORD, whose name is Jealous, is a jealous God; **Num. 11:2** when Moses prayed unto the LORD, the fire was quenched; **11:11-12** and Moses said unto the LORD, Wherefore hast thou afflicted thy servant? and wherefore have I not found favour in thy sight, that thou layest the burden of all this people upon me? Have I conceived all this people? have I begotten them, that thou shouldest say unto me, Carry them in thy bosom, as a nursing father beareth the sucking child, unto the land which thou swarest unto their fathers; **1 Sam. 1:10** she was in bitterness of soul, and prayed unto the LORD, and wept sore; **1 Kgs. 8:28-29** yet have thou respect unto the prayer of thy servant, and to his supplication, O LORD my God, to hearken unto the cry and to the prayer, which thy servant prayeth before thee to day: That thine eyes may be open toward this house night and day, even toward the place of which thou hast said, My name shall be there: that thou mayest hearken unto the prayer which thy servant shall make toward this place; **8:44-45** if thy people go out to battle against their enemy, whithersoever thou shalt send them, and shall pray unto the LORD toward the city which thou hast chosen, and toward the house that I have built for thy name: Then hear thou in heaven their prayer and their supplication, and maintain their cause; **8:49** hear thou their prayer and their supplication in heaven thy dwelling place, and maintain their cause; **22:5** *i.*, I pray thee, at the word of the LORD to day; **2 Kgs. 22:13** go ye, *i.* of the LORD for me, and for the people, and for all Judah, concerning the words of this book that is found; **1 Chron. 14:10** David *i.* of God, saying, Shall I go up against the Philistines? and wilt thou deliver them into mine hand? And the LORD said unto him, Go up; for I will deliver them into thine hand; **14:14** David *i.* again of God; and God said unto him, Go not up after them; turn away from them, and come upon them over against the mulberry trees; **17:18-26** what can David speak more to thee for the honour of thy servant? for thou knowest thy servant. O LORD, for thy servants sake, and according to thine own heart, hast thou done all this greatness, in making known all these great things. O LORD, there is none like thee, neither is there any God beside thee, according to all that we have heard with our ears; **2 Chron. 34:21** go, *i.* of the LORD for me, and for them that are left in Israel and in Judah, concerning the words of the book that is found: for great is the wrath of the LORD that is poured out upon us, because our fathers have not kept the word of the LORD, to do after all that is written in this book; **34:26** the king of Judah, who sent you to *i.* of the LORD, so shall ye say unto him, Thus saith the LORD God of Israel concerning the words which thou hast heard; **Ps. 6:9** the LORD hath heard my supplication; the LORD will receive my prayer; **109:4** for my love they are my adversaries: but I give myself unto prayer; **Ezek. 14:7** a prophet to *i.* of him concerning me; I the LORD will answer him by myself; **20:1** certain of the elders of Israel came to *i.* of the LORD, and sat before me. Then came the word of the LORD unto me, saying, Son of man, speak unto the elders of Israel, and say unto them, Thus saith the Lord GOD; Are ye come to *i.* of me? As I live, saith the Lord GOD, I will not be *i.* of by you; **Dan. 2:18** that they would desire mercies of the God of heaven concerning this secret; **2:23** I thank thee, and praise thee, O thou God of my fathers, who hast given me wisdom and might, and hast made known unto me now what we desired of thee.

INSPIRATION, INSPIRE (*see also* Guide, Comforter, Holy Ghost, Prophecy, Testimony, Revelation)

All scripture is given by inspiration of God, and is profitable for doctrine, for reproof, for correction, for instruction in righteousness: That the man of God may be perfect, throughly furnished unto all good works. 2 Tim. 3:16-17 (*see also* Perfect, Scripture, Works)

INSTRUCT, INSTRUCTION (*see also* Command, Counsel, Edify, Preach, Teach)

Hear instruction, and be wise, and refuse it not. Prov. 8:33 (*see also* Wise)

Whoso loveth instruction loveth knowledge: but he that hateth reproof is brutish. Prov. 12:1 (*see also* Correct, Know)

Poverty and shame shall be to him that refuseth instruction: but he that regardeth reproof shall be honoured. Prov. 13:18 (*see also* Refuse)

Cease, my son, to hear the instruction that causeth to err from the words of knowledge. Prov. 19:27 (*see also* Hear, Know)

He is in the way of life that keepeth instruction: but he that refuseth reproof erreth. Prov. 10:17 (*see also* Reproof, Way)

Buy the truth, and sell it not; also wisdom, and instruction, and understanding. Prov. 23:23 (*see also* True, Understand, Wisdom)

The fear of the LORD is the beginning of knowledge: but fools despise wisdom and and instruction. Prov. 1:7 (*see also* Beginning, Wisdom)

Prov. 1:7 the fear of the LORD is the beginning of knowledge: but fools despise wisdom and *i.*; **1:22** how long, ye simple ones, will ye love simplicity? and the scorners delight in their scorning, and fools hate knowledge; **1:30-31** they would none of my counsel: they despised all my reproof. Therefore shall they eat of the fruit of their own way, and be filled with their own devices; **8:33** hear *i.*, and be wise, and refuse it not; **12:1** whoso loveth *i.* loveth knowledge: but he that hateth reproof is brutish; **15:5** a fool despiseth his fathers *i.*: but he that regardeth reproof is prudent; **15:32** he that refuseth *i.* despiseth his own soul: but he that heareth reproof getteth understanding; **Jer. 17:23** they obeyed not, neither inclined their ear, but made their neck stiff, that they might not hear, nor receive *i.*; **Zeph. 3:7** thou wilt fear me, thou wilt receive *i.*

Take fast hold of instruction; let her not go: keep her; for she is thy life. Prov. 4:13

Prov. 4:13 take fast hold of *i.*; let her not go: keep her; for she is thy life; **5:12** how have I hated *i.*, and my heart despised reproof; **8:10** receive my *i.*, and not silver; and knowledge rather than choice gold.

Hear the instruction of thy father, and forsake not the law of thy mother. Prov. 1:8 (*see also* Law)

Prov. 1:8-9 hear the *i.* of thy father, and forsake not the law of thy mother: For they shall be an ornament of grace unto thy head; **6:20-23** keep thy fathers commandment, and forsake not the law of thy mother: Bind them continually upon thine heart, and tie them about thy neck; **8:33** hear *i.*, and be wise, and refuse it not; **13:1** a wise son heareth his fathers *i.*: but a scorner heareth not rebuke; **15:20** a wise son maketh a glad father: but a foolish man despiseth his mother; **19:26** he that wasteth his father, and chaseth away his mother, is a son that causeth shame, and bringeth reproach; **23:22** hearken unto thy father that begat thee, and despise not thy mother when she is old.

INSTRUMENT (*see also* Call, Serve)

Neither yield ye your members as instruments of unrighteousness unto sin: but yield yourselves unto God, as those that are alive from the dead, and your members as instruments of righteousness unto God. Rom. 6:13 (*see also* Will, Yield)

INTEGRITY (*see also* Honest, Perfect, Righteous, Uprightness)

Walk before me, as David thy father walked, in integrity of heart, and in uprightness, to do according to all that I have commanded thee, and wilt keep my statutes and my judgments. 1 Kgs. 9:4 (*see also* Heart)

The just man walketh in his integrity: his children are blessed after him. Prov. 20:7 (*see also* Walk)

Ps. 25:21 let *i.* and uprightness preserve me; for I wait on thee; **26:1** judge me, O LORD; for I have walked in mine *i.*: I have trusted also in the LORD; therefore I shall not slide; **26:11-12** I will walk in mine *i.*: redeem me, and be merciful unto me; **Prov. 11:3** the *i.* of the upright shall guide them: but the perverseness of transgressors shall destroy them; **20:7** the just man walketh in his *i.*: his children are blessed after him.

INTEND, INTENT (*see also* Desire)

INTERPRET, INTERPRETATION (*see also* Gift, Holy Ghost, Language, Prophecy, Reveal, Seer, Teach, Tongues)

Now the wise men, the astrologers, have been brought in before me, that they should read this writing, and make known unto me the interpretation thereof: but they could not shew the interpretation of the thing. Dan 5:15 (*see also* Astrologer, Dream, Magician)

I would that ye all spake with tongues, but rather that ye prophesied: for greater is he that prophesieth than he that speaketh with tongues, except he interpret, that the church may receive edifying. 1 Cor. 14:5 (*see also* Gift, Prophecy, Tongues)

The secret which the king hath demanded cannot the wise men, the astrologers, the magicians, the soothsayers, shew unto the king; But there is a God in heaven that revealeth secrets, and maketh known to the king Nebuchadnezzar what shall be in the latter days. Dan. 1:27-28 (*see also* Dream, Secret)

God hath set some in the church, first apostles, secondarily prophets, thirdly teachers, after that miracles, then gifts of healings, helps, governments, diversities of tongues. Are all apostles? are all prophets? are all teachers? are all workers of miracles? Have all the gifts of healing? do all speak with tongues? do all interpret? But covet earnestly the best gifts: and yet shew I unto you a more excellent way. 1 Cor. 12:28-31 (*see also* Excellent, Gift, Government, Prophet, Way)

INVITE (*see also* Ask, Beseech, Entreat)

ISRAEL (*see also* Adopt, Genealogy, Gathering, Latter Days, Restore)

Be it known unto you all, and to all the people of Israel, that by the name of Jesus Christ of Nazareth, whom ye crucified, whom God raised from the dead, even by him doth this man stand here before you whole. This is the stone which was set at nought of you builders, which is become the head of the corner. Neither is there salvation in any other: for there is none other name under heaven given among men, whereby we must be saved. Acts 4:10-12 (*see also* Corner, Jesus Christ, Name, Saved, Stone)

There shall be no more any vain vision nor flattering divination within the house of Israel. Ezek. 12:24 (*see also* Divination, Vision)

It is a light thing that thou shouldest be my servant to raise up the tribes of Jacob, and to restore the preserved of Israel: I will also give thee for a light to the Gentiles, that thou mayest be my salvation unto the end of the earth. Isa. 49:6 (*see also* Restoration)

JEALOUS, JEALOUSY (*see also* Covet, Envious)

They provoked him to jealousy with strange gods, with abominations provoked they him to anger. Duet 32:16 (*see also* Abomination)

They provoked him to anger with their high places, and moved him to jealousy with their graven images. Ps. 78:58 (*see also* Graven Image)

Do we provoke the Lord to jealousy? are we stronger than he? 1 Cor. 10:22

Thou shalt not bow down thyself to them, nor serve them: for I the LORD thy God am a jealous God, visiting the iniquities of the fathers upon the children unto the third and fourth generation of them that hate me. Ex. 20:5 (*see also* Children, Thou Shalt Not)

JEHOVAH (*see also* Christ, God, Lord, Jesus Christ, Messiah, Redeemer, Savior)

Let them be confounded and troubled for ever; yea, let them be put to shame, and

perish: That men may know that thou, whose name alone is JEHOVAH, art the most high over all the earth. Ps. 83:18 (*see also* Name)

JERUSALEM (*see also* New Jerusalem)

Pray for the peace of Jerusalem: they shall prosper that love thee. Ps. 122:6 (*see also* Love, Peace)

Ye that make mention of the LORD, keep not silence, And give him no rest, till he establish, and till he make Jerusalem a praise in the earth. Isa. 62:6-7 (*see also* Establish, Mention)

Son of man, cause Jerusalem to know her abominations. Ezek. 16:2 (*see also* Abomination)

Come, and let us go up to the mountain of the LORD, and to the house of the God of Jacob; and he will teach us of his ways, and we will walk in his paths; for the law shall go forth of Zion, and the word of the LORD from Jerusalem. Micah 4:2 (*see also* House, Law, Mountain, Ways, Word, Zion)

Ye are come unto mount Sion, and unto the city of the living God, the heavenly Jerusalem, and to an innumerable company of angels. Heb. 12:22 (*see also* Zion)

Shake thyself from the dust; arise, and sit down, O Jerusalem: loose thyself from the bands of thy neck, O captive daughter of Zion. Isa. 52:2 (*see also* Loose)

O Jerusalem, wash thine heart from wickedness, that thou mayest be saved. Jer. 4:14 (*see also* Wash, Wickedness)

JESUS CHRIST (*see also* Atone, Christ, God, Jehovah, Judge, Lord, Mediator, Messiah, Redeemer, Salvation, Save, Savior)

His head and his hairs were white like wool, as white as snow; and his eyes were as a flame of fire; And his feet like unto fine brass, as if they burned in a furnace; and his voice as the sound of many waters. Rev. 1:15 (*see also* Brass, Voice)

This is life eternal, that they might know thee the only true God, and Jesus Christ, whom thou hast sent. John 17:3 (*see also* Eternal)

Put ye on the Lord Jesus Christ, and make not provision for the flesh, to fulfil the lusts thereof. Rom. 13:14 (see also Flesh, Lust)

I know that he shall rise again in the resurrection at the last day. Jesus said unto her, I am the resurrection, and the life: he that believeth in me, though he were dead, yet shall he live. John 11:24-25 (see also Death, Resurrection)

Gird up the loins of your mind, be sober, and hope to the end for the grace that is to be brought unto you at the revelation of Jesus Christ. 1 Pet. 1:13 (see also Grace, Hope, Mind)

Let all the house of Israel know assuredly, that God hath made that same Jesus, whom ye have crucified, both Lord and Christ. Acts 2:36 (see also Assure, Testify)

Happy is that people, that is in such a case: yea, happy is that people, whose God is the LORD. Ps. 144:15 (see also Happiness)

Wherefore also it is contained in the scripture, Behold, I lay in Sion a chief corner stone, elect, precious: and he that believeth on him shall not be confounded. 1 Pet. 2:6 (see also Cornerstone, Zion)

Knowing that Christ being raised from the dead dieth no more; death hath no more dominion over him. For in that he died, he died unto sin once: but in that he liveth, he liveth unto God. Likewise reckon ye also yourselves to be dead indeed unto sin, but alive unto God through Jesus Christ our Lord. Romans 6:9-11 (see also Alive, Sin)

Jesus increased in wisdom and stature, and in favour with God and man. Luke 2:52 (see also Favor, Increase, Stature, Wisdom)

[Look] unto Jesus the author and finisher of our faith; who for the joy that was set before him endured the cross, despising the shame, and is set down at the right hand of the throne of God. Heb. 12:2 (see also Author, Faith, Finisher)

There is neither Jew nor Greek, there is neither bond nor free, there is neither male nor female: for ye are all one in Christ Jesus. Gal. 3:28 (see also Bond, Equality, Female, Male, One)

Grace be unto you, and peace, from him which is, and which was, and which is to come; and from the seven Spirits which are before his throne; And from Jesus Christ, who is the faithful witness, and the first begotten of the dead, and the prince of the kings of the earth. Unto him that loved us, and washed us from our sins in his own blood, And hath made us kings and priests unto God and his Father; to him be glory and dominion for ever and ever. Amen. Rev. 1:4-6 (see also Begotten, Blood, Glory)

Be not ye called Rabbi: for one is your Master, even Christ; and all ye are brethren. Matt. 23:8 (see also Call, Rabbi)

Be likeminded one toward another according to Christ Jesus: That ye may with one mind and one mouth glorify God, even the Father of our Lord Jesus Christ. Rom. 15:5-6 (see also Likeminded, One, Unity)

Be it known unto you all, and to all the people of Israel, that by the name of Jesus Christ of Nazareth, whom ye crucified, whom God raised from the dead, even by him doth this man stand here before you whole. This is the stone which was set at nought of you builders, which is become the head of the corner. Neither is there salvation in any other: for there is none other name under heaven given among men, whereby we must be saved. Acts 4:10-12 (see also Corner, Israel, Name, Saved, Stone)

They shall mock him, and shall scourge him, and shall spit upon him, and shall kill him: and the third day he shall rise again. Mark 10:34 (see also Mock)

To you who are troubled rest with us, when the Lord Jesus shall be revealed from heaven with his mighty angels, In flaming fire taking vengeance on them that know not God, and that obey not the gospel of our Lord Jesus Christ. 2 Thes. 1:7-8 (see also Gospel)

Repent, and be baptized every one of you in the name of Jesus Christ for the remission of sins, and ye shall receive the gift of the Holy Ghost. Acts 2:38 (see also Baptize, Repent)

These are written, that ye might believe that Jesus is the Christ, the Son of God; and that believing ye might have life through his name. John 20:31 (see also Belief, Name)

We command you, brethren, in the name of our Lord Jesus Christ, that ye withdraw yourselves from every brother that walketh disorderly, and not after the tradition which he received of us. 2Thes 3:6 (*see also* Unruly)

These are written, that ye might believe that Jesus is the Christ, the Son of God; and that believing ye might have life through his name. John 20:31 (*see also* Belief)

Ye also, as lively stones, are built up a spiritual house, an holy priesthood, to offer up spiritual sacrifices, acceptable to God by Jesus Christ. 1 Pet. 2:5 (*see also* Priesthood, Offer, Sacrifice)

We also joy in God through our Lord Jesus Christ, by whom we have now received the atonement. Rom. 5:11 (*see also* Atonement, Rejoice)

Paul, being grieved, turned and said to the spirit, I command thee in the name of Jesus Christ to come out of her. And he came out the same hour. Acts 16:18 (*see also* Command, Hour, Unclean)

Ye are no more strangers and foreigners, but fellowcitizens with the saints, and of the household of God; And are built upon the foundation of the apostles and prophets, Jesus Christ himself being the chief corner stone. Eph. 2:19-20 (*see also* Apostle, Cornerstone, Prophet, Saint)

JOIN, JOINED (*see also* Unite)

Have ye not read, that he which made them at the beginning made them male and female, And said, For this cause shall a man leave father and mother, and shall cleave to his wife: and they twain shall be one flesh? Wherefore they are no more twain, but one flesh. What therefore God hath joined together, let not man put asunder. Matt. 19:4-6 (*see also* Flesh, Marriage)

JOY, JOYFUL, JOYFULLY (*see also* Cheerful, Delight, Glad, Happiness)

Blessed is the people that know the joyful sound: they shall walk, O LORD, in the light of thy countenance. Ps. 89:15 (*see also* Countenance)

In the day of prosperity be joyful. Eccl. 7:14 (*see also* Prosper)

I will greatly rejoice in the LORD, my soul shall be joyful in my God; for he hath clothed me with the garments of salvation, he hath covered me with the robe of righteousness. Isa. 61:10 (*see also* Soul)

Live joyfully with the wife whom thou lovest all the days of the life of thy vanity, which he hath given thee under the sun, all the days of thy vanity: for that is thy portion in this life, and in thy labour which thou takest under the sun. Eccl. 9:9 (*see also* Live, Wife)

Eccl. 9:9 live joyfully with the wife whom thou lovest all the days of the life of thy vanity, which he hath given thee under the sun, all the days of thy vanity: for that is thy portion in this life, and in thy labour which thou takest under the sun.

The ransomed of the LORD shall return, and come to Zion with songs and everlasting joy upon their heads: they shall obtain joy and gladness, and sorrow and sighing shall flee away. Isa. 35:10 (*see also* Song)

Isa. 35:10 the ransomed of the LORD shall return, and come to Zion with songs and everlasting *j.* upon their heads: they shall obtain *j.* and gladness, and sorrow and sighing shall flee away.

JUDGE, JUDGMENT (*see also* Accuse, Bishop, Condemn, Justice)

Let us not therefore judge one another any more: but judge this rather, that no man put a stumbling block or an occasion to fall in his brother's way. Rom. 14:13 (*see also* Stumble)

He commanded us to preach unto the people, and to testify that it is he which was ordained of God to be the Judge of quick and dead. To him give all the prophets witness, that through his name whosoever believeth in him shall receive remission of sins. Acts 10:43 (*see also* Believe, Remission)

We must all appear before the judgment seat of Christ; that every one may receive the things done in his body, according to that he hath done, whether it be good or bad. 2 Cor. 5:10 (*see also* Appear, Bad, Body)

After the wisdom of thy God, that is in thine hand, set magistrates and judges, which may judge all the people that are beyond the river, all such as know the laws of thy God; and teach ye them that know them not. Ezra 7:25 (*see also* Government)

Ex. 18:18-26 Moses chose able men out of all Israel, and made them heads over the people, rulers of thousands, rulers of hundreds, rulers of fifties, and rulers of tens. And they *j.* the people at all seasons: the hard causes they brought unto Moses, but every small matter they *j.* themselves; **2 Chron. 1:10-11** give me now wisdom and knowledge, that I may go out and come in before this people; **Ezra 7:25** after the wisdom of thy God, that is in thine hand, set magistrates and *j.*, which may *j.* all the people that are beyond the river, all such as know the laws of thy God; and teach ye them that know them not; **Ps. 119:85** the proud have digged pits for me, which are not after thy law.

Ye shall do no unrighteousness in judgment: thou shalt not respect the person of the poor, nor honor the person of the mighty: but in righteousness shalt thou judge thy neighbour. Lev. 19:15 (*see also* Righteous)

Lev. 19:15 ye shall do no unrighteousness in *j.*: thou shalt not respect the person of the poor, nor honour the person of the mighty: but in righteousness shalt thou *j.* thy neighbour; **19:35-36** ye shall do no unrighteousness in *j.*; **Deut. 1:16-17** hear the causes between your brethren, and *j.* righteously between every man and his brother, and the stranger that is with him; **25:1** if there be a controversy between men, and they come unto *j.*, that the *j.* may *j.* them; then they shall justify the righteous, and condemn the wicked; **1 Chron. 18:14** David reigned over all Israel, and executed *j.* and justice among all his people; **2 Chron. 6:23** hear thou from heaven, and do, and *j.* thy servants, by requiting the wicked, by recompensing his way upon his own head; and by justifying the righteous; **Job 17:9** the righteous also shall hold on his way, and he that hath clean hands shall be stronger and stronger; **Ps. 7:3-5** if there be iniquity in my hands; If I have rewarded evil unto him that was at peace with me; [yea, I have delivered him that without cause is mine enemy:] Let the enemy persecute my soul, and take it; **7:8** the LORD shall *j.* the people: *j.* me, O LORD, according to my righteousness, and according to mine integrity that is in me; **37:30-31** the mouth of the righteous speaketh wisdom, and his tongue

talketh of *j.*; **58:1** do ye indeed speak righteousness, O congregation? do ye *j.* uprightly, O ye sons of men; **72:1-2** five the king thy *j.*, O God, and thy righteousness unto the kings son. He shall *j.* thy people with righteousness, and thy poor with *j.*; **75:2** when I shall receive the congregation I will *j.* uprightly; **82:2** how long will ye *j.* unjustly, and accept the persons of the wicked; **97:11** light is sown for the righteous, and gladness for the upright in heart; **106:3** blessed are they that keep *j.*, and he that doeth righteousness at all times; **119:66** teach me good *j.* and knowledge: for I have believed thy commandments; **Prov. 8:20** I lead in the way of righteousness, in the midst of the paths of *j.*; **29:14** the king that faithfully *j.* the poor, his throne shall be established for ever; **31:9** open thy mouth, *j.* righteously, and plead the cause of the poor and needy; **Isa. 11:3-4** he shall not *j.* after the sight of his eyes, neither reprove after the hearing of his ears: But with righteousness shall he *j.* the poor, and reprove with equity for the meek of the earth; **Jer. 7:5** throughly execute *j.* between a man and his neighbour; **Ezek. 16:52** bear thine own shame for thy sins that thou hast committed more abominable than they: they are more righteous than thou: yea, be thou confounded also, and bear thy shame; **16:63** remember, and be confounded, and never open thy mouth any more because of thy shame, when I am pacified toward thee for all that thou hast done.

Learn to do well; seek judgment, relieve the oppressed, judge the fatherless, plead for the widow. Isa. 1:17 (*see also* Do, Learn, Plead, Relieve)

Isa. 1:17 learn to do well; seek *j.* relieve the oppressed, *j.* the fatherless, plead for the widow; **1:23** thy princes are rebellious, and companions of thieves: every one loveth gifts, and followeth after rewards: they *j.* not the fatherless, neither doth the cause of the widow come unto them; **Jer. 22:3-5** execute ye *j.* and righteousness, and deliver the spoiled out of the hand of the oppressor: and do no wrong, do no violence to the stranger, the fatherless, nor the widow.

O inhabitants of Jerusalem, and men of Judah, judge, I pray you, betwixt me and my vineyard. What could have been done more to my vineyard, that I have not done in it? Isa. 5:3-4 (*see also* Do)

Isa. 3:7 in that day shall he swear, saying, I will not be an healer; for in my house is neither bread nor clothing: make me not a ruler of the people; **5:3-4** *j.*, I pray you, betwixt me and my vineyard. What could have been done more to my vineyard, that I have not done in it? wherefore, when I looked that it should bring forth grapes, brought it forth wild grapes.

It is not good to accept the person of the wicked, to overthrow the righteous in judgment. Prov. 18:5

Prov. 18:5 it is not good to accept the person of the wicked, to overthrow the righteous in *j.*; **Jer. 22:3-5** execute ye *j.* and righteousness, and deliver the spoiled out of the hand of the oppressor: and do no wrong, do no violence; **Ezek. 18:8** he that hath not given forth upon usury, neither hath taken any increase, that hath withdrawn his hand from iniquity, hath executed true *j.* between man and man.

It is not good to have respect of persons in judgment. Prov. 24:23 (*see also* Respect)

Prov. 24:23 these things also belong to the wise. It is not good to have respect of persons in *j.*; **28:21** to have respect of persons is not good: for for a piece of bread that man will transgress.

Execute ye judgment and righteousness. Jer. 22:3-5 (*see also* Righteous)

Jer. 22:3-5 execute ye *j.* and righteousness, and deliver the spoiled out of the hand of the oppressor: and do no wrong, do no violence; **22:15-16** did not thy father eat and drink, and do *j.* and justice, and then it was well with him? He *j.* the cause of the poor and needy; then it was well with him: was not this to know me? saith the LORD.

The house of Israel rebelled against me in the wilderness: they walked not in my statutes, and they despised my judgments, which if a man do, he shall even live in them; and my sabbaths they greatly polluted. Ezek. 20:13 (*see also* Rebel)

Ezek. 20:13 the house of Israel rebelled against me in the wilderness: they walked not in my statutes, and they despised my *j.*, which if a man do, he shall even live in them; and my sabbaths they greatly polluted; **20:16** they despised my *j.*, and walked not in my statutes, but polluted my sabbaths: for their heart went after their idols.

Judge not according to the appearance, but judge righteous judgment. John 7:24 (*see also* Appear)

Matt. 7:3-5 *j.* not, that ye be not *j.*. For with what *j.* ye *j.*, ye shall be *j.*: and with what measure ye mete, it shall be measured to you again. And why beholdest thou the mote that is in thy brother's eye, but considerest not the beam that is in thine own eye? Or how wilt thou say to thy brother, Let me pull out the mote out of thine eye; and, behold, a beam is in thine own eye? Thou hypocrite, first cast out the beam out of thine own eye; and then shalt thou see clearly to cast out the mote out of thy brother's eye; **Luke 6:37** *j.* not, and ye shall not be *j.*: condemn not, and ye shall not be condemned: forgive, and ye shall be forgive; **12:56-57** ye hypocrites, ye can discern the face of the sky and of the earth; but how is it that ye do not discern this time? Yea, and why even of yourselves *j.* ye not what is right; **John 5:30** I can of mine own self do nothing: as I hear, I *j.*: and my *j.* is just; because I seek not mine own will, but the will of the Father which hath sent me; **7:24** *j.* not according to the appearance, but *j.* righteous *j.*; **8:15** ye *j.* after the flesh; I *j.* no man. And yet if I *j.*, my *j.* is true: for I am not alone, but I and the Father that sent me. It is also written in your law, that the testimony of two men is true; **12:48** he that rejecteth me, and receiveth not my words, hath one that *j.* him: the word that I have spoken, the same shall *j.* him in the last day; **Acts 4:19** but Peter and John answered and said unto them, Whether it be right in the sight of God to hearken unto you more than unto God, *j.* ye; **Rom. 2:1-2** whosoever thou art that *j.*: for wherein thou *j.* another, thou condemnest thyself; for thou that *j.* doest the same things. But we are sure that the *j.* of God is according to truth against them which commit such things; **2:27** shall not uncircumcision which is by nature, if it fulfil the law, *j.* thee, who by the letter and circumcision dost transgress the law; **14:4** who art thou that *j.* another man's servant? to his own master he standeth or falleth. Yea, he shall be holden up: for God is able to make him stand; **14:10-13** why dost thou *j.* thy brother? or why dost thou set at nought thy brother? for we shall all stand before the *j.* seat of Christ; For it is written, As I live, saith the Lord, every knee shall bow to me, and every tongue shall confess to God. So then every one of us shall give account of himself to God. Let us not therefore *j.* one another any more: but *j.* this rather, that no man put a stumblingblock or an occasion to fall in his brother's way; **1 Cor. 2:15-16** he that is spiritual *j.* all things, yet he himself is *j.* of no man. For who hath known the mind of the Lord, that he may instruct him? But we have the mind of Christ; **4:3-5** it is a very small thing that I should be *j.* of you, or of man's *j.*: yea, I *j.* not mine own self. For I know nothing by myself; yet am I not hereby justified: but he that *j.* me is the Lord. Therefore *j.* nothing before the time, until the Lord come, who both will bring to light the hidden things of darkness, and will make manifest the counsels of the hearts: and then shall every man have praise of God; **6:2-5** do ye not know that the saints shall *j.* the world? and if the world shall be *j.* by you, are ye unworthy to *j.* the smallest matters? Know ye not that we shall *j.* angels? how much more things that pertain to this life? If then ye have *j.* of things pertaining to this life, set them to *j.* who are least esteemed in the church. I speak to your shame. Is it so, that there is not a wise man among you? no, not one that shall be able to *j.* between his brethren; **James 4:11-12** speak not evil one of another, brethren. He that speaketh evil of his brother, and *j.* his brother, speaketh evil of the law, and *j.* the law: but if thou *j.* the law, thou art not a doer of the law, but a *j.*. There is one lawgiver, who is able to save and to destroy: who art thou that *j.* another.

JUST, JUSTICE, JUSTIFICATION, JUSTIFY, JUSTLY (*see also* Atone, Equal, Law, Mercy, Punish)

Masters, give unto your servants that which is just and equal; knowing that ye also have a Master in heaven. Col. 4:1 (*see also* Servant)

O man, what is good; and what doth the LORD require of thee, but to do justly, and to love mercy, and to walk humbly with thy God? Micah 6:8 (*see also* Humble, Merciful)

I know your manifold transgressions and your mighty sins: they afflict the just, they take a bribe, and they turn aside the poor in the gate from their right. Amos 5:12 (*see also* Afflict)

The terrible one is brought to nought, and the scorner is consummed, and all that watch for iniquity are cut off: That make a man an offender for a word, and lay a snare for him that reproveth in the gate, and turn aside the just thing for a thing of nought. Isa. 29:20-21 (*see also* Offend, Word)

A false balance is abomination to the LORD: but a just weight is his delight. Prov. 11:1 (*see also* Balance, Weight)

He that justifieth the wicked, and he that condemneth the just, even they both are abomination to the LORD. Prov. 17:15 (*see also* Condemn, Wicked)

Prov. 17:15 he that *j.* the wicked, and he that condemneth the just, even they both are abomination to the LORD; **17:26** to punish the *j.* is not good, nor to strike princes for equity; **Isa. 59:4** none calleth for justice, nor any pleadeth for truth: they trust in vanity, and speak lies; they conceive mischief, and bring forth iniquity.

Be just. 2 Sam. 23:3

Gen. 6:9 Noah was a *j.* man and perfect in his generations, and Noah walked with God; **Lev. 19:36** *j.* balances, *j.* weights, a *j.* ephah, and a *j.* hin, shall ye have: I am the LORD your God; **Deut. 16:18** judges and officers shalt thou make thee in all thy gates, which the LORD thy God giveth thee, throughout thy tribes: and they shall judge the people with *j.* judgment; **16:20** that which is altogether *j.* shalt thou follow, that thou mayest live, and inherit the land which the LORD thy God giveth thee; **25:15** thou shalt have a perfect and *j.* weight, a perfect and *j.* measure shalt thou have: that thy days may be lengthened in the land which the LORD thy God giveth thee; **32:4** he is the Rock, his work is perfect: for all his ways are judgment: a God of truth and without iniquity, *j.* and right is he; **2 Sam. 23:3** he that ruleth over men must be *j.*, ruling in the fear of God; **Ps. 7:9** let the wickedness of the wicked come to an end; but establish the *j.*: for the righteous God trieth the hearts and reins; **94:15** judgment shall return unto righteousness: and all the upright in heart shall follow it; **119:121** I have done judgment and justice: leave me not to mine oppressors; **Prov. 3:33** the curse of the LORD is in the house of the wicked: but he blesseth the habitation of the *j.*; **4:18** the path of the *j.* is as the shining light, that shineth more and more unto the perfect day; **9:9** give instruction to a wise man, and he will be yet wiser: teach a *j.* man, and he will increase in learning; **10:7** the memory of the *j.* is blessed: but the name of the wicked shall rot; **10:20** the tongue of the *j.* is as choice silver: the heart of the wicked is little worth; **10:31** the mouth of the *j.* bringeth forth wisdom: but the froward tongue shall be cut out; **11:1** a false balance is abomination to the LORD: but a *j.* weight is his delight; **11:9** through knowledge shall the *j.* be delivered; **12:13** the wicked is snared by the transgression of his lips: but the *j.* shall come out of trouble; **12:21** there shall no evil happen to the *j.*: but the wicked shall be filled with mischief; **20:7** the *j.* man walketh in his integrity: his children are blessed after him; **21:15** it is joy to the *j.* to do judgment: but destruction shall be to the workers of iniquity; **29:10** the bloodthirsty hate the upright: but the *j.* seek his soul; **Eccl. 7:20** there is not a *j.* man upon earth, that doeth good, and sinneth not; **Isa. 26:7** the way of the *j.* is uprightness: thou, most upright, dost weigh the path of the *j.*; **56:1** keep ye judgment, and do justice: for my salvation is near to come, and my righteousness to be revealed; **Ezek. 18:5-9** if a man be *j.*, and do that which is lawful and right... he is *j.*, he shall surely live, saith the Lord GOD; **45:9** remove violence and spoil, and execute judgment and justice, take away your exactions from my people, saith the Lord GOD; **Micah 6:8** what doth the LORD require of thee, but to do *j.*, and to love mercy, and to walk humbly with thy God; **Haba 2:4** his soul which is lifted up is not upright in him: but the *j.* shall live by his faith.

Ye are witnesses, and God also, how holily and just and unblameably we behaved ourselves among you that believe. 1 Thes. 2:10 (*see also* Witness)

Matt. 1:19 then Joseph her husband, being a *j.* man, and not willing to make her a publick example, was minded to put her away privily; **27:19** he was set down on the judgment seat, his wife sent unto him, saying, Have thou nothing to do with that *j.* man: for I have suffered many things this day in a dream because of him; **27:24** he took water, and washed his hands before the multitude, saying, I am innocent of the blood of this *j.* person: see ye to it; **Acts 10:22** Cornelius the centurion, a *j.* man, and one that feareth God, and of good report among all the nation of the Jews, was warned from God by an holy angel to send for thee into his house, and to hear words of thee; **Gal. 3:11** no man is justified by the law in the sight of God, it is evident: for, The *j.* shall live by faith; **1 Thes. 2:10** ye are witnesses, and God also, how holily and *j.* and unblameably we behaved ourselves among you that believe.

KEEP (*see also* Obey, Observe, Retain)

If thou wilt enter into life, keep the command-ments. Matt. 19:17 (*see also* Commandment)

Keep the way of the Lord. Gen. 18:19 (*see also* Way)

Wait on the LORD, and keep his way and he shall exalt thee to inherit the land. Ps. 37:34 (*see also* Wait)

Thou hast commanded us to keep thy precepts diligently. Ps. 119:4 (*see also* Precepts)

I have refrained my feet from every evil way, that I might keep thy word. Ps. 119:101 (*see also* Evil, Word)

Keep the law. Prov. 28:4 (*see also* Law)

Keep thy solemn feasts, perform thy vows. Nahum 1:15 (*see also* Feast, Vow)

Only take heed to thyself, and keep thy soul diligently, lest thou forget the things which thine eyes have seen, and lest they depart from thine heart all the days of thy life: but teach them thy sons, and thy sons sons. Deut. 4:9 (*see also* Forget, Take, Testimony)

Ye have not kept my ways, but have been partial in the law. Mal. 2:9 (*see also* Law, Way)

Mal. 2:9 I [have] also made you contemptible and base before all the people, according as ye have not kept my ways, but have been partial in the law.

Thou hast avouched the LORD this day to be thy God, and to walk in his ways, and to keep his statutes, and his commandments, and his judgments, and to hearken unto his voice. Deut. 26:17 (*see also* Hearken, Way)

Deut. 8:6 thou shalt *k.* the commandments of the LORD thy God, to walk in his ways, and to fear him; **26:17-18** thou hast avouched the LORD this day to be thy God, and to walk in his ways, and to *k.* his statutes, and his commandments, and his judgments, and to hearken unto his voice; **27:10** thou shalt therefore obey the voice of the LORD thy God, and do his commandments and his statutes; **28:1** if thou shalt hearken diligently unto the voice of the LORD thy God, to observe and to do all his commandments which I command thee this day, that the LORD thy God will set thee on high; **28:9** the LORD shall establish thee an holy people unto himself, as he hath sworn unto thee, if thou shalt *k.* the commandments of the LORD thy God; **30:16** I command thee this day to love the LORD thy God, to walk in his ways, and to *k.* his commandments and his statutes and his judgments; **Judg. 2:19-20** the anger of the LORD was hot against Israel; and he said, Because that this people hath transgressed my covenant which I commanded their fathers, and have not hearkened unto my voice; **2:22** through them I may prove Israel, whether they will *k.* the way of the LORD to walk therein; **1 Sam. 2:25** they hearkened not unto the voice of their father, because the LORD would slay them; **1 Kgs. 2:3** *k.* the charge of the LORD thy God, to walk in his ways, to *k.* his statutes, and his commandments; **8:58** he may incline our hearts unto him, to walk in all his ways, and to *k.* his commandments, and his statutes, and his judgments, which he commanded our fathers; **2 Chron. 17:6** his heart was lifted up in the ways of the LORD: moreover he took away the high places and groves; **Ps. 81:13-16** oh that my people had hearkened unto me, and Israel had walked in my ways! I should soon have subdued their enemies, and turned my hand against their adversaries; **103:18** to such as *k.* his covenant, and to those that remember his commandments to do them; **119:3** they also do no iniquity: they walk in his ways; **119:10-11** with my whole heart have I sought thee: O let me not wander from thy commandments. Thy word have I hid in mine heart, that I might not sin against thee; **Prov. 1:33** whoso hearkeneth unto me shall dwell safely, and shall be quiet from fear of evil; **Isa. 42:24** they would not walk in his ways, neither were they obedient unto his law; **48:12** hearken unto me, O Jacob and Israel, my called; I am he; I am the first, I also am the last; **Jer. 26:4** thus saith the LORD; If ye will not hearken to me, to walk in my law, which I have set before you; **32:33** they have turned unto me the back, and not the face: though I taught them, rising up early and teaching them, yet they have not hearkened to receive instruction; **Ezek. 7:4** mine eye shall not spare thee, neither will I have pity: but I will recompense thy ways upon thee, and thine abominations shall be in the midst of thee: and ye shall know that I am the LORD; **Hosea 9:17** my God will cast them away, because they did not hearken unto him.

KEY, KEYS (*see also* Authority, Priesthood)

Woe unto you, lawyers! for ye have taken away the key of knowledge: ye entered not in yourselves, and them that were entering in ye hindered. Luke 11:52 (*see also* Hinder)

KILL (*see also* Blood, Death, Murder, Persecute, Smite)

Thou shalt not kill. Ex. 20:13 (*see also* Thou Shalt Not)

Gen. 4:8-15 what hast thou done? the voice of thy brothers blood crieth unto me from the ground. And now art thou cursed from the earth, which hath opened her mouth to receive thy brothers blood from thy hand; **9:6** whoso sheddeth mans blood, by man shall his blood be shed; **27:41-42** Esau hated Jacob because of the blessing wherewith his father blessed him: and Esau said in his heart, The days of mourning for my father are at hand; then will I slay my brother Jacob; **37:18-22** they conspired against him to slay him. And they said one to another, Behold, this dreamer cometh. Come now therefore, and let us slay him, and cast him into some pit; **Ex. 20:13** thou shalt not *k.*; **21:12-14** he that smiteth a man, so that he die, shall be surely put to death; **Lev. 24:17** he that *k.* any man shall surely be put to death; **24:21** he that *k.* a man, he shall be put to death; **Deut. 5:17** thou shalt not *k.*; **19:10** that innocent blood be not shed in thy land, which the LORD thy God giveth thee for an inheritance, and so blood be upon thee; **2 Sam. 21:4** neither for us shalt thou *k.* any man in Israel; **1 Chron. 22:8** thou shalt not build an house unto my name, because thou hast shed much blood upon the earth in my sight; **28:3** thou shalt not build an house for my name, because thou hast been a man of war, and hast shed blood; **Job 24:14** the murderer rising with the light *k.* the poor and needy, and in the night is as a thief; **Ps. 10:8** he sitteth in the lurking places of the villages: in the secret places doth he murder the innocent; **94:5-6** they slay the widow and the stranger, and murder the fatherless; **106:37-40** they sacrificed their sons and their daughters unto devils, And shed innocent blood... and the land was polluted with blood... Therefore was the wrath of the LORD kindled against his people; **Prov. 1:15-16** walk not thou in the way with them; refrain thy foot from their path: For their feet run to evil, and make haste to shed blood; **6:16-17** these six things doth the LORD hate: yea, seven are an abomination unto him: A proud look, a lying tongue, and hands that shed innocent blood; **Jer. 4:31** woe is me now! for my soul is wearied because of murderers; **7:6** oppress not the stranger, the fatherless, and the widow, and shed not innocent blood in this place; **22:3** do no wrong, do no violence to the stranger, the fatherless, nor the widow, neither shed innocent blood in this place;

Joel 3:19 [there] shall be a desolation... for the violence against the children of Judah, because they have shed innocent blood in their land; **Amos 1:11** I will not turn away the punishment thereof; because he did pursue his brother with the sword, and did cast off all pity, and his anger did tear perpetually, and he kept his wrath for ever; **1:13** I will not turn away the punishment thereof; because they have ripped up the women with child; **Matt. 5:21** ye have heard that it was said by them of old time, Thou shalt not *k.*; and whosoever shall *k.* shall be in danger of the judgment; **14:3-10** give me here John Baptist's head in a charger. And the king was sorry: nevertheless for the oath's sake, and them which sat with him at meat, he commanded it to be given her. And he sent, and beheaded John in the prison; **15:19-20** for out of the heart proceed evil thoughts, murders, adulteries, fornications, thefts, false witness, blasphemies: These are the things which defile a man; **19:18** thou shalt do no murder; **22:7** he sent forth his armies, and destroyed those murderers, and burned up their city; **Mark 10:19** (Luke 18:20, Rom. 13:9) do not *k.*; **10:34** they shall mock him, and shall scourge him, and shall spit upon him, and shall *k.* him.

KIND, KINDNESS (*see also* Compassion, Good, Mercy)

She openeth her mouth with wisdom; and in her tongue is the law of kindness. Prov. 31:26

Prov. 19:22 the desire of a man is his kindness; **31:26** she openeth her mouth with wisdom; and in her tongue is the law of *k.*

Be ye kind one to another, tenderhearted, forgiving one another, even as God for Christ's sake hath forgiven you. Eph. 4:32 (*see also* Forgive)

1 Cor 13:4 charity suffereth long, and is *k.*; charity envieth not; charity vaunteth not itself, is not puffed up; **2 Cor. 6:6** by pureness, by knowledge, by longsuffering, by *k.*, by the Holy Ghost, by love unfeigned; **Eph. 4:32** be ye *k.* one to another, tenderhearted, forgiving one another, even as God for Christ's sake hath forgiven you; **Col. 3:12** put on therefore, as the elect of God, holy and beloved, bowels of mercies, *k.*, humbleness of mind, meekness, longsuffering; **2 Pet 1:7** to godliness brotherly *k.*; and to brotherly kindness charity.

KING (*see also* Compassion, Good, Mercy)

The LORD is the true God, he is the living God, and an everlasting king: at his wrath the earth shall tremble, and the nations shall not be able to abide his indignation. Jer. 10:10 (*see also* God, True)

Let the children of Zion be joyful in their King. Ps. 149:2

Ps. 149:2-4 let Israel rejoice in him that made him: let the children of Zion be joyful in their *K.* Let them praise his name in the dance: let them sing praises unto him; **Isa. 40:9** O Zion, that bringest good tidings, get thee up into the high mountain; O Jerusalem, that bringest good tidings, lift up thy voice with strength; lift it up, be not afraid; say unto the cities of Judah, Behold your God.

Let Israel rejoice in him that made him: let the children of Zion be joyful in their King. Let them praise his name in the dance: let them sing praises unto him with the timbrel and harp. Ps. 149:2-3 (*see also* Rejoice)

Ps. 44:4 thou art my *K.*, O God: command deliverances for Jacob; **46:7** the LORD of hosts is with us; the God of Jacob is our refuge; **46:11** the LORD of hosts is with us; the God of Jacob is our refuge; **48:14** this God is our God for ever and ever: he will be our guide even unto death; **68:20** he that is our God is the God of salvation; and unto GOD the Lord belong the issues from death; **74:12** God is my *k.* of old, work. salvation in the midst of the earth; **89:18** the LORD is our defence; and the Holy One of Israel is our *k.*; **95:3** the LORD is a great God, and a great *k.* above all gods; **144:15** happy is that people, that is in such a case: yea, happy is that people, whose God is the LORD; **146:5** happy is he that hath the God of Jacob for his help, whose hope is in the LORD his God; **146:7** which executeth judgment for the oppressed: which giveth food to the hungry. The LORD looseth the prisoners; **149:2-4** let Israel rejoice in him that made him: let the children of Zion be joyful in their *k.*. Let them praise his name in the dance: let them sing praises unto him; **Zech. 8:8** I will bring them, and they shall dwell in the midst of Jerusalem: and they shall be my people, and I will be their God, in truth and in righteousness.

KINGDOM (*see also* Celestial, Church, Zion)

Blessed are the poor in spirit: for theirs is the kingdom of heaven. Matt 5:3 (*see also* Poor)

Blessed are they which are persecuted for righteousness' sake: for theirs is the kingdom of heaven. Matt. 5:10 (*see also* Persecute)

Except ye be converted, and become as little children, ye shall not enter into the kingdom of heaven. Matt. 18:3 (*see also* Child, Convert)

Another parable put he forth unto them, saying, The kingdom of heaven is like to a grain of mustard seed, which a man took, and sowed in his field. Matt. 13:31 (*see also* Grain, Sow)

Speak of the glory of thy kingdom, and talk of thy power; To make known to the sons of men his mighty acts, and the glorious majesty of his kingdom Ps. 145:11-12 (*see also* Testify)

Ye shut up the kingdom of heaven against men: for ye neither go in yourselves, neither suffer ye them that are entering to go in. Matt. 23:13 (*see also* Go)

Solomon determined to build an house for the name of the LORD, and an house for his kingdom. 2 Chron. 2:1 (*see also* House, Name)

Seek ye first the kingdom of God, and his righteousness; and all these things shall be added unto you. Matt. 6:33-34 (*see also* Seek)

Matt. 6:33-34 seek ye first the *k.* of God, and his righteousness; and all these things shall be added unto you. Take therefore no thought for the morrow: for the morrow shall take thought for the things of itself. Sufficient unto the day is the evil thereof; **13:31-32** (Mark 4:31-32) the *k.* of heaven is like to a grain of mustard seed, which a man took, and sowed in his field: Which indeed is the least of all seeds: but when it is grown, it is the greatest among herbs, and becometh a tree, so that the birds of the air come and lodge in the branches thereof; **13:33** the *k.* of heaven is like unto leaven, which a woman took, and hid in three measures of meal, till the whole was leavened; **13:44** the *k.* of heaven is like unto treasure hid in a field; the which when a man hath found, he hideth, and for joy thereof goeth and selleth all that he hath, and buyeth that field; **13:45-48** the *k.* of heaven is like unto a merchant man, seeking goodly pearls: Who, when he had found one pearl of great price, went and sold all that he had, and bought it. Again, the *k.* of heaven is like unto a net, that was cast into the sea, and gathered of every kind: Which, when it was full, they drew to shore, and sat down, and gathered the good into vessels, but cast the bad away; **20:1-14** the *k.* of heaven is like unto a man that is an householder, which went out early in the morning to hire labourers into his vineyard; **21:42-43** Jesus saith unto them, Did ye never read in the scriptures, The stone which the builders rejected, the same is become the head of the corner: this is the Lord's doing, and it is marvelous in our eyes? Therefore say I unto you, The *k.* of God shall be taken from you, and given to a nation bringing forth the fruits thereof; **22:2** the *k.* of heaven is like unto a certain king, which made a marriage for his son; **25:14** the *k.* of heaven is as a man travelling into a far country, who called his own servants, and delivered unto them his goods; **Mark 4:26** so is the *k.* of God, as if a man should cast seed into the ground; **9:1** (Luke 9:27) there be some of them that stand here, which shall not taste of death, till they have seen the *k.* of God come with power; **10:14** suffer the little children to come unto me, and forbid them not: for of such is the *k.* of God; **10:25** (18:25) it is easier for a camel to go through the eye of a needle, than for a rich man to enter into the *k.* of God; **12:32-34** thou art not far from the *k.* of God. And no man after that durst ask him any question; **14:25** I will drink no more of the fruit of the vine, until that day that I drink it new in the *k.* of God; **15:43** Joseph of Arimathaea, an honourable counsellor, which also waited for the *k.* of God, came, and went in boldly unto Pilate, and craved the body of Jesus; **Luke 1:33** he shall reign over the house of Jacob for ever; and of his *k.* there shall be no end; **8:1** he went throughout every city and village, preaching and shewing the glad tidings of the *k.* of God; **9:11** he received them, and spake unto them of the *k.* of God, and healed them that had need of healing; **9:59-62** let the dead bury their dead: but go thou and preach the *k.* of God. And another also said, Lord, I will follow thee; but let me first go bid them farewell, which are at home at my house. And Jesus said unto him, No man, having put his hand to the plough, and looking back, is fit for the *k.* of God; **11:9** ask, and it shall be given you; seek, and ye shall find; knock, and it shall be opened you; **10:11** even the very dust of your city, which cleaveth on us, we do wipe off against you: notwithstanding be ye sure of this, that the *k.* of God is come nigh unto you; **11:20** but if I with the finger of God cast out devils, no doubt the *k.* of

God is come upon you; **12:30-33** For all these things do the nations of the world seek after: and your Father knoweth that ye have need of these things. But rather seek ye the *k.* of God; and all these things shall be added unto you; **13:18-21** unto what is the *k.* of God like? and whereunto shall I resemble it? It is like a grain of mustard seed, which a man took, and cast into his garden; and it grew, and waxed a great tree; and the fowls of the air lodged in the branches of it. And again he said, Whereunto shall I liken the *k.* of God? It is like leaven, which a woman took and hid in three measures of meal, till the whole was leavened; **13:28-29** there shall be weeping and gnashing of teeth, when ye shall see Abraham, and Isaac, and Jacob, and all the prophets, in the *k.* of God, and you yourselves thrust out. And they shall come from the east, and from the west, and from the north, and from the south, and shall sit down in the *k.* of God; **14:15** blessed is he that shall eat bread in the *k.* of God; **16:16-17** the law and the prophets were until John: since that time the *k.* of God is tittle of the law to fail; **17:20-25** he was demanded of the Pharisees, when the *k.* of God should come, he answered them and said, The *k.* of God cometh not with observation: Neither preached, and every man presseth into it. And it is easier for heaven and earth to pass, than one shall they say, Lo here! or, lo there! for, behold, the *k.* of God is within you; **18:17** whosoever shall not receive the *k.* of God as a little child shall in no wise enter therein; **19:11** because they thought that the *k.* of God should immediately appear; **21:31** so likewise ye, when ye see these things come to pass, know ye that the *k.* of God is nigh at hand; **22:16** I say unto you, I will not any more eat thereof, until it be fulfilled in the *k.* of God; **22:28-30** ye are they which have continued with me in my temptations. And I appoint unto you a *k.*, as my Father hath appointed unto me; That ye may eat and drink at my table in my *k.*, and sit on thrones judging the twelve tribes of Israel; **23:42** Lord, remember me when thou comest into thy *k.*; **23:51** who also himself waited for the *k.* of God; **John 3:3** Jesus answered and said unto him, Verily, verily, I say unto thee, Except a man be born again, he cannot see the *k.* of God; **3:5-6** except a man be born of water and of the Spirit, he cannot enter into the *k.* of God; **Acts 1:3** he shewed himself alive after his passion by many infallible proofs, being seen of them forty days, and speaking of the things pertaining to the *k.* of God; **Rom. 14:15-18** the *k.* of God is not meat and drink; but righteousness, and peace, and joy in the Holy Ghost. For he that in these things serveth Christ is acceptable to

God, and approved of men; **15:24-25** then cometh the end, when he shall have delivered up the *k.* to God, even the Father; when he shall have put down all rule and all authority and power. For he must reign, till he hath put all enemies under his feet; **Philip. 2:20-21** I have no man likeminded, who will naturally care for your state. For all seek their own, not the things which are Jesus Christ's; **Heb. 11:13-16** but now they desire a better country, that is, an heavenly: wherefore God is not ashamed to be called their God: for he hath prepared for them a city; **James 4:8** draw nigh to God, and he will draw nigh to you. Cleanse your hands, ye sinners; and purify your hearts, ye double minded.

KISS (*see also* Greet, Love, Respect)

[She] stood at his feet behind him weeping, and began to wash his feet with tears, and did wipe them with the hairs of her head, and kissed his feet, and anointed them with the ointment. Luke 7:38 (*see also* Feet)

KNEE (*see also* Humble)

I have sworn by myself, the word is gone out of my mouth in righteousness, and shall not return, That unto me every knee shall bow, every tongue shall swear. Isa 45:23

For it is written, As I live, saith the Lord, every knee shall bow to me, and every tongue shall confess to God. Rom 14:11 (*see also* Confess)

KNEEL (*see also* Bow, Humble, Pray)

Come, let us worship and bow down: let us kneel before the LORD our maker. Ps. 95:6 (*see also* Bow, Worship)

KNOCK (*see also* Ask, Inquire, Pray)

Ask, and it shall be given you; seek, and ye shall find; knock, and it shall be opened unto you. Luke 11:9 (*see also* Ask, Seek)

KNOW, KNOWLEDGE, KNOWN (*see also* Discern, Inspire, Reveal, Testify, Wisdom, Witness)

Whoso loveth instruction loveth knowledge: but he that hateth reproof is brutish. Prov. 12:1 (*see also* Correct, Instruct)

Go from the presence of a foolish man, when thou preceivest not in him the lips of knowledge. **Prov. 14:7** (*see also* Fool)

Be still, and know that I am God. **Ps. 46:10**

Cease, my son, to hear the instruction that causeth to err from the words of knowledge. **Prov. 19:27** (*see also* Hear, Instruct)

I applied mine heart to know, and to search, and to seek out wisdom, and the reason of things, and to know the wickedness of folly, even of foolishness and madness. **Eccl. 7:25** (*see also* Apply, Heart, Reason, Seek, Wisdom)

Know the LORD: for they shall all know me, from the least of them unto the greatest of them, saith the LORD; for I will forgive their iniquity, and I will remember their sin no more. **Jer. 31:34**

LORD, thou hast searched me, and known me. Thou knowest my downsitting and mine uprising, thou understandest my thought afar off. Thou compassest my path and my lying down, and art acquainted with all my ways. For there is not a word in my tongue, but, lo, O LORD, thou knowest it altogether. **Ps. 139:1-5** (*see also* All Things)

According as his divine power hath given unto us all things that pertain unto life and godliness, through the knowledge of him that hath called us to glory and virtue: Whereby we are given unto us exceeding great and precious promises: that by these ye might be partakers of the divine nature, having escaped the corruption that is in the world through lust. **2 Pet. 1:3-4** (*see also* All Things, Divine Nature, Lust, Promise)

Bow down thine ear, and hear the words of the wise, and apply thine heart unto my knowledge. **Prov. 22:17** (*see also* Bow, Wise)

We speak the wisdom of God in a mystery, even the hidden wisdom, which God ordained before the world unto our glory. **1 Cor. 2:7** (*see also* Mysteries)

The priests lips should keep knowledge, and they should seek the law at his mouth: for he is the messenger of the LORD of hosts. **Mal. 2:7** (*see also* Messenger, Priest)

Know ye that the LORD he is God. **Ps. 100:3** (*see also* Lord)

Know the righteousness of the LORD. **Micah 6:5** (*see also* Righteous)

Micah 6:5 O my people, remember now what Balak king of Moab consulted, and what Balaam the son of Beor answered him from Shittim unto Gilgal; that ye may *k.* the righteousness of the LORD.

For precept must be upon precept, precept upon precept; line upon line, line upon line; here a little, and there a little: For with stammering lips and another tongue will he speak to this people. **Isa. 28:10** (*see also* Learn, Precept, Understand)

Isa. 28:10 for precept must be upon precept, precept upon precept; line upon line, line upon line; here a little, and there a little; **28:13** the word of the LORD was unto them precept upon precept, precept upon precept; line upon line, line upon line; here a little, and there a little.

Be it according to thy word: that thou mayest know that there is none like unto the LORD our God. **Ex. 8:10**

Ex. 8:10 be it according to thy word: that thou mayest *k.* that there is none like unto the LORD our God; **9:13-14** the LORD said unto Moses, Rise up early in the morning, and stand before Pharaoh, and say unto him, Thus saith the LORD God of the Hebrews, Let my people go, that they may serve me. For I will at this time send all my plagues upon thine heart, and upon thy servants, and upon thy people; that thou mayest *k.* that there is none like me in all the earth; **2 Chron. 13:10** as for us, the LORD is our God, and we have not forsaken him; **Ps. 90:2** before the mountains were brought forth, or ever thou hadst formed the earth and the world, even from everlasting to everlasting, thou art God; **94:14** the LORD will not cast off his people, neither will he forsake his inheritance; **Isa. 46:9** remember the former things of old: for I am God, and there is none else; I am God, and there is none like me.

I will behold thy face in righteousness: I shall be satisfied, when I awake, with thy likeness. **Ps. 17:15** (*see also* Likeness)

Ps. 16:11 thou wilt shew me the path of life: in thy presence is fulness of joy; at thy right hand there are pleasures for evermore; **17:15** I will

behold thy face in righteousness: I shall
be satisfied, when I awake, with thy likeness;
24:6 this is the generation of them that seek him,
that seek thy face, O Jacob; **27:8-9** seek ye my
face; my heart said unto thee, Thy face, LORD,
will I seek. Hide not thy face far from me; put
not thy servant away in anger: thou hast been my
help; leave me not, neither forsake me, O God of
my salvation; **27:11** teach me thy way, O LORD,
and lead me in a plain path, because of mine
enemies; **69:32** the humble shall see this, and be
glad: and your heart shall live that seek God;
76:1 in Judah is God known: his name is great in
Israel; **105:3-4** glory ye in his holy name: let the
heart of them rejoice that seek the LORD. Seek
the LORD, and his strength: seek his face
evermore; **119:10-11** with my whole heart have I
sought thee: O let me not wander from thy
commandments. Thy word have I hid in mine
heart, that I might not sin against thee; **Jer. 9:6**
thine habitation is in the midst of deceit; through
deceit they refuse to *k.* me, saith the LORD let
him that glorieth glory in this, that he
understandeth and *k.* me, that I am the LORD
which exercise lovingkindness, judgment, and
righteousness, in the earth: for in these things I
delight.

**I have filled him with the spirit of God, in
wisdom, in understanding, and in knowledge,
and in all manner of workmanship. Ex. 31:3**
(*see also* Understand, Wisdom)

Ex. 31:3-5 I have filled him with the spirit of
God, in wisdom, and in understanding, and in *k.*,
and in all manner of workmanship; **35:31** he hath
filled him with the spirit of God, in wisdom, in
understanding, and in *k.*, and in all manner of
workmanship; **35:35** them hath he filled with
wisdom of heart, to work all manner of work;
36:1 then wrought... every wise hearted man, in
whom the LORD put wisdom and understanding
to *k.* how to work all manner of work for the
service of the sanctuary, according to all that the
LORD had commanded; **1 Sam. 2:3** talk no more
so exceeding proudly; let not arrogancy come out
of your mouth: for the LORD is a God of *k.*, and
by him actions are weighed; **1 Kgs. 3:9** give
therefore thy servant an understanding heart to
judge thy people, that I may discern between
good and bad; **3:12** I have given thee a wise and
an understanding heart; so that there was none
like thee before thee, neither after thee shall any
arise like unto thee; **4:29** God gave Solomon
wisdom and understanding exceeding much, and
largeness of heart; **5:7** blessed be the LORD this
day, which hath given unto David a wise son

over this great people; **10:7-8** happy are thy men,
happy are these thy servants, which stand
continually before thee, and that hear thy
wisdom; **10:24** all the earth sought to Solomon,
to hear his wisdom, which God had put in his
heart; **1 Chron. 22:12** only the LORD give thee
wisdom and understanding, and give thee
charge... that thou mayest keep the law of the
LORD thy God; **2 Chron. 1:11-12** wisdom and *k.*
is granted unto thee; and I will give thee riches,
and wealth, and honour; **2:12** blessed be the
LORD God of Israel, that made heaven and earth,
who hath given to David the king a wise son,
endued with prudence and understanding; **9:1-7**
when she was come to Solomon, she communed
with him of all that was in her heart. And
Solomon told her all her questions: and there was
nothing hid from Solomon which he told her not.
And... [she] had seen the wisdom of Solomon;
9:22-23 king Solomon passed all the kings of the
earth in riches and wisdom. And all the kings of
the earth sought the presence of Solomon, to hear
his wisdom, that God had put in his heart; **26:5**
as long as he sought the LORD, God made him to
prosper; **Neh. 8:12-13** all the people went their
way to eat, and to drink, and to send portions,
and to make great mirth, because they had
understood the words that were declared unto
them; **Job 12:12-13** with the ancient is wisdom;
and in length of days understanding. With him is
wisdom and strength, he hath counsel and
understanding; **28:12-28** the fear of the Lord,
that is wisdom; and to depart from evil is
understanding; **32:8-9** there is a spirit in man:
and the inspiration of the Almighty giveth them
understanding. Great men are not always wise:
neither do the aged understand judgment; **33:3**
my words shall be of the uprightness of my
heart: and my lips shall utter *k.* clearly; **34:33**
should it be according to thy mind? he will
recompense it, whether thou refuse, or whether
thou choose; and not I: therefore speak what thou
k.; **35:11** who teacheth us more than the beasts of
the earth, and maketh us wiser than the fowls of
heaven; **36:2-5** I will shew thee that I have yet to
speak on Gods behalf. I will fetch my *k.* from
afar, and will ascribe righteousness to my Maker.
For truly my words shall not be false: he that is
perfect in *k.* is with thee; **Ps. 32:8-9** I will
instruct thee and teach thee in the way which
thou shalt go: I will guide thee with mine eye;
49:3 my mouth shall speak of wisdom; and the
meditation of my heart shall be of understanding;
49:20 man that is in honour, and understandeth
not, is like the beasts that perish; **51:6** thou
desirest truth in the inward parts: and in the
hidden part thou shalt make me to *k.* wisdom;

107:43 whoso is wise, and will observe these things, even they shall understand the lovingkindness of the LORD; **111:10** the fear of the LORD is the beginning of wisdom: a good understanding have all they that do his commandments; **119:25-27** teach me thy statutes. Make me to understand the way of thy precepts: so shall I talk of thy wondrous works; **119:29** remove from me the way of lying: and grant me thy law graciously; **119:34** give me understanding, and I shall keep thy law; yea, I shall observe it with my whole heart; **119:104** through thy precepts I get understanding: therefore I hate every false way; **119:108** accept, I beseech thee, the freewill offerings of my mouth, O LORD, and teach me thy judgments; **119:125** I am thy servant; give me understanding, that I may *k.* thy testimonies; **119:130** the entrance of thy words giveth light; it giveth understanding unto the simple; **119:144** the righteousness of thy testimonies is everlasting: give me understanding, and I shall live; **119:169** let my cry come near before thee, O LORD: give me understanding according to thy word; **Prov. 1:1-5** a wise man will hear, and will increase learning; and a man of understanding shall attain unto wise counsels; **2:2-5** incline thine ear unto wisdom, and apply thine heart to understanding; Yea, if thou criest after *k.*, and liftest up thy voice for understanding... Then shalt thou understand the fear of the LORD, and find the *k.* of God; **2:10-12** when wisdom entereth into thine heart, and *k.* is pleasant unto thy soul; Discretion shall preserve thee, understanding shall keep thee; **3:13-18** happy is the man that findeth wisdom, and the man that getteth understanding; **3:35** the wise shall inherit glory: but shame shall be the promotion of fools; **4:1** hear, ye children, the instruction of a father, and attend to *k.* understanding; **4:5-10** get wisdom, get understanding: forget it not; neither decline from the words of my mouth; **8:11-12** wisdom is better than rubies; and all the things that may be desired are not to be compared to it; **9:2-4** whoso is simple, let him turn in hither; **9:8-12** rebuke a wise man, and he will love thee. Give instruction to a wise man, and he will be yet wiser: teach a just man, and he will increase in learning; **10:13** in the lips of him that hath understanding wisdom is found: but a rod is for the back of him that is void of understanding; **10:23** it is as sport to a fool to do mischief: but a man of understanding hath wisdom; **12:8** a man shall be commended according to his wisdom: but he that is of a perverse heart shall be despised; **13:10** by pride cometh contention: but with the well advised is wisdom; **13:14-15** the

law of the wise is a fountain of life, to depart from the snares of death; **14:3** in the mouth of the foolish is a rod of pride: but the lips of the wise shall preserve them; **14:6** a scorner seeketh wisdom, and findeth it not: but *k.* is easy unto him that understandeth; **14:33** wisdom resteth in the heart of him that hath understanding: but that which is in the midst of fools is made *k.*; **15:2** the tongue of the wise useth *k.* aright: but the mouth of fools poureth out foolishness; **15:7** the lips of the wise disperse *k.*: but the heart of the foolish doeth not so; **15:20** a wise son maketh a glad father: but a foolish man despiseth his mother; **15:24-25** the way of life is above to the wise, that he may depart from hell beneath; **16:16** how much better is it to get wisdom than gold! and to get understanding rather to be chosen than silver; **16:22** understanding is a wellspring of life unto him that hath it: but the instruction of fools is folly; **17:18** a man void of understanding striketh hands, and becometh surety in the presence of his friend; **17:24** wisdom is before him that hath understanding; but the eyes of a fool are in the ends of the earth; **18:1** through desire a man, having separated himself, seeketh and intermeddleth with all wisdom; **18:4** the words of a mans mouth are as deep waters, and the wellspring of wisdom as a flowing brook; **18:15** the heart of the prudent getteth *k.*; and the ear of the wise seeketh *k.*; **19:2** that the soul be without *k.*, it is not good; and he that hasteth with his feet sinneth; **19:8** he that getteth wisdom loveth his own soul: he that keepeth understanding shall find good; **19:25** smite a scorner, and the simple will beware: and reprove one that hath understanding, and he will understand *k.*; **20:5** counsel in the heart of man is like deep water; but a man of understanding will draw it out; **20:15** the lips of *k.* are a precious jewel; **21:11-12** when the scorner is punished, the simple is made wise: and when the wise is instructed, he receiveth *k.*; **21:20** there is treasure to be desired and oil in the dwelling of the wise; but a foolish man spendeth it up; **21:22** a wise man scaleth the city of the mighty, and casteth down the strength of the confidence thereof; **21:30** there is no wisdom nor understanding nor counsel against the LORD; **23:15** if thine heart be wise, my heart shall rejoice, even mine; **23:19** be wise, and guide thine heart in the way; **23:23** buy the truth, and sell it not; also wisdom, and instruction, and understanding; **24:5** a wise man is strong; yea, a man of *k.* increaseth strength; **24:13-14** the *k.* of wisdom [shall be sweet] unto thy soul: when thou hast found it, then there shall be a reward; **27:11** be wise, and make my heart glad, that I may answer him that reproacheth me; **28:2** by a man of understanding and *k.* the state thereof shall be prolonged; **29:8** scornful men bring a city into a snare: but wise men turn away wrath; **Eccl. 1:13** I gave my heart to seek and search out by wisdom concerning all things that are done under heaven; **1:16-18** my heart had great experience of wisdom and *k..* And I gave my heart to *k.* wisdom, and to *k.* madness and folly; **2:3** I sought in mine heart to give myself unto wine, yet acquainting mine heart with wisdom; and to lay hold on folly; **2:12-13** I saw that wisdom excelleth folly, as far as light excelleth darkness; **2:26** God giveth to a man that is good in his sight wisdom, and *k.*, and joy: but to the sinner he giveth travail; **4:13** better is a poor and a wise child than an old and foolish king, who will no more be admonished; **6:8** what hath the wise more than the fool? what hath the poor, that *k.* to walk before the living; **7:11-12** wisdom is a defence, and money is a defence: but the excellency of *k.* is, that wisdom giveth life to them that have it; **7:19** wisdom strengtheneth the wise more than ten mighty men which are in the city; **7:23-24** all this have I proved by wisdom: I said, I will be wise; but it was far from me; **8:1** who is as the wise man? and who *k.* the interpretation of a thing? a mans wisdom maketh his face to shine; **8:16** I applied mine heart to *k.* wisdom, and to see the business that is done upon the earth; **9:16-18** wisdom is better than strength: nevertheless the poor mans wisdom is despised, and his words are not heard. The words of wise men are heard in quiet more than the cry of him that ruleth among fools; **10:1-2** so doth a little folly him that is in reputation for wisdom and honour. A wise mans heart is at his right hand; but a fools heart at his left; **10:10** if the iron be blunt, and he do not whet the edge, then must he put to more strength: but wisdom is profitable to direct; **10:12** the words of a wise mans mouth are gracious; but the lips of a fool will swallow up himself; **12:9** because the preacher was wise, he still taught the people *k.*; yea, he gave good heed, and sought out, and set in order many proverbs; **Isa. 5:13** my people are gone into captivity, because they have no *k.*; **27:11** it is a people of no understanding: therefore he that made them will not have mercy on them, and he that formed them will shew them no favour; **28:9-10** whom shall he teach *k.*? and whom shall he make to understand doctrine? them that are weaned from the milk... For precept must be upon precept, precept upon precept; line upon line, line upon line; here a little, and there a little; **32:4** the heart also of the rash shall understand *k.*, and the tongue of the stammerers shall be ready to speak plainly; **33:6**

wisdom and *k.* shall be the stability of thy times, and strength of salvation; **Jer. 3:15** I will give you pastors according to mine heart, which shall feed you with *k.* and understanding; **3:22** return, ye backsliding children, and I will heal your backslidings. Behold, we come unto thee; for thou art the LORD our God; **Dan. 2:21** he giveth wisdom unto the wise, and *k.* to them that *k.* understanding; **12:4** many shall run to and fro, and *k.* shall be increased; **12:10** none of the wicked shall understand; but the wise shall understand; **Hosea 4:14** the people that doth not understand shall fall; **6:6** I desired mercy, and not sacrifice; and the *k.* of God more than burnt offerings.

Who is this that darkeneth counsel by words without knowledge? Job 38:2 (*see also* Word)

Job 35:16 Job [doth] open his mouth in vain; he multiplieth words without *k.*; **38:1-2** the LORD answered Job out of the whirlwind, and said, Who is this that darkeneth counsel by words without *k.*; **42:3** who is he that hideth counsel without *k.*? therefore have I uttered that I understood not; things too wonderful for me, which I *k.* not.

If ye know these things, happy are ye if ye do them. John 13:17 (*see also* Happiness)

John 4:42 we believe, not because of thy saying: for we have heard him ourselves, and *k.* that this is indeed the Christ, the Saviour of the world; **8:55** ye have not *k.* him; but I *k.* him: and if I should say, I *k.* him not, I shall be a liar like unto you: but I *k.* him, and keep his saying; **13:17** if ye *k.* these things, happy are ye if ye do them.

Walk worthy of the Lord unto all pleasing, being fruitful in every good work, and increasing in the knowledge of God. Col. 1:10 (*see also* Walk, Worthy)

Rom. 10:2 I bear them record that they have a zeal of God, but not according to *k.*; **11:34** who hath *k.* the mind of the Lord? or who hath been his counsellor; **15:14** ye also are full of goodness, filled with all *k.*, able also to admonish one another; **1 Cor. 1:5** in every thing ye are enriched by him, in all utterance, and in all *k.*; **8:2** if any man think that he *k.* any thing, he *k.* nothing yet as he ought to *k.*; **10:1** I would not that ye should be ignorant, how that all our fathers were under the cloud, and all passed through the sea; **Eph. 3:19-20** unto him that is able to do exceeding abundantly above all that we ask or think, according to the power that worketh in us; **Philip. 1:9** I pray, that your love may abound yet more and more in *k.* and in all judgment; **3:8** I count all things but loss for the excellency of the *k.* of Christ Jesus my Lord: for whom I have suffered the loss of all things, and do count them but dung, that I may win Christ; **3:10** that I may *k.* him, and the power of his resurrection, and the fellowship of his sufferings, being made conformable unto his death; **Col. 1:10** walk worthy of the Lord unto all pleasing, being fruitful in every good work, and increasing in the *k.* of God; **2:3** in whom are hid all the treasures of wisdom and *k.*; **3:10** put on the new man, which is renewed in *k.* after the image of him that created him.

Incline thine ear unto wisdom, and apply thine heart to understanding. Prov. 2:2 (*see also* Understand)

Prov. 2:2 incline thine ear unto wisdom, and apply thine heart to understanding; **2:5** then shalt thou understand the fear of the LORD, and find the knowledge of God; **7:4** say unto wisdom, Thou art my sister; and call understanding thy kinswoman; **8:9-10** they are all plain to him that understandeth, and right to them that find *k.*. Receive my instruction, and not silver; and *k.* rather than choice gold; **8:12** I wisdom dwell with prudence, and find out *k.* of witty inventions; **8:17-21** I love them that love me; and those that seek me early shall find me; **8:35** whoso findeth me findeth life, and shall obtain favour of the LORD; **14:6** a scorner seeketh wisdom, and findeth it not: but *k.* is easy unto him that understandeth; **15:14** the heart of him that hath understanding seeketh *k.*: but the mouth of fools feedeth on foolishness; **19:23** the fear of the LORD tendeth to life: and he that hath it shall abide satisfied; he shall not be visited with evil; **25:2** it is the glory of God to conceal a thing: but the honour of kings is to search out a matter; **28:11** the rich man is wise in his own conceit; but the poor that hath understanding searcheth him out; **Isa.** should not a people seek unto their God? for the living to the dead; **11:2-3** the spirit of the LORD shall rest upon him, the spirit of wisdom and understanding, the spirit of counsel and might, the spirit of *k.* and of the fear of the LORD; **11:9** they shall not hurt nor destroy in all my holy mountain: for the earth shall be full of the *k.* of the LORD; **31:1** woe to them that go down to Egypt for help; and stay on horses, and trust in chariots... but they look not unto the Holy One of Israel, neither seek the LORD; **43:10** ye may *k.* and believe me, and understand that I am

he: before me there was no God formed, neither shall there be after me; **Jer. 22:16** he judged the cause of the poor and needy; then it was well with him: was not this to *k.* me? saith the LORD; **24:7** I will give them an heart to *k.* me, that I am the LORD: and they shall be my people, and I will be their God; **Hosea 4:1-6** hear the word of the LORD, ye children of Israel: for the LORD hath a controversy with the inhabitants of the land, because there is no truth, nor mercy, nor *k.* of God in the land; **Zeph. 1:6** them that are turned back from the LORD; and those that have not sought the LORD, nor enquired for him.

LABOR, LABORED, LABORING (*see also* Calling, Industrious, Wage, Work)

He that tilleth his land shall have plenty of bread: but he that followeth after vain persons shall have poverty enough. Prov. 28:19 (*see also* Vain)

Labour not to be rich: cease from thin own wisdom. Prov. 23:4 (*see also* Rich, Wisdom)

Come unto me, all ye that labour and are heavy laden, and I will give you rest. Take my yoke upon you, and learn of me; for I am meek and lowly in heart: and ye shall find rest unto your souls. For my yoke is easy, and my burden is light. Matt. 11:28-30 (*see also* Come, Rest, Yoke)

Remember the sabbath day, to keep it holy. Six days shalt thou labour, and do all thy work: But the seventh day is the sabbath of the LORD thy God: in it thou shalt not do any work, thou, nor thy son, nor thy daughter, thy manservant, nor thy maidservant, nor thy cattle, nor thy stranger that is within thy gates: For in six days the LORD made heaven and earth, the sea, and all that in them is, and rested the seventh day: wherefore the LORD blessed the sabbath day, and hallowed it. Ex. 20:8-11 (*see also* Sabbath, Thou Shalt, Work)

What profit hath he that hath laboured for the wind? Eccl. 5:16-20 (*see also* Worth)

The labour of the righteous tendeth to life: the fruit of the wicked to sin. Prov. 10:16 (*see also* Righteous)

Prov. 10:16 the *l.* of the righteous tendeth to life: the fruit of the wicked to sin; **14:23** in all *l.* there is profit: but the talk of the lips tendeth only to penury.

I have laboured in vain, I have spent my strength for nought, and in vain: yet surely my judgment is with the LORD, and my work with my God. Isa. 49:4 (*see also* Worth)

Isa. 49:4 I have *l.* in vain, I have spent my strength for nought, and in vain: yet surely my judgment is with the LORD, and my work with my God; **55:2** wherefore do ye spend money for that which is not bread? and your *l.* for that which satisfieth not? hearken diligently unto me, and eat ye that which is good; **Jer. 2:8** the priests said not, Where is the LORD? and they that handle the law knew me not: the pastors also transgressed against me, and the prophets prophesied by Baal, and walked after things that do not profit.

Every man should eat and drink, and enjoy the good of all his labor, it is the gift of God. Eccl. 3:13 (*see also* Gift)

Eccl. 2:24 there is nothing better for a man, than that he should eat and drink, and that he should make his soul enjoy good in his *l.*; **3:13** every man should eat and drink, and enjoy the good of all his *l.*, it is the gift of God; **5:20** he shall not much remember the days of his life; because God answereth him in the joy of his heart; **9:7** go thy way, eat thy bread with joy, and drink thy wine with a merry heart; for God now accepteth thy works.

Labour not for the meat which perisheth, but for that meat which endureth unto everlasting life. John 6:27 (*see also* Everlasting Life)

John 6:27 *l.* not for the meat which perisheth, but for that meat which endureth unto everlasting life, which the Son of man shall give unto you: for him hath God the Father sealed; **1 Cor. 15:10** by the grace of God I am what I am: and his grace which was bestowed upon me was not in vain; but I *l.* more abundantly than they all: yet not I, but the grace of God which was with me; **1 Tim. 6:7** for we brought nothing into this world, and it is certain we can carry nothing out; **Rev. 2:3** hast borne, and hast patience, and for my name's sake hast *l.*, and hast not fainted.

LACK

Then Jesus beholding him loved him, and said unto him, One thing thou lackest: go thy way, sell whatsoever thou hast, and give to the poor, and thou shalt have treasure in heaven: and come, take up the cross, and follow me. Mark 10:21 (*see also* Follow, Treasure, Luke 18:22)

If any of you lack wisdom, let him ask of God, that giveth to all men liberally, and upbraideth not; and it shall be given him. But let him ask in faith, nothing wavering. For he that wavereth is like a wave of the sea driven with the wind and tossed. James 1:5-6 (*see also* Ask, Waver, Wisdom, JSH 1:11)

LASCIVIOUS, LASCIVIOUSNESS (*see also* Carnal, Fallen, Lust, Wicked)

That which cometh out of the man, that defileth the man. For from within, out of the heart of men, proceed evil thoughts, adulteries, fornications, murders, Thefts, covetousness, wickedness, deceit, lasciviousness, an evil eye, blasphemy, pride, foolishness: All these evil things come from within, and defile the man. Mark 7:20-23 (*see also* Defile, Evil, Things)

Who being past feeling have given themselves over unto lasciviousness, to work all uncleanness with greediness? Eph. 4:19 (*see also* Unclean)

LANDMARK

Remove not the ancient landmark, which thy fathers have set. Prov. 22:28

Prov. 22:28 remove not the ancient *l.*, which thy fathers have set; **23:10-11** remove not the old *l.*; and enter not into the fields of the fatherless: For their redeemer is mighty; he shall plead their cause with thee.

LAST DAYS (*see also* End, Second Coming)

This know also, that in the last days perilous times shall come. 2 Tim. 3:1 (*see also* Perilous)

Now the Spirit speaketh expressly, that in the latter times some shall depart from the faith, giving heed to seducing spirits, and doctrines of devils; Speaking lies in hypocrisy; having their conscience seared with a hot iron; Forbidding to marry, and commanding to abstain from meats, which God hath created to be received with thanksgiving of them which believe and know the truth. 1 Tim. 4:1-3 (*see also* Abstain, Conscience, Food, Marriage, Meat, Thanksgiving)

LAUGH, LAUGHTER (*see also* Happiness, Joy, Scorn, Sing)

LAW, LAWFUL, LAWFULLY (*see also* Accountable, Commandment, Covenant, Decree, Statute)

Whoso keepeth the law is a wise son: but he that is a companion of riotous men shameth his father. **Prov. 28:7** (*see also* Riotous)

But we know that the law is good, if a man use it lawfully. **1 Tim 1:8** (*see also* Use)

Where there is no vision, the people perish: but he that keepeth the law, happy is he. **Prov. 29:18** (*see also* Vision, Perish)

Understand the words of the law. **Neh. 8:13** (*see also* Word)

Come, and let us go up to the mountain of the LORD, and to the house of the God of Jacob; and he will teach us of his ways, and we will walk in his paths; for the law shall go forth of Zion, and the word of the LORD from Jerusalem. **Micah 4:2** (*see also* House, Jerusalem, Mountain, Ways, Word, Zion)

We know that the law is good, if a man use it lawfully. **1 Tim. 1:8**

Put them in mind to be subject to principalities and powers, to obey magistrates, to be ready to every good work. **Titus 3:1** (*see also* Obey)

His delight is in the law of the LORD; and in his law doth he mediate day and night. **Ps. 1:2** (*see also* Meditate)

Hear the instruction of thy father, and forsake not the law of thy mother. **Prov. 1:8** (*see also* Instruct)

Bind up the testimony, seal the law among my disciples. **Isa. 8:16** (*see also* Testify)

He that turneth away his ear from hearing the law, even his prayer shall be abomination. **Prov. 28:9** (*see also* Pray)

Ye have not kept my ways, but have been partial in the law. **Mal. 2:9** (*see also* Keep, Way)

Woe unto you, scribes and Pharisees, hypocrites! for ye pay tithe of mint and anise and cummin, and have omitted the weightier matters of the law, judgment, mercy, and faith: these ought ye to have done, and not to leave the other undone. **Matt. 23:23** (*see also* Hypocrite, Worth)

I delight to do thy will, O my God: yea, thy law is within my heart. **Ps. 40:8** (*see also* Delight)

Ps. 37:31 the *l.* of his God is in his heart; none of his steps shall slide; **40:8** I delight to do thy will, O my God: yea, thy *l.* is within my heart; **Isa. 51:7** hearken unto me, ye that know righteousness, the people in whose heart is my *l.*; fear ye not the reproach of men.

Ye shall have one manner of law, as well for the stranger, as for one of your own country: for I am the LORD your God. **Lev. 24:22** (*see also* Stranger)

Lev. 24:22 ye shall have one manner of *l.*, as well for the stranger, as for one of your own country: for I am the LORD your God; **Isa. 24:5** the earth also is defiled under the inhabitants thereof; because they have transgressed the *l.*, changed the ordinance, broken the everlasting covenant.

Give me understanding, and I shall keep thy law; yea, I shall observe it with my whole heart. **Ps. 119:34** (*see also* Understand)

Ps. 119:34-35 give me understanding, and I shall keep thy *l.*; yea, I shall observe it with my whole heart; **119:70** I delight in thy *l.*; **119:174** I have longed for thy salvation, O LORD; and thy *l.* is my delight.

As the fire devoureth the stubble, and the flame consumeth the chaff, so their root shall be as rottenness, and their blossom shall go up as dust: because they have cast away the law of the LORD of hosts, and despised the word of the Holy One of Israel. Isa. 5:24 (*see also* Word)

Isa. 5:24 as the fire devoureth the stubble, and the flame consumeth the chaff, so their root shall be as rottenness, and their blossom shall go up as dust: because they have cast away the *l.* of the LORD of hosts.

Keep the law. Prov. 28:4 (*see also* Keep)

Prov. 28:4 they that forsake the law praise the wicked: but such as keep the *l.* contend with them; **28:7** whoso keepeth the *l.* is a wise son: but he that is a companion of riotous men shameth his father; **Isa. 42:24** who gave Jacob for a spoil, and Israel to the robbers? did not the LORD, he against whom we have sinned? for they would not walk in his ways, neither were they obedient unto his *l.*

He hath done that which is lawful and right; he shall surely live. Ezek. 33:16 (*see also* Right)

Ezek. 33:16 none of his sins that he hath committed shall be mentioned unto him: he hath done that which is *l.* and right; he shall surely live; **Dan. 2:11** it is a rare thing that the king requireth, and there is none other that can shew it before the king, except the gods, whose dwelling is not with flesh.

[Obey] the voice of the LORD our God, to walk in his laws, which he set before us by his servants the prophets. Dan. 9:10 (*see also* Prophet, Voice)

Dan. 9:10-11 neither have we obeyed the voice of the LORD our God, to walk in his *l.*, which he set before us by his servants the prophets.

Give ear unto the law of our God. Isa. 1:10

2 Chron. 12:1 when Rehoboam had established the kingdom, and had strengthened himself, he forsook the *l.* of the LORD, and all Israel with him; **12:5** thus saith the LORD, Ye have forsaken me, and therefore have I also left you in the hand of Shishak; **13:11** we keep the charge of the LORD our God; but ye have forsaken him; **15:2** the LORD is with you, while ye be with him; and

if ye seek him, he will be found of you; but if ye forsake him, he will forsake you; **24:24** the army of the Syrians came with a small company of men, and the LORD delivered a very great host into their hand, because they had forsaken the LORD God of their fathers; **Neh. 10:34** we cast the lots among the priests, the Levites, and the people, for the wood offering, to bring it into the house of our God... to burn upon the altar of the LORD our God, as it is written in the *l.*; **10:39** we will not forsake the house of our God; **Ps. 119:87** they had almost consumed me upon earth; but I forsook not thy precepts; **Prov. 4:2** I give you good doctrine, forsake ye not my *l.*; **15:10** correction is grievous unto him that forsaketh the way: and he that hateth reproof shall die; **29:18** where there is no vision, the people perish: but he that keepeth the *l.*, happy is he; **Isa. 1:10** hear the word of the LORD, ye rulers of Sodom; give ear unto the *l.* of our God, ye people of Gomorrah; **Jer. 2:13** my people have committed two evils; they have forsaken me the fountain of living waters, and hewed them out cisterns, broken cisterns, that can hold no water; **5:19** then shalt thou answer them, Like as ye have forsaken me, and served strange gods in your land, so shall ye serve strangers in a land that is not yours; **9:13** the LORD saith... they have forsaken my *l.* which I set before them, and have not obeyed my voice, neither walked therein; **16:11** your fathers have forsaken me, saith the LORD, and have walked after other gods, and have served them, and have worshipped them, and have forsaken me, and have not kept my *l.*; **16:13** I [will] cast you out of this land into a land that ye know not, neither ye nor your fathers; and there shall ye serve other gods day and night; where I will not shew you favour; **31:33** after those days, saith the LORD, I will put my *l.* in their inward parts, and write it in their hearts; and will be their God, and they shall be my people; **44:10-11** they are not humbled even unto this day, neither have they feared, nor walked in my *l.*, nor in my statutes, that I set before you and before your fathers. Therefore thus saith the LORD of hosts, the God of Israel; Behold, I will set my face against you for evil; **44:23** because ye have sinned against the LORD, and have not obeyed the voice of the LORD, nor walked in his *l.*, nor in his statutes, nor in his testimonies; therefore this evil is happened unto you; **Hosea 8:1** he shall come as an eagle against the house of the LORD, because they have transgressed my covenant, and trespassed against my *l.*

LAY ASIDE

Seeing we also are compassed about with so great a cloud of witnesses, let us lay aside every weight, and the sin which doth so easily beset us, and let us run with patience the race that is set before us. Heb. 12:1 (see also Beset, Patience, Race, Run, Sin, Weight, Witness)

LAYING ON OF HANDS (see also Authority, Bless, Heal, Holy Ghost, Miracle, Priesthood)

[Peter and John] then laid they their hands on them, and they received the Holy Ghost. Acts 8:17 (see also Holy Ghost)

Therefore leaving the principles of the doctrine of Christ, let us go on unto perfection; not laying again the foundation of repentance from dead works, and of faith toward God, Of the doctrine of baptisms, and of laying on of hands, and of resurrection of the dead, and of eternal judgment. Heb. 6:1-2 (see also Authority, Call, Go, Principle)

All they that had any sick with divers diseases brought them unto him; and he laid his hands on every one of them, and healed them. Luke 4:40 (see also Heal)

Mark 10:13 they brought young children to him, that he should touch them; 10:16 he took them up in his arms, put his hands upon them, and blessed them; 16:18 they shall take up serpents; and if they drink any deadly thing, it shall not hurt them: they shall lay hands on the sick, and they shall recover; Luke 4:40 all they that had any sick with divers diseases brought them unto him; and he laid his hands on every one of them, and healed them; 13:13 he laid his hands on her: and immediately she was made straight, and glorified God; 18:15 they brought unto him also infants, that he would touch them; Acts 13:3 when they had fasted and prayed, and laid their hands on them, they sent them away.

LAY UP (see also Prepare, Store)

Lay not up for yourselves treasures upon earth, where moth and rust doth corrupt, and where thieves break through and steal: But lay up for yourselves treasures in heaven, where neither moth nor rust doth corrupt, and where thieves do not break through nor steal: For where your treasure is, there will your heart be also. Matt. 6:19-21 (see also Heart, Heaven, Steal, Treasure)

LAZINESS, LAZY (see Slothful)

LEAD, LEADER, LEADERSHIP, LED (see also Holy Ghost, Know, Search, Seek, Study)

As many as are led by the Spirit of God, they are the sons of God. Rom. 8:14 (see also Holy Spirit)

The leaders of this people cause them to err; and they that are led of them are destroyed. Isa. 9:16 (see also Err)

LEARN, LEARNED, LEARNING (see also Holy Ghost, Know, Search, Seek, Study)

Learn to do well; seek judgment, relieve the oppressed, judge the fatherless, plead for the widow. Isa. 1:17 (see also Do, Judge, Plead, Relieve)

For precept must be upon precept, precept upon precept; line upon line, line upon line; here a little, and there a little: For with stammering lips and another tongue will he speak to this people. Isa. 28:10 (see also Know, Precept, Understand)

With my soul have I desired thee in the night; yea, with my spirit within me will I seek thee early: for when thy judgments are in the earth, the inhabitants of the world will learn righteousness. Isa. 26:9 (see also Righteous)

I have yet many things to say unto you, but ye cannot bear them now. John 16:12 (see also Mysteries)

Mark 10:5 Jesus answered and said unto them, For the hardness of your heart he wrote you this precept; John 16:12 I have yet many things to say unto you, but ye cannot bear them now.

Come unto me, all ye that labour and are heavy laden, and I will give you rest. Take my yoke upon you, and learn of me; for I am meek and lowly in heart: and ye shall find rest unto your souls. Matt. 11:28-29 (see also Heart, Heavy, Lowly, Meek, Seek)

Matt. 8:5 when Jesus was entered into Capernaum, there came unto him a centurion, beseeching him; 9:10 as Jesus sat at meat in the house, behold, many publicans and sinners came and sat down with him and his disciples; 11:27 all things are delivered unto me of my Father: and no man knoweth the Son, but the Father;

neither knoweth any man the Father, save the Son, and he to whomsoever the Son will reveal him; **11:29** take my yoke upon you, and learn of me; for I am meek and lowly in heart: and ye shall find rest unto your souls; **13:54** he taught them in their synagogue, insomuch that they were astonished, and said, Whence hath this man this wisdom, and these mighty works; **14:13** when the people had heard thereof, they followed him on foot out of the cities; **28:5** fear not ye: for I know that ye seek Jesus, which was crucified; **Luke 10:22** all things are delivered to me of my Father: and no man knoweth who the Son is, but the Father; and who the Father is, but the Son, and he to whom the Son will reveal him; **John 16:3** these things will they do unto you, because they have not known the Father, nor me; **16:12** I have yet many things to say unto you, but ye cannot bear them now; **17:3** this is life eternal, that they might know thee the only true God, and Jesus Christ, whom thou hast sent; **Acts 15:17** the residue of men might seek after the Lord, and all the Gentiles, upon whom my name is called, saith the Lord, who doeth all these things; **17:27** seek the Lord, if haply they might feel after him, and find him, though he be not far from every one of us; **Rom. 14:11** I live, saith the Lord, every knee shall bow to me, and every tongue shall confess to God; **Heb. 11:6** without faith it is impossible to please him: for he that cometh to God must believe that he is, and that he is a rewarder of them that diligently seek him.

LEAVE, LEFT (*see also* Depart, Go)

Discretion shall preserve thee, understanding shall keep thee; To deliver thee from the way of the evil man, from the man that speaketh froward things; who leave the paths of righteousness, to walk in the ways of darkness. Prov. 2:11-13 (*see also* Dark, Righteous, Walk, Way)

LEND, LENT (*see also* Borrow)

When thou dost lend thy brother any thing, thou shalt not go into his house to fetch his pledge. Deut. 24:10 (*see also* Pledge)

LEWD, LEWDNESS (*see also* Evil, Lascivious, Wicked)

Cause lewdness to cease out of the land. Ezek. 23:48

Ezek. 22:9 in thee are men that carry tales to shed blood: and in thee they eat upon the mountains: in the midst of thee they commit *l.*; **22:11** one hath committed abomination with his neighbour's wife; and another hath *l.* defiled his daughter in law; and another in thee hath humbled his sister, his fathers daughter; **23:48-49** I [will] cause *l.* to cease out of the land, that all women may be taught not to do after your *l.*. And they shall recompense your *l.* upon you, and ye shall bear the sins of your idols; **24:13** in thy filthiness is *l.*: because I have purged thee, and thou wast not purged, thou shalt not be purged from thy filthiness any more, till I have caused my fury to rest upon thee; **Hosea 6:9** as troops of robbers wait for a man, so the company of priests murder in the way by consent: for they commit *l.*

LIAR, LIE, LYING (*see also* Gossip, Talebearer)

The getting of treasures by a lying tongue is a vanity tossed to and fro of them that seek death. Prov. 21:6 (*see also* Treasure)

There shall in no wise enter into [the temple] any thing that defileth, neither whatsoever worketh abomination, or maketh a lie: but they which are written in the Lamb's book of life. Rev. 21:27 (*see also* Defile, Temple)

If a ruler hearken to lies, all his servants are wicked. Prov. 29:12 (*see also* Hearken)

God shall send them strong delusion, that they should believe a lie: That they all might be damned who believed not the truth, but had pleasure in unrighteousness. 2 Thes. 2:11-12 (*see also* Pleasure, Unrighteousness)

Let the lying lips be put to silence; which speak grievous things proudly and contemptuously against the righteous. Ps. 31:18 (*see also* Silence, Speak)

Let the lying lips be put to silence; which speak grievous things proudly and contemptuously against the righteous. Ps. 31:18 (*see also* Grieve)

As for our iniquities, we know them: in transgressing and lying against the LORD, and departing away from our God, speaking oppression and revolt, conceiving and uttering from the heart words of falsehood. Isa. 59:12-13 (*see also* Transgress)

He that hideth hatred with lying lips, and he that uttereth a slander, is a fool. Prov. 10:18 (*see also* Hate, Slander)

Who is a liar but he that denieth that Jesus is the Christ? He is antichrist, that denieth the Father and the Son. 1 Jn. 2:22-23 (*see also* Deny)

Trust ye not in lying words. Jer. 7:4 (*see also* Trust)

Jer. 7:4 trust ye not in *l.* words; 7:8 ye trust in *l.* words, that cannot profit.

The mouth of them that speak lies shall be stopped. Ps. 63:11 (*see also* Mouth)

Ps. 62:4 they only consult to cast him down from his excellency: they delight in *l.*: they bless with their mouth, but they curse inwardly; 63:11 the king shall rejoice in God; every one that sweareth by him shall glory: but the mouth of them that speak *l.* shall be stopped; Isa. 44:25 that frustrateth the tokens of the *l.*, and maketh diviners mad; that turneth wise men backward, and maketh their knowledge foolish.

Thou shalt not live; for thou speakest lies in the name of the LORD. Zech. 13:3 (*see also* Name)

Zech. 13:3-3 when any shall yet prophesy, then his father and his mother that begat him shall say unto him, Thou shalt not live; for thou speakest *l.* in the name of the LORD.

These six things doth the LORD hate: yea, seven are an abomination unto him: A proud look, a lying tongue, and hands that shed innocent blood, An heart that deviseth wicked imaginations, feet that be swift in running to mischief, A false witness that speaketh lies, and he that soweth discord among brethren. Prov. 6:16-19 (*see also* Discord, False Witness, Imagine, Innocent, Mischief, Pride)

Ps. 119:163 I hate and abhor *l.*; Prov. 6:16-19 these six things doth the LORD hate: yea, seven are an abomination unto him: A proud look, a *l.* tongue, and hands that shed innocent blood, An heart that deviseth wicked imaginations, feet that be swift in running to mischief, A false witness that speaketh *l.*, and he that soweth discord among brethren.

Lie not one to another, seeing that ye have put off the old man with his deeds. Col. 3:9

Matt. 28:12-15 then they were assembled with the elders, and had taken counsel, they gave large money unto the soldiers, Saying, Say ye, His disciples came by night, and stole him away while we slept. And if this come to the governor's ears, we will persuade him, and secure you. So they took the money, and did as they were taught: and this saying is commonly reported among the Jews until this day; Acts 5:3 why hath Satan filled thine heart to lie to the Holy Ghost, and to keep back part of the price of the land; 5:8-10 tell me whether ye sold the land for so much? And she said, Yea, for so much. Then Peter said unto her, How is it that ye have agreed together to tempt the Spirit of the Lord? behold, the feet of them which have buried thy husband are at the door, and shall carry thee out. Then fell she down straightway at his feet, and yielded up the ghost: and the young men came in, and found her dead, and, carrying her forth, buried her by her husband; Eph. 4:25 putting away *l.*, speak every man truth with his neighbour: for we are members one of another; Col. 3:9 *l.* not one to another, seeing that ye have put off the old man with his deeds; 1 Tim. 4:2 speaking *l.* in hypocrisy; having their conscience seared with a hot iron; James 3:14 if ye have bitter envying and strife in your hearts, glory not, and *l.* not against the truth; Rev. 3:9 I will make them of the synagogue of Satan, which say they are Jews, and are not, but do *l.*

A false witness shall not be unpunished, and he that speaketh lies shall not escape. Prov. 19:5 (*see also* Accusation, Deceive, False Witness)

Gen. 39:13-18 the Hebrew servant, which thou hast brought unto us, came in unto me to mock me: And it came to pass, as I lifted up my voice and cried, that he left his garment with me, and fled out; Lev. 6:2-5 if a soul sin, and commit a trespass against the LORD, and *l.* unto his neighbour in that which was delivered him to keep, or in fellowship, or in a thing taken away by violence, or hath deceived his neighbour; Or have found that which was lost, and *l.* concerning it, and sweareth falsely; in any of all these that a man doeth, sinning therein; 19:11 ye shall not steal, neither deal falsely, neither *l.* one to another; Ps. 31:6 I have hated them that regard *l.* vanities: but I trust in the LORD; 31:18 let the *l.* lips be put to silence; which speak grievous things proudly and contemptuously against the righteous; **40:4** blessed is that man that maketh the LORD his trust, and respecteth not the proud, nor such as turn aside to *l.*; **52:3** thou lovest evil more than good; and *l.* rather than to speak righteousness; **58:3** the wicked are estranged from the womb: they go astray as soon as they be born, speaking *l.*; **116:11** I said in my haste, All men are liars; **119:29** remove from me the way of *l.*: and grant me thy law graciously; **Prov. 12:19** the lip of truth shall be established for ever: but a *l.* tongue is but for a moment; **12:22** *l.* lips are abomination to the LORD: but they that deal truly are his delight; **13:5** a righteous man hateth *l.*: but a wicked man is loathsome, and cometh to shame; **17:4** a wicked doer giveth heed to false lips; and a liar giveth ear to a naughty tongue; **17:7** excellent speech becometh not a fool: much less do *l.* lips a prince; **19:5** a false witness shall not be unpunished, and he that speaketh *l.* shall not escape; **19:9** a false witness shall not be unpunished, and he that speaketh *l.* shall perish; **Isa. 28:15** we have made a covenant with death, and with hell are we at agreement; when the overflowing scourge shall pass through, it shall not come unto us: for we have made *l.* our refuge, and under falsehood have we hid ourselves; **28:17** the hail shall sweep away the refuge of *l.*, and the waters shall overflow the hiding place; **30:9-11** this is a rebellious people, *l.* children, children that will not hear the law of the LORD: Which say to the seers, See not; and to the prophets, Prophesy not unto us right things, speak unto us smooth things, prophesy deceits: Get you out of the way, turn aside out of the path, cause the Holy ne of Israel to cease from before us; **32:7** the instruments also of the churl are evil: he deviseth wicked devices to destroy the poor with *l.* words, even when the needy speaketh right; **44:25-28** that frustrateth the tokens of the liars, and maketh diviners mad; that turneth wise men backward, and maketh their knowledge foolish; **50:11** all ye that kindle a fire, that compass yourselves about with sparks: walk in the light of your fire, and in the sparks that ye have kindled. This shall ye have of mine hand; ye shall *l.* down in sorrow; **57:11** of whom hast thou been afraid or feared, that thou hast *l.*, and hast not remembered me, nor laid it to thy heart?; **59:3-4** our hands are defiled with blood, and your fingers with iniquity; your lips have spoken *l.*, your tongue hath muttered perverseness. None calleth for justice, nor any pleadeth for truth: they trust in vanity, and speak *l.*; they conceive mischief, and bring forth iniquity; **63:8** surely they are my people,

children that will not *l.*: so he was their Saviour; **Jer. 9:3** they bend their tongues like their bow for *l.*: but they are not valiant for the truth upon the earth; for they proceed from evil to evil, and they know not me, saith the LORD; **9:5** hey will deceive every one his neighbour, and will not speak the truth: they have taught their tongue to speak *l.*, and weary themselves to commit iniquity; **23:14** I have seen also in the prophets of Jerusalem an horrible thing: they commit adultery, and walk in *l.*; **50:36** a sword is upon the liars; and they shall dote: a sword is upon her mighty men; and they shall be dismayed; **Ezek. 13:19** will ye pollute me among my people for handfuls of barley and for pieces of bread, to slay the souls that should not die, and to save the souls alive that should not live, by your *l.* to my people that hear your *l.*; **Dan. 11:27** both these kings hearts shall be to do mischief, and they shall speak *l.* at one table; but it shall not prosper: for yet the end shall be at the time appointed; **Hosea 4:1-5** the LORD hath a controversy with the inhabitants of the land, because there is no truth, nor mercy, nor knowledge of God in the land. By s wearing, and *l.*, and killing, and stealing, and committing adultery, they break out, and blood toucheth blood. Therefore shall the land mourn, and every one that dwelleth therein shall languish, with the beasts of the field, and with the fowls of heaven; yea, the fishes of the sea also shall be taken away; **7:3** they make the king glad with their wickedness, and the princes with their *l.*; **12:1** he daily increaseth *l.* and desolation; **Amos 2:4** they have despised the law of the LORD, and have not kept his commandments, and their *l.* caused them to err, after the which their fathers have walked; **Micah 6:12** the rich men thereof are full of violence, and the inhabitants thereof have spoken *l.*, and their tongue is deceitful in their mouth; **Nahum 3:1** woe to the bloody city! it is all full of *l.* and robbery; the prey departeth not; **Zeph. 3:13** the remnant of Israel shall not do iniquity, nor speak *l.*; neither shall a deceitful tongue be found in their mouth: for they shall feed and lie down, and none shall make them afraid.

LIBERTY (*see also* Choice, Constitution, Righteousness)

Stand fast therefore in the liberty wherewith Christ hath made us free, and be not entangled again with the yoke of bondage. Gal. 5:1 (*see also* Fall, Stand)

So is the will of God, that with well doing ye may put to silence the ignorance of foolish men: As free, and not using your liberty for a cloke of maliciousness, but as the servants of God. **1 Pet. 2:15-16** (*see also* Do, Servant, Will)

Ye have not hearkened unto me, in proclaiming liberty, every one to his brother, and every man to his neighbour: behold, I proclaim a liberty for you, saith the LORD, to the sword, to the pestilence, and to the famine; and I will make you to be removed into all the kingdoms of the earth. **Jer. 34:17** (*see also* Proclaim)

Proclaim liberty to the captives, and the opening of the prison to them that are bound. **Isa. 61:1** (*see also* Prison, Proclaim)

Isa. 61:1 the Spirit of the Lord GOD is upon me; because the LORD hath anointed me to preach good tidings unto the meek... to proclaim *l.* to the captives, and the opening of the prison to them that are bound; **61:3** appoint unto them that mourn in Zion, to give unto them beauty for ashes, the oil of joy for mourning, the garment of praise for the spirit of heaviness; that they might be called trees of righteousness, the planting of the LORD, that he might be glorified.

Ye have not hearkened unto me, in proclaiming liberty, every one to his brother, and every man to his neighbour: behold, I proclaim a liberty for you, saith the LORD. **Jer. 34:15-17** (*see also* Proclaim)

Gen. 14:12-16 when Abram heard that his brother was taken captive... he divided himself against them, he and his servants, by night, and smote them, and pursued them; **Neh. 4:14** be not ye afraid of them: remember the Lord, which is great and terrible, and fight for your brethren, your sons, and your daughters, your wives, and your houses; **4:16** half of my servants wrought in the work, and the other half of them held both the spears, the shields, and the bows, and the habergeons; **Isa. 61:1** he hath sent me to bind up the brokenhearted, to proclaim *l.* to the captives, and the opening of the prison to them that are bound; **Jer. 34:15-17** ye have not hearkened unto me, in proclaiming *l.*, every one to his brother, and every man to his neighbour: behold, I proclaim a liberty for you, saith the LORD.

The Spirit of the Lord is upon me, because he hath anointed me to preach the gospel to the poor; he hath sent me to heal the brokenhearted, to preach deliverance to the captives, and recovering of sight to the blind, to set at liberty them that are bruised, To preach the acceptable year of the Lord. **Luke 4:18-19** (*see also* Preach)

Luke 4:18-19 the Spirit of the Lord is upon me, because he hath anointed me to preach the gospel to the poor; he hath sent me to heal the brokenhearted, to preach deliverance to the captives, and recovering of sight to the blind, to set at *l.* them that are bruised, to preach the acceptable year of the Lord; **Rom. 8:2** the creature itself also shall be delivered from the bondage of corruption into the glorious *l.* of the children of God; **2 Cor. 3:17** Now the Lord is that Spirit: and where the Spirit of the Lord is, there is *l.*; **Gal. 5:1** Stand fast therefore in the *l.* wherewith Christ hath made us free, and be not entangled again with the yoke of bondage.

LIFE, LIVES (*see also* Atonement, Eternal Life, Redeem, Resurrection, Soul, Spirit)

Lead a quiet and peaceable life in all godliness and honesty. **1 Tim. 2:2** (*see also* Godliness, Honest, Peace)

Whosoever will save his life shall lose it; but whosoever shall lose his life for my sake and the gospel's, the same shall save it. For what shall it profit a man, if he shall gain the whole world, and lose his own soul? **Mark 8:36** (*see also* Gain, Save, Soul)

He that followeth after righteousness and mercy, findeth life, righteousness, and honour. **Prov. 21:21** (*see also* Follow, Mercy, Righteousness)

LIFT (*see also* Exalt, Magnify)

Thine heart was lifted up because of thy beauty, thou hast corrupted thy wisdom by reason of thy brightness: I will cast thee to the ground. **Ezek. 28:17** (*see also* Beautiful)

Lift up a standard for the people. **Isa. 62:10** (*see also* Standard)

Isa. 62:10 go through, go through the gates; prepare ye the way of the people; cast up, cast up the highway; gather out the stones; *l.* up a standard for the people; **Jer. 4:6** set up the standard toward Zion: retire, stay not: for I will bring evil from the north, and a great destruction.

LIGHT (*see also* Candle, Discern, Enlighten, Example, Holy Ghost, Scripture, Truth, Word)

Commit thy way unto the Lord; trust also in Him; and He shall bring it to pass. And he shall bring forth thy righteousness as the light, and thy judgment as the noonday. Ps. 37:5-6 (*see also* Commit, Trust, Way)

It is a light thing that thou shouldest be my servant to raise up the tribes of Jacob, and to restore the preserved of Israel: I will also give thee for a light to the Gentiles, that thou mayest be my salvation unto the end of the earth. Isa. 49:6 (*see also* Earth, Gentile, Salvation)

Let us therefore cast off the works of darkness, and let us put on the armor of light. Rom. 13:12 (*see also* Armor)

Arise, shine; for thy light is come, and the glory of the LORD is risen upon thee. Isa. 60:1 (*see also* Arise)

Ye were sometimes darkness, but now are ye light in the Lord: walk as children of light. Eph. 5:8 (*see also* Walk)

Eph. 5:8 ye were sometimes darkness, but now are ye light in the Lord: walk as children of light.

Come ye, and let us walk in the light of the LORD. Isa. 2:5 (*see also* Walk)

Ps. 56:13 thou hast delivered my soul from death: wilt not thou deliver my feet from falling, that I may walk before God in the *l.* of the living; **119:105** thy word is a lamp unto my feet, and a *l.* unto my path; **119:130** the entrance of thy words giveth *l.*; it giveth understanding unto the simple; **Isa. 2:5** come ye, and let us walk in the *l.* of the LORD.

Let your light so shine before men, that they may see your good works, and glorify your Father which is in heaven. Matt. 5:16 (*see also* Candle, Example)

Matt. 5:16 let your *l.* so shine before men, that they may see your good works, and glorify your Father which is in heaven; **Luke 11:33-36** the *l.* of the body is the eye: therefore when thine eye

is single, thy whole body also is full of *l.*; but when thine eye is evil, thy body also is full of darkness.

LIKEMINDED (*see also* One, Think, United)

Be likeminded one toward another according to Christ Jesus: That ye may with one mind and one mouth glorify God, even the Father of our Lord Jesus Christ. Rom. 15:5-6 (*see also* Jesus Christ, One, Unity)

Rom. 15:5-6 the God of patience and consolation grant you to be *l.* one toward another according to Christ Jesus: That ye may with one mind and one mouth glorify God, even the Father of our Lord Jesus Christ; **1 Cor. 1:10** I beseech you, brethren, by the name of our Lord Jesus Christ, that ye all speak the same thing, and that there be no divisions among you; but that ye be perfectly joined together in the same mind and in the same judgment; **Philip. 2:2** fulfil ye my joy, that ye be *l.*, having the same love, being of one accord, of one mind.

LIKEN (*see also* Apply)

Shall I not, as I have done unto Samaria and her idols, so do to Jerusalem and her idols? Isa. 10:11 (*see also* Idol)

LIKENESS (*see also* Image)

I will behold thy face in righteousness: I shall be satisfied, when I awake, with thy likeness. Ps. 17:15 (*see also* Know)

LIMIT (*see also* Unbelief)

They turned back and tempted God, and limited the Holy One of Israel. Ps. 78:41 (*see also* Tempt)

LIPS (*see also* Mouth, Speak, Tongue)

Put away from thee a froward mouth, and perverse lips put far from thee. Prov. 4:24 (*see also* Froward, Perverse)

My lips shall not speak wickedness, nor my tongue utter deceit. Job 27:4 (*see also* Speak)

My son, attend unto my wisdom, and bow thine ear to my understanding: That thou mayest regard discretion and *that* thy lips may keep knowledge. Prov. 5:2 (*see also* Discrete, Mouth)

Prov. 5:2 regard discretion... that thy *l.* may keep knowledge; **10:19** in the multitude of words there wanteth not sin: but he that refraineth his *l.* is wise; **12:14** a man shall be satisfied with good by the fruit of his mouth: and the recompence of a mans hands shall be rendered unto him; **15:23** a man hath joy by the answer of his mouth: and a word spoken in due season, how good is it; **16:13** righteous *l.* are the delight of kings; and they love him that speaketh right; **16:23** the heart of the wise teacheth his mouth, and addeth learning to his *l.*; **17:27-28** he that hath knowledge spareth his words: and a man of understanding is of an excellent spirit. Even a fool, when he holdeth his peace, is counted wise: and he that shutteth his *l.* is esteemed a man of understanding; **18:20-21** a mans belly shall be satisfied with the fruit of his mouth; and with the increase of his *l.* shall he be filled; **20:15** the *l.* of knowledge are a precious jewel; **23:16** my reins shall rejoice, when thy *l.* speak right things.

LIST, LISTED, LISTETH (*see also* Listen, Obey)

But I say unto you, That Elias is come already, and they knew him not, but have done unto him whatsoever they listed. Likewise shall also the Son of man suffer of them. Then the disciples understood that he spake unto them of John the Baptist. Matt. 17:12-13

LISTEN, LISTENING (*see* Communicate, Ear, Hear, List, Understand)

LIVE, LIVING (*see also* Abide, Alive, Dwell, Life)

Man shall not live by bread alone, but by every word that proceedeth out of the mouth of God. Matt. 4:4 (*see also* Bread, Proceed, Word)

Live joyfully with the wife whom thou lovest all the days of the life of thy vanity, which he hath given thee under the sun, all the days of thy vanity: for that is thy portion in this life, and in thy labour which thou takest under the sun. Eccl. 9:9 (*see also* Joyfully, Wife)

The LORD liveth; and blessed be my rock; and let the God of my salvation be exalted. Ps. 18:46

LOATHE, LOATHSOME (*see also* Abomination, Hate, Wicked)

A righteous man hateth lying: but a wicked man is loathsome, and cometh to shame. Prov. 13:5

LOFTINESS, LOFTY (*see also* Highminded, Pride, Vanity)

The mean man shall be brought down, and the mighty man shall be humbled, and the eyes of the lofty shall be humbled. Isa. 5:15 (*see also* Humble, Mean)

LONGSUFFERING (*see also* Endurance, Patience, Suffer)

LORD, thou knowest: remember me, and visit me, and revenge me of my persecutors; take me not away in thy longsuffering: know that for thy sake I have suffered rebuke. Jer. 15:15 (*see also* Sake, Remember)

LOOK (*see also* Behold, Eye, See, Watch)

Look on every one that is proud, and bring him low; and tread down the wicked in their place. Job 40:12 (*see also* Pride, Wicked)

He shall not look to the altars, the work of his hands, neither shall respect that which his fingers have made, either the groves, or the images. Isa. 17:8 (*see also* Image)

Look unto me, and be ye saved, all the ends of the earth: for I am God, and there is none else. Isa. 45:22 (*see also* Save)

LOOSE

Shake thyself from the dust; arise, and sit down, O Jerusalem: loose thyself from the bands of thy neck, O captive daughter of Zion. Isa. 52:2 (*see also* Jerusalem)

LORD (*see also* Christ, God, Jesus Christ, Messiah, Redeemer, Savior)

I will bear the indignation of the LORD, because I have sinned against him, until he plead my cause, and execute judgment for me: he will bring me forth to the light, and I shall behold his righteousness. Micah 7:9-10 (*see also* Bear, Indignation)

Know ye that the LORD he is God. Ps. 100:3 (*see also* Know)

Ps. 100:3 know ye that the LORD he is God; 144:12-15 happy is that people, that is in such a case: yea, happy is that people, whose God is the LORD.

LOT (*see also* Cast, Choice)

The lot causeth contensions to cease, and parteth between the mighty. Prov. 18:18 (*see also* Contend)

LOVE, LOVINGKINDNESS (*see also* Affection, Charity, Friendship, Kindness)

Pray for the peace of Jerusalem: they shall prosper that love thee. Ps. 122:6 (*see also* Jerusalem, Peace)

Jesus said unto him, Thous shalt love the Lord thy God with all thy heart, and with all thy soul, and with all thy mind. This is the first and great commandment. And the second is like unto it, Thou shalt love thy neighbour as thyself. On these two commandments, hang all the law and the prophets. Matt 22:37-40 (*see also* Commandment, Hang, Thous Shalt)

I will worship toward thy holy temple, and praise thy name for thy lovingkindness and for thy truth: for thou hast magnified thy word above all thy name. Ps. 138:2 (*see also* Temple, Worship)

By love, serve one another. Gal. 5:13 (*see also* Serve)

Who shall separate us from the love of Christ? shall tribulation, or distress, or persecution, or famine, or nakedness, or peril, or sword? Rom. 8:35 (*see also* Separate)

He that loveth pleasure shall be a poor man: he that loveth wine and oil shall not be rich. Prov. 21:17 (*see also* Pleasure)

Better is a dinner of herbs where love is, than a stalled ox and hatred therewith. Prov. 15:17 (*see also* Hate)

Their husbands love their wives, and their wives love their husbands; and their husbands and their wives love their children. Jacob 3:7 (*see also* Husband, Wife)

Love your enemies, bless them that curse you, do good to them that hate you, and pray for them which despitefully use you, and persecute you. Matt. 5:44 (*see also* Curse, Enemy, Persecute, Spite)

Love not the world, neither the things that are in the world. 1 Jn. 2:15 (*see also* Things, World)

Owe no man any thing, but to love one another: for he that loveth another hath fulfilled the law. Rom. 13:8 (*see also* Debt, Owe)

He that loveth silver shall not be satisfied with silver; nor he that loveth abundance with increase: this is also vanity. Eccl. 5:10 (*see also* Silver, Vain)

Husbands, love your wives, even as Christ also loved the church, and gave himself for it. That he might sanctify and cleanse it with the washing of water by the word, That he might present it to himself a glorious church, not having spot, or wrinkle, or any such thing; but that it should be holy and without blemish. So ought men to love their wives as their own bodies. He that loveth his wife loveth himself. Eph. 5:25-28 (*see also* Church, Husband)

Let none of you imagine evil in your hearts against his neighbour; and love no false oath: for all these are things that I hate, saith the LORD. Zech. 8:17 (*see also* Imagine, Oath)

Thou shalt not avenge, nor bear any grudge against the children of thy people, but thou shalt love thy neighbour as thyself: I *am* the LORD. Lev. 19:18 (*see also* Neighbor)

Lev. 19:18 thou shalt not avenge, nor bear any grudge against the children of thy people, but thou shalt *l.* thy neighbour as thyself: I am the LORD; Deut. 10:19 *l.* ye therefore the stranger: for ye were strangers in the land of Egypt; Prov. 17:17 a friend loveth at all times, and a brother is born for adversity; Zech. 8:17 let none of you imagine evil in your hearts against his neighbour.

Love the name of the LORD. Isa. 56:6 (*see also* Name)

Ps. 69:36 they that *l.* his name shall dwell therein; 119:132 look thou upon me, and be merciful unto me, as thou usest to do unto those that *l.* thy name; **Isa. 56:6-7** [they that] *l.* the name of the LORD, to be his servants, every one that keepeth the sabbath from polluting it, and taketh hold of my covenant; Even them will I bring to my holy mountain, and make them joyful.

Mention the lovingkindness of the LORD, and the praises of the LORD, according to all that the LORD, hath bestowed on us, and the great goodness toward the house of Israel, which he hath bestowed on them according to his mercies, and according to the multitude of his lovingkindness. Isa. 63:7 (*see also* Mention)

Isa. 63:7 I will mention the *l.* of the LORD, and the praises of the LORD, according to all that the LORD hath bestowed on us, and the great goodness toward the house of Israel; **Jer. 9:24** let him that glorieth glory in this, that he understandeth and knoweth me, that I am the LORD which exercise *l.*, judgment, and righteousness, in the earth: for in these things I delight.

Thou shalt love the LORD thy God with all thine heart, and with all thy soul, and with all thy might. Deut. 6:5 (*see also* Thou Shalt)

Ex. 20:6 shewing mercy unto thousands of them that *l.* me, and keep my commandments; **Deut. 5:10** shewing mercy unto thousands of them that *l.* me and keep my commandments; **6:5** thou shalt *l.* the LORD thy God with all thine heart, and with all thy soul, and with all thy might; **7:9** the LORD thy God, he is God, the faithful God, which keepeth covenant and mercy with them that *l.* him and keep his commandments; **10:12** what doth the LORD thy God require of thee, but to fear the LORD thy God, to walk in all his ways, and to *l.* him, and to serve the LORD thy God with all thy heart and with all thy soul; **10:15** the LORD had a delight in thy fathers to *l.* them; **11:1** thou shalt *l.* the LORD thy God, and keep his charge, and his statutes, and his judgments, and his commandments; **11:13** ye shall hearken diligently unto my commandments which I command you this day, to *l.* the LORD your God, and to serve him with all your heart and with all your soul; **11:22-25** if ye shall diligently keep all these commandments which I command you, to do them, to *l.* the LORD your God, to walk in all his ways, and to cleave unto him; Then will the LORD drive out all these nations from before you; **13:3-4** the LORD your God proveth you, to know whether ye *l.* the LORD your God with all your heart and with all your soul; **19:9** if thou shalt

keep all these commandments to do them, which I command thee this day, to *l.* the LORD thy God, and to walk ever in his ways; then shalt thou add three cities more for thee; **30:6** the LORD thy God will circumcise thine heart, and the heart of thy seed, to *l.* the LORD thy God with all thine heart, and with all thy soul; **30:16** I command thee this day to *l.* the LORD thy God; **30:20** *l.* the LORD thy God, and that thou mayest obey his voice, and that thou mayest cleave unto him; **Josh.22:5** take diligent heed to do the commandment and the law, which Moses the servant of the LORD charged you, to *l.* the LORD your God; **23:11** take good heed therefore unto yourselves, that ye *l.* the LORD your God; **Judg. 5:31** let them that *l.* him be as the sun when he goeth forth in his might; **1 Kgs. 8:48** return unto thee with all their heart, and with all their soul; **2 Kgs. 23:25** like unto him was there no king before him, that turned to the LORD with all his heart, and with all his soul, and with all his might; **Ps. 5:11** let them also that *l.* thy name be joyful in thee; **18:1** I will *l.* thee, O LORD, my strength; **31:23** *l.* the LORD, all ye his saints: for the LORD preserveth the faithful; **69:36** they that *l.* his name shall dwell therein; **116:1** I I *l.* the LORD, because he hath heard my voice and my supplications; **145:20** the LORD preserveth all them that *l.* him; **Prov. 8:17** I I *l.* them that *l.* me; and those that seek me early shall find me; **8:21** I may cause those that *l.* me to inherit substance; and I will fill their treasures; **10:12** hatred stirreth up strifes: but *l.* covereth all sins.

How excellent is thy lovingkindness, O God! therefore the children of men put their trust under the shadow of thy wings. Ps. 36:7 (*see also* Trust)

Ps. 36:7-10 how excellent is thy *l.*, O God! therefore the children of men put their trust under the shadow of thy wings; **40:11** withhold not thou thy tender mercies from me, O LORD: let thy *l.* and thy truth continually preserve me; **48:9** we have thought of thy *l.*, O God, in the midst of thy temple; **63:3** because thy *l.* is better than life, my lips shall praise thee; **69:16** hear me, O LORD; for thy *l.* is good: turn unto me according to the multitude of thy tender mercies; **119:65** thou hast dealt well with thy servant, O LORD, according unto thy word; **119:88** quicken me after thy *l.*; so shall I keep the testimony of thy mouth; **119:149** hear my voice according unto thy *l.*: O LORD, quicken me according to thy judgment; **119:159** consider how I *l.* thy precepts: quicken me, O LORD, according to thy *l.*; **138:2** I will worship toward thy holy temple, and praise thy name for thy *l.* and for thy truth; **143:8** cause me to hear thy *l.* in the morning; for in thee do I trust; **Jer. 31:3** the LORD hath appeared of old unto me, saying, Yea, I have *l.* thee with an everlasting *l.*: therefore with *l.* have I drawn thee; **32:18** thou shewest *l.* unto thousands, and recompensest the iniquity of the fathers into the bosom of their children after them.

Thou shalt love the Lord thy God with all thy heart, and with all thy soul, and with all thy mind. Matt. 22:37 (*see also* Thou Shalt)

Matt. 22:37 Jesus said unto him, Thou shalt *l.* the Lord thy God with all thy heart, and with all thy soul, and with all thy mind; **22:40** on these two commandments hang all the law and the prophets; **Mark 12:28-31** Which is the first commandment of all? And Jesus answered him, The first of all the commandments is, Hear, O Israel; The Lord our God is one Lord: And thou shalt *l.* the Lord thy God with all thy heart, and with all thy soul, and with all thy mind, and with all thy strength: this is the first commandment. And the second is like, namely this, Thou shalt *l.* thy neighbour as thyself. There is none other commandment greater than these; **Luke 10:27-28** Thou shalt *l.* the Lord thy God with all thy heart, and with all thy soul, and with all thy strength, and with all thy mind; and thy neighbour as thyself. And he said unto him, Thou hast answered right: this do, and thou shalt live; **John 8:42** Jesus said unto them, If God were your Father, ye would *l.* me: for I proceeded forth and came from God; neither came I of myself, but he sent me; **14:15-16** if ye *l.* me, keep my commandments. And I will pray the Father, and he shall give you another Comforter, that he may abide with you for ever; **15:10** as the Father hath *l.* me, so have I *l.* you: continue ye in my *l.*. If ye keep my commandments, ye shall abide in my *l.*; even as I have kept my Father's commandments, and abide in his *l.*; **21:15-16** Jesus saith to Simon Peter, Simon, son of Jonas, *l.* thou me more than these? He saith unto him, Yea, Lord; thou knowest that I *l.* thee. He saith unto him, Feed my lambs. He saith to him again the second time, Simon, son of Jonas, *l.* thou me? He saith unto him, Yea, Lord; thou knowest that I *l.* thee. He saith unto him, Feed my sheep; **1 Cor. 16:22** if any man *l.* not the Lord Jesus Christ, let him be Anathema Maran-atha; **Philemon 1:5** hearing of thy *l.* and faith, which thou hast toward the Lord Jesus, and toward all saints; **1 Jn. 4:20** if a man say, I *l.* God, and hateth his brother, he is a liar: for he

that *l.* not his brother whom he hath seen, how can he *l.* God whom he hath not seen; **1 Jn. 5:2-3** by this we know that we *l.* the children of God, when we *l.* God, and keep his commandments. For this is the *l.* of God, that we keep his commandments: and his commandments are not grievous.

Thou shalt love thy neighbor as thyself. Matt. 22:39 (*see also* Thou Shalt)

Matt. 22:37-40 Jesus said unto him, Thou shalt *l.* the Lord thy God with all thy heart, and with all thy soul, and with all thy mind. This is the first and great commandment. And the second is like unto it, Thou shalt *l.* thy neighbour as thyself. On these two commandments hang all the law and the prophets; **Mark 12:31** the second is like, namely this, Thou shalt *l.* thy neighbour as thyself. There is none other commandment greater than these; **12:33** to *l.* him with all the heart, and with all the understanding, and with all the soul, and with all the strength, and to *l.* his neighbour as himself, is more than all whole burnt offerings and sacrifices; **Luke 10:27-28** Thou shalt *l.* the Lord thy God with all thy heart, and with all thy soul, and with all thy strength, and with all thy mind; and thy neighbour as thyself. And he said unto him, Thou hast answered right: this do, and thou shalt live; **John 13:34-35** a new commandment I give unto you, That ye *l.* one another; as I have *l.* you, that ye also *l.* one another. By this shall all men know that ye are my disciples, if ye have *l.* one to another; **15:12-13** this is my commandment, That ye *l.* one another, as I have *l.* you. Greater *l.* hath no man than this, that a man lay down his life for his friends; **15:17** these things I command you, that ye *l.* one another; **Rom. 12:10** be kindly affectioned one to another with brotherly *l.*; in honour preferring one another; **13:9** thou shalt not commit adultery, Thou shalt not kill, Thou shalt not steal, Thou shalt not bear false witness, Thou shalt not covet; and if there be any other commandment, it is briefly comprehended in this saying, namely, Thou shalt *l.* thy neighbour as thyself; **1 Cor. 16:24** my *l.* be with you all in Christ Jesus; **2 Cor. 2:7-8** I beseech you that ye would confirm your *l.* toward him; **Gal. 5:14** for all the law is fulfilled in one word, even in this; Thou shalt *l.* thy neighbour as thyself; **1 Thes. 3:12** the Lord make you to increase and abound in *l.* one toward another, and toward all men, even as we do toward you; **4:9-10** as touching brotherly *l.* ye need not that I write unto you: for ye yourselves are taught of God to *l.* one another. And indeed ye do it toward all the brethren which are in all Macedonia: but we beseech you, brethren, that ye increase more and more; **2 Thes. 1:3** it is meet, because that your faith groweth exceedingly, and the charity of every one of you all toward each other aboundeth; **Titus 2:4-5** teach the young women to be sober, to *l.* their husbands, to *l.* their children, To be discreet, chaste, keepers at home, good, obedient to their own husbands, that the word of God be not blasphemed; **Phillip 1:5** hearing of thy *l.* and faith, which thou hast toward the Lord Jesus, and toward all saints; **1:7** we have great joy and consolation in thy *l.*, because the bowels of the saints are refreshed by thee, brother; **Heb. 13:1** let brotherly *l.* continue; **James 2:8** if ye fulfil the royal law according to the scripture, Thou shalt *l.* thy neighbour as thyself, ye do well; **1 Pet. 1:22** seeing ye have purified your souls in obeying the truth through the Spirit unto unfeigned *l.* of the brethren, see that ye *l.* one another with a pure heart fervently; **3:8** be ye all of one mind, having compassion one of another, *l.* as brethren, be pitiful, be courteous; **1 Jn. 2:9-10** he that saith he is in the light, and hateth his brother, is in darkness even until now. He that *l.* his brother abideth in the light, and there is none occasion of stumbling in him; **3:10-11** the children of the devil: whosoever doeth not righteousness is not of God, neither he that *l.* not his brother. For this is the message that ye heard from the beginning, that we should *l.* one another; **3:14** we know that we have passed from death unto life, because we *l.* the brethren. He that *l.* not his brother abideth in death; **4:6-11** let us *l.* one another: for *l.* is of God; and every one that *l.* is born of God, and knoweth God. He that *l.* not knoweth not God; for God is *l.* In this was manifested the *l.* of God toward us, because that God sent his only begotten Son into the world, that we might live through him. Herein is *l.*, not that we *l.* God, but that he *l.* us, and sent his Son to be the propitiation for our sins. Beloved, if God so *l.* us, we ought also to *l.* one another; **4:12** if we *l.* one another, God dwelleth in us, and his *l.* is perfected in us; **4:16** we have known and believed the *l.* that God hath to us. God is *l.*; and he that dwelleth in *l.* dwelleth in God, and God in him; **4:20-21** if a man say, I *l.* God, and hateth his brother, he is a liar: for he that *l.* not his brother whom he hath seen, how can he *l.* God whom he hath not seen? And this commandment have we from him, That he who *l.* God *l.* his brother also; **2 Jn. 1:5** I wrote a new commandment unto thee, but that which we had from the beginning, that we *l.* one another; **3 Jn.**

1:1 the elder unto the wellbeloved Gaius, whom I *l.* in the truth.

Thou shalt love the Lord thy God with all thy heart, and with all thy soul, and with all thy mind, and with all thy strength: this is the first commandment. Mark 12:30 (*see also* Commandment, Thou Shalt)

Mark 12:30 thou shalt *l.* the Lord thy God with all thy heart, and with all thy soul, and with all thy mind, and with all thy strength: this is the first commandment; **John 14:23-24** if a man *l.* me, he will keep my words: and my Father will *l.* him, and we will come unto him, and make our abode with him. He that *l.* me not keepeth not my sayings: and the word which ye hear is not mine, but the Father's which sent me; **14:31** that the world may know that I *l.* the Father; and as the Father gave me commandment, even so I do; **15:9** as the Father hath *l.* me, so have I *l.* you: continue ye in my *l.*; **16:27** the Father himself *l.* you, because ye have *l.* me, and have believed that I came out from God; **Rom. 8:28** we know that all things work together for good to them that *l.* God, to them who are the called according to his purpose; **8:35** who shall separate us from the *l.* of Christ? shall tribulation, or distress, or persecution, or famine, or nakedness, or peril, or sword; **8:39** nor height, nor depth, nor any other creature, shall be able to separate us from the *l.* of God, which is in Christ Jesus our Lord; **1 Cor. 2:9** but as it is written, Eye hath not seen, nor ear heard, neither have entered into the heart of man, the things which God hath prepared for them that *l.* him; **8:3** if any man *l.* God, the same is known of him; **2 Tim. 4:8** henceforth there is laid up for me a crown of righteousness, which the Lord, the righteous judge, shall give me at that day: and not to me only, but unto all them also that *l.* his appearing; **James 1:12** blessed is the man that endureth temptation: for when he is tried, he shall receive the crown of life, which the Lord hath promised to them that *l.* him; **2:5** hath not God chosen the poor of this world rich in faith, and heirs of the kingdom which he hath promised to them that *l.* him.

LOW, LOWLINESS, LOWLY (*see also* Humility, Meek)

Let nothing be done through strife or vainglory; but in lowliness of mind let each esteem other better than themselves. Philip. 2:3 (*see also* Esteem)

Come unto me, all ye that labour and are heavy laden, and I will give you rest. Take my yoke upon you, and learn of me; for I am meek and lowly in heart: and ye shall find rest unto your souls. **Matt. 11:28-29** (*see also* Heart, Heavy, Learn, Meek, Seek)

He scorneth the scorners: but he giveth grace unto the lowly. **Prov. 3:34** (*see also* Heart)

Job 5:11 set up on high those that be *l*.; that those which mourn may be exalted to safety; **Ps. 138:6** though the LORD be high, yet hath he respect unto the *l*.: but the proud he knoweth afar; **Prov. 3:34** he scorneth the scorners: but he giveth grace unto the *l*.; **11:1-2** a false balance is abomination to the LORD: but a just weight is his delight. When pride cometh, then cometh shame: but with the *l*. is wisdom; **13:7** there is that maketh himself rich, yet hath nothing: there is that maketh himself poor, yet hath great riches.

LOYAL, LOYALTY (*see also* Faithfulness, Obedience, Steadfast, Trustworthiness)

As the LORD liveth, and as my lord the king liveth, surely in what place my lord the king shall be, whether in death or life, even there also will thy servant be. **2 Sam 15:21** (*see also* Serve)

Ruth 1:11-18 Ruth said, Intreat me not to leave thee, or to return from following after thee: for whither thou goest, I will go; and where thou lodgest, I will lodge: thy people shall be my people, and thy God my God; **2 Sam. 15:21** as the LORD liveth, and as my lord the king liveth, surely in what place my lord the king shall be, whether in death or life, even there also will thy servant be; **2 Kgs. 2:1-8** as the LORD liveth, and as thy soul liveth, I will not leave thee; **4:30** as the LORD liveth, and as thy soul liveth, I will not leave thee. And he arose, and followed her.

LUCIFER (*see* Devil, Evil, Satan, Wicked)

LUCRE (*see* Money, Riches, Wealth)

LUST (*see also* Adultery, Carnal, Desire, Fornication, Pleasure)

Flee also youthful lusts: but follow righteousness, faith, charity, peace, with them that call on the Lord out of a pure heart. **2 Tim. 2:22** (*see also* Flee, Peace, Pure)

They tempted God in their heart by asking meat for their lust. **Ps. 78:18** (*see also* Tempt)

Ye ask, and receive not, because ye ask amiss, that ye may consume it upon your lusts. **James 4:3** (*see also* Ask, Consume)

According as his divine power hath given unto us all things that pertain unto life and godliness, through the knowledge of him that hath called us to glory and virtue: Whereby we are given unto us exceeding great and precious promises: that by these ye might be partakers of the divine nature, having escaped the corruption that is in the world through lust. **2 Pet. 1:3-4** (*see also* All Things, Divine Nature, Knowledge, Promise)

God also gave them up to uncleanness through the lusts of their own hearts, to dishonour their own bodies between themselves. **Rom. 1:24** (*see also* Dishonor)

Likewise also the men, leaving the natural use of the woman, burned in their lust one toward another; men with men working that which is unseemly, and receiving in themselves that recompence of their error which was meet. **Rom. 1:27** (*see also* Natural, Men, Women)

Put ye on the Lord Jesus Christ, and make not provision for the flesh, to fulfil the lusts thereof. **Rom. 13:14** (*see also* Flesh, Jesus Christ)

Mark 4:19 the cares of this world, and the deceitfulness of riches, and the *l*. of other things entering in, choke the word, and it becometh unfruitful; **Rom. 6:12** let not sin therefore reign in your mortal body, that ye should obey it in the *l*. thereof; **13:14** put ye on the Lord Jesus Christ, and make not provision for the flesh, to fulfil the *l*. thereof; **1 Cor. 10:6** these things were our examples, to the intent we should not *l*. after evil things, as they also *l*.; **Eph. 2:3** we all had our conversation in times past in the *l*. of our flesh, fulfilling the desires of the flesh and of the mind; and were by nature the children of wrath, even as others; **Col. 3:2** set your affection on things above, not on things on the earth; **2 Tim. 2:22** flee also youthful *l*.: but follow righteousness, faith, charity, peace, with them that call on the Lord out of a pure heart; **Titus 2:12** teaching us that, denying ungodliness and worldly *l*., we should live soberly, righteously, and godly, in this present world; **James 1:14-16** every man is tempted, when he is drawn away of his own *l*., and enticed. Then when lust hath conceived, it bringeth forth sin: and sin, when it is finished, bringeth forth death. Do not err, my beloved brethren; **4:2** ye *l.*, and have not: ye kill, and desire to have, and cannot obtain: ye fight and war, yet ye have not, because ye ask not; **4:5** do ye think that the scripture saith in vain, The spirit that dwelleth in us lusteth to envy; **1 Pet. 2:11** I beseech you as strangers and pilgrims, abstain from fleshly *l.*, which war against the soul; **2 Pet. 2:18** when they speak great swelling words of vanity, they allure through the *l.* of the flesh, through much wantonness, those that were clean escaped from them who live in error; **3:3** there shall come in the last days scoffers, walking after their own *l.*; **1 Jn. 2:16** all that is in the world, the *l.* of the flesh, and the *l.* of the eyes, and the pride of life, is not of the Father, but is of the world; **Jude 1:16** these are murmurers, complainers, walking after their own *l.*; and their mouth speaketh great swelling words, having men's persons in admiration because of advantage; **1:18** there should be mockers in the last time, who should walk after their own ungodly *l.*; **Rev. 18:13-14** the fruits that thy soul *l.* after are departed from thee, and all things which were dainty and goodly are departed from thee.

MAGIC, MAGICIAN (*see also* Sorcery, Superstitious, Witchcraft, Wizardry)

Now the wise men, the astrologers, have been brought in before me, that they should read this writing, and make known unto me the interpretation thereof: but they could not shew the interpretation of the thing. Dan 5:15 (*see also* Astrologer, Dream, Interpretation)

Dan. 2:2 the king commanded to call the *m.* and the astrologers, and the sorcerers, and the Chaldeans, for to shew the king his dreams. So they came and stood before the king; **2:5** the thing is gone from me: if ye will not make known unto me the dream, with the interpretation thereof, ye shall be cut in pieces, and your houses shall be made a dunghill; **2:9-10** ye have prepared lying and corrupt words to speak before me, till the time be changed: therefore tell me the dream, and I shall know that ye can shew me the interpretation thereof; **4:6-7** I [made] a decree to bring in all the wise men of Babylon before me, that they might make known unto me the interpretation of the dream. Then came in the *m.*, the astrologers, the Chaldeans,

and the sooth-sayers; **5:15** now the wise men, the astrologers, have been brought in before me, that they should read this writing, and make known unto me the interpretation thereof: but they could not shew the interpretation of the thing.

MAGNIFY (*see also* Calling, Exalt, Glorify, Praise)

Magnify not thyself against the Lord. Jer. 48:26 (*see also* Against)

MAKE KNOWN (*see also* Declare, Reveal)

Give thanks unto the Lord, call upon his name, make known his deeds among the people. 1 Chron. 16:8 (*see also* Call, Thank)

MALE (*see also* Brethren, Man, Priesthood)

There is neither Jew nor Greek, there is neither bond nor free, there is neither male nor female: for ye are all one in Christ Jesus. Gal. 3:28 (*see also* Bond, Equality, Female, One)

MAN (*see also* Brethren)

And the Lord God formed man of the dust of the ground, and breathed into his nostrils the breath of life; and man became a living soul. Gen 2:7 (*see also* Dust)

MANSION (*see also* House)

In my Father's house are many mansions: if it were not so, I would have told you. I go to prepare a place for you. John 14:2

MARK (*see also* Landmark, Sign)

This one thing I do, forgetting those things which are behind, and reaching forth unto those things which are before, I press toward the mark for the prize of the high calling of God in Christ Jesus. Philip 3:13-14 (*see also* Do, Prize, Reach)

And the Lord said unto them - Go through the midst of the city, through the midst of Jerusalem, and set a mark upon the foreheads of the men that sigh and that cry for all the abominations that be done in the midst thereof. Ezek. 9:4 (*see also* Abomination, Cry)

MARRIAGE (*see also* Children, Family, Father, Husband, Wife)

Marriage is honourable in all, and the bed undefiled: but whoremongers and adulterers God will judge. Heb. 13:4 (*see also* Undefiled)

Now the Spirit speaketh expressly, that in the latter times some shall depart from the faith, giving heed to seducing spirits, and doctrines of devils; Speaking lies in hypocrisy; having their conscience seared with a hot iron; Forbidding to marry, and commanding to abstain from meats, which God hath created to be received with thanksgiving of them which believe and know the truth. 1 Tim. 4:1-3 (*see also* Abstain, Conscience, Food, Latter Day, Meat, Thanksgiving)

Have ye not read, that he which made them at the beginning made them male and female, And said, For this cause shall a man leave father and mother, and shall cleave to his wife: and they twain shall be one flesh? Wherefore they are no more twain, but one flesh. What therefore God hath joined together, let not man put asunder. Matt. 19:4-6 (*see also* Flesh, Join)

Matt. 19:3-6 the Pharisees also came unto him, tempting him, and saying unto him, Is it lawful for a man to put away his wife for every cause? And he answered and said unto them, Have ye not read, that he which made them at the beginning made them male and female, And said, For this cause shall a man leave father and mother, and shall cleave to his wife: and they twain shall be one flesh? Wherefore they are no more twain, but one flesh. What therefore God hath joined together, let not man put asunder; Mark 10:9 what therefore God hath joined together, let not man put asunder.

MASTER (*see also* Lord, Teacher)

Neither be ye called masters: for one is your Master, *even* Christ. Matt. 23:10 (*see also* Call)

No man can serve two masters: for either he will hate the one, and love the other; or else he will hold to the one, and despise the other. Ye cannot serve God and mammon. Matt. 6:24 (*see also* Servant)

MATTER

He that handleth a matter wisely shall find good: and whoso trusteth in the LORD, happy is he. Prov. 16:20 (*see also* Trust, Wise)

But let none of you suffer as a murderer, or as a thief, or as an evildoer, or as a busybody in other men's matters. 1 Pet. 4:15 (*see also* Busybody)

He that answereth a matter before he heareth it, it is folly and shame unto him. Prov. 18:13 (*see also* Answer)

MEAN (*see also* Evil, Wicked)

The mean man shall be brought down, and the mighty man shall be humbled, and the eyes of the lofty shall be humbled. Isa. 5:15 (*see also* Humble, Lofty)

MEAT (*see also* Eat, Flesh, Food, Knowledge)

For when for the time ye ought to be teachers, ye have need that one teach you again which be the first principles of the oracles of God; and are become such as have need of milk, and not of strong meat. Heb 5:12 (*see also* Milk, Principle, Teach)

Now the Spirit speaketh expressly, that in the latter times some shall depart from the faith, giving heed to seducing spirits, and doctrines of devils; Speaking lies in hypocrisy; having their conscience seared with a hot iron; Forbidding to marry, and commanding to abstain from meats, which God hath created to be received with thanksgiving of them which believe and know the truth. 1 Tim. 4:1-3 (*see also* Abstain, Conscience, Food, Latter Day, Marriage, Thanksgiving)

MEDDLE (*see also* Gossip, Talebearer)

Fear thou the LORD and the king: and meddle not with them that are given to change: For their calamity shall rise suddenly; and who knoweth the ruin of them both? Prov. 24:21 (*see also* Change)

MEDIATOR (*see* Jesus Christ, Redeemer, Remission)

MEDITATE (*see also* Consider, Ponder, Think)

Meditate upon these things; give thyself wholly to them; that thy profiting may appear to all. 1 Tim. 4:15 (*see also* Give, Ponder)

I will meditate in thy precepts, and have respect unto thy ways. Ps. 119:15 (*see also* Precept, Way)

This book of the law shall not depart out of thy mouth; but thou shalt meditate therein day and night, that thou mayest observe to do according to all that is written therein: for then thou shalt make thy way prosperous, and then thou shalt have good success. Josh. 1:8 (*see also* Book, Do, Prosperous, Success)

His delight is in the law of the LORD; and in his law doth he mediate day and night. Ps. 1:2 (*see also* Law)

Ps. 1:2-3 his delight is in the law of the LORD; and in his law doth he *m.* day and night; **104:34** my *m.* of him shall be sweet: I will be glad in the LORD; **112:1** praise ye the LORD. Blessed is the man that feareth the LORD, that delighteth greatly in his commandments; **119:16** I will delight myself in thy statutes: I will not forget thy word; **119:23** princes also did sit and speak against me: but thy servant did *m.* in thy statutes; **119:47-48** I will delight myself in thy commandments, which I have loved. My hands also will I lift up unto thy commandments, which I have loved; and I will *m.* in thy statutes; **119:70** their heart is as fat as grease; but I delight in thy law; **119:72** the law of thy mouth is better unto me than thousands of gold and silver; **119:77-78** let thy tender mercies come unto me, that I may live: for thy law is my delight. Let the proud be ashamed; for they dealt perversely with me without a cause: but I will *m.* in thy precepts; **119:97-99** how love I thy law! it is my *m.* all the day. Thou through thy commandments hast made me wiser than mine enemies: for they are ever with me; **119:103** how sweet are thy words unto my taste! yea, sweeter than honey to my mouth; **119:148** mine eyes prevent the night watches, that I might *m.* in thy word; **143:5** I remember the days of old; I *m.* on all thy works; I muse on the work of thy hands.

MEEK, MEEKNESS (*see also* Contrite, Humble, Teachable)

Blessed are the meek: for they shall inherit the earth. Matt. 5:5

Speak evil of no man, to be no brawlers, but gentle, shewing all meekness unto all men. Titus 3:2 (*see also* Gossip, Speak)

The Spirit of the Lord GOD is upon me; because the LORD hath anointed me to preach good tidings unto the meek. Isa. 61:1 (*see also* Preach)

Isa. 61:1-7 the Spirit of the Lord GOD is upon me; because the LORD hath anointed me to preach good tidings unto the *m*; he hath sent me to bind up the brokenhearted, to proclaim liberty to the captives, and the opening of the prison to them that are bound.

Seek ye the LORD, all ye meek of the earth, which have wrought his judgment; seek righteousness, seek meekness: it may be ye shall be hid in the day of the LORD's anger. Zeph. 2:3 (*see also* Seek)

Ps. 22:26 the *m.* shall eat and be satisfied: they shall praise the LORD that seek him: your heart shall live for ever; **25:9** the *m.* will he guide in judgment: and the *m.* will he teach his way; **37:11** the *m.* shall inherit the earth; and shall delight themselves in the abundance of peace; **72:12-13** he shall deliver the needy when he crieth; the poor also, and him that hath no helper. He shall spare the poor and needy, and shall save the souls of the needy; **74:21** let not the oppressed return ashamed: let the poor and needy praise thy name; **76:9** when God arose to judgment, to save all the *m.* of the earth; **147:6** the LORD lifteth up the *m.:* he casteth the wicked down to the ground; **149:4** the LORD taketh pleasure in his people: he will beautify the *m.* with salvation; **Isa. 29:19** the *m.* also shall increase their joy in the LORD, and the poor among men shall rejoice in the Holy One of Israel; **Zeph. 2:3** seek ye the LORD, all ye *m.* of the earth, which have wrought his judgment; seek righteousness, seek *m.:* it may be ye shall be hid in the day of the LORD's anger.

Come unto me, all ye that labour and are heavy laden, and I will give you rest. Take my yoke upon you, and learn of me; for I am meek and lowly in heart: and ye shall find rest unto your souls. Matt. 11:28-29 (*see also* Heart, Heavy, Learn, Lowly, Seek)

Matt. 5:5 blessed are the *m.:* for they shall inherit the earth; **11:29** take my yoke upon you, and learn of me; for I am *m.* and lowly in heart: and ye shall find rest unto your souls; **21:5-6** thy

King cometh unto thee, *m.*, and sitting upon an ass, and a colt the foal of an ass; **Luke 6:20** he lifted up his eyes on his disciples, and said, Blessed be ye poor: for yours is the kingdom of God; **2 Cor. 10:1** I Paul myself beseech you by the *m.* and gentleness of Christ, who in presence am base among you, but being absent am bold toward you; **Gal. 6:1** if a man be overtaken in a fault, ye which are spiritual, restore such an one in the spirit of *m.*; considering thyself, lest thou also be tempted; **Eph. 4:1-2** walk worthy of the vocation wherewith ye are called, With all lowliness and *m.*; **Col. 3:12** put on therefore, as the elect of God, holy and beloved, bowels of mercies, kindness, humbleness of mind, *m.*, longsuffering; **1 Tim. 6:11** O man of God, flee these things; and follow after righteousness, godliness, faith, love, patience, *m.*; **2 Tim. 2:25** in meekness instructing those that oppose themselves; if God peradventure will give them repentance to the acknowledging of the truth; **Titus 3:2** speak evil of no man, to be no brawlers, but gentle, shewing all *m.* unto all men; **James 3:13** let him shew out of a good conversation his works with *m.* of wisdom.

MEET, MEETING (*see also* Assemble, Church, Worship)

Prepare to meet thy God, O Israel. Amos 4:12 (*see also* Prepare)

MELCHISEDEC (*see also* High Priest)

That by two immutable things, in which it was impossible for God to lie, we might have a strong consolation, who have fled for refuge to lay hold upon the hope set before us: Which hope we have as an anchor of the soul, both sure and stedfast, and which entereth into that within the veil; Whither the forerunner is for us entered, even Jesus, made an high priest for ever after the order of Melchisedec. Heb. 6:18-19 (*see also* High Priest, Hope, Impossible)

MEN (*see also* Brethren, Male)

Likewise also the men, leaving the natural use of the woman, burned in their lust one toward another; men with men working that which is unseemly, and receiving in themselves that recompence of their error which was meet. Rom. 1:27 (*see also* Lust, Natural, Women)

MENTION (*see also* Declare, Say)

Ye that make mention of the LORD, keep not silence, And give him no rest, till he establish, and till he make Jerusalem a praise in the earth. Isa. 62:6-7 (*see also* Establish, Jerusalem)

Mention the lovingkindness of the LORD, and the praises of the LORD, according to all that the LORD, hath bestowed on us, and the great goodness toward the house of Israel, which he hath bestowed on them according to his mercies, and according to the multitude of his lovingkindness. Isa. 63:7 (*see also* Loving-kindness)

MERCIFUL, MERCY (*see also* Compassion, Forgive, Justice, Grace, Kindness, Love)

Blessed are the merciful: for they shall obtain mercy. Matt. 5:7

Let them now that fear the LORD say, that his mercy endureth forever. Ps. 118:4

The LORD is good to all: and his tender mercies are over all his works. Ps. 145:9 (*see also* Good)

He that covereth his sins shall not prosper: but whoso confesseth and forsaketh them shall have mercy. Prov. 28:13 (*see also* Confess, Forsake, Sin)

Let thy mercies come also unto me, O LORD, even thy salvation, according to thy word. So shall I have wherewith to answer him that reproacheth me: for I trust in thy word. Ps. 119:41-42 (*see also* Trust, Word)

Let not mercy and truth forsake thee: bind them about thy neck: write them upon the table of thine heart; So shalt thou find favour and good understanding in the sight of God and man. Prov. 3:3-4 (*see also* Bind, Heart, True, Write)

He that followeth after righteousness and mercy, findeth life, righteousness, and honour. Prov. 21:21 (*see also* Follow, Life, Righteousness)

The merciful man doeth good to his own soul: but he that is cruel troubleth his own flesh. Prov. 11:17 (*see also* Cruel)

O man, what is good; and what doth the LORD require of thee, but to do justly, and to love mercy, and to walk humbly with thy God? Micah 6:8 (*see also* Humble, Just)

Also unto thee, O Lord, belongeth mercy: for thou renderest to every man according to his work. Ps. 62:12 (*see also* Render, Work)

The wicked borroweth, and payeth not again: but the righteous sheweth mercy, and giveth. Ps. 37:21 (*see also* Borrow)

Ps. 18:25 with the *m.* thou wilt shew thyself *m.*; with an upright man thou wilt shew thyself upright; **18:50** great deliverance giveth he to his king; and sheweth *m.* to his anointed; **37:21** the wicked borroweth, and payeth not again: but the righteous sheweth *m.*, and giveth; **56:1** be *m.* unto me, O God: for man would swallow me up; he fighting daily oppresseth me; **Prov. 11:17** the *m.* man doeth good to his own soul: but he that is cruel troubleth his own flesh; **14:21** he that despiseth his neighbour sinneth: but he that hath *m.* on the poor, happy is he; **14:31** he that oppresseth the poor reproacheth his Maker: but he that honoureth him hath *m.* on the poor; **20:28** *m.* and truth preserve the king: and his throne is upholden by *m.*; **24:21-22** fear thou the LORD and the king: and meddle not with them that are given to change; **Isa. 16:3-5** in *m.* shall the throne be established: and he shall sit upon it in truth in the tabernacle of David, judging, and seeking judgment, and hasting righteousness; **Dan. 4:27** let my counsel be acceptable unto thee, and break off thy sins by righteousness, and thine iniquities by shewing *m.* to the poor; **Hosea 4:1-5** the LORD hath a controversy with the inhabitants of the land, because there is no truth, nor *m.*, nor knowledge of God in the land; **Zech. 7:9** thus speaketh the LORD of hosts, saying, Execute true judgment, and shew *m.* and compassions every man to his brother.

Be ye therefore merciful, as your Father also is merciful. Luke 6:36

Matt. 5:7 blessed are the *m.*: for they shall obtain *m.*; **20:30-31** have *m.* on us, O Lord, thou Son of David; **Luke 6:36** be ye therefore *m.*, as your Father also is *m.*; **10:33-34** a certain Samaritan, as he journeyed, came where he was: and when he saw him, he had compassion on him, And went to him, and bound up his wounds, pouring in oil and wine, and set him on his own beast, and brought him to an inn, and took care of him; **10:37** he that shewed *m.* on him. Then

said Jesus unto him, Go, and do thou likewise; **18:39** he cried so much the more, Thou Son of David, have *m.* on me; **Acts 7:60** he kneeled down, and cried with a loud voice, Lord, lay not this sin to their charge. And when he had said this, he fell asleep; **Rom. 9:16** so then it is not of him that willeth, nor of him that runneth, but of God that sheweth *m.*; **11:32** God hath concluded them all in unbelief, that he might have *m.* upon all; **15:9** the Gentiles might glorify God for his *m.*; as it is written, For this cause I will confess to thee among the Gentiles, and sing unto thy name; **2 Cor. 4:1** seeing we have this ministry, as we have received *m.*, we faint not; **Gal. 6:1** if a man be overtaken in a fault, ye which are spiritual, restore such an one in the spirit of meekness; considering thyself, lest thou also be tempted; **Eph. 2:4** God, who is rich in *m.*, for his great love wherewith he loved us; **Philip. 2:26-27** he was sick nigh unto death: but God had *m.* on him; and not on him only, but on me also, lest I should have sorrow upon sorrow; **James 2:13** he shall have judgment without *m.*, that hath shewed no *m.*; and *m.* rejoiceth against judgment; **3:17** the wisdom that is from above is first pure, then peaceable, gentle, and easy to be intreated, full of *m.* and good fruits, without partiality, and without hypocrisy; **5:11** we count them happy which endure. Ye have heard of the patience of Job, and have seen the end of the Lord; that the Lord is very pitiful, and of tender *m.*

I am like a green olive tree in the house of God: I trust in the mercy of God for ever and ever. Ps. 52:8 (*see also* Trust)

Ps. 23:6 goodness and *m.* shall follow me all the days of my life: and I will dwell in the house of the LORD for ever; **33:18-19** the eye of the LORD is upon them that fear him, upon them that hope in his *m.*; To deliver their soul from death; **33:22** let thy *m.*, O LORD, be upon us, according as we hope in thee; **38:15** in thee, O LORD, do I hope: thou wilt hear, O LORD my God; **52:8** I am like a green olive tree in the house of God: I trust in the *m.* of God for ever and ever; **59:17** God is my defence, and the God of my *m.*; **71:14** I will hope continually, and will yet praise thee more and more; **103:15-17** the *m.* of the LORD is from everlasting to everlasting upon them that fear him, and his righteousness unto childrens children; **111:7** the works of his hands are verity and judgment; all his commandments are sure; **119:124** deal with thy servant according unto thy *m.*, and teach me thy statutes; **Hosea 6:6** I desired *m.*, and not sacrifice; and the knowledge of God more than burnt offerings; **10:12** sow to yourselves in righteousness, reap in *m.*; break up your fallow ground: for it is time to seek the LORD, till he come and rain righteousness upon you.

MERRY (*see also* Happiness, Joy, Wonderful)

Is any merry? Let him sing psalms. James 5:13 (*see also* Sing)

A merry heart doeth good *like* **a medicine: but a broken spirit drieth the bones. Prov. 17:22**

2 Chron. 7:10 he sent the people away into their tents, glad and *m.* in heart for the goodness that the LORD had shewed; **Prov. 17:22** a *m.* heart doeth good like a medicine: but a broken spirit drieth the bones.

MESSENGER (*see also* Angel, Apostle, Disciple, Prophet, Servant)

The priests lips should keep knowledge, and they should seek the law at his mouth: for he is the messenger of the LORD of hosts. Mal. 2:7 (*see also* Know, Priest)

They mocked the messengers of God, and despised his words, and misused his prophets, until the wrath of the LORD arose against his people, till there was no remedy. 2 Chron. 36:16 (*see also* Mock, Persecute, Prophet)

2 Chron. 36:16 they mocked the *m.* of God, and despised his words, and misused his prophets, until the wrath of the LORD arose against his people, till there was no remedy; **Neh. 4:1** when Sanballat heard that we builded the wall, he was wroth, and took great indignation, and *m.* the Jews; **Ps. 2:2** the kings of the earth set themselves, and the rulers take counsel together, against the LORD, and against his anointed; **Prov. 13:13** whoso despiseth the word shall be destroyed: but he that feareth the commandment shall be rewarded; **17:5** whoso *m.* the poor reproacheth his Maker: and he that is glad at calamities shall not be unpunished; **19:16** he that keepeth the commandment keepeth his own soul; but he that despiseth his ways shall die; **Isa. 28:22** be ye not *m.*, lest your bands be made strong: for I have heard from the Lord GOD of hosts a consumption, even determined upon the whole earth; **Jer. 15:17** I sat not in the assembly of the *m.*, nor rejoiced.

MESSIAH (*see also* Christ, Jesus Christ, Lord, Savior)

The woman saith unto him, I know that Messias cometh, which is called Christ: when he is come, he will tell us all things. John 4:25 (*see also* All Things)

MIGHT, MIGHTILY, MIGHTY (*see also* Great, Strength)

Whatever thy hand findeth to do, do it with thy might; for there is no work, nor device, nor knowledge, nor wisdom, in the grave, whither thou goest. Eccl. 9:10 (*see also* Hand)

MILE

Whosoever shall compel thee to go a mile, go with him twain. Matt. 5:41 (*see also* Compel)

MILK (*see also* Food, Knowledge)

For when for the time ye ought to be teachers, ye have need that one teach you again which be the first principles of the oracles of God; and are become such as have need of milk, and not of strong meat. Heb 5:12 (*see also* Meat, Principle, Teach)

MIND, MINDED, MINDFUL (*see also* Intelligence, Learn, Study)

They received the word with all readiness of mind, and searched the scriptures daily, whether those things were so. Acts 17:11 (*see also* Daily, Readiness, Receive, Scripture, Search, Word)

Young men likewise exhort to be sober minded. Titus 2:6 (*see also* Sober)

Be spiritually minded. Rom. 8:6 (*see also* Spiritually)

Be of one mind. 2 Cor. 13:11 (*see also* One, Unity)

Gird up the loins of your mind, be sober, and hope to the end for the grace that is to be brought unto you at the revelation of Jesus Christ. 1 Pet. 1:13 (*see also* Grace, Hope, Jesus Christ)

Be ye transformed by the renewing of your mind, that ye may prove what is that good, and acceptable, and perfect, will of God. Rom. 12:2 (*see also* Prove, Renew, Transform)

He is proud, knowing nothing, but doting about questions and strifes of words, whereof cometh envy, strife, railings, evil surmisings, Perverse disputings of men of corrupt minds, and destitute of the truth, supposing that gain is godliness: from such withdraw thyself. 1 Tim. 6:4-5 (*see also* Question, Strife, Pride, True)

They that are after the flesh do mind the things of the flesh; but they that are after the Spirit the things of the Spirit. For to be carnally minded is death; but to be spiritually minded is life and peace. Rom. 8:5-6 (*see also* Flesh, Spirit)

Rom. 8:6-7 to be carnally *m.* is death; but to be spiritually *m.* is life and peace. Because the carnal *m.* is enmity against God: for it is not subject to the law of God, neither indeed can be; 8:11 if the Spirit of him that raised up Jesus from the dead dwell in you, he that raised up Christ from the dead shall also quicken your mortal bodies by his Spirit that dwelleth in you; Gal. 2:20 I am crucified with Christ: nevertheless I live; yet not I, but Christ liveth in me: and the life which I now live in the flesh I live by the faith of the Son of God, who loved me, and gave himself for me; 6:1 if a man be overtaken in a fault, ye which are spiritual, restore such an one in the spirit of meekness; considering thyself, lest thou also be tempted; Col. 1:21 you, that were sometime alienated and enemies in your *m.* by wicked works, yet now hath he reconcile.

A double minded man is unstable in all his ways. James 1:8 (*see also* Double Minded, Unsteady, Way)

James 1:8 a double *m.* man is unstable in all his ways; 3:9-13 therewith bless we God, even the Father; and therewith curse we men, which are made after the similitude of God. Out of the same mouth proceedeth blessing and cursing. My brethren, these things ought not so to be. Doth a fountain send forth at the same place sweet water and bitter? Can the fig tree, my brethren, bear olive berries? either a vine, figs? so can no fountain both yield salt water and fresh; 4:8 purify your hearts, ye double *m.*

MINISTER, MINISTERING, MINISTRY (*see also* Angel, Compassion, Priesthood, Serve, Steward)

Even as the Son of man came not to be ministered unto, but to minister, and to give his life a ransom for many. Matt. 20:28 (*see also* Ransom)

Take heed to the ministry which thou hast received in the Lord, that thou fulfill it. Col. 4:17 (*see also* Call)

If thou put the brethren in remembrance of these things, thou shalt be a good minister of Jesus Christ, nourished up in the words of faith and of good doctrine, whereunto thou hast attained. 1 Tim. 4:6 (*see also* Remember, Nourish)

Minister unto the saints. Rom. 15:25

Rom. 15:25 now I go unto Jerusalem to *m.* unto the saints; 2 Tim. 1:16-18 the Lord grant unto him that he may find mercy of the Lord in that day: and in how many things he *m.* unto me at Ephesus, thou knowest very well.

MIRACLE, MIRACULOUS (*see also* Bless, Gift, Heal)

How shall we escape, if we neglect so great salvation; which at the first began to be spoken by the Lord, and was confirmed unto us by them that heard him; God also bearing them witness, both with signs and wonders, and with divers miracles, and gifts of the Holy Ghost, according to his own will? Heb. 2:3-4 (*see also* Escape, Salvation, Witness)

[They] were beyond measure astonished, saying, He hath done all things well: he maketh both the deaf to hear, and the dumb to speak. Mark 7:37 (*see also* Deaf, Dumb)

Where be all his miracles which our fathers told us? Judg. 6:13 (*see also* Belief)

Ex. 7:9 shew a *m.* for you: then thou shalt say unto Aaron, Take thy rod, and cast it before Pharaoh, and it shall become a serpent; 14:21-22 Moses stretched out his hand over the sea; and the LORD caused the sea to go back by a strong east wind all that night, and made the sea dry land, and the waters were divided. And the children of Israel went into the midst of the sea upon the dry ground: and the waters were a wall unto them on their right hand, and on their left; **15:25** the LORD shewed him a tree, which when he had cast into the waters, the waters were made sweet: there he made for them a statute and an ordinance, and there he proved them; **Num. 14:22** all those men which have seen my glory, and my *m.*, which I did in Egypt and in the wilderness, and have tempted me now these ten times, and have not hearkened to my voice; **21:9** Moses made a serpent of brass, and put it upon a pole, and it came to pass, that if a serpent had bitten any man, when he beheld the serpent of brass, he lived; **Deut. 11:3** his *m.*, and his acts, which he did in the midst of Egypt unto Pharaoh the king of Egypt, and unto all his land; **Judg. 6:13** where be all his *m.* which our fathers told us of, saying, Did not the LORD bring us up from Egypt; **1 Kgs. 17:13-16** thus saith the LORD God of Israel, The barrel of meal shall not waste, neither shall the cruse of oil fail, until the day that the LORD sendeth rain upon the earth. And she went and did according to the saying of Elijah: and she, and he, and her house, did eat many days. And the barrel of meal wasted not, neither did the cruse of oil fail, according to the word of the LORD, which he spake by Elijah; **2 Kgs. 5:8-14** go and wash in Jordan seven times, and thy flesh shall come again to thee, and thou shalt be clean... according to the saying of the man of God: and his flesh came again like unto the flesh of a little child, and he was clean.

All the multitude kept silence, and gave audience to Barnabas and Paul, declaring what miracles and wonders God had wrought among the Gentiles by them. Acts 15:12 (*see also* Declare)

Matt. 4:24 they brought unto him all sick people that were taken with divers diseases and torments, and those which were possessed with devils, and those which were lunatick, and those that had the palsy; and he healed them; **8:2-3** (Mark 1:40-41, Luke 5:12-13) there came a leper and worshipped him, saying, Lord, if thou wilt, thou canst make me clean. And Jesus put forth his hand, and touched him, saying, I will; be thou clean. And immediately his leprosy was cleansed; **8:6-8** Lord, my servant lieth at home sick of the palsy, grievously tormented. And Jesus saith unto him, I will come and heal him. The centurion answered and said, Lord, I am not worthy that thou shouldest come under my roof: but speak the word only, and my servant shall be healed; **8:13** Jesus said unto the centurion, Go thy way; and as thou hast believed, so be it done unto thee. And his servant was healed in the

selfsame hour; **8:14-15** (Mark 1:30-31, Luke 4:38-39) when Jesus was come into Peter's house, he saw his wife's mother laid, and sick of a fever. And he touched her hand, and the fever left her: and she arose, and ministered unto them; **8:26** why are ye fearful, O ye of little faith? Then he arose, and rebuked the winds and the sea; and there was a great calm; **8:28-32** he said unto them, Go. And when they were come out, they went into the herd of swine: and, behold, the whole herd of swine ran violently down a steep place into the sea, and perished in the waters; **9:2-6** they brought to him a man sick of the palsy, lying on a bed: and Jesus seeing their faith said unto the sick of the palsy; Son, be of good cheer; thy sins be forgiven thee; **9:24-25** give place: for the maid is not dead, but sleepeth. And they laughed him to scorn. But when the people were put forth, he went in, and took her by the hand, and the maid arose; **9:27-31** two blind men followed him, crying, and saying, Thou Son of David, have mercy on us. And when he was come into the house, the blind men came to him: and Jesus saith unto them, Believe ye that I am able to do this? They said unto him, Yea, Lord. Then touched he their eyes, saying, According to your faith be it unto you. And their eyes were opened; **9:32-33** they brought to him a dumb man possessed with a devil. And when the devil was cast out, the dumb spake: and the multitudes marvelled, saying, It was never so seen in Israel; **9:35** Jesus went about all the cities and villages... healing every sickness and every disease among the people; **12:13** stretch forth thine hand. And he stretched it forth; and it was restored whole, like as the other; **12:22** one possessed with a devil, blind, and dumb: and he healed him, insomuch that the blind and dumb both spake and saw; **14:15-21** (Mark 6:37-44, Luke 9:16-17, John 6:4-12) And they did all eat, and were filled: and they took up of the fragments that remained twelve baskets full. And they that had eaten were about five thousand men, beside women and children **14:23-25** in the fourth watch of the night Jesus went unto them, walking on the sea; **14:34-36** (Mark 6:53-56) they sent out into all that country round about, and brought unto him all that were diseased; And besought him that they might only touch the hem of his garment: and as many as touched were made perfectly whole; **15:28** O woman, great is thy faith: be it unto thee even as thou wilt. And her daughter was made whole from that very hour; **15:30-31** great multitudes came unto him, having with them those that were lame, blind, dumb, maimed, and many others, and cast them down at Jesus' feet; and he healed them; **15:32-**

39 (Mark 8:4-9) he took the seven loaves and the fishes, and gave thanks, and brake them, and gave to his disciples, and the disciples to the multitude. And they did all eat, and were filled: and they took up of the broken meat that was left seven baskets full. And they that did eat were four thousand men, beside women and children. **17:18** Jesus rebuked the devil; and he departed out of him: and the child was cured from that very hour; **17:27** lest we should offend them, go thou to the sea, and cast an hook, and take up the fish that first cometh up; and when thou hast opened his mouth, thou shalt find a piece of money: that take, and give unto them for me and thee; **19:2** great multitudes followed him; and he healed them there; **20:32-34** Lord, that our eyes may be opened. So Jesus had compassion on them, and touched their eyes: and immediately their eyes received sight, and they followed him; **21:14** the blind and the lame came to him in the temple; and he healed them; **27:52** the graves were opened; and many bodies of the saints which slept arose; **Mark 1:32-34** he healed many that were sick of divers diseases, and cast out many devils; and suffered not the devils to speak, because they knew him; **2:8-11** (Luke 5:24-25) that ye may know that the Son of man hath power on earth to forgive sins, (he saith to the sick of the palsy,) I say unto thee, Arise, and take up thy bed, and go thy way into thine house; **3:10-12** he had healed many; insomuch that they pressed upon him for to touch him, as many as had plagues. And unclean spirits, when they saw him, fell down before him, and cried, saying, Thou art the Son of God. And he straitly charged them that they should not make him known; **5:36-39** when he was come in, he saith unto them, Why make ye this ado, and weep? the damsel is not dead, but sleepeth; **5:41-42** he took the damsel by the hand, and said unto her, Talitha cumi; which is, being interpreted, Damsel, I say unto thee, arise. And straightway the damsel arose, and walked; **7:32-36** looking up to heaven, he sighed, and saith unto him, Ephphatha, that is, Be opened. And straightway his ears were opened, and the string of his tongue was loosed, and he spake plain; **8:22-25** he took the blind man by the hand, and led him out of the town; and when he had spit on his eyes, and put his hands upon him, he asked him if he saw ought. And he looked up, and said, I see men as trees, walking. After that he put his hands again upon his eyes, and made him look up: and he was restored, and saw every man clearly; **9:23** if thou canst believe, all things are possible to him that believeth; **9:38-39** forbid him not: for there is no man which shall do a *m.* in my name, that

can lightly speak evil of me; **Luke 5:15** great multitudes came together to hear, and to be healed by him of their infirmities; **5:17** the power of the Lord was present to heal them; **6:17-19** they that were vexed with unclean spirits: and they were healed. And the whole multitude sought to touch him: for there went virtue out of him, and healed them all; **7:10** they that were sent, returning to the house, found the servant whole that had been sick; **7:12-15** he said, Young man, I say unto thee, Arise. And he that was dead sat up, and began to speak. And he delivered him to his mother; **7:21** in that same hour he cured many of their infirmities and plagues, and of evil spirits; and unto many that were blind he gave sight; **7:22** go your way, and tell John what things ye have seen and heard; how that the blind see, the lame walk, the lepers are cleansed, the deaf hear, the dead are raised, to the poor the gospel is preached; **8:49-50** fear not: believe only, and she shall be made whole; **9:1** he called his twelve disciples together, and gave them power and authority over all devils, and to cure diseases; **9:6** they departed, and went through the towns, preaching the gospel, and healing every where; **9:37-42** O faithless and perverse generation, how long shall I be with you, and suffer you? Bring thy son hither. And as he was yet a coming, the devil threw him down, and tare him. And Jesus rebuked the unclean spirit, and healed the child, and delivered him again to his father; **11:14** he was casting out a devil, and it was dumb. And it came to pass, when the devil was gone out, the dumb spake; and the people wondered; **13:11-13** he laid his hands on her: and immediately she was made straight, and glorified God; **22:51** he touched his ear, and healed him; **John 2:1-10** every man at the beginning doth set forth good wine; and when men have well drunk, then that which is worse: but thou hast kept the good wine until now; **2:11** this beginning of *m.* did Jesus in Cana of Galilee, and manifested forth his glory; and his disciples believed on him; **3:2** Rabbi, we know that thou art a teacher come from God: for no man can do these *m.* that thou doest, except God be with him; **4:46-54** then enquired he of them the hour when he began to amend. And they said unto him, Yesterday at the seventh hour the fever left him. So the father knew that it was at the same hour, in the which Jesus said unto him, Thy son liveth: and himself believed, and his whole house; **5:8-9** rise, take up thy bed, and walk. And immediately the man was made whole, and took up his bed, and walked: and on the same day was the sabbath; **6:2** a great multitude followed him, because they saw his *m.*

which he did on them that were diseased; **6:14** when they had seen the *m.* that Jesus did, said, This is of a truth that prophet that should come into the world; **6:26** ye seek me, not because ye saw the *m.*, but because ye did eat of the loaves, and were filled; **7:30-31** when Christ cometh, will he do more *m.* than these which this man hath done; **9:6-9** When he had thus spoken, he spat on the ground, and made clay of the spittle, and he anointed the eyes of the blind man with the clay; **9:16** this man is not of God, because he keepeth not the sabbath day. Others said, How can a man that is a sinner do such *m.*; **10:41** many resorted unto him, and said, John did no *m.*: but all things that John spake of this man were true; **11:43-44** he cried with a loud voice, Lazarus, come forth. And he that was dead came forth, bound hand and foot with graveclothes: and his face was bound about with a napkin. Jesus saith unto them, Loose him, and let him go; **11:47** then gathered the chief priests and the Pharisees a council, and said, What do we? for this man doeth many *m.*; **12:1-2** Lazarus was which had been dead, whom he raised from the dead. There they made him a supper; and Martha served: but Lazarus was one of them that sat at the table with him; **12:18** the people also met him, for that they heard that he had done this *m.*; **12:37** though he had done so many *m.* before them, yet they believed not on him; **Acts 2:22** Jesus of Nazareth, a man approved of God among you by *m.* and wonders and signs, which God did by him in the midst of you, as ye yourselves also know; **2:43** fear came upon every soul: and many wonders and signs were done by the apostles; **3:2-8** a certain man lame from his mother's womb was carried, whom they laid daily at the gate of the temple which is called Beautiful; **4:14** beholding the man which was healed standing with them, they could say nothing against it; **4:16** a notable *m.* hath been done by them is manifest to all them that dwell in Jerusalem; and we cannot deny it; **4:22** the man was above forty years old, on whom this *m.* of healing was shewed; **4:30** by stretching forth thine hand to heal; and that signs and wonders may be done by the name of thy holy child Jesus; **5:12** the hands of the apostles were many signs and wonders wrought among the people; **5:15-16** insomuch that they brought forth the sick into the streets, and laid them on beds and couches, that at the least the shadow of Peter passing by might overshadow some of them; **5:23** the prison truly found we shut with all safety, and the keepers standing without before the doors: but when we had opened, we found no man within; **6:8** Stephen, full of faith and power,

did great wonders and *m.* among the people; **7:36** he had shewed wonders and signs in the land of Egypt, and in the Red sea, and in the wilderness forty years; **8:6** the people with one accord gave heed unto those things which Philip spake, hearing and seeing the *m.* which he did; **8:13** he continued with Philip, and wondered, beholding the *m.* and signs which were done; **9:37-42** Peter put them all forth, and kneeled down, and prayed; and turning him to the body said, Tabitha, arise. And she opened her eyes: and when she saw Peter, she sat up; **15:12** all the multitude kept silence, and gave audience to Barnabas and Paul, declaring what *m.* and wonders God had wrought among the Gentiles by them; **19:11-12** God wrought special *m.* by the hands of Paul; **20:9-12** Paul went down, and fell on him, and embracing him said, Trouble not yourselves; for his life is in him; **28:3-6** they looked when he should have swollen, or fallen down dead suddenly: but after they had looked a great while, and saw no harm come to him, they changed their minds, and said that he was a god; **1 Cor. 12:10** to another the working of *m.*; to another prophecy; **14:22-25** tongues are for a sign, not to them that believe, but to them that believe not: but prophesying serveth not for them that believe not, but for them which believe; **14:31-32** ye may all prophesy one by one, that all may learn, and all may be comforted. And the spirits of the prophets are subject to the prophets; **2 Cor. 12:12** the signs of an apostle were wrought among you in all patience, in signs, and wonders, and mighty deeds.

MISCHIEF (*see also* Harm, Rebel)

These six things doth the LORD hate: yea, seven are an abomination unto him: A proud look, a lying tongue, and hands that shed innocent blood, An heart that deviseth wicked imaginations, feet that be swift in running to mischief, A false witness that speaketh lies, and he that soweth discord among brethren. Prov. 6:16-19 (*see also* Discord, False Witness, Imagine, Innocent, Pride)

O full of all subtilty and all mischief, thou child of the devil, thou enemy of all righteousness, wilt thou not cease to pervert the right ways of the Lord. Acts 13:10 (*see also* Pervert, Subtle, Way)

His mischief shall return upon his own head, and his violent dealing shall come down upon his own pate. Ps. 7:16 (*see also* Head, Return, Violent)

Oppress not the widow, nor the fatherless, the stranger, nor the poor; and let none of you imagine evil against his brother in your heart. Zech. 7:10 (*see also* Heart, Imagine)

He that diligently seeketh good procureth favour: but he that seeketh mischief, it shall come unto him. Prov. 11:27

Prov. 10:23 it is as sport to a fool to do *m.*: but a man of understanding hath wisdom; **11:27** he that diligently seeketh good procureth favour: but he that seeketh *m.*, it shall come unto him.

None calleth for justice, nor any pleadeth for truth: they trust in vanity, and speak lies; they conceive mischief, and bring forth iniquity. Isa. 59:4 (*see also* Conceive)

Isa. 59:4-5 none calleth for justice, nor any pleadeth for truth: they trust in vanity, and speak lies; they conceive *m.*, and bring forth iniquity; **Ezek. 11:2** said he unto me, Son of man, these are the men that devise *m.*, and give wicked counsel in this city; **Dan. 11:27** both these kings hearts shall be to do *m.*, and they shall speak lies at one table; but it shall not prosper: for yet the end shall be at the time appointed.

MISERABLE, MISERY (*see* Adversity, Despair, Hate, Pain)

MISSIONARY WORK (*see also* Baptize, Declare, Exhort, Minister, Messenger, Preach, Seventy, Teach, Warn)

The Lord appointed other seventy also, and sent them two by two before his face into every city and place, whither he himself would come. Luke 10:1 (*see also* Seventy)

MOCK, MOCKING, MOCERY (*see also* Persecute, Profane)

They mocked the messengers of God, and despised his words, and misused his prophets, until the wrath of the LORD arose against his people, till there was no remedy. 2 Chron. 36:16 (*see also* Messenger, Persecute, Prophet)

They shall mock him, and shall scourge him, and shall spit upon him, and shall kill him: and the third day he shall rise again. Mark 10:34 (*see also* Jesus Christ)

Matt. 20:19 shall deliver him to the Gentiles to *m.*, and to scourge, and to crucify him: and the third day he shall rise again; **27:26-31** they stripped him, and put on him a scarlet robe. And when they had platted a crown of thorns, they put it upon his head, and a reed in his right hand: and they bowed the knee before him, and *m.* him, saying, Hail, King of the Jews! And they spit upon him, and took the reed, and smote him on the head. And after that they had *m.* him, they took the robe off from him, and put his own raiment on him, and led him away to crucify him; **27:41-43** the chief priests *m.* him, with the scribes and elders, said, He saved others; himself he cannot save. If he be the King of Israel, let him now come down from the cross, and we will believe him. He trusted in God; let him deliver him now, if he will have him: for he said, I am the Son of God; **Mark 10:34** they shall *m.* him, and shall scourge him, and shall spit upon him, and shall kill him: and the third day he shall rise again; **15:15-20** they clothed him with purple, and platted a crown of thorns, and put it about his head, And began to salute him, Hail, King of the Jews! And they smote him on the head with a reed, and did spit upon him, and bowing their knees worshipped him. And when they had *m.* him, they took off the purple from him, and put his own clothes on him, and led him out to crucify him; **15:29-30** they that passed by railed on him, wagging their heads, and saying, Ah, thou that destroyest the temple, and buildest it in three days, Save thyself, and come down from the cross; **15:32** let Christ the King of Israel descend now from the cross, that we may see and believe. And they that were crucified with him reviled him; **Luke 14:29** after he hath laid the foundation, and is not able to finish it, all that behold it begin to *m.* him; **John 19:1-3** Pilate therefore took Jesus, and scourged him. And the soldiers platted a crown of thorns, and put it on his head, and they put on him a purple robe, And said, Hail, King of the Jews! and they smote him with their hands; **Rom. 2:23** thou that makest thy boast of the law, through breaking the law dishonourest thou God.

MODEST, MODESTY (*see also* Apparel)

In like manner also, that women adorn themselves in modest apparel, with shame-facedness and sobriety; not with broided hair, or gold, or pearls, or costly array; but (which becometh women professing godliness) with good works. 1 Tim. 2:9-10 (*see also* Apparel)

MONEY (*see also* Bribe, Debt, Riches, Treasure, Wealth)

The love of money is the root of all evil: which while some coveted after, they have erred from the faith, and pierced themselves through with many sorrows. 1 Tim. 6:9 (*see also* Evil, Sorrow)

MORTAL, MORTALITY (*see also* Blood, Fallen, Flesh)

MOTHER (*see also* Child, Family, Marriage, Parent)

Whoso curseth his father or his mother, his lamp shall be put out in obscure darkness. Prov. 20:20 (*see also* Curse, Father)

Honour thy father and thy mother, as the LORD thy God hath commanded thee; that thy days may be prolonged, and that it may go well with thee, in the land which the LORD thy God giveth thee. Deut. 5:16 (*see also* Father, Go, Honor)

MOUNTAIN

How beautiful upon the mountains are the feet of him that bringeth good tidings, that publisheth peace; that bringeth good tidings of good, that publisheth salvation; that saith unto Zion, Thy God reigneth! Isa. 52:7 (*see also* Good, Peace, Publish, Zion)

Come, and let us go up to the mountain of the LORD, and to the house of the God of Jacob; and he will teach us of his ways, and we will walk in his paths; for the law shall go forth of Zion, and the word of the LORD from Jerusalem. Micah 4:2 (*see also* House, Jerusalem, Law, Ways, Word, Zion)

Isa. 2:2 the *m.* of the LORD's house shall be established in the top of the *m.*, and shall be exalted above the hills; and all nations shall flow unto it; **Micah 4:2** come, and let us go up to the mountain of the LORD, and to the house of the

God of Jacob; and he will teach us of his ways, and we will walk in his paths.

MOURN, MOURNING (*see also* Despair, Grief, Sorrow)

Blessed are they that mourn; for they shall be comforted. Matt. 5:4

Proclaim the acceptable year of the Lord, and the day of vengeance of our God; to comfort all that mourn. Isa. 61:2 (*see also* Comfort, Proclaim, Year)

When the righteous are in authority, the people rejoice: but when the wicked beareth rule, the people mourn. Prov. 29:2 (*see also* Authority, Righteous, Rule, Wicked)

MOUTH (*see also* Lips, Speak, Tongue, Voice)

Do not ye yet understand, that whatsoever entereth in at the mouth goeth into the belly, and is cast out into the draught? But those things which proceed out of the mouth come froth from the heart; and they defile the man. For out of the heart proceed evil thoughts, murders, adulteries, fornications, thefts, false witness, blasphemies: These are the things which defile a man: but to eat with unwashen hands defileth not a man. Matt: 17-20 (*see also* Defile, Heart, Proceed)

My son, attend unto my wisdom, and bow thine ear to my understanding: That thou mayest regard discretion and *that* thy lips may keep knowledge. Prov. 5:2 (*see also* Discrete, Lips)

Out of the same mouth proceedeth blessing and cursing. My brethren, these things ought not so to be. James 3:10 (*see also* Proceed)

Take heed to speak that which the Lord hath put in thy mouth. Num. 23:12 (*see also* Speak)

He spake by the mouth of his holy prophets, which have been since the world began. Luke 1:70 (*see also* Prophet)

The mouth of them that speak lies shall be stopped. Ps. 63:11 (*see also* Liar)

Suffer not thy mouth to cause thy flesh to sin; neither say thou before the angel, that it was an error. Eccl. 5:6 (*see also* Sin)

Ye hypocrites, well did Esaias prophesy of you, saying, This people draweth nigh unto me with their mouth, and honoureth me with their lips; but their heart is far from me. Matt. 15:7-8 (*see also* Hypocrite)

Be not rash with thy mouth, and let not thine heart be hasty to utter any thing before God: for God is in heaven, and thou upon earth: therefore let thy words be few. Eccl. 5:2-3 (*see also* Haste)

MOVE, MOVED (*see also* Inspired)

For the prophecy came not in old time by the will of man: but holy men of God spake as they were moved by the Holy Ghost. 2 Pet. 1:21 (*see also* Holy Ghost, Prophecy)

Cast thy burden upon the LORD, and he shall sustain thee: he shall never suffer the righteous to be moved. Ps. 55:22 (*see also* Burden)

MULTIPLY (*see also* Increase)

Be fruitful, and multiply, and replenish the earth, and subdue it. Gen. 1:28 (*see also* Replenish)

Gen. 1:22 be fruitful, and *m.*, and fill the waters in the seas, and let fowl *m.* in the earth; **1:28** be fruitful, and *m.*, and replenish the earth, and subdue it; **4:1-2** Eve bare Cain, and said, I have gotten a man from the LORD; **4:25** she bare Seth: For God, hath appointed me another seed; **6:1** men began to *m.* on the face of the earth; **6:4** the sons of God came in unto the daughters of men, and they bare children to them; **8:17** every living thing that is with thee, *m.* upon the earth; **9:1** be fruitful, and *m.*, and replenish the earth; **9:7** bring forth abundantly in the earth, and *m.* therein; **35:11** be fruitful and *m.*; **47:27** Israel... grew, and *m.* exceedingly; **Ex. 1:7** the children of Israel were fruitful, and increased abundantly, and *m.*, and waxed exceeding mighty; **1:20** God dealt well with the midwives: and the people *m.*, and waxed very mighty; **Deut. 8:1** live, and *m.*, and go in and possess the land which the LORD sware unto your fathers; **Job 29:18** I shall *m.* my days as the sand; **Jer. 23:3** they shall be fruitful and increase.

MULTITUDE

And above all things have fervent charity among yourselves: for charity shall cover the multitude of sins. 1 Pet 4:8 (*see also* Charity, Sin)

MURDER (*see* Blood, Kill)

MURMUR, MURMURING (*see also* Dispute, Gossip, Rebel)

Do all things without murmurings and disputings: That ye may be blameless and harmless, the sons of God, without rebuke, in the midst of a crooked and perverse nation, among whom ye shine as lights in the world. Philip. 2:14-15 (*see also* All Things, Dispute)

John 6:43 Jesus therefore answered and said unto them, *M.* not among yourselves; **1 Cor. 10:10** neither murmur ye, as some of them also murmured, and were destroyed of the destroyer; **Philip. 2:13-15** it is God which worketh in you both to will and to do of his good pleasure. Do all things without *m.* and disputings: That ye may be blameless and harmless, the sons of God, without rebuke, in the midst of a crooked and perverse nation, among whom ye shine as lights in the world; **4:11** Not that I speak in respect of want: for I have learned, in whatsoever state I am, therewith to be content.

The LORD heareth your murmurings which ye murmur against him: and what are we? your murmurings are not against us, but against the LORD. Ex. 16:8

Ex. 16:2 the whole congregation of the children of Israel *m.* against Moses and Aaron in the wilderness; **16:7-8** ye shall see the glory of the LORD; for that he heareth your *m.* against the LORD: and what are we, that ye *m.* against us? And Moses said, This shall be, when the LORD shall give you in the evening flesh to eat, and in the morning bread to the full; for that the LORD heareth your *m.* which ye *m.* against him: and what are we? your *m.* are not against us, but against the LORD; **Num. 14:26-27** how long shall I bear with this evil congregation, which *m.* against me? I have heard the *m.* of the children of Israel, which they *m.* against me; **Ps. 106:25-26** but *m.* in their tents, and hearkened not unto the voice of the LORD. Therefore he lifted up his hand against them, to overthrow them in the wilderness.

MYSTERIES, MYSTERY (*see also* Knowledge)

I have yet many things to say unto you, but ye cannot bear them now. John 16:12 (*see also* Learn)

Eye hath not seen, nor ear heard, neither have entered into the heart of man, the things which God hath prepared for them that love him. But God hath reveled them unto us by his Spirit; for the Spirit searcheth all things, yea, the deep things of God. 1 Cor. 2:9-10 (*see also* Enter, Search, Spirit)

And he said unto them, Unto you it is given to know the mystery of the kingdom of God: but unto them that are without, all these things are done in parables. Mark 4:11 (*see also* Parable)

Call unto me, and I will answer thee, and shew thee great and mighty things, which thou knowest not. Jer. 33:3 (*see also* Call, Reveal)

Ps. 119:18 open thou mine eyes, that I may behold wondrous things out of thy law; **119:23** princes also did sit and speak against me: but thy servant did meditate in thy statutes; **Jer. 33:3** call unto me, and I will answer thee, and shew thee great and mighty things, which thou knowest not; **Dan. 7:28** my cogitations much troubled me, and my countenance changed in me: but I kept the matter in my heart; **8:26-27** the vision of the evening and the morning which was told is true: wherefore shut thou up the vision; for it shall be for many days.

We speak the wisdom of God in a mystery, even the hidden wisdom, which God ordained before the world unto our glory. 1 Cor. 2:7 (*see also* Know)

Luke 8:10 it is given to know the *m.* of the kingdom of God: but to others in parables; that seeing they might not see, and hearing they might not understand; **1 Cor. 2:7** we speak the wisdom of God in a *m.*, even the hidden wisdom, which God ordained before the world unto our glory; **Eph. 3:4** when ye read, ye may understand my knowledge in the *m.* of Christ; **Col. 1:26-27** even the *m.* which hath been hid from ages and from generations, but now is made manifest to his saints: To whom God would make known what is the riches of the glory of this *m.* among the Gentiles; which is

Christ in you, the hope of glory; **2:2** that their hearts might be comforted, being knit together in love, and unto all riches of the full assurance of understanding, to the acknowledgment of the *m.* of God, and of the Father, and of Christ; **1 Tim. 3:9** holding the *m.* of the faith in a pure conscience; **3:16** without controversy great is the *m.* of godliness: God was manifest in the flesh, justified in the Spirit, seen of angels, preached unto the Gentiles, believed on in the world, received up into glory; **Rev. 1:20** the *m.* of the seven stars which thou sawest in my right hand, and the seven golden candlesticks. The seven stars are the angels of the seven churches: and the seven candlesticks which thou sawest are the seven churches; **10:7** in the days of the voice of the seventh angel, when he shall begin to sound, the *m.* of God should be finished, as he hath declared to his servants the prophets.

NAKED, NAKEDNESS

Is it not to deal thy bread to the hungry, and that thou bring the poor that are cast out to thy house? when thou seest the naked, that thou cover him; and that thou hide not thyself from thine own flesh? Isa. 58:7 (*see also* Cast, Cover)

NAME

Love the name of the LORD. Isa. 56:6 (*see also* Love)

Thou shalt not live; for thou speakest lies in the name of the LORD. Zech. 13:3 (*see also* Liar)

Be it known unto you all, and to all the people of Israel, that by the name of Jesus Christ of Nazareth, whom ye crucified, whom God raised from the dead, even by him doth this man stand here before you whole. This is the stone which was set at nought of you builders, which is become the head of the corner. Neither is there salvation in any other: for there is none other name under heaven given among men, whereby we must be saved. Acts 4:10-12 (*see also* Corner, Israel, Jesus Christ, Saved, Stone)

Let them be confounded and troubled for ever; yea, let them be put to shame, and perish: That men may know that thou, whose name alone is JEHOVAH, art the most high over all the earth. Ps. 83:18 (*see also* Jehovah)

Praise ye the name of the LORD. Ps. 135:1 (*see also* Praise)

Whatsoever ye do in word or deed, do all in the name of the Lord Jesus, giving thanks to God and the Father by him. Col. 3:17 (*see also* Do)

These are written, that ye might believe that Jesus is the Christ, the Son of God; and that believing ye might have life through his name. John 20:31 (*see also* Belief)

Solomon determined to build an house for the name of the LORD, and an house for his kingdom. 2 Chron. 2:1 (*see also* House, Kingdom)

The place of my throne, and the place of the soles of my feet, where I will dwell in the midst of the children of Israel for ever, and my holy name, shall the house of Israel no more defile. Ezek. 43:7 (*see also* Holy)

Yea, in the way of thy judgments, O LORD, have we waited for thee; the desire of our soul is to thy name, and to the remembrance of thee. Isa. 26:8 (*see also* Desire)

A good name is rather to be chosen than great riches, and loving favour rather than silver and gold. Prov. 22:1 (*see also* Rich)

These signs shall follow them that believe; In my name shall they cast out devils; they shall speak with new tongues; They shall take up serpents; and if they drink any deadly thing it shall not hurt them; they shall lay hands on the sick and they shall recover. Mark 16:17-18 (*see also* Cast, Deadly, Devil, Sign, Tongues)

When he seeth his children, the work of mine hands, in the midst of him, they shall sanctify my name, and sanctify the Holy One of Jacob, and shall fear the God of Israel. Isa. 29:23 (*see also* Sanctified)

Isa. 29:23 when he seeth his children, the work of mine hands, in the midst of him, they shall sanctify my *n*., and sanctify the Holy One of Jacob, and shall fear the God of Israel.

Walk in the name of the LORD our God for ever and ever. Micah 4:5 (*see also* Walk)

Micah 4:5 all people will walk every one in the *n*. of his god, and we will walk in the *n*. of the LORD our God for ever and ever; Zech. 10:12 I will strengthen them in the LORD; and they shall walk up and down in his *n*., saith the LORD.

Thou shalt not take the name of the LORD thy God in vain; for the LORD will not hold him guiltless that taketh his name in vain. Ex. 20:7 (*see also* Thou Shalt Not, Vain)

Ex. 20:7 thou shalt not take the *n*. of the LORD thy God in vain; for the LORD will not hold him guiltless that taketh his *n*. in vain; Lev. 18:21 thou shalt not let any of thy seed pass through the fire to Molech, neither shalt thou profane the *n*. of thy God; Deut. 5:11 thou shalt not take the *n*. of the LORD thy God in vain: for the LORD will not hold him guiltless that taketh his *n*. in vain; Ps. 139:20 they speak against thee wickedly, and thine enemies take thy *n*. in vain; Prov. 30:9 lest I be poor, and steal, and take the *n*. of my God in vain; Isa. 5:18 woe unto them that draw iniquity with cords of vanity; Jer. 2:5 what iniquity have your fathers found in me, that they are gone far from me, and have walked after vanity, and are become vain.

Remember the name of the LORD our God. Ps. 20:7 (*see also* Remember)

Ps. 20:7 we will remember the *n*. of the LORD our God; 22:27 all the ends of the world shall remember and turn unto the LORD: and all the kindreds of the nations shall worship before thee; 45:17 I will make thy *n*. to be remembered in all generations: therefore shall the people praise thee for ever and ever; 119:55 I have remembered thy *n*., O LORD, in the night, and have kept thy law; Isa. 57:11-12 of whom hast thou been afraid or feared, that thou hast lied, and hast not remembered me, nor laid it to thy heart? have not I held my peace even of old, and thou fearest me not.

The name of the LORD is a strong tower: the righteous runneth into it, and is safe. Prov. 18:10 (*see also* Trust)

Prov. 18:10 the *n*. of the LORD is a strong tower: the righteous runneth into it, and is safe; Mal. 1:11 from the rising of the sun even unto the going down of the same my *n*. shall be great among the Gentiles; and in every place incense shall be offered unto my *n*., and a pure offering: for my *n*. shall be great among the heathen, saith the LORD of hosts.

NARROW (*see also* Path)

Enter ye in at the strait gate; for wide is the gate, and broad is the way, that leadeth to destruction, and many there be which go in thereat; Because strait is the gate, and narrow is the way, which leadeth to life, and few be there that find it. Matt. 7:13-14 (*see also* Few, Gate, Strait, Work)

NATION (*see also* Israel)

Let the heavens be glad, and the earth rejoice: and let men say among the nations, the LORD reigneth. 1 Chron. 16:31 (*see also* Rejoice)

And before him shall be gathered all nations: and he shall separate them one from another, as a shepherd divideth his sheep from the goats. Matt. 25:32 (*see also* Gather, Separate)

Open ye the gates, that the righteous nation which keepeth the truth may enter in. Isa. 26:2 (*see also* Gate, Righteous, Truth)

NATURAL

Likewise also the men, leaving the natural use of the woman, burned in their lust one toward another; men with men working that which is unseemly, and receiving in themselves that recompence of their error which was meet. Rom. 1:27 (*see also* Lust, Women)

NATURAL MAN (*see also* Carnal, Death, Fallen)

The natural man receiveth not the things of the Spirit of God: for they are foolishness unto him: neither can he know them, because they are spiritually discerned. 1 Cor. 2:14 (*see also* Foolish, Spirit)

1 Cor. 2:14 the natural man receiveth not the things of the Spirit of God: for they are foolishness unto him: neither can he know them, because they are spiritually discerned; **Col. 3:5-7** mortify therefore your members which are upon the earth; fornication, uncleanness, inordinate affection, evil concupiscence, and covetousness, which is idolatry: For which things' sake the wrath of God cometh on the children of disobedience: In the which ye also walked some time, when ye lived in them.

NECK (*see also* Stiffnecked)

He, that being often reproved hardeneth his neck, shall suddenly be destroyed, and that without remedy. Prov. 29:1 (*see also* Reprove)

Prov. 29:1 he, that being often reproved hardeneth his *n.*, shall suddenly be destroyed, and that without remedy; **Ezek. 3:7** the house of Israel will not hearken unto thee; for they will not hearken unto me: for all the house of Israel are impudent and hardhearted.

They dealt proudly, and hearkened not unto thy commandments, but sinned against thy judgments, (which if a man do, he shall live in them;) and withdrew the shoulder, and hardened their neck. Neh. 9:29 (*see also* Pride)

2 Kgs. 17:14 they would not hear, but hardened their *n.*, like to the *n.* of their fathers, that did not believe in the LORD their God; **2 Chron. 36:13** he stiffened his *n.*, and hardened his heart from turning unto the LORD God of Israel; **Neh. 9:17** [they] refused to obey, neither were mindful of thy wonders that thou didst among them; but hardened their *n.*, and in their rebellion appointed a captain to return to their bondage; **9:29** they dealt proudly, and hearkened not unto thy commandments, but sinned against thy judgments, [which if a man do, he shall live in them;] and withdrew the shoulder, and hardened their *n.*; **Ps. 95:8** harden not your heart, as in the provocation, and as in the day of temptation in the wilderness; **Prov. 28:14** happy is the man that feareth alway: but he that hardeneth his heart shall fall into mischief; **Jer. 7:26** they hearkened not unto me, nor inclined their ear, but hardened their *n.*; **19:15** I will bring upon this city and upon all her towns all the evil that I have pronounced against it, because they have hardened their *n.*, that they might not hear my words; **Zech. 7:12-13** they made their hearts as an adamant stone, lest they should hear the law, and the words which the LORD of hosts hath sent in his spirit by the former prophets: therefore came a great wrath from the LORD.

NEED, NEEDFUL, NEEDY (*see also* Beg, Poor)

For the poor shall never cease out of the land: therefore I command thee, saying, thou shalt open thine hand wide unto thy brother, to thy poor, and to thy needy, in the land. Deut. 15:11 (*see also* Hand, Poor)

NEGLECT, NEGLIGENT (*see also* Account, Forget)

Neglect not the gift that is in thee. 1 Tim. 4:14 (*see also* Gift)

Be not now negligent: for the LORD hath chosen you to stand before him, to serve him, and that ye should minister unto him. 2 Chron. 29:11 (*see also* Serve)

NEIGHBOR (*see also* Brother Sister)

Thou shalt not bear false witness against thy neighbour. Ex. 20:16 (*see also* Thou Shalt Not, Witness)

Thou shalt not avenge, nor bear any grudge against the children of thy people, but thou shalt love thy neighbour as thyself: I *am* the LORD. Lev. 19:18 (*see also* Love, Thous Shalt Not)

Withdraw thy foot from thy neighbour's house; lest he be weary of thee, and so hate thee. Prov. 25:17 (*see also* Weary)

NEW (*see also* Covenant)

Moreover I will make a covenant of peace with them; it shall be an everlasting covenant with them: and I will place them, and multiply them, and will set my sanctuary in the midst of them for evermore. Ezek. 37:26

Behold, the days come, saith the LORD, that I will make a new covenant with the house of Israel, and with the house of Judah. Jer. 31:31

NIGHT (*see also* Darkness)

I must work the works of him that sent me, while it is day: the night cometh, when no man can work. John. 9:4 (*see also* Day, Work)

NOTHING, NOTHINGNESS (*see also* Darkness, Humility)

For with God nothing shall be impossible. Luke 1:37 (*see also* Do, Impossible)

I am the vine, yea are the branches: He that abideth in me, and I in him, the same bringeth forth much fruit: for without me ye can do nothing. John 15:5 (*see also* Abide, Do, Fruit, Vine)

If ye have faith as a grain of mustard seed, ye shall say unto this mountain, Remove hence to yonder place; and it shall remove; and nothing shall be impossible unto you. Matt. 17:20 (*see also* Faith, Grain, Impossible, Seed)

NOURISH, NOURISHMENT (*see also* Eat)

If thou put the brethren in remembrance of these things, thou shalt be a good minister of Jesus Christ, nourished up in the words of faith and of good doctrine, whereunto thou hast attained. 1 Tim. 4:6 (*see also* Minister, Remember)

NURTURE (*see also* Care, Compassion, Heal, Kindness, Serve, Teach)

Ye fathers, provoke not your children to wrath: but bring them up in the nurture and admonition of the Lord. Eph. 6:4 (*see also* Admonition, Children)

OATH (*see also* Covenant, Pledge, Promise, Swear, Vow)

Let none of you imagine evil in your hearts against his neighbour; and love no false oath: for all these are things that I hate, saith the LORD. Zech. 8:17 (*see also* Imagine, Love)

Swear not, neither by heaven, neither by the earth, neither by any other oath: but let your yea be yea; and your nay, nay; lest ye fall into condemnation. James 5:12 (*see also* Swear)

OBEDIENCE, OBEDIENT, OBEY (*see also* Diligence, Hearken, Observe, Steadfast, Submit)

Children, obey your parents in all things: for this is well pleasing unto the Lord. Col. 3:20 (*see also* Child)

Put them in mind to be subject to principalities and powers, to obey magistrates, to be ready to every good work. Titus 3:1 (*see also* Law)

Obey, I beseech thee, the voice of the LORD, which I speak unto thee: so it shall be well unto thee, and thy soul shall live. Jer. 38:20 (*see also* Speak, Voice)

Unto them that are contentious, and do not obey the truth, but obey unrighteousness, indignation and wrath. Rom. 2:8 (*see also* Contention)

Who is among you that feareth the LORD, that obeyeth the voice of his servant, that walketh in darkness, and hath no light? let him trust in the name of the LORD, and stay upon his God. Isa. 50:10 (*see also* Prophet, Servant)

Teach the young women to be sober, to love their husbands, to love their children, To be discreet, chaste, keepers at home, good, obedient to their own husbands, that the word of God be not blasphemed. Titus 2:4-5 (*see also* Teach)

Obey my voice indeed, and keep my covenant. Ex. 19:5 (*see also* Covenant)

Ex. 19:5 *o.* my voice indeed, and keep my covenant, then ye shall be a peculiar treasure unto me above all people; 1 Sam. 15:22 hath the LORD as great delight in burnt offerings and sacrifices, as in *o.* the voice of the LORD? Behold, to obey is better than sacrifice.

If ye be willing and obedient, ye shall eat the good of the land: But if ye refuse and rebel, ye shall be devoured with the sword. Isa. 1:19-20 (*see also* Rebel, Will)

Ezra 9:13 we are not able to stand without, neither is this a work of one day or two: for we are many that have transgressed in this thing; Job 34:11 the work of a man shall he render unto him, and cause every man to find according to his ways; 36:11 if they *o.* and serve him, they shall spend their days in prosperity, and their years in pleasures; Ps. 1:2-3 his delight is in the law of the LORD; and in his law doth he meditate day and night; 18:20 the LORD rewarded me according to my righteousness; according to the cleanness of my hands hath he recompensed me; 18:24 therefore hath the LORD recompensed me according to my righteousness, according to the cleanness of my hands in his eyesight; Isa. 1:19-20 if ye be willing and *o.*, ye shall eat the good of the land: But if ye refuse and rebel, ye shall be devoured with the sword.

Obey my voice, and I will be your God, and ye shall be my people: and walk ye in all the ways that I have commanded you, that it may be well unto you. Jer. 7:23 (*see also* Commandment)

Gen. 26:4-5 I will make thy seed to multiply as the stars of heaven, and will give unto thy seed all these countries; and in thy seed shall all the nations of the earth be blessed; Because that Abraham *o.* my voice, and kept my charge, my commandments, my statutes, and my laws; Ex. 5:2 who is the LORD, that I should *o.* his voice to let Israel go? I know not the LORD, neither will I let Israel go; 19:5-6 if ye will *o.* my voice indeed, and keep my covenant, then ye shall be a peculiar treasure unto me above all people: for all the earth is mine: And ye shall be unto me a kingdom of priests, and an holy nation; 19:8 all that the LORD hath spoken we will do; 23:22 if thou shalt indeed *o.* his voice, and do all that I speak; then I will be an enemy unto thine enemies, and an adversary unto thine adversaries; Lev. 19:37 observe all my statutes, and all my judgments, and do them: I am the LORD; Deut. 8:20 the nations which the LORD destroyeth before your face, so shall ye perish; because ye would not be obedient unto the voice of the LORD your God; 13:4 ye shall walk after the LORD your God, and fear him, and keep his commandments, and *o.* his voice, and ye shall serve him, and cleave unto him; 30:2 return unto the LORD thy God, and shalt *o.* his voice according to all that I command thee this day, thou and thy children, with all thine heart, and with all thy soul; 30:20 thou mayest love the LORD thy God, and that thou mayest *o.* his voice, and that thou mayest cleave unto him: for he is thy life, and the length of thy days; 1 Sam. 12:14-15 if ye will fear the LORD, and serve him, and *o.* his voice, and not rebel against the commandment of the LORD, then shall both ye and also the king that reigneth over you continue following the LORD your God: But if ye will not *o.* the voice of the LORD, but rebel against the commandment of the LORD, then shall the hand of the LORD be against you, as it was against your fathers; 15:22 to *o.* is better than sacrifice, and to hearken than the fat of rams; 2 Kgs. 18:11-12 because they *o.* not the voice of the LORD their God, but transgressed his covenant, and all that Moses the servant of the LORD commanded, and would not hear them, nor do them; Job 36:11-12 if they *o.* and serve him, they shall spend their days in prosperity, and their years in pleasures. But if they *o.* not, they shall perish by the sword, and they shall die without knowledge; Ps. 18:22 all his judgments were before me, and I did not put away his statutes from me; 19:11 in keeping of them there is great reward; 119:8 I will keep thy statutes: O forsake me not utterly; 119:17 deal bountifully with thy servant, that I may live, and keep thy word; Jer. 3:25 we have sinned against the LORD our God, we and our fathers, from our youth even unto this day, and have not *o.* the voice of the LORD our God; 7:23 *o.* my voice, and I will be your God, and ye shall be my people: and walk ye in all the ways that I have commanded you, that it may be well unto you; **7:28** this is a nation that *o.* not the voice of the LORD their God, nor receiveth correction: truth is perished, and is cut off from their mouth; **9:13** because they have forsaken my law which I set before them, and have not *o.* my voice, neither walked therein; **11:4** *o.* my voice, and do them, according to all which I command you: so shall ye be my people, and I will be your God; **11:7-8** *o.* my voice. Yet they *o.* not, nor inclined their ear, but walked every one in the imagination of their evil heart; **12:17** if they will not *o.*, I will utterly pluck up and destroy that nation, saith the LORD; **18:10** if it do evil in my sight, that it *o.* not my voice; **26:13** amend your ways and your doings, and *o.* the voice of the LORD your God; and the LORD will repent him of the evil that he hath pronounced against you; **32:23** hey *o.* not thy voice, neither walked in thy law; they have done nothing of all that thou commandedst them to do: therefore thou hast caused all this evil to come upon them; **40:3** ye have sinned against the LORD, and have not *o.* his voice, therefore this thing is come upon you; **42:5-6** whether it be good, or whether it be evil, we will *o.* the voice of the LORD our God, to whom we send thee; that it may be well with us, when we *o.* the voice of the LORD our God; **44:23** because ye have sinned against the LORD, and have not *o.* the voice of the LORD, nor walked in his law, nor in his statutes, nor in his testimonies; therefore this evil is happened unto you, as at this day; **Ezek. 5:6-8** have not walked in my statutes, neither have kept my judgments, neither have done according to the judgments of the nations that are round about you; Therefore thus saith the Lord GOD; Behold, I, even I, am against thee, and will execute judgments in the midst of thee in the sight of the nations; **36:27-30** I will put my spirit within you, and cause you to walk in my statutes, and ye shall keep my judgments, and do them; **37:24-26** walk in my judgments, and observe my statutes, and do them; **Dan. 7:27** the greatness of the kingdom under the whole heaven, shall be given to the people of the saints of the most High, whose kingdom is an everlasting kingdom, and all dominions shall serve and *o.* him; **9:10** neither have we *o.* the voice of the LORD our God, to walk in his laws, which he set before us by his servants the prophets; **9:14** the LORD our God is righteous in all his works which he doeth: for we *o.* not his voice; **Zeph. 3:2** she *o.* not the voice; she received not correction; she trusted not in the LORD; she drew not near to her God; **Hag. 1:12** the people, *o.* the voice of the LORD

their God, and the words of Haggai the prophet, as the LORD their God had sent him, and the people did fear before the LORD; **Zech. 6:15** if ye will diligently *o.* the voice of the LORD your God.

Be obedient in all things. 2 Cor. 2:9 (*see also* All Things)

Acts 6:7 a great company of the priests were *o.* to the faith; **Rom. 15:18** to make the Gentiles *o.*, by word and deed; **2 Cor. 2:9** for to this end also did I write, that I might know the proof of you, whether ye be *o.* in all things; **Eph. 6:5** servants, be *o.* to them that are your masters according to the flesh, with fear and trembling, in singleness of your heart, as unto Christ; **Philip. 2:8** being found in fashion as a man, he humbled himself, and became *o.* unto death, even the death of the cross; **1 Pet. 1:14** as *o.* children, not fashioning yourselves according to the former lusts in your ignorance.

Servants, be obedient to them that are your masters according to the flesh, with fear and trembling, in singleness of your heart, as unto Christ. Eph. 6:5 (*see also* Servant)

Eph 6:5 servants, be *o.* to them that are your masters according to the flesh, with fear and trembling, in singleness of your heart, as unto they that have believing masters, let them not despise them, because they are brethren; but rather do them service, because they are faithful and beloved, partakers of the benefit. These things teach and exhort; **Titus 2:9-10** exhort Christ; **6:8-9** whatsoever good thing any man doeth, the same shall he receive of the Lord, whether he be bond or free; **1 Tim. 6:1-2** let as many servants as are under the yoke count their own masters worthy of all honour, that the name of God and his doctrine be not blasphemed. And servants to be *o.* unto their own masters, and to please them well in all things; not answering again; Not purloining, but shewing all good fidelity; that they may adorn the doctrine of God our Saviour in all things; **1 Pet. 2:18-20** servants, be subject to your masters with all fear; not only to the good and gentle, but also to the froward. For this is thankworthy, if a man for conscience toward God endure grief, suffering wrongfully. For what glory is it, if, when ye be buffeted for your faults, ye shall take it patiently? but if, when ye do well, and suffer for it, ye take it patiently, this is acceptable with God.

Though we walk in the flesh, we do not war after the flesh: Casting down imaginations, and every high thing that exalteth itself against the knowledge of God, and bringing into captivity every thought to the obedience of Christ. **2 Cor. 10:3,5** (*see also* Flesh, Imagination, Thought)

Rom. 1:21 when they knew God, they glorified him not as God, neither were thankful; but became vain in their imaginations, and their foolish heart was darkened; **2 Cor. 10:5** casting down imaginations, and every high thing that exalteth itself against the knowledge of God, and bringing into captivity every thought to the *o.* of Christ; **Eph. 4:17-18** I say therefore, and testify in the Lord, that ye henceforth walk not as other Gentiles walk, in the vanity of their mind, Having the understanding darkened, being alienated from the life of God through the ignorance that is in them, because of the blindness of their heart; **2 Pet. 2:18** they speak great swelling words of vanity, they allure through the lusts of the flesh, through much wantonness, those that were clean escaped from them who live in error.

Take heed unto thyself, and unto the doctrine; continue in them: for in doing this thou shalt both save thyself, and them that hear thee. 1 Tim. 4:16 (*see also* Gospel)

Rom. 2:16 in the day when God shall judge the secrets of men by Jesus Christ according to my gospel; **1 Cor. 9:14** even so hath the Lord ordained that they which preach the gospel should live of the gospel; **Eph. 3:6** the Gentiles should be fellowheirs, and of the same body, and partakers of his promise in Christ by the gospel; **6:15** your feet shod with the preparation of the gospel of peace; **2 Thes. 1:8-10** in flaming fire taking vengeance on them that know not God, and that *o.* not the gospel of our Lord Jesus Christ: Who shall be punished with everlasting destruction from the presence of the Lord, and from the glory of his power; **2:14-15** therefore, brethren, stand fast, and hold the traditions which ye have been taught, whether by word, or our epistle; **3:14-16** if any man *o.* not our word by this epistle, note that man, and have no company with him, that he may be ashamed. Yet count him not as an enemy, but admonish him as a brother; **1 Tim. 4:16** take heed unto thyself, and unto the doctrine; continue in them: for in doing this thou shalt both save thyself, and them that hear thee.

OBSERVE, OBSERVATION (*see also* Behold, Keep, Obey, See)

Only be thou strong and very courageous, that thou mayest observe to do according to all the law. Josh. 1:7

Josh.1:6-7 be strong and of a good courage: for unto this people shalt thou divide for an inheritance the land, which I sware unto their fathers to give them. Only be thou strong and very courageous, that thou mayest *o.* to do according to all the law; **1 Chron. 22:13** be strong, and of good courage; dread not, nor be dismayed; **2 Chron. 15:7** be ye strong therefore, and let not your hands be weak: for your work shall be rewarded; **Ps. 31:24** be of good courage, and he shall strengthen your heart, all ye that hope in the LORD.

OBSTINATE (*see also* Hardhearted, Stiffnecked, Steadfast)

Thou art obstinate, and thy neck is an iron sinew, and thy brow brass. Isa. 48:4

Isa. 48:4 I knew that thou art *o.,* and thy neck is an iron sinew, and thy brow brass; **Jer. 6:16-17** thus saith the LORD, Stand ye in the ways, and see, and ask for the old paths, where is the good way, and walk therein, and ye shall find rest for your souls. But they said, We will not walk therein.

OBTAIN (*see also* Find, Receive)

OFFEND, OFFENDER, OFFENSE (*see also* Mock, Persecute)

Approve things that are excellent; that ye may be sincere and without offense till the day of Christ. Philip. 1:10 (*see also* Approve, Excellent)

Whosoever shall be ashamed of me and of my words, of him shall the Son of man be ashamed, when he shall come in his own glory, and in his Father's, and of the holy angels. Luke 9:26 (*see also* Ashamed)

I exercise myself, to have always a conscience void of offense toward God, and toward men. Acts 24:16 (*see also* Conscience)

A brother offended is harder to be won than a strong city: and their contentions are like the bars of a castle. Prov. 18:19 (*see also* Contend)

Wherefore if thy hand or thy foot offend thee, cut them off, and cast them from thee: it is better for thee to enter into life halt or maimed, rather than having two hands or two feet to be cast into everlasting fire. Matt. 18:8 (*see also* Cut, Everlasting Fire)

The terrible one is brought to nought, and the scorner is consummed, and all that watch for iniquity are cut off: That make a man an offender for a word, and lay a snare for him that reproveth in the gate, and turn aside the just thing for a thing of nought. Isa. 29:20-21 (*see also* Just, Word)

If thy hand offend thee, cut it off: it is better for thee to enter into life maimed, than having two hands to go into hell, into the fire that never shall be quenched. Mark 9:43 (*see also* Hell)

Mark 9:43 if thy hand offend thee, cut it off: it is better for thee to enter into life maimed, than having two hands to go into hell, into the fire that never shall be quenched; **9:45-50** if thy foot offend thee, cut it off: it is better for thee to enter halt into life, than having two feet to be cast into hell.

Give none offense, neither to the Jews, nor to the Gentiles, nor to the church of God. 1 Cor. 10:32

1 Cor 10:32 give none *o.*, neither to the Jews, nor to the Gentiles, nor to the church of God; **2 Cor. 6:3** giving no *o.* in any thing, that the ministry be not blamed; **Philip. 1:10** that ye may be sincere and without *o.* till the day of Christ.

Blessed is he, whosoever shall not be offended in me. Matt. 11:6

Matt. 11:6 blessed is he, whosoever shall not be *o.* in me; **13:54-57** he taught them in their synagogue, insomuch that they were astonished, and said, Whence hath this man this wisdom, and these mighty works? Is not this the carpenter's son; **15:12** knowest thou that the Pharisees were *o.*, after they heard this saying; **26:33** though all men shall be *o.* because of thee, yet will I never be *o.*; **Mark 4:17** have no root in themselves, and so endure but for a time: afterward, when affliction or persecution ariseth for the word's sake, immediately they are *o.*; **6:3** they were *o.* at him; **14:27** All ye shall be *o.* because of me this night: for it is written, I will smite the shepherd, and the sheep shall be scattered; **14:29** Peter said

unto him, Although all shall be *o.*, yet will not I; **Luke 4:28-29** all they in the synagogue, when they heard these things, were filled with wrath, And rose up, and thrust him out of the city, and led him unto the brow of the hill whereon their city was built, that they might cast him down headlong; **7:23** blessed is he, whosoever shall not be *o.* in me; **9:26** whosoever shall be ashamed of me and of my words, of him shall the Son of man be ashamed, when he shall come in his own glory, and in his Father's, and of the holy angels.

If any man offend not in word, the same is a perfect man, and able also to bridle the whole body. James 3:2-8 (*see also* Body, Bridle, Perfect)

James 3:2-8 for in many things we *o.* all. If any man *o.* not in word, the same is a perfect man, and able also to bridle the whole body. Behold, we put bits in the horses' mouths, that they may obey us; and we turn about their whole body. Behold also the ships, which though they be so great, and are driven of fierce winds, yet are they turned about with a very small helm, whithersoever the governor listeth. Even so the tongue is a little member, and boasteth great things. Behold, how great a matter a little fire kindleth! And the tongue is a fire, a world of iniquity: so is the tongue among our members, that it defileth the whole body, and setteth on fire the course of nature; and it is set on fire of hell. For every kind of beasts, and of birds, and of serpents, and of things in the sea, is tamed, and hath been tamed of mankind: But the tongue can no man tame; it is an unruly evil, full of deadly poison.

OFFER, OFFERING (*see also* Give, Sacrifice)

If thou bring thy gift to the altar, and there rememberest that thy brother hath ought against thee; Leave there thy gift before the altar, and go thy way; first be reconciled to thy brother, and then come and offer thy gift. Matt. 5:23-24 (*see also* Gift, Reconcile)

Bring an offering in a clean vessel into the house of the LORD. Isa. 66:20 (*see also* House)

Isa. 66:20 they shall bring all your brethren for an *o.* unto the LORD out of all nations... as the children of Israel bring an *o.* in a clean vessel into the house of the LORD.

Ye also, as lively stones, are built up a spiritual house, an holy priesthood, to offer up spiritual sacrifices, acceptable to God by Jesus Christ. 1 Pet. 2:5 (*see also* Jesus Christ, Priesthood, Sacrifice)

Rom. 12:1 present your bodies a living sacrifice, holy, acceptable unto God, which is your reasonable service; **Philip. 4:17** if I be offered upon the sacrifice and service of your faith, I joy, and rejoice with you all; **Heb. 13:15** let us offer the sacrifice of praise to God continually, that is, the fruit of our lips giving thanks to his name; **1 Pet. 2:5** as lively stones, are built up a spiritual house, an holy priesthood, to offer up spiritual sacrifices, acceptable to God by Jesus Christ.

Give unto the LORD the glory due unto his name: bring an offering, and come before him: worship the LORD in the beauty of holiness. 1 Chron. 16:29 (*see also* Beauty, Glory)

Gen. 4:3-5 Cain brought of the fruit of the ground an *o.* unto the LORD. And Abel, he also brought of the firstlings of his flock and of the fat thereof. And the LORD had respect unto Abel and to his *o.*: But unto Cain and to his *o.* he had not respect; **Ex. 10:25** thou must give us also sacrifices and burnt *o.*, that we may sacrifice unto the LORD our God; **18:12** Jethro... took a burnt *o.* and sacrifices for God: and Aaron came, and all the elders of Israel, to eat bread with [him] before God; **24:5** he sent young men of the children of Israel, which *o.* burnt *o.*, and sacrificed peace *o.* of oxen unto the LORD; **25:2** bring me an *o.*: of every man that giveth it willingly with his heart ye shall take my *o.*; **29:28** it is an heave *o.*: and it shall be an heave *o.* from the children of Israel of the sacrifice of their peace *o.*, even their heave *o.* unto the LORD; **2 Sam. 24:24** the king said... neither will I *o.* burnt *o.* unto the LORD my God of that which doth cost me nothing; **1 Chron. 16:29** give unto the LORD the glory due unto his name: bring an *o.*, and come before him: worship the LORD in the beauty of holiness; **29:9** the people rejoiced, for that they *o.* willingly, because with perfect heart they *o.* willingly to the LORD; **29:14-15** who am I, and what is my people, that we should be able to *o.* so willingly after this sort? for all things come of thee, and of thine own have we given thee; **29:17** in the uprightness of mine heart I have willingly *o.* all these things: and now have I seen with joy thy people, which are present here, to *o.* willingly unto thee; **Ezra 7:16** all the silver and gold that

thou canst find... with the freewill *o.* of the people, and of the priests, *o.* willingly for the house of their God; **Ps. 4:5** *o.* the sacrifices of righteousness, and put your trust in the LORD; **110:3** thy people shall be willing in the day of thy power, in the beauties of holiness from the womb of the morning; **Prov. 23:26** give me thine heart, and let thine eyes observe my ways; **Isa. 44:3** I will pour water upon him that is thirsty, and floods upon the dry ground: I will pour my spirit upon thy seed, and my blessing upon thine offspring; **57:7-8** [go] thou up to *o.* sacrifice; **Dan. 6:7** [the rulers have decreed that] whosoever shall ask a petition of any God or man for thirty days, save of thee, O king, he shall be cast into the den of lions; **Jonah 2:9** I will sacrifice unto thee with the voice of thanksgiving; I will pay that that I have vowed; **Mal. 3:3** he shall purify [them], and purge them as gold and silver, that they may *o.* unto the LORD an *o.* in righteousness.

OIL (*see also* Anoint, Bless, Call, Heal)

Is any sick among you? let him call for the elders of the church; and let them pray over him, anointing him with oil in the name of the Lord: And the prayer of faith shall save the sick, and the Lord shall raise him up; and if he have committed sins, they shall be forgiven him. James 5:14-15 (*see also* Anoint, Elder, Heal)

OMEGA (*see also* End, Jesus Christ)

I am Alpha and Omega, the beginning and the ending, saith the Lord, which is, and which was, and which is to come, the Almighty. Rev. 1:8 (*see also* Alpha)

ONE (*see also* Celestial, Join, United)

There is neither Jew nor Greek, there is neither bond nor free, there is neither male nor female: for ye are all one in Christ Jesus. Gal. 3:28 (*see also* Bond, Equality, Female, Male)

Let your conversation be as it becometh the gospel of Christ: that whether I come and see you, or else be absent, I may hear of your affairs, that ye stand fast in one spirit, with one mind striving together for the faith of the gospel. Philip. 1:27 (*see also* Become, Conversation, Gospel)

Consider it in thine heart, that the LORD he is God in heaven above, and upon the earth beneath: there is none else. Deut. 4:39 (*see also* Heart)

I will give them one heart, and I will put a new spirit within you; and I will take the stony heart out of their flesh, and will give them an heart of flesh: That they may walk in my statutes, and keep mine ordinances, and do them: and they shall be my people, and I will be their God. Ezek. 11:19-20 (*see also* Commandment, Heart)

Be likeminded one toward another according to Christ Jesus: That ye may with one mind and one mouth glorify God, even the Father of our Lord Jesus Christ. Rom. 15:5-6 (*see also* Jesus Christ, Likeminded, Unity)

Who is this King of glory? The LORD of hosts, he is the King of glory. Ps. 24:8 (*see also* Glorify)

Ps. 18:31 who is God save the LORD? or who is a rock save our God; 24:8 who is this King of glory? The LORD strong and mighty, the LORD mighty in battle; 24:10 who is this King of glory? The LORD of hosts, he is the King of glory; Jer. 2:18 the children gather wood, and the fathers kindle the fire, and the women knead their dough, to make cakes to the queen of heaven, and to pour out drink offerings unto other gods, that they may provoke me to anger.

Be of one mind. 2 Cor. 13:11 (*see also* Mind, Unity)

Matt. 12:25 every kingdom divided against itself is brought to desolation; and every city or house divided against itself shall not stand; Mark 3:24-25 if a kingdom be divided against itself, that kingdom cannot stand. And if a house be divided against itself, that house cannot stand; John 17:11 Holy Father, keep through thine own name those whom thou hast given me, that they may be *o.*, as we are; 17:21-22 that they all may be *o.*; as thou, Father, art in me, and I in thee, that they also may be *o.* in us: that the world may believe that thou hast sent me. And the glory which thou gavest me I have given them; that they may be *o.*, even as we are *o.*; Acts 2:44-45 all that believed were together, and had all things common; And sold their possessions and goods, and parted them to all men, as every man had need; 4:32 the multitude of them that believed were of *o.* heart and of *o.* soul: neither said any

of them that ought of the things which he possessed was his own; but they had all things common; 12:5 Peter therefore was kept in prison: but prayer was made without ceasing of the church unto God for him; 15:25-27 it seemed good unto us, being assembled with *o.* accord; Rom. 15:6 that ye may with *o.* mind and *o.* mouth glorify God, even the Father of our Lord Jesus Christ; 1 Cor. 12:26 whether *o.* member suffer, all the members suffer with it; or *o.* member be honoured, all the members rejoice with it; 2 Cor. 13:11 be perfect, be of good comfort, be of *o.* mind, live in peace; and the God of love and peace shall be with you; **Philip.** 1:27 let your conversation be as it becometh the gospel of Christ: that whether I come and see you, or else be absent, I may hear of your affairs, that ye stand fast in *o.* spirit, with *o.* mind striving together for the faith of the gospel; 2:1-2 if there be therefore any consolation in Christ, if any comfort of love, if any fellowship of the Spirit, if any bowels and mercies, Fulfil ye my joy, that ye be likeminded, having the same love, being of *o.* accord, of *o.* mind; 3:16-17 let us walk by the same rule, let us mind the same thing. Brethren, be followers together of me, and mark them which walk so as ye have us for an ensample; Col. 2:2 that their hearts might be comforted, being knit together in love, and unto all riches of the full assurance of understanding, to the acknowledgement of the mystery of God, and of the Father, and of Christ; 1 Pet. 3:8 be ye all of *o.* mind, having compassion *o.* of another, love as brethren, be pitiful, be courteous.

ONLY BEGOTTEN (*see* Christ, Jesus Christ, Lord, Messiah, Savior, Redeemer)

OPEN, OPENED (*see also* Reveal)

They said one to another, Did not our heart burn within us, while he talked with us by the way, and while he opened to us the scriptures? Luke 24:32 (*see also* Burn)

Behold, I stand at the door, and knock: if any man hear my voice, and open the door, I will come in to him, and will sup with him, and he with me. Rev. 3:20 (*see also* Door)

OPERATION

Because they regard not the works of the LORD, nor the operation of his hands, he shall destroy them, and not build them up. Ps. 28:5 (*see also* Regard, Works)

OPINION (*see also* Belief, Hope)

Elijah came unto all the people, and said, How long halt ye between two opinions? if the LORD be God, follow him: but if Baal, then follow him. And the people answered him not a word. **1 Kgs. 18:21**

OPPOSE, OPPOSITE, OPPOSITION (*see* Afflict, Oppress, Persecute)

OPPRESS, OPPRESSED, OPPRESSION (*see also* Affliction, Cruel, Despise, Injustice, Persecute)

Because ye despise this word, and trust in oppression or perverseness, and stay thereon: Therefore this iniquity shall be to you as a breach ready to fall, swelling out in a high wall, whose breaking cometh suddenly at an instant. **Isa. 30:12-13** (*see also* Despise, Perverse, Word)

Oppress not the widow, nor the fatherless, the stranger, nor the poor; and let none of you imagine evil against his brother in your heart. **Zech. 7:10** (*see also* Fatherless, Stranger, Widow)

Trust not in oppression, and become not vain in robbery: if riches increase, set not your heart upon them. **Ps. 62:10** (*see also* Heart, Increase, Rich, Rob, Trust)

Ps. 62:10 trust not in oppression, and become not vain in robbery; **Prov. 22:16** he that *o.* the poor to increase his riches, and he that giveth to the rich, shall surely come to want.

He that oppresseth the poor to increase his riches, and he that giveth to the rich, shall surely come to want. **Prov. 22:16** (*see also* Poor, Rich)

Prov. 22:16 he that oppresseth the poor to increase his riches, and he that giveth to the rich, shall surely come to want; **22:22** rob not the poor, because he is poor: neither *o.* the afflicted; **28:3** a poor man that *o.* the poor is like a sweeping rain which leaveth no food.

As for our iniquities, we know them: in transgressing and lying against the LORD, and departing away from our God, speaking oppression and revolt, conceiving and uttering from the heart words of falsehood. **Isa. 59:12-13** (*see also* Revolt)

Isa. 59:13 in transgressing and lying against the LORD, and departing away from our God, speaking oppression and revolt, conceiving and uttering from the heart words of falsehood; **Jer. 6:6** thus hath the LORD of hosts said, Hew ye down trees, and cast a mount against Jerusalem: this is the city to be visited; she is wholly *o.* in the midst of her.

He that walketh righteously, and speaketh uprightly; he that despiseth the gain of oppressions, that shaketh his hands from holding of bribes, that stoppeth his ears from hearing of blood, and shutteth his eyes from seeing evil; He shall dwell on high: his defence shall be the munitions of rocks: bread shall be given him; his waters shall be sure. **Isa. 33:15-16** (*see also* Gain, Hear, Righteous, See, Speak, Uprightly, Walk)

Isa. 33:15-16 he that walketh righteously, and speaketh uprightly; he that despiseth the gain of oppressions, that shaketh his hands from holding of bribes... He shall dwell on high; **Jer. 22:17** thine eyes and thine heart are not but for thy covetousness, and for to shed innocent blood, and for *o.*, and for violence, to do it; **Ezek. 22:27** her princes in the midst thereof are like wolves ravening the prey, to shed blood, and to destroy souls, to get dishonest gain; **Micah 2:2** they covet fields, and take them by violence; and houses, and take them away: so they *o.* a man and his house, even a man and his heritage.

Ye shall not therefore oppress one another; but thou shalt fear thy God: for I am the LORD your God. **Lev. 25:17**

Ex. 3:9 the cry of the children of Israel is come unto me: and I have also seen the oppression wherewith the Egyptians *o.* them; **22:21** thou shalt neither vex a stranger, nor *o.* him; **23:9** thou shalt not *o.* a stranger: for ye know the heart of a stranger; **Lev. 25:14** if thou sell ought unto thy neighbour, or buyest ought of thy neighbour's hand, ye shall not *o.* one another; **25:17** ye shall not therefore *o.* one another; but thou shalt fear thy God: for I am the LORD your God; **Deut. 23:15-16** thou shalt not deliver unto his master the servant which is escaped from his master unto thee: He shall dwell with thee, even among you... thou shalt not *o.* him; **24:14** thou shalt not *o.* an hired servant that is poor and needy, whether he be of thy brethren, or of thy strangers that are in thy land within thy gates; **Ps. 10:18** to judge the fatherless and the *o.*, that the man of the earth may no more *o*.; **Prov. 14:31** he that *o*. the poor reproacheth his Maker: but he that honoureth him hath mercy on the poor; **22:16** he that *o*. the poor to increase his riches, and he that giveth to the rich, shall surely come to want; **22:22** rob not the poor, because he is poor: neither *o*. the afflicted in the gate; **Eccl. 7:7** surely *o*. maketh a wise man mad; and a gift destroyeth the heart; **Isa. 3:5** the people shall be *o*., every one by another, and every one by his neighbour; **30:12** because ye despise this word, and trust in *o*. and perverseness, and stay thereon; **49:26** I will feed them that *o*. thee with their own flesh; and they shall be drunken with their own blood; **Jer. 7:6-7** if ye *o*. not the stranger, the fatherless, and the widow, and shed not innocent blood in this place, neither walk after other gods to your hurt: Then will I cause you to dwell in this place; **21:12** execute judgment in the morning, and deliver him that is spoiled out of the hand of the *o*., lest my fury go out like fire; **30:20** their children also shall be as aforetime, and their congregation shall be established before me, and I will punish all that *o*. them; **Ezek. 18:7** hath not *o*. any, but hath restored to the debtor his pledge, hath spoiled none by violence, hath given his bread to the hungry, and hath covered the naked with a garment; **22:7** in the midst of thee have they dealt by *o*. with the stranger: in thee have they vexed the fatherless and the widow; **22:29** the people of the land have used *o*., and exercised robbery, and have vexed the poor and needy: yea, they have *o*. the stranger wrongfully; **Zech. 7:10** *o*. not the widow, nor the fatherless, the stranger, nor the poor; and let none of you imagine evil against his brother in your heart; **Mal. 3:5** I will come near to you to judgment; and I will be a swift witness against the sorcerers, and against the adulterers, and against false swearers, and against those that *o*. the hireling in his wages.

ORDER (*see also* Govern, Law, Peace, Priesthood, Statue, Unity, Zion)

Let all things be done decently and in order. 1 Cor. 14:40 (*see also* All Things)

God is not the author of confusion, but of peace, as in all churches of the saints. 1 Cor. 14:33 (*see also* Peace)

If a man know not how to rule his own house, how shall he take care of the church of God? 1 Tim. 3:4-5 (*see also* Rule)

1 Tim. 3:4-5 one that ruleth well his own house, having his children in subjection with all gravity; For if a man know not how to rule his own house, how shall he take care of the church of God.

Set in order the things that are wanting, and ordain elders in every city, as I had appointed thee. Titus 1:5 (*see also* Elder)

Acts 6:2-3 look ye out among you seven men of honest report, full of the Holy Ghost and wisdom, whom we may appoint over this business; **15:25** it seemed good unto us, being assembled with one accord; **15:36** let us go again and visit our brethren in every city where we have preached the word of the Lord, and see how they do; **15:41** he went through Syria and Cilicia, confirming the churches; **20:28** to all the flock, over the which the Holy Ghost hath made you overseers, to feed the church of God, which he hath purchased with his own blood; **1 Cor. 16:1** now concerning the collection for the saints, as I have given *o*. to the churches of Galatia, even so do ye; **Titus 1:5** set in *o*. the things that are wanting, and ordain elders in every city, as I had appointed thee.

ORDINANCE (*see also* Administer, Baptism, Covenant, Law, Laying on of Hands, Marriage, Priesthood, Sacrament, Statute)

The earth also is defiled under the inhabitants thereof; because they have transgressed the laws, changed the ordinance, broken the everlasting covenant. Isa. 24:5 (*see also* Everlasting Covenant)

They seek me daily, and delight to know my ways, as a nation that did righteousness, and forsook not the ordinance of their God: they ask of me the ordinances of justice; they take delight in approaching to God. Isa. 58:2

Isa. 58:2 they seek me daily, and delight to know my ways, as a nation that did righteousness, and forsook not the ordinance of their God: they ask of me the *o*. of justice; they take delight in approaching to God; **Jer. 31:36-37** if those *o*. depart from before me, saith the LORD, then the seed of Israel also shall cease from being a nation before me for ever; **Ezek. 43:11** shew them... all the *o*. thereof, and all the forms thereof, and all the laws thereof: and write it in their sight, that they may keep the whole form thereof, and all the *o*. thereof, and do them; **44:5** the LORD said unto me, Son of man, mark well, and behold with thine eyes, and hear with thine ears all that I say unto thee concerning all the *o.* of the house of the Lord, and all the laws thereof; **Mal. 3:7** from the days of your fathers ye are gone away from mine *o.*, and have not kept them. Return unto me, and I will return unto you, saith the Lord of hosts; **3:14** ye have said, It is vain to serve God: and what profit is it that we have kept his *o.*, and that we have walked mournfully before the Lord of hosts.

Submit yourselves to every ordinance of man for the Lord's sake: whether it be to the king, as supreme. 1 Pet. 2:13 (*see also* Submit)

Luke 1:6 they were both righteous before God, walking in all the commandments and *o.* of the Lord blameless; **1 Cor. 11:2** remember me in all things, and keep the *o.*, as I delivered them to you; **Heb. 9:1** the first covenant had also *o.* of divine service, and a worldly sanctuary; **1 Pet. 2:13** submit yourselves to every *o.* of man for the Lord's sake: whether it be to the king, as supreme.

ORPHAN (*see also* Adopt)

We are orphans and fatherless, our mothers are as widows. Lam. 5:3

OUTCAST (*see also* Beggar, Needy, Persecute, Poor)

Hide the outcasts; bewray not him that wandereth. Isa. 16:3-5 (*see also* Wander)

OVERCAME, OVERCOME (*see also* Endure)

If after they have escaped the pollutions of the world through the knowledge of the Lord and Savior Jesus Christ, they are again entangled therein, and overcome, the latter end is worse with them than the beginning. For it had been better for them not to have known the way of righteousness, than, after they have known it, to turn from the holy commandment delivered unto them. But it is happened unto them according to the true proverb, The dog is turned to his own vomit again; and the sow that was washed to her wallowing in the mire. 2 Pet. 2:20-22 (*see also* Entangle, Vomit, Way)

He that overcometh shall inherit all things; and I will be his God, and he shall be my son. But the fearful, and unbelieving, and the abominable, and murderers, and whore-mongers, and sorcerers, and idolaters, and all liars, shall have their part in the lake which burneth with fire and brimstone: which is the second death. Rev. 21:7 (*see also* All Things, Death, Inherit, Second, Unbelief)

Be not overcome of evil, but overcome evil with good. Rom. 12:21 (*see also* Evil)

Rom. 12:21 be not *o.* of evil, but *o.* evil with good; **Rev. 2:7** to him that *o.* will I give to eat of the tree of life, which is in the midst of the paradise of God; **2:17** to him that *o.* will I give to eat of the hidden manna, and will give him a white stone, and in the stone a new name written, which no man knoweth saving he that receiveth it; **3:5** he that *o.*, the same shall be clothed in white raiment; and I will not blot out his name out of the book of life, but I will confess his name before my Father, and before his angels; **3:12** him that *o.* will I make a pillar in the temple of my God, and he shall go no more out: and I will write upon him the name of my God, and the name of the city of my God, which is new Jerusalem, which cometh down out of heaven from my God: and I will write upon him my new name; **3: 21** to him that *o.* will I grant to sit with me in my throne, even as I also *o.*, and am set down with my Father in his throne; **21:7** he that *o.* shall inherit all things; and I will be his God, and he shall be my son.

OWE (*see also* Bind, Bondage, Borrow, Debt)

Owe no man any thing, but to love one another: for he that loveth another hath fulfilled the law. Rom. 13:8 (*see also* Debt, Love)

OWN

Let no man seek his own, but every man another's wealth. 1 Cor. 10:24 (*see also* Own, Wealth)

PAIN (*see also* Adversity, Afflict, Persecute)

PARABLE (*see also* Teach)

And he said unto them, Unto you it is given to know the mystery of the kingdom of God: but unto them that are without, all these things are done in parables. **Mark 4:11** (*see also* Mystery)

Matt. 13:3 he spake many things unto them in parables, saying, Behold, a sower went forth to sow; **Mark 4:11** unto you it is given to know the mystery of the kingdom of God: but unto them that are without, all these things are done in parables; **Luke 8:10** Unto you it is given to know the mysteries of the kingdom of God: but to others in parables; that seeing they might not see, and hearing they might not understand.

PARDON (*see also* Forgive)

Let the wicked forsake his way, and the unrighteous man his thoughts: and let him return unto the LORD, and he will have mercy upon him; and to our God, for he will abundantly pardon. **Isa. 55:7** (*see also* Forsake, Return)

PARENT (*see* Child, Family, Father, Marriage, Mother)

PART

If any man shall take away from the words of the book of this prophecy, God shall take away his part out of the book of life, and out of the holy city, and from the things which are written in this book **Rev. 22:19** (*see also* Book, Written)

PARTIAL, PARTIALITY (*see also* Equal, Favor)

I charge thee before God, and the Lord Jesus Christ, and the elect angels, that thou observe these things without preferring one before another, doing nothing by partiality. **1 Tim. 5:21** (*see also* Equal, Respect)

PATH (*see also* Way, Straight)

Come ye, and let us go to the mountain of the LORD to the house of the God of Jacob; and he will teach us of his ways and we will walk in his paths: for out of Zion shall go forth the law, and the word of the LORD from Jerusalem. **Isa. 2:3** (*see also* Go, House, Way)

Enter not into the paths of the wicked, and go not in the way of evil men. Avoid it, pass not by it, turn from it, and pass away. **Prov. 4:14-15** (*see also* Avoid, Enter)

Ps. 17:4 concerning the works of men, by the word of thy lips I have kept me from the paths of the destroyer; **23:3** he restoreth my soul: he leadeth me in the *p.* of righteousness for his names sake; **Prov. 4:14-16** enter not into the *p.* of the wicked, and go not in the way of evil men. Avoid it, pass not by it, turn from it, and pass away; **13:9** the light of the righteous rejoiceth: but the lamp of the wicked shall be put out.

PATIENCE, PATIENT, PATIENTLY (*see also* Endurance, Longsuffering)

Be patient therefore, brethren, unto the coming of the Lord. **James 5:7**

Many are the afflictions of the righteous: but the LORD delivereth him out of them all **Ps. 34:19** (*see also* Afflict)

Warn them that are unruly, comfort the feebleminded, support the weak, be patient toward all men. **1 Thes. 5:14** (*see also* Treat, Warn)

He that is slow to wrath is of great understanding: but he that is hasty of spirit exalteth folly. **Prov. 14:29** (*see also* Haste)

Better is the end of a thing than the beginning thereof: and the patient in spirit is better than the proud in spirit. **Eccl. 7:8** (*see also* Pride)

Seeing we also are compassed about with so great a cloud of witnesses, let us lay aside every weight, and the sin which doth so easily beset us, and let us run with patience the race that is set before us. **Heb. 12:1** (*see also* Beset, Lay Aide, Race, Run, Sin, Weight, Witness)

Luke 8:15 on the good ground are they, which in an honest and good heart, having heard the word, keep it, and bring forth fruit with *p.*; **21:19** in your *p.* possess ye your souls; **Rom. 2:7** to them who by *p.* continuance in well doing seek for glory and honour and immortality, eternal life; **5:3-4** we glory in tribulations also: knowing that tribulation worketh *p.*; And *p.*, experience; and experience, hope; **8:26** if we hope for that we see not, then do we with *p.* wait for it; **12:12** rejoicing in hope; *p.* in tribulation; continuing instant in prayer; **2 Cor. 6:4** in all things approving ourselves as the ministers of God, in much *p.*, in afflictions, in necessities, in distresses; **Col. 1:11** strengthened with all might, according to his glorious power, unto all *p.* and longsuffering with joyfulness; **3:12** put on therefore, as the elect of God, holy and beloved, bowels of mercies, kindness, humbleness of mind, meekness, longsuffering; **1 Tim. 1:16** for this cause I obtained mercy, that in me first Jesus Christ might shew forth all longsuffering, for a pattern to them which should hereafter believe on him to life everlasting; **3:2-3** *p.*, not a brawler, not covetous; **6:11** O man of God, flee these things; and follow after righteousness, godliness, faith, love, *p.*, meekness; **2 Tim. 3:10** thou hast fully known my doctrine, manner of life, purpose, faith, longsuffering, charity, *p.*; **4:2** reprove, rebuke, exhort with all longsuffering and doctrine; **Heb. 10:36** ye have need of *p.*, that, after ye have done the will of God, ye might receive the promise; **12:1** let us lay aside every weight, and the sin which doth so easily beset us, and let us run with *p.* the race that is set before us; **James 1:2-4** count it all joy when ye fall into divers temptations; Knowing this, that the trying of your faith worketh *p.*. But let *p.* have her perfect work, that ye may be perfect and entire, wanting nothing; **5:7-8** be ye also *p.*; stablish your hearts: for the coming of the Lord draweth nigh; **1 Pet. 2:20-21** what glory is it, if, when ye be buffeted for your faults, ye shall take it *p.*? but if, when ye do well, and suffer for it, ye take it *p.*, this is acceptable with God. For even hereunto were ye called: because Christ also suffered for us, leaving us an example, that ye should follow his steps; **2 Pet. 1:5-6** giving all diligence, add to your faith virtue; and to virtue knowledge; And to knowledge temperance; and to temperance *p.*; and to *p.* godliness; **3:9** the Lord is not slack concerning his promise, as some men count slackness; but is longsuffering to us-ward, not willing that any should perish, but that all should come to repentance; **3:15** the longsuffering of our Lord is salvation; even as our beloved brother Paul also according to the wisdom given unto him hath written unto you; **Rev. 2:2** I know thy works, and thy labour, and thy *p.*

PATTERN (*see also* Example, Image)

In all things shewing thyself a pattern of good works: in doctrine shewing uncorruptness, gravity, sincerity, Sound speech, that cannot be condemned; that he that is of the contrary part may be ashamed, having no evil thing to say of you. Titus 2:7-8 (*see also* Good, Speak, Works)

PAID, PAY, PAYMENT (*see also* Give, Reward, Promise, Priesthood)

When thou vowest a vow unto God, defer not to pay it; for he hath no pleasure in fools: pay that which thou hast vowed. Eccl. 5:4 (*see also* Defer, Vow)

When thou shalt vow a vow unto the LORD thy God, thou shalt not slack to pay it: for the LORD thy God will surely require it of thee; and it would be sin in thee. Deut. 23:21 (*see also* Sin, Vow)

PEACE, PEACABLE (*see also* Comfort, Order, Rest, Silence)

God is not the author of confusion, but of peace, as in all churches of the saints. 1 Cor. 14:33 (*see also* Order)

Blessed are the peacemakers: for they shall be called the children of God. Matt. 5:9 (*see also* Child)

Let him eschew evil, and do good; let him seek peace, and ensue it. 1 Pet. 3:11 (*see also* Eschew)

Let the peace of God rule in your hearts, to the which also ye are called in one body; and be ye thankful. Col. 3:15 (*see also* Thank)

For he that will love life, and see good days, let him refrain his tongue from evil, and his lips that they speak no guile: Let him eschew evil, and do good; let him seek peace, and ensue it. 1 Pet. 3:10-11 (*see also* Guile, Speak)

There is no peace, saith my God, to the wicked. Isa. 57:21 (*see also* Wicked)

If it be possible, as much as lieth in you, live peaceably with all men. Rom. 12:18 (*see also* Possible)

Pray for the peace of Jerusalem: they shall prosper that love thee. Ps. 122:6 (*see also* Jerusalem, Love)

Peace be within thy walls, and prosperity within thy palaces. For my bretheren and companions' sakes, I will now say, Peace be within thee. Ps. 122:7-8 (*see also* House, Mountain)

For unto us a child is born, unto us a son is given: and the government shall be upon his shoulder: and his name shall be called, Wonderful, Counsellor, The mighty God, The everlasting Father, The Prince of Peace. Isa. 9:6 (*see also* Counselor, Father, Government, Wonderful)

How beautiful upon the mountains are the feet of him that bringeth good tidings, that publisheth peace; that bringeth good tidings of good, that publisheth salvation; that saith unto Zion, Thy God reigneth! Isa. 52:7 (*see also* Good, Publish, Zion)

Hold thy peace at the presence of the LORD God: for the day of the LORD is at hand: for the LORD hath prepared a sacrifice, he hath bid his guests. Zeph. 1:7 (*see also* Day, Presence)

Love the truth and peace. Zech. 8:19 (*see also* True)

The law of truth was in his mouth, and iniquity was not found in his lips: he walked with me in peace and equity, and did turn many away from iniquity. Mal. 2:6 (*see also* Equal)

Seek peace, and pursue it. Ps. 34:14

Ps. 34:14 seek *p.* and pursue it; **37:11** the meek shall inherit the earth; and shall delight themselves in the abundance of *p.*; **122:7** *p.* be within thy walls, and prosperity within thy palace.

Flee also youthful lusts: but follow righteousness, faith, charity, peace, with them that call on the Lord out of a pure heart. 2 Tim. 2:22 (*see also* Flee, Lust, Pure)

A man of understanding holdeth his peace. Prov. 11:12 (*see also* Understand)

Prov. 11:12 he that is void of wisdom despiseth his neighbour: but a man of understanding holdeth his *p.*; **17:28** even a fool, when he holdeth his *p.*, is counted wise: and he that shutteth his lips is esteemed a man of understanding.

Lead a quiet and peaceable life in all godliness and honesty. 1 Tim. 2:2 (*see also* Godliness, Honest, Life)

1 Tim 2:2 for kings, and for all that are in authority; that we may lead a quiet and *p.* life in all godliness and honesty; **Heb. 13:18** pray for us: for we trust we have a good conscience, in all things willing to live honestly.

Follow peace with all men, and holiness, without which no man shall see the Lord. Heb. 12:14 (*see also* Holiness)

Matt. 5:9 blessed are the peacemakers: for they shall be called the children of God; **Mark 9:50** have salt in yourselves, and have *p.* one with another; **Luke 1:79** give light to them that sit in darkness and in the shadow of death, to guide our feet into the way of *p.*; **Rom. 5:1** being justified by faith, we have *p.* with God through our wherewith one may edify another; **1 Cor. 14:33** God is not the author of confusion, but of *p.*, as in all churches of the saints; **2 Cor. 13:11** be perfect, be of good comfort, be of one mind, live in *p.*; and the God of love and *p.* shall be Lord Jesus Christ; **14:19** let us therefore follow after the things which make for *p.*; **Heb. 12:14** follow *p.* with all men, and holiness, without which no man shall see the Lord; **1 Pet. 3:11** let him eschew evil, and do good; let him seek *p.*, and ensue it.

Let the peace of God rule in your hearts. Col. 3:15 (*see also* Rule)

Eph 2:14-15 for he is our *p.*, who hath made both one, and hath broken down the middle wall of partition between us; Having abolished in his flesh the enmity, even the law of commandments contained in ordinances; for to make in himself of twain one new man, so making *p.*; **2:17** came and preached *p.* to you which were afar off, and to them that were nigh; **4:1-3** walk worthy of the vocation wherewith ye are called, With all lowliness and meekness, with longsuffering, forbearing one another in love; Endeavouring to keep the unity of the Spirit in the bond of *p.*; **Col. 3:15** let the *p.* of God rule in your hearts, to the which also ye are called in one body; and be ye thankful; **1 Thes. 1:1, 2 Thes. 1:2** Grace be unto you, and *p.*, from God our Father, and the Lord Jesus Christ; **3:16** now the Lord of *p.* himself give you *p.* always by all means. The Lord be with you all.

Follow after the things which make for peace, and things wherewith one may edify another. Rom. 14:19 (*see also* Edify)

Rom. 14:19 follow after the things which make for *p.*, and things wherewith one may edify another; **15:2** let every one of us please his neighbour for his good to edification; **1 Thes. 5:11** comfort yourselves together, and edify one another, even as also ye do.

PEARL (*see also* Blessing, Gift, Knowledge, Mystery, Revelation, Sacred, Testimony)

Give not that which is holy unto the dogs, neither cast ye your pearls before swine, lest they trample them under their feet, and turn again and rend you. Matt. 7:6 (*see also* Holy)

PERIL, PERILOUS (*see also* Danger)

This know also, that in the last days perilous times shall come. 2 Tim. 3:1 (*see also* Last Days)

PERFECT, PERFECTION, PERFECTLY (*see also* Father, Godliness, Integrity, Jesus Christ, Just)

If any man offend not in word, the same is a perfect man, and able also to bridle the whole body. James 3:2-8 (*see also* Bridle, Offend)

The eyes of the LORD run to and fro throughout the whole earth, to shew himself strong in the behalf of them whose heart is perfect toward him. 2 Chron. 16:9 (*see also* Heart)

If thou wilt be perfect, go and sell that thou hast, and give to the poor, and thou shalt have treasure in heaven: and come and follow me. Matt. 19:21-22 (*see also* Follow, Sacrifice, Treasure)

I will walk within my house with a perfect heart. Ps. 101:2 (*see also* Heart)

Above all things, put on charity, which is the bond of perfectness. Col. 3:14 (*see also* Charity)

All scripture is given by inspiration of God, and is profitable for doctrine, for reproof, for correction, for instruction in righteousness: That the man of God may be perfect, throughly furnished unto all good works. 2 Tim. 3:16-17 (*see also* Inspiration, Scripture, Works)

And he gave some, apostles; and some, prophets; and some, evangelists; and some, pastors and teachers; For the perfecting of the saints, for the work of the ministry, for the edifying of the body of Christ: Till we all come in the unity of the faith, and of the knowledge of the Son of God, unto a perfect man, unto the measure of the stature of the fulness of Christ. Eph. 4:11-13 (*see also* Apostle, Prophet, Unity)

Be ye therefore perfect, even as your Father in heaven is perfect. Matt. 5:48 (*see also* Father)

Matt. 5:48 be ye therefore *p.*, even as your Father which is in heaven is *p.*; **Luke 6:40** the disciple is not above his master: but every one that is *p.* shall be as his master; **2 Cor. 13:11** be *p.*, be of good comfort, be of one mind, live in peace; and the God of love and peace shall be with you; **Eph. 4:12-13** for the *p.* of the saints, for the work of the ministry, for the edifying of the body of Christ: Till we all come in the unity of the faith, and of the knowledge of the Son of God, unto a *p.* man, unto the measure of the stature of the fulness of Christ; **2 Tim. 3:16-17** all scripture is given by inspiration of God, and is profitable for doctrine, for reproof, for correction, for instruction in righteousness: That the man of God may be *p.*, throughly furnished unto all good works.

Know thou the God of thy father, and serve him with a perfect heart and with a willing mind: for the LORD searcheth all hearts, and understandeth all the imaginations of the thoughts. 1 Chron. 28:9 (*see also* Imagine)

Gen. 6:9 Noah was a just man and *p.* in his generations, and Noah walked with God; **17:1** I am the Almighty God; walk before me, and be thou *p.*; **Deut. 18:13** thou shalt be *p.* with the LORD thy God; **1 Kgs. 8:61** let your heart therefore be *p.* with the LORD our God, to walk in his statutes, and to keep his commandments; **11:4** (15:3) his heart was not *p.* with the LORD his God, as was the heart of David his father; **15:14** the high places were not removed: nevertheless Asas heart was *p.* with the LORD all his days; **2 Kgs. 20:3** I beseech thee, O LORD, remember now how I have walked before thee in truth and with a *p.* heart, and have done that which is good in thy sight; **1 Chron. 28:9** know thou the God of thy father, and serve him with a *p.* heart and with a willing mind: for the LORD searcheth all hearts, and understandeth all the imaginations of the thoughts; **29:9** the people rejoiced, for that they offered willingly, because with *p.* heart they offered willingly to the LORD; **29:19** give unto Solomon my son a *p.* heart, to keep thy commandments, thy testimonies, and thy statutes, and to do all these things; **2 Chron. 8:16** the house of the LORD was *p.*; **16:9** the eyes of the LORD run to and fro throughout the whole earth, to shew himself strong in the behalf of them whose heart is *p.* toward him; **19:9** thus shall ye do in the fear of the LORD, faithfully, and with a *p.* heart; **25:2** he did that which was right in the sight of the LORD, but not with a *p.* heart; **Job 1:1** Job... was *p.* and upright, and one that feared God, and eschewed evil; **1:8** hast thou considered my servant Job, that there is none like him in the earth, a *p.* and an upright man, one that feareth God, and escheweth evil; **2:3** hast thou considered my servant Job, that there is none like him in the earth, a *p.* and an upright man, one that feareth God, and escheweth evil; **8:20** God will not cast away a *p.* man, neither will he help the evil doers; **22:3** is it any pleasure to the Almighty, that thou art righteous? or is it gain to him, that thou makest thy ways *p.*; **Ps. 18:30-32** As for God, his way is *p.*: the word of the LORD is tried: he is a buckler to all those that trust in him... It is God that girdeth me with strength, and maketh my way *p.*; **37:37** mark the *p.* man, and behold the upright: for the end of that man is peace; **101:2** I will behave myself wisely in a *p.* way. O when wilt thou come unto me? I will walk within my house with a *p.* heart; **101:6** mine eyes shall be upon the faithful of the land, that they may dwell with me: he that walketh in a *p.* way, he shall serve me; **Prov. 2:21** the upright shall dwell in the land, and the *p.* shall remain in it; **Isa. 38:3-5** remember now, O LORD, I beseech thee, how I have walked before thee in truth and with a *p.* heart, and have done that which is good in thy sight.

I am the Almighty God; walk before me, and be thou perfect. Gen. 17:1 (*see also* Walk)

Gen. 6:9 Noah was a just man and *p.* in his generations, and Noah walked with God; **17:1-2** I am the Almighty God; walk before me, and be thou *p.*; **Deut. 18:13** thou shalt be *p.* with the

LORD thy God; **25:15** thou shalt have a *p.* and just weight, a *p.* and just measure shalt thou have; **2 Sam. 22:33** God is my strength and power: and he maketh my way *p.*; **1 Kgs. 2:4** if thy children take heed to their way, to walk before me in truth with all their heart and with all their soul, there shall not fail thee; **8:23-25** there is no God like thee, in heaven above, or on earth beneath, who keepest covenant and mercy with thy servants that walk before thee with all their heart; **8:36** teach them the good way wherein they should walk; **8:61** let your heart therefore be *p.* with the LORD our God, to walk in his statutes, and to keep his commandments; **9:4** walk before me... in integrity of heart, and in uprightness, to do according to all that I have commanded thee, and wilt keep my statutes and my judgments; **11:4** his heart was not *p.* with the LORD his God; **15:3** and his heart was not *p.* with the LORD his God; **15:14** Asas heart was *p.* with the LORD all his days; **2 Kgs. 20:3** I beseech thee, O LORD, remember now how I have walked before thee in truth and with a *p.* heart, and have done that which is good in thy sight; **1 Chron. 12:38** these men of war... came with a *p.* heart to Hebron, to make David king over all Israel; **28:9** know thou the God of thy father, and serve him with a *p.* heart and with a willing mind; **29:9** the people rejoiced, for that they offered willingly, because with *p.* heart they offered willingly to the LORD; **29:19** give unto Solomon my son a *p.* heart, to keep thy commandments, thy testimonies, and thy statutes, and to do all these things; **2 Chron. 6:14** there is no God like thee in the heaven, nor in the earth; which keepest covenant, and shewest mercy unto thy servants, that walk before thee with all their hearts; **7:17** walk before me, as David thy father walked, and do according to all that I have commanded thee, and shalt observe my statutes and my judgments; **8:16** the house of the LORD was *p.*; **15:17** the heart of Asa was *p.* all his days; **16:9** the eyes of the LORD run to and fro throughout the whole earth, to shew himself strong in the behalf of them whose heart is *p.* toward him; **19:9** thus shall ye do in the fear of the LORD, faithfully, and with a *p.* heart; **25:2** he did that which was right in the sight of the LORD, but not with a *p.* heart; **Job 1:1** there was a man... whose name was Job; and that man was *p.* and upright, and one that feared God, and eschewed evil; **1:8** hast thou considered my servant Job, that there is none like him in the earth, a *p.* and an upright man, one that feareth God, and escheweth evil; **2:3** hast thou considered my servant Job, that there is none like him in the earth, a *p.* and an upright man, one that feareth God, and escheweth evil; **8:20** God will not cast away a *p.* man, neither will he help the evil doers; **24:13** they are of those that rebel against the light; they know not the ways thereof, nor abide in the paths thereof; **31:7** if my step hath turned out of the way, and mine heart walked after mine eyes, and if any blot hath cleaved to mine hands; **36:4** he that is *p.* in knowledge is with thee; **Ps. 18:30-32** his way is *p.*: the word of the LORD is tried: he is a buckler to all those that trust in him... It is God that girdeth me with strength, and maketh my way *p.*; **37:37** mark the *p.* man, and behold the upright: for the end of that man is peace; **101:2** I will behave myself wisely in a *p.* way... I will walk within my house with a *p.* heart; **101:6** he that walketh in a *p.* way, he shall serve me; **Prov. 11:5** the righteousness of the *p.* shall direct his way; **Isa. 38:3-6** remember now, O LORD, I beseech thee, how I have walked before thee in truth and with a *p.* heart, and have done that which is good in thy sight; **Jer. 6:16** stand ye in the ways, and see, and ask for the old paths, where is the good way, and walk therein, and ye shall find rest for your souls.

PERFORM, PERFORMANCE (*see also* Accomplish, Do, Fulfill, Keep)

I have inclined mine heart to perform thy statutes always, even unto the end. Ps. 119:112 (*see also* Statute)

PERISH (*see also* Death)

Where there is no vision, the people perish: but he that keepeth the law, happy is he. Prov. 29:18 (*see also* Law, Vision)

PERSECUTE, PERSECUTION (*see also* Adversity, Affliction, Chasten, Cruelty, Despise, Enemy, Hate, Kill, Murder, Oppress, Reject, Revile, Suffer, Tribulation)

Blessed are they which are persecuted for righteousness' sake: for theirs is the kingdom of heaven. Matt. 5:10 (*see also* Kingdom)

Blessed are ye, when men shall revile you, and persecute you, and shall say all manner of evil against you falsely, for my sake. Rejoice, and be exceeding glad: for great is your reward in heaven: for so persecuted they the prophets which were before you. Matt 5:11-12 (*see also* Prophet, Reward)

I gave my back to the smiters and my cheeks to them that plucked off the hair: I hid not my face from shame and spitting. For the Lord GOD will help me; therefore shall I not be confounded. Isa. 50:6-7 (*see also* Endure, Smite)

They mocked the messengers of God, and despised his words, and misused his prophets, until the wrath of the LORD arose against his people, till there was no remedy. 2 Chron. 36:16 (*see also* Messenger, Mock, Prophet)

Woe be unto the pastors that destroy and scatter the sheep of my pasture! saith the LORD. Jer. 23:1 (*see also* Destroy, Scatter)

Isa. 51:23 I will put it into the hand of them that afflict thee; which have said to thy soul, Bow down, that we may go over: and thou hast laid thy body as the ground, and as the street, to them that went over; **Jer. 17:18** let them be confounded that *p.* me, but let not me be confounded: let them be dismayed, but let not me be dismayed: bring upon them the day of evil, and destroy them with double destruction; **20:11** the LORD is with me as a mighty terrible one: therefore my *p.* shall stumble, and they shall not prevail: they shall be greatly ashamed; **23:1** woe be unto the pastors that destroy and scatter the sheep of my pasture! saith the LORD.

Therefore also said the wisdom of God, I will send them prophets and apostles, and some of them they shall slay and persecute: That the blood of all the prophets, which was shed from the foundation of the world, may be required of this generation. Luke 11:49-50 (*see also* Blood, Prophet, Wisdom)

Matt. 23:30-31 if we had been in the days of our fathers, we would not have been partakers with them in the blood of the prophets. Wherefore ye be witnesses unto yourselves, that ye are the children of them which killed the prophets; **23:34-35** (Luke 11:49-51) send unto you prophets, and wise men, and scribes: and some of them ye shall kill and crucify; and some of them shall ye scourge in your synagogues, and *p.* them from city to city: That upon you may come all the righteous blood shed upon the earth, from the blood of righteous Abel unto the blood of Zacharias son of Barachias, whom ye slew between the temple and the altar; **Acts 9:2** if he found any of this way, whether they were men or women, he might bring them bound unto Jerusalem; **12:1-3** Herod the king stretched forth his hands to vex certain of the church. And he killed James the brother of John with the sword. And because he saw it pleased the Jews, he proceeded further to take Peter also; **13:50-51** the Jews stirred up the devout and honourable women, and the chief men of the city, and raised *p.* against Paul and Barnabas, and expelled them out of their coasts; **14:19-20** there came thither certain Jews from Antioch and Iconium, who persuaded the people, and, having stoned Paul, drew him out **23:13** they were more than forty which had made this conspiracy; **1 Thes. 2:15** who both killed the Lord Jesus, and their own prophets, and have *p.* us; and they please not God, and are contrary to all men**; Rev. 16:6** for they have shed the blood of saints and prophets, and thou hast given them blood to drink; for they are of the city, supposing he had been dead. Howbeit, as the disciples stood round about him, he rose up, and came into the city: and the next day he departed with Barnabas to Derbe; worthy; **17:6** I saw the woman drunken with the blood of the saints, and with the blood of the martyrs of Jesus: and when I saw her, I wondered with great admiration.

Love your enemies, bless them that curse you, do good to them that hate you, and pray for them which despitefully use you, and persecute you. Matt. 5:44 (*see also* Curse, Enemy, Love, Spite)

Matt. 5:44 (Luke 6:27-28) love your enemies, bless them that curse you, do good to them that hate you, and pray for them which despitefully use you, and *p.* you; **5:46** if ye love them which love you, what reward have ye? do not even the publicans the same; **10:22-23** ye shall be hated of all men for my name's sake: but he that endureth to the end shall be saved. But when they *p.* you in this city, flee ye into another: for verily I say unto you, Ye shall not have gone over the cities of Israel, till the Son of man be come; **24:9** then shall they deliver you up to be afflicted, and shall kill you: and ye shall be hated of all nations for my name's sake; **Mark 4:17** have no root in themselves, and so endure but for a time: afterward, when affliction or *p.* ariseth for the word's sake, immediately they are offended; **13:9** take heed to yourselves: for they shall deliver you up to councils; and in the synagogues ye shall be beaten: and ye shall be brought before rulers and kings for my sake, for a testimony against them; **13:11-13** when they shall lead you, and deliver you up, take no thought beforehand what ye shall speak, neither do ye premeditate: but whatsoever shall be given

you in that hour, that speak ye: for it is not ye that speak, but the Holy Ghost. Now the brother shall betray the brother to death, and the father the son; and children shall rise up against their parents, and shall cause them to be put to death. And ye shall be hated of all men for my name's sake: but he that shall endure unto the end, the same shall be saved; **Luke 6:22** blessed are ye, when men shall hate you, and when they shall separate you from their company, and shall reproach you, and cast out your name as evil, for the Son of man's sake; **6:29** unto him that smiteth thee on the one cheek offer also the other; and him that taketh away thy cloke forbid not to take thy coat also; **6:32** if ye love them which love you, what thank have ye? for sinners also love those that love them; **6:35** love ye your enemies, and do good, and lend, hoping for nothing again; and your reward shall be great, and ye shall be the children of the Highest: for he is kind unto the unthankful and to the evil; **12:20** therefore if thine enemy hunger, feed him; if he thirst, give him drink: for in so doing thou shalt heap coals of fire on his head; **18:7** shall not God avenge his own elect, which cry day and night unto him, though he bear long with them; **21:12-20** they shall lay their hands on you, and *p.* you, delivering you up to the synagogues, and into prisons, being brought before kings and rulers for my name's sake. And it shall turn to you for a testimony. Settle it therefore in your hearts, not to meditate before what ye shall answer: For I will give you a mouth and wisdom, which all your adversaries shall not be able to gainsay nor resist. And ye shall be betrayed both by parents, and brethren, and kinsfolks, and friends; and some of you shall they cause to be put to death. And ye shall be hated of all men for my name's sake. But there shall not an hair of your head perish. In your patience possess ye your souls; **22:33** Lord, I am ready to go with thee, both into prison, and to death; **John 11:16** let us also go, that we may die with him; **Acts 5:41** they departed from the presence of the council, rejoicing that they were counted worthy to suffer shame for his name; **7:52** which of the prophets have not your fathers *p.*? and they have slain them which shewed before of the coming of the Just One; of whom ye have been now the betrayers and murderers; **7:58** cast him out of the city, and stoned him: and the witnesses laid down their clothes at a young man's feet, whose name was Saul; **9:1-2** breathing out threatenings and slaughter against the disciples of the Lord, went unto the high priest, And desired of him letters to Damascus to the synagogues, that if he found any of this way, whether they were men or women, he might bring them bound unto Jerusalem; **14:5** there was an assault made both of the Gentiles, and also of the Jews with their rulers, to use them despitefully, and to stone them; **14:19** there came thither certain Jews from Antioch and Iconium, who persuaded the people, and, having stoned Paul, drew him out of the city, supposing he had been dead; **14:22** confirming the souls of the disciples, and exhorting them to continue in the faith, and that we must through much tribulation enter into the kingdom of God; **15:26** men that have hazarded their lives for the name of our Lord Jesus Christ; **16:22-26** the multitude rose up together against them: and the magistrates rent off their clothes, and commanded to beat them. And when they had laid many stripes upon them, they cast them into prison, charging the jailor to keep them safely: Who, having received such a charge, thrust them into the inner prison, and made their feet fast in the stocks. And at midnight Paul and Silas prayed, and sang praises unto God: and the prisoners heard them. And suddenly there was a great earthquake, so that the foundations of the prison were shaken: and immediately all the doors were opened, and every one's bands were loosed; **26:7** which promise our twelve tribes, instantly serving God day and night, hope to come. For which hope's sake, king Agrippa, I am accused of the Jews; **Rom. 5:3** we glory in tribulations also: knowing that tribulation worketh patience; **8:17-19** if so be that we suffer with him, that we may be also glorified together. For I reckon that the sufferings of this present time are not worthy to be compared with the glory which shall be revealed in us. For the earnest expectation of the creature waiteth for the manifestation of the sons of God; **8:28** we know that all things work together for good to them that love God, to them who are the called according to his purpose; **8:35-39** who shall separate us from the love of Christ? shall tribulation, or distress, or *p.*, or famine, or nakedness, or peril, or sword? As it is written, For thy sake we are killed all the day long; we are accounted as sheep for the slaughter. Nay, in all these things we are more than conquerors through him that loved us. For I am persuaded, that neither death, nor life, nor angels, nor principalities, nor powers, nor things present, nor things to come, Nor height, nor depth, nor any other creature, shall be able to separate us from the love of God, which is in Christ Jesus our Lord; **1 Cor. 4:10-12** we are fools for Christ's sake, but ye are wise in Christ; we are weak, but ye are strong; ye are honourable, but we are despised. Even unto this present hour we both

hunger, and thirst, and are naked, and are buffeted, and have no certain dwellingplace; And labour, working with our own hands: being reviled, we bless; being *p.*, we suffer it; **13:4** charity suffereth long, and is kind; charity envieth not; charity vaunteth not itself, is not puffed up; **2 Cor. 1:5** for as the sufferings of Christ abound in us, so our consolation also aboundeth by Christ; **1:7** our hope of you is stedfast, knowing, that as ye are partakers of the sufferings, so shall ye be also of the consolation; **1:8-10** we would not, brethren, have you ignorant of our trouble which came to us in Asia, that we were pressed out of measure, above strength, insomuch that we despaired even of life: But we had the sentence of death in ourselves, that we should not trust in ourselves, but in God which raiseth the dead: Who delivered us from so great a death, and doth deliver: in whom we trust that he will yet deliver us; **2:5** if any have caused grief, he hath not grieved me, but in part: that I may not overcharge you all; **4:8-9** we are troubled on every side, yet not distressed; we are perplexed, but not in despair; *p.*, but not forsaken; cast down, but not destroyed; **4:15-18** all things are for your sakes, that the abundant grace might through the thanksgiving of many redound to the glory of God. For which cause we faint not; but though our outward man perish, yet the inward man is renewed day by day. For our light affliction, which is but for a moment, worketh for us a far more exceeding and eternal weight of glory; While we look not at the things which are seen, but at the things which are not seen: for the things which are seen are temporal; but the things which are not seen are eternal; **5:4-6** we that are in this tabernacle do groan, being burdened: not for that we would be unclothed, but clothed upon, that mortality might be swallowed up of life. Now he that hath wrought us for the selfsame thing is God, who also hath given unto us the earnest of the Spirit. Therefore we are always confident, knowing that, whilst we are at home in the body, we are absent from the Lord; **7:6** nevertheless God, that comforteth those that are cast down, comforted us by the coming of Titus; **8:2** how that in a great trial of affliction the abundance of their joy and their deep poverty abounded unto the riches of their liberality; **11:20-28** for ye suffer, if a man bring you into bondage, if a man devour you, if a man take of you, if a man exalt himself, if a man smite you on the face. I speak as concerning reproach, as though we had been weak. Howbeit whereinsoever any is bold, (I speak foolishly,) I am bold also. Are they Hebrews? so am I. Are they Israelites? so am I. Are they the seed of Abraham? so am I. Are they ministers of Christ? (I speak as a fool) I am more; in labours more abundant, in stripes above measure, in prisons more frequent, in deaths oft. Of the Jews five times received I forty stripes save one. Thrice was I beaten with rods, once was I stoned, thrice I suffered shipwreck, a night and a day I have been in the deep; In journeyings often, in perils of waters, in perils of robbers, in perils by mine own countrymen, in perils by the heathen, in perils in the city, in perils in the wilderness, in perils in the sea, in perils among false brethren; In weariness and painfulness, in watchings often, in hunger and thirst, in fastings often, in cold and nakedness. Beside those things that are without, that which cometh upon me daily, the care of all the churches; **12:5** of such an one will I glory: yet of myself I will not glory, but in mine infirmities; **12: 9-10** my grace is sufficient for thee: for my strength is made perfect in weakness. Most gladly therefore will I rather glory in my infirmities, that the power of Christ may rest upon me. And he said unto me, My grace is sufficient for thee: for my strength is made perfect in weakness. Most gladly therefore will I rather glory in my infirmities, that the power of Christ may rest upon me; **Gal. 4:13** ye know how through infirmity of the flesh I preached the gospel unto you at the first; **6:10** as we have therefore opportunity, let us do good unto all men, especially unto them who are of the household of faith; **6:17-18** from henceforth let no man trouble me: for I bear in my body the marks of the Lord Jesus; **Eph. 3:13** I desire that ye faint not at my tribulations for you, which is your glory; **Philip. 1:12-19** the things which happened unto me have fallen out rather unto the furtherance of the gospel; So that my bonds in Christ are manifest in all the palace, and in all other places; And many of the brethren in the Lord, waxing confident by my bonds, are much more bold to speak the word without fear. Some indeed preach Christ even of envy and strife; and some also of good will: The one preach Christ of contention, not sincerely, supposing to add affliction to my bonds: But the other of love, knowing that I am set for the defence of the gospel. What then? notwithstanding, every way, whether in pretence, or in truth, Christ is preached; and I therein do rejoice, yea, and will rejoice. For I know that this shall turn to my salvation through your prayer, and the supply of the Spirit of Jesus Christ; **1:28-30** in nothing terrified by your adversaries: which is to them an evident token of perdition, but to you of salvation, and that of God; **3:8** I count all things

but loss for the excellency of the knowledge of Christ Jesus my Lord: for whom I have suffered the loss of all things, and do count them but dung, that I may win Christ; **Col. 1:24** who now rejoice in my sufferings for you, and fill up that which is behind of the afflictions of Christ in my flesh for his body's sake, which is the church; **1 Thes. 1:6** ye became followers of us, and of the Lord, having received the word in much affliction, with joy of the Holy Ghost; **2:2** even after that we had suffered before, and were shamefully entreated, as ye know, at Philippi, we were bold in our God to speak unto you the gospel of God with much contention; **2:14** ye, brethren, became followers of the churches of God which in Judaea are in Christ Jesus: for ye also have suffered like things of your own countrymen, even as they have of the Jews; **3:3-4** no man should be moved by these afflictions: for yourselves know that we are appointed thereunto. For verily, when we were with you, we told you before that we should suffer tribulation; even as it came to pass, and ye know; **3:7** we were comforted over you in all our affliction and distress by your faith; **2 Thes. 1:4-5** we ourselves glory in you in the churches of God for your patience and faith in all your *p.* and tribulations that ye endure: Which is a manifest token of the righteous judgment of God, that ye may be counted worthy of the kingdom of God, for which ye also suffer; **4:10** we both labour and suffer reproach, because we trust in the living God, who is the Saviour of all men, specially of those that believe; **2 Tim. 1:8** be not thou therefore ashamed of the testimony of our Lord, nor of me his prisoner: but be thou partaker of the afflictions of the gospel according to the power of God; **2:3** endure hardness, as a good soldier of Jesus Christ; **2:9** wherein I suffer trouble, as an evil doer, even unto bonds; but the word of God is not bound; **3:11-12** *p.*, afflictions, which came unto me at Antioch, at Iconium, at Lystra; what *p.* I endured: but out of them all the Lord delivered me. Yea, and all that will live godly in Christ Jesus shall suffer persecution; **4:5** watch thou in all things, endure afflictions, do the work of an evangelist, make full proof of thy ministry; **Heb. 5:8** yet afflictions; Partly, whilst ye were made a gazingstock both by reproaches and afflictions; and partly, whilst ye became companions of them that were so used. For ye had compassion learned he obedience by the things which he suffered; **10:32-35** ye endured a great fight of me in my bonds, and took joyfully the spoiling of your goods, knowing in yourselves that ye have in heaven a better and an enduring substance.

Cast not away therefore your confidence, which hath great recompence of reward; **11:25** choosing rather to suffer affliction with the people of God, than to enjoy the pleasures of sin for a season; **11:27** by faith he forsook Egypt, not fearing the wrath of the king: for he endured, as seeing him who is invisible; **11:35-38** others had trial of cruel mockings and scourgings, yea, moreover of bonds and imprisonment: They were stoned, they were sawn asunder, were tempted, were slain with the sword; **13:3** remember them that are in bonds, as bound with them; and them which suffer adversity; **James 5:10-11** Take, my brethren, the prophets, who have spoken in the name of the Lord, for an example of suffering affliction, and of patience. Behold, we count them happy which endure. Ye have heard of the patience of Job, and have seen the end of the Lord; that the Lord is very pitiful, and of tender mercy; **5:13** is any among you afflicted? let him pray; **1 Pet. 2:19** this is thankworthy, if a man for conscience toward God endure grief, suffering wrongfully; **2:20** what glory is it, if, when ye be buffeted for your faults, ye shall take it patiently? but if, when ye do well, and suffer for it, ye take it patiently, this is acceptable with God; **2:23** who, when he was reviled, reviled not again; when he suffered, he threatened not; but committed himself to him that judgeth righteously; **3:14** if ye suffer for righteousness' sake, happy are ye: and be not afraid of their terror, neither be troubled; **3:17** it is better, if the will of God be so, that ye suffer for well doing, than for evil doing; **4:12-14** think it not strange concerning the fiery trial which is to try you, as though some strange thing happened unto you: But rejoice, inasmuch as ye are partakers of Christ's sufferings; that, when his glory shall be revealed, ye may be glad also with exceeding joy. If ye be reproached for the name of Christ, happy are ye; for the spirit of glory and of God resteth upon you: on their part he is evil spoken of, but on your part he is glorified; **4:16-19** if any man suffer as a Christian, let him not be ashamed; but let him glorify God on this behalf. For the time is come that judgment must begin at the house of God: and if it first begin at us, what shall the end be of them that obey not the gospel of God? And if the righteous scarcely be saved, where shall the ungodly and the sinner appear? Wherefore let them that suffer according to the will of God commit the keeping of their souls to him in well doing, as unto a faithful Creator; **1 Jn. 3:13** marvel not, my brethren, if the world hate you; **3:16** hereby perceive we the love of God, because he laid down his life for us: and we ought to lay down our lives for the brethren; **Rev. 1:9** companion in tribulation, and in the kingdom and patience of Jesus Christ, was in the isle that is called Patmos; **2:3** hast borne, and hast patience, and for my name's sake hast laboured, and hast not fainted; **2:9-10** fear none of those things which thou shalt suffer: behold, the devil shall cast some of you into prison, that ye may be tried; and ye shall have tribulation ten days: be thou faithful unto death, and I will give thee a crown of life; **6: 9-11** how long, O Lord, holy and true, dost thou not judge and avenge our blood on them that dwell on the earth?; **7: 14** these are they which came out of great tribulation, and have washed their robes, and made them white in the blood of the Lamb; **13:15** as many as would not worship the image of the beast should be killed; **19:2** hath avenged the blood of his servants at her hand; **20:4** I saw the souls of them that were beheaded for the witness of Jesus, and for the word of God, and which had not worshipped the beast, neither his image, neither had received his mark upon their foreheads, or in their hands; and they lived and reigned with Christ a thousand years.

Be sober, be vigilant; because your adversary the devil, as a roaring lion, walketh about, seeking whom he may devour; Whom resist stedfast in the faith, knowing that the same afflictions are accomplished in your brethren that are in the world. But the God of all grace, who hath called us unto his eternal glory by Christ Jesus, after that ye have suffered a while, make you perfect, stablish, strengthen, settle you. 1 Pet. 5:8-10 (*see also* Vigilant)

PERSERVERANCE, PERSEVERE (*see* Diligence, Endure, Steadfast)

PERSUADE (*see also* Converse)

Do I now persuade men, or God? or do I seek to please men? for if I yet pleased men, I should not be the servant of Christ. Gal. 1:10 (*see also* Please, Servant)

He reasoned in the synagogue every sabbath, and persuaded the Jews and the Greeks. Acts 18:4

Acts 18:4 he reasoned in the synagogue every sabbath, and *p.* the Jews and the Greeks; **18:28** he mightily convinced the Jews, and that publickly, shewing by the scriptures that Jesus was Christ; **19:8-9** he went into the synagogue, and spake boldly for the space of three months, disputing and *p.* the things concerning the kingdom of God; **2 Cor. 5:10** knowing therefore the terror of the Lord, we *p.* men; but we are made manifest unto God; and I trust also are made manifest in your consciences.

PERVERSE (*see also* Pervert)

Put away from thee a froward mouth, and perverse lips put far from thee. Prov. 4:24 (*see also* Froward, Lips)

A wholesome tongue is a tree of life: but perverseness therein is a breach in the spirit. Prov. 15:4 (*see also* Tongue, Wholesome)

Because ye despise this word, and trust in oppression or perverseness, and stay thereon: Therefore this iniquity shall be to you as a breach ready to fall, swelling out in a high wall, whose breaking cometh suddenly at an instant. Isa. 30:12-13 (*see also* Despise, Oppress, Word)

PERVERT (*see also* Change, Corrupt, Falsehood, Perverse)

The burden of the LORD shall ye mention no more: for every man's word shall be his burden; for ye have perverted the words of the living God. Jer. 23:36 (*see also* Word)

Thou hast trusted in thy wickedness: thou hast said, None seeth me. Thy wisdom and thy knowledge, it hath perverted thee; and thou hast said in thine heart, I am, and none else beside me. Isa. 47:10 (*see also* Trust, Wicked)

O full of all subtilty and all mischief, thou child of the devil, thou enemy of all righteousness, wilt thou not cease to pervert the right ways of the Lord. Acts 13:10 (*see also* Mischief, Subtle, Way)

Acts 13:10 O full of all subtilty and all mischief, thou child of the devil, thou enemy of all righteousness, wilt thou not cease to *p.* the right ways of the Lord; **Gal. 1:7-9** though we, or an angel from heaven, preach any other gospel unto you than that which we have preached unto you, let him be accursed.

PETITION (*see* Ask, Beg, Beseech, Inquire)

PITIFUL, PITY (*see also* Comparison, Kindness, Mercy)

To him that is afflicted, pity should be shewed from his friend. Job 6:14 (*see also* Afflict)

Job 6:14 to him that is afflicted *p.* should be shewed from his friend; **19:21** have *p.* upon me, have *p.* upon me, O ye my friends; for the hand of God hath touched me.

PLAGUE (*see also* Sickness)

I saw another sign in heaven, great and marvellous, seven angels having the seven last plagues; for in them is filled up the wrath of God. Rev. 15:1 (*see also* Angel, Seven, Sign)

PLAIN, PLAINLY, PLAINNESS (*see also* Clear, Hear, See, Simple, Truth)

These things have I spoken unto you in proverbs: but the time cometh, when I shall no more speak unto you in proverbs, but I shall shew you plainly of the Father. John 16:25 (*see also* Father, Speak)

John 11:14 then said Jesus unto them *p.,* Lazarus is dead. And I am glad for your sakes that I was not there, to the intent ye may believe; nevertheless let us go unto him; **16:25** these things have I spoken unto you in proverbs: but the time cometh, when I shall no more speak unto you in proverbs, but I shall shew you *p.* of the Father; **16:29** his disciples said unto him, Lo, now speakest thou *p.,* and speakest no proverb; **18:20** Jesus answered him, I spake openly to the world; I ever taught in the synagogue, and in the temple, whither the Jews always resort; and in secret have I said nothing; **Acts 20:20** I kept back nothing that was profitable unto you, but have shewed you, and have taught you publickly, and from house to house; **2 Cor. 2:17** we are not as many, which corrupt the word of God: but as of sincerity, but as of God, in the sight of God speak we in Christ; **3:13** seeing then that we have such hope, we use great *p.* of speech.

PLEAD (*see also* Ask, Beg, Beseech, Entreat)

Learn to do well; seek judgment, relieve the oppressed, judge the fatherless, plead for the widow. Isa. 1:17 (*see also* Do, Learn, Judge, Relieve)

PLEASANT, PLEASE, PLEASURE (*see also* Delight, Happiness, Lust)

He that loveth pleasure shall be a poor man: he that loveth wine and oil shall not be rich. **Prov. 21:17** (*see also* Love)

But without faith it is impossible to please him: for he that cometh to God must believe that he is, and that he is a rewarder of them that diligently seek him. **Heb. 11:6** (*see also* Believe, Diligently, Faith, Impossible, Reward, Seek)

Hear now this, thou that art given to pleasures, that dwellest carelessly, that sayest in thine heart, I am, and none else beside me. **Isa. 47:8**

God shall send them strong delusion, that they should believe a lie: That they all might be damned who believed not the truth, but had pleasure in unrighteousness. **2 Thes. 2:11-12** (*see also* Lie, Unrighteousness)

Do I now persuade men, or God? or do I seek to please men? for if I yet pleased men, I should not be the servant of Christ. **Gal. 1:10** (*see also* Persuade, Servant)

1 Cor 10:33 even as I please all men in all things, not seeking mine own profit, but the profit of many, that they may be saved; **Gal. 1:10** for do I now persuade men, or God? or do I seek to please men? for if I yet pleased men, I should not be the servant of Christ.

PLEDGE (*see also* Covenant, Oath, Promise)

When thou dost lend thy brother any thing, thou shalt not go into his house to fetch his pledge. **Deut. 24:10** (*see also* Lend)

POLLUTE, POLLUTION (*see also* Corrupt, Defile, Filthiness, Profane)

The children of Judah have done evil in my sight, saith the LORD: they have set their abominations in the house which is called by my name, to pollute it. **Jer. 7:30** (*see also* Abomination, Defile, House)

PONDER (*see also* Consider, Meditate, Think)

Meditate upon these things; give thyself wholly to them; that thy profiting may appear to all. **1 Tim. 4:15** (*see also* Give, Meditate)

Mary kept all these things, and pondered them in her heart. **Luke 2:19** (*see also* Heart)

Luke 2:19 Mary kept all these things, and *p.* them in her heart; **2:33** Joseph and his mother marvelled at those things which were spoken of him; **2:51** his mother kept all these sayings in her heart; **5:21-22** what reason ye in your hearts.

POOR (*see also* Afflict, Alms, Charity, Meek, Needy)

Blessed are the poor in spirit: for theirs is the kingdom of heaven. **Matt 5:3** (*see also* Kingdom)

If there be among you a poor man of one of thy brethren within any of thy gates in thy land which the LORD thy God giveth thee, thou shalt not harden thine heart, nor shut thine hand from thy poor brother. **Deut. 15:7** (*see also* Heart)

The righteous considereth the cause of the poor: but the wicked regardeth not to know it. **Prov. 29:7** (*see also* Righteous)

We then that are strong ought to bear the infirmities of the weak, and not to please ourselves. **Rom. 15:1** (*see also* Burden)

Matt. 19:21 if thou wilt be perfect, go and sell that thou hast, and give to the *p.*, and thou shalt have treasure in heaven: and come and follow me; **Mark 10:21** go thy way, sell whatsoever thou hast, and give to the *p.*, and thou shalt have treasure in heaven: and come, take up the cross, and follow me; **12:41-44** this *p.* widow hath cast more in, than all they which have cast into the treasury: For they all did cast in of their abundance; but she of her want did cast in all that she had, even all her living; **14:7** for ye have the *p.* with you always, and whensoever ye will ye may do them good: but me ye have not always; **15:21** they compel one Simon a Cyrenian, who passed by, coming out of the country, the father of Alexander and Rufus, to bear his cross; **Luke 14:12-14** when thou makest a feast, call the *p.*, the maimed, the lame, the blind: And thou shalt be blessed; for they cannot recompense thee: for thou shalt be recompensed at the resurrection of the just; **19:8-9** Lord, the half of my goods I give to the *p.*; and if I have taken any thing from any man by false accusation, I restore him fourfold. And Jesus said unto him, This day is salvation come to this house, forsomuch as he also is a son of

Abraham; **Acts 11:29** then the disciples, every man according to his ability, determined to send relief unto the brethren which dwelt in Judaea; **20:35** I have shewed you all things, how that so labouring ye ought to support the weak, and to remember the words of the Lord Jesus, how he said, It is more blessed to give than to receive; **Rom. 15:1** we then that are strong ought to bear the infirmities of the weak, and not to please ourselves; **2 Cor. 9:7** every man according as he purposeth in his heart, so let him give; not grudgingly, or of necessity: for God loveth a cheerful giver; **Gal. 2:10** only they would that we should remember the *p.*; the same which I also was forward to do; **6:2** bear ye one another's burdens, and so fulfil the law of Christ; **1 Thes. 4:12** ye may walk honestly toward them that are without, and that ye may have lack of nothing; **1 Tim. 5:16** if any man or woman that believeth have widows, let them relieve them, and let not the church be charged; that it may relieve them that are widows indeed.

He that oppresseth the poor to increase his riches, and he that giveth to the rich, shall surely come to want. Prov. 22:16 (*see also* Oppress, Rich)

Prov. 14:31 he that oppresseth the *p.* reproacheth his Maker: but he that honoureth him hath mercy on the *p.*; **22:16** he that oppresseth the *p.* to increase his riches, and he that giveth to the rich, shall surely come to want; **30:14** there is a generation, whose teeth are as swords, and their jaw teeth as knives, to devour the *p.* from off the earth, and the needy from among men.

Rob not the poor, because he is poor. Prov. 22:22

Prov. 22:22-23 rob not the *p.*, because he is *p.*: neither oppress the afflicted; **Isa. 17:12-14** God shall rebuke them, and they shall flee far off, and shall be chased as the chaff of the mountains before the wind... This is the portion of them that spoil us, and the lot of them that rob us.

For the poor shall never cease out of the land: therefore I command thee, saying, thou shalt open thine hand wide unto thy brother, to thy poor, and to thy needy, in the land. Deut. 15:11 (*see also* Hand, Needy)

Ex. 22:25 if thou lend money to any of my people that is *p.* by thee, thou shalt not be to him as an usurer, neither shalt thou lay upon him usury; **23:3** neither shalt thou countenance a *p.*

man in his cause; **23:6** thou shalt not wres t the judgment of thy *p.* in his cause; **Lev. 23:22** neither shalt thou gather any gleaning of thy harvest: thou shalt leave them unto the *p.*, and to the stranger; **25:35** if thy brother be waxen *p.*, and fallen in decay with thee; then thou shalt relieve him: yea, though he be a stranger, or a sojourner; that he may live with thee; **Deut. 15:7** if there be among you a *p.* man of one of thy brethren within any of thy gates in thy land which the LORD thy God giveth thee, thou shalt not harden thine heart, nor shut thine hand from thy *p.* brother; **15:9** beware that... thine eye be evil against thy *p.* brother, and thou givest him nought; and he cry unto the LORD against thee, and it be sin unto thee; **15:11** the *p.* shall never cease out of the land: therefore I command thee, saying, Thou shalt open thine hand wide unto thy brother, to thy *p.*, and to thy needy, in thy land; **24:14-15** thou shalt not oppress an hired servant that is *p.* and needy, whether he be of thy brethren, or of thy strangers that are in thy land within thy gates; **Job 5:15-16** he saveth the *p.* from the sword, from their mouth, and from the hand of the mighty; **20:18-19** he hath oppressed and hath forsaken the *p.*; **22:5-11** thou hast sent widows away empty, and the arms of the fatherless have been broken. Therefore snares are round about thee, and sudden fear troubleth thee; **29:12-13** I delivered the *p.* that cried, and the fatherless, and him that had none to help him; **29:15-16** I was eyes to the blind, and feet was I to the lame. I was a father to the *p.*: and the cause which I knew not I searched out; **29:25** I chose out their way, and sat chief, and dwelt as a king in the army, as one that comforteth the mourners; **30:25** did not I weep for him that was in trouble? was not my soul grieved for the *p.*; **31:16-22** if I have withheld the *p.* from their desire... Then let mine arm fall from my shoulder blade, and mine arm be broken from the bone; **34:28** they cause the cry of the *p.* to come unto him, and he heareth the cry of the afflicted; **36:15** he delivereth the *p.* in his affliction, and openeth their ears in oppression; **Ps. 9:18** the needy shall not alway be forgotten: the expectation of the *p.* shall not perish for ever; **10:2** the wicked in his pride doth persecute the *p.*: let them be taken in the devices that they have imagined; **12:5** gor the oppression of the *p.*, for the sighing of the needy, now will I arise, saith the LORD; **37:14** the wicked have drawn out the sword, and have bent their bow, to cast down the *p.* and needy; **41:1-3** blessed is he that considereth the *p.*: the LORD will deliver him in time of trouble; **74:19** forget not the congregation of thy *p.* for ever; **74:21** let not the oppressed return ashamed: let the *p.* and needy praise thy name; **82:3-4** defend the *p.* and fatherless: do justice to the afflicted and needy. Deliver the *p.* and needy: rid them out of the hand of the wicked; **Prov. 14:20-21** he that despiseth his neighbour sinneth: but he that hath mercy on the *p.*, happy is he; **14:31** he that oppresseth the *p.* reproacheth his Maker: but he that honoureth him hath mercy on the *p.*; **17:5** whoso mocketh the *p.* reproacheth his Maker: and he that is glad at calamities shall not be unpunished; **19:17** he that hath pity upon the *p.* lendeth unto the LORD; and that which he hath given will he pay him again; **21:13** whoso stoppeth his ears at the cry of the *p.*, he also shall cry himself, but shall not be heard; **21:26** he coveteth greedily all the day long: but the righteous giveth and spareth not; **22:9** he that hath a bountiful eye shall be blessed; for he giveth of his bread to the *p.*; **22:16** he that oppresseth the *p.* to increase his riches, and he that giveth to the rich, shall surely come to want; **22:22** rob not the *p.*, because he is *p.*: neither oppress the afflicted in the gate; **28:3** a *p.* man that oppresseth the *p.* is like a sweeping rain which leaveth no food; **28:27** he that giveth unto the *p.* shall not lack: but he that hideth his eyes shall have many a curse; **29:7** the righteous considereth the cause of the *p.*: but the wicked regardeth not to know it; **31:9** plead the cause of the *p.* and needy; **31:20** she stretcheth out her hand to the *p.*; yea, she reacheth forth her hands to the needy; **Eccl. 5:8** if thou seest the oppression of the *p.*, and violent perverting of judgment and justice in a province, marvel not at the matter; **Isa. 14:30** the firstborn of the *p.* shall feed, and the needy shall lie down in safety; **14:32** what shall one then answer the messengers of the nation? That the LORD hath founded Zion, and the *p.* of his people shall trust in it; **25:4** thou hast been a strength to the *p.*, a strength to the needy in his distress; **32:7** he deviseth wicked devices to destroy the *p.* with lying words, even when the needy speaketh right; **58:6-7** is it not to deal thy bread to the hungry, and that thou bring the *p.* that are cast out to thy house? when thou seest the naked, that thou cover him; and that thou hide not thyself from thine own flesh; **Ezek. 16:49** neither did she strengthen the hand of the *p.* and needy; **18:12** hath oppressed the *p.* and needy, hath spoiled by violence, hath not restored the pledge, and hath lifted up his eyes to the idols, hath committed abomination; **22:29** the people of the land have used oppression, and exercised robbery, and have vexed the *p.* and needy: yea, they have oppressed the stranger wrongfully; **Dan. 4:27** break off thy sins by righteousness, and thine iniquities by shewing

mercy to the *p.*; **Amos 4:1** hear this word, ye kine of Bashan, that are in the mountain of Samaria, which oppress the *p.*, which crush the needy; **5:11-12** I know your manifold transgressions and your mighty sins: they afflict the just, they take a bribe, and they turn aside the *p.* in the gate from their right; **8:4** hear this, O ye that swallow up the needy, even to make the *p.* of the land to fail; **Zech. 7:10** oppress not the widow, nor the fatherless, the stranger, nor the *p.*; and let none of you imagine evil against his brother in your heart.

POSSIBLE (*see also* Belief)

The things which are impossible with men are possible with God. Luke 18:27 (*see also* All Things)

If it be possible, as much as lieth in you, live peaceably with all men. Rom. 12:18 (*see also* Peace)

Trust in him at all times; ye people, pour out your heart before him: God is a refuge for us. Ps. 62:8 (*see also* Trust)

1 Sam. 1:15 I have drunk neither wine nor strong drink, but have *p.* out my soul before the LORD; **Ps. 62:8** trust in him at all times; ye people, *p.* out your heart before him: God is a refuge for us.

PRAISE (*see also* Exalt, Glorify, Honor, Hymn, Psalms, Song, Thank)

How can ye believe, which receive honour one of another, and seek not the honour that cometh from God only? John 5:44 (*see also* Glorify, Honor)

Praise the LORD, call upon his name, declare his doings among the people, make mention that his name is exalted. Isa. 12:4 (*see also* Call, Declare)

Sing praise to the name of the LORD most high. Ps. 7:17 (*see also* Sing)

In God we boast all the day long, and praise thy name for ever. Ps. 44:8 (*see also* Boast)

Praise ye the name of the LORD. Ps. 135:1 (*see also* Name)

Ps. 135:1 *p.* ye the LORD. *p.* ye the name of the LORD; *p.* him; **135:3** *p.* the LORD; for the LORD is good: sing *p.* unto his name; for it is pleasant.

Let another man praise thee, and not thine own mouth; a stranger, and not thine own lips. Prov. 27:2 (*see also* Boast)

Prov. 27:2 let another man *p.* thee, and not thine own mouth; a stranger, and not thine own lips; **27:21** as the fining pot for silver, and the furnace for gold; so is a man to his *p.*

Thank and praise the LORD God of Israel. 1 Chron. 16:4 (*see also* Thank)

Gen. 29:35 now will I *p.* the LORD: therefore she called his name Judah; and left bearing; **Ex. 15:1** sing unto the Lord; **Lev. 19:24** all the fruit thereof shall be holy to *p.* the LORD withal; **Judg. 5:2-3** I, will sing unto the LORD; I will sing *p.* to the LORD God of Israel; **2 Sam. 22:50** I will give thanks unto thee, O LORD, among the heathen, and I will sing *p.* unto thy name; **1 Chron. 16:4** he appointed certain of the Levites to minister before the ark of the LORD, and to record, and to thank and *p.* the LORD God of Israel; **16:7-12** give thanks unto the LORD, call upon his name, make known his deeds among the people. Sing unto him, sing psalms unto him, talk ye of all his wondrous works. Glory ye in his holy name; **16:25** great is the LORD, and greatly to be *p.*: he also is to be feared above all gods; **16:34-36** save us, O God of our salvation, and gather us together, and deliver us from the heathen, that we may give thanks to thy holy name, and glory in thy *p.*; **16:41** give thanks to the LORD, because his mercy endureth for ever; **23:5** four thousand *p.* the LORD with the instruments which I made, said David, to *p.* therewith; **23:30** stand every morning to thank and *p.* the LORD, and likewise at even; **25:3** give thanks and to *p.* the LORD; **29:13** our God, we thank thee, and *p.* thy glorious name; **2 Chron. 5:13** the trumpeters and singers were as one, to make one sound to be heard in praising and thanking the LORD; **7:3** they bowed themselves with their faces to the ground upon the pavement, and worshipped, and *p.* the LORD; **7:6** the priests waited on their offices: the Levites also with instruments of musick of the LORD, which David the king had made to *p.* the LORD; **20:19** the Levites, of the children of the Kohathites, and of the children of the Korhites, stood up to *p.* the LORD God of Israel with a loud voice; **20:21** he appointed singers unto the LORD, and that should *p.* the beauty of holiness, as they went out before the

army, and to say, *p.* the LORD; **20:21-22** he appointed singers unto the LORD, and that should *p.* the beauty of holiness, as they went out before the army, and to say, *p.* the LORD; for his mercy endureth for ever; **29:30** they sang *p.* with gladness, and they bowed their heads and worshipped; **30:21** the Levites and the priests *p.* the LORD day by day, singing with loud instruments unto the LORD; **Ezra 3:10-11** they sang together by course in praising and giving thanks unto the LORD; because he is good; **Neh. 5:13** the congregation said, Amen, and *p.* the LORD; **Job 36:3** I will fetch my knowledge from afar, and will ascribe righteousness to my Maker; **Ps. 7:17** I will *p.* the LORD according to his righteousness: and will sing *p.* to the name of the LORD most high; **8:9** LORD our Lord, how excellent is thy name in all the earth; **9:1-2** I will *p.* thee, O LORD, with my whole heart; I will shew forth all thy marvellous works. I will be glad and rejoice in thee: I will sing *p.* to thy name; **9:11** sing *p.* to the LORD, which dwelleth in Zion; **18:3** I will call upon the LORD, who is worthy to be *p.*; **18:49** I [will] give thanks unto thee, O LORD, among the heathen, and sing *p.* unto thy name; **22:3** thou art holy, O thou that inhabitest the *p.* of Israel; **22:22-23** I will declare thy name unto my brethren: in the midst of the congregation will I *p.* thee. Ye that fear the LORD, *p.* him; all ye the seed of Jacob, glorify him; **27:6** therefore will I offer in his tabernacle sacrifices of joy; I will sing, yea, I will sing *p.* unto the LORD; **28:7** the LORD is my strength and my shield; my heart trusted in him, and I am helped: therefore my heart greatly rejoiceth; and with my song will I *p.* him; **30:12** my glory may sing *p.* to thee, and not be silent. O LORD my God, I will give thanks unto thee for ever; **33:2** *p.* the LORD with harp: sing unto him with the psaltery and an instrument of ten strings; **34:1-3** I will bless the LORD at all times: his *p.* shall continually be in my mouth; **35:18** I will give thee thanks in the great congregation: I will *p.* thee among much people; **35:27-28** let the LORD be magnified, which hath pleasure in the prosperity of his servant. And my tongue shall speak of thy righteousness and of thy *p.* all the day long; **40:3** he hath put a new song in my mouth, even *p.* unto our God: many shall see it, and fear, and shall trust in the LORD; **42:5** why art thou cast down, O my soul? and why art thou disquieted in me? hope thou in God: for I shall yet *p.* him for the help of his countenance; **42:11** why art thou cast down, O my soul? and why art thou disquieted within me? hope thou in God: for I shall yet *p.* him, who is the health of my countenance, and my God; **43:4-5** upon the harp will I *p.* thee, O God my God. Why art thou cast down, O my soul? and why art thou disquieted within me? hope in God: for I shall yet *p.* him; **44:8** in God we boast all the day long, and *p.* thy name for ever; **45:17** I will make thy name to be remembered in all generations: therefore shall the people *p.* thee for ever and ever; **47:5-7** sing *p.* to God, sing *p.*: sing *p.* unto our King, sing *p.*. For God is the King of all the earth: sing ye *p.*; **48:1** great is the LORD, and greatly to be *p.* in the city of our God, in the mountain of his holiness; **50:23** whoso offereth *p.* glorifieth me: and to him that ordereth his conversation aright will I shew the salvation of God; **51:15** Lord, open thou my lips; and my mouth shall shew forth thy *p.*; **52:9** I will *p.* thee for ever, because thou hast done it: and I will wait on thy name; for it is good before thy saints; **54:6** I will freely sacrifice unto thee: I will *p.* thy name, O LORD; for it is good; **56:4** in God I will *p.* his word, in God I have put my trust; I will not fear what flesh can do unto me; **56:10** in God will I *p.* his word: in the LORD will I *p.* his word; **56:12** thy vows are upon me, O God: I will render *p.* unto thee; **57:5** be thou exalted, O God, above the heavens; let thy glory be above all the earth; **57:7** my heart is fixed, O God, my heart is fixed: I will sing and give *p.*; **61:8** I [will] sing *p.* unto thy name for ever, that I may daily perform my vows; **63:3** because thy lovingkindness is better than life, my lips shall *p.* thee; **63:5** my mouth shall *p.* thee with joyful lips; **66:1-2** make a joyful noise unto God, all ye lands: Sing forth the honour of his name: make his *p.* glorious; **66:8** bless our God, ye people, and make the voice of his *p.* to be heard; **67:3** let the people *p.* thee, O God; let all the people *p.* thee; **67:5** let the people *p.* thee, O God; let all the people *p.* thee; **68:4** sing unto God, sing *p.* to his name: extol him that rideth upon the heavens; **68:32** sing unto God, ye kingdoms of the earth; O sing *p.* unto the Lord; **69:30** I will *p.* the name of God with a song, and will magnify him with thanksgiving; **71:8** let my mouth be filled with thy *p.* and with thy honour all the day; **71:14** I will hope continually, and will yet *p.* thee more and more; **71:22** I will also *p.* thee with the psaltery, even thy truth, O my God: unto thee will I sing with the harp, O thou Holy One of Israel; **72:15** prayer also shall be made for him continually; and daily shall he be *p.*; **74:21** let not the oppressed return ashamed: let the poor and needy *p.* thy name; **75:1** unto thee, O God, do we give thanks, unto thee do we give thanks; **75:9** I will declare for ever; I will sing *p.* to the God of Jacob; **76:10** the wrath of man shall *p.* thee: the remainder of wrath shalt thou restrain;

78:4 we will not hide them from their children, shewing to the generation to come the *p.* of the LORD, and his strength, and his wonderful works; **79:13** we thy people and sheep of thy pasture will give thee thanks for ever: we will shew forth thy *p.* to all generations; **86:12** I will *p.* thee, O Lord my God, with all my heart: and I will glorify thy name for evermore; **89:5** the heavens shall *p.* thy wonders, O LORD: thy faithfulness also in the congregation of the saints; **92:1-4** it is a good thing to give thanks unto the LORD, and to sing *p.* unto thy name, O most High; **96:4** the LORD is great, and greatly to be *p.*: he is to be feared above all gods; **97:12** rejoice in the LORD, ye righteous; and give thanks at the remembrance of his holiness; **98:4** make a joyful noise unto the LORD, all the earth: make a loud noise, and rejoice, and sing *p.*; **99:3** let them *p.* thy great and terrible name; for it is holy; **100:4** enter into his gates with thanksgiving, and into his courts with *p.*: be thankful unto him, and bless his name; **102:18** the people which shall be created shall *p.* the LORD; **104:33** I will sing unto the LORD as long as I live: I will sing *p.* to my God while I have my being; **104:35** bless thou the LORD, O my soul. *p.* ye the LORD; **105:1** give thanks unto the LORD; call upon his name: make known his deeds among the people; **105:45** *p.* ye the LORD; **106:1** *p.* ye the LORD. O give thanks unto the LORD; for he is good: for his mercy endureth for ever; **106:12** believed they his words; they sang his *p.*; **106:47-48** blessed be the LORD God of Israel from everlasting to everlasting: and let all the people say, Amen. *p.* ye the LORD; **107:1-2** give thanks unto the LORD, for he is good: for his mercy endureth for ever; **107:8-9** that men would *p.* the LORD for his goodness, and for his wonderful works to the children of men; **107:15** that men would *p.* the LORD for his goodness, and for his wonderful works to the children of men; **107:21-22** that men would *p.* the LORD for his goodness, and for his wonderful works to the children of men! And let them sacrifice the sacrifices of thanksgiving, and declare his works with rejoicing; **107:31-32** that men would *p.* the LORD for his goodness, and for his wonderful works to the children of men! Let them exalt him also in the congregation of the people, and *p.* him; **108:1** God, my heart is fixed; I will sing and give *p.*, even with my glory; **108:3-5** I will *p.* thee, O LORD, among the people: and I will sing *p.* unto thee among the nations; **109:1** hold not thy peace, O God of my *p.*; **109:30** I will greatly *p.* the LORD with my mouth; yea, I will *p.* him among the multitude; **111:1** *p.* ye the LORD. I will *p.* the LORD with my whole heart, in the assembly of the upright, and in the congregation; **112:1** *p.* ye the LORD. Blessed is the man that feareth the LORD, that delighteth greatly in his commandments; **113:1-3** *p.* ye the LORD. *p.*, O ye servants of the LORD, *p.* the name of the LORD; **113:9** *p.* ye the LORD; **115:18** we will bless the LORD from this time forth and for evermore. *p.* the LORD; **116:19** *p.* ye the LORD; **117:1-2** *p.* the LORD, all ye nations: *p.* him, all ye people. For his merciful kindness is great toward us: and the truth of the LORD endureth for ever. *p.* ye the LORD; **118:1** give thanks unto the LORD; for he is good: because his mercy endureth for ever; **118:19** open to me the gates of righteousness: I will go into them, and I will *p.* the LORD; **118:21** I will *p.* thee: for thou hast heard me, and art become my salvation; **118:28-29** thou art my God, and I will *p.* thee: thou art my God, I will exalt thee. O give thanks unto the LORD; for he is good; **119:7** I will *p.* thee with uprightness of heart, when I shall have learned thy righteous judgments; **119:62** at midnight I will rise to give thanks unto thee because of thy righteous judgments; **119:164** seven times a day do I *p.* thee because of thy righteous judgments; **119:171** my lips shall utter *p.*, when thou hast taught me thy statutes; **119:175** let my soul live, and it shall *p.* thee; and let thy judgments help me; **122:4** give thanks unto the name of the LORD; **135:1-3** *p.* ye the LORD. *p.* ye the name of the LORD; *p.* him, O ye servants of the LORD. Ye that stand in the house of the LORD, in the courts of the house of our God, *p.* the LORD; **135:19-21** bless the LORD, O house of Israel: bless the LORD, O house of Aaron: Bless the LORD, O house of Levi: ye that fear the LORD, bless the LORD; **136:1-3** give thanks unto the LORD; for he is good: for his mercy endureth for ever; **136:26** give thanks unto the God of heaven: for his mercy endureth for ever; **138:1-2** I will *p.* thee with my whole heart: before the gods will I sing *p.* unto thee. I will worship toward thy holy temple; **138:4** all the kings of the earth shall *p.* thee, O LORD, when they hear the words of thy mouth; **139:14** I will *p.* thee; for I am fearfully and wonderfully made: marvellous are thy works; and that my soul knoweth right well; **140:13** the righteous shall give thanks unto thy name: the upright shall dwell in thy presence; **142:7** bring my soul out of prison, that I may *p.* thy name: the righteous shall compass me about; for thou shalt deal bountifully with me; **144:9** I will sing a new song unto thee, O God: upon a psaltery and an instrument of ten strings will I sing *p.* unto thee; **145:1-4** I will extol thee, my God, O king; and I will bless thy name for ever and ever. Every day will I bless thee; and I will

p. thy name for ever and ever; **145:21** my mouth shall speak the *p.* of the LORD: and let all flesh bless his holy name for ever and ever; **146:1-2** *p.* ye the LORD. *p.* the LORD, O my soul. While I live will I *p.* the LORD: I will sing *p.* unto my God while I have any being; **146:10** the LORD shall reign for ever, even thy God, O Zion, unto all generations. *p.* ye the LORD; **147:1** *p.* ye the LORD: for it is good to sing *p.* unto our God; for it is pleasant; and *p.* is comely; **147:5** great is our Lord, and of great power: his understanding is infinite; **147:7** sing unto the LORD with thanksgiving; sing *p.* upon the harp unto our God; **147:12** *p.* the LORD, O Jerusalem; *p.* thy God, O Zion; **147:20** he hath not dealt so with any nation: and as for his judgments, they have not known them. *p.* ye the LORD; **148:1-14** *p.* ye the LORD. *p.* ye the LORD from the heavens: *p.* him in the heights. *p.* ye him, all his angels: *p.* ye him, all his hosts; **149:1** *p.* ye the LORD. Sing unto the LORD a new song, and his *p.* in the congregation of saints; **149:3** let them *p.* his name in the dance: let them sing *p.* unto him with the timbrel and harp; **149:9** to execute upon them the judgment written: this honour have all his saints. *p.* ye the LORD; **150:1-6** *p.* ye the LORD. *p.* God in his sanctuary: *p.* him in the firmament of his power. *p.* him for his mighty acts: *p.* him according to his excellent greatness; **Isa. 12:1** O LORD, I will *p.* thee: though thou wast angry with me, thine anger is turned away, and thou comfortedst me; **12:4** *p.* the LORD, call upon his name, declare his doings among the people, make mention that his name is exalted; **25:1** O LORD, thou art my God; I will exalt thee, I will *p.* thy name; for thou hast done wonderful things; **25:9** this is our God; we have waited for him, and he will save us: this is the LORD; we have waited for him, we will be glad and rejoice in his salvation; **60:6** they shall shew forth the *p.* of the LORD; **62:9** they that have gathered it shall eat it, and *p.* the LORD; **Jer. 20:13** sing unto the LORD, *p.* ye the LORD: for he hath delivered the soul of the poor from the hand of evildoers; **31:7** sing with gladness for Jacob, and shout among the chief of the nations: publish ye, *p.* ye, and say, O LORD, save thy people, the remnant of Israel; **31:12-14** they shall come and sing in the height of Zion, and shall flow together to the goodness of the LORD; **33:11** *p.* the LORD of hosts: for the LORD is good; for his mercy endureth for ever; **Dan. 2:19-20** blessed be the name of God for ever and ever: for wisdom and might are his; **2:23** I thank thee, and *p.* thee, O thou God of my fathers, who hast given me wisdom and might, and hast made known unto me now what we desired of thee; **4:34** I blessed the most High, and I *p.* and honoured him that liveth for ever, whose dominion is an everlasting dominion, and his kingdom is from generation to generation; **4:37** I Nebuchadnezzar *p.* and extol and honour the King of heaven, all whose works are truth; **Joel 2:26-27** *p.* the name of the LORD your God, that hath dealt wondrously with you: and my people shall never be ashamed; **Haba 3:3** his glory covered the heavens, and the earth was full of his *p.*

PRAY, PRAYER (*see also* Ask, Communicate, Seek)

When ye fast, be not, as the hypocrites, of a sad countenance: for they disfigure their faces, that they may appear unto men to fast. Verily I say unto you, They have their reward. Matt. 6:16 (*see also* Fast)

[She] served God with fasting and prayers night and day. Luke 2:37 (*see also* Fast)

Confess your faults one to another, and ray one for another, that ye may be healed. The effectual fervent prayer of a righteous man availeth much. James 5:16 (*see also* Confess, Heal)

O LORD, attend unto my cry, give ear unto my prayer, that goeth not out of feigned lips. Ps. 17:1 (*see also* Feign)

He that turneth away his ear from hearing the law, even his prayer shall be abomination. Prov. 28:9 (*see also* Law)

When thou prayest, enter into thy closet, and when thou hast shut thy door, pray to thy Father which is in secret; and thy Father which seeth in secret shall reward thee openly. Matt. 6:6 (*see also* Closet, Secret)

In trouble have they visited thee, they poured out a prayer when thy chastening was upon them. Isa. 26:16 (*see also* Chasten)

All this evil is come upon us: yet made we not our prayer before the LORD our God, that we might turn from our iniquities and understand thy truth. Dan. 9:13 (*see also* Iniquity)

The LORD turned the captivity of Job, when he prayed for his friends. Job 42:10

Job 42:8 go to my servant Job, and offer up for yourselves a burnt offering; and my servant Job shall *p.* for you: for him will I accept; **42:10** the LORD turned the captivity of Job, when he *p.* for his friends; **Ps. 119:136** rivers of waters run down mine eyes, because they keep not thy law.

Be merciful unto me, O Lord: for I cry unto thee daily. Rejoice the soul of thy servant: for unto thee, O Lord, do I lift up my soul. Ps. 86:3-5 (*see also* Cry, Daily)

Neh. 1:6 let thine ear now be attentive, and thine eyes open, that thou mayest hear the *p.* of thy servant, which I *p.* before thee now, day and night; **1:11** Lord, I beseech thee, let now thine ear be attentive to the *p.* of thy servant, and to the *p.* of thy servants, who desire to fear thy name; **2:4** the king said unto me, For what dost thou make request? So I *p.* to the God of heaven; **4:9** we made our *p.* unto our God, and set a watch against them day and night, because of them; **Job 16:17** not for any injustice in mine hands: also my *p.* is pure; **Ps. 5:3** my voice shalt thou hear in the morning, O LORD; in the morning will I direct my *p.* unto thee, and will look up; **32:6** for this shall every one that is godly *p.* unto thee in a time when thou mayest be found; **69:13** as for me, my *p.* is unto thee, O LORD, in an acceptable time: O God, in the multitude of thy mercy hear me, in the truth of thy salvation; **86:3-5** be merciful unto me, O Lord: for I cry unto thee daily. Rejoice the soul of thy servant: for unto thee, O Lord, do I lift up my soul; **88:1-2** O LORD God of my salvation, I have cried day and night before thee: Let my *p.* come before thee: incline thine ear unto my cry; **88:9** mine eye mourneth by reason of affliction: LORD, I have called daily upon thee, I have stretched out my hands unto thee; **145:18** the LORD is nigh unto all them that call upon him, to all that call upon him in truth; **Isa. 58:2** they seek me daily, and delight to know my ways, as a nation that did righteousness, and forsook not the ordinance of their God: they ask of me the ordinances of justice; they take delight in approaching to God.

Men ought always to pray, and not to faint. Luke 18:1 (*see also* Always, Faint)

Matt. 5:44, Luke 6:28 *p.* for them which despitefully use you, and persecute you; **6:5-8** when thou *p.*, thou shalt not be as the hypocrites are: for they love to *p.* standing in the synagogues and in the corners of the streets, that they may be seen of men. Verily I say unto you, They have their reward; when thou *p.*, enter into thy closet, and when thou hast shut thy door, *p.* to thy Father which is in secret; and thy Father which seeth in secret shall reward thee openly; when ye *p.*, use not vain repetitions, as the heathen do: for they think that they shall be heard for their much speaking; be not ye therefore like unto them: for your Father knoweth what things ye have need of, before ye ask him; **6:9-13** (Luke 11:1-4) after this manner therefore *p.* ye: Our Father which art in heaven, Hallowed be thy name. Thy kingdom come. Thy will be done in earth, as it is in heaven. Give us this day our daily bread. And forgive us our debts, as we forgive our debtors. And lead us not into temptation, but deliver us from evil: For thine is the kingdom, and the power, and the glory, for ever. Amen; **9:38** (Luke 10:2) *p.* ye therefore the Lord of the harvest, that he will send forth labourers into his harvest; **15:8** this people draweth nigh unto me with their mouth, and honoureth me with their lips; but their heart is far from me; **21:13** my house shall be called the house of *p.*; but ye have made it a den of thieves; **21:22** all things, whatsoever ye shall ask in *p.*, believing, ye shall receive; **24:20, Mark 13:18** *p.* ye that your flight be not in the winter, neither on the sabbath day; **26:39** he went a little further, and fell on his face, and *p.*, saying, O my Father, if it be possible, let this cup pass from me: nevertheless not as I will, but as thou wilt; **26:41** watch and *p.*, that ye enter not into temptation: the spirit indeed is willing, but the flesh is weak; **26:42** he went away again the second time, and *p.*; **26:44** *p.* the third time, saying the same words; **26:53** thinkest thou that I cannot now *p.* to my Father, and he shall presently give me more than twelve legions of angels; **Mark 1:35** rising up a great while before day, he went out, and departed into a solitary place, and there *p.*; **6:46** he departed into a mountain to *p.*; **9:29** this kind can come forth by nothing, but by *p.* and fasting; **11:24** what things soever ye desire, when ye *p.*, believe that ye receive them, and ye shall have them; **13:33** take ye heed, watch and *p.*: for ye know not when the time is; **14:32** they came to a place which was named Gethsemane: and he saith to his disciples, Sit ye here, while I shall *p.*; **14:35** he went forward a little, and fell on the ground, and *p.* that, if it were possible, the hour might pass from him; **14:38** watch ye and *p.*, lest ye enter into temptation. The spirit truly is ready, but the flesh is weak; **14:39** he went away, and *p.*, and spake the same words; **15:34** at the ninth hour Jesus cried with a loud voice, saying, Eloi, Eloi, lama sabachthani? which is, being interpreted, My God, my God, why hast thou forsaken me;

Luke 1:10 the whole multitude of the people were *p.* without; **1:13** the angel said unto him, Fear not, Zacharias: for thy *p.* is heard; **3:21** Jesus also being baptized, and *p.*, the heaven was opened; **5:16** he withdrew himself into the wilderness, and *p.*; **5:33** why do the disciples of John fast often, and make *p.*, and likewise the disciples of the Pharisees; **6:12** he went out into a mountain to *p.*, and continued all night in *p.* to God **9:28-29** he took Peter and John and James, and went up into a mountain to *p.*. And as he *p.*, the fashion of his countenance was altered, and his raiment was white and glistering; **10:21** Jesus rejoiced in spirit, and said, I thank thee, O Father, Lord of heaven and earth, that thou hast hid these things from the wise and prudent, and hast revealed them unto babes: even so, Father; for so it seemed good in thy sight; **18:1-8** men ought always to *p.*, and not to faint; **21:36** watch ye therefore, and *p.* always, that ye may be accounted worthy to escape all these things that shall come to pass, and to stand before the Son of man; **22:40-46** *p.* that ye enter not into temptation; **John 11:41-42** Jesus lifted up his eyes, and said, Father, I thank thee that thou hast heard me. And I knew that thou hearest me always: but because of the people which stand by I said it, that they may believe that thou hast sent me; **17:9** I *p.* for them: I *p.* not for the world, but for them which thou hast given me; for they are thine; **Acts 1:14** these all continued with one accord in *p.* and supplication; **2:42** they continued stedfastly in the apostles' doctrine and fellowship, and in breaking of bread, and in *p.*; **3:1** Peter and John went up together into the temple at the hour of *p.*, being the ninth hour; **4:31** when they had *p.*, the place was shaken where they were assembled together; and they were all filled with the Holy Ghost, and they spake the word of God with boldness; **6:4** we will give ourselves continually to *p.*, and to the ministry of the word; **8:15** they were come down, *p.* for them, that they might receive the Holy Ghost; **8:24** *p.* ye to the Lord for me, that none of these things which ye have spoken come upon me; **10:2** a devout man, and one that feared God with all his house, which gave much alms to the people, and *p.* to God alway; **10:4** thy *p.* and thine alms are come up for a memorial before God; **10:9** Peter went up upon the housetop to *p.* about the sixth hour; **10:31** thy *p.* is heard, and thine alms are had in remembrance in the sight of God; **12:5-6** Peter therefore was kept in prison: but *p.* was made without ceasing of the church unto God for him; **12:12** many were gathered together *p.*; **20:36-37** he kneeled down, and *p.* with them all; **21:5** we kneeled down on the shore, and *p.*; **Rom. 1:9** without ceasing I make mention of you always in my *p.*; **8:15** ye have received the Spirit of adoption, whereby we cry, Abba, Father; **8:26** the Spirit also helpeth our infirmities: for we know not what we should *p.* for as we ought: but the Spirit itself maketh intercession for us with groanings which cannot be uttered; **10:1** my heart's desire and *p.* to God for Israel is, that they might be saved; **10:12-13** there is no difference between the Jew and the Greek: for the same Lord over all is rich unto all that call upon him. For whosoever shall call upon the name of the Lord shall be saved; **12:12** rejoicing in hope; patient in tribulation; continuing instant in *p.*; **1 Cor. 1:4** I thank my God always on your behalf, for the grace of God which is given you by Jesus Christ; **2 Cor. 1:11** ye also helping together by *p.* for us, that for the gift bestowed upon us by the means of many persons thanks may be given by many on our behalf; **Eph. 1:16** cease not to give thanks for you, making mention of you in my *p.*; **6:18** *p.* always with all *p.* and supplication in the Spirit, and watching thereunto with all perseverance and supplication for all saints; **Philip. 1:3-4** I thank my God upon every remembrance of you, Always in every *p.* of mine for you all making request with joy; **4:6-7** be careful for nothing; but in every thing by *p.* and supplication with thanksgiving let your requests be made known unto God. And the peace of God, which passeth all understanding, shall keep your hearts and minds through Christ Jesus; **Col. 1:3-9** give thanks to God and the Father of our Lord Jesus Christ, *p.* always for you; **4:2-4** continue in *p.*, and watch in the same with thanksgiving; Withal *p.* also for us, that God would open unto us a door of utterance, to speak the mystery of Christ; **1 Thes. 1:2** give thanks to God always for you all, making mention of you in our *p.*; **3:10** Night and day *p.* exceedingly that we might see your face, and might perfect that which is lacking in your faith; **5:17** *p.* without ceasing; **5:25** *p.* for us; **2 Thes. 1:11** we *p.* always for you, that our God would count you worthy of this calling, and fulfil all the good pleasure of his goodness, and the work of faith with power; **2:13** we are bound to give thanks alway to God for you; **3:1-2** *p.* for us, that the word of the Lord may have free course, and be glorified, even as it is with you: And that we may be delivered from unreasonable and wicked men: for all men have not faith; **1 Tim. 2:1-2** supplications, *p.*, intercessions, and giving of thanks, be made for all men; **2:8** *p.* every where, lifting up holy hands, without wrath and doubting; **4:5** it is sanctified by the word of God and *p.*; **5:5** trusteth

in God, and continueth in supplications and *p.* night and day; **2 Tim. 1:3** without ceasing I have remembrance of thee in my *p.* night and day; **Philem 1:4** I thank my God, making mention of thee always in my *p.*; **Heb. 4:15-16** let us therefore come boldly unto the throne of grace, that we may obtain mercy, and find grace to help in time of need; **5:7** he had offered up *p.* and supplications with strong crying and tears unto him that was able to save him from death; **13:18** *p.* for us: for we trust we have a good conscience, in all things willing to live honestly; **James 5:13-18** is any among you afflicted? let him *p.*; is any sick among you? let him call for the elders of the church; and let them *p.* over him, anointing him with oil in the name of the Lord; the *p.* of faith shall save the sick, and the Lord shall raise him up; and if he have committed sins, they shall be forgiven him; *p.* one for another, that ye may be healed. The effectual fervent *p.* of a righteous man availeth much; he *p.* earnestly that it might not rain: and it rained not on the earth by the space of three years and six months. And he *p.* again, and the heaven gave rain, and the earth brought forth her fruit; **1 Pet. 3:7** ye husbands, dwell with them according to knowledge, giving honour unto the wife, as unto the weaker vessel, and as being heirs together of the grace of life; that your *p.* be not hindered; **3:12** the eyes of the Lord are over the righteous, and his ears are open unto their *p.*; **4:7** be ye therefore sober, and watch unto *p.*; **1 Jn. 3:22** whatsoever we ask, we receive of him, because we keep his commandments, and do those things that are pleasing in his sight; **Jude 1:20** building up yourselves on your most holy faith, *p.* in the Holy Ghost; **Rev. 8:4** the smoke of the incense, which came with the *p.* of the saints, ascended up before God out of the angel's hand.

PREACH (*see also* Declare, Exhort, Proclaim, Publish, Teach, Testify)

I have preached righteousness in the great congregation: lo, I have not refrained my lips, O LORD, thou knowest. Ps. 40:9 (*see also* Refrain)

The Spirit of the Lord is upon me, because he hath anointed me to preach the gospel to the poor; he hath sent me to heal the broken-hearted, to preach deliverance to the captives, and recovering of sight to the blind, to set at liberty them that are bruised, To preach the acceptable year of the Lord. Luke 4:18-19 (*see also* Liberty)

Go ye into all the world, and preach the gospel to every creature. **Mark 16:15** (*see also* Gospel)

THE Spirit of the Lord GOD is upon me; because the LORD hath anointed me to preach good tidings unto the meek. **Isa. 61:1** (*see also* Meek)

He called his twelve disciples together, and gave them power and authority over all devils, and to cure diseases. And he sent them to preach the kingdom of God, and to heal the sick. **Luke 9:1-2** (*see also* Authority)

Matt. 7:28-29 (Mark 1:21-22) when Jesus had ended these sayings, the people were astonished at his doctrine; he taught them as one having authority, and not as the scribes; **21:23-27** Jesus answered and said unto them, I also will ask you one thing, which if ye tell me, I in like wise will tell you by what authority I do these things; **22:29** Jesus answered and said unto them, Ye do err, not knowing the scriptures, nor the power of God; **28:18-19** Jesus came and spake unto them, saying, All power is given unto me in heaven and in earth. Go ye therefore, and teach all nations, baptizing them in the name of the Father, and of the Son, and of the Holy Ghost; **Mark 1:27** they were all amazed, insomuch that they questioned among themselves, saying, What thing is this? what new doctrine is this? for with authority commandeth he even the unclean spirits, and they do obey him; **2:7-11** that ye may know that the Son of man hath power on earth to forgive sins, (he saith to the sick of the palsy,) I say unto thee, Arise, and take up thy bed, and go thy way into thine house; **3:14** he ordained twelve, that they should be with him, and that he might send them forth to preach; **6:7** he called unto him the twelve, and began to send them forth by two and two; and gave them power over unclean spirits; **11:28-33** (Luke 20:2-8) By what authority doest thou these things? and who gave thee this authority to do these things? And Jesus answered and said unto them, I will also ask of you one question, and answer me, and I will tell you by what authority I do these things. The baptism of John, was it from heaven, or of men? answer me. And they reasoned with themselves, saying, If we shall say, From heaven; he will say, Why then did ye not believe him? But if we shall say, Of men; they feared the people: for all men counted John, that he was a prophet indeed. And they answered and said unto Jesus, We cannot tell. And Jesus answering saith unto them, Neither do I tell you by what

authority I do these things; **Luke 4:32** they were astonished at his doctrine: for his word was with power; **9:1-2** he called his twelve disciples together, and gave them power and authority over all devils, and to cure diseases. And he sent them to preach the kingdom of God, and to heal the sick; **10:19** I give unto you power to tread on serpents and scorpions, and over all the power of the enemy: and nothing shall by any means hurt you; **20:2** tell us, by what authority doest thou these things? or who is he that gave thee this authority; **John 21:17** Simon, son of Jonas, lovest thou me? Peter was grieved because he said unto him the third time, Lovest thou me? And he said unto him, Lord, thou knowest all things; thou knowest that I love thee. Jesus saith unto him, Feed my sheep; **Acts 4:2** preached through Jesus the resurrection from the dead; **4:7** by what power, or by what name, have ye done this; **4:33-36** with great power gave the apostles witness of the resurrection of the Lord Jesus: and great grace was upon them all; **4:41** devils also came out of many, crying out, and saying, Thou art Christ the Son of God. And he rebuking them suffered them not to speak: for they knew that he was Christ; **5:20** go, stand and speak in the temple to the people all the words of this life; **13:9-10** then Saul, (who also is called Paul,) filled with the Holy Ghost, set his eyes on him; **2 Cor. 12:19** we speak before God in Christ: but we do all things, dearly beloved, for your edifying; **1 Tim. 4:11** these things command and teach; **Titus 2:15** these things speak, and exhort, and rebuke with all authority. Let no man despise thee; **1 Pet. 1:12** it was revealed, that not unto themselves, but unto us they did minister the things, which are now reported unto you by them that have preached the gospel unto you with the Holy Ghost sent down from heaven; which things the angels desire to look into; **1 Jn. 2:27** the anointing which ye have received of him abideth in you, and ye need not that any man teach you: but as the same anointing teacheth you of all things, and is truth, and is no lie, and even as it hath taught you, ye shall abide in him.

PRECEPT (*see also* Doctrine, Law, Statute)

For precept must be upon precept, precept upon precept; line upon line, line upon line; here a little, and there a little: For with stammering lips and another tongue will he speak to this people. **Isa. 28:10** (*see also* Learn, Know, Understand)

I esteem all thy precepts concerning all things to be right; and I hate every false way. Ps. 119:128

Ps. 119:128 I esteem all thy *p.* concerning all things to be right; and I hate every false way; **119:173** let thine hand help me; for I have chosen thy *p.*

I will meditate in thy precepts, and have respect unto thy ways. Ps. 119:15 (*see also* Meditate, Way)

Thou hast commanded us to keep thy precepts diligently. Ps. 119:4 (*see also* Keep)

Ps. 119:4 thou hast commanded us to keep thy *p.* diligently; **119:6** I [shall] not be ashamed, when I have respect unto all thy commandments; **119:40** I have longed after thy *p.*: quicken me in thy righteousness; **119:45** I will walk at liberty: for I seek thy *p.*; **119:56** this I had, because I kept thy *p.*; **119:63** I am a companion of all them that fear thee, and of them that keep thy *p.*; **119:69** the proud have forged a lie against me: but I will keep thy *p.* with my whole heart; **119:93-94** I will never forget thy *p.*: for with them thou hast quickened me. I am thine, save me; for I have sought thy *p.*; **119:109-110** my soul is continually in my hand: yet do I not forget thy law. The wicked have laid a snare for me: yet I erred not from thy *p.*; **119:134** deliver me from the oppression of man: so will I keep thy *p.*; **119:168** I have kept thy *p.* and thy testimonies: for all my ways are before thee; **Prov. 13:4** the soul of the sluggard desireth, and hath nothing: but the soul of the diligent shall be made fat.

PREMORTAL LIFE

When he prepared the heavens, I was there. Prov. 8:27

PREPARE, PREPARATION (*see also* Ready)

If a man therefore purge himself from these, he shall be a vessel unto honour, sanctified, and meet for the master's use, and prepared unto every good work. 2 Tim. 2:21 (*see also* Sanctified, Work)

Be thou prepared, and prepare for thyself, thou, and all thy company that are assembled unto thee, and be thou a guard unto them. Ezek. 38:7 (*see also* Guard)

Prepare to meet thy God, O Israel. Amos 4:12 (*see also* Meet)

The horse is prepared against the day of battle; but safety is of the LORD. Prov. 21:31 (*see also* Battle)

Prepare ye the way of the Lord, make straight in the desert a highway for our God. Isa. 40:3 (*see also* Way)

Isa. 40:3-5 *p.* ye the way of the LORD, make straight in the desert a highway for our God; **57:14** cast ye up, *p.* the way, take up the stumblingblock out of the way of my people.

Prepare ye the way of the Lord, make his paths straight. Luke 3:4 (*see also* Way)

Matt. 3:3 *p.* ye the way of the Lord, make his paths straight; **Mark 1:2-3** send my messenger before thy face, which shall *p.* thy way before thee. The voice of one crying in the wilderness, *p.* ye the way of the Lord, make his paths straight; **1:7** there cometh one mightier than I after me, the latchet of whose shoes I am not worthy to stoop down and unloose; **Luke 1:17** turn the hearts of the fathers to the children, and the disobedient to the wisdom of the just; to make ready a people *p.* for the Lord; **1:76** thou, child, shalt be called the prophet of the Highest: for thou shalt go before the face of the Lord to *p.* his ways; **3:4** the voice of one crying in the wilderness, *p.* ye the way of the Lord, make his paths straight; **John 1:23** make straight the way of the Lord, as said the prophet Esaias.

PRESENCE (*see also* Feel, See)

Hold thy peace at the presence of the LORD God: for the day of the LORD is at hand: for the LORD hath prepared a sacrifice, he hath bid his guests. Zeph. 1:7 (*see also* Day, Peace)

PRICE (*see also* Worth)

Ye that is called in the Lord, being a servant is the Lord's freeman: likewise also he that is called, being free, is Christ's servant. Ye are bought with a price; be not ye the servants of men. 1 Cor 7:22-23 (*see also* Called, Servant)

PRIDE, PROUD (*see also* Arrogance, Boast, Conceit, Envy, Hardhearted, Haughty, Vain)

These six things doth the LORD hate: yea, seven are an abomination unto him: A proud look, a lying tongue, and hands that shed innocent blood, An heart that deviseth wicked imaginations, feet that be swift in running to mischief, A false witness that speaketh lies, and he that soweth discord among brethren. **Prov. 6:16-19** (*see also* Discord, False Witness, Imagine, Innocent, Mischief)

They dealt proudly, and hearkened not unto thy commandments, but sinned against thy judgments, (which if a man do, he shall live in them;) and withdrew the shoulder, and hardened their neck. **Neh. 9:29** (*see also* Neck)

Better is the end of a thing than the beginning thereof: and the patient in spirit is better than the proud in spirit. **Eccl. 7:8** (*see also* Patience)

He is proud, knowing nothing, but doting about questions and strifes of words, whereof cometh envy, strife, railings, evil surmisings, Perverse disputings of men of corrupt minds, and destitute of the truth, supposing that gain is godliness: from such withdraw thyself. **1 Tim. 6:4-5** (*see also* Question, Strife, Mind, True)

The wicked, through the pride of his countenance, will not seek after God: God is not in all his thoughts. **Ps. 10:4** (*see also* Seek, Thought, Wicked)

Thou shouldest not have looked on the day of thy brother in the day that he became a stranger; neither shouldest thou have rejoiced over the children of Judah in the day of their destruction; neither shouldest thou have spoken proudly in the day of distress. **Obad. 1:12** (*see also* Speak)

God resisteth the proud, but giveth grace unto the humble. **James 4:6** (*see also* Grace, Humble)

Mark 7:21-23 from within, out of the heart of men, proceed evil thoughts, adulteries, fornications, murders, thefts, covetousness, wickedness, deceit, lasciviousness, an evil eye, blasphemy, *p.*, foolishness: All these evil things come from within, and defile the man; **Luke 1:51** he hath scattered the *p.* in the imagination of their hearts; **John 9:34** thou wast altogether

born in sins, and dost thou teach us? And they cast him out; **1 Cor. 13:4** charity suffereth long, and is kind; charity envieth not; charity vaunteth not itself, is not puffed up; **1 Tim. 3:6** not a novice, lest being lifted up with *p.* he fall into the condemnation of the devil; **2 Tim. 3:2** for men shall be lovers of their own selves, covetous, boasters, *p.*, blasphemers, disobedient to parents, unthankful, unholy; **James 4:6** God resisteth the *p.*, but giveth grace unto the humble.

Look on every one that is proud, and bring him low; and tread down the wicked in their place. **Job 40:12** (*see also* Look, Wicked)

Job 40:12 look on every one that is *p.*, and bring him low; and tread down the wicked in their place; **Ps. 31:18** let the lying lips be put to silence; which speak grievous things *p.* and contemptuously against the righteous; **40:4** blessed is that man that maketh the LORD his trust, and respecteth not the *p.*, nor such as turn aside to lies; **94:2** lift up thyself, thou judge of the earth: render a reward to the *p.*; **119:69-70** the *p.* have forged a lie against me: but I will keep thy precepts with my whole heart; **119:78** let the *p.* be ashamed; for they dealt perversely with me without a cause; **119:122** be surety for thy servant for good: let not the *p.* oppress me; **Prov. 15:25** the LORD will destroy the house of the *p.*: but he will establish the border of the widow; **Isa. 2:12-17** the day of the LORD of hosts shall be upon every one that is *p.* and lofty, and upon every one that is lifted up; and he shall be brought low... the loftiness of man shall be bowed down, and the haughtiness of men shall be made low: and the LORD alone shall be exalted; **3:5** the people shall be oppressed, every one by another, and every one by his neighbour: the child shall behave himself *p.* against the ancient, and the base against the honourable; **5:15** the mean man shall be brought down, and the mighty man shall be humbled, and the eyes of the lofty shall be humbled; **57:21** there is no peace, saith my God, to the wicked; **Mal. 4:1** the day cometh, that shall burn as an oven; and all the *p.*, yea, and all that do wickedly, shall be stubble.

Pride goeth before destruction, and an haughty spirit before a fall. **Prov. 16:18** (*see also* Haughtiness)

Ps. 131:1 LORD, my heart is not haughty, nor mine *e.* lofty: neither do I exercise myself in great matters, or in things too high for me; **Prov.**

16:18 pride goeth before destruction, and an haughty spirit before a fall; **18:12** before destruction the heart of man is haughty, and before honour is humility; **Isa. 3:16-26** because the daughters of Zion are haughty, and walk with stretched forth necks and wanton *e.*, walking and mincing as they go, and making a tinkling with their feet: Therefore the Lord will smite with a scab the crown of the head of the daughters of Zion; **10:33** the LORD of hosts, shall lop the bough with terror: and the high ones of stature shall be hewn down, and the haughty shall be humbled; **13:11** I will punish the world for their evil, and the wicked for their iniquity; and I will cause the arrogancy of the proud to cease, and will lay low the haughtiness of the terrible; **16:6** we have heard of the pride of Moab; he is very proud: even of his haughtiness, and his pride, and his wrath: but his lies shall not be so; **16:9-10** gladness is taken away, and joy out of the plentiful field; and in the vineyards there shall be no singing, neither shall there be shouting: the treaders shall tread out no wine in their presses; I have made their vintage shouting to cease; **16:12** it shall come to pass, when it is seen that Moab is weary on the high place, that he shall come to his sanctuary to pray; but he shall not prevail; **16:14** the LORD hath spoken, saying, Within three years, as the years of an hireling, and the glory of Moab shall be contemned, with all that great multitude; and the remnant shall be very small and feeble; **24:4** the earth mourneth and fadeth away, the world languisheth and fadeth away, the haughty people of the earth do languish.

Hear ye, and give ear; be not proud: for the LORD hath spoken. Jer. 13:15 (*see also* Hear)

Ex. 18:11 I know that the LORD is greater than all gods: for in the thing wherein they dealt *p.* he was above them; **Lev. 26:19** I will break the *p.* of your power; and I will make your heaven as iron, and your earth as brass; **2 Chron. 26:16** when he was strong, his heart was lifted up to his destruction: for he transgressed against the LORD his God; **32:26** Hezekiah humbled himself for the *p.* of his heart, both he and the inhabitants of Jerusalem, so that the wrath of the LORD came not upon them; **Neh. 9:10** thou knewest that they dealt *p.* against them; **9:16** they and our fathers dealt *p.*, and hardened their necks, and hearkened not to thy commandments; **9:29** that thou mightest bring them again unto thy law: yet they dealt *p.*, and hearkened not unto thy commandments, but sinned against thy judgments; **Job 31:25** if I rejoiced because my wealth was great, and because mine hand had gotten much; **40:11-**

12 behold every one that is *p.*, and abase him. Look on every one that is *p.*, and bring him low; and tread down the wicked in their place; **Ps. 10:2-4** the wicked in his *p.* doth persecute the poor: let them be taken in the devices that they have imagined. For the wicked boasteth of his hearts desire, and blesseth the covetous, whom the LORD abhorreth; **12:3** the LORD shall cut off all flattering lips, and the tongue that speaketh *p.* things; **18:27** thou wilt save the afflicted people; but wilt bring down high looks; **31:20** thou shalt hide them in the secret of thy presence from the *p.* of man: thou shalt keep them secretly in a pavilion from the strife of tongues; **36:2** he flattereth himself in his own eyes, until his iniquity be found to be hateful; **36:11** let not the foot of *p.* come against me, and let not the hand of the wicked remove me; **40:4** blessed is that man that maketh the LORD his trust, and respecteth not the *p.*, nor such as turn aside to lies; **59:12-13** the sin of their mouth and the words of their lips let them even be taken in their *p.*: and for cursing and lying which they speak; **101:5** him that hath an high look and a *p.* heart will not I suffer; **119:21** thou hast rebuked the *p.* that are cursed, which do err from thy commandments; **119:78** let the *p.* be ashamed; for they dealt perversely with me without a cause: but I will meditate in thy precepts; **Prov. 6:16-17** these six things doth the LORD hate: yea, seven are an abomination unto him: A *p.* look, a lying tongue, and hands that shed innocent blood; **8:13** the fear of the LORD is to hate evil: *p.*, and arrogancy, and the evil way, and the froward mouth, do I hate; **11:2** when *p.* cometh, then cometh shame: but with the lowly is wisdom; **13:10** by *p.* cometh contention: but with the well advised is wisdom; **14:3** in the mouth of the foolish is a rod of *p.*: but the lips of the wise shall preserve them; **15:25** the LORD will destroy the house of the *p.*; **16:5** every one that is *p.* in heart is an abomination to the LORD; **16:18-19** *p.* goeth before destruction, and an haughty spirit before a fall. Better it is to be of an humble spirit with the lowly, than to divide the spoil with the *p.*; **21:4** an high look, and a *p.* heart, and the plowing of the wicked, is sin; **28:25** he that is of a *p.* heart stirreth up strife: but he that putteth his trust in the LORD shall be made fat; **29:23** a mans *p.* shall bring him low: but honour shall uphold the humble in spirit; **30:13** O how lofty are their eyes! and their eyelids are lifted up; **Eccl. 7:8** the patient in spirit is better than the *p.* in spirit; **Isa. 2:12** the day of the LORD of hosts shall be upon every one that is *p.* and lofty, and upon every one that is lifted up; and he shall be brought low; **13:11** I will punish the world for their evil, and the wicked for their iniquity; and I will cause the arrogancy of the *p.* to cease, and will lay low the haughtiness of the terrible; **14:11** thy pomp is brought down to the grave, and the noise of thy viols: the worm is spread under thee, and the worms cover thee; **16:6-7** we have heard of the *p.* of Moab; he is very *p.*: even of his haughtiness, and his *p.*, and his wrath: but his lies shall not be so. Therefore shall Moab howl for Moab; **16:9-10** gladness is taken away, and joy out of the plentiful field; and in the vineyards there shall be no singing, neither shall there be shouting: the treaders shall tread out no wine in their presses; I have made their vintage shouting to cease; **16:12** when it is seen that Moab is weary on the high place, that he shall come to his sanctuary to pray; but he shall not prevail; **16:14** the LORD hath spoken, saying, Within three years, as the years of an hireling, and the glory of Moab shall be contemned, with all that great multitude; **23:9** the LORD of hosts hath purposed it, to stain the *p.* of all glory, and to bring into contempt all the honourable of the earth; **25:11** he shall bring down their *p.* together with the spoils of their hands; **26:5** he bringeth down them that dwell on high; the lofty city, he layeth it low; he layeth it low, even to the ground; **28:1** woe to the crown of *p.*, to the drunkards of Ephraim, whose glorious beauty is a fading flower; **28:3-4** the crown of *p.*, the drunkards of Ephraim, shall be trodden under feet: And the glorious beauty, which is on the head of the fat valley, shall be a fading flower; **28:7** the priest and the prophet have erred through

strong drink, they are swallowed up of wine, they are out of the way through strong drink; they err in vision, they stumble in judgment; **Jer. 13:9** thus saith the LORD, After this manner will I mar the *p.* of Judah, and the great *p.* of Jerusalem; **13:15** hear ye, and give ear; be not *p.*: for the LORD hath spoken; **13:17** if ye will not hear it, my soul shall weep in secret places for your *p.*; and mine eye shall weep sore, and run down with tears; **48:29** we have heard the *p.* of Moab, [he is exceeding *p.*] his loftiness, and his arrogancy, and his *p.*, and the haughtiness of his heart; **48:33** joy and gladness is taken from the plentiful field, and from the land of Moab; and I have caused wine to fail from the winepresses: none shall tread with shouting; their shouting shall be no shouting; **48:37-38** there shall be lamentation generally upon all the housetops of Moab, and in the streets thereof: for I have broken Moab like a vessel wherein is no pleasure, saith the LORD; **48:46** woe be unto thee, O Moab! the people of Chemosh perisheth: for thy sons are taken captives, and thy daughters

captives; **50:29-32** let none thereof escape: recompense her according to her work; according to all that she hath done, do unto her: for she hath been *p.* against the LORD, against the Holy One of Israel; **Ezek. 7:10-11** the morning is gone forth; the rod hath blossomed, *p.* hath budded. Violence is risen up into a rod of wickedness: none of them shall remain, nor of their multitude, nor of any of theirs; **7:24** I will bring the worst of the heathen, and they shall possess their houses: I will also make the pomp of the strong to cease; and their holy places shall be defiled; **16:49** this was the iniquity of thy sister Sodom, *p.*, fulness of bread, and abundance of idleness was in her and in her daughters, neither did she strengthen the hand of the poor and needy; **16:56** thy sister Sodom was not mentioned by thy mouth in the day of thy *p.*; **28:2** thus saith the Lord GOD; Because thine heart is lifted up, and thou hast said, I am a God, I sit in the seat of God, in the midst of the seas; yet thou art a man, and not God, though thou set thine heart as the heart of God; **30:6** thus saith the LORD; They also that uphold Egypt shall fall; and the *p.* of her power shall come down: from the tower of Syene shall they fall in it by the sword; **Dan. 4:37** those that walk in *p.* he is able to abase; **5:20-21** when his heart was lifted up, and his mind hardened in *p.*, he was deposed from his kingly throne, and they took his glory from him; **Hosea 5:5** the *p.* of Israel doth testify to his face: therefore shall Israel and Ephraim fall in their iniquity; **Haba 2:4-5** his soul which is lifted up is not upright in him: but the just shall live by his faith; **Zeph. 2:9-10** the residue of my people shall spoil them, and the remnant of my people shall possess them. This shall they have for their *p.*, because they have reproached and magnified themselves against the people of the LORD of hosts; **3:11** I will take away out of the midst of thee them that rejoice in thy *p.*, and thou shalt no more be haughty because of my holy mountain; **Zech. 9:6** I will cut off the *p.* of the Philistines; **10:11** the *p.* of Assyria shall be brought down, and the sceptre of Egypt shall depart away; **Mal. 3:15** now we call the *p.* happy; yea, they that work wickedness are set up; **4:1** the day cometh, that shall burn as an oven; and all the *p.*, yea, and all that do wickedly, shall be stubble.

PRIEST

Let thy priests be clothed with righteousness. Ps. 132:9 (*see also* Righteous)

The priests lips should keep knowledge, and they should seek the law at his mouth: for he is the messenger of the LORD of hosts. Mal. 2:7 (*see also* Know, Messenger)

PRIEST DUTIES (Old Testament)

Gen. 14:18 and he [was] the *p.* of the most high God; **Ex. 2:16** the *p.* of Midian had seven daughters: and they came and drew [water], and filled the troughs to water their father's flock; **3:1** kept the flock of Jethro his father in law, the *p.* of Midian; **18:1** the *p.* of Midian, Moses' father in law, heard of all that God had done for Moses, and for Israel his people; **29:30** that son that is *p.* in his stead shall put them on seven days; **31:10** the cloths of service, and the holy garments for Aaron the *p.*, and the garments of his sons, to minister in the *p.*'s office; **35:19** the holy garments for Aaron the *p.*, and the garments of his sons, to minister in the *p.*'s office; **38:21** [for] the service of the Levites, by the hand of Ithamar, son to Aaron the *p.*; **39:41** the holy garments for Aaron the *p.*, and his sons' garments, to minister in the *p.*'s office; **Lev. 1:7** the sons of Aaron the *p.* shall put fire upon the altar; **1:9** the *p.* shall burn all on the altar, [to be] a burnt sacrifice; **1:12** the *p.* shall lay them in order on the wood that [is] on the fire which [is] upon the altar; **1:13** the *p.* shall bring [it] all, and burn [it] upon the altar; **1:15** the *p.* shall bring it unto the altar, and wring off his head, and burn [it] on the altar; 1:17 the *p.* shall burn it upon the altar, upon the wood that [is] upon the fire; **2:2** the *p.* shall burn the memorial of it upon the altar, [to be] an offering made by fire, of a sweet savour unto the LORD; **2:8** when it is presented unto the *p.*, he shall bring it unto the altar; **2:9** the *p.* shall take from the meat offering a memorial thereof, and shall burn [it] upon the altar; **2:16** the *p.* shall burn the memorial of it; **3:11** the *p.* shall burn it upon the altar: [it is] the food of the offering made by fire unto the LORD; **3:16** the *p.* shall burn them upon the altar: [it is] the food of the offering made by fire for a sweet savour; **4:3-7** if the *p.* that is anointed do sin according to the sin of the people; then let him bring for his sin; **4:10** the *p.* shall burn them upon the altar of the burnt offering; **4:16-35** the *p.* that is anointed shall bring of the bullock's blood to the tabernacle of the congregation; **5:6-18** the *p.* shall make an atonement for him concerning his sin; **6:6-7** *p.* shall make an atonement for him before the LORD; 6:10 *p.* shall put on his linen garment, and his linen breeches shall he put upon his flesh; **6:12** the *p.* shall burn wood on it every morning, and lay the burnt

offering in order upon it; **6:22-26** the *p.* of his sons that is anointed in his stead shall offer it; **7:5** the *p.* shall burn them upon the altar [for] an offering made by fire unto the LORD; **7:7** the *p.* that maketh atonement therewith shall have [it]; **7:8** [even] the *p.* shall have to himself the skin of the burnt offering which he hath offered; **7:31** the *p.* shall burn the fat upon the altar: but the breast shall be Aaron's and his sons; **7:32** the right shoulder shall ye give unto the *p.* [for] an heave offering of the sacrifices of your peace offerings; **7:34** given them unto Aaron the *p.* and unto his sons by a statute for ever from among the children of Israel; **12:6** for a sin offering, unto the door of the tabernacle of the congregation, unto the *p.*; **12:8** the *p.* shall make an atonement for her, and she shall be clean; **13:2** he shall be brought unto Aaron the *p.*, or unto one of his sons the *p.*; **13:3-28** it [is] a plague of leprosy: and the *p.* shall look on him, and pronounce him unclean; **13:30-37** the *p.* shall pronounce him unclean: it [is] a dry scall, [even] a leprosy upon the head or beard; **13:39-14:2** he is a leprous man, he [is] unclean: the *p.* shall pronounce him utterly unclean; his plague [is] in his head; **14:2-5** the law of the leper in the day of his cleansing: He shall be brought unto the *p.*; **14:11** the *p.* that maketh [him] clean shall present the man that is to be made clean, and those things, before the LORD; **14:12** the *p.* shall take one he lamb, and offer him for a trespass offering; **14:14** the *p.* shall take [some] of the blood of the trespass offering, and the *p.* shall put [it] upon the tip of the right ear of him that is to be cleansed; **14:15** the *p.* shall take [some] of the log of oil, and pour [it] into the palm of his own left hand; **14:16** *p.* shall dip his right finger in the oil that [is] in his left hand; **14:17-18** the rest of the oil that [is] in his hand shall the *p.* put upon the tip of the right ear of him that is to be cleansed; **14:19-20** the *p.* shall offer the sin offering, and make an atonement for him that is to be cleansed from his uncleanness; **14:23-31** he shall bring them on the eighth day for his cleansing unto the *p.*, unto the door of the tabernacle of the congregation, before the LORD; **14:35-48** he that owneth the house shall come and tell the *p.*, saying, It seemeth to me [there is] as it were a plague in the house; **15:14** two turtledoves, or two young pigeons, and come before the LORD unto the door of the tabernacle of the congregation, and give them unto the *p.*; **15:15** the *p.* shall offer them, the one [for] a sin offering, and the other [for] a burnt offering; **15:29** two turtles, or two young pigeons, and bring them unto the *p.*, to the door of the tabernacle of the congregation; 15:30 the *p.* shall offer the one [for] a sin offering, and the other [for] a burnt offering; **16:30** on that day shall [the *p.*] make an atonement for you, to cleanse you; **16:32** the *p.*, whom he shall anoint, and whom he shall consecrate to minister in the *p.*'s office in his father's stead, shall make the atonement; **17:5** unto the door of the tabernacle of the congregation, unto the *p.*, and offer them [for] peace offerings unto the LORD; **17:6** the *p.* shall sprinkle the blood upon the altar of the LORD [at] the door of the tabernacle of the congregation; **19:22** the *p.* shall make an atonement for him with the ram of the trespass offering before the LORD for his sin which he hath done; **21:9** the daughter of any *p.*, if she profane herself by playing the whore, she profaneth her father; **21:21** no man that hath a blemish of the seed of Aaron the *p.* shall come nigh to offer the offerings of the LORD made by fire; **22:10** a sojourner of the *p.*, or an hired servant, shall not eat [of] the holy thing; **22:11** if the *p.* buy [any] soul with his money, he shall eat of it; **22:14** shall give [it] unto the *p.* with the holy thing; **23:10** then ye shall bring a sheaf of the firstfruits of your harvest unto the *p.*; **23:11** on the morrow after the sabbath the *p.* shall wave it; **23:20** the *p.* shall wave them with the bread of the firstfruits [for] a wave offering before the LORD; **27:8** if he be poorer than thy estimation, then he shall present himself before the *p.*; **27:11** then he shall present the beast before the *p.*; **27:12** the *p.* shall value it, whether it be good or bad; **27:14** when a man shall sanctify his house [to be] holy unto the LORD, then the *p.* shall estimate it, whether it be good or bad; **27:18** if he sanctify his field after the jubile, then the *p.* shall reckon unto him the money according to the years that remain; **27:23** the *p.* shall reckon unto him the worth of thy estimation; **Num. 3:6** present them before Aaron the *p.*, that they may minister unto him; **4:16** the office of Eleazar the son of Aaron the *p.* [pertaineth] the oil for the light, and the sweet incense, and the daily meat offering; **4:28** their charge [shall be] under the hand of Ithamar the son of Aaron the *p.*; **4:33** according to all their service, in the tabernacle of the congregation, under the hand of Ithamar the son of Aaron the *p.*; **5:8** let the trespass be recompensed unto the LORD, [even] to the *p.*; **5:9** every offering of all the holy things of the children of Israel, which they bring unto the *p.*; **5:10** whatsoever any man giveth the *p.*, it shall be his; **5:15** shall the man bring his wife unto the *p.*, and he shall bring her offering for her; **5:16** *p.* shall bring her near, and set her before the LORD; **5:17** the *p.* shall take holy water in an earthen vessel; **5:18** the *p.* shall set the woman before the

LORD, and uncover the woman's head, and put the offering of memorial in her hands; **5:19** the *p.* shall charge her by an oath, and say unto the woman; **5:21** the *p.* shall charge the woman with an oath of cursing; **5:23** the *p.* shall write these curses in a book, and he shall blot [them] out with the bitter water; **5:25** the *p.* shall take the jealousy offering out of the woman's hand, and shall wave the offering before the LORD; **5:26** the *p.* shall take an handful of the offering, [even] the memorial thereof, and burn [it] upon the altar; **5:30** the *p.* shall execute upon her all this law; **6:10** he shall bring two turtles, or two young pigeons, to the *p.*, to the door of the tabernacle of the congregation; **6:11** the *p.* shall offer the one for a sin offering, and the other for a burnt offering; **6:16** the *p.* shall bring [them] before the LORD, and shall offer his sin offering, and his burnt offering; **6:17** the *p.* shall offer also his meat offering, and his drink offering; **6:19** the *p.* shall take the sodden shoulder of the ram, and one unleavened cake out of the basket; **6:20** the *p.* shall wave them [for] a wave offering before the LORD; **15:25** the *p.* shall make an atonement for all the congregation of the children of Israel, and it shall be forgiven them; **15:28** the *p.* shall make an atonement for the soul that sinneth ignorantly; **16:37** speak unto Eleazar the son of Aaron the *p.*, that he take up the censers out of the burning; **16:39** Eleazar the *p.* took the brasen censers, wherewith they that were burnt had offered; **18:28** ye shall give thereof the LORD'S heave offering to Aaron the *p.*; **19:3** ye shall give her unto Eleazar the *p.*, that he may bring her forth without the camp; **19:4** Eleazar the *p.* shall take of her blood with his finger, and sprinkle of her blood directly before the tabernacle of the congregation seven times; **19:6** the *p.* shall take cedar wood, and hyssop, and scarlet, and cast [it] into the midst of the burning of the heifer; **19:7** the *p.* shall wash his clothes, and he shall bathe his flesh in water; **26:1** after the plague, that the LORD spake unto Moses and unto Eleazar the son of Aaron the *p.*; **26:3** Moses and Eleazar the *p.* spake with them in the plains of Moab; **26:63** these [are] they that were numbered by Moses and Eleazar the *p.*; **26:64** among these there was not a man of them whom Moses and Aaron the *p.* numbered; **27:2** they stood before Moses, and before Eleazar the *p.*, and before the princes and all the congregation; **27:19** set him before Eleazar the *p.*, and before all the congregation; **27:21** he shall stand before Eleazar the *p.*, who shall ask [counsel] for him after the judgment of Urim before the LORD; **27:22** he took Joshua, and set him before Eleazar the *p.*, and before all the congregation; **31:12** they brought the captives, and the prey, and the spoil, unto Moses, and Eleazar the *p.*; **31:13** Moses, and Eleazar the *p.*, and all the princes of the congregation, went forth to meet them without the camp; **31:21** the *p.* said unto the men of war which went to the battle, This [is] the ordinance of the law which the LORD commanded Moses; **31:26** take the sum of the prey that was taken, [both] of man and of beast, thou, and Eleazar the *p.*; **31:29** give it unto Eleazar the *p.*, [for] an heave offering of the LORD; **31:31** Eleazar the *p.* did as the LORD commanded Moses; **31:41** Moses gave the tribute, [which was] the LORD'S heave offering, unto Eleazar the *p.*; **31:51** Moses and Eleazar the *p.* took the gold of them; **31:54** the *p.* took the gold of the captains of thousands and of hundreds, and brought it into the tabernacle of the congregation; **32:2** the children of Gad and the children of Reuben came and spake unto Moses, and to Eleazar the *p.*; **32:28** concerning them Moses commanded Eleazar the *p.*; **33:38** Aaron the *p.* went up into mount Hor at the command-ment of the LORD; **34:17** the men which shall divide the land unto you: Eleazar the *p.*, and Joshua the son of Nun; **35:32** he should come again to dwell in the land, until the death of the *p.*; **Deut. 17:12** the man that will do presumptuously, and will not hearken unto the *p.* that standeth to minister there before the LORD thy God; **18:3** this shall be the *p.*'s due from the people, from them that offer a sacrifice; **20:2** the *p.* shall approach and speak unto the people; **26:3** go unto the *p.* that shall be in those days, and say unto him, I profess this day unto the LORD thy God; **26:4** the *p.* shall take the basket out of thine hand, and set it down before the altar of the LORD thy God; **Josh. 14:1** Eleazar the *p.*, and Joshua the son of Nun, and the heads of the fathers of the tribes of the children of Israel, distributed for inheritance to them; **17:4** they came near before Eleazar the *p.*, and before Joshua the son of Nun, and before the princes, saying; **19:51** Eleazar the *p.*, and Joshua the son of Nun, and the heads of the fathers of the tribes of the children of Israel, divided for an inheritance by lot in Shiloh before the LORD; **21:1** came near the heads of the fathers of the Levites unto Eleazar the *p.*; **21:4** the lot came out for the families of the Kohathites: and the children of Aaron the *p.*, [which were] of the Levites; **21:13** they gave to the children of Aaron the *p.* Hebron with her suburbs; **22:30** Phinehas the *p.*, and the princes of the congregation and heads of the thousands of Israel which [were] with him, heard the words; **22:31** Phinehas the son of Eleazar the *p.* said unto the children of

Reuben; **22:32** the *p.*, and the princes, returned from the children of Reuben, and from the children of Gad, out of the land of Gilead; **Judges 17:5** consecrated one of his sons, who became his *p.*; **17:10** Micah said unto him, Dwell with me, and be unto me a father and a *p.*; **17:12** the young man became his *p.*, and was in the house of Micah; **17:13** the LORD will do me good, seeing I have a Levite to [my] *p.*; **18:4** dealeth Micah with me, and hath hired me, and I am his *p.*; **18:6** the *p.* said unto them, Go in peace; **18:17** the *p.* stood in the entering of the gate with the six hundred men [that were] appointed with weapons of war; **18:18** then said the *p.* unto them, What do ye; **18:19** hold thy peace, lay thine hand upon thy mouth, and go with us, and be to us a father and a *p.*; **18:24** ye have taken away my gods which I made, and the *p.*, and ye are gone away: and what have I more; **18:27** they took [the things] which Micah had made, and the *p.* which he had; **1 Sam. 1:9** Eli the *p.* sat upon a seat by a post of the temple of the LORD; **2:11** the child did minister unto the LORD before Eli the *p.*; **2:14** he struck [it] into the pan, or kettle, or caldron, or pot; all that the fleshhook brought up the *p.* took for himself; **2:15** before they burnt the fat, the *p.*'s servant came, and said to the man that sacrificed; **2:28** did I choose him out of all the tribes of Israel [to be] my *p.*, to offer upon mine altar, to burn incense, to wear an ephod before me; **2:35** I will raise me up a faithful *p.*, [that] shall do according to [that] which [is] in mine heart and in my mind; **14:19** Saul said unto the *p.*, Withdraw thine hand; **14:36** then said the *p.*, Let us draw near hither unto God; **21:1** came David to Nob to Ahimelech the *p.*; **21:2** David said unto Ahimelech the *p.*, The king hath commanded me a business; **21:4** the *p.* answered David, and said, [There is] no common bread under mine hand, but there is hallowed bread; **21:5** David answered the *p.*, and said unto him, Of a truth women [have been] kept from us about these three days; **21:6** the *p.* gave him hallowed [bread]; **21:9** the *p.* said, The sword of Goliath the Philistine, whom thou slewest in the valley of Elah, behold, it [is here] wrapped in a cloth behind the ephod; **22:11** the king sent to call Ahimelech the *p.*; **30:7** (23:9) David said to Abiathar the *p.*, Ahimelech's son, I pray thee, bring me hither the ephod; **2 Sam. 15:27** the king said also unto Zadok the *p.*, [Art not] thou a seer; **1 Kgs. 1:7** he conferred with Joab the son of Zeruiah, and with Abiathar the *p.*; **1:8** Zadok the *p.*, and Benaiah the son of Jehoiada, and Nathan the prophet, and Shimei, and Rei, and the mighty men which [belonged] to David; **1:19** he hath slain oxen and fat cattle and sheep in abundance, and hath called all the sons of the king, and Abiathar the p.; **1:25** hath called all the king's sons, and the captains of the host, and Abiathar the p.; and, behold, they eat and drink before him; **1:26** Zadok the p., and Benaiah the son of Jehoiada, and thy servant Solomon, hath he not called; **1:32** king David said, Call me Zadok the p., and Nathan the prophet, and Benaiah the son of Jehoiada; **1:34** let Zadok the p. and Nathan the prophet anoint him there king over Israel; **1:38** Zadok the p., and Nathan the prophet, and Benaiah the son of Jehoiada, and the Cherethites, and the Pelethites, went down; **1:39** Zadok the p. took an horn of oil out of the tabernacle, and anointed Solomon; **1:42** while he yet spake, behold, Jonathan the son of Abiathar the p. came; **1:44** the king hath sent with him Zadok the p., and Nathan the prophet; **1:45** Zadok the p. and Nathan the prophet have anointed him king in Gihon; **2:22** ask for him the kingdom also; for he [is] mine elder brother; even for him, and for Abiathar the p.; **2:26** unto Abiathar the p. said the king, Get thee to Anathoth, unto thine own fields; for thou [art] worthy of death; **2:27** Solomon thrust out Abiathar from being p. unto the LORD; **2:35** Zadok the p. did the king put in the room of Abiathar; **4:2** these [were] the princes which he had; Azariah the son of Zadok the p.; **2 Kgs. 11:9** with them that should go out on the sabbath, and came to Jehoiada the p.; **11:10** to the captains over hundreds did the p. give king David's spears and shields, that [were] in the temple of the LORD; **11:15** Jehoiada the p. commanded the captains of the hundreds, the officers of the host; **11:18** the p. appointed officers over the house of the LORD; **12:2** Jehoash did [that which was] right in the sight of the LORD all his days wherein Jehoiada the p. instructed him; **12:7** king Jehoash called for Jehoiada the p., and the [other] p., and said unto them, Why repair ye not the breaches of the house; **12:9** Jehoiada the p. took a chest, and bored a hole in the lid of it, and set it beside the altar, on the right side as one cometh into the house of the LORD; **16:10** king Ahaz sent to Urijah the p. the fashion of the altar, and the pattern of it, according to all the workmanship thereof; **16:11** Urijah the p. built an altar according to all that king Ahaz had sent from Damascus; **16:15** king Ahaz commanded Urijah the p., saying, Upon the great altar burn the morning burnt offering; **16:16** thus did Urijah the p., according to all that king Ahaz commanded; **22:10** Hilkiah the p. hath delivered me a book; **22:12** the king commanded Hilkiah the p.; **22:14** Hilkiah the p., and Ahikam, and Achbor, and Shaphan, and Asahiah, went unto Huldah the prophetess; **23:4** the king commanded Hilkiah the high p., and the p. of the second order, and the keepers of the door, to bring forth out of the temple of the LORD; **23:24** he might perform the words of the law which were written in the book that Hilkiah the p. found in the house of the LORD; **25:18** the captain of the guard took Seraiah the chief p., and Zephaniah the second p.; **1 Chr. 16:39** Zadok the p., and his brethren the p., before the tabernacle of the LORD; **24:6** [before] the chief of the fathers of the p. and Levites; **27:5** the third captain of the host for the third month [was] Benaiah the son of Jehoiada, a chief p.; **29:22** anointed [him] unto the LORD [to be] the chief governor, and Zadok [to be] p.; **2 Chr. 13:9** have ye not cast out the p. of the LORD, the sons of Aaron, and the Levites, and have made you p. after the manner of the nations of [other] lands; **15:3** for a long season Israel [hath been] without the true God, and without a teaching p., and without law; **19:11** Amariah the chief p. [is] over you in all matters of the LORD; **23:8** the Levites and all Judah did according to all things that Jehoiada the p. had commanded; **23:9** the p. delivered to the captains of hundreds spears, and bucklers, and shields, that [had been] king David's; **23:14** Jehoiada the p. brought out the captains of hundreds that were set over the host; **23:17** brake his altars and his images in pieces, and slew Mattan the p. of Baal before the altars; **24:2** Joash did [that which was] right in the sight of the LORD all the days of Jehoiada the p.; **24:20** the Spirit of God came upon Zechariah the son of Jehoiada the p., which stood above the people; **24:25** his own servants conspired against him for the blood of the sons of Jehoiada the p., and slew him on his bed; **26:17** Azariah the p. went in after him, and with him fourscore p. of the LORD, [that were] valiant men; **26:20** Azariah the chief p., and all the p., looked upon him, and, behold, he [was] leprous in his forehead; **31:10** Azariah the chief p. of the house of Zadok answered him, and said, Since [the people] began to bring the offerings into the house of the LORD, we have had enough to eat; **34:14** Hilkiah the p. found a book of the law of the LORD [given] by Moses; **34:18** Shaphan the scribe told the king, saying, Hilkiah the p. hath given me a book; **Ezra 2:63** they should not eat of the most holy things, till there stood up a p. with Urim and with Thummim; **7:11** this [is] the copy of the letter that the king Artaxerxes gave unto Ezra the p., the scribe; **7:12** unto Ezra the p., a scribe of the law of the God of heaven, perfect [peace], and at such a time; **7:21** whatsoever Ezra the *p.*, the scribe of the law of the God of heaven, shall require of you, it be done speedily; **8:33** was the silver and the gold and the vessels weighed in the house of our God by the hand of Meremoth the son of Uriah the *p.*; **10:10** Ezra the *p.* stood up, and said unto them, Ye have transgressed, and have taken strange wives, to increase the trespass of Israel; **10:16** Ezra the *p.*, [with] certain chief of the fathers, after the house of their fathers, and all of them by [their] names, were separated; **Neh. 7:65** they should not eat of the most holy things, till there stood [up] a *p.* with Urim and Thummim; **8:2** Ezra the *p.* brought the law before the congregation both of men and women; **8:9** Ezra the *p.* the scribe, and the Levites that taught the people, said unto all the people, This day [is] holy unto the LORD your God; **10:38** the *p.* the son of Aaron shall be with the Levites, when the Levites take tithes; **12:26** in the days of Nehemiah the governor, and of Ezra the *p.*, the scribe; **13:4** Eliashib the *p.*, having the oversight of the chamber of the house of our God; **13:13** I made treasurers over the treasuries, Shelemiah the *p.*, and Zadok the scribe; Ps. **110:4** thou [art] a *p.* for ever after the order of Melchizedek; **Isa. 8:2** I took unto me faithful witnesses to record, Uriah the *p.*, and Zechariah the son of Jeberechiah; **24:2** it shall be, as with the people, so with the *p.*; **28:7** the *p.* and the prophet have erred through strong drink; **Jer. 6:13** from the prophet even unto the *p.* every one dealeth falsely; **8:10** every one from the least even unto the greatest is given to covetousness, from the prophet even unto the *p.* every one dealeth falsely; **14:18** both the prophet and the *p.* go about into a land that they know not; **18:18** the law shall not perish from the *p.*, nor counsel from the wise, nor the word from the prophet; **20:1** the son of Immer the *p.*, who [was] also chief governor in the house of the LORD, heard that Jeremiah prophesied these things; **21:1** king Zedekiah sent unto him Pashur the son of Melchiah, and Zephaniah the son of Maaseiah the *p.*; **23:11** both prophet and *p.* are profane; yea, in my house have I found their wickedness, saith the LORD; **23:33** when this people, or the prophet, or a *p.*, shall ask thee, saying, What [is] the burden of the LORD; **23:34** the prophet, and the *p.*, and the people, that shall say, The burden of the LORD, I will even punish that man and his house; **29:25** to Zephaniah the son of Maaseiah the *p.*, and to all the *p.*, saying; **29:26** the

LORD hath made thee *p.* in the stead of Jehoiada the *p.*, that ye should be officers in the house of the LORD; **29:29** Zephaniah the *p.* read this letter in the ears of Jeremiah the prophet; **37:3** Zephaniah the son of Maaseiah the *p.* to the prophet Jeremiah, saying, Pray now unto the LORD our God for us; **52:24** the captain of the guard took Seraiah the chief *p.*; **Lam. 2:6** hath despised in the indignation of his anger the king and the *p.*; **2:20** shall the *p.* and the prophet be slain in the sanctuary of the Lord; **Ezek. 1:3** the word of the LORD came expressly unto Ezekiel the *p.*; **7:26** the law shall perish from the *p.*, and counsel from the ancients; **44:13** they shall not come near unto me, to do the office of a *p.* unto me; **44:21** neither shall any *p.* drink wine, when they enter into the inner court; **44:30** every oblation of all, of every [sort] of your oblations, shall be the *p.*'s; **45:19** the *p.* shall take of the blood of the sin offering, and put [it] upon the posts of the house; **Hosea 4:4** thy people [are] as they that strive with the *p.*; **4:6** I will also reject thee, that thou shalt be no *p.* to me: seeing thou hast forgotten the law of thy God; **4:9** there shall be, like people, like *p.*: and I will punish them for their ways, and reward them their doings; Amos **7:10** Amaziah the *p.* of Bethel sent to Jeroboam king of Israel; Zech. **6:13** he shall bear the glory, and shall sit and rule upon his throne; and he shall be a *p.* upon his throne.

PRIESTCRAFT (*see also* False, False Prophet, False Teacher)

Not every one that saith unto me, Lord, Lord, shall enter into the kingdom of heaven; but he that doeth the will of my Father who is in heaven. Many will say to me in that day: Lord, Lord, have we not prophesied in thy name, and in thy name have cast out devils, and in thy name done many wonderful works? And then will I profess unto them: I never knew you; depart from me, ye that work iniquity. Matt. 7:21-23 (*see also* Enter, False Prophets, Father, Will, Wonderful)

PRIESTHOOD (*see also* Deacon, Elder, High Priest, Melchesdec, Priest, Seventy, Teacher)

Ye also, as lively stones, are built up a spiritual house, an holy priesthood, to offer up spiritual sacrifices, acceptable to God by Jesus Christ. 1 Pet. 2:5 (*see also* Jesus Christ, Offer, Sacrifice)

Seek ye the priesthood also. Num. 16:10 (*see also* Seek)

Ex. 40:15 their anointing shall surely be an everlasting priesthood through hout their generations; **Num. 16:10** seek ye the priesthood also; **18:1** thou and thy sons with thee shall bear the iniquity of your priesthood; **25:13** he shall have it, and his seed after him, [even] the covenant of an everlasting priesthood; **Josh. 18:7** the Levites have no part among you; for the priesthood of the LORD [is] their inheritance.

PRINCIPLE (*see also* Commandment, Doctrine, Exhort, Preach, Publish)

Therefore leaving the principles of the doctrine of Christ, let us go on unto perfection; not laying again the foundation of repentance from dead works, and of faith toward God, Of the doctrine of baptisms, and of laying on of hands, and of resurrection of the dead, and of eternal judgment. Heb. 6:1-2 (*see also* Authority, Call, Go, Laying on of Hands)

For when for the time ye ought to be teachers, ye have need that one teach you again which be the first principles of the oracles of God; and are become such as have need of milk, and not of strong meat. Heb 5:12 (*see also* Meat, Milk, Teach)

PRISON, PRISONER (*see also* Death, Hell)

Proclaim liberty to the captives, and the opening of the prison to them that are bound. Isa. 61:1 (*see also* Liberty, Proclaim)

PRIZE

This one thing I do, forgetting those things which are behind, and reaching forth unto those things which are before, I press toward the mark for the prize of the high calling of God in Christ Jesus. Philip 3:13-14 (*see also* Do, Mark, Reach)

PROCEED

He humbled thee, and suffered thee to hunger, and fed thee with manna, which thou knewest not, neither did thy fathers know; that he might make thee know that man doth not live by bread only, but by every word that proceedeth out of the mouth of the LORD doth man live. Deut. 8:3 (*see also* Bread, Word)

Man shall not live by bread alone, but by every word that proceedeth out of the mouth of God. Matt. 4:4 (*see also* Bread, Live, Word)

Do not ye yet understand, that whatsoever entereth in at the mouth goeth into the belly, and is cast out into the draught? But those things which proceed out of the mouth come froth from the heart; and they defile the man. For out of the heart proceed evil thoughts, murders, adulteries, fornications, thefts, false witness, blasphemies: These are the things which defile a man: but to eat with unwashen hands defileth not a man. Matt: 17-20 (*see also* Defile, Heart, Mouth)

Out of the same mouth proceedeth blessing and cursing. My brethren, these things ought not so to be. James 3:10 (*see also* Mouth)

PROCLAIM (*see also* Declare, Exhort, Preach, Publish)

Ye have not hearkened unto me, in proclaiming liberty, every one to his brother, and every man to his neighbour: behold, I proclaim a liberty for you, saith the LORD. Jer. 34:15-17 (*see also* Liberty)

Most men will proclaim every one his own goodness: but a faithful man who can find? Prov. 20:6 (*see also* Good)

Ye have not hearkened unto me, in proclaiming liberty, every one to his brother, and every man to his neighbour: behold, I proclaim a liberty for you, saith the LORD, to the sword, to the pestilence, and to the famine; and I will make you to be removed into all the kingdoms of the earth. Jer. 34:17 (*see also* Liberty)

Proclaim liberty to the captives, and the opening of the prison to them that are bound. Isa. 61:1 (*see also* Liberty, Prison)

Proclaim the acceptable year of the Lord, and the day of vengeance of our God, to comfort all that mourn. Isa. 61:2 (*see also* Comfort, Mourn, Year)

Isa. 61:2-3 *p.* the acceptable year of the LORD, and the day of vengeance of our God; to comfort all that mourn; To appoint unto them that mourn in Zion; **62:11** the LORD hath *p.* unto the end of the world, Say ye to the daughter of Zion,

Behold, thy salvation cometh; behold, his reward is with him, and his work before him; **63:3-6** the day of vengeance is in mine heart, and the year of my redeemed is come. And I looked, and there was none to help; and I wondered that there was none to uphold: therefore mine own arm brought salvation unto me.

Stand in the gate of the LORD's house, and proclaim there this word, and say, Hear the word of the LORD. Jer. 7:2 (*see also* House, Word)

Jer. 7:2 stand in the gate of the LORD's house, and *p.* there this word, and say, Hear the word of the LORD; **Ezek. 20:3** thus saith the Lord GOD; Are ye come to enquire of me? As I live, saith the Lord GOD, I will not be enquired of by you.

PROFANE, PROFANITY (*see also* Blaspheme, Corrupt, Defile, Lips, Mouth, Pollute, Speak, Swear, Tongue)

An abomination is committed in Israel and in Jerusalem; for Judah hath profaned the holiness of the LORD which he loved, and hath married the daughter of a strange god. Mal. 2:11 (*see also* Holiness)

Neither shalt thou profane the name of God; I am LORD. Lev. 18:21

Lev. 18:21 neither shalt thou *p.* the name of thy God: I am the LORD; **19:12** ye shall not swear by my name falsely, neither shalt thou *p.* the name of thy God: I am the LORDLORD; **20:3** I will set my face against that man, and will cut him off from among his people; because he hath given of his seed unto Molech, to defile my sanctuary, and to *p.* my holy name; **21:6** they shall be holy unto their God, and not *p.* the name of their God; **22:1-2** *p.* not my holy name in those things which they hallow unto me: I am the LORD; **22:32** neither shall ye *p.* my holy name; but I will be hallowed among the children of Israel: I am the LORD which hallow you; **Ezek. 36:20-23** they *p.* my holy name, when they said to them, These are the people of the LORD, and are gone forth out of his land. But I had pity for mine holy name, which the house of Israel had *p.*; **Amos 2:8** they lay themselves down upon clothes laid to pledge by every altar, and they drink the wine of the condemned in the house of their god; **Mal. 1:12-13** ye have *p.* it, in that ye say, The table of the LORD is polluted; and the fruit thereof, even his meat, is contemptible.

PROFESS, PROFESSION (*see also* Testify, Witness)

Let us hold fast the profession of our faith without wavering; (for he is faithful that promised). Heb. 10:23 (*see also* Wavering)

PROFIT (*see also* Benefit, Bless)

My people have changed their glory for that which doth not profit. Jer. 2:8 (*see also* Glory, Walk)

Treasures of wickedness profit nothing; but righteousness delivereth from death. Prov. 10:2 (*see also* Righteous, Treasure, Wickedness)

What doth it profit, my brethren, though a man say he hath faith, and have not works? can faith save him? James. 2:14 (*see also* Faith, Save, Works)

For unto us was the gospel preached, as well as unto them: but the word preached did not profit them, not being mixed with faith in them that heard it. Heb. 4:2 (*see also* Faith)

Of these things put them in remembrance, charging them before the Lord that they strive not about words to no profit, but to the subverting of the hearers. 2 Tim. 2:14 (*see also* Strive, Words)

For what is a man profited, if he shall gain the whole world, and lose his own soul? or what shall a man give in exchange for his soul? Matt.16:26 (*see also* Gain, Soul, World)

PROLONG (*see also* Consequence, Covenant, Oath, Reward, Vow)

Ye shall walk in all the ways which the LORD your God hath commanded you, that ye may live, and that ye may prolong your days in the land which ye shall posses. Deut. 5:33 (*see also* Day, Walk, Way)

PROMISE (*see also* Consequence, Covenant, Oath, Reward, Vow)

He staggered not at the promise of God through unbelief; but was strong in faith, giving glory to God; And being fully persuaded that, what he had promised, he was able also to perform. And therefore it was imputed to him for righteousness. Rom. 4:20-22 (*see also* Belief)

Be not slothful, but followers of them who through faith and patience inherit the promises. **Heb. 6:12** (*see also* Slothful)

According as his divine power hath given unto us all things that pertain unto life and godliness, through the knowledge of him that hath called us to glory and virtue: Whereby we are given unto us exceeding great and precious promises: that by these ye might be partakers of the divine nature, having escaped the corruption that is in the world through lust. **2 Pet. 1:3-4** (*see also* All Things, Divine Nature, Knowledge, Lust)

That which is gone out of thy lips thou shalt keep and perform; even a freewill offering, according as thou has vowed unto the LORD thy God, which thou hast promised with thy mouth. **Deut. 23:23** (*see also* Vow)

PROPHECY, PROPHESY (*see also* Declare, Gift, Holy Ghost, Inspiration, Revelation)

For the prophecy came not in old time by the will of man: but holy men of God spake as they were moved by the Holy Ghost. **2 Pet. 1:21** (*see also* Holy Ghost, Moved)

I am thy fellowservant, and of thy brethren that have the testimony of Jesus: worship God: for the testimony of Jesus is the spirit of prophecy. **Rev. 19:10** (*see also* Testimony)

I would that ye all spake with tongues, but rather that ye prophesied: for greater is he that prophesieth than he that speaketh with tongues, except he interpret, that the church may receive edifying. **1 Cor. 14:5** (*see also* Gift, Interpret, Tongues)

Having then gifts differing according to the grace that is given to us, whether prophecy, let us prophesy according to the proportion of faith. **Rom. 12:6** (*see also* Gift)

Acts 19:6 when Paul had laid his hands upon them, the Holy Ghost came on them; and they spake with tongues, and *p.*; **21:9** the same man had four daughters, virgins, which did *p.*; **Rom. 12:6** having then gifts differing according to the grace that is given to us, whether *p.*, let us *p.* according to the proportion of faith; **1 Cor. 14:1** follow after charity, and desire spiritual gifts, but rather that ye may *p.*; **14:3-4** he that *p.* speaketh unto men to edification, and exhortation, and

comfort. He that speaketh in an unknown tongue edifieth himself; but he that *p.* edifieth the church; **14:5** I would that ye all spake with tongues, but rather that ye *p.*: for greater is he that *p.* than he that speaketh with tongues, except he interpret, that the church may receive edifying; **1 Thes. 5:20** despise not *p.*; **1 Tim. 4:14** neglect not the gift that is in thee, which was given thee by *p.*, with the laying on of the hands of the presbytery; **2 Pet. 1:19-20** we have also a more sure word of *p.*; whereunto ye do well that ye take heed, as unto a light that shineth in a dark place, until the day dawn, and the day star arise in your hearts: Knowing this first, that no *p.* of the scripture is of any private interpretation; **3:4** where is the promise of his coming? for since the fathers fell asleep, all things continue as they were from the beginning of the creation; **Rev. 4:1** after this I looked, and, behold, a door was opened in heaven: and the first voice which I heard was as it were of a trumpet talking with me; which said, Come up hither, and I will shew thee things which must be hereafter; **10:11** thou must *p.* again before many peoples, and nations, and tongues, and kings; **11:3** I will give power unto my two witnesses, and they shall *p.* a thousand two hundred and threescore days; **19:10** I am thy fellowservant, and of thy brethren that have the testimony of Jesus: worship God: for the testimony of Jesus is the spirit of *p.*

The Spirit of God came upon him, and he prophecied among them. **1 Sam. 10:10**

Num. 11:25-27 when the spirit rested upon them, they *p.* and did not cease; **1 Sam. 10:1-13** it was so, that when he had turned his back to go from Samuel, God gave him another heart: and all those signs came to pass that day... and the Spirit of God came upon him, and he *p.* among them; **18:10** it came to pass on the morrow, that the evil spirit from God came upon Saul, and he *p.* in the midst of the house; **19:20-24** when they saw the company of the prophets *p.*, and Samuel standing as appointed over them, the Spirit of God was upon the messengers of Saul, and they also *p.*; **28:19-20** the LORD will also deliver Israel with thee into the hand of the Philistines: and to morrow shalt thou and thy sons be with me: the LORD also shall deliver the host of Israel; **30:7-8** David inquired at the LORD, saying, Shall I pursue after this troop? shall I overtake them? And he answered him, Pursue: for thou shalt surely overtake them, and without fail recover all; **1 Kgs. 18:29** they *p.* until the time of the offering of the evening sacrifice, that there was neither voice, nor any to answer, nor any that regarded; **22:8** there is yet one man, Micaiah the son of Imlah, by whom we may enquire of the LORD: but I hate him; for he doth not *p.* good concerning me, but evil; **22:24-25** which way went the Spirit of the LORD from me to speak unto thee? And Micaiah said, Behold, thou shalt see in that day, when thou shalt go into an inner chamber to hide thyself; **2 Kgs. 4:43-44** give the people, that they may eat: for thus saith the LORD, They shall eat, and shall leave thereof; **1 Chron. 25:1-3** David and the captains of the host separated to the service of the sons of Asaph, and of Heman, and of Jeduthun, who should *p.* with harps, with psalteries, and with cymbals; **2 Chron. 9:29** the acts of Solomon, first and last, are they not written in the book of Nathan the prophet, and I n the *p.* of Ahijah the Shilonite, and in the visions of Iddo the seer against Jeroboam the son of Nebat; **15:1-8** when Asa heard these words, and the *p.* of Oded the prophet, he took courage, and put away the abominable idols out of all the land; **20:37** Eliezer the son of Dodavah of Mareshah *p.* against Jehoshaphat, saying, Because thou hast joined thyself with Ahaziah, the LORD hath broken thy works; **21:12-15** there came a writing to him from Elijah the prophet, saying, Thus saith the LORD God of David thy father; **Ezra 5:1** the prophets, Haggai the prophet, and Zechariah the son of Iddo, *p.* unto the Jews that were in Judah and Jerusalem in the name of the God of Israel; **Jer. 19:14-15** then came Jeremiah from Tophet, whither the LORD had sent him to *p.*; and he stood in the court of the LORD's house.

PROPHET (*see also* Disciple, Lead, Priesthood, Revelation, Seer, Witness)

Blessed are ye, when men shall revile you, and persecute you, and shall say all manner of evil against you falsely, for my sake. Rejoice, and be exceeding glad: for great is your reward in heaven: for so persecuted they the prophets which were before you. Matt 5:11-12 (*see also* Persecute, Reward)

Therefore also said the wisdom of God, I will send them prophets and apostles, and some of them they shall slay and persecute: That the blood of all the prophets, which was shed from the foundation of the world, may be required of this generation. Luke 11:49-50 (*see also* Blood, Persecute, Wisdom)

God hath set some in the church, first apostles, secondarily prophets, thirdly teachers, after that miracles, then gifts of healings, helps, governments, diversities of tongues. Are all apostles? are all prophets? are all teachers? are all workers of miracles? Have all the gifts of healing? do all speak with tongues? do all interpret? But covet earnestly the best gifts: and yet shew I unto you a more excellent way. 1 Cor. 12:28-31 (*see also* Excellent, Gift, Government, Interpret, Way)

He that receiveth you receiveth me, and he that receiveth me receiveth him that sent me. He that receiveth a prophet in the name of a prophet shall receive a prophet's reward; and he that receiveth a righteous man in the name of a righteous man shall receive a righteous man's reward. Matt. 10:40-41 (*see also* Receive, Reward, Serve)

He spake by the mouth of his holy prophets, which have been since the world began. Luke 1:70 (*see also* Mouth)

Who is among you that feareth the LORD, that obeyeth the voice of his servant, that walketh in darkness, and hath no light? let him trust in the name of the LORD, and stay upon his God. Isa. 50:10 (*see also* Obey, Servant)

Ye are no more strangers and foreigners, but fellowcitizens with the saints, and of the household of God; And are built upon the foundation of the apostles and prophets, Jesus Christ himself being the chief corner stone. Eph. 2:19-20 (*see also* Apostle, Cornerstone, Jesus Christ, Saint)

They mocked the messengers of God, and despised his words, and misused his prophets, until the wrath of the LORD arose against his people, till there was no remedy. 2 Chron. 36:16 (*see also* Messenger, Mock, Persecute)

[Obey] the voice of the Lord our God, to walk in his laws, which he set before us by his servants the prophets. Dan. 9:10 (*see also* Law, Voice)

Should ye not hear the words which the LORD hath cried by the former prophets, when Jerusalem was inhabited and in prosperity, and the cities thereof round about her, when men inhabited the south and the plain? Zech. 7:7 (*see also* Hear, Word)

The prophet that hath a dream, let him tell a dream. **Jer. 23:28** (*see also* Dream)

Hearken to the words of my servants the prophets, whom I sent unto you, both rising up early, and sending them, but ye have not hearkened. **Jer. 26:5** (*see also* Hearken)

Is there not here a prophet of the LORD, that we may inquire of the LORD by him? **2 Kgs. 3:11** (*see also* Inquire)

And he gave some, apostles; and some, prophets; and some, evangelists; and some, pastors and teachers; For the perfecting of the saints, for the work of the ministry, for the edifying of the body of Christ: Till we all come in the unity of the faith, and of the knowledge of the Son of God, unto a perfect man, unto the measure of the stature of the fulness of Christ. **Eph. 4:11-13** (*see also* Apostle, Perfection, Unity)

Believe in the LORD your God, so shall ye be established; believe his prophets, so shall ye prosper. **2 Chron. 20:20** (*see also* Belief, Establish, Hearken, Prosper)

Ex. 16:19-20 Moses said, Let no man leave of it till the morning. Notwithstanding they hearkened not unto Moses; but some of them left of it until the morning, and it bred worms, and stank: and Moses was wroth with them; **Lev. 26:21** if ye walk contrary unto me, and will not hearken unto me; I will bring seven times more plagues upon you according to your sins; **26:27** if ye will not for all this hearken unto me, but walk contrary unto me; **Num. 12:6** hear now my words: If there be a prophet among you, I the LORD will make myself known unto him in a vision, and will speak unto him in a dream; **12:14** the LORD said unto Moses, If her father had but spit in her face, should she not be ashamed seven days? let her be shut out from the camp seven days, and after that let her be received in again; **Deut. 4:1** hearken, O Israel, unto the statutes and unto the judgments, which I teach you, for to do them, that ye may live, and go in and possess the land which the LORD God of your fathers giveth you; **32:46** set your hearts unto all the words which I testify among you this day, which ye shall command your children to observe to do, all the words of this law; **34:9** Joshua the son of Nun was full of the spirit of wisdom; for Moses had laid his hands upon him: and the children of Israel hearkened unto him, and did as the LORD commanded Moses; **Josh.1:16-18** all that thou

commandest us we will do, and whithersoever thou sendest us, we will go; **1 Sam. 9:6** behold now, there is in this city a man of God, and he is an honourable man; all that he saith cometh surely to pass: now let us go thither; peradventure he can shew us our way that we should go; **9:9** beforetime in Israel, when a man went to enquire of God, thus he spake, Come, and let us go to the seer: for he that is now called a *P.* was beforetime called a Seer; **1 Kgs. 22:7** is there not here a *p.* of the LORD besides, that we might enquire of him; **22:15** go, and prosper: for the LORD shall deliver it into the hand of the king; **2 Kgs. 3:11** is there not here a *p.* of the LORD, that we may enquire of the LORD by him; **17:23** until the LORD removed Israel out of his sight, as he had said by all his servants the *p.*; **1 Chron. 11:3** they anointed David king over Israel, according to the word of the LORD by Samuel; **2 Chron. 18:13** as the LORD liveth, even what my God saith, that will I speak; **18:15** how many times shall I adjure thee that thou say nothing but the truth to me in the name of the LORD; **20:20** believe in the LORD your God, so shall ye be established; believe his *p.*, so shall ye prosper; **24:19** yet he sent *p.* to them, to bring them again unto the LORD; and they testified against them: but they would not give ear; **25:16** then the *p.* forbare, and said, I know that God hath determined to destroy thee, because thou hast done this, and hast not hearkened unto my counsel; **26:5** he sought God in the days of Zechariah, who had understanding in the visions of God: and as long as he sought the LORD, God made him to prosper; **29:25** according to the commandment of David, and of Gad the kings seer, and Nathan the *p.*: for so was the commandment of the LORD by his *p.*; **Ezra 7:21** whatsoever Ezra the priest, the scribe of the law of the God of heaven, shall require of you, it be done speedily; **9:11** thou hast commanded by thy servants the *p.*, saying, The land, unto which ye go to possess it, is an unclean land with the filthiness of the people of the lands, with their abominations, which have filled it from one end to another with their uncleanness; **10:12** all the congregation answered and said with a loud voice, As thou hast said, so must we do; **Neh. 9:30** testifiedst against them by thy spirit in thy *p.*: yet would they not give ear: therefore gavest thou them into the hand of the people of the lands; **Ps. 103:20** bless the LORD, ye his angels, that excel in strength, that do his commandments, hearkening unto the voice of his word; **106:25** hearkened not unto the voice of the LORD; **Isa. 28:23** give ye ear, and hear my voice; hearken, and hear my speech; **34:1** come near, ye nations, to hear; and hearken, ye people: let the earth hear, and all that is therein; the world, and all things that come forth of it; **51:1** hearken to me, ye that follow after righteousness, ye that seek the LORD: look unto the rock whence ye are hewn, and to the hole of the pit whence ye are digged; **51:4** hearken unto me, my people; and give ear unto me, O my nation: for a law shall proceed from me, and I will make my judgment to rest for a light of the people; **51:7** hearken unto me, ye that know righteousness, the people in whose heart is my law; **Jer. 6:19** I will bring evil upon this people, even the fruit of their thoughts, because they have not hearkened unto my words, nor to my law, but rejected it; **7:24** they hearkened not, nor inclined their ear, but walked in the counsels and in the imagination of their evil heart, and went backward, and not forward; **7:26** they hearkened not unto me, nor inclined their ear, but hardened their neck: they did worse than their fathers; **18:18** let us devise devices against Jeremiah; for the law shall not perish from the priest, nor counsel from the wise, nor the word from the *p.*. Come, and let us smite him with the tongue, and let us not give heed to any of his words; **23:4** I will set up shepherds over them which shall feed them: and they shall fear no more, nor be dismayed, neither shall they be lacking, saith the LORD; **23:22** if they had stood in my counsel, and had caused my people to hear my words, then they should have turned them from their evil way, and from the evil of their doings; **25:3-4** the LORD hath sent unto you all his servants the *p.*, rising early and sending them; but ye have not hearkened, nor inclined your ear to hear; **25:7** ye have not hearkened unto me, saith the LORD; that ye might provoke me to anger with the works of your hands to your own hurt; **27:18** if they be *p.*, and if the word of the LORD be with them, let them now make intercession to the LORD of hosts; **28:2-9** thus speaketh the LORD of hosts, the God of Israel, saying... the *p.* that have been before me and before thee of old prophesied both against many countries, and against great kingdoms, of war, and of evil, and of pestilence. The *p.* which prophesieth of peace, when the word of the *p.* shall come to pass, then shall the *p.* be known, that the LORD hath truly sent him; **29:18-19** because they have not hearkened to my words, saith the LORD, which I sent unto them by my servants the *p.*, rising up early and sending them; but ye would not hear, saith the LORD; **32:19-22** pray for us unto the LORD our God; and according unto all that the LORD our God shall say, so declare unto us, and we will do it; **32:33** they have turned unto me the back, and not the face: though I taught them, rising up early and teaching them, yet they have not hearkened to receive instruction; **35:15** I have sent also unto you all my servants the *p.*, rising up early and sending them; **37:2** neither he, nor his servants, nor the people of the land, did hearken unto the words of the LORD, which he spake by the *p.* Jeremiah; **37:17** is there any word from the LORD? And Jeremiah said, There is: for, said he, thou shalt be delivered into the hand of the king of Babylon; **38:2** thus saith the LORD, He that remaineth in this city shall die by the sword, by the famine, and by the pestilence: but he that goeth forth to the Chaldeans shall live; for he shall have his life for a prey, and shall live; **38:14-18** took Jeremiah the *p.* unto him into the third entry that is in the house of the LORD: and the king said unto Jeremiah, I will ask thee a thing; hide nothing from me; **39:12** take him, and look well to him, and do him no harm; but do unto him even as he shall say unto thee; **42:2-4** said unto Jeremiah the *p.*, Let, we beseech thee, our supplication be accepted before thee, and pray for us unto the LORD thy God, even for all this remnant; **42:7** the word of the LORD came unto Jeremiah; **42:9** thus saith the LORD, the God of Israel, unto whom ye sent me to present your supplication before him; **43:1-2** when Jeremiah had made an end of speaking unto all the people all the words of the LORD their God, for which the LORD their God had sent him to them, even all these words; **43:4-5** all the people, obeyed not the voice of the LORD, to dwell in the land of Judah; **44:4-5** howbeit I sent unto you all my servants the *p.*, rising early and sending them; **44:16** as for the word that thou hast spoken unto us in the name of the LORD, we will not hearken unto thee; **44:25** thus saith the LORD of hosts, the God of Israel, saying; Ye and your wives have both spoken with your mouths, and fulfilled with your hand, saying, We will surely perform our vows that we have vowed, to burn incense to the queen of heaven, and to pour out drink offerings unto her: ye will surely accomplish your vows, and surely perform your vows; **Ezek. 2:5** and they, whether they will hear, or whether they will forbear, [for they are a rebellious house,] yet shall know that there hath been a *p.* among them; **Dan. 9:6** neither have we hearkened unto thy servants the *p.*, which spake in thy name to our kings, our princes, and our fathers, and to all the people of the land; **Hosea 9:17** my God will cast them away, because they did not hearken unto him: and they shall be wanderers among the nations; **12:10** I have also spoken by the *p.*, and I have multiplied visions, and used similitudes, by the ministry of the *p.*; **12:13** by a *p.* the LORD brought Israel out of Egypt, and by a *p.* was he preserved; **Amos 2:11-12** I raised up of your sons for *p.*, and of your young men for Nazarites; **3:7** surely the Lord GOD will do nothing, but he revealeth his secret unto his servants the *p.*; **Micah 3:9** hear this, I pray you, ye heads of the house of Jacob, and princes of the house of Israel, that abhor judgment, and pervert all equity; **Haba 1:1** the burden which Habakkuk the *p.* did see; **Hag. 1:1** came the word of the LORD by Haggai the *p.* unto Zerubbabel the son of Shealtiel, governor of Judah; **1:13** then spake Haggai the LORD's messenger in the LORD's message unto the people, saying, I am with you, saith the LORD; **Zech. 1:1** came the word of the LORD unto Zechariah, the son of Berechiah, the son of Iddo the *p.*; **1:6** my words and my statutes, which I commanded my servants the *p.*, did they not take hold of your fathers? and they returned and said, Like as the LORD of hosts thought to do unto us, according to our ways, and according to our doings, so hath he dealt with us; **7:3** to speak unto the priests which were in the house of the LORD of hosts, and to the *p.*, saying, Should I weep in the fifth month, separating myself, as I have done these so many years.

Touch not mine anointed, and do my prophets no harm. 1 Chron. 16:22 (*see also* Persecute)

1 Chron. 16:22 touch not mine anointed, and do my prophets no harm; **2 Chron. 24:21** they conspired against him, and stoned him with stones at the commandment of the king in the court of the house of the LORD; **36:16** they mocked the messengers of God, and despised his words, and misused his *p.*, until the wrath of the LORD arose against his people, till there was no remedy; **Neh. 9:26** they were disobedient, and rebelled against thee, and cast thy law behind their backs, and slew thy *p.* which testified against them to turn them to thee, and they wrought great provocations; **Ps. 105:15** touch not mine anointed, and do my *p.* no harm; **Jer. 18:18** said they, Come, and let us devise devices against Jeremiah; for the law shall not perish from the priest, nor counsel from the wise, nor the word from the *p.*; **26:16** then said the princes and all the people unto the priests and to the *p.*; This man is not worthy to die: for he hath spoken to us in the name of the LORD our God; **33:1** the word of the LORD came unto Jeremiah the second time, while he was yet shut up in the court of the prison; **37:18-21** Jeremiah said unto king Zedekiah, What have I offended against thee, or against thy servants, or against this people, that

ye have put me in prison? Where are now your *p.* which prophesied unto you, saying, The king of Babylon shall not come against you, nor against this land; **38:6** then took they Jeremiah, and cast him into the dungeon of Malchiah; **38:9** my lord the king, these men have done evil in all that they have done to Jeremiah the *p.*, whom they have cast into the dungeon; and he is like to die for hunger in the place where he is.

Hearken not unto the words of [false] prophets that prophecy unto you; they make you vain; they speak a vision of their own heart and not out of the mouth of the LORD. Jer. 23:16 (*see also* False)

Jer. 14:13-18 the prophets say unto them, Ye shall not see the sword, neither shall ye have famine; but I will give you assured peace in this place. Then the LORD said unto me, The *p.* prophesy lies in my name; **23:16** hearken not unto the words of [false] prophets that prophecy unto you; they make you vain; they speak a vision of their own heart and not out of the mouth of the LORD; **27:14-17** hearken not unto the words of the *p.* that speak unto you, saying, Ye shall not serve the king of Babylon: for they prophesy a lie unto you. For I have not sent them, saith the LORD; **28:11** Hananiah spake in the presence of all the people, saying, Thus saith the LORD; Even so will I break the yoke of Nebuchadnezzar king of Babylon from the neck of all nations within the space of two full years; **28:13** go and tell Hananiah, saying, Thus saith the LORD; Thou hast broken the yokes of wood; but thou shalt make for them yokes of iron; **28:15** said the *p.* Jeremiah unto Hananiah the *p.*, Hear now, Hananiah; The LORD hath not sent thee; but thou makest this people to trust in a lie; **Jer.** (*see also* False)**29:8-9** let not your *p.* and your diviners, that be in the midst of you, deceive you, neither hearken to your dreams which ye cause to be dreamed. For they prophesy falsely unto you in my name; **29:23** they have committed villany in Israel, and have committed adultery with their neighbour's wives, and have spoken lying words in my name, which I have not commanded them; even I know, and am a witness; **29:26** every man that is mad, and maketh himself a *p.*, that thou shouldest put him in prison, and in the stocks; **29:31-32** because that Shemaiah hath prophesied unto you, and I sent him not, and he caused you to trust in a lie: Therefore thus saith the LORD; Behold, I will punish Shemaiah; **37:9** thus saith the LORD; Deceive not yourselves, saying, The Chaldeans shall surely depart from us: for they shall not depart; **37:19** where are now your *p.* which prophesied unto you, saying, The king of Babylon shall not come against you, nor against this land; **Lam. 2:9** her gates are sunk into the ground; he hath destroyed and broken her bars: her king and her princes are among the Gentiles: the law is no more; her *p.* also find no vision from the LORD; **2:14** thy *p.* have seen vain and foolish things for thee: and they have not discovered thine iniquity, to turn away thy captivity; but have seen for thee false burdens and causes of banishment; **3:37** who is he that saith, and it cometh to pass, when the Lord commandeth it not; **Ezek. 12:24** there shall be no more any vain vision nor flattering divination within the house of Israel; **13:3-11** thus saith the Lord GOD; Because ye have spoken vanity, and seen lies, therefore, behold, I am against you, saith the Lord GOD And mine hand shall be upon the *p.* that see vanity, and that divine lies; **13:16-17** the *p.* of Israel which prophesy concerning Jerusalem, and which see visions of peace for her, and there is no peace, saith the Lord GOD; **13:19-23** with lies ye have made the heart of the righteous sad, whom I have not made sad; and strengthened the hands of the wicked, that he should not return from his wicked way, by promising him life: Therefore ye shall see no more vanity, nor divine divinations; **14:10-11** they shall bear the punishment of their iniquity: the punishment of the *p.* shall be even as the punishment of him that seeketh unto him; That the house of Israel may go no more astray from me; **21:23** it shall be unto them as a false divination in their sight, to them that have sworn oaths: but he will call to remembrance the iniquity, that they may be taken; **22:25** there is a conspiracy of her *p.* in the midst thereof, like a roaring lion ravening the prey; they have devoured souls; they have taken the treasure and precious things; they have made her many widows in the midst thereof; **22:28** her *p.* have daubed them with untempered morter, seeing vanity, and divining lies unto them, saying, Thus saith the Lord GOD, when the LORD hath not spoken; **Hosea 9:8-9** the watchman of Ephraim was with my God: but the *p.* is a snare of a fowler in all his ways, and hatred in the house of his God; **Micah 2:11** if a man walking in the spirit and falsehood do lie, saying, I will prophesy unto thee of wine and of strong drink; he shall even be the *p.* of this people; **3:5-7** then shall the seers be ashamed, and the diviners confounded: yea, they shall all cover their lips; for there is no answer of God; **3:11** the heads thereof judge for reward, and the priests thereof teach for hire, and the *p.* thereof divine for

money; **Zeph. 3:4** her *p.* are light and treacherous persons: her priests have polluted the sanctuary, they have done violence to the law; **Zech. 10:2-4** (11:3) the idols have spoken vanity, and the diviners have seen a lie, and have told false dreams; they comfort in vain: therefore they went their way as a flock, they were troubled, because there was no shepherd; **11:17** woe to the idol shepherd that leaveth the flock! the sword shall be upon his arm, and upon his right eye: his arm shall be clean dried up, and his right eye shall be utterly darkened; **13:2-4** thou speakest lies in the name of the LORD; **Mal. 1:14** cursed be the deceiver, which hath in his flock a male, and voweth, and sacrificeth unto the Lord a corrupt thing; **2:7-8** the priests lips should keep knowledge, and they should seek the law at his mouth: for he is the messenger of the LORD of hosts.

Believest thou the prophets? Acts 26:27 (*see also* Believe)

Luke 13: 34 O Jerusalem, Jerusalem, which killest the *p.*, and stonest them that are sent unto thee; how often would I have gathered thy children together, as a hen doth gather her brood under her wings, and ye would not; **16:27-30** they have Moses and the *p.*; let them hear them. And he said, Nay, father Abraham: but if one went unto them from the dead, they will repent; **20:9-14** what shall I do? I will send my beloved son: it may be they will reverence him when they see him; **Luke 24:27** beginning at Moses and all the *p.*, he expounded unto them in all the scriptures the things concerning himself; **24:44** these are the words which I spake unto you, while I was yet with you, that all things must be fulfilled, which were written in the law of Moses, and in the *p.*, and in the psalms, concerning me; **John 1:6-7** there was a man sent from God, whose name was John. The same came for a witness, to bear witness of the Light, that all men through him might believe; **3:11-12** we speak that we do know, and testify that we have seen; and ye receive not our witness. If I have told you earthly things, and ye believe not, how shall ye believe, if I tell you of heavenly things; **11:13** who shall tell thee words, whereby thou and all thy house shall be saved; **13:40** beware therefore, lest that come upon you, which is spoken of in the *p.*; **26:27** King Agrippa, believest thou the *p.*? I know that thou believest; **27:21** ye should have hearkened unto me; **Acts 3:21-24** God hath spoken by the mouth of all his holy *p.* since the world began; **5:12-13** by the hands of the apostles were many signs and wonders wrought among the people; **4:4** many of them which heard the word believed; **5:45-47** for had ye believed Moses, ye would have believed me: for he wrote of me. But if ye believe not his writings, how shall ye believe my words; **7:52** which of the *p.* have not your fathers persecuted; **26:27** believest thou the *p.*; **Rom. 1:2** which he had promised afore by his *p.* in the holy scriptures; **1 Cor. 11:1** be ye followers of me, even as I also am of Christ; **15:11** whether it were I or they, so we preach, and so ye believed; **Eph. 2:20** are built upon the foundation of the apostles and *p.*, Jesus Christ himself being the chief corner stone; **2 Thes. 1:10** when he shall come to be glorified in his saints, and to be admired in all them that believe (because our testimony among you was believed) in that day; **James 5:10** take, my brethren, the *p.*, who have spoken in the name of the Lord, for an example of suffering affliction, and of patience; **Rev. 1:1** the **Rev.** of Jesus Christ, which God gave unto him, to shew unto his servants things which must shortly come to pass; and he sent and signified it by his angel unto his servant John; **10:7** in the days of the voice of the seventh angel, when he shall begin to sound, the mystery of God should be finished, as he hath declared to his servants the *p.*; **10:11** he said unto me, Thou must prophesy again before many peoples, and nations, and tongues, and kings; **11:10** they that dwell upon the earth shall rejoice over them, and make merry, and shall send gifts one to another; because these two *p.* tormented them that dwelt on the earth; **11:18** thou shouldest give reward unto thy servants the *p.*, and to the saints, and them that fear thy name, small and great; **22:9** see thou do it not: for I am thy fellowservant, and of thy brethren the *p.*, and of them which keep the sayings of this book: worship God.

PROSPER, PROSPERITY, PROSPEROUS
(*see also* Blessing, Increase)

This book of the law shall not depart out of thy mouth; but thou shalt meditate therein day and night, that thou mayest observe to do according to all that is written therein: for then thou shalt make thy way prosperous, and then thou shalt have good success. Josh. 1:8 (*see also* Book, Do, Meditate, Success)

In the day of prosperity be joyful. Eccl. 7:14 (*see also* Joy)

Fight ye not against the Lord God of your fathers; for ye shall not prosper. 2 Chron. 13:12 (*see also* Fight)

Believe in the Lord your God, so shall ye be established; believe his prophets, so shall ye prosper. 2 Chron. 20:20 (*see also* Believe, Establish, Hearken, Prophet)

PROSTITUTE (*see also* Fornication, Harlot, Whore)

Do not prostitute thy daughters, to cause her to be a whore; lest the land fall into whoredom, and the land become full of wickedness. Lev. 19:29 (*see also* Whore)

PROVE (*see also* Experiment, Try)

Prove all things; hold fast that which is good. 1 Thes. 5:21 (*see also* Good)

Bring ye all the tithes into the storehouse, that there may be meat in mine house, and prove me now herewith, saith the LORD of hosts, if I will not open you the windows of heaven, and pour you out a blessing. Mal. 3:8-12 (*see also* Storehouse, Tithe)

Be ye transformed by the renewing of your mind, that ye may prove what is that good, and acceptable, and perfect, will of God. Rom. 12:2 (*see also* Mind, Renew, Transform)

Examine me, O LORD, and prove me; try my reins and my heart. Ps. 26:2 (*see also* Heart)

Harden not your heart, as in the provocation, and as in the day of temptation in the wilderness:When your fathers tempted me, proved me, and saw my work. Ps. 95:9 (*see also* Harden)

PROVOKE (*see also* Anger)

Charity suffereth long, and is kind; charity envieth not; charity vaunteth not itself, is not puffed up, Doth not behave itself unseemly, seeketh not her own, is not easily provoked, thinketh no evil; Rejoiceth not in iniquity, but rejoiceth in the truth; Beareth all things, believeth all things, hopeth all things, endureth all things. 1 Cor. 13:4-7 (*see also* All Things, Believe, Charity, Endure, Hope, Rejoice, Seek, Suffer, Think)

They made Israel to sin, in provoking the LORD God of Israel to anger with their vanities. 1 Kgs. 16:13 (*see also* Vain)

PRUDENT (*see also* Know, Understand, Wise)

The simple believeth every word: but the prudent man looketh well to his going. Prov. 14:15 (*see also* Time)

Woe unto them that are wise in their own eyes, and prudent in their own sight! Isa. 5:21 (*see also* Wise)

The wisdom of the prudent is to understand his way: but the folly of fools is deceit. Prov. 14:8 (*see also* Way, Wisdom)

Prov. 12:16 a fool's wrath is presently known: but a *p.* man covereth shame; **13:16** every *p.* man dealeth with knowledge: but a fool layeth open his folly; **14:8** the wisdom of the *p.* is to understand his way: but the folly of fools is deceit; **14:15** the simple believeth every word: but the *p.* man looketh well to his going; **14:18** the simple inherit folly: but the *p.* are crowned with knowledge; **22:3** (27:12) a *p.* man foreseeth the evil, and hideth himself: but the simple pass on, and are punished.

PSALMS (*see also* Hymn, Sing, Song)

Let us come before his presence with thanksgiving and take a joyful noise unto him with psalms. Ps. 95:2 (*see also* Thanksgiving)

Let the word of Christ dwell in you richly in all wisdom; teaching and admonishing one another in psalms and hymns and spiritual songs, singing with grace in your hearts to the Lord. Col. 3:16 (*see also* Admonish, Grace, Hymn, Sing, Wisdom, Word)

PUBLISH (*see also* Declare, Preach, Teach)

The word of the Lord was published throughout all the region. Acts 13:49

I will publish the name of the LORD: ascribe ye greatness unto our God. Deut. 32:3 (*see also* Great)

How beautiful upon the mountains are the feet of him that bringeth good tidings, that publisheth peace; that bringeth good tidings of good, that publisheth salvation; that saith unto Zion, Thy God reigneth! Isa. 52:7 (*see also* Beautiful, Good, Mountain, Peace, Zion)

PUNISH, PUNISHMENT (*see* Accountability, Chasten, Judgment, Prison, Promise)

PURE, PURIFIED, PURIFY (*see also* Chastity, Cleanliness, Holy, Sanctify, Virtue, Wash)

Love pureness of heart. Prov. 22:11

Flee also youthful lusts: but follow righteousness, faith, charity, peace, with them that call on the Lord out of a pure heart. 2 Tim. 2:22 (*see also* Flee, Lust, Peace)

Blessed are the pure in heart: for they shall see God. Matt. 5:8 (*see also* Heart)

Let no man despise thy youth; but be thou an example of the believers, in word, in conversation, in charity, in spirit, in faith, in purity. 1 Tim. 4:12 (*see also* Believe, Charity, Conversation, Despise, Example)

There is a generation that are pure in their own eyes, an yet is not washed from their filthiness. Prov. 30:12 (*see also* Filthiness, Wash)

Who can say, I have made my heart clean, I am pure from my sin? Prov. 20:9 (*see also* Heart)

Ps. 18:26 with the *p.* thou wilt shew thyself *p.*; and with the froward thou wilt shew thyself froward; **24:4** he that hath clean hands, and a *p.* heart; who hath not lifted up his soul unto vanity, nor sworn deceitfully; **Prov. 15:26** the thoughts of the wicked are an abomination to the LORD: but the words of the *p.* are pleasant words; **20:9** who can say, I have made my heart clean, I am *p.* from my sin; **20:11** even a child is known by his doings, whether his work be *p.*, and whether it be right; **21:8** the way of man is froward and strange: but as for the *p.*, his work is right.

Keep thyself pure. 1 Tim. 5:22

Acts 20:26 I take you to record this day, that I am *p.* from the blood of all men; **2 Cor. 6:4-6** in all things approving ourselves as the ministers of God, in much patience, in afflictions, in necessities, in distresses, In stripes, in imprisonments, in tumults, in labours,in watchings, in fastings; By *p.*, by knowledge, by longsuffering, by kindness, by the Holy Ghost, by love unfeigned; **1 Tim. 5:22** keep thyself *p.*; **Titus 1:15** unto the *p.* all things are *p.*: but unto them that are defiled and unbelieving is nothing *p.*; but even their mind and conscience is defiled; **James 4:8** cleanse your hands, ye sinners; and *p.* your hearts, ye double minded; **1 Jn. 3:3-4** every man that hath this hope in him purifieth himself, even as he is *p.*; **Rev. 3:4** thou hast a few names even in Sardis which have not defiled their garments; and they shall walk with me in white: for they are worthy.

PURPOSE (*see also* Desire, Will, Works)

To every thing there is a season, and a time to every purpose under heaven; A time to be born, and a time to die; a time to plant, and a time to pluck up that which is planted; A time to kill, and a time to heal; a time to break down, and a time to build up; A time to weep, and a time to laugh; a time to mourn, and a time to dance; A time to cast away stones, and a time to father stones together; a time to embrace, and a time to refrain from embracing; A time to get, and a time to lose; a time to keep, and a time to cast away; A time to rend, and a time to sew; a time to keep silence, and a time to speak; A time to love, and a time to hate; a time of war, and a time of peace. Eccl. 3:1-8 (*see also* Season, Time)

QUENCH (*see also* Satisfy)

Quench not the Spirit. 1 Thes. 5:19 (*see also* Spirit)

QUESTION (*see also* Ask, Inquire, Pray)

He is proud, knowing nothing, but doting about questions and strifes of words, whereof cometh envy, strife, railings, evil surmisings, Perverse disputings of men of corrupt minds, and destitute of the truth, supposing that gain is godliness: from such withdraw thyself. 1 Tim. 6:4-5 (*see also* Strife, Mind, Pride, True)

QUIET (*see also* Silent)

Study to be quiet, and to do your own business, and to work with your own hands, as we commanded you; 1 Thes 4:11

Let it be the hidden man of the heart, in that which is not corruptible, even the ornament of a meek and quiet spirit, which is in the sight of God of great price. 1 Pet. 3:4

RABBI (*see also* Master, Teacher)

Be not ye called Rabbi: for one is your Master, *even* Christ; and all ye are brethren. Matt. 23:8 (*see also* Call)

RACE (*see also* Run)

Seeing we also are compassed about with so great a cloud of witnesses, let us lay aside every weight, and the sin which doth so easily beset us, and let us run with patience the race that is set before us. Heb. 12:1 (*see also* Beset, Lay Aside, Patience, Run, Sin, Weight, Witness)

RAINBOW (*see also* Covenant, Promise)

And God said, This is the token of the covenant which I make between me and you and every living creature that is with you, for perpetual generations: I do set my bow in the cloud, and it shall be for a token of a covenant between me and the earth. And it shall come to pass, when I bring a cloud over the earth, that the bow shall be seen in the cloud: And I will remember my covenant, which is between me and you and every living creature of all flesh; and the waters shall no more become a flood to destroy all flesh. Gen. 9:13 (*see also* Covenant)

RANSOM (*see also* Sacrifice)

Even as the Son of man came not to be ministered unto, but to minister, and to give his life a ransom for many. Matt. 20:28 (*see also* Minister)

Matt. 20:28 even as the Son of man came not to be ministered unto, but to minister, and to give his life a ransom for man.

REACH

This one thing I do, forgetting those things which are behind, and reaching forth unto those things which are before, I press toward the mark for the prize of the high calling of God in Christ Jesus. **Philip 3:13-14** (*see also* Do, Mark, Prize)

READ (*see* Book, Know, Ponder, Scripture, Seek, Understand)

READINESS, READY (*see also* Prepare)

Sanctify the Lord God in your heats; and be ready always to give an answer to every man that asketh you a reason of the hope that is in you with meekness and fear: Having a good conscience; that, whereas they speak evil of you, as of evildoers, they may be ashamed that falsely accuse your good conversation in Christ. **1 Pet. 3:15-16** (*see also* Answer, Conversation, Hope, Reason, Sanctify)

They received the word with all readiness of mind, and searched the scriptures daily, whether those things were so. **Acts 17:11** (*see also* Daily, Mind, Receive, Scripture, Search, Word)

REAP (*see also* Promise, Reward, Sow)

Be not deceived; God is not mocked: for whatsoever a man soweth, that shall he also reap. **Galtians 6:7** (*see also* Deceive, Sow)

He which soweth sparingly shall reap also sparingly; and he which soweth bountifully shall reap also bountifully. **2 Cor. 9:6** (*see also* Sow, Sparingly)

Sow to yourselves in righteousness, reap in mercy; break up your fallow ground: for it is time to seek the LORD, till he come and rain righteousness upon you. **Hosea 10:12** (*see also* Heart, Seek)

He that soweth to his flesh shall of the flesh reap corruption; but he that soweth to the Spirit shall of the Spirit reap life everlasting. **Gal. 6:8** (*see also* Flesh, Sow, Spirit)

REASON (*see also* Communicate, Cause, Counsel, Think)

I applied mine heart to know, and to search, and to seek out wisdom, and the reason of things, and to know the wickedness of folly, even of foolishness and madness. **Eccl. 7:25** (*see also* Apply, Heart, Know, Seek, Wisdom)

Sanctify the Lord God in your heats; and be ready always to give an answer to every man that asketh you a reason of the hope that is in you with meekness and fear: Having a good conscience; that, whereas they speak evil of you, as of evildoers, they may be ashamed that falsely accuse your good conversation in Christ. **1 Pet. 3:15-16** (*see also* Answer, Conversation, Hope, Ready, Sanctify)

Paul, as his manner was, went in unto them, and three sabbath days reasoned with them out of the scriptures. **Acts 17:2** (*see also* Scripture)

Acts 17:2 Paul, as his manner was, went in unto them, and three sabbath days *r.* with them out of the scriptures; **17:17** disputed he in the synagogue with the Jews, and with the devout persons, and in the market daily with them that met with him; **18:19** he himself entered into the synagogue, and *r.* with the Jews; **18:28** for he mightily convinced the Jews, and that publickly, shewing by the scriptures that Jesus was Christ; **19:8-9** he went into the synagogue, and spake boldly for the space of three months, disputing and persuading the things concerning the kingdom of God.

REBEL, REBELLION, REBELLIOUS (*see also* Apostasy, Contend, Disobey, Hardhearted, Murmur, Riotous, Revolt, Stiffnecked, Unpardonable)

If ye be willing and obedient, ye shall eat the good of the land: But if ye refuse and rebel, ye shall be devoured with the sword. **Isa. 1:19-20** (*see also* Obedience, Will)

For rebellion is as the sin of witchcraft, and stubbornness is as iniquity and idolatry. Because thou hast rejected the word of the LORD, he hath also rejected thee from being king. **1 Sam 15:23** (*see also* Idolatry, Stubborn, Witchcraft)

Let not the rebellious exalt themselves. Ps. 66:7 (*see also* Exalt)

An evil man seeketh only rebellion: therefore a cruel messenger shall be sent against him. Prov. 17:11

The house of Israel rebelled against me in the wilderness: they walked not in my statutes, and they despised my judgments, which if a man do, he shall even live in them; and my sabbaths they greatly polluted. Ezek. 20:13 (*see also* Judge)

I will cast thee from off the face of the earth: this year thou shalt die, because thou hast taught rebellion against the LORD. Jer. 28:16 (*see also* Teach)

Jer. 28:16 I will cast thee from off the face of the earth: this year thou shalt die, because thou hast taught *r.* against the LORD; **29:32** I will punish Shemaiah the Nehelamite, and his seed: he shall not have a man to dwell among this people; neither shall he behold the good that I will do for my people, saith the LORD; because he hath taught *r.* against the LORD; **50:24** I have laid a snare for thee, and thou art also taken, O Babylon, and thou wast not aware: thou art found, and also caught, because thou hast striven against the LORD.

Rebel not ye against the LORD. Num. 14:9

Num. 14:9 *r.* not ye against the LORD, neither fear ye the people of the land; for they are bread for us; **27:14** ye *r.* against my commandment in the desert of Zin, in the strife of the congregation; **Deut. 1:26** ye would not go up, but *r.* against the commandment of the LORD your God; **1:43** I spake unto you; and ye would not hear, but *r.* against the commandment of the LORD; **9:7** forget not, how thou provokedst the LORD thy God to wrath in the wilderness... ye have been *r.* against the LORD; **9:23** ye *r.* against the commandment of the LORD your God, and ye believed him not, nor hearkened to his voice; **9:24** ye have been *r.* against the LORD from the day that I knew you; **21:18-21** if a man have a stubborn and *r.* son... [then] all the men of his city shall stone him with stones, that he die: so shalt thou put evil away from among you; **31:27** I know thy *r.*, and thy stiff neck: behold, while I am yet alive with you this day, ye have been *r.* against the LORD; and how much more after my death; **Josh.1:18** whosoever he be that doth *r.* against thy commandment, and

will not hearken unto thy words in all that thou commandest him, he shall be put to death; **22:18-19** it will be, seeing ye *r.* to day against the LORD, that to morrow he will be wroth with the whole congregation of Israel; **22:29** God forbid that we should *r.* against the LORD, and turn this day from following the LORD; **1 Sam. 12:14-15** if ye will fear the LORD, and serve him, and obey his voice, and not *r.* against the commandment of the LORD, then shall both ye and also the king that reigneth over you continue following the LORD; **15:23** *r.* is as the sin of witchcraft, and stubbornness is as iniquity and idolatry; **Ezra 4:12** the Jews which came up from thee to us are come unto Jerusalem, building the *r.* and the bad city, and have set up the walls thereof; **4:15** so shalt thou find in the book of the records, and know that this city is a *r.* city, and hurtful unto kings and provinces; **Neh. 9:26-27** they were disobedient, and *r.* against thee, and cast thy law behind their backs, and slew thy prophets which testified against them to turn them to thee, and they wrought great provocations. Therefore thou deliveredst them into the hand of their enemies; **Job 24:13** they are of those that *r.* against the light; they know not the ways thereof, nor abide in the paths thereof; **Ps. 5:10** destroy thou them, O God; let them fall by their own counsels; cast them out in the multitude of their transgressions; for they have *r.* against thee; **66:7** he ruleth by his power for ever; his eyes behold the nations: let not the *r.* exalt themselves; **68:6** God setteth the solitary in families: he bringeth out those which are bound with chains: but the *r.* dwell in a dry land; **68:18** thou hast ascended on high, thou hast led captivity captive: thou hast received gifts for men; yea, for the *r.* also, that the LORD God might dwell among them; **78:8** might not be as their fathers, a stubborn and *r.* generation; a generation that set not their heart aright, and whose spirit was not stedfast with God; **105:28** he sent darkness, and made it dark; and they *r.* not against his word; **107:11** they *r.* against the words of God, and contemned the counsel of the most High; **Prov. 17:11** an evil man seeketh only *r.*: therefore a cruel messenger shall be sent against him; **Isa. 1:2-3** I have nourished and brought up children, and they have *r.* against me; **1:20** if ye refuse and *r.*, ye shall be devoured with the sword: for the mouth of the LORD hath spoken it; **1:23** thy princes are *r.*, and companions of thieves: every one loveth gifts, and followeth after rewards; **30:1** woe to the *r.* children, saith the LORD, that take counsel, but not of me; **30:9** this is a *r.* people, lying children, children that will not hear the law of the LORD;

50:5 the Lord GOD hath opened mine ear, and I was not *r.*, neither turned away back; **63:10** they *r.*, and vexed his holy Spirit: therefore he was turned to be their enemy, and he fought against them; **65:2** I have spread out my hands all the day unto a *r.* people, which walketh in a way that was not good, after their own thoughts; **Jer. 4:17** they [are] against her round about; because she hath been *r.* against me, saith the LORD; **5:23** this people hath a revolting and a *r.* heart; they are revolted and gone; **28:16** I will cast thee from off the face of the earth: this year thou shalt die, because thou hast taught *r.* against the LORD; **Lam. 1:18** the LORD is righteous; for I have *r.* against his commandment: hear, I pray you, all people, and behold my sorrow; **1:20** I am in distress: my bowels are troubled; mine heart is turned within me; for I have grievously *r.*; **3:40-42** let us lift up our heart with our hands unto God in the heavens. We have transgressed and have *r.*: thou hast not pardoned; **Ezek. 2:3-8** thou shalt speak my words unto them, whether they will hear, or whether they will forbear: for they are most *r.*. But thou, son of man, hear what I say unto thee; Be not thou *r.*; **3:9** as an adamant harder than flint have I made thy forehead: fear them not, neither be dismayed at their looks, though they be a *r.* house; **3:26-27** I will make thy tongue cleave to the roof of thy mouth, that thou shalt be dumb, and shalt not be to them a reprover: for they are a *r.* house; **12:2-3** thou dwellest in the midst of a *r.* house, which have eyes to see, and see not; they have ears to hear, and hear not: for they are a *r.* house; **12:9-11** hath not the house of Israel, the *r.* house, said unto thee, What doest thou? Say thou unto them, Thus saith the Lord GOD; **12:25** O *r.* house, will I say the word, and will perform it, saith the Lord GOD; **17:12** say now to the *r.* house, Know ye not what these things mean; **20:8** they *r.* against me, and would not hearken unto me... I will pour out my fury upon them; **20:13** the house of Israel *r.* against me in the wilderness: they walked not in my statutes, and they despised my judgments, which if a man do, he shall even live in them; **20:38** I will purge out from among you the *r.*s, and them that transgress against me; **24:3** utter a parable unto the *r.* house, and say unto them, Thus saith the Lord GOD; Set on a pot, set it on, and also pour water into it; **44:6** thou shalt say to the *r.*, even to the house of Israel, Thus saith the Lord GOD; O ye house of Israel, let it suffice you of all your abominations; **Dan. 2:3** I send thee to the children of Israel, to a *r.* nation that hath *r.* against me: they and their fathers have transgressed against me; **2:5** whether they will hear, or whether they will forbear, [for they are a

r. house,] yet shall know that there hath been a prophet among them; **2:7-8** thou shalt speak my words unto them, whether they will hear, or whether they will forbear: for they are most *r.*; **9:5** we have sinned, and have committed iniquity, and have done wickedly, and have *r.*, even by departing from thy precepts and from thy judgments; **9:9** to the Lord our God belong mercies and forgivenesses, though we have *r.* against him; **Hosea 7:14** they have not cried unto me with their heart, when they howled upon their beds: they assemble themselves for corn and wine, and they *r.* against me; **13:15-16** Samaria shall become desolate; for she hath *r.* against her God: they shall fall by the sword.

God forbid that we should rebel against the LORD, and turn this day from following the LORD. Josh 22:29 (*see also* Turn)

Num. 14:9 *r.* not ye against the LORD, neither fear ye the people of the land; **20:24** he shall not enter into the land which I have given unto the children of Israel, because ye *r.* against my word; **27:14** ye *r.* against my commandment in the desert of Zin, in the strife of the congregation, to sanctify me at the water before their eyes; **Deut. 1:26** ye would not go up, but *r.* against the commandment of the LORD your God; **1:43** I spake unto you; and ye would not hear, but *r.* against the commandment of the LORD; **9:7** forget not, how thou provokedst the LORD thy God to wrath in the wilderness: from the day that thou didst depart out of the land of Egypt, until ye came unto this place, ye have been *r.* against the LORD; **9:23-24** ye *r.* against the commandment of the LORD your God, and ye believed him not, nor hearkened to his voice. Ye have been *r.* against the LORD from the day that I knew you; **21:18-20** they shall say unto the elders of his city, This our son is stubborn and *r.*, he will not obey our voice; he is a glutton, and a drunkard; **31:27** I know thy *r.*, and thy stiff neck: behold, while I am yet alive with you this day, ye have been *r.* against the LORD; and how much more after my death; **Josh. 1:18** whosoever he be that doth *r.* against thy commandment, and will not hearken unto thy words in all that thou commandest him, he shall be put to death; **22:16-19** what trespass is this that ye have committed against the God of Israel, to turn away this day from following the LORD, in that ye have builded you an altar, that ye might *r.* this day against the LORD; **22:29** God forbid that we should *r.* against the LORD, and turn this day from following the LORD; **Judg. 2:19** they returned, and corrupted themselves more than their fathers, in following other gods to serve them, and to bow down unto them; they ceased not from their own doings, nor from their stubborn way; **1 Sam. 12:14-15** if ye will fear the LORD, and serve him, and obey his voice, and not *r*. against the commandment of the LORD, then shall both ye and also the king that reigneth over you continue following the LORD; **Ezra 4:12** the Jews which came up from thee to us are come unto Jerusalem, building the *r*. and the bad city, and have set up the walls thereof; **4:15** know that this city is a *r*. city, and hurtful unto kings and provinces, and that they have moved sedition within the same of old time; **Neh. 9:26** they were disobedient, and *r*. against thee, and cast thy law behind their backs; **Job 24:13** they are of those that *r*. against the light; they know not the ways thereof, nor abide in the paths thereof; **Ps. 5:10** destroy thou them, O God; let them fall by their own counsels; cast them out in the multitude of their transgressions; for they have *r*. against thee; **66:7** he ruleth by his power for ever; his eyes behold the nations: let not the *r*. exalt themselves; **68:6** God setteth the solitary in families: he bringeth out those which are bound with chains: but the *r*. dwell in a dry land; **78:8** might not be as their fathers, a stubborn and *r*. generation; a generation that set not their heart aright, and whose spirit was not stedfast with God; **107:11** they *r*. against the words of God, and contemned the counsel of the most High; **Prov. 7:11-12** she is loud and stubborn; her feet abide not in her house: Now is she without, now in the streets, and lieth in wait at every corner; **23:21** the drunkard and the glutton shall come to poverty: and drowsiness shall clothe a man with rags; **26:9** as a thorn goeth up into the hand of a drunkard, so is a parable in the mouth of fools; **Eccl. 10:17** blessed art thou, O land, when thy king is the son of nobles, and thy princes eat in due season, for strength, and not for drunkenness; **Isa. 1:2** the LORD hath spoken, I have nourished and brought up children, and they have *r*. against me; **1:20** if ye refuse and *r*., ye shall be devoured with the sword: for the mouth of the LORD hath spoken it; **1:23** thy princes are *r*., and companions of thieves: every one loveth gifts, and followeth after rewards; **5:11** woe unto them that rise up early in the morning, that they may follow strong drink; that continue until night, till wine inflame them; **22:13** behold joy and gladness, slaying oxen, and killing sheep, eating flesh, and drinking wine: let us eat and drink; for to morrow we shall die; **28:1** woe to the crown of pride, to the drunkards of Ephraim, whose glorious beauty is a fading flower, which are on the head of the fat valleys

of them that are overcome with wine; **28:3-4** the crown of pride, the drunkards of Ephraim, shall be trodden under feet; **28:7** they also have erred through wine, and through strong drink are out of the way; the priest and the prophet have erred through strong drink, they are swallowed up of wine; **30:1** woe to the *r*. children, saith the LORD, that take counsel, but not of me; **30:9** this is a *r*. people, lying children, children that will not hear the law of the LORD; **30:12** ye despise this word, and trust in oppression and perverseness, and stay thereon; **50:5** the Lord GOD hath opened mine ear, and I was not *r*., neither turned away back; **63:10** they *r*., and vexed his holy Spirit: therefore he was turned to be their enemy, and he fought against them; **65:2** I have spread out my hands all the day unto a *r*. people, which walketh in a way that was not good, after their own thoughts; **Jer. 4:17** as keepers of a field, are they against her round about; because she hath been *r*. against me, saith the LORD; **5:23** this people hath a revolting and a *r*. heart; they are revolted and gone; **Lam. 1:18** the LORD is righteous; for I have *r*. against his commandment: hear, I pray you, all people, and behold my sorrow; **1:20** I am in distress: my bowels are troubled; mine heart is turned within me; for I have grievously *r*.; **3:42** we have transgressed and have *r*.: thou hast not pardoned; **Ezek. 2:3-8** I send thee to the children of Israel, to a *r*. nation that hath *r*. against me: they and their fathers have transgressed against me; **3:9** fear them not, neither be dismayed at their looks, though they be a *r*. house; **3:26-27** I will make thy tongue cleave to the roof of thy mouth, that thou shalt be dumb, and shalt not be to them a reprover: for they are a *r*. house; **12:2-3** thou dwellest in the midst of a *r*. house, which have eyes to see, and see not; they have ears to hear, and hear not: for they are a *r*. house; **12:9** hath not the house of Israel, the *r*. house, said unto thee, What doest thou; **17:12** say now to the *r*. house, Know ye not what these things mean; **20:8** they *r*. against me, and would not hearken unto me: they did not every man cast away the abominations of their eyes, neither did they forsake the idols of Egypt: then I said, I will pour out my fury upon them; **20:21** the children *r*. against me: they walked not in my statutes, neither kept my judgments to do them, which if a man do, he shall even live in them; **20:38** I will purge out from among you the *r*.s, and them that transgress against me; **44:6** thou shalt say to the *r*., even to the house of Israel, Thus saith the Lord GOD; O ye house of Israel, let it suffice you of all your abominations; **Dan. 9:5** we have sinned, and have committed iniquity, and have done wickedly, and have *r.*, even by departing from thy precepts and from thy judgments; **9:9** to the Lord our God belong mercies and forgivenesses, though we have *r.* against him; **Hosea 7:14** they have not cried unto me with their heart, when they howled upon their beds: they assemble themselves for corn and wine, and they *r.* against me; **13:16** Samaria shall become desolate; for she hath *r.* against her God: they shall fall by the sword; **Joel 1:5** awake, ye drunkards, and weep; and howl, all ye drinkers of wine, because of the new wine; for it is cut off from your mouth.

REBUKE (*see also* Chasten, Reproach)

Rebuke not an elder, but intreat him as a father; and the younger men as brethren; The elder women as mothers; the younger as sisters, with all purity. 1 Tim. 5 1-2 (*see also* Elder, Entreat, Young)

When Jesus saw that the people came running together, he rebuked the foul spirit, saying unto him, Thou dumb and deaf spirit, I charge thee, come out of him, and enter no more into him. Mark 9:25 (*see also* Deaf, Dumb)

This witness is true. Wherefore rebuke them sharply, that they may be sound in the faith. Titus 1:13 (*see also* Sound)

It is better to hear the rebuke of the wise, than for a man to hear the song of fools. Eccl. 7:5 (*see also* Better)

Prov. 24:24-25 to them that *r.* him shall be delight, and a good blessing shall come upon them; **27:5** open *r.* is better than secret love; **28:23** he that *r.* a man afterwards shall find more favour than he that flattereth with the tongue; **Eccl. 7:5** it is better to hear the *r.* of the wise, than for a man to hear the song of fools.

Them that sin rebuke before all, that others also may fear. 1 Tim. 5:20

1 Tim 5:20 them that sin *r.* before all, that others also may fear; **Titus 1:13** This witness is true. Wherefore *r.* them sharply, that they may be sound in the faith.

LORD, **thou knowest: remember me, and visit me, and revenge me of my persecutors; take me not away in thy longsuffering: know that for thy sake I have suffered rebuke. Jer. 15:15** (*see also* Longsuffering, Sake, Remember)

Jer. 15:15 LORD, thou knowest: remember me, and visit me, and revenge me of my persecutors; take me not away in thy longsuffering: know that for thy sake I have suffered *r.* **15:20-21** they shall fight against thee, but they shall not prevail against thee: for I am with thee to save thee and to deliver thee, saith the LORD. And I will deliver thee out of the hand of the wicked.

RECEIVE

They received the word with all readiness of mind, and searched the scriptures daily, whether those things were so. Acts 17:11 (*see also* Daily, Mind, Readiness, Scripture, Search, Word)

He that receiveth you receiveth me, and he that receiveth me receiveth him that sent me. He that receiveth a prophet in the name of a prophet shall receive a prophet's reward; and he that receiveth a righteous man in the name of a righteous man shall receive a righteous man's reward. Matt. 10:40-41 (*see also* Prophet, Reward, Serve)

RECKON (*see also* Account, Record)

My God put into mine heart to gather together the nobles, and the rulers, and the people, that they might be reckoned by genealogy. Neh. 7:5 (*see also* Genealogy)

Knowing that Christ being raised from the dead dieth no more; death hath no more dominion over him. For in that he died, he died unto sin once: but in that he liveth, he liveth unto God. Likewise reckon ye also yourselves to be dead indeed unto sin, but alive unto God through Jesus Christ our Lord. Rom. 6:9-11 (*see also* Alive, Jesus Christ, Sin)

RECOMPENSE (*see also* Avenge, Pay, Render, Reward, Vengeance)

Flee out of the midst of Babylon, and deliver every man his soul; be not cut off in her iniquity; for this is the time of the LORD's **vengeance; he will render unto her a recompense. Jer. 51:6** (*see also* Iniquity)

Thou hast not remembered the days of thy youth, but hast fretted me in all these things; behold, therefore I also will recompense thy way upon thine head, saith the Lord GOD. **Ezek. 16:43** (*see also* Remember, Youth)

Say not thou, I will recompense evil; but wait on the LORD, and he shall save thee. Prov. 20:22

Prov. 20:22 say not thou, I will *r.* evil; but wait on the LORD, and he shall save thee; **Isa. 64:4** since the beginning of the world men have not heard, nor perceived by the ear, neither hath the eye seen, O God, beside thee, what he hath prepared for him that waiteth for him; **Jer. 18:20** shall evil be *r.* for good? for they have digged a pit for my soul; **Ezek. 25:12-13** because that Edom hath dealt against the house of Judah by taking vengeance, and hath greatly offended, and revenged himself upon them; Therefore thus saith the Lord GOD; I will also stretch out mine hand upon Edom, and will cut off man and beast from it; **25:15** thus saith the Lord GOD... the Philistines have dealt by revenge, and have taken vengeance with a despiteful heart, to destroy it for the old hatred.

RECONCILE, RECONCILED, RECONCILIATION (*see also* Atone, Redeem)

Be ye reconciled to God. 2 Cor. 5:20

Unto the married I command, yet not I, but the Lord, Let not the wife depart from her husband: But and if she depart, let her remain unmarried, or be reconciled to her husband: and let not the husband put away his wife. 1 Cor. 7:10-11 (*see also* Husband, Wife)

If thou bring thy gift to the altar, and there rememberest that thy brother hath ought against thee; Leave there thy gift before the altar, and go thy way; first be reconciled to thy brother, and then come and offer thy gift. Matt. 5:23-24 (*see also* Gift, Offer)

RECORD, RECORDED (*see also* Account, Book, Sayings, Scripture, Write)

Many other signs truly did Jesus in the presence of his disciples, which are not written in this book: But these are written, that ye might believe that Jesus is the Christ, the Son of God; and that believing ye might have life through his name. John 20:30-31 (*see also* Belief)

Matt. 13:52 every scribe which is instructed unto the kingdom of heaven is like unto a man that is an householder, which bringeth forth out of his treasure things new and old; **John 20:30-**

31 many other signs truly did Jesus in the presence of his disciples, which are not written in this book: But these are written, that ye might believe that Jesus is the Christ, the Son of God; and that believing ye might have life through his name; **21:24-25** this is the disciple which testifieth of these things, and wrote these things: and we know that his testimony is true. And there are also many other things which Jesus did, the which, if they should be written every one, I suppose that even the world itself could not contain the books that should be written; **2 Cor. 13:10** I write these things being absent, lest being present I should use sharpness, according to the power which the Lord hath given me to edification, and not to destruction; **2 Tim. 4:13** the cloke that I left at Troas with Carpus, when thou comest, bring with thee, and the books, but especially the parchments; **Rev. 1:11** I am Alpha and Omega, the first and the last: and, What thou seest, write in a book, and send it unto the seven churches which are in Asia; **1:19** write the things which thou hast seen, and the things which are, and the things which shall be hereafter; **19:9** he saith unto me, Write, Blessed are they which are called unto the marriage supper of the Lamb. And he saith unto me, These are the true sayings of God; **21:5** write: for these words are true and faithful; **22:7-10** blessed is he that keepeth the sayings of the prophecy of this book. And I John saw these things, and heard them... then saith he unto me, See thou do it not: for I am thy fellowservant, and of thy brethren the prophets, and of them which keep the sayings of this book: worship God. And he saith unto me, Seal not the sayings of the prophecy of this book: for the time is at hand.

Now go, write it before them in a table, and note it in a book, that it may be before the time to come for ever and ever. Isa. 30:8 (*see also* Write)

Gen. 5:1 this is the book of the generations of Adam; **Ex. 17:14** write this for a memorial in a book, and rehearse it in the ears of Joshua; **24:4** Moses wrote all the words of the LORD; **24:7** he took the book of the covenant, and read in the audience of the people; **34:27** write thou these words: for after the tenor of these words I have made a covenant with thee and with Israel; **Num. 33:2** Moses wrote their goings out according to their journeys by the commandment of the LORD; **Deut. 17:18** he shall write him a copy of this law in a book; **27:3** thou shalt write upon them all the words of this law, when thou art passed over, that thou mayest go in unto the land which the

LORD thy God giveth thee; **27:8** thou shalt write upon the stones all the words of this law very plainly; **30:19** I call heaven and earth to record this day against you, that I have set before you life and death, blessing and cursing; **31:19** write ye this song for you, and teach it the children of Israel: put it in their mouths, that this song may be a witness for me against the children of Israel; **31:24-26** when Moses had made an end of writing the words of this law in a book... Moses commanded the Levites, which bare the ark of the covenant of the LORD, saying, Take this book of the law; **Josh.24:26** Joshua wrote these words in the book of the law of God; **1 Chron. 16:4** he appointed certain of the Levites to minister before the ark of the LORD, and to *r.*, and to thank and praise the LORD God of Israel; **Ezra 4:15** that search may be made in the book of the *r.* of thy fathers: so shalt thou find in the book of the *r.*; **5:17** let there be search made in the kings treasure house, which is there at Babylon, whether it be so... and let the king send his pleasure to us concerning this matter; **6:1-2** search was made in the house of the rolls, where the treasures were laid up in Babylon. And there was found... in the palace... a roll, and therein was a *r.* thus written; **Neh. 9:38** because of all this we make a sure covenant, and write it; and... seal unto it; **Esther 6:1** he commanded to bring the book of *r.* of the chronicles; and they were read before the king; **Job 16:19** my witness is in heaven, and my *r.* is on high; **19:23-24** oh that my words were now written! oh that they were printed in a book! That they were graven with an iron pen and lead in the rock for ever; **Ps. 76:11** in Judah is God known:

his name is great in Israel; **Prov. 3:3** let not mercy and truth forsake thee: bind them about thy neck; write them upon the table of thine heart; **7:3** bind them upon thy fingers, write them upon the table of thine heart; **Isa. 8:1-2** the LORD said unto me, Take thee a great roll, and write in it with a mans pen... And I took unto me faithful witnesses to *r.*; **8:16** bind up the testimony, seal the law among my disciples; **30:8** go, write it before them in a table, and note it in a book, that it may be for the time to come for ever and ever; **Jer. 25:13** I will bring upon that land all my words which I have pronounced against it, even all that is written in this book; **30:2** write thee all the words that I have spoken unto thee in a book; **36:2-6** take thee a roll of a book, and write therein all the words that I have spoken unto thee against Israel, and against Judah, and against all the nations, from the day I spake unto thee; **36:14** take in thine hand the roll wherein thou hast read in the ears of the people, and come;

36:17-18 he pronounced all these words unto me with his mouth, and I wrote them with ink in the book; **36:28** take thee again another roll, and write in it all the former words that were in the first roll; **36:32** [he] wrote therein from the mouth of Jeremiah all the words of the book which... had burned in the fire: and there were added besides unto them many like words; **45:1-5** the word that Jeremiah the prophet spake... when he had written these words in a book at the mouth of Jeremiah; **Ezek. 2:9-10** when I looked, behold, an hand was sent unto me; and, lo, a roll of a book was therein; And he spread it before me; and it was written within and without; **9:11** the man clothed with linen, which had the inkhorn by his side, reported the matter, saying, I have done as thou hast commanded me; **10:2** go in between the wheels, even under the cherub, and fill thine hand with coals of fire from between the cherubims, and scatter them over the city; **10:6** take fire from between the wheels, from between the cherubims; then he went in, and stood beside the wheels; **13:9** they shall not be in the assembly of my people, neither shall they be written in the writing of the house of Israel; **37:16** take thee one stick, and write upon it, For Judah, and for the children of Israel his companions: then take another stick, and write upon it, For Joseph, the stick of Ephraim, and for all the house of Israel his companions; **43:11** write it in their sight, that they may keep the whole form thereof, and all the ordinances thereof, and do them; **Dan. 7:10** ten thousand times ten thousand stood before him: the judgment was set, and the books were opened; **10:21** I will shew thee that which is noted in the scripture of truth; **Haba 2:2** write the vision, and make it plain upon tables, that he may run that readeth it; **Mal. 3:16** a book of remembrance was written before him for them that feared the LORD.

REDEEM, REDEEMER, REDEMPTION
(*see also* Deliver, Jesus Christ, Restore, Save)

Ye know that ye were not redeemed with corruptible things, as silver and gold, from your vain conversation received by tradition from your fathers. 1 Pet. 1:18 (*see also* Conversation, Corrupt, Tradition)

They that trust in their wealth, and boast themselves in the multitude of their riches; None of them can by any means redeem his brother. Ps. 49:6-7 (*see also* Boast, Rich)

REFINE, REFINER (*see also* Affliction, Purify, Sanctify)

Behold, I have refined thee, but not with silver; I have chosen thee in the furnace of affliction. Isa. 48:10 (*see also* Afflict, Furnace)

REFRAIN (*see also* Repent, Turn)

I have preached righteousness in the great congregation: lo, I have not refrained my lips, O LORD, thou knowest. Ps. 40:9 (*see also* Preach)

REFUSE (*see also* Reject)

Poverty and shame shall be to him that refuseth instruction: but he that regardeth reproof shall be honoured. Prov. 13:18 (*see also* Instruct)

REGARD (*see also* Hearken, Heed, Respect)

How much less to him that accepteth not the persons of princes, nor regard the rich more than the poor? for they all are the work of his hands. Job 34:19 (*see also* Equal)

Because they regard not the works of the LORD, nor the operation of his hands, he shall destroy them, and not build them up. Ps. 28:5 (*see also* Operation, Works)

REJECT (*see also* Apostasy, Disobey, Refuse, Repent)

Full well ye reject the commandment of God, that ye may keep your own traditions. Mark 7:9 (*see also* Tradition)

The wise men are ashamed, they are dismayed and taken: lo, they have rejected the word of the LORD; and what wisdom is in them? Jer. 8:9 (*see also* Word)

REJOICE (*see also* Joy, Glory, Happiness, Praise, Sing)

Let Israel rejoice in him that made him: let the children of Zion be joyful in their King. Let them praise his name in the dance: let them sing praises unto him with the timbrel and harp. Ps. 149:2-3 (*see also* King)

This is the day which the LORD hath made; we will rejoice and be glad in it. Ps. 118:24 (*see also* Day, Today)

Rejoice [not] to do evil, and delight in the frowardness of the wicked. Prov. 2:14 (*see also* Evil)

Rejoice not when thine enemy falleth, and let not thine heart be glad when he stumbleth: Lest the LORD see it, and it displease him, and he turn away his wrath from him. Prov. 24:17-18 (*see also* Enemy, Fail)

I perceive that there is nothing better, than that a man should rejoice in his own works. Eccl. 3:22 (*see also* Work)

Rejoice, O young man in thy youth; and let thy heart cheer thee in the days of thy youth, and walk in the ways of thine heart, and in the sight of thine eyes. Eccl. 11:9 (*see also* Walk, Youth)

Thou shouldest not have looked on the day of thy brother in the day that he became a stranger; neither shouldest thou have rejoiced over the children of Judah in the day of their destruction; neither shouldest thou have spoken proudly in the day of distress. Obad. 1:12 (*see also* Destroy)

Charity suffereth long, and is kind; charity envieth not; charity vaunteth not itself, is not puffed up, Doth not behave itself unseemly, seeketh not her own, is not easily provoked, thinketh no evil; Rejoiceth not in iniquity, but rejoiceth in the truth; Beareth all things, believeth all things, hopeth all things, endureth all things. 1 Cor. 13:4-7 (*see also* All Things, Bear, Believe, Charity, Endure, Hope, Provoke, Seek, Suffer, Think)

Let the heavens be glad, and the earth rejoice: and let men say among the nations, the LORD reigneth. 1 Chron. 16:31 (*see also* Nation)

1 Chron. 16:31-33 let the heavens be glad, and let the earth *r.*: and let men say among the nations, The LORD reigneth; **2 Chron. 6:41** arise, O LORD God, into thy resting place, thou, and the ark of thy strength: let thy priests, O LORD God, be clothed with salvation, and let thy saints *r.* in goodness; **30:21** the children of Israel that were present at Jerusalem kept the feast of unleavened bread seven days with great gladness: and the Levites and the priests praised the LORD day by day; **30:23** the whole assembly took counsel to keep other seven days: and they kept other seven days with gladness; **Ezra 3:12-13** many shouted aloud for joy: So that the people could not discern the noise of the shout of joy from the noise of the weeping of the people; **Job 38:7** the morning stars sang together, and all the sons of God shouted for joy; **Ps. 5:11** let all those that put their trust in thee *r.*: let them ever shout for joy, because thou defendest them: let them also that love thy name be joyful in thee; **16:9** my heart is glad, and my glory *r.*: my flesh also shall rest in hope; **21:1** the king shall joy in thy strength, O LORD; and in thy salvation how greatly shall he *r.*; **32:11** be glad in the LORD, and *r.*, ye righteous: and shout for joy, all ye that are upright in heart; **33:1** *r.* in the LORD, O ye righteous: for praise is comely for the upright; **64:10** the righteous shall be glad in the LORD, and shall trust in him; and all the upright in heart shall glory; **68:3** let the righteous be glad; let them *r.* before God: yea, let them exceedingly *r.*; **70:4** let all those that seek thee *r.* and be glad in thee: and let such as love thy salvation say continually, Let God be magnified; **89:16** in thy name shall they *r.* all the day: and in thy righteousness shall they be exalted; **90:14** satisfy us early with thy mercy; that we may *r.* and be glad all our days; **96:11-12** let the heavens *r.*, and let the earth be glad; let the sea roar, and the fulness thereof. Let the field be joyful, and all that is therein: then shall all the trees of the wood *r.*; **97:1** the LORD reigneth; let the earth *r.*; let the multitude of isles be glad thereof; **97:8** Zion heard, and was glad; and the daughters of Judah *r.* because of thy judgments, O LORD; **98:4-9** make a joyful noise unto the LORD, all the earth: make a loud noise, and *r.*, and sing praise; **149:2** let Israel *r.* in him that made him: let the children of Zion be joyful in their King; **Prov. 28:12** when righteous men do *r.*, there is great glory: but when the wicked rise, a man is hidden; **Isa. 41:16** thou shalt fan them, and the wind shall carry them away, and the whirlwind shall scatter them: and thou shalt *r.* in the LORD, and shalt glory in the Holy One of Israel; **61:10** I will greatly *r.* in the LORD, my soul shall be joyful in my God; for he hath clothed me with the garments of salvation, he hath covered me with the robe of righteousness; **65:18** be ye glad and *r.* for ever in that which I create: for, behold, I create Jerusalem a *r.*, and her people a joy; **66:10-11** *r.* ye with Jerusalem, and be glad with her, all ye that love her: *r.* for joy with her, all ye that mourn for her; **Joel 2:23-25** be glad then, ye children of Zion, and *r.* in the LORD your God; **Zech. 9:9** *r.* greatly, O daughter of Zion; shout, O daughter of Jerusalem: behold, thy King cometh unto thee; **10:7** their heart shall *r.* as through wine: yea, their children shall see it, and be glad; their heart shall *r.* in the LORD.

Rejoice in goodness. 2 Chron. 6:41 (*see also* Goodness)

2 Chron. 6:41 arise, O LORD God, into thy resting place, thou, and the ark of thy strength: let thy priests, O LORD God, be clothed with salvation, and let thy saints *r.* in goodness; **Ps. 23:6** goodness and mercy shall follow me all the days of my life: and I will dwell in the house of the LORD for ever; **Haba 3:18** I will *r.* in the LORD, I will joy in the God of my salvation.

My soul shall be joyful in the LORD: it shall rejoice in his salvation. Ps. 35:9 (*see also* Salvation)

Ps. 35:9 my soul shall be joyful in the LORD: it shall *r.* in his salvation; **38:22** make haste to help me, O Lord my salvation; **40:16** let all those that seek thee *r.* and be glad in thee: let such as love thy salvation say continually, The LORD be magnified; **78:22** they believed not in God, and trusted not in his salvation; **118:14-15** the LORD is my strength and song, and is become my salvation. The voice of *r.* and salvation is in the tabernacles of the righteous; **118:21** I will praise thee: for thou hast heard me, and art become my salvation; **119:81** my soul fainteth for thy salvation: but I hope in thy word; **Jer. 3:23** truly in vain is salvation hoped for from the hills, and from the multitude of mountains: truly in the LORD our God is the salvation of Israel.

We also joy in God through our Lord Jesus Christ, by whom we have now received the atonement. Rom. 5:11

Matt. 2:9 when they saw the star, they *r.* with exceeding great joy; **13:20** the kingdom of heaven is like unto treasure hid in a field; the which when a man hath found, he hideth, and for joy thereof goeth and selleth all that he hath, and buyeth that field; **Mark 11:7-9** they that followed, cried, saying, Hosanna; Blessed is he that cometh in the name of the Lord; **Luke 1:64** his mouth was opened immediately, and his tongue loosed, and he spake, and praised God; **2:13** suddenly there was with the angel a multitude of the heavenly host praising God; **2:28** then took he him up in his arms, and blessed God; **2:38** she coming in that instant gave thanks likewise unto the Lord, and spake of him to all them that looked for redemption in Jerusalem; **6:23** *r.* ye in that day, and leap for joy: for, behold, your reward is great in heaven: for in the like manner did their fathers unto the prophets; **13:35** blessed is he that cometh in the name of the Lord; **17:15-17** with a loud voice glorified God, And fell down on his face at his feet, giving him thanks; **19:37-40** blessed be the King that cometh in the name of the Lord: peace in heaven, and glory in the highest. And some of the Pharisees from among the multitude said unto him, Master, rebuke thy disciples. And he answered and said unto them, I tell you that, if these should hold their peace, the stones would immediately cry out; **John 3:29** *r.* greatly because of the bridegroom's voice: this my joy therefore is fulfilled; **16:20-24** whatsoever ye shall ask the Father in my name, he will give it you. Hitherto have ye asked nothing in my name: ask, and ye shall receive, that your joy may be full; **12:16** these things understood not his disciples at the first: but when Jesus was glorified, then remembered they that these things were written of him, and that they had done these things unto him; **17:13-14** I speak in the world, that they might have my joy fulfilled in themselves; **Acts 2:28** thou hast made known to me the ways of life; thou shalt make me full of joy with thy countenance; **2:47** praising God, and having favour with all the people. And the Lord added to the church daily such as should be saved; **3:8-9** he leaping up stood, and walked, and entered with them into the temple, walking, and leaping, and praising God. And all the people saw him walking and praising God; **4:21** all men glorified God for that which was done; **4:24** they lifted up their voice to God with one accord, and said, Lord, thou art God, which hast made heaven, and earth, and the sea, and all that in them is; **5:41** they departed from the presence of the council, rejoicing that they were counted worthy to suffer shame for his name; **8:39** And when they were come up out of the water, the Spirit of the Lord caught away Philip, that the eunuch saw him no more: and he went on his way rejoicing; **10:46** they heard them speak with tongues, and magnify God; **11:18** when they heard these things, they held their peace, and glorified God, saying, Then hath God also to the Gentiles granted repentance unto life; **13:48** when the Gentiles heard this, they were glad, and glorified the word of the Lord: and as many as were ordained to eternal life believed; **13:52** the disciples were filled with joy, and with the Holy Ghost; **15:3** declaring the conversion of the Gentiles: and they caused great joy unto all the brethren; **15:31** when they had read, they *r.* for the consolation; **16:25** at midnight Paul and Silas prayed, and sang praises unto God: and the prisoners heard them; **16:34** he set meat before them, and *r.*, believing in God with all his house; **21:20** when they heard it, they glorified the

Lord; **28:15** when Paul saw, he thanked God, and took courage; **Rom. 1:8** I thank my God through Jesus Christ for you all, that your faith is spoken of throughout the whole world; **5:11** we also joy in God through our Lord Jesus Christ, by whom we have now received the atonement; **7:22** I delight in the law of God after the inward man; **7:25** I thank God through Jesus Christ our Lord; **11:36** for of him, and through him, and to him, are all things: to whom be glory for ever; **14:6** he that regardeth the day, regardeth it unto the Lord; and he that regardeth not the day, to the Lord he doth not regard it. He that eateth, eateth to the Lord, for he giveth God thanks; and he that eateth not, to the Lord he eateth not, and giveth God thanks; **15:9-11** the Gentiles might glorify God for his mercy; as it is written, For this cause I will confess to thee among the Gentiles, and sing unto thy name. And again he saith, *r.*, ye Gentiles, with his people. And again, Praise the Lord, all ye Gentiles; and laud him, all ye people; **1 Cor. 1:4** I thank my God always on your behalf, for the grace of God which is given you by Jesus Christ; **6:20** ye are bought with a price: therefore glorify God in your body, and in your spirit, which are God's; **15:57** thanks be to God, which giveth us the victory through our Lord Jesus Christ; **2 Cor. 1:3** blessed be God, even the Father of our Lord Jesus Christ, the Father of mercies, and the God of all comfort; **1:10** who delivered us from so great a death, and doth deliver: in whom we trust that he will yet deliver us; **2:14** thanks be unto God, which always causeth us to triumph in Christ, and maketh manifest the savour of his knowledge by us in every place; **6:10** sorrowful, yet alway rejoicing; as poor, yet making many rich; as having nothing, and yet possessing all things; being enriched in every thing to all bountifulness, which causeth through us thanksgiving to God. For the administration of this service not only supplieth the want of the saints, but is abundant also by many thanksgivings unto God; **10:17** he that glorieth, let him glory in the Lord; **11:10** as the truth of Christ is in me, no man shall stop me of this boasting; **12:1** it is not expedient for me doubtless to glory. I will come to visions and revelations of the Lord; **Gal. 1:5** to whom be glory for ever and ever; **Eph. 1:12** we should be to the praise of his glory, who first trusted in Christ; **3:21** unto him be glory in the church by Christ Jesus throughout all ages, world without end; **5:4** giving of thanks; **5:19-20** speaking to yourselves in psalms and hymns and spiritual songs, singing and making melody in your heart to the Lord; Giving thanks always for all things unto God and the Father in the name of our Lord Jesus Christ; **Philip. 1:4** I thank my God, making mention of thee always in my prayers; **1:26** that your rejoicing may be more abundant in Jesus Christ for me by my coming to you again; **2:16** holding forth the word of life; that I may *r.* in the day of Christ, that I have not run in vain, neither laboured in vain; **3:1** *r.* in the Lord; **4:4** *r.* in the Lord alway: and again I say, *r*; **4:10** I *r.* in the Lord greatly, that now at the last your care of me hath flourished again; **4:20** now unto God and our Father be glory for ever and ever; **Col. 1:3** we give thanks to God and the Father of our Lord Jesus Christ, praying always for you; **1:12-13** giving thanks unto the Father, which hath made us meet to be partakers of the inheritance of the saints in light; **2:7** rooted and built up in him, and stablished in the faith, as ye have been taught, abounding therein with thanksgiving; **3:15** let the peace of God rule in your hearts, to the which also ye are called in one body; and be ye thankful; **1 Thes. 1:2** we give thanks to God always for you all, making mention of you in our prayers; **3:9** what thanks can we render to God again for you, for all the joy wherewith we joy for your sakes before our God; **1 Tim. 1:17** now unto the King eternal, immortal, invisible, the only wise God, be honour and glory for ever and ever; **2:1** first of all, supplications, prayers, intercessions, and giving of thanks, be made for all men; **Heb. 13:15** let us offer the sacrifice of praise to God continually, that is, the fruit of our lips giving thanks to his name; **James 3:7-9** bless we God, even the Father; and therewith curse we men, which are made after the similitude of God; **1 Pet. 5:11** be glory and dominion for ever and ever; **Jude 1:25** to the only wise God our Saviour, be glory and majesty, dominion and power, both now and ever; **Rev. 4:11** receive glory and honour and power; **5:12-13** blessing, and honour, and glory, and power, be unto him that sitteth upon the throne, and unto the Lamb for ever and ever; **11:16-17** we give thee thanks, O Lord God Almighty, which art, and wast, and art to come; because thou hast taken to thee thy great power, and hast reigned; **14:7** worship him that made heaven, and earth, and the sea, and the fountains of waters; **15:3** great and marvellous are thy works, Lord God Almighty; just and true are thy ways, thou King of saints; **19:1** I heard a great voice of much people in heaven, saying, Alleluia; Salvation, and glory, and honour, and power, unto the Lord our God; **19:5** praise our God, all ye his servants, and ye that fear him, both small and great; **19:7** give honour to him:

for the marriage of the Lamb is come, and his wife hath made herself ready.

RELIEF, RELIEVE (*see also* Almsgiving, Charity, Serve)

Learn to do well; seek judgment, relieve the oppressed, judge the fatherless, plead for the widow. Isa. 1:17 (*see also* Do, Learn, Judge, Plead)

Isa. 1:17 learn to do well; seek judgment, relieve the oppressed, judge the fatherless, plead for the widow; **10:2** to turn aside the needy from judgment, and to take away the right from the poor of my people, that widows may be their prey, and that they may rob the fatherless.

REMEMBER, REMEMBERANCE

Remember ye the law of Moses my servant, which I commanded unto him in Horeb for all Israel, with the statutes and judgments. Mal. 4:4 (*see also* Command)

Remember his holy covenant. Luke 1:72 (*see also* Covenant)

Remember the name of the LORD our God. Ps. 20:7 (*see also* Name)

Remember these, O Jacob and Israel; for thou art my servant: I have formed thee; thou art my servant; O Israel, thou shalt not be forgotten of me. Isa. 44:21 (*see also* Servant)

These things have I spoken unto you, being yet present with you. But the Comforter, which is the Holy Ghost, whom the Father will send in my name, he shall teach you all things, and bring all things to your remembrance, whatsoever I have said unto you. John 14:25-26 (*see also* All Things, Comforter, Holy Ghost)

Remember the former things of old: for I *am* God, and *there* is none else; I *am* God, and *there* is none like me, Declaring the end from the beginning, and from ancient times *the things* that are not yet done, saying, My counsel shall stand, and I will do all my pleasure: Calling a ravenous bird from the east, the man that executeth my counsel from a far county: yea, I have spoken *it*, I will also bring it to pass; I have purposed *it*, I will also do it. Isa. 46:9-11 (*see also* Counsel)

If they shall confess their iniquity, and the iniquity of their fathers, with their trespass which they trespassed against me, and that also they have walked contrary unto me; And that I also have walked contrary unto them, and have brought them into the land of their enemies; if then their uncircumcised hearts be humbled, and they then accept of the punishment of their iniquity: Then will I remember my covenant with Jacob, and also my covenant with Isaac, and also my covenant with Abraham will I remember; and I will remember the land. Lev. 26:40-42 (*see also* Confess, Iniquity, Repent)

Remember his marvelous works that he hath done; his wonders, and the judgments of his mouth. Ps. 105:5 (*see also* Works)

Ps. 63:6 I *r.* thee upon my bed, and meditate on thee in the night watches; 78:42 they *r.* not his hand, nor the day when he delivered them from the enemy; 105:5 *r.* his marvellous works that he hath done; his wonders, and the judgments of his mouth; 111:4 he hath made his wonderful works to be *r.*: the LORD is gracious and full of compassion; 143:5 I *r.* the days of old; I meditate on all thy works; I muse on the work of thy hands.

Remember now thy creator in the days of thy youth. Eccl. 12:1 (*see also* Youth)

Eccl. 12:1 *r.* now thy Creator in the days of thy youth, while the evil days come not, nor the years draw nigh; Jer. 51:50 ye that have escaped the sword, go away, stand not still: *r.* the LORD afar off, and let Jerusalem come into your mind.

Thou hast not remembered the days of thy youth, but hast fretted me in all these things; behold, therefore I also will recompense thy way upon thine head, saith the Lord GOD. Ezek. 16:43 (*see also* Recompense, Youth)

Ezek. 16:22 in all thine abominations and thy whoredoms thou hast not *r.* the days of thy youth, when thou wast naked and bare, and wast polluted in thy blood; 16:43 thou hast not *r.* the days of thy youth, but hast fretted me in all these things; behold, therefore I also will recompense thy way upon thine head, saith the Lord GOD.

If thou put the brethren in remembrance of these things, thou shalt be a good minister of Jesus Christ, nourished up in the words of faith and of good doctrine, whereunto thou hast attained. 1 Tim. 4:6 (*see also* Minister, Nourish)

1 Cor 15:2 by which also ye are saved, if ye keep in memory what I preached unto you, unless ye have believed in vain; Philip. 4:9 those things, which ye have both learned, and received, and heard, and seen in me, do: and the God of peace shall be with you; 1 Tim. 4:6 if thou put the brethren in *r.* of these things, thou shalt be a good minister of Jesus Christ, nourished up in the words of faith and of good doctrine, whereunto thou hast attained; 2 Pet. 1:15 I will endeavour that ye may be able after my decease to have these things always in *r.*; 3:1-2 I stir up your pure minds by way of *r.*: That ye may be mindful of the words which were spoken before by the holy prophets, and of the commandment of us the apostles of the Lord and Saviour; Jude 1:5-7 I will therefore put you in *r.*, though ye once knew this, how that the Lord, having saved the people out of the land of Egypt, afterward destroyed them that believed not.

REMISSION (*see* Baptize, Forgive, Holy Ghost, Repent, Sin)

And he took the cup, and gave thanks, and gave it to them, saying, Drink ye all of it; For this is my blood of the new testament, which is shed for many for the remission of sins. Matt. 26:28 (*see also* Blood)

He commanded us to preach unto the people, and to testify that it is he which was ordained of God to be the Judge of quick and dead. To him give all the prophets witness, that through his name whosoever believeth in him shall receive remission of sins. Acts 10:43 (*see also* Believe, Judge)

Almost all things are by the law purged with blood; and without shedding of blood is no remission. Heb. 9:22 (*see also* Blood)

John did baptize in the wilderness, and preach the baptism of repentance for the remission of sins. Mark 1:4 (*see also* Baptize)

Repent, and be baptized every one of you in the name of Jesus Christ for the remission of sins, and ye shall receive the gift of the Holy Ghost. Acts 2:38 (*see also* Baptize, Repent)

REMOVE

Turn not to the right hand nor to the left: remove thy foot from evil. **Prov. 4:27** (*see also* Evil, Foot)

RENDER (*see also* Charity, Give, Serve)

Also unto thee, O Lord, belongeth mercy: for thou renderest to every man according to his work. **Ps. 62:12** (*see also* Mercy, Work)

See that none render evil for evil unto any man; but ever follow that which is good, both among yourselves, and to all men. **1 Thes. 5:15** (*see also* Evil)

Say not, I will do so to him as he hath done to me; I will render to the man according to his work. **Prov. 24:29** (*see also* Do, Work)

Render therefore unto Caesar the things which are Caesar's, and unto God the things that are God's. **Matt. 22:21** (*see also* Tax)

Matt. 22:21 *r.* therefore unto Caesar the things which are Caesar's; and unto God the things that are God's; **Mark 12:14-17** (Luke 20:22-25) Is it lawful to give tribute to Caesar, or not? Shall we give, or shall we not give? But he, knowing their hypocrisy, said unto them, Why tempt ye me? bring me a penny, that I may see it. And they brought it. And he saith unto them, Whose is this image and superscription? And they said unto him, Caesar's. And Jesus answering said unto them, *r.* to Caesar the things that are Caesar's, and to God the things that are God's.

RENEW (*see also* Born Again, Commit)

They that wait upon the Lord shall renew their strength; they shall mount up with wings as eagles; they shall run, and not be weary; and they shall walk, and not faint. **Isa. 40:31** (*see also* Strength, Wait)

Be ye transformed by the renewing of your mind, that ye may prove what is that good, and acceptable, and perfect, will of God. **Rom. 12:2** (*see also* Mind, Prove, Transform)

REPAIR (*see* Repent)

Gather of all Israel money to repair the house of your God from year to year. **2 Chron. 24:4-5** (*see also* House)

REPENT, REPENTANCE (*see also* Baptism, Purify, Redeem, Remission, Return, Sin, Turn)

Repent, and be baptized every one of you in the name of Jesus Christ for the remission of sins, and ye shall receive the gift of the Holy Ghost. **Acts 2:38** (*see also* Baptize, Remission)

Make merry, and be glad: for this thy brother was dead, and is alive again; and was lost, and is found. **Luke 15:32**

I will declare mine iniquity; I will be sorry for my sin. **Ps. 38:18** (*see also* Iniquity, Sin)

Let us search and try our ways, and turn again to the LORD. **Lam. 3:40** (*see also* Search, Try, Turn, Way)

Repent, and turn yourselves from your idols. **Ezek. 14:6** (*see also* Idol)

Let the wicked forsake his way, and the unrighteous man his thoughts: and let him return unto the LORD, and he will have mercy upon him; and to our God, for he will abundantly pardon. **Isa. 55:7** (*see also* Way)

They should repent and turn to God, and do works meet for repentance. **Acts 26:20** (*see also* Fruit)

If they shall confess their iniquity, and the iniquity of their fathers, with their trespass which they trespassed against me, and that also they have walked contrary unto me; And that I also have walked contrary unto them, and have brought them into the land of their enemies; if then their uncircumcised hearts be humbled, and they then accept of the punishment of their iniquity: Then will I remember my covenant with Jacob, and also my covenant with Isaac, and also my covenant with Abraham will I remember; and I will remember the land. **Lev. 26:40-42** (*see also* Confess, Iniquity, Remember)

Lev. 26:40-42 if they shall confess their iniquity, and the iniquity of their fathers, with their trespass which they trespassed against me... Then will I remember my covenant; **1 Kgs. 8:47** repent, and make supplication unto thee in the land of them that carried them captives, saying, We have sinned, and have done perversely, we have committed wickedness; **1 Chron. 21:8** I have sinned greatly, because I have done this thing: but now, I beseech thee, do away the iniquity of thy servant; for I have done very foolishly; **21:17** even I it is that have sinned and done evil indeed; but as for these sheep, what have they done? let thine hand, I pray thee, O LORD my God, be on me, and on my fathers house; but not on thy people; **2 Chron. 6:24-25** if thy people... shall return and confess thy name, and pray and make supplication before thee in this house; Then hear thou from the heavens, and forgive the sin of thy people Israel; **6:26-27** they have sinned against thee; yet if they pray toward this place, and confess thy name, and turn from their sin, when thou dost afflict them; Then hear thou from heaven, and forgive the sin of thy servants; **6:37-38** we have sinned, we have done amiss, and have dealt wickedly; If they return to thee with all their heart and with all their soul; **33:15-16** he repaired the altar of the LORD, and sacrificed thereon peace offerings and thank offerings, and commanded Judah to serve the LORD God of Israel; **Ezra 10:1** when he had confessed, weeping and casting himself down before the house of God, there assembled unto him out of Israel a very great congregation; **Job 33:27-28** if any say, I have sinned, and perverted that which was right, and it profited me not; He will deliver his soul from going into the pit; **42:6** I abhor myself, and *r.* in dust and ashes; **Ps. 19:12-14** cleanse thou me from secret faults. Keep back thy servant also from presumptuous sins; let them not have dominion over me: then shall I be upright, and I shall be innocent from the great transgression; **25:11** O LORD, pardon mine iniquity; for it is great; **25:18** look upon mine affliction and my pain; and forgive all my sins; **31:9** have mercy upon me, O LORD, for I am in trouble: mine eye is consumed with grief; **32:1** blessed is he whose transgression is forgiven, whose sin is covered; **38:1-10** Lord, all my desire is before thee; and my groaning is not hid from thee. My heart panteth, my strength faileth me: as for the light of mine eyes, it also is gone from me; **38:17-18** I am ready to halt, and my sorrow is continually before me. For I will declare mine iniquity; I will be sorry for my sin; **51:1-12** have mercy upon me, O God, according to thy lovingkindness: according unto the multitude of thy tender mercies blot out my transgressions; **60:1** O God, thou hast cast us off, thou hast scattered us, thou hast been displeased; O turn thyself to us again; **68:21** God shall wound the head of his enemies, and the hairy scalp of such an one as goeth on still in his trespasses; **79:9** help us, O God of our salvation, for the glory of thy name: and deliver us, and purge away our sins; **80:7** turn us again, O God of hosts, and cause thy face to shine; and we

shall be saved; **80:14** return, we beseech thee, O God of hosts: look down from heaven, and behold, and visit this vine; **119:59** I thought on my ways, and turned my feet unto thy testimonies; **119:176** I have gone astray like a lost sheep; seek thy servant; for I do not forget thy commandments; **Isa. 1:18** let us reason together, saith the LORD: though your sins be as scarlet, they shall be as white as snow; though they be red like crimson, they shall be as wool; **55:7** let the wicked forsake his way, and the unrighteous man his thoughts: and let him return unto the LORD, and he will have mercy upon him; **Jer. 3:4** wilt thou not from this time cry unto me, My father, thou art the guide of my youth; **3:12-13** return, thou backsliding Israel, saith the LORD; and I will not cause mine anger to fall upon you: for I am merciful, saith the LORD, and I will not keep anger for ever; **8:6-7** no man *r.* him of his wickedness, saying, What have I done? every one turned to his course; **9:1** oh that my head were waters, and mine eyes a fountain of tears, that I might weep day and night for the slain of the daughter of my people; **9:18** let them make haste, and take up a wailing for us, that our eyes may run down with tears, and our eyelids gush out with waters; **9:20-21** hear the word of the LORD, O ye women, and let your ear receive the word of his mouth, and teach your daughters wailing, and every one her neighbour lamentation; **14:20-21** we acknowledge, O LORD, our wickedness, and the iniquity of our fathers: for we have sinned against thee; **15:11** verily it shall be well with thy remnant; verily I will cause the enemy to entreat thee well in the time of evil and in the time of affliction; **15:19** if thou return, then will I bring thee again, and thou shalt stand before me; **18:11** return ye now every one from his evil way, and make your ways and your doings good; **31:19** I *r.*; and after that I was instructed, I smote upon my thigh: I was ashamed, yea, even confounded, because I did bear the reproach of my youth; **31:21** set thine heart toward the highway, even the way which thou wentest: turn again, O virgin of Israel, turn again to these thy cities; **33:7-8** I will cleanse them from all their iniquity, whereby they have sinned against me; and I will pardon all their iniquities, whereby they have sinned; **36:7** it may be they will present their supplication before the LORD, and will return every one from his evil way: for great is the anger and the fury that the LORD hath pronounced; **Lam. 1:11** see, O LORD, and consider; for I am become vile; **Ezek. 14:6** *r.*, and turn yourselves from your idols; and turn away your faces from all your abominations;

18:21-22 if the wicked will turn from all his sins that he hath committed, and keep all my statutes, and do that which is lawful and right, he shall surely live, he shall not die; **18:27-28** when the wicked man turneth away from his wickedness that he hath committed, and doeth that which is lawful and right, he shall save his soul alive; **18:31-32** cast away from you all your transgressions, whereby ye have transgressed; and make you a new heart and a new spirit; **20:43** there shall ye remember your ways, and all your doings, wherein ye have been defiled; and ye shall lothe yourselves in your own sight for all your evils that ye have committed; **Dan. 9:5** we have sinned, and have committed iniquity, and have done wickedly, and have rebelled, even by departing from thy precepts and from thy judgments; **9:15-19** we have sinned, we have done wickedly. O Lord, according to all thy righteousness, I beseech thee, let thine anger and thy fury be turned away from thy city Jerusalem; **Hosea 6:1-3** let us return unto the LORD: for he hath torn, and he will heal us; he hath smitten, and he will bind us up; **7:10** the pride of Israel testifieth to his face: and they do not return to the LORD their God, nor seek him for all this; **7:16** they return, but not to the most High: they are like a deceitful bow: their princes shall fall by the sword for the rage of their tongue; **14:1-4** return unto the LORD thy God; for thou hast fallen by thine iniquity. Take with you words, and turn to the LORD: say unto him, Take away all iniquity, and receive us graciously.

The time is fulfilled, and the kingdom of God is at hand: repent ye, and believe the gospel. Mark 1:15 (*see also* Gospel)

Matt. 3:2 (4:17) *r.* ye: for the kingdom of heaven is at hand; **9:13** (Mark 2:17, Luke 5:31-32) I am not come to call the righteous, but sinners to *r.*; **11:20-24** then began he to upbraid the cities wherein most of his mighty works were done, because they *r.* not; **12:41** the men of Nineveh shall rise in judgment with this generation, and shall condemn it: because they *r.* at the preaching of Jonas; **21:29** he answered and said, I will not: but afterward he *r.*, and went; **21:32** ye believed him not: but the publicans and the harlots believed him: and ye, when ye had seen it, *r.* not afterward, that ye might believe him; **Mark 1:15** the time is fulfilled, and the kingdom of God is at hand: *r.* ye, and believe the gospel; **6:12** they went out, and preached that men should *r.*; **Luke 7:37-38** a woman in the city, which was a sinner, when she knew that Jesus sat at meat in the Pharisee's house, brought an alabaster box of ointment, And stood at his feet behind him weeping, and began to wash his feet with tears, and did wipe them with the hairs of her head, and kissed his feet, and anointed them with the ointment; **7:41-43** there was a certain creditor which had two debtors: the one owed five hundred pence, and the other fifty. And when they had nothing to pay, he frankly forgave them both; **7:47** her sins, which are many, are forgiven; for she loved much: but to whom little is forgiven, the same loveth little; **13:1-5** except ye *r.*, ye shall all likewise perish; **13:34-35** O Jerusalem, Jerusalem, which killest the prophets, and stonest them that are sent unto thee; how often would I have gathered thy children together, as a hen doth gather her brood under her wings, and ye would not! Behold, your house is left unto you desolate: and verily I say unto you, Ye shall not see me, until the time come when ye shall say, Blessed is he that cometh in the name of the Lord; **15:4-7** I say unto you, that likewise joy shall be in heaven over one sinner that *r.*, more than over ninety and nine just persons, which need no *r.*; **15:8-10** there is joy in the presence of the angels of God over one sinner that *r.*; **15:19-32** he said unto him, Son, thou art ever with me, and all that I have is thine. It was meet that we should make merry, and be glad: for this thy brother was dead, and is alive again; and was lost, and is found; **16:19-31** they have Moses and the prophets; let them hear them. And he said, Nay, father Abraham: but if one went unto them from the dead, they will *r.*. And he said unto him, If they hear not Moses and the prophets, neither will they be persuaded, though one rose from the dead; **17:3-4** if thy brother trespass against thee, rebuke him; and if he *r.*, forgive him. And if he trespass against thee seven times in a day, and seven times in a day turn again to thee, saying, I *r.*; thou shalt forgive him; **24:46-47** *r.* and remission of sins should be preached in his name among all nations, beginning at Jerusalem; **Acts 2:38** *r.*, and be baptized every one of you in the name of Jesus Christ for the remission of sins, and ye shall receive the gift of the Holy Ghost; **3:19** *r.* ye therefore, and be converted, that your sins may be blotted out, when the times of refreshing shall come from the presence of the Lord; **5:31** him hath God exalted with his right hand to be a Prince and a Saviour, for to give *r.* to Israel, and forgiveness of sins; **8:21-22** *r.* therefore of this thy wickedness, and pray God, if perhaps the thought of thine heart may be forgiven thee; **17:30** the times of this ignorance God winked at; but now commandeth all men every where to *r.*; **20:21** testifying both to the

Jews, and also to the Greeks, *r.* toward God, and faith toward our Lord Jesus Christ; **26:18** open their eyes, and to turn them from darkness to light, and from the power of Satan unto God, that they may receive forgiveness of sins, and inheritance among them which are sanctified by faith that is in me; **26:20** they should *r.* and turn to God, and do works meet for *r.*; **Rom. 4:7** blessed are they whose iniquities are forgiven, and whose sins are covered; **5:12** as by one man sin entered into the world, and death by sin; and so death passed upon all men, for that all have sinned; **6:20-23** when ye were the servants of sin, ye were free from righteousness. What fruit had ye then in those things whereof ye are now ashamed? for the end of those things is death. But now being made free from sin, and become servants to God, ye have your fruit unto holiness, and the end everlasting life. For the wages of sin is death; but the gift of God is eternal life through Jesus Christ our Lord; **1 Cor. 6:9-11** know ye not that the unrighteous shall not inherit the kingdom of God? Be not deceived: neither fornicators, nor idolaters, nor adulterers, nor effeminate, nor abusers of themselves with mankind, Nor thieves, nor covetous, nor drunkards, nor revilers, nor extortioners, shall inherit the kingdom of God; **2 Cor. 5:18-20** we are ambassadors for Christ, as though God did beseech you by us: we pray you in Christ's stead, be ye reconciled to God; **7:8-11** for godly sorrow worketh *r.* to salvation not to be *r.* of: but the sorrow of the world worketh death; **12:21** God will humble me among you, and that I shall bewail many which have sinned already, and have not *r.* of the uncleanness and fornication and lasciviousness which they have committed; **Gal. 1:6** I marvel that ye are so soon removed from him that called you into the grace of Christ unto another gospel; **Eph. 2:1-5** you hath he quickened, who were dead in trespasses and sins; Even when we were dead in sins, hath quickened us together with Christ; **4:28** let him that stole steal no more: but rather let him labour, working with his hands the thing which is good, that he may have to give to him that needeth; **Col. 1:14** in whom we have redemption through his blood, even the forgiveness of sins; **2:13** you, being dead in your sins and the uncircumcision of your flesh, hath he quickened together with him, having forgiven you all trespasses; **2 Tim. 2:25-26** if God peradventure will give them *r.* to the acknowledging of the truth; And that they may recover themselves out of the snare of the devil, who are taken captive by him at his will; **Titus 3:3-5** we ourselves also were sometimes foolish, disobedient, deceived, serving divers lusts and pleasures, living in malice and envy, hateful, and hating one another. But after that the kindness and love of God our Saviour toward man appeared, Not by works of righteousness which we have done, but according to his mercy he saved us, by the washing of regeneration, and renewing of the Holy Ghost; **8:12** I will be merciful to their unrighteousness, and their sins and their iniquities will I remember no more; **9:28** Christ was once offered to bear the sins of many; and unto them that look for him shall he appear the second time without sin unto salvation; **10:12** after he had offered one sacrifice for sins for ever, sat down on the right hand of God; **10:17-20** their sins and iniquities will I remember no more. Now where remission of these is, there is no more offering for sin. Having therefore, brethren, boldness to enter into the holiest by the blood of Jesus, By a new and living way, which he hath consecrated for us, through the veil, that is to say, his flesh; **12:1** let us lay aside every weight, and the sin which doth so easily beset us, and let us run with patience the race tha t is set before us; **James 4:8-10** be afflicted, and mourn, and weep: let your laughter be turned to mourning, and your joy to heaviness; **5:16** confess your faults one to another, and pray one for another, that ye may be healed; **5:19-20** he which converteth the sinner from the error of his way shall save a soul from death, and shall hide a multitude of sins; **1 Pet. 2:24** who his own self bare our sins in his own body on the tree, that we, being dead to sins, should live unto righteousness: by whose stripes ye were healed; **2 Pet. 3:9** the Lord is not slack concerning his promise, as some men count slackness; but is longsuffering to us-ward, not willing that any should perish, but that all should come to *r.*; **1 Jn. 1:8-10** if we say that we have no sin, we deceive ourselves, and the truth is not in us. If we confess our sins, he is faithful and just to forgive us our sins, and to cleanse us from all unrighteousness; **2:1** if any man sin, we have an advocate with the Father, Jesus Christ the righteous; **Rev. 1:5** unto him that loved us, and washed us from our sins in his own blood; **2:4-5** I will come unto thee quickly, and will remove thy candlestick out of his place, except thou *r.*; **2:7** to him that overcometh will I give to eat of the tree of life, which is in the midst of the paradise of God; **2:11** he that overcometh shall not be hurt of the second death; **2:16** *r.*; or else I will come unto thee quickly, and will fight against them with the sword of my mouth; **2:17** him that overcometh will I give to eat of the hidden manna, and will give him a white stone, and in the stone a new name written, which no man knoweth saving he that receiveth it; **2:21-22** I gave her space to *r.* of her fornication; and she *r.* not. Behold, I will cast her into a bed, and them that commit adultery with her into great tribulation, except they *r.* of their deeds; **2:26** and he that overcometh, and keepeth my works unto the end, to him will I give power over the nations; **3:3** hold fast, and *r.*. If therefore thou shalt not watch, I will come on thee as a thief, and thou shalt not know what hour I will come upon thee; **3:19** as many as I love, I rebuke and chasten; be zealous therefore, and *r.*; **6:16** and said to the mountains and rocks, Fall on us, and hide us from the face of him that sitteth on the throne, and from the wrath of the Lamb; **7:14** these are they which came out of great tribulation, and have washed their robes, and made them white in the blood of the Lamb; **16:9** (16:11) men were scorched with great heat, and blasphemed the name of God, which hath power over these plagues: and they *r.* not to give him glory.

REPLENISH (*see also* Restore)

Be fruitful, and multiply, and replenish the earth, and subdue it. Gen. 1:28 (*see also* Multiply)

REPROACH (*see also* Punish)

He that backbiteth not with his tongue, nor doeth evil to his neighbour, nor taketh up a reproach against his neighbour [shall abide in thy tabernacle]. Ps. 15:3 (*see also* Backbite)

Fear ye not the reproach of men, neither be ye afraid of their revilings. Isa. 51:7 (*see also* Fear)

Render unto our neighbours sevenfold into their bosom their reproach, wherewith they have reproached thee, O Lord. Ps. 79:12

Ps. 74:22 arise, O God, plead thine own cause: remember how the foolish man reproacheth thee daily; **79:12** render unto our neighbours sevenfold into their bosom their *r.*, wherewith they have *r.* thee, O Lord; **Isa. 37:4** the king of Assyria his master hath sent to *r.* the living God, and will reprove the words which the LORD thy God hath heard: wherefore lift up thy prayer for the remnant that is left; **Jer. 6:10** their ear is uncircumcised, and they cannot hearken: behold, the word of the LORD is unto them a reproach; they have no delight in it.

REPROOF, REPROVE (*see also* Chasten, Exhort, Holy Ghost, Punish, Rebuke, Teach)

He, that being often reproved hardeneth his neck, shall suddenly be destroyed, and that without remedy. Prov. 29:1 (*see also* Neck)

All scripture is given by inspiration of God, and is profitable for doctrine, for reproof, for correction, for instruction in righteousness: That the man of God may be perfect, throughly furnished unto all good works. 2 Tim. 3:16-17 (*see also* Inspiration, Perfect, Scripture, Works)

Correction is grievous unto him that forsaketh the way: and he that hateth reproof shall die. Prov. 15:10 (*see also* Way)

He is in the way of life that keepeth instruction: but he that refuseth reproof erreth. Prov. 10:17 (*see also* Instruct, Way)

Prov. 10:17 he is in the way of life that keepeth instruction: but he that refuseth *r.* erreth; **13:18** poverty and shame shall be to him that refuseth instruction: but he that regardeth *r.* shall be honoured; **15:5** a fool despiseth his fathers instruction: but he that regardeth *r.* is prudent; **15:31-32** the ear that heareth the *r.* of life abideth among the wise. He that refuseth instruction despiseth his own soul: but he that heareth *r.* getteth understanding.

As an earring of gold, and an ornament of fine gold, so is a wise reprover upon an obedient ear. Prov. 25:12 (*see also* Wisdom)

Prov. 25:12 as an earring of gold, and an ornament of fine gold, so is a wise *r.* upon an obedient ear; **29:15** the rod and *r.* give wisdom: but a child left to himself bringeth his mother to shame.

RESPECT (*see also* Esteem, Honor, Love, Obey)

At that day shall a man look to his Maker, and his eyes shall have respect to the Holy One of Israel. Isa. 17:7

I charge thee before God, and the Lord Jesus Christ, and the elect angels, that thou observe these things without preferring one before another, doing nothing by partiality. 1 Tim. 5:21 (*see also* Equal, Partial)

Regardest not the person of men. Matt. 22:16 (*see also* Equal)

It is not good to have respect of persons in judgment. Prov. 24:23 (*see also* Judge)

REST (*see also* Peace, Sabbath)

Come unto me, all ye that labour and are heavy laden, and I will give you rest. Take my yoke upon you, and learn of me; for I am meek and lowly in heart: and ye shall find rest unto your souls. For my yoke is easy, and my burden is light. Matt. 11:28-30 (*see also* Come, Labor, Yoke)

They returned, and prepared spices and ointments; and rested the sabbath day according to the commandment. Luke 23:56 (*see also* Sabbath)

Rest in the LORD, and wait patiently for Him. Ps. 37:7 (*see also* Wait)

Ps. 37:7 *r.* in the LORD, and wait patiently for him; 123:2 our eyes wait upon the LORD our God, until that he have mercy upon us; 130:6 my soul waiteth for the Lord more than they that watch for the morning: I say, more than they that watch for the morning.

RESTORATION, RESTORE, RESTORED (*see also* Cure, Gospel, Heal, Redeem, Replenish)

It is a light thing that thou shouldest be my servant to raise up the tribes of Jacob, and to restore the preserved of Israel: I will also give thee for a light to the Gentiles, that thou mayest be my salvation unto the end of the earth. Isa. 49:6 (*see also* Israel)

RESURRECT, RESURRECTION (*see also* Eternal Life, Jesus Christ, Second Coming)

There are also celestial bodies, and bodies terrestrial: but the glory of the celestial is one, and the glory of the terrestrial is another. There is one glory of the sun, and another glory of the moon, and another glory of the stars: for one star differeth from another star in glory. So also is the resurrection of the dead. 1 Cor. 15:40-42 (*see also* Celestial, Dead, Glory, Terrestrial)

I know that he shall rise again in the resurrection at the last day. Jesus said unto her, I am the resurrection, and the life: he that believeth in me, though he were dead, yet shall he live. John 11:24-25 (*see also* Death, Jesus Christ)

RETAIN (*see also* Hold, Keep, Remember)

Even as they did not like to retain God in their knowledge, God gave them over to a reprobate mind, to do those things which are not convenient. Rom. 1:28

RETURN

His mischief shall return upon his own head, and his violent dealing shall come down upon his own pate. Ps. 7:16 (*see also* Head, Mischief, Violent)

Return unto me and I will return unto you, saith the Lord of Hosts. But ye said, Wherein shall we return? Will a man rob God? Yet ye have robbed me. But ye say, Wherein have we robbed thee? In tithes and offerings. Mal. 3:7 (*see also* Rob, Tithe)

Let the wicked forsake his way, and the unrighteous man his thoughts: and let him return unto the LORD, and he will have mercy upon him; and to our God, for he will abundantly pardon. Isa. 55:7 (*see also* Forsake, Pardon)

If ye do return unto the LORD with all your hearts, then put away the strange gods and Ashtaroth from among you, and prepare your hearts unto the LORD, and serve him only: and he will deliver you out of the hand of the Philistines. 1 Sam. 7:3 (*see also* Deliver)

I will give them an heart to know me, that I am the LORD: and they shall be my people, and I will be their God: for they shall return unto me with their whole heart. Jer. 24:7 (*see also* Heart)

Deut. 30:2 shalt *r.* unto the LORD thy God, and shalt obey his voice according to all that I command thee this day, thou and thy children, with all thine heart, and with all thy soul; 30:8 thou shalt *r.* and obey the voice of the LORD, and do all his commandments which I command thee this day; 1 Sam. 7:3 if ye do *r.* unto the LORD with all your hearts... and prepare your hearts unto the LORD, and serve him only: and he will deliver you out of the hand of the Philistines; **1 Kgs. 8:48** *r.* unto thee with all their heart, and with all their soul, in the land of their enemies; **2 Chron. 6:24-25** if thy people Israel... shall *r.* and confess thy name, and pray and make supplication before thee in this house; Then hear thou from the heavens, and forgive the sin of thy people Israel; **6:38** *r.* to thee with all their heart and with all their soul in the land of their captivity; **Job 22:23** if thou *r.* to the Almighty, thou shalt be built up, thou shalt put away iniquity far from thy tabernacles; **Isa. 19:22** the LORD shall smite Egypt: he shall smite and heal it: and they shall *r.* even to the LORD, and he shall be intreated of them, and shall heal them; **Jer. 3:1** thou hast played the harlot with many lovers; yet *r.* again to me, saith the LORD; **3:12** *r.*, thou backsliding Israel, saith the LORD; and I will not cause mine anger to fall upon you: for I am merciful, saith the LORD, and I will not keep anger for ever; **4:1** if thou wilt *r.*, O Israel, saith the LORD, *r.* unto me: and if thou wilt put away thine abominations out of my sight, then shalt thou not remove; **15:19** thus saith the LORD, If thou *r.*, then will I bring thee again, and thou shalt stand before me; **24:7** I will give them an heart to know me, that I am the LORD: and they shall be my people, and I will be their God: for they shall *r.* unto me with their whole heart; **Hosea 3:5** afterward shall the children of Israel *r.*, and seek the LORD their God, and David their king; and shall fear the LORD and his goodness in the latter days; **6:1** let us *r.* unto the LORD: for he hath torn, and he will heal us; he hath smitten, and he will bind us up; **7:10** the pride of Israel testifieth to his face: and they do not *r.* to the LORD their God, nor seek him for all this; **14:1** O Israel, *r.* unto the LORD thy God; for thou hast fallen by thine iniquity; **Amos 4:6-11** I have overthrown some of you, as God overthrew Sodom and Gomorrah, and ye were as a firebrand plucked out of the burning: yet have ye not *r.* unto me, saith the LORD; **Mal. 3:7** *r.* unto me, and I will *r.* unto you, saith the LORD of hosts.

REVEAL, REVELATION (*see also* Divine, Dream, Guidance, Inspiration, Prophecy, Testimony, Vision, Witness)

I will pour out my spirit upon all flesh; and your sons and your daughters shall prophesy, your old men shall dream dreams, your young men shall see visions. Joel 2:28 (*see also* Dream, Vision)

I neither received it of man, neither was I taught it, but by the revelation of Jesus Christ. Gal. 1:12

Call unto me, and I will answer thee, and shew thee great and mighty things, which thou knowest not. Jer. 33:3 (*see also* Call, Mysteries)

There is a God in heaven that revealeth secrets. Dan. 2:28 (*see also* Secret)

Dan. 2:26-28 Daniel answered in the presence of the king, and said, The secret which the king hath demanded cannot the wise men, the astrologers, the magicians, the soothsayers, shew unto the king; But there is a God in heaven that revealeth secrets.

The God of our Lord Jesus Christ, the Father of glory, may give unto you the spirit of wisdom and revelation in the knowledge of him: The eyes of your understanding being enlightened; that ye may know what is the hope of his calling, and what the riches of the glory of his inheritance in the saints. Eph. 1:17-18 (*see also* Father, Hope, Wisdom)

Matt. 1:20 while he thought on these things, behold, the angel of the Lord appeared unto him in a dream, saying, Joseph, thou son of David, fear not to take unto thee Mary thy wife: for that which is conceived in her is of the Holy Ghost; **2:12** being warned of God in a dream that they should not return to Herod, they departed into their own country another way; **2:13** the angel of the Lord appeareth to Joseph in a dream, saying, Arise, and take the young child and his mother, and flee into Egypt, and be thou there until I bring thee word: for Herod will seek the young child to destroy him; **2:19** when Herod was dead, behold, an angel of the Lord appeareth in a dream to Joseph in Egypt; **Luke 2:9** the angel of the Lord came upon them, and the glory of the Lord shone round about them: and they were sore; **2:15** as the angels were gone away from them into heaven, the shepherds said one to another, Let us now go even unto Bethlehem, and see this thing which is come to pass, which the Lord hath made known unto us; **2:26** it was revealed unto him by the Holy Ghost, that he should not see death, before he had seen the Lord's Christ; **Acts 18:9** then spake the Lord to Paul in the night by a vision, Be not afraid, but speak, and hold not thy peace; **Rom. 8:16** the Spirit itself beareth witness with our spirit, that we are the children of God; **Gal. 2:2** I went up by *r.*, and communicated unto them that gospel which I preach among the Gentiles; **Eph. 1:9** having made known unto us the mystery of his will, according to his good pleasure which he hath purposed in himself; **1:17-18** the God of our Lord Jesus Christ, the Father of glory, may give unto you the spirit of wisdom and *r.* in the knowledge of him: The eyes of your understanding being enlightened; that ye may know what is the hope of his calling, and what the riches of the glory of his inheritance in the saints; **3:2-3** if ye have heard of the dispensation of the grace of God which is given me to you-ward: How that by *r.* he made known unto me the mystery; **3:5** in other ages was not made known unto the sons of men, as it is now revealed unto his holy apostles and prophets by the Spirit; **Rev. 1:1-2** the *r.* of Jesus Christ, which God gave unto him, to shew unto his servants things which must shortly come to pass; and he sent and signified it by his angel unto his servant John; who bare record of the word of God, and of the testimony of Jesus Christ, and of all things that he saw.

REVENGE (*see* Avenge, Hate, Vengeance)

REVILE, REVILING (*see* Backbite, Gossip, Hate, Persecute, Strife)

REVOLT (*see also* Rebel, Riotous)

As for our iniquities, we know them: in transgressing and lying against the LORD, and departing away from our God, speaking oppression and revolt, conceiving and uttering from the heart words of falsehood. **Isa. 59:12-13** (*see also* Oppress)

REWARD (*see also* Abundance, Bless, Inherit, Justice, Promise, Wage)

Say ye to the daughter of Zion, Behold, thy salvation cometh; behold, his reward is with him, and his work before him. **Isa. 62:11** (*see also* Say, Zion)

He that receiveth you receiveth me, and he that receiveth me receiveth him that sent me. He that receiveth a prophet in the name of a prophet shall receive a prophet's reward; and he that receiveth a righteous man in the name of a righteous man shall receive a righteous man's reward. **Matt. 10:40-41** (*see also* Prophet, Receive, Serve)

Blessed are ye, when men shall revile you, and persecute you, and shall say all manner of evil against you falsely, for my sake. Rejoice, and be exceeding glad: for great is your reward in heaven: for so persecuted they the prophets which were before you. **Matt 5:11-12** (*see also* Persecute, Prophet)

The LORD rewarded me according to my righteousness; according to the cleanness of my hands hath he recompensed me. **Ps. 18:20** (*see also* Clean, Hand, Righteous)

But without faith it is impossible to please him: for he that cometh to God must believe that he is, and that he is a rewarder of them that diligently seek him. **Heb. 11:6** (*see also* Believe, Diligently, Faith, Impossible, Please, Seek)

Whoso rewardeth evil for good, evil shall not depart from his house. **Prov. 17:13** (*see also* House)

Ps. 35:12 they *r.* me evil for good to the spoiling of my soul; **109:5** they have *r.* me evil for good, and hatred for my love; **Prov. 17:13** whoso *r.* evil for good, evil shall not depart from his house; **Isa. 33:1** woe to thee that spoilest, and thou wast not spoiled; and dealest treacherously, and they dealt not treacherously with thee! when thou shalt cease to spoil, thou shalt be spoiled.

RICH, RICHES, RICHLY (*see also* Abundance, Bless, Money, Wealth)

A good name is rather to be chosen than great riches, and loving favour rather than silver and gold. **Prov. 22:1** (*see also* Name)

It is easier for a camel to go through the eye of a needle, than for a rich man to enter into the kingdom of God. **Matt 19:24** (*see also* Enter)

Charge them that are rich in this world, that they be not highminded, nor trust in uncertain riches, but in the living God, who giveth us richly all things to enjoy. **1 Tim. 6:17** (*see also* Highminded)

He that oppresseth the poor to increase his riches, and he that giveth to the rich, shall surely come to want. **Prov. 22:16** (*see also* Oppress, Poor)

Be rich in good works, ready to distribute, willing to communicate. 1 Tim. 6:18 (*see also* Communicate)

A faithful man shall abound with blessings: but he that maketh haste to be rich shall not be innocent. Prov. 28:20 (*see also* Haste)

He that hasteth to be rich hath an evil eye, and considereth not that poverty shall come upon him. Prov. 28:22 (*see also* Haste)

As the partridge sitteth on eggs, and hatcheth them not; so he that getteth riches, and not by right, shall leave them in the midst of his days, and at his end shall be a fool. Jer. 17:11 (*see also* Day, Right)

Trust not in oppression, and become not vain in robbery: if riches increase, set not your heart upon them. Ps. 62:10 (*see also* Heart, Increase, Oppress, Rob, Trust)

Better is a little with righteousness than great revenues without right. Prov. 16:8 (*see also* Right)

Labour not to be rich: cease from thin own wisdom. Prov. 23:4 (*see also* Labor)

Ps. 39:6 every man walketh in a vain shew: surely they are disquieted in vain: he heapeth up *r.*, and knoweth not who shall gather them; **49:10** he seeth that wise men die, likewise the fool and the brutish person perish, and leave their wealth to others; **Prov. 11:4** *r.* profit not in the day of wrath: but righteousness delivereth from death; **13:7** there is that maketh himself *r.*, yet hath nothing: there is that maketh himself poor, yet hath great *r.*; **23:4** labour not to be *r.*: cease from thine own wisdom; **Eccl. 5:12** the sleep of a labouring man is sweet, whether he eat little or much: but the abundance of the *r.* will not suffer him to sleep.

They that trust in their wealth, and boast themselves in the multitude of their riches; None of them can by any means redeem his brother. Ps. 49:6-7 (*see also* Boast, Redeem)

Ps. 49:6-7 they that trust in their wealth, and boast themselves in the multitude of their *r.*; None of them can by any means redeem his brother; **49:10** wise men die, likewise the fool and the brutish person perish, and leave their wealth to others; **49:12** nevertheless man being in honour abideth not: he is like the beasts that

perish; **52:1** why boastest thou thyself in mischief, O mighty man? the goodness of God endureth continually; **52:7** this is the man that made not God his strength; but trusted in the abundance of his *r.*, and strengthened himself in his wickedness; **94:4** how long shall they utter and speak hard things? and all the workers of iniquity boast themselves; **Prov. 11:28** he that trusteth in his *r.* shall fall: but the righteous shall flourish as a branch; **18:11** the *r.* mans wealth is his strong city, and as an high wall in his own conceit; **20:14** it is naught, it is naught, saith the buyer: but when he is gone his way, then he boasteth; **30:32** if thou hast done foolishly in lifting up thyself, or if thou hast thought evil, lay thine hand upon thy mouth.

Be not highminded, nor trust in uncertain riches, but in the living God, who giveth us richly all things to enjoy. 1 Tim. 6:17-19 (*see also* Highminded, Trust)

Matt. 6:31-33 seek ye first the kingdom of God, and his righteousness; and all these things shall be added unto you; **13:22** the care of this world, and the deceitfulness of *r.*, choke the word, and he becometh unfruitful; **Mark 4:19** the cares of this world, and the deceitfulness of *r.*, and the lusts of other things entering in, choke the word, and it becometh unfruitful; **8:36** what shall it profit a man, if he shall gain the whole world, and lose his own soul; **10:22** he was sad at that saying, and went away grieved: for he had great possessions; **10:24** how hard is it for them that trust in *r.* to enter into the kingdom of God; **Luke 6:24** woe unto you that are *r.*! for ye have received your consolation; **8:14** choked with cares and *r.* and pleasures of this life, and bring no fruit to perfection; **16:11-13** if therefore ye have not been faithful in the unrighteous mammon, who will commit to your trust the true *r.*; **18:23-24** how hardly shall they that have *r.* enter into the kingdom of God; **Rom. 11:12** if the fall of them be the *r.* of the world, and the diminishing of them the *r.* of the Gentiles; how much more their fulness; **1 Tim. 6:17-19** charge them that are *r.* in this world, that they be not highminded, nor trust in uncertain *r.*, but in the living God, who giveth us *r.* all things to enjoy; That they do good, that they be *r.* in good works, ready to distribute, willing to communicate; Laying up in store for themselves a good foundation against the time to come, that they may lay hold on eternal life; **James 1:10-11** but the *r.*, in that he is made low: because as the flower of the grass he shall pass away. For the sun is no sooner risen with a burning heat, but it withereth the grass, and the flower thereof falleth, and the grace of the fashion of it perisheth: so also shall the *r.* man fade away in his ways; **5:2** your *r.* are corrupted, and your garments are motheaten. Your gold and silver is cankered; and the rust of them shall be a witness against you, and shall eat your flesh as it were fire. Ye have heaped treasure together for the last days; **Rev. 18:17-19** that great city, wherein were made *r.* all that had ships in the sea by reason of her costliness! for in one hour is she made desolate.

RIGHT, RIGHTEOUS, RIGHTEOUSNESS
(*see also* Equal, Good, Honest, Jesus Christ, Judge, Just, Sanctification, Truth, Way)

Open ye the gates, that the righteous nation which keepeth the truth may enter in. **Isa. 26:2** (*see also* Gate, Nation, Truth)

Know the righteousness of the LORD. **Micah 6:5** (*see also* Know)

Ye shall do no unrighteousness in judgment: thou shalt not respect the person of the poor, nor honor the person of the mighty: but in righteousness shalt thou judge thy neighbour. **Lev. 19:15** (*see also* Judge)

Better is a little with righteousness than great revenues without right. **Prov. 16:8** (*see also* Rich)

The labour of the righteous tendeth to life: the fruit of the wicked to sin. **Prov. 10:16** (*see also* Labor)

A righteous man falling down before the wicked is as a troubled fountain, and a corrupt spring. **Prov. 25:26** (*see also* Wicked)

Thou shalt do that which is right and good in the sight of the LORD: that it may be well with thee, and that thou mayest go in and possess the good land which the LORD sware unto thy fathers, To cast out all thine enemies from before thee, as the LORD hath spoken. **Deut. 6:18-19** (*see also* Good)

Discretion shall preserve thee, understanding shall keep thee; to deliver thee from the way of the evil man, from the man that speaketh froward things; who leave the paths of righteousness, to walk in the ways of darkness. **Prov. 2:11-13** (*see also* Dark, Leave, Walk, Way)

The righteous considereth the cause of the poor: but the wicked regardeth not to know it. **Prov. 29:7** (*see also* Poor)

Take away the wicked from before the king, and his throne shall be established in righteousness. **Prov. 25:5** (*see also* Wicked)

With my soul have I desired thee in the night; yea, with my spirit within me will I seek thee early: for when thy judgments are in the earth, the inhabitants of the world will learn righteousness. **Isa. 26:9** (*see also* Learn)

Hearken unto me, ye stouthearted, that are far from righteousness. **Isa. 46:12** (*see also* Hearken, Stouthearted)

Blessed are they that keep judgment, and he that doeth righteousness at all times. **Ps. 106:3** (*see also* Blessed)

I will greatly rejoice in the LORD, my soul shall be joyful in my God; for he hath clothed me with the garments of salvation, he hath covered me with the robe of righteousness. **Isa. 61:10** (*see also* Garments, Robe)

When the righteous are in authority, the people rejoice: but when the wicked beareth rule, the people mourn. **Prov. 29:2** (*see also* Authority, Mourn, Rule, Wicked)

Execute ye judgment and righteousness. **Jer. 22:3-5** (*see also* Judge)

As the partridge sitteth on eggs, and hatcheth them not; so he that getteth riches, and not by right, shall leave them in the midst of his days, and at his end shall be a fool. **Jer. 17:11** (*see also* Day, Rich)

He hath done that which is lawful and right; he shall surely live. **Ezek. 33:16** (*see also* Law)

Delight thyself also in the LORD; and he shall give thee the desires of thine heart. **Ps. 37:4** (*see also* Delight, Desire)

Lay not wait, O wicked man, against the dwelling of the righteous; spoil not his resting place: For a just man falleth seven times, and riseth up again: but the wicked shall fall into mischief. **Prov. 24:15-16** (*see also* Spoil)

Whoso causeth the righteous to go astray in an evil way, he shall fall himself into his own pits; but the upright shall have good things in possession. Prov. 28:10 (*see also* Astray, Way)

Be not righteous over much; neither make thyself over wise: why shouldest thou destroy thyself? Eccl. 7:16 (*see also* Wise)

When a righteous man turneth away from his right-eousness, and committeth iniquity, and dieth in them; for his iniquity that he hath done shall he die. Ezek. 18:26 (*see also* Death, Iniquity, Turn)

Ezel 18:24 when the *r.* turneth away from his *r.*, and committeth iniquity, and doeth according to all the abominations that the wicked man doeth, shall he live?; 18:26 when a *r.* man turneth away from his *r.*, and committeth iniquity, and dieth in them; for his iniquity that he hath done shall he die.

He did that which was right in the sight of the LORD. 2 Chron. 29:2 (*see also* Do)

1 Kgs. 15:30 the sins of Jeroboam which he sinned, and which he made Israel sin, by his provocation wherewith he provoked the LORD God of Israel to anger; 2 Chron. 29:2 he did that which was *r.* in the sight of the LORD, according to all that David his father had done; Ps. 78:37 their heart was not *r.* with him, neither were they stedfast in his covenant.

He that walketh righteously, and speaketh uprightly; he that despiseth the gain of oppressions, that shaketh his hands from holding of bribes, that stoppeth his ears from hearing of blood, and shutteth his eyes from seeing evil; He shall dwell on high: his defence shall be the munitions of rocks: bread shall be given him; his waters shall be sure. Isa. 33:15-16 (*see also* Gain, Hear, Oppress, See, Speak, Uprightly, Walk)

Isa. 33:15-16 he that walketh *r.*, and speaketh uprightly; he that despiseth the gain of oppressions... He shall dwell on high; 57:2 he shall enter into peace: they shall rest in their beds, each one walking in his uprightness; Amos 5:10 they hate him that rebuketh in the gate, and they abhor him that speaketh uprightly.

Let them shout for joy, and be glad, that favour my righteous cause: yea, let them say continually, Let the LORD be magnified, which hath pleasure in the prosperity of his servant. Ps. 35:27 (*see also* Cause)

Ps. 35:27 let them shout for joy, and be glad, that favour my *r.* cause: yea, let them say continually, Let the LORD be magnified, which hath pleasure in the prosperity of his servant; 132:9 let thy priests be clothed with *r.*; and let thy saints shout for joy.

If thou warn the righteous man, that the righteous sin not, and he doth not sin, he shall surely live, because he is warned; also thou hast delivered thy soul. Ezek. 3:21 (*see also* Sin, Warn)

Ezek. 3:20-21 if thou warn the *r.* man, that the *r.* sin not, and he doth not sin, he shall surely live, because he is warned; also thou hast delivered thy soul; 33:12-13 when I shall say to the *r.*, that he shall surely live; if he trust to his own *r.*, and commit iniquity, all his *r.* shall not be remembered; 33:18 when the *r.* turneth from his *r.*, and committeth iniquity, he shall even die thereby.

I have set the LORD always before me: because he is at my right hand, I shall not be moved. Ps. 16:8 (*see also* Steadfast)

Ps. 15:5 he that putteth not out his money to usury, nor taketh reward against the innocent. He that doeth these things shall never be moved; 16:8 I have set the LORD always before me: because he is at my *r.* hand, I shall not be moved; 17:15 I will behold thy face in *r.*: I shall be satisfied, when I awake, with thy likeness; Eccl. 10:4 if the spirit of the ruler rise up against thee, leave not thy place; for yielding pacifieth great offences; Isa. 27:5 let him take hold of my strength, that he may make peace with me; and he shall make peace with me.

Let thy priests be clothed with righteousness. Ps. 132:9 (*see also* Priest)

Ps. 132:9 let thy priests be clothed with *r.*; 132:16-17 I will also clothe her priests with salvation: and her saints shall shout aloud for joy.

The LORD rewarded me according to my righteousness; according to the cleanness of my hands hath he recompensed me. **Ps. 18:20** (*see also* Clean, Hand, Reward)

Job 29:14 I put on *r.*, and it clothed me: my judgment was as a robe; **Ps. 11:7** the *r.* LORD loveth *r.*; his countenance doth behold the upright; **17:15** I will behold thy face in *r.*: I shall be satisfied, when I awake, with thy likeness; **18:20** the LORD rewarded me according to my *r.*; according to the cleanness of my hands hath he recompensed me; **18:24** the LORD [hath] recompensed me according to my *r.*, according to the cleanness of my hands in his eyesight; **33:5** he loveth *r.* and judgment: the earth is full of the goodness of the LORD; **37:39-40** the salvation of the *r.* is of the LORD: he is their strength in the time of trouble. And the LORD shall help them, and deliver them.

Go in the strength of the Lord GOD: I will make mention of thy righteousness, even of thine only. Ps. 71:16 (*see also* Go, Strength)

Ps. 71:15-18 my mouth shall shew forth thy *r.* and thy salvation all the day; for I know not the numbers thereof. I will go in the strength of the Lord GOD: I will make mention of thy *r.*; **71:24** my tongue also shall talk of thy *r.* all the day long: for they are confounded, for they are brought unto shame, that seek my hurt.

Treasures of wickedness profit nothing; but righteousness delivereth from death. Prov. 10:2 (*see also* Treasure, Wicked)

Prov. 10:2-3 treasures of wickedness profit nothing: but *r.* delivereth from death; **15:16** better is little with the fear of the LORD than great treasure and trouble therewith; **Jer. 48:7-8** because thou hast trusted in thy works and in thy treasures, thou shalt also be taken; **50:37** a sword is upon their horses, and upon their chariots, and upon all the mingled people that are in the midst of her; and they shall become as women: a sword is upon her treasures; and they shall be robbed; **50:39** the wild beasts of the desert with the wild beasts of the islands shall dwell there, and the owls shall dwell therein: and it shall be no more inhabited for ever; neither shall it be dwelt in.

He that followeth after righteousness and mercy, findeth life, righteousness, and honour. **Prov. 21:21** (*see also* Follow, Life, Mercy)

Job 27:6 my *r.* I hold fast, and will not let it go: my heart shall not reproach me so long as I live; **Ps. 11:7** the *r.* LORD loveth *r.*; his countenance doth behold the upright; **26:1** judge me, O LORD; for I have walked in mine integrity: I have trusted also in the LORD; therefore I shall not slide; **33:5** he loveth *r.* and judgment: the earth is full of the goodness of the LORD; **37:16** a little that a *r.* man hath is better than the riches of many wicked; **37:29** the *r.* shall inherit the land, and dwell therein for ever; **65:5** by terrible things in *r.* wilt thou answer us, O God of our salvation; who art the confidence of all the ends of the earth, and of them that are afar off upon the sea; **92:12** the *r.* shall flourish like the palm tree: he shall grow like a cedar in Lebanon; **107:42** the *r.* shall see it, and rejoice: and all iniquity shall stop her; **118:19-20** open to me the gates of *r.*: I will go into them, and I will praise the LORD: This gate of the LORD, into which the *r.* shall enter; **146:8** the LORD openeth the eyes of the blind: the LORD raiseth them that are bowed down: the LORD loveth the *r.*; **Prov. 2:7** he layeth up sound wisdom for the *r.*: he is a buckler to them that walk uprightly; **10:21** the lips of the *r.* feed many: but fools die for want of wisdom; **10:24-25** the fear of the wicked, it shall come upon him: but the desire of the *r.* shall be granted. As the whirlwind passeth, so is the wicked no more: but the *r.* is an everlasting foundation; **10:28-30** the hope of the *r.* shall be gladness: but the expectation of the wicked shall perish; **10:32** the lips of the *r.* know what is acceptable: but the mouth of the wicked speaketh frowardness; **11:4-6** the *r.* of the perfect shall direct his way: but the wicked shall fall by his own wickedness. The *r.* of the upright shall deliver them: but transgressors shall be taken in their own naughtiness; **11:8** the *r.* is delivered out of trouble, and the wicked cometh in his stead; **11:10** when it goeth well with the *r.*, the city rejoiceth: and when the wicked perish, there is shouting; **11:18-19** the wicked worketh a deceitful work: but to him that soweth *r.* shall be a sure reward. As *r.* tendeth to life: so he that pursueth evil pursueth it to his own death; **11:21** though hand join in hand, the wicked shall not be unpunished: but the seed of the *r.* shall be delivered; **11:23** the desire of the *r.* is only good: but the expectation of the wicked is wrath;

11:28-31 the fruit of the *r.* is a tree of life; and he that winneth souls is wise. Behold, the *r.* shall be recompensed in the earth: much more the wicked and the sinner; **12:3** a man shall not be established by wickedness: but the root of the *r.* shall not be moved; **12:5** the thoughts of the *r.* are right: but the counsels of the wicked are deceit; **12:7** the wicked are overthrown, and are not: but the house of the *r.* shall stand; **12:12** the wicked desireth the net of evil men: but the root of the *r.* yieldeth fruit; **12:28** in the way of *r.* is life; and in the pathway thereof there is no death; **13:5-6** a *r.* man hateth lying: but a wicked man is loathsome, and cometh to shame. *R.* keepeth him that is upright in the way: but wickedness overthroweth the sinner; **13:21** evil pursueth sinners: but to the *r.* good shall be repayed; **13:25** the *r.* eateth to the satisfying of his soul: but the belly of the wicked shall want; **15:6** in the house of the *r.* is much treasure: but in the revenues of the wicked is trouble; **15:9** the way of the wicked is an abomination unto the LORD: but he loveth him that followeth after *r.*; **15:19** the way of the slothful man is as an hedge of thorns: but the way of the *r.* is made plain; **15:29** the LORD is far from the wicked: but he heareth the prayer of the *r.*; **16:8** better is a little with *r.* than great revenues without right; **21:21** he that followeth after *r.* and mercy findeth life, *r.*, and honour; **23:23-24** the father of the *r.* shall greatly rejoice: and he that begetteth a wise child shall have joy of him; **28:1** the wicked flee when no man pursueth: but the *r.* are bold as a lion; **28:28** when the wicked rise, men hide themselves: but when they perish, the *r.* increase; **29:2** when the *r.* are in authority, the people rejoice: but when the wicked beareth rule, the people mourn; **Isa. 3:10** say ye to the *r.*, that it shall be well with him: for they shall eat the fruit of their doings; **11:4-5** with *r.* shall he judge the poor, and reprove with equity for the meek of the earth: and he shall smite the earth with the rod of his mouth, and with the breath of his lips shall he slay the wicked; **32:16-18** judgment shall dwell in the wilderness, and *r.* remain in the fruitful field. And the work of *r.* shall be peace; and the effect of *r.* quietness and assurance for ever; **45:13** I have raised him up in *r.*, and I will direct all his ways: he shall build my city, and he shall let go my captives, not for price nor reward, saith the LORD; **51:1-2** hearken to me, ye that follow after *r.*, ye that seek the LORD: look unto the rock whence ye are hewn, and to the hole of the pit whence ye are digged; **59:16-17** his arm brought salvation unto him; and his *r.*, it sustained him. For he put on *r.* as a breastplate, and an helmet of salvation upon his head; **60:21** thy people also

shall be all *r.*: they shall inherit the land for ever, the branch of my planting, the work of my hands, that I may be glorified; **61:10-11** I will greatly rejoice in the LORD, my soul shall be joyful in my God; for he hath clothed me with the garments of salvation, he hath covered me with the robe of *r.*; **62:2** the Gentiles shall see thy *r.*, and all kings thy glory: and thou shalt be called by a new name, which the mouth of the LORD shall name; **64:5-6** thou meetest him that rejoiceth and worketh *r.*, those that remember thee in thy ways: behold, thou art wroth; for we have sinned: in those is continuance, and we shall be saved; **Jer. 17:18** let them be confounded that persecute me, but let not me be confounded: let them be dismayed, but let not me be dismayed: bring upon them the day of evil, and destroy them with double destruction; **33:16** in those days shall Judah be saved, and Jerusalem shall dwell safely: and this is the name wherewith she shall be called, The LORD our *r.*; **Ezek. 33:18** when the *r.* turneth from his *r.*, and committeth iniquity, he shall even die thereby; **Hosea 10:12** sow to yourselves in *r.*, reap in mercy; break up your fallow ground: for it is time to seek the LORD, till he come and rain *r.* upon you; **Zeph. 2:3** seek ye the LORD, all ye meek of the earth, which have wrought his judgment; seek *r.*, seek meekness: it may be ye shall be hid in the day of the LORDs anger; **3:19-20** at that time I will undo all that afflict thee: and I will save her that halteth, and gather her that was driven out; and I will get them praise and fame in every land where they have been put to shame.

Blessed are they which do hunger and thirst after righteousness: for they shall be filled. Matt. 5:6 (*see also* Hunger, Thirst)

Matt. 5:6 (5:20) except your *r.* shall exceed the *r.* of the scribes and Pharisees, ye shall in no case enter into the kingdom of heaven; **6:33-34** seek ye first the kingdom of God, and his *r.*; and all these things shall be added unto you. Take therefore no thought for the morrow: for the morrow shall take thought for the things of itself. Sufficient unto the day is the evil thereof; **9:13** (Mark 2:17, Luke 5:31-32) go ye and learn what that meaneth, I will have mercy, and not sacrifice: for I am not come to call the *r.*, but sinners to repentance; **10:41** he that receiveth a prophet in the name of a prophet shall receive a prophet's reward; and he that receiveth a *r.* man in the name of a *r.* man shall receive a *r.* man's reward; **13:17** many prophets and *r.* men have desired to see those things which ye see, and have not seen them; and to hear those things which ye hear, and have not heard them; **13:43** then shall the *r.* shine forth as the sun in the kingdom of their Father. Who hath ears to hear, let him hear; **21:32** John came unto you in the way of *r.*, and ye believed him not: but the publicans and the harlots believed him: and ye, when ye had seen it, repented not afterward, that ye might believe him; **24:22** (Mark 13:20) except those days should be shortened, there should no flesh be saved: but for the elect's sake those days shall be shortened; **25:33-37** he shall set the sheep on his right hand, but the goats on the left. Then shall the King say unto them on his right hand, Come, ye blessed of my Father, inherit the kingdom prepared for you from the foundation of the world; **25:46** these shall go away into everlasting punishment: but the *r.* into life eternal; **Luke 1:6** they were both *r.* before God, walking in all the commandments and ordinances of the Lord blameless; **1:53** he hath filled the hungry with good things; and the rich he hath sent empty away; **1:74-75** he would grant unto us, that we being delivered out of the hand of our enemies might serve him without fear, In holiness and *r.* before him, all the days of our life; **6:20-21** he lifted up his eyes on his disciples, and said, Blessed be ye poor: for yours is the kingdom of God. Blessed are ye that hunger now: for ye shall be filled. Blessed are ye that weep now: for ye shall laugh; **23:47** when the centurion saw what was done, he glorified God, saying, Certainly this was a *r.* man; **John 7:18** he that speaketh of himself seeketh his own glory: but he that seeketh his glory that sent him, the same is true, and no unr. is in him; **8:34** whosoever committeth sin is the servant of sin; **8:47** he that is of God heareth God's words: ye therefore hear them not, because ye are not of God; **Acts 4:19** whether it be right in the sight of God to hearken unto you more than unto God, judge ye; **10:35** every nation he that feareth him, and worketh *r.*, is accepted with him; **Rom. 1:17** therein is the *r.* of God revealed from faith to faith: as it is written, The just shall live by faith; **3:21-22** the *r.* of God without the law is manifested, being witnessed by the law and the prophets; Even the *r.* of God which is by faith of Jesus Christ unto all and upon all them that believe: for there is no difference; **3:23-24** all have sinned, and come short of the glory of God; Being justified freely by his grace through the redemption that is in Christ Jesus; **4:3** Abraham believed God, and it was counted unto him for *r.*; **4:9** cometh this blessedness then upon the circumcision only, or upon the uncircumcision also? for we say that faith was reckoned to

Abraham for *r.*; **4:11** he received the sign of circumcision, a seal of the *r.* of the faith which he had yet being uncircumcised: that he might be the father of all them that believe, though they be not circumcised; that *r.* might be imputed unto them also; **4:13** the promise, that he should be the heir of the world, was not to Abraham, or to his seed, through the law, but through the *r.* of faith; **4:22-24** it was imputed to him for *r.*. Now it was not written for his sake alone, that it was imputed to him; But for us also, to whom it shall be imputed, if we believe on him that raised up Jesus our Lord from the dead; **5:19** by one man's disobedience many were made sinners, so by the obedience of one shall many be made *r.*; **5:21** as sin hath reigned unto death, even so might grace reign through *r.* unto eternal life by Jesus Christ our Lord; **6:13** neither yield ye your members as instruments of unr. unto sin: but yield yourselves unto God, as those that are alive from the dead, and your members as instruments of *r.* unto God; **6:16** know ye not, that to whom ye yield yourselves servants to obey, his servants ye are to whom ye obey; whether of sin unto death, or of obedience unto *r.*; **7:14** For we know that the law is spiritual: but I am carnal, sold under sin; **8:9-10** but ye are not in the flesh, but in the Spirit, if so be that the Spirit of God dwell in you. Now if any man have not the Spirit of Christ, he is none of his. And if Christ be in you, the body is dead because of sin; but the Spirit is life because of *r.*; **9:30** what shall we say then? That the Gentiles, which followed not after *r.*, have attained to *r.*, even the *r.* which is of faith; **9:31** Israel, which followed after the law of *r.*, hath not attained to the law of *r.*; **10:3-4** they being ignorant of God's *r.*, and going about to establish their own *r.*, have not submitted themselves unto the *r.* of God. For Christ is the end of the law for *r.* to every one that believeth; **10:6** the *r.* which is of faith speaketh on this wise, Say not in thine heart, Who shall ascend into heaven? (that is, to bring Christ down from above); **10:10** with the heart man believeth unto *r.*; and with the mouth confession is made unto salvation; **14:15-18** if thy brother be grieved with thy meat, now walkest thou not charitably. Destroy not him with thy meat, for whom Christ died. Let not then your good be evil spoken of: For the kingdom of God is not meat and drink; but *r.*, and peace, and joy in the Holy Ghost. For he that in these things serveth Christ is acceptable to God, and approved of men; **1 Cor. 6:9** know ye not that the unrighteous shall not inherit the kingdom of God? Be not deceived: neither fornicators, nor idolaters, nor adulterers, nor effeminate, nor abusers of themselves with mankind; **15:34** awake to *r.*, and sin not; for some have not the knowledge of God: I speak this to your shame; **2 Cor. 3:9** if the ministration of condemnation be glory, much more doth the ministration of *r.* exceed in glory; **5:21** he hath made him to be sin for us, who knew no sin; that we might be made the *r.* of God in him; **6:7** the word of truth, by the power of God, by the armour of *r.* on the right hand and on the left; **9:9** he hath given to the poor: his *r.* remaineth for ever; **Gal. 3:6** even as Abraham believed God, and it was accounted to him for *r.*; **3:21** is the law then against the promises of God? God forbid: for if there had been a law given which could have given life, verily *r.* should have been by the law; **5:5** For we through the Spirit wait for the hope of *r.* by faith; **Eph. 4:24** put on the new man, which after God is created in *r.* and true holiness; **5:9** (For the fruit of the Spirit is in all goodness and *r.* and truth); **Philip. 1:11** being filled with the fruits of *r.*, which are by Jesus Christ, unto the glory and praise of God; **3:9** be found in him, not having mine own *r.*, which is of the law, but that which is through the faith of Christ, the *r.* which is of God by faith; **1 Tim. 6:11** O man of God, flee these things; and follow after *r.*, godliness, faith, love, patience, meekness; **2 Tim. 2:22** flee also youthful lusts: but follow *r.*, faith, charity, peace, with them that call on the Lord out of a pure heart; **3:16** all scripture is given by inspiration of God, and is profitable for doctrine, for reproof, for correction, for instruction in *r.*; **Titus 2:12** teaching us that, denying ungodliness and worldly lusts, we should live soberly, *r.*, and godly, in this present world; **Heb. 1:9** thou hast loved *r.*, and hated iniquity; therefore God, even thy God, hath anointed thee with the oil of gladness above thy fellows; **3:2** who was faithful to him that appointed him, as also Moses was faithful in all his house; **5:12-14** for when for the time ye ought to be teachers, ye have need that one teach you again which be the first principles of the oracles of God; and are become such as have need of milk, and not of strong meat. For every one that useth milk is unskilful in the word of *r.*: for he is a babe. But strong meat belongeth to them that are of full age, even those who by reason of use have their senses exercised to discern both good and evil; **11:7** by faith Noah, being warned of God of things not seen as yet, moved with fear, prepared an ark to the saving of his house; by the which he condemn-

ed the world, and became heir of the *r.* which is by faith; **11:33** who through faith subdued kingdoms, wrought *r.*, obtained promises, stopped the mouths of lions; **12:11** now no chastening for the present seemeth to be joyous, but grievous: nevertheless afterward it yieldeth the peaceable fruit of *r.* unto them which are exercised thereby; **James 1:20** the wrath of man worketh not the *r.* of God; **2:23** the scripture was fulfilled which saith, Abraham believed God, and it was imputed unto him for *r.*: and he was called the Friend of God; **3:18** the fruit of *r.* is sown in peace of them that make peace; **5:16-18** the effectual fervent prayer of a *r.* man availeth much. Elias was a man subject to like passions as we are, and he prayed earnestly that it might not rain: and it rained not on the earth by the space of three years and six months. And he prayed again, and the heaven gave rain, and the earth brought forth her fruit; **1 Pet. 2:24** who his own self bare our sins in his own body on the tree, that we, being dead to sins, should live unto *r.*: by whose stripes ye were healed; **3:7-13** let him eschew evil, and do good; let him seek peace, and ensue it. For the eyes of the Lord are over the *r.*, and his ears are open unto their prayers: but the face of the Lord is against them that do evil; **3:14** But and if ye suffer for *r.'* sake, happy are ye: and be not afraid of their terror, neither be troubled; **4:18** if the *r.* scarcely be saved, where shall the ungodly and the sinner appear; **2 Pet. 1:1** Simon Peter, a servant and an apostle of Jesus Christ, to them that have obtained like precious faith with us through the *r.* of God and our Saviour Jesus Christ; **2:5** spared not the old world, but saved Noah the eighth person, a preacher of *r.*, bringing in the flood upon the world of the ungodly; **3:14** seeing that ye look for such things, be diligent that ye may be found of him in peace, without spot, and blameless; **1 Jn. 2:29** if ye know that he is *r.*, ye know that every one that doeth *r.* is born of him; **3:10** In this the children of God are manifest, and the children of the devil: whosoever doeth not *r.* is not of God, neither he that loveth not his brother.

RIGHT WAY (*see* Righteousness, Way)

RIOTING, RIOTOUS (*see also* Drunk, Rebel, Revolt, Unruly)

Whoso keepeth the law is a wise son: but he that is a companion of riotous men shameth his father. Prov. 28:7 (*see also* Law)

RISE, RISEN, ROSE (*see also* Arise)

Rise up, ye women that are at ease; hear my voice, ye careless daughters; give ear unto my speech. Many days and years shall ye be troubled, ye careless women: for the vintage shall fail, the gathering shall not come. Isa. 32:9-10 (*see also* Hear)

ROB, ROBBERY (*see also* Steal)

Trust not in oppression, and become not vain in robbery: if riches increase, set not your heart upon them. Ps. 62:10 (*see also* Heart, Increase, Oppress, Rich, Trust)

Whoso robbeth his father or his mother, and saith, It is no transgression; the same is the companion of a destroyer. Prov. 28:24 (*see also* Transgress)

Return unto me and I will return unto you, saith the Lord of Hosts. But ye said, Wherein shall we return? Will a man rob God? Yet ye have robbed me. But ye say, Wherein have we robbed thee? In tithes and offerings. Mal. 3:7 (*see also* Rob, Tithe)

ROBE (*see also* Garment)

I will greatly rejoice in the LORD, my soul shall be joyful in my God; for he hath clothed me with the garments of salvation, he hath covered me with the robe of righteousness. Isa. 61:10 (*see also* Garments, Righteous)

ROCK (*see also* Cornerstone, Foundation, Jesus Christ, Revelation, Stone)

ROD (*see also* Gospel, Word)

Feed thy people with thy rod, the flock of thine heritage, which dwell solitarily in the wood. Micah 7:14 (*see also* Feed)

RULE, RULER (*see also* Authority, Dominion, Government, King, Unrighteous Dominion)

The merciful man doeth good to his own soul: but he that is cruel troubleth his own flesh. Prov. 11:17 (*see also* Cruel, Force, Merciful)

He that hath no rule over his own spirit is like a city that is broken down and without walls. Prov. 25:28 (*see also* Self Control, Spirit)

If a man know not how to rule his own house, how shall he take care of the church of God? 1 Tim. 3:4-5 (*see also* Order)

When the righteous are in authority, the people rejoice: but when the wicked beareth rule, the people mourn. Prov. 29:2 (*see also* Authority, Mourn, Righteous, Wicked)

Let the peace of God rule in your hearts. Col. 3:15 (*see also* Peace)

He that is slow to anger is better than the mighty; and he that ruleth his spirit than he that taketh a city. Prov. 16:32 (*see also* Anger, Spirit)

Prov. 16:32 he that is slow to anger is better than the mighty; and he that *r.* his spirit than he that taketh a city; 25:28 he that hath no *r.* over his own spirit is like a city that is broken down, and without walls.

RUN (*see also* Diligence, Race)

Seeing we also are compassed about with so great a cloud of witnesses, let us lay aside every weight, and the sin which doth so easily beset us, and let us run with patience the race that is set before us. Heb. 12:1 (*see also* Beset, Lay Aside, Patience, Race, Sin, Weight, Witness)

Heb 12:1 seeing we also are compassed about with so great a cloud of witnesses, let us lay aside every weight, and the sin which doth so easily beset us, and let us *r.* with patience the race that is set before us; **Philip. 2:16** holding forth the word of life; that I may rejoice in the day of Christ, that I have not *r.* in vain, neither laboured in vain.

SABBATH (*see also* Church, Day, Holy, Peace, Rest)

Hallow the sabbath day, to do no work therein. Jer. 17:24 (*see also* Hallow)

The seventh day is the sabbath of the LORD thy God: in it thou shalt not do any work, thou, nor thy son, nor thy daughter, thy manservant, nor thy maidservant, nor thy cattle, nor thy stranger that is within thy gates: Ex. 20:10 (*see also* Seventh, Thou Shalt Not, Work)

Thou hast despised mine holy things, and hast profaned my sabbaths. Ezek. 22:8 (*see also* Holiness)

The sabbath was made for man, and not man for the sabbath: Therefore the Son of man is Lord also of the sabbath. Mark 2:27-28

If thou turn away thy foot from the sabbath, from doing thy pleasure on my holy day; and call the sabbath a delight, the holy of the LORD, honorable; and shalt honor him, not doing thy own ways, nor finding thine own pleasure, nor speaking thine own words: Then shalt thou delight thyself in the LORD; and I will cause thee to ride upon the high places of the earth, and feed thee with the heritage of Jacob thy father: for the mouth of the LORD hath spoken it. Isa. 58:13-14 (*see also* Delight, Honor)

Remember the sabbath day, to keep it holy. Six days shalt thou labour, and do all thy work: But the seventh day is the sabbath of the LORD thy God: in it thou shalt not do any work, thou, nor thy son, nor thy daughter, thy manservant, nor thy maidservant, nor thy cattle, nor thy stranger that is within thy gates: For in six days the LORD made heaven and earth, the sea, and all that in them is, and rested the seventh day: wherefore the LORD blessed the sabbath day, and hallowed it. Ex. 20:8-11 (*see also* Labor, Thou Shalt, Work)

Gen. 2:3 God blessed the seventh day, and sanctified it; Ex. 16:23 this is that which the LORD hath said, To morrow is the rest of the holy s. unto the LORD; 16:25-27 six days ye shall gather it; but on the seventh day, which is the s., in it there shall be none; 16:29-30 he giveth you on the sixth day the bread of two days; let no man go out of his place on the seventh day. So the people rested on the seventh day; 20:8-11 remember the s. day, to keep it holy. the seventh day is the s. of the LORD thy God: in it thou shalt not do any work, the LORD blessed the s. day, and hallowed it; 23:12 six days thou shalt do thy work, and on the seventh day thou shalt rest; 31:13-17 my s. ye shall keep: Ye shall keep the s. it is holy unto you: in the seventh is the s. of rest, holy to the LORD: the children of Israel shall keep the s., for a perpetual covenant; 35:2-3 on the seventh day there shall be to you an holy day, a s. of rest to the LORD: Ye shall kindle no fire throughout your habitations upon the s. day; Lev. 19:3 ye shall keep my s.: I am the LORD your God; 19:30 ye shall keep my s.; 23:3 six

days shall work be done: but the seventh day is the s. of rest, an holy convocation; ye shall do no work therein: it is the s. of the LORD in all your dwellings; 25:2 when ye come into the land which I give you, then shall the land keep a s. unto the LORD; 25:4-6 in the seventh year shall be a s. of rest unto the land, the s. of the land shall be meat for you; 25:8 thou shalt number seven s. of years unto thee; 26:2 ye shall keep my s., and reverence my sanctuary: I am the LORD; Deut. 5:12-15 keep the s. day to sanctify it, as the LORD thy God hath commanded thee. the seventh day is the s. of the LORD thy God: the LORD thy God commanded thee to keep the s. day; 2 Chron. 36:21 to fulfil the word of the LORD, until the land had enjoyed her s.; Neh. 9:14 known unto them thy holy s.; 10:31 we would not buy it of them on the s.; 13:16-22 ye bring more wrath upon Israel by profaning the s.; Isa. 56:2 blessed is the man that... keepeth the s. from polluting it, and keepeth his hand from doing any evil; 56:4 thus saith the LORD unto [those] that keep my s., and choose the things that please me, and take hold of my covenant; 56:6-7 every one that keepeth the s. from polluting it, and taketh hold of my covenant; Even them will I bring to my holy mountain, and make them joyful; 58:13-14 if thou turn away thy foot from the s., from doing thy pleasure on my holy day; and call the s. a delight, the holy of the LORD, honourable; and shalt honour him, not doing thine own ways, nor finding thine own pleasure, nor speaking thine own words: Then shalt thou delight thyself in the LORD; 66:23 from one s. to another, shall all flesh come to worship before me; Jer. 17:21-22 bear no burden on the s. day, nor bring it in by the gates of Jerusalem; Neither carry forth a burden out of your houses on the s. day, neither do ye any work, but hallow ye the s. day; 17:24 bring in no burden through the gates of this city on the s. day, but hallow the s. day, to do no work therein; Ezek. 20:12-13 I gave them my s., to be a sign between me and them, that they might know that I am the LORD that sanctify them. But the house of Israel rebelled against me in the wilderness: they walked not in my statutes, and they despised my judgments... and my s. they greatly polluted; 20:20-21 hallow my s.; and they shall be a sign between me and you, that ye may know that I am the LORD your God; 20:24 they had not executed my judgments, but had despised my statutes, and had polluted my s.; 22:8 thou hast despised mine holy things, and hast profaned my s.; 22:26 [they] have profaned mine holy things: they have put no difference between the holy and profane, neither have they shewed difference between the unclean and the clean, and have hid their eyes from my *s.*, and I am profaned among them; **23:38** they have defiled my sanctuary in the same day, and have profaned my *s.*; **44:24** they shall keep my laws and my statutes in all mine assemblies; and they shall hallow my *s.*

They returned, and prepared spices and ointments; and rested the sabbath day according to the commandment. Luke 23:56 (*see also* Rest)

Mark 3:1-3 they watched him, whether he would heal him on the *s.* day; that they might accuse him. And he saith unto the man which had the withered hand, Stand forth; **Luke 4:31** taught them on the *s.* days; **13:14-17** the ruler of the synagogue answered with indignation, because that Jesus had healed on the *s.* day, and said unto the people, There are six days in which men ought to work: in them therefore come and be healed, and not on the *s.* day. The Lord then answered him, and said, Thou hypocrite, doth not each one of you on the *s.* loose his ox or his ass from the stall, and lead him away to watering?; **14:3-5** is it lawful to heal on the *s.* day? And they held their peace. And he took him, and healed him, and let him go; And answered them, saying, Which of you shall have an ass or an ox fallen into a pit, and will not straightway pull him out on the *s.* day; **23:56** they returned, and prepared spices and ointments; and rested the *s.* day according to the commandment; **John 5:16-17** therefore did the Jews persecute Jesus, and sought to slay him, because he had done these things on the *s.* day. But Jesus answered them, My Father worketh hitherto, and I work; **7:23** if a man on the *s.* day receive circumcision, that the law of Moses should not be broken; are ye angry at me, because I have made a man every whit whole on the *s.* day; **9:14** it was the *s.* day when Jesus made the clay, and opened his eyes; **9:16** said some of the Pharisees, This man is not of God, because he keepeth not the *s.* day; **Heb. 4:4-11** he spake in a certain place of the seventh day on this wise, And God did rest the seventh day from all his works.

Do well on the sabbath days. Matt. 12:12 (*see also* Do)

Matt. 12:1-8 (Luke 6:2-5) Jesus went on the *s.* day through the corn; and his disciples were an hungred, and began to pluck the ears of corn, and to eat. But when the Pharisees saw it, they said unto him, Behold, thy disciples do that which is not lawful to do upon the *s.* day. But he said unto them, Have ye not read what David did, when he was an hungred, and they that were with him; How he entered into the house of God, and did eat the shewbread, which was not lawful for him to eat, neither for them which were with him, but only for the priests? Or have ye not read in the law, how that on the *s.* days the priests in the temple profane the *s.*, and are blameless? But I say unto you, That in this place is one greater than the temple. But if ye had known what this meaneth, I will have mercy, and not sacrifice, ye would not have condemned the guiltless. For the Son of man is Lord even of the *s.* day; **12:10-12** there was a man which had his hand withered. And they asked him, saying, Is it lawful to heal on the *s.* days? that they might accuse him. And he said unto them, What man shall there be among you, that shall have one sheep, and if it fall into a pit on the *s.* day, will he not lay hold on it, and lift it out? How much then is a man better than a sheep? Wherefore it is lawful to do well on the *s.* days; **24:20** pray ye that your flight be not in the winter, neither on the *s.* day; **Mark 3:2-4** they watched him, whether he would heal him on the *s.* day; that they might accuse him. And he saith unto the man which had the withered hand, Stand forth. And he saith unto them, Is it lawful to do good on the *s.* days, or to do evil? to save life, or to kill? But they held their peace; **6:2** when the *s.* day was come, he began to teach in the synagogue; **Luke 6:6-10** And it came to pass also on another *s.*, that he entered into the synagogue and taught: and there was a man whose right hand was withered. And the scribes and Pharisees watched him, whether he would heal on the *s.* day; that they might find an accusation against him. But he knew their thoughts, and said to the man which had the withered hand, Rise up, and stand forth in the midst. And he arose and stood forth. Then said Jesus unto them, I will ask you one thing; Is it lawful on the *s.* days to do good, or to do evil? to save life, or to destroy it? And looking round about upon them all, he said unto the man, Stretch forth thy hand. And he did so: and his hand was restored whole as the other; **13:13-16** the ruler of the synagogue answered with indignation, because that Jesus had healed on the *s.* day, and said unto the people, There are six days in which men ought to work: in them therefore come and be healed, and not on the *s.* day. The Lord then answered him, and said, Thou hypocrite, doth not each one of you on the *s.* loose his ox or his ass from the stall, and lead him away to watering? And ought not this woman, being a daughter of Abraham, whom

Satan hath bound, lo, these eighteen years, be loosed from this bond on the *s.* day; **14:3-5** is it lawful to heal on the *s.* day? And they held their peace. And he took him, and healed him, and let him go; And answered them, saying, Which of you shall have an ass or an ox fallen into a pit, and will not straightway pull him out on the *s.* day; **John 5:10-12** the Jews therefore said unto him that was cured, It is the *s.* day: it is not lawful for thee to carry thy bed. He answered them, He that made me whole, the same said unto me, Take up thy bed, and walk. Then asked they him, What man is that which said unto thee, Take up thy bed, and walk; **9:14-16** it was the *s.* day when Jesus made the clay, and opened his eyes. Then again the Pharisees also asked him how he had received his sight. He said unto them, He put clay upon mine eyes, and I washed, and do see. Therefore said some of the Pharisees, This man is not of God, because he keepeth not the *s.* day. Others said, How can a man that is a sinner do such miracles? And there was a division among them.

SACRAMENT (*see also* Atonement, Bread, Jesus Christ, Name, Water)

Whosoever shall eat this bread, and drink this cup of the Lord, unworthily, shall be guilty of the body and blood of the Lord. But let a man examine himself, and so let him eat of that bread, and drink of that cup. For he that eateth and drinketh unworthily, eateth and drinketh damnation to himself, not discerning the Lord's body. 1 Cor. 11:27-29 (*see also* Examine, Unworthiness, Worthy)

The Lord Jesus the same night in which he was betrayed took bread: And when he had given thanks, he brake it, and said, Take, eat: this is my body, which is broken for you: this do in remembrance of me. After the same manner also he took the cup, when he had supped, saying, This cup is the new testament in my blood: this do ye, as oft as ye drink it, in remembrance of me. For as often as ye eat this bread, and drink this cup, ye do shew the Lord's death till he come. 1 Cor. 11:23-26

Matt. 26:26-28 (Mark 14:22-24, Luke 22:19-20, 1 Cor. 11:23-26) Jesus took bread, and blessed it, and brake it, and gave it to the disciples, and said, Take, eat; this is my body. And he took the cup, and gave thanks, and gave it to them, saying, Drink ye all of it. For this is my blood of the new testament, which is shed for many for the remission of sins; **John 6:53-56** except ye eat the flesh of the Son of man, and drink his blood, ye have no life in you. Whoso eateth my flesh, and drinketh my blood, hath eternal life; and I will raise him up at the last day. For my flesh is meat indeed, and my blood is drink indeed. He that eateth my flesh, and drinketh my blood, dwelleth in me, and I in him; **Acts 2:42** they continued stedfastly in the apostles' doctrine and fellowship, and in breaking of bread, and in prayers; **1 Cor. 10:16-17** the cup of blessing which we bless, is it not the communion of the blood of Christ? The bread which we break, is it not the communion of the body of Christ? For we being many are one bread, and one body: for we are all partakers of that one bread.

SACRED (*see* Holiness, Sanctified, Virtue)

SACRIFICE (*see also* Atone, Blood, Charity, Jesus Christ, Offer, Redeem, Save, Serve)

Ye also, as lively stones, are built up a spiritual house, an holy priesthood, to offer up spiritual sacrifices, acceptable to God by Jesus Christ. 1 Pet. 2:5 (*see also* Jesus Christ, Offer, Priesthood)

I will offer to thee the sacrifice of thanksgiving, and will call upon the name of the Lord. Ps. 116:17 (*see also* Thank)

Offer sacrifices of righteousness. Deut. 33:19 (*see also* Offer)

Gen. 8:20 Noah... took of every clean beast, and of every clean fowl, and offered burnt offerings on the altar; **46:1** Israel took his journey with all that he had... and offered *s.* unto the God of his father; **Ex. 10:25** thou must give us also *s.* and burnt offerings, that we may *s.* unto the LORD our God; **18:12** Jethro... took a burnt offering and *s.* for God; **Deut. 33:19** they shall offer *s.* of righteousness; **1 Sam. 6:15** [they] offered burnt offerings and *s. s.* the same day unto the LORD; **11:15** they *s. s.* of peace offerings before the LORD; **2 Kgs. 10:24** they went in to offer *s.* and burnt offerings; **1 Chron. 16:1** they offered burnt *s.* and peace offerings before God; **23:31** offer all burnt *s.* unto the LORD in the sabbaths, in the new moons, and on the set feasts, by number, according to the order commanded unto them; **29:21** they *s. s.* unto the LORD, and offered burnt offerings unto the LORD; **2 Chron. 7:4** the king and all the people offered *s.* before the LORD; **13:11** they burn unto the LORD every morning and every evening burnt *s.* and sweet incense; **29:31** come near and bring *s.* and thank offerings into the house of the LORD; **Ezra 6:9-10** they may offer *s.* of sweet savours unto the God of heaven, and pray for the life of the king, and of his sons; **Neh. 12:43** they offered great *s.*, and rejoiced: for God had made them rejoice with great joy; **Ps. 4:5** offer the *s.* of righteousness, and put your trust in the LORD; **27:6** I [will] offer in his tabernacle *s.* of joy; I will sing, yea, I will sing praises unto the LORD; **50:8** I will not reprove thee for thy *s.* or thy burnt offerings, to have been continually before me; **51:17-19** The *s.* of God are a broken spirit: a broken and a contrite heart... Then shalt thou be pleased with the *s.* of righteousness; **66:15** I will offer unto thee burnt *s.* of fatlings, with the incense of rams; **107:22** let them *s.* the *s.* of thanksgiving; **Isa. 43:23-24** neither hast thou filled me with the fat of thy *s.*: but thou hast made me to serve with thy sins, thou hast wearied me with thine iniquities; **56:7** them will I bring to my holy mountain, and make them joyful in my house of prayer: their burnt offerings and their *s.* shall be accepted upon mine altar; **Jer. 6:20** your burnt offerings are not acceptable, nor your *s.* sweet unto me; **7:21-22** put your burnt offerings unto your *s.*, and eat flesh; **17:26** they shall come... bringing burnt offerings, and *s.*, and meat offerings, and incense, and bringing *s.* of praise, unto the house of the LORD; **Ezek. 20:28** they offered there their *s.*, and there they presented the provocation of their offering; **Hosea 8:13** they *s.* flesh for the *s.* of mine offerings, and eat it; but the LORD accepteth them not; **Amos 4:4** bring your *s.* every morning, and your tithes after three years.

When ye offer your gifts, when ye make your sons to pass through the fire, ye pollute yourselves with all your idols, even unto this day. Ezek. 20:31 (*see also* False)

Jer. 7:31-34 they have built the high places... to burn their sons and their daughters in the fire; which I commanded them not, neither came it into my heart; **19:5-11** they have built also the high places of Baal, to burn their sons with fire for burnt offerings unto Baal, which I commanded not, nor spake it, neither came it into my mind; **32:35** they built the high places... to cause their sons and their daughters to pass through the fire unto Molech; which I commanded them not, neither came it into my mind, that they should do this abomination; **Ezek. 16:20-21** is this of thy whoredoms a small matter, That thou hast slain my children, and delivered them to cause them to pass through the fire for them; **16:36-42** thy filthiness was poured

out, and thy nakedness discovered through thy whoredoms with thy lovers, and with all the idols of thy abominations, and by the blood of thy children, which thou didst give unto them; Behold, therefore... I will judge thee; **20:28** when I had brought them into the land, for the which I lifted up mine hand to give it to them, then they saw every high hill, and all the thick trees, and they offered there their sacrifices; **20:31** when ye offer your gifts, when ye make your sons to pass through the fire, ye pollute yourselves with all your idols, even unto this day; **23:37** blood is in their hands, and with their idols have they committed adultery, and have also caused their sons, whom they bare unto me, to pass for them through the fire, to devour them; **Hosea 4:19** the wind hath bound her up in her wings, and they shall be ashamed because of their *s.*

If thou wilt be perfect, go and sell that thou hast, and give to the poor, and thou shalt have treasure in heaven: and come and follow me. Matt. 19:21-22 (*see also* Follow, Perfect, Treasure)

Matt. 19:21-22 if thou wilt be perfect, go and sell that thou hast, and give to the poor, and thou shalt have treasure in heaven: and come and follow me; **19:27** behold, we have forsaken all, and followed thee; what shall we have therefore; **19:29** every one that hath forsaken houses, or brethren, or sisters, or father, or mother, or wife, or children, or lands, for my name's sake, shall receive an hundredfold, and shall inherit everlasting life; **Mark 10:21** one thing thou lackest: go thy way, sell whatsoever thou hast, and give to the poor, and thou shalt have treasure in heaven: and come, take up the cross, and follow me; **10:29-30** there is no man that hath left house, or brethren, or sisters, or father, or mother, or wife, or children, or lands, for my sake, and the gospel's, But he shall receive an hundredfold now in this time, houses, and brethren, and sisters, and mothers, and children, and lands, with persecutions; and in the world to come eternal life; **12:41-44** (Luke 21:1-4) this poor widow hath cast more in, than all they which have cast into the treasury: For all they did cast in of their abundance; but she of her want did cast in all that she had, even all her living; **Luke 14:33** likewise, whosoever he be of you that forsaketh not all that he hath, he cannot be my disciple; **8:22-23** yet lackest thou one thing: sell all that thou hast, and distribute unto the poor, and thou shalt have treasure in heaven: and come, follow me; **18:28-30** we have left all, and followed thee. And he said unto them, Verily

I say unto you, There is no man that hath left house, or parents, or brethren, or wife, or children, for the kingdom of God's sake, Who shall not receive manifold more in this present time, and in the world to come life everlasting; **Acts 2:45** sold their possessions and goods, and parted them to all men, as every man had need; **21:13** what mean ye to weep and to break mine heart? for I am ready not to be bound only, but also to die at Jerusalem for the name of the Lord Jesus; **1 Pet. 2:5** ye also, as lively stones, are built up a spiritual house, an holy priesthood, to offer up spiritual *s.*, acceptable to God by Jesus Christ.

SAINTS (*see also* Church, Holy, Sheep)

Beloved, when I gave all diligence to write unto you of the common salvation, it was needful for me to write unto you, and exhort you that ye should earnestly contend for the faith which was once delivered unto the saints. Jude 1:3 (*see also* Contend, Earnestly)

Ye are no more strangers and foreigners, but fellowcitizens with the saints, and of the household of God; And are built upon the foundation of the apostles and prophets, Jesus Christ himself being the chief corner stone. Eph. 2:19-20 (*see also* Apostle, Cornerstone, Jesus Christ, Prophet)

Matt. 27:52 the graves were opened; and many bodies of the *s.* which slept arose; **Rom. 16:15** salute Philologus, and Julia, Nereus, and his sister, and Olympas, and all the *s.* which are with them; **1 Cor. 1:2** unto the church of God which is at Corinth, to them that are sanctified in Christ Jesus, called to be *s.*, with all that in every place call upon the name of Jesus Christ our Lord, both theirs and ours; **Eph. 2:19-20** now therefore ye are no more strangers and foreigners, but fellowcitizens with the *s.*, and of the household of God; And are built upon the foundation of the apostles and prophets, Jesus Christ himself being the chief corner stone; **3:8** unto me, who am less than the least of all *s.*, is this grace given, that I should preach among the Gentiles the unsearchable riches of Christ; **Philip. 1:1** to all the *s.* in Christ Jesus which are at Philippi, with the bishops and deacons; **Col. 1:2** to the *s.* and faithful brethren in Christ which are at Colosse; **1:4** since we heard of your faith in Christ Jesus, and of the love which ye have to all the *s.*; **1:26**

even the mystery which hath been hid from ages and from generations, but now is made manifest to his *s.*; **Heb. 13:24** salute all them that have the rule over you, and all the *s.*; **1 Pet. 2:9-10** ye are a chosen generation, a royal priesthood, an holy nation, a peculiar people; that ye should shew forth the praises of him who hath called you out of darkness into his marvellous light: Which in time past were not a people, but are now the people of God: which had not obtained mercy, but now have obtained mercy; **Jude 1:3** it was needful for me to write unto you, and exhort you that ye should earnestly contend for the faith which was once delivered unto the *s.*; **1:14** the Lord cometh with ten thousands of his *s.*; **Rev. 11:18** thy wrath is come, and the time of the dead, that they should be judged, and that thou shouldest give reward unto thy servants the prophets, and to the *s.*, and them that fear thy name, small and great; and shouldest destroy them which destroy the earth; **13:7-8** it was given unto him to make war with the *s.*, and to overcome them: and power was given him over all kindreds, and tongues, and nations. And all that dwell upon the earth shall worship him, whose names are not written in the book of life of the Lamb slain from the foundation of the world; **13:10** he that leadeth into captivity shall go into captivity: he that killeth with the sword must be killed with the sword. Here is the patience and the faith of the *s.*

SAKE

LORD, thou knowest: remember me, and visit me, and revenge me of my persecutors; take me not away in thy longsuffering: know that for thy sake I have suffered rebuke. Jer. 15:15 (*see also* Longsuffering, Rebuke)

SALT (*see also* Example, Testimony, Worthiness)

Ye are the salt of the earth: but if the salt have lost his savour, wherewith shall it be salted? it is thenceforth good for nothing, but to be cast out, and to be trodden under foot of men. Matt. 5:13

Matt. 5:13 Ye are the *s.* of the earth: but if the *s.* have lost his savour, wherewith shall it be *s.*? it is thenceforth good for nothing, but to be cast out, and to be trodden under foot of men.

SALUTE, SALUTATION (*see also* Greet)

SALVATION (*see also* Baptism, Deliver, Grace, Jesus Christ, Redeem, Repent, Save, Savior)

How shall we escape, if we neglect so great salvation; which at the first began to be spoken by the Lord, and was confirmed unto us by them that heard him; God also bearing them witness, both with signs and wonders, and with divers miracles, and gifts of the Holy Ghost, according to his own will? Heb. 2:3-4 (*see also* Escape, Miracle, Witness)

My soul shall be joyful in the Lord: it shall rejoice in his salvation. Ps. 35:9 (*see also* Rejoice)

It is a light thing that thou shouldest be my servant to raise up the tribes of Jacob, and to restore the preserved of Israel: I will also give thee for a light to the Gentiles, that thou mayest be my salvation unto the end of the earth. Isa. 49:6 (*see also* Earth, Gentile, Light)

Work out your own salvation in fear and trembling. Philip. 2:12

Luke 9:56 the Son of man is not come to destroy men's lives, but to save them. And they went to another village; **John 5:34** I receive not testimony from man: but these things I say, that ye might be saved; **15:4** abide in me, and I in you. As the branch cannot bear fruit of itself, except it abide in the vine; no more can ye, except ye abide in me; **Acts 5:31** him hath God exalted with his right hand to be a Prince and a Saviour, for to give repentance to Israel, and forgiveness of sins; **13:26** men and brethren, children of the stock of Abraham, and whosoever among you feareth God, to you is the word of this *s.* sent; **15:11** we believe that through the grace of the Lord Jesus Christ we shall be saved, even as they; **16:30-31** sirs, what must I do to be saved? And they said, Believe on the Lord Jesus Christ, and thou shalt be saved, and thy house; **26:18** open their eyes, and to turn them from darkness to light, and from the power of Satan unto God, that they may receive forgiveness of sins, and inheritance among them which are sanctified by faith that is in me; **Rom. 1:16** I am not ashamed of the gospel of Christ: for it is the power of God unto *s.* to every one that believeth; to the Jew first, and also to the Greek; **5:10** if, when we were enemies, we were reconciled to God by the death of his Son, much

more, being reconciled, we shall be saved by his life; **11:11** through their fall *s.* is come unto the Gentiles; **13:11** knowing the time, that now it is high time to awake out of sleep: for now is our *s.* nearer than when we believed; **1 Cor. 15:2** by which also ye are saved, if ye keep in memory what I preached unto you, unless ye have believed in vain; **2 Cor. 6:2** I have heard thee in a time accepted, and in the day of *s.* have I succoured thee: behold, now is the accepted time; behold, now is the day of *s.*; **Gal. 6:5** for every man shall bear his own burden; **Eph. 2:8-9** for by grace are ye saved through faith; and that not of yourselves: it is the gift of God: Not of works, lest any man should boast; **Philip. 1:20** according to my earnest expectation and my hope, that in nothing I shall be ashamed, but that with all boldness, as always, so now also Christ shall be magnified in my body, whether it be by life, or by death; **2:12** ye have always obeyed, not as in my presence only, but now much more in my absence, work out your own *s.* with fear and trembling; **1 Thes. 5:10** who died for us, that, whether we wake or sleep, we should live together with him; **2 Tim. 2:10** I endure all things for the elect's sakes, that they may also obtain the *s.* which is in Christ Jesus with eternal glory; **3:15** from a child thou hast known the holy scriptures, which are able to make thee wise unto *s.* through faith which is in Christ Jesus; **Heb. 2:3** how shall we escape, if we neglect so great *s.*; **2:10-12** he that sanctifieth and they who are sanctified are all of one: for which cause he is not ashamed to call them brethren; **Rev. 12:10** I heard a loud voice saying in heaven, Now is come *s.*, and strength, and the kingdom of our God, and the power of his Christ.

God hath from the beginning chosen you to salvation through sanctification of the Spirit and belief of the truth. 2 Thes. 2:13 (*see also* Believe, True)

John 8:45-47 because I tell you the truth, ye believe me not. Which of you convinceth me of sin? And if I say the truth, why do ye not believe me? He that is of God heareth God's words: ye therefore hear them not, because ye are not of God; **14:29** I have told you before it come to pass, that, when it is come to pass, ye might believe; **1 Thes. 2:13** for this cause also thank we God without ceasing, because, when ye received the word of God which ye heard of us, ye received it not as the word of men, but as it is in truth, the word of God, which effectually worketh also in you that believe; **2 Thes. 2:13** God hath from the beginning chosen you to *s.*

through sanctification of the Spirit and belief of the truth; **2 Tim. 4:4** they shall turn away their ears from the truth, and shall be turned unto fables.

SAME (*see* Familiar, One, United)

SANCTIFICATION, SANCTIFIED, SANCTIFY (*see also* Atone, Baptism, Born Again, Holy Ghost, Purify)

Sanctify the Lord God in your heats; and be ready always to give an answer to every man that asketh you a reason of the hope that is in you with meekness and fear: Having a good conscience; that, whereas they speak evil of you, as of evildoers, they may be ashamed that falsely accuse your good conversation in Christ. 1 Pet. 3:15-16 (*see also* Answer, Conversation, Hope, Ready, Reason)

Sanctify yourselves therefore, and be ye holy: for I am the LORD your God. Lev. 20:7-8

Ex. 19:22 let the priests also, which come near to the LORD, *s.* themselves, lest the LORD break forth upon them; **31:13** my sabbaths ye shall keep: for it is a sign between me and you throughout your generations; that ye may know that I am the LORD that doth *s.* you; **Lev. 8:11-12** he sprinkled thereof upon the altar seven times, and anointed the altar and all his vessels, both the laver and his foot, to *s.* them; **11:44** I am the LORD your God: ye shall therefore *s.* yourselves, and ye shall be holy; for I am holy; **20:7-8** *s.* yourselves therefore, and be ye holy: for I am the LORD your God. And ye shall keep my statutes, and do them: I am the LORD which *s.* you; **21:8** thou shalt *s.* him therefore; for he offereth the bread of thy God: he shall be holy unto thee: for I the LORD, which *s.* you, am holy; **Josh. 3:5** *s.* yourselves: for to morrow the LORD will do wonders among you; **7:13** *s.* yourselves against to morrow: for thus saith the LORD God of Israel; **1 Sam. 16:5** I am come to sacrifice unto the LORD: *s.* yourselves, and come with me to the sacrifice; **1 Chron. 15:12** *s.* yourselves, both ye and your brethren, that ye may bring up the ark of the LORD God of Israel unto the place that I have prepared for it; **2 Chron. 29:5** *s.* now yourselves, and *s.* the house of the LORD God of your fathers, and carry forth the filthiness out of the holy place; **29:15-19** they gathered their brethren, and *s.* themselves, and came, according to the commandment of the king, by the words of the LORD; **30:17** there were many in the congregation that were not *s.*: therefore the

Levites had the charge of the killing of the passovers for every one that was not clean, to *s.* them unto the LORD; **31:18** in their set office they *s.* themselves in holiness; **35:6** *s.* yourselves, and prepare your brethren, that they may do according to the word of the LORD; **Ezek. 28:25-26** they shall dwell with confidence, when I have executed judgments upon all those that despise them round about them; and they shall know that I am the LORD their God.

When he seeth his children, the work of mine hands, in the midst of him, they shall sanctify my name, and sanctify the Holy One of Jacob, and shall fear the God of Israel. Isa. 29:23 (*see also* Name)

Isa. 29:23 when he seeth his children, the work of mine hands, in the midst of him, they shall *s.* my name, and sanctify the Holy One of Jacob, and shall fear the God of Israel; **Ezek. 36:23** I will *s.* my great name, which was profaned among the heathen, which ye have profaned in the midst of them; and the heathen shall know that I am the LORD.

If a man therefore purge himself from these, he shall be a vessel unto honour, sanctified, and meet for the master's use, and prepared unto every good work. 2 Tim. 2:21 (*see also* Prepare, Work)

John 17:17 *s.* them through thy truth: thy word is truth; **17:20** for their sakes I *s.* myself, that they also might be *s.* through the truth; **1 Cor. 6:11** ye are washed, but ye are *s.*, but ye are justified in the name of the Lord Jesus, and by the Spirit of our God; **Eph. 2:22** in whom ye also are builded together for an habitation of God through the Spirit; **1 Thes. 5:23** the very God of peace *s.* you wholly; and I pray God your whole spirit and soul and body be preserved blameless unto the coming of our Lord Jesus Christ; **2 Tim. 2:21** if a man therefore purge himself from these, he shall be a vessel unto honour, *s.*, and meet for the master's use, and prepared unto every good work.

SANCTUARY (*see also* Abode, House, Tabernacle, Temple)

We are confounded, because we have heard reproach: shame hath covered our faces: for strangers are come into the sanctuaries of the LORD 's house. Jer. 51:51 (*see also* House)

Thou hast defiled thy sanctuaries by the multitude of thine iniquities, by the iniquity of thy traffick; therefore will I bring forth a fire from the midst of thee, it shall devour thee. Ezek. 28:18-19 (see also Defile, Iniquity)

Thus saith the Lord GOD; No stranger uncircumcised in heart, nor circumcised in flesh, shall enter into my sanctuary, of any strangers that is among the children of Israel. Ezek. 44:9 (see also Circumcise, Uncircumcised)

SATAN (see Adversary, Devil, Evil, Fallen, False, Lucifer, Wicked)

SATISFIED, SATISFY (see Pay)

SAVE, SAVED (see also Born, Again, Deliver, Redeem, Salvation)

Whosoever will save his life shall lose it; but whosoever shall lose his life for my sake and the gospel's, the same shall save it. For what shall it profit a man, if he shall gain the whole world, and lose his own soul? Mark 8:36 (see also Gain, Life, Soul)

What doth it profit, my brethren, though a man say he hath faith, and have not works? can faith save him? James. 2:14 (see also Faith, Profit, Works)

Be it known unto you all, and to all the people of Israel, that by the name of Jesus Christ of Nazareth, whom ye crucified, whom God raised from the dead, even by him doth this man stand here before you whole. This is the stone which was set at nought of you builders, which is become the head of the corner. Neither is there salvation in any other: for there is none other name under heaven given among men, whereby we must be saved. Acts 4:10-12 (see also Corner, Israel, Jesus Christ, Name, Stone)

Look unto me, and be ye saved, all the ends of the earth: for I am God, and there is none else. Isa. 45:22 (see also Look)

Strengthen ye the weak hands, and confirm the feeble knees. Say to them that are of a fearful heart, Be strong, fear not: behold, your God will come with vengeance, even God with a recompense; he will come and save you. Isa. 35:3-4 (see also Feeble, Strengthen)

Save yourselves from this untoward generation. Acts 2:40 (see also Generation)

Matt. 3:7 O generation of vipers, who hath warned you to flee from the wrath to come; Acts 2:40 with many other words did he testify and exhort, saying, S. yourselves from this untoward generation.

SAVIOR (see also Atone, Christ, God, Jesus Christ, Lord, Messiah, Redeemer)

I am the LORD thy God from the land of Egypt, and thou shalt know no god but me: for there is no saviour beside me. Hosea 13:4 (see also God)

Trust in the living God, who is the Saviour of all men, specially of those that believe. 1 Tim. 4:10 (see also Believe, Trust)

SAVOR (see also Taste)

He rebuked Peter, saying, Get thee behind me, Satan: for thou savourest not the things that be of God, but the things that be of men. Mark 8:33 (see also Things)

Matt. 16:22-23 get thee behind me, Satan: thou art an offence unto me: for thou s. not the things that be of God, but those that be of men; Mark 8:33 he rebuked Peter, saying, Get thee behind me, Satan: for thou s. not the things that be of God, but the things that be of men.

SAY, SAYINGS (see also Declare, Speak)

It shall come to pass at that time, that I will search Jerusalem with candles, and punish the men that are settled on their lees: that say in their heart, The LORD will not do good, neither will he do evil. Zeph. 1:12 (see also Evil, Good)

My son, attend to my words; incline thine ear unto my sayings. Let them not depart from thine eyes; keep them in the midst of thine heart. For they are life unto those that find them, and health to all their flesh. Prov. 4:20-22 (see also Attend, Incline, Word)

Say ye to the daughter of Zion, Behold, thy salvation cometh; behold, his reward is with him, and his work before him. Isa. 62:11 (see also Reward, Zion)

Zion said, the LORD hath forsaken me, and my LORD hath forgotten me. Can a woman forget her sucking child, that she should not have compassion on the son of her womb? yea, they may forget, yet will I not forget thee. **Isa. 49:14-15** (*see also* Forget, Forsake)

Say among the heathen that the LORD reigneth. **Ps. 96:10**

They shall call on my name, and I will hear them: I will say, It is my people: and they shall say, The LORD is my God. **Zech. 13:9** (*see also* Name)

Zech. 13:9 they shall call on my name, and I will hear them: I will *s.*, It is my people: and they shall *s.*, The LORD is my God; **14:9** the LORD shall be king over all the earth: in that day shall there be one LORD, and his name one.

SCATTER (*see also* Israel)

Woe be unto the pastors that destroy and scatter the sheep of my pasture! saith the LORD. **Jer. 23:1** (*see also* Destroy, Persecute)

SCORN, SCORNER, SCORNFUL (*see also* Laugh, Mock, Reproach, Reprove)

Cast out the scorner, and contention shall go out; yea, strife and reproach shall cease. **Prov. 22:10** (*see also* Cast, Contend)

Blessed is the man that walketh not in the counsel of the ungodly, nor standeth in the way of sinners, nor sitteth in the seat of the scornful. **Ps. 1:1** (*see also* Walk)

Ps. 1:1 blessed is the man that walketh not in the counsel of the ungodly, nor standeth in the way of sinners, nor sitteth in the seat of the *s.*; **1:4-6** the way of the ungodly shall perish; **Prov. 3:34** he *s.* the *s.*: but he giveth grace unto the lowly; **15:12** a *s.* loveth not one that reproveth him: neither will he go unto the wise; **19:25** smite a *s.*, and the simple will beware: and reprove one that hath under-standing; **21:11** when the *s.* is punished, the simple is made wise: and when the wise is instructed, he receiveth knowledge; **21:24** proud and haughty *s.* is his name, who dealeth in proud wrath; **Isa. 28:14** hear the word of the LORD, ye *s.* men; **57:21** there is no peace, saith my God, to the wicked.

If thou be wise, thou shalt be wise for thyself; but if thou scornest, thou alone shalt bear it. **Prov. 9:12** (*see also* Wise)

Prov. 9:12 if thou be wise, thou shalt be wise for thyself: but if thou *s.*, thou alone shalt bear it; **13:1** a wise son heareth his fathers instruction: but a *s.* heareth not rebuke; **15:12** a *s.* loveth not one that reproveth him: neither will he go unto the wise; **19:29** judgments are prepared for *s.*, and stripes for the back of fools; **21:24** proud and haughty *s.* is his name, who dealeth in proud wrath; **24:9** the thought of foolishness is sin: and the *s.* is an abomination to men; **29:8** *s.* men bring a city into a snare: but wise men turn away wrath.

SCRIPTURE (*see also* Book, Knowledge, Record, Study, Word, Write)

They received the word with all readiness of mind, and searched the scriptures daily, whether those things were so. **Acts 17:11** (*see also* Daily, Mind, Readiness, Receive, Search, Word)

All scripture is given by inspiration of God, and is profitable for doctrine, for reproof, for correction, for instruction in righteousness: That the man of God may be perfect, throughly furnished unto all good works. **2 Tim. 3:16-17** (*see also* Inspiration, Perfect, Works)

Paul, as his manner was, went in unto them, and three sabbath days reasoned with them out of the scriptures. **Acts 17:2** (*see also* Reason)

When therefore he was risen from the dead, his disciples remembered that he had said this unto them; and they believed the scripture, and the word which Jesus had said. **John 2:22** (*see also* Believe)

Search the scriptures; for in them ye think ye have eternal life: and they are they which testify of me. **John 5:39** (*see also* Eternal Life, Search)

Matt. 22:29 ye do err, not knowing the *s.*, nor the power of God; **24:15** (Mark 13:14) when ye therefore shall see the abomination of desolation, spoken of by Daniel the prophet, stand in the holy place, (whoso readeth, let him understand); **Mark 12:10** have ye not read this *s.*; The stone which the builders rejected is become the head of the corner; **12:24** do ye not therefore err, because ye know not the *s.*, neither the power of God; **12:26** have ye not read in the book of Moses, how in the bush God spake unto him; **14:49** I was daily with you in the temple teaching, and ye took me not: but the *s.* must be fulfilled; **15:28** the *s.* was fulfilled, which saith, And he was numbered with the transgressors; **Luke 4:21** this day is this *s.* fulfilled in your ears; **8:11** the parable is this: The seed is the word of God; **24:27** beginning at Moses and all the prophets, he expounded unto them in all the *s.* the things concerning himself; **24:32** did not our heart burn within us, while he talked with us by the way, and while he opened to us the *s.*; **24:45** then opened he their understanding, that they might understand the *s.*; **John 2:22** he was risen from the dead, his disciples remembered that he had said this unto them; and they believed the *s.*, and the word which Jesus had said; **4:14** whosoever drinketh of the water that I shall give him shall never thirst; but the water that I shall give him shall be in him a well of water springing up into everlasting life; **5:39** search the *s.*; for in them ye think ye have eternal life: and they are they which testify of me; **7:38** He that believeth on me, as the *s.* hath said, out of his belly shall flow rivers of living water; **8:31** if ye continue in my word, then are ye my disciples indeed; **10:34-35** is it not written in your law, I said, Ye are gods? If he called them gods, unto whom the word of God came, and the *s.* cannot be broken; **Acts 17:11-12** they received the word with all readiness of mind, and searched the *s.* daily; **18:24** an eloquent man, and mighty in the *s.*, came to Ephesus; **18:28** he mightily convinced the Jews, and that publickly, shewing by the *s.* that Jesus was Christ; **Rom. 15:4** whatsoever things were written aforetime were written for our learning, that we through patience and comfort of the *s.* might have hope; **2 Tim. 3:15** the holy *s.*, which are able to make thee wise unto salvation through faith which is in Christ Jesus; **3:16-17** all *s.* is given by inspiration of God, and is profitable for doctrine, for reproof, for correction, for instruction in righteousness: That the man of God may be perfect, throughly furnished unto all good works; **2 Pet 3:16** in all his epistles, speaking in them of these things; in which are some things hard to be understood, which they that are unlearned and unstable wrest, as they do also the other *s.*, unto their own destruction; **1 Jn. 1:4** these things write we unto

you, that your joy may be full; **2 Jn. 1:12** having many things to write unto you, I would not write with paper and ink: but I trust to come unto you, and speak face to face, that our joy may be full; **3 Jn. 1:13-14** I had many things to write, but I will not with ink and pen write unto thee; **Rev. 1:3** blessed is he that readeth, and they that hear the words of this prophecy, and keep those things which are written therein: for the time is at hand; **1:11** what thou seest, write in a book, and send it unto the seven churches which are in Asia.

SEAL, SEALED

Grieve not the holy Spirit of God, whereby ye are sealed unto the day of redemption. Eph. 4:30 (*see also* Grieve, Holy Spirit)

SEARCH (*see also* Ask, Inquire, Seek, Scripture, Study)

They received the word with all readiness of mind, and searched the scriptures daily, whether those things were so. Acts 17:11 (*see also* Daily, Mind, Readiness, Receive, Scripture, Word)

Let us search and try our ways, and turn again to the Lord. Lam. 3:40 (*see also* Repent, Try, Turn, Way)

Eye hath not seen, nor ear heard, neither have entered into the heart of man, the things which God hath prepared for them that love him. But God hath reveled them unto us by his Spirit; for the Spirit searcheth all things, yea, the deep things of God. 1 Cor. 2:9-10 (*see also* Enter, Mysteries, Spirit)

Search the scriptures; for in them ye think ye have eternal life: and they are they which testify of me. John 5:39 (*see also* Eternal Life, Scripture)

The rich man is wise in his own conceit; but the poor that hath understanding searcheth him out. Prov. 28:11 (*see also* Conceit)

Prov. 28:11 the rich man is wise in his own conceit; but the poor that hath understanding *s.* him out; **Jer. 29:12-14** ye [shall] call upon me, and ye shall go and pray unto me, and I will hearken unto you. And ye shall seek me, and find me, when ye shall *s.* for me with all your heart.

SEASON (*see also* Time)

The Lord GOD hath given me the tongue of the learned, that I should know how to speak a word in season to him that is weary. Isa. 50:4 (*see also* Speak, Tongue, Weary)

If ye walk in my statutes and keep my commandments, and do them; Then I will give you rain in due season, and the land shall yield her increase, and the trees of the field shall yield her fruit. Lev. 26:3-4 (*see also* Commandment, Fruit)

A man hath joy by the answer of his mouth: and a word spoken in due season, how good is it. Prov. 15:23 (*see also* Answer, Word)

To every thing there is a season, and a time to every purpose under heaven; A time to be born, and a time to die; a time to plant, and a time to pluck up that which is planted; A time to kill, and a time to heal; a time to break down, and a time to build up; A time to weep, and a time to laugh; a time to mourn, and a time to dance; A time to cast away stones, and a time to father stones together; a time to embrace, and a time to refrain from embracing; A time to get, and a time to lose; a time to keep, and a time to cast away; A time to rend, and a time to sew; a time to keep silence, and a time to speak; A time to love, and a time to hate; a time of war, and a time of peace. Eccl. 3:1-8 (*see also* Purpose, Time)

SECOND COMFORTER

If ye love me, keep my commandments. And I will pray the Father, and he shall give you another Comforter, that he may abide with you for ever; Even the Spirit of truth; whom the world cannot receive, because it seeth him not, neither knoweth him: but ye know him; for he dweleth with you, and shall be in you. John 14:16 (*see also* Commandment)

SECOND COMING (*see also* Jesus Christ, Millennium, Resurrection)

We which are alive and remain shall be caught up together with them in the clouds, to meet the Lord in the air: and so shall we ever be with the Lord. 1 Thes. 4:17 (*see also* Caught)

Heaven and earth shall pass away, but my words shall not pass away. But of that day and hour knoweth no man, no, not the angels of heaven, by my Father only. Matt 24:36 (*see also* Day, Hour)

Let no man deceive you by any means: for that day shall not come, except there come a falling away first, and that man of sin be revealed, the son of perdition; who opposeth and exalteth himself above all that is called God, or that is worshiped; so that he as God sitteth in the temple of God, shewing himself that he is God. 2 Thes. 2:3-4 (*see also* Apostasy, Falling Away)

SECOND DEATH (*see also* Death, Hell)

He that overcometh shall inherit all things; and I will be his God, and he shall be my son. But the fearful, and unbelieving, and the abominable, and murderers, and whoremongers, and sorcerers, and idolaters, and all liars, shall have their part in the lake which burneth with fire and brimstone: which is the second death. Rev. 21:7 (*see also* All Things, Death, Inherit, Unbelief)

For it is impossible for those who were once enlightened, and have tasted of the heavenly gift, and were made partakers of the Holy Ghost, And have tasted the good word of God, and the powers of the world to come, If they shall fall away, to renew them again unto repentance; seeing they crucify to themselves the Son of God afresh, and put him to an open shame. Heb. 6:4 (*see also* Enlightened, Holy Ghost, Impossible)

SECRET (*see also* Mysteries)

There is a God in heaven that revealeth secrets. Dan. 2:28 (*see also* Reveal)

Debate thy cause with thy neighbour *himself*; and discover not a secret to another: lest he that heareth *it* put thee to shame, and thine infamy turn not away. Prov. 25:9-10 (*see also* Debate, Gossip)

When thou fasteth, anoint thine head, and wash thy face; That thou appear not unto men to fast, but unto thy Father which is in secret; and thy Father, which seeth in secret, shall reward thee openly. Matt. 6:17-18 (*see also* Appear, Fast)

When thou prayest, enter into thy closet, and when thou hast shut thy door, pray to thy Father which is in secret; and thy Father which seeth in secret shall reward thee openly. Matt. 6:6 (*see also* Closet, Prayer)

The secret which the king hath demanded cannot the wise men, the astrologers, the magicians, the soothsayers, shew unto the king; But there is a God in heaven that revealeth secrets, and maketh known to the king Nebuchadnezzar what shall be in the latter days. Dan. 1:27-28 (*see also* Dream, Interpretation)

SEE, SEEN, SAW (*see also* Behold, Eye, Look, Observe, Watch)

O taste and see that the LORD is good: blessed is the man that trusteth in him. Ps. 34:8 (*see also* Taste, Trust)

All ye inhabitants of the world, and dwellers on the earth, see ye, when he lifted up an ensign on the mountains; and when he bloweth a trumpet, hear ye. Isa. 18:3 (*see also* Hear)

He that walketh righteously, and speaketh uprightly; he that despiseth the gain of oppressions, that shaketh his hands from holding of bribes, that stoppeth his ears from hearing of blood, and shutteth his eyes from seeing evil; He shall dwell on high: his defence shall be the munitions of rocks: bread shall be given him; his waters shall be sure. Isa. 33:15-16 (*see also* Gain, Hear, Oppress, Righteous, Speak, Uprightly, Walk)

Make the heart of this people fat, and make their ears heavy, and shut their eyes; lest they see with their eyes, and hear with their ears, and understand with their heart, and convert, and be healed. Isa. 6:10 (*see also* Convert, Heal)

[Do not] say, Let him make speed, and hasten his work, that we may see it: and let the counsel of the Holy One of Israel draw nigh and come, that we may know it! Isa. 5:19 (*see also* Sign)

Isa. 5:12 they regard not the work of the LORD, neither consider the operation of his hands; 5:19 [do not] say, Let him make speed, and hasten his work, that we may see it: and let the counsel of

the Holy One of Israel draw nigh and come, that we may know it.

I have seen God face to face, and my life is preserved. Jer. Gen. 32:24-30 (*see also* Face)

Gen. 5:22 Enoch walked with God; 5:24 Enoch walked with God: and he was not; for God took him; 6:9 Noah was a just man and perfect in his generations, and Noah walked with God; 12:7 there builded he an altar unto the LORD, who appeared unto him; 15:5 he brought him forth abroad, and said, Look now toward heaven, and tell the stars, if thou be able to number them: and he said, So shall thy seed be; 18:1-5 the LORD appeared unto him in the plains; 18:10 I will certainly return unto thee according to the time of life; and, lo, Sarah thy wife shall have a son. And Sarah heard it in the tent door; 18:18 Abraham shall surely become a great and mighty nation, and all the nations of the earth shall be blessed in him; 18:22-33 Abraham stood yet before the LORD... [and they spoke]... And the LORD went his way, as soon as he had left communing with Abraham: and Abraham returned unto his place; 26:3 sojourn in this land, and I will be with thee, and will bless thee; 26:24 the LORD appeared unto him the same night, and said, I am the God of Abraham thy father: fear not, for I am with thee, and will bless thee; 32:24-30 Jacob called the name of the place Peniel: for I have seen God face to face, and my life is preserved; 35:9 God appeared unto Jacob again... and blessed him; 35:13 God went up from him in the place where he talked with him; 48:3 Jacob said unto Joseph, God Almighty appeared unto me... and blessed me; 48:15-16 he blessed Joseph, and said, God, before whom my fathers Abraham and Isaac did walk, the God which fed me all my life long unto this day; Ex. 4:1-5 believe that the LORD God of their fathers, the God of Abraham, the God of Isaac, and the God of Jacob, hath appeared unto thee; 6:3 I appeared unto Abraham, unto Isaac, and unto Jacob, by the name of God Almighty, but by my name JEHOVAH was I not known to them; Job 19:26 in my flesh shall I see God; 42:5 I have heard of thee by the hearing of the ear: but now mine eye seeth thee; Ps. 27:13 I had fainted, unless I had believed to see the goodness of the LORD in the land of the living; 68:24 they have seen thy goings, O God; even the goings of my God, my King; Isa. 53:1 who hath believed our report? and to whom is the arm of the LORD revealed; Jer. 1:9-10 the LORD put forth his hand, and touched my mouth; Ezek. 3:22-23 then I arose, and went forth into the plain: and, behold, the glory of the LORD stood there.

SEER (*see* Interpret, Prophet, Reveal)

SEDUCE (*see also* Carnal, Deceive, Lust)

False Christs and false prophets shall rise, and shall shew signs and wonders, to seduce, if it were possible, even the elect. Mark 13:22 (*see also* Elect, False Christ, False Prophet, Sign, Wonder)

SEED (*see also* Heir, Inherit)

If ye have faith as a grain of mustard seed, ye shall say unto this mountain, Remove hence to yonder place; and it shall remove; and nothing shall be impossible unto you. Matt. 17:20 (*see also* Faith, Impossible)

SEEK, SOUGHT (*see also* Ask, Inquire, Ponder, Pray, Search, Study)

But without faith it is impossible to please him: for he that cometh to God must believe that he is, and that he is a rewarder of them that diligently seek him. Heb. 11:6 (*see also* Believe, Diligently, Faith, Impossible, Reward)

Charity suffereth long, and is kind; charity envieth not; charity vaunteth not itself, is not puffed up, Doth not behave itself unseemly, seeketh not her own, is not easily provoked, thinketh no evil; Rejoiceth not in iniquity, but rejoiceth in the truth; Beareth all things, believeth all things, hopeth all things, endureth all things. 1 Cor. 13:4-7 (*see also* All Things, Bear, Believe, Charity, Endure, Hope, Provoke, Rejoice, Suffer, Think)

Seek the LORD, and his strength: seek his face evermore. Ps. 105:3-4 (*see also* Face)

The wicked, through the pride of his countenance, will not seek after God: God is not in all his thoughts. Ps. 10:4 (*see also* Pride, Thought, Wicked)

Woe unto them that seek deep to hide their counsel from the LORD and their works are in the dark, and they say, Who seeth us? and who knoweth us? Isa. 29:15 (*see also* Counsel)

Seek ye the priesthood also. Num. 16:10 (*see also* Priesthood)

Sow to yourselves in righteousness, reap in mercy; break up your fallow ground: for it is time to seek the LORD, till he come and rain righteousness upon you. Hosea 10:12 (*see also* Heart, Reap)

Seek ye the LORD, all ye meek of the earth, which have wrought his judgment; seek righteousness, seek meekness: it may be ye shall be hid in the day of the LORD's anger. Zeph. 2:3 (*see also* Meek)

When they shall say unto you, Seek unto them that have familiar spirits, and unto wizards that peep, and that mutter: should not a people seek unto their God? Isa. 8:19 (*see also* Familiar, Wizards)

Draw nigh to God, and he will draw nigh to you. James 4:8 (*see also* Draw)

Evil men understand not judgment: but they that seek the LORD understand all things. Prov. 28:5 (*see also* All Things, Understand)

Seek ye first the kingdom of God, and his righteousness; and all these things shall be added unto you. Matt. 6:33-34 (*see also* Kingdom)

Come unto me, all ye that labour and are heavy laden, and I will give you rest. Take my yoke upon you, and learn of me; for I am meek and lowly in heart: and ye shall find rest unto your souls. Matt. 11:28-29 (*see also* Heart, Heavy, Learn, Lowly, Meek)

In the day of my trouble I will call upon thee: for thou wilt answer me. Ps. 86:7 (*see also* Call, Trouble)

I applied mine heart to know, and to search, and to seek out wisdom, and the reason of things, and to know the wickedness of folly, even of foolishness and madness. Eccl. 7:25 (*see also* Apply, Heart, Know, Reason, Wisdom)

Ask, and it shall be given you; seek, and ye shall find; knock, and it shall be opened unto you. Luke 11:9 (*see also* Ask, Knock)

Seek after wisdom. 1 Cor. 1:22 (*see also* Wisdom)

An evil and adulterous generation seeketh after a sign; and there shall no sign be given to it, but the sign of the prophet Jonas. Matt. 12:38-39 (*see also* Sign)

Thou shalt seek the LORD thy God, thou shalt find him, if thou seek him with all thy heart and with all thy soul. Deut. 4:29 (*see also* Find, Thou Shalt)

Deut. 4:29-31 if from thence thou shalt *s.* the LORD thy God, thou shalt find him, if thou *s.* him with all thy heart and with all thy soul; **1 Chron. 16:10-11** let the heart of them rejoice that *s.* the LORD. *s.* the LORD and his strength, *s.* his face continually; **22:19** set your heart and your soul to *s.* the LORD your God; **2 Chron. 11:16** after them out of all the tribes of Israel such as set their hearts to *s.* the LORD God of Israel came to Jerusalem; **12:14** he did evil, because he prepared not his heart to *s.* the LORD; **14:4** commanded Judah to *s.* the LORD God of their fathers, and to do the law and the commandment; **15:12-13** they entered into a covenant to *s.* the LORD God of their fathers with all their heart and with all their soul; That whosoever would not *s.* the LORD God of Israel should be put to death; **20:3-4** Jehoshaphat feared, and set himself to *s.* the LORD, and proclaimed a fast; **Ezra 6:21** the children of Israel, which were come again out of captivity, and all such as had separated themselves unto them from the filthiness of the heathen of the land, to *s.* the LORD God of Israel, did eat; **Ps. 9:10** they that know thy name will put their trust in thee: for thou, LORD, hast not forsaken them that *s.* thee; **14:2** the LORD looked down from heaven upon the children of men, to see if there were any that did understand, and seek God; **34:4** I sought the LORD, and he heard me, and delivered me from all my fears; **34:10** they that *s.* the LORD shall not want any good thing; **34:10** they that *s.* the LORD shall not want any good thing; **42:1-3** as the hart panteth after the water brooks, so panteth my soul after thee, O God. My soul thirsteth for God, for the living God: when shall I come and appear before God; **105:3-4** let the heart of them rejoice that *s.* the LORD. *s.* the LORD, and his strength: *s.* his face evermore; **119:2** blessed are they that keep his testimonies, and that *s.* him with the whole heart; **Prov. 28:5** they that *s.* the LORD understand all things; **Isa. 9:13** the people turneth not unto him that smiteth them, neither do they *s.* the LORD of hosts; **31:1** they look not unto the Holy One of Israel, neither *s.* the LORD; **51:1** hearken to me, ye that follow after righteousness, ye that *s.* the LORD: look unto the rock whence ye are hewn;

Jer. 10:21 the pastors are become brutish, and have not sought the LORD: therefore they shall not prosper; **29:12-14** ye shall *s.* me, and find me, when ye shall searcheth for me with all your heart; **50:4** the children of Israel shall come, they and the children of Judah together, going and weeping: they shall go, and *s.* the LORD their God; **Hosea 3:5** the children of Israel [shall] return, and *s.* the LORD their God, and David their king; and shall fear the LORD and his goodness in the latter days; **5:6** they shall go with their flocks and with their herds to *s.* the LORD; but they shall not find him; **10:12** it is time to *s.* the LORD, till he come and rain righteousness upon you; **Amos 5:4-10** *s.* the LORD, and ye shall live; lest he break out like fire in the house of Joseph, and devour it; **Zeph. 2:3** *s.* ye the LORD, all ye meek of the earth, which have wrought his judgment; *s.* righteousness, *s.* meekness; **Zech. 8:22-23** many people and strong nations shall come to *s.* the LORD of hosts in Jerusalem; **Mal. 3:1-3** the Lord, whom ye *s.*, shall suddenly come to his temple, even the messenger of the covenant, whom ye delight in.

O GOD, thou art my God; early will I seek thee: my soul thirsteth for thee. Ps. 63:1 (*see also* Early)

Ps. 63:1 O God, thou art my God; early will I *s.* thee: my soul thirsteth for thee; **108:2** awake, psaltery and harp: I myself will awake early; **Prov. 8:17-21** I love them that love me; and those that *s.* me early shall find me; **Isa. 26:9** with my soul have I desired thee in the night; yea, with my spirit within me will I *s.* thee early.

In the day of my trouble I will call upon thee: for thou wilt answer me. Ps. 86:7 (*see also* Call, Seek)

Ps. 77:2 in the day of my *t.* I seek the Lord: my sore ran in the night, and ceased not: my soul refused to be comforted; **81:7** thou calledst in *t.*, and I delivered thee; **86:7** in the day of my *t.* I will call upon thee: for thou wilt answer me; **88:3** my soul is full of *t.*: and my life draweth nigh unto the grave; **138:3** in the day when I cried thou answeredst me, and strengthenedst me with strength in my soul; **142:2** I poured out my complaint before him; I shewed before him my *t.*; **142:4** I looked on my right hand, and beheld, but there was no man that would know me: refuge failed me; no man cared for my soul; **143:11** quicken me, O LORD, for thy names sake: for thy righteousness sake bring my soul out of *t.*; **Jer. 2:27** they have turned their back unto me, and not their face: but in the time of their *t*. they will say, Arise, and save us.

SELF CONTROL (*see also* Ask, Inquire, Ponder, Pray, Search, Study)

He that hath no rule over his own spirit is like a city that is broken down and without walls. **Prov. 25:28** (*see also* Rule, Spirit)

SELFISH, SELFISHNESS (*see* Covet, Greed, Lust, Pride)

SENSUAL, SENSUOUS (*see* Carnal, Lust, Natural Man)

SEPARATE

Your iniquities have separated between you and your God, and your sins have hid his face from you, that he will not hear. **Isa. 59:2** (*see also* Face, Iniquity)

Who shall separate us from the love of Christ? shall tribulation, or distress, or persecution, or famine, or nakedness, or peril, or sword? **Rom. 8:35** (*see also* Love)

And before him shall be gathered all nations: and he shall separate them one from another, as a shepherd divideth his sheep from the goats. **Matt. 25:32** (*see also* Gather, Nation)

SERVANT (*see also* Minister, Priesthood, Serve, Steward)

Whosoever will be chief among you, let him be your servant. **Matt. 20:27** (*see also* Chief)

Masters, give unto your servants that which is just and equal; knowing that ye also have a Master in heaven. **Col. 4:1** (*see also* Just)

Do I now persuade men, or God? or do I seek to please men? for if I yet pleased men, I should not be the servant of Christ. **Gal. 1:10** (*see also* Persuade, Please)

Blessed be he that cometh in the name of the LORD: we have blessed you out of the house of the LORD. **Ps. 118:26** (*see also* House)

Ye that is called in the Lord, being a servant is the Lord's freeman: likewise also he that is called, being free, is Christ's servant. Ye are bought with a price; be not ye the servants of men. **1 Cor 7:22-23** (*see also* Called, Price)

As the LORD liveth, and as my lord the king liveth, surely in what place my lord the king shall be, whether in death or life, even there also will thy servant be. **2 Sam 15:21** (*see also* Loyal)

So is the will of God, that with well doing ye may put to silence the ignorance of foolish men: As free, and not using your liberty for a cloke of maliciousness, but as the servants of God. **1 Pet. 2:15-16** (*see also* Do, Liberty, Will)

Servants, be obedient to them that are your masters according to the flesh, with fear and trembling, in singleness of your heart, as unto Christ. **Eph. 6:5** (*see also* Obedient)

If thou wilt be a servant. unto this people this day, and wilt serve them, and answer them, and speak good words to them, then they will be thy servants for ever. **1 Kgs. 12:7** (*see also* Word)

Remember these, O Jacob and Israel; for thou art my servant: I have formed thee; thou art my servant; O Israel, thou shalt not be forgotten of me. **Isa. 44:21** (*see also* Remember)

Who is among you that feareth the LORD, that obeyeth the voice of his servant, that walketh in darkness, and hath no light? let him trust in the name of the LORD, and stay upon his God. **Isa. 50:10** (*see also* Obey, Prophet)

Blessed be the God of Shadrach, Meshach, and Abed-nego, who hath sent his angel, and delivered his servants that trusted in him, and have changed the king's word, and yielded their bodies, that they might not serve nor worship any god, except their own God. **Dan. 3:28** (*see also* Angel, Courage, Idol, Worship)

He that receiveth you receiveth me, and he that receiveth me receiveth him that sent me. He that receiveth a prophet in the name of a prophet shall receive a prophet's reward; and he that receiveth a righteous man in the name of a righteous man shall receive a righteous man's reward. **Matt. 10:40-41** (*see also* Prophet, Receive, Reward, Serve)

Matt. 10:40-42 he that receiveth you receiveth me, and he that receiveth me receiveth him that sent me. He that receiveth a prophet in the name of a prophet shall receive a prophet's reward; and he that receiveth a righteous man in the name of a righteous man shall receive a righteous man's reward. And whosoever shall give to drink unto one of these little ones a cup of cold water only in the name of a disciple, verily I say unto you, he shall in no wise lose his reward; **Luke 10:11-15** the kingdom of God is come nigh unto you; **John 13:20** he that receiveth whomsoever I send receiveth me; and he that receiveth me receiveth him that sent me; **Eph. 6:6** as the servants of Christ, doing the will of God from the heart; **1 Thes. 2:13** for this cause also thank we God without ceasing, because, when ye received the word of God which ye heard of us, ye received it not as the word of men, but as it is in truth, the word of God, which effectually worketh also in you that believe; **3 Jn. 1:10** if I come, I will remember his deeds which he doeth, prating against us with malicious words: and not content therewith, neither doth he himself receive the brethren, and forbiddeth them that would, and casteth them out of the church. thirsty, and ye gave me drink: I was a stranger, and ye took me in; **25:40** inasmuch as ye have done it unto one of the least of these my brethren, ye have done it unto me; **25:42-46** I was an hungred, and ye gave me no meat: I was thirsty, and ye gave me no drink: I was a stranger, and ye took me not in: naked, and ye clothed me not: sick, and in prison, and ye visited me not. Then shall they also answer him, saying, Lord, when saw we thee an hungred, or athirst, or a stranger, or naked, or sick, or in prison, and did not minister unto thee? Then shall he answer them, saying, Verily I say unto you, Inasmuch as ye did it not to one of the least of these, ye did it not to me. And these shall go away into everlasting punishment: but the righteous into life eternal; **Mark 9:35** he sat down, and called the twelve, and saith unto them, If any man desire to be first, the same shall be last of all, and servant of all; **10:41-45** ye know that they which are accounted to rule over the Gentiles exercise lordship over them; and their great ones exercise authority upon them. But so shall it not be among you: but whosoever will be great among you, shall be your minister: And whosoever of you will be the chiefest, shall be servant of all. For even the Son of man came not to be ministered unto, but to minister, and to give his life a ransom for many; **Luke 22:24-27** there was also a strife among them, which of them should be accounted the greatest. And he said unto them, The kings of the Gentiles exercise lordship over them; and they that exercise authority upon them are called benefactors. But ye shall not be so: but he that is greatest among you, let him be as the younger;

and he that is chief, as he that doth *s.*. For whether is greater, he that sitteth at meat, or he that *s.*? is not he that sitteth at meat? but I am among you as he that *s.*; **Rom. 15:2** let every one of us please his neighbour for his good to edification; **1 Cor. 9:19** though I be free from all men, yet have I made myself servant unto all, that I might gain the more; **2 Cor. 1:24** but are helpers of your joy: for by faith ye stand; **Gal. 5:13** ye have been called unto liberty; only use not liberty for an occasion to the flesh, but by love *s.* one another; **Philip. 2:16-17** if I be offered upon the sacrifice and *s.* of your faith, I joy, and rejoice with you all.

SERVE, SERVICE (*see also* Priesthood, Work, Worship)

Turn not aside from following the LORD, but serve the LORD with all your heart. 1 Sam 12:20 (*see also* Follow, Turn)

Thy God whom thou servest continually, he will deliver thee. Dan. 6:16 (*see also* Deliver)

[Serve] the LORD thy God with joyfulness, and with gladness of heart, for the abundance of all things. Deut. 28:47 (*see also* Abundance)

Thou shalt fear the lord thy God; Him shalt thou serve, and to Him shalt thou cleave, and swear by His name. Deut. 10:20 (*see also* Fear)

Be not now negligent: for the LORD hath chosen you to stand before him, to serve him, and that ye should minister unto him. 2 Chron. 29:11 (*see also* Neglect)

Woe unto him that buildeth his house in unrighteousness, and his chambers by wrong; that useth his neighbour's service without wages, and giveth him not for his work. Jer. 22:13 (*see also* House, Wage, Work)

By love, serve one another. Gal. 5:13 (*see also* Love)

Matt. 20:25-27 whosoever will be great among you, let him be your minister; And whosoever will be chief among you, let him be your servant; **23:11** he that is greatest among you shall be your servant; **24:46-47** blessed is that servant, whom his lord when he cometh shall find so doing. Verily I say unto you, That he shall make him ruler over all his goods; **25:35** I was an hungred, and ye gave me meat; **Gal. 5:13** by love, serve one another.

No man can serve two masters: for either he will hate the one, and love the other; or else he will hold to the one, and despise the other. Ye cannot serve God and mammon. Matt. 6:24 (*see also* Hate, Master)

Matt. 6:24 (Luke 16:13) no man can *s.* two masters: for either he will hate the one, and love the other; or else he will hold to the one, and despise the other. Ye cannot *s.* God and mammon; **1 Cor. 7:35** I speak for your own profit; not that I may cast a snare upon you, but for that which is comely, and that ye may attend upon the Lord without distraction; **15:58** be ye stedfast, unmoveable, always abounding in the work of the Lord, forasmuch as ye know that your labour is not in vain in the Lord; **16:10** see that he may be with you without fear: for he worketh the work of the Lord, as I also do.

If it seem evil unto you to serve the LORD, choose you this day whom ye will serve; whether the gods which your fathers served that were on the other side of the flood, or the gods of the Amorites, in whose land ye dwell: but as for me and my house, we will serve the LORD. Josh. 24:15 (*see also* Choice)

Ex. 10:7-8 go, *s.* the LORD your God; **10:11** go now ye that are men, and *s.* the LORD; for that ye did desire; **10:24-26** Moses said... there shall not an hoof be left behind; for thereof must we take to *s.* the LORD our God; and we know not with what we must *s.* the LORD, until we come thither; **12:31** rise up, and get you forth from among my people, both ye and the children of Israel; and go, *s.* the LORD, as ye have said; **23:25** ye shall *s.* the LORD your God, and he shall bless thy bread, and thy water; and I will take sickness away from the midst of thee; **Deut. 10:12** what doth the LORD thy God require of thee, but to fear the LORD thy God, to walk in all his ways, and to love him, and to *s.* the LORD thy God with all thy heart and with all thy soul; **Josh.24:15** if it seem evil unto you to *s.* the LORD, choose you this day whom ye will *s.*...but as for me and my house, we will *s.* the LORD; **24:18-21** the LORD drave out from before us all the people, even the Amorites which dwelt in the land: therefore will we also *s.* the LORD; for he is our God; **24:31** Israel *s.*d the LORD all the days of Joshua, and all the days of the elders that overlived Joshua, and which had known all the works of the LORD; **1 Sam. 12:20** fear not: ye have done all this wickedness: yet turn not aside from following the LORD, but *s.* the LORD with all your heart; **2 Sam. 15:8** thy *s.* vowed a vow while I abode at

Geshur in Syria, saying, If the LORD shall bring me again indeed to Jerusalem, then I will *s.* the LORD; **1 Kgs. 18:21** if the LORD be God, follow him; **1 Chron. 28:9** know thou the God of thy father, and *s.* him with a perfect heart and with a willing mind; **2 Chron. 30:8** *s.* the LORD your God, that the fierceness of his wrath may turn away from you; **33:16** he repaired the altar of the LORD, and sacrificed thereon peace offerings and thank offerings, and commanded Judah to *s.* the LORD God of Israel; **34:33** Josiah took away all the abominations out of all the countries that pertained to the children of Israel, and made all that were present in Israel to *s.*, even to *s.* the LORD their God; **Ps. 2:11** *s.* the LORD with fear, and rejoice with trembling; **33:12** blessed is the nation whose God is the LORD: and the people whom he hath chosen for his own inheritance; **100:2** *s.* the LORD with gladness: come before his presence with singing; **102:22** when the people are gathered together, and the kingdoms, to *s.* the LORD; **127:1** except the LORD build the house, they labour in vain that build it; **Isa. 54:13-17** all thy children shall be taught of the LORD; and great shall be the peace of thy children. In righteousness shalt thou be established... This is the heritage of the *s.* of the LORD, and their righteousness is of me; **Jer. 30:9** they shall *s.* the LORD their God, and David their king, whom I will raise up unto them.

Ye shall serve the LORD your God, and he shall bless thy bread, and thy water; and I will take sickness away from the midst of thee. Ex. 23:25 (*see also* Abundance)

Ex. 10:7-8 let the men go, that they may serve the LORD their God; **10:11** go now ye that are men, and *s.* the LORD; **10:24** go ye, *s.* the LORD; **10:26** we know not with what we must *s.* the LORD, until we come thither; **12:31** go, *s.* the LORD, as ye have said; **23:25** ye shall *s.* the LORD your God, and he shall bless thy bread, and thy water; **24:3** all the people answered with one voice, and said, All the words which the LORD hath said will we do; **Deut. 10:12** what doth the LORD thy God require of thee, but to fear the LORD thy God, to walk in all his ways, and to love him, and to *s.* the LORD thy God with all thy heart and with all thy soul; **28:47** because thou *s.* not the LORD thy God with joyfulness, and with gladness of heart, for the abundance of all things; **Josh.22:5** take diligent heed to do the commandment and the law, which Moses the servant of the LORD charged you, to love the LORD your God, and to walk in all his ways, and to keep his commandments, and to cleave unto him, and to *s.* him with all your heart and with all your soul; **24:14** fear the LORD, and *s.* him in sincerity and in truth; **24:21** we will *s.* the LORD; **24:24** the LORD our God will we *s.*, and his voice will we obey; **24:31** Israel *s.* the LORD all the days of Joshua; **1 Sam. 12:10** deliver us out of the hand of our enemies, and we will *s.* thee; **12:14-15** if ye will fear the LORD, and *s.* him, and obey his voice, and not rebel against the commandment of the LORD, then shall both ye and also the king that reigneth over you continue following the LORD your God; **12:20-22** turn not aside from following the LORD, but *s.* the LORD with all your heart; **12:24** fear the LORD, and *s.* him in truth with all your heart; **2 Sam. 15:8** thy servant vowed a vow while I abode at Geshur in Syria, saying, If the LORD shall bring me again indeed to Jerusalem, then I will *s.* the LORD; **1 Chron. 28:9** know thou the God of thy father, and *s.* him with a perfect heart and with a willing mind; **2 Chron. 29:11** the LORD hath chosen you to stand before him, to *s.* him; **30:8** yield yourselves unto the LORD, and enter into his sanctuary, which he hath sanctified for ever: and *s.* the LORD your God; **33:16** he repaired the altar of the LORD, and sacrificed thereon peace offerings and thank offerings, and commanded Judah to *s.* the LORD God of Israel; **34:33** Josiah... made all that were present in Israel to *s.*, even to *s.* the LORD their God; **35:3** *s.* now the LORD your God, and his people Israel; **Job 36:11-12** if they obey and *s.* him, they shall spend their days in prosperity, and their years in pleasures; **Ps. 2:11** *s.* the LORD with fear, and rejoice with trembling; **72:11** all kings shall fall down before him: all nations shall *s.* him; **100:2** *s.* the LORD with gladness: come before his presence with singing; **102:22** when the people are gathered together, and the kingdoms, to *s.* the LORD; **116:16** O LORD, truly I am thy servant; I am thy servant; **143:12** of thy mercy cut off mine enemies, and destroy all them that afflict my soul: for I am thy servant; **Isa. 49:3** thou art my servant, O Israel, in whom I will be glorified; **54:17** this is the heritage of the servants of the LORD, and their righteousness is of me, saith the LORD; **61:5-10** I the LORD love judgment, I hate robbery for burnt offering; and I will direct their work in truth, and I will make an everlasting covenant with them; **65:13-15** my servants shall eat, but ye shall be hungry: behold, my servants shall drink, but ye shall be thirsty: behold, my servants shall rejoice, but ye shall be ashamed; **65:23-24** they shall not labour in vain, nor bring forth for trouble; for they are the seed of the blessed of the LORD; **66:14** when ye see this, your heart shall rejoice, and your bones shall

flourish like an herb: and the hand of the LORD shall be known toward his servants; **Jer. 30:9** they shall *s.* the LORD their God; **30:17** I will restore health unto thee, and I will heal thee of thy wounds, saith the LORD; **30:22** ye shall be my people, and I will be your God; **Mal. 3:14** ye have said, It is vain to *s.* God: and what profit is it that we have kept his ordinance, and that we have walked mournfully before the LORD of hosts; **3:17-18** then shall ye return, and discern between the righteous and the wicked, between him that *s.* God and him that *s.* him not.

Serve the living and true God. 1 Thes. 1:9

Matt. 9:37 the harvest truly is plenteous, but the labourers are few; Pray ye therefore the Lord of the harvest, that he will send forth labourers into his harvest; **24:45-47** who then is a faithful and wise servant, whom his lord hath made ruler over his household, to give them meat in due season? Blessed is that servant, whom his lord when he cometh shall find so doing. Verily I say unto you, That he shall make him ruler over all his goods; **Mark 9:35** if any man desire to be first, the same shall be last of all, and servant of all; **Luke 1:74** he would grant unto us, that we being delivered out of the hand of our enemies might *s.* him without fear; **4:8** get thee behind me, Satan: for it is written, Thou shalt worship the Lord thy God, and him only shalt thou *s.*; **9:24** whosoever will save his life shall lose it: but whosoever will lose his life for my sake, the same shall save it; **10:7** the labourer is worthy of his hire; **12:37-38** blessed are those servants, whom the lord when he cometh shall find watching: verily I say unto you, that he shall gird himself, and make them to sit down to meat, and will come forth and *s.* them. And if he shall come in the second watch, or come in the third watch, and find them so, blessed are those servants; **12:42-43** who then is that faithful and wise steward, whom his lord shall make ruler over his household, to give them their portion of meat in due season? Blessed is that servant, whom his lord when he cometh shall find so doing; **17:7-10** when ye shall have done all those things which are commanded you, say, We are unprofitable servants: we have done that which was our duty to do; **17:33** whosoever shall seek to save his life shall lose it; and whosoever shall lose his life shall preserve it; **22:24-26** there was also a strife among them, which of them should be accounted the greatest; **John 12:25-26** he that loveth his life shall lose it; and he that hateth his life in this world shall keep it unto life eternal. If any man *s.* me, let him follow me; and where I am, there shall also my servant be: if any man *s.* me, him will my Father honour; **15:20** the servant is not greater than his lord. If they have persecuted me, they will also persecute you; if they have kept my saying, they will keep yours also; **Acts 7:7** the nation to whom they shall be in bondage will I judge, said God: and after that shall they come forth, and *s.* me in this place; **20:19** serving the Lord with all humility of mind, and with many tears, and temptations; **Rom. 1:1** Paul, a servant of Jesus Christ, called to be an apostle, separated unto the gospel of God; **1:9** for God is my witness, whom I *s.* with my spirit in the gospel of his Son, that without ceasing I make mention of you always in my prayers; **6:16** to whom ye yield yourselves servants to obey, his servants ye are to whom ye obey; whether of sin unto death, or of obedience unto righteousness; **6:17** ye were the servants of sin, but ye have obeyed from the heart that form of doctrine which was delivered you; **6:19** as ye have yielded your members servants to uncleanness and to iniquity unto iniquity; even so now yield your members servants to righteousness unto holiness; **6:22** being made free from sin, and become servants to God, ye have your fruit unto holiness, and the end everlasting life; **12:1** present your bodies a living sacrifice, holy, acceptable unto God, which is your reasonable *s.*; **14:18** he that in these things *s.* Christ is acceptable to God, and approved of men; **1 Cor. 7: 22** he that is called in the Lord, being a servant, is the Lord's freeman: likewise also he that is called, being free, is Christ's servant; **2 Cor. 4:5** we preach not ourselves, but Christ Jesus the Lord; and ourselves your servants for Jesus' sake; **Eph. 6:6-8** as the servants of Christ, doing the will of God from the heart; With good will doing *s.*, as to the Lord, and not to men: Knowing that whatsoever good thing any man doeth, the same shall he receive of the Lord, whether he be bond or free; **Col. 3:23-24** whatsoever ye do, do it heartily, as to the Lord, and not unto men; Knowing that of the Lord ye shall receive the reward of the inheritance: for ye *s.* the Lord Christ; **1Thes 1:9** (Morm. 9:28) ye turned to God from idols to *s.* the living and true God; **1 Tim. 3:1** this is a true saying, If a man desire the office of a bishop, he desireth a good work; **4:10** we both labour and suffer reproach, because we trust in the living God, who is the Saviour of all men, specially of those that believe; **2 Tim. 2:21** if a man therefore purge himself from these, he shall be a vessel unto honour, sanctified, and meet for the master's use, and prepared unto every good work; **2:24** the servant of the Lord must not strive; but be

gentle unto all men, apt to teach, patient; **12:28** let us have grace, whereby we may *s.* God acceptably with reverence and godly fear; **Rev. 7:15-17** therefore are they before the throne of God, and *s.* him day and night in his temple: and he that sitteth on the throne shall dwell among them. They shall hunger no more, neither thirst any more; neither shall the sun light on them, nor any heat. For the Lamb which is in the midst of the throne shall feed them, and shall lead them unto living fountains of waters: and God shall wipe away all tears from their eyes.

SERVITUDE (*see* Bind, Bondage)

SEVEN, SEVENTH

I saw another sign in heaven, great and marvellous, seven angels having the seven last plagues; for in them is filled up the wrath of God. Rev. 15:1 (*see also* Angel, Plague, Sign)

The seventh day is the sabbath of the LORD thy God: in it thou shalt not do any work, thou, nor thy son, nor thy daughter, thy manservant, nor thy maidservant, nor thy cattle, nor thy stranger that is within thy gates: Ex. 20:10 (*see also* Sabbath, Thou Shalt Not, Work)

Then came Peter to him, and said, Lord, how oft shall my brother sin against me, and I forgive him? till seven times? Jesus saith unto him, I say not unto thee, Until seven times: but, until seventy times seven. Matt. 18:21-22 (*see also* Forgive)

SEVENTY (*see also* Missionary Work, Priesthood)

The Lord appointed other seventy also, and sent them two by two before his face into every city and place, whither he himself would come. Luke 10:1 (*see also* Missionary Work)

SHEEP (*see* Family, Neighbor, Saint)

Feed my sheep. John 21:16 (*see* John 21:15-17)

My sheep hear my voice, and I know them, and they follow me; And I give unto them eternal life; and they shall never perish, neither shall any man pluck them our of my hand. John 10:27 (*see also* Eternal Life, Sheep, Voice)

Woe be unto the pastors that destroy and scatter the sheep of my pasture! saith the LORD. Jer. 23:1 (*see also* Destroy, Persecute, Scatter)

Beware of false prophets, which come to you in sheep's clothing, but inwardly they are ravening wolves. Ye shall know them by their fruits. Matt. 7:15-16 (*see also* False Prophet)

And before him shall be gathered all nations: and he shall separate them one from another, as a shepherd divideth his sheep from the goats. Matt. 25:32 (*see also* Gather, Nation, Separate)

SHEPHERD (*see also* Jesus Christ, Lead, Minister, Priesthood)

When the chief Shepherd shall appear, ye shall receive a crown of glory that fadeth not away. 1 Pet. 5:4 (*see also* Appear, Crown)

SICK, SICKNESS (*see also* Administer, Bless, Heal, Miracle, Plague)

SIGN (*see also* Holy Ghost, Miracle)

Therefore shall ye lay up these my words in your heart and in your soul, and bind them for a sign upon your hand, that they may be as frontlets between your eyes. Deut. 11:18 (*see also* Heart, Word)

I saw another sign in heaven, great and marvellous, seven angels having the seven last plagues; for in them is filled up the wrath of God. Rev. 15:1 (*see also* Angel, Plague, Seven)

These signs shall follow them that believe; In my name shall they cast out devils; they shall speak with new tongues; They shall take up serpents; and if they drink any deadly thing it shall not hurt them; they shall lay hands on the sick and they shall recover. Mark 16:17-18 (*see also* Cast, Deadly, Devil, Name, Tongues)

[Do not] say, Let him make speed, and hasten his work, that we may see it: and let the counsel of the Holy One of Israel draw nigh and come, that we may know it! Isa. 5:19 (*see also* See)

Thus saith the Lord, learn not the way of the heathen, and be not dismayed at the signs of heaven; for the heathen are dismayed at them. Jer. 10:2 (*see also* Heathen, Heaven, Way)

False Christs and false prophets shall rise, and shall shew signs and wonders, to seduce, if it were possible, even the elect. Mark 13:22 (*see also* Elect, False Christ, False Prophet, Seduce, Wonder)

Discern the signs of the times. Matt. 16:3 (*see also* Discern)

Matt. 16:3 in the morning, It will be foul weather to day: for the sky is red and lowring, O ye hypocrites, ye can discern the face of the sky; but can ye not discern the *s.* of the times.

An evil and adulterous generation seeketh after a sign; and there shall no sign be given to it, but the sign of the prophet Jonas. Matt. 12:38-39 (*see also* Seek)

Matt. 12:38-39 certain of the scribes and of the Pharisees answered, saying, Master, we would see a *s.* from thee. But he answered and said unto them, An evil and adulterous generation seeketh after a *s.*; and there shall no *s.* be given to it, but the *s.* of the prophet Jonas; 16:1-4 the Pharisees also with the Sadducees came, and tempting desired him that he would shew them a *s.* from heaven; 27:42 he saved others; himself he cannot save. If he be the King of Israel, let him now come down from the cross, and we will believe him; 27:48-49, Mark 15:36 straightway one of them ran, and took a spunge, and filled it with vinegar, and put it on a reed, and gave him to drink. The rest said, Let be, let us see whether Elias will come to save him; Mark 8:11 the Pharisees came forth, and began to question with him, seeking of him a *s.* from heaven, tempting him; 8:12-13 he sighed deeply in his spirit, and saith, Why doth this generation seek after a *s.*? verily I say unto you, There shall no *s.* be given unto this generation; 15:32 let Christ the King of Israel descend now from the cross, that we may see and believe. And they that were crucified with him reviled him; Luke 11:16 others, tempting him, sought of him a *s.* from heaven; 11:29-30 when the people were gathered thick together, he began to say, This is an evil generation: they seek a *s.*; and there shall no *s.* be given it, but the *s.* of Jonas the prophet. For as Jonas was a *s.* unto the Ninevites, so shall also the Son of man be to this generation; 23:8-9 when Herod saw Jesus, he was exceeding glad: for he was desirous to see him of a long season, because he had heard many things of him; and he hoped to have seen some miracle done by him. Then he questioned with him in many words; but he answered him nothing; **John 4:48** except ye see *s.* and wonders, ye will not believe.

Watch therefore: for ye know not what hour your Lord doth come. Matt. 24:42 (*see also* Hour, Watch)

Matt. 24:6-8 ye shall hear of wars and rumours of wars: see that ye be not troubled: for all these things must come to pass, but the end is not yet. For nation shall rise against nation, and kingdom against kingdom: and there shall be famines, and pestilences, and earthquakes, in divers places. All these are the beginning of sorrows; **24:14** this gospel of the kingdom shall be preached in all the world for a witness unto all nations; and then shall the end come; **24:32-33** (Mark 13:28-30) learn a parable of the fig tree; When his branch is yet tender, and putteth forth leaves, ye know that summer is nigh: So likewise ye, when ye shall see all these things, know that it is near, even at the doors; **24:42-43** watch therefore: for ye know not what hour your Lord doth come. But know this, that if the goodman of the house had known in what watch the thief would come, he would have watched, and would not have suffered his house to be broken up; **Mark 13:33-36** take ye heed, watch and pray: for ye know not when the time is; **Luke 12:37-40** blessed are those servants, whom the lord when he cometh shall find watching: verily I say unto you, that he shall gird himself, and make them to sit down to meat, and will come forth and serve them... and this know, that if the goodman of the house had known what hour the thief would come, he would have watched, and not have suffered his house to be broken through. Be ye therefore ready also: for the Son of man cometh at an hour when ye think not; **12:42-48** And the Lord said, Who then is that faithful and wise steward, whom his lord shall make ruler over his household, to give them their portion of meat in due season? Blessed is that servant, whom his lord when he cometh shall find so doing. Of a truth I say unto you, that he will make him ruler over all that he hath. But and if that servant say in his heart, My lord delayeth his coming; and shall begin to beat the menservants and maidens, and to eat and drink, and to be drunken; The lord of that servant will come in a day when he looketh not for him, and at an hour when he is not aware, and will cut him in sunder, and will appoint him his portion with the unbelievers. And that servant, which knew his lord's will, and prepared not himself, neither did according to his will, shall be beaten with many stripes. But he that knew not, and did

commit things worthy of stripes, shall be beaten with few stripes. For unto whomsoever much is given, of him shall be much required: and to whom men have committed much, of him they will ask the more; **12:55** when ye see the south wind blow, ye say, There will be heat; and it cometh to pass; **13:25-27** When once the master of the house is risen up, and hath shut to the door, and ye begin to stand without, and to knock at the door, saying, Lord, Lord, open unto us; and he shall answer and say unto you, I know you not whence ye are: Then shall ye begin to say, We have eaten and drunk in thy presence, and thou hast taught in our streets. But he shall say, I tell you, I know you not whence ye are; depart from me, all ye workers of iniquity; **21:8-11** many shall come in my name, saying, I am Christ; and the time draweth near: go ye not therefore after them. But when ye shall hear of wars and commotions, be not terrified: for these things must first come to pass; but the end is not by and by. Then said he unto them, Nation shall rise against nation, and kingdom against kingdom: And great earthquakes shall be in divers places, and famines, and pestilences; and fearful sights and great *s.* shall there be from heaven; **21:20-28** when ye shall see Jerusalem compassed with armies, then know that the desolation thereof is nigh. Then let them which are in Judaea flee to the mountains; and let them which are in the midst of it depart out; and let not them that are in the countries enter thereinto. For these be the days of vengeance, that all things which are written may be fulfilled. But woe unto them that are with child, and to them that give suck, in those days! for there shall be great distress in the land, and wrath upon this people. And they shall fall by the edge of the sword, and shall be led away captive into all nations: and Jerusalem shall be trodden down of the Gentiles, until the times of the Gentiles be fulfilled. And there shall be *s.* in the sun, and in the moon, and in the stars; and upon the earth distress of nations, with perplexity; the sea and the waves roaring; Men's hearts failing them for fear, and for looking after those things which are coming on the earth: for the powers of heaven shall be shaken. And then shall they see the Son of man coming in a cloud with power and great glory. And when these things begin to come to pass, then look up, and lift up your heads; for your redemption draweth nigh; **Rom. 8:19** the earnest expectation of the creature waiteth for the manifestation of the sons of God; **1 Cor. 1:7-8** So that ye come behind in no gift; waiting for the coming of our Lord Jesus Christ: Who shall also confirm you unto the end, that ye may be blameless in the day of our Lord Jesus Christ; **10:11** all these things happened unto them for ensamples: and they are written for our admonition, upon whom the ends of the world are come; **Gal. 4:4** when the fulness of the time was come, God sent forth his Son, made of a woman, made under the law; **1 Thes. 1:10** to wait for his Son from heaven, whom he raised from the dead, even Jesus, which delivered us from the wrath to come; **5:6** let us not sleep, as do others; but let us watch and be sober; **2 Thes. 2:1-6** that day shall not come, except there come a falling away first, and that man of sin be revealed, the son of perdition; **3:5** the Lord direct your hearts into the love of God, and into the patient waiting for Christ; **1 Tim. 4:1-3** the Spirit speaketh expressly, that in the latter times some shall depart from the faith, giving heed to seducing spirits, and doctrines of devils; Speaking lies in hypocrisy; having their conscience seared with a hot iron; Forbidding to marry, and commanding to abstain from meats, which God hath created to be received with thanksgiving of them which believe and know the truth; **2 Tim. 3:1-3** this know also, that in the last days perilous times shall come. For men shall be lovers of their own selves, covetous, boasters, proud, blasphemers, disobedient to parents, unthankful, unholy, Without natural affection, trucebreakers, false accusers, incontinent, fierce, despisers of those that are good; **4:8** there is laid up for me a crown of righteousness, which the Lord, the righteous judge, shall give me at that day: and not to me only, but unto all them also that love his appearing; **Titus 2:13** looking for that blessed hope, and the glorious appearing of the great God and our Saviour Jesus Christ; **2 Pet. 3:13-14** we, according to his promise, look for new heavens and a new earth, wherein dwelleth righteousness. Wherefore, beloved, seeing that ye look for such things, be diligent that ye may be found of him in peace, without spot, and blameless; **Jude 1:14** Enoch also, the seventh from Adam, prophesied of these, saying, Behold, the Lord cometh with ten thousands of his saints; **Rev. 1:7** he cometh with clouds; and every eye shall see him, and they also which pierced him: and all kindreds of the earth shall wail because of him; **6:12-16** I beheld when he had opened the sixth seal... the kings of the earth, and the great men, and the rich men, and the chief captains, and the mighty men, and every bondman, and every free man, hid themselves in the dens and in the rocks of the mountains; And said to the mountains and rocks, Fall on us, and hide us from the face of him that sitteth on the throne, and from the wrath of the

Lamb; **8:6-13** I beheld, and heard an angel flying through the midst of heaven, saying with a loud voice, Woe, woe, woe, to the inhabiters of the earth by reason of the other voices of the trumpet of the three angels, which are yet to sound; **9:6** in those days shall men seek death, and shall not find it; and shall desire to die, and death shall flee from them; **9:7-18** by these three was the third part of men killed, by the fire, and by the smoke, and by the brimstone, which issued out of their mouths; **11:15** the seventh angel sounded; and there were great voices in heaven, saying, The kingdoms of this world are become the kingdoms of our Lord, and of his Christ; and he shall reign for ever and ever; **11:19** the temple of God was opened in heaven, and there was seen in his temple the ark of his testament: and there were lightnings, and voices, and thunderings, and an earthquake, and great hail; **15:1** I saw another *s.* in heaven, great and marvellous, seven angels having the seven last plagues; for in them is filled up the wrath of God; **16:14** they are the spirits of devils, working miracles, which go forth unto the kings of the earth and of the whole world, to gather them to the battle of that great day of God Almighty; **16:19** the great city was divided into three parts, and the cities of the nations fell: and great Babylon came in remembrance before God, to give unto her the cup of the wine of the fierceness of his wrath.

SILENCE, SILENT (*see also* Peace, Quiet)

But the LORD is in his holy temple: let all the earth keep silence before him. Hab. 2:20 (*see also* Earth, Temple)

Be silent, O all flesh, before the LORD: for he is raised up out of his holy habitation. Zech. 2:13 (*see also* Holy)

Let the lying lips be put to silence; which speak grievous things proudly and contemptuously against the righteous. Ps. 31:18 (*see also* Lie, Speak)

SILVER (*see also* Rich)

He that loveth silver shall not be satisfied with silver; nor he that loveth abundance with increase: this is also vanity. Eccl. 5:10 (*see also* Love, Vain)

Eccl. 5:10-15 he that loveth *s.* shall not be satisfied with *s.*; nor he that loveth abundance with increase: this is also vanity; **Isa. 1:22** thy *s.*

is become dross, thy wine mixed with water; **2:7** their land also is full of *s.* and gold, neither is there any end of their treasures; **Ezek. 7:19** they shall cast their *s.* in the streets, and their gold shall be removed: their *s.* and their gold shall not be able to deliver them in the day of the wrath of the LORD.

SIMPLE, SIMPLENESS (*see* Easy)

SIN (*see also* Abomination, Apostasy, Blaspheme, Carnal, Corrupt, Contend, Darkness, Death, Devil, Disobey, Evil, Fall, Iniquity, Natural Man, Offend, Transgress, Trespass, Wickedness)

Seeing we also are compassed about with so great a cloud of witnesses, let us lay aside every weight, and the sin which doth so easily beset us, and let us run with patience the race that is set before us. Heb. 12:1 (*see also* Beset, Patience, Run, Weight, Witness)

And above all things have fervent charity among yourselves: for charity shall cover the multitude of sins. 1 Pet 4:8 (*see also* Charity, Multitude)

When thou shalt vow a vow unto the LORD thy God, thou shalt not slack to pay it: for the LORD thy God will surely require it of thee; and it would be sin in thee. Deut. 23:21 (*see also* Pay, Vow)

Knowing that Christ being raised from the dead dieth no more; death hath no more dominion over him. For in that he died, he died unto sin once: but in that he liveth, he liveth unto God. Likewise reckon ye also yourselves to be dead indeed unto sin, but alive unto God through Jesus Christ our Lord. Rom. 6:9-11 (*see also* Alive, Jesus Christ, Reckon)

I will declare mine iniquity; I will be sorry for my sin. Ps. 38:18 (*see also* Iniquity, Repent)

He that covereth his sins shall not prosper: but whoso confesseth and forsaketh them shall have mercy. Prov. 28:13 (*see also* Confess, Forsake, Mercy)

Cry aloud, spare not, lift up thy voice like a trumpet, and shew my people their transgression, and the house of Jacob their sins. Isa. 58:1 (*see also* Cry, Voice)

If thou warn the righteous man, that the righteous sin not, and he doth not sin, he shall surely live, because he is warned; also thou hast delivered thy soul. Ezek. 3:21 (*see also* Righteous, Warn)

Suffer not thy mouth to cause thy flesh to sin; neither say thou before the angel, that it was an error. Eccl. 5:6 (*see also* Mouth)

Sin not. Ex. 20:20

Ex. 20:20 fear not: for God is come to prove you, and that his fear may be before your faces, that ye *s.* not; **1 Sam. 14:34** *s.* not against the LORD; **Ps. 4:4** stand in awe, and *s.* not: commune with your own heart upon your bed, and be still; **39:1** I will take heed to my ways, that I *s.* not with my tongue: I will keep my mouth with a bridle, while the wicked is before me.

Woe unto them that draw iniquity with cords of vanity, and sin as it were with a cart rope. Isa. 5:18 (*see also* Iniquity, Vanity)

1 Kgs. 15:30 because of the *s.* of Jeroboam which he *s.*, and which he made Israel *s.*, by his provocation wherewith he provoked the LORD God of Israel to anger; **15:34** he did evil in the sight of the LORD, and walked in the way of Jeroboam, and in his *s.* wherewith he made Israel to *s.*; **16:19** his *s.* which he *s.* in doing evil in the sight of the LORD, in walking in the way of Jeroboam, and in his *s.* which he did, to make Israel to *s.*; **16:26** he walked in all the way of Jeroboam the son of Nebat, and in his *s.* wherewith he made Israel to *s.*, to provoke the LORD God of Israel to anger with their vanities; **21:22** [I] will make thine house like the house of Jeroboam the son of Nebat... for the provocation wherewith thou hast provoked me to anger, and made Israel to *s.*; **Prov. 14:34-35** righteousness exalteth a nation: but *s.* is a reproach to any people; **Isa. 5:18** woe unto them that draw iniquity with cords of vanity, and *s.* as it were with a cart rope.

Turn from transgression. Isa. 59:20 (*see also* Transgress)

2 Chron. 6:26-27 if they pray toward this place, and confess thy name, and turn from their *s.*, when thou dost afflict them; Then hear thou from heaven, and forgive the *s.* of thy servants; **6:37-38** if they... turn and pray unto thee in the land of their captivity, saying, We have *s.*, we have done amiss, and have dealt wickedly; If they return to thee with all their heart and with all their soul in the land of their captivity; **Job 1:22** in all this Job *s.* not, nor charged God foolishly; **2:10** what? shall we receive good at the hand of God, and shall we not receive evil? In all this did not Job *s.* with his lips; **24:19** drought and heat consume the snow waters: so doth the grave those which have *s.*; **Ps. 85:8** I will hear what God the Lord will speak: for he will speak peace unto his people, and to his saints: but let them not turn again to folly; **Prov. 13:21-22** evil pursueth *s.*: but to the righteous good shall be repayed. A good man leaveth an inheritance to his childrens children: and the wealth of the *s.* is laid up for the just; **Isa. 59:20** the Redeemer shall come to Zion, and unto them that turn from transgression in Jacob; **Jer. 3:14-16** turn, O backsliding children, saith the Lord; for I am married unto you: and I will take you one of a city, and two of a family, and I will bring you to Zion; **3:22** return, ye backsliding children, and I will heal your backslidings. Behold, we come unto thee; for thou art the Lord our God; **5:25** your iniquities have turned away these things, and your *s.* have withholden good things from you; **25:5** turn ye again now every one from his evil way, and from the evil of your doings, and dwell in the land that the Lord hath given unto you and to your fathers for ever and ever; **Jonah 3:8** let them turn every one from his evil way, and from the violence that is in their hands.

He that sinneth against me wrongeth his own soul: all they that hate me love death. Prov. 8:36 (*see also* Hate)

Prov. 8:36 he that *s.* against me wrongeth his own soul: all they that hate me love death; **Jer. 3:25** we lie down in our shame, and our confusion covereth us: for we have *s.* against the Lord our God; **8:14-15** the Lord our God hath put us to silence, and given us water of gall to drink, because we have *s.* against the Lord; **50:14-15** put yourselves in array against Babylon round about: all ye that bend the bow, shoot at her, spare no arrows: for she hath *s.* against the Lord.

Bear thine own shame for thy sins that thou hast committed. Ezek. 16:52

Ezek. 16:52 bear thine own shame for thy *s.* that thou hast committed more abominable than they: they are more righteous than thou: yea, be thou confounded also, and bear thy shame; **16:54** thou mayest bear thine own shame, and mayest be confounded in all that thou hast done, in that

thou art a comfort unto them; **16:58** thou hast borne thy lewdness and thine abominations, saith the Lord; **16:63** thou mayest remember, and be confounded, and never open thy mouth any more because of thy shame, when I am pacified toward thee for all that thou hast done, saith the Lord God.

SINCERE, SINCERITY (*see also* Honest, Integrity, Pure)

Approve things that are excellent; that ye may be sincere and without offense till the day of Christ. Philip. 1:10 (*see also* Approve, Excellent, Offense)

As newborn babes, desire the sincere milk of the word, that ye may grow thereby. 1 Pet. 2:2 (*see also* Desire, Word)

SING, SONG (*see also* Hymn, Music, Praise, Psalms, Rejoice, Testify, Thanks, Worship)

Let the word of Christ dwell in you richly in all wisdom; teaching and admonishing one another in psalms and hymns and spiritual songs, singing with grace in your hearts to the Lord. Col. 3:16 (*see also* Admonish, Grace, Hymn, Psalm, Wisdom, Word)

The ransomed of the Lord shall return, and come to Zion with songs and everlasting joy upon their heads: they shall obtain joy and gladness, and sorrow and sighing shall flee away. Isa. 35:10 (*see also* Joy)

Is any merry? Let him sing psalms. James 5:13 (*see also* Merry, Psalms)

Mark 14:26 when they had sung an hymn, they went out into the mount of Olives; **Rom. 15:9** I will confess to thee among the Gentiles, and sing unto thy name; **1 Cor. 14:15** I will sing with the spirit, and I will sing with the understanding also; **James 5:13** is any merry? let him sing psalms; **Rev. 14:3** they sung as it were a new song before the throne, and before the four beasts, and the elders.

Sing praise to the name of the Lord most high. Ps. 7:17 (*see also* Praise)

Ex. 15:1 then *s.* Moses and the children of Israel this *s.* unto the Lord, and spake, saying, I will *s.* unto the Lord, for he hath triumphed gloriously; **15:21** *s.* ye to the Lord, for he hath triumphed gloriously; the horse and his rider hath he thrown into the sea; **32:18** it is not the voice of them that shout for mastery, neither is it the voice of them that cry for being overcome: but the noise of them that *s.* do I hear; **Judg. 5:3** hear, O ye kings; give ear, O ye princes; I, even I, will *s.* unto the LORD; I will *s.* praise to the LORD God of Israel; **2 Sam. 22:50** I will give thanks unto thee, O LORD, among the heathen, and I will *s.* praises unto thy name; **1 Chron. 16:9** *s.* unto him, *s.* psalms unto him, talk ye of all his wondrous works; **16:23** *s.* unto the LORD, all the earth; shew forth from day to day his salvation; **16:33** then shall the trees of the wood *s.* out at the presence of the LORD, because he cometh to judge the earth; **2 Chron. 29:30** they *s.* praises with gladness, and they bowed their heads and worshipped; **Ps. 7:17** I will praise the LORD according to his righteousness: and will *s.* praise to the name of the LORD most high; **9:2** I will be glad and rejoice in thee: I will *s.* praise to thy name, O thou most High; **9:11** *s.* praises to the LORD, which dwelleth in Zion: declare among the people his doings; **13:6** I will *s.* unto the LORD, because he hath dealt bountifully with me; **18:49** I give thanks unto thee, O LORD, among the heathen, and *s.* praises unto thy name; **21:13** be thou exalted, LORD, in thine own strength: so will we *s.* and praise thy power; **27:6** shall mine head be lifted up above mine enemies round about me: therefore will I offer in his tabernacle sacrifices of joy; I will *s.*, yea, I will *s.* praises unto the LORD; **30:4** *s.* unto the LORD, O ye saints of his, and give thanks at the remembrance of his holiness; **30:12** to the end that my glory may *s.* praise to thee, and not be silent. O LORD my God, I will give thanks unto thee for ever; **33:3** *s.* unto him a new song; play skilfully with a loud noise; **47:5-7** God is gone up with a shout, the LORD with the sound of a trumpet. *S.* praises to God, *s.* praises: *s.* praises unto our King, *s.* praises. For God is the King of all the earth: *s.* ye praises with understanding; **57:9** I will praise thee, O Lord, among the people: I will *s.* unto thee among the nations; **59:16-17** I will *s.* of thy power; yea, I will *s.* aloud of thy mercy in the morning: for thou hast been my defence and refuge in the day of my trouble. Unto thee, O my strength, will I *s.*: for God is my defence, and the God of my mercy; **61:8** so will I *s.* praise unto thy name for ever, that I may daily perform my vows; **68:4** *s.* unto God, *s.* praises to his name: extol him that rideth upon the heavens by his name JAH, and rejoice before him; **68:32** *s.* unto God, ye kingdoms of the earth; O *s.* praises unto the Lord; **71:22-23** I will also praise thee with the psaltery, even thy truth, O my God: unto thee will I *s.* with the harp, O thou Holy One of Israel.

My lips shall greatly rejoice when I *s.* unto thee; and my soul, which thou hast redeemed; **75:9** I will declare for ever; I will *s.* praises to the God of Jacob; **81:1-4** *s.* aloud unto God our strength: make a joyful noise unto the God of Jacob. Take a psalm, and bring hither the timbrel, the pleasant harp with the psaltery; **92:1** it is a good thing to give thanks unto the LORD, and to *s.* praises unto thy name, O most High; **95:1-2** O come, let us *s.* unto the LORD: let us make a joyful noise to the rock of our salvation. Let us come before his presence with thanksgiving, and make a joyful noise unto him with psalms; **96:1-2** O *s.* unto the LORD a new song: *s.* unto the LORD, all the earth. *S.* unto the LORD, bless his name; shew forth his salvation from day to day; **98:1** O *s.* unto the LORD a new song; for he hath done marvelous things: his right hand, and his holy arm, hath gotten him the victory; **98:4** make a joyful noise unto the LORD, all the earth: make a loud noise, and rejoice, and *s.* praise; **100:1-2** make a joyful noise unto the LORD, all ye lands. Serve the LORD with gladness: come before his presence with *s.*; **101:1** I will *s.* of mercy and judgment: unto thee, O LORD, will I *s.*; **104:33** I will *s.* unto the LORD as long as I live: I will *s.* praise to my God while I have my being; **108:3** I will praise thee, O LORD, among the people: and I will *s.* praises unto thee among the nations; **119:54** thy statutes have been my songs in the house of my pilgrimage; **135:3** praise the LORD; for the LORD is good: *s.* praises unto his name; for it is pleasant; **137:3-4** they that carried us away captive required of us a song; and they that wasted us required of us mirth, saying, *S.* us one of the songs of Zion. How shall we *s.* the LORD's *s.* in a strange land; **138:1** I will praise thee with my whole heart: before the gods will I *s.* praise unto thee; **138:5** they shall *s.* in the ways of the LORD: for great is the glory of the; **144:9** I will *s.* a new *s.* unto thee, O God: upon a psaltery and an instrument of ten strings will I *s.* praises unto thee; **146:2** I live will I praise the LORD: I will *s.* praises unto my God while I have any being; **147:1** praise ye the LORD: for it is good to *s.* praises unto our God; for it is pleasant; and praise is comely; **147:7** *s.* unto the LORD with thanksgiving; *s.* praise upon the harp unto our God; **149:1** praise ye the LORD. *S.* unto the LORD a new song, and his praise in the congregation of; **149:3** praise his name in the dance: let them *s.* praises unto him with the timbrel and harp; **Isa. 12:5-6** *s.* unto the LORD; for he hath done excellent things: this is known in all the earth. Cry out and shout, thou inhabitant of Zion: for great is the Holy One of Israel in the midst of thee; **14:7** the whole earth is at rest, and is quiet:

they break forth into *s.*; **35:2** rejoice even with joy and *s.*; **35:10** come to Zion with songs and everlasting joy upon their heads: they shall obtain joy and gladness, and sorrow and sighing shall flee away; **38:20** we will *s.* my songs to the stringed instruments all the days of our life in the house of the LORD; **42:10-11** *s.* unto the LORD a new song, and his praise from the end of the earth, ye that go down to the sea, and all that is therein; the isles, and the inhabitants thereof. Let the wilderness and the cities thereof lift up their voice, the villages that Kedar doth inhabit: let the inhabitants of the rock *s.*, let them shout from the top of the mountains; **44:23** *s.*, O ye heavens; for the LORD hath done it: shout, ye lower parts of the earth: break forth into *s.*, ye mountains, O forest, and every tree therein: for the LORD hath redeemed Jacob, and glorified himself in Israel; **49:13** *s.*, O heavens; and be joyful, O earth; and break forth into *s.*, O mountains: for the LORD hath comforted his people, and will have mercy upon his afflicted; **52:8-9** thy watchmen shall lift up the voice; with the voice together shall they *s.*: for they shall see eye to eye, when the LORD shall bring again Zion. Break forth into joy, *s.* together, ye waste places of Jerusalem: for the LORD hath comforted his people, and will have mercy upon his people, hath redeemed Jerusalem; **54:1** break forth into *s.*, and cry aloud, thou that didst not travail with child; **Jer. 20:13** *s.* unto the LORD, praise ye the LORD: for he hath delivered the soul of the poor from the hand of evildoers; **Zeph. 3:14** *s.*, O daughter of Zion; shout, O Israel; be glad and rejoice with all the heart, O daughter of Jerusalem; **3:17** the LORD thy God in the midst of thee is mighty; he will save, he will rejoice over thee with joy; he will rest in his love, he will joy over thee with *s.*; **Zech. 2:10** *s.* and rejoice, O daughter of Zion: for, lo, I come, and I will dwell in the midst of thee, saith the LORD.

SISTER (*see also* Brethren, Child, Family, Fellowship, Neighbor, Wife)

He stretched forth his hand toward his disciples, and said, Behold my mother and my brethren! For whosoever shall do the will of m Father which is in heaven, the same is my brother, and sister, and mother. Matt. 12:49-50 (*see also* Brethren, Will, Mark 3:35)

SLACK, SLAKEN (*see also* Lazy, Slothful)

In that day it shall be said to Jerusalem, Fear thou not: and to Zion, Let not thine hands be slack. Zeph. 3:16 (*see also* Hand)

SLANDER (*see* Backbite, Deceive, False, Gossip, Lie, Talebearer)

He that hideth hatred with lying lips, and he that uttereth a slander, is a fool. Prov. 10:18 (*see also* Hate, Liar)

SLEEP, SLEPT (*see also* Death, Idle, Laziness)

Love not sleep, lest thou come to poverty. Prov. 20:13

SLOTHFUL, SLOTHFULNESS (*see also* Idle, Laziness)

Be not slothful, but followers of them who through faith and patience inherit the promises. Heb. 6:12 (*see also* Promise)

Rom. 12:11 not *s.* in business; fervent in spirit; serving the Lord; **Heb. 6:12** be not *s.*, but followers of them who through faith and patience inherit the promises.

He also that is slothful in his work is brother to him that is a great waster. Prov. 18:9 (*see also* Waste)

Prov. 12:24 the hand of the diligent shall bear rule: but the *s.* shall be under tribute; **15:19** the way of the *s.* man is as an hedge of thorns: but the way of the righteous is made plain; **18:9** he also that is *s.* in his work is brother to him that is a great waster; **19:15** *s.* casteth into a deep sleep; and an idle soul shall suffer hunger; **19:24** a *s.* man hideth his hand in his bosom, and will not so much as bring it to his mouth again; **20:4** the sluggard will not plow by reason of the cold; therefore shall he beg in harvest, and have nothing; **21:25** the desire of the *s.* killeth him; for his hands refuse to labour; **22:13** the *s.* man saith, There is a lion without, I shall be slain in the streets; **24:32-33** I saw, and considered it well: I looked upon it, and received instruction. Yet a little sleep, a little slumber, a little folding of the hands to sleep; **26:13-15** the *s.* man saith, There is a lion in the way; a lion is in the streets. As the door turneth upon his hinges, so doth the *s.* upon his bed; **Eccl. 10:18** by much *s.* the building decayeth; and through idleness of the hands the house droppeth through.

SMITE, SMITTEN, SMOTE (*see also* Kill, Murder, Strike)

I gave my back to the smiters and my cheeks to them that plucked off the hair: I hid not my face from shame and spitting. For the Lord GOD will help me; therefore shall I not be confounded. **Isa. 50:6-7** (*see also* Endure, Persecute)

I say unto you, That ye resist not evil: but whosoever shall smite thee on thy right cheek, turn to him the other also. **Matt. 5:39** (*see also* Cheek)

SNARE (*see* Deceive, Entangle)

SOBER, SOBERNESS (*see also* Drunk, Strong Drink)

Be sober, be vigilant; because your adversary the devil, as a roaring lion, walketh about, seeking whom he may devour: **1 Pet. 5:8** (*see also* Adversary, Vigilant)

Young men likewise exhort to be sober minded. **Titus 2:6** (*see also* Mind)

Rom. 12:3 through the grace given unto me, to every man that is among you, not to think of himself more highly than he ought to think; but to think *s.*, according as God hath dealt to every man the measure of faith; **Philip. 4:8-9** whatsoever things are true, whatsoever things are honest, whatsoever things are just, whatsoever things are pure, whatsoever things are lovely, whatsoever things are of good report; if there be any virtue, and if there be any praise, think on these things. Those things, which ye have both learned, and received, and heard, and seen in me, do: and the God of peace shall be with you; **1 Tim. 3:11** even so must their wives be grave, not slanderers, *s.*, faithful in all things; **Titus 2:6** young men likewise exhort to be *s.* minded; **2:12** teaching us that, denying ungodliness and worldly lusts, we should live *s.*, righteously, and godly, in this present world; **1 Pet. 1:13** gird up the loins of your mind, be *s.*, and hope to the end for the grace that is to be brought unto you at the **Rev.** of Jesus Christ; **4:7** be ye therefore *s.*, and watch unto prayer; **5:8** be *s.*, be vigilant; because your adversary the devil, as a roaring lion, walketh about, seeking whom he may devour.

SOLEMN, SOLEMNITIES, SOLEMNITY (*see also* Blessing, Gift, Mystery, Sincerity)

In the multitude of my thoughts within me thy comforts delight my soul. **Ps. 94:19** (*see also* Thought)

SOOTHSAYER (*see* False Prophet, Magic, Sorcery, Wizardry)

SORCERER, SORCERY (*see also* False Prophet, Magic, Superstitious, Wizardry)

Hearken not ye to your prophets, nor to your diviners, nor to your dreamers, nor to your enchantments, nor to your sorcerers, which speak unto you, saying, Ye shall not serve the king of Babylon: For they prophesy a lie unto you. **Jer. 27:9-10** (*see also* Enchantments)

By thy sorceries were all nations deceived. **Rev. 18:23** (*see also* Deceive)

Acts 8:9 a certain man, called Simon, which beforetime in the same city used *s.*, and bewitched the people of Samaria, giving out that himself was some great one; **19:17-20** many of them also which used curious arts brought their books together, and burned them before all men; **Rev. 9:21** neither repented they of their murders, nor of their *s.*, nor of their fornication, nor of their thefts; **18:23** the light of a candle shall shine no more at all in thee... for thy merchants were the great men of the earth; for by thy *s.* were all nations deceived.

SORROW, SORROWFUL (*see also* Adversity, Anguish, Despair, Grief, Misery, Mourn, Pain, Tribulation, Trouble)

The love of money is the root of all evil: which while some coveted after, they have erred from the faith, and pierced themselves through with many sorrows. **1 Tim. 6:9** (*see also* Evil, Money)

All these are the beginning of sorrows. Then shall they deliver you up to be afflicted, and shall kill you: and ye shall be hated of all nations for my name's sake. And then shall many be offended, and shall betray one another, and shall hate one another. **Matt. 24:8-10** (*see also* Betray)

SOUL (*see also* Heart, Spirit)

Whosoever will save his life shall lose it; but whosoever shall lose his life for my sake and the gospel's, the same shall save it. For what shall it profit a man, if he shall gain the whole world, and lose his own soul? **Mark 8:36** (*see also* Gain, Life, Save)

If thou draw out thy soul to the hungry, and satisfy the afflicted soul; then shall thy light rise in obscurity, and thy darkness be as the noonday: And the LORD shall guide thee continually. **Isa. 58:10** (*see also* Afflict, Hunger)

I will greatly rejoice in the LORD, my soul shall be joyful in my God; for he hath clothed me with the garments of salvation, he hath covered me with the robe of righteousness. **Isa. 61:10** (*see also* Garments, Joy)

Thorns and snares are in the way of the froward: he that doth keep his soul shall be far from them. **Prov. 22:5** (*see also* Froward, Way)

Fear not them which kill the body, but are not able to kill the soul: but rather fear him which is able to destroy both soul and body in hell. **Matt. 10:28** (*see also* Fear)

SOUND (*see also* Understand)

This witness is true. Wherefore rebuke them sharply, that they may be sound in the faith. **Titus 1:13** (*see also* Rebuke)

Speak thou the things which become sound doctrine: That the aged men be sober, grave, temperate, sound in faith, in charity, in patience. **Titus 2:1-2** (*see also* Doctrine)

Hold fast the form of sound words, which thou hast heard of me, in faith and love which is in Christ Jesus. **2 Tim. 1:13** (*see also* Hold Fast, Word)

SOW, SOWER, SOWN (*see also* Diligence, Do, Serve, Teach)

Break up your fallow ground, and sow not among thorns. **Jer. 4:3**

He that soweth to his flesh shall of the flesh reap corruption; but he that soweth to the Spirit shall of the Spirit reap life everlasting. **Gal. 6:8** (*see also* Flesh, Reap, Spirit)

He that soweth iniquity shall reap vanity: and the rod of his anger shall fail. **Prov. 22:8** (*see also* Iniquity)

He which soweth sparingly shall reap also sparingly; and he which soweth bountifully shall reap also bountifully. **2 Cor. 9:6** (*see also* Reap, Sparingly)

Another parable put he forth unto them, saying, The kingdom of heaven is like to a grain of mustard seed, which a man took, and sowed in his field. **Matt. 13:31** (*see also* Grain, Kingdom)

Be not deceived; God is not mocked: for whatsoever a man soweth, that shall he also reap. **Galtians 6:7** (*see also* Deceive, Reap)

Matt. 13:3-8 behold, a sower went forth to sow; And when he *s.*, some seeds fell by the way side, and the fowls came and devoured them up: Some fell upon stony places, where they had not much earth: and forthwith they sprung up, because they had no deepness of earth: And when the sun was up, they were scorched; and because they had no root, they withered away. And some fell among thorns; and the thorns sprung up, and choked them: But other fell into good ground, and brought forth fruit; **13:18-23** hear ye therefore the parable of the *s.*. When any one heareth the word of the kingdom, and understandeth it not, then cometh the wicked one, and catcheth away that which was sown in his heart. This is he which received seed by the way side. But he that received the seed into stony places, the same is he that heareth the word, and anon with joy receiveth it; Yet hath he not root in himself, but dureth for a while: for when tribulation or persecution ariseth because of the word, by and by he is offended. He also that received seed among the thorns is he that heareth the word; and the care of this world, and the deceitfulness of riches, choke the word, and he becometh unfruitful. But he that received seed into the good ground is he that heareth the word, and understandeth it; **Mark 4:3-8** hearken; Behold, there went out a *s.* to *s.*; **Luke 5-15** a *s.* went out to sow his seed: and as he *s.*, some fell by the way side; **19:21-22** out of thine own mouth will I judge thee, thou wicked servant. Thou knewest that I was an austere man, taking up that I laid not down, and reaping that I did not *s.*; **2 Cor. 9:6** he which soweth sparingly shall reap also sparingly; and he which *s.* bountifully shall reap also bountifully; **Gal. 6:7** be not deceived; God is not mocked: for whatsoever a man *s.*, that shall he also reap.

SPARE, SPARED, SPARINGLY

He which soweth sparingly shall reap also sparingly; and he which soweth bountifully shall reap also bountifully. 2 Cor. 9:6 (*see also* Reap, Sow)

SPEAK, SPOKEN (*see also* Declare, Preach, Say)

Though I speak with the tongues of men and of angels, and have not charity, I am become as sounding brass, or a tinkling cymbal. 1 Cor. 13:1 (*see also* Brass, Charity)

Speak not with a stiff neck. Ps. 75:5 (*see also* Stiffnecked)

He that speaketh flattery to his friends, even the eyes of his children shall fail. Job 17:5 (*see also* Flatter)

These things have I spoken unto you in proverbs: but the time cometh, when I shall no more speak unto you in proverbs, but I shall shew you plainly of the Father. John 16:25 (*see also* Father, Plain)

Let every man be swift to hear, slow to speak, slow to wrath. James 1:19 (*see also* Hear, Wrath)

The Lord GOD hath given me the tongue of the learned, that I should know how to speak a word in season to him that is weary. Isa. 50:4 (*see also* Season, Tongue, Weary)

Take no thought how or what ye shall speak: for it shall be given you in that same hour what ye shall speak. For it is not ye that speak, but the Spirit of your Father which speaketh in you. Matt. 10:19-20 (*see also* Hour, Spirit, Thought)

Do violence to no man, neither accuse any falsely; and be content with your wages. Luke 3:14 (*see also* Accuse, False)

He that walketh righteously, and speaketh uprightly; he that despiseth the gain of oppressions, that shaketh his hands from holding of bribes, that stoppeth his ears from hearing of blood, and shutteth his eyes from seeing evil; He shall dwell on high: his defence shall be the munitions of rocks: bread shall be given him; his waters shall be sure. Isa. 33:15-16 (*see also* Gain, Hear, Oppress, Righteous, See, Uprightly, Walk)

Speaketh truth. Prov. 12:17 (*see also* True)

A word fitly spoken is like apples of gold in pictures of silver. Prov. 25:11 (*see also* Word)

In all things shewing thyself a pattern of good works: in doctrine shewing uncorruptness, gravity, sincerity, Sound speech, that cannot be condemned; that he that is of the contrary part may be ashamed, having no evil thing to say of you. Titus 2:7-8 (*see also* Good, Pattern, Works)

Let no corrupt communication proceed out of your mouth, but that which is good to the use of edifying, that it may minister grace unto the hearers. Eph. 4:29 (*see also* Edify, Grace)

Hear; for I will speak of excellent things; and the opening of my lips shall be right things. For my mouth shall speak truth; and wickedness is an abomination to my lips. Prov. 6:7 (*see also* True)

Let your speech be alway with grace, seasoned with salt, that ye may know how ye ought to answer every man. Col. 4:6 (*see also* Grace)

Say not, I am a child: for thou shalt go to all that I shall send thee, and whatsoever I command thee thou shalt speak. Be not afraid of their faces: for I am with thee to deliver thee, saith the LORD. Jer. 1:7-8 (*see also* Belief)

He that hath my word, let him speak my word faithfully. Jer. 23:28 (*see also* Faith, Word)

They speak vanity every one with his neighbour: with flattering lips and with a double heart. Ps. 12:2 (*see also* Double, Heart)

Speak ye every man the truth to his neighbour; execute the judgment of truth and peace in your gates. Zech. 8:16 (*see also* Truth)

Keep thy tongue from evil, and thy lips from speaking guile. Ps. 34:13 (*see also* Guile, Iniquity)

Obey, I beseech thee, the voice of the LORD, which I speak unto thee: so it shall be well unto thee, and thy soul shall live. Jer. 38:20 (*see also* Obey, Voice)

Let the lying lips be put to silence; which speak grievous things proudly and contemptuously against the righteous. Ps. 31:18 (*see also* Lie, Silence)

Ps. 31:18 let the lying lips be put to silence; which *s.* grievous things proudly and contemptuously against the righteous; **Prov. 18:3** when the wicked cometh, then cometh also contempt, and with ignominy reproach.

Stand in the court of the LORD'S house, and speak unto all the cities of Judah, which come to worship in the LORD's house, all the words that I command thee to speak unto them; diminish not a word. Jer. 26:2 (*see also* Word)

Jer. 26:2 stand in the court of the LORD's house, and *s.* unto all the cities of Judah, which come to worship in the LORD's house, all the words that I command thee to *s.* unto them; diminish not a word; **26:7-8** it came to pass, when Jeremiah had made an end of *s.* all that the LORD had commanded him to *s.* unto all the people, that the priests and the prophets and all the people took him, saying, Thou shalt surely die.

For he that will love life, and see good days, let him refrain his tongue from evil, and his lips that they speak no guile: Let him eschew evil, and do good; let him seek peace, and ensue it. 1 Pet. 3:10-11 (*see also* Guile, Peace)

Mark 7:15 there is nothing from without a man, that entering into him can defile him: but the things which come out of him, those are they that defile the man; **7:22-23** thefts, covetousness, wickedness, deceit, lascivious-ness, an evil eye, blasphemy, pride, foolishness: All these evil things come from within, and defile the man; **Col. 4:6** let your *s.* be alway with grace, seasoned with salt, that ye may know how ye ought to answer every man; **1 Pet. 3:10** he that will love life, and see good days, let him refrain his tongue from evil, and his lips that they *s.* no guile.

My lips shall not speak wickedness, nor my tongue utter deceit. Job 27:4 (*see also* Lips)

Job 27:4 my lips shall not speak wickedness, nor my tongue utter deceit; **Ps. 5:10** destroy thou them, O God; let them fall by their own counsels; cast them out in the multitude of their transgressions; for they have rebelled against thee; **10:7** his mouth is full of cursing and deceit and fraud: under his tongue is mischief and vanity; **34:13** keep thy tongue from evil, and thy lips from *s.* guile; **36:3** the words of his mouth are iniquity and deceit: he hath left off to be wise, and to do good; **101:7** he that worketh deceit shall not dwell within my house: he that telleth lies shall not tarry in my sight; **Prov. 20:17** bread of deceit is sweet to a man; but afterwards his mouth shall be filled with gravel; **26:18-19** as a mad man who casteth firebrands, arrows, and death, So is the man that deceiveth his neighbour; **27:6** faithful are the wounds of a friend; but the kisses of an enemy are deceitful; **Jer. 22:22** the wind shall eat up all thy pastors, and thy lovers shall go into captivity: surely then shalt thou be ashamed and confounded for all thy wickedness.

Speak evil of no man, to be no brawlers, but gentle, shewing all meekness unto all men. Titus 3:2 (*see also* Gossip, Meek)

Titus 3:2 *s.* evil of no man, to be no brawlers, but gentle, shewing all meekness unto all men; **James 4:11-12** *s.* not evil one of another, brethren. He that *s.* evil of his brother, and judgeth his brother, *s.* evil of the law, and judgeth the law: but if thou judge the law, thou art not a doer of the law, but a judge.

Speak forth the words of truth and soberness. Acts 26:25 (*see also* True)

Matt. 12:34-37 O generation of vipers, how can ye, being evil, *s.* good things? for out of the abundance of the heart the mouth *s.*. But I say unto you, That every idle word that men shall *s.*, they shall give account thereof in the day of judgment. For by thy words thou shalt be justified, and by thy words thou shalt be condemned; **Mark 7:15** there is nothing from without a man, that entering into him can defile him: but the things which come out of him, those are they that defile the man; **Luke 6:45** a good man out of the good treasure of his heart bringeth forth that which is good; and an evil man out of the evil treasure of his heart bringeth forth that which is evil: for of the abundance of the heart his mouth *s*.; **John 8:40** but now ye seek to kill me, a man that hath told you the truth, which I have heard of God: this did not Abraham; **8:45** because I tell you the truth, ye believe me not; **Acts 18:26** he began to *s*. boldly in the synagogue: whom when Aquila and Priscilla had heard, they took him unto them, and expounded unto him the way of God more perfectly; **26:25** I am not mad, most noble Festus; but *s*. forth the words of truth and soberness; **Rom. 9:1** I say the truth in Christ, I lie not, my conscience also bearing me witness in the Holy Ghost; **2 Cor. 2:17** we are not as many, which corrupt the word of God: but as of sincerity, but as of God, in the sight of God *s*. we in Christ; **4:2** have renounced the hidden things of dishonesty, not walking in craftiness, nor handling the word of God deceitfully; but by manifestation of the truth commending ourselves to every man's conscience in the sight of God; **7:14** if I have boasted any thing to him of you, I am not ashamed; but as we spake all things to you in truth, even so our boasting, which I made before Titus, is found a truth; **13:8** we can do nothing against the truth, but for the truth; **Gal. 4:16** am I therefore become your enemy, because I tell you the truth; **Eph. 4:15** *s*. the truth in love, may grow up into him in all things, which is the head, even Christ; **4:25** putting away lying, *s*. every man truth with his neighbour: for we are members one of another; **5:4** neither filthiness, nor foolish talking, nor jesting, which are not convenient: but rather giving of thanks; **Titus 2:3** they be in behaviour as becometh holiness, not false accusers, not given to much wine, teachers of good things.

Take heed to speak that which the Lord hath put in thy mouth. Num. 23:12 (*see also* Mouth)

Ex. 6:10-11 the LORD *s*. unto Moses, saying, Go in, speak unto Pharaoh king of Egypt, that he let the children of Israel go out of his land; **6:29** the LORD spake unto Moses, saying, I am the LORD: *s*. thou unto Pharaoh king of Egypt all that I say unto thee; **7:2** thou shalt *s*. all that I command thee: and Aaron thy brother shall *s*. unto Pharaoh; **12:1-3** *s*. ye unto all the congregation of Israel; **14:1-2** the LORD spake unto Moses, saying, *s*. unto the children of Israel; **14:15** the LORD said unto Moses, Wherefore criest thou unto me? *s*. unto the children of Israel, that they go forward; **16:11-12** the LORD spake unto Moses, saying, I have heard the murmurings of the children of Israel: *s*. unto them; **19:6** ye shall be unto me a kingdom of priests, and an holy

nation. These are the words which thou shalt *s*. unto the children of Israel; **25:1-2** the LORD spake unto Moses, saying, *s*. unto the children of Israel, that they bring me an offering; **31:12-13** the LORD spake unto Moses, saying, *s*. thou also unto the children of Israel, saying, Verily my sabbaths ye shall keep; **Lev. 1:1-2** the LORD called unto Moses, and spake unto him out of the tabernacle of the congregation, saying, *s*. unto the children of Israel; **4:1-2** the LORD spake unto Moses, saying, *s*. unto the children of Israel; **6:24-25** the LORD spake unto Moses, saying, *s*. unto Aaron and to his sons, saying, This is the law of the sin offering; **7:22-23** the LORD spake unto Moses, saying, *s*. unto the children of Israel; **7:28-29** the LORD spake unto Moses, saying, *s*. unto the children of Israel; **11:1-2** the LORD spake unto Moses and to Aaron, saying unto them, *s*. unto the children of Israel; **12:1-2** the LORD spake unto Moses, saying, *s*. unto the children of Israel; **15:1-2** the LORD spake unto Moses and to Aaron, saying, *s*. unto the children of Israel; **16:2** the LORD said unto Moses, *s*. unto Aaron thy brother, that he come not at all times into the holy place within the vail before the mercy seat; **17:1-2** the LORD spake unto Moses, saying, *s*. unto Aaron, and unto his sons, and unto all the children of Israel, and say unto them; This is the thing which the LORD hath commanded; **18:1-2** the LORD spake unto Moses, saying, *s*. unto the children of Israel, and say unto them, I am the LORD your God; **19:1-2** the LORD spake unto Moses, saying, *s*. unto all the congregation of the children of Israel, and say unto them, Ye shall be holy: for I the LORD your God am holy; **21:1** the LORD said unto Moses, *s*. unto the priests the sons of Aaron, and say unto them, There shall none be defiled for the dead among his people; **21:16-17** the LORD spake unto Moses, saying, *s*. unto Aaron, saying, Whosoever he be of thy seed in their generations that hath any blemish, let him not approach to offer the bread of his God; **22:1-2** the LORD spake unto Moses, saying, *s*. unto Aaron and to his sons, that they separate themselves from the holy things of the children of Israel; **23:1-2** the LORD spake unto Moses, saying, *s*. unto the children of Israel; **23:9-10** the LORD spake unto Moses, saying, *s*. unto the children of Israel; **23:23-24** the LORD spake unto Moses, saying, *s*. unto the children of Israel; **23:33-34** the LORD spake unto Moses, saying, *s*. unto the children of Israel, saying, Whosoever curseth his God shall bear his sin; **25:1-2** the LORD spake unto Moses in mount Sinai, saying, *s*. unto the children of Israel; **27:1-2** the LORD spake unto Moses, saying, *s.* unto the children of Israel; **Num. 5:5-6** the LORD spake unto Moses, saying, *s.* unto the children of Israel; **5:11-12** the LORD spake unto Moses, saying, *s.* unto the children of Israel; **6:1-2** the LORD spake unto Moses, saying, *s.* unto the children of Israel; **6:22-23** the LORD spake unto Moses, saying, *s.* unto Aaron and unto his sons, saying, On this wise ye shall bless the children of Israel, saying unto them; **8:1-2** the LORD spake unto Moses, saying, *s.* unto Aaron, and say unto him, When thou lightest the lamps, the seven lamps shall give light over against the candlestick; **9:9-10** the LORD spake unto Moses, saying, *s.* unto the children of Israel; **15:1-2** the LORD spake unto Moses, saying, *s.* unto the children of Israel; **15:17-18** the LORD spake unto Moses, saying, *s.* unto the children of Israel; **15:37-38** the LORD spake unto Moses, saying, *s.* unto the children of Israel; **16:23-24** the LORD spake unto Moses, saying, *s.* unto the congregation; **16:36-37** the LORD spake unto Moses, saying, *s.* unto Eleazar the son of Aaron the priest, that he take up the censers out of the burning; **17:1-2** the LORD spake unto Moses, saying, *s.* unto the children of Israel; **18:25-26** the LORD spake unto Moses, saying, Thus *s.* unto the Levites, and say unto them; **19:2** *s.* unto the children of Israel, that they bring thee a red heifer without spot; **22:8** he said unto them, Lodge here this night, and I will bring you word again, as the LORD shall *s.* unto me; **22:35** the angel of the LORD said unto Balaam, Go with the men: but only the word that I shall *s.* unto thee, that thou shalt *s.*; **22:38** I am come unto thee: have I now any power at all to say any thing? the word that God putteth in my mouth, that shall I *s.*; **23:5** the LORD put a word in Balaams mouth, and said, Return unto Balak, and thus thou shalt *s.*; **23:12** he answered and said, Must I not take heed to *s.* that which the LORD hath put in my mouth; **23:26** all that the LORD *s.*eth, that I must do; **24:13** I cannot go beyond the commandment of the LORDLORD, to do either good or bad of mine own mind; but what the LORD saith, that will I *s.*; **33:50-51** the LORD spake unto Moses in the plains of Moab by Jordan near Jericho, saying, *s.* unto the children of Israel; **35:9-10** the LORD spake unto Moses, saying, *s.* unto the children of Israel; **Deut. 18:17-20** the LORD said unto me, They have well spoken that which they have spoken. I will raise them up a Prophet from among their brethren, like unto thee, and will put my words in his mouth; **Josh. 20:1-2** the LORD also spake unto Joshua, saying, *s.* to the children of Israel; **1 Kgs. 21:19** thou shalt *s.* unto him, saying, Thus saith the LORD, Hast thou killed, and also taken possession? And thou shalt *s.* unto

him, saying, Thus saith the LORD; **22:14** as the LORD liveth, what the LORD saith unto me, that will I *s.*; **2 Chron. 11:2-3** the word of the LORD came to Shemaiah the man of God, saying, *s.* unto Rehoboam the son of Solomon, king of Judah, and to all Israel; **Job 27:3-5** all the while my breath is in me, and the spirit of God is in my nostrils; My lips shall not *s.* wickedness, nor my tongue utter deceit; **29:21-22** unto me men gave ear, and waited, and kept silence at my counsel. After my words they spake not again; and my speech dropped upon them; **36:2** I will shew thee that I have yet to *s.* on Gods behalf; **Ps. 119:172** my tongue shall *s.* of thy word: for all thy commandments are righteousness; **Eccl. 12:9** because the preacher was wise, he still taught the people knowledge; yea, he gave good heed, and sought out, and set in order many proverbs; **Jer. 1:7** the LORD said unto me, Say not, I am a child: for thou shalt go to all that I shall send thee, and whatsoever I command thee thou shalt *s.*; **1:17** gird up thy loins, and arise, and *s.* unto them all that I command thee; **7:27** thou shalt *s.* all these words unto them; but they will not hearken to thee: thou shalt also call unto them; but they will not answer thee; **9:22** *s.*, Thus saith the LORD, Even the carcases of men shall fall as dung upon the open field; **11:2-3** *s.* unto the men of Judah, and to the inhabitants of Jerusalem; And say thou unto them, Thus saith the LORD God of Israel; **13:12** thou shalt *s.* unto them this word; Thus saith the LORD God of Israel; **26:2** stand in the court of the LORD's house, and *s.* unto all the cities of Judah, which come to worship in the LORD's house, all the words that I command thee to *s.* unto them; **26:8** Jeremiah had made an end of *s.* all that the LORD had commanded him to *s.* unto all the people; **26:15** the LORD hath sent me unto you to *s.* all these words in your ears; **29:24-25** thus shalt thou also *s.* to Shemaiah the Nehelamite, saying, Thus *s.*eth the LORD of hosts, the God of Israel; **34:2** go and *s.* to Zedekiah king of Judah, and tell him, Thus saith the LORD; **35:1-2** go unto the house of the Rechabites, and *s.* unto them; **39:15-16** the word of the LORD came unto Jeremiah, while he was shut up in the court of the prison, saying, Go and *s.*; **Ezek. 2:7** thou shalt *s.* my words unto them, whether they will hear, or whether they will forbear; **3:1** go *s.* unto the house of Israel; **3:4** go, get thee unto the house of Israel, and *s.* with my words unto them; **3:10-11** all my words that I shall *s.* unto thee receive in thine heart, and hear with thine ears. And go, get thee to them of the captivity, unto the children of thy people, and *s.* unto them, and tell them; **11:5** the Spirit of the LORD fell upon me, and said unto me, *s.*; Thus saith the LORD; **14:4** *s.* unto them, and say unto them, Thus saith the Lord GOD; **20:2-3** *s.* unto the elders of Israel, and say unto them, Thus saith the Lord GOD; **20:27** *s.* unto the house of Israel, and say unto them, Thus saith the Lord GOD; **24:20-21** the word of the LORD came unto me, saying, *s.* unto the house of Israel, Thus saith the Lord GOD; **29:3** *s.*, and say, Thus saith the Lord GOD; Behold, I am against thee, Pharaoh king of Egypt; **31:1-2** the word of the LORD came unto me, saying, Son of man, *s.* unto Pharaoh king of Egypt, and to his multitude; **33:1-2** the word of the LORD came unto me, saying, Son of man, *s.* to the children of thy people; **33:10-12** *s.* unto the house of Israel; Thus ye *s.*, saying, If our transgressions and our sins be upon us, and we pine away in them, how should we then live; **39:17** thus saith the Lord GOD; *s.* unto every feathered fowl, and to every beast of the field, Assemble yourselves, and come; **Zech. 6:12** *s.* unto him, saying, Thus *s.*eth the LORD of hosts; **7:4-5** then came the word of the LORD of hosts unto me, saying, *s.* unto all the people of the land, and to the priests.

SPEECH (*see* Communicate, Language, Speak)

SPIRIT (*see also* Holy Ghost, Holy Spirit)

They that are after the flesh do mind the things of the flesh; but they that are after the Spirit the things of the Spirit. For to be carnally minded is death; but to be spiritually minded is life and peace. **Rom. 8:5-6** (*see also* Flesh, Mind)

Jesus answered, Verily, verily, I say unto thee, Except a man be born of water and of the Spirit, he cannot enter into the kingdom of God. **John 3:5** (*see also* Born, Enter, Water)

He that is slow to anger is better than the mighty; and he that ruleth his spirit than he that taketh a city. **Prov. 16:32** (*see also* Anger, Rule)

Eye hath not seen, nor ear heard, neither have entered into the heart of man, the things which God hath prepared for them that love him. But God hath reveled them unto us by his Spirit; for the Spirit searcheth all things, yea, the deep things of God. **1 Cor. 2:9-10** (*see also* Enter, Mysteries, Search)

He that soweth to his flesh shall of the flesh reap corruption; but he that soweth to the Spirit shall of the Spirit reap life everlasting. **Gal. 6:8** (*see also* Flesh, Sow)

The natural man receiveth not the things of the Spirit of God: for they are foolishness unto him: neither can he know them, because they are spiritually discerned. **1 Cor. 2:14** (*see also* Foolish, Natural Man)

Take no thought how or what ye shall speak: for it shall be given you in that same hour what ye shall speak. For it is not ye that speak, but the Spirit of your Father which speaketh in you. **Matt. 10:19-20** (*see also* Speak, Thought)

Be not drunk with wine, wherein is excess; but be filled with the Spirit. **Eph. 5:18** (*see also* Excess, Wine)

Quench not the spirit. **1 Thes. 5:19** (*see also* Quench)

He that hath no rule over his own spirit is like a city that is broken down and without walls. **Prov. 25:28** (*see also* Rule, Self Control)

SPIRITUAL, SPIRITUALITY, SPIRITUALLY (*see also* Righteousness)

Be spiritually minded. **Rom. 8:6** (*see also* Minded)

SPITE (*see also* Hate, Pride)

Love your enemies, bless them that curse you, do good to them that hate you, and pray for them which despitefully use you, and persecute you. **Matt. 5:44** (*see also* Curse, Enemy, Love, Persecute)

SPOIL (*see also* Persecute, Steal)

Lay not wait, O wicked man, against the dwelling of the righteous; spoil not his resting place: For a just man falleth seven times, and riseth up again: but the wicked shall fall into mischief. **Prov. 24:15-16** (*see also* Righteous)

Prov. 24:15-16 lay not wait, O wicked man, against the dwelling of the righteous; *s.* not his resting place; **Isa. 33:1** woe to thee that *s.*, and thou wast not *s.*; and dealest treacherously, and they dealt not treacherously with thee! when thou shalt cease to *s.*, thou shalt be *s.*

SPRANG, SPRINGING, SPRUNG

But whosoever drinketh of the water that I shall give him shall never thirst; but the water that I shall give him shall be in him a well of water springing up into everlasting life. John 4:14 (*see also* Everlasting Life, Thirst)

SPURN (*see* Rebel, Reject)

STAKES (*see also* Church, Order)

Enlarge the place of thy tent, and let them stretch forth the curtains of thine habitations; spare not, lengthen the cords, and strengthen thy stakes. Isa. 54:2-3 (*see also* Cord, Strengthen)

STAND, STAND FAST, STEADFAST (*see also* Diligence, Endure, Faithful, Integrity, Obedient, Persevere)

The grass withereth, the flower fadeth: but the word of our God shall stand for ever. Isa. 40:8 (*see also* Word)

Thus saith the LORD, Stand ye in the ways, and see, and ask for the old paths, where is the good way, and walk therein, and ye shall find rest for your souls. Jer. 6:16 (*see also* Walk, Ways)

I have set the LORD always before me: because he is at my right hand, I shall not be moved. Ps. 16:8 (*see also* Righteous)

Be ye stedfast, unmoveable, always abounding in the work of the Lord, forasmuch as ye know that your labour is not in vain in the Lord. 1 Cor. 15:58 (*see also* Work)

Stand fast therefore in the liberty wherewith Christ hath made us free, and be not entangled again in the yoke of bondage. Gal. 5:1 (*see also* Fall, Liberty)

Gal 5:1 stand fast therefore in the liberty wherewith Christ hath made us free, and be not entangled again with the yoke of bondage; **Philip. 3:14-15** I press toward the mark for the prize of the high calling of God in Christ Jesus. Let us therefore, as many as be perfect, be thus minded: and if in any thing ye be otherwise minded, God shall reveal even this unto you; **Col. 2:5** though I be absent in the flesh, yet am I with you in the spirit, joying and beholding your order, and the *s.* of your faith in Christ; **1 Thes. 3:5** I could no longer forbear, I sent to know your faith, lest by some means the tempter have tempted you, and our labour be in vain; **3:13** to the end he may stablish your hearts unblameable in holiness before God, even our Father, at the coming of our Lord Jesus Christ with all his saints; **1 Pet. 5:9-10** whom resist *s.* in the faith, knowing that the same afflictions are accomplished in your brethren that are in the world. But the God of all grace, who hath called us unto his eternal glory by Christ Jesus, after that ye have suffered a while, make you perfect, stablish, strengthen, settle you; **2 Pet. 3:17** beware lest ye also, being led away with the error of the wicked, fall from your own *s.*; **Jude 1:3** exhort you that ye should earnestly contend for the faith which was once delivered unto the saints; **Rev. 2:13** I know thy works, and where thou dwellest, even where Satan's seat is: and thou holdest fast my name, and hast not denied my faith.

STANDARD (*see also* Example, Jesus Christ, Righteous)

Lift up a standard for the people. Isa. 62:10 (*see also* Lift)

STATURE

Jesus increased in wisdom and stature, and in favour with God and man. Luke 2:52 (*see also* Favor, Increase, Jesus Christ, Wisdom)

STATUTE (*see also* Commandment, Decree, Law, Order, Ordinance, Precept)

I have inclined mine heart to perform thy statutes always, even unto the end. Ps. 119:112 (*see also* Perform)

STEAL (*see also* Rob, Thief)

Lay not up for yourselves treasures upon earth, where moth and rust doth corrupt, and where thieves break through and steal: But lay up for yourselves treasures in heaven, where neither moth nor rust doth corrupt, and where thieves do not break through nor steal: For where your treasure is, there will your heart be also. Matt. 6:19-21 (*see also* Heart, Heaven, Lay Up, Treasure)

Thou shalt not steal. Ex. 20:15 (*see also* Thou Shalt Not)

Ex. 20:15 thou shalt not *s*.; **21:16** he that *s*. a man, and selleth him, or if he be found in his hand, he shall surely be put to death; **22:1** if a man shall *s*. an ox, or a sheep, and kill it, or sell it; he shall restore five oxen for an ox, and four sheep for a sheep; **22:7-8** if a man shall deliver unto his neighbour money or stuff to keep, and it be stolen out of the mans house; if the thief be found, let him pay double; **Lev. 19:11** ye shall not *s*.; **Deut. 5:19** neither shalt thou *s*.; **1 Sam. 12:3** whose ox have I taken? or whose ass have I taken? or whom have I defrauded? whom have I oppressed? or of whose hand have I received any bribe to blind mine eyes therewith? and I will restore it you; **Job 24:14** the murderer rising with the light killeth the poor and needy, and in the night is as a thief; **Prov. 6:30** men do not despise a thief, if he *s*. to satisfy his soul when he is hungry; **29:24** whoso is partner with a thief hateth his own soul; **Jer. 2:26** as the thief is ashamed when he is found, so is the house of Israel ashamed; **7:9** will ye *s*., murder, and commit adultery, and swear falsely; **Amos 3:10** they know not to do right, saith the LORD, who store up violence and robbery in their palaces; **Nahum 3:1** woe to the bloody city! it is all full of lies and robbery; **Zech. 5:3** every one that *s*. shall be cut off as on this side according to it; **Matt. 19:18** (Mark 10:19, Luke 18:20) thou shalt not *s*.; **Rom. 13:9** thou shalt not *s*... and if there be any other commandment, it is briefly comprehended in this saying, namely, Thou shalt love thy neighbour as thyself; **1 Cor. 6:10** nor thieves, nor covetous, nor drunkards, nor revilers, nor extortioners, shall inherit the kingdom of God.

STEWARD, STEWARDSHIP (*see also* Accountability, Calling)

Unto whomsoever much is given, of him shall be much required: and to whom men have committed much, of him they will ask the more. Luke 12:48 (*see also* Accountable)

His lord said unto him: Well done, thou good and faithful servant: thou hast been faithful over a few things, I will make thee ruler over many things: enter thou into the joy of thy lord. Matt. 25:21 (*see also* Accountable)

Matt. 25:14-30 for the kingdom of heaven is as a man travelling into a far country, who called his own servants, and delivered unto them his goods. And unto one he gave five talents, to another two, and to another one; to every man according to his several ability; and straightway took his journey; **Luke 19:12-27** unto every one which hath shall be given; and from him that hath not, even that he hath shall be taken away from him.

STICK (*see also* Gospel, Record, Scripture, Word)

Moreover, thou son of man, take thee one stick, and write upon it, For Judah, and for the children of Israel his companions: then take another stick, and write upon it For Joseph, the stick of Ephraim, and for all the house of Israel his companions: And join them one to another into one stick; and they shall become one in thine hand. Ezek. 37:16-17 (*see also* Bible)

STIFFNECKED, STIFFNECKEDNESS

Speak not with a stiff neck. Ps. 75:5 (*see also* Speak)

Be ye not stiffnecked, as your fathers were, but yield yourselves unto the Lord. 2 Chron. 30:8 (*see also* Yield)

Ex. 32:9 I have seen this people, and, behold, it is a *s*. people; **33:3** I will not go up in the midst of thee; for thou art a *s*. people: lest I consume thee in the way; **33:5** ye are a *s*. people: I will come up into the midst of thee in a moment, and consume thee; **34:9** let my Lord, I pray thee, go among us; for it is a *s*. people; and pardon our iniquity and our sin, and take us for thine inheritance; **Deut. 9:6** the LORD thy God giveth thee not this good land to possess it for thy righteousness; for thou art a *s*. people; **9:13** the LORD spake unto me, saying, I have seen this people, and, behold, it is a *s*. people; **10:16** be no more *s*.; **2 Chron. 30:8** be ye not *s*., as your fathers were, but yield yourselves unto the LORD; **Ps. 75:5** lift not up your horn on high: speak not with a *s*.; **Ezek. 2:4** they are impudent children and stiffhearted. I do send thee unto them.

STONE (*see also* Cornerstone, Foundation, Jesus Christ, Rock)

Have ye not read this scripture; The stone which the builders rejected is become the head of the corner? Mark 12:10 (*see also* Corner)

Be it known unto you all, and to all the people of Israel, that by the name of Jesus Christ of Nazareth, whom ye crucified, whom God raised from the dead, even by him doth this man stand here before you whole. This is the stone which was set at nought of you builders, which is become the head of the corner. Neither is there salvation in any other: for there is none other name under heaven given among men, whereby we must be saved. Acts 4:10-12 (*see also* Cornerstone, Israel, Jesus Christ, Name, Saved)

STORE, STOREHOUSE (*see also* Lay Up, Prepare)

Bring ye all the tithes into the storehouse, that there may be meat in mine house, and prove me now herewith, saith the Lord of hosts, if I will not open you the windows of heaven, and pour you out a blessing. Mal. 3:8-12 (*see also* Prove, Tithe)

STOUT, STOUTHEARTED (*see also* Hardhearted, Haughty, Pride, Vain)

Hearken unto me, ye stouthearted, that are far from righteousness. Isa. 46:12 (*see also* Hearken, Righteous)

STRAIGHT, STRAIT (*see also* Gate, Path, Way)

Strive to enter in at the strait gate: for many, I say unto you, will seek to enter in, and shall not be able. Luke 13:24 (*see also* Enter, Gate, Strive)

I will go before thee, and make the crooked places straight: I will break in pieces the gates of brass, and cut in sunder the bars of iron. Isa. 45:2 (*see also* Crooked, Go)

Enter ye in at the strait gate; for wide is the gate, and broad is the way, that leadeth to destruction, and many there be which go in thereat; Because strait is the gate, and narrow is the way, which leadeth to life, and few be there that find it. Matt. 7:13-14 (*see also* Few, Gate, Narrow, Work)

STRANGER (*see also* Neighbor)

Ye shall have one manner of law, as well for the stranger, as for one of your own country: for I am the Lord your God. Lev. 24:22 (*see also* Law)

Oppress not the widow, nor the fatherless, the stranger, nor the poor; and let none of you imagine evil against his brother in your heart. Zech. 7:10 (*see also* Fatherless, Oppress, Widow)

Be not forgetful to entertain strangers: for thereby some have entertained angels unawares. Heb. 13:2 (*see also* Angel)

If a stranger sojourn with thee in your land, ye shall not vex him, But the stranger that dwelleth with you shall be unto you as one born among you, and thou shalt love him as thyself. Lev. 19:33-34

Gen. 37:1 Jacob dwelt in the land wherein his father was a *s*.; **Ex. 22:21** thou shalt neither vex a *s*., nor oppress him; **23:9** thou shalt not oppress a *s*.: for ye know the heart of a *s*.; **Lev. 19:33-34** if a *s*. sojourn with thee in your land, ye shall not vex him. But the *s*. that dwelleth with you shall be unto you as one born among you, and thou shalt love him as thyself; **25:6** the sabbath of the land shall be meat for you; for thee, and for thy servant, and for thy maid, and for thy hired servant, and for thy *s*. that sojourneth with thee; **Num. 9:14** if a *s*. shall sojourn among you, and will keep the passover unto the Lord; according to the ordinance of the passover, and according to the manner thereof, so shall he do: ye shall have one ordinance, both for the *s*., and for him that was born in the land; **Deut. 10:18-19** he doth execute the judgment of the fatherless and widow, and loveth the *s*., in giving him food and raiment. Love ye therefore the *s*.; **Ruth 2:10** she fell on her face, and bowed herself to the ground, and said unto him, Why have I found grace in thine eyes, that thou shouldest take knowledge of me, seeing I am a *s*.; **Job 31:32** the *s*. did not lodge in the street: but I opened my doors to the traveller; **Jer. 7:6-7** if ye oppress not the *s*., the fatherless, and the widow, and shed not innocent blood in this place, neither walk after other gods to your hurt: Then will I cause you to dwell in this place; **22:3** execute ye judgment and righteousness, and deliver the spoiled out of the hand of the oppressor: and do no wrong, do no violence to the *s*.; **Ezek. 22:7** in the midst of thee have they dealt by oppression with the *s*.: in thee have they vexed the fatherless and the widow; **47:23** in what tribe the *s*. sojourneth, there shall ye give him his inheritance, saith the Lord God; **Zech. 7:10** oppress not the widow, nor the fatherless, the *s*., nor the poor; and let none of you imagine evil against his brother in your heart.

STRENGTH, STRENGTHEN (*see also* Courage, Might, Priesthood)

I can do all things through Christ which strengtheneth me. Philip. 4:13 (*see also* All Things)

They that wait upon the Lord shall renew their strength; they shall mount up with wings as eagles; they shall run, and not be weary; and they shall walk, and not faint. Isa. 40:31 (*see also* Renew, Wait)

Enlarge the place of thy tent, and let them stretch forth the curtains of thine habitations; spare not, lengthen the cords, and strengthen thy stakes. Isa. 54:2-3 (*see also* Cord, Stake)

Go in the strength of the Lord GOD: I will make mention of thy righteousness, even of thine only. Ps. 71:16 (*see also* Go, Righteous)

Give not thy strength to women, nor thy ways to that which destroyeth kings. Prov. 31:3 (*see also* Ways, Woman)

Ascribe ye strength unto God; his excellency is over Israel, and his strength is in the clouds. Ps. 68:34 (*see also* Ascribe, Glorify)

Ps. 68:34-35 ascribe ye *s.* unto God: his excellency is over Israel, and his *s.* is in the clouds; **118:14** the LORD is my *s.* and song, and is become my salvation; **Isa. 49:5** though Israel be not gathered, yet shall I be glorious in the eyes of the LORD, and my God shall be my *s.*; **Amos 6:13-14** have we not taken to us horns by our own *s.*? But, behold, I will raise up against you a nation, O house of Israel, saith the LORD the God of hosts; and they shall afflict you.

Strengthen ye the weak hands, and confirm the feeble knees. Say to them that are of a fearful heart, Be strong, fear not: behold, your God will come with vengeance, even God with a recompense; he will come and save you. Isa. 35:3-4 (*see also* Feeble, Save)

Job 4:3-4 thou hast instructed many, and thou hast *s.* the weak hands. Thy words have upholden him that was falling, and thou hast *s.* the feeble knees; **16:4-5** I also could speak as ye do: if your soul were in my souls stead, I could heap up words against you, and shake

mine head at you. But I would *s.* you with my mouth, and the moving of my lips should asswage your grief; **Isa. 35:3-4** *s.* ye the weak hands, and confirm the feeble knees. Say to them that are of a fearful heart, Be strong, fear not: behold, your God will come with vengeance.

STRICT (*see* Plain)

STRIFE (*see also* Adversity, Persecution)

For where envying and strife is, there is confusion and every evil work. James 3:16 (*see also* Confusion, Envy)

Walk honestly, as in the day; not in rioting and drunkenness, not in chambering and wantonness, not in strife and envying. Rom. 13:13 (*see also* Envy)

He is proud, knowing nothing, but doting about questions and strifes of words, whereof cometh envy, strife, railings, evil surmisings, Perverse disputings of men of corrupt minds, and destitute of the truth, supposing that gain is godliness: from such withdraw thyself. 1 Tim. 6:4-5 (*see also* Question, Mind, Pride, True)

Let there be no strife, I pray thee, between me and thee, and between my herdmen and thy herdmen; for we be brethren. Gen. 13:8 (*see also* Contend)

Gen. 13:7-8 let there be no *s.*, I pray thee, between me and thee, and between my herdmen and thy herdmen; for we be brethren; **Ps. 31:20** thou shalt keep them secretly in a pavilion from the *s.* of tongues; **Prov. 15:18** a wrathful man stirreth up *s.*: but he that is slow to anger appeaseth *s.*; **16:28** a froward man soweth *s.*: and a whisperer separateth chief friends; **16:30** he shutteth his eyes to devise froward things: moving his lips he bringeth evil to pass; **17:19** he loveth transgression that loveth *s.*: and he that exalteth his gate seeketh destruction; **20:3** it is an honour for a man to cease from *s.*; **22:10** cast out the scorner, and contention shall go out; yea, *s.* and reproach shall cease; **26:17-21** he that... meddleth with *s.* belonging not to him; **28:25** he that is of a proud heart stirreth up *s.*: but he that putteth his trust in the LORD shall be made fat; **29:22** an angry man stirreth up *s.*, and a furious man aboundeth in transgression.

STRIKE

Be not thou one of them that strike hands, or of them that are sureties for debts. Prov. 22:26 (*see also* Debt)

STRIVE, STROVE (*see also* Diligence, Endure)

Go not hastily to strive, lest thou know not what to do in the end thereof, when thy neighbour hath put thee to shame. Prov. 25:8 (*see also* Haste)

Of these things put them in remembrance, charging them before the Lord that they strive not about words to no profit, but to the subverting of the hearers. 2 Tim. 2:14 (*see also* Profit, Words)

Woe unto him that striveth with his Maker! Isa. 45:9

Strive to enter in at the strait gate: for many, I say unto you, will seek to enter in, and shall not be able. Luke 13:24 (*see also* Enter, Gate, Strait)

STRONG, STRONGER, STRONGEST (*see also* Courage, Strength)

Be strong, all ye people of the land, saith the Lord, and work: for I am with you, saith the Lord of hosts. Hag. 2:4 (*see also* Work)

Wine is a mocker, strong drink is raging: and whosoever is deceived thereby is not wise. Prov. 20:1 (*see also* Deceive, Wine)

STRONG DRINK (*see* Drunk, Wine)

STRONGHOLD (*see* Gospel, House, Jesus Christ, Temple)

STUBBORN, STUBBORNESS

For rebellion is as the sin of witchcraft, and stubbornness is as iniquity and idolatry. Because thou hast rejected the word of the Lord, he hath also rejected thee from being king. 1 Sam 15:23 (*see also* Idolatry, Rebellion, Witchcraft)

STUDY (*see also* Knowledge, Learn, Ponder, Read, Scripture, Understand, Wisdom)

Study to shew thyself approved unto God, a workman that needeth not to be ashamed, rightly dividing the word of truth. 2 Tim. 2:15 (*see also* Approved)

The heart of the righteous studieth to answer: but the mouth of the wicked poureth out evil things. Prov. 15:28 (*see also* Answer, Heart)

STUMBLE, STUMBLING BLOCK

Let us not therefore judge one another any more: but judge this rather, that no man put a stumbling block or an occasion to fall in his brother's way. Rom. 14:13 (*see also* Judge)

Rom. 14:13 let us not therefore judge one another any more: but judge this rather, that no man put a *s.* block or an occasion to fall in his brother's way; 14:21 it is good neither to eat flesh, nor to drink wine, nor any thing whereby thy brother *s.*, or is offended, or is made weak; Rev. 2:14 I have a few things against thee, because thou hast there them that hold the doctrine of Balaam, who taught Balac to cast a *s.* block before the children of Israel, to eat things sacrificed unto idols, and to commit fornication.

SUBJECT, SUBJECTION (*see also* Obedience, Submit, Yield)

I keep under my body, and bring it into subjection: lest that by any means, when I have preached to others, I myself should be a castaway. 1 Cor. 9:27 (*see also* Body, Flesh, Will)

SUBMIT (*see also* Humble, Obey, Subject, Yield)

Submit yourselves to every ordinance of man for the Lord's sake: whether it be to the king, as supreme. 1 Pet. 2:13 (*see also* Ordinance)

Likewise, ye younger, submit yourselves unto the elder. Yea, all of you be subject one to another, and be clothed with humility: for God resisteth the proud, and giveth grace to the humble. 1 Pet. 5:5 (*see also* Grace, Humble, Young)

Wives, submit yourselves unto your own husbands as unto the Lord. For the husband is the head of the wife, even as Christ is the head of the church: and he is the saviour of the body. Therefore as the church is subject unto Christ, so let the wives be to their own husbands in every thing. Eph. 5:22-24 (*see also* Wife)

Eph 5:22-24 wives, *s.* yourselves unto your own husbands, as unto the Lord. For the husband is the head of the wife, even as Christ is the head of the church: and he is the saviour of the body. Therefore as the church is subject unto Christ, so let the wives be to their own husbands in every thing; 5:33 let every one of you in particular so love his wife even as himself; and the wife see that she reverence her husband; Col. 3:18 wives, *s.* yourselves unto your own husbands, as it is fit in the Lord; Titus 2:4-5 teach the young women to be sober, to love their husbands, to love their children, To be discreet, chaste, keepers at home, good, obedient to their own husbands, that the word of God be not blasphemed; 1 Pet. 3:1 likewise, ye wives, be in subjection to your own husbands; that, if any obey not the word, they also may without the word be won by the conversation of the wives; 3:2-6 holy women also, who trusted in God, adorned themselves, being in subjection unto their own husbands: Even as Sara obeyed Abraham, calling him lord: whose daughters ye are, as long as ye do well, and are not afraid with any amazement.

SUBSTANCE (*see also* Almsgiving)

Honour the Lord with thy substance, and with the first fruits of all thine increase. Prov. 3:9-10 (*see also* Fruit)

SUBTLE, SUBTLETY (*see also* Deceit, Guile)

O full of all subtilty and all mischief, thou child of the devil, thou enemy of all righteousness, wilt thou not cease to pervert the right ways of the Lord. Acts 13:10 (*see also* Mischief, Pervert, Way)

SUCCESS (*see also* Bless, Promise, Reward)

This book of the law shall not depart out of thy mouth; but thou shalt meditate therein day and night, that thou mayest observe to do according to all that is written therein: for then thou shalt make thy way prosperous, and then thou shalt have good success. Josh. 1:8 (*see also* Book, Do, Meditate, Prosperous)

SUE (*see also* Law)

If any man will sue thee at the law, and take away thy coat, let him have thy cloke also. Matt. 5:40

SUFFER, SUFFERING (*see* Adversity, Afflict, Chasten, Despair, Longsuffering, Pain)

SUFFICIENT (*see also* Abundance)

Eat so much as is sufficient for thee, lest thou be filled therewith, and vomit it. Prov. 25:16 (*see also* Eat)

SUPERSTITIOUS (*see also* Belief, Idolatry, Sorcery, Wizard)

Paul stood in the midst of Mars' hill, and said, Ye men of Athens, I perceive that in all things ye are too superstitious. Acts 17:22

SUPPLICATION (*see* Humble, Pray)

SWEAR, SWORN (*see also* Blaspheme, Covenant, Oath, Profanity, Promise, Vow)

Woe unto you, ye blind guides, which say, Whosoever shall swear by the temple, it is nothing; but whosoever shall swear by the gold of the temple, he is a debtor! Ye fools and blind: for whether is greater, the gold, or the temple that sanctifieth the gold? And, Whosoever shall swear by the altar, it is nothing; but whosoever sweareth by the gift that is upon it, he is guilty. Matt. 23:16-18 (*see also* Guide)

The Lord hath a controversy with the inhabitants of the land, because there is no truth, nor mercy, nor knowledge of God in the land. By swearing, and lying, and killing, and stealing, and committing adultery, they break out, and blood toucheth blood. Hosea 4:1-2 (*see also* Darkness)

Jer. 5:2 though they say, The Lord liveth; surely they *s.* falsely; Hosea 4:1-5 the Lord hath a controversy with the inhabitants of the land, because there is no truth, nor mercy, nor knowledge of God in the land. By *s.*, and lying, and killing, and stealing, and committing adultery, they break out, and blood toucheth blood.

Swear not, neither by heaven, neither by the earth, neither by any other oath: but let your yea be yea; and your nay, nay; lest ye fall into condemnation. James 5:12 (*see also* Oath)

Matt. 5:34-35 *s.* not at all; neither by heaven; for it is God's throne: Nor by the earth; for it is his footstool: neither by Jerusalem; for it is the city of the great King; **5:36** neither shalt thou *s.* by thy head, because thou canst not make one hair white or black; **5:37** let your communication be, Yea, yea; Nay, nay: for whatsoever is more than these cometh of evil; **23:16-18** woe unto you, ye blind guides, which say, Whosoever shall *s.* by the temple, it is nothing; but whosoever shall *s.* by the gold of the temple, he is a debtor! Ye fools and blind: for whether is greater, the gold, or the temple that sanctifieth the gold? And, Whosoever shall *s.* by the altar, it is nothing; but whosoever *s.*eth by the gift that is upon it, he is guilty; **23:20-21** whoso therefore shall *s.* by the altar, *s.* by it, and by all things thereon. And whoso shall *s.* by the temple, *s.* by it, and by him that dwelleth therein; **James 5:12** above all things, my brethren, *s.* not, neither by heaven, neither by the earth, neither by any other oath: but let your yea be yea; and your nay, nay; lest ye fall into condemnation.

SWEET

Woe unto them that call evil good, and good evil; that put darkness for light, and light for darkness; that put bitter for sweet and sweet for bitter! Isa. 5:20 (*see also* Evil, Good)

SWORD

Be ye afraid of the sword: for wrath bringeth the punishments of the sword, that ye may know there is a judgment. Job 19:29 (*see also* Afraid)

TABERNACLE (*see also* Abode, Body, House, Temple)

LORD, who shall abide in thy tabernacle? Who shall dwell in thy holy hill? He that walketh uprightly, and worketh righteousness, and speaketh the truth in his heart. Ps. 15:1-2 (*see also* Truth)

TAKE, TAKEN, TOOK

Take no thought how or what ye shall speak: for it shall be given you in that same hour what ye shall speak. For it is not ye that speak, but the Spirit of your Father which speaketh in you. Matt. 10:19-20 (*see also* Speak, Spirit, Thought)

Friend, I do thee no wrong: didst not thou agree with me for a penny? Take that thine is, and go thy way: I will give unto this last, even as unto thee. Matt. 20:1-14 (*see also* Agree)

Only take heed to thyself, and keep thy soul diligently, lest thou forget the things which thine eyes have seen, and lest they depart from thine heart all the days of thy life: but teach them thy sons, and thy sons sons. Deut. 4:9 (*see also* Forget, Keep, Testimony)

There hath no temptation. taken you but such as is common to man: but God is faithful, who will not suffer you to be tempted above that ye are able; but will with the temptation also make a way to escape, that ye may be able to bear it. 1 Cor. 10:13 (*see also* Bear, Escape, Temptation)

TALEBEARER (*see also* False, Gossip, Lie)

Thou shalt not go up and down as a talebearer among thy people. Lev. 19:16 (*see also* Gossip)

Lev. **19:16** thou shalt not go up and down as a *t.* among thy people; **Prov. 11:13** a *t.* revealeth secrets: but he that is of a faithful spirit concealeth the matter; **16:28** a froward man soweth strife: and a whisperer separateth chief friends; **18:8** the words of a *t.* are as wounds; **20:19** he that goeth about as a *t.* revealeth secrets: therefore meddle not with him that flattereth with his lips; **26:20** where there is no *t.*, the strife ceaseth; **26:22** the words of a *t.* are as wounds; **Isa. 50:11** walk in the light of your fire, and in the sparks that ye have kindled. This shall ye have of mine hand; ye shall lie down in sorrow.

TALENT (*see also* Gift)

Well done thou good and faithful servant: thou hast been faithful over a few things, I will make thee ruler over many things; enter thou into the joy of thy lord. Matt. 25:21

Matt 25:14-30 (Luke 19:13) well done thou food and faithful servant: thou hast been faithful over a few things, I will make thee ruler ver many things; enter thou into the joy of thy lord.

TALK (*see also* Communicate, Converse, Cry, Speak, Utter)

When I speak with thee, I will open thy mouth, and thou shalt say unto them, Thus saith the Lord GOD; He that heareth, let him hear; and he that forbeareth, let him forbear. Ezek. 3:27 (*see also* Belief)

TASTE (*see also* Eat, Savor)

O taste and see that the LORD is good: blessed is the man that trusteth in him. Ps. 34:8 (*see also* See, Trust)

TAX (*see also* Burden, Law)

Render therefore unto Caesar the things which are Caesar's, and unto God the things that are God's. Matt. 22:21 (*see also* Render)

TEACH, TEACHABLE, TEACHER (*see also* Believe, Edify, Holy Ghost, Learn, Spirit)

Teach the young women to be sober, to love their husbands, to love their children, To be discreet, chaste, keepers at home, good, obedient to their own husbands, that the word of God be not blasphemed. Titus 2:4-5 (*see also* Obedient)

The servant of the Lord must not strive; but be gentle unto all men, apt to teach, patient. 2 Tim. 2:24 (*see also* Gentle)

For when for the time ye ought to be teachers, ye have need that one teach you again which be the first principles of the oracles of God; and are become such as have need of milk, and not of strong meat. Heb 5:12 (*see also* Meat, Milk, Principle)

There shall be false teachers among you, who privily shall bring in damnable heresies. 2 Pet. 2:1 (*see also* False)

I will cast thee from off the face of the earth: this year thou shalt die, because thou hast taught rebellion against the LORD. Jer. 28:16 (*see also* Rebel)

They that have believeing masters, let them not despise them, because they are brethren; but rather do them service, because they are faithful and beloved, partakers of the benefit. These things teach and exhort. 1 Tim 6:3 (*see also* Exhort)

Teach my people the difference between the holy and profane, and cause them to discern between the unclean and the clean. Ezek. 44:23 (*see also* Clean, Holy)

And these words, which I command thee this day, shall be in thine heart: And thou shalt teach them diligently unto thy children, and shalt talk of them when thou sittest in thine house, and when thou walkest by the way and when thou liest down, and when thou risest up. And thou shalt bind them for a sign upon thine hand, and they shalt be as frontlets between thine eyes. And thou shalt write them upon the posts of thy house, and on thy gates. Deut. 6:6-9 (*see also* Children, Diligence, Word)

This people draweth nigh unto me with their mouth, and honoureth me with their lips; but their heart is far from me. But in vain they do worship me, teaching for doctrines the commandments of men. Matt. 15:8-9 (*see also* Doctrine)

Be not carried about with divers and strange doctrines. For it is a good thing that the heart be established with grace; not with meats, which have not profited them that have been occupied therein. Heb. 13:9 (*see also* Doctrine, False Doctrine)

Thou shalt teach them ordinances and laws, and shalt shew them the way wherein they must walk, and the work that they must do. Ex. 18:20 (*see also* Way)

Ex. 18:20 thou shalt *t*. them ordinances and laws, and shalt shew them the way wherein they must walk, and the work that they must do;

24:12 I will give thee tables of stone, and a law, and commandments which I have written; that thou mayest *t.* them; **Lev. 10:11** that ye may *t.* the children of Israel all the statutes which the Lord hath spoken unto them by the hand of Moses; **Deut. 4:5** I have taught you statutes and judgments, even as the Lord my God commanded me; **4:9-10** *t.* them thy sons, and thy sons sons... that they may learn to fear me all the days that they shall live upon the earth, and that they may *t.* their children; **4:14** the Lord commanded me at that time to *t.* you statutes and judgments, that ye might do them in the land whither ye go over to possess it; **5:31** stand thou here by me, and I will speak unto thee all the commandments, and the statutes, and the judgments, which thou shalt *t.* them, that they may do them; **6:1** these are the commandments, the statutes, and the judgments, which the Lord your God commanded to *t.* you, that ye might do them; **6:7** thou shalt *t.* them diligently unto thy children, and shalt talk of them when thou sittest in thine house, and when thou walkest by the way, and when thou liest down, and when thou risest up; **1 Sam. 12:23** God forbid that I should sin against the Lord in ceasing to pray for you: but I will *t.* you the good and the right way; **1 Kgs. 8:36** *t.* them the good way wherein they should walk; **2 Kgs. 17:27-28** let him *t.* them the manner of the God of the land; **2 Chron. 6:27** forgive the sin of thy servants, and of thy people Israel, when thou hast taught them the good way, wherein they should walk; **30:22** Hezekiah spake comfortably unto all the Levites that taught the good knowledge of the Lord; **Ezra 7:10** Ezra had prepared his heart to seek the law of the Lord, and to do it, and to *t.* in Israel statutes and judgments; **7:25** Ezra, after the wisdom of thy God, that is in thine hand, set magistrates and judges... all such as know the laws of thy God; and *t.* ye them that know them not; **Ps. 32:8** I will instruct thee and *t.* thee in the way which thou shalt go: I will guide thee with mine eye; **34:11** come, ye children, hearken unto me: I will *t.* you the fear of the Lord; **51:13** then will I *t.* transgressors thy ways; and sinners shall be converted unto thee; **Prov. 4:11** I have taught thee in the way of wisdom; I have led thee in right paths; **9:9** give instruction to a wise man, and he will be yet wiser: *t.* a just man, and he will increase in learning; **Eccl. 12:9** because the preacher was wise, he still taught the people knowledge; yea, he gave good heed, and sought out, and set in order many proverbs; **Jer. 32:33** though I *t.* them, rising up early and *t.* them, yet they have not hearkened to receive instruction; **Ezek. 44:23** they shall *t.* my people the

difference between the holy and profane, and cause them to discern between the unclean and the clean.

TEMPERANCE, TEMPERATE

Every man that striveth for the mastery is temperate in all things. 1 Cor. 9:25 (*see also* All Things)

Acts 24:25 And as he reasoned of righteousness, *t.*, and judgment to come, Felix trembled, and answered, Go thy way for this time; when I have a convenient season, I will call for thee; **1 Cor. 9:25** every man that striveth for the mastery is *t.* in all things. Now they do it to obtain a corruptible crown; but we an incorruptible; **Philip. 4:5-7** let your moderation be known unto all men. The Lord is at hand; **Titus 1:8** but a lover of hospitality, a lover of good men, sober, just, holy, *t.*; **2:2** that the aged men be sober, grave, *t.*, sound in faith, in charity, in patience; **2 Pet. 1:6** and [add] to knowledge *t.*; and to *t.* patience; and to patience godliness.

TEMPLE (*see also* Abode, Body, House, Sanctuary, Tabernacle)

One thing have I desired of the Lord, that will I seek after; that I may dwell in the house of the Lord all the days of my life, to behold the beauty of the Lord, and to enquire in his temple. Ps. 27:4 (*see also* Inquire)

They, continuing daily with one accord in the temple, and breaking bread from house to house, did eat their meat with gladness and singleness of heart. Acts 2:46 (*see also* Eat)

But the Lord is in his holy temple: let all the earth keep silence before him. Hab. 2:20 (*see also* Earth, Silence)

Thou oughtest to behave thyself in the house of God, which is the church of the living God, the pillar and ground of the truth. 1 Tim. 3:15 (*see also* Behave, House)

What? Know ye not that your body is a temple of the Holy Ghost which is in you, which ye have of God, and ye are not your own? For ye are bought with a price: therefore glorify God in your body, and in your spirit, which are God's. 1 Cor. 6:20 (*see also* Body, Bought, Holy Ghost)

There shall in no wise enter into [the temple] any thing that defileth, neither whatsoever worketh abomination, or maketh a lie: but they which are written in the Lamb's book of life. **Rev. 21:27** (*see also* Defile, Lie)

Matt. 21:12 (Mark 11:15-17, Luke 19:45, John 2:14-17) Jesus went into the *t.* of God, and cast out all them that sold and bought in the *t.*, and overthrew the tables of the moneychangers, and the seats of them that sold doves, And said unto them, It is written, My house shall be called the house of prayer; but ye have made it a den of thieves; **Luke 20:1** as he taught the people in the *t.*, and preached the gospel, the chief priests and the scribes came upon him with the elders; **Acts 7:48** the most High dwelleth not in temple made with hands; as saith the prophet; **Rev. 11:1-2** rise, and measure the *t.* of God, and the altar, and them that worship therein; **21:23-27** the city had no need of the sun, neither of the moon, to shine in it: for the glory of God did lighten it, and the Lamb is the light thereof. And the nations of them which are saved shall walk in the light of it: and the kings of the earth do bring their glory and honour into it. And the gates of it shall not be shut at all by day: for there shall be no night there. And they shall bring the glory and honour of the nations into it. And there shall in no wise enter into it any thing that defileth, neither whatsoever worketh abomination, or maketh a lie: but they which are written in the Lamb's book of life.

I will worship toward thy holy temple, and praise thy name for thy lovingkindness and for thy truth: for thou hast magnified thy word above all thy name. **Ps. 138:2** (*see also* Lovingkindness, Worship)

Ps. 5:7 I will come into thy house in the multitude of thy mercy: and in thy fear will I worship toward thy holy *t.*; **18:6** in my distress I called upon the LORD, and cried unto my God: he heard my voice out of his *t.*, and my cry came before him, even into his ears; **27:6** now shall mine head be lifted up above mine enemies round about me: therefore will I offer in his tabernacle sacrifices of joy; **138:2** I will worship toward thy holy *t.*, and praise thy name for thy lovingkindness and for thy truth: for thou hast magnified thy word above all thy name.

TEMPT, TEMPTATION, TEMPTED (*see also* Devil, Entice, Fall, Prove, Sin, Try, Trial)

They turned back and tempted God, and limited the Holy One of Israel. **Ps. 78:41** (*see also* Limit)

Harden not your hearts, as in the provocation, in the day of temptation in the wilderness: When your fathers tempted me, proved me, and saw my works forty years. **Heb. 3:8** (*see also* Heart)

There hath no temptation. taken you but such as is common to man: but God is faithful, who will not suffer you to be tempted above that ye are able; but will with the temptation also make a way to escape, that ye may be able to bear it. **1 Cor. 10:13** (*see also* Bear, Escape, Taken)

Endureth temptation. James 1:12-15 (*see also* Endure)

Mark 14:38 watch ye and pray, lest ye enter into *t.*. The spirit truly is ready, but the flesh is weak; **Luke 4:13** when the devil had ended all the *t.*, he departed from him for a season; **8:13** they on the rock are they, which, when they hear, receive the word with joy; and these have no root, which for a while believe, and in time of *t.* fall away; **1 Cor. 10:13** there hath no *t.* taken you but such as is common to man: but God is faithful, who will not suffer you to be *t.* above that ye are able; but will with the *t.* also make a way to escape, that ye may be able to bear it; **Gal. 6:1** if a man be overtaken in a fault, ye which are spiritual, restore such an one in the spirit of meekness; considering thyself, lest thou also be *t.*; **Heb. 3:8** harden not your hearts, as in the provocation, in the day of *t.* in the wilderness; **James 1:12-15** blessed is the man that endureth *t.*: for when he is tried, he shall receive the crown of life, which the Lord hath promised to them that love him. Let no man say when he is *t.*, I am *t.* of God: for God cannot be *t.* with evil, neither *t.* he any man: But every man is *t.*, when he is drawn away of his own lust, and enticed. Then when lust hath conceived, it bringeth forth sin: and sin, when it is finished, bringeth forth death; **Rev. 3:10** thou hast kept the word of my patience, I also will keep thee from the hour of *t.*, which shall come upon all the world, to try them that dwell upon the earth.

Thou shalt not tempt the Lord thy God. Luke 4:12 (*see also* Thou Shalt Not)

Matt. 4:6-7 if thou be the Son of God, cast thyself down: for it is written, He shall give his angels charge concerning thee: and in their hands they shall bear thee up, lest at any time thou dash thy foot against a stone. Jesus said unto him, It is written again, Thou shalt not *t.* the Lord thy God; **22:18** Jesus perceived their wickedness, and said, Why *t.* ye me, ye hypocrites; **22:35** one of them, which was a lawyer, asked him a question, *t.* him; **27:40** thou that destroyest the temple, and buildest it in three days, save thyself. If thou be the Son of God, come down from the cross; **Mark 8:11** the Pharisees came forth, and began to question with him, seeking of him a sign from heaven, *t.* him; **10:2** the Pharisees came to him, and asked him, Is it lawful for a man to put away his wife? *t.* him; **12:15** shall we give, or shall we not give? But he, knowing their hypocrisy, said unto them, Why *t.* ye me? bring me a penny, that I may see it; **15:31** the chief priests mocking said among themselves with the scribes, He saved others; himself he cannot save; **Luke 4:9** set him on a pinnacle of the temple, and said unto him, If thou be the Son of God, cast thyself down from hence; **4:12** thou shalt not *t.* the Lord thy God; **11:16** others, *t.* him, sought of him a sign from heaven; **20:23** he perceived their craftiness, and said unto them, Why *t.* ye me; **John 8:6** this they said, *t.* him, that they might have to accuse him. But Jesus stooped down, and with his finger wrote on the ground, as though he heard them not; **Acts 5:9-10** how is it that ye have agreed together to *t.* the Spirit of the Lord? behold, the feet of them which have buried thy husband are at the door, and shall carry thee out. Then fell she down straightway at his feet, and yielded up the ghost: and the young men came in, and found her dead, and, carrying her forth, buried her by her husband; **15:10** why *t.* ye God, to put a yoke upon the neck of the disciples, which neither our fathers nor we were able to bear; **1 Cor. 10:9** neither let us *t.* Christ, as some of them also *t.*, and were destroyed of serpents.

They tempted God in their heart by asking meat for their lust. Ps. 78:18 (*see also* Lust)

Ex. 17:2 Moses said unto them, Why chide ye with me? wherefore do ye *t.* the LORD; **17:7** he called the name of the place Massah, and Meribah, because of the chiding of the children of Israel, and because they *t.* the LORD, saying, Is the LORD among us, or not; **Deut. 6:16** ye shall not *t.* the LORD your God; **Ps. 78:18** they *t.* God in their heart by asking meat for their lust; **78:41** they turned back and *t.* God, and limited the Holy One of Israel; **78:56** they *t.* and provoked the most high God, and kept not his testimonies; **106:14** lusted exceedingly in the wilderness, and *t.* God in the desert; **Isa. 7:11-13** I will not ask, neither will I *t.* the LORD.

TERRESTRIAL (*see also* Glory, Kingdom)

There are also celestial bodies, and bodies terrestrial: but the glory of the celestial is one, and the glory of the terrestrial is another. There is one glory of the sun, and another glory of the moon, and another glory of the stars: for one star differeth from another star in glory. So also is the resurrection of the dead. 1 Cor. 15:40-42 (*see also* Celestial, Dead, Glory, Resurrection)

TESTIFY, TESTIMONY (*see also* Comforter, Declare, Gift, Holy Ghost, Preach, Reveal, Teach, Witness)

I am thy fellowservant, and of thy brethren that have the testimony of Jesus: worship God: for the testimony of Jesus is the spirit of prophecy. Rev. 19:10 (*see also* Prophecy)

Only take heed to thyself, and keep thy soul diligently, lest thou forget the things which thine eyes have seen, and lest they depart from thine heart all the days of thy life: but teach them thy sons, and thy sons sons. Deut. 4:9 (*see also* Forget, Keep, Take)

There was a man sent from God, whose name was John. The same came for a witness, to bear witness of the Light, that all men through him might believe. John 1:7 (*see also* Witness)

Let all the house of Israel know assuredly, that God hath made that same Jesus, whom ye have crucified, both Lord and Christ. Acts 2:36 (*see also* Assure, Jesus Christ)

Whosoever shall confess that Jesus is the Son of God, God dwelleth in him, and he in God. 1 Jn. 4:15 (*see also* Dwell)

Bind up the testimony, seal the law among my disciples. Isa. 8:16 (*see also* Law)

Be not thou therefore ashamed of the testimony of our Lord. 2 Tim. 1:8 (*see also* Ashamed)

Acts 13:23 this man's seed hath God according to his promise raised unto Israel a Saviour, Jesus; **18:5** Paul was pressed in the spirit, and *t.* to the Jews that Jesus was Christ; **Rom. 1:16** I am not ashamed of the gospel of Christ: for it is the power of God unto salvation to every one that believeth; to the Jew first, and also to the Greek; **1 Cor. 1:6** even as the *t.* of Christ was confirmed in you; **2 Tim. 1:8-12** be not thou therefore ashamed of the *t.* of our Lord, nor of me his prisoner: but be thou partaker of the afflictions of the gospel according to the power of God; **2:12** if we suffer, we shall also reign with him: if we deny him, he also will deny us.

I will speak of thy testimonies also before kings, and will not be ashamed. Ps. 119:46 (*see also* Ashamed)

Ps. 119:46 I will speak of thy *t.* also before kings, and will not be ashamed; **145:6-7** men shall speak of the might of thy terrible acts: and I will declare thy greatness; **145:12** make known to the sons of men his mighty acts, and the glorious majesty of his kingdom.

Speak of the glory of thy kingdom, and talk of thy power; To make known to the sons of men his mighty acts, and the glorious majesty of his kingdom Ps. 145:11-12 (*see also* Kingdom)

1 Kgs. 10:1-6 she said to the king, It was a true report that I heard in mine own land of thy acts and of thy wisdom; **2 Chron. 24:19** he sent prophets to them, to bring them again unto the LORD; and they *t.* against them: but they would not give ear; **33:13** prayed unto him: and he was intreated of him, and heard his supplication, and brought him again to Jerusalem into his kingdom. Then Manasseh knew that the LORD he was God; **Job 19:23-26** that my words were now written! oh that they were printed in a book! That they were graven with an iron pen and lead in the rock for ever! For I know that my redeemer liveth; **Ps. 26:7-8** that I may publish with the voice of thanksgiving, and tell of all thy wondrous works; **66:16** come and hear, all ye that fear God, and I will declare what he hath done for my soul; **81:8** hear, O my people, and I will *t.* unto thee: O Israel, if thou wilt hearken

unto me; **81:10** I am the LORD thy God, which brought thee out of the land of Egypt: open thy mouth wide, and I will fill it; **145:6-7** men shall speak of the might of thy terrible acts: and I will declare thy greatness. They shall abundantly utter the memory of thy great goodness, and shall sing of thy righteousness; **145:11-12** they shall speak of the glory of thy kingdom, and talk of thy power; To make known to the sons of men his mighty acts, and the glorious majesty of his kingdom; **Prov. 14:25** a true witness delivereth souls: but a deceitful witness speaketh lies; **Ezek. 11:24-25** the spirit took me up, and brought me in a vision by the Spirit of God... So the vision that I had seen went up from me. Then I spake unto them of the captivity all the things that the LORD had shewed me; **Dan. 4:1-2** I thought it good to shew the signs and wonders that the high God hath wrought toward me.

Blessed are they that keep his testimonies, and that seek him with the whole heart. Ps. 119:2 (*see also* Heart)

Ps. 78:56 they tempted and provoked the most high God, and kept not his *t.*; **99:7** he spake unto them in the cloudy pillar: they kept his *t.*, and the ordinance that he gave them; **119:2** blessed are they that keep his *t.*, and that seek him with the whole heart; **119:14** I have rejoiced in the way of thy *t.*, as much as in all riches; **119:22** remove from me reproach and contempt; for I have kept thy *t.*; **119:24** thy *t.* also are my delight and my counsellors; **119:31** I have stuck unto thy *t.*: O LORD, put me not to shame; **119:36** incline my heart unto thy *t.*, and not to covetousness; **119:46** I will speak of thy *t.* also before kings, and will not be ashamed; **119:88** quicken me after thy lovingkindness; so shall I keep the *t.* of thy mouth; **119:95** the wicked have waited for me to destroy me: but I will consider thy *t.*; **119:111** thy *t.* have I taken as an heritage for ever: for they are the rejoicing of my heart; **119:119** thou puttest away all the wicked of the earth like dross: therefore I love thy *t.*; **119:129** thy *t.* are wonderful: therefore doth my soul keep them; **119:138** thy *t.* that thou hast commanded are righteous and very faithful; **119:152** concerning thy *t.*, I have known of old that thou hast founded them for ever; **119:157** many are my persecutors and mine enemies; yet do I not decline from thy *t.*; **119:167-168** my soul hath kept thy *t.*; and I love them exceedingly. I have kept thy precepts and thy *t.*: for all my ways are before thee; **132:12** if thy children will keep my covenant and my *t.* that I shall teach them, their children shall also sit upon thy throne for evermore; **Jer.**

44:23 ye have sinned against the LORD, and have not obeyed the voice of the LORD, nor walked in his law, nor in his statutes, nor in his *t.*; therefore this evil is happened unto you.

THANK. THANFUL, THANKS, THANKSGIVING (*see also* Grateful, Praise, Prayer, Rejoice)

I will offer to thee the sacrifice of thanksgiving, and will call upon the name of the Lord. Ps. 116:17 (*see also* Sacrifice)

Now the Spirit speaketh expressly, that in the latter times some shall depart from the faith, giving heed to seducing spirits, and doctrines of devils; Speaking lies in hypocrisy; having their conscience seared with a hot iron; Forbidding to marry, and commanding to abstain from meats, which God hath created to be received with thanksgiving of them which believe and know the truth. 1 Tim. 4:1-3 (*see also* Abstain, Conscience, Food, Latter Day, Marriage, Meat)

Thank and praise the LORD God of Israel. 1 Chron. 16:4 (*see also* Praise)

Offer unto God thanksgiving; and pay thy vows unto the most High: And call upon me in the day of trouble: I will deliver thee and thou shalt glorify me. Ps. 50:14-15 (*see also* Call)

Every creature of God is good, and nothing to be refused, if it be received with thanksgiving: For it is sanctified by the word of God and prayer. 1 Tim. 4:4-5 (*see also* Food)

Let the peace of God rule in your hearts, to the which also ye are called in one body; and be ye thankful. Col. 3:15 (*see also* Peace)

In everything give thanks: for this is the will of God in Christ Jesus concerning you. 1 Thes. 5:18 (*see also* Will)

1 Thes 5:18 in every thing give *t.*: for this is the will of God in Christ Jesus concerning you; **2 Thes. 1:3** we are bound to *t.* God always for you, brethren, as it is meet, because that your faith groweth exceedingly, and the charity of every one of you all toward each other aboundeth; **1 Tim. 6:8** having food and raiment let us be therewith content.

Give thanks unto the LORD, call upon his name, make known his deeds among the people. 1 Chron. 16:8 (*see also* Call, Make Known)

1 Chron. 16:8-12 give *t.* unto the LORD, call upon his name, make known his deeds among the people; **16:34-36** give *t.* unto the LORD; for he is good: for his mercy endureth for ever; **Ps. 35:18** I will give thee *t.* in the great congregation: I will praise thee among much people; **105:1** give *t.* unto the LORD; call upon his name: make known his deeds among the people; **106:1** praise ye the LORD. O give *t.* unto the LORD; for he is good: for his mercy endureth for ever; **122:4** the tribes go up, the tribes of the LORD, unto the testimony of Israel, to give *t.* unto the name of the LORD.

THIEF (*see also* Steal)

Do not despise a thief, if he steal to satisfy his soul when he is hungry. Prov. 6:30-31

Whoso is partner with a thief hateth his own soul. Prov. 29:24

THINGS (*see also* All Things)

Love not the world, neither the things that are in the world. 1 Jn. 2:15 (*see also* Love, World)

He rebuked Peter, saying, Get thee behind me, Satan: for thou savourest not the things that be of God, but the things that be of men. Mark 8:33 (*see also* Savor)

THINK, THOUGHT (*see also* Counsel, Imagine, Meditate, Reason)

The thoughts of the wicked are an abomination to the LORD: but the words of the pure are pleasant words. Prov. 15:26 (*see also* Abomination, Wicked, Word)

Take no thought how or what ye shall speak: for it shall be given you in that same hour what ye shall speak. For it is not ye that speak, but the Spirit of your Father which speaketh in you. Matt. 10:19-20 (*see also* Speak, Spirit, Take)

Matt. 10:17-20 when they deliver you up, take no thought how or what ye shall speak: for it shall be given you in that same hour what ye shall speak. For it is not ye that speak, but the

Spirit of your Father which speaketh in you; **Acts 18:25** this man was instructed in the way of the Lord; and being fervent in the spirit, he spake and taught diligently the things of the Lord, knowing only the baptism of John.

Though we walk in the flesh, we do not war after the flesh: Casting down imaginations, and every high thing that exalteth itself against the knowledge of God, and bringing into captivity every thought to the obedience of Christ. 2 Cor. 10:3,5 (*see also* Flesh, Imagination, Obedient)

The wicked, through the pride of his countenance, will not seek after God: God is not in all his thoughts. Ps. 10:4 (*see also* Pride, Seek, Wicked)

If thou hast done foolishly in lifting up thyself, or if thou has thought evil, lay thine hand upon thy mouth. Prov. 30:32 (*see also* Evil)

How long shall thy vain thoughts lodge within thee? Jer. 4:14 (*see also* Vain)

Ps. 119:113 I hate vain *t.*: but thy law do I love; **Jer. 4:14** wash thine heart from wickedness, that thou mayest be saved. How long shall thy vain *t.* lodge within thee.

That which cometh out of the man, that defileth the man. For from within, out of the heart of men, proceed evil thoughts, adulteries, fornications, murders, Thefts, covetousness, wickedness, deceit, lasciviousness, an evil eye, blasphemy, pride, foolishness: All these evil things come from within, and defile the man. Mark 7:20-23 (*see also* Defile, Evil, Lasciviousness)

Matt. 9:4 wherefore *t.* ye evil in your hearts? **Mark 7:21-23** from within, out of the heart of men, proceed evil *t.*, adulteries, fornications, murders, thefts, covetousness, wickedness, deceit, lasciviousness, an evil eye, blasphemy, pride, foolishness: All these evil things come from within, and defile the man; **Luke 6:11** they were filled with madness; and communed one with another what they might do to Jesus; **Rom. 1:28** even as they did not like to retain God in their knowledge, God gave them over to a reprobate mind, to do those things which are not convenient.

Commit thy works unto the LORD, and thy thoughts shall be established. Prov. 16:3 (*see also* Work)

Prov. 16:3 commit thy works unto the LORD, and thy *t.* shall be established; **24:12** doth not he that pondereth the heart consider it? and he that keepeth thy soul, doth not he know it? and shall not he render to every man according to his works.

GOD saw that the wickedness of man was great in the earth, and that every imagination of the thoughts of his heart was only evil continually. Gen. 6:5 (*see also* Imagine)

Gen. 6:5 GOD saw that the wickedness of man was great in the earth, and that every imagination of the *t.* of his heart was only evil continually; **8:21** the LORD smelled a sweet savour; and the LORD said in his heart, I will not again curse the ground any more for mans sake; for the imagination of mans heart is evil from his youth; **Deut. 29:19** he bless himself in his heart, saying, I shall have peace, though I walk in the imagination of mine heart, to add drunkenness to thirst; **1 Kgs. 8:39** hear thou in heaven thy dwelling place, and forgive, and do, and give to every man according to his ways, whose heart thou knowest; [for thou, even thou only, knowest the hearts of all the children of men;; **1 Chron. 28:9** know thou the God of thy father, and serve him with a perfect heart and with a willing mind: for the LORD searcheth all hearts, and understandeth all the imaginations of the *t.*; **29:18** O LORD God... keep this for ever in the imagination of the *t.* of the heart of thy people, and prepare their heart unto thee; **2 Chron. 6:30** hear thou from heaven thy dwelling place, and forgive, and render unto every man according unto all his ways, whose heart thou knowest; [for thou only knowest the hearts of the children of men:; **Neh. 6:8** there are no such things done as thou sayest, but thou feignest them out of thine own heart; **Job 21:27** I know your *t.*, and the devices which ye wrongfully imagine against me; **Ps. 2:1** why do the heathen rage, and the people imagine a vain thing; **10:4** the wicked, through the pride of his countenance, will not seek after God: God is not in all his *t.*; **35:25** let them not say in their hearts, Ah, so would we have it: let them not say, We have swallowed him up; **56:5** every day they wrest my words: all their *t.* are against me for evil; **74:8** they said in their hearts, Let us destroy them together: they have burned up all the synagogues of God in the land; **94:11** the LORD knoweth the *t.* of man, that they are vanity; **119:113** I hate vain *t.*: but thy law do I love; **139:23** search me, O God, and know my heart: try me, and know my *t.*; **Prov. 6:16-19** these six things doth the LORD hate: yea, seven are an abomination unto him: A proud look, a lying tongue, and hands that shed innocent blood, An heart that deviseth wicked imaginations; **12:5** the *t.* of the righteous are right: but the counsels of the wicked are deceit; **12:20** deceit is in the heart of them that imagine evil: but to the counsellors of peace is joy; **15:26** the *t.* of the wicked are an abomination to the LORD: but the words of the pure are pleasant words; **16:9** a mans heart deviseth his way: but the LORD directeth his steps; **21:5** the *t.* of the diligent tend only to plenteousness; but of every one that is hasty only to want; **Isa. 9:17** every one is an hypocrite and an evildoer, and every mouth speaketh folly; **55:7-9** let the wicked forsake his way, and the unrighteous man his *t.*....For my *t.* are not your *t.*, neither are your ways my ways, saith the LORD; **59:7** their feet run to evil, and they make haste to shed innocent blood: their *t.* are *t.* of iniquity; wasting and destruction are in their paths; **66:18** I know their works and their *t.*: it shall come, that I will gather all nations and tongues; and they shall come, and see my glory; **Jer. 4:14** how long shall thy vain *t.* lodge within thee; **6:19** hear, O earth: behold, I will bring evil upon this people, even the fruit of their *t.*, because they have not hearkened unto my words, nor to my law, but rejected it; **7:24** they hearkened not, nor inclined their ear, but walked in the counsels and in the imagination of their evil heart, and went backward, and not forward; **13:10** this evil people, which refuse to hear my words, which walk in the imagination of their heart, and walk after other gods, to serve them, and to worship them, shall even be as this girdle; **Lam. 3:60-61** thou hast seen all their vengeance and all their imaginations against me. Thou hast heard their reproach, O LORD, and all their imaginations against me; **Dan. 11:27** both these kings hearts shall be to do mischief, and they shall speak lies at one table; but it shall not prosper; **Hosea 7:15** I have bound and strengthened their arms, yet do they imagine mischief against me; **Zech. 8:17** let none of you imagine evil in your hearts against his neighbour; and love no false oath: for all these are things that I hate, saith the LORD.

I know that thou canst do every thing, and that no thought can be withholden from thee. Job 42:2 (*see also* Belief)

Job 42:2 I know that thou canst do every thing, and that no *t.* can be withholden from thee; **Ps. 139:1-2** O LORD, thou hast searched me, and known me. Thou knowest my downsitting and mine uprising, thou understandest my *t.* afar off; **139:23** O God, and know my heart: try me, and know my *t.*

In the multitude of my thoughts within me thy comforts delight my soul. Ps. 94:19 (*see also* Solemnity)

Ps. 94:19 in the multitude of my *t.* within me thy comforts delight my soul; **119:15** I will meditate in thy precepts, and have respect unto thy ways; **119:18** open thou mine eyes, that I may behold wondrous things out of thy law; **119:23** princes also did sit and speak against me: but thy servant did meditate in thy statutes; **119:35** make me to go in the path of thy commandments; for therein do I delight; **139:17-18** how precious also are thy *t.* unto me, O God! how great is the sum of them; **Isa. 40:1** comfort ye, comfort ye my people, saith your God; **43:18-19** remember ye not the former things, neither consider the things of old. Behold, I will do a new thing; now it shall spring forth; shall ye not know it; **48:6-8** thou hast heard, see all this; and will not ye declare it? I have shewed thee new things from this time, even hidden things, and thou didst not know them.

THIRST (*see also* Hunger, Water)

Blessed are they which do hunger and thirst after righteousness: for they shall be filled. Matt. 5:6 (*see also* Hunger, Righteousness)

But whosoever drinketh of the water that I shall give him shall never thirst; but the water that I shall give him shall be in him a well of water springing up into everlasting life. John 4:14 (*see also* Everlasting Life, Springing)

THOU SHALT (*see also* Commandment, Do)

Thou shalt love the LORD thy God with all thine heart, and with all thy soul, and with all thy might. Deut. 6:5 (*see also* Love)

Thou shalt love thy neighbor as thyself. Matt. 22:39 (*see also* Love)

Jesus said unto him, Thous shalt love the Lord thy God with all thy heart, and with all thy soul, and with all thy mind. This is the first and great commandment. And the second is like unto it, Thou shalt love thy neighbour as thyself. On these two commandments, hang all the law and the prophets. Matt 22:37-40 (*see also* Commandment, Hang, Love)

Thou shalt love the Lord thy God with all thy heart, and with all thy soul, and with all thy mind, and with all thy strength: this is the first commandment. Mark 12:30 (*see also* Commandment, Love, Matt. 22:37)

Thou shalt seek the LORD thy God, thou shalt find him, if thou seek him with all thy heart and with all thy soul. Deut. 4:29 (*see also* Find, Seek)

Remember the sabbath day, to keep it holy. Six days shalt thou labour, and do all thy work: But the seventh day is the sabbath of the LORD thy God: in it thou shalt not do any work, thou, nor thy son, nor thy daughter, thy manservant, nor thy maidservant, nor thy cattle, nor thy stranger that is within thy gates: For in six days the LORD made heaven and earth, the sea, and all that in them is, and rested the seventh day: wherefore the LORD blessed the sabbath day, and hallowed it. Ex. 20:8-11 (*see also* Labor, Sabbath, Work)

Honour thy father and thy mother: that thy days may be long upon the land which the LORD thy God giveth thee. Ex. 20:12 (*see also* Father, Honor, Mother)

Thou shalt have no other gods before me. Ex. 20:3 (*see also* God, Idol)

Thou shalt worship the Lord thy God, and him only shalt thou serve. Luke 4:8 (*see also* Worship)

Thou shalt keep my covenant therefore, thou, and thy seed after thee in their generations. Gen. 17:9 (*see also* Covenant)

THOU SHALT NOT (*see also* Commandment)

Thou shalt not take the name of the LORD thy God in vain; for the LORD will not hold him guiltless that taketh his name in vain. Ex. 20:7 (*see also* Name, Vain)

Thou shalt not kill. Ex. 20:13 (*see also* Kill, Mosiah 13:21)

Thou shalt not commit adultery. Ex. 20:14 (*see also* Adultery, Mosiah 13:22)

Thou shalt not steal. Ex. 20:15(*see also* Steal, Mosiah 13:22)

Thou shalt have no other gods before me. Ex. 20:3 (*see also* God, Idol)

The seventh day is the sabbath of the LORD thy God: in it thou shalt not do any work, thou, nor thy son, nor thy daughter, thy manservant, nor thy maidservant, nor thy cattle, nor thy stranger that is within thy gates: Ex. 20:10 (*see also* Sabbath, Seventh, Work)

Thou shalt not bow down thyself to them, nor serve them: for I the LORD thy God am a jealous God, visiting the iniquities of the fathers upon the children unto the third and fourth generation of them that hate me. Ex. 20:5 (*see also* Children, Jealous)

Thou shalt not bear false witness against thy neighbour. Ex. 20:16 (*see also* False, Witness)

Thou shalt not tempt the Lord thy God. Luke 4:12 (*see also* Tempt)

Thou shalt not lie with mankind, as with womankind: it is abomination. Lev. 18:22 (*see also* Abomination)

Thou shat not covet thy neighbour's house, thou shalt not covet thy neighbour's wife, nor his manservant, nor his maidservant, nor his ox, nor his ass, nor anything that is thy neighbour's. Ex. 20:17 (*see also* Covet, Mosiah 13:24)

Thou shalt not defraud thy neighbour, neither rob him. Lev. 19:13 (*see also* Defraud)

Thou shalt not avenge, nor bear any grudge against the children of thy people, but thou shalt love thy neighbour as thyself: I *am* the LORD. Lev. 19:18 (*see also* Love, Neighbor)

Thou shalt not hate thy brother in thine heart: thou shalt in any wise rebuke thy neighbour and not suffer sin upon him. Lev. 19:17 (*see also* Hate)

Thou shalt not make unto thee any graven image, or any likeness of any thing that is in heaven above, or that is in the earth beneath, or that is in the water under the earth. Thou shalt not bow down thyself to them, nor serve them: For I the LORD thy God am a jealous God, visiting the iniquity of the fathers upon the children unto the third and fourth generation of them that hate me; And shewing mercy unto thousands of them that love me, and keep my commandments. Ex. 20:4-6 (*see also* Graven Image, Idol)

TIME (*see also* Day, Eternity, House, Season, Today)

The simple believeth every word: but the prudent man looketh well to his going. Prov. 14:15 (*see also* Prudent)

Be not over much wicked, neither be thou foolish: why shouldest thou die before thy time? Eccl. 7:17 (*see also* Fool, Wicked)

Walk in wisdom toward them that are without, redeeming the time. Col. 4:5 (*see also* Walk, Wisdom)

Humble yourselves therefore under the mighty hand of God, that he may exalt you in due time. 1 Pet. 5:5-6 (*see also* Humble)

Write the vision, and make it plain upon tables, that he may run that readeth it. For the vision is yet for an appointed time. Haba 2:2-3 (*see also* Vision, Write)

To every thing there is a season, and a time to every purpose under heaven; A time to be born, and a time to die; a time to plant, and a time to pluck up that which is planted; A time to kill, and a time to heal; a time to break down, and a time to build up; A time to weep, and a time to laugh; a time to mourn, and a time to dance; A time to cast away stones, and a time to father stones together; a time to embrace, and a time to refrain from embracing; A time to get, and a time to lose; a time to keep, and a time to cast away; A time to rend, and a time to sew; a time to keep silence, and a time to speak; A time to love, and a time to hate; a time of war, and a time of peace. Eccl. 3:1-8 (*see also* Purpose, Season)

TITHE, TITHING (*see also* Offer, Sacrifice)

Honour the LORD with thy substance, and with the firstfruits of all thine increase. Prov. 3:9 (*see also* Honor)

Return unto me and I will return unto you, saith the Lord of Hosts. But ye said, Wherein shall we return? Will a man rob God? Yet ye have robbed me. But ye say, Wherein have we robbed thee? In tithes and offerings. Mal. 3:7 (*see also* Rob, Tithe)

The sons of Levi, who receive the office of the priesthood, have a commandment to take tithes of the people according to the law. Heb. 7:5

Heb 7:2 to whom also Abraham gave a tenth part of all; 7:4 now consider how great this man was, unto whom even the patriarch Abraham gave the tenth of the spoils; 7:5 the sons of Levi, who receive the office of the priesthood, have a commandment to take *t.* of the people according to the law; 7:9 For every high priest taken from among men is ordained for men in things pertaining to God, that he may offer both gifts and sacrifices for sins.

Bring ye all the tithes into the storehouse, that there may be meat in mine house, and prove me now herewith, saith the LORD of hosts, if I will not open you the windows of heaven, and pour you out a blessing. Mal. 3:8-12 (*see also* Prove, Storehouse)

Gen. 14:20-24 he gave him *t.* of all; 28:22 of all that thou shalt give me I will surely give the tenth unto thee; Lev. 27:30 all the *t.* of the land, whether of the seed of the land, or of the fruit of the tree, is the LORD's; Num. 18:24-29 out of all your gifts ye shall offer every heave offering of the LORD, of all the best thereof, even the hallowed part thereof out of it; Deut. 12:6 ye shall bring your burnt offerings, and your sacrifices, and your *t.*, and heave offerings of your hand; 12:11 thither shall ye bring all that I command you; your burnt offerings, and your sacrifices, your *t.*, and the heave offering of your hand; 14:23 thou shalt eat before the LORD thy God, in the place which he shall choose to place his name there, the *t.* of thy corn, of thy wine, and of thine oil, and the firstlings of thy herds and of thy flocks; 26:12 [make] an end of *t.* all the *t.* of thine increase the third year, which is the year of *t.*; 1 Chron. 29:14-17 who am

I, and what is my people, that we should be able to offer so willingly after this sort? for all things come of thee, and of thine own have we given thee; **2 Chron. 31:5-6** [they] brought in abundance the firstfruits of corn, wine, and oil, and honey, and of all the increase of the field; and the *t.* of all things brought they in abundantly; **31:10** since the people began to bring the offerings into the house of the LORD, we have had enough to eat, and have left plenty: for the LORD hath blessed his people; **31:12** [bring] in the offerings and the *t.* and the dedicated things faithfully; **Neh. 10:37-38** we... shall bring up the *t.* of the *t.* unto the house of our God, to the chambers, into the treasure house; **12:44** some [were] appointed over the chambers for the treasures, for the offerings, for the firstfruits, and for the *t.*, to gather into them; **13:5** he had prepared for him a great chamber, where aforetime they laid the meat offerings, the frankincense, and the vessels, and the *t.* of the corn, the new wine, and the oil; **13:12** all Judah [brought] the *t.* of the corn and the new wine and the oil unto the treasuries; **Ps. 116:14** I will pay my vows unto the LORD now in the presence of all his people; **116:18-19** I will pay my vows unto the LORD now in the presence of all his people; **Prov. 3:9-10** honour the LORD with thy substance, and with the firstfruits of all thine increase; **Amos 4:4-7** bring your sacrifices every morning, and your *t.* after three years; **Jonah 2:9** I will sacrifice unto thee with the voice of thanksgiving; I will pay that that I have vowed; **Mal. 3:8-12** bring ye all the *t.* into the storehouse, that there may be meat in mine house, and prove me now herewith, saith the LORD of hosts, if I will not open you the windows of heaven, and pour you out a blessing.

TODAY (*see also* Day, Time)

This is the day which the LORD hath made; we will rejoice and be glad in it. Ps. 118:24 (*see also* Day, Rejoice)

TOLERANCE (*see also* Patience, Understand)

For what knowest thou, O wife, whether thou shalt save thy husband? or how knowest thou, O man, whether thou shalt save thy wife? 1 Cor. 7:16 (*see also* Belief)

TOMORROW (*see also* Day, Time)

Boast not thyself of tomorrow; for thou knowest not what a day may bring forth. Prov. 27:1 (*see also* Boast)

TONGUE, TONGUES (*see also* Interpret, Language, Lips, Mouth, Speak)

A wholesome tongue is a tree of life: but perverseness therein is a breach in the spirit. Prov. 15:4 (*see also* Perverse, Wholesome)

He that hath a froward heart findeth no good: and he that hath a perverse tongue falleth into mischief. Prov 17:20 (*see also* Froward, Heart)

The Lord GOD hath given me the tongue of the learned, that I should know how to speak a word in season to him that is weary. Isa. 50:4 (*see also* Season, Speak, Weary)

Keep thy tongue from evil, and thy lips from speaking guile. Ps. 34:13 (*see also* Evil, Guile)

My tongue shall speak of thy word: for all thy commandments are righteousness. Ps. 119:172 (*see also* Word)

These signs shall follow them that believe; In my name shall they cast out devils; they shall speak with new tongues; They shall take up serpents; and if they drink any deadly thing it shall not hurt them; they shall lay hands on the sick and they shall recover. Mark 16:17-18 (*see also* Cast, Deadly, Devil, Name, Sign)

I would that ye all spake with tongues, but rather that ye prophesied: for greater is he that prophesieth than he that speaketh with tongues, except he interpret, that the church may receive edifying. 1 Cor. 14:5 (*see also* Gift, Interpret, Prophecy)

Acts 2:6 the multitude came together, and were confounded, because that every man heard them speak in his own language; **10:46** they heard them speak with *t.*, and magnify God; **19:6** when Paul had laid his hands upon them, the Holy Ghost came on them; and they spake with *t.*, and prophesied; **1 Cor. 14:2** he that speaketh in an unknown *t.* speaketh not unto men, but unto God: for no man understandeth him; howbeit in the spirit he speaketh mysteries; **14:5-6** I would that ye all spake with *t.*, but rather that ye prophesied: for greater is he that prophesieth than he that speaketh with *t.*, except he interpret, that the church may receive edifying. Now, brethren, if I come unto you speaking with *t.*, what shall I profit you, except I shall speak to you either by revelation, or by knowledge, or by prophesying, or by doctrine; **14:9** except ye utter by the *t.* words easy to be understood, how shall it be known what is spoken? for ye shall speak into the air; **14:14-19** if I pray in an unknown *t.*, my spirit prayeth, but my understanding is unfruitful. What is it then? I will pray with the spirit, and I will pray with the understanding also: I will sing with the spirit, and I will sing with the understanding also. Else when thou shalt bless with the spirit, how shall he that occupieth the room of the unlearned say Amen at thy giving of thanks, seeing he understandeth not what thou sayest? For thou verily givest thanks well, but the other is not edified. I thank my God, I speak with *t.* more than ye all: Yet in the church I had rather speak five words with my understanding, that by my voice I might teach others also, than ten thousand words in an unknown *t.*; **14:22** *t.* are for a sign, not to them that believe, but to them that believe not: but prophesying serveth not for them that believe not, but for them which believe; **14:26** how is it then, brethren? when ye come together, every one of you hath a psalm, hath a doctrine, hath a *t.*, hath a revelation, hath an interpretation. Let all things be done unto edifying; **14:28** if there be no interpreter, let him keep silence in the church; and let him speak to himself, and to God.

TRADITION (*see also* Way, World)

We command you, brethren, in the name of our Lord Jesus Christ, that ye withdraw yourselves from every brother that walketh disorderly, and not after the tradition which he received of us. 2 Thes. 3:6 (*see also* Disorderly)

Ye know that ye were not redeemed with corruptible things, as silver and gold, from your vain conversation received by tradition from your fathers. 1 Pet. 1:18 (*see also* Conversation, Corrupt, Redeem)

Full well ye reject the commandment of God, that ye may keep your own traditions. Mark 7:9 (*see also* Reject)

Mark 7:3-5 except they wash their hands oft, eat not, holding the *t.* of the elders. And when they come from the market, except they wash, they eat not; **7:8-13** laying aside the commandment of God, ye hold the *t.* of men, as the washing of pots and cups: and many other such like things ye do. And he said unto them, Full well ye reject the commandment of God, that ye may keep your own *t.*

TRAIN (*see also* Teach)

Train up a child in the way he should go: and when he is old, he will not depart from it. Prov. 22:6 (*see also* Child, Depart, Way)

TRAMPLE (*see* Blaspheme, Deny, Mock, Rebel, Reject)

TRANSFORM (*see also* Born Again, Change, Renew)

Be ye transformed by the renewing of your mind, that ye may prove what is that good, and acceptable, and perfect, will of God. Rom. 12:2 (*see also* Mind, Prove, Renew)

Rom. 12:2 be not conformed to this world: but be ye *t.* by the renewing of your mind, that ye may prove what is that good, and acceptable, and perfect, will of God; **2 Cor. 5:17** if any man be in Christ, he is a new creature: old things are passed away; behold, all things are become new; **Gal. 1:23-24** that he which persecuted us in times past now preacheth the faith which once he destroyed; **6:15-16** for in Christ Jesus neither circumcision availeth any thing, nor uncircumcision, but a new creature. And as many as walk according to this rule, peace be on them, and mercy, and upon the Israel of God; **Eph. 4:22-24** put off concerning the former conversation the old man, which is corrupt according to the deceitful lusts; And be renewed in the spirit of your mind; And that ye put on the new man, which after God is created in righteousness and true holiness; **Col. 3:16** let the word of Christ dwell in you richly in all wisdom; teaching and admonishing one another in psalms and hymns and spiritual songs, singing with grace in your hearts to the Lord in Christ, he is a new creature: old things are passed away; behold, all things are become new.

TRANSGRESS, TRANSGRESSION (*see also* Evil, Iniquity, Offend, Sin, Trespass, Wicked)

As for our iniquities, we know them: in transgressing and lying against the LORD, and departing away from our God, speaking oppression and revolt, conceiving and uttering from the heart words of falsehood. Isa. 59:12-13 (*see also* Liar)

Whoso robbeth his father or his mother, and saith, It is no transgression; the same is the companion of a destroyer. Prov. 28:24 (*see also* Rob)

Turn from transgression. Isa. 59:20 (*see also* Sin)

Cast away from you all your transgressions, whereby ye have transgressed; and make you a new heart and a new spirit; for why will ye die, O house of Israel? Ezek. 18:31 (*see also* Heart)

It is no good report that I hear: ye make the LORD's people to transgress. 1 Sam. 2:24

Judg. 2:20 the anger of the LORD was hot against Israel; and he said, Because that this people hath *t.* my covenant which I commanded their fathers, and have not hearkened unto my voice; 1 Sam. 2:24 it is no good report that I hear: ye make the LORD's people to *t.*; Jer. 5:6 every one that goeth out thence shall be torn in pieces: because their *t.* are many, and their backslidings are increased.

TREASURE (*see also* Promise, Reward, Riches, Wealth)

If thou wilt be perfect, go and sell that thou hast, and give to the poor, and thou shalt have treasure in heaven: and come and follow me. Matt. 19:21-22 (*see also* Follow, Perfect, Sacrifice, Luke 18:22)

Incline thine ear unto wisdom, and apply thine heart to understanding. Prov. 2:2 (*see also* Apply, Know, Understand)

Treasures of wickedness profit nothing; but righteousness delivereth from death. Prov. 10:2 (*see also* Profit, Righteous, Wickedness)

Then Jesus beholding him loved him, and said unto him, One thing thou lackest: go thy way, sell whatsoever thou hast, and give to the poor, and thou shalt have treasure in heaven: and come, take up the cross, and follow me. Mark 10:21 (*see also* Follow, Lack)

The getting of treasures by a lying tongue is a vanity tossed to and fro of them that seek death. Prov. 21:6 (*see also* Liar)

Because thou hast trusted in thy works and in thy treasure thou shalt also be taken. Jer. 48:7 (*see also* Works)

Jer. 48:7 because thou hast trusted in thy works and in thy *t.* thou shalt also be taken; 49:4 wherefore gloriest thou in the valleys, thy flowing valley, O backsliding daughter? that trusted in her *t.*, saying, Who shall come unto me.

Lay not up for yourselves treasures upon earth, where moth and rust doth corrupt, and where thieves break through and steal: But lay up for yourselves treasures in heaven, where neither moth nor rust doth corrupt, and where thieves do not break through nor steal: For where your treasure is, there will your heart be also. Matt. 6:19-21 (*see also* Heart, Heaven, Lay Up, Steal)

Matt. 6:19-21 lay not up for yourselves *t.* upon earth, where moth and rust doth corrupt, and where thieves break through and steal: But lay up for yourselves *t.* in heaven, where neither moth nor rust doth corrupt, and where thieves do not break through nor steal: For where your *t.* is, there will your heart be also; 12:33-34 sell that ye have, and give alms; provide yourselves bags which wax not old, a *t.* in the heavens that faileth not, where no thief approacheth, neither moth corrupteth. For where your *t.* is, there will your heart be also; 16:11 if therefore ye have not been faithful in the unrighteous mammon, who will commit to your trust the true riches; Rev. 3:17 because thou sayest, I am rich, and increased with goods, and have need of nothing; and knowest not that thou art wretched, and miserable, and poor, and blind, and naked.

TREAT, TREATMENT (*see also* Care, Do, Give)

Let the husband render unto the render unto the wife due benevolence: and likewise also the wife unto the husband. 1 Cor. 7:3-5 (*see also* Husband, Wife)

Warn them that are unruly, comfort the feebleminded, support the weak, be patient toward all men. 1 Thes. 5:14 (*see also* Patience, Warn)

1 Thes 5:14 warn them that are unruly, comfort the feebleminded, support the weak, be patient toward all men; **2 Thes. 1:4** we ourselves glory in you in the churches of God for your patience and faith in all your persecutions and tribulations that ye endure; **2 Tim. 2:24** the servant of the Lord must not strive; but be gentle unto all men, apt to teach, patient; **Titus 2:2** aged men be sober, grave, temperate, sound in faith, in charity, in patience.

TRESPASS (*see also* Offend, Sin, Transgress)

If thy brother shall trespass against thee, go and tell him his faults between thee and him alone. Matt. 18:15 (*see also* Forgive)

Matt. 18:15-17 if thy brother shall *t.* against thee, go and tell him his fault between thee and him alone: if he shall hear thee, thou hast gained thy brother. But if he will not hear thee, then take with thee one or two more, that in the mouth of two or three witnesses every word may be established.

TRIAL, TRIED

Fear none of those things which thou shalt suffer: behold, the devil shall cast some of you into prison, that ye may be tried; and ye shall have tribulation ten days: be thou faithful unto death, and I will give thee a crown of life. Rev. 2:10 (*see also* Crown, Fear, Tribulation)

TRIBULATION (*see also* Affliction, Trouble, Persecution)

Blessed be God, even the Father of our Lord Jesus Christ, the Father of mercies, and the God of all comfort; Who comforteth us in all our tribulation, that we may be able to comfort them which are in any trouble, by the comfort wherewith we ourselves are comforted of God. For as the sufferings of Christ abound in us, so our consolation also aboundeth by Christ. 2 Cor. 1:3-5 (*see also* Comfort, Empathize)

Fear none of those things which thou shalt suffer: behold, the devil shall cast some of you into prison, that ye may be tried; and ye shall have tribulation ten days: be thou faithful unto death, and I will give thee a crown of life. Rev. 2:10 (*see also* Crown, Fear, Trial)

TROUBLE, TROUBLED (*see* Afflict, Anguish, Grief, Misery, Sorrow, Tribulation)

Let not your hearts be troubled, neither let it be afraid. John 14:27 (*see also* Fear)

In the day of my trouble I will call upon thee: for thou wilt answer me. Ps. 86:7 (*see also* Call, Seek)

Ps. 77:2 in the day of my trouble I *s.* the Lord: my sore ran in the night, and ceased not: my soul refused to be comforted; **81:7** thou calledst in trouble, and I delivered thee; **86:7** in the day of my trouble I will call upon thee: for thou wilt answer me; **88:3** my soul is full of troubles: and my life draweth nigh unto the grave; **138:3** in the day when I cried thou answeredst me, and strengthenedst me with strength in my soul; **142:2** I poured out my complaint before him; I shewed before him my trouble; **142:4** I looked on my right hand, and beheld, but there was no man that would know me: refuge failed me; no man cared for my soul; **143:11** quicken me, O LORD, for thy names sake: for thy righteousness sake bring my soul out of trouble; **Jer. 2:27** they have turned their back unto me, and not their face: but in the time of their trouble they will say, Arise, and save us.

TRUE, TRUTH (*see also* Gospel, Honest, Righteous, Upright)

He is proud, knowing nothing, but doting about questions and strifes of words, whereof cometh envy, strife, railings, evil surmisings, Perverse disputings of men of corrupt minds, and destitute of the truth, supposing that gain is godliness: from such withdraw thyself. 1 Tim. 6:4-5 (*see also* Question, Strife, Mind, Pride)

The LORD is the true God, he is the living God, and an everlasting king: at his wrath the earth shall tremble, and the nations shall not be able to abide his indignation. Jer. 10:10 (*see also* God, King)

LORD, who shall abide in thy tabernacle? Who shall dwell in thy holy hill? He that walketh uprightly, and worketh righteousness, and speaketh the truth in his heart. Ps. 15:1-2 (*see also* Tabernacle)

Teach me thy way, O LORD; I will walk in thy truth: unite my heart to fear thy name. Ps. 86:11 (*see also* Fear, Way)

Buy the truth, and sell it not; also wisdom, and instruction, and understanding. **Prov. 23:23** (*see also* Instruct, Understand, Wisdom)

Open ye the gates, that the righteous nation which keepeth the truth may enter in. **Isa. 26:2** (*see also* Gate, Nation, Righteous)

None calleth for justice, nor any pleadeth for truth: they trust in vanity, and speak lies; they conceive mischief, and bring forth iniquity. **Isa. 59:4** (*see also* Justice)

Let not mercy and truth forsake thee: bind them about thy neck: write them upon the table of thine heart; So shalt thou find favour and good understanding in the sight of God and man. **Prov. 3:3-4** (*see also* Bind, Heart, Merciful, Write)

Speak ye every man the truth to his neighbour; execute the judgment of truth and peace in your gates. **Zech. 8:16** (*see also* Speak)

Love the truth and peace. **Zech. 8:19** (*see also* Peace)

Hear; for I will speak of excellent things; and the opening of my lips shall be right things. For my mouth shall speak truth; and wickedness is an abomination to my lips. **Prov. 6:7** (*see also* Speak)

I have chosen the way of truth. **Ps. 119:30** (*see also* Way)

Speaketh truth. **Prov. 12:17** (*see also* Speak)

Prov. 12:17 he that speaketh *t.* sheweth forth righteousness: but a false witness deceit; **12:19** the lip of *t.* shall be established for ever: but a lying tongue is but for a moment.

They are not valiant for the truth upon the earth, for they proceed from evil to evil, and they know not me, saith the LORD. **Jer. 9:3** (*see also* Evil, Valiant)

God hath from the beginning chosen you to salvation through sanctification of the Spirit and belief of the truth. **2 Thes. 2:13** (*see also* Believe, Salvation)

Speak forth the words of truth and soberness. **Acts 26:25** (*see also* Speak)

TRUST, TRUSTWORTHINESS, TRUSTWORTHY (*see also* Believe, Depend, Faith, Jesus Christ, Obey, Scripture)

Be not highminded, nor trust in uncertain riches, but in the living God, who giveth us richly all things to enjoy. **1 Tim. 6:17-19** (*see also* Highminded, Rich)

Trust not in oppression, and become not vain in robbery: if riches increase, set not your heart upon them. **Ps. 62:10** (*see also* Heart, Increase, Oppress, Rich, Rob)

Trust in him at all times; ye people, pour out your heart before him: God is a refuge for us. **Ps. 62:8** (*see also* Pour)

Commit thy way unto the Lord; trust also in Him; and He shall bring it to pass. And he shall bring forth thy righteousness as the light, and thy judgment as the noonday. **Ps. 37:5-6** (*see also* Commit, Light, Way)

O my God, I trust in thee: let me not be ashamed, let not mine enemies triumph over me. Yea, let none that wait on thee be ashamed: let them be ashamed which transgress without cause **Ps. 25:2** (*see also* Ashamed)

Blessed be the God of Shadrach, Meshach, and Abed-nego, who hath sent his angel, and delivered his servants that trusted in him, and have changed the kings word, and yielded their bodies, that they might not serve nor worship any god, except their own God. **Dan. 3:28** (*see also* Idol, Serve, Worship)

The name of the LORD is a strong tower: the righteous runneth into it, and is safe. **Prov. 18:10** (*see also* Name)

This is thy lot, the portion of thy measures from me, saith the LORD; because thou hast forgotten me, and trusted in falsehood. **Jer. 13:25** (*see also* False)

He that handleth a matter wisely shall find good: and whoso trusteth in the LORD, happy is he. **Prov. 16:20** (*see also* Matter, Wise)

I am like a green olive tree in the house of God: I trust in the mercy of God for ever and ever. **Ps. 52:8** (*see also* Merciful)

Let thy mercies come also unto me, O LORD, even thy salvation, according to thy word. So shall I have wherewith to answer him that reproacheth me: for I trust in thy word. Ps. 119:41-42 (*see also* Mercy, Word)

Trust in the LORD with all thine heart; and lean not unto thine own understanding. Prov. 3:5 (*see also* Heart, Understand)

None calleth for justice, nor any pleadeth for truth: they trust in vanity, and speak lies; they conceive mischief, and bring forth iniquity. Isa. 59:4 (*see also* Vanity)

Trust ye not in lying words. Jer. 7:4 (*see also* Liar)

Cursed be the man that trusteth in man, and maketh flesh his arm, and whose heart departeth from the LORD. Jer. 17:5 (*see also* Flesh, Heart)

He that trusteth in his own heart is a fool: but whoso walketh wisely, he shall be delivered. Prov. 28:26 (*see also* Heart)

He shall not be afraid of evil tidings: his heart is fixed, trusting in the LORD. His heart is established, he shall not be afraid. Ps. 112:7-8 (*see also* Establish, Evil)

O taste and see that the LORD is good: blessed is the man that trusteth in him. Ps. 34:8 (*see also* See, Taste)

How excellent is thy lovingkindness, O God! therefore the children of men put their trust under the shadow of thy wings. Ps. 36:7 (*see also* Lovingkindness)

Thou hast trusted in thy wickedness: thou hast said, None seeth me. Thy wisdom and thy knowledge, it hath perverted thee; and thou hast said in thine heart, I am, and none else beside me. Isa. 47:10 (*see also* Pervert, Wicked)

Trust in the living God, who is the Saviour of all men, specially of those that believe. 1 Tim. 4:10 (*see also* Believe, Savior)

Matt. 12:21 in his name shall the Gentiles *t*.; 1 Cor. 6:14 God hath both raised up the Lord, and will also raise up us by his own power; 2 Cor. 1:10 who delivered us from so great a death, and

doth deliver: in whom we *t.* that he will yet deliver us; 2:14-17 thanks be unto God, which always causeth us to triumph in Christ, and maketh manifest the savour of his knowledge by us in every place; 3:4-5 such *t.* have we through Christ to God-ward: Not that we are sufficient of ourselves to think any thing as of ourselves; but our sufficiency is of God; Eph. 1:12-13 we should be to the praise of his glory, who first *t.* in Christ. In whom ye also *t.* after that ye heard the word of truth, the gospel of your salvation: in whom also after that ye believed, ye were sealed with that holy Spirit of promise; Philip. 2:19 I *t.* in the Lord Jesus to send Timotheus shortly unto you, that I also may be of good comfort, when I know your state; 2:24 I *t.* in the Lord that I also myself shall come shortly; 2 Thes. 3:4 we have confidence in the Lord touching you, that ye both do and will do the things which we command you; 1 Tim. 4:10 we both labour and suffer reproach, because we *t.* in the living God, who is the Saviour of all men, specially of those that believe; 5:5 now she that is a widow indeed, and desolate, *t.* in God, and continueth in supplications and prayers night and day; 6:17 charge them that are rich in this world, that they be not highminded, nor *t.* in uncertain riches, but in the living God, who giveth us richly all things to enjoy; 2 Tim. 1:12 I am not ashamed: for I know whom I have believed, and am persuaded that he is able to keep that which I have committed unto him against that day; 3:11 persecutions, afflictions, which came unto me at Antioch, at Iconium, at Lystra; what persecutions I endured: but out of them all the Lord delivered me; 4:17-18 notwithstanding the Lord stood with me, and strengthened me; that by me the preaching might be fully known, and that all the Gentiles might hear: and I was delivered out of the mouth of the lion; Heb. 2:13 I will put my *t.* in him. And again, Behold I and the children which God hath given me; 1 Pet. 5:7 casting all your care upon him; for he careth for you.

Vain is the help of man. Ps. 60:11 (*see also* Flesh)

Ps. 60:11 (108:12) give us help from trouble: for vain is the help of man; 146:3-4 put not your *t.* in princes, nor in the son of man, in whom there is no help; Isa. 36:9 how then wilt thou turn away the face of one captain of the least of my masters servants, and put thy *t.* on Egypt for chariots and for horsemen; 36:15-16 make an agreement with me by a present, and come out to me: and eat ye every one of his vine, and every one of his fig tree, and drink ye every one the waters of his own cistern; **Jer. 14:22** are there any among the vanities of the Gentiles that can cause rain? or can the heavens give showers? art not thou he, O LORD our God;**17:5-6** cursed be the man that *t.* in man, and maketh flesh his arm, and whose heart departeth from the LORD; **46:25** I will punish the multitude of No, and Pharaoh, and Egypt, with their gods, and their kings; even Pharaoh, and all them that *t.* in him; **Hosea 10:13** ye have plowed wickedness, ye have reaped iniquity; ye have eaten the fruit of lies: because thou didst *t.* in thy way, in the multitude of thy mighty men.

Trust in the LORD, and do good. Ps. 37:3 (*see also* Do, Good)

2 Kgs. 18:5 he *t.* in the LORD God of Israel; so that after him was none like him among all the kings of Judah, nor any that were before him; **1 Chron. 5:20** they cried to God in the battle, and he was intreated of them; because they put their *t.* in him; **19:13** be of good courage, and let us behave ourselves valiantly for our people, and for the cities of our God: and let the LORD do that which is good in his sight; **2 Chron. 32:8** with him is an arm of flesh; but with us is the LORD our God to help us, and to fight our battles; **Job 13:14-15** wherefore do I take my flesh in my teeth, and put my life in mine hand? Though he slay me, yet will I *t.* in him; **30:23** I know that thou wilt bring me to death, and to the house appointed for all living; **35:14** although thou sayest thou shalt not see him, yet judgment is before him; therefore *t.* thou in him; **Ps. 2:12** blessed are all they that put their *t.* in him; **3:3-7** thou, O LORD, art a shield for me; my glory, and the lifter up of mine head. I cried unto the LORD with my voice, and he heard me out of his holy hill; **4:5** offer the sacrifices of righteousness, and put your *t.* in the LORD; **7:1** O LORD my God, in thee do I put my *t.*: save me from all them that persecute me, and deliver me; **9:9-10** the LORD also will be a refuge for the oppressed, a refuge in times of trouble. And they that know thy name will put their *t.* in thee: for thou, LORD, hast not forsaken them that seek thee; **11:1** in the LORD put I my *t.*: How say ye to my soul, Flee as a bird to your mountain; **13:5** I have *t.* in thy mercy; my heart shall rejoice in thy salvation; **16:1** preserve me, O God: for in thee do I put my *t.*; **17:7-9** shew thy marvellous lovingkindness, O thou that savest by thy right hand them which put their *t.* in thee from those that rise up against them; **17:13** arise, O LORD, disappoint him, cast him down: deliver my soul from the wicked, which is thy sword; **18:2** the LORD is my

rock, and my fortress, and my deliverer; my God, my strength, in whom I will *t.*; my buckler, and the horn of my salvation, and my high tower; **18:17-18** he delivered me from my strong enemy, and from them which hated me: for they were too strong for me. They prevented me in the day of my calamity: but the LORD was my stay; **18:27-43** as for God, his way is perfect: the word of the LORD is tried: he is a buckler to all those that *t.* in him. For who is God save the LORD; **19:7** the law of the LORD is perfect, converting the soul: the testimony of the LORD is sure, making wise the simple; **20:7** some *t.* in chariots, and some in horses: but we will remember the name of the LORD our God; **21:7** the king *t.* in the LORD, and through the mercy of the most High he shall not be moved; **22:4-5** our fathers *t.* in thee: they *t.*, and thou didst deliver them. They cried unto thee, and were delivered: they *t.* in thee, and were not confounded; **25:2** my God, I *t.* in thee: let me not be ashamed, let not mine enemies triumph over me; **26:1** judge me, O LORD; for I have walked in mine integrity: I have *t.* also in the LORD; therefore I shall not slide; **28:7** the LORD is my strength and my shield; my heart *t.* in him, and I am helped: therefore my heart greatly rejoiceth; and with my *s.* will I praise him; **31:1** in thee, O LORD, do I put my *t.*; let me never be ashamed: deliver me in thy righteousness; **31:3-7** I *t.* in the LORD. I will be glad and rejoice in thy mercy: for thou hast considered my trouble; thou hast known my soul in adversities; **31:14** I *t.* in thee, O LORD: I said, Thou art my God; **31:19** how great is thy goodness, which thou hast laid up for them that fear thee; which thou hast wrought for them that *t.* in thee before the sons of men; **32:7-10** many sorrows shall be to the wicked: but he that *t.* in the LORD, mercy shall compass him about; **33:21** our heart shall rejoice in him, because we have *t.* in his holy name; **34:8** taste and see that the LORD is good: blessed is the man that *t.* in him; **34:22** the LORD redeemeth the soul of his servants: and none of them that *t.* in him shall be desolate; **37:3** *t.* in the LORD, and do good; so shalt thou dwell in the land, and verily thou shalt be fed; **37:5-6** commit thy way unto the LORD; *t.* also in him; and he shall bring it to pass; **37:40** the LORD shall help them, and deliver them: he shall deliver them from the wicked, and save them, because they *t.* in him; **40:3-4** blessed is that man that maketh the LORD his *t.*, and respecteth not the proud, nor such as turn aside to lies; **40:17** I am poor and needy; yet the Lord thinketh upon me: thou art my help and my deliverer; make no tarrying, O my God; **41:10-11** O LORD, be merciful unto me, and raise me up, that I may requite them. By this I know that thou favourest me, because mine enemy doth not triumph over me; **44:6-8** I will not *t.* in my bow, neither shall my sword save me. But thou hast saved us from our enemies, and hast put them to shame that hated us. In God we boast all the day long; **56:4** in God I will praise his word, in God I have put my *t.*; I will not fear what flesh can do unto me; **57:1** be merciful unto me, O God, be merciful unto me: for my soul *t.* in thee: yea, in the shadow of thy wings will I make my refuge, until these calamities be overpast; **61:4** I will abide in thy tabernacle for ever: I will *t.* in the covert of thy wings; **62:8** *t.* in him at all times; ye people, pour out your heart before him: God is a refuge for us; **71:1-3** in thee, O LORD, do I put my *t.*: let me never be put to confusion. Deliver me in thy righteousness, and cause me to escape: incline thine ear unto me, and save me; **71:5-6** thou art my hope, O Lord GOD: thou art my *t.* from my youth. By thee have I been holden up from the womb; **73:24-26** whom have I in heaven but thee? and there is none upon earth that I desire beside thee. My flesh and my heart faileth: but God is the strength of my heart, and my portion for ever; **84:12 O** LORD of hosts, blessed is the man that *t.* in thee; **85:13** righteousness shall go before him; and shall set us in the way of his steps; **86:2** preserve my soul; for I am holy: O thou my God, save thy servant that *t.* in thee; **91:1-16** I will say of the LORD, He is my refuge and my fortress: my God; in him will I *t.*. Surely he shall deliver thee; **92:4** thou, LORD, hast made me glad through thy work: I will triumph in the works of thy hands; **94:22** the LORD is my defence; and my God is the rock of my refuge; **112:7** he shall not be afraid of evil tidings: his heart is fixed, *t.* in the LORD; **112:9** he hath dispersed, he hath given to the poor; his righteousness endureth for ever; his horn shall be exalted with honour; **115:9-11** *t.* thou in the LORD: he is their help and their shield. O house of Aaron, *t.* in the LORD: he is their help and their shield. Ye that fear the LORD, *t.* in the LORD: he is their help and their shield; **118:8-9** it is better to *t.* in the LORD than to put confidence in man. It is better to *t.* in the LORD than to put confidence in princes; **119:39** turn away my reproach which I fear: for thy judgments are good; **121:5-8** the LORD is thy keeper: the LORD is thy shade upon thy right hand. The sun shall not smite thee by day, nor the moon by night. The LORD shall preserve thee from all evil: he shall preserve thy soul; **124:6-8** blessed be the LORD, who hath not given us as a prey to their teeth; **125:1-2** they that *t.* in the LORD shall be as mount Zion, which cannot be removed, but

abideth for ever; **125:5** as for such as turn aside unto their crooked ways, the LORD shall lead them forth with the workers of iniquity: but peace shall be upon Israel; **126:2** then was our mouth filled with laughter, and our tongue with singing: then said they among the heathen, The LORD hath done great things for them; **127:1** except the LORD build the house, they labour in vain that build it: except the LORD keep the city, the watchman waketh but in vain; **141:8** mine eyes are unto thee, O GOD the Lord: in thee is my *t.*; leave not my soul destitute; **142:5** I cried unto thee, O LORD: I said, Thou art my refuge and my portion in the land of the living; **143:8** cause me to hear thy lovingkindness in the morning; for in thee do I *t.*: cause me to know the way wherein I should walk; for I lift up my soul unto thee; **144:2** my goodness, and my fortress; my high tower, and my deliverer; my shield, and he in whom I *t.*; who subdueth my people under me; **144:10-15** happy is that people, that is in such a case: yea, happy is that people, whose God is the LORD; **145:14** the LORD upholdeth all that fall, and raiseth up all those that be bowed down; **147:5** great is our Lord, and of great power: his understanding is infinite; **Prov. 16:20** he that handleth a matter wisely shall find good: and whoso *t.* in the LORD, happy is he; **21:31** the horse is prepared against the day of battle: but safety is of the LORD; **22:19** that thy *t.* may be in the LORD, I have made known to thee this day; **28:25** he that is of a proud heart stirreth up strife: but he that putteth his *t.* in the LORD shall be made fat; **29:25** the fear of man bringeth a snare: but whoso putteth his *t.* in the LORD shall be safe; **30:5** every word of God is pure: he is a shield unto them that put their *t.* in him; **Isa. 9:2-4** the people that walked in darkness have seen a great light: they that dwell in the land of the shadow of death, upon them hath the light shined... For thou hast broken the yoke of his burden, and the staff of his shoulder, the rod of his oppressor; **12:2** God is my salvation; I will *t.*, and not be afraid: for the LORD JEHOVAH is my strength and my song; he also is become my salvation; **14:32** the LORD hath founded Zion, and the poor of his people shall *t.* in it; **19:22** the LORD shall smite Egypt: he shall smite and heal it: and they shall return even to the LORD, and he shall be intreated of them, and shall heal them; **26:3-4** thou wilt keep him in perfect peace, whose mind is stayed on thee: because he *t.* in thee. *T.* ye in the LORD for ever: for in the LORD JEHOVAH is everlasting strength; **33:22** the LORD is our judge, the LORD is our lawgiver, the LORD is our king; he will save us; **36:4-7** we *t.* in the LORD o ur God: is it not he, whose high places and whose altars Hezekiah hath taken away, and said to Judah and to Jerusalem, Ye shall worship before this altar; **36:10** am I now come up without the LORD against this land to destroy it? the LORD said unto me, Go up against this land, and destroy it; **36:15-21** neither let Hezekiah make you *t.* in the LORD, saying, The LORD will surely deliver us: this city shall not be delivered into the hand of the king of Assyria; **41:10** fear thou not; for I am with thee: be not dismayed; for I am thy God: I will strengthen thee; yea, I will help thee; yea, I will uphold thee with the right hand of my righteousness; **41:13-14** I the LORD thy God will hold thy right hand, saying unto thee, Fear not; I will help thee. Fear not, thou worm Jacob, and ye men of Israel; I will help thee, saith the LORD; **45:3-5** I will give thee the treasures of darkness, and hidden riches of secret places, that thou mayest know that I, the LORD, which call thee by thy name, am the God of Israel; **45:14** surely God is in thee; and there is none else, there is no God; **46:4** even to your old age I am he; and even to hoar hairs will I carry you: I have made, and I will bear; even I will carry, and will deliver you; **49:7-10** thus saith the LORD, In an acceptable time have I heard thee, and in a day of salvation have I helped thee: and I will preserve thee, and give thee for a covenant of the people; **49:15-16** yet will I not forget thee. Behold, I have graven thee upon the palms of my hands; thy walls are continually before me; **49:18** as I live, saith the LORD, thou shalt surely clothe thee with them all, as with an ornament, and bind them on thee, as a bride doeth; **50:8-10** who is among you that feareth the LORD, that obeyeth the voice of his servant, that walketh in darkness, and hath no light? let him *t.* in the name of the LORD, and stay upon his God; **52:12** ye shall not go out with haste, nor go by flight: for the LORD will go before you; and the God of Israel will be your rereward; **55:11** so shall my word be that goeth forth out of my mouth: it shall not return unto me void, but it shall accomplish that which I please, and it shall prosper in the thing whereto I sent it; **57:13** when thou criest, let thy companies deliver thee; but the wind shall carry them all away; vanity shall take them: but he that putteth his *t.* in me shall possess the land; **57:18** I have seen his ways, and will heal him: I will lead him also, and restore comforts unto him and to his mourners; **59:19** so shall they fear the name of the LORD from the west, and his glory from

the rising of the sun. When the enemy shall come in like a flood, the Spirit of the LORD shall lift up a standard against him; **60:19** the LORD shall be unto thee an everlasting light, and thy God thy glory; **61:4-6** ye shall be named the Priests of the LORD: men shall call you the Ministers of our God: ye shall eat the riches of the Gentiles, and in their glory shall ye boast yourselves; **Jer. 1:18-19** they shall fight against thee; but they shall not prevail against thee; for I am with thee, saith the LORD, to deliver thee; **17:7-8** blessed is the man that *t.* in the LORD, and whose hope the LORD is; **20:11** the LORD is with me as a mighty terrible one: therefore my persecutors shall stumble, and they shall not prevail: they shall be greatly ashamed; for they shall not prosper; **31:18** thou hast chastised me, and I was chastised, as a bullock unaccustomed to the yoke: turn thou me, and I shall be turned; for thou art the LORD my God; **39:17-18** I will deliver thee in that day, saith the LORD: and thou shalt not be given into the hand of the men of whom thou art afraid. For I will surely deliver thee... because thou hast put thy *t.* in me; **46:27** fear not thou, O my servant Jacob, and be not dismayed, O Israel: for, behold, I will save thee from afar off, and thy seed from the land of their captivity; **Dan. 3:17** if it be so, our God whom we serve is able to deliver us from the burning fiery furnace, and he will deliver us out of thine hand, O king; **3:28** blessed be the God of Shadrach, Meshach, and Abed-nego, who hath sent his angel, and delivered his servants that *t.* in him, and have changed the kings word, and yielded their bodies; **6:16** the king commanded, and they brought Daniel, and cast him into the den of lions. Now the king spake and said unto Daniel, Thy God whom thou servest continually, he will deliver thee; **6:20** Daniel, servant of the living God, is thy God, whom thou servest continually, able to deliver thee from the lions; **6:23** Daniel was taken up out of the den, and no manner of hurt was found upon him, because he believed in his God; **Nahum 1:7** the LORD is good, a strong hold in the day of trouble; and he knoweth them that *t.* in him; **Zeph. 3:2** she obeyed not the voice; she received not correction; she *t.* not in the LORD; she drew not near to her God.

TRY (*see also* Experiment, Prove, Tempt)

Let us search and try our ways, and turn again to the Lord. Lam. 3:40 (*see also* Repent, Search, Turn, Way)

TURN (*see also* Change, Repent, Return)

Hear what God the LORD will speak: for he will speak peace unto his people, and to his saints: but let them not turn again to folly. Ps. 85:8 (*see also* Folly)

God forbid that we should rebel against the LORD, and turn this day from following the LORD. Josh 22:29 (*see also* Rebel)

When a righteous man turneth away from his right-eousness, and committeth iniquity, and dieth in them; for his iniquity that he hath done shall he die. Ezek. 18:26 (*see also* Death, Iniquity, Righteousness)

Turn ye again now every one from his evil way, and from the evil of your doings, and dwell in the land that the LORD hath given unto you and to your fathers for ever and ever. Jer. 25:5 (*see also* Evil, Way)

Turn not aside from following the LORD, but serve the LORD with all your heart. 1 Sam 12:20 (*see also* Follow, Serve)

I marvel that ye are so soon removed from him that called you into the grace of Christ unto another gospel. Gal. 1:6 (*see also* Gospel)

Set thee up waymarks, make thee high heaps: set thine heart toward the highway, even the way which thou wentest: turn again. Jer. 31:21 (*see also* Heart, Way)

Turn ye even to me with all your heart, and with fasting, and with weeping, and with mourning: And rend your heart, and not your garments, and turn unto the LORD your God: for he is gracious and merciful, slow to anger, and of great kindness, and repenteth him of the evil. Joel 2:12-13 (*see also* Heart)

Let us search and try our ways, and turn again to the Lord. Lam. 3:40 (*see also* Repent, Search, Try, Way)

Ye should turn from these vanities unto the living God, which made heaven, and earth, and the sea, and all things that are therein. Acts 14:15 (*see also* Vain)

Luke 1:16-17 many of the children of Israel shall he *t.* to the Lord their God; **Acts 11:21** the hand of the Lord was with them: and a great number believed, and *t.* unto the Lord; **14:15** ye

should *t.* from these vanities unto the living God, which made heaven, and earth, and the sea, and all things that are therein; **26:18-20** *t.* them from darkness to light, and from the power of Satan unto God, that they may receive forgiveness of sins, and inheritance among them which are sanctified by faith that is in me; **2 Cor. 3:16** when it shall *t.* to the Lord, the vail shall be taken away; **Philip. 1:19** I know that this shall *t.* to my salvation through your prayer, and the supply of the Spirit of Jesus Christ.

He shall turn the heart of the fathers to the children, and the heart of the children to their fathers, lest I come and smite the earth with a curse. Mal. 4:6 (*see also* Heart)

UNANIMOUS (*see* One, United, Voice)

UNBELIEF, UNBELIEVING (*see also* Doubt, Faithless, Fear, Hardhearted, Pride, Stiffnecked)

Then saith he to Thomas, Reach hither thy finger, and behold my hands; and reach hither thy hand, and thrust it into my side: and be not faithless, but believing. John 20:27 (*see also* Faithless)

He that overcometh shall inherit all things; and I will be his God, and he shall be my son. But the fearful, and unbelieving, and the abominable, and murderers, and whore-mongers, and sorcerers, and idolaters, and all liars, shall have their part in the lake which burneth with fire and brimstone: which is the second death. Rev. 21:7 (*see also* All Things, Death, Inherit, Second)

Matt. 13:28 he did not many mighty works there because of their *u.*; **21:32** John came unto you in the way of righteousness, and ye believed him not: but the publicans and the harlots believed him: and ye, when ye had seen it, repented not afterward, that ye might believe him; **Mark 9:24** and straightway the father of the child cried out, and said with tears, Lord, I believe; help thou mine *u.*; **16:14** afterward he appeared unto the eleven as they sat at meat, and upbraided them with their *u.* and hardness of heart, because they believed not them which had seen him after he was risen; **John 14:29** I have told you before it come to pass, that, when it is come to pass, ye might believe; **Rom. 11:23** if they abide not still in *u.*, shall be graffed in: for God is able to graff them in again; **11:30-31** as ye in times past have not believed God, yet have now obtained mercy through their *u.*: Even so have these also now not believed, that through your mercy they also may obtain mercy; **1 Cor. 7:13** the woman which hath an husband that believeth not, and if he be pleased to dwell with her, let her not leave him. For the *u.* husband is sanctified by the wife, and the *u.* wife is sanctified by the husband: else were your children unclean; but now are they holy. But if the *u.* depart, let him depart. A brother or a sister is not under bondage in such cases: but God hath called us to peace; **1 Tim. 1:12-15** I thank Christ Jesus our Lord, who hath enabled me, for that he counted me faithful, putting me into the ministry; Who was before a blasphemer, and a persecutor, and injurious: but I obtained mercy, because I did it ignorantly in *u..* And the grace of our Lord was exceeding abundant with faith and love which is in Christ Jesus; **Titus 1:15** unto the pure all things are pure: but unto them that are defiled and *u.* is nothing pure; but even their mind and conscience is defiled; **Heb. 3:12** take heed, brethren, lest there be in any of you an evil heart of *u.*, in departing from the living God; **Rev. 21:7** he that overcometh shall inherit all things; and I will be his God, and he shall be my son. But the fearful, and *u.*, and the abominable, and murderers, and whoremongers, and sorcerers, and idolaters, and all liars, shall have their part in the lake which burneth with fire and brimstone: which is the second death.

UNCIRCUMCISED (*see also* Circumcise)

Thus saith the Lord GOD; No stranger uncircumcised in heart, nor circumcised in flesh, shall enter into my sanctuary, of any strangers that is among the children of Israel. Ezek. 44:9 (*see also* Circumcise, Sanctuary)

UNCLEAN, UNCLEANESS, UNCLEANLINESS (*see also* Defile, Evil, Filthiness, Unworthy)

Paul, being grieved, turned and said to the spirit, I command thee in the name of Jesus Christ to come out of her. And he came out the same hour. Acts 16:18 (*see also* Authority)

He set the porters at the gates of the house of the LORD, that none which was unclean in any thing should enter in. 2 Chron. 23:19 (*see also* House)

Who being past feeling have given themselves over unto lasciviousness, to work all uncleanness with greediness? Eph. 4:19 (*see also* Lascivious)

Depart ye, depart ye, go ye out from thence, touch no unclean *thing*; go ye out of the midst of her; be ye clean, that bear the vessels of the LORD. Isa. 52:11 (*see also* Clean, Vessels)

Teach my people the difference between the holy and profane, and cause them to discern between the unclean and the clean. Ezek. 44:23 (*see also* Clean, Holy, Teach)

Come out from among them, and be ye separate, saith the Lord, and touch not the unclean thing; and I will receive you, And will be a Father unto you, and ye shall be my sons and daughters. 2 Cor. 6:17 (*see also* Father)

2 Cor 6:17-18 come out from among them, and be ye separate, saith the Lord, and touch not the *u.* thing; and I will receive you, And will be a Father unto you, and ye shall be my sons and daughters; **Eph. 5:3** but fornication, and all *u.*, or covetousness, let it not be once named among you, as becometh saints.

UNDEFILED (*see also* Clean, Pure)

Marriage is honourable in all, and the bed undefiled: but whoremongers and adulterers God will judge. Heb. 13:4 (*see also* Marriage)

UNDERSTAND, UNDERSTANDING (*see also* Discern, Know, Learn, Scripture, Study, Search, Truth, Wisdom)

Give me understanding, and I shall keep thy law; yea, I shall observe it with my whole heart. Ps. 119:34 (*see also* Law)

He that received seed into the good ground is he that heareth the word, and understandeth it; which also beareth fruit, and bringeth forth, some an hundredfold, some sixty, some thirty. Matt. 13:23 (*see also* Hear)

Incline thine ear unto wisdom, and apply thine heart to understanding. Prov. 2:2 (*see also* Apply, Wisdom)

Be ye of an understanding heart. Prov. 8:5 (*see also* Heart)

Trust in the LORD with all thine heart; and lean not unto thine own understanding. Prov. 3:5 (*see also* Heart, Trust)

Forsake the foolish, and live; and go in the way of understanding. Prov. 9:6 (*see also* Fool, Way)

A man of understanding holdeth his peace. Prov. 11:12 (*see also* Peace)

The man that wandereth out of the way of understanding shall remain in the congregation of the dead. Prov. 21:16 (*see also* Way)

Buy the truth, and sell it not; also wisdom, and instruction, and understanding. Prov. 23:23 (*see also* Instruct, True, Wisdom)

Through wisdom is an house builded; and by understanding it is established: And by knowledge shall the chambers be filled with all precious and pleasant riches. Prov. 24:3-4 (*see also* House, Wisdom)

Evil men understand not judgment: but they that seek the LORD understand all things. Prov. 28:5 (*see also* All Things, Seek)

I have filled him with the spirit of God, in wisdom, in understanding, and in knowledge, and in all manner of workmanship. Ex. 31:3 (*see also* Know, Wisdom)

For precept must be upon precept, precept upon precept; line upon line, line upon line; here a little, and there a little: For with stammering lips and another tongue will he speak to this people. Isa. 28:10 (*see also* Know, Learn, Precept)

From the first day that thou didst set thine heart to understand, and to chasten thyself before thy God, thy words were heard, and I am come for thy words. Dan. 10:12 (*see also* Chasten)

He sought God in the days of Zechariah, who had understanding in the visions of God: and as long as he sought the LORD, God made him to prosper. 2 Chron. 26:5 (*see also* Vision)

2 Chron. 26:5 he sought God in the days of Zechariah, who had *u.* in the visions of God: and as long as he sought the LORD, God made him to prosper; Ps. 119:27 make me to *u.* the way of thy precepts: so shall I talk of thy wondrous works; Prov. 3:13 happy is the man that findeth wisdom, and the man that getteth *u.*

Be ye not as the horse, or as the mule, which have no understanding: whose mouth must be held in with bit and bridle, lest they come near unto thee. Ps. 32:9 (*see also* Be)

Ps. 32:9 be ye not as the horse, or as the mule, which have no *u.*: whose mouth must be held in with bit and bridle, lest they come near unto thee; 82:5 they know not, neither will they understand; they walk on in darkness.

UNITE, UNITED, UNITY (*see also* Fellowship, Likeminded, Love, One)

Be of one mind. 2 Cor. 13:11 (*see also* One)

And he gave some, apostles; and some, prophets; and some, evangelists; and some, pastors and teachers; For the perfecting of the saints, for the work of the ministry, for the edifying of the body of Christ: Till we all come in the unity of the faith, and of the knowledge of the Son of God, unto a perfect man, unto the measure of the stature of the fulness of Christ. Eph. 4:11-13 (*see also* Apostle, Perfection, Prophet)

Be likeminded one toward another according to Christ Jesus: That ye may with one mind and one mouth glorify God, even the Father of our Lord Jesus Christ. Rom. 15:5-6 (*see also* Jesus Christ, Likeminded, One)

How good and how pleasant it is for brethren to dwell together in unity! Ps. 133:1 (*see also* Dwell)

UNRIGHTEOUS, UNRIGTEOUSNESS (*see also* Evil, Unrighteous Dominion, Wickedness)

WOE unto them that decree unrighteous decrees, and that write grievousness which they have prescribed. Isa. 10:1 (*see also* Decree)

Know ye not that the unrighteous shall not inherit the kingdom of God? Be not deceived: neither fornicators, nor idolaters, nor adulterers, nor effeminate, nor abusers of themselves with mankind, Nor thieves, nor covetous, nor drunkards, nor revilers, nor extortioners, shall inherit the kingdom of God. 1 Cor. 6:9-10 (*see also* Extort, Inherit)

God shall send them strong delusion, that they should believe a lie: That they all might be damned who believed not the truth, but had pleasure in unrighteousness. 2 Thes. 2:11-12 (*see also* Lie, Pleasure)

UNSTEADY (*see also* Double Minded)

A double minded man is unstable in all his ways. James 1:8 (*see also* Double Minded, Mind, Way)

UNRULY (*see also* Contend, Rebellious)

We command you, brethren, in the name of our Lord Jesus Christ, that ye withdraw yourselves from every brother that walketh disorderly, and not after the tradition which he received of us. 2Thes 3:6 (*see also* Jesus Christ)

1 Thes 5:14 warn them that are *u.*, comfort the feebleminded, support the weak, be patient toward all men; 2 Thes. 3:6 we command you, brethren, in the name of our Lord Jesus Christ, that ye withdraw yourselves from every brother that walketh disorderly, and not after the tradition which he received of us.

UNWORTHINESS, UNWORTHILY, UNWORTHY (*see also* Good, Honest, Integrity, Righteous)

It was necessary that the word of God should first have been spoken to you: but seeing ye put it from you, and judge yourselves unworthy of everlasting life, lo, we turn to the Gentiles. Acts 13:46 (*see also* Word)

Whosoever shall eat this bread, and drink this cup of the Lord, unworthily, shall be guilty of the body and blood of the Lord. But let a man examine himself, and so let him eat of that bread, and drink of that cup. For he that eateth and drinketh unworthily, eateth and drinketh damnation to himself, not discerning the Lord's body. 1 Cor. 11:27-29 (*see also* Examine, Sacrament, Worthy)

UPRIGHT, UPRIGHTLY, UPRIGHTNESS (*see also* Good, Honest, Integrity, Righteous)

He that walketh righteously, and speaketh uprightly; he that despiseth the gain of oppressions, that shaketh his hands from holding of bribes, that stoppeth his ears from hearing of blood, and shutteth his eyes from seeing evil; He shall dwell on high: his defence shall be the munitions of rocks: bread shall be given him; his waters shall be sure. Isa. 33:15-16 (*see also* Gain, Hear, Oppress, Righteous, See, Speak, Walk)

USE (*see also* Act, Diligence, Do, Exercise, Labor, Works)

But we know that the law is good, if a man use it lawfully. 1 Tim 1:8 (*see also* Law)

UTTER, UTTERANCE (*see also* Cry, Declare, Speak, Talk)

The vile person will speak villany, and his heart will work iniquity, to practise hypocrisy, and to utter error against the LORD, to make empty the soul of the hungry. Isa. 32:6 (*see also* Error)

VAIN, VANITY (*see also* Arrogance, Foolish, Haughty, Highminded, Pride)

Thou shalt not take the name of the LORD thy God in vain; for the LORD will not hold him guiltless that taketh his name in vain. Ex. 20:7 (*see also* Name, Thou Shalt Not)

I have not sat with vain persons, neither will I go in with dissemblers. I have hated the congregation of evil doers; and will not sit with the wicked. Ps. 26:4-5 (*see also* Evil)

Let no man beguile you of your reward in a voluntary humility and worshiping of angels, intruding into those things which he hath not seen, vainly puffed up by his fleshly mind. Col. 2:18 (*see also* Angel, Beguile)

Woe unto them that draw iniquity with cords of vanity, and sin as it were with a cart rope. Isa. 5:18 (*see also* Iniquity, Sin)

How long shall thy vain thoughts lodge within thee? Jer. 4:14 (*see also* Thought)

Ye should turn from these vanities unto the living God, which made heaven, and earth, and the sea, and all things that are therein. Acts 14:15 (*see also* Turn)

He that tilleth his land shall have plenty of bread: but he that followeth after vain persons shall have poverty enough. Prov. 28:19 (*see also* Labor)

He that loveth silver shall not be satisfied with silver; nor he that loveth abundance with increase: this is also vanity. Eccl. 5:10 (*see also* Love, Silver)

Turn away mine eyes from beholding vanity; and quicken thou me in thy way. Ps. 119:37 (*see also* Way)

None calleth for justice, nor any pleadeth for truth: they trust in vanity, and speak lies; they conceive mischief, and bring forth iniquity. Isa. 59:4 (*see also* Trust)

Isa. 59:4 none calleth for justice, nor any pleadeth for truth: they trust in *v.*, and speak lies; they conceive mischief, and bring forth iniquity; Jer. 51:18 they are *v.*, the work of errors: in the time of their visitation they shall perish.

They made Israel to sin, in provoking the LORD God of Israel to anger with their vanities. 1 Kgs. 16:13 (*see also* Provoke)

1 Kgs. 16:13 they sinned, and... they made Israel to sin, in provoking the LORD God of Israel to anger with their *v.*; 16:26 he walked in all the way of Jeroboam the son of Nebat, and in his sin wherewith he made Israel to sin, to provoking the LORD God of Israel to anger with their *v.*; 2 Kgs. 17:15 they rejected his statutes, and his covenant that he made with their fathers, and his testimonies which he testified against them; and they followed *v.*, and became vain; Job 31:5 if I have walked with *v.*, or if my foot hath hasted to deceit; 35:13 God will not hear *v.*, neither will the Almighty regard it; Ps. 4:2 ye sons of men, how long will ye turn my glory into shame? how long will ye love *v.*, and seek after leasing; 12:2 they speak *v.* every one with his neighbour: with flattering lips and with a double heart do they speak; 24:4 he that hath clean hands, and a pure heart; who hath not lifted up his soul unto *v.*, nor sworn deceitfully; 31:6 I have hated them that

regard lying *v.*: but I trust in the LORD; 144:8 whose mouth speaketh *v.*, and their right hand is a right hand of falsehood; 144:11 rid me, and deliver me from the hand of strange children, whose mouth speaketh *v.*, and their right hand is a right hand of falsehood; Haba 2:13 is it not of the LORD of hosts that the people shall labour in the very fire, and the people shall weary themselves for very *v.*.

VALIANT (*see also* Courage)

They are not valiant for the truth upon the earth, for they proceed from evil to evil, and they know not me, saith the LORD. Jer. 9:3 (*see also* Evil, True)

VENGEANCE (*see also* Punish, Revenge)

Declare in Zion the vengeance of the LORD our God, the vengeance of His temple. Jer. 50:28 (*see also* Declare, Zion)

VESSELS

Depart ye, depart ye, go ye out from thence, touch no unclean *thing*; go ye out of the midst of her; be ye clean, that bear the vessels of the LORD. Isa. 52:11 (*see also* Clean, Unclean)

VIGILANT (*see also* Diligence)

Be sober, be vigilant; because your adversary the devil, as a roaring lion, walketh about, seeking whom he may devour: 1 Pet. 5:8 (*see also* Adversary, Sober)

A bishop then must be blameless, the husband of one wife, vigilant, sober, of good behaviour, given to hospitality, apt to teach. 1 Tim. 3:2 (*see also* Bishop, Wife)

VINE, VINEYARD (*see also* Genealogy, Inheritance, Israel)

I am the vine, yea are the branches: He that abideth in me, and I in him, the same bringeth forth much fruit: for without me ye can do nothing. John 15:5 (*see also* Abide, Do, Fruit, Nothing)

VIOLENT, VIOLENCE (*see also* Contend, Kill, Murder, Persecute, Strike)

A violent man enticeth his neighbour, and leadeth him into the way that is not good. Prov. 16:29 (*see also* Way)

His mischief shall return upon his own head, and his violent dealing shall come down upon his own pate. Ps. 7:16 (*see also* Head, Mischief, Return)

Do violence to no man, neither accuse any falsely; and be content with your wages. Luke 3:14 (*see also* Accuse)

Luke 3:14 the soldiers likewise demanded of him, saying, And what shall we do? And he said unto them, Do *v.* to no man, neither accuse any falsely; and be content with your wages; **Acts 21:35** when he came upon the stairs, so it was, that he was borne of the soldiers for the *v.* of the people.

A man that doeth violence to the blood of any person shall flee to the pit. Prov. 28:17 (*see also* Blood, Kill)

Prov. 16:29 a *v.* man enticeth his neighbour, and leadeth him into the way that is not good; **28:17** a man that doeth *v.* to the blood of any person shall flee to the pit; **Isa. 59:6** neither shall they cover themselves with their works: their works are works of iniquity, and the act of *v.* is in their hands; **Jer. 22:17** thine eyes and thine heart are not but for thy covetousness, and for to shed innocent blood, and for oppression, and for *v.*, to do it; **Ezek. 8:17** is it a light thing... that they commit the abominations which they commit here? for they have filled the land with *v.*, and have returned to provoke me to anger; **18:7** hath not oppressed any, but hath restored to the debtor his pledge, hath spoiled none by *v.*, hath given his bread to the hungry, and hath covered the naked with a garment; **28:16** By the multitude of thy merchandise they have filled the midst of thee with *v.*, and thou hast sinned: therefore I will cast thee as profane out of the mountain of God: and I will destroy thee; **45:9** thus saith the Lord GOD; Let it suffice you, O princes of Israel: remove *v.* and spoil, and execute judgment and justice, take away your exactions from my people; **Amos 3:10** they know not to do right, saith the LORD, who store up *v.* and robbery in their palaces; **6:3** ye that put far away the evil day, and cause the seat of *v.* to come near; **Obad. 1:10** thy *v.* against thy brother Jacob shame shall cover thee, and thou shalt be cut off for ever; **Jonah 3:8** let them turn every one from his evil way, and from the *v.* that is in their hands; **Micah 2:1-2** woe to them that devise iniquity, and work evil upon their beds! when the morning is light, they practise it, because it is in the power of their hand. And they covet fields, and take

them by *v.*; **6:12** the rich men thereof are full of *v.*, and the inhabitants thereof have spoken lies, and their tongue is deceitful in their mouth; **Zeph. 1:9** in the same day also will I punish all those that leap on the threshold, which fill their masters houses with *v.* and deceit.

VIRTUE, VIRTUOUS (*see also* Chastity, Clean, Good, Holiness, Modesty, Pure, Sacred)

A virtuous woman is a crown to her husband: but she that maketh ashamed is as rottenness in his bones. Prov. 12:4 (*see also* Wife)

Who can find a virtuous woman? for her price is far above rubies. The heart of her husband doth safely trust in her, so that he shall have no need of spoil. She will do him good and not evil all the days of her life. Prov. 31:10-12 (*see also* Wife)

Prov. 31:10-12 (*see also* verses 13-31) who can find a *v.* woman? for her price is far above rubies. The heart of her husband doth safely trust in her, so that he shall have no need of spoil. She will do him good and not evil all the days of her life.

VISION, VISONARY (*see also* Dream, Holy Ghost, Know, Prophecy, Revelation, See)

Where there is no vision, the people perish: but he that keepeth the law, happy is he. Prov. 29:18 (*see also* Law, Perish)

There shall be no more any vain vision nor flattering divination within the house of Israel. Ezek. 12:24 (*see also* Divination, Israel)

He sought God in the days of Zechariah, who had understanding in the visions of God: and as long as he sought the LORD, God made him to prosper. 2 Chron. 26:5 (*see also* Understanding)

I will pour out my spirit upon all flesh; and your sons and your daughters shall prophesy, your old men shall dream dreams, your young men shall see visions. Joel 2:28 (*see also* Dream, Reveal)

Write the vision, and make it plain upon tables, that he may run that readeth it. For the vision is yet for an appointed time. Haba 2:2-3 (*see also* Time, Write)

Gen. 15:1 the word of the LORD came unto Abram in a *v.*; **Num. 12:6** if there be a prophet among you, I the LORD will make myself known unto him in a *v.*, and will speak unto him in a dream; **24:4** he... saw the *v.* of the Almighty, falling into a trance, but having his eyes open; **24:16** he... saw the *v.* of the Almighty, falling into a trance, but having his eyes open; **Isa. 1:1** the *v.* of Isaiah the son of Amoz, which he saw; **Ezek. 11:24** the spirit took me up, and brought me in a *v.* by the Spirit of God; **Dan. 2:19** the secret [was] revealed unto Daniel in a night *v.*; **7:2** Daniel spake and said, I saw in my *v.* by night; **8:1-2** a *v.* appeared unto me, even unto me Daniel, after that which appeared unto me at the first; **8:13-17** I, even I Daniel, had seen the *v.*, and sought for the meaning; **9:21-24** whiles I was speaking in prayer, even the man Gabriel, whom I had seen in the *v.* at the beginning, being caused to fly swiftly, touched me about the time of the evening oblation; **10:7-8** I Daniel alone saw the *v.*: for the men that were with me saw not the *v.*... I was left alone, and saw this great *v.*, and there remained no strength in me; **Haba 2:2-3** write the *v.*, and make it plain upon tables, that he may run that readeth it. For the *v.* is yet for an appointed time.

When he came out, he could not speak unto them: and they perceived that he had seen a vision in the temple: for he beckoned unto them, and remained speechless. Luke 1:22 (*see also* Temple)

Matt. 17:9 as they came down from the mountain, Jesus charged them, saying, Tell the *v.* to no man, until the Son of man be risen again from the dead; **Luke 1:22** when he came out, he could not speak unto them: and they perceived that he had seen a *v.* in the temple: for he beckoned unto them, and remained speechless; **24:23** when they found not his body, they came, saying, that they had also seen a *v.* of angels, which said that he was alive; **Acts 10:3** he saw in a *v.* evidently about the ninth hour of the day an angel of God coming in to him, and saying unto him, Cornelius; **10:10-11** he fell into a trance, And saw heaven opened, and a certain vessel descending unto him, as it had been a great sheet knit at the four corners, and let down to the earth; **10:19** while Peter thought on the *v.*, the Spirit said unto him, Behold, three men seek thee; **11:5** I was in the city of Joppa praying: and in a trance I saw a *v.*, A certain vessel descend, as it had been a great sheet, let down from heaven by four corners; and it came even to me; **16:10** after he had seen the *v.*, immediately we endeavoured to

go into Macedonia, assuredly gathering that the Lord had called us for to preach the gospel unto them; **18:9** then spake the Lord to Paul in the night by a *v.*, Be not afraid, but speak, and hold not thy peace; **22:17-18** when I was come again to Jerusalem, even while I prayed in the temple, I was in a trance; And saw him saying unto me, Make haste, and get thee quickly out of Jerusalem: for they will not receive thy testimony concerning me; **26:19** whereupon, O king Agrippa, I was not disobedient unto the heavenly *v.*; **Rev. 9:17** thus I saw the horses in the *v.*, and them that sat on them, having breastplates of fire.

VOCATION (*see also* Labor, Work)

Walk worthy of the vocation wherewith ye are called. Eph. 4:1 (*see also* Call)

Eph 4:1 I therefore, the prisoner of the Lord, beseech you that ye walk worthy of the *v.* wherewith ye are called; **Col. 4:17** take heed to the ministry which thou hast received in the Lord, that thou fulfil it.

VOICE (*see also* Lips, Mouth, Speak)

Obey, I beseech thee, the voice of the LORD, which I speak unto thee: so it shall be well unto thee, and thy soul shall live. Jer. 38:20 (*see also* Obey, Speak)

His head and his hairs were white like wool, as white as snow; and his eyes were as a flame of fire; And his feet like unto fine brass, as if they burned in a furnace; and his voice as the sound of many waters. Rev. 1:15 (*see also* Brass, Jesus Christ)

Cry aloud, spare not, lift up thy voice like a trumpet, and shew my people their transgression, and the house of Jacob their sins. Isa. 58:1 (*see also* Cry, Sin)

My sheep hear my voice, and I know them, and they follow me; And I give unto them eternal life; and they shall never perish, neither shall any man pluck them our of my hand. John 10:27 (*see also* Eternal Life, Sheep)

[Obey] the voice of the Lord our God, to walk in his laws, which he set before us by his servants the prophets. Dan. 9:10 (*see also* Law, Prophet)

VOMIT

If after they have escaped the pollutions of the world through the knowledge of the Lord and Savior Jesus Christ, they are again entangled therein, and overcome, the latter end is worse with them than the beginning. For it had been better for them not to have known the way of righteousness, than, after they have known it, to turn from the holy commandment delivered unto them. But it is happened unto them according to the true proverb, The dog is turned to his own vomit again; and the sow that was washed to her wallowing in the mire. 2 Pet. 2:20-22 (*see also* Entangle, Way)

VOW (*see also* Covenant, Oath, Pledge, Promise, Swear)

When thou shalt vow a vow unto the LORD thy God, thou shalt not slack to pay it: for the LORD thy God will surely require it of thee; and it would be sin in thee. Deut. 23:21 (*see also* Pay, Sin)

When thou vowest a vow unto God, defer not to pay it; for he hath no pleasure in fools: pay that which thou hast vowed. Eccl. 5:4 (*see also* Defer, Pay)

Keep thy solemn feasts, perform thy vows. Nahum 1:15 (*see also* Feast, Keep)

That which is gone out of thy lips thou shalt keep and perform; even a freewill offering, according as thou has vowed unto the LORD thy God, which thou hast promised with thy mouth. Deut. 23:23 (*see also* Promise)

Gen. 28:20 Jacob vowed a *v.*, saying, If God will be with me, and will keep me in this way that I go; **31:13** I am the God of Beth-el, where thou anointedst the pillar, and where thou *v.*st a *v.* unto me: now arise, get thee out from this land; **Lev. 22:18-23** whosoever offereth a sacrifice of peace offerings unto the LORD to accomplish his *v.*, or a freewill offering in beeves or sheep, it shall be perfect to be accepted; **23:38** beside the sabbaths of the LORD, and beside your gifts, and beside all your *v.*, and beside all your freewill offerings, which ye give unto the LORD; **Num. 15:3** will make an offering by fire unto the LORD, a burnt offering, or a sacrifice in performing a *v.*, or in a freewill offering, or in your solemn feasts, to make a sweet savour unto the LORD; **29:39** these things ye shall do unto the LORD in your set feasts, beside your *v.*, and your

freewill offerings, for your burnt offerings; **30:2-14** if a man *v.* a *v.* unto the LORD, or swear an oath to bind his soul with a bond; he shall not break his word, he shall do according to all that proceedeth out of his mouth; **Deut. 4:13** he declared unto you his covenant, which he commanded you to perform, even ten commandments; and he wrote them upon two tables of stone; **12:6** thither ye shall bring your burnt offerings, and your sacrifices, and your tithes, and heave offerings of your hand, and your *v.*, and your freewill offerings; **12:11** thither shall ye bring all that I command you; your burnt offerings, and your sacrifices, your tithes, and the heave offering of your hand, and all your choice *v.* which ye *v.* unto the LORD; **12:17** thou mayest not eat within thy gates the tithe of thy corn, or of thy wine, or of thy oil, or the firstlings of thy herds or of thy flock, nor any of thy *v.* which thou *v.*est, nor thy freewill offerings; **12:26** only thy holy things which thou hast, and thy *v.*, thou shalt take, and go unto the place which the LORD shall choose; **16:10** thou shalt keep the feast of weeks unto the LORD thy God with a tribute of a freewill offering of thine hand, which thou shalt give unto the LORD thy God; **23:21-23** when thou shalt *v.* a *v.* unto the LORD thy God, thou shalt not slack to pay it: for the LORD thy God will surely require it of thee; and it would be sin in thee; **Judg. 11:30-31** Jephthah *v.* a *v.* unto the LORD, and said, If thou shalt without fail deliver the children of Ammon into mine hands, Then it shall be, that whatsoever cometh forth of the doors of my house to meet me, when I return in peace from the children of Ammon, shall surely be the LORD s; **1 Sam. 1:11** she *v.* a *v.*, and said, O LORD of hosts, if thou wilt indeed look on the affliction of thine handmaid, and remember me, and not forget thine handmaid, but wilt give unto thine handmaid a man child, then I will give him unto the LORD all the days of his life; **1:22** Hannah went not up; for she said unto her husband, I will not go up until the child be weaned, and then I will bring him, that he may appear before the LORD; **1:25-28** for this child I prayed; and the LORD hath given me my petition which I asked of him: Therefore also I have lent him to the LORD; as long as he liveth he shall be lent to the LORD; **2 Sam. 15:7-9** Absalom said unto the king, I pray thee, let me go and pay my *v.*, which I have *v.* unto the LORD; **2 Chron. 34:31** the king stood in his place, and made a covenant before the LORD, to walk after the LORD, and to keep his commandments; **Ezra 1:4** whosoever remaineth in any place where he sojourneth, let the men of his place help him with silver, and with gold, and with goods, and with beasts, beside the freewill offering for the house of God; **3:5** afterward offered the continual burnt offering, both of the new moons, and of all the set feasts of the LORD that were consecrated, and of every one that willingly offered a freewill offering unto the LORD; **7:16** all the silver and gold that thou canst find in all the province of Babylon, with the freewill offering of the people, and of the priests, offering willingly for the house of their God which is in Jerusalem; **8:28** ye are holy unto the LORD; the vessels are holy also; and the silver and the gold are a freewill offering unto the LORD God of your fathers; **Job 22:27** thou shalt make thy prayer unto him, and he shall hear thee, and thou shalt pay thy *v.*; **Ps. 22:25** my praise shall be of thee in the great congregation: I will pay my *v.* before them that fear him; **50:14** offer unto God thanksgiving; and pay thy *v.* unto the most High; **56:12** thy *v.* are upon me, O God: I will render praises unto thee; **61:5** thou, O God, hast heard my *v.*: thou hast given me the heritage of those that fear thy name; **61:8** so will I sing praise unto thy name for ever, that I may daily perform my *v.*; **65:1** praise waiteth for thee, O God, in Sion: and unto thee shall the *v.* be performed; **66:13-14** I will go into thy house with burnt offerings: I will pay thee my *v.*, Which my lips have uttered, and my mouth hath spoken, when I was in trouble; **76:11** *v.*, and pay unto the LORD your God: let all that be round about him bring presents unto him that ought to be feared; **116:14** I will pay my *v.* unto the LORD now in the presence of all his people; **116:18-19** I will pay my *v.* unto the LORD now in the presence of all his people; **132:1-5** LORD, remember David, and all his afflictions: How he sware unto the LORD, and *v.* unto the mighty God of Jacob; **Prov. 7:14** I have peace offerings with me; this day have I payed my *v.*; **Eccl. 5:4-5** when thou *v.*est a *v.* unto God, defer not to pay it; for he hath no pleasure in fools: pay that which thou hast *v.*; **Isa. 19:21** they shall *v.* a *v.* unto the LORD, and perform it; **Jer. 44:25** we will surely perform our *v.* that we have *v.*; **Jonah 1:16** the men feared the LORD exceedingly, and offered a sacrifice unto the LORD, and made *v.*; **2:9** I will sacrifice unto thee with the voice of thanksgiving; I will pay that that I have *v.*; **Nahum 1:15** keep thy solemn feasts, perform thy *v.*: for the wicked shall no more pass through thee; he is utterly cut off.

WAGE, WAGES (*see also* Blessing, Money, Payment, Recompense, Reward)

Woe unto him that buildeth his house in unrighteousness, and his chambers by wrong; that useth his neighbour's service without wages, and giveth him not for his work. Jer. 22:13 (*see also* House, Serve, Work)

Be content with your wages. Luke 3:14

Luke 3:14 do violence to no man, neither accuse any falsely; and be content with your *w.*; **Philip. 4:11** not that I speak in respect of want: for I have learned, in whatsoever state I am, therewith to be content.

WAIT

They that wait upon the Lord shall renew their strength; they shall mount up with wings as eagles; they shall run, and not be weary; and they shall walk, and not faint. Isa. 40:31 (*see also* Renew, Strength)

Rest in the LORD, and wait patiently for Him. Ps. 37:7 (*see also* Rest)

Wait on the LORD: be of good courage, and he shall strengthen thine heart: wait, I say, on the LORD. Ps. 27:14 (*see also* Faint)

Ps. 27:13-14 I had fainted, unless I had believed to see the goodness of the LORD in the land of the living. *W.* on the LORD: be of good courage, and he shall strengthen thine heart: *w.*, I say, on the LORD; **40:12** innumerable evils have compassed me about: mine iniquities have taken hold upon me, so that I am not able to look up; they are more than the hairs of mine head: therefore my heart faileth me.

Wait on the LORD, and keep his way and he shall exalt thee to inherit the land. Ps. 37:34 (*see also* Keep)

Ps. 25:5 lead me in thy truth, and teach me: for thou art the God of my salvation; on thee do I wait all the day; **25:21** let integrity and uprightness preserve me; for I *w.* on thee; **33:20** our soul *w.* for the LORD: he is our help and our shield; **37:9** evildoers shall be cut off: but those that *w.* upon the LORD, they shall inherit the earth; **37:34** *w.* on the LORD, and keep his way, and he shall exalt thee to inherit the land: when the wicked are cut off, thou shalt see it; **40:1-2** I *w.* patiently for the LORD; and he inclined unto me, and heard my cry; **59:9-10** because of his strength will I *w.* upon thee: for God is my defence; **62:1** my soul *w.* upon God: from him cometh my salvation; **62:5-7** my soul, *w.* thou only upon God; for my expectation is from him. He only is my rock and my salvation: he is my defence; I shall not be moved; **69:1-5** I am weary of my crying: my throat is dried: mine eyes fail while I *w.* for my God; **106:13** they soon forgat his works; they *w.* not for his counsel; **130:6** my soul *w.* for the Lord more than they that watch for the morning; **145:15** the eyes of all *w.* upon thee; and thou givest them their meat in due season; **Prov. 8:34-35** blessed is the man that heareth me, watching daily at my gates, *w.* at the posts of my doors. For whoso findeth me findeth life, and shall obtain favour of the LORD; **20:22** say not thou, I will recompense evil; but *w.* on the LORD, and he shall save thee; **27:18** he that *w.* on his master shall be honoured; **Isa. 8:17** I will *w.* upon the LORD, that hideth his face from the house of Jacob, and I will look for him; **26:8** in the way of thy judgments, O LORD, have we *w.* for thee; the desire of our soul is to thy name, and to the remembrance of thee; **30:18** the LORD is a God of judgment: blessed are all they that *w.* for him; **30:20-23** though the Lord give you the bread of adversity, and the water of affliction, yet shall not thy teachers be removed into a corner any more, but thine eyes shall see thy teachers: And thine ears shall hear a word behind thee, saying, This is the way, walk ye in it; **33:2** O LORD, be gracious unto us; we have *w.* for thee: be thou their arm every morning, our salvation also in the time of trouble; **40:29-31** they that *w.* upon the LORD shall renew their strength; they shall mount up with wings as eagles; they shall run, and not be weary; and they shall walk, and not faint; **49:23** they shall bow down to thee with their face toward the earth, and lick up the dust of thy feet; and thou shalt know that I am the LORD: for they shall not be ashamed that *w.* for me; **51:5** my righteousness is near; my salvation is gone forth, and mine arms shall judge the people; the isles shall *w.* upon me, and on mine arm shall they trust; **Lam. 3:25-26** the LORD is good unto them that *w.* for him, to the soul that seeketh him. It is good that a man should both hope and quietly *w.* for the salvation of the LORD; **Hosea 12:6** turn thou to thy God: keep mercy and judgment, and *w.* on thy God continually; **Zeph. 3:8** *w.* ye upon me, saith the LORD, until the day that I rise up to the

prey: for my determination is to gather the nations; **Zech. 11:11** the poor of the flock that *w.* upon me knew that it was the word of the LORD.

WALK (*see also* Behave, Follow, Live, Path, Way)

Let us walk honestly, as in the day; not in rioting and drunkenness, not in chambering and wantonness, not in strife and envying. Rom. 13:13 (*see also* Honest)

Walk in wisdom toward them that are without, redeeming the time. Col. 4:5 (*see also* Time, Wisdom)

Ye shall walk in all the ways which the LORD your God hath commanded you, that ye may live, and that ye may prolong your days in the land which ye shall posses. Deut. 5:33 (*see also* Day, Prolong, Way)

Walk worthy of the Lord unto all pleasing, being fruitful in every good work, and increasing in the knowledge of God. Col. 1:10 (*see also* Know, Worthy)

Rejoice, O young man in thy youth; and let thy heart cheer thee in the days of thy youth, and walk in the ways of thine heart, and in the sight of thine eyes. Eccl. 11:9 (*see also* Rejoice, Youth)

Walk not after the flesh, but after the Spirit. Rom. 8:4 (*see also* Flesh)

Ye were sometimes darkness, but now are ye light in the Lord: walk as children of light. Eph. 5:8 (*see also* Light)

I am the Almighty God; walk before me, and be thou perfect. Gen. 17:1 (*see also* Perfect)

Blessed is the man that walketh not in the counsel of the ungodly, nor standeth in the way of sinners, nor sitteth in the seat of the scornful. Ps. 1:1 (*see also* Scorn)

The just man walketh in his integrity: his children are blessed after him. Prov. 20:7 (*see also* Integrity)

Thus saith the LORD, Stand ye in the ways, and see, and ask for the old paths, where is the good way, and walk therein, and ye shall find rest for your souls. Jer. 6:16 (*see also* Stand, Way)

Come ye, and let us walk in the light of the LORD. Isa. 2:5 (*see also* Light)

Discretion shall preserve thee, understanding shall keep thee; to deliver thee from the way of the evil man, from the man that speaketh froward things; who leave the paths of righteousness, to walk in the ways of darkness. Prov. 2:11-13 (*see also* Dark, Leave, Righteous, Way)

There is a way which seemeth right unto a man, but the end thereof are the ways of death. Prov. 14:12 (*see also* Way)

He that walketh righteously, and speaketh uprightly; he that despiseth the gain of oppressions, that shaketh his hands from holding of bribes, that stoppeth his ears from hearing of blood, and shutteth his eyes from seeing evil; He shall dwell on high: his defence shall be the munitions of rocks: bread shall be given him; his waters shall be sure. Isa. 33:15-16 (*see also* Gain, Hear, Oppress, Righteous, See, Speak, Uprightly)

Walk in the ways of good men, and keep the paths of the righteous. Prov. 2:20 (*see also* Good, Way)

Neither shall they walk any more after the imagination of their evil heart. Jer. 3:17 (*see also* Heart, Imagine)

They said, There is no hope: but we will walk after our own devises, and we will every one do the imagination of his evil heart. Jer. 18:12 (*see also* Device, Imagine)

As for them whose heart walketh after the heart of their detestable things and their abominations, I will recompense their way upon their own heads, saith the Lord GOD. Ezek. 11:21 (*see also* Heart)

Walk in the name of the LORD our God for ever and ever. Micah 4:5 (*see also* Name)

He that walketh with wise men shall be wise: but a companion of fools shall be destroyed. Prov. 13:20 (*see also* Fool, Wise)

My people have changed their glory for that which doth not profit. Jer. 2:8 (*see also* Glory, Profit)

Jer. 2:8 the priests said not, Where is the LORD? and they that handle the law knew me not: the pastors also transgressed against me, and the prophets prophesied by Baal, and *w.* after things that do not profit; 2:11 hath a nation changed their gods, which are yet no gods? but my people have changed their glory for that which doth not profit.

He that saith he abideth in him ought himself also so to walk, even as he walked. 1 Jn. 2:6 (*see also* Example)

John 15:20-21 the servant is not greater than his lord. If they have persecuted me, they will also persecute you; if they have kept my saying, they will keep yours also; Rom. 15:19-20 through mighty signs and wonders, by the power of the Spirit of God; so that from Jerusalem, and round about unto Illyricum, I have fully preached the gospel of Christ; Eph. 5:1-2 be ye therefore followers of God, as dear children; And *w.* in love, as Christ also hath loved us, and hath given himself for us an offering and a sacrifice to God for a sweetsmelling savour; Philip. 3:12 not as though I had already attained, either were already perfect: but I follow after, if that I may apprehend that for which also I am apprehended of Christ Jesus; Col. 2:6 as ye have therefore received Christ Jesus the Lord, so *w.* ye in him; 1 Pet. 1:15-16 as he which hath called you is holy, so be ye holy in all manner of conversation; Because it is written, Be ye holy; for I am holy; 2:21-22 Christ also suffered for us, leaving us an example, that ye should follow his steps: Who did no sin, neither was guile found in his mouth; 3:13 who is he that will harm you, if ye be followers of that which is good; 3:17-18 it is better, if the will of God be so, that ye suffer for well doing, than for evil doing. For Christ also hath once suffered for sins, the just for the unjust, that he might bring us to God, being put to death in the flesh, but quickened by the Spirit; 4:1 as Christ hath suffered for us in the flesh, arm yourselves likewise with the same mind: for he that hath suffered in the flesh hath ceased from sin; 1 Jn. 2:6 he that saith he abideth in him ought himself also so to *w.*, even as he *w.*

WANDER, WANDERER (*see also* Astray)

Hide the outcasts; bewray not him that wandereth. Isa. 16:3-5 (*see also* Outcast)

WAR (*see also* Adversary, Battle, Blood, Defend, Destroy, Fight, Persecute)

Scatter thou the people that delight in war. Ps. 68:30

Ps. 68:30 rebuke the company of spearmen, the multitude of the bulls, with the calves of the people, till every one submit himself with pieces of silver: scatter thou the people that delight in war; **120:6-7** my soul hath long dwelt with him that hateth peace. I am for peace: but when I speak, they are for *w.*

WARN, WARNINGS (*see also* Admonish, Cry, Rebuke, Reprove, Testify, Witness)

Warn the wicked from his wicked way. Ezek. 3:18-19 (*see also* Wicked)

Warn them that are unruly, comfort the feebleminded, support the weak, be patient toward all men. 1 Thes. 5:14 (*see also* Patience, Treat)

If thou warn the righteous man, that the righteous sin not, and he doth not sin, he shall surely live, because he is warned; also thou hast delivered thy soul. Ezek. 3:21 (*see also* Righteous, Sin)

WASH, WASHINGS (*see also* Baptism, Clean, Feet, Purify)

There is a generation that are pure in their own eyes, an yet is not washed from their filthiness. Prov. 30:12 (*see also* Filthiness, Pure)

O Jerusalem, wash thine heart from wickedness, that thou mayest be saved. Jer. 4:14 (*see also* Jerusalem, Wicked)

If I then, your Lord and Master, have ashed your feet; ye also ought to wash one another's feet. For I have given you an example, that ye should do as I have done to you. John 13:14-15 (*see also* Do, Example, Feet)

John 13:12 so after he had *w.* their feet, and had taken his garments, and was set down again, he said unto them, Know ye what I have done to you; **13:14-15** if I then, your Lord and Master, have *w.* your feet; ye also ought to *w.* one another's feet. For I have given you an example, that ye should do as I have done to you.

WASTE (*see also* Idle, Laziness, Slothful)

He also that is slothful in his work is brother to him that is a great waster. Prov. 18:9 (*see also* Slothful)

WATCH, WATCHFUL, WATCHFULNESS (*see also* Diligence, Look, Observe, See, Vigilant)

We made our prayer unto our God, and set a watch against them day and night. Neh. 4:9 (*see also* Enemy)

Watch therefore: for ye know not what hour your Lord doth come. Matt. 24:42 (*see also* Signs)

Matt. 24:6-8 ye shall hear of wars and rumours of wars: see that ye be not troubled: for all these things must come to pass, but the end is not yet. For nation shall rise against nation, and kingdom against kingdom: and there shall be famines, and pestilences, and earthquakes, in divers places. All these are the beginning of sorrows; **24:14** this gospel of the kingdom shall be preached in all the world for a witness unto all nations; and then shall the end come; **24:32-33** (Mark 13:28-30) learn a parable of the fig tree; When his branch is yet tender, and putteth forth leaves, ye know that summer is nigh: So likewise ye, when ye shall see all these things, know that it is near, even at the doors; **24:42-43** *w.* therefore: for ye know not what hour your Lord doth come. But know this, that if the goodman of the house had known in what *w.* the thief would come, he would have *w.*, and would not have suffered his house to be broken up; **Mark 13:33-36** take ye heed, *w.* and pray: for ye know not when the time is; **Luke 12:37-40** blessed are those servants, whom the lord when he cometh shall find *w.*: verily I say unto you, that he shall gird himself, and make them to sit down to meat, and will come forth and serve them… and this know, that if the goodman of the house had known what hour the thief would come, he would have *w.*, and not have suffered his house to be broken through. Be ye therefore ready also: for the Son of man cometh at an hour when ye think not; **12:42-48** And the Lord said, Who then is that faithful and wise steward, whom his lord shall make ruler over his household, to give them their portion of meat in due season? Blessed is that servant, whom his lord when he cometh shall find so doing. Of a truth I say unto you, that he will make him ruler over all that he hath. But and if that servant say in his heart, My lord delayeth his coming; and shall begin to beat the menservants and maidens, and to eat and drink, and to be drunken; The lord of that servant will come in a day when he looketh not for him, and at an hour when he is not aware, and will cut him in sunder, and will appoint him his portion with the unbelievers. And that servant, which knew his lord's will, and prepared not himself, neither did according to his will, shall be beaten with many stripes. But he that knew not, and did commit things worthy of stripes, shall be beaten with few stripes. For unto whomsoever much is given, of him shall be much required: and to whom men have committed much, of him they will ask the more; **12:55** when ye see the south wind blow, ye say, There will be heat; and it cometh to pass; **13:25-27** When once the master of the house is risen up, and hath shut to the door, and ye begin to stand without, and to knock at the door, saying, Lord, Lord, open unto us; and he shall answer and say unto you, I know you not whence ye are: Then shall ye begin to say, We have eaten and drunk in thy presence, and thou hast taught in our streets. But he shall say, I tell you, I know you not whence ye are; depart from me, all ye workers of iniquity; **21:8-11** many shall come in my name, saying, I am Christ; and the time draweth near: go ye not therefore after them. But when ye shall hear of wars and commotions, be not terrified: for these things must first come to pass; but the end is not by and by. Then said he unto them, Nation shall rise against nation, and kingdom against kingdom: And great earthquakes shall be in divers places, and famines, and pestilences; and fearful sights and great signs shall there be from heaven; **21:20-28** when ye shall see Jerusalem compassed with armies, then know that the desolation thereof is nigh. Then let them which are in Judaea flee to the mountains; and let them which are in the midst of it depart out; and let not them that are in the countries enter thereinto. For these be the days of vengeance, that all things which are written may be fulfilled. But woe unto them that are with child, and to them that give suck, in those days! for there shall be great distress in the land, and wrath upon this people. And they shall fall by the edge of the sword, and shall be led away captive into all nations: and Jerusalem shall be trodden down of the Gentiles, until the times of the Gentiles be fulfilled. And there shall be signs in the sun, and in the moon, and in the stars; and upon the earth distress of nations, with perplexity; the sea and the waves roaring; Men's hearts failing them for fear, and for looking after those things which are coming on the earth: for the powers of heaven shall be shaken. And then shall they see the Son of man coming in a cloud with power and great glory. And when these things begin to come to pass, then look up, and lift up your heads; for your redemption draweth nigh; **Rom. 8:19** the earnest expectation of the creature waiteth for the manifestation of the sons of God; **1 Cor. 1:7-8** So that ye come behind in no gift; waiting for the coming of our Lord Jesus Christ: Who shall also confirm you unto the end, that ye may be blameless in the day of our Lord Jesus Christ; **10:11** all these things happened unto them for ensamples: and they are written for our admonition, upon whom the ends of the world are come; **Gal. 4:4** when the fulness of the time was come, God sent forth his Son, made of a woman, made under the law; **1 Thes. 1:10** to wait for his Son from heaven, whom he raised from the dead, even Jesus, which delivered us from the wrath to come; **5:6** let us not sleep, as do others; but let us w. and be sober; **2 Thes. 2:1-6** that day shall not come, except there come a falling away first, and that man of sin be revealed, the son of perdition; **3:5** the Lord direct your hearts into the love of God, and into the patient waiting for Christ; **1 Tim. 4:1-3** the Spirit speaketh expressly, that in the latter times some shall depart from the faith, giving heed to seducing spirits, and doctrines of devils; Speaking lies in hypocrisy; having their conscience seared with a hot iron; Forbidding to marry, and commanding to abstain from meats, which God hath created to be received with thanksgiving of them which believe and know the truth; **2 Tim. 3:1-3** this know also, that in the last days perilous times shall come. For men shall be lovers of their own selves, covetous, boasters, proud, blasphemers, disobedient to parents, unthankful, unholy, Without natural affection, trucebreakers, false accusers, incontinent, fierce, despisers of those that are good; **4:8** there is laid up for me a crown of righteousness, which the Lord, the righteous judge, shall give me at that day: and not to me only, but unto all them also that love his appearing; **Titus 2:13** looking for that blessed hope, and the glorious appearing of the great God and our Saviour Jesus Christ; **2 Pet. 3:13-14** we, according to his promise, look for new heavens and a new earth, wherein dwelleth righteousness. Wherefore, beloved, seeing that ye look for such things, be diligent that ye may be found of him in peace, without spot, and blameless; **Jude 1:14** Enoch also, the seventh from Adam, prophesied of these, saying, Behold, the Lord cometh with ten thousands of his saints; **Rev. 1:7** he cometh with clouds; and every eye shall see him, and they also which pierced him: and all kindreds of the earth shall wail because of him; **6:12-16** I beheld when he had opened the sixth seal... the kings of the earth, and the great men, and the rich men, and the chief captains, and the mighty men, and every bondman, and every free man, hid themselves in the dens and in the rocks of the mountains; And said to the mountains and rocks, Fall on us, and hide us from the face of him that sitteth on the throne, and from the wrath of the Lamb; **8:6-13** I beheld, and heard an angel flying through the midst of heaven, saying with a loud voice, Woe, woe, woe, to the inhabiters of the earth by reason of the other voices of the trumpet of the three angels, which are yet to sound; **9:6** in those days shall men seek death, and shall not find it; and shall desire to die, and death shall flee from them; **9:7-18** by these three was the third part of men killed, by the fire, and by the smoke, and by the brimstone, which issued out of their mouths; **11:15** the seventh angel sounded; and there were great voices in heaven, saying, The kingdoms of this world are become the kingdoms of our Lord, and of his Christ; and he shall reign for ever and ever; **11:19** the temple of God was opened in heaven, and there was seen in his temple the ark of his testament: and there were lightnings, and voices, and thunderings, and an earthquake, and great hail; **15:1** I saw another sign in heaven, great and marvellous, seven angels having the seven last plagues; for in them is filled up the wrath of God; **16:14** they are the spirits of devils, working miracles, which go forth unto the kings of the earth and of the whole world, to gather them to the battle of that great day of God Almighty; **16:19** the great city was divided into three parts, and the cities of the nations fell: and great Babylon came in remembrance before God, to give unto her the cup of the wine of the fierceness of his wrath.

WATER (*see also* Baptism, Sacrament, Wash)

Jesus answered, Verily, verily, I say unto thee, Except a man be born of water and of the Spirit, he cannot enter into the kingdom of God. John 3:5 (*see also* Born, Enter, Spirit)

WAVER, WAVERING (*see also* Change)

Let us hold fast the profession of our faith without wavering; (for he is faithful that promised). Heb. 10:23 (*see also* Profession)

If any of you lack wisdom, let him ask of God, that giveth to all men liberally, and upbraideth not; and it shall be given him. But let him ask in faith, nothing wavering. For he that wavereth is like a wave of the sea driven with the wind and tossed. James 1:5-6 (*see also* Ask, Lack, Wisdom, JSH 1:11)

WAY, WAYS (*see also* Do, Example, Path, Righteousness, Right Way, Walk)

Turn away mine eyes from beholding vanity; and quicken thou me in thy way. Ps. 119:37 (*see also* Vain)

A double minded man is unstable in all his ways. James 1:8 (*see also* Double Minded, Mind, Unsteady)

Forsake the foolish, and live; and go in the way of understanding. Prov. 9:6 (*see also* Foolish, Understand)

God hath set some in the church, first apostles, secondarily prophets, thirdly teachers, after that miracles, then gifts of healings, helps, governments, diversities of tongues. Are all apostles? are all prophets? are all teachers? are all workers of miracles? Have all the gifts of healing? do all speak with tongues? do all interpret? But covet earnestly the best gifts: and yet shew I unto you a more excellent way. 1 Cor. 12:28-31 (*see also* Excellent, Prophet)

Thou hast avouched the LORD this day to be thy God, and to walk in his ways, and to keep his statutes, and his commandments, and his judgments, and to hearken unto his voice. Deut. 26:17 (*see also* Hearken, Keep)

Thorns and snares are in the way of the froward: he that doth keep his soul shall be far from them. Prov. 22:5 (*see also* Froward, Soul)

The wisdom of the prudent is to understand his way: but the folly of fools is deceit. Prov. 14:8 (*see also* Prudent, Wisdom)

I proclaimed a fast there, at the river of Ahava, that we might afflict ourselves before our God, to seek of him a right way for us, and for our little ones, and for all our substance. Ezra 8:21-23 (*see also* Fast)

If after they have escaped the pollutions of the world through the knowledge of the Lord and Savior Jesus Christ, they are again entangled therein, and overcome, the latter end is worse with them than the beginning. For it had been better for them not to have known the way of righteousness, than, after they have known it, to turn from the holy commandment delivered unto them. But it is happened unto them according to the true proverb, The dog is turned to his own vomit again; and the sow that was washed to her wallowing in the mire. 2 Pet. 2:20-22 (*see also* Entangle, Vomit)

Envy not the oppressor, and choose none of his ways. Prov. 3:31-32 (*see also* Envy)

I will get me unto the great men, and will speak unto them; for they have known the way of the LORD, and the judgment of their God: but these have altogether broken the yoke, and burst the bonds. Jer. 5:5 (*see also* Iniquity)

Come, and let us go up to the mountain of the LORD, and to the house of the God of Jacob; and he will teach us of his ways, and we will walk in his paths; for the law shall go forth of Zion, and the word of the LORD from Jerusalem. Micah 4:2 (*see also* House, Jerusalem, Law, Mountain, Word, Zion)

Teach me thy way, O LORD; I will walk in thy truth: unite my heart to fear thy name. Ps. 86:11 (*see also* Fear, Truth)

Thou shalt teach them ordinances and laws, and shalt shew them the way wherein they must walk, and the work that they must do. Ex. 18:20 (*see also* Teach)

Prepare ye the way of the Lord, make his paths straight. Luke 3:4 (*see also* Prepare)

Train up a child in the way he should go: and when he is old, he will not depart from it. Prov. 22:6 (*see also* Child, Depart, Train)

Enter ye in at the strait gate: for wide is the gate, and broad is the way, that leadeth to destruction, and many there be which go in thereat: Because strait is the gate, and narrow is the way, which leadeth unto life, and few there be that find it. Matt. 7:13-14 (*see also* Baptism, Go)

O full of all subtilty and all mischief, thou child of the devil, thou enemy of all righteousness, wilt thou not cease to pervert the right ways of the Lord. Acts 13:10 (*see also* Mischief, Pervert, Subtle)

Walk in the ways of good men, and keep the paths of the righteous. Prov. 2:20 (*see also* Good, Walk)

He is in the way of life that keepeth instruction: but he that refuseth reproof erreth. Prov. 10:17 (*see also* Instruct, Reproof)

In all thy ways acknowledge him, and he shall direct thy paths. Prov. 3:6 (*see also* Acknowledge, Direct)

Make no friendship with an angry man; and with a furious man thou shalt not go: Lest thou learn his ways, and get a snare to thy soul. Prov. 22:24-25 (*see also* Anger)

Give not thy strength to women, nor thy ways to that which destroyeth kings. Prov. 31:3 (*see also* Strength, Woman)

Hear thou, my son, and be wise, and guide thine heart in the way. Prov. 23:19 (*see also* Heart)

Thus saith the LORD of hosts, the God of Israel, Amend your ways and your doings, and I will cause you to dwell in this place. Jer. 7:3 (*see also* Amend)

Be ye not as your fathers, unto whom the former prophets have cried, saying, Thus saith the LORD of hosts; Turn ye now from your evil ways, and from your evil doings: but they did not hear, nor hearken unto me, saith the LORD. Zech. 1:4 (*see also* Evil, Hear)

Ye have not kept my ways, but have been partial in the law. Mal. 2:9 (*see also* Keep, Law)

Let us search and try our ways, and turn again to the Lord. Lam. 3:40 (*see also* Repent, Search, Try, Turn)

Be ashamed and confounded for your own ways, O house of Israel. Ezek. 36:32 (*see also* Iniquity)

Come and let us go up to the mountain of the Lord, and to the house of the God of Jacob; and he will teach us of his ways, and we will walk in his paths; for the law shall go forth of Zion and the word of the Lord from Jerusalem. **Micah 4:2** (*see also* Jerusalem, Law, Mountain, Word, Zion)

The man that wandereth out of the way of understanding shall remain in the congregation of the dead. **Prov. 21:16** (*see also* Understand)

Whoso causeth the righteous to go astray in an evil way, he shall fall himself into his own pits; but the upright shall have good things in possession. **Prov. 28:10** (*see also* Astray, Righteous)

Prepare ye the way of the Lord, make straight in the desert a highway for our God. **Isa. 40:3** (*see also* Prepare)

Let the wicked forsake his way, and the unrighteous man his thoughts: and let him return unto the Lord, and he will have mercy upon him; and to our God, for he will abundantly pardon. **Isa. 55:7** (*see also* Repent)

I have chosen the way of truth. **Ps. 119:30** (*see also* True)

Thus saith the Lord, learn not the way of the heathen, and be not dismayed at the signs of heaven; for the heathen are dismayed at them. **Jer. 10:2** (*see also* Heathen, Heaven, Sign)

Return ye now every one from his evil way, and make your ways and your doings good. **Jer. 18:11** (*see also* Evil, Good)

Turn ye again now every one from his evil way, and from the evil of your doings, and dwell in the land that the LORD hath given unto you and to your fathers for ever and ever. **Jer. 25:5** (*see also* Evil, Turn)

Set thee up waymarks, make thee high heaps: set thine heart toward the highway, even the way which thou wentest: turn again. **Jer. 31:21** (*see also* Heart, Turn)

Through thy precepts I get understanding: therefore I hate every false way. **Ps. 119:104** (*see also* Hate)

Surely these are poor; they are foolish: for they know not the way of the LORD, nor the judgment of their God. **Jer. 5:4** (*see also* Fool)

Thus saith the LORD, Stand ye in the ways, and see, and ask for the old paths, where is the good way, and walk therein, and ye shall find rest for your souls. **Jer. 6:16** (*see also* Stand, Walk)

Correction is grievous unto him that forsaketh the way: and he that hateth reproof shall die. **Prov. 15:10** (*see also* Reproof)

Ponder the path of thy feet and let all thy ways be established. **Prov. 4:26** (*see also* Establish, Feet, Ponder)

Thus saith the Lord of Hosts; Consider your ways. **Hag. 1:4-5** (*see also* Consider)
The way of life is above to the wise, that he may depart from hell beneath. **Prov. 15:24** (*see also* Wise)

I will meditate in thy precepts, and have respect unto thy ways. **Ps. 119:15** (*see also* Meditate, Precept)

Ps. 119:15 I will meditate in thy precepts, and have respect unto thy *w.*; **119:117-118** I will have respect unto thy statutes continually.

A violent man enticeth his neighbour, and leadeth him into the way that is not good. **Prov. 16:29** (*see also* Violent)

Prov. 16:29 a violent man enticeth his neighbour, and leadeth him into the *w.* that is not good; **Jer. 18:11** thus saith the LORD; Behold, I frame evil against you, and devise a device against you: return ye now every one from his evil *w.*, and make your *w.* and your doings good; **Ezek. 16:47** thou [hast] not walked after their *w.*, nor done after their abominations: but, as if that were a very little thing, thou wast corrupted more than they in all thy *w.*

Commit thy way unto the Lord; trust also in Him; and He shall bring it to pass. And he shall bring forth thy righteousness as the light, and thy judgment as the noonday. Ps. 37:5-6 (*see also* Commit, Light, Trust)

Ps. 37:5-6 commit thy *w.* unto the LORD; trust also in him; and he shall bring it to pass. And he shall bring forth thy righteousness as the light, and thy judgment as the noonday; **139:24** see if there be any wicked *w.* in me, and lead me in the *w.* everlasting.

There is a way which seemeth right unto a man, but the end thereof are the ways of death. Prov. 14:12 (*see also* Walk)

Prov. 14:12 there is a *w.* which seemeth right unto a man, but the end thereof are the *w.* of death; **14:14** the backslider in heart shall be filled with his own *w.*: and a good man shall be satisfied from himself; **Isa. 66:3** they have chosen their own *w.*, and their soul delighteth in their abominations.

It is a people that do err in their heart, and they have not known my ways. Ps. 95:10 (*see also* Err, Heart)

Job 21:14 they say unto God, Depart from us; for we desire not the knowledge of thy *w.*; **22:21-22** acquaint now thyself with him, and be at peace: thereby good shall come unto thee. Receive, I pray thee, the law from his mouth, and lay up his words in thine heart; **Ps. 95:10** it is a people that do err in their heart, and they have not known my *w.*; **111:2-4** the works of the LORD are great, sought out of all them that have pleasure therein.

Keep the way of the Lord. Gen. 18:19 (*see also* Keep)

Gen. 18:19 they shall keep the *w.* of the LORD, to do justice and judgment; **Judg. 2:22** through them I may prove Israel, whether they will keep the *w.* of the LORD to walk therein; **Ps. 25:4** shew me thy *w.*, O LORD; teach me thy paths; **85:13** righteousness shall go before him; and shall set us in the *w.* of his steps; **86:11** teach me thy *w.*, O LORD; I will walk in thy truth; **Prov. 8:20** I lead in the *w.* of righteousness, in the midst of the paths of judgment; **10:29** the *w.* of the LORD is strength to the upright: but destruction shall be to the workers of iniquity; **12:28** in the *w.* of righteousness is life; and in the pathway thereof

there is no death; **13:6** righteousness keepeth him that is upright in the *w.*: but wickedness overthroweth the sinner; **Jer. 5:4-5** surely these are poor; they are foolish: for they know not the *w.* of the LORD, nor the judgment of their God; **6:16** stand ye in the *w.*, and see, and ask for the old paths, where is the good *w.*, and walk therein, and ye shall find rest for your souls.

Discretion shall preserve thee, understanding shall keep thee; To deliver thee from the way of the evil man, from the man that speaketh froward things; who leave the paths of righteousness, to walk in the ways of darkness. Prov. 2:11-13 (*see also* Dark, Leave, Righteous, Walk)

Prov. 2:13 who leave the paths of uprightness, to walk in the *w.* of darkness; **Jer. 15:7-8** I will destroy my people, since they return not from their *w.*; **18:15** my people hath forgotten me, they have burned incense to vanity, and they have caused them to stumble in their *w.* from the ancient paths, to walk in paths, in a *w.* not cast up; **18:17** I will scatter them as with an east wind before the enemy: I will shew them the back, and not the face, in the day of their calamity.

Ye shall walk in all the ways which the LORD your God hath commanded you, that ye may live, and that ye may prolong your days in the land which ye shall posses. Deut. 5:33 (*see also* Day, Prolong, Walk)

Deut. 5:33 ye shall walk in all the *w.* which the LORD your God hath commanded you, that ye may live, and that it may be well with you; **11:22** ye shall diligently keep all these commandments which I command you, to do them, to love the LORD your God, to walk in all his *w.*, and to cleave unto him; **1 Kgs. 8:39** hear thou in heaven thy dwelling place, and forgive, and do, and give to every man according to his *w.*, whose heart thou knowest; **8:58** he may incline our hearts unto him, to walk in all his *w.*, and to keep his commandments, and his statutes, and his judgments; **2 Kgs. 10:31** Jehu took no heed to walk in the law of the LORD God of Israel with all his heart: for he departed not from the sins; **23:3** the king stood by a pillar, and made a covenant before the LORD, to walk after the LORD, and to keep his commandments and his testimonies and his statutes with all their heart and all their soul; **2 Chron. 6:31** that they may fear thee, to walk in thy *w.*, so long as they live in the land; **Neh. 5:9** ought ye not to walk in the fear of our God because of the reproach of the heathen our enemies; **5:15** the former governors that had been before me were chargeable unto the people, and had taken of them bread and wine, beside forty shekels of silver; yea, even their servants bare rule over the people: but so did not I, because of the fear of God; **Job 23:11** my foot hath held his steps, his *w.* have I kept, and not declined; **Ps. 18:21** I have kept the *w.* of the LORD, and have not wickedly departed from my God; **26:3** thy lovingkindness is before mine eyes: and I have walked in thy truth; **56:13** thou hast delivered my soul from death: wilt not thou deliver my feet from falling, that I may walk before God in the light of the living; **119:1** blessed are the undefiled in the *w.*, who walk in the law of the LORD; **119:3-5** they also do no iniquity: they walk in his *w.*. Thou hast commanded us to keep thy precepts diligently. O that my *w.* were directed to keep thy statutes; **128:1-2** blessed is every one that feareth the LORD; that walketh in his *w.*; **138:5** they shall sing in the *w.* of the LORD: for great is the glory of the LORD; **Prov. 2:20** that thou mayest walk in the *w.* of good men, and keep the paths of the righteous; **8:32** blessed are they that keep my *w.*; **16:7** when a mans *w.* please the LORD, he maketh even his enemies to be at peace with him; **Isa. 42:24** they would not walk in his *w.*, neither were they obedient unto his law; **64:5** thou meetest him that rejoiceth and worketh righteousness, those that remember thee in thy *w.*: behold, thou art wroth; for we have sinned; **Jer. 7:23** obey my voice, and I will be your God, and ye shall be my people: and walk ye in all the *w.* that I have commanded you; **10:23** O LORD, I know that the *w.* of man is not in himself: it is not in man that walketh to direct his steps; **17:10** I the LORD search the heart, I try the reins, even to give every man according to his *w.*; **Zech. 3:7** if thou wilt walk in my *w.*, and if thou wilt keep my charge, then thou shalt also judge my house, and shalt also keep my courts.

WEALTH, WEALTHY (*see also* Lucre, Money, Riches)

Let no man seek his own, but every man another's wealth. 1 Cor. 10:24 (*see also* Own)

WEARINESS, WEARY

Withdraw thy foot from thy neighbour's house; lest he be weary of thee, and so hate thee. Prov. 25:17 (*see also* Neighbor)

The Lord GOD hath given me the tongue of the learned, that I should know how to speak a word in season to him that is weary. Isa. 50:4 (*see also* Season, Speak, Tongue)

Ye have wearied the LORD with your words. Yet ye say, Wherein have we wearied him? When ye say, Every one that doeth evil is good in the sight of the LORD. Mal. 2:17 (*see also* Evil, Good)

Isa. 43:22 thou hast not called upon me, O Jacob; but thou hast been *w.* of me, O Israel; **43:24** thou hast made me to serve with thy sins, thou hast *w.* me with thine iniquities; **Micah 2:10** arise ye, and depart; for this is not your rest: because it is polluted, it shall destroy you, even with a sore destruction; **Jer. 31:25-26** I have satiated the *w.* soul, and I have replenished every sorrowful soul. Upon this I awaked, and beheld; and my sleep was sweet unto me; **Mal. 2:17** ye have *w.* the LORD with your words. Yet ye say, Wherein have we *w.* him? When ye say, Every one that doeth evil is good in the sight of the LORD.

WEEP (*see* Cry, Mourn, Sorrow)

WEIGH, WEIGHT

A false balance is abomination to the LORD: but a just weight is his delight. Prov. 11:1 (*see also* Balance, Just)

Seeing we also are compassed about with so great a cloud of witnesses, let us lay aside every weight, and the sin which doth so easily beset us, and let us run with patience the race that is set before us. Heb. 12:1 (*see also* Beset, Patience, Run, Sin, Witness)

WHOLE

Wilt thou be made whole? John. 5:6 (*see also* Heal)

WHOLESOME (*see also* Clean, Modest, Pure)

A wholesome tongue is a tree of life: but perverseness therein is a breach in the spirit. Prov. 15:4 (*see also* Perverse, Tongue)

WHORE, WHOREMONGER, WHOREDOM (*see also* Adultery, Carnal, Filthiness, Fornication, Harlot, Idolatry, Lust)

Do not prostitute thy daughters, to cause her to be a whore; lest the land fall into whoredom, and the land become full of wickedness. Lev. 19:29 (*see also* Prostitute)

Lev. 19:29 do not prostitute thy daughter, to cause her to be a whore; lest the land fall to whoredom, and the land become full of wickedness; **20:6** the soul that turneth after such as have familiar spirits, and after wizards, to go a whoring after them, I will even set my face against that soul; **Num. 25:1-4** the people began to commit whoredom with the daughters of Moab... and the anger of the LORD was kindled against Israel; **Deut. 22:21** they shall bring out the damsel to the door of her fathers house, and the men of her city shall stone her with stones that she die: because she hath wrought folly in Israel, to play the whore in her fathers house; **23:17** there shall be no whore of the daughters of Israel, nor a sodomite of the sons of Israel; **Jer. 3:1-2** if a man put away his wife, and she go from him, and become another mans, shall he return unto her again? shall not that land be greatly polluted; **Ezek. 16:24-39** because thy filthiness was poured out, and thy nakedness discovered through thy *w.* with thy lovers... I will even gather them round about against thee, and will discover thy nakedness unto them; **23:7-35** she committed her *w.* with them, with all them that were the chosen men of Assyria, and with all on whom she doted: with all their idols she defiled herself; **43:7** shall the house of Israel no more defile, neither they, nor their kings, by their whoredom; **43:9** let them put away their whoredom, and the carcases of their kings, far from me, and I will dwell in the midst of them for ever; **Hosea 1:2** go, take unto thee a wife of *w.* and children of *w.*: for the land hath committed great *w.*, departing from the LORD; **2:2-11** let her therefore put away her *w.* out of her sight, and her adulteries from between her breasts; Lest I strip her naked, and set her as in the day that she was born, and make her as a wilderness, and set her like a dry land, and slay her with thirst; **4:11-13** the spirit of *w.* hath caused them to err, and they have gone a whoring from under their God; **4:18-19** they have committed *w.* continually: her rulers with shame do love; **5:3-4** thou committest *w.*, and Israel is defiled. They will not frame their doings to turn unto their God: for the spirit of *w.* is in the midst of them, and they have not known the LORD; **6:10** I have seen an horrible thing in the house of Israel: there is the *w.* of Ephraim, Israel is defiled; **9:1-4** rejoice not, O Israel, for joy, as other people: for thou hast gone a whoring from thy God, thou hast loved a reward upon every cornfloor; **Nahum 3:3-6** they stumble upon their corpses: Because of the multitude of the *w.* of the wellfavoured harlot, the mistress of witchcrafts, that selleth nations through her *w.*; **3:10** she went into captivity: her young children also were dashed in pieces at the top of all the streets: and they cast lots for her honourable men, and all her great men were bound in chains.

WICKED, WICKEDNESS (*see also* Backbiting, Contention, Deceit, Devil, Disobey, Evil, Filthiness, Fornication, Hell, Iniquity, Sin, Transgression)

When the righteous are in authority, the people rejoice: but when the wicked beareth rule, the people mourn. Prov. 29:2 (*see also* Authority, Mourn, Righteous, Rule)

For we wrestle not against flesh and blood, but against principalities, against powers, against the rulers of the darkness of this world, against spiritual wickedness in high places. Eph. 6:12 (*see also* Wrestle)

The wicked, through the pride of his countenance, will not seek after God: God is not in all his thoughts. Ps. 10:4 (*see also* Pride, Seek, Thought)

The thoughts of the wicked are an abomination to the LORD: but the words of the pure are pleasant words. Prov. 15:26 (*see also* Abomination, Thought, Word)

Look on every one that is proud, and bring him low; and tread down the wicked in their place. Job 40:12 (*see also* Look, Pride)

The wicked shall be turned into hell, and all the nations that forget God. Ps. 9:17 (*see also* Forget)

Treasures of wickedness profit nothing; but righteousness delivereth from death. Prov. 10:2 (*see also* Profit, Righteous, Treasure)

O Jerusalem, wash thine heart from wickedness, that thou mayest be saved. Jer. 4:14 (*see also* Jerusalem, Wash)

Thou hast trusted in thy wickedness: thou hast said, None seeth me. Thy wisdom and thy knowledge, it hath perverted thee; and thou hast said in thine heart, I am, and none else beside me. Isa. 47:10 (*see also* Pervert, Trust)

He that justifieth the wicked, and he that condemneth the just, even they both are abomination to the LORD. Prov. 17:15 (*see also* Justify)

Take away the wicked from before the king, and his throne shall be established in righteousness. Prov. 25:5 (*see also* Righteous)

A righteous man falling down before the wicked is as a troubled fountain, and a corrupt spring. Prov. 25:26 (*see also* Righteous)

Be not over much wicked, neither be thou foolish: why shouldest thou die before thy time? Eccl. 7:17 (*see also* Fool, Time)

Warn the wicked from his wicked way. Ezek. 3:18-19 (*see also* Warn)

Ezek. 3:18-19 if thou warn the *w.*, and he turn not from his *w.*, nor from his *w.* way, he shall die in his iniquity; but thou hast delivered thy soul; 33:6-12 if thou warn the *w.* of his way to turn from it; if he do not turn from his way, he shall die in his iniquity; but thou hast delivered thy soul.

There is no peace, saith my God, to the wicked. Isa. 57:21 (*see also* Peace)

Ps. 92:7 when the *w.* spring as the grass, and when all the workers of iniquity do flourish; it is that they shall be destroyed for ever; Gen. 6:5-6 GOD saw that the *w.* of man was great in the earth, and that every imagination of the thoughts of his heart was only evil continually... and it grieved him at his heart; 6:11-12 God looked upon the earth, and, behold, it was corrupt; for all flesh had corrupted his way upon the earth; 18:20 the cry of Sodom and Gomorrah is great, and... their sin is very grievous; 19:7 I pray you, brethren, do not so *w.*ly; 19:15 the angels hastened Lot, saying, Arise, take thy wife, and thy two daughters, which are here; lest thou be consumed in the iniquity of the city; Ex. 15:7-8 in the greatness of thine excellency thou hast overthrown them that rose up against thee: thou sentest forth thy wrath, which consumed them as stubble; 1 Chron. 21:1-3 why will he be a cause

of trespass to Israel; 2 Chron. 22:3 he also walked in the ways of the house of Ahab: for his mother was his counsellor to do *w.*ly; Job 4:8 they that plow iniquity, and sow *w.*, reap the same; 11:20 the eyes of the *w.* shall fail, and they shall not escape, and their hope shall be as the giving up of the ghost; 18:5-21 the light of the *w.* shall be put out, and the spark of his fire shall not shine. The light shall be dark in his tabernacle, and his candle shall be put out with him; 20:5 the triumphing of the *w.* is short, and the joy of the hypocrite but for a moment; 20:12-29 though *w.* be sweet in his mouth, though he hide it under his tongue; Though he spare it, and forsake it not; but keep it still within his mouth: Yet his meat in his bowels is turned, it is the gall of asps within him; 21:13-14 they spend their days in wealth, and in a moment go down to the grave. Therefore they say unto God, Depart from us; for we desire not the knowledge of thy ways; 21:18 they are as stubble before the wind, and as chaff that the storm carrieth away; 21:24-26 another dieth in the bitterness of his soul, and never eateth with pleasure. They shall lie down alike in the dust, and the worms shall cover them; 21:30 the *w.* is reserved to the day of destruction... they shall be brought forth to the day of wrath; 21:33 the clods of the valley shall be sweet unto him, and every man shall draw after him, as there are innumerable before him; 22:18 the counsel of the *w.* is far from me; 24:23-24 they are exalted for a little while, but are gone and brought low; they are taken out of the way as all other; 27:10-23 behold, all ye yourselves have seen it; why then are ye thus altogether vain? This is the portion of a *w.* man with God, and the heritage of oppressors, which they shall receive of the Almighty; 31:3 is not destruction to the *w.*? and a strange punishment to the workers of iniquity; 34:10 far be it from God, that he should do *w.*; and from the Almighty, that he should commit iniquity; 34:22 there is no darkness, nor shadow of death, where the workers of iniquity may hide themselves; 34:25 he knoweth their works, and he overturneth them in the night, so that they are destroyed; 38:15 from the *w.* their light is withholden, and the high arm shall be broken; Ps. 5:9-10 there is no faithfulness in their mouth; their inward part is very *w.*; their throat is an open sepulchre; they flatter with their tongue. Destroy thou them, O God; 7:11 God judgeth the righteous, and God is angry with the *w.* every day; 7:14-16 his mischief shall return upon his own head, and his violent dealing shall come down upon his own pate; 9:5-6 thou hast rebuked the heathen, thou hast destroyed the *w.*, thou hast put out their name for ever and ever;

9:16-17 the LORD is known by the judgment which he executeth: the *w.* is snared in the work of his own hands... The *w.* shall be turned into hell, and all the nations that forget God; **10:2-3** the *w.* in his pride doth persecute the poor: let them be taken in the devices that they have imagined; **10:5-7** he hath said in his heart, I shall not be moved: for I shall never be in adversity. His mouth is full of cursing and deceit and fraud: under his tongue is mischief and vanity; **10:13-15** break thou the arm of the *w.* and the evil man: seek out his *w.* till thou find none; **11:2** the *w.* bend their bow, they make ready their arrow upon the string, that they may privily shoot at the upright in heart; **11:5-6** the LORD trieth the righteous: but the *w.* and him that loveth violence his soul hateth; **26:9-10** gather not my soul with sinners, nor my life with bloody men; **28:4** give them according to their deeds, and according to the *w.* of their endeavours; **31:17** let me not be ashamed, O LORD; for I have called upon thee: let the *w.* be ashamed, and let them be silent in the grave; **34:21** evil shall slay the *w.*: and they that hate the righteous shall be desolate; **37:14-16** [the] sword [of the *w.*] shall enter into their own heart, and their bows shall be broken; **37:20-22** the *w.* shall perish, and the enemies of the LORD shall be as the fat of lambs: they shall consume; into smoke shall they consume away; **37:28** the LORD loveth judgment, and forsaketh not his saints; they are preserved for ever: but the seed of the *w.* shall be cut off; **37:32** the *w.* watcheth the righteous, and seeketh to slay him; **37:35-36** I have seen the *w.* in great power, and spreading himself like a green bay tree. Yet he passed away, and, lo, he was not; **37:38** the transgressors shall be destroyed together: the end of the *w.* shall be cut off; **39:11** when thou with rebukes dost correct man for iniquity, thou makest his beauty to consume away like a moth; **40:14-15** let them be ashamed and confounded together that seek after my soul to destroy it; let them be driven backward and put to shame that wish me evil; **50:17-20** thou givest thy mouth to evil, and thy tongue frameth deceit; **52:3** thou lovest evil more than good; and lying rather than to speak righteousness; **53:1** the fool hath said in his heart, There is no God. Corrupt are they, and have done abominable iniquity: there is none that doeth good; **53:3-5** every one of them is gone back: they are altogether become filthy; there is none that doeth good, no, not one; **54:5** he shall reward evil unto mine enemies: cut them off in thy truth; **55:3** they cast iniquity upon me, and in wrath they hate me; **55:11-15** it was not an enemy that reproached me; then I could have borne it: neither was it he that hated me that did

magnify himself against me; then I would have hid myself from him: But it was thou; **55:23** thou, O God, shalt bring them down into the pit of destruction: bloody and deceitful men shall not live out half their days; **56:2** mine enemies would daily swallow me up: for they be many that fight against me; **56:5** every day they wrest my words: all their thoughts are against me for evil; **58:2-10** he shall take [the *w.*] away as with a whirlwind, both living, and in his wrath. The righteous shall rejoice when he seeth the vengeance: he shall wash his feet in the blood of the *w.*; **59:5** O LORD God of hosts, the God of Israel, awake to visit all the heathen: be not merciful to any *w.* transgressors; **59:15** let them wander up and down for meat, and grudge if they be not satisfied; **64:6-8** God shall shoot at them with an arrow; suddenly shall they be wounded. So they shall make their own tongue to fall upon themselves; **68:1-2** let God arise, let his enemies be scattered: let them also that hate him flee before him; **68:6** God setteth the solitary in families: he bringeth out those which are bound with chains: but the rebellious dwell in a dry land; **69:23-28** add iniquity unto their iniquity: and let them not come into thy righteousness. Let them be blotted out of the book of the living, and not be written with the righteous; **70:2** let them be ashamed and confounded that seek after my soul: let them be turned backward, and put to confusion; **74:3-4** lift up thy feet unto the perpetual desolations; even all that the enemy hath done *w.*ly in the sanctuary; **74:7** they have cast fire into thy sanctuary, they have defiled by casting down the dwelling place of thy name to the ground; **74:23** forget not the voice of thine enemies: the tumult of those that rise up against thee increaseth continually; **75:8** the dregs thereof, all the *w.* of the earth shall wring them out, and drink them; **79:1-2** the heathen are come into thine inheritance; thy holy temple have they defiled; they have laid Jerusalem on heaps; **83:2** thine enemies make a tumult: and they that hate thee have lifted up the head; **83:17** let them be confounded and troubled for ever; yea, let them be put to shame, and perish; **88:5** the slain that lie in the grave, whom thou rememberest no more: and they are cut off from thy hand; **89:30-32** if his children forsake my law, and walk not in my judgments; If they break my statutes, and keep not my commandments; Then will I visit their transgression with the rod; **91:8** only with thine eyes shalt thou behold and see the reward of the *w.*; **92:9** thine enemies shall perish; all the workers of iniquity shall be scattered; **94:3** how long shall the *w.*, how long shall the *w.* triumph; **94:13** thou mayest give him rest from the days of adversity, until the pit be digged for the *w*.; **94:21** they gather themselves together against the soul of the righteous, and condemn the innocent blood; **94:23** he shall bring upon them their own iniquity, and shall cut them off in their own *w*.; **99:1** the LORD reigneth; let the people tremble; **101:3** I will set no *w*. thing before mine eyes: I hate the work of them that turn aside; **101:8** I will early destroy all the *w*. of the land; that I may cut off all *w*. doers; **102:15** the heathen shall fear the name of the LORD; **104:35** let the sinners be consumed out of the earth, and let the *w*. be no more; **106:6-7** we have committed iniquity, we have done *w*.; **106:18** a fire was kindled in their company; the flame burned up the *w*.; **106:43** they provoked him with their counsel, and were brought low for their iniquity; **107:17-18** fools because of their transgression, and because of their iniquities, are afflicted; **107:34** a fruitful land into barrenness, for the *w*. of them that dwell therein; **107:42** the righteous shall see it, and rejoice: and all iniquity shall stop her mouth; **109:2-20** when he shall be judged, let him be condemned: and let his prayer become sin. Let his days be few; and let another take his office; **109:29** let mine adversaries be clothed with shame, and let them cover themselves with their own confusion; **112:10** the *w*. shall see it, and be grieved... the desire of the *w*. shall perish; **115:2-7** wherefore should the heathen say, Where is now their God? But our God is in the heavens: he hath done whatsoever he hath pleased; **115:17** the dead praise not the LORD, neither any that go down into silence; **119:21** thou hast rebuked the proud that are cursed; **119:118-119** thou hast trodden down all them that err from thy statutes: for their deceit is falsehood. Thou puttest away all the *w*. of the earth like dross; **119:145** hear me, O LORD: I will keep thy statutes; **119:150** they draw nigh that follow after mischief: they are far from thy law; **119:155** salvation is far from the *w*.: for they seek not thy statutes; **119:158** I beheld the transgressors, and was grieved; because they kept not thy word; **124:2-5** if it had not been the LORD who was on our side, when men rose up against us: Then they had swallowed us up quick, when their wrath was kindled against us; **125:3** the rod of the *w*. shall not rest upon the lot of the righteous; lest the righteous put forth their hands unto iniquity; **125:5** as for such as turn aside unto their crooked ways, the LORD shall lead them forth with the workers of iniquity; **129:4** the LORD is righteous: he hath cut asunder the cords of the *w*.; **137:8-9** happy shall he be, that rewardeth thee as thou hast served us; **139:19-21** thou wilt slay the *w*., O God: depart

from me therefore, ye bloody men; **140:1-4** keep me, O LORD, from the hands of the *w*.; preserve me from the violent man; who have purposed to overthrow my goings; **140:9** let the mischief of their own lips cover them; **140:11** let not an evil speaker be established in the earth; **146:9** the LORD preserveth the strangers; he relieveth the fatherless and widow: but the way of the *w*. he turneth upside down; **147:6** the LORD lifteth up the meek: he casteth the *w*. down to the ground; **Prov. 1:16-18** their feet run to evil, and make haste to shed blood; **2:15** whose ways are crooked, and they froward in their paths; **2:22** the *w*. shall be cut off from the earth, and the transgressors shall be rooted out of it; **3:33** the curse of the LORD is in the house of the *w*.: but he blesseth the habitation of the just; **3:35** the wise shall inherit glory: but shame shall be the promotion of fools; **4:16-17** they sleep not, except they have done mischief; and their sleep is taken away; **4:19** the way of the *w*. is as darkness: they know not at what they stumble; **5:3-5** her feet go down to death; her steps take hold on hell; **5:22-23** his own iniquities shall take the *w*. himself, and he shall be holden with the cords of his sins; **6:23** the commandment is a lamp; and the law is light; and reproofs of instruction are the way of life; **10:6** blessings are upon the head of the just: but violence covereth the mouth of the *w*.; **10:11** the mouth of a righteous man is a well of life: but violence covereth the mouth of the *w*.; **10:16** the labour of the righteous tendeth to life: the fruit of the *w*. to sin; **10:20** the tongue of the just is as choice silver: the heart of the *w*. is little worth; **10:24-25** the fear of the *w*., it shall come upon him: but the desire of the righteous shall be granted; **10:27-30** the fear of the LORD prolongeth days: but the years of the *w*. shall be shortened. The hope of the righteous shall be gladness: but the expectation of the *w*. shall perish; **10:32** the lips of the righteous know what is acceptable: but the mouth of the *w*. speaketh frowardness; **11:5-11** the righteousness of the perfect shall direct his way: but the *w*. shall fall by his own *w*.. The righteousness of the upright shall deliver them: but transgressors shall be taken in their own naughtiness; **11:18** the *w*. worketh a deceitful work: but to him that soweth righteousness shall be a sure reward; **11:21** the *w*. shall not be unpunished: but the seed of the righteous shall be delivered; **11:23** the desire of the righteous is only good: but the expectation of the *w*. is wrath; **11:31** the righteous shall be recompensed in the earth: much more the *w*. and the sinner; **12:3** a man shall not be established by *w*.: but the root of the righteous shall not be moved; **12:5-7** the *w.* are overthrown, and are not: but the house of the righteous shall stand; **12:10** a righteous man regardeth the life of his beast: but the tender mercies of the *w.* are cruel; **12:12-13** the *w.* is snared by the transgression of his lips: but the just shall come out of trouble; **12:21** there shall no evil happen to the just: but the *w.* shall be filled with mischief; **12:26** the righteous is more excellent than his neighbour: but the way of the *w.* seduceth them; **13:2** a man shall eat good by the fruit of his mouth: but the soul of the transgressors shall eat violence; **13:5-6** righteousness keepeth him that is upright in the way: but *w.* overthroweth the sinner; **13:9** the light of the righteous rejoiceth: but the lamp of the *w.* shall be put out; **13:15** good understanding giveth favour: but the way of transgressors is hard; **13:17** a *w.* messenger falleth into mischief: but a faithful ambassador is health; **13:25** the righteous eateth to the satisfying of his soul: but the belly of the *w.* shall want; **14:11** the house of the *w.* shall be overthrown: but the tabernacle of the upright shall flourish; **14:17-19** the evil bow before the good; and the *w.* at the gates of the righteous; **14:32** the *w.* is driven away in his *w.*: but the righteous hath hope in his death; **14:34** righteousness exalteth a nation: but sin is a reproach to any people; **15:6** in the house of the righteous is much treasure: but in the revenues of the *w.* is trouble; **15:8-9** the way of the *w.* is an abomination unto the LORD: but he loveth him that followeth after righteousness; **15:28-29** the LORD is far from the *w.*: but he heareth the prayer of the righteous; **16:12** it is an abomination to kings to commit *w.*: for the throne is established by righteousness; **16:27** an ungodly man diggeth up evil: and in his lips there is as a burning fire; **16:30** he shutteth his eyes to devise froward things: moving his lips he bringeth evil to pass; **17:4** a *w.* doer giveth heed to false lips; and a liar giveth ear to a naughty tongue; **17:11** an evil man seeketh only rebellion: therefore a cruel messenger shall be sent against him; **17:19** he loveth transgression that loveth strife: and he that exalteth his gate seeketh destruction; **17:23** a *w.* man taketh a gift out of the bosom to pervert the ways of judgment; **18:3** when the *w.* cometh, then cometh also contempt; **19:28** an ungodly witness scorneth judgment: and the mouth of the *w.* devoureth iniquity; **20:26** a wise king scattereth the *w.*, and bringeth the wheel over them; **21:7** the robbery of the *w.* shall destroy them; because they refuse to do judgment; **21:10** the soul of the *w.* desireth evil: his neighbour findeth no favour in his eyes; **21:12** the righteous man wisely considereth the house of the *w.*: but

God overthroweth the *w.* for their *w.*; **21:18** the *w.* shall be a ransom for the righteous, and the transgressor for the upright; **21:27** the sacrifice of the *w.* is abomination: how much more, when he bringeth it with a *w.* mind; **21:29** a *w.* man hardeneth his face: but as for the upright, he directeth his way; **24:16** the *w.* shall fall into mischief; **26:2** as the bird by wandering, as the swallow by flying, so the curse causeless shall not come; **26:10** the great God that formed all things both rewardeth the fool, and rewardeth transgressors; **27:20** Hell and destruction are never full; so the eyes of man are never satisfied; **28:1** the *w.* flee when no man pursueth: but righteous are bold as a lion; **28:15** as a roaring lion, and a ranging bear; so is a *w.* ruler over the poor people; **29:6** in the transgression of an evil man there is a snare: but the righteous doth sing and rejoice; **29:16** when the *w.* are multiplied, transgression increaseth: but the righteous shall see their fall; **29:22** an angry man stirreth up strife, and a furious man aboundeth in transgression; **29:27** an unjust man is an abomination to the just: and he that is upright in the way is abomination to the *w.*; **Eccl. 2:26** to the sinner he giveth travail, to gather and to heap up, that he may give to him that is good before God; **3:17** God shall judge the righteous and the *w.*: for there is a time there for every purpose and for every work; **4:3** better is he than both they, which hath not yet been, who hath not seen the evil work that is done under the sun; **8:8** there is no man that hath power over the spirit to retain the spirit... neither shall *w.* deliver those that are given to it; **8:10-13** it shall be well with them that fear God, which fear before him: But it shall not be well with the *w.*, neither shall he prolong his days; **9:3** the heart of the sons of men is full of evil, and madness is in their heart while they live, and after that they go to the dead; **9:5-6** the living know that they shall die: but the dead know not any thing, neither have they any more a reward; for the memory of them is forgotten; **9:18** wisdom is better than weapons of war: but one sinner destroyeth much good; **Isa. 1:4-7** sinful nation, a people laden with iniquity, a seed of evildoers, children that are corrupters: they have forsaken the LORD; **1:15** when ye make many prayers, I will not hear: your hands are full of blood; **1:21** how is the faithful city become an harlot! it was full of judgment; **1:28-31** destruction of the transgressors and of the sinners shall be together, and they that forsake the LORD shall be consumed; **2:11** lofty looks of man shall be humbled, and the haughtiness of men shall be bowed down; **3:8-9** their tongue and their doings are against the LORD, to provoke the eyes of his glory... they have rewarded evil unto themselves; **3:11** woe unto the *w.*! it shall be ill with him: for the reward of his hands shall be given him; **5:14** hell hath enlarged herself, and opened her mouth without measure: and their glory, and their multitude, and their pomp, and he that rejoiceth, shall descend into it; **5:18** woe unto them that draw iniquity with cords of vanity, and sin as it were with a cart rope; **5:23-25** they have cast away the law of the LORD of hosts, and despised the word of the Holy One of Israel; **8:9-10** take counsel together, and it shall come to nought; speak the word, and it shall not stand; **8:22** trouble and darkness, dimness of anguish; and they shall be driven to darkness; **9:12-13** the people turneth not unto him that smiteth them, neither do they seek the LORD of hosts; **9:20** he shall snatch on the right hand, and be hungry; and he shall eat on the left hand, and they shall not be satisfied: they shall eat every man the flesh of his own arm; **10:4** they shall bow down under the prisoners, and they shall fall under the slain; **11:4** he shall smite the earth with the rod of his mouth, and with the breath of his lips shall he slay the *w.*; **13:7-11** therefore shall all hands be faint, and every mans heart shall melt: And they shall be afraid: pangs and sorrows shall take hold of them; **14:5** the LORD hath broken the staff of the *w.*; **14:12-17** thou shalt be brought down to hell, to the sides of the pit. They that see thee shall narrowly look upon thee, and consider thee, saying, Is this the man that made the earth to tremble, that did shake kingdoms; that made the world as a wilderness, and destroyed the cities thereof; that opened not the house of his prisoners; **15:3** they shall gird themselves with sackcloth: on the tops of their houses, and in their streets, every one shall howl, weeping abundantly; **17:1** taken away from being a city, and it shall be a ruinous heap; **17:4-6** the glory of Jacob shall be made thin, and the fatness of his flesh shall wax lean; **19:6** they shall turn the rivers far away; and the brooks of defence shall be emptied and dried up: the reeds and flags shall wither; **24:16-17** the treacherous dealers have dealt treacherously; **26:14** thou visited and destroyed them, and made all their memory to perish; **26:21** the LORD cometh out of his place to punish the inhabitants of the earth for their iniquity: the earth also shall disclose her blood, and shall no more cover her slain; **28:8** for all tables are full of vomit and filthiness, so that there is no place clean; **28:15** we have made a covenant with death, and with hell are we at agreement; when the overflowing scourge shall pass through, it shall not come unto us: for we have made lies our refuge, and under falsehood

have we hid ourselves; **28:18** your covenant with death shall be disannulled, and your agreement with hell shall not stand; when the overflowing scourge shall pass through, then ye shall be trodden down by it; **29:20** the terrible one is brought to nought, and the scorner is consumed, and all that watch for iniquity are cut off; **30:13-14** this iniquity shall be to you as a breach ready to fall, swelling out in a high wall, whose breaking cometh suddenly at an instant; **30:28** there shall be a bridle in the jaws of the people, causing them to err; **31:2-3** arise against the house of the evildoers, and against the help of them that work iniquity; **32:6-7** the vile person will speak villany, and his heart will work iniquity, to practise hypocrisy, and to utter error against the LORD, to make empty the soul of the hungry, and he will cause the drink of the thirsty to fail; **33:9** the earth mourneth and languisheth; **33:11-12** ye shall conceive chaff, ye shall bring forth stubble: your breath, as fire, shall devour you; **38:18** the grave cannot praise thee, death can not celebrate thee: they that go down into the pit cannot hope for thy truth; **40:2** she hath received of the LORD's hand double for all her sins; **41:21-23** do good, or do evil, that we may be dismayed, and behold it together; **41:29** they are all vanity; their works are nothing: their molten images are wind and confusion; **42:13** the LORD shall go forth as a mighty man, he shall stir up jealousy like a man of war: he shall cry, yea, roar; he shall prevail against his enemies; **42:24-25** he hath poured upon him the fury of his anger, and the strength of battle: and it hath set him on fire round about; **43:24** thou hast made me to serve with thy sins, thou hast wearied me with thine iniquities; **47:9-11** thou hast trusted in thy *w.*: thou hast said, None seeth me; **48:22** there is no peace, saith the LORD, unto the *w.*; **49:17-20** thy children shall make haste; thy destroyers and they that made thee waste shall go forth of thee; **49:26** I will feed them that oppress thee with their own flesh; and they shall be drunken with their own blood, as with sweet wine; **50:1** for your iniquities have ye sold yourselves, and for your transgressions is your mother put away; **51:23** I will put it into the hand of them that afflict thee; which have said to thy soul, Bow down, that we may go over: and thou hast laid thy body as the ground, and as the street, to them that went over; **55:7** let the *w.* forsake his way, and the unrighteous man his thoughts: and let him return unto the LORD, and he will have mercy upon him; and to our God, for he will abundantly pardon; **56:10-12** [they] are blind: they are all ignorant, they are all dumb dogs, they cannot bark; sleeping, lying down, loving to slumber. Yea, they are greedy dogs which can never have enough; **57:3-9** [are ye] a seed of falsehood, Enflaming yourselves with idols under every green tree, slaying the children in the valleys under the clifts of the rocks; **57:20-21** the *w.* are like the troubled sea, when it cannot rest, whose waters cast up mire and dirt. There is no peace, saith my God, to the *w.*; **59:2-4** your iniquities have separated between you and your God, and your sins have hid his face from you, that he will not hear; **59:6-12** their works are works of iniquity, and the act of violence is in their hands. Their feet run to evil, and they make haste to shed innocent blood: their thoughts are thoughts of iniquity; wasting and destruction are in their paths; **59:21** my words which I have put in thy mouth, shall not depart out of thy mouth, nor out of the mouth of thy seed, nor out of the mouth of thy seeds seed; **64:6-7** we are all as an unclean thing, and all our righteousnesses are as filthy rags; and we all do fade as a leaf; and our iniquities, like the wind, have taken us away; **65:6** I will not keep silence, but will recompense, even recompense into their bosom; **65:11-15** ye shall leave your name for a curse unto my chosen: for the Lord GOD shall slay thee, and call his servants by another name; **66:4** I also will choose their delusions, and will bring their fears upon them; **66:14** the hand of the LORD shall be known toward his servants, and his indignation toward his enemies; **66:17** [they] shall be consumed together; **66:24** look upon the carcases of the men that have transgressed against me: for their worm shall not die, neither shall their fire be quenched; and they shall be an abhorring unto all flesh; **Jer. 1:14** evil shall break forth upon all the inhabitants of the land; **1:16** judgments against them touching all their *w.*, who have forsaken me, and have burned incense unto other gods, and worshipped the works of their own hands; **2:8** the pastors also transgressed against me, and the prophets prophesied by Baal, and walked after things that do not profit; **2:12** be astonished, O ye heavens, at this, and be horribly afraid, be ye very desolate, saith the LORD; **2:19-23** thine own *w.* shall correct thee, and thy backslidings shall reprove thee: know therefore and see that it is an evil thing and bitter, that thou hast forsaken the LORD thy God, and that my fear is not in thee; **3:2-5** the showers have been withholden, and there hath been no latter rain; and thou hadst a whores forehead, thou refusedst to be ashamed; **4:4** my fury come forth like fire, and burn that none can quench it, because of the evil of your doings; **4:18-20** thy way and thy doings have procured these things unto thee... destruction

upon destruction is cried; for the whole land is spoiled: suddenly are my tents spoiled, and my curtains in a moment; **5:6** every one that goeth out thence shall be torn in pieces: because their transgressions are many, and their backslidings are increased; **5:28** they are waxen fat, they shine: yea, they overpass the deeds of the *w.*: they judge not the cause, the cause of the fatherless, yet they prosper; and the right of the needy do they not judge; **6:7-8** as a fountain casteth out her waters, so she casteth out her *w.*: violence and spoil is heard in her; before me continually is grief and wounds; **6:24-26** we have heard the fame thereof: our hands wax feeble: anguish hath taken hold of us, and pain, as of a woman in travail; **7:12-16** see what I did... for the *w.* of my people Israel. And now, because ye have done all these works, saith the LORD... Therefore will I do unto this house; **7:27** thou shalt speak all these words unto them; but they will not hearken to thee: thou shalt also call unto them; but they will not answer thee; **8:2-3** they shall not be gathered, nor be buried; they shall be for dung upon the face of the earth. And death shall be chosen rather than life by all the residue of them that remain of this evil family; **11:15** what hath my beloved to do in mine house, seeing she hath wrought lewdness with many, and the holy flesh is passed from thee? when thou doest evil, then thou rejoicest; **12:1-2** wherefore doth the way of the *w.* prosper? wherefore are all they happy that deal very treacherously; **12:10-11** many pastors have destroyed my vineyard, they have trodden my portion under foot, they have made my pleasant portion a desolate wilderness; **12:14** thus saith the LORD against all mine evil neighbours... I will pluck them out of their land, and pluck out the house of Judah from among them; **13:16** give glory to the LORD your God, before he cause darkness, and before your feet stumble upon the dark mountains, and, while ye look for light, he turn it into the shadow of death; **13:22** for the greatness of thine iniquity are thy skirts discovered, and thy heels made bare; **14:7** O LORD, though our iniquities testify against us, do thou it for thy names sake: for our backslidings are many; we have sinned against thee; **15:1-3** though Moses and Samuel stood before me, yet my mind could not be toward this people: cast them out of my sight, and let them go forth; **15:7-9** I will fan them with a fan in the gates of the land; I will bereave them of children, I will destroy my people, since they return not from their ways; **15:13-14** thy substance and thy treasures will I give to the spoil without price, and that for all thy sins, even in all thy borders.

And I will make thee to pass with thine enemies into a land which thou knowest not; **16:3-4** they shall die of grievous deaths; they shall not be lamented; neither shall they be buried; but they shall be as dung upon the face of the earth: and they shall be consumed by the sword, and by famine; **16:9** I will cause to cease out of this place in your eyes, and in your days, the voice of mirth, and the voice of gladness, the voice of the bridegroom, and the voice of the bride; **16:13-14** I [will] cast you out of this land into a land that ye know not, neither ye nor your fathers; and there shall ye serve other gods day and night; where I will not shew you favour; **17:4** thou... shalt discontinue from thine heritage that I gave thee; and I will cause thee to serve thine enemies in the land which thou knowest not: for ye have kindled a fire in mine anger, which shall burn for ever; **17:9** the heart is deceitful above all things, and desperately *w.*: who can know it; **17:18** let them be confounded that persecute me, but let not me be confounded: let them be dismayed, but let not me be dismayed: bring upon them the day of evil, and destroy them with double destruction; **17:23** they obeyed not, neither inclined their ear, but made their neck stiff, that they might not hear, nor receive instruction; **18:18** come, and let us devise devices against Jeremiah; for the law shall not perish from the priest, nor counsel from the wise, nor the word from the prophet... let us smite him with the tongue, and let us not give heed to any of his words; **18:21-22** deliver up their children to the famine, and pour out their blood by the force of the sword; and let their wives be bereaved of their children, and be widows; and let their men be put to death; let their young men be slain by the sword in battle; **20:11** the LORD is with me as a mighty terrible one: therefore my persecutors shall stumble, and they shall not prevail: they shall be greatly ashamed; for they shall not prosper; **21:7** he shall smite them with the edge of the sword; he shall not spare them, neither have pity, nor have mercy; **21:12** execute judgment in the morning, and deliver him that is spoiled out of the hand of the oppressor, lest my fury go out like fire, and burn that none can quench it, because of the evil of your doings; **22:22** the wind shall eat up all thy pastors, and thy lovers shall go into captivity: surely then shalt thou be ashamed and confounded for all thy *w.*; **23:2** ye have scattered my flock, and driven them away, and have not visited them: behold, I will visit upon you the evil of your doings, saith the LORD; **23:11-14** both prophet and priest are profane; yea, in my house have I found their *w.*, saith the LORD. Wherefore their way shall be

unto them as slippery ways in the darkness... for I will bring evil upon them, even the year of their visitation, saith the LORD; **23:19** a whirlwind of the LORD is gone forth in fury, even a grievous whirlwind: it shall fall grievously upon the head of the *w.*; **23:38-40** I have sent unto you, saying, Ye shall not say, The burden of the LORD; Therefore, behold, I, even I, will utterly forget you, and I will forsake you, and the city that I gave you and your fathers, and cast you out of my presence: And I will bring an everlasting reproach upon you, and a perpetual shame, which shall not be forgotten; **24:2** one basket had very good figs, even like the figs that are first ripe: and the other basket had very naughty figs, which could not be eaten, they were so bad; **24:9-10** I will deliver them to be removed into all the kingdoms of the earth for their hurt, to be a reproach and a proverb, a taunt and a curse, in all places whither I shall drive them; **25:12** I will punish the king of Babylon, and that nation, saith the LORD, for their iniquity, and the land of the Chaldeans, and will make it perpetual desolations; **25:31-34** the LORD hath a controversy with the nations, he will plead with all flesh; he will give them that are *w.* to the sword, saith the LORD; **26:8** when Jeremiah had made an end of speaking all that the LORD had commanded him to speak unto all the people... the priests and the prophets and all the people took him, saying, Thou shalt surely die; **26:23** they fetched forth Urijah... and brought him unto... the king; who slew him with the sword, and cast his dead body into the graves of the common people; **29:17-18** I will send upon them the sword, the famine, and the pestilence, and will make them like vile figs, that cannot be eaten, they are so evil; **30:14-15** why criest thou for thine affliction? thy sorrow is incurable for the multitude of thine iniquity: because thy sins were increased, I have done these things unto thee; **30:23** the whirlwind of the LORD goeth forth with fury, a continuing whirlwind: it shall fall with pain upon the head of the *w.*; **31:30** every one shall die for his own iniquity: every man that eateth the sour grape, his teeth shall be set on edge; **36:31** I will punish him and his seed and his servants for their iniquity; and I will bring upon them, and upon the inhabitants of Jerusalem, and upon the men of Judah, all the evil that I have pronounced against them; **41:11-12** when [they] heard of all the evil that Ishmael the son of Nethaniah had done, Then they took all the men, and went to fight; **44:2-3** ye have seen all the evil that I have brought upon Jerusalem, and upon all the cities of Judah; and, behold, this day they are a desolation, and no man dwelleth therein, Because of their *w.*; **44:9** have ye forgotten the *w.* of your fathers, and the *w.* of the kings... and the *w.* of their wives, and your own *w.*, and the *w.* of your wives, which they have committed...; **44:22** the LORD could no longer bear, because of the evil of your doings, and because of the abominations which ye have committed; therefore is your land a desolation, and an astonishment, and a curse; **46:10** this is the day of the Lord GOD of hosts, a day of vengeance, that he may avenge him of his adversaries: and the sword shall devour, and it shall be satiate and made drunk with their blood; **46:21-26** the LORD of hosts, the God of Israel, saith; Behold, I will punish the multitude... with their gods, and their kings; even Pharaoh, and all them that trust in him; **48:1-5** Moab is destroyed; her little ones have caused a cry to be heard. For in the going up of Luhith continual weeping shall go up; for in the going down of Horonaim the enemies have heard a cry of destruction; **48:16-18** the calamity of Moab is near to come, and his affliction hasteth fast. All ye that are about him, bemoan him; and all ye that know his name, say, How is the strong staff broken, and the beautiful rod; **48:20** Moab is confounded; for it is broken down: howl and cry; tell ye it in Arnon, that Moab is spoiled; **48:46** woe be unto thee, O Moab! the people of Chemosh perisheth: for thy sons are taken captives, and thy daughters captives; **49:2** I will cause an alarm of war to be heard in Rabbah of the Ammonites; and it shall be a desolate heap, and her daughters shall be burned with fire: then shall Israel be heir unto them that were his heirs; **49:12** they whose judgment was not to drink of the cup have assuredly drunken; and art thou he that shall altogether go unpunished? thou shalt not go unpunished, but thou shalt surely drink of it; **49:15-17** I will make thee small among the heathen, and despised among men. Thy terribleness hath deceived thee, and the pride of thine heart; **49:20-22** surely the least of the flock shall draw them out: surely he shall make their habitations desolate with them. The earth is moved at the noise of their fall, at the cry the noise thereof was heard in the Red sea; **49:32** their camels shall be a booty, and the multitude of their cattle a spoil: and I will scatter into all winds them that are in the utmost corners; and I will bring their calamity from all sides thereof, saith the LORD; **49:36-37** I will cause Elam to be dismayed before their enemies, and before them that seek their life: and I will bring evil upon them, even my fierce anger, saith the LORD; **50:46** at the noise of the taking of Babylon the earth is moved, and the cry is heard among the nations; **51:49** as Babylon hath caused the slain of Israel to fall, so at Babylon shall fall the slain of all the earth; **51:55** the LORD hath spoiled Babylon, and destroyed out of her the great voice; when her waves do roar like great waters, a noise of their voice is uttered; **Lam. 1:2-5** she weepeth sore in the night, and her tears are on her cheeks: among all her lovers she hath none to comfort her: all her friends have dealt treacherously with her, they are become her enemies; **1:8-9** Jerusalem hath grievously sinned; therefore she is removed: all that honoured her despise her, because they have seen her nakedness: yea, she sigheth, and turneth backward; **1:12** behold, and see if there be any sorrow like unto my sorrow, which is done unto me, wherewith the LORD hath afflicted me in the day of his fierce anger; **1:16** I weep; mine eye, mine eye runneth down with water, because the comforter that should relieve my soul is far from me: my children are desolate, because the enemy prevailed; **1:22** let all their *w.* come before thee; and do unto them, as thou hast done unto me for all my transgressions: for my sighs are many, and my heart is faint; **3:1-66** render unto them a recompence, O LORD, according to the work of their hands. Give them sorrow of heart, thy curse unto them. Persecute and destroy them in anger from under the heavens of the LORD; **4:8-9** their visage is blacker than a coal; they are not known in the streets: their skin cleaveth to their bones; it is withered, it is become like a stick; **Ezek. 4:15-17** they shall eat bread by weight, and with care; and they shall drink water by measure, and with astonishment: That they may want bread and water, and be astonied one with another, and consume away for their iniquity; **5:9-10** I will do in thee that which I have not done, and whereunto I will not do any more the like, because of all thine abominations... I will execute judgments in thee, and the whole remnant of thee will I scatter into all the winds; **5:14-17** I shall execute judgments in thee in anger and in fury and in furious rebukes. I the LORD have spoken it; **6:9** they that escape of you shall remember me among the nations whither they shall be carried captives... and they shall lothe themselves for the evils which they have committed in all their abominations; **6:12** he that is far off shall die of the pestilence; and he that is near shall fall by the sword; and he that remaineth and is besieged shall die by the famine: thus will I accomplish my fury upon them; **7:11-20** violence is risen up into a rod of *w.*: none of them shall remain, nor of their multitude, nor of any of theirs: neither shall there be wailing for them; **7:25** destruction cometh;

and they shall seek peace, and there shall be none; **8:9** go in, and behold the *w.* abominations that they do here; **8:15** turn thee yet again, and thou shalt see greater abominations than these; **8:17** is it a light thing to the house of Judah that they commit the abominations which they commit here? for they have filled the land with violence, and have returned to provoke me to anger; **16:23** after all thy *w.*, [woe, woe unto thee! saith the Lord GOD;; **18:8** he that hath not given forth upon usury, neither hath taken any increase, that hath withdrawn his hand from iniquity, hath executed true judgment between man and man; **18:12-13** [if he] hath... committed abomination, Hath given forth upon usury, and hath taken increase: shall he then live? he shall not live: he hath done all these abominations; he shall surely die; his blood shall be upon him; **18:16-20** [he that] hath walked in my statutes; he shall not die for the iniquity of his father, he shall surely live. As for his father, because he cruelly oppressed, spoiled his brother by violence, and did that which is not good among his people, lo, even he shall die in his iniquity; **20:30** are ye polluted after the manner of your fathers? and commit ye whoredom after their abominations; **21:3** I am against thee, and will draw forth my sword out of his sheath, and will cut off from thee the righteous and the *w.*; **21:12** cry and howl, son of man: for it shall be upon my people, it shall be upon all the princes of Israel: terrors by reason of the sword shall be upon my people; **21:15** I have set the point of the sword against all their gates, that their heart may faint, and their ruins be multiplied; **21:23** it shall be unto them as a false divination in their sight, to them that have sworn oaths: but he will call to remembrance the iniquity, that they may be taken; **21:25** profane *w.* prince of Israel, whose day is come, when iniquity shall have an end; **21:31-32** I will pour out mine indignation upon thee, I will blow against thee in the fire of my wrath, and deliver thee into the hand of brutish men, and skilful to destroy; **22:15-16** I will scatter thee among the heathen, and disperse thee in the countries, and will consume thy filthiness out of thee; **22:20-21** I [will] gather you in mine anger and in my fury, and I will leave you there, and melt you. Yea, I will gather you, and blow upon you in the fire of my wrath, and ye shall be melted in the midst thereof; **24:23** your tires shall be upon your heads, and your shoes upon your feet: ye shall not mourn nor weep; but ye shall pine away for your iniquities, and mourn one toward another; **24:25** shall it not be in the day when I take from them their strength, the joy of their glory, the desire of their eyes, and that

whereupon they set their minds, their sons and their daughters; **25:6-7** I will stretch out mine hand upon thee, and will deliver thee for a spoil to the heathen; and I will cut thee off from the people, and I will cause thee to perish out of the countries: I will destroy thee; and thou shalt know that I am the LORD; **25:10-11** I will execute judgments upon Moab; and they shall know that I am the LORD; **26:5-14** her daughters which are in the field shall be slain by the sword; and they shall know that I am the LORD; **26:21** I will make thee a terror, and thou shalt be no more: though thou be sought for, yet shalt thou never be found again; **27:27-31** [all] shall fall into the midst of the seas in the day of thy ruin... And shall cause their voice to be heard against thee, and shall cry bitterly, and shall cast up dust upon their heads, they shall wallow themselves in the ashes; **28:16** thou hast sinned: therefore I will cast thee as profane out of the mountain of God: and I will destroy thee; **31:11-14** I have therefore delivered him into the hand of the mighty one of the heathen; he shall surely deal with him: I have driven him out for his *w.*; **31:17-18** they also went down into hell with him unto them that be slain with the sword; and they that were his arm, that dwelt under his shadow in the midst of the heathen; **32:10** I will make many people amazed at thee, and their kings shall be horribly afraid for thee, when I shall brandish my sword before them; and they shall tremble at every moment; **32:12** I [will] cause thy multitude to fall, the terrible of the nations, all of them... and all the multitude thereof shall be destroyed; **33:9-11** if thou warn the *w.* of his way to turn from it; if he do not turn from his way, he shall die in his iniquity; but thou hast delivered thy soul; **33:15** if the *w.* restore the pledge, give again that he had robbed, walk in the statutes of life, without committing iniquity; he shall surely live, he shall not die; **33:19** if the *w.* turn from his *w.*, and do that which is lawful and right, he shall live thereby; **35:3-5** I am against thee, and I will stretch out mine hand against thee, and I will make thee most desolate. I will lay thy cities waste, and thou shalt be desolate, and thou shalt know that I am the LORD; **38:3-4** I will turn thee back, and put hooks into thy jaws, and I will bring thee forth, and all thine army; **39:23-24** the house of Israel went into captivity for their iniquity: because they trespassed against me, therefore hid I my face from them, and gave them into the hand of their enemies; **Dan. 9:14-15** the LORD watched upon the evil, and brought it upon us: for the LORD our God is righteous in all his works which he doeth: for we obeyed not his voice; **12:10** many shall be purified, and made white, and tried; but the *w*. shall do *w*.: and none of the *w*. shall understand; but the wise shall understand; **Hosea 5:5** the pride of Israel doth testify to his face: therefore shall Israel and Ephraim fall in their iniquity; **7:2** they consider not in their hearts that I remember all their *w*.: now their own doings have beset them about; they are before my face; **9:14-15** for the *w*. of their doings I will drive them out of mine house, I will love them no more; **10:8** the sin of Israel, shall be destroyed: the thorn and the thistle shall come up on their altars; and they shall say to the mountains, Cover us; and to the hills, Fall on us; **10:13** ye have plowed *w*., ye have reaped iniquity; ye have eaten the fruit of lies: because thou didst trust in thy way, in the multitude of thy mighty men; **12:14** Ephraim provoked him to anger most bitterly: therefore shall he leave his blood upon him, and his reproach shall his Lord return unto him; **13:9** O Israel, thou hast destroyed thyself; but in me is thine help; **Joel 1:9** the meat offering and the drink offering is cut off from the house of the LORD; the priests, the LORD's ministers, mourn; **1:11-12** be ye ashamed, O ye husbandmen; howl, O ye vinedressers, for the wheat and for the barley; because the harvest of the field is perished; **1:17-18** the seed is rotten under their clods, the garners are laid desolate, the barns are broken down; for the corn is withered; **3:13** put ye in the sickle, for the harvest is ripe: come, get you down; for the press is full, the fats overflow; for their *w*. is great; **Amos 2:14-16** the flight shall perish from the swift, and the strong shall not strengthen his force, neither shall the mighty deliver himself... he that is courageous among the mighty shall flee away naked in that day; **3:2** you only have I known of all the families of the earth: therefore I will punish you for all your iniquities; **3:14-15** I shall visit the transgressions of Israel upon him... the horns of the altar shall be cut off, and fall to the ground... and the great houses shall have an end, saith the LORD; **6:12** shall horses run upon the rock? will one plow there with oxen? for ye have turned judgment into gall, and the fruit of righteousness into hemlock; **9:8** the eyes of the Lord GOD are upon the sinful kingdom, and I will destroy it from off the face of the earth; saving that I will not utterly destroy the house of Jacob; **9:10** all the sinners of my people shall die by the sword, which say, The evil shall not overtake nor prevent us; **Jonah 1:2** arise, go to Nineveh, that great city, and cry against it; for their *w*. is come up before me; **Micah 3:2, 4** [they] who hate the good, and love the evil... shall..cry unto the LORD, but he will not hear them: he will even hide his face from

them at that time, as they have behaved themselves ill in their doings; **6:10-16** the rich men thereof are full of violence, and the inhabitants thereof have spoken lies, and their tongue is deceitful in their mouth. Therefore also will I make thee sick in smiting thee, in making thee desolate because of thy sins; **7:2** the good man is perished out of the earth: and there is none upright among men: they all lie in wait for blood; they hunt every man his brother with a net; **7:4** the best of them is as a brier: the most upright is sharper than a thorn hedge: the day of thy watchmen and thy visitation cometh; now shall be their perplexity; **7:13** the land shall be desolate because of them that dwell therein, for the fruit of their doings; **Nahum 1:2-3** God is jealous, and the LORD revengeth; the LORD revengeth, and is furious; the LORD will take vengeance on his adversaries, and he reserveth wrath for his enemies; **2:5** they shall stumble in their walk; they shall make haste to the wall thereof, and the defence shall be prepared; **2:8-12** she is empty, and void, and waste: and the heart melteth, and the knees smite together, and much pain is in all loins, and the faces of them all gather blackness; **Hab. 3:12-13** thou didst march through the land in indignation, thou dids t thresh the heathen in anger. Thou wentest forth for the salvation of thy people, even for salvation with thine anointed; **Zeph. 1:17-18** I will bring distress upon men, that they shall walk like blind men, because they have sinned against the LORD: and their blood shall be poured out as dust, and their flesh as the dung; **2:9** surely Moab shall be as Sodom, and the children of Ammon as Gomorrah... a perpetual desolation: the residue of my people shall spoil them, and the remnant of my people shall possess them; **3:5** the just LORD is in the midst thereof; he will not do iniquity: every morning doth he bring his judgment to light, he faileth not; **Zech. 9:5** [they] shall see it, and fear... and be very sorrowful... for her expectation shall be ashamed; and the king shall perish from Gaza, and Ashkelon shall not be inhabited; **14:12** their flesh shall consume away while they stand upon their feet, and their eyes shall consume away in their holes, and their tongue shall consume away in their mouth; **Mal. 1:4** thus saith the LORD of hosts, They shall build, but I will throw down; and they shall call them, The border of *w*., and, The people against whom the LORD hath indignation for ever; **4:1** the day cometh, that shall burn as an oven; and all the proud, yea, and all that do *w*.ly, shall be stubble; **4:3** ye shall tread down the *w*.; for they shall be ashes under the soles of your feet in the day that I shall do this.

WIDOW (*see also* Poor)

Oppress not the widow, nor the fatherless, the stranger, nor the poor; and let none of you imagine evil against his brother in your heart. Zech. 7:10 (*see also* Fatherless, Oppress, Stranger)

Pure religion and undefiled before God and the Father is this, To visit the fatherless and widows in their affliction, and to keep himself unspotted from the world. James 1:27 (*see also* Fatherless)

1 Tim 5:3-4 honour *w.* that are widows indeed. But if any *w.* have children or nephews, let them learn first to shew piety at home, and to requite their parents: for that is good and acceptable before God; **James 1:27** pure religion and undefiled before God and the Father is this, To visit the fatherless and *w.* in their affliction, and to keep himself unspotted from the world.

WIFE, WIVES (*see also* Marriage)

Whoso findeth a wife findeth a good thing, and obtaineth favour of the LORD. Prov. 18:22 (*see also* Favor)

A virtuous woman is a crown to her husband: but she that maketh ashamed is as rottenness in his bones. Prov. 12:4 (*see also* Virtue)

Let the husband render unto the render unto the wife due benevolence: and likewise also the wife unto the husband. 1 Cor. 7:3-5 (*see also* Husband, Treatment)

A bishop then must be blameless, the husband of one wife, vigilant, sober, of good behaviour, given to hospitality, apt to teach. 1 Tim. 3:2 (*see also* Bishop, Vigilant)

For this cause shall a man leave his father and mother, and cleave to his wife; And they twain shall be one flesh: so then they are no more twain, but one flesh. Mark 10:7-8 (*see also* Cleave)

Who can find a virtuous woman? for her price is far above rubies. The heart of her husband doth safely trust in her, so that he shall have no need of spoil. She will do him good and not evil all the days of her life. Prov. 31:10-12 (*see also* Virtue)

He that is unmarried careth for the things that belong to the Lord, how he may please the Lord: But he that is married careth for the things that are of the world, how he may please his wife. 1 Cor. 7:32-33 (*see also* Care)

Live joyfully with the wife whom thou lovest all the days of the life of thy vanity, which he hath given thee under the sun, all the days of thy vanity: for that is thy portion in this life, and in thy labour which thou takest under the sun. Eccl. 9:9 (*see also* Joyfully, Live)

Wives, submit yourselves unto your own husbands as unto the Lord. For the husband is the head of the wife, even as Christ is the head of the church: and he is the saviour of the body. Therefore as the church is subject unto Christ, so let the wives be to their own husbands in every thing. Eph. 5:22-24 (*see also* Submit)

WILL, WILLING, WILLINGLY (*see also* Desire, Diligence, Purpose)

So is the will of God, that with well doing ye may put to silence the ignorance of foolish men: As free, and not using your liberty for a cloke of maliciousness, but as the servants of God. 1 Pet. 2:15-16 (*see also* Do, Liberty, Servant)

In everything give thanks: for this is the will of God in Christ Jesus concerning you. 1 Thes. 5:18 (*see also* Thank)

He stretched forth his hand toward his disciples, and said, Behold my mother and my brethren! For whosoever shall do the will of m Father which is in heaven, the same is my brother, and sister, and mother. Matt. 12:49-50 (*see also* Brethren, Sister, Mark 3:35)

I keep under my body, and bring it into subjection: lest that by any means, when I have preached to others, I myself should be a castaway. 1 Cor. 9:27 (*see also* Body, Flesh, Subject)

If ye be willing and obedient, ye shall eat the good of the land: But if ye refuse and rebel, ye shall be devoured with the sword. Isa. 1:19-20 (*see also* Obedience, Rebel)

Not every one that saith unto me, Lord, Lord, shall enter into the kingdom of heaven; but he that doeth the will of my Father who is in heaven. Many will say to me in that day: Lord, Lord, have we not prophesied in thy name, and in thy name have cast out devils, and in thy name done many wonderful works? And then will I profess unto them: I never knew you; depart from me, ye that work iniquity. Matt. 7:21-23 (*see also* False Prophets, Father, Priestcraft, Wonderful)

Do after the will of your God. Ezra 7:18 (*see also* Do)

Ezra 7:18 whatsoever shall seem good to thee, and to thy brethren, to do with the rest of the silver and the gold, that do after the *w.* of your God; Ps. 40:8 I delight to do thy *w.*, O my God: yea, thy law is within my heart; 143:10 teach me to do thy *w.*; for thou art my God: thy spirit is good; lead me into the land of uprightness; Ezek. 33:32 thou art unto them as a very lovely song of one that hath a pleasant voice, and can play well on an instrument: for they hear thy words, but they do them not.

Neither yield ye your members as instruments of unrighteousness unto sin: but yield yourselves unto God, as those that are alive from the dead, and your members as instruments of righteousness unto God. Rom. 6:13 (*see also* Instrument, Yield)

Matt. 7:21-23 not every one that saith unto me, Lord, Lord, shall enter into the kingdom of heaven; but he that doeth the *w.* of my Father which is in heaven. Many *w.* say to me in that day, Lord, Lord, have we not prophesied in thy name? and in thy name have cast out devils? and in thy name done many wonderful works? And then *w.* I profess unto them, I never knew you: depart from me, ye that work iniquity; 12:48-50 (Mark 3:32-35) whosoever shall do the *w.* of my Father which is in heaven, the same is my brother, and sister, and mother; 15:19-20 for out of the heart proceed evil thoughts, murders, adulteries, fornications, thefts, false witness, blasphemies: These are the things which defile a man: but to eat with unwashen hands defileth not a man; 16:24 then said Jesus unto his disciples, If any man *w.* come after me, let him deny himself, and take up his cross, and follow me; 21:29-31 the publicans and the harlots go into the kingdom of God before you; 26:39 if it be possible, let this cup pass from me: nevertheless not as I *w.*, but as thou wilt; 26:42 if this cup

may not pass away from me, except I drink it, thy *w.* be done; Mark 14:36 Abba, Father, all things are possible unto thee; take away this cup from me: nevertheless not what I *w.*, but what thou wilt; Luke 2:48-49 how is it that ye sought me? wist ye not that I must be about my Father's business; 22:42 Father, if thou be *w.*, remove this cup from me: nevertheless not my *w.*, but thine, be done; John 1:13 which were born, not of blood, nor of the *w.* of the flesh, nor of the *w.* of man, but of God; 4:32-34 Jesus saith unto them, My meat is to do the *w.* of him that sent me, and to finish his work; 5:19 the Son can do nothing of himself, but what he seeth the Father do: for what things soever he doeth, these also doeth the Son likewise; 5:30 I can of mine own self do nothing: as I hear, I judge: and my judgment is just; because I seek not mine own *w.*, but the *w.* of the Father which hath sent me; 5:36 I have greater witness than that of John: for the works which the Father hath given me to finish, the same works that I do, bear witness of me, that the Father hath sent me; 6:38-40 I came down from heaven, not to do mine own *w.*, but the *w.* of him that sent me. And this is the Father's *w.* which hath sent me, that of all which he hath given me I should lose nothing, but should raise it up again at the last day. And this is the *w.* of him that sent me, that every one which seeth the Son, and believeth on him, may have everlasting life: and I *w.* raise him up at the last day; 7:16-17 my doctrine is not mine, but his that sent me. If any man *w.* do his *w.*, he shall know of the doctrine, whether it be of God, or whether I speak of myself; 8:25-29 Jesus unto them, When ye have lifted up the Son of man, then shall ye know that I am he, and that I do nothing of myself; but as my Father hath taught me, I speak these things. And he that sent me is with me: the Father hath not left me alone; for I do always those things that please him; 8:49-50 Jesus answered, I have not a devil; but I honour my Father, and ye do dishonour me. And I seek not mine own glory: there is one that seeketh and judgeth; 9:31 now we know that God heareth not sinners: but if any man be a worshipper of God, and doeth his *w.*, him he heareth; 12:49-50 I have not spoken of myself; but the Father which sent me, he gave me a commandment, what I should say, and what I should speak. And I know that his commandment is life everlasting: whatsoever I speak therefore, even as the Father said unto me, so I speak; 14:31 that the world may know that I love the Father; and as the Father gave me commandment, even so I do; 17:4 I have glorified thee on the earth: I have finished the work which thou gavest me to do;

17:12 while I was with them in the world, I kept them in thy name: those that thou gavest me I have kept, and none of them is lost, but the son of perdition; that the scripture might be fulfilled; **18:10-11** then said Jesus unto Peter, Put up thy sword into the sheath: the cup which my Father hath given me, shall I not drink it; **18:37** Jesus answered, Thou sayest that I am a king. To this end was I born, and for this cause came I into the world, that I should bear witness unto the truth. Every one that is of the truth heareth my voice; **20:21** peace be unto you: as my Father hath sent me, even so send I you; **Acts 18:21** I *w.* return again unto you, if God *w.*; **20:24** none of these things move me, neither count I my life dear unto myself, so that I might finish my course with joy, and the ministry, which I have received of the Lord Jesus, to testify the gospel of the grace of God; **21:14** when he would not be persuaded, we ceased, saying, The *w.* of the Lord be done; **Rom. 1:10** for God is my witness, whom I serve with my spirit in the gospel of his Son, that without ceasing I make mention of you always in my prayers; **1:29-32** being filled with all unrighteousness, fornication, wickedness, covetousness, maliciousness; full of envy, murder, debate, deceit, malignity; whisperers, Backbiters, haters of God, despiteful, proud, boasters, inventors of evil things, disobedient to parents, Without understanding, covenantbreakers, without natural affection, implacable, unmerciful: Who knowing the judgment of God, that they which commit such things are worthy of death, not only do the same, but have pleasure in them that do them; **6:13** neither yield ye your members as instruments of unrighteousness unto sin: but yield yourselves unto God, as those that are alive from the dead, and your members as instruments of righteousness unto God; **6:19** as ye have yielded your members servants to uncleanness and to iniquity unto iniquity; even so now yield your members servants to righteousness unto holiness; **6:22** become servants to God, ye have your fruit unto holiness, and the end everlasting life; **8:28** we know that all things work together for good to them that love God, to them who are the called according to his purpose; **10:3** being ignorant of God's righteousness, and going about to establish their own righteousness, have not submitted themselves unto the righteousness of God; **12:2** be not conformed to this world: but be ye transformed by the renewing of your mind, that ye may prove what is that good, and acceptable, and perfect, *w.* of God; **13:1-2** let every soul be subject unto the higher powers. For there is no power but of God: the powers that be are ordained of God. Whosoever therefore resisteth the power, resisteth the ordinance of God: and they that resist shall receive to themselves damnation; **1 Cor. 1:1** Paul, called to be an apostle of Jesus Christ through the *w.* of God; **6:17** he that is joined unto the Lord is one spirit; **15:58** be ye stedfast, unmoveable, always abounding in the work of the Lord, forasmuch as ye know that your labour is not in vain in the Lord; **2 Cor. 8:5** this they did, not as we hoped, but first gave their own selves to the Lord, and unto us by the *w.* of God; **Eph. 5:17** be ye not unwise, but understanding what the *w.* of the Lord is; **6:6** not with eyeservice, as menpleasers; but as the servants of Christ, doing the *w.* of God from the heart; **Philip. 1:20-21** Christ shall be magnified in my body, whether it be by life, or by death. For to me to live is Christ, and to die is gain; **2:30** the work of Christ he was nigh unto death, not regarding his life, to supply your lack of service toward me; **Col. 3:24** knowing that of the Lord ye shall receive the reward of the inheritance: for ye serve the Lord Christ; **4:12** that ye may stand perfect and complete in all the *w.* of God; **1 Thes. 4:4** every one of you should know how to possess his vessel in sanctification and honour; **2 Thes. 2:10-12** with all deceivableness of unrighteousness in them that perish; because they received not the love of the truth, that they might be saved; **3:4** we have confidence in the Lord touching you, that ye both do and *w.* do the things which we command you; **Heb. 5:4** no man taketh this honour unto himself, but he that is called of God, as was Aaron; **10:36** ye have need of patience, that, after ye have done the *w.* of God, ye might receive the promise; **12:9** shall we not much rather be in subjection unto the Father of spirits, and live; **13:20-21** brought again from the dead our Lord Jesus, that great shepherd of the sheep, through the blood of the everlasting covenant, Make you perfect in every good work to do his *w.*, working in you that which is wellpleasing in his sight, through Jesus Christ; to whom be glory; **James 4:15** ye ought to say, If the Lord *w.*, we shall live, and do this, or that; **1 Pet. 2:13-14** submit yourselves to every ordinance of man for the Lord's sake: whether it be to the king, as supreme; Or unto governors, as unto them that are sent by him for the punishment of evildoers, and for the praise of them that do well; **1 Jn. 2:17** the world passeth away, and the lust thereof: but he that doeth the *w.* of God abideth for ever; **Rev. 22:3** there shall be no more curse: but the throne of God and of the Lamb shall be in it; and his servants shall serve him.

WINE (*see also* Drunkenness)

Be not drunk with wine, wherein is excess; but be filled with the Spirit. Eph. 5:18 (*see also* Drunk, Excess, Spirit)

Eph 5:18 be not drunk with *w.*, wherein is excess; but be filled with the Spirit; **1 Tim. 3:8** likewise must the deacons be grave, not doubletongued, not given to much *w.*, not greedy of filthy lucre; **Titus 2:2-3** aged men be sober, grave, temperate, sound in faith, in charity, in patience. The aged women likewise, that they be in behaviour as becometh holiness, not false accusers, not given to much *w.*, teachers of good things.

Wine is a mocker, strong drink is raging: and whosoever is deceived thereby is not wise. Prov. 20:1 (*see also* Deceive, Strong Drink)

Prov. 20:1 wine is a mocker, strong drink is raging: and whosoever is deceived thereby is not wise; **21:17** he that loveth pleasure shall be a poor man: he that loveth *w.* and oil shall not be rich; **31:4-7** it is not for kings to drink *w.*; nor for princes strong drink: Lest they drink, and forget the law, and pervert the judgment of any of the afflicted; **Eccl. 2:3** I sought in mine heart to give myself unto wine, yet acquainting mine heart with wisdom; and to lay hold on folly, till I might see what was that good for the sons of men; **Isa. 5:11** woe unto them that rise up early in the morning, that they may follow strong drink; that continue until night, till *w.* inflame them; **5:22** woe unto them that are mighty to drink *w.*, and men of strength to mingle strong drink; **24:9** they shall not drink *w.* with a song; strong drink shall be bitter to them that drink it; **Hosea 4:11** whoredom and *w.* and new *w.* take away the heart.

Be not among winebibbers; among riotous eaters of flesh: for the drunkard and the glutton shall come to poverty: and drowsiness shall clothe a man with rags. Prov. 23:20-21 (*see also* Be, Drunk)

Prov. 23:20-21 be not among winebibbers; among riotous eaters of flesh: For the drunkard and the glutton shall come to poverty: and drowsiness shall clothe a man with rags; **23:29-35** who hath woe? who hath sorrow? who hath contentions? who hath babbling? who hath wounds without cause? who hath redness of eyes? They that tarry long at the *w.*; they that go to seek mixed *w.*; **Isa. 28:1** woe to the crown of

pride, to the drunkards of Ephraim, whose glorious beauty is a fading flower, which are on the head of the fat valleys of them that are overcome with *w.*; **Amos 6:4-7** [they] drink *w.* in bowls, and anoint themselves with the chief ointments: but they are not grieved for the affliction of Joseph. Therefore now shall they go captive with the first that go captive, and the banquet of them that stretched themselves shall be removed.

WISDOM, WISE, WISELY (*see also* Discern, Gift, Holy Ghost, Intelligence, Learn, Prudent, Understand)

A wise man will hear, and will increase learning; and a man of understanding shall attain unto wise counsels. Prov. 1:5 (*see also* Counsel)

The wisdom of the prudent is to understand his way: but the folly of fools is deceit. Prov. 14:8 (*see also* Prudent, Way)

If any of you lack wisdom, let him ask of God, that giveth to all men liberally, and upbraideth not; and it shall be given him. But let him ask in faith, nothing wavering. For he that wavereth is like a wave of the sea driven with the wind and tossed. James 1:5-6 (*see also* Ask, Lack, Waver, JSH 1:11)

Jesus increased in wisdom and stature, and in favour with God and man. Luke 2:52 (*see also* Favor, Increase, Jesus Christ, Stature)

Be not righteous over much; neither make thyself over wise: why shouldest thou destroy thyself? Eccl. 7:16 (*see also* Righteous)

The God of our Lord Jesus Christ, the Father of glory, may give unto you the spirit of wisdom and revelation in the knowledge of him: The eyes of your understanding being enlightened; that ye may know what is the hope of his calling, and what the riches of the glory of his inheritance in the saints. Eph. 1:17-18 (*see also* Father, Hope, Reveal)

He that handleth a matter wisely shall find good: and whoso trusteth in the LORD, happy is he. Prov. 16:20 (*see also* Matter, Trust)

I have filled him with the spirit of God, in wisdom, in understanding, and in knowledge, and in all manner of workmanship. Ex. 31:3 (*see also* Know, Understand)

Therefore also said the wisdom of God, I will send them prophets and apostles, and some of them they shall slay and persecute: That the blood of all the prophets, which was shed from the foundation of the world, may be required of this generation. Luke 11:49-50 (*see also* Blood, Persecute, Prophet)

Let the word of Christ dwell in you richly in all wisdom; teaching and admonishing one another in psalms and hymns and spiritual songs, singing with grace in your hearts to the Lord. Col. 3:16 (*see also* Admonish, Grace, Hymn, Psalm, Sing, Word)

Thus saith the LORD, Let not the wise man glory in his wisdom, neither let the mighty man glory in his might, let not the rich man glory in his riches: But let him that glorieth glory in this, that he understandeth and knoweth me Jer. 9:23-24 (*see also* Glorify)

Walk in wisdom toward them that are without, redeeming the time. Col. 4:5 (*see also* Walk)

The fear of the LORD is the beginning of knowledge: but fools despise wisdom and and instruction. Prov. 1:7 (*see also* Beginning, Instruction)

Incline thine ear unto wisdom, and apply thine heart to understanding. Prov. 2:2 (*see also* Apply, Know, Understand)

Keep sound wisdom and discretion: So shall they be life unto thy soul, and grace to thy neck. Prov. 3:21-22 (*see also* Discrete)

Speak not in the ears of a fool: for he will despise the wisdom of thy words. Prov. 23:9 (*see also* Fool)

Buy the truth, and sell it not; also wisdom, and instruction, and understanding. Prov. 23:23 (*see also* Instruct, True, Understand)

Through wisdom is an house builded; and by understanding it is established: And by knowledge shall the chambers be filled with all precious and pleasant riches. Prov. 24:3-4 (*see also* House, Understand)

As an earring of gold, and an ornament of fine gold, so is a wise reprover upon an obedient ear. Prov. 25:12 (*see also* Reprove)

I applied mine heart to know, and to search, and to seek out wisdom, and the reason of things, and to know the wickedness of folly, even of foolishness and madness. Eccl. 7:25 (*see also* Apply, Heart, Know, Reason, Seek)

Be not wise in thine own eyes: fear the Lord, and depart from evil. It shall be health in thy navel, and marrow to thy bones. Prov. 3:7-8 (*see also* Fear)

Hear instruction, and be wise, and refuse it not. Prov. 8:33 (*see also* Instruction)

If thou be wise, thou shalt be wise for thyself; but if thou scornest, thou alone shalt bear it. Prov. 9:12 (*see also* Scorn, Scorner)

The wise in heart will receive commandments: but a prating fool shall fall. Prov. 10:8 (*see also* Heart)

He that walketh with wise men shall be wise: but a companion of fools shall be destroyed. Prov. 13:20 (*see also* Fool, Walk)

The way of life is above to the wise, that he may depart from hell beneath. Prov. 15:24 (*see also* Way)

Bow down thine ear and hear the words of the wise, and apply thine heart unto my knowledge. Prov. 22:17 (*see also* Bow, Know)

Hear thou, my son, and be wise, and guide thine heart in the way. Prov. 23:19 (*see also* Guide, Hear, Heart)

Woe unto them that are wise in their own eyes, and prudent in their own sight! Isa. 5:21 (*see also* Prudent)

For wisdom is better than rubies; and all the things that may be desired are not to be compared to it. Prov. 8:11 (*see also* Desire)

Labour not to be rich: cease from thin own wisdom. Prov. 23:4 (*see also* Labor, Rich)

Teach us to number our days, that we may apply our hearts unto wisdom. Ps. 90:12 (*see also* Day)

Ps. 90:12 teach us to number our days, that we may apply our hearts unto wisdom; Prov. 31:26 she openeth her mouth with *w*.; and in her tongue is the law of kindness.

Be ye therefore wise as serpents and harmless as doves. Matt. 10:16 (*see also* Be, Harmless)

Matt. 10:16 I send you forth as sheep in the midst of wolves: be ye therefore *w.* as serpents, and harmless as doves; **Eph. 5:15-16** see then that ye walk circumspectly, not as fools, but as *w.*, Redeeming the time, because the days are evil.

Seek after wisdom. 1 Cor. 1:22 (*see also* Seek)

Matt. 10:16 I send you forth as sheep in the midst of wolves: be ye therefore *w.* as serpents, and harmless as doves; **11:19** *w.* is justified of her children; **12:42** (Luke 11:31) she came from the uttermost parts of the earth to hear the *w.* of Solomon; and, behold, a greater than Solomon is here; **25:8-9** the foolish said unto the *w.*, Give us of your oil; for our lamps are gone out. But the *w.* answered, saying, Not so; lest there be not enough for us and you: but go ye rather to them that sell, and buy for yourselves; **Luke 2:40** the child grew, and waxed strong in spirit, filled with *w.*: and the grace of God was upon him; **2:52** Jesus increased in *w.* and stature, and in favour with God and man; **7:35** *w.* is justified of all her children; **Acts 6:3** look ye out among you seven men of honest report, full of the Holy Ghost and *w.*, whom we may appoint over this business; **Rom. 11:33** O the depth of the riches both of the *w.* and knowledge of God! how unsearchable are his judgments, and his ways past finding out; **1 Cor. 1:22** seek after *w.*; **1:25** because the foolishness of God is *w.* than men; and the weakness of God is stronger than men; **2:6-8** howbeit we speak *w.* among them that are perfect: yet not the *w.* of this world, nor of the princes of this world, that come to nought: But we speak the *w.* of God in a mystery, even the hidden *w.*, which God ordained before the world unto our glory: Which none of the princes of this world knew: for had they known it, they would not have crucified the Lord of glory; **Eph. 1:17** the God of our Lord Jesus Christ, the Father of glory, may give unto you the spirit of *w.* and revelation in the knowledge of him; **Col. 1:9** do not cease to pray for you, and to desire that ye might be filled with the knowledge of his will in all *w.* and spiritual understanding; **1:28** we preach, warning every man, and teaching every man in all *w.*; that we may present every man perfect in Christ Jesus; **2:3** in whom are hid all the treasures of *w.* and knowledge; **2 Tim. 3:15** from a child thou hast known the holy scriptures, which are able to make thee *w.* unto salvation through faith which is in Christ Jesus; **James**

1:5-6 If any of you lack *w.*, let him ask of God, that giveth to all men liberally, and upbraideth not; and it shall be given him. But let him ask in faith, nothing wavering. For he that wavereth is like a wave of the sea driven with the wind and tossed; **3:13** who is a *w.* man and endued with knowledge among you? let him shew out of a good conversation his works with meekness of *w.*; **3:17** the *w.* that is from above is first pure, then peaceable, gentle, and easy to be intreated, full of mercy and good fruits, without partiality, and without hypocrisy.

WITCH, WITCHCRAFT (*see also* Enchantment, Evil, False Prophet, Sorcery, Superstitious, Wizardry)

For rebellion is as the sin of witchcraft, and stubbornness is as iniquity and idolatry. Because thou hast rejected the word of the LORD, he hath also rejected thee from being king. 1 Sam 15:23 (*see also* Idolatry, Rebellion, Stubborn)

WITNESS (*see also* Apostle, Confess, Holy Ghost, Prophet, Testify)

How shall we escape, if we neglect so great salvation; which at the first began to be spoken by the Lord, and was confirmed unto us by them that heard him; God also bearing them witness, both with signs and wonders, and with divers miracles, and gifts of the Holy Ghost, according to his own will? Heb. 2:3-4 (*see also* Escape, Miracle, Salvation)

Seeing we also are compassed about with so great a cloud of witnesses, let us lay aside every weight, and the sin which doth so easily beset us, and let us run with patience the race that is set before us. Heb. 12:1 (*see also* Beset, Patience, Run, Sin, Weight)

Against an elder, receive not an accusation but before two or three witnesses. 1 Tim. 5:19 (*see also* Accuse, Elder)

Ye are my witnesses, saith the Lord, that I am God. Isa. 43:9-12

Isa. 43:9-12 ye are my witnesses, saith the LORD, and my servant whom I have chosen: that ye may know and believe me, and understand that I am he: before me there was no God formed, neither shall there be after me; **44:8** fear ye not, neither be afraid: have not I told thee from that time, and have declared it? ye are even my *w.*. Is there a God beside me? yea, there is no God; I know not any.

There was a man sent from God, whose name was John. The same came for a witness, to bear witness of the Light, that all men through him might believe. John 1:7 (*see also* Testify)

Matt. 8:4 (Luke 5:14) see thou tell no man; but go thy way, shew thyself to the priest, and offer the gift that Moses commanded, for a testimony unto them; **9:30-31** see that no man know it. But they, when they were departed, spread abroad his fame in all that country; **10:32** whosoever therefore shall confess me before men, him will I confess also before my Father which is in heaven; **14:33** they that were in the ship came and worshipped him, saying, Of a truth thou art the Son of God; **16:16** and Simon Peter answered and said, Thou art the Christ, the Son of the living God; **Mark 4:21-22** (Luke 8:16-17) is a candle brought to be put under a bushel, or under a bed? and not to be set on a candlestick? For there is nothing hid, which shall not be manifested; neither was any thing kept secret, but that it should come abroad; **5:19** go home to thy friends, and tell them how great things the Lord hath done for thee, and hath had compassion on thee; **15:39** when the centurion, which stood over against him, saw that he so cried out, and gave up the ghost, he said, Truly this man was the Son of God; **16:6-7** be not affrighted: Ye seek Jesus of Nazareth, which was crucified: he is risen; he is not here: behold the place where they laid him. But go your way, tell his disciples and Peter that he goeth before you into Galilee: there shall ye see him, as he said unto you; **Luke 1:1-2** forasmuch as many have taken in hand to set forth in order a declaration of those things which are most surely believed among us, Even as they delivered them unto us, which from the beginning were eyewitnesses, and ministers of the word; **1:4** that thou mightest know the certainty of those things, wherein thou hast been instructed; **1:48-49** he that is mighty hath done to me great things; and holy is his name; **8:39** return to thine own house, and shew how great things God hath done unto thee. And he went his way, and published throughout the whole city how great things Jesus had done unto him; **9:19-20** but whom say ye that I am? Peter answering said, The Christ of God; **10:17** the seventy returned again with joy, saying, Lord, even the devils are subject unto us through thy name; **12:8** whosoever shall confess me before men, him shall the Son of man also confess

before the angels of God; **24:10-12** their words seemed to them as idle tales, and they believed them not. Then arose Peter, and ran unto the sepulchre; and stooping down, he beheld the linen clothes laid by themselves, and departed, wondering in himself at that which was come to pass; **24:19** Jesus of Nazareth, which was a prophet mighty in deed and word before God and all the people; **24:34** the Lord is risen indeed, and hath appeared to Simon; **24:35** they told what things were done in the way, and how he was known of them in breaking of bread; **24:48** ye are *w.* of these things; **John 1:7** the same came for a *w.*, to bear *w.* of the Light, that all men through him might believe; **1:8** he was not that Light, but was sent to bear *w.* of that Light; **1:15** John bare *w.* of him, and cried, saying, This was he of whom I spake, He that cometh after me is preferred before me: for he was before me; **1:18** no man hath seen God at any time; the only begotten Son, which is in the bosom of the Father, he hath declared him; **1:25-27** I baptize with water: but there standeth one among you, whom ye know not; He it is, who coming after me is preferred before me, whose shoe's latchet I am not worthy to unloose; **1:29** the next day John seeth Jesus coming unto him, and saith, Behold the Lamb of God, which taketh away the sin of the world; **1:35-36** looking upon Jesus as he walked, he saith, Behold the Lamb of God; **1:48-49** whence knowest thou me? Jesus answered and said unto him, Before that Philip called thee, when thou wast under the fig tree, I saw thee. Nathanael answered and saith unto him, Rabbi, thou art the Son of God; thou art the King of Israel; **3:26-29** John answered and said, A man can receive nothing, except it be given him from heaven. Ye yourselves bear me *w.*, that I said, I am not the Christ, but that I am sent before him; **3:31-32** he that cometh from above is above all: he that is of the earth is earthly, and speaketh of the earth: he that cometh from heaven is above all. And what he hath seen and heard, that he testifieth; and no man receiveth his testimony; **4:29** come, see a man, which told me all things that ever I did: is not this the Christ; **4:42** now we believe, not because of thy saying: for we have heard him ourselves, and know that this is indeed the Christ, the Saviour of the world; **5:31-33** if I bear *w.* of myself, my *w.* is not true. There is another that beareth *w.* of me; and I know that the *w.* which he *w.* of me is true. Ye sent unto John, and he bare *w.* unto the truth; **5:36** I have greater *w.* than that of John: for the works which the Father hath given me to finish, the same works that I do, bear *w.* of me, that the Father hath sent me; **7:28-29** ye both know me, and ye know whence I am: and I am not come of myself, but he that sent me is true, whom ye know not. But I know him: for I am from him, and he hath sent me; **7:40-41** of a truth this is the Prophet. Others said, This is the Christ. But some said, Shall Christ come out of Galilee; **7:46** the officers answered, Never man spake like this man; **9:10-11** how were thine eyes opened? He answered and said, A man that is called Jesus made clay, and anointed mine eyes, and said unto me, Go to the pool of Siloam, and wash: and I went and washed, and I received sight; **9:15** he said unto them, He put clay upon mine eyes, and I washed, and do see; **9:17-21** they say unto the blind man again, What sayest thou of him, that he hath opened thine eyes? He said, He is a prophet; **9:25** whether he be a sinner or no, I know not: one thing I know, that, whereas I was blind, now I see; **9:27** I have told you already, and ye did not hear: wherefore would ye hear it again? will ye also be his disciples; **9:30** why herein is a marvellous thing, that ye know not from whence he is, and yet he hath opened mine eyes; **9:32-33** since the world began was it not heard that any man opened the eyes of one that was born blind. If this man were not of God, he could do nothing; **10:11** I am the good shepherd: the good shepherd giveth his life for the sheep; **11:27** yea, Lord: I believe that thou art the Christ, the Son of God, which should come into the world; **12:17** the people therefore that was with him when he called Lazarus out of his grave, and raised him from the dead, bare record; **12:42** among the chief rulers also many believed on him; but because of the Pharisees they did not confess him, lest they should be put out of the synagogue; **12:49** I have not spoken of myself; but the Father which sent me, he gave me a commandment, what I should say, and what I should speak; **15:1** I am the true vine, and my Father is the husbandman; **15:27** ye also shall bear *w.*, because ye have been with me from the beginning; **18:37** to this end was I born, and for this cause came I into the world, that I should bear *w.* unto the truth. Every one that is of the truth heareth my voice; **21:17** Lord, thou knowest all things; thou knowest that I love thee. Jesus saith unto him, Feed my sheep; **21:24** Lord, thou knowest all things; thou knowest that I love thee. Jesus saith unto him, Feed my sheep; **Acts 1:3** to whom also he shewed himself alive after his passion by many infallible proofs, being seen of them forty days, and speaking of the things pertaining to the kingdom of God; **1:8** ye shall receive power, after that the Holy Ghost is come upon you: and ye shall be *w.* unto me both in Jerusalem, and in all Judaea, and in Samaria,

and unto the uttermost part of the earth; **1:22** beginning from the baptism of John, unto that same day that he was taken up from us, must one be ordained to be a *w.* with us of his resurrection; **2:32** this Jesus hath God raised up, whereof we all are *w.*; **2:36** let all the house of Israel know assuredly, that God hath made that same Jesus, whom ye have crucified, both Lord and Christ; **2:40** with many other words did he testify and exhort, saying, Save yourselves from this untoward generation; **3:8** he leaping up stood, and walked, and entered with them into the temple, walking, and leaping, and praising God; **3:15** killed the Prince of life, whom God hath raised from the dead; whereof we are *w.*; **3:20** he shall send Jesus Christ, which before was preached unto you; **4:9-11** be it known unto you all, and to all the people of Israel, that by the name of Jesus Christ of Nazareth, whom ye crucified, whom God raised from the dead, even by him doth this man stand here before you whole. This is the stone which was set at nought of you builders, which is become the head of the corner; **4:13** now when they saw the boldness of Peter and John, and perceived that they were unlearned and ignorant men, they marvelled; and they took knowledge of them, that they had been with Jesus; **4:20** we cannot but speak the things which we have seen and heard; **4:33** with great power gave the apostles *w.* of the resurrection of the Lord Jesus: and great grace was upon them all; **5:32** we are his *w.* of these things; and so is also the Holy Ghost, whom God hath given to them that obey him; **6:10** they were not able to resist the wisdom and the spirit by which he spake; **7:37** this is that Moses, which said unto the children of Israel, A prophet shall the Lord your God raise up unto you of your brethren, like unto me; him shall ye hear; **9:20** straightway he preached Christ in the synagogues, that he is the Son of God; **10:39** we are *w.* of all things which he did both in the land of the Jews, and in Jerusalem; whom they slew and hanged on a tree; **10:41** not to all the people, but unto *w.* chosen before of God, even to us, who did eat and drink with him after he rose from the dead; **10:42** he commanded us to preach unto the people, and to testify that it is he which was ordained of God to be the Judge of quick and dead; **12:11** when Peter was come to himself, he said, Now I know of a surety, that the Lord hath sent his angel, and hath delivered me out of the hand of Herod, and from all the expectation of the people of the Jews; **13:22** he raised up unto them David to be their king; to whom also he gave testimony, and said, I have found David the son of Jesse, a man after mine own heart, which shall fulfil all my will; **13:25** as John fulfilled his course, he said, Whom think ye that I am? I am not he. But, behold, there cometh one after me, whose shoes of his feet I am not worthy to loose; **13:30-32** God raised him from the dead: And he was seen many days of them which came up with him from Galilee to Jerusalem, who are his *w.* unto the people. And we declare unto you glad tidings, how that the promise which was made unto the fathers; **14:3** speaking boldly in the Lord, which gave testimony unto the word of his grace, and granted signs and wonders to be done by their hands; **14:27** they rehearsed all that God had done with them, and how he had opened the door of faith unto the Gentiles; **15:4** they declared all things that God had done with them; **15:32** being prophets also themselves, exhorted the brethren with many words, and confirmed them; **17:2** Paul, as his manner was, went in unto them, and three sabbath days reasoned with them out of the scriptures; **17:23** as I passed by, and beheld your devotions, I found an altar with this inscription, TO THE UNKNOWN GOD. Whom therefore ye ignorantly worship, him declare I unto you; **18:5** Paul was pressed in the spirit, and testified to the Jews that Jesus was Christ; **20:24** none of these things move me, neither count I my life dear unto myself, so that I might finish my course with joy, and the ministry, which I have received of the Lord Jesus, to testify the gospel of the grace of God; **20:27** I have not shunned to declare unto you all the counsel of God; **21:13** I am ready not to be bound only, but also to die at Jerusalem for the name of the Lord Jesus; **21:39** I beseech thee, suffer me to speak unto the people; **22:1** men, brethren, and fathers, hear ye my defence which I make now unto you; **22:4-14** Saul, why persecutest thou me? And I answered, Who art thou, Lord? And he said unto me, I am Jesus of Nazareth, whom thou persecutest; **26:10-15** I heard a voice speaking unto me, and saying in the Hebrew tongue, Saul, Saul, why persecutest thou me? it is hard for thee to kick against the pricks. And I said, Who art thou, Lord? And he said, I am Jesus whom thou persecutest; **26:22-23** I continue unto this day, *w.* both to small and great, saying none other things than those which the prophets and Moses did say should come; **26:29** I would to God, that not only thou, but also all that hear me this day, were both almost, and altogether such as I am, except these bonds; **28:23-24** to whom he expounded and testified the kingdom of God, persuading them concerning Jesus, both out of the law of Moses, and out of the prophets, from morning till evening. And some believed the things which

were spoken, and some believed not; **Rom. 1:11** I long to see you, that I may impart unto you some spiritual gift, to the end ye may be established; **10:9** if thou shalt confess with thy mouth the Lord Jesus, and shalt believe in thine heart that God hath raised him from the dead, thou shalt be saved; **14:5** one man esteemeth one day above another: another esteemeth every day alike. Let every man be fully persuaded in his own mind; **1 Cor. 2:1** when I came to you, came not with excellency of speech or of wisdom, declaring unto you the testimony of God; **2:1-5** my speech and my preaching was not with enticing words of man's wisdom, but in demonstration of the Spirit and of power: That your faith should not stand in the wisdom of men, but in the power of God; **8: 6** there is but one God, the Father, of whom are all things, and we in him; and one Lord Jesus Christ, by whom are all things, and we by him; **12: 3** no man speaking by the Spirit of God calleth Jesus accursed: and that no man can say that Jesus is the Lord, but by the Holy Ghost; **15:1-4** I declare unto you the gospel which I preached unto you, which also ye have received, and wherein ye stand; **15:6** he was seen of above five hundred brethren at once; **15:8** last of all he was seen of me also, as of one born out of due time; **2 Cor. 4:2-3** have renounced the hidden things of dishonesty, not walking in craftiness, nor handling the word of God deceitfully; but by manifestation of the truth commending ourselves to every man's conscience in the sight of God. But if our gospel be hid, it is hid to them that are lost; **4:6-7** God, who commanded the light to shine out of darkness, hath shined in our hearts, to give the light of the knowledge of the glory of God in the face of Jesus Christ; **Gal. 1:13-20** the things which I write unto you, behold, before God, I lie not; **Eph. 4:17** this I say therefore, and testify in the Lord, that ye henceforth walk not as other Gentiles walk, in the vanity of their mind; **Philip. 1:7** in the defence and confirmation of the gospel, ye all are partakers of my grace; **2:11** every tongue should confess that Jesus Christ is Lord, to the glory of God the Father; **1 Tim. 6:12** fight the good fight of faith, lay hold on eternal life, whereunto thou art also called, and hast professed a good profession before many *w.*; **Titus 3:8** this is a faithful saying, and these things I will that thou affirm constantly, that they which have believed in God might be careful to maintain good works. These things are good and profitable unto men; **Heb. 10:15** the Holy Ghost also is a *w.* to us: for after that he had said before; **1 Pet. 3:15** sanctify the Lord God in your hearts: and be ready always to give an answer to every man that asketh you a reason of the hope that is in you with meekness and fear; **5:12** I have written briefly, exhorting, and testifying that this is the true grace of God wherein ye stand; **2 Pet. 1:16-18** we made known unto you the power and coming of our Lord Jesus Christ, but were eyewitnesses of his majesty. For he received from God the Father honour and glory, when there came such a voice to him from the excellent glory, This is my beloved Son, in whom I am well pleased. And this voice which came from heaven we heard, when we were with him in the holy mount; **1 Jn. 1:1-4** that which we have seen and heard declare we unto you; **2:8** a new commandment I write unto you, which thing is true in him and in you: because the darkness is past, and the true light now shineth; **2:23-26** whosoever denieth the Son, the same hath not the Father: [but] he that acknowledgeth the Son hath the Father also; **4:2** hereby know ye the Spirit of God: Every spirit that confesseth that Jesus Christ is come in the flesh is of God; **4:14-15** we have seen and do testify that the Father sent the Son to be the Saviour of the world; **5:7-10** there are three that bear record in heaven, the Father, the Word, and the Holy Ghost: and these three are one. And there are three that bear *w.* in earth, the Spirit, and the water, and the blood: and these three agree in one. If we receive the *w.* of men, the *w.* of God is greater: for this is the *w.* of God which he hath testified of his Son. He that believeth on the Son of God hath the *w.* in himself: he that believeth not God hath made him a liar; because he believeth not the record that God gave of his Son; **5:19-20** we know that we are of God, and the whole world lieth in wickedness. And we know that the Son of God is come, and hath given us an understanding, that we may know him that is true, and we are in him that is true, even in his Son Jesus Christ. This is the true God, and eternal life; **3 Jn. 1:3** I rejoiced greatly, when the brethren came and testified of the truth that is in thee, even as thou walkest in the truth; **1:12** we also bear record; and ye know that our record is true; **Rev. 1:2** who bare record of the word of God, and of the testimony of Jesus Christ, and of all things that he saw; **1:9-10** for the testimony of Jesus Christ. I was in the Spirit on the Lord's day, and heard behind me a great voice, as of a trumpet; **6:9** when he had opened the fifth seal, I saw under the altar the souls of them that were slain for the word of God, and for the testimony which they held; **11:7** when they shall have

finished their testimony, the beast that ascendeth out of the bottomless pit shall make war against them, and shall overcome them, and kill them; **12:17** the dragon was wroth with the woman, and went to make war with the remnant of her seed, which keep the commandments of God, and have the testimony of Jesus Christ; **19:9-10** I am thy fellowservant, and of thy brethren that have the testimony of Jesus: worship God: for the testimony of Jesus is the spirit of prophecy; **22:18-19** I testify unto every man that heareth the words of the prophecy of this book, If any man shall add unto these things, God shall add unto him the plagues that are written in this book.

WIZARD, WIZARDRY (*see also* Sorcery, Superstitious)

When they shall say unto you, Seek unto them that have familiar spirits, and unto wizards that peep, and that mutter: should not a people seek unto their God? Isa. 8:19 (*see also* Familiar, Seek)

WOLF, WOLVES

Beware of false prophets, which come to you in sheep's clothing, but inwardly they are ravening wolves. Ye shall know them by their fruits. Matt. 7:15-16 (*see also* False Prophet, Sheep)

WOMAN, WOMANHOOD, WOMEN (*see also* Female, Marriage, Wife)

Likewise also the men, leaving the natural use of the woman, burned in their lust one toward another; men with men working that which is unseemly, and receiving in themselves that recompence of their error which was meet. Rom. 1:27 (*see also* Lust, Men, Natural)

Give not thy strength to women, nor thy ways to that which destroyeth kings. Prov. 31:3 (*see also* Strength, Way)

The woman shall not wear that which pertaineth unto a man, neither shall a man put on a women's garment: for all that do so are abomination unto the LORD thy God. Deut. 22:5 (*see also* Garments)

WONDER, WONDERS, WONDROUS (*see* Miracle, Sign)

False Christs and false prophets shall rise, and shall shew signs and wonders, to seduce, if it were possible, even the elect. Mark 13:22 (*see also* Elect, False Christ, False Prophet, Seduce, Sign)

WONDERFUL (*see also* Charity, Compassionate, Jesus Christ, Joy, Kind)

For unto us a child is born, unto us a son is given: and the government shall be upon his shoulder: and his name shall be called, Wonderful, Counsellor, The mighty God, The everlasting Father, The Prince of Peace. Isa. 9:6 (*see also* Counselor, Father, Government, Peace, Wonderful)

Not every one that saith unto me, Lord, Lord, shall enter into the kingdom of heaven; but he that doeth the will of my Father who is in heaven. Many will say to me in that day: Lord, Lord, have we not prophesied in thy name, and in thy name have cast out devils, and in thy name done many wonderful works? And then will I profess unto them: I never knew you; depart from me, ye that work iniquity. Matt. 7:21-23 (*see also* Enter Father, Priestcraft, Will)

WORD, WORDS (*see also* Jesus Christ, Record, Revelation, Scripture)

In the beginning was the Word, and the Word was with God, and the Word was God. John 1:1 (*see also* Beginning, God)

The grass withereth, the flower fadeth: but the word of our God shall stand for ever. Isa. 40:8 (*see also* Stand)

Hold fast the form of sound words, which thou hast heard of me, in faith and love which is in Christ Jesus. 2 Tim. 1:13 (*see also* Hold Fast, Sound)

Feed thy people with thy rod, the flock of thine heritage, which dwell solitarily in the wood. Micah 7:14 (*see also* Feed, Rod)

Of these things put them in remembrance, charging them before the Lord that they strive not about words to no profit, but to the subverting of the hearers. 2 Tim. 2:14 (*see also* Profit, Strive)

It was necessary that the word of God should first have been spoken to you: but seeing ye put it from you, and judge yourselves unworthy of everlasting life, lo, we turn to the Gentiles. Acts 13:46 (*see also* Unworthy)

Come, and let us go up to the mountain of the LORD, and to the house of the God of Jacob; and he will teach us of his ways, and we will walk in his paths; for the law shall go forth of Zion, and the word of the LORD from Jerusalem. Micah 4:2 (*see also* House, Jerusalem, Law, Mountain, Ways, Zion)

Ye shall not add unto the word which I command you, neither shall ye diminish ought from it, that ye may keep the commandments of the LORD your God which I command you. Deut. 4:2 (*see also* Add, Diminish)

Stand in the court of the LORD's house, and speak unto all the cities of Judah, which come to worship in the LORD's house, all the words that I command thee to speak unto them; diminish not a word. Jer. 26:2 (*see also* Speak)

I have refrained my feet from every evil way, that I might keep thy word. Ps. 119:101 (*see also* Evil, Keep)

The simple believeth every word: but the prudent man looketh well to his going. Prov. 14:15 (*see also* Belief)

The eyes of them that see shall not be dim, and the ears of them that hear shall hearken. Isa. 32:3 (*see also* Eye)

As newborn babes, desire the sincere milk of the word, that ye may grow thereby. 1 Pet. 2:2 (*see also* Desire, Sincere)

Let the word of Christ dwell in you richly in all wisdom; teaching and admonishing one another in psalms and hymns and spiritual songs, singing with grace in your hearts to the Lord. Col. 3:16 (*see also* Admonish, Grace, Hymn, Psalm, Sing, Wisdom)

My mother and my brethren are these which hear the word of God, and do it. Luke 8:21 (*see also* Hear)

Many of the brethren in the Lord, waxing confident by my bonds, are much more bold to speak the word without fear. Philip. 1:14 (*see also* Fear)

As the fire devoureth the stubble, and the flame consumeth the chaff, so their root shall be as rottenness, and their blossom shall go up as dust: because they have cast away the law of the LORD of hosts, and despised the word of the Holy One of Israel. Isa. 5:24 (*see also* Law)

As for our iniquities, we know them: in transgressing and lying against the LORD, and departing away from our God, speaking oppression and revolt, conceiving and uttering from the heart words of falsehood. Isa. 59:12-13 (*see also* False, Heart)

The burden of the LORD shall ye mention no more: for every man's word shall be his burden; for ye have perverted the words of the living God. Jer. 23:36 (*see also* Pervert)

Should ye not hear the words which the LORD hath cried by the former prophets, when Jerusalem was inhabited and in prosperity, and the cities thereof round about her, when men inhabited the south and the plain? Zech. 7:7 (*see also* Hear, Prophet)

Stand in the court of the LORD'S house, and speak unto all the cities of Judah, which come to worship in the LORD's house, all the words that I command thee to speak unto them; diminish not a word. Jer. 26:2 (*see also* Speak)

Hear ye the word of the LORD, O house of Jacob, and all the families of the house of Israel. Jer. 2:4 (*see also* Hear)

Ye have wearied the LORD with your words. Yet ye say, Wherein have we wearied him? When ye say, Every one that doeth evil is good in the sight of the LORD, and he delighteth in them. Mal. 2:17 (*see also* Evil)

Stand in the gate of the LORD's house, and proclaim there this word, and say, Hear the word of the LORD. Jer. 7:2 (*see also* Proclaim)

The wise men are ashamed, they are dismayed and taken: lo, they have rejected the word of the LORD; and what wisdom is in them? Jer. 8:9 (*see also* Reject)

Stand in the court of the LORD's house, and speak unto all the cities of Judah, which come to worship in the LORD's house, all the words that I command thee to speak unto them; diminish not a word. Jer. 26:2 (*see also* Speak)

He that hath my word, let him speak my word faithfully. Jer. 23:28 (*see also* Faith, Speak)

A word fitly spoken is like apples of gold in pictures of silver. Prov. 25:11 (*see also* Speak)

The terrible one is brought to nought, and the scorner is consumed, and all that watch for iniquity are cut off: That make a man an offender for a word, and lay a snare for him that reproveth in the gate, and turn aside the just thing for a thing of nought. Isa. 29:20-21 (*see also* Just, Offend)

Who is this that darkeneth counsel by words without knowledge? Job 38:2 (*see also* Know)

Give ear, O my people, to my law: incline your ears to the words of my mouth. Ps. 78:1 (*see also* Ear)

My tongue shall speak of thy word: for all thy commandments are righteousness. Ps. 119:172 (*see also* Tongue)

The preacher sought to find out acceptable words: and that which was written was upright, even words of truth. Eccl. 12:10-11 (*see also* Written)

My soul fainteth for thy salvation: but I hope in thy word. Ps. 119:81 (*see also* Hope)

Seest thou a man that is hasty in his words? there is more hope of a fool than of him. Prov. 29:20 (*see also* Haste)

Because ye despise this word, and trust in oppression or perverseness, and stay thereon: Therefore this iniquity shall be to you as a breach ready to fall, swelling out in a high wall, whose breaking cometh suddenly at an instant. Isa. 30:12-13 (*see also* Despise, Oppress, Perverse)

Be ye doers of the word, and not hearers only, deceiving your own selves. For if any be a hearer of the word, and not a doer, he is like unto a man beholding his natural face in a glass: For he beholdeth himself, and goeth his way, and straightway forgetteth what manner of man he was. James 1:22-24 (*see also* Do, Hear)

The thoughts of the wicked are an abomination to the LORD: but the words of the pure are pleasant words. Prov. 15:26 (*see also* Abomination, Thought, Wicked)

Prov. 15:26 the thoughts of the wicked are an abomination to the LORD: but the *w.* of the pure are pleasant *w.;* **16:24** pleasant words are as an honeycomb, sweet to the soul, and health to the bones.

My son, attend to my words; incline thine ear unto my sayings. Let them not depart from thine eyes; keep them in the midst of thine heart. For they are life unto those that find them, and health to all their flesh. Prov. 4:20-22 (*see also* Attend, Incline, Say)

Prov. 4:20-22 attend to my *w.;* incline thine ear unto my sayings. Let them not depart from thine eyes; keep them in the midst of thine heart. For they are life unto those that find them, and health to all their flesh; **7:1** keep my *w.*, and lay up my commandments with thee.

A man hath joy by the answer of his mouth: and a word spoken in due season, how good is it. Prov. 15:23 (*see also* Answer, Season)

Prov. 15:23 a man hath joy by the answer of his mouth: and a *w.* spoken in due season, how good is it; **Eccl. 3:7** a time to rend, and a time to sew; a time to keep silence, and a time to speak; **Amos 5:10** they hate him that rebuketh in the gate, and they abhor him that speaketh uprightly.

I cannot go beyond the word of the LORD my God, to do less or more. Num. 22:18

Num. 22:18 I cannot go beyond the *w.* of the LORD my God, to do less or more; **24:13** I cannot go beyond the commandment of the LORD, to do either good or bad of mine own mind; but what the LORD saith, that will I speak; **Ps. 119:28** my soul melteth for heaviness: strengthen thou me according unto thy *w.;* **Isa. 40:8** the flower fadeth: but the *w.* of our God shall stand for ever.

He humbled thee, and suffered thee to hunger, and fed thee with manna, which thou knewest not, neither did thy fathers know; that he might make thee know that man doth not live by bread only, but by every word that proceedeth out of the mouth of the LORD doth man live. Deut. 8:3 (*see also* Bread, Proceed)

Deut. 8:3 he humbled thee, and suffered thee to hunger, and fed thee with manna, which thou knewest not, neither did thy fathers know; that he might make thee know that man doth not live by bread only, but by every word that proceedeth out of the mouth of the LORD doth man live; **Prov. 30:5** every *w.* of God is pure: he is a shield unto them that put their trust in him; **Isa. 40:8** the grass withereth, the flower fadeth: but the *w.* of our God shall stand for ever; **Jer. 23:28** he that hath my *w.*, let him speak my *w.* faithfully.

Let thy mercies come also unto me, O LORD, even thy salvation, according to thy word. So shall I have wherewith to answer him that reproacheth me: for I trust in thy word. Ps. 119:41-42 (*see also* Mercy, Trust)

Ps. 119:41-42 let thy mercies come also unto me, O LORD, even thy salvation, according to thy *w.* So shall I have wherewith to answer him that reproacheth me: for I trust in thy *w.;* **119:170** let my supplication come before thee: deliver me according to thy *w.;* **Isa. 55:11** so shall my *w.* be that goeth forth out of my mouth: it shall not return unto me void, but it shall accomplish that which I please.

Therefore shall ye lay up these my words in your heart and in your soul, and bind them for a sign upon your hand, that they may be as frontlets between your eyes. Deut. 11:18 (*see also* Heart, Sign)

Deut. 6:8 thou shalt bind them for a sign upon thine hand, and they shall be as frontlets between thine eyes; **11:18** therefore shall ye lay up these my *w.* in your heart and in your soul, and bind them for a sign upon your hand; **Isa. 32:3** the eyes of them that see shall not be dim, and the ears of them that hear shall hearken; **55:11** so shall my *w.* be that goeth forth out of my mouth: it shall not return unto me void, but it shall accomplish that which I please.

Man shall not live by bread alone, but by every word that proceedeth out of the mouth of God. Matt. 4:4 (*see also* Bread, Live, Proceed)

Matt. 4:3-4 man shall not live by bread alone, but by every *w.* that proceedeth out of the mouth of God; **Luke 4:3-4** man shall not live by bread alone, but by every *w.* of God; **6:47** whosoever cometh to me, and heareth my sayings, and doeth them, I will shew you to whom he is like; **Eph. 6:17** take the helmet of salvation, and the sword of the Spirit, which is the *w.* of God; **James 1:21** lay apart all filthiness and superfluity of naughtiness, and receive with meekness the engrafted *w.*, which is able to save your souls.

Hear the word, and receive it, and bring forth fruit. Mark 4:20 (*see also* Bring, Fruit)

Mark 4:20 these are they which are sown on good ground; such as hear the *w.*, and receive it, and bring forth fruit, some thirtyfold, some sixty, and some an hundred; **Acts 11:14** who shall tell thee *w.*, whereby thou and all thy house shall be saved; **1 Pet. 1:25** the *w.* of the Lord endureth for ever. And this is the *w.* which by the gospel is preached unto you.

They received the word with all readiness of mind, and searched the scriptures daily, whether those things were so. Acts 17:11 (*see also* Daily, Mind, Readiness, Receive, Scripture, Search)

Acts 16:14 whose heart the Lord opened, that she attended unto the things which were spoken of Paul; **17:11** they received the *w.* with all readiness of mind, and searched the scriptures daily, whether those things were so; **Rom. 8:27** he that searcheth the hearts knoweth what is the mind of the Spirit, because he maketh intercession for the saints according to the will of God.

We ought to give the more earnest heed to the things which we have heard, lest at any time we should let them slip. Heb. 2:1 (*see also* Earnest, Heed)

Heb 2:1 we ought to give the more earnest heed to the things which we have heard, lest at any time we should let them slip; **James 1:22-24** be ye doers of the *w.*, and not hearers only, deceiving your own selves. For if any be a hearer of the *w.*, and not a doer, he is like unto a man beholding his natural face in a glass: For he beholdeth himself, and goeth his way, and straightway forgetteth what manner of man he was; **1 Pet. 1:25** the *w.* of the Lord endureth for ever. And this is the *w.* which by the gospel is preached unto you.

Understand the words of the law. Neh. 8:13 (*see also* Law)

Neh. 8:2 Ezra the priest brought the law before the congregation both of men and women, and all that could hear with understanding; **8:5** Ezra opened the book in the sight of all the people; [for he was above all the people]; **8:13** on the second day were gathered together the chief of the fathers of all the people, the priests, and the Levites, unto Ezra the scribe, even to understand the words of the law; **8:18** day by day, from the first day unto the last day, he read in the book of the law of God; **Jer. 36:6** go thou, and read in the roll, which thou hast written from my mouth, the *w.* of the LORD in the ears of the people in the LORD's house upon the fasting day; **36:8** Baruch the son of Neriah did according to all that Jeremiah the prophet commanded him, reading in the book the *w.* of the LORD in the LORD's house; **36:15** they said unto him, Sit down now, and read it in our ears. So Baruch read it in their ears; **36:21** the king sent Jehudi to fetch the roll: and he took it out of Elishama the scribes chamber. And Jehudi read it in the ears of the king, and in the ears of all the princes.

And these words, which I command thee this day, shall be in thine heart: And thou shalt teach them diligently unto thy children, and shalt talk of them when thou sittest in thine house, and when thou walkest by the way and when thou liest down, and when thou risest up. And thou shalt bind them for a sign upon thine hand, and they shalt be as frontlets between thine eyes. And thou shalt write them upon the posts of thy house, and on thy gates. Deut. 6:6-9 (*see also* Children, Diligence, Teach)

Deut. 6:6-9 these words, which I command thee this day, shall be in thine heart: And thou shalt teach them diligently unto thy children, and shalt talk of them when thou sittest in thine house, and when thou walkest by the way, and when thou liest down, and when thou risest up; **11:19-21** ye shall teach them your children, speaking of them when thou sittest in thine house, and when thou walkest by the way, when thou liest down, and when thou risest up; **Ezra 7:10** Ezra had prepared his heart to seek the law of the LORD, and to do it, and to teach in Israel statutes and judgments; **7:25** set magistrates and judges, which may judge all the people that are beyond the river, all such as know the laws of thy God; and teach ye them that know them not; **Ps. 34:11** come, ye children, hearken unto me: I will teach you the fear of the LORD; **78:4-8** we will not hide them from their children, shewing to the generation to come the praises of the LORD, and his strength, and his wonderful works that he hath done; **145:4-5** one generation shall praise thy works to another, and shall declare thy mighty acts; **Prov. 17:6** childrens children are the crown of old men; and the glory of children are their fathers; **Isa. 54:13** all thy children shall be taught of the LORD; and great shall be the peace of thy children; **Mal. 1:5** your eyes shall see, and ye shall say, The LORD will be magnified.

WORK, WORKS (*see also* Diligence, Industry, Labor, Serve)

What doth it profit, my brethren, though a man say he hath faith, and have not works? can faith save him? **James. 2:14** (*see also* Faith, Profit, Save)

I must work the works of him that sent me, while it is day: the night cometh, when no man can work. **John. 9:4** (*see also* Day, Night)

Remember the sabbath day, to keep it holy. Six days shalt thou labour, and do all thy work: But the seventh day is the sabbath of the LORD thy God: in it thou shalt not do any work, thou, nor thy son, nor thy daughter, thy manservant, nor thy maidservant, nor thy cattle, nor thy stranger that is within thy gates: For in six days the LORD made heaven and earth, the sea, and all that in them is, and rested the seventh day: wherefore the LORD blessed the sabbath day, and hallowed it. **Ex. 20:8-11** (*see also* Labor, Sabbath, Thou Shalt)

Cursed be he that doeth the the work of the LORD deceitfully. **Jer. 48:10** (*see also* Deceive)

Say not, I will do so to him as he hath done to me; I will render to the man according to his work. **Prov. 24:29** (*see also* Do, Render)

Because they regard not the works of the LORD, nor the operation of his hands, he shall destroy them, and not build them up. **Ps. 28:5** (*see also* Operation, Regard)

In all things shewing thyself a pattern of good works: in doctrine shewing uncorruptness, gravity, sincerity, Sound speech, that cannot be condemned; that he that is of the contrary part may be ashamed, having no evil thing to say of you. **Titus 2:7-8** (*see also* Good, Pattern, Speak)

I perceive that there is nothing better, than that a man should rejoice in his own works. **Eccl. 3:22** (*see also* Rejoice)

Enter ye in at the strait gate; for wide is the gate, and broad is the way, that leadeth to destruction, and many there be which go in thereat; Because strait is the gate, and narrow is the way, which leadeth to life, and few be there that find it. **Matt. 7:13-14** (*see also* Few, Gate, Narrow, Strait)

All scripture is given by inspiration of God, and is profitable for doctrine, for reproof, for correction, for instruction in righteousness: That the man of God may be perfect, throughly furnished unto all good works. **2 Tim. 3:16-17** (*see also* Inspiration, Perfect, Scripture)

Because thou hast trusted in thy works and in thy treasure thou shalt also be taken. **Jer. 48:7** (*see also* Treasure)

Remember his marvelous works that he hath done; his wonders, and the judgments of his mouth. **Ps. 105:5** (*see also* Remember)

If a man therefore purge himself from these, he shall be a vessel unto honour, sanctified, and meet for the master's use, and prepared unto every good work. **2 Tim. 2:21** (*see also* Prepare, Sanctified)

Woe unto him that buildeth his house in unrighteousness, and his chambers by wrong; that useth his neighbour's service without wages, and giveth him not for his work. **Jer. 22:13** (*see also* Serve, Wage)

Be strong, all ye people of the land, saith the LORD, and work: for I am with you, saith the LORD of hosts. **Hag. 2:4** (*see also* Strong)

They regard not the work of the LORD, neither consider the operation of his hands. **Isa. 5:12** (*see also* Hand)

For as the body without the spirit is dead, so faith without works is dead also. **James 2:26** (*see also* Faith)

Be ye stedfast, unmoveable, always abounding in the work of the Lord, forasmuch as ye know that your labour is not in vain in the Lord. **1 Cor. 15:58** (*see also* Stand fast)

Stand still and consider the wondrous works of God. Job 37:14 (*see also* Consider)

Commit thy works unto the LORD, and thy thoughts shall be established. Prov. 16:3 (*see also* Think)

Also unto thee, O Lord, belongeth mercy: for thou renderest to every man according to his work. Ps. 62:12 (*see also* Mercy, Render)

Neh. 4:6 built we the wall; and all the wall was joined together unto the half thereof: for the people had a mind to *w.*; **Ps. 62:12** unto thee, O Lord, belongeth mercy: for thou renderest to every man according to his *w.*

Their land also is full of idols; they worship the work of their own hands, that which their own fingers have made own fingers have made. Isa. 2:8 (*see also* Idol, Worship)

Isa. 2:8 their land also is full of idols; they worship the work of their own hands, that which their own fingers have made; **Jer. 1:16** I will utter my judgments against them touching all their wickedness, who have forsaken me, and have burned incense unto other gods, and worshipped the *w.* of their own hands.

For even when we were with you, this we commanded you, that if any would not work, neither should he eat. 2 Thes. 3:10 (*see also* Eat)

1 Thes 4:11 ye study to be quiet, and to do your own business, and to *w.* with your own hands, as we commanded you; **2 Thes. 3:8-10** if any would not *w.*, neither should he eat; **1 Tim. 5:8** if any provide not for his own, and specially for those of his own house, he hath denied the faith, and is worse than an infidel.

Work the works of God. John 6:28 (*see also* Do, God)

Matt. 10:8 heal the sick, cleanse the lepers, raise the dead, cast out devils: freely ye have received, freely give; **11:1** when Jesus had made an end of commanding his twelve disciples, he departed thence to teach and to preach in their cities; **12:15** Jesus knew it, he withdrew himself from thence: and great multitudes followed him, and he healed them all; **14:14** Jesus went forth, and saw a great multitude, and was moved with compassion toward them, and he healed their sick; **Mark 6:13** they cast out many devils, and anointed with oil many that were sick, and healed them; **6:30** the apostles gathered themselves together unto Jesus, and told him all things, both what they had done, and what they had taught; **7:36** he hath done all things well: he maketh both the deaf to hear, and the dumb to speak; **8:2-9** I have compassion on the multitude, because they have now been with me three days, and have nothing to eat: And if I send them away fasting to their own houses, they will faint by the way; **Luke 9:1** he called his twelve disciples together, and gave them power and authority over all devils, and to cure diseases; **9:49-50** we saw one casting out devils in thy name; and we forbad him, because he followeth not with us. And Jesus said unto him, Forbid him not: for he that is not against us is for us; **10:5** whatsoever house ye enter, first say, Peace be to this house; **10:17** seventy returned again with joy, saying, Lord, even the devils are subject unto us through thy name; **10:19** I give unto you power to tread on serpents and scorpions, and over all the power of the enemy: and nothing shall by any means hurt you; **John 6:28-29** what shall we do, that we might *w.* the *w.* of God? Jesus answered and said unto them, This is the *w.* of God, that ye believe on him whom he hath sent; **17:26** ye seek me, not because ye saw the miracles, but because ye did eat of the loaves, and were filled; **21:25** there are also many other things which Jesus did, the which, if they should be written every one, I suppose that even the world itself could not contain the books that should be written; **Acts 9:40** Peter put them all forth, and kneeled down, and prayed; and turning him to the body said, Tabitha, arise. And she opened her eyes: and when she saw Peter, she sat up; **10:38** God anointed Jesus of Nazareth with the Holy Ghost and with power: who went about doing good, and healing all that were oppressed of the devil; for God was with him; **Rom. 15:19** through mighty signs and wonders, by the power of the Spirit of God; so that from Jerusalem, and round about unto Illyricum, I have fully preached the gospel of Christ; **Heb. 5:1-3** every high priest taken from among men is ordained for men in things pertaining to God, that he may offer both gifts and sacrifices for sins; **1 Pet. 4:19** let them that suffer according to the will of God commit the keeping of their souls to him in well doing, as unto a faithful Creator.

WORLD, WORLDLINESS, WORLDLY (*see also* Creation, Earth, Fallen)

Know that an idol is nothing in the world, and that there is none other God but one. 1 Cor. 8:4 (*see also* Idol)

Love not the world, neither the things that are in the world. 1 Jn. 2:15 (*see also* Love, Things)

John 17:14-16 I have given them thy word; and the *w.* hath hated them, because they are not of the *w.*, even as I am not of the *w.*. I pray not that thou shouldest take them out of the *w.*, but that thou shouldest keep them from the evil. They are not of the *w.*, even as I am not of the *w.*; **Col. 3:1-2** if ye then be risen with Christ, seek those things which are above, where Christ sitteth on the right hand of God. Set your affection on things above, not on things on the earth; **1 Tim. 6:7** we brought nothing into this *w.*, and it is certain we can carry nothing out; **2 Tim. 2:4** no man that warreth entangleth himself with the affairs of this life; that he may please him who hath chosen him to be a soldier; **James 4:4** ye adulterers and adulteresses, know yenot that the friendship of the *w.* is enmity with God? whosoever therefore will be a friend of the *w.* is the enemy of God; **1 Jn. 2:15** love not the *w.*, neither the things that are in the *w.*. If any man love the *w.*, the love of the Father is not in him; **4:4-5** ye are of God, little children, and have overcome them: because greater is he that is in you, than he that is in the *w.*. They are of the *w.*: therefore speak they of the *w.*, and the *w.* heareth them; **5:4** whatsoever is born of God overcometh the *w.*: and this is the victory that overcometh the *w.*, even our faith; **Rev. 18:4** come out of her, my people, that ye be not partakers of her sins, and that ye receive not of her plagues; **18:11** the merchants of the earth shall weep and mourn over her; for no man buyeth their merchandise any more; **18:17** for in one hour so great riches is come to nought.

WORSHIP (*see also* Church, Idolatry, Meet, Praise, Serve)

Blessed be the God of Shadrach, Meshach, and Abed-nego, who hath sent his angel, and delivered his servants that trusted in him, and have changed the king's word, and yielded their bodies, that they might not serve nor worship any god, except their own God. Dan. 3:28 (*see also* Angel, Courage, Idol, Serve, Trust)

Their land also is full of idols; they worship the work of their own hands, that which their own fingers have made own fingers have made. Isa. 2:8 (*see also* Idol, Work)

I will worship toward thy holy temple, and praise thy name for thy lovingkindness and for thy truth: for thou hast magnified thy word above all thy name. Ps. 138:2 (*see also* Lovingkindness, Temple)

Thy graven images also will I cut off, and thy standing images out of the midst of thee; and thou shalt no more worship the work of thine hands. Micah 5:13 (*see also* Graven Images, Hand)

Come, let us worship and bow down: let us kneel before the Lord our maker. Ps. 95:6 (*see also* Bow, Kneel)

Give unto the Lord the glory due unto his name; worship the Lord in the beauty of holiness. Ps. 29:2 (*see also* Glory)

Gen. 24:26 the man bowed down his head, and *w.* the Lord; **24:48** I bowed down my head, and *w.* the Lord, and blessed the Lord God of my master Abraham; **24:52** when Abrahams servant heard their words, he *w.* the Lord, bowing himself to the earth; **Ex. 23:13** make no mention of the name of other gods, neither let it be heard out of thy mouth; **1 Sam. 15:25** I pray thee, pardon my sin, and turn again with me, that I may *w.* the Lord; **15:30** I have sinned: yet honour me now, I pray thee, before the elders of my people, and before Israel, and turn again with me, that I may *w.* the Lord thy God; **1 Chron. 16:29** *w.* the Lord in the beauty of holiness; **Neh. 8:6** all the people answered, Amen, Amen, with lifting up their hands: and they bowed their heads, and *w.* the Lord; **9:3** another fourth part they confessed, and *w.* the Lord their God; **9:6** thou, art Lord alone; thou hast made heaven, the heaven of heavens, with all their host, the earth, and all things that are therein... and the host of heaven *w.* thee; **Job 1:20** Job arose, and rent his mantle, and shaved his head, and fell down upon the ground, and *w.*; **Ps. 29:2** give unto the Lord the glory due unto his name; *w.* the Lord in the beauty of holiness; **66:4** all the earth shall *w.* thee, and shall sing unto thee; they shall sing to thy name; **86:9** all nations whom thou hast made shall come and *w.* before thee, O Lord; and shall glorify thy name; **96:9** O *w.* the Lord in the beauty of holiness; **97:12** rejoice in the Lord, ye righteous; and give thanks at the remembrance of his holiness; **99:5** exalt ye the LORD our God, and *w.* at his footstool; **108:7** God hath spoken in his holiness; I will rejoice; **110:3** thy people shall be willing in the day of thy power, in the beauties of holiness from the womb of the morning; **Isa. 27:13** they... shall *w.* the LORD in the holy mount at Jerusalem; **Jer. 7:2** hear the word of the LORD, all ye of Judah, that enter in at these gates to *w.* the LORD; **Ezek. 11:20** that they may walk in my statutes, and keep mine ordinances, and do them: and they shall be my people, and I will be their God; **Zech. 14:16-18** whoso will not come up of all the families of the earth unto Jerusalem to *w.* the King, the LORD of hosts, even upon them shall be no rain.

Thou shalt worship the Lord thy God, and him only shalt thou serve. Luke 4:8 (*see also* Thou Shalt)

Matt. 2:11 they saw the young child with Mary his mother, and fell down, and *w.* him: and when they had opened their treasures, they present- ed unto him gifts; gold, and frankincense, and myrrh; **4:8-10, Luke 4:5-8** get thee hence, Satan: for it is written, Thou shalt *w.* the Lord thy God, and him only shalt thou serve; **8:2** there came a leper and *w.* him, saying, Lord, if thou wilt, thou canst make me clean; **9:18** there came a certain ruler, and *w.* him, saying, My daughter is even now dead: but come and lay thy hand upon her, and she shall live; **14:33** they that were in the ship came and *w.* him, saying, Of a truth thou art the Son of God; **15:25** *w.* him, saying, Lord, help me; **26:10-13** why trouble ye the woman? for she hath wrought a good work upon me. For ye have the poor always with you; but me ye have not always; **28:8-9** they came and held him by the feet, and *w.* him; **28:17** when they saw him, they *w.* him: but some doubted; **Mark 7:25** a certain woman, whose young daughter had an unclean spirit, heard of him, and came and fell at his feet; **Luke 7:38** stood at his feet behind him weeping, and began to wash his feet with tears, and did wipe them with the hairs of her head, and kissed his feet, and anointed them with the ointment; **7:44-46** I entered into thine house, thou gavest me no water for my feet: but she hath washed my feet with tears, and wiped them with the hairs of her head. Thou gavest me no kiss: but this woman since the time I came in hath not ceased to kiss my feet. My head with oil thou didst not anoint: but this woman hath anointed my feet with ointment;

24:51-53 while he blessed them, he was parted from them, and carried up into heaven. And they *w.* him, and r eturned to Jerusalem with great joy: And were continually in the temple, praising and blessing God; **John 4:23-24** the true *w.* shall *w.* the Father in spirit and in truth: for the Father seeketh such to *w.* him. God is a Spirit: and they that *w.* him must *w.* him in spirit and in truth; **9:38** Lord, I believe. And he *w.* him; **12:16** when Jesus was glorified, then remembered they that these things were written of him, and that they had done these things unto him; **12:20** there were certain Greeks among them that came up to *w.* at the feast; **Acts 2:46-47** the Lord added to the church daily such as should be saved; **18:7** entered into a certain man's house, named Justus, one that *w.* God, whose house joined hard to the synagogue; **Rev. 5:14** the four and twenty elders fell down and *w.* him that liveth for ever and ever; **14:7** *w.* him that made heaven, and earth, and the sea, and the fountains of waters; **22:9** I am thy fellowservant, and of thy brethren the prophets, and of them which keep the sayings of this book: *w.* God.

WORTH

I have laboured in vain, I have spent my strength for nought, and in vain: yet surely my judgment is with the LORD, and my work with my God. Isa. 49:4 (*see also* Labor)

Woe unto you, scribes and Pharisees, hypocrites! for ye pay tithe of mint and anise and cummin, and have omitted the weightier matters of the law, judgment, mercy, and faith: these ought ye to have done, and not to leave the other undone. Matt. 23:23 (*see also* Hypocrite, Law)

What profit hath he that hath laboured for the wind? Eccl. 5:16-20 (*see also* Labor)

Eccl. 5:16-20 what profit hath he that hath laboured for the wind? All his days also he eateth in darkness, and he hath much sorrow and wrath with his sickness; **6:3-6** he cometh in with vanity, and departeth in darkness, and his name shall be covered with darkness. Moreover he hath not seen the sun, nor known any thing; **6:12** who knoweth what is good for man in this life, all the days of his vain life which he spendeth as a shadow.

WORTHINESS, WORTHY (*see also* Clean, Dependable, Faithful, Honorable, Priesthood, Pure, Repentance)

Whosoever shall eat this bread, and drink this cup of the Lord, unworthily, shall be guilty of the body and blood of the Lord. But let a man examine himself, and so let him eat of that bread, and drink of that cup. For he that eateth and drinketh unworthily, eateth and drinketh damnation to himself, not discerning the Lord's body. **1 Cor. 11:27-29** (*see also* Examine, Sacrament, Unworthiness)

Walk worthy of the Lord unto all pleasing, being fruitful in every good work, and increasing in the knowledge of God. **Col. 1:10** (*see also* Know, Walk)

WRATH (*see also* Anger, Hate, Revenge, Smite, Vengeance)

Let every man be swift to hear, slow to speak, slow to wrath. **James 1:19** (*see also* Hear, Speak)

A SOFT answer turneth away wrath: but grievous words stir up anger. **Prov. 15:1** (*see also* Answer)

Surely the churning of milk bringeth forth butter, and the wringing of the nose bringeth forth blood: so the forcing of wrath bringeth forth strife. **Prov. 30:33** (*see also* Force)

Cease from anger, and forsake wrath: fret not thyself in any wise to do evil. **Ps. 37:8** (*see also* Anger)
He that is slow to wrath is of great understanding: but he that is hasty of spirit exalteth folly. **Prov. 14:29**

A stone is heavy, and the sand weighty; but a fool's wrath is heavier than them both. **Prov. 27:3** (*see also* Heavy)

Wrath killeth the foolish man, and envy slayeth the silly one. **Job 5:2** (*see also* Envy)

Job 5:2 wrath killeth the foolish man, and envy slayeth the silly one; **Prov. 16:14** the *w.* of a king is as messengers of death: but a wise man will pacify it; **19:19** a man of great *w.* shall suffer punishment: for if thou deliver him, yet thou must do it again.

WRESTLE, WRESTLED, WRESTLING

Jacob was left alone; and there wrestled a man with him until the breaking of the day. **Gen. 32:24**

For we wrestle not against flesh and blood, but against principalities, against powers, against the rulers of the darkness of this world, against spiritual wickedness in high places. **Eph. 6:12** (*see also* Wickedness)

WRITE, WRITTEN (*see also* Language, Record, Scripture, Word)

Now go, write it before them in a table, and note it in a book, that it may be before the time to come for ever and ever. **Isa. 30:8** (*see also* Record)

If any man shall take away from the words of the book of this prophecy, God shall take away his part out of the book of life, and out of the holy city, and from the things which are written in this book **Rev. 22:19** (*see also* Book, Part)

The preacher sought to find out acceptable words: and that which was written was upright, even words of truth. **Eccl. 12:10-11** (*see also* Word)

Write the vision, and make it plain upon tables, that he may run that readeth it. For the vision is yet for an appointed time. **Haba 2:2-3** (*see also* Time, Vision)

Let not mercy and truth forsake thee: bind them about thy neck: write them upon the table of thine heart; So shalt thou find favour and good understanding in the sight of God and man. **Prov. 3:3-4** (*see also* Bind, Heart, Merciful, True)

WRONG (*see* Evil, False, Injustice, Lie, Wicked)

YEAR (*see also* Day, Time)

Proclaim the acceptable year of the Lord, and the day of vengeance of our God; to comfort all that mourn. **Isa. 61:2** (*see also* Comfort, Mourn, Proclaim)

YIELD (*see also* Humble, Meek, Submit)

Be ye not stiffnecked, as your fathers were, but yield yourselves unto the Lord. 2 Chron. 30:8 (*see also* Stiffnecked)

Neither yield ye your members as instruments of unrighteousness unto sin: but yield yourselves unto God, as those that are alive from the dead, and your members as instruments of righteousness unto God. Rom. 6:13 (*see also* Instrument, Will)

YOKE (*see also* Bind, Bondage, Debt, Owe)

Come unto me, all ye that labour and are heavy laden, and I will give you rest. Take my yoke upon you, and learn of me; for I am meek and lowly in heart: and ye shall find rest unto your souls. For my yoke is easy, and my burden is light. Matt. 11:28-30 (*see also* Come, Labor, Rest)

Be ye not unequally yoked together with unbelievers: for what fellowship hath righteousness with unrighteousness? and what communion hath light with darkness. 2 Cor. 6:14 (*see also* Fellowship)

Luke 12:46 at an hour when he is not aware, and will cut him in sunder, and will appoint him his portion with the unbelievers; 2 Cor. 6:14 be ye not unequally *y.* together with unbelievers: for what fellowship hath righteousness with unrighteousness? and what communion hath light with darkness.

YOUNG (*see also* Child, Youth)

Likewise, ye younger, submit yourselves unto the elder. Yea, all of you be subject one to another, and be clothed with humility: for God resisteth the proud, and giveth grace to the humble. 1 Pet. 5:5 (*see also* Humble, Submit)

Rebuke not an elder, but intreat him as a father; and the younger men as brethren; The elder women as mothers; the younger as sisters, with all purity. 1 Tim. 5 1-2 (*see also* Elder, Entreat, Rebuke)

YOUTH (*see also* Child, Young)

Remember now thy creator in the days of thy youth. Eccl. 12:1 (*see also* Remember)

Thou hast not remembered the days of thy youth, but hast fretted me in all these things; behold, therefore I also will recompense thy way upon thine head, saith the Lord GOD. Ezek. 16:43 (*see also* Recompense, Remember)

Rejoice, O young man in thy youth; and let thy heart cheer thee in the days of thy youth, and walk in the ways of thine heart, and in the sight of thine eyes. Eccl. 11:9 (*see also* Rejoice, Walk)

ZION (*see also* Jerusalem, Kingdom, Pure)

Let us declare in Zion the work of the LORD our God. Jer. 51:10 (*see also* Declare)

Come, and let us go up to the mountain of the LORD, and to the house of the God of Jacob; and he will teach us of his ways, and we will walk in his paths; for the law shall go forth of Zion, and the word of the LORD from Jerusalem. Micah 4:2 (*see also* House, Jerusalem, Law, Mountain, Ways, Word)

Wherefore also it is contained in the scripture, Behold, I lay in Sion a chief corner stone, elect, precious: and he that believeth on him shall not be confounded. 1 Pet. 2:6 (*see also* Cornerstone, Jesus Christ)

Let them all be confounded and turned back that hate Zion. Ps. 129:5

It shall even be as when an hungry man dreameth, and, behold, he eateth; but he awaketh, and his soul is empty: or as when a thirsty man dreameth, and, behold, he drinketh; but he awaketh, and, behold, he is faint, and his soul hath appetite: so shall the multitude of all the nations be, that fight against mount Zion. Isa. 29:8 (*see also* Fight)

How beautiful upon the mountains are the feet of him that bringeth good tidings, that publisheth peace; that bringeth good tidings of good, that publisheth salvation; that saith unto Zion, Thy God reigneth! Isa. 52:7 (*see also* Good, Mountain, Peace, Publish)

Say ye to the daughter of Zion, Behold, thy salvation cometh; behold, his reward is with him, and his work before him. Isa. 62:11 (*see also* Reward, Say)

Arise ye, and let us go up to Zion unto the LORD our God. Jer. 31:6 (*see also* Arise)

They shall ask the way to Zion with their faces thitherward, *saying,* Come, and let us join ourselves to the LORD in a perpetual covenant that shall not be forgotten. Jer. 50:5 (*see also* Ask, Covenant)

Declare in Zion the vengeance of the LORD our God, the vengeance of His temple. Jer. 50:28 (*see also* Declare, Vengeance)

Blow ye the trumpet in Zion, and sound an alarm in my holy mountain: let all the inhabitants of the land tremble: for the day of the Lord cometh, for *it is* nigh at hand. Joel 2:1 (*see also* Day)

Joel 2:1 blow ye the trumpet in Z., and sound an alarm in my holy mountain: let all the inhabitants of the land tremble: for the day of the LORD cometh, for it is nigh at hand; **2:15-17** blow the trumpet in z., sanctify a fast, call a solemn assembly: Gather the people, sanctify the congregation, assemble the elders, gather the children.

Ye are come unto mount Sion, and unto the city of the living God, the heavenly Jerusalem, and to an innumerable company of angels. Heb. 12:22 (*see also* Jerusalem)

Rom. 11:26 shall come out of Sion the Deliverer; **Heb. 12:22** ye are come unto mount Sion, and unto the city of the living God, the heavenly Jerusalem, and to an innumerable company of angels.

If ye know these things,
happy are ye if ye do them.

John 13:17

PRINCIPLES WITH PROMISE
OLD TESTAMENT
NEW TESTAMENT

TOPICAL INDEX

ISBN 978-0-9786815-4-8

52295

9 780978 681548

www.ingramcontent.com/pod-product-compliance
Lightning Source LLC
Chambersburg PA
CBHW060235100426
42742CB00011B/1531